CHI 2014
One of a CHInd

Conference Proceedings

Toronto, Canada | April 26 - May 1, 2014

Association for Computing Machinery

SIGCHI
Special Interest Group Computer Human Interaction

The 32nd Annual ACM Conference on Human Factors in Computing Systems

Association for
Computing Machinery

Advancing Computing as a Science & Profession

The Association for Computing Machinery
2 Penn Plaza, Suite 701
New York, New York 10121-0701

Notice to Past Authors of ACM-Published Articles
ACM intends to create a complete electronic archive of all articles and/or other material previously published by ACM. If you have written a work that has been previously published by ACM in any journal or conference proceedings prior to 1978, or any SIG Newsletter at any time, and you do NOT want this work to appear in the ACM Digital Library, please inform permissions@acm.org, stating the title of the work, the author(s), and where and when published.

ISBN: 978-1-4503-2473-1 (Digital)

ISBN: 978-1-4503-3289-7 (Print)

Additional copies may be ordered prepaid from:

ACM Order Department
PO Box 30777
New York, NY 10087-0777, USA

Phone: 1-800-342-6626 (USA and Canada)
+1-212-626-0500 (Global)
Fax: +1-212-944-1318
E-mail: acmhelp@acm.org
Hours of Operation: 8:30 am – 4:30 pm ET

Printed in the USA

Welcome to CHI 2014!

CHI is more than a conference, it is an international community of researchers and practitioners who want to make a difference. Everything we do is focused on uncovering, critiquing and celebrating radically new ways for people and technology to evolve together. People in their everyday contexts, in diverse regions of the world, from very different backgrounds, with alternative outlooks on life drive this innovation. As you take part in the conference sessions we really hope you will experience how powerful this people-centred approach to technological transformation can be. CHI as a conference is now in its 32nd year and has grown to become the premier international forum on human-computer interaction, gathering us all to share innovative interactive insights that shape people's lives. CHI draws together a multidisciplinary community from around the globe.

Our great strength is our ability to bring together students and experts, researchers and practitioners, scientists, designers and engineers, drawing from their rich perspectives to create new visions of humancomputer interaction. This year's conference theme is One of a CHInd. We chose this nearly two years ago as we began planning for this event. It has helped us focus our efforts and we hope you will use it to keep your eyes open to the bigger picture amongst all the excitement, range of presentations and activities at the conference.

CHI 2014 is One of CHInd because it is a celebration of the conference's one of a kind diversity; from the broad range of backgrounds of its attendees, to the diverse spectrum of communities and fields that the conference and its research have an impact on. CHI 2014 will take place at the Metro Toronto Convention Centre in Toronto, Canada, a city itself known for its one of a kind cultural diversity. But, CHI 2014 is more than a celebration of the diversity of our community and conference setting.

We hope that this year's event, more than anything, reminds you that the "people," "participants," "users" or "humans" that you hear described throughout this week are actually uniquely wonderful individuals full of hopes, concerns, joys and frustrations. CHI is here to serve all of these one of a kinds.

CHI 2014 features two outstanding keynote speakers: Booker prize winning author, Margaret Atwood and leading UX designer, Scott Jenson.

New for CHI 2014, we have Provoke! Wisdom! Impact! plenary talks first thing each morning on Tuesday, Wednesday and Thursday. Come along, join the crowd and be energised by our speakers who will each bring in their experience of the Big Picture to inspire us. The talks will be short - twenty minutes - and then the rest of the day's programme will begin.

We are also delighted to host a timely retrospective exhibition on wearable technology curated by Thad Starner and Clint Zeagler. CHI 2014 also includes two days of focused workshops and four days of technical content, including CHI's prestigious technical program, with 16 parallel sessions of rigorously reviewed research Papers, engaging Panels, Case Studies and Special Interest Groups (SIGs), an extensive Course program and invited talks from SIGCHI's award winners: Steve Whittaker, Gillian Grampton Smith and Richard Ladner.

We also host student research, design, and game competitions, provocative alt.chi presentations and last-minute SIGs for discussing current topics. Interactivity hands-on demonstrations showcase the best of interactive technology. We also highlight over 241 Work-In-Progress posters: this year we have added some features to these sessions to better help you get the most out of the exciting, early stage work on show; do go along and engage with the authors about their work. Evening events include the CHI 2014 conference reception, Sponsors and University events, local performances and the Job Fair.

We received over 3200 submissions and accepted nearly 1000 that will appear in the ACM Digital Library. To help you navigate through this immense program, there are a number of online and digital resources from the conference website to our mobile apps. You can also browse the videos, papers and extended abstracts on the CHI 2014 USB Key. But, CHI 2014 is about being in Toronto so perhaps the best way to select from and experience the event is by asking for pointers and chatting with your fellow attendees, our wonderful student volunteers, the information desk helpers or any of this year's committee.

We are all here to make your experience as useful and enjoyable as possible. We are deeply indebted to our vast number of volunteers, without whom CHI 2014 would not be possible, including over 3800 reviewers, over 180 senior members of the program committee, nearly 100 members of the CHI 2014 conference committee and, of course, the more than 180 student volunteers. We thank you all! We are honored and excited by the opportunity to host CHI 2014 and wish you a productive and enjoyable stay in Toronto!

Matt Jones,
Swansea University, Wales, UK
CHI 2014 General Conference Co-Chair

Philippe Palanque
Université Paul Sabatier
CHI 2014 General Conference Co-Chair

Albrecht Schmidt
University of Stuttgart, Germany
CHI 2014 Technical Program Co-Chair

Tovi Grossman
Autodesk Research, Canada
CHI 2014 Technical Program Co-Chair

From ACM SIGCHI's President and Vice President for Conferences

SIGCHI is proud to sponsor the premier annual conference in the field of human-computer interaction. We are extremely grateful to the CHI 2014 Conference Chairs Matt Jones and Philippe Palanque , to Technical Program Chairs Albrecht Schmidt and Tovi Grossman, and to their wonderful crew, who succeeded to build an impressive program and experience.

CHI 2014 is back in Toronto, Canada, returning to the same location of CHI 1987, 5 years after the first conference, on Human Factors in Computer Systems, in Gaithersburg, MD, March 1982. That first conference in Gaithersburg drew over 900 attendees, and since then CHI, with the official name: "ACM Conference on Human Factors in Computing Systems", has continued to grow and broaden its range of topics and contributing disciplines: the founding psychologists and software engineers began to meet new visions from ethnography, sociology, communication sciences and arts, among others. Relevant industries, as well as research institutes and academia, showed an increasing - and often long-lasting - interest and involvement (through volunteers and through sponsorship for conference expenses).

CHI is an ideal forum for people to meet formally as well as informally, to exchange knowledge and views, to share experiences, and to learn. The CHI conference brings together professionals from research and practice; people from industry, academia, and from government; long-term veterans of HCI, young professionals and students; all in an environment designed to encourage interaction. We invite you to actively participate in that interaction: introduce yourself to people, interact with presenters and speakers, renew old friendships and make new ones.

CHI is organized on behalf of ACM's Special Interest Group on Computer-Human Interaction (SIGCHI), an international community of professionals who share an interest in the many diverse facets of HCI. SIGCHI is committed both to advancing the field of HCI, to facilitate exchange of information within the SIGCHI community, and to support students to enter the domain.

The CHI conference is arguably the single most visible activity of SIGCHI, but we also sponsor and support a wide range of specialized conferences and workshops in areas ranging from interactive systems design to user interface technology to computer-supported cooperative work to "intelligent" user interfaces. Visit the SIGCHI website at **http://www.sigchi.org** to find our conference schedule, listing upcoming as well as past conferences.

SIGCHI and ACM produce some of the most respected publications in the field. All members receive interactions, a highly-acclaimed magazine covering the broad field of HCI and user interface design. ACM Transactions on Computer-Human Interactions (ToCHI), now in its 21st year, is our flagship journal - a quarterly publication with the top-quality archival research aimed at researchers and those translating research into practice.

SIGCHI is truly an international organization, with over 30 local chapters and 3 student chapters in 25 countries on 6 continents. We encourage all SIGCHI members to join their local chapter - or if there isn't one in your area, we would love to help you create one. And don't forget virtual communities! SIGCHI hosts dozens of electronic mailing lists on topics ranging from HCI and the Web, to HCI educations, to public policy and beyond. Those lists range from dozens of subscribers to thousands, and are an excellent way to keep up with the field and with friends and colleagues.

Finally, on behalf of ACM SGICHI, we again want to thank the conference committee and all of the hundreds of volunteers who make this conference possible. Their work makes this a rewarding experience for all of us.

Gerrit C. van der Veer
SIGCHI President

John "Scooter" Morris
SIGCHI Vice-President for Conferences

CHI 2014 Papers and Notes Chairs' Welcome

The CHI Papers and Notes programme is continuing to grow and this year we received more than 2000 submissions for the first time. We are pleased that CHI is still the leading conference for research in humancomputer interaction.

CHI 2014 continued the use of subcommittees to manage the review process. Authors selected the subcommittee they believed was best qualified to review their work: Due to the changing pattern of submissions we split some subcommittees into more manageable sizes and coalesced others. We are pleased with the subcommittee process: By dividing the work, each paper received much more careful discussion than would otherwise have been possible.

This year we considered 2036 submissions, including 1428 papers and 608 notes, representing a 4% growth over last year. We accepted 465 submissions (23%): 382 papers and 83 notes.

The CHI review process demands a tremendous amount of work from all areas of the human computer interaction community. As co-chairs of the process, we are amazed at the ability of the community to organize itself to accomplish this task. We would like to thank the 2866 individual reviewers for their careful consideration of these papers. We also deeply appreciate the huge amount of time donated to this process by the 205-member program committee, who paid their own way to attend the face-to-face program committee meeting, an event larger than the average ACM conference.

We are proud of the work of the CHI 2014 program committee and hope that you enjoy these papers and notes, which represent the best research in human-computer interaction.

Stephen Brewster,
Glasgow University
CHI 2014 Papers and Notes Chairs

Andy Cockburn,
University of Canterbury
CHI 2014 Papers and Notes Chairs

Table of Contents

April 29th, 2014 – Volume 2a

Interactive Visualization and Visual Elements

Session Chair: Eytan Adar , *University of Michigan*

Understanding and Designing Games

Session Chair: Lennart Nacke , *University of Ontario Institute of Technology*

Personal Values and Preferences

Session Chair: Katharina Reinecke , *University of Michigan*

April 29th, 2014 – Volume 2b

Studying Visualization

Session Chair: Pierre Dragicevic , *INRIA*

Exploring Exergames

Session Chair: Darren Edge , *Microsoft Research Asia*

Narratives and Storytelling

Session Chair: Aisling Kelliher , *Carnegie Mellon University*

Designing for Older Adults and Demographic Change

Session Chair: Vicki Hanson , *University of Dundee*

Learning and Education

Session Chair: Deborah Tatar , *Virginia Polytechnic Institute and State University*

April 30th, 2014 – Volume 3a

Telepresence and Connecting over Video

Session Chair: Kori Inkpen , *Microsoft Research*

Exergame Design

Session Chair: Sean Munson , *University of Washington*

April 30th, 2014 – Volume 3b

Question and Answer Systems

Session Chair: Jeffrey Nichols , *IBM Research*

Cross-Device Interaction

Session Chair: Fabio Paternò , *CNR-ISTI*

Exergaming for Health and Fitness

Session Chair: Dan Morris , *Microsoft Research*

Sensory Experiences: Smell and Taste

Session Chair: Jettie Hoonhout , *Philips Research*

Multitouch Interaction

Session Chair: Sebastian Boring , *University of Copenhagen*

Authentication and Passwords

Session Chair: Serge Egelman , *University of California, Berkeley*

Policies and Practice: Doing the Right Thing

Session Chair: Volker Wulf , *University of Siegen and Fraunhofer FIT*

Journalism and Social News

Session Chair: Coye Cheshire , *University of California, Berkeley*

Interruptions and Distractions

Session Chair: Jason Alexander , *Lancaster University*

Lost and Found in Translation

Session Chair: Tiago Guerreiro , *University of Lisbon*

Participatory Design

Session Chair: Mona Leigh Guha , *University of Maryland*

Brain Computer Interfaces

Session Chair: Lynne Baillie , *Glasgow Caledonian University*

3D Printing and Fabrication

Session Chair: Alex Olwal , *Google [x]*

CHI 2014 Conference Organization

General Chair:
Matt Jones, *Swansea University, Wales, UK*
Philippe Palanque, *Université Paul Sabatier, France*

Technical Program

Technical Program Co-Chairs:
Albrecht Schmidt, *University of Stuttgart , Germany*
Tovi Grossman, *Autodesk Research, Canada*

Technical Program Chair Assistant:
Michael Glueck, *Autodesk Research, Canada*

Papers and Notes:
Stephen Brewster, *University of Glasgow, UK*
Andy Cockburn, *University of Canterbrury, New Zealand*

Panels:
Gillian Hayes, *University of California, Irvine, USA*
Khai Truong, *University of Toronto, Canada*

Case Studies:
Jonathan Arnowitz, *Google, USA*
DJ Hoets, *SAP, USA*
Michael Arent, *Rivendel Consulting, USA*
KAIST, Republic of Korea in Henderson, *Flipside, The Netherlands*

Courses:
Regina Bernhaupt, *Ruwido, France*
Elizabeth Churchill, *eBay Research Labs, USA*

Interactivity:
Steven Benford, *University of Nottingham, UK*
Julie Rico Williamson, *University of Glasgow, Scotland, UK*

Video Showcase:
Jinwook Seo, *Seoul National University, Korea*
Nicolas Roussel, *INRIA, France*

SIGs:
Enrico Rukzio, *Ulm University, Germany*
Henry Duh, *University of Tasmania, Australia*

Doctoral Consortium:
Manfred Tscheligi, *University of Salzburg, Austria*
Katherine Isbister, *New York University, USA*

Workshops:
Nadir Weibel, *University of California, San Diego, USA*
Juergen Steimle, *Max Planck Institute, Germany*

Works in Progress:
Shelly Farnham, *Microsoft, USA*
Shamsi Iqbal, *Microsoft, USA*
Shaun Lawson, *University of Lincoln, USA*

Student Research Competition:
Celine Latulipe, *UNC Charlotte, USA*
Floyd Muller, *University in Melbourne, Australia*

Student Design Competition:
Thecla Schiphorst, *Simon Fraser University, Canada*
Youn-Kyung Lim, *KAIST, Korea*

Student Game Competition: Seth Cooper, *University of Washington, USA*
Alessandro Canossa, *Northeastern University, USA*

alt.chi: Daniela Rosner, *University of Washington, USA*
Lilly Irani, *UC San Diego, USA*

TOCHI Papers: Jeffrey Nichols, *IBM Research, USA*

Best of CHI Awards: Daniel Wigdor, *University of Toronto, Canada*
Karyn Moffatt, *McGill School of Information, Canada*

Spotlights

Spotlights Chairs: Kristina Höök, *Royal Institute of Technology, Sweden*
Ed Chi, *Google Research, USA*

Games & Entertainment: Magy Seif El-Nasr, *Northeastern University, USA*
Heather Desurvire, *Behavioristics, Inc, USA*
Lennart Nacke, *University of Ontario, Canada*

HCI For Development (HCI4D): Melissa Densmore, *Microsoft Research, USA*
Matthew Kam, *Carnegie Mellon University, USA*
Ban Al-Ani, *University of California, Irvine, USA*

Interaction Science: Andrew Howes, *University of Birmingham, UK*
Benjamin R. Cowan, *University of Birmingham, UK*
Stephen J. Payne, *University of Oxford, UK*
Paul Cairns, *University of York, UK*
Christian P. Janssen, *The Smith-Kettlewell Eye Research Institute, USA*
Anna L Cox, *University College London, UK*
Anthony J. Hornof, *University of Oregon, USA*
Peter Pirolli, *Palo Alto Research Center (PARC), USA*

Making Cultures: Jeffrey Bardzell, *University Bloomington, USA*
Shaowen Bardzell, *Shaowen Bardzell, USA*
Carl DiSalvo, *Georgia Institute of Technology, USA*
Ann Light, *Northumbria University, UK*
Daniela Rosner, *University of Washington, USA*

Art and Interaction: David England, *John Moores University, UK*
Joceyn Spence, *University of Surrey, UK*

Operations

Student Volunteer Coordinators: Lindsay Reynolds, *Cornell University, USA*
Jon Haber, *University of Calgary, Canada*

Technology Liaisons: Scooter Morris, *University of California, San Francisco, USA*
Sara Drenner, *University of Minnesota-Twin Cities, USA*

Webmaster: Liam Betsworth, *Swansea University, Wales, UK*

Social Media: Max Wilson, *Nottingham University, UK*
Katie Panciera, *University of Minnesota, USA*

Proceedings: Marco Winckler, *Université Paul Sabatier, France*
Yann Riche, *Microsoft, USA*
Stéphane Conversy, *ENAC, France*

Infrastructure Accessibility Chair: Jennifer Rode, *Drexel University, USA*

Digital Accessibility Chair: Jonathan Lazar, *Towson University, USA*

Community Sourcing & Scheduling: Paul André, *Facebook, USA*
Anant Bhardwaj, *MIT, USA*
Lydia Chilton, *University of Washington, USA*
Juho Kim, *MIT, USA*
Steven Dow, *Carnegie Mellon University, USA*
Rob Miller, *MIT, USA*
Haoqi Zhang, *Northwestern University, USA*

Mobile Apps: Stephen Oney, *Carnegie Mellon University, USA*
Eiji Hayashi, *Carnegie Mellon University, USA*
Jason Wiese, *Carnegie Mellon University, USA*
Célia Martinie, *Université Paul Sabatier, France*

Video Previews: Gene Golovchinsky *[in memory]*
Gonzalo Ramos, *University of Toronto, Canada*
Fanny Chevalier, *INRIA, France*

Conference Management: Janeé Pelletier, *Conference & Logistics Consultants, USA*
Allison Perrelli, *Conference & Logistics Consultants, USA*

Sponsors, Exhibits & Recruitment: Carol Klyver, *Foundations of Excellence, USA*

Registration: Yvonne Lopez, *Executive Events, Inc. USA*
Brooke Daley, *Executive Events, Inc. USA*

PCS Liaisons: Max van Kleek, *University of Southampton, UK*
Carol Klyver, *Foundations of Excellence, USA*
Scooter Morris, *University of California, San Francisco, USA*

Women's Breakfast Event: Allison Druin, *University of Maryland, USA*

CHI 2014 Papers and Notes Subcommittee & Associate Chairs

Subcommittee Chairs:

Mark Ackerman, *University of Michigan, USA*
Victoria Bellotti, *Xerox PARC, USA*
Laura Dabbish, *Carnegie Mellon University, USA*
Stephen Fairclough, *Liverpool John Moores University, UK*
Steven Feiner, *Columbia University, USA*
Jon Froelich, *University of Maryland, USA*
Vicki Hanson, *IBM Research, USA*
Jettie Hoonhout, *Philips Research, The Netherlands*
Hilary Hutchinson, *Google Research, USA*
Shahram Izadi, *Microsoft Research, UK*
David Kirk, *Newcastle University, UK*
Antonio Krueger, *DFKI, Germany*
Myriam Lewkowicz, *Université de Technologie de Troyes, France*
Youn-Kyung Lim, *KAIST, South Korea*
Joanna McGrenere, *University of British Columbia, Canada*
Bilge Mutlu, *University of Wisconsin-Madison, USA*
Fabio Paterno, *CNR ISTI, Italy*
Wanda Pratt, *University of Washington, USA*
mc schraefel, *University of Southampton, UK*
Sriram Subramanian, *University of Bristol, UK*
Bill Thies, *Microsoft Research, India*
Manfred Tscheligi, *CURE, Austria*
Ron Wakkary, *Simon Fraser University, Canada*
John Zimmerman, *Carnegie Mellon University, USA*

Associate Chairs:

Eytan Adar, *University of Michigan, USA*
Jason Alexander, *Lancaster University, UK*
Paul André, *Carnegie Mellon University, USA*
Judd Antin, *Yahoo! Research, USA*
Alissa Antle, *Simon Fraser University, Canada*
Paul Aoki, *Intel Labs, USA*
Daniel Ashbrook, *Nokia Research Center Hollywood, USA*
Gabriela Avram, *University of Limerick, Ireland*
Brian Bailey, *University of Illinois, USA*
Lynne Baillie, *Glasgow Caledonian University, UK*
Ravin Balakrishnan, *University of Toronto, Canada*
Jeffrey Bardzell, *Indiana University Bloomington, USA*
Richard Beckwith, *Intel Research, USA*
Hrvoje Benko, *Microsoft Research, USA*
Timothy Bickmore, *Northeastern University, USA*
Jeffrey Bigham, *Carnegie Mellon University, USA*
Mark Blythe, *Northumbria University, UK*
Alexander Boden, *University of Siegen, Germany*
Sebastian Boring, *University of Copenhagen, Denmark*
Duncan Brumby, *University College London, UK*
A.j. Brush, *Microsoft Research, USA*
Andreas Bulling, *Max-Planck Institut Für Informatik, Germany*
Daniela Busse, *Samsung Research America (SRA), USA*
Andreas Butz, *Ludwig-Maximilians-Universität München, Germany*
John Canny, *UC Berkley, USA*
Xiang Cao, *Lenovo Research & Technology, China*
Erin Carroll, *University of Rochester, USA*
Nicholas Chen, *University of Maryland, UK*
Yunan Chen, *University of California, USA*
Coye Cheshire, *UC Berkeley, USA*
Fanny Chevalier, *University of Toronto, Canada*
Keith Cheverst, *Lancaster University, England, UK*
Luigina Ciolfi, *Sheffield Hallam University, UK*
Rob Comber, *Newcastle University, UK*
Lorrie Cranor, *Carnegie Mellon University, USA*
Scott Davidoff, *Jet Propulsion Laboratory, USA*
Antonella de Angeli, *University of Trento, Italy*
Alexander de Luca, *University of Munich, Germany*
Rogerio de Paula, *IBM Research, Brazil*
Marco de Sá, *Facebook, USA*
Morgan Dixon, *University of Washington, USA*
Steven Dow, *Carnegie Mellon University, USA*
Pierre Dragicevic, *INRIA, France*
Mark Dunlop, *University of Strathclyde, Scotland, UK*
Darren Edge, *Microsoft Research Asia, China*
Serge Egelman, *University of California, USA*
Niklas Elmqvist, *Purdue University, USA*
Ylva Fernaeus, *KTH, Sweden*
Clifton Forlines, *Draper Laboratory, USA*
Jodi Forlizzi, *Carnegie Mellon University, USA*
Zhiyong Fu, *Information Art and Design Department, China*
Dominic Furniss, *University College London, UK*
Susan Fussell, *Cornell University, USA*

Associate Chairs: Natasa Milic-Frayling, *Microsoft Research Ltd, UK*
Robert Miller, *The Pennsylvania State University, USA*
Karyn Moffatt, *McGill University, Canada*
Tom Moher, *University of Illinois at Chicago, USA*
Wendy Moncur, *University of Dundee, Scotland,*
Dan Morris, *Microsoft Research, USA*
Tomer Moscovich, *INRIA, France*
Ingrid Mulder, *Delft University of Technology, The Netherlands*
Michael Muller, *Alexander Von Humboldt Institute for Internet and Society, USA*
Jörg Müller, *University of Arts, Berlin, Germany*
Sean Munson, *University of Washington, USA*
Lennart Nacke, *University of Ontario Institute of Technology, Canada*
Michael Nebeling, *ETH Zurich, Switzerland*
Carman Neustaedter, *Simon Fraser University, Canada*
Jeffrey Nichols, *IBM Research, USA*
Ian Oakley, *Ulsan National Institute of Science and Technology, South Korea*
Marianna Obrist, *Newcastle University, UK*
William Odom, *Carnegie Mellon University, USA*
Amy Ogan, *Carnegie Mellon University, USA*
Patrick Olivier, *Newcastle University, UK*
Alex Olwal, *Royal Institute of Technology (KTH), USA*
Claire O'malley, *University of Nottingham, UK*
Antti Oulasvirta, *Max-Planck Institut Für Informatik, Germany*
Andrea Parker, *Northeastern University, USA*
Sameer Patil, *Aalto University, Finland*
Mark Perry, *Brunel University, UK*
Christopher Power, *University of York, UK*
Aaron Quigley, *University of St. Andrews, UK*
Chris Quintana, *University of Michigan, USA*
Emilee Rader, *Michigan State University, USA*
David Randall, *University of Siegen, UK*
Pei-Luen Patrick Rau, *Tsinghua University, China*
Stuart Reeves, *University of Nottingham, England*
Katharina Reinecke, *Harvard University, USA*
Anne Roudaut, *University of Bristol, Germany*
Mark Rouncefield, *Lancaster University, UK*
Daniel Russell, *Google, USA*
Nithya Sambasivan, *University of California, USA*
Corina Sas, *Lancaster University, UK*
Martina Angela Sasse, *University College London (UCL), UK*
Christina Satchell, *The University of Melbourne, Australia*
James Scott, *Microsoft Research, UK*
Andrew Sears, *Rochester Institute of Technology, USA*
Abigail Sellen, *Microsoft Research, UK*
N. Sadat Shami, *IBM Research, USA*
Rajinder Sodhi, *University of Illinois at Urbana-Champaign, USA*
Erin Solovey, *Drexel University, USA*
Danae Stanton Fraser, *University of Bath, UK*
Jürgen Steimle, *Massachusetts Institute of Technology, USA*
Wolfgang Stuerzlinger, *York University, Canada*
Hironobu Takagi, *IBM Research, Japan*
Yuichiro Takeuchi, *Sony Computer Science Laboratories, Japan*
Deborah Tatar, *Virginia Tech,*

Associate Chairs: Jaime Teevan, *Microsoft Research, USA*
John Thomas, *IBM T.J. Watson Research Center, USA*
Melanie Tory, *University of Victoria, Canada*
Zachary Toups, *New Mexico State University, USA*Deborah Tatar, *Virginia Tech*
Elise Van Den Hoven, *University of Technology Sydney, Australia*
John Vines, *Newcastle University, UK*
Daniel Vogel, *University of Waterloo, Canada*
Amy Voida, *Indiana University, USA*
Annalu Waller, *University of Dundee, Scotland, UK*
Hao-Chuan Wang, *National Tsing Hua University, Taiwan*
Nadir Weibel, *University of California San Diego, USA*
Daniel Wigdor, *University of Toronto, Canada*
Lauren Wilcox, *Georgia Institute of Technology, USA*
Maria Wolters, *University of Edinburgh, UK*
Volker Wulf, *University of Siegen and Fraunhofer FIT, Germany*
Sarita Yardi Schoenebeck, *University of Michigan, USA*
Svetlana Yarosh, *AT&T Research Labs, USA*
Thorsten Zander, *TU Berlin, Germany*
Shengdong Zhao, *National University of Singapore, Singapore*
Michelle Zhou, *IBM Research - Almaden, USA*
Xiaomu Zhou, *Rutgers University, USA*

CHI 2014 Papers and Notes Reviewers

Konstantin Aal, *University of Siegen, Germany*
Parham Aarabi, *University of Toronto, Canada*
Francisco Abad, *Universitat Politècnica de València, Spain*
Julio Abascal, *University of the Basque Country, Spain*
Evgeniy Abdulin, *Texas State University, USA*
Saeed Abdullah, *Cornell University, USA*
Troy Abel, *Virginia Tech, USA*
Gregory Abowd, *Georgia Institute of Technology, USA*
Alessandro Acquisti, *Carnegie Mellon University, USA*
Lada Adamic, *University of Michigan, USA*
Anne Adams, *UCL Interaction Centre, USA*
Anne Adams, *Simplec, UK*
Dustin Adams, *University of California, USA*
Kim Adams, *University of Alberta, Canada*
Phil Adams, *Cornell University, USA*
Idris Adjerid, *Carnegie Mellon University, USA*
Rachel Adler, *Northeastern Illinois University, USA*
Tamara Adlin, *USA*
Daniel Afergan, *Tufts University, USA*
Ana Afonso, *Universidade de Lisboa, Portugal*
Stefan Agamanolis, *Akron Children's Hospital, USA*
Maneesh Agrawala, *University of California, USA*
David Ahlström, *Alpen-Adria Universität Klagenfurt, Austria*
Salman Ahmad, *Stanford University, USA*
Teemu Ahmaniemi, *Nokia Research Center, Finland*
June Ahn, *University of Maryland, USA*
Aino Ahtinen, *VTT Technical Research Centre, Finland*
David Akers, *Stanford University, USA*
Devdatta Akhawe, *UC Berkeley, USA*
Abdullah Al Mahmud, *Delft University of Technology, Netherlands*
Vicent Alabau, *Universidad Politécnica de Valencia (UPV), Spain*
Amro Al-Akkad, *Fraunhofer Institute for Applied Information Technology (FIT), Germany*
Gazihan Alankus, *Washington University In St. Louis, USA*
Turadg Aleahmad, *Coursera, USA*
Saleem Alhabash, *Michigan State University, USA*
Abir Al-Hajri, *UBC, Canada*
Dzmitry Aliakseyeu, *Philips Research, The Netherlands*
Doris Allhutter, *Institute of Technology Assessment, Austria*
Sonya Allin, *University of Toronto, Canada*
Norman Alm, *University of Dundee, UK*
Abdullah Al-Mahmud, *Delft University of Technology, The Netherlands*
Omar Alonso, *Microsoft, USA*
Basak Alper, *University of California Santa Barbara, USA*
Mohammad Al-Smadi, *Tallinn University, Estonia*
Florian Alt, *University of Munich, Germany*
Bashar Altakrouri, *University of Luebeck, Germany*
Reem Alzahabi, *Michigan State University, USA*
Saleema Amershi, *Microsoft Research, USA*

Morgan Ames, *Stanford University, USA*
Oliver Amft, *TU Eindhoven, Netherlands*
Farshid Amirabdollahian, *University of Hertfordshire, UK*
Swamy Ananthanarayan, *University of Colorado, USA*
Margarita Anastassova, *CEA, France*
Nazanin Andalibi, *Drexel University, USA*
Erik Andersen, *University of Washington, USA*
Fraser Anderson, *University of Alberta, Canada*
Ken Anderson, *Intel Corporation, USA*
Nazareno Andrade, *Universidade Federal de Campina Grande, Brazil*
Adrienne Andrew, *University of Washington, USA*
Christopher Andrews, *Virginia Polytechnic Institute and State University, USA*
Sean Andrist, *University of Wisconsin--Madison, USA*
Marvin Andujar, *Clemson University, USA*
Leonardo Angelini, *University of Applied Sciences Western Switzerland, Svizzera*
Michelle Annett, *University of Alberta, Canada*
Craig Anslow, *Victoria University of Wellington, New Zealand*
Lisa Anthony, *University of Florida, USA*
Thomas Apperley, *The University of New South Wales, Australia*
Caroline Appert, *Université Paris-Sud, France*
Bruno Araujo, *INESC-ID, Portugal*
Daniel Archambault, *Swansea University, UK*
Carmelo Ardito, *University of Bari, Italy*
Ahmed Arif, *Ryerson University, Canada*
John Arnott, *University of Dundee, UK*
Rosa Arriaga, *Georgia Institute of Technology, USA*
Kate Arrington, *Lehigh University, USA*
Thierry Artieres, *Université Pierre Et Marie Curie, France*
Mariam Asad, *Georgia Institute of Technology, USA*
Chieko Asakawa, *IBM Research - Tokyo, Japan*
Felix-Robinson Aschoff, *University of Zurich, Switzerland*
Debi Ashenden, *Cranfield University, UK*
Maryam Ashoori, *IBM, Canada*
Ilhan Aslan, *Universität Salzburg, Austria*
Zeina Atrash, *Northwestern University, USA*
Alan Au, *University of Washington, USA*
Anne Aula, *Google, USA*
Hane Aung, *University College London, UK*
Nikolaos Avouris, *University of Patras, Greece*
Daniel Avrahami, *Intel, USA*
Katerina Avramides, *London Knowledge Lab, UK*
Yuji Ayatsuka, *Koozyt, Japan*
Matthew Aylett, *Cereproc Ltd., UK*
Ruth Aylett, *Heriot-Watt University, UK*
Mobolaji Ayoade, *Glasgow Caledonian University, UK*
Phillip Ayoub, *Pennsylvania State University, USA*
Yadid Ayzenberg, *MIT, USA*
Shiri Azenkot, *University of Washington, USA*
Maryam Azh, *National University of Singapore, Singapore*
Tamara Babaian, *Bentley College, USA*
Chris Baber, *The University of Birmingham, UK*

Benjamin Bach, *INRIA, France*
Paula Bach, *The Pennsylvania State University, USA*
Myroslav Bachynskyi, *Max-Planck Institut Für Informatik, Germany*
Jonathan Back, *University College London, UK*
Maribeth Back, *FX Palo Alto Laboratory, USA*
Norm Badler, *University of Pennsylvania, USA*
Sangwon Bae, *Yonsei University, Seoul*
Seok-Hyung Bae, *KAIST, Republic of Korea*
Ronald Baecker, *University of Toronto, Canada*
Naveen Bagalkot, *IT University of Copenhagen, Denmark*
Zhen Bai, *University of Cambridge, UK*
Gilles Bailly, *CNRS, France*
Ryan Baker, *Teachers College, USA*
Suzanne Bakken, *Columbia University, USA*
Saskia Bakker, *Eindhoven University of Technology, The Netherlands*
Eytan Bakshy, *Facebook, USA*
Madeline Balaam, *Newcastle University, UK*
Aruna Balakrishnan, *Google, USA*
Guha Balakrishnan, *MIT, USA*
Matthias Baldauf, *FTW Telecommunications Research Center, Austria*
Rebecca Balebako, *Carnegie Mellon University, USA*
Elizabeth Bales, *University of Washington, USA*
Robert Ball, *Stephen F. KAIST, Republic of Korea in State University, USA*
Stinne Ballegaard, *KORA, Denmark*
Till Ballendat, *University of Munich, Germany*
Liam Bannon, *University of Limerick, Ireland*
Nikola Banovic, *Carnegie Mellon University, USA*
Francesco Banterle, *ISTI-CNR, Italy*
Xuan Bao, *Duke University, USA*
Evan Barba, *Georgetown University, USA*
Simone Barbosa, *Pontifical Catholic University of Rio de Janeiro (PUC-Rio), Brasil*
Jakob Bardram, *IT University of Copenhagen, Denmark*
Shaowen Bardzell, *Indiana University Bloomington, USA*
Javier Bargas-Avila, *Google, Switzerland*
Louise Barkhuus, *Stockholm University, Sweden*
Connelly Barnes, *Princeton University, USA*
Douglas Barnes
Pippin Barr, *University of Malta, Malta*
Barbara Barricelli, *University of West London, UK*
Barbara Barry, *MIT Media Lab, USA*
Tom Bartindale, *Newcastle University, UK*
Christoph Bartneck, *University of Canterbury, New Zealand*
Thomas Bartoschek, *University of Münster, Germany*
Lyn Bartram, *Simon Fraser University, Canada*
Santosh Basapur, *Illinois Institute of Technology, USA*
Rahul Basole, *Georgia Institute of Technology, USA*
Arianna Bassoli, *London School of Economics, UK*
Archer Batcheller, *University of Michigan, USA*
Scott Bateman, *University of Prince Edward Island, Canada*
Oliver Bates, *Lancaster University, UK*
Agathe Battestini, *Nokia, USA*
Olivier Bau, *Samsung Research America, USA*
Patrick Baudisch, *Hasso Plattner Institute, Germany*

Christine Bauer, *Vienna University of Economics and Business, Austria*
Jared Bauer, *University of Washington, USA*
Lujo Bauer, *Carnegie Mellon University, USA*
Eric Baumer, *Cornell University, USA*
Gordon Baxter, *University of St Andrews, UK*
Philip Beaman, *University of Reading, UK*
David Beattie, *Glasgow Caledonian University, Scotland, Uk*
Michel Beaudouin-Lafon, *Université Paris-Sud, France*
Elke Beck, *University of Salzburg, Austria*
S. Ann Becker, *Florida Tech, USA*
Benjamin Bederson, *University of Maryland, USA*
Roman Bednarik, *University of Eastern Finland, Finland*
Jenay Beer, *University of South Carolina, USA*
Andrew Begel, *Microsoft Research, USA*
Marios Belk, *University of Cyprus, Cyprus*
Rachel Bellamy, *IBM Research, USA*
Francesco Bellotti, *University of Genoa, Italy*
Raquel Benbunan-Fich, *Baruch College, USA*
Peter Benda, *The University of Melbourne, Australia*
Zinaida Benenson, *University of Erlangen-Nuremberg, Germany*
Steve Benford, *University of Nottingham, UK*
Mike Bennett, *Microsoft, USA*
Peter Bennett, *University of Bristol, UK*
Frank Bentley, *Motorola Mobility Inc., USA*
David Benyon, *Edinburgh Napier University, UK*
François Bérard, *CLIPS-IMAG, France*
Bettina Berendt, *KU Leuven, Belgium*
Alistair Beresford, *University of Cambridge, England*
Ofer Bergman, *Bar-Ilan University, Israel*
Kirsten Bergmann, *Bielefeld University, Germany*
Shane Bergsma, *Johns Hopkins University, USA*
Joanna Bergstrom-Lehtovirta, *Helsinki Institute for Information Technology HIIT, Finland*
Shlomo Berkovsky, *NICTA, Australia*
Gunilla Berndtsson, *Ericsson AB, Sweden*
Regina Bernhaupt, *IRIT, France*
Olav Bertelsen, *Aarhus University, Denmark*
Florent Berthaut, *INRIA, France*
Andrew Besmer, *UNC Charlotte, USA*
Michael Best, *Georgia Institute of Technology, USA*
Katrien Beuls, *Vrije Universiteit Brussel, Belgium*
Chris Bevan, *University of Bath, UK*
Nigel Bevan, *Professional Usability Services, UK*
Anastasia Bezerianos, *Université de Paris-Sud, France*
Konstantin Beznosov, *University of British Columbia, Canada*
Anant Bhardwaj, *Massachusetts Institute of Technology, USA*
Samit Bhattacharya, *IIT Guwahati, India*
Xiaojun Bi, *Google, USA*
Andrea Bianchi, *KAIST, Republic of Korea*
Nadia Bianchi-Berthouze, *University College London, UK*
Peter Bibby, *University of Nottingham, UK*
Nicola Bidwell, *CSIR-Meraka, South Africa*
Gerald Bieber, *Fraunhofer IGD, Germany*

Ralf Biedert, *German Research Center for Artificial Intelligence (DFKI), Germany*
Jacob Biehl, *FX Palo Alto Laboratory, USA*
Matthew Bietz, *University of California, USA*
Lukas Biewald, *CrowdFlower, USA*
Ali Bigdelou, *Technical University of Munich, Germany*
Dania Bilal, *University of Tennessee, USA*
Mark Billinghurst, *University of Canterbury, New Zealand*
Dorrit Billman, *NASA Ames, USA*
Jens Binder, *University of Manchester, UK*
Jon Bird, *City University London, UK*
Max Birk, *University of Saskatchewan, Canada*
Jeremy Birnholtz, *Northwestern University, USA*
Walter Bischof, *University of Alberta, Canada*
Pradipta Biswas, *University of Cambridge, England*
Staffan Björk, *University of Gothenburg, Sweden*
Pernille Bjorn, *IT University of Copenhagen, Denmark*
Alan Blackwell, *University of Cambridge, UK*
Rachel Blagojevic, *University of Auckland, New Zealand*
Renaud Blanch, *Université Grenoble I, France*
Ann Blandford, *University College London, UK*
Benjamin Blankertz, *Berlin Institute of Technology, Germany*
Eli Blevis, *The Hong Kong Polytechnic University, USA*
Brett Bligh, *Lancaster University, UK*
Jan Blom, *Nokia Research Center, Switzerland*
Katherine Blondon, *University of Washington, USA*
Marco Blumendorf, *Yetu AG, Germany*
Susanne Bødker, *Aarhus University, Denmark*
Mads Boedker, *Copenhagen Business School, Denmark*
Kirsten Boehner, *Cornell University, USA*
Cristian Bogdan, *KTH, Sweden*
Matthias Böhmer, *German Research Center for Artificial Intelligence (DFKI), Germany*
Susanne Boll, *University of Oldenburg, Germany*
Albertus Bongers, *University Technology Sydney, Australia*
Joe Bonneau, *USA*
Matthew Bonner, *Georgia Institute of Technology, USA*
David Bonnet, *Université Paris-Sud & CNRS, France*
Elizabeth Bonsignore, *University of Maryland, USA*
Kellogg Booth, *University of British Columbia, Canada*
Jan Borchers, *RWTH Aachen University, Germany*
Silvia Bordin, *TrentoRise, Italy*
Marcela Borge, *Penn State, USA*
Michelle Borkin, *Harvard University, USA*
Alan Borning, *University of Washington, USA*
Nis Bornoe, *Aalborg University, Denmark*
Gaetano Borriello, *University of Washington, USA*
Brennon Bortz, *Virginia Polytechnic Institute and State University, USA*
Nathan Bos, *University of Michigan, USA*
Claus Bossen, *University of Aarhus, Denmark*
Paolo Bottoni, *University of Rome - 'la Sapienza', Italy*
Matt-Mouley Bouamrane, *University of Glasgow, UK*
Stephane Bouchard, *Université Du Quebec En Outaouais, Canada*
Andy Boucher, *Goldsmiths College, UK*

Nadia Boukhelifa, *INRIA Saclay, France*
Anders Bouwer, *University of Amsterdam, Netherlands*
Judy Bowen, *The University of Waikato, New Zealand*
Chris Bowers, *University of Birmingham, UK*
John Bowers, *Newcastle University, UK*
Geoffrey Bowker, *UC Irvine, USA*
Doug Bowman, *Virginia Polytechnic Institute and State University, USA*
John Boyd, *Google, Na*
Erin Bradner, *Autodesk, USA*
Erin Brady, *University of Rochester, USA*
Andrew Bragdon, *Microsoft, USA*
Jonathan Bragg, *University of Washington, USA*
Giorgio Brajnik, *University of Udine, Italy*
Pedro Branco, *University of Minho, Portugal*
Joel Brandt, *Adobe Research, USA*
Stacy Branham, *Virginia Tech, USA*
Tone Bratteteig, *University of Oslo, Norway*
Cristian Bravo-Lillo, *Carnegie Mellon University, USA*
Matthew Brehmer, *University of British Columbia, Canada*
Margot Brereton, *Queensland University of Technology, Australia*
Robert Brewer, *University of Hawaii at Manoa, USA*
Jo Briggs, *Northumbria University, UK*
Pam Briggs, *Northumbria University, UK*
Willem-Paul Brinkman, *Delft University of Technology, The Netherlands*
Katie Brittain, *Newcastle University, UK*
Juliana Brixey, *UT Health Science Center at Houston, USA*
Anke Brock, *IRIT, France*
Eric Brockmeyer, *Disney Research, USA*
Gregor Broll, *DOCOMO Euro-Labs, Germany*
Geert Brone, *University of Leuven - Campus Antwerp, Belgium*
Jonas Brönstrup, *Technical University of Berlin, Germany*
Andy Brooks, *University of California, USA*
Mark Brosnan, *University of Bath, UK*
Ryan Brotman, *Intel Corporation, USA*
Anne-Marie Brouwer, *TNO Human Factors, Netherlands*
Barry Brown, *University of California San Diego, USA*
Deana Brown, *Georgia Institute of Technology, USA*
Michael Brown, *The University of Nottingham, UK*
Jed Brubaker, *University of California, USA*
Amy Bruckman, *Georgia Institute of Technology, USA*
Gerd Bruder, *University of Würzburg, Germany*
Pascal Bruegger, *University of Applied Sciences, Switzerland*
Clemens Brunner, *Graz University of Technology, Austria*
Miguel Bruns Alonso, *Eindhoven University of Technology, The Netherlands*
Anders Bruun, *Aalborg University, Denmark*
Nick Bryan-Kinns, *Queen Mary, UK*
Martin Brynskov, *Aarhus University, Denmark*
Michael Brzozowski, *Google, USA*
George Buchanan, *City University London, UK*
Sarah Buchanan, *University of Central Florida, USA*
Karolina Buchner, *Yahoo! Labs, USA*
Elizabeth Buie, *Northumbria University, UK*
Andrea Bunt, *University of Manitoba, Canada*

Cody Buntain, *University of Maryland, USA*
Judee Burgoon, *University of Arizona, USA*
Stefano Burigat, *University of Udine, Italy*
Moira Burke, *Facebook, USA*
Gary Burnett, *University of Nottingham, UK*
Margaret Burnett, *Oregon State University, USA*
Jesse Burstyn, *Queen's University, Canada*
Chris Burton, *University of Edinburgh, UK*
Jerry Busby, *Lancaster University, UK*
Marc Busch, *CURE - Center for Usability Research & Engineering, Austria*
Georg Buscher, *Microsoft, USA*
Monika Buscher, *Lancaster University, UK*
Stefano Bussolon, *Università di Trento, Italy*
Brian Butler, *UMD, USA*
D. Alex Butler, *Microsoft Research, UK*
Fabio Buttussi, *University of Udine, Italy*
Ayse Buyuktur, *University of Michigan, USA*
Daragh Byrne, *Arizona State University, USA*
Michael Byrne, *Rice University, USA*
Béatrice Cahour, *CNRS Télécom Paristech, France*
Kelly Caine, *Clemson University, USA*
Paul Cairns, *University of York, UK*
Maya Cakmak, *University of Washington, USA*
Jeffrey Calcaterra, *IBM Corporation, USA*
Roberto Calderon, *University of British Columbia, Canada*
André Calero Valdez, *RWTH Aachen University, Germany*
Janko Calic, *CVSS, UK*
Chris Callison-Burch, *Johns Hopkins University, USA*
Gaelle Calvary, *Grenoble Institute of Technology, France*
Licia Calvi, *NHTV Breda University of Applied Sciences, The Netherlands*
L Jean Camp, *Indiana University, USA*
Jose Campos, *Universidade do Minho, Portugal*
Heloisa Candello, *University of Brighton, UK*
Angelo Cangelosi, *Plymouth University, UK*
Cristina Cannone, *Università degli Studi di Milano, Italy*
Robert Capra, *University of North Carolina at Chapel Hill, USA*
Baptiste Caramiaux, *Goldsmiths College, London*
Giuseppe Carenini, *University of British Columbia, Canada*
Stefan Carmien, *University of Colorado, Spain*
Davide Carneiro, *University of Minho, Portugal*
Sheelagh Carpendale, *University of Calgary, Canada*
Luis Carriço, *University of Lisbon, Portugal*
John Carroll, *The Pennsylvania State University, USA*
Scott Carter, *FX Palo Alto Laboratory, USA*
Thomas Carter, *University of Bristol, UK*
Samuel Carton, *Northwestern University, USA*
Mark Cartwright, *Northwestern University, USA*
Géry Casiez, *University of Lille & INRIA Lille, France*
Alvaro Cassinelli, *University of Tokyo (todai), Japan*
Steven Castellucci, *York University, Canada*
Marcelo Cataldo, *Carnegie Mellon University, USA*
Grevet Catherine, *GVU Center, USA*
Abigail Cauchi, *Swansea University, UK*

Marc Cavazza, *University of Tesside, UK*
James Caverlee, *Texas A&M University, USA*
Melissa Cefkin, *IBM Research, USA*
Robert Cercos, *RMIT University, Australia*
Daniel Cernea, *University of Kaiserslautern, Germany*
Matteo Cesana, *Politecnico di Milano, Italy*
Pablo Cesar, *CWI, The Netherlands*
Ruy Cevantes, *UC Irvine, USA*
Elizabeth Cha, *Personal Robotics Lab, USA*
Samidh Chakrabarti, *Google, USA*
Matthew Chalmers, *University of Glasgow, UK*
Teresa Chambel, *University of Lisbon, Portugal*
Alan Chamberlain, *The University of Nottingham, UK*
Erik Champion, *Curtin University, Australia*
Deborah Chan, *University Health Network, Canada*
Joel Chan, *University of Pittsburgh, USA*
Liwei Chan, *Academia Sinica, Taiwan*
Angela Chang, *MIT Media Lab, USA*
Keng-Hao Chang, *University of California, Berkeley*
Remco Chang, *Tufts University, USA*
Peter Chapman, *University of Nottingham, UK*
Olivier Chapuis, *Université Paris-Sud, France*
Catherine Chase, *Carnegie Mellon University, USA*
Duen Horng (polo) Chau, *Georgia Institute of Technology, USA*
Beenish Chaudry, *Indiana University, USA*
Fang Chen, *Tsinghua University, Spain*
Gaowei Chen, *Pittsburg University,*
Hsiang-Ting Chen, *University of Tokyo, Taiwan*
Jay Chen, *New York University, USA*
Jilin Chen, *IBM Research, USA*
Judy Chen, *University of California, USA*
Liming Chen, *University of Ulster, UK*
Monchu Chen, *University of Madeira, Portugal*
Xiang 'Anthony' Chen, *Carnegie Mellon University, USA*
Yi-Shin Chen, *National Tsing Hua University, Taiwan*
Britte Cheng, *SRI International, USA*
Kai-Yin Cheng, *Microsoft Research Asia, Taiwan*
Lung-Pan Cheng, *National Taiwan University, Germany*
Shiwei Cheng, *Zhejiang University of Technology, China*
Mauro Cherubini, *Telefonica Research, Italy*
Marshini Chetty, *University of Maryland, USA*
Gifford Cheung, *University of Washington, USA*
Ed Chi, *Google, USA*
Pei-Yu Chi, *University of California, USA*
Sonia Chiasson, *Carleton University, Canada*
Mark Chignell, *University of Toronto, Canada*
Parmit Chilana, *University of Waterloo, USA*
Lydia Chilton, *MIT CSAIL, USA*
Alvin Chin, *Nokia Research Center, China*
George Chin, *Pacific Northwest National Laboratory, USA*
Clark Chinn, *Rutgers University,*
Winyu Chinthammit, *University of Tasmania, KAIST, Republic of Korea*
Eun Kyoung Choe, *University of Washington, USA*
Erik Choi, *Rutgers University, USA*

Ming Ki Chong, *Lancaster University, UK*
Wen Huei Chou, *Yunline University of Science and Technology, Taiwan*
Tanzeem Choudhury, *Dartmouth College, USA*
Ellen Christiansen, *Mads Clausen Institute, Denmark*
Georgios Christou, *Cyprus College, Cyprus*
Hao-Hua Chu, *National Taiwan University, Taiwan*
Jason Chuang, *University of Washington, USA*
Tyng-Ruey Chuang, *Academia Sinica, Taiwan*
Chia-Fang Chung, *University of Washington, USA*
Eunki Chung, *Carnegie Mellon University, USA*
Karen Church, *Telefonica Research, Spain*
Elizabeth Churchill, *eBay Research Lab, USA*
Marcelo Cicconet, *New York University, USA*
Jesse Cirimele, *Stanford University, USA*
Gabriel Cirio
Adrian Clark, *University of Canterbury, New Zealand*
Alan Clark, *Northwestern University, USA*
Lillian Clark, *University of Portsmouth, UK*
Rachel Clarke, *Newcastle University, UK*
James Clawson, *Georgia Institute of Technology, USA*
Adrian Clear, *Lancaster University, UK*
Tamara Clegg, *University of Maryland, USA*
Torkil Clemmensen, *Copenhagen Business School, Denmark*
Sue Cobb, *University of Nottingham, UK*
Michael Coburn, *RMIT University, Australia*
Gilbert Cockton, *Northumbria University, UK*
Gabe Cohn, *University of Washington, USA*
Marisa Cohn, *University of California Irvine, USA*
Michael Cohn, *Compukol Communications LLC, USA*
Jared Cole, *Carnegie Mellon University, USA*
Heather Cole-Lewis, *Columbia University, USA*
Lizzie Coles-Kemp, *Royal Holloway, UK*
Christopher Collins, *University of Ontario Institute of Technology, Canada*
Kevyn Collins-Thompson, *University of Michigan, USA*
Sébastien Combéfis, *Université Catholique de Louvain, Belgium*
Cristina Conati, *University of British Columbia, Canada*
Karin Coninx, *Hasselt University, Belgium*
Kay Connelly, *Indiana University Bloomington, USA*
Sunny Consolvo, *Google, USA*
Stéphane Conversy, *ENAC, France*
Gregorio Convertino, *Xerox Research Center Europe, Italy*
Perry Cook, *Princeton Computer Science, USA*
Michael Cooke, *Trinity College Dublin, Ireland*
Kovila Coopamootoo, *Newcastle University, UK*
Seth Cooper, *University of Washington, USA*
Andrew Cordar, *University of Florida, USA*
Raymundo Cornejo, *CICESE, Mexico*
Nicola Corradi, *Università di Padova, Italy*
Dan Cosley, *Cornell University, USA*
Joao Costa, *University of Ontario Institute of Technology, Canada*
Marc Cavazza, *University of Tesside, UK*
Gennaro Costagliola, *University of Salerno, Italy*
Enrico Costanza, *University of Southampton, UK*
James Coughlan, *Smith-Kettlewell Eye Research Institute, USA*

Tim Coughlan, *The University of Nottingham, UK*
Paul Coulton, *Lancaster University, UK*
Scott Counts, *Microsoft Research, USA*
Céline Coutrix, *Université Joseph Fourier, France*
Lynne Coventry, *University of Northumbria, UK*
Benjamin Cowan, *University of Birmingham, UK*
Anna Cox, *University College London, UK*
David Coyle, *University of Bristol, UK*
Michael Crabb, *University of Dundee, Scotland, UK*
Claire Craig, *Sheffield Hallam University, UK*
Scotty Craig, *Arizona State University,*
Henriette Cramer, *Yahoo! Labs, USA*
Meg Cramer, *UC Irvine, USA*
Angela Crandall, *iHub, Kenya*
Justin Cranshaw, *Carnegie Mellon University, USA*
Charles Crook, *University of Nottingham, UK*
Andrew Crossan, *University of Glasgow, UK*
R. Jordan Crouser, *Tufts University, USA*
Kevin Crowston, *Syracuse University, USA*
David Crundall, *University of Nottingham, UK*
Weiwei Cui, *Microsoft Research Asia, China*
Yanqing Cui, *Nokia Research Center, Finland*
Franco Curmi, *Lancaster University, UK*
Simone Cutini, *Università di Padova, Italy*
Edward Cutrell, *Microsoft Research India, India*
Chandrika Cycil, *Brunel University, UK*
Allen Cypher, *IBM Research - Almaden, USA*
Mary Czerwinski, *Microsoft Research, USA*
Alexei Czeskis, *Google, USA*
Raimund Dachselt, *Technische Universität Dresden, Germany*
Palle Dahlstedt, *Chalmers,*
Peng Dai, *Google, USA*
Florian Daiber, *DFKI German Research Center for AI, Germany*
Peter Dalsgaard, *Aarhus University, Denmark*
Ruth Dalton, *Northumbria University, UK*
Sashikanth Damaraju, *Texas A&M University, USA*
Chi Tai Dang, *University of Augsburg, Germany*
Andreea Danielescu, *Arizona State University, USA*
Darcy Dapra, *Google, USA*
Sauvik Das, *Carnegie Mellon University, USA*
Jennifer Davidson, *Oregon State University, USA*
Nigel Davies, *Lancaster University, UK*
James Davis, *UC Santa Cruz, USA*
Janet Davis, *Grinnell College, USA*
Katie Davis, *University of Washington,*
Richard Davis, *Singapore Management University, Singapore*
Rahmad Dawood, *Universitas Syiah Kuala, Indonesia*
Munmun de Choudhury, *Microsoft Research, USA*
Tjerk de Greef, *Delft University of Technology, The Netherlands*
Edward de Guzman, *Autodesk, USA*
Martin de Jode, *University College London, UK*
Daniele de Massari, *Fondazione Ospedale San Camillo, Italy*
Clarisse de Souza, *PUC-Rio, Brazil*

Cleidson de Souza, *Universidade Federal do Pará, Brazil*
David Dearman, *Twitter, USA*
Rob Deline, *Microsoft Research, USA*
Nicola Dell, *University of Washington, USA*
Robert Deloatch, *University of Illinois at Urbana-Champaign, USA*
Cagatay Demiralp, *Stanford University, USA*
Carrie Demmans Epp, *University of Toronto, Canada*
Nick Depalma, *Massachusetts Institute of Technology, USA*
Jan Derboven, *IBBT-KU Leuven, Belgium*
Katie Derthick, *University of Washington, USA*
Parag Deshpande, *Umeå Institute of Design, Sweden*
Audrey Desjardins, *Simon Fraser University, Canada*
Heather Desurvire, *Behavioristics, USA*
Sebastian Deterding, *Hans Bredow Institute for Media Research, Germany*
Laura Devendorf, *UC Berkeley, USA*
Guy Dewsbury, *Gdewsbury, UK*
Anind Dey, *Carnegie Mellon University, USA*
Barbara di Eugenio, *University of Illinois, USA*
Nicholas Diakopoulos, *Rutgers University, USA*
E.ilana Diamant, *University of Pittsburgh, USA*
Michael Dickard, *Ohio University, USA*
Margaret Dickey-Kurdziolek, *Virginia Tech, USA*
Sarah Diefenbach, *Folkwang University of the Arts, Germany*
Paul Dietz, *Microsoft, USA*
Tawanna Dillahunt, *Carnegie Mellon University, USA*
Jill Dimond, *Sassafras Tech Collective, USA*
Christian Dindler, *Aarhus University, Denmark*
Xianghua Ding, *Fudan University, China*
Abdigani Diriye, *Carnegie Mellon University, USA*
Betsy Disalvo, *Georgia Institute of Technology, USA*
Carl Disalvo, *Georgia Institute of Technology, USA*
Anke Dittmar, *University of Rostock, Germany*
Stephen Diverdi, *Adobe Systems Inc, USA*
Alan Dix, *Lancaster University, UK*
Sidney D'mello, *University of Notre Dame, USA*
Chuong do, *Coursera,*
Gavin Doherty, *Trinity College Dublin, Ireland*
Lynn Dombrowski, *University of California Irvine, USA*
Judith Donath, *MIT, USA*
Tao Dong, *University of Michigan, USA*
Birsen Donmez, *University of Toronto, Canada*
Marco Donnarumma, *Goldsmiths College, UK*
Jonathan Donner, *Microsoft Research India, USA*
Mira Dontcheva, *Adobe Research, USA*
James Doodson, *University of Leicester, England, UK*
Tanja Döring, *University of Bremen, Germany*
Marian Dörk, *Newcastle University, UK*
Brian Dorn, *University of Nebraska at Omaha, USA*
Michael Dorsch, *University of Michigan, USA*
Afsaneh Doryab, *Carnegie Mellon University, USA*
Jakub Dostal, *University of St Andrews, UK*
Wenwen Dou, *University of North Carolina at Charlotte, USA*
Andre Doucette, *University of Saskatchewan, Canada*

Audubon Dougherty, *MIT, USA*
Mark Doughty, *University of Lincoln, UK*
Paul Dourish, *University of California, USA*
John Downs, *The University of Melbourne, Australia*
Julie Downs, *Carnegie Mellon University, USA*
Toby Dragon, *Ithaca College, USA*
Christoph Draxler, *LMU München, Germany*
Martha Driessnack, *Oregon Health & Science University, USA*
Laurie Dringus, *Nova Southeastern University, USA*
Milena Droumeva, *Simon Fraser University, Canada*
Steven Drucker, *Microsoft Research, USA*
Allison Druin, *University of Maryland, USA*
Honglu Du, *Palo Alto Research Center, USA*
Ruofei Du, *Microsoft Research Asia, China*
Tina Du, *University of South KAIST, Republic of Korea ralia, Australia*
Carlos Duarte, *Universidade de Lisboa, Portugal*
Luís Duarte, *University of Lisbon, Portugal*
Emmanuel Dubois, *University of Toulouse, France*
Nicolas Ducheneaut, *Palo Alto Research Center, USA*
Andrew Duchowski, *Clemson University, USA*
Tobias Duckworth, *University of Salford, UK*
Casey Dugan, *IBM, USA*
Geoffrey Duggan, *University of Exeter, UK*
Susan Dumais, *Microsoft Research, USA*
Bruno Dumas, *Vrije Universiteit Brussel, Belgium*
Sean Duncan, *Indiana University, USA*
Lucy Dunne, *University College Dublin, Ireland*
Paul Dunphy, *Newcastle University, UK*
Andreas Dünser, *CSIRO - CCI, Australia*
Sophie Dupuy-Chessa, *University of Grenoble, France*
Shree Durga, *University of Wisconsin, USA*
Abigail Durrant, *Newcastle University, UK*
Erik Duval, *KU Leuven, Belgium*
Tim Dwyer, *Monash University, Australia*
Jason Dykes, *City University London, UK*
James Eagan, *Télécom-Paristech, France*
Sarah Eagle, *University of Bristol, UK*
David Ebert, *Purdue University, USA*
Florian Echtler, *Siemens Corporate Technology, Germany*
Dean Eckles, *Stanford University, USA*
Ernest Edmonds, *De Montfort University, UK*
Alistair Edwards, *University of York, UK*
Keith Edwards, *Georgia Institute of Technology, USA*
Kate Ehrlich, *IBM, USA*
Michael Eisenberg, *University of Colorado, USA*
Inger Ekman, *Aalto School of Economics, Finland*
Rana El Kaliouby, *University of Cambridge, UK*
Irene Eleta, *University of Maryland, USA*
Gunnar Ellingsen, *University of Tromsø, Norway*
Dan Ellis, *Columbia University, USA*
Geoff Ellis, *Lancaster University, UK*
Nicole Ellison, *University of Michigan, USA*
Lia Emanuel, *University of Bath,*
Bernadette Emsenhuber, *Johannes Kepler University of Linz, Austria*

Alex Endert, *Pacific Northwest National Laboratory, USA*
Klaus-Peter Engelbrecht, *Telekom Innovation Laboratories, Germany*
David England, *Liverpool John Moores University, UK*
Arvid Engström, *Mobile Life @ Stockholm University, Sweden*
Johan Engström, *Volvo Group Trucks Technology, Sweden*
Barrett Ens, *University of Manitoba, Canada*
Clayton Epp, *University of Saskatchewan, Canada*
Daniel Epstein, *University of Washington, USA*
Sheena Erete, *Northwestern University, USA*
Ingrid Erickson, *Rutgers University, USA*
Thomas Erickson, *IBM Research - T. J. Watson, USA*
Elina Eriksson, *KTH, Sweden*
Eva Eriksson, *Chalmers University of Technology, Sweden*
Lizbeth Escobedo, *Universidad Autonoma de Baja California, Mexico*
Parisa Eslambolchilar, *Future Interaction Technologies Lab, UK*
Sergio Espana, *Universitat Politecnica de Valencia, Spain*
Augusto Esteves, *University of Madeira, Portugal*
Michael Evans, *British Broadcasting Corporation, UK*
Vanessa Evers, *University of Twente, The Netherlands*
Marc Fabri, *Leeds Metropolitan University, UK*
Jerry Fails, *Montclair State University, USA*
Shamal Faily, *University of Oxford, UK*
Anthony Faiola, *Indiana University (IUPUI), USA*
Fiona Fairlie, *Glasgow Caledonian University, UK*
Majdi Faleh
Josef Faller, *Graz University of Technology, Austria*
Daniel Fallman, *Umeå University, Sweden*
Min Fan, *Simon Fraser University Surrey, Canada*
Xianyong Fang, *Anhui University, China*
Jill Fantauzza, *Georgia Institute of Technology, USA*
Jan Erik Farbrot, *Institute for Energy Technology / OECD Halden Reactor Project, Norway*
Elisabetta Farella, *DEIS - University of Bologna, Italy*
Shelly Farnham, *Microsoft Research, USA*
Umer Farooq, *The Pennsylvania State University, USA*
Karen Farris, *University of Michigan, USA*
Michael Farrugia, *UCD Dublin, Luxembourg*
Rosta Farzan, *University of Pittsburgh, USA*
Haakon Faste, *California College of the Arts, USA*
Andrew Faulring, *Carnegie Mellon University, USA*
Stu Favilla, *Swinburne University of Technology, Australia*
Melanie Feinberg, *University of Texas at KAIST, Republic of Korea in, USA*
Jean-Daniel Fekete, *INRIA, France*
Niels Feldmann, *Karlsruhe Institute of Technology (KIT), Germany*
Karla Felix Navarro, *University of Technology Sydney, Australia*
Deborah Fels, *Ryerson University, Canada*
Sidney Fels, *University of British Columbia, Canada*
Adrienne Felt, *Google, USA*
Jinjuan Feng, *University of Maryland, USA*
Robert Ferguson, *McGill University, Canada*
Jennifer Fernquist, *Google,*
Denzil Ferreira, *University of Oulu, Finland*
Pedro Ferreira, *Mobile Life @ KTH, Sweden*

Suely Fragoso, *Federal University of Rio Grande do Sul (UFRGS), Brazil*
Anders Frank, *Swedish National Defence College, Sweden*
Mario Frank, *UC Berkeley, Germany*
Mike Fraser, *University of Bristol, UK*
Christopher Frauenberger, *University of Sussex, UK*
Dustin Freeman, *University of Toronto, Canada*
Euan Freeman, *University of Glasgow, Scotland, UK*
Andre Freire, *Universidade de Lisboa, Brazil*
Luanne Freund, *University of British Columbia, Canada*
Jill Freyne, *CSIRO, Australia*
Sarah-Christin Freytag, *Berlin Institute of Technology, Germany*
Enrique Frias-Martinez, *Telefonica Research, Spain*
Adrian Friday, *Lancaster University, UK*
Doron Friedman, *The Interdisciplinary Center, Israel*
Mathias Frisch, *MID Gmbh, Germany*
Chris Frisina, *Virginia Tech, USA*
Jonas Fritsch, *Aarhus University, Denmark*
Mario Fritz, *MPI Informatik, Germany*
Thomas Fritz, *University of Zurich, Switzerland*
Bernd Froehlich, *Bauhaus Universität Weimar, Germany*
Jon Froehlich, *University of Maryland, USA*
David Frohlich, *University of Surrey, UK*
Peter Fröhlich, *FTW Telecommunications Research Center, Austria*
Erik Frøkjær, *Københavns Universitet, Denmark*
Mads Frost, *IT University of Copenhagen, Denmark*
Wai-Tat Fu, *University of Illinois at Urbana-Champaign, USA*
Georg Fuchs, *Fraunhofer Institute Intelligent Analysis and Information Systems IAIS, Germany*
Johannes Fuchs, *University, Germany*
Verena Fuchsberger, *ICT&S Center, Austria*
Kaori Fujinami, *Tokyo University of Agriculture and Technology, Japan*
Kentarou Fukuda, *IBM Research - Tokyo, Japan*
Benjamin Fung, *McGill University, Canada*
Mathias Funk, *Eindhoven University of Technology, The Netherlands*
Silvia Gabrielli, *Create-Net, Italy*
Hind Gacem, *Télécom-Paristech, France*
Martin Gaedke, *Technische Universität Chemnitz, Germany*
Andrea Gaggioli, *Catholic University of Milan, Italy*
Sarah Gallacher, *UCL, UK*
Teresa Galvão, *Universidade do Porto, Portugal*
Maribeth Gandy, *Georgia Institute of Technology, USA*
Eva Ganglbauer, *Vienna University of Technology, Austria*
Ge Gao, *Cornell University, USA*
Ruth García-Gavilanes, *Universitat Pompeu Fabra, Spain*
Simson Garfinkel, *MIT, USA*
R. Kelly Garrett, *Ohio State University, USA*
Daniel Gartenberg, *George Mason University, USA*
Franca Garzotto, *HOC-Politecnico di Milano, Italy*
Nadia Gauducheau, *ICD-CNRS, France*
Steffen Gauglitz, *University of California, USA*
Paul Gault, *University of Dundee, UK*
William Gaver, *Goldsmiths College, UK*
Tom Gedeon, *KAIST, Republic of Korea ralian National University, Australia*

Nils Gehlenborg, *Harvard Medical School, USA*
Sven Gehring, *German Research Center for Artificial Intelligence (DFKI), Germany*
Johanna Gelderblom, *University of Pretoria, South Africa*
Hans Gellersen, *Lancaster University, UK*
Aaron Genest, *University of Saskatchewan, Canada*
Kallirroi Georgila, *University of Southern California, USA*
Elizabeth Gerber, *Northwestern University, USA*
Peter Gerjets, *Knowledge Media Research Center*
Jens Gerken, *ICT Innovative Communication Technologies AG, Germany*
Kathrin Gerling, *University of Lincoln, UK*
David Gerritsen, *Carnegie Mellon University, USA*
Paul Gestwicki, *Ball State University, USA*
Luc Geurts, *KU Leuven, Belgium*
Werner Geyer, *IBM Research - T. J. Watson, USA*
Giuseppe Ghiani, *ISTI-CNR, Italy*
George Ghinea, *Brunel University, UK*
Emilien Ghomi, *Université Paris-Sud, France*
Maysam Ghovanloo, *Georgia Institute of Technology, USA*
Alicia Gibb, *Nycresistor, USA*
Lorna Gibson, *University of Dundee, UK*
Eric Gilbert, *Georgia Institute of Technology, USA*
Kathleen Gilbert, *Indiana University, USA*
Alastair Gill, *University of Surrey, UK*
Kiel Gilleade, *Liverpool John Moores University, UK*
Nicholas Gillian, *MIT Media Lab, USA*
Stephen Gilroy, *Teesside University, UK*
Shuli Gilutz, *Interdisciplinary Center (IDC) Herzliya, Israel*
Shiry Ginosar, *University of California, USA*
Jeffrey Girard, *University of Pittsburgh, USA*
Audrey Girouard, *Carleton University, Canada*
Voula Gkatzidou, *Brunel University, UK*
Dylan Glas, *ATR, Japan*
Marie Glasemann, *Aalborg University, Denmark*
Michael Glueck, *University of Toronto, Canada*
Janet Go, *Autodesk, USA*
Kentaro Go, *University of Yamanashi, Japan*
Fernand Gobet, *University of Liverpool, UK*
Mayank Goel, *University of Washington, USA*
Anja Goeritz, *University of Freiburg, Germany*
Sean Goggins, *University of Missouri, USA*
Wooi Boon Goh, *Nanyang Technological University, Singapore*
Sergio Goldenberg, *Georgia Institute of Technology, USA*
Scott Golder, *Cornell University, USA*
Ilya Goldin, *Carnegie Mellon University, USA*
Dan Goldman, *Adobe, USA*
David Golightly, *Experian UK, UK*
Connie Golsteijn, *Eindhoven University of Technology, Netherlands*
Evan Golub, *University of Maryland, USA*
Richard Gomer, *University of Southampton, UK*
Antonio Gomes, *Queen's University, Canada*
Rafael Gomez, *Queensland University of Technology, Australia*
Steven Gomez, *Brown University, USA*

Jorge Goncalves, *Instituto Superior Técnico, Finland*
Daniel Gonçalves, *University of Oulu, Portugal*
Tiago Gonçalves, *FCUL, Portugal*
Nan-Wei Gong, *Massachusetts Institute of Technology, USA*
Amy Gonzales, *Indiana University, USA*
Berto Gonzalez, *University of North Carolina at Charlotte, USA*
Victor Gonzalez, *University of Manchester, UK*
Walkyria Goode, *SPARK Experience, USA*
Elizabeth Goodman, *UC Berkeley, USA*
Paul Gorman, *Oregon Health & Science University, USA*
Sandy Gould, *University College London, UK*
Rúben Gouveia, *University of Madeira, Portugal*
Nitesh Goyal, *Cornell University, USA*
Kazjon Grace, *UNC Charlotte, USA*
Michele Graffeo, *University of Trento, Italy*
Connor Graham, *National University of Singapore, Singapore*
Martin Graham, *Napier University, UK*
Nicholas Graham, *Queen's University, Canada*
Klaus Gramann, *Berlin Institute of Technology, Germany*
Dimitris Grammenos, *Foundation for Research and Technology - Hellas, Greece*
Sukeshini Grandhi, *Eastern Connecticut State University, USA*
Laura Granka, *Google, USA*
Raphael Grasset, *Graz University of Technology, Austria*
Colin Gray, *Indiana University, USA*
Rebecca Gray, *Michigan State University, USA*
David Green, *Newcastle University, UK*
Keith Green, *Clemson University, USA*
Michael Greenberg, *Northwestern University, USA*
Saul Greenberg, *University of Calgary, Canada*
Chris Greenhalgh, *The University of Nottingham, UK*
Peggy Gregory, *University of Central Lancashire, UK*
Catherine Grevet, *Georgia Institute of Technology, USA*
Harry Griffin, *University College London, UK*
Erin Griffiths, *University of Virginia, USA*
Thomas Grill, *University of Salzburg, Austria*
Rebecca Grinter, *Georgia Institute of Technology, USA*
Laurent Grisoni, *University Lille, France*
Alex Groce, *Oregon State University, USA*
Georg Groh, *TU Muenchen, Germany*
Diane Gromala, *Simon Fraser University, Canada*
Kaj Grønbæk, *University of Aarhus, Denmark*
Erik Grönvall, *IT University of Copenhagen, Denmark*
Mark Gross, *Carnegie Mellon University, USA*
Shad Gross, *Indiana University Bloomington, USA*
Tom Gross, *University of Bamberg, Germany*
Jens Grossklags, *The Pennsylvania State University, USA*
Jens Grubert, *University of Technology Graz, Austria*
Shion Guha, *Cornell University, USA*
Yves Guiard, *Télécom-Paristech CNRS, France*
François Guimbretière, *Cornell University, USA*
Rebecca Gulotta, *Carnegie Mellon University, USA*
Hatice Gunes, *University of Technology, Australia*
Philip Guo, *Stanford University, USA*

Ankit Gupta, *University of Washington, USA*
Sidhant Gupta, *University of Washington, USA*
David Gurzick, *Hood College, USA*
Sean Gustafson, *Hasso Plattner Institute, Germany*
Mattia Gustarini, *University of Geneva, Switzerland*
Francisco Luis Gutiérrez Vela, *University of Granada, España*
Ricardo Gutierrez-Osuna, *Texas A&M University, USA*
Mark Guzdial, *Georgia Institute of Technology, USA*
Tajin Ha, *KAIST, S. Korea*
Joerg Haake, *Fernuniversitaet Hagen, Germany*
Eija Haapalainen Ferreira, *University of Oulu, Finland*
Eben Haber, *IBM Research - Almaden, USA*
Jonathan Haber, *University of Calgary, Canada*
Martin Hachet, *Labri-INRIA University of Bordeaux, France*
Mieke Haesen, *Hasselt University - Tul - Iminds, Belgium*
Joshua Hailpern, *Hewlett Packard, USA*
Oliver Haimson, *University of California, USA*
Julia Haines, *University of California, USA*
Maria Håkansson, *Chalmers University of Technology, Sweden*
David Hakken, *Indiana University Bloomongton, USA*
Jonna Hakkila, *University of Oulu, Finland*
Jonna Häkkilä, *Soul4design, Finland*
Jukka Häkkinen, *Aalto University School of Science and Technology, Finland*
Timothy Hale, *Partners Healthcare Inc., USA*
Aaron Halfaker, *University of Minnesota, USA*
Joseph Hall, *The Center for Democracy & Technology, USA*
Michael Haller, *University of Applied Sciences Upper KAIST, Republic of Korea ria, Austria*
Lars Hallnäs, *Chalmers University of Technology, Sweden*
John Halloran, *Coventry University, UK*
Kim Halskov, *Aarhus University, Denmark*
Christine Halverson, *IBM Research - T. J. Watson, USA*
Tim Halverson, *Air Force Research Laboratory, USA*
Martin Halvey, *Glasgow Caledonian University, UK*
Perttu Hämäläinen, *Aalto University, Finland*
William Hamilton, *Texas A&M University, USA*
Jessica Hammer, *Carnegie Mellon University, USA*
Nils Hammerla, *Newcastle University, UK*
Tracy Hammond, *Texas A&M University, USA*
Jaehyun Han, *KAIST, Republic of Korea*
Jeonghye Han, *Computer Education, Republic of Korea*
Kyungsik (keith) Han, *The Pennsylvania State University, USA*
Teng Han, *University of Bristol, China*
Jeff Hancock, *Cornell University, USA*
Mark Handel, *The Boeing Company, USA*
Alina Hang, *University of Munich, Germany*
Benjamin Hanrahan, *Virginia Polytechnic Institute and State University, France*
Derek Hansen, *Brigham Young University, USA*
John Paulin Hansen, *IT University of Copenhagen, Denmark*
Kotaro Hara, *University of Maryland, USA*
Mona Haraty, *University of British Columbia, Canada*
Marian Harbach, *Leibniz University Hannover, Germany*

Gunnar Harboe, *University of Zurich, Switzerland*
Ellie Harmon, *UC Irvine, USA*
Morten Harning, *Dialogical ApS, Denmark*
Franklin Harper, *University of Minnesota, USA*
Richard Harper, *Microsoft Research, UK*
Simon Harper, *University of Manchester, UK*
Erik Harpstead, *Carnegie Mellon University, USA*
Rikard Harr, *Umeå University, Sweden*
Chris Harrison, *Carnegie Mellon University, USA*
Daniel Harrison, *University College London, UK*
Lane Harrison, *University of North Carolina at Charlotte, USA*
Jennefer Hart, *Lancaster University, UK*
Casper Harteveld, *Northeastern University, USA*
Björn Hartmann, *University of California, USA*
Mark Hartswood, *University of Edinburgh, UK*
Andrea Hartzler, *University of Washington, USA*
Catherine Harvey, *University of Nottingham, UK*
Khalad Hasan, *University of Manitoba, Canada*
Chelsea Hash, *Polytechnic Institute of NYU, USA*
Mitsuyo Hashida, *Soai Uiversity, Japan*
Marc Hassenzahl, *Folkwang University of the Arts, Germany*
Doris Hausen, *University of Munich, Germany*
Sabrina Hauser, *Simon Fraser University, Canada*
Kirstie Hawkey, *Dalhousie University, Canada*
Eiji Hayashi, *Carnegie Mellon University, USA*
Gillian Hayes, *University of California, USA*
Helen He, *University of Calgary, Canada*
Marti Hearst, *UC Berkeley, USA*
Brent Hecht, *University of Minnesota, USA*
Per-Olof Hedvall, *Lund University, Sweden*
Jaimee Heffner, *Fred Hutchinson Cancer Research Center, USA*
Tomi Heimonen, *University of Tampere, Finland*
Eric Hekler, *Arizona State University, USA*
Robert Held, *University of California, USA*
Bradley Hemminger, *University of North Carolina, USA*
Niels Hendriks, *University of Leuven, Belgium*
David Hendry, *University of Washington, USA*
Fabian Hennecke, *University of Munich, Germany*
Nathalie Henry Riche, *Microsoft Research, USA*
Niels Henze, *University of Stuttgart, Germany*
Cormac Herley, *Microsoft Research, Ghjhj*
Hamilton Hernandez, *Queen's University, Canada*
Davinia Hernandez-Leo, *Universitat Pompeu Fabra, Spain*
Marc Herrlich, *University of Bremen, Germany*
Morten Hertzum, *University of Copenhagen, Denmark*
Philipp Herzig, *SAP Research CEC Dresden, Germany*
Phil Heslop, *Newcastle University, UK*
Luke Hespanhol, *University of Sydney, Australia*
Jan Hess, *University of Siegen, Germany*
Susan Hessey, *Brithish Telecom, UK*
Wilko Heuten, *OFFIS - Institute for Information Technology, Germany*
Clint Heyer, *IT University of Copenhagen, Denmark*
Nadja Heym, *University of Nottingham, UK*

Jutta Hild, *Fraunhofer IOSB, Germany*
Benjamin Mako Hill, *University of Washington, USA*
Serena Hillman, *Simon Fraser University, Canada*
Juan David Hincapié-Ramos, *IT University of Copenhagen, Canada*
Ken Hinckley, *Microsoft Research, USA*
Jon Hindmarsh, *King's College London, UK*
Uta Hinrichs, *University of St Andrews, UK*
Sen Hirano, *University of California, USA*
Matthew Hirsch, *MIT Media Lab, USA*
Tad Hirsch, *University of Washington, USA*
Leanne Hirshfield, *Hamilton College, USA*
Chaya Hiruncharoenvate, *Georgia Institute of Technology, USA*
Christina Hochleitner, *CURE - Center for Usability Research & Engineering, Austria*
Nadia Hocine, *Montpellier 2 University, France*
Duncan Hodges, *University of Oxford, UK*
Gray Hodgkinson, *Massey University, New Zealand*
Orland Hoeber, *University of Regina, Canada*
Jesse Hoey, *University of Waterloo, Canada*
Guy Hoffman, *IDC Herzliya, Israel*
Bernie Hogan, *University of Toronto, Canada*
Trevor Hogan, *Cork Institute of Technology, Ireland*
Andrew Hogue, *University of Ontario Institute of Technology, Canada*
James Hollan, *UCSD, USA*
Simon Holland, *The Open University, UK*
Tobias Hollerer, *University of California, USA*
Nic Hollinworth, *University of Reading, UK*
Caitlin Holman, *University of Michigan, USA*
David Holman, *Queen's University, Canada*
Hrönn Holmer, *Cornell University, USA*
Stefan Holmlid, *Linköpings universitet, Sweden*
Lars Erik Holmquist, *Indep. Consultant, USA*
Kenneth Holmqvist, *Lund University, Sweden*
Bree Holtz, *Information Studies and Media, USA*
Christian Holz, *Yahoo! Labs, USA*
Andreas Holzinger, *Graz Medical University, Austria*
Hwajung Hong, *Georgia Institute of Technology, USA*
Jason Hong, *Carnegie Mellon University, USA*
Jin-Hyuk Hong, *Carnegie Mellon University, USA*
Lichan Hong, *Google, USA*
Kristina Höök, *KTH, Sweden*
Mohammed Hoque, *University of Rochester, USA*
Michael Horn, *Northwestern University, USA*
John Horton, *Harvard University, USA*
Matthew Horton, *Child Computer Interaction Group, UK*
Simo Hosio, *University of Oulu, Finland*
Steven Houben, *IT University of Copenhagen, Denmark*
Kirralie Houghton, *Queensland University of Technology, Australia*
Robert Houghton, *The University of Nottingham, UK*
Juan Pablo Hourcade, *University of Iowa, USA*
Rachid Hourizi, *University of Bath, UK*
Aaron Houssian, *Philips Research, The Netherlands*
Andrew Howes, *University of Manchester, UK*

James Howison, *Carnegie Mellon University, USA*
Kate Howland, *University of Sussex, UK*
Iris Howley, *Carnegie Mellon University, USA*
Idris Hsi, *Microsoft, USA*
Yi-Ta Hsieh, *University of Helsinki, Finland*
Chang Hu, *Microsoft, USA*
Jun Hu, *Eindhoven University of Technology, Netherlands*
Mengdie Hu, *Georgia Institute of Technology, USA*
Y. Charlie Hu, *Purdue University, USA*
Yuheng Hu, *Arizona State University, USA*
Chung-Ching Huang, *Indiana University, USA*
Haosheng Huang, *Research Group Cartography, Austria*
Jeff Huang, *University of Washington, USA*
Kevin Huang, *Georgia Institute of Technology, USA*
Shih-Wen Huang, *University of Washington, USA*
Jochen Huber, *MIT Media Lab, USA*
Bernardo Huberman, *HP Labs, USA*
Matthew Hudson, *The University of York, UK*
Scott Hudson, *Carnegie Mellon University, USA*
David Huffaker, *Google, USA*
Amanda Hughes, *Utah State University, USA*
Julie Hui, *Northwestern University, USA*
Alina Huldtgren, *Delft University of Technology, Germany*
Jessica Hullman, *University of Michigan, USA*
Shah Rukh Humayoun, *University of Kaiserslautern, Germany*
Seth Hunter, *MIT Media Lab, USA*
Stephane Huot, *Université Paris-Sud, France*
Annika Hupfeld, *University of Nottingham, UK*
Amy Hurst, *Carnegie Mellon University, USA*
Wolfgang Hürst, *Utrecht University, The Netherlands*
Christophe Hurter, *University of Toulouse, France*
Heinrich Hussmann, *Ludwig-Maximilians-Universität München, Germany*
Dugald Hutchings, *Elon University, USA*
John Hutchinson, *Lancaster University, UK*
C.j. Hutto, *Georgia Institute of Technology, USA*
Luke Hutton, *University of St Andrews, UK*
Ebba Thora Hvannberg, *University of Iceland, Iceland*
Inseok Hwang, *KAIST, South Korea*
Sungjae Hwang, *KAIST, South Korea*
Aulikki Hyrskykari, *University of Tampere, Finland*
Ioanna Iacovides, *UCL, UK*
Djilali Idoughi, *University A. Mira of Bejaia, Algeria*
Takeo Igarashi, *The University of Tokyo, Japan*
Klas Ihme, *University of Leipzig, Germany*
Masahiko Inami, *KMD, Japan*
Todd Ingalls, *Arizona State University, USA*
Stephen Intille, *Northeastern University, USA*
Alexandra Ion, *University of Applied Sciences Upper KAIST, Republic of Korea ria, Austria*
Iulia Ion, *Google, USA*
Panos Ipeirotis, *New York University, New York*
Shamsi Iqbal, *Microsoft Research, USA*
Ellen Isaacs, *PARC, USA*

Katherine Isbister, *Polytechnic Institute of New York University, USA*
Tobias Isenberg, *INRIA, France*
Kentaro Ishii, *The University of Tokyo, Japan*
Poika Isokoski, *University of Tampere, Finland*
Ali Israr, *Disney Research, USA*
Howell Istance, *De Montfort University, UK*
Yuichi Itoh, *Osaka University, Japan*
Bret Jackson, *University of New Mexico, USA*
Daniel Jackson, *Newcastle University, UK*
Steven Jackson, *Cornell University, USA*
Tanner Jackson, *Princeton, USA*
Robert Jacob, *Tufts University, USA*
Mattias Jacobsson, *Mobile Life @ SICS, Sweden*
Nassim Jafarinaimi, *Georgia Institute of Technology, USA*
Nils Jäger, *University of Nottingham, UK*
Mohit Jain, *University of Toronto, Canada*
Sharad Jaiswal, *Bell Labs India, India*
Timo Jakobi, *University of Siegen, Germany*
Mikkel Jakobsen, *University of Copenhagen, Denmark*
Hamid R. Jamali, *Kharazmi University, Iran*
Anthony Jameson, *German Research Center for Artificial Intelligence (DFKI), Germany*
Jacek Jankowski, *Digital Enterprise Research Institute, France*
Maddy Janse, *Philips Research, The Netherlands*
Bernard Jansen, *The Pennsylvania State University, USA*
Yvonne Jansen, *Université Paris-Sud, France*
Christian Janssen, *Smith-Kettlewell Eye Research Institute, USA*
Joris Janssen, *Eindhoven University of Technology, The Netherlands*
Ryan Janzen, *University of Toronto, Canada*
Tim Jay, *University of Bristol, UK*
K. Neil Jenkings, *Newcastle University, UK*
Tom Jenkins, *Georgia Institute of Technology, USA*
Carlos Jensen, *Oregon State University, USA*
Jennifer Jenson, *York University, Canada*
Seokhee Jeon, *ETH Zurich, Switzerland*
Jin-Woo Jeong, *Hanyang University, Republic of Korea*
Hans-Christian Jetter, *University of Konstanz, UK*
Jiepu Jiang, *University of Massachusetts Amherst, USA*
Nan Jiang, *Bournemouth University, UK*
Marina Jirotka, *University of Oxford, UK*
Kazuhiro Jo, *IAMAS, Japan*
Bonnie John, *IBM Research, USA*
Andrew Johnson, *University of Illinois at Chicago, USA*
Gabe Johnson, *Blank Slate Systems, USA*
Jeff Johnson, *UI Wizards, USA*
Kimberly Johnson, *Google, USA*
Maritza Johnson, *University of California, USA*
Mikael Johnson, *Helsinki University of Technology, Finland*
Steven Johnson, *Temple U., USA*
Aditya Johri, *Virginia Tech, USA*
Tero Jokela, *Nokia Research Center, Finland*
Brett Jones, *University of Illinois at Urbana-Champaign, USA*
J. Adam Jones, *University of Southern California, USA*

Malcolm Jones, *Northumbria University, UK*
Matt Jones, *Swansea University, Wales, UK*
Steve Jones, *University of Waikato, New Zealand*
William Jones, *University of Washington, USA*
Martin Jonsson, *Södertörn University, Sweden*
Sergi Jorda, *Universitat Pompeu Fabra, Spain*
Joaquim Jorge, *INESC-ID, Portugal*
Rui Jose, *Universidade do Minho, Portugal*
Anirudha Joshi, *Indian Institute of Technology, India*
Neel Joshi, *Microsoft, USA*
Ricardo Jota, *University of Toronto, Portugal*
M.-Carmen Juan, *UPV, Spain*
Oskar Juhlin, *Mobile Life @ Stockholm University, Sweden*
Satu Jumisko-Pyykkö, *Tampere University of Technology, Finland*
Heekyoung Jung, *University of Cincinnati, USA*
Malte Jung, *Cornell University, USA*
Tzyy-Ping Jung, *UCSD, USA*
Yumi Jung, *Michigan State University, USA*
Beyerer Jürgen, *Karlsruhe Institute of Technology (KIT), Germany*
Marko Jurmu, *University of Oulu, Finland*
Mike Just, *Glasgow Caledonian University, UK*
Antti Jylhä, *University of Helsinki, Finland*
Dennis Kafura, *Virginia Tech, USA*
Anne Kaikkonen, *Nokia Corporation, Finland*
Sanjay Kairam, *Stanford University, USA*
Yasuaki Kakehi, *Keio University, Japan*
Matthew Kam, *American Institutes for Research, USA*
Noreen Kamal, *University of British Columbia, Canada*
Alexander Kan, *The University of Melbourne, Australia*
Sean Kandel, *Stanford University, USA*
Eser Kandogan, *IBM, USA*
Bridget Kane, *Trinity College Dublin, Ireland*
Shaun Kane, *University of Maryland Baltimore County, USA*
Ruogu Kang, *Carnegie Mellon University, USA*
Marije Kanis, *Brunel University, UK*
Gopinaath Kannabiran, *Indiana University, USA*
Anne Marie Kanstrup, *Aalborg University, Denmark*
Ashish Kapoor, *Microsoft Research, USA*
Dennis Kappen, *University of Ontario Institute of Technology, Canada*
Evangelos Kapros, *Trinity College Dublin, Ireland*
Maurits Kaptein, *Eindhoven University of Technology, The Netherlands*
Victor Kaptelinin, *Umeå University, Sweden*
Mustafa Karagozler, *Disney Research, USA*
Karrie Karahalios, *University of Illinois, USA*
Amela Karahasanovic, *SINTEF ICT, Norway*
John Karat, *IBM Research - T. J. Watson, USA*
David Karger, *MIT, USA*
Thorsten Karrer, *RWTH Aachen University, Germany*
Christos Katsanos, *Hellenic Open University, Greece*
Brian Katz, *LIMSI-CNRS, France*
Larry Katz, *University of Calgary, Canada*
Andrea Kavanaugh, *Virginia Tech, USA*
Fahim Kawsar, *Phd Candidate, Japan*

Matthew Kay, *University of Waterloo, Canada*
Joseph 'jofish' Kaye, *Nokia, USA*
Gabriella Kazai, *Microsoft Research, UK*
Konstantinos Kazakos, *Newcastle University, UK*
Rubaiat Habib Kazi, *National University of Singapore, Canada*
Elizabeth Kaziunas, *University of Michigan, USA*
Wendy Keay-Bright, *University of Wales Institute, Wales, UK*
Daniel Keefe, *University of Minnesota, USA*
Brian Keegan, *Northeastern University, USA*
Flavius Kehr, *University of Koblenz-Landau, Germany*
Caitlin Kelleher, *Washington University, USA*
Wendy Kellogg, *IBM Research - T. J. Watson, USA*
Diane Kelly, *University of North Carolina, USA*
Ryan Kelly, *University of Bath, UK*
Logan Kendall, *University of Washington, USA*
Denisa Kera, *National University of Singapore, Singapore*
Dagmar Kern, *Bertrandt Ingenieurbüro Gmbh, Germany*
Andruid Kerne, *Texas A&M University, USA*
Andreas Kerren, *Linnaeus University, Sweden*
Karina Kervin, *University of Michigan, USA*
Cem Keskin, *Microsoft Research, UK*
Rilla Khaled, *University of Malta, Malta*
Mohammadreza Khalilbeigi, *Darmstadt University of Technology, Germany*
Vassilis-Javed Khan, *NHTV Breda University of Applied Sciences, The Netherlands*
Ahmed Kharrufa, *Newcastle University, UK*
Rohit Khot, *RMIT University, Australia*
Vera Khovanskaya, *Cornell University, USA*
Emre Kiciman, *Microsoft Research, USA*
Wolf Kienzle, *Microsoft Research, USA*
Johan Kildal, *Nokia, Finland*
Dongwhan Kim, *Seoul National University, Republic of Korea*
Hyang-Sook Kim, *St. Norbert's College, USA*
Hyung Nam Kim, *Northwestern University, USA*
Joy Kim, *Stanford University, USA*
Juho Kim, *Massachusetts Institute of Technology, USA*
Ju-Whan Kim, *KAIST, Republic of Korea*
Kibum Kim, *Kochi University of Technology, Japan*
Seung Wook Kim, *Samsung R&D Center Silicon Valley, USA*
Seungjun Kim, *Carnegie Mellon University, USA*
Si Jung Kim, *University of Central Florida, USA*
Sung-Hee Kim, *Purdue University, USA*
Sunyoung Kim, *Carnegie Mellon University, USA*
Taemie Kim, *Sociometric Solutions, USA*
Kenrick Kin, *University of California, USA*
Jennifer King, *University of California, USA*
Michael Kipp, *Augsburg University of Applied Sciences, Germany*
Reuben Kirkham, *Nottingham University, England*
Iacovos Kirlappos, *University College London, UK*
Alex Kirlik, *University of Illinois at Urbana, USA*
Ben Kirman, *University of Lincoln, UK*
Paul Kirschner, *Open Universiteit, Nederland*
David Kirsh, *University of California, USA*

Christopher Kirwan, *Parsons The New School for Design, USA*
Yoshifumi Kitamura, *Tohoku University, Japan*
Kris Kitani, *Carnegie Mellon University, USA*
Aniket Kittur, *Carnegie Mellon University, USA*
Funda Kivran-Swaine, *Rutgers University, USA*
René Kizilcec, *Stanford University, USA*
Scott Klemmer, *UC San Diego, USA*
Jayne Klenner, *King's College, USA*
Clemens Klokmose, *Aarhus University, Denmark*
Eric Klopfer, *MIT, USA*
Jarrod Knibbe, *University of Bristol, UK*
Bart Knijnenburg, *University of California, The Netherlands*
Cory Knobel, *University of California, USA*
Hendrik Knoche, *EPFL, Switzerland*
Bran Knowles, *Lancaster University, UK*
Masatomo Kobayashi, *IBM Research - Tokyo, Japan*
Michael Koch, *Bundeswehr University Munich, Germany*
Kenneth Koedinger, *Carnegie Mellon University, USA*
Lone Koefoed Hansen, *Aarhus University, Denmark*
Christian Koehler, *Carnegie Mellon University, USA*
Hyunseung Koh, *Indiana University, USA*
Kyle Koh, *Seoul National University, South Korea*
Hideki Koike, *University of Electro-Communications, Japan*
Mario Kolberg, *University of Stirling, UK*
Boriana Koleva, *The University of Nottingham, UK*
Beth Kolko, *University of Washington, USA*
Jon Kolko, *Frog Design, USA*
Thomas Költringer, *Ventum Consulting, Austria*
Steven Komarov, *Harvard University, USA*
Anita Komlodi, *University of Maryland, USA*
Andreas Komninos, *University of Strathclyde, UK*
Joseph Konstan, *University of Minnesota, USA*
Matthias Korn, *Aarhus University, Denmark*
Oliver Korn, *University of Applied Sciences Esslingen, Germany*
Gerd Kortuem, *The Open University, UK*
Robert Kosara, *Tableau Software, USA*
Timothy Koschmann, *Southern Illinois University, USA*
Ilpo Koskinen, *University of Art and Design Helsinki, Finland*
Vassilis Kostakos, *University of Oulu, Finland*
Ilkka Kosunen, *University of Helsinki, Finland*
Theodora Koulouri, *Brunel University,*
Matthias Kovatsch, *ETH Zurich, Switzerland*
Yong Ming Kow, *University of California Irvine, Hong Kong Sar*
Nicole Kraemer, *University of Duisburg-Essen,*
Adam Kramer, *Facebook, USA*
Jan-Peter Krämer, *RWTH Aachen University, Germany*
Matthias Kranz, *University of Passau, Germany*
Sven Kratz, *University of Munich, Germany*
Robert Kraut, *Carnegie Mellon University, USA*
Christian Kray, *University of Münster, Germany*
Shivsubramani Krishnamoorthy, *Amrita University, USA*
Ernst Kruijff, *Graz University of Technology, Austria*
John Krumm, *Microsoft Research, USA*
Erin Krupka, *University of Michigan, USA*

Ravi Kuber, *UMBC, USA*
Sebastien Kubicki, *CERV - Centre Européen de Réalité Virtuelle, France*
Alex Kuhn, *University of Michigan, USA*
Kai Kuikkaniemi, *Helsinki Institute for Information Technology HIIT, Finland*
Sari Kujala, *Aalto University, Finland*
Tuomo Kujala, *University of Jyväskylä, Finland*
Hannu Kukka, *University of Oulu, Finland*
Anand Kulkarni, *University of California, USA*
Chinmay Kulkarni, *Stanford University, USA*
Anuj Kumar, *Carnegie Mellon University, USA*
Arun Kumar, *IBM Research, India*
Neha Kumar, *University of California, USA*
Ranjitha Kumar, *Stanford University, USA*
Santosh Kumar, *University of Memphis, USA*
Ponnurangam Kumaraguru, *IIIT-Delhi, India*
Andrew Kun, *University of New Hampshire, USA*
Andreas Kunz, *Swiss Federal Institute of Technology Zurich, Switzerland*
Kai Kunze, *Osaka Prefecture University, Japan*
Liisa Kuparinen, *University of Jyväskylä, Finland*
Sri Kurniawan, *University of California, USA*
Gordon Kurtenbach, *Autodesk, Canada*
Arma an Kuru, *Middle East Technical University, Turkey*
Raja Kushalnagar, *Rochester Institute of Technology, USA*
Diana Kusunoki, *Drexel University, USA*
Kari Kuutti, *University of Oulu, Finland*
Stacey Kuznetsov, *Carnegie Mellon University, USA*
Youngshin Kwak, *Ulsan National Institute of Science and Technology, South Korea*
Bum Chul Kwon, *University of Konstanz, Germany*
Gyu Hyun Kwon, *Virginia Polytechnic Institute and State University, USA*
Jarmo Laaksolahti, *Swedish Institute of Computer Science, Sweden*
Richard Ladner, *University of Washington, USA*
Ben Lafreniere, *University of Waterloo, Canada*
Carl Lagoze, *University of Michigan, USA*
Susan Lai, *San Jose Gateway, Canada*
Denis Lalanne, *University of Fribourg, Switzerland*
Mary Lalomia, *Philips Medical, USA*
Shyong Lam, *Google, USA*
Anthony Lamarca, *Intel Research Seattle, USA*
Kristin Lamberty, *University of Minnesota, USA*
Cliff Lampe, *University of Michigan, USA*
Airi Lampinen, *Helsinki Institute for Information Technology HIIT, Finland*
James Landay, *University of Washington, USA*
Richard Landers, *Old Dominion University, USA*
Monica Landoni, *University of Lugano, Switzerland*
Pascal Landry, *Universitat Pompeu Fabra, Spain*
Steven Landry, *Purdue University, USA*
Peter Landwehr, *Carnegie Mellon University, USA*
Nicholas Lane, *Microsoft, China*
Patrick Langdon, *University of Cambridge, UK*
Marc Langheinrich, *Università Della Svizzera Italiana, Switzerland*
Joel Lanir, *University of Haifa, Israel*

Edward Lank, *University of Waterloo, Canada*
Rosa Lanzillotti, *Università di Bari, Italy*
Astrid Larssen, *Ashesi University College, Ghana*
Walter Lasecki, *University of Rochester Computer Science, USA*
Nancy Latham, *Boston University School of Public Health, USA*
Thomas Latoza, *UC Irvine, USA*
Celine Latulipe, *University of North Carolina at Charlotte, USA*
Manfred Lau, *Lancaster University, UK*
Felix Lauber, *University of Munich, Germany*
Carolyn Lauckner, *Michigan State University, USA*
Gael Laurans, *Delft University of Technology, The Netherlands*
Eric Laurier, *University of Edinburgh, UK*
Yann Laurillau, *University of Grenoble, France*
Debra Lauterbach, *Google, USA*
Joseph Laviola Jr., *University of Central Florida, USA*
Joseph Lawrance, *Oregon State University, USA*
Shaun Lawson, *University of Lincoln, UK*
Shawn Lawson, *Rensselaer Polytechnic Institute, USA*
Amanda Lazar, *University of Washington, USA*
Jonathan Lazar, *Towson University, USA*
Marco Lazzari, *University of Bergamo, Italy*
Lucian Leahu, *SICS, Sweden*
Alex Leavitt, *University of Southern California, USA*
Eric Lecolinet, *Télécom-Paristech, France*
Kerstin Leder Mackley, *Loughborough University, UK*
David Ledo, *University of Calgary, Canada*
Bongshin Lee, *Microsoft Research, USA*
Charlotte Lee, *University of Washington, USA*
Geehyuk Lee, *KAIST, Korea*
Joon Suk Lee, *Virginia Tech, USA*
Joyce Lee, *University of Michigan, USA*
Matthew Lee, *Philips Research, USA*
Michael Lee, *University of Washington, USA*
Min Kyung Lee, *Carnegie Mellon University, USA*
Stephanie Lee, *University of Washington, USA*
Uichin Lee, *KAIST, South Korea*
Young Lee, *Motorola Research, USA*
Colby Leider, *University of Miami, USA*
Darren Leigh, *USA*
Iolanda Leite, *Instituto Superior Técnico, Portugal*
Daniel Leithinger, *Massachusetts Institute of Technology, USA*
Luis A. Leiva, *Universitat Politècnica de València, Spain*
Eva Lenz, *Folkwang University of the Arts, Germany*
Pedro Leon, *Carnegie Mellon University, USA*
Chiara Leonardi, *Fondazione Bruno Kessler, Italy*
Stefania Leone, *University of South Carolina, USA*
Tuck Leong, *University of Technology, Australia*
George Lepouras, *University of Peloponnese, Greece*
Gilly Leshed, *Cornell University, USA*
Catherine Letondal, *ENAC, France*
Rock Leung, *University of British Columbia, Canada*
Vincent Levesque, *Immersion, Canada*
Peter Levin, *Intel Corporation, USA*

Vincent Lewandowski, *KTH, Sweden*
Clayton Lewis, *University of Colorado, USA*
Caroline Leygue, *University of Nottingham, UK*
Ian Li, *Carnegie Mellon University, USA*
Karen Li
Na Li, *Pennsylvania State University, USA*
Nan Li, *EPFL, Switzerland*
Wei Li, *Autodesk Research, Canada*
Hai-Ning Liang, *Xi'an Jiaotong-Liverpool University, China*
Rung-Huei Liang, *National Taiwan University of Science and Technology, Taiwan (r.o.c.)*
Fotis Liarokapis, *Coventry University, UK*
Ilaria Liccardi, *INRIA Paris, France*
Henry Lieberman, *Massachusetts Institute of Technology, USA*
Michael Liegl, *Lancaster University, UK*
Ann Light, *Northumbria University, UK*
Lassi Liikkanen, *Helsinki Institute for Information Technology HIIT, Finland*
Brian Lim, *Fraunhofer Center for Sustainable Energy Systems, USA*
Sohye Lim, *Ewha Womans University, Republic of Korea*
James Lin, *Google, USA*
Jialiu Lin, *Carnegie Mellon University, USA*
Min Lin, *Samsung Electronics, P. R. China*
Per Linde, *Malmö University,*
Robert Lindeman, *Worcester Polytechnic Institute, USA*
Rhema Linder, *Texas A&M University, USA*
Gitte Lindgaard, *Carleton University, Canada*
Siân Lindley, *Microsoft Research, UK*
Janne Lindqvist, *Rutgers University, USA*
Stephen Lindsay, *Swansea University, Wales, UK*
Conor Linehan, *University of Lincoln, UK*
Jessica Lingel, *Microsoft Research, USA*
Heather Lipford, *University of North Carolina at Charlotte, USA*
Roman Lissermann, *Technische Universität Darmstadt, Germany*
Eden Litt, *Northwestern University, USA*
Greg Little, *Massachusetts Institute of Technology, USA*
Linda Little, *Northumbria University, UK*
Jin Liu, *Cornell University, USA*
Leslie Liu, *University of Washington, USA*
Tracy Liu, *University of Michigan, USA*
Wei Liu, *Delft University of Technology, Netherlands*
Yefeng Liu, *Waseda University, Japan*
Ying Liu, *Charles Sturt University, Australia*
Ying Hsang Liu, *Intel, China*
Yun-En Liu, *University of Washington, USA*
Zhicheng Liu, *Georgia Institute of Technology, USA*
Zhicheng Liu, *Georgia Institute of Technology, USA*
Mark Livingston, *Naval Research Laboratory, USA*
Avishay Livne, *The University of Michigan, USA*
Sara Ljungblad, *LOTS Design AB, Sweden*
Markus Löchtefeld, *German Research Center for Artificial Intelligence (DFKI), Germany*
Dan Lockton, *University of Warwick, UK*

Thomas Lodato, *Georgia Institute of Technology, USA*
Courtney Loder, *UC Irvine, USA*
Sebastian Loehmann, *University of Munich, Germany*
Steffen Lohmann, *University of Stuttgart, Germany*
Benjamin Lok, *University of Florida, USA*
Lian Loke, *University of Sydney, Australia*
Derek Lomas, *Carnegie Mellon University, USA*
Benjamin Long, *Bristol University, UK*
Kiel Long, *Lancaster University, England, UK*
Chee Kit Looi, *NTU, Singapore*
Jack Loomis, *UCSB, USA*
Arminda Lopes, *Instituto Politecnico de Castelo Branco, Portugal*
Pedro Lopes, *Hasso Plattner Institute, Germany*
Fabien Lotte, *INRIA Bordeaux Sud-Ouest, France*
Danielle Lottridge, *San Francisco State University, USA*
Sandy Louchart, *Heriot-Watt University, Scotland, UK*
Oriana J Love, *Pacific Northwest National Laboratory, USA*
Hao Lu, *Intel, USA*
Hong Lu, *IBM Research, USA*
Jie Lu, *Samsung, USA*
Mei Lu, *CUNY Graduate Center, USA*
Pengfei Lu, *Fudan University, USA*
Tun Lu, *University of Washington, China*
Hao Lü, *Google, USA*
Andrés Lucero, *Nokia Research Center, Finland*
Bernd Ludwig, *University of Regensburg, Germany*
Patrick Lühne, *Hasso Plattner Institute, Germany*
Rowena Luk, *AMITA Telemedicine, Canada*
Kristian Lukander, *Finnish Institute of Occupational Health, Finland*
Jonathan Lukens, *University of Tennessee, USA*
Stephan Lukosch, *Delft University of Technology, The Netherlands*
Jay Lundell, *Intel Research, USA*
Kurt Luther, *Carnegie Mellon University, USA*
Wayne Lutters, *UMBC, USA*
Marianne Lykke, *Aalborg University, Denmark*
Peter Lyle, *Queensland University of Technology, Australia*
Leilah Lyons, *University of Illinois at Chicago, USA*
Michael Lyons, *Ritsumeikan University, Japan*
Heikki Lyytinen, *University of Jyväskylä, Finland*
Xiaojuan Ma, *Noah's Ark Lab, Hong Kong, China*
Catriona Macaulay, *University of Dundee, UK*
Craig Macdonald, *Pratt Institute, USA*
Carolyn Macgregor, *University of Waterloo, Canada*
Cristiano Maciel, *Universidade Federal de Mato Grosso, Brazil*
Giuliano Maciocci, *Qualcomm Research Cambridge, UK*
Wendy Mackay, *INRIA, France*
Scott Mackenzie, *York University, Canada*
Allan Maclean, *Image Semantics Ltd, UK*
Karon Maclean, *University of British Columbia, Canada*
Christopher Maclellan, *Carnegie Mellon University, USA*
Andrew Macvean, *Heriot-Watt University, Edinburgh*
Rui Madeira, *ESTSetúbal/IPS, Portugal*
Pattie Maes, *Massachusetts Institute of Technology, USA*

Rachel Magee, *Drexel University, USA*
Charlotte Magnusson, *Lund University, Sweden*
Mary Lou Maher, *University of Sydney, Australia*
Jalal Mahmud, *IBM Research - Almaden, USA*
Nasim Mahmud, *Hasselt University - Tul - IBBT, Belgium*
Angela Mahr, *German Research Center for Artificial Intelligence (DFKI), Germany*
Scott Mainwaring, *Intel Research, USA*
Julie Maitland, *Populus Global Solutions Inc., Canada*
Päivi Majaranta, *University of Tampere, Finland*
Yasutoshi Makino, *Keio University, Japan*
Sylvain Malacria, *University of Canterbury, France*
Miguel Malheiros, *University College London, UK*
Alessio Malizia, *University 'la Sapienza' of Rome, Italy*
Lone Malmborg, *IT University of Copenhagen, Denmark*
Lena Mamykina, *Columbia University, USA*
Hiroyuki Manabe, *NTT DOCOMO, Japan*
Clara Mancini, *The Open University, UK*
Regan Mandryk, *University of Saskatchewan, Canada*
Jennifer Mankoff, *Carnegie Mellon University, USA*
Daniela Mapelli, *Università di Padoa,*
Valérie Maquil, *Public Research Center Henri Tudor, Luxembourg*
Gabriela Marcu, *Carnegie Mellon University, USA*
Adam Marcus, *MIT CSAIL, USA*
Georgios Marentakis, *Institute for Electronic Music and Acoustics - Graz, Austria*
Gloria Mark, *University of California, USA*
Anders Markussen, *University of Copenhagen, Denmark*
Thomas Markussen, *Kolding School of Design, Denmark*
Jennifer Marlow, *Carnegie Mellon University, USA*
Elena Márquez Segura, *Uppsala University, Sweden*
Gary Marsden, *University of Cape Town, South Africa*
Andrea Marshall, *Drexel University Ischool, USA*
Catherine Marshall, *Microsoft, USA*
Joe Marshall, *University of Nottingham, UK*
Mark Marshall, *Sheffield Hallam University, UK*
Stuart Marshall, *Victoria University of Wellington, New Zealand*
Jean-Bernard Martens, *Eindhoven University of Technology, The Netherlands*
Stefan Marti, *Harman International, USA*
Anna Lisa Martin, *Zurich University of the Arts, Switzerland*
Aqueasha Martin, *Clemson University, USA*
Benoît Martin, *Université de Lorraine, France*
David Martin, *Xerox Research Center Europe, France*
Taylor Martin, *USU, USA*
Sarah Martindale, *The University of Nottingham, UK*
Diego Martinez Plasencia, *University of Bristol, UK*
Célia Martinie, *University Toulouse 3, France*
Misa Maruyama, *University of Hawaii at Manoa, USA*
Sergio Mascetti, *University of Milan, Italy*
Afra Mashhadi, *Alcatel-Lucent, Ireland*
Mikhil Masli, *Grouplens Research, USA*
Winter Mason, *Stevens Institute of Technology, USA*
Justin Matejka, *Autodesk, Canada*

Anijo Mathew, *Illinois Institute of Technology, USA*
Akhil Mathur, *University of Toronto, Canada*
Ben Matthews, *The University of Queensland, Australia*
Mark Matthews, *Cornell University, USA*
Tara Matthews, *IBM Research - Almaden, USA*
Denys Matthies, *University of Munich, Germany*
Frank Maurer, *University of Calgary, Canada*
Max-Emanuel Maurer, *University of Munich, Germany*
Deborah Maxwell, *University of Edinburgh, UK*
Aaron May, *Simon Fraser University, Canada*
Simon Mayer, *ETH Zurich, Switzerland*
Christopher Mayhorn, *North Carolina State University, USA*
Walterio Mayol-Cuevas, *University of Bristol, UK*
Oscar Mayora, *ITESM Cuernavaca, Mexico*
Rene Mayrhofer, *Lancaster University, UK*
Ali Mazalek, *Georgia Institute of Technology, USA*
Melissa Mazmanian, *University of California, USA*
Michelle Mazurek, *Carnegie Mellon University, USA*
Emanuela Mazzone, *University of Central Lancashire, Spain*
Victoria Mcarthur, *York University, Canada*
Simon Mccallum, *Gjøvik University College, Norway*
John Mccarthy, *University College Cork, Ireland*
Scott Mccrickard, *Virginia Tech, USA*
Sean Mcdirmid, *Microsoft Advanced Technology Center, Peoples Republic of China*
David Mcdonald, *University of Washington, USA*
Nora Mcdonald, *Drexel University, USA*
Mary F Mcdonough
Daniel Mcduff, *MIT Media Lab, USA*
Gregor Mcewan, *University of Saskatchewan, Canada*
Daniel Mcfarlane, *Lockheed Martin Advanced Technology Laboratories, USA*
Kevin Mcgee, *National University of Singapore, Singapore*
Mark Mcgill, *University of Glasgow, UK*
William Mcgrath, *Stanford University, USA*
Joanna Mcgrenere, *University of British Columbia, Canada*
Michael Mcguffin, *École de Technologie Supérieure, Canada*
Ross Mclachlan, *University of Glasgow, Scotland, UK*
Ryan Mcmahan, *University of Texas at Dallas, USA*
Donald Mcmillan, *SICS, Sweden*
Indrani Medhi-Thies, *Microsoft Research, India*
Richard Medland, *Queensland University of Technology, Australia*
Ben Medler, *EA, USA*
Elisa Mekler, *University of Basel, Switzerland*
Volkamer Melanie, *TU Darmstadt, Germany*
David Mellis, *Massachusetts Institute of Technology, USA*
Gustavo Mello Machado, *University of Stuttgart, Germany*
Nemanja Memarovic, *Universita Della Svizzera Italiana, Switzerland*
Maria Menendez, *University of Trento, Italy*
Sarah Mennicken, *University of Zurich, Switzerland*
Rachel Menzies, *University of Dundee, UK*
Emma Mercier, *University of Illinois at Urbana-Champaign, USA*
David Merrill, *Massachusetts Institute of Technology, USA*
Ronald Metoyer, *Oregon State University, USA*

Johanna Meurer, *University, Germany*
Jochen Meyer, *OFFIS - Institute for Information Technology, Germany*
Miriah Meyer, *University of Utah, USA*
Haipeng Mi, *Tsinghua University, China*
Nicholas Micallef, *Glasgow Caledonian University, UK*
Martin Mihajlov, *Ss. Cyril and Methodius University, Macedonia*
Silvia Miksch, *Vienna University of Technology, Austria*
David Millen, *IBM Research, USA*
Andrew Miller, *University of British Columbia, USA*
Gregor Miller, *Massachusetts Institute of Technology, Canada*
Scarlett Miller (herring), *Georgia Institute of Technology, USA*
Michael Minge, *Berlin University of Technology, Germany*
Aliaksei Miniukovich, *University of Trento, Italy*
Andrea Minuto, *University of Twente, The Netherlands*
Pejman Mirza-Babaei, *University of Ontario Institute of Technology, Canada*
Sonali Mishra, *University of Michigan, USA*
Taniya Mishra, *AT&T, USA*
Alex Mitchell, *National University of Singapore, Singapore*
Tanushree Mitra, *Georgia Institute of Technology, USA*
Tracy Mitzner, *Georgia Institute of Technology, USA*
Takahiro Miura, *The University of Tokyo, Japan*
Takashi Miyaki, *Inria, France*
Bart Moens, *Ghent University, Belgium*
Andrew Molineux, *Lancaster University, England*
Andreas Möller, *Technische Universität München, Germany*
Max Möllers, *RWTH Aachen University, Germany*
David Molyneaux, *Microsoft Research, England, UK*
Arthur Money, *Brunel University, UK*
Andrew Monk, *University of York, UK*
Andres Monroy-Hernandez, *Massachusetts Institute of Technology, USA*
Toni-Jan Keith Monserrat, *National University of Singapore, Philippines*
Kyle Montague, *University of Dundee, Scotland, UK*
Bob Moore, *PARC, USA*
Simone Mora, *Norwegian University of Science and Technology, Norway*
Stuart Moran, *University of Nottingham, UK*
Neema Moraveji, *Microsoft Research Asia, China*
Guillaume Moreau, *Ecole Centrale de Nantes, France*
Lourdes Moreno, *Universidad Carlos III de Madrid, Spain*
Jonathan Morgan, *University of Washington, USA*
Giulio Mori, *ISTI-CNR, Italy*
Joji Mori, *The University of Melbourne, Australia*
Carlos Morimoto, *University of Sao Paulo, Brazil*
Janine Morley, *Lancaster University, UK*
Fabio Morreale, *University of Trento, Italy*
Patricia Morreale, *Kean University, USA*
Margaret Morris, *Intel Corporation, USA*
Meredith Morris, *Microsoft Research, USA*
Ann Morrison, *Aalborg University, Denmark*
Cecily Morrison, *Microsoft Research, UK*
Richard Mortier, *The University of Nottingham, UK*
Lee Morton, *Glasgow Caledonian University, UK*
Christiane Moser, *ICT&S Center, Austria*
Vicki Moulder, *Simon Fraser University, Canada*

Christos Mousas, *University of Sussex, England, UK*
Mu Mu, *Lancaster University, UK*
Omar Mubin, *University of Western Sydney, Australia*
Christian Muehl, *Inria Bordeaux, France*
Florian "Floyd" Mueller, *Exertion Games Lab, Australia*
Stefanie Mueller, *Hasso Plattner Institute, Germany*
Christian Mueller-Tomfelde, *CSIRO ICT Centre, Australia*
Max Mühlhäuser, *TU Darmstadt, Germany*
Adiyan Mujibiya, *The University of Tokyo, Japan*
Heiko Müller, *IBM Research, Germany*
Gernot Müller-Putz, *Graz University of Technology, Austria*
Alessandro Mulloni, *Qualcomm Research KAIST, Republic of Korea ria, Austria*
Cosmin Munteanu, *National Research Council Canada, Canada*
Helmut Munz, *RMIT University, Austria*
Martin Murer, *University of Salzburg, Austria*
Dianne Murray, *Indep. Consultant, UK*
Ildar Muslukhov, *University of British Columbia, Canada*
Mirco Musolesi, *University of Birmingham, UK*
Brad Myers, *Carnegie Mellon University, USA*
Elizabeth Mynatt, *Georgia Institute of Technology, USA*
Mor Naaman, *Cornell University, USA*
Miguel Nacenta, *University of St Andrews, UK*
Frank Nack, *University of Amsterdam (uva), The Netherlands*
Till Nagel, *University of Applied Sciences Potsdam, Germany*
Tobias Nägeli, *ETH Zurich, Switzerland*
Hideyuki Nakanishi, *Osaka University, Japan*
Kevin Nam, *University of Michigan, USA*
Suranga Nanayakkara, *Singapore University of Technology and Design, USA*
Mathieu Nancel, *University of Canterbury, France*
Nitya Narasimhan, *edupreneur, USA*
Bonnie Nardi, *University of California, USA*
Amani Naseem, *RMIT University, Australia*
Chris Nash, *University of Cambridge, UK*
Meena Natarajan, *UC Berkeley, USA*
Lisa Nathan, *University of British Columbia, Canada*
David Navarre, *IRIT, France*
Elena Nazzi, *IT University of Copenhagen, Denmark*
Mark Neerincx, *TNO Human Factors, Netherlands*
Michael Neff, *UC Davis, USA*
Paolo Negri
Matei Negulescu, *University of Waterloo, Canada*
Matti Nelimarkka, *Helsinki Institute for Information Technology HIIT, Finland*
Les Nelson, *PARC, USA*
Cornelius Neufeldt, *University of Siegen, Germany*
Alena Neviarouskaya, *University of Tokyo, Japan*
Alan Newell, *Dundee University, Scotland, UK*
Mark Newman, *University of Michigan, USA*
Victor Ng-Thow-Hing, *Honda Research Institute USA, USA*
David Nguyen, *Nokia Research Center, USA*
Duyen Nguyen, *Cornell University, USA*
James Nicholson, *Northumbria University, England, UK*

Hugo Nicolau, *University of Dundee, UK*
Lene Nielsen, *IT University of Copenhagen, Denmark*
Gerrit Niezen, *Swansea University, UK*
Femke Nijboer, *University of Twente, The Netherlands*
Valentina Nisi, *University of Madeira, Portugal*
Xi Niu, *Indiana University, USA*
Sylvie Noël, *Universita di Trento, Italy*
Pedro Nogueira, *LIACC - Artificial Intelligence and Computer Science Laboratory, Portugal*
A. Imran Nordin, *University of York, UK*
Mie Nørgaard, *Aarhus School of Architecture, Denmark*
Francesco Nori
Maria Normark, *Södertörn University, Sweden*
Lauren Norrie, *University of Glasgow, Scotland, UK*
Chris North, *Virginia Polytechnic Institute and State University, USA*
Oded Nov, *Polytechnic Institute of New York University, USA*
Laurie Novak, *Vanderbilt University, USA*
Francisco Nunes, *Vienna University of Technology, Austria*
Petteri Nurmi, *Helsinki Institute for Information Technology HIIT, Finland*
Andreas Nürnberger, *Otto-Von-Guericke-University Magdeburg, Germany*
Stina Nylander, *Swedish Institute of Computer Science, Sweden*
Heather O'brien, *University of British Columbia, Canada*
Marita O'brien, *University of Alabama-Huntsville, USA*
Brendan O'connor, *Carnegie Mellon University, USA*
Lora Oehlberg, *INRIA, USA*
Anne Oeldorf-Hirsch, *University of Connecticut, USA*
Eyal Ofek, *Microsoft Research, USA*
Corinna Ogonowski, *University of Siegen, Germany*
Alice Oh, *KAIST, Republic of Korea*
Jonghwan Oh, *Seoul National University, Republic of Korea*
Kenton O'hara, *Microsoft Research, UK*
Harri Oinas-Kukkonen, *University of Oulu, Finland*
Aisling O'kane, *University College London, UK*
Bugra Oktay, *University of Nevada, USA*
Patrick Oladimeji, *Swansea University, UK*
Halla Olafsdottir, *Université Paris-Sud, France*
Erica Olmsted-Hawala, *U.S. Census Bureau, USA*
Dan Olsen, *Brigham Young University, USA*
Gary Olson, *University of California, USA*
Judith Olson, *U of Michigan, USA*
Katherine Olson, *Georgia Institute of Technology, USA*
Thomas Olsson, *Tampere University of Technology, Finland*
Sile O'modhrain, *University of Michigan, USA*
Jacki O'neill, *XRCE, France*
Stephen Oney, *Carnegie Mellon University, USA*
Wei Tsang Ooi, *National University of Singapore, Singapore*
Elisa Oreglia, *University of California Berkeley, USA*
Tihomir Orehovacki, *University of Zagreb, Croatia*
Eleanor O'rourke, *University of Washington, USA*
Valeria Orso, *University of Padova, Italy*
Martin Ortlieb, *Google, Switzerland*
Keith Ostfeld, *Children's Museum of Houston, USA*
Nuno Otero, *Linnæus University, Sweden*
Tom Ouyang, *MIT, USA*

Derya Özçelik, *Eindhoven University of Technology, The Netherlands*
Jeni Paay, *Aalborg University, Denmark*
Tyler Pace, *Indiana University Bloomington, USA*
Tim Paek, *Microsoft Research, USA*
Michel Pahud, *Microsoft Research, USA*
Helen Pain, *University of Edinburgh, UK*
Drew Paine, *University of Washington, USA*
Aditya Pal, *IBM Research - Almaden, USA*
Philippe Palanque, *ICS-IRIT, France*
Leysia Palen, *University of Colorado, USA*
Henri Palleis, *Ludwig-Maximilians-Universität München, Germany*
Susan Palmiter, *Design Technologies, USA*
Viktoria Pammer, *Know-Center, Austria*
Yingxin Pan, *IBM Research - China, China*
Yue Pan, *Indiana University Bloomington, USA*
Zhengzheng Pan, *Facebook, USA*
Katherine Panciera, *University of Minnesota, USA*
Sabrina Panëels, *McGill University, France*
Carolyn Pang, *Simon Fraser University, Canada*
Saurabh Panjwani, *Microsoft Research India, India*
Katrina Panovich, *MIT, USA*
Nadia Pantidi, *The University of Nottingham, UK*
Caroline Pantofaru, *Willow Garage, USA*
Eleftherios Papachristos, *University of Patras, Greece*
Savvas Papaioannou, *University of Oxford, UK*
Joseph Paradiso, *MIT Media Laboratory, USA*
Aditya Parameswaran, *Stanford University, USA*
Zachary Pardos, *UC Berkeley, USA*
Pablo Paredes, *University of Berkeley, USA*
Narcis Pares, *Universitat Pompeu Fabra, Spain*
Tapan Parikh, *UC Berkeley, USA*
Minsu Park, *KAIST, South Korea*
Souneil Park, *Univ. of Michigan, USA*
Sun Young Park, *University of California, USA*
Taiwoo Park, *KAIST, South Korea*
Young-Woo Park, *KAIST, South Korea*
Chris Parnin, *Georgia Institute of Technology, USA*
Kurt Partridge, *Google, USA*
Gaurav Paruthi, *University of Michigan, USA*
Marco Pasch, *University of Lugano, Switzerland*
Gert Pasman, *Delft University of Technology, The Netherlands*
Jerome Pasquero, *Research In Motion Limited, Canada*
Kayur Patel, *University of Washington, USA*
Nirmal Patel, *Georgia Institute of Technology, USA*
Rupa Patel, *University of Washington, USA*
Rupal Patel, *Northeastern University, USA*
Shwetak Patel, *University of Washington, USA*
Jessica Pater, *Georgia Institute of Technology, USA*
Andrew Patrick, *Carleton University, Canada*
Donald Patterson, *University of California Irvine, USA*
Sharoda Paul, *GE Global Research, USA*
Eric Paulos, *University of California, USA*
Dana Pavel, *University of Essex, UK*

Ioannis Pavlidis, *University of Houston, USA*
Andriy Pavlovych, *York University, Canada*
Stephen Payne, *University of Bath, UK*
Jennifer Pearson, *Swansea University, UK*
Fabrizio Pece, *University College London, UK*
Evan Peck, *Tufts University, USA*
Sonja Pedell, *Swinburne University of Technology, Australia*
Sonjs Pedell, *Swinburne University of Technology, Australia*
Esben Pedersen, *University of Copenhagen, Danmark*
Thomas Pederson, *IT University of Copenhagen, Denmark*
Peter Peltonen, *University of Helsinki, Finland*
Jorge Peña, *University of California, USA*
Wei Peng, *Information Studies, USA*
Gerald Penn, *University of Toronto, Canada*
Kylie Peppler, *Indiana University, USA*
Lucas Pereira, *Madeira Interactive Technologies Institute, Portugal*
Adam Perer, *IBM Research, USA*
Manuel Perez-Quinones, *Virginia Tech, USA*
Charles Perin, *INRIA Saclay, France*
Trevor Pering, *Intel Research, USA*
Ken Perlin, *New York University, USA*
Simon Perrault, *National University of Singapore, Singapore*
Daniel Perry, *University of Washington, USA*
Florian Perteneder, *University of Applied Sciences Upper KAIST, Republic of Korea ria, Austria*
Marianne Graves Petersen, *Aarhus University, Denmark*
Daniela Petrelli, *Sheffield Hallam University, UK*
Helen Petrie, *University of York, UK*
Tamara Peyton, *Penn State University, USA*
Laura Pfeifer Vardoulakis, *Google, USA*
Max Pfeiffer, *Leibniz Universität Hannover, Germany*
Thies Pfeiffer, *Bielefeld University, Germany*
Bastian Pfleging, *University of Stuttgart, Germany*
Martin Pielot, *Telefonica Research, Spain*
James Pierce, *Carnegie Mellon University, USA*
Jeffrey Pierce, *Samsung UX Innovations Lab, USA*
Emmanuel Pietriga, *INRIA, France*
Mary Pietrowicz, *National Center for Supercomputing Applications, USA*
Thomas Pietrzak, *University of Lille, France*
Hannah Pileggi, *Georgia Institute of Technology, USA*
Clément Pillias, *CNAM, France*
Laura Pina, *'UCSD' As In University of California at San Diego, USA*
Fabiano Pinatti, *Institute of Design and Assessment of Technology, Austria*
Kathleen Pine, *University of California, USA*
Claudio Pinhanez, *IBM Brazil, Brazil*
Volkmar Pipek, *University of Siegen, Germany*
Anne Marie Piper, *Northwestern University, USA*
Michael Pirker, *Ruwido KAIST, Republic of Korea ria Gmbh, Austria*
Peter Pirolli, *PARC, USA*
Catherine Plaisant, *University of Maryland, USA*
Andreas Pleuss, *University of Limerick, Ireland*
Bernd Ploderer, *The University of Melbourne, Australia*
Thomas Ploetz, *Newcastle University, UK*

Barry Po, *HSBC, Canada*
Henning Pohl, *University of Hannover, Germany*
Margit Pohl, *Vienna University of Technology, Austria*
Anna Pohlmeyer, *Delft University of Technology, Netherlands*
Ioannis Politis, *Eindhoven University of Technology, Netherlands*
John Pollak, *Cornell University, USA*
Marc Pomplun, *University of Massachusetts Boston, USA*
Heather Pon-Barry, *Informatics, USA*
Suporn Pongnumkul, *University of Washington, USA*
Erika Poole, *Penn State University, USA*
Alan Pope, *NASA Langley Research Center, USA*
Ana-Maria Popescu, *Pinterest, USA*
Leslie Poppe, *University of Washington, USA*
Kristi Potter, *University of Oregon, USA*
Tania Pouli, *Technicolor, France*
Ivan Poupyrev, *Disney Research, USA*
Sören Preibusch, *Microsoft Research, UK*
Chris Preist, *University of Bristol, UK*
Nora Presson, *University of Pittsburgh, USA*
Mike Preuss, *WWU Münster, Germany*
Blaine Price, *The Open University, UK*
Sara Price, *Institute of Education, UK*
Reid Priedhorsky, *Los Alamos National Laboratory, USA*
Rafael Prikladnicki, *Pucrs, Brazil*
Michael Prilla, *University of Bochum, Germany*
Suzanne Prior, *Media and Computer Games, UK*
Kathrin Probst, *University of Applied Sciences Upper KAIST, Republic of Korea ria, Austria*
Jason Procyk, *Simon Fraser University, Canada*
Halley Profita, *University of Colorado, USA*
Sebastian Prost, *CURE - Center for Usability Research & Engineering, Austria*
Janna Protzak, *Berlin Institute of Technology, Germany*
Emily Provost, *University of Michigan, USA*
John Pruitt, *Microsoft, USA*
Larissa Pschetz, *Microsoft Research Asia, Midlothian*
Deborah Ptak, *University of Toronto, Canada*
Pearl Pu, *EPFL, Switzerland*
Andreas Pusch, *Julius-Maximilians-Universität, Germany*
Cynthia Putnam, *Depaul University, USA*
Pardha Pyla, *Virginia Tech, India*
Huamin Qu, *HKUST, Hong Kong*
Novi Quadrianto, *University of Cambridge, UK*
Daniele Quercia, *Yahoo! Research, UK*
Whitney Quesenbery, *Whitney Interactcive Design, USA*
Alexander Quinn, *University of Maryland, USA*
Philip Quinn, *University of Canterbury, New Zealand*
Pablo-Alejandro Quinones, *University of Michigan, USA*
Andrew Quitmeyer, *Georgia Institute of Technology, USA*
Pernilla Qvarfordt, *FX Palo Alto Laboratory, USA*
Daphne Raban, *University of Haifa, Israel*
Mashfiqui Rabbi, *Cornell University, USA*
Robert Racadio, *University of Washington, USA*
Irene Rae, *University of Wisconsin, USA*

Matthew Rafalow, *University of California Irvine, USA*
Nikunj Raghuvanshi, *Microsoft Research, USA*
Tauhidur Rahman, *Cornell University, USA*
Kari-Jouko Räihä, *University of Tampere, Finland*
Andrew Raij, *University of South Florida, USA*
Roope Raisamo, *University of Tampere, Finland*
Eeva Raita, *Helsinki Institute for Information Technology HIIT, Finland*
Mikko Rajanen, *University of Oulu, Finland*
Thusha Rajendran, *UK*
Nitendra Rajput, *IBM Research, India*
Ismo Rakkolainen, *University of Tampere, Finland*
Raf Ramakers, *Hasselt University - Tul - Iminds, Belgium*
Ernesto Ramirez, *University of California, USA*
Gonzalo Ramos, *Microsoft, USA*
Adriane Randolph, *Kennesaw State University, USA*
Nimmi Rangaswamy, *Microsoft Research India, India*
Juhi Ranjan, *University of Virginia, USA*
Dimitrios Raptis, *Aalborg University, Denmark*
Umar Rashid, *University of Kent, UK*
Kirsten Rassmus-Gröhn, *Lund University, Sweden*
Rabindra Ratan, *Information Studies, USA*
Matt Ratto, *University of Toronto, Toronto*
Martina Rau, *University of Wisconsin, USA*
Janet Read, *University of Central Lancashire, England*
Kyle Rector, *University of Washington, USA*
Madhu Reddy, *Penn State University, USA*
Fiona Redhead, *Queensland University of Technology, Australia*
Johan Redström, *Umeå Institute of Design, Sweden*
Darren Reed, *University of York, UK*
Robert Reeder, *Google, USA*
Sarah Reeder, *Indiana University, USA*
Tim Regan, *Microsoft, UK*
Holger Regenbrecht, *University of Otago, New Zealand*
Derek Reilly, *Dalhousie University, Canada*
Peter Reimann, *University of Sydney, Australia*
Bryan Reimer, *MIT, USA*
Sofia Reis, *Universidade Nova de Lisboa, Portugal*
Wolfgang Reitberger, *Vienna University of Technology, Austria*
Harald Reiterer, *University, Germany*
Thomas Reitmaier, *UCT Centre In ICT4D, South Africa*
Jun Rekimoto, *University of Tokyo / Sony CSL, Japan*
Christian Remy, *University of Zurich, Switzerland*
Gang Ren, *University of Bath, UK*
Xiangshi Ren, *Kochi University of Technology, Japan*
Yuqing Ren, *Carnegie Mellon University, USA*
Karen Renaud, *University of Glasgow, UK*
Christian Rendl, *University of Applied Sciences Upper KAIST, Republic of Korea ria, Austria*
Stefan Rennick-Egglestone, *The University of Nottingham, UK*
Ronald Rensink, *University of British Columbia, Canada*
Paul Resnick, *University of Michigan, USA*
Glenda Revelle, *University of Arkansas, USA*
Gabriel Reyes, *Georgia Institute of Technology, USA*
Lindsay Reynolds, *Cornell University, USA*

Mark Rice, *Institute of Infocomm Research, Singapore*
Alex Richardson, *The KAIST, Republic of Korea ralian National University, Australia*
Alexander Richter, *Unibwm, Germany*
Jochen Rick, *Saarland University, Germany*
Angela Riechers, *School of Visual Arts, USA*
Jens Riegelsberger, *University College London, UK*
Soo Young Rieh, *University of Michigan, USA*
Andreas Riener, *Johannes Kepler University, Austria*
Alexander Rind, *Vienna University of Technology, Austria*
Lazlo Ring, *Northeastern University, USA*
Mikko Rissanen, *Move Correctly, Singapore*
Tobias Ritschel, *MPI Informatik, Germany*
Giuseppe Riva, *Università Cattolica Del Sacro Cuore, Italy*
Christopher Roast, *Sheffield Hallam University, UK*
Lionel Robert, *University of Michigan, USA*
Jonathan Roberts, *Bangor University, UK*
Judy Robertson, *Heriot-Watt University, UK*
Scott Robertson, *University of Hawaii at Manoa, USA*
Toni Robertson, *University of Technology, Australia*
Jeffrey Robins, *Google, USA*
Simon Robinson, *Swansea University, UK*
Carsten Röcker, *RWTH Aachen University, Germany*
Tom Rodden, *University of Nottingham, UK*
Edgar Rodriguez, *Wellington, New Zealand*
David Roedl, *Indiana University, USA*
Yvonne Rogers, *University College London, UK*
Daniel Roggen, *Newcastle University, UK*
Markus Rohde, *International Institute for Socio-Informatics, Germany*
Michael Rohs, *University of Hannover, Germany*
Daniel Romero, *Northwestern University, USA*
Mario Romero, *Delft University of Technology, Sweden*
Natalia Romero Herrera, *KTH, The Netherlands*
John Rooksby, *University of St Andrews, UK*
Chris Rooney, *Middlesex University, UK*
Carolyn Rose, *Carnegie Mellon University, USA*
Asta Roseway, *Microsoft Research, USA*
Joel Ross, *University of California, USA*
Chiara Rossitto, *Stockholm University, Sweden*
Mattias Rost, *Mobile Life @ SICS, Sweden*
Robert Roth, *University of Wisconsin-Madison, USA*
Virpi Roto, *University of Helsinki, Finland*
Nicolas Roussel, *Inria, France*
Maria Roussou, *Makebelieve Design & Consulting, Greece*
Debjani Roy, *IIT Bombay, India*
Quentin Roy, *CNRS LTCI UMR 5141, France*
Agata Rozga, *Georgia Institute of Technology, USA*
Elisa Rubegni, *Universita Della Svizzera Italiana, Switzerland*
Steve Rubin, *University of California, USA*
Michael Rubinstein, *MIT, USA*
Stefan Rüger, *The Open University, UK*
Jaime Ruiz, *Colorado State University, USA*
Enrico Rukzio, *Lancaster University, Germany*

Sonja Rümelin, *University of Munich, Germany*
Tuukka Ruotsalo, *Aalto University, Finland*
Derek Ruths, *McGill University, Canada*
Kimiko Ryokai, *MIT Media Laboratory, USA*
Jeffrey Rzeszotarski, *Carnegie Mellon University, USA*
Daniel Saakes, *Delft University of Technology, The Netherlands*
Selma Sabanovic, *Indiana University, USA*
Andreas Sackl, *FTW Telecommunications Research Center, Austria*
Ramik Sadana, *Georgia Institute of Technology, USA*
Alireza Sahami Shirazi, *University of Stuttgart, Germany*
Arnaud Sahuguet, *Google, USA*
Alan Said, *CWI, The Netherlands*
Daisuke Sakamoto, *The University of Tokyo, Japan*
Mona Sakr, *Institute of Education, UK*
Ben Salem, *Northumbria University, UK*
Pascal Salembier, *University of Technology of Troyes, France*
Mariana Salgado, *Laurea University of Applied Sciences, Finland*
Guarionex Salivia, *Minnesota State University, USA*
Eva Lotta Sallnäs Pysander, *Royal Institute of Technology, Sweden*
Katri Salminen, *University of Tampere, Finland*
Antti Salovaara, *Aalto University, Finland*
Anastasia Salter, *University of Baltimore, USA*
Frode Sandnes, *Oslo University College, Norway*
Aditya Sankar, *University of Washington, India*
Vagner Santana, *State University of Campinas, Brazil*
Pedro Santana-Mancilla, *University of Colima, Mexico*
Carmen Santoro, *ISTI-CNR, Italy*
T. Saponas, *Microsoft Research, USA*
Aleksandra Sarcevic, *Drexel University, USA*
Makoto Sasaki, *Iwate University, Japan*
Daisuke Sato, *IBM Research - Tokyo, Japan*
Munehiko Sato, *Disney Research, USA*
Yoichi Sato, *The University of Tokyo, Japan*
Debra Satterfield, *Iowa State University, USA*
Allison Sauppé, *University of Wisconsin-Madison, USA*
Valkyrie Savage, *University of California, USA*
Nadav Savio, *Google.org, USA*
Pete Sawyer, *Lancaster University, UK*
Walt Scacchi, *University of California, USA*
Christopher Scaffidi, *Carnegie Mellon University, USA*
Joey Scarr, *University of Canterbury, New Zealand*
Christopher Schaefbauer, *University of Colorado, USA*
Patricia Schank, *SRI International, USA*
Raimund Schatz, *Forschungszentrum Telekommunikation Wien (ftw.), Austria*
Florian Schaub, *Carnegie Mellon University, USA*
Benjamin Scheibehenne, *University of Basel, Switzerland*
Jesse Schell, *Carnegie Mellon University, USA*
Ansgar Scherp, *Business Informatics and Business Mathematics, Germany*
Gianluca Schiavo, *University of Trento & FBK, Italy*
Markus Schilling, *Simon Fraser University, Canada*
Thecla Schiphorst, *Simon Fraser University, Canada*
Steven Schirra, *Massachusetts Institute of Technology, USA*
Chris Schmandt, *Massachusetts Institute of Technology, USA*

Dominik Schmidt, *Hasso Plattner Institute, Germany*
Holger Schnädelbach, *University of Nottingham, UK*
Jodi Schneider, *National University of Ireland, Ireland*
Guy Schofield, *Newcastle University, UK*
Jean Scholtz, *Pacific Northwest Laboratory, USA*
Johannes Schöning, *Hasselt University - Tul - Iminds, Belgium*
Marén Schorch, *University of Siegen, Germany*
Falk Schreiber
Ronald Schroeter, *Queensland University of Technology, Australia*
Kai Schubert, *University of Siegen, Germany*
Daniel Schultheiss, *Ilmenau University of Technology, Germany*
Timothy Schultz, *Drexel University, USA*
Victoria Schwanda Sosik, *Cornell University, USA*
Tobias Schwartz, *Fraunhofer FIT, Germany*
Julia Schwarz, *University of Washington, USA*
Lauren Scissors, *Northwestern University, USA*
Stacey Scott, *University of Waterloo, Canada*
Peter Scupelli, *Carnegie Mellon University, USA*
Sue Ann Seah, *University of Bristol, UK*
A. Fleming Seay, *Carnegie Mellon University, USA*
Michael Sedlmair, *University of Vienna, Austria*
Magy Seif El-Nasr, *Northeastern University, USA*
Julian Seifert, *Ulm University, Germany*
Susanne Seitinger, *MIT Media Lab, USA*
James Self, *UNIST, South Korea*
Kate Sellen, *OCAD University, Canada*
Katherine Sellen, *University of Toronto, Canada*
Bryan Semaan, *University of Hawaii at Manoa, USA*
Shilad Sen, *University of Minnesota, USA*
Phoebe Sengers, *Cornell University, USA*
Sepandar Sepehr, *McMaster University, Canada*
Marcos Serrano, *IRIT, France*
Lauren Sessions Goulet, *Facebook, USA*
Leslie Setlock, *Cornell University, USA*
Burr Settles, *Carnegie Mellon University, USA*
Teddy Seyed, *University of Calgary, Canada*
Aviv Shachak, *University of Toronto, Canada*
Orit Shaer, *Tufts University, USA*
David Shaffer, *University of Wisconsin, USA*
Chirag Shah, *Rutgers University, USA*
Priti Shah, *University of Michigan, USA*
Qonita Shahab, *Eindhoven University of Technology, The Netherlands*
Noor Shaker, *IT University of Copenhagen, Denmark*
David Shamma, *Yahoo!, USA*
Ben Shapiro, *Tufts,*
Ehud Sharlin, *University of Calgary, Canada*
Moushumi Sharmin, *University of Memphis, USA*
Sarah Sharples, *University of Nottingham, UK*
Wes Sharrock, *Manchester University, UK*
Aaron Shaw, *Northwestern University, USA*
Richard Shay, *Carnegie Mellon University, USA*
John Shearer, *Newcastle University, UK*
Mohamed Sheik-Nainar, *Synaptics Inc, USA*
Chia Shen, *Harvard University, USA*

Dawei Shen, *Massachusetts Institute of Technology, USA*
S. Andrew Sheppard, *University of Minnesota, USA*
Yuanchun Shi, *Tsinghua University, China*
Patrick Shih, *The Pennsylvania State University, USA*
Choonsung Shin, *Carnegie Mellon University, USA*
Hiroyuki Shinoda, *The University of Tokyo, Japan*
Frank Shipman, *Texas A&M University, USA*
Sajad Shirali-Shahreza, *University of Toronto, Canada*
Mariya Shiyko, *Northeastern University, USA*
Buntarou Shizuki, *University of Tsukuba, Japan*
Irina Shklovski, *IT University of Copenhagen, Denmark*
Garth Shoemaker, *Google, USA*
Milad Shokouhi, *Microsoft Research, UK*
Jamie Shotton, *Microsoft Research Cambridge, UK*
Mark Shovman, *Yahoo! Inc., Israel*
George Siemens, *Athabasca University, Canada*
Beat Signer, *Vrije Universiteit Brussel, Belgium*
Six Silberman, *Bureau of Economic Interpretation, USA*
Elizabeth Sillence, *Northumbria University, UK*
Liz Sillence, *Northumbria University, UK*
Paula Alexandra Silva, *University of Hawaii at Manoa, Portugal*
Johanna Silvennoinen, *University of Jyväskylä, Finland*
Adalberto Simeone, *Lancaster University, UK*
David Simmons, *University of Glasgow, UK*
Ian Simon, *University of Washington, USA*
Judge Simon, *RAT Group, UK*
Laurent Simon, *University of Cambridge, UK*
Jolynna Sinanan, *The University of Melbourne, Australia*
Leif Singer, *University of Victoria, Canada*
Karan Singh, *University of Toronto, Canada*
Supriya Singh, *Royal Melbourne Institute of Technology, Australia*
Vikash Singh, *University of North Carolina at Charlotte, USA*
Valentina Sintsova, *EPFL, Switzerland*
Behzod Sirjani, *Northwestern University, USA*
David Sirkin, *Stanford University, USA*
Daniel Sjölie, *Umeå University, Sweden*
Mikael B. Skov, *Aalborg University, Denmark*
Marjorie Skubic, *University of Missouri, USA*
Roger Slack, *Bangor University, Wales, UK*
Bernhard Slawik, *University of Munich, Germany*
Manya Sleeper, *Carnegie Mellon University, USA*
Karin Slegers, *KU Leuven, Belgium*
James D. Slotta, *University of Toronto, Canada*
Petr Slovák, *Vienna University of Technology, Austria*
Jan Smeddinck, *University of Bremen, Germany*
Joshua Smith, *University of Washington, USA*
Madeline Smith, *Cornell University, USA*
Matthew Smith, *Leibniz Universität Hannover, Germany*
Ross Smith, *University of South KAIST, Republic of Korea ralia, Australia*
Thomas Smith, *Newcastle University, UK*
Michael Smyth, *Edinburgh Napier University, UK*
Jaime Snyder, *Syracuse University, USA*
Timothy Sohn, *Google, USA*
Tomas Sokoler, *IT University of Copenhagen, Denmark*

Jacob Solomon, *Michigan State University, USA*
Andreas Sonderegger, *University of Fribourg, Switzerland*
Hyunyoung Song, *University of Maryland, USA*
Junehwa Song, *KAIST, Korea*
Yale Song, *MIT CSAIL, USA*
Diane Sonnenwald, *UCD, Ireland*
Daniel Sonntag, *DFKI German Research Center for AI, Germany*
Vladimir Soroka, *IBM Haifa Research Lab, Israel*
Alexander Sorokin, *CrowdFlower, USA*
Iris Soute, *Eindhoven University of Technology, The Netherlands*
Caleb Southern, *Georgia Institute of Technology, USA*
Michiel Sovijärvi-Spape, *Aalto University, Finland*
Anna Spagnolli, *University of Padova, Italy*
Oleg Spakov, *University of Tampere, Finland*
Lucio Davide Spano, *University of Cagliari, Italy*
Mirjana Spasojevic, *Nokia, USA*
Chris Speed, *Edinburgh College of Art, UK*
Tess Speelpenning, *Philips Research, The Netherlands*
Wolfgang Spiessl, *BMW Research and Technology, Germany*
Tasos Spiliotopoulos, *Madeira Interactive Technologies Institute, Portugal*
Martin Spindler, *University of Magdeburg, Germany*
Adam Sporka, *Czech Technical University In Prague, Czech Republic*
Mary Ann Sprague, *Xerox, USA*
Srinath Sridhar, *Max-Planck Institut Für Informatik, Germany*
Saurabh Srivastava, *IBM India Research Laboratory, India*
Robert St. Amant, *North Carolina State University, USA*
Tad Stach, *Queen's University, Canada*
Frank Stajano, *University of Cambridge, UK*
Jeannie Stamberger, *Carnegie Mellon University, USA*
Brodie Stanfield, *University of Ontario Institute of Technology, Canada*
Kevin Stanley, *University of Saskatchewan, Canada*
Pieter Jan Stappers, *Delft University of Technology, The Netherlands*
Kate Starbird, *University of Washington, USA*
Thad Starner, *Georgia Institute of Technology, USA*
John Stasko, *Georgia Institute of Technology, USA*
Bogdan State, *Stanford University, USA*
Ian Stavness, *University of Saskatchewan, Canada*
Anthony Steed, *University College London, UK*
Ann Steele, *The University of Texas at KAIST, Republic of Korea in, USA*
Daniel Steffen, *German Research Center for Artificial Intelligence (DFKI), Germany*
Ben Steichen, *University of British Columbia, Canada*
Martin Stein, *University of Siegen, Germany*
Sebastian Stein, *University of Dundee, Scotland, UK*
Fabius Steinberger, *University of Technology, Australia*
Thomas Steiner, *Hamburg, Germany*
Aaron Steinfeld, *Carnegie Mellon University, USA*
Frank Steinicke, *University of Würzburg, Germany*
Sophie Stellmach, *Technische Universität Dresden, Germany*
Amanda Stent, *Yahoo! Labs, USA*
William Steptoe, *UCL, UK*
Sarah Stevenage
Gunnar Stevens, *University of Siegen, Germany*
Craig Stewart, *University of Glasgow, Scotland, UK*

Michael Stewart, *Virginia Polytechnic Institute and State University, USA*
Rainer Stiefelhagen, *Universität Karlsruhe (TH), Germany*
Jeremiah Still, *Missouri Western State University, USA*
David Stillwell, *University of Nottingham, UK*
Greg Stoddard, *Northwestern, USA*
Erik Stolterman, *Indiana University Bloomington, USA*
Margaret-Anne Storey, *University of Victoria,*
Cristiano Storni, *University of Limerick, Ireland*
Steven Strachan, *CEA, France*
Daniel Strazzulla, *INRIA, France*
Yolande Strengers, *AHURI-RMIT Research Centre, Australia*
Dagny Stuedahl, *University of Oslo, Norway*
Simone Stumpf, *City University London, UK*
Christian Sturm, *Hamm-Lippstadt University of Applied Sciences, Germany*
Norman Su, *University College Dublin, Ireland*
Ozge Subasi, *Vienna University of Technology, Austria*
Sriram Subramanian, *University of Bristol, UK*
Yusuke Sugano, *The University of Tokyo, Japan*
Masanori Sugimoto, *Hokkaido University, Japan*
Bongwon Suh, *Seoul National University, Republic of Korea*
Hyeon-Jeong Suk, *KAIST, South Korea*
Piyawadee Sukaviriya, *IBM Research - T. J. Watson, USA*
Gita Sukthankar, *University of Central Florida, USA*
Evan Suma, *University of Southern California, USA*
Chengzheng Sun, *Nanyang Technological University, Singapore*
David Sun, *UC Berkeley, USA*
Huatong Sun, *University of Washington Tacoma, USA*
Xiao Hua Sun, *IBM Research China, China*
Hari Sundaram, *Arizona State University, USA*
Petra Sundström, *Mobile Life @ SICS, Sweden*
Ja-Young Sung, *Georgia Institute of Technology, USA*
Siddharth Suri, *Microsoft Research, USA*
Alistair Sutcliffe, *The University of Manchester, UK*
Dag Svænes, *NTNU, Norway*
David Swallow, *University of York, UK*
Colin Swindells, *University of Victoria, Canada*
Cristina Sylla, *University of Minho, Portugal*
Anna-Liisa Syrjänen, *University of Oulu, Finland*
Daniel Szafir, *University of Wisconsin, USA*
Agnieszka (aga) Szostek, *Warsaw School of Social Psychology, Poland*
Gerd Szwillus, *Universität Paderborn, Germany*
Aurélien Tabard, *University of Munich, Germany*
Leila Takayama, *Willow Garage, USA*
Justin Talbot, *Stanford University, USA*
Chek Tien Tan, *University of Technology, Australia*
Hong Tan, *Microsoft Research Asia, China*
Kumiko Tanaka-Ishii, *University of Tokyo, Japan*
Joshua Tanenbaum, *Simon Fraser University, Canada*
Karen Tanenbaum, *Simon Fraser University, USA*
Anthony Tang, *University of Calgary, Canada*
Charlotte Tang, *University of British Columbia, Canada*
John Tang, *Microsoft Research, USA*
Stefano Targher, *University of Trento, Italy*
Andrea Tartaro, *Furman University, USA*

Craig Tashman, *Georgia Institute of Technology, USA*
Dan Tasse, *Carnegie Mellon University, USA*
Sarah Tausch, *University of Munich, Germany*
Alex Taylor, *Microsoft Research, UK*
Nick Taylor, *University of Dundee, UK*
Robyn Taylor, *Newcastle University, UK*
Stuart Taylor, *Microsoft Research, UK*
Robert Teather, *McMaster University, Canada*
Kimberly Tee, *SMART Technologies, USA*
Daniel Teibel, *Cassia, USA*
Paul Tennent, *The University of Nottingham, UK*
Monica Tentori, *UABC, Mexico*
Leong-Hwee Teo, *Carnegie Mellon University, Singapore*
Lucia Terrenghi, *Google, Switzerland*
Michael Terry, *University of Waterloo, Canada*
Loren Terveen, *University of Minnesota, USA*
Ambuj Tewari, *University of Michigan, USA*
Anuj Tewari, *UC Berkeley, USA*
Anja Thieme, *Newcastle University, UK*
Harold Thimbleby, *University of Swansea, Wales, UK*
Elizabeth Thiry, *Pennsylvania State University, USA*
Jennifer Thom, *Amazon, USA*
Katherine Thomas, *University of North Texas, USA*
Edison Thomaz, *Georgia Institute of Technology, USA*
Bart Thomee, *Yahoo Labs, Spain*
Robin Thompson, *Newcastle University, UK*
Feng Tian, *Chinese Academy of Sciences, P.r. China*
Lorenza Tiberio, *National Research Council of Italy (CNR), Italia*
Rob Tieben, *Eindhoven University of Technology, Netherlands*
Janko Timmermann, *OFFIS - Institute for Information Technology, Germany*
Nava Tintarev, *University of Aberdeen, Scotland, UK*
Mike Tissenbaum, *University of Toronto, Canada*
Hiroaki Tobita, *Sony CSL Paris, Tokyo*
Eran Toch, *Tel Aviv University, Israel*
Lisa Tolentino, *Arizona State University, USA*
Konrad Tollmar, *KTH, Sweden*
Peter Tolmie, *University of Nottingham, UK*
Catalina Toma, *University of Wisconsin-Madison, USA*
Christian Tominski, *University of Rostock, Germany*
Martin Tomitsch, *Vienna University of Technology, Australia*
Bill Tomlinson, *University of California, USA*
James Tompkin, *MPI Informatik, Germany*
KAIST, Republic of Korea in Toombs, *Indiana University Bloomington, USA*
Mercan Topkara, *IBM Research, USA*
Tammy Toscos, *Indiana University-Purdue University, USA*
Chad Tossell, *Rice University, USA*
W. Ben Towne, *Carnegie Mellon University, USA*
Cuong Tran, *University of California, USA*
Minh-Triet Tran, *University of Science, Vietnam*
Matthias Treder, *Technische Universität Berlin, Germany*
Jeffrey Treem, *Northwestern University, USA*
Shari Trewin, *IBM Research - T. J. Watson, USA*

Ha Trinh, *University of Dundee, UK*
Giovanni Maria Troiano, *Universitat Pompeu Fabra, Spain*
Khai Truong, *University of Toronto, Canada*
Janice Tsai, *Microsoft Research, USA*
Theophanis Tsandilas, *Inria, France*
Jason Tsay, *Carnegie Mellon University, USA*
Edward Tse, *SMART Technologies, Canada*
Nikolaos Tselios, *University of Patras, Greece*
Yuan-Chi Tseng, *National Cheng Kung University, Taiwan*
Jessica Tsimeris, *KAIST, Republic of Korea ralian National University, Australia*
Gill Tsouri, *Rochester Institute of Technology, USA*
Katherine Tsui, *University of Massachusetts Lowell, USA*
Oren Tsur, *Harvard University, USA*
Huawei Tu, *Swansea University, UK*
Alexandre Tuch, *University of Basel, Switzerland*
Zeynep Tufekci, *University of North Carolina, USA*
Kathleen Tuite, *University of Washington, USA*
Marcello Turconi, *University of Trieste, Italy*
Jayson Turner, *Lancaster University, UK*
Thea Turner, *USA*
Lisa Tweedie, *Tweedie Consulting, UK*
Michael Twidale, *University of Illinois at Urbana-Champaign, USA*
George Tzanetakis, *University of Victoria, Canada*
Brygg Ullmer, *Louisiana State University, USA*
Kent Unruh, *University of Washington, USA*
Connor Upton, *Intel Labs Europe, Ireland*
Blase Ur, *Carnegie Mellon University, USA*
Dina Utami
Stephen Uzor, *Glasgow Caledonian University, UK*
Kaisa Väänänen-Vainio-Mattila, *Tampere University of Technology, Finland*
Heli Väätäjä, *Tampere University of Technology, Finland*
Philip Vahey, *SRI International, USA*
Rajan Vaish, *University of California, USA*
Consuelo Valdes, *Wellesley College, USA*
Dimitar Valkov, *University of Muenster, Germany*
Anna Vallgårda, *IT University of Copenhagen, Denmark*
Philip Van Allen, *Art Center College of Design, USA*
Bram Van de Laar, *University of Twente,*
Robin Van Den Akker, *Belgium*
Jan Van Den Bergh, *Hasselt University - Tul - Iminds, Belgium*
Bart Van Den Hooff, *VU University Amsterdam, The Netherlands*
Janet Van Der Linden, *The Open University, UK*
Jelle Van Dijk, *Eindhoven University of Technology, Netherlands*
Aart Van Halteren, *Philips Research, Netherlands*
Frank Van Ham, *IBM Research, USA*
Nancy Van House, *University of California, USA*
Max Van Kleek, *MIT, UK*
Kristof Van Laerhoven, *TU Darmstadt, Germany*
Jos Van Leeuwen, *University of Madeira, Portugal*
Christof Van Nimwegen, *Utrecht University, The Netherlands*
Paul Van Schaik, *Teesside University, UK*

Peter Van Waart, *Rotterdam University of Applied Sciences, The Netherlands*
Davy Vanacken, *Hasselt University - Tul - Iminds, Belgium*
Jeroen Vanattenhoven, *KU Leuven, Belgium*
Andrew Vande Moere, *KU Leuven, Belgium*
Jean Vanderdonckt, *Université Catholique de Louvain (UCL), Belgium*
Kami Vaniea, *Carnegie Mellon University, USA*
Elina Vartiainen, *Nokia Research Center, Sweden*
Asimina Vasalou, *University of Birmingham, UK*
Radu-Daniel Vatavu, *University Stefan Cel Mare of Suceava, Romania*
Yolanda Vazquez-Alvarez, *University of Glasgow, UK*
Eduardo Veas, *Graz University of Technology, Austria*
Rajesh Veeraraghavan, *UC Berkeley, USA*
Laurian Vega, *Virginia Tech, USA*
Tiffany Veinot, *University of Michigan, USA*
Eduardo Velloso, *Lancaster University, UK*
Gina Venolia, *Microsoft Research, USA*
Colin Venters, *University of Huddersfield, UK*
Nervo Verdezoto, *Aarhus University, Denmark*
Arnold Vermeeren, *Delft University of Technology, The Netherlands*
Amber Vermeesch, *Michigan State University, USA*
Jo Vermeulen, *Hasselt University - Tul - Iminds, Belgium*
Frederic Vernier, *Université Paris XI, France*
Keith Vertanen, *Montana Tech, USA*
Roel Vertegaal, *Queen's University, Canada*
Janet Vertesi, *Princeton University, USA*
Carla Verwijs, *In Transition, Canada*
Chi Vi, *University of Bristol, UK*
Melodie Vidal, *Lancaster University, UK*
Timothy Vidas, *Carnegie Mellon University, USA*
Sarah Vieweg, *Qatar Computing Research Institute, Qatar*
Markel Vigo, *University of Manchester, UK*
Nicolas Villar, *Microsoft Research, UK*
Vinayak, *Purdue University, USA*
Jussi Virkkala
Jessica Vitak, *University of Maryland, USA*
Lisa Vizer, *University of Maryland, USA*
Vasillis Vlachokyriakos, *Newcastle University, UK*
Simon Voelker, *RWTH-Aachen University, Germany*
Christian Vogler, *Gallaudet University, USA*
Stephen Voida, *Indiana University, USA*
Martin Voigt, *TU Dresden, Germany*
Dirk Vom Lehn, *King's College London, Great Britain*
Ulrich Von Zadow, *Archimedes Exhibitions Gmbh, Germany*
Emanuel Von Zezschwitz, *University of Munich, Germany*
Mihaela Vorvoreanu, *Purdue University, USA*
Hana Vrzakova, *University of Eastern Finland, Finland*
Romain Vuillemot, *Harvard University, USA*
Dhaval Vyas, *University of Twente, The Netherlands*
Katarzyna Wac, *Carnegie Mellon University, USA*
Chat Wacharamanotham, *RWTH Aachen University, Germany*
Juan P. Wachs, *Purdue University, USA*
Greg Wadley, *The University of Melbourne, Australia*

Johanna Wagner, *Graz University of Technology, Austria*
Julie Wagner, *INRIA, Germany*
Patrick Wagstrom, *Carnegie Mellon University, USA*
Shahtab Wahid, *Virginia Tech, USA*
Brendan Walker, *The University of Nottingham, England, UK*
Bruce Walker, *Georgia Institute of Technology, USA*
Erin Walker, *Arizona State University, USA*
I Walker, *University of Bath, UK*
Lorna Wall, *UCL, UK*
Steven Wall, *System Concepts Ltd, UK*
James Wallace, *University of Waterloo, Canada*
Jayne Wallace, *University of Dundee, UK*
Guenter Wallner, *University of Applied Arts Vienna, Austria*
Jagoda Walny, *University of Calgary, Canada*
Greg Walsh, *University of Maryland, USA*
Tanja Walsh, *Tampere University of Technology, Finland*
Robert Walter, *Telekom Innovation Laboratories, Germany*
Lin Wan, *University of Siegen, Germany*
Chaoli Wang, *Michigan Technological University, USA*
Fei Wang, *IBM Research - Almaden, USA*
Jing Wang, *The Pennsylvania State University, USA*
Jingtao Wang, *University of Pittsburgh, USA*
Liang Wang, *Microsoft, USA*
Robert Wang, *Massachusetts Institute of Technology, USA*
Rongrong Wang, *Samsung Research America, USA*
Xiaoyu Wang, *University of North Carolina at Charlotte, USA*
Yang Wang, *Syracuse University, USA*
Yi-Chia Wang, *Carnegie Mellon University, USA*
Yuchen Wang, *University of Alberta, Canada*
Colin Ware, *University of New Hampshire, USA*
Andrew Warr, *Google, USA*
Rick Wash, *Michigan State University, USA*
Gloria Washington, *Clemson University, USA*
Takayuki Watanabe, *Tokyo Woman's Christian University, Japan*
Kari Watkins, *Georgia Institute of Technology, USA*
Diane Watson, *University of Waterloo, Canada*
Martin Wattenberg, *IBM Research, USA*
Leon Watts, *University of Bath, UK*
Jenny Waycott, *The University of Melbourne, Australia*
Kimberly Weaver, *Georgia Institute of Technology, USA*
Gerhard Weber, *Technische Universität Dresden, Germany*
Michael Weber, *University of Ulm, Germany*
Ina Wechsung, *TU Berlin, Germany*
Rina Wehbe, *University of Ontario Institute of Technology, Canada*
Xuetao Wei, *University of Cincinnati, USA*
Anne Weibert, *University of Siegen, Germany*
Christian Weichel, *Lancaster University, UK*
Karl-Heinz Weidmann, *Fachhochschule Vorarlberg, KAIST, Republic of Korea ria/Europe*
Alexandra Weilenmann, *IT-University of Göteborg, Sweden*
Tino Weinkauf, *Max-Planck Institut Für Informatik, Germany*
Astrid Weiss, *Vienna University of Technology, Austria*
Stephan Wensveen, *Eindhoven University of Technology, The Netherlands*

Elizabeth Wenzel, *NASA Ames Research Center, USA*
Wayne Westerman, *Apple, USA*
Adam Westerski, *Universidad Politecnica de Madrid, Spain*
Tara Whalen, *Dalhousie University, Canada*
Joseph Wherton, *Barts and The London School of Medicine and Dentistry, UK*
Brandyn White, *University of Maryland: College Park, USA*
Kevin White, *University of Maryland Baltimore County, USA*
Sean White, *Nokia, USA*
Anthony Whitehead, *Carleton University, Canada*
Michael Whitney, *University of North Carolina at Charlotte, USA*
Steve Whittaker, *University of California Santa Cruz, USA*
Jon Whittle, *Infolab21, UK*
Mikael Wiberg, *Umeå University, Sweden*
Hadley Wickham, *Rstudio, USA*
Josef Wiemeyer, *Sport Science, Germany*
Jason Wiese, *Carnegie Mellon University, USA*
Alexander Wiethoff, *University of Munich, Germany*
Andrea Wiggins, *University of New Mexico, USA*
Danielle Wilde, *Rmit University, Australia*
Erik Wilde, *UC Berkeley, USA*
Oliver Wilder-Smith, *Northeastern University, USA*
David Wilfinger, *University of Salzburg, Austria*
Wesley Willett, *INRIA, France*
Amanda Williams, *Wyld Collective Ltd., Canada*
Amanda Marisa Williams, *University of California, Canada*
Joseph Williams, *Stanford University, USA*
Kaiton Williams, *Cornell University, USA*
John Williamson, *University of Glasgow, UK*
Julie Williamson, *University of Glasgow, UK*
Andrew Wilson, *Microsoft Research, USA*
Graham Wilson, *University of Glasgow, Scotland, UK*
Mathew Wilson, *Swansea University, UK*
Max Wilson, *Swansea University, UK*
Raphael Wimmer, *University of Munich, Germany*
Marco Winckler, *ICS-IRIT, France*
Christian Winkler, *Ulm University, Germany*
Sarah Wiseman, *University College London, UK*
Pamela Wisniewski, *The Pennsylvania State University, USA*
Jason Wither, *Microsoft, USA*
Jens Witkowski, *Albert-Ludwigs-Universität Freiburg, Germany*
Dan Witzner Hansen, *IT University of Copenhagen, Denmark*
Jacob Wobbrock, *University of Washington, USA*
Jill Woelfer, *University of Washington, USA*
Donghee Yvette Wohn, *Northwestern University, USA*
Katrin Wolf, *Deutsche Telekom Laboratories, Germany*
Peter Wolkerstorfer, *CURE - Center for Usability Research & Engineering, Austria*
B.l. William Wong, *Middlesex University, UK*
Nelson Wong, *University of Saskatchewan, Canada*
Krist Wongsuphasawat, *University of Maryland, USA*
Gavin Wood, *Newcastle University, UK*
Simon Wood, *ABC, Australia*
Emma Woodberry, *Addenbrooke's Hospital, UK*

Rob Woodbury, *Simon Fraser University, Canada*
Allison Woodruff, *Intel Research, USA*
Kirk Woolford, *University of Surrey, UK*
Marcel Worring, *University of Amsterdam, The Netherlands*
Rita Wouhaybi, *Intel Corporation, USA*
Julie Wright, *Umass Boston, USA*
Michael Wright, *University of Bath, UK*
Peter Wright, *Newcastle University, UK*
Andy Wu, *Georgia Institute of Technology, USA*
Anna Wu, *Pennsylvania State University, USA*
Jiayu Wu, *Tsinghua University, China*
Mike Wu, *The University of Toronto, Canada*
Shaomei Wu, *Information Science, USA*
Yu Wu, *The Pennsylvania State University, USA*
Daniela Wurhofer, *University of Salzburg, Austria*
Susan Wyche, *Michigan State University, USA*
Peta Wyeth, *Queensland University of Technology, Australia*
Ruth Wylie, *Arizona State University, USA*
Lonce Wyse, *National University of Singapore, Singapore*
Robert Xiao, *Carnegie Mellon University, USA*
Xiao Xiao, *Massachusetts Institute of Technology, USA*
Xing Xie, *Microsoft Research Asia, China*
Anbang Xu, *University of Illinois at Urbana-Champaign, USA*
Heng Xu, *The Pennsylvania State University, USA*
Yan Xu, *Intel Labs, USA*
Kota Yamaguchi, *University of Tokyo, Japan*
Katsu Yamane, *Disney Research, USA*
Naomi Yamashita, *NTT Communication Science Laboratories, Japan*
Hirotake Yamazoe, *Osaka University, Japan*
de-Nian Yang, *Academia Sinica, Taipei*
Huahai Yang, *IBM Research - Almaden, USA*
Jiang Yang, *University of Michigan, USA*
Rayoung Yang, *University of Michigan, USA*
Rui Yang
Stephen Yang, *SUNY Cortland, USA*
Xing-Dong Yang, *University of Alberta, Canada*
Koji Yatani, *Microsoft Research Asia, China*
Yina Ye, *Helsinki Institute for Information Technology HIIT, Finland*
Nick Yee, *PARC, USA*
Tom Yeh, *University of Colorado, USA*
Yeliz Yesilada, *University of Manchester, UK*
Jude Yew, *National University of Singapore, Singapore*
Samantha Yglesias, *Virginia Tech, Montgomery*
Ji Soo Yi, *Purdue University, USA*
Emine Yilmaz, *University College London, UK*
Langxuan Yin, *Northeastern University, USA*
Ming Yin, *Harvard University, USA*
Jason Yip, *University of Maryland, USA*
Salu Ylirisku, *Aalto University, Finland*
Christian Yoder, *University of California, USA*
Daisy Yoo, *Carnegie Mellon University, USA*
Hyoseok Yoon, *KAIST, Korea*
Chuang-Wen You, *Academia Sinica, Taiwan*

Alyson Young, *UMBC, USA*
James Young, *University of Manitoba, Canada*
Chun Yu, *Tsinghua University, China*
Lixiu Yu, *Carnegie Mellon University, USA*
Michael Yu, *Carnegie Mellon University, USA*
Neng-Hao Yu, *National Taiwan University, Taiwan*
Zhiwen Yu, *School of Computer Science Xi'an, China*
Chien Wen Yuan, *Cornell University, USA*
Nicholas Yuan, *Microsoft Research Asia, China*
Beste Yuksel, *Tufts University, USA*
Stanislaw Zabramski, *Uppsala University, Sweden*
Lisl Zach, *Drexel University, USA*
Jose Zagal, *Georgia Institute of Technology, USA*
Panagiotis Zaharias, *Athens University of Economics and Business, Greece*
Bieke Zaman, *IBBT-KU Leuven, Belgium*
Massimo Zancanaro, *FBK-Irst, Italy*
Richard Zanibbi, *Rochester Institute of Technology, USA*
Michael Zarro, *Drexel University, USA*
Polle Zellweger, *Maczell Consulting, USA*
Shumin Zhai, *Research @ Google, USA*
Cheng Zhang, *Georgia Institute of Technology, USA*
Haimo Zhang, *National University of Singapore, Singapore*
Haoqi Zhang, *Harvard University, USA*
Pei Zhang, *Carnegie Mellon University, USA*
Tao Zhang, *North Carolina State University, USA*
Yan Zhang, *University of Texas at KAIST, Republic of Korea in, USA*
Yanxia Zhang, *Lancaster University, UK*
Chen Zhao, *Alibaba International UED, USA*
Dejin Zhao, *PSU, USA*
Jian Zhao, *University of Toronto, Canada*
Xuan Zhao, *University of Michigan, USA*
Bin Zheng, *University of Alberta, Canada*
Yangshuo Zheng, *Tsinghua University, China*
Jia Zhou, *Chongqing, China*
Lina Zhou, *University of Maryland, USA*
Yajin Zhou, *Raleigh, USA*
Bin Zhu, *Microsoft Research Asia, China*
Haiyi Zhu, *Carnegie Mellon University, USA*
Mengxiao Zhu, *Rutgers University, USA*
Zhigang Zhu, *The City College of New York, USA*
Martina Ziefle, *Rwth Aachen University, Germany*
Juergen Ziegler, *University of Duisburg-Essen, Germany*
Caroline Ziemkiewicz, *Brown University, USA*
Roshanak Zilouchian Moghaddam, *University of Illinois at Urbana-Champaign, USA*
Ryder Ziola, *University of Washington, USA*
Miriam Zisook, *Northeastern University, USA*
Hadar Ziv, *University of California, USA*
Goranka Zoric, *Stockholm University, Sweden*
Jo Zucco, *University of South KAIST, Republic of Korea ralia, Australia*
Sacha Zyto, *MIT, USA*

Special thanks for the financial support provided by the following sponsors:

CHI Champion Sponsors

AUTODESK®

Bloomberg

Google

Graphisme, animation et nouveaux médias
GRAND
Graphics, Animation and New Media

Microsoft

NAVER

Computer Science
UNIVERSITY OF TORONTO

CHI Contributing Sponsors

facebook

NSF

YAHOO! LABS

Friends of CHI

Disney Research   Newcastle University

Printed on Rolland Enviro 100
100% post-consumer fiber
Certified EcoLogo
Processed chlorine free
Manufactured using biogas energy
Printed using soy-based inks

Remote Handshaking: Touch Enhances Video-Mediated Social Telepresence

Hideyuki Nakanishi[1], Kazuaki Tanaka[1,2], Yuya Wada[1]
[1]Department of Adaptive Machine Systems, Osaka University
[2]CREST, Japan Science and Technology Agency
2-1 Yamadaoka, Suita, Osaka 565-0871, Japan
{nakanishi, tanaka, yuya.wada}@ams.eng.osaka-u.ac.jp

ABSTRACT
Since past studies on haptic and visual communication have tended to be isolated from each other, it has remained unclear whether a touch channel can still enrich mediated communication where video and audio channels are already available. To clarify this, we analyzed remote handshaking in which a robot hand that was attached just under a videoconferencing terminal's display moved according to the opening and closing motion of a conversation partner's hand. Combining touch and video channels raises a question as to whether the partner's action of touching a haptic device should be visible to the user. If it can be invisible, the action may be unnecessary, and a unilaterally controlled device may be enough to establish an effective touch channel. Our analysis revealed that the feeling of being close to the partner can be enhanced by mutual touch in which the partner's action needs to occur but should be invisible.

Author Keywords
Haptic devices; humanoid robots; social touch; social telepresence; videoconferencing; video-mediated communication; social interaction.

ACM Classification Keywords
H.5.3 Information interfaces and presentation (e.g., HCI): Group and Organization Interfaces - Computer-supported cooperative work.

INTRODUCTION
Social telepresence is an illusion that users who are actually in geographically separated places feel as if they were meeting face to face with each other. Various ways to produce and strengthen this illusion have been extensively studied, since a lack of the illusion is regarded as a bottleneck in replacing a face-to-face meeting with a teleconference. A live video connection is a basic method for producing the feeling of meeting face to face [10,16], which is strengthened if the setup of cameras and displays allows eye contact to be established [4,22]. A past study found that the quality of telepresence is improved when the picture of a conversation partner is stereoscopic or life-size [26]. Recent studies reported that a moving point of view, which can be implemented as a remote camera that moves according to the position of a user's eyes [13], enhances social telepresence [19,20]. It is also reported that a picture of a conversation partner's upper body produces a stronger sense of oneness than a picture that included only the partner's head [23], and the physical movement of a display that shows the upper body enhances social telepresence [21]. All of these techniques depend on a live video connection and do not use any other communication channel. Between video-mediated and face-to-face situation, there is an inherent difference, i.e., a haptic communication channel.

Although mediated social touch, which is a haptic sensation transmitted between geographically separated users, has been extensively studied [14], those studies have paid limited attention to social telepresence. Since it's almost impossible to create a single all-purpose device that can imitate all kinds of touch, some studies devoted most of their efforts to developing a device that is tailored to transmit a specific kind of haptic sensation [5,11,12,15,18,24,33]. Since social touch cannot send explicit messages that can be delivered by texts or audio, other studies focused on analyzing how social touch is used as an additional nonverbal communication channel to deliver emotional states or simple reactions [1,6,8,25,31,32]. As a result, a moderate number of studies have observed the effects of touch on social telepresence. One of the studies found various effects of social touch but failed to find its effects specifically on social telepresence [28]. Another study successfully observed that social touch was able to strengthen social telepresence [3], though this result seems somewhat obvious, since each pair of subjects in that study was not connected by any other communication channel, e.g., audio or video. Recently, it was reported that audio communication accompanied by a touch channel was superior to audio-only communication in producing social telepresence [34]. Eventually, it has remained unclear whether the addition of touch can enhance

CHI 2014, April 26 - May 01 2014, Toronto, ON, Canada

ACM 978-1-4503-2473-1/14/04...$15.00.
http://dx.doi.org/10.1145/2556288.2557169

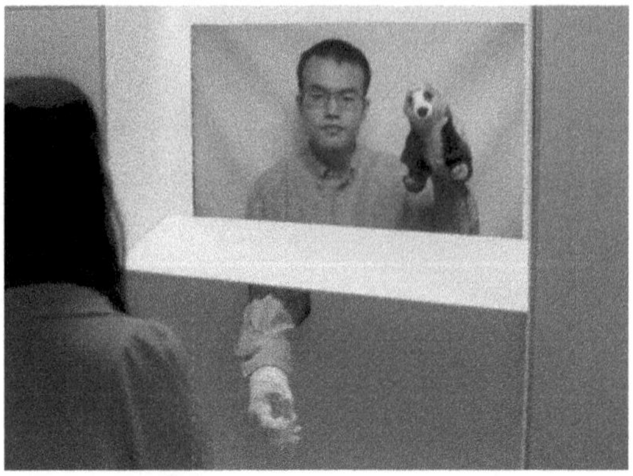

Figure 1. Snapshot of the system

video-mediated communication, which is a standard means of social telepresence.

As shown in Figure 1, we developed a system that integrates a touch channel into video-mediated communication (http://www.diginfo.tv/v/12-0045-r-en.php). And we observed the touch channel's contribution to social telepresence in a situation where both audio and video channels are available to users. A previous study showed that a video chat system that had a social touch function produced significantly higher social telepresence than a normal system [29]. This is an interesting result but it has not been sufficiently examined. Since the subjects in that study compared a simple video chat environment with a combination of that environment and a special haptic device after experiencing both of them, this comparison seemed to suggest rating the latter condition higher. Furthermore, the baseline to appraise social touch was low enough to make it easy to find significant effects of social touch, since the small-size display of the video chat environment was able to show only a conversation partner's head that was smaller than life-size, which leads to a low-level social telepresence [23,26]. In contrast to this previous study, we conducted a between-subjects experiment to make haptic and video-only conditions rated by a separated group of subjects, and we used a large-size display to show a nearly life-size picture of a human upper body.

DESIGNS

How to Integrate Social Touch

There are several possible ways to integrate social touch into video-mediated communication. In mediated social touch, each of the two geographically separated users has devices for input and output. A user's touching action is captured by the input device, and the output device provides the other user a haptic sensation. The integration with video-mediated communication confuses this situation, since the live video connection can provide visual feedback that corresponds to the touching action and also visual information that complements the haptic sensation. Moreover, it must be taken into account that the visual feedback enables social touch without any haptic sensation, which is purely remote control of the output device. The presence or absence of visual feedback, visual information, and haptic sensation gives birth to a variety of integration methods.

This study adopted a handshake as a representative example of social touch, because a handshake is a mutual touching action that appears in a field of view. Namely, a person triggers his/her own action and recognizes the other's action simultaneously, and can see both actions at once. This kind of touching action is suitable to study the diversity that is attributed to the presence or absence of visual feedback, visual information, and haptic sensation. An additional reason to adopt a handshake is that it is the form of social touch that most naturally occurs between strangers. We thought that a function to remotely shake hands would match well with videoconferencing.

We developed a humanlike robot hand that specialized in a handshake and that could also be attached to a videoconferencing terminal as illustrated in Figure 2, which shows five conditions for remote handshaking: (a) the user grasps the robot hand and supposes that the other user remotely controls it (invisible one-way), (b) the user grasps the robot hand and sees that the other user remotely controls it (visible one-way), (c) the user controls the robot hand that is installed in the other user's room (non-haptic one-way), (d) the user grasps the robot hand and supposes that the other user grasps another robot hand that is invisible (invisible two-way), and (e) the user grasps the robot hand and sees that the other user grasps another robot hand (visible two-way). We compared these conditions in the experiments described later.

The conditions described above vary in the combinations of visual feedback, visual information, and haptic sensation. The non-haptic one-way and visible two-way conditions provide visual feedback that enables a user to recognize the

(a) Invisible one-way **(b) Visible one-way** **(c) Non-haptic one-way** **(d) Invisible two-way** **(e) Visible two-way**

Figure 2. Five conditions for remote handshaking

robot hand installed in the other user's room moving according to the opening and closing motion of the user's hand. The visible one-way and visible two-way conditions provide visual information that enables a user to recognize the robot hand moving according to the motion of the other user's hand. All the conditions except the non-haptic one-way condition, in which a user's hand opens and closes in the air, provide a haptic sensation.

How to Construct the Robot Hand

Before this study, we conducted pilot studies in which we repeated developing and testing a prototype of the robot hand. Figure 3 shows one of those prototypes, which was a wooden manikin hand attached to a linear positioning table and could move upward and downward to shake hands. This prototype was ineffective mainly due to the inability to grasp, and also due to its coldness and hardness. Unexpectedly, its ability to shake hands was not very effective. Thus, for this study, we developed a robot hand that had three features as described below. These features distinguish it from conventional humanlike robot hands.

Grip Force

Our robot hand has sufficient grip force for a user to feel as if the user's hand were being grasped by a person. The grip force of conventional humanlike robot hands is usually weaker than ours, because most of them are designed just to express a humanlike motion and not to generate a humanlike force. Figure 4(a) shows the mechanism to move the fingers and thumb. Wires are attached to the inside and outside of each finger/thumb. The servomotor pulls the inside wire to bend the finger/thumb, and pulls the outside wire to stretch the finger/thumb. The wire is enclosed in a corrugated tube to reduce friction. To generate a constant grip force continuously, a spring is inserted into the inside wire.

Body Temperature

Our robot hand becomes warm to imitate the human body temperature. When a user grasps the robot hand, the user can sense the temperature through the contact surface between the user's hand and the robot hand. Since conventional robot hands do not have this function, their coldness may give a user the impression that the robot hand

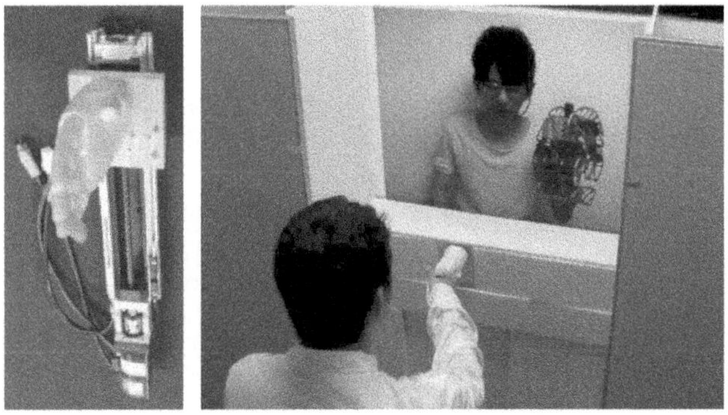

Figure 3. A previous prototype of the robot hand

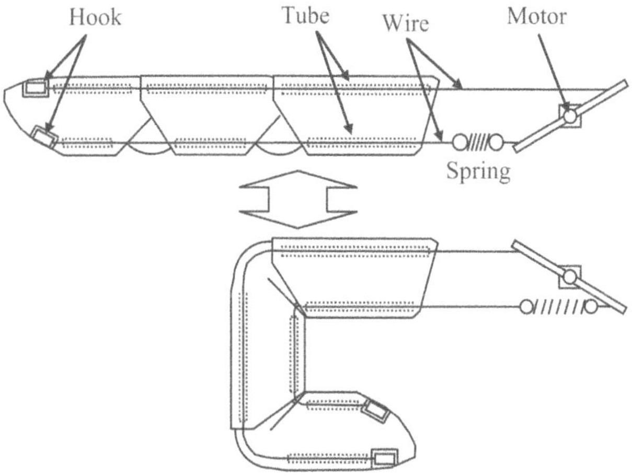

(a) Grip force

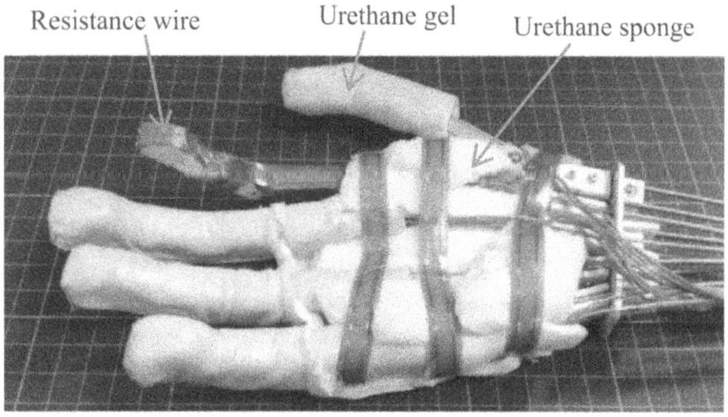

(b) Body temperature and skin softness

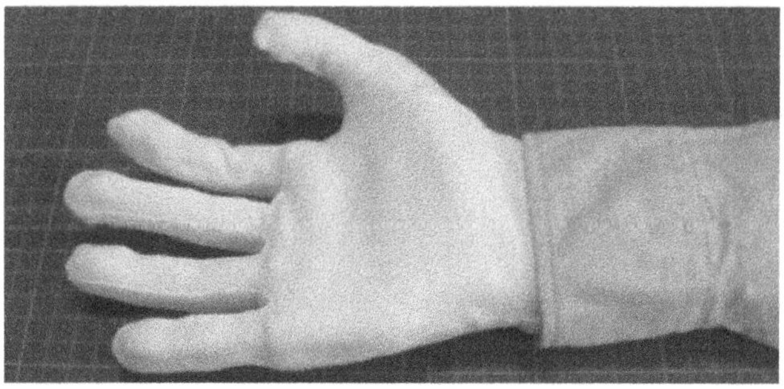

(c) Outside appearance

Figure 4. The robot hand for this study

is a machine and very different from a human hand. This kind of impression is harmful to social telepresence and thus should be avoided. As shown in Figure 4(b), to warm the whole hand, a resistance wire twines round the fingers, thumb, and palm. This picture shows the inside structure of the hand, and its outside appearance is natural as shown in Figure 4(c).

Skin Softness

Our robot hand is wrapped in artificial skin. Conventional robot hands that are wrapped in artificial skin usually make use of the skin to show a humanlike appearance. On the other hand, the skin of our robot hand is intended to provide a humanlike haptic sensation in the following two ways: the softness of the skin mitigates a mechanical feeling that is caused by the hardness of a robot hand, and the yielding ability of the skin reduces a gap that appears between human and robot hands when the robot hand is grasped. Figure 4(b) shows our robot hand being wrapped in two different materials to provide both softness and a yielding ability. The fingers and thumb are wrapped in urethane gel, which has a humanlike softness, whereas the palm is wrapped in urethane sponge so that the palm can yield to pressure very well.

EXPERIMENTS

Goal

We aimed to examine whether remote handshaking enhances social telepresence even when a live video connection provides users both audio and video channels. To do so, it's necessary to show that having a conversation that includes the events of handshaking is better than just having a conversation (no-handshake condition) in video-mediated communication. An experiment to compare them must be between-subjects, since subjects would rate a conversation with the handshaking events higher than a simple conversation after they had both kinds of conversations. The problem here is that there are five conditions for remote handshaking as illustrated in Figure 2, thus a lot of subjects are necessary to enable a between-subjects design. Therefore, we first clarified which of the five conditions is the most effective in producing social telepresence, and then compared it with the no-handshake condition.

The comparison of the conditions for remote handshaking could be within-subjects, since all the conditions included the handshaking events. However, we did not ask the same subject to experience all the conditions, because the explanation to a subject about how to move the robot hand was slightly different between the one-way and two-way conditions. In the one-way conditions, a sensor on a finger captured the motion of a human hand as you can see in Figure 6. The purpose of using the sensor was to make a subject believe that the robot hand truly moved according to the human hand motion. In the two-way conditions we didn't use the sensor, since it might prevent the subject from feeling the temperature and softness of the robot hand. This was not a problem in the one-way conditions where the subject did not need to wear the sensor and grasp the robot hand simultaneously. Thus, the experiment to compare the one-way conditions and the experiment to compare the two-way conditions were separately planned.

In the first experiment, which compared the one-way conditions, we explained to the subjects that the robot hand moved according to the data obtained by the sensor. Since this experiment showed the invisible one-way condition to be the most effective, we compared the condition with the two two-way conditions in the second experiment. In this experiment we briefly explained to the subjects that a person's grasping action triggers the grasping action of the robot hand installed in the other room, though the robot hands were actually controlled by a keyboard in the presenter's room. It was easy to include the invisible one-way condition in the second experiment, since the latter explanation worked well for the condition. Since the invisible two-way condition was the most effective in the second experiment, we compared the condition with the no-handshake condition in the third experiment.

Task

To conduct a controlled experiment, the experiences of talking through the display and paying attention to the display should not differ across the subjects. To satisfy this requirement, a member of our research group played the role of a presenter who gave the subjects the same presentation in which the presenter showed the subject a stuffed toy animal as shown in Figure 1 and asked the subject several questions about the animal.

In all conditions the presentation began and ended with a greeting. In the five handshaking conditions, these greetings included a handshake as follows. In the greeting at the beginning, when the presenter said, "How do you do?" he stretched his hand out forward. When the subject began closing the subject's hand, the presenter said, "Nice to meet you," and closed his hand. When the subject replied to the greeting, the presenter opened his hand and stopped stretching his hand out. Then, the presenter began explaining the stuffed toy. In the greeting at the end, when the presenter said, "Thank you for your attention," he stretched his hand out forward. When the subject began closing the subject's hand, the presenter said, "See you again," and closed his hand. When the subject replied to the greeting, the presenter opened his hand and stopped stretching his hand out. This ended the presentation. The presence or absence of handshakes was only the difference between the no-handshake and the handshaking conditions and the way to exchange greetings was the same in all conditions. The handshakes did not greatly change the period of time spent greeting, so the length of the presentation was almost the same in all conditions.

Setup

Figure 5 depicts the structure of the rooms used for the experiments. As shown in Figure 5(a), the robot hand was attached just under the display, since we hoped that a subject would feel as if the presenter's real hand were sticking out of the terminal. To facilitate this illusion, the color of the clothes of the presenter and the robot hand was the same. We constructed a kiosk terminal so that the subject could shake hands with the presenter naturally. As you can see in Figure 5(b), the presenter was actually seated, but all the subjects thought that he was standing. We used a 28-inch wide-screen display to show a nearly life-size picture of the presenter's upper body. We set the field of view to 30 vertical degrees so that the subjects could

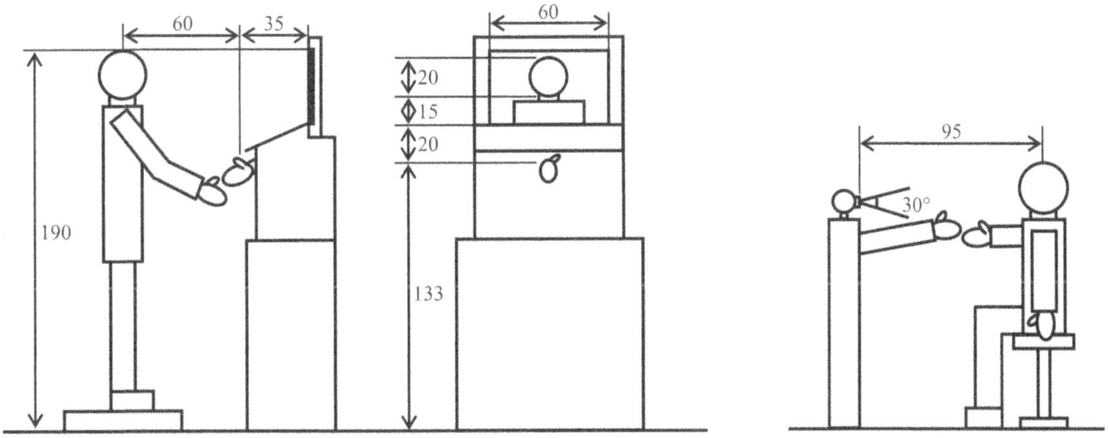

(a) Subject's room (b) Presenter's room

Figure 5. The structure of the rooms used for the experiments (length unit: centimeters)

recognize the presenter stretching his hand out forward even in the two invisible conditions. The height of the base on which the subject stood was adjusted to make the subject's eyes level with the presenter's eyes.

The figure shows the rooms in the case of the visible two-way condition. We didn't use the robot hand in the no-handshake condition, and installed the robot hand only in the presenter's room in the non-haptic one-way condition. In the invisible one-way, the visible one-way, and also the invisible two-way conditions, only the subject's room had the robot hand. So, the setup of the invisible two-way condition was totally identical to that of the invisible one-way condition, and only the verbal explanation about handshaking differed between the two conditions. In the invisible two-way condition, the subject was taught that the presenter shakes hands with another robot hand that was installed in his room, but he did not actually grasp the robot hand in order to make his arm and shoulder motion, which was visible to the subject through the display, completely the same across the two invisible conditions. This contrivance enabled us to see the psychological effects caused by just the subjects' supposition that the handshake was bidirectional in the invisible two-way condition.

Questionnaire

As described below, the questionnaire included several statements and asked the extent to which the statements matched the impression the subject had.

We expected that remote handshaking would increase the degree of social telepresence since two people must be physically collocated in the same space when they shake hands with each other. It was reported that physical accessibility changed the activities of mirror neurons in monkeys' brains [7]. Different neurons discharged when the distance between a monkey and an object differed. And the neuron that discharged when the distance was long also discharged when the distance was short if there was a transparent barrier between the monkey and the object. This situation seems similar to a videoconference, where a transparent barrier, i.e., a display, divides the users. So, we thought that remote handshaking would be able to produce pseudo physical accessibility, which would significantly differentiate the degree of social telepresence. To confirm this, the questionnaire included the following statement:

- I felt as if I were close to the presenter in the same room.

Since a handshake is not just a physical touch but reinforces social bonding, we expected remote handshaking would increase the degree of social bonding. A handshake is a common means of greeting others, a ritual to initiate human relationships, and a basis for initial impressions. It is known that a handshake can nonverbally communicate information of a person's personality [9,30,35], and produce a feeling of being friendly [2]. So, we thought that remote handshaking would be able to produce a similar psychological effect. To confirm this, the questionnaire included the following statement:

- I felt that the presenter was friendly.

In the first and second experiments we asked the subject to answer a second questionnaire, which included a statement about the reality of the handshakes. The subject didn't know that there was another questionnaire before finishing the first questionnaire described above. We separated the questionnaires, because it seems unfair to make the subject unnecessarily pay attention to the handshakes when answering the degree of social telepresence and bonding. The second questionnaire included the following statement:

- I felt as if I were shaking hands with the presenter in real life.

In the third experiment we didn't use the second questionnaire, since we didn't need to compare the reality of the handshakes. In this experiment, we added statements about the quality of the presentation to the first questionnaire. This experiment was between-subjects, so we were afraid that individual differences might cause undesirable differences in the perceived quality of the presentation, which might affect the degrees of social

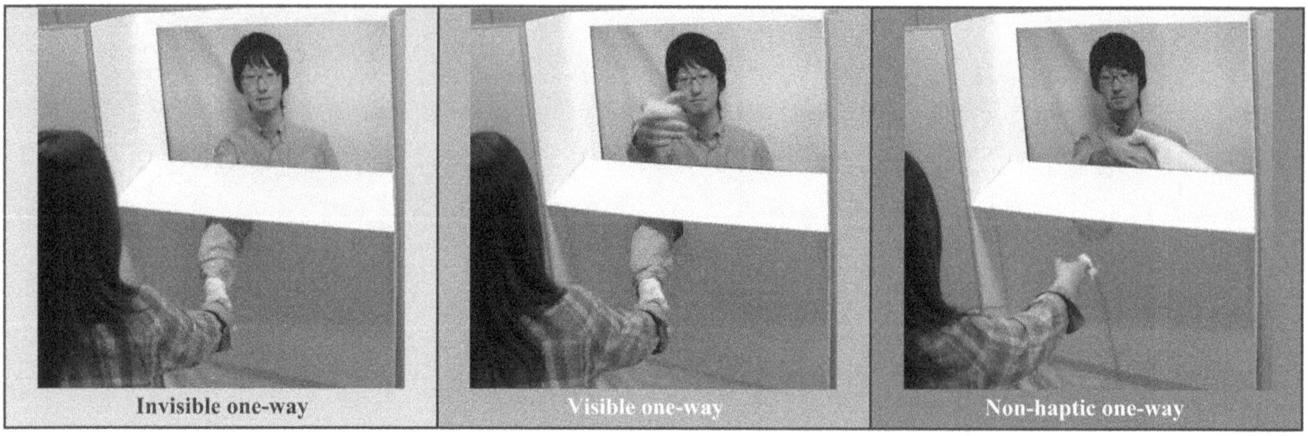

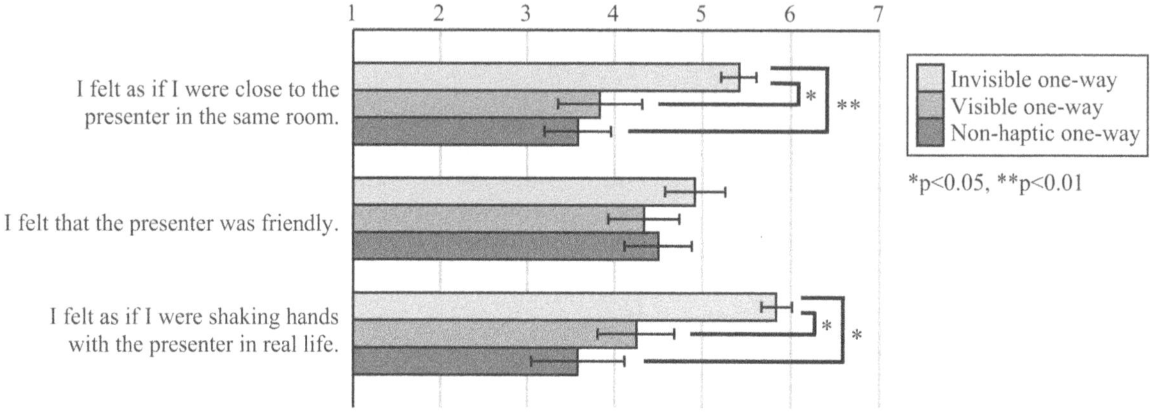

Figure 6. Results of the first experiment

telepresence and bonding. We added the following statements:

- The video was sufficiently clear.
- The audio was sufficiently clear.
- The presentation was intelligible.

In the first and second experiments the subjects answered the two questionnaires after they experienced all three conditions. The order of experiencing was counterbalanced. The subjects rated the statements for each condition. In the third experiment the subjects answered only the first questionnaire. They rated the statements for the condition they experienced.

In the first and second experiments, the statements were rated on a 7-point Likert scale where 1 = strongly disagree, 4 = neutral, and 7 = strongly agree. In the third experiment, the statements were rated on a 9-point Likert scale where 1 = strongly disagree, 5 = neutral, and 9 = strongly agree. We collected open-ended responses in order to infer what determined the scores. All the statements were accompanied with an entry column where the subjects rationalized their scores.

Subjects

The subjects were undergraduate students whose ages ranged from eighteen to twenty-four years. Twelve subjects, consisting of six females and six males, participated in the first experiment. Fifteen subjects, consisting of nine females and six males, participated in the second experiment. Twenty-six subjects participated in the third experiment. This experiment was between-subjects and had two conditions, so thirteen subjects, consisting of six females and seven males, participated in each condition. In total, fifty-three subjects participated in our experiments.

RESULTS

The results of the three experiments are shown in Figures 6, 7, and 8 respectively, in which each box represents the mean value of the responses to each statement, and each bar represents the standard error of the mean value. We used Kolmogorov-Smirnov test to confirm that all the scores obtained in the three experiments are normally distributed.

Figure 6 shows a comparison of the invisible, visible and non-haptic one-way conditions by repeated-measures ANOVA followed by Bonferroni's test. We found a significant difference in the feeling of being close to the presenter in the same room ($F(2,22)=8.084$, $p<.01$). Multiple comparisons showed that this feeling was significantly stronger in the invisible one-way condition than the visible one-way ($p<.05$) and the non-haptic one-way ($p<.01$) conditions. We also found a significant difference in the feeling of shaking hands with the presenter in real life ($F(2,22)= 7.675$, $p<.01$). Multiple comparisons showed that this feeling was significantly stronger in the

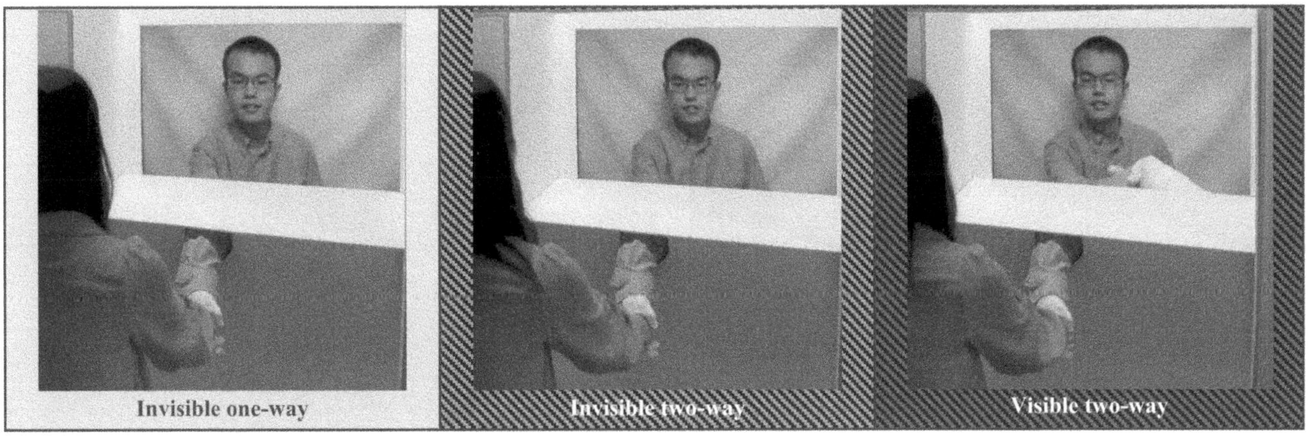

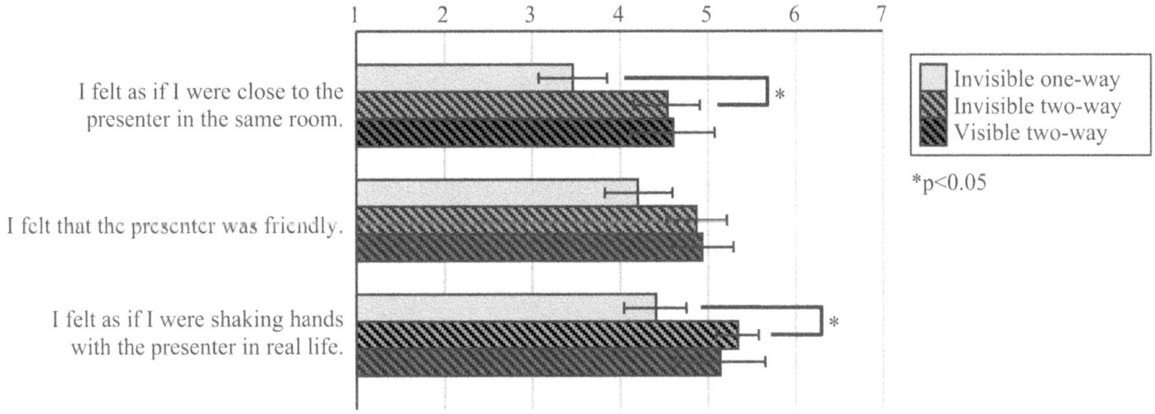

Figure 7. Results of the second experiment

invisible one-way condition than the visible one-way ($p<.05$) and the non-haptic one-way ($p<.05$) conditions. There was no significant difference between the visible one-way and non-haptic one-way conditions. The open-ended responses indicated that the duplication of the presenter's hand degraded the visible one-way condition. Six of the twelve subjects commented that it was strange to see the two presenter's hands, which were the robot hand under the display and the presenter's hand in the display. It was also indicated that the lack of haptic sensation degraded the non-haptic one-way condition. Nine subjects commented that shaking hands in the air was unrealistic.

Figure 7 shows a comparison of the invisible one-way, invisible two-way, and visible two-way conditions by repeated-measures ANOVA followed by Bonferroni's test. We found significant differences in the feeling of being close to the presenter in the same room ($F(2,28)=4.191$, $p<.05$) and the feeling of shaking hands with the presenter in real life ($F(2,28)=3.341$, $p<.05$). Multiple comparisons showed that both feelings were significantly stronger in the invisible two-way condition than the invisible one-way condition ($p<.05$). There was no significant difference between the visible two-way condition and the other conditions. Although the mean values in the two two-way conditions are similar to each other, only the invisible condition was significantly better than the one-way condition. The large variance of the dispersed scores in the visible condition makes it insignificantly differ from the one-way condition. The open-ended responses revealed the scores to be polarized by the visibility of the presenter's action of grasping the robot hand. Seven of the fifteen subjects positively commented on the visibility and five subjects negatively commented on it.

There was no significant difference in the feeling that the presenter was friendly in the first experiment ($F(2,22)=.749$, *n.s.*) and also the second experiment ($F(2,28)=2.127$, *n.s.*). In the open-ended responses, four subjects in each experiment explicitly commented that the difference in the way of shaking hands did not strongly influence the friendliness.

Figure 8 shows a comparison of the invisible two-way condition and the no-handshake condition by a one-tailed t-test. We found a significant difference in the feeling of being close to the presenter in the same room ($t(24)=1.791$, $p<.05$), and also the feeling that the presenter was friendly ($t(24)=2.434$, $p<.05$). Both feelings were significantly stronger in the invisible two-way condition than the no-handshake condition. The open-ended responses indicated that the handshakes, especially the warmth of the robot hand, caused this difference. Six of the thirteen subjects in the invisible two-way condition commented that the handshakes improved the feeling of being close. Three of

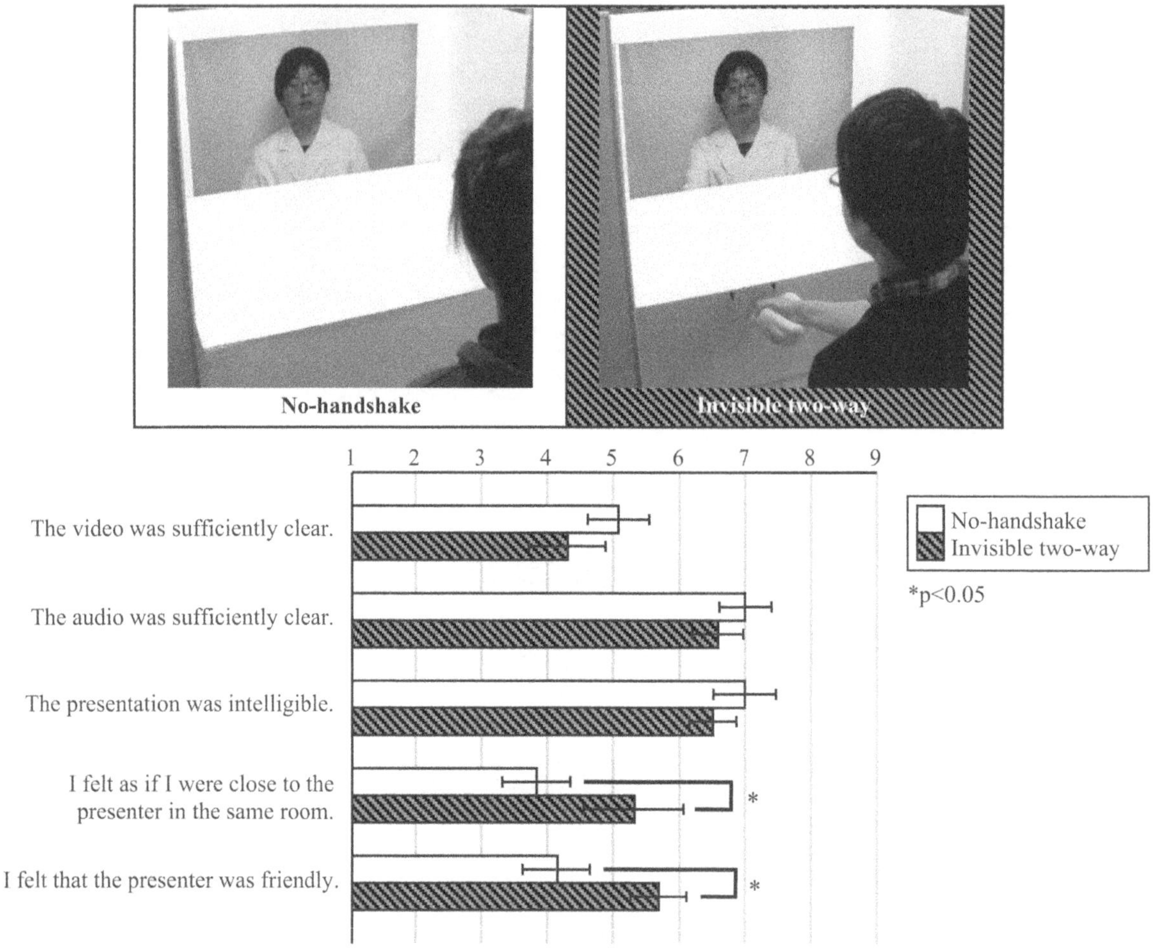

Figure 8. Results of the third experiment

the six subjects also commented that the warmth greatly facilitated the improvement. There was no significant difference in the perceived clearness of the live video and the audio, and in the perceived intelligibility of the presentation, so the audio-visual quality and the quality of the presentation seemed not to affect the results.

DISCUSSION

Overall, the results are convincing. We found that haptic sensation is essential to mediated social touch and should be mutually shared among users, and observed that the mutually shared haptic sensation enhanced social telepresence in video-mediated communication. However, the results of the first experiment were a little surprising, since the most effective condition, which was the invisible one-way condition, was obviously inferior to the visible one-way condition in the visibility of the synchronization between the movements of the robot hand and the presenter's hand. The subjects did not favor the visibility also in the second experiment as follows. The visible two-way condition, in which the subject could see the synchronization, was not better than the invisible two-way condition, in which the subject could not see it. Furthermore, the visible two-way condition was not significantly better than even the invisible one-way condition, which was revealed to be significantly worse than the invisible two-way condition. The visibility of the synchronization itself might be able to provide good effects, but the visibility of the presenter's hand seemed to give rise to the strange duplication and cancel the effects. According to the subjects' comments, the problem seemed to be the duplication itself rather than the discrepancy in appearance between the robot hand and the presenter's hand. It is a topic for future work to explore a way to show the synchronization without showing the duplication.

Probably, a handshake is a mixture of the touch that is a physical access to each other's body and the ritual that expresses an affirmative attitude toward others, and the quality of a user interface for remote handshaking mainly influences the reality of the touch. The results imply that social telepresence can be strengthened by a touch, whereas social bonding can be strengthened by a ritual. The ritual changed the degree of social bonding in the third experiment. There is a possibility that the ritual also changed the degree of social telepresence in the third experiment. However, it seems not to be true that the touch was a secondary factor, since the difference in the design of touch significantly changed the degree of social

Figure 9. Snapshots of our exhibition booth

telepresence in the first and second experiments. It is a topic for future work to separate the effects of the touch and the ritual.

The open-ended responses indicated that the humanlikeness of the robot hand was impressive for the subjects and contributed to the reality of interacting with a real person. This reality may be related to the uncanny valley according to our observation in scientific exhibitions for the general public where we exhibited the hand. In those exhibitions a lot of families visited our booth and experienced grasping the hand as shown in Figure 9. We observed that both children and adults were scared by the hand to some extent but the way of being scared clearly differed between them. Children seemed to expect a real human hand. So, they first were scared by the fact that the hand was not connected with a human body but attached to the wall. Next, they were scared by the difference of a tactile impression between the hand and a real human hand. On the other hand, adults seemed to expect a robot hand that is usually hard and cool. So, they first were surprised by the softness and the warmth of the hand. Next, they were scared by those realistic sensations.

In this study we embodied the minimum part of a human body, which was a hand. A humanoid robot that embodies the entire body of a human operator is an opposite approach [27]. The entire embodiment seems to be superior to the minimum embodiment in mediating diverse kinds of social touch. However, the entire embodiment has a serious unsuitability for producing social telepresence, since it cannot display the human operator's current appearance, which can be delivered by a live video connection. The minimum embodiment makes it possible to mix a visual representation and a physical representation of a human body. This study showed that the mixed representation is superior to a pure visual representation. Comparing the mixed representation with a pure physical representation is a topic for future work.

In this study we attached a robotic device to a videoconferencing terminal. A telepresence robot, which is a videoconferencing terminal mounted on a robotic base [17], is a similar combination, but just enables a user to move around a physical space and does not enable physical interaction as our robot hand can do. The combination of a robotic capability and video-mediated communication is still an unexplored design space and has a lot of possibilities.

CONCLUSION

The attempt to equip a videoconferencing system with a haptic device resulted in creating a user interface that is better than either a videoconferencing system or a haptic device, and also facilitated our understanding of mediated social touch as follows. We found that social touch should be mutual: a physical touch between a user and a robotic imitation of the other user's body should be accompanied with another physical touch between the other user and a robotic imitation of the user's body. We also found that social touch should not be duplicated: the other user's touching the imitation of the user's body should not be visible to the user, since it's unnatural to be simultaneously engaged in the physical touch occurring in front of the display and the visual touch occurring within the display. The user should be engaged only in the physical touch, since it's more realistic than the visual touch. We hope that this study reduces the distance between the studies on video-mediated and touch-mediated communication.

ACKNOWLEDGMENTS

We thank Gaku Senoo for helping this study. This study was supported by JSPS Grants-in-Aid for Scientific Research No. 21680013 "Telerobotic media for supporting social telepresence", No. 20220002 "Representation of human presence by using tele-operated androids", JST CREST "Studies on cellphone-type teleoperated androids transmitting human presence" and Global COE Program "Center of human-friendly robotics based on cognitive neuroscience."

REFERENCES

1. Bailenson, J.N., Yee, N., Brave, S., Merget, D. and Koslow, D. Virtual Interpersonal Touch: Expressing and Recognizing Emotions through Haptic Devices. *Human-Computer Interaction*, 22(3), (2007), 325-353.
2. Bardeen, J.P. Interpersonal Perception through the Tactile, Verbal, and Visual Modes. *International Communication Association Convention*, (1971).
3. Basdogan, C., Ho, C., Srinivasan, M.A. and Slater, M. An Experimental Study on the Role of Touch in Shared Virtual Environments. *Human-Computer Interaction*, 7(4), (2000), 443-460.
4. Bondareva, Y. and Bouwhuis, D. Determinants of Social Presence in Videoconferencing. *Proc. AVI 2004 Workshop on Environments for Personalized Information Access*, (2004), 1-9.
5. Brave, S., Ishii, H. and Dahley, A. Tangible Interfaces for Remote Collaboration and Communication. *Proc. CSCW 98*, (1998), 169-178.

6. Brown, L.M., Sellen, A., Krishna, R. and Harper, R. Exploring the Potential of Audio-Tactile Messaging for Remote Interpersonal Communication, *Proc. CHI2009*, (2009), 1527-1530.

7. Caggiano, V., Fogassi, L., Rizzolatti, G., Thier, P. and Casile, A. Mirror Neurons Differentially Encode the Peripersonal and Extrapersonal Space of Monkeys. *Science*, 324(5925), (2009), 403-406.

8. Chang, A., O'Modhrain, S., Jacob, R., Gunther, E. and Ishii, H. ComTouch: Design of a Vibrotactile Communication Device. *Proc. DIS 2002*, (2002), 312-320.

9. Chaplin, W.F., Phillips, J.B., Brown, J.D., Clanton, N.R. and Stein, J.L. Handshaking, Gender, Personality, and First Impressions. *Journal of Personality and Social Psychology*, 79(1), (2000), 110-117.

10. de Greef, P. and IJsselsteijn, W. Social Presence in a Home Tele-Application. *CyberPsychology & Behavior*, 4(2), (2001), 307-315.

11. Fogg, B.J., Cutler, L.D., Arnold, P. and Eisbach, C. HandJive: A Device for Interpersonal Haptic Entertainment, *Proc. CHI 98*, (1998), 57-64.

12. Furukawa, M., Kajimoto, H. and Tachi, S. KUSUGURI: A Shared Tactile Interface for Bidirectional Tickling. *Proc. AH 2012*, (2012), 9:1-9:8

13. Gaver, W.W., Smets, G. and Overbeeke, K. A Virtual Window on Media Space. *Proc. CHI 95*, (1995), 257-264.

14. Haans, A. and IJsselsteijn, W Mediated Social Touch: a Review of Current Research and Future Directions. *Virtual Reality*, 9(2), (2006), 149-159.

15. Hashimoto, H. and Manoratkul, S. Tele-Handshake through the Internet. *Proc. ROMAN 96*, (1996), 90-95.

16. Isaacs, E.A. and Tang, J.C. What Video Can and Can't Do for Collaboration: a Case Study. *Multimedia Systems*, 2(2), (1994), 63-73.

17. Lee, M.K. and Takayama, L. "Now, I Have a Body": Uses and Social Norms for Mobile Remote Presence in the Workplace. *Proc. CHI 2011*, (2011), 33-42.

18. Morikawa, O., Hashimoto, S., Munakata, T. and Okunaka, J. Embrace System for Remote Counseling. *Proc. ICMI 2006*, (2006), 318-325.

19. Nakanishi, H., Murakami, Y., Nogami, D. and Ishiguro, H. Minimum Movement Matters: Impact of Robot-Mounted Cameras on Social Telepresence. *Proc. CSCW 2008*, (2008), 303-312.

20. Nakanishi, H., Murakami, Y. and Kato, K. Movable Cameras Enhance Social Telepresence in Media Spaces. *Proc. CHI 2009*, (2009), 433-442.

21. Nakanishi, H., Kato, K. and Ishiguro, H. Zoom Cameras and Movable Displays Enhance Social Telepresence. *Proc. CHI2011*, (2011), 63-72.

22. Nguyen, D.T. and Canny, J. Multiview: Improving Trust in Group Video Conferencing through Spatial Faithfulness. *Proc. CHI 2007*, (2007), 1465-1474.

23. Nguyen, D.T. and Canny, J. More than Face-to-Face: Empathy Effects of Video Framing. *Proc. CHI 2009*, (2009), 423-432.

24. O'Brien, S. and Mueller, F. Holding Hands Over a Distance: Technology Probes in an Intimate, Mobile Context. *Proc. OZCHI 2006*, (2006), 293-296.

25. Park, Y.W., Baek, K.M. and Nam, T.J. The Roles of Touch during Phone Conversations: Long-Distance Couples' Use of POKE in Their Homes. *Proc. CHI 2013*, (2013), 1679-1688.

26. Prussog, A., Muhlbach, L. and Bocker, M. Telepresence in Videocommunications. *Proc. Annual Meeting of Human Factors and Ergonomics Society*, (1994), 25-38.

27. Sakamoto, D., Kanda, T., Ono, T., Ishiguro, H. and Hagita, N. Android as a Telecommunication Medium with a Human-like Presence. *Proc. HRI 2007*, (2007), 193-200.

28. Sallnas, E.-L., Rassmus-Grohn, K. and Sjostrom, C. Supporting Presence in Collaborative Environments by Haptic Force Feedback. *Transactions on Computer-Human Interaction*, 7(4), (2000), 461-476.

29. Samani, H.A., Parsani, R., Rodriguez, L.T., Saadatian, E., Dissanayake, K.H. and Cheok, A.D. Kissenger: Design of a Kiss Transmission Device. *Proc. DIS 2012*, (2012), 48-57.

30. Shipps, E.M. and Freeman H.R. Handshake: Its Relation to First Impressions and Measured Personality Traits. *Psi Chi Journal of Undergraduate Research*, 8(4), (2003), 144-148.

31. Smith, J. and MacLean, K. Communicating Emotion through a Haptic Link: Design Space and Methodology. *International Journal of Human-Computer Studies*, 65(4), (2007), 376-387.

32. Suhonen K., Vaananen-Vainio-Mattila, K. and Makela, K. User Experiences and Expectations of Vibrotactile, Thermal and Squeeze Feedback in Interpersonal Communication. *Proc. BCS-HCI 2012*, (2012), 205-214.

33. Vetere, F., Gibbs, M.R., Kjeldskov, J., Howard, S., Mueller, F., Pedell, S., Mecoles, K. and Bunyan, M. Mediating Intimacy: Designing Technologies to Support Strong-Tie Relationships. *Proc. CHI 2005*, (2005), 471-480.

34. Wang, R., Quek, F., Tatar, D., Teh, J.K.S. and Cheok, A.D. Keep in Touch: Channel, Expectation and Experience. *Proc. CHI 2012*, (2012), 139-148.

35. Wesson, D.A. The Handshake as Non-verbal Communication in Business. *Marketing Intelligence & Planning*, 10(9), (1992), 41-46.

Bodies in Motion: Mobility, Presence, and Task Awareness in Telepresence

Irene Rae
University of Wisconsin–Madison
1210 West Dayton Street
Madison, WI 53706, USA
irene@cs.wisc.edu

Bilge Mutlu
University of Wisconsin–Madison
1210 West Dayton Street
Madison, WI 53706, USA
bilge@cs.wisc.edu

Leila Takayama*
Willow Garage, Inc.
68 Willow Road
Menlo Park, CA 94025, USA
takayama@willowgarage.com

ABSTRACT
Robotic telepresence systems—videoconferencing systems that allow a remote user to drive around in another location—provide an alternative to video-mediated communications as a way of interacting over distances. These systems, which are seeing increasing use in business and medical settings, are unique in their ability to grant the remote user the ability to maneuver in a distant location. While this mobility promises increased feelings of "being there" for remote users and thus greater support for task collaboration, whether these promises are borne out, providing benefits in task performance, is unknown. To better understand the role that mobility plays in shaping the remote user's sense of presence and its potential benefits, we conducted a two-by-two (system mobility: stationary vs. mobile; task demands for mobility: low vs. high) controlled laboratory experiment. We asked participants ($N = 40$) to collaborate in a construction task with a confederate via a robotic telepresence system. Our results showed that mobility significantly increased the remote user's feelings of presence, particularly in tasks with high mobility requirements, but decreased task performance. Our findings highlight the positive effects of mobility on feelings of "being there," while illustrating the need to design support for effective use of mobility in high-mobility tasks.

Author Keywords
Remote collaboration; robotic telepresence; robot-mediated communication; mobility; presence; task awareness

ACM Classification Keywords
H.4.3 Information Systems Applications: Communications Applications—*computer conferencing, teleconferencing, and videoconferencing*

INTRODUCTION
Videoconferencing systems have seen use as early as the 1970s [43]. Since that time, researchers, inventors, and designers have sought to bring video-mediated communications closer to face-to-face interactions, to simulate the sensation of actually "being there." A common approach to achieving this goal has been to improve audio [38] and visual connections [9] between remote communication partners. Another approach has been to augment videoconferencing systems with robotic platforms, also known as robotic telepresence systems [16, 29]. By enhancing the sensation of "being there" in the remote location, or *presence*, these systems promise to impart some of the same benefits that being physically present would provide, such as increased coordination and awareness. Through capabilities such system maneuverability, laser pointers as

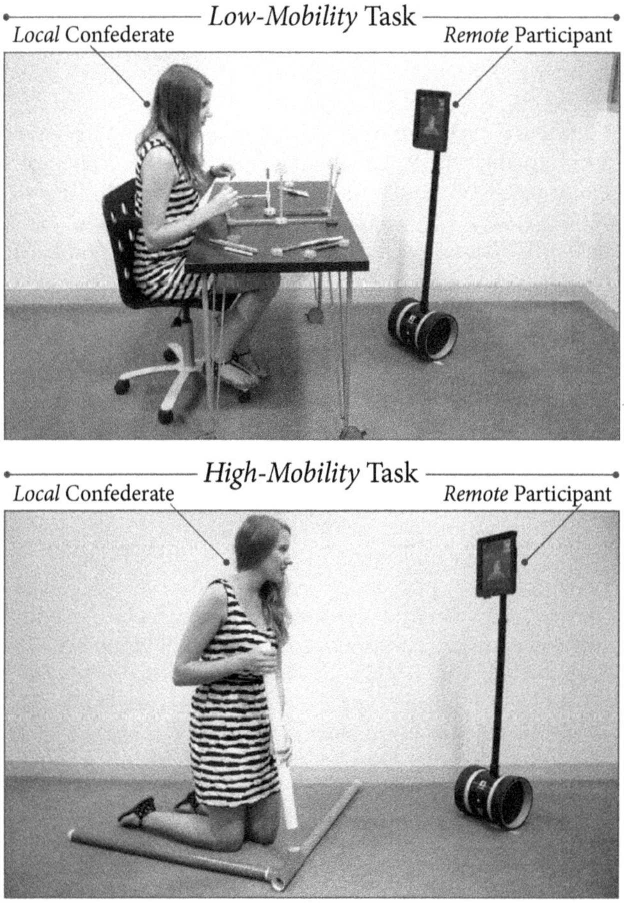

Figure 1. Participants remotely collaborated with a local confederate in a construction task that either took up a small amount of desk space, requiring *low* levels of mobility, or a large amount of space, requiring *high* levels of mobility, in the room.

*Author now at Google[x], takayama@google.com

CHI 2014, April 26–May 1, 2014, Toronto, Ontario, Canada.

ACM 978-1-4503-2473-1/14/04..$15.00.
http://dx.doi.org/10.1145/2556288.2557047

deictic indicators, and the provision of a physical embodiment, research on robotic telepresence systems has explored ways to support increased presence for remote users. For example, past studies have demonstrated that robotic telepresence systems increased the local users' feelings of the remote user's presence, improving collaborative team outcomes [23, 31, 41]. However, few studies have examined the effects that these systems may have on the remote user's, the *remote's*, perceptions of their own presence in the local environment.

In domains such as manufacturing, construction, or exploration, the ability to change perspectives and maneuver in the environment may not only enable the remote user to offer the local user guidance and instruction, but may also directly contribute to task completion. By enabling the remote user to interact with the surrounding space, these systems may increase the remote's awareness of the physical environment, facilitating task-oriented actions, such as mapping an area, locating objects, and conducting visual checks. However, because many of these systems have been designed for use in office settings [2, 11, 17, 33, 34, 42], previous literature has primarily focused on the contexts of conversation and collaborative meetings. In these scenarios, once the system has been positioned in front of the local user, the *local*, the mobility of the system no longer plays a key role, and the robotic platform becomes the equivalent of a videoconferencing display. As a result, how mobility affects the remote's sense of presence and contribution to task outcomes, particularly in settings where maneuverability directly impacts task completion, is unclear.

Our goal in this study is to investigate the role that mobility plays in instilling a sense of presence in the remote user and to increase our understanding of how it may improve team performance in physically oriented tasks. Specifically, we seek to gain a better understanding of how mobility supports the remote user's contributions in tasks that require different levels of mobility (Figure 1)—in tasks that are visible from a single view, requiring *low* levels of mobility, and tasks where the ability to maneuver gives the remote user greater latitude to participate in the completion of team goals, i.e., tasks with *high* requirements for mobility. By exploring these questions, we hope to inform the future design of mobility features for robotic telepresence systems and to deepen our understanding of how mobility shapes remote collaboration.

The next section provides an overview of related work on remote collaboration, focusing specifically on presence and task awareness. This overview is followed by a description of our hypotheses and our study design. We then present our results and discuss their implications for design and research. Finally, we summarize the study's limitations, areas for future work, and our conclusions.

RELATED WORK

Previous work on supporting remotely distributed teams has focused on the importance of *workspace awareness*—how knowledge and awareness of where others are working and what they are doing might facilitate the coordination of action [20]—and on supporting *grounding*—the process of creating common ground to achieve mutual understanding [5]. For both workspace awareness and grounding, the ability to track the presence and spatial positioning of others is key for successful collaboration. In this section, we provide an overview of work that has examined presence and task awareness in both virtual and physical telepresence environments.

Presence

The domain of workspace awareness in computer-supported cooperative work focuses on improving collaborative outcomes by simulating a physical workspace in a virtual environment. By designing tools that provide users with timely information about the task at hand, such as who is present, where they are working, and what they are doing, these systems translate the affordances found in physically shared workspaces into online tools that support group work [8, 14, 18, 20]. For example, by using digital representations of user arms to create a sense of where they are active in a virtual workspace [12], providing historical logs of past exchanges [13], and preserving spatial relationships [36], these systems facilitate coordination between users and improve group efficiency. In these examples, indicators of collaborator presence are implemented as representations of information, such as positioning and availability, that users would have access to in a non-virtual workspace.

Previous research on robotic telepresence has examined how having a physical embodiment might support the remote user's presence in the local user's environment. Findings from this work have demonstrated that these platforms improve the local users' sense of the remote user's presence, increasing the frequency of informal interactions between co-workers—shown to be critical for organizational coordination [22]—and the remote user's ability to participate in meetings [23, 41]. Additional research has examined how other aspects of robotic telepresence systems shape interactions, such as the effects that embodiment and control have on the development of trust between users in negotiation tasks [31], how the height of the system shapes the local's perceptions of the remote user's persuasiveness [32], and the role that system appearance plays on the local's feelings of team membership toward the remote user [30]. Previous work has also explored manipulating the camera's mobility in a telepresence system to increase the remote user's feelings of presence; however, the stationary nature of the task and the camera's limitations resulted in few users utilizing this capability, making it difficult to draw definitive conclusions [28].

While this past research illustrates how various aspects of robotic telepresence systems affect and improve the local user's perceptions of the remote user's presence [1], we lack a clear understanding of whether these systems truly improve the remote user's sense of "being there" in the local environment.

Task Awareness

Research in workspace awareness has explored different ways of conveying critical information and supporting grounding by informing users about movement within the online workspace. For example, prior work has explored the use of workspace miniatures to show the location and activity of others in the workspace [19] and the use of indicators of availability [8] to aid in collaborative coordination.

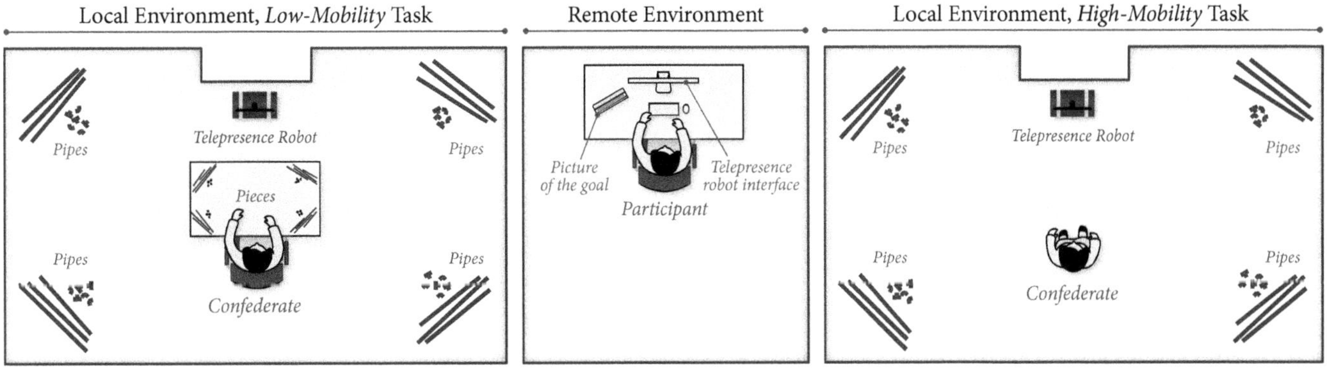

Figure 2. The physical arrangements of the study room in the *low-mobility* task condition, the participant's environment, and the study room in the *high-mobility* task condition on the left, center, and right, respectively.

Within the sphere of robotic telepresence, prior literature has sought to understand user needs for movement and awareness within specific contexts, such as office [23, 40], medical [6, 39] and educational [15] settings. Research in teleoperation has explored the design of control interfaces that aid remote users in being aware of their surroundings to accomplish solo exploration tasks, including the avoidance of obstacles and successful navigation [16, 24, 26]. While these bodies of work inform the design of interfaces that more effectively support mobility in the remote environment, they do little to aid us in understanding how such mobility facilitates task awareness, coordination, and feelings of presence. Mobile telepresence systems offer a unique opportunity for remote users to not only benefit from the tools developed in workspace awareness research and teleoperation, but also to directly contribute to tasks in a physical workspace.

In our study, we seek to understand the contribution that mobility may have in supporting remote users' feelings of presence, facilitating their ability to contribute to task completion. To this end, we focus on two types of tasks: tasks where mobility requirements are low and movement does not aid in the completion of goals, such as conversations, negotiations, and activities limited to a small workspace, and tasks where the requirements are high and the ability to move in the physical space facilitates performance, such as construction, manufacturing, and exploration. In other words, when does mobility matter?

HYPOTHESES

Informed by previous research in workspace awareness and robotic telepresence systems, we formed two hypotheses predicting the role that the mobility of the system would play in different task types.

Hypothesis 1. Remote users will report more presence in the local's environment when the system is mobile than when the system is stationary.

Hypothesis 2. In a task that requires high levels of mobility, using a mobile system will improve collaborative outcomes over using a stationary system, while mobility of the system will not affect these outcomes in a task that requires low levels of mobility.

METHOD

To test these hypotheses, we designed a controlled laboratory experiment in which remote participants worked with a local confederate in a collaborative construction task. In the study, we manipulated the mobility of the robotic telepresence system and the movement or mobility required by the task. We measured the effects of these manipulations on the participant's sense of presence in the local environment and team task performance outcomes, such as completion time and errors. The paragraphs below provide further detail on our study design, participants, measurements, and analyses.

Study Design

Our study followed a two-by-two between-participants design. The independent variables were *mobility*, varied by the use of a stationary or mobile robotic telepresence system, and the levels of *mobility or movement* required by the task, low vs. high. In order to maintain consistency across participants, we developed a task to construct an object that could be built on a small scale with TinkerToys, or on a large scale with PVC pipes. When built on a small scale, the completed object measured approximately 22 inches (55.88 cm) in length and 3.5 inches (8.89 cm) in height, fitting on a table that was fully visible from the telepresence system's camera. When constructed on a large scale, the completed object measured approximately 7 feet (182.88 cm) in length and 3 feet (91.44 cm) in height, requiring it to be built in a clear floor space that was not easily visible from the telepresence system's camera. The construction of small-scale and large-scale objects served as *low-mobility* and *high-mobility* tasks, respectively. Figure 2 illustrates the arrangement of the study environment across the task manipulation.

Although both local and remote users of a telepresence robot may benefit from the level of mobility that the remote user has, we were chiefly interested in the remote user's experience and perspective for two reasons. First, prior work has primarily been dedicated to understanding robotic telepresence interactions from the local user's perspective [30, 32, 1]. Second, because face-to-face interaction participants have the ability to move in the environment, we expected that providing the remote user with the ability to maneuver would have a greater impact on the remote user's experience. To this end, we asked participants to act as the remote user and used a

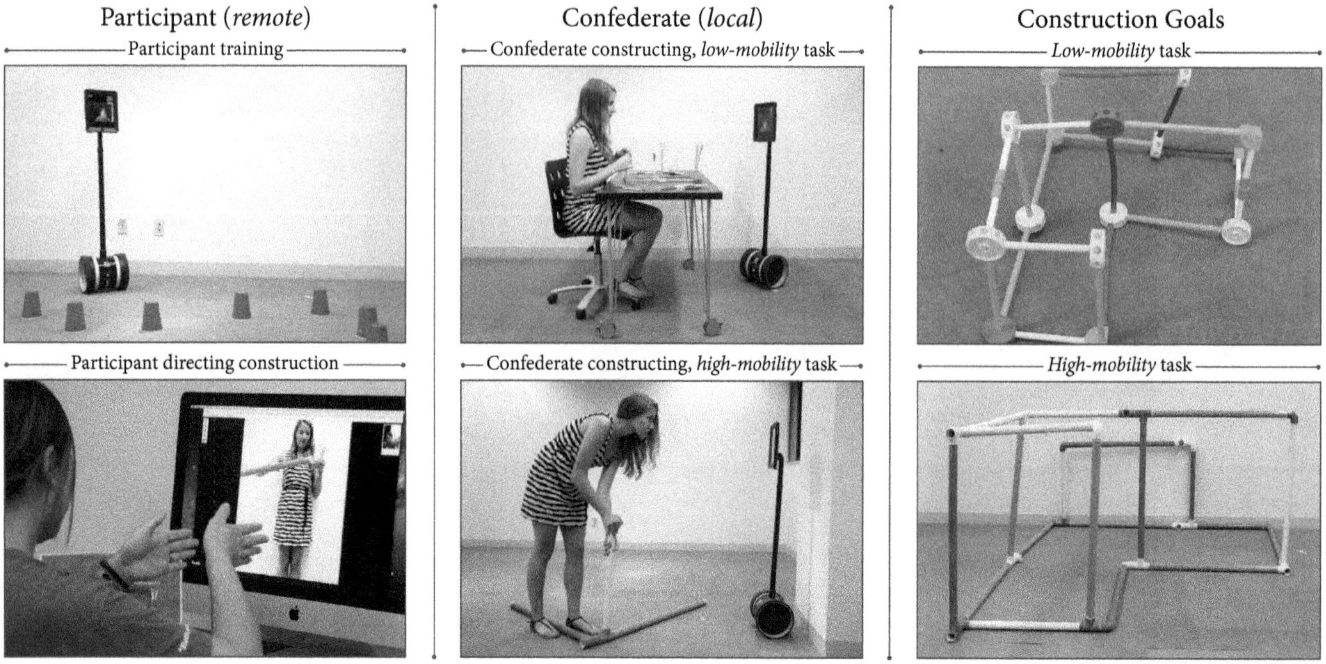

Figure 3. *Left*: participant controlling the telepresence robot in the training phase and the remote setup in which they provided the confederate with instructions. *Center*: the local setup for the low mobility and high mobility task conditions in which the confederate carried out the construction of the object. *Right*: pictures of the completed objects for the small and large tasks provided to the participant.

confederate—one of our experimenters, who pretended to be a participant—as the local user in our task. The locations of the participant and the confederate are illustrated in Figure 2.

System

Both stationary and mobile interactions in our study took place via a Double telepresence robot[1] (shown in Figure 1), which has a weight of 15 pounds and an height that is adjustable to either 47 inches or 60 inches (101.6cm to 152.4cm). The Double allows remote users to drive in the local's environment, switch between a front and bottom-view camera, and adjust the height to two different settings. The telepresence robot's screen was an Apple iPad 2 tablet computer[2] with a diagonal screen size of 9.7 inches (24.64 cm) and a screen resolution of 2048×1536 and 264 ppi. The front camera of the tablet computer provided a video stream of what the system was facing to aid with communication, and the back camera showed the immediate surroundings of the robot using a mirror directed toward the ground to aid with navigation.

The participant and the confederate communicated via the Double videoconferencing interface, shown in Figure 3. In the stationary condition, participants were not instructed on the controls for moving the system and the system was plugged into the wall, preventing movement. In the mobile condition, participants were provided with an instruction sheet on the controls for moving the system and were able to freely maneuver around in the experiment room.

Construction Task

In our study, participants engaged in a construction task with a confederate where the pieces were either small, 3.35 inches (8.51cm) to 10.85 inches (27.56cm) in length, or large, 2 feet (60.96cm) to 3 feet (91.44cm) in length. The completed object had a total of 35 parts—22 straight pieces and 13 connecting joints—with varying orientations and colors. Participants were told that they would be working together with another study participant to build the object, that they would have the instructions, and that the other person would have the parts. We motivated participants to work as quickly and accurately as possible by adding an incentive; if they were able to build the correct object faster than any other teams from the study, they would receive an extra dollar. They were also told that they could begin the task as soon as the timer was started and that the timer would stop when they told the experimenter that they were finished. Participants received a picture of the completed object that they were not allowed to show to the confederate, as shown on the right in Figure 3.

[1]http://www.doublerobotics.com/
[2]http://www.apple.com/ipad/

Measures

To measure the collaborative outcomes of the construction task, we utilized a number of objective and subjective measures.

Measures of Presence

In order to measure the remote user's feelings of presence, we asked participants to mark where they and their partner worked during the task on a map of the rooms. Figure 4 shows example data from this measure. Markings on the map were coded as "in-room" if participants noted that they and the confederate were in the room where the object was being constructed. They were coded as "separate" if participants marked that they and the confederate operated from separate rooms. In order to avoid biasing participants, the map of the room was not changed between conditions, but participants were warned that the layout of the rooms or the objects included on the map may not be accurate.

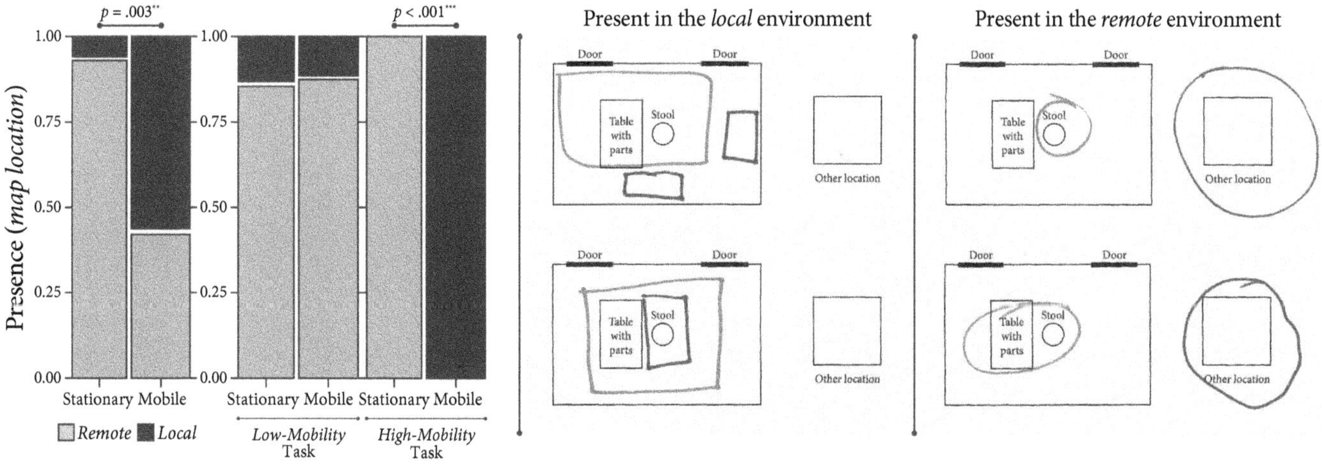

Figure 4. *Left*: Data from the measures of presence across mobile and stationary conditions and broken down to tasks requiring low and high levels of mobility. (***) and (**) denote $p < .001$ and $p < .01$, respectively. *Center and right*: Example data from the presence measure, participants used blue to circle the area that they worked in and green to circle the area that their partner worked in. The examples in the center illustrate data from participants who felt present in the room where they were tele-present, rather than the "other location" where they were physically located, and those on the right illustrate data from participants who felt present where they were physically located.

Measures of Task Performance

We used the time taken to complete the construction of the object as a measure of task efficiency. Time was marked in seconds from when the timer was started to when the participant opened the door of the study room and announced that they were finished. The number of mistakes in the completed object, i.e., errors in the orientation or position of the pieces, served as a measure of task accuracy.

Other Measures

While we did not pose any specific hypotheses about subjective evaluations, we created an exploratory post-experiment questionnaire to better understand the effects that the mobility of the system might have on the remote user's perceptions of teamwork, team recovery, workspace awareness, and environmental awareness. Participants were asked to rate their agreement on a five-point Likert scale, 1 = Strongly disagree, 5 = Strongly agree, with 34 statements (e.g., "I was aware of my position in the room," "We made fewer errors than other teams," "I was able to prevent errors from being made during the task," and so on). Statements were modified from items in the Networked Minds Measure of Social Presence [7] and NASA's Situational Awareness Rating Technique [37]. In addition, participants were asked to rate their feelings of closeness with their partner using the Inclusion of Other in the Self Scale [3].

Procedure

An experimenter greeted the participant at the entrance of our laboratory and obtained informed consent. The experimenter then seated the participant in front of a computer and gave the participant up to 10 minutes to practice either driving the telepresence robot around (in the mobile condition) or practice moving through a maze (in the stationary condition). Once 10 minutes had elapsed or the participant announced that they were finished with the practice, the experimenter disconnected the participant's terminal from the robotic telepresence system (in the mobile condition), instructed the participant on the construction task, and provided the participant with a picture of the finished object, as shown on the right in Figure 3. Following these steps, the experimenter reconnected to the robotic telepresence system and introduced the confederate as another participant in the study. The participant was reminded that they could begin when the timer was started and to open the door and announce when they were finished. After answering any questions, the experimenter started the timer and exited the room. During the task, the confederate did not initiate actions or provide guidance, acting only to complete participant instructions; this was to prevent affecting the speed of task completion or the number of mistakes. The confederate also limited her responses to a scripted list (e.g., "Like this?," "What next?," "Here?," "That's it? Great!") to maintain consistency across participants. Once the participant had opened the door of the experiment room and announced that the task was completed, the experimenter re-entered, turned off the timer, told the confederate to log out of the system, and administered the post-study questionnaire. Each session took approximately 30 minutes.

Participants

A total of 32 adults (four males and four females per condition), whose ages ranged between 18 and 30 years, $M = 20.9$, $SD = 2.37$, volunteered to participate in the study. We recruited from the University of Wisconsin–Madison campus community using online job postings and in-person recruitment. Participants reported that they were familiar with videoconferencing, $M = 4.8$, $SD = 1.7$ (1 = not very familiar, 7 = very familiar) and on average used videoconferencing once a month, $M = 2.2$, $SD = 0.8$ (1 = I did not use videoconferencing in the past 6 months, 2 = I used videoconferencing at least once a month in the past 6 months, 3 = I used videoconferencing at least once a week in the past 6 months, 4 = I used videoconferencing at least once a day in the past 6 months). Although we told participants that they would receive an extra dollar if they were the fastest team to complete the task correctly in order to motivate faster completion times, all participants received a total of $5, which included the completion bonus.

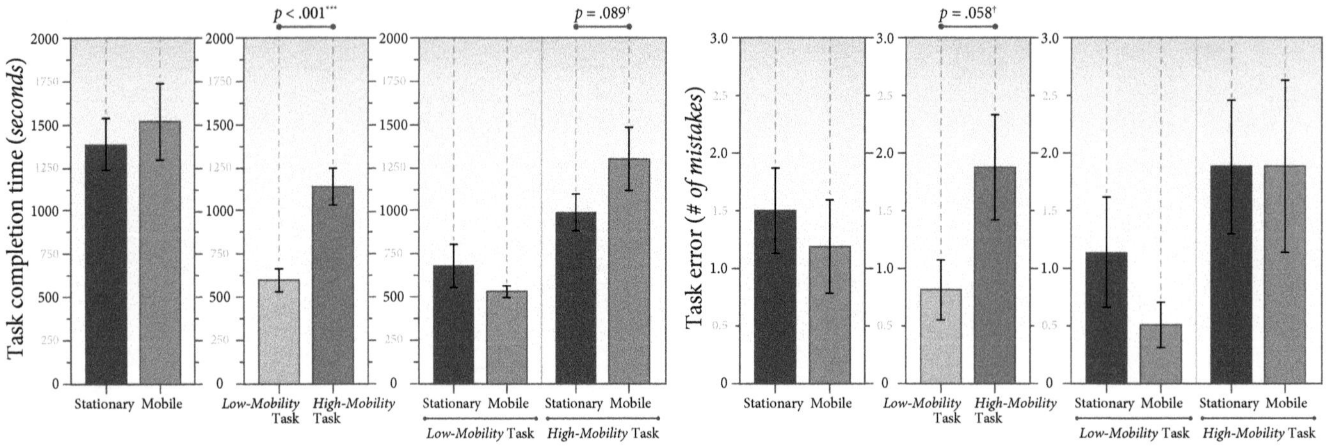

Figure 5. Data from measures of task completion time and task error. (***) and (†) denote $p < .001$ and $p < .10$, respectively. On the left, the high-mobility task took significantly longer to complete than the low-mobility task, and participants in the high-mobility task took marginally longer to complete the task when using the mobile vs. the stationary system. On the right, participants made marginally more mistakes in the high-mobility task than the low-mobility task.

Analyses

We tested age, gender, and videoconferencing experience as potential covariates and found that none had a significant effect ($p > .05$). A two-way fixed-effects analysis of variance (ANOVA) was conducted with the mobility of the system and task mobility requirements as input variables and completion time and number of mistakes as response variables. Planned comparisons in all tests used the Scheffé method. A Pearson's Chi-squared test was used to determine the effects of mobility on the participant's feelings of presence in the drawn map measure.

To construct scales from items in our questionnaire, we conducted an exploratory factor analysis, which resulted in four factors that corresponded to scales of teamwork (four items; Cronbach's $\alpha = .84$), team recovery (four items; Cronbach's $\alpha = .71$), workspace awareness (two items; Cronbach's $\alpha = .70$), and awareness of the environment (two items; Cronbach's $\alpha = .70$).

RESULTS

Our first hypothesis predicted that remote users would feel more present in the local environment when communicating with the confederate using a mobile system than when they used a stationary system. We found full support for this hypothesis; remote users reported themselves as present in the room with the confederate significantly more frequently when they used a mobile system than when they used a stationary system, $\chi^2(1, n = 31) = 8.7$, $p = .003$. A closer examination of these results showed that, when engaged in the low-mobility task, system mobility had no effect on feelings of presence, $\chi^2(1, n = 15) = .10$, $p = .73$. However, in the high-mobility task, all participants using a mobile system reported themselves as being present in the room with the confederate (where the object was being constructed), while all participants that used a stationary system reported themselves as being in a separate room (where they were physically seated), $\chi^2(1, n = 16) = 16.0$, $p < .001$. Figure 4 illustrates these results and provides examples of responses from participants who felt present in the room with the confederate and those who felt separate, i.e., present in the room where they were physically located.

Our second hypothesis posited that mobility would improve task performance in a high-mobility task but not in a low-mobility task. Our results did not provide support for this hypothesis. First, we found that it took participants significantly more time to complete the high-mobility task, $M = 1138.31$, $SD = 497.84$, than the low-mobility task, $M = 601.94$, $SD = 497.84$, $F(1, 28) = 18.57$, $p < .001$. There was also a marginal difference in the number of errors made between tasks, participants making more mistakes in the high-mobility task, $M = 1.88$, $SD = 2.15$, than in the low-mobility task, $M = 0.81$, $SD = 2.15$, $F(1, 28) = 3.91$, $p = .06$.

We found no main effect of system mobility on completion time or the number of errors. There was no significant difference in the time it took participants to complete tasks using the stationary system, $M = 829.50$, $SD = 497.82$, versus the mobile system, $M = 910.75$, $SD = 497.82$, $F(1, 28) = 0.43$, $p = .52$. There was also no significant difference between the number of errors made when the system was stationary, $M = 1.50$, $SD = 2.15$, versus when the system was mobile, $M = 1.19$, $SD = 2.15$, $F(1, 28) = 0.34$, $p = .57$.

However, we found that mobility had a marginal interaction effect between the mobility of the system and the mobility requirements of the task, $F(1, 28) = 3.39$, $p = .08$. The

Measure	*F* ratio	*p* value
Completion times		
System mobility	0.426 (1, 28)	.52
Task mobility	18.573 (1, 28)	.00***
System mobility × task mobility	3.389 (1, 28)	.08†
Mistakes		
System mobility	0.338 (1, 28)	.57
Task mobility	3.913 (1, 28)	.06
System mobility × task mobility	0.338 (1, 28)	.57†

Figure 6. Effects of system mobility and mobility required by the task on completion times and the number of mistakes. (†) and (***) denote $p < .10$ and $p < .001$, respectively.

high-mobility task took marginally longer when using the mobile system, $M = 1293.50$, $SD = 514.48$, than when using a stationary system, $M = 983.13$, $SD = 295.53$, $F(1, 28) = 3.11$, $p = .09$. There was no difference in the time it took participants to complete the low-mobility task between using the mobile system, $M = 528.00$, $SD = 94.50$, and the stationary system, $M = 675.88$, $SD = 367.03$, $F(1, 28) = 0.71$, $p = .41$.

We found no interaction effects for the mobility of the system and the mobility requirements of the task on the number of errors. Planned comparisons showed that participants using a mobile system made marginally more mistakes in the high-mobility task, $M = 1.88$, $SD = 2.10$, than in the low-mobility task, $M = 0.50$, $SD = 0.54$, $F(1, 28) = 3.28$, $p = .08$.

Finally, we found no significant effects of system mobility or the mobility required by the task on the remote user's perceptions of teamwork, team recovery, workspace awareness, and environmental awareness.

DISCUSSION

Consistent with our first hypothesis, our results showed that system mobility significantly improved the remote's feelings of being present in the local's location, particularly when the task required high levels of mobility. In these situations, we observed that all participants using the mobile system not only actively moved in the task space, but also exhibited more present behaviors. For instance, when constructing the large object, participants who were driving the system used language that referred to themselves in space, such as "Where am I?" and "I'm just trying to get into a position where I can see the corner." However, when using a stationary system or in the low-mobility task, we observed requests and statements by the remote user that referred to actions of the local confederate, such as "Can you push the object back please?" and "I can't see what you're doing, can you hold it up?"

Contrary to the predictions of our second hypothesis, greater mobility did not increase task efficiency or accuracy. Using a mobile system was actually detrimental to task performance in the high-mobility task and had no effect in the low-mobility task. We believe that the reasons for this outcome fall into two primary categories: a high burden of attention for the remote user and an instability in the remote user's frame of reference, which are discussed in the paragraphs below.

Burden of Attention

During the task, we observed a number of behaviors that seemed to indicate that participants found performing the task and maneuvering the telepresence robot to require high levels of attention. In their comments in the post-study survey, participants illustrated task difficulties with comments such as "It was hard to communicate everything you wanted to say using non-verbal actions and more directions verbally instead," "[It was] difficult describing connectors," and "I'm pretty horrible at this [the construction task]." Many users were unfamiliar with the shapes of the joints and had trouble articulating differences between pieces and directions for the construction. Participants also reported difficulties with translating the photograph into three dimensional space, sometimes resulting in an object that was a mirror image of the one in the instructions.

We also observed participants having difficulties with maneuvering the telepresence robot. Although users were given 10 minutes to train with the system and were provided with an instruction sheet explaining the controls (the four arrow keys on the keyboard for moving in four possible directions), users still experienced challenges. For example, participants were observed to back into walls, run into pipes on the ground, or to move extremely slowly to avoid collisions. These difficulties resulted in one user tipping the system over during the training period and crashing it, such that the system had to be recovered from a prone position on the floor.

In NASA's Situational Awareness Rating Technique (SART) [37], the primary factors for understanding a user's situational awareness include the user's division of attention, spare mental capacity, concentration, and familiarity with the situation. While each of these factors individually may not have been a problem for participants, our observations were that the combination of being presented with an unfamiliar control system, coping with the task, having to divide attention between the photograph and the video of the other room, the pressure of competing in time and accuracy, and the concentration needed to interact with the local confederate, may have been overwhelming for users in the mobile system condition. This high cognitive load may have resulted in an inability to take full advantage of the system's mobility, decreasing their ability to work quickly. This effect may have been particularly strong in the high-mobility task, as the low-mobility task did not require participants to move.

Instability of Reference Points

Psychological research on spatial cognition has studied the cognitive techniques that people use to understand their own positioning and the positioning of objects in their environment [27]. In this work, spatial reference systems are divided into three categories, *egocentric reference systems*, where location is specified with respect to the observer, *environmental reference systems*, in which locations are specified with respect to other objects, and *intrinsic reference systems*, when people learn a particular spatial layout of objects or a pattern [27]. This work provides strong evidence that memories of room-sized layouts are mentally represented in terms of egocentric reference systems (e.g., to my left [10]) or intrinsic reference systems, particularly when objects may be grouped into higher-order clusters [27].

In our task, when participants were not able to maneuver around the environment, their frame of reference was fixed in an egocentric view, where their spatial understanding was limited to object positioning in relation to the robotic telepresence system, or "themselves." However, when the mobility of the system enabled participants to change their field of view, their mental model for understanding object positioning may have changed to an intrinsic reference system. This may have led them to attempt to gauge where objects were in relation to other features in the environment (e.g., "the red piece behind the chair"), causing problems for the three reasons discussed below.

First, the system provided the remote user with a narrow field of view, making it challenging for participants to see multiple objects at a time. As a result, once the participant had moved in space, relating new objects to old ones became increasingly difficult. During the high-mobility task, participants using the mobile system occasionally asked the confederate for help in relating the objects that they could see at that moment with the locations that they had previously been, (e.g., "Is this the orange piece from the corner you just added the green thingy to?" and "Wait, is this the one across from the red pipe?").

Second, when physically present, people may rely on a number of environmental and kinesthetic cues to estimate their changes in position. In the robotic telepresence system that we used, no feedback was provided for how far the system had rotated or the distance that it had moved, creating distortions in egocentric frames of reference. Exacerbating this situation was our decision to remove all distinguishing characteristics from the study room in order to minimize distractions from the task at hand. While there were several features (such as doors, windows, and furniture) which would be common in an office or factory setting, the environment was not as rich in cues as more naturalistic settings might be. We observed participants in the mobile condition moving the system forward, then pausing to turn back and forth to get a better understanding of their position and surroundings. In some cases, participants would back up to their previous position and make remarks such as "Ok, so that's there..." before driving forward again, leading us to the conclusion that they were searching for objects in the environment to use as navigational aids. We also observed occasions in which the participant rotated the system and lost track of how far they had gone, ending in their facing a wall and having to ask the confederate, "Where are you now?"

Third, the most distinguishing objects in the room were the pieces for constructing the object and the confederate. As required by the task, both the pieces and the confederate were in constant movement under the direction provided by the participant. When using the stationary system, we often observed participants referring to the confederate's position when the confederate was not in view of the camera, as in the statements "There should be a green joint on your left and a red one on your right..." and "Yeah, right where you are now." In contrast, when using a mobile system, participants appeared disoriented about the confederate's location in relation to their own, leading to backing repeatedly into walls while trying to locate the confederate or the object.

Previous work in computer-mediated communication has identified that the remote user's inability to understand how they are situated in the local user's environment can cause problems or frictions between users [21]. When viewed from the perspective of robotic telepresence systems, this lack of positional awareness significantly limits the ability of these systems to support task collaboration and has the potential to render them unusable. While the ability to navigate has shown dividends in creating an orientation-free mental representation of the environment versus an orientation-dependent representation developed from a map or photographs [35], our results highlight the gap between having the ability to move and the user actually benefitting from the capability.

One potential solution for supporting the remote user's navigational needs is to leverage heads-up displays to create a realistic three dimensional representation of a virtual environment, such as a recreation of the local's surroundings, and to simulate a correct perspective for the user by monitoring the relative position of the user's eyes or head [25, 4]. However, head mounted displays introduce other challenges for users of robotic telepresence systems, as they obfuscate the remote user's face.

DESIGN IMPLICATIONS

Our findings suggest that while the addition of mobility may provide remote users with a greater sense of presence in the local's environment, simply providing them with the ability to maneuver is not enough. The ability to drive the telepresence system not only adds the burden of understanding its spatial positioning in relation to other objects in the environment, but also divides the remote user's attention, significantly increasing cognitive load. Walking and talking becomes a much more difficult proposition when trying to interact with others through a mobile system.

While these problems are not insurmountable, our research points to the need for designers to consider ways of supporting the remote user's efforts. For example, providing the remote user with a wider field of view may allow them to gain a better intrinsic understanding of the location of obstacles in the environment. Adding indicators in telepresence interfaces that show the distance traveled, the degrees of rotation turned, or the position of the telepresence robot on a simple map of the local environment, such as those provided in gaming interfaces, may aid in maintaining an egocentric view of the system's position. Providing the remote user with the ability to offload the controls for movement, either by providing pre-planned paths or more intuitively mapped control systems, such as game or gesture-based controllers, may reduce cognitive load, allowing the remote user to more fully focus on the task at hand.

LIMITATIONS AND FUTURE WORK

Based on our study, we believe that there are informative lessons learned and fruitful paths forward for future work. First, to control for the difficulty of maneuvering the robotic telepresence system, it is critical for future studies to provide a flexible training period that allows participants to become comfortable and agile with the system. This lengthened training period would enable achieving a certain skill level instead of training for a set period of time. Alternatively, a longer-term study could examine task performance over time. Second, to be able to make broader claims about the use of robotic telepresence systems in spatially-oriented tasks, it is important for future work to explore a wider variety of tasks, such as collaborative exploration, search and rescue, and so on. Third, providing a richer, more naturalistic environment with stable reference points, such as additional furniture or wall hangings, may not only improve overall task performance with the robotic telepresence system, but may also offer greater external validity. While we chose to use a commercial system for our study to more accurately simulate real-world conditions, the use of a custom system in follow-up studies would allow greater latitude for a deeper investigation into how mobility might best be supported. Furthermore, there are always limitations of a study's participant pool in terms of how representative it is of a broader population of people with diverse educational, professional, and cultural backgrounds, which may be addressed by conducting follow-up studies, e.g., across different professional environments or cultural contexts. For this purpose, we have sought to provide sufficient detail in the Methods Section to allow future repeatability of our study.

CONCLUSION

Our work explored the effects of mobility on collaborative outcomes in two different task scenarios—a "small" task that required low levels of mobility and a "large" task with high mobility requirements—seeking to answer the question, "When does mobility matter?" To this end, we conducted a controlled laboratory experiment that followed a two-by-two (system mobility: stationary vs. mobile; task mobility requirements: low vs. high) between-participants design in which participants acted as the remote user and a confederate acted as the local user. Our results showed that the mobility of the system significantly improved the remote user's feelings of presence, particularly in tasks requiring high levels of mobility. However, contrary to our prediction, we found that mobility lowered task performance in measures of efficiency in high-mobility tasks. Our results suggest that, although the ability to maneuver the system provides remote users with immediate benefits such as a greater sense of presence, there is an often overlooked burden that controlling a mobile system adds to the remote user's cognitive load. These findings not only have implications for creating awareness of the potential consequences of providing the remote user with additional functionalities, such as mobility, but also highlight new opportunities for designing tools to support remote users. Robotic telepresence systems offer the unique chance to participate in and to directly contribute to physically situated tasks. However, our findings highlight the need for a deeper understanding of how mobility may be integrated in the design of robotic telepresence systems to best support the demands that such tasks place on the remote users.

ACKNOWLEDGMENTS

We would like to thank Jilana Boston, Brandi Hefty, and Ross Luo for their help with conducting the study. This research was supported by National Science Foundation award 1117652.

REFERENCES

1. Adalgeirsson, S. O., and Breazeal, C. Mebot: a robotic platform for socially embodied presence. In *Proc. of the 5th ACM/IEEE international conference on Human-robot interaction*, HRI '10, IEEE Press (Piscataway, NJ, USA, 2010), 15–22.
2. Anybots, Inc. Qb, 2012 (accessed September 8, 2012). https://www.anybots.com.
3. Aron, A., Aron, E. N., and Smollan, D. Inclusion of other in the self scale and the structure of interpersonal closeness. *Journal of personality and social psychology 63*, 4 (1992), 596.
4. Arthur, K. W., Booth, K. S., and Ware, C. Evaluating 3d task performance for fish tank virtual worlds. *ACM Transactions on Information Systems (TOIS) 11*, 3 (1993), 239–265.
5. Baker, M., Hansen, T., Joiner, R., and Traum, D. The role of grounding in collaborative learning tasks. *Collaborative learning: Cognitive and computational approaches* (1999), 31–63.
6. Beer, J. M., and Takayama, L. Mobile remote presence systems for older adults: acceptance, benefits, and concerns. In *Proc. of the 6th international conference on Human-robot interaction*, ACM Press (2011), 19–26.
7. Biocca, F., Harms, C., and Gregg, J. The networked minds measure of social presence: pilot test of the factor structure and concurrent validity. *Media Interface and Network Design Lab* (2001).
8. Brush, A. B., Meyers, B. R., Scott, J., and Venolia, G. Exploring awareness needs and information display preferences between coworkers. In *Proc. of the 2009 annual conference on Human factors in computing systems*, ACM Press (2009), 2091–2094.
9. Chen, M. Leveraging the asymmetric sensitivity of eye contact for videoconference. In *Proc. of the 2002 annual conference on Human factors in computing systems*, ACM Press (2002), 49–56.
10. Diwadkar, V. A., and McNamara, T. P. Viewpoint dependence in scene recognition. *Psychological Science 8*, 4 (1997), 302–307.
11. Double Robotics. Double, 2012 (accessed September 8, 2012). http://www.doublerobotics.com/.
12. Doucette, A., Mandryk, R. L., Gutwin, C., Nacenta, M., and Pavlovych, A. The effects of tactile feedback and movement alteration on interaction and awareness with digital embodiments. In *Proc. of the SIGCHI Conference on Human Factors in Computing Systems*, CHI '13, ACM (New York, NY, USA, 2013), 1891–1900.
13. Dourish, P., and Bellotti, V. Awareness and coordination in shared workspaces. In *Proc. of the 1992 ACM conference on Computer-supported cooperative work*, CSCW '92, ACM (New York, NY, USA, 1992), 107–114.
14. Ellis, C. A., Gibbs, S. J., and Rein, G. Groupware: some issues and experiences. *Commun. ACM 34*, 1 (Jan. 1991), 39–58.
15. Fels, D. I., Waalen, J. K., Zhai, S., and Weiss, P. Telepresence under exceptional circumstances: Enriching the connection to school for sick children. In *Proc. Interact 2001* (2001), 617–624.
16. Fong, T., and Thorpe, C. Vehicle teleoperation interfaces. *Autonomous robots 11*, 1 (2001), 9–18.
17. Giraff Technologies AB. Giraff, 2012 (accessed September 8, 2012). http://www.giraff.org/om-giraff/.
18. Grudin, J. Groupware and social dynamics: eight challenges for developers. *Commun. ACM 37*, 1 (Jan. 1994), 92–105.

19. Gutwin, C., and Greenberg, S. The effects of workspace awareness support on the usability of real-time distributed groupware. *ACM Trans. Comput.-Hum. Interact. 6*, 3 (Sept. 1999), 243–281.

20. Gutwin, C., and Greenberg, S. A descriptive framework of workspace awareness for real-time groupware. *Computer Supported Cooperative Work (CSCW) 11*, 3-4 (2002), 411–446.

21. Heath, C., and Luff, P. Disembodied conduct: communication through video in a multi-media office environment. In *Proc. of the 1991 annual conference on Human factors in computing systems*, ACM Press (1991), 99–103.

22. Kraut, R. E., Fish, R. S., Root, R. W., and Chalfonte, B. L. Informal communication in organizations: Form, function, and technology. In *Human reactions to technology: Claremont symposium on applied social psychology*, Citeseer (1990), 145–199.

23. Lee, M. K., and Takayama, L. "Now, I have a body": uses and social norms for mobile remote presence in the workplace. In *Proc. of the 2011 annual conference on Human factors in computing systems*, ACM Press (2011), 33–42.

24. McGovern, D. E. Human interfaces in remote driving. Tech. rep., Sandia National Labs., Albuquerque, NM (USA), 1988.

25. McKenna, M. Interactive viewpoint control and three-dimensional operations. In *Proc. of the 1992 symposium on Interactive 3D graphics*, ACM (1992), 53–56.

26. Michaud, F., Boissy, P., Corriveau, H., Grant, A., Lauria, M., Labonte, D., Cloutier, R., Roux, M., Royer, M., and Iannuzzi, D. Telepresence robot for home care assistance. In *Proc. of AAAI Spring Symposium on Multidisciplinary Collaboration for Socially Assistive Robotics* (2007), 50–56.

27. Mou, W., and McNamara, T. P. Intrinsic frames of reference in spatial memory. *Journal of Experimental Psychology: Learning, Memory, and Cognition 28*, 1 (2002), 162.

28. Nakanishi, H., Murakami, Y., Nogami, D., and Ishiguro, H. Minimum movement matters: impact of robot-mounted cameras on social telepresence. In *Proc. of the 2008 ACM conference on Computer supported cooperative work*, CSCW '08, ACM (New York, NY, USA, 2008), 303–312.

29. Paulos, E., and Canny, J. Prop: personal roving presence. In *Proc. of the 1998 annual conference on Human factors in computing systems*, ACM Press (1998), 296–303.

30. Rae, I., Takayama, L., and Mutlu, B. One of the gang: supporting in-group behavior for embodied mediated communication. In *Proc. of the 2012 annual conference on Human factors in computing systems*, ACM Press (2012), 3091–3100.

31. Rae, I., Takayama, L., and Mutlu, B. In-body experiences: embodiment, control, and trust in robot-mediated communication. In *Proc. of the SIGCHI Conference on Human Factors in Computing Systems*, CHI '13, ACM (New York, NY, USA, 2013), 1921–1930.

32. Rae, I., Takayama, L., and Mutlu, B. The influence of height in robot-mediated communication. In *Proc. of the 8th ACM/IEEE international conference on Human-robot interaction*, HRI '13, IEEE Press (Piscataway, NJ, USA, 2013), 1–8.

33. RoboDynamics. Luna, 2012 (accessed September 8, 2012). http://robodynamics.com/.

34. Suitable Technologies. Beam, 2012 (accessed September 15, 2013). https://www.suitabletech.com/beam/.

35. Sun, H.-J., Chan, G. S., and Campos, J. L. Active navigation and orientation-free spatial representations. *Memory & Cognition 32*, 1 (2004), 51–71.

36. Tang, A., Pahud, M., Inkpen, K., Benko, H., Tang, J. C., and Buxton, B. Three's company: understanding communication channels in three-way distributed collaboration. In *Proc. of the 2010 ACM conference on Computer supported cooperative work*, ACM Press (2010), 271–280.

37. Taylor, R. Situational awareness rating technique(sart): The development of a tool for aircrew systems design. *AGARD, Situational Awareness in Aerospace Operations 17 p(SEE N 90-28972 23-53)* (1990).

38. Toshima, I., Aoki, S., and Hirahara, T. Sound localization using an acoustical telepresence robot: Telehead ii. *Presence: Teleoperators and Virtual Environments 17*, 4 (2008), 392–404.

39. Tsui, K., and Yanco, H. Assistive, rehabilitation, and surgical robots from the perspective of medical and healthcare professionals. In *AAAI 2007 Workshop on Human Implications of Human-Robot Interaction*, Technical Report WS-07-07 Papers from the AAAI 2007 Workshop on Human Implications of HRI (2007).

40. Tsui, K. M., Desai, M., Yanco, H. A., and Uhlik, C. Exploring use cases for telepresence robots. In *Proc. of the 6th international conference on Human-robot interaction*, ACM Press (2011), 11–18.

41. Venolia, G., Tang, J., Cervantes, R., Bly, S., Robertson, G., Lee, B., and Inkpen, K. Embodied social proxy: mediating interpersonal connection in hub-and-satellite teams. In *Proc. of the 2010 annual conference on Human factors in computing systems*, ACM Press (2010), 1049–1058.

42. VGo Communications, Inc. Vgo, 2012 (accessed September 8, 2012). http://www.vgocom.com/.

43. Weeks, G. D., and Chapanis, A. Cooperative versus conflictive problem solving in three telecommunication modes. *Perceptual and motor skills 42*, 3 (06/01; 2012/09 1976), 879–917.

Exploring Video Streaming in Public Settings: Shared Geocaching Over Distance Using Mobile Video Chat

Jason Procyk[1], Carman Neustaedter[1], Carolyn Pang[1], Anthony Tang[2], and Tejinder K. Judge[3]

Simon Fraser University[1]
250-13450 102nd Avenue
Surrey, BC, Canada
[first_secondname]@sfu.ca

University of Calgary[2]
2500 University Drive NW
Calgary, AB, Canada
tonyt@ucalgary.ca

Google Inc. [3]
1900 Charleston Rd
Mountain View, CA, USA
tkjudge@google.com

ABSTRACT
Our research explores the use of mobile video chat in public spaces by people participating in *parallel experiences*, where both a local and remote person are doing the same activity together at the same time. We prototyped a wearable video chat experience and had pairs of friends and family members participate in 'shared geocaching' over distance. Our results show that video streaming works best for navigation tasks but is more challenging to use for fine-grained searching tasks. Video streaming also creates a very intimate experience with a remote partner, but this can lead to distraction from the 'real world' and even safety concerns. Overall, privacy concerns with streaming from a public space were not typically an issue; however, people tended to rely on assumptions of what were acceptable. The implications are that designers should consider appropriate feedback, user disembodiment, and asymmetry when designing for parallel experiences.

ACM Classification Keywords
H.5.3 [Information interfaces and presentation]: Group and Organization Interfaces - Computer Supported Cooperative Work

Author Keywords
Shared experiences; video communication; Geocaching

INTRODUCTION
With the proliferation of smartphones and mobile video streaming technologies (e.g., Google Glass), we will soon see an increasing amount of usage of mobile video streaming and mobile video chat from public settings. Yet this is a largely unchartered territory where we do not yet know how people will react to and use such technologies.

Our overarching research goal was to understand how mobile video communication systems could support the sharing of everyday outdoor activities between people who were geographically separated and how people would react to such experiences. We were particularly interested in *parallel experiences*: situations where *both* the local and remote family member or friend were doing the same activity in parallel together, rather than one person passively watching the activity from home. This reflects many situations in life where co-located people go out and do an activity, in parallel, together (e.g., walking, running, playing sports, site-seeing). In these situations, people may not be actively doing the exact same thing together, but they are in essence participating in the same general activity at the same time and in the same location (e.g., similar to parallel play amongst children [34]).

To explore this scenario, we used commercial software and hardware along with a wearable component to create a technology probe [17] that provides two-way video exchange via a smartphone and head-mounted mobile camera. We then conducted a study of the GPS-based treasure hunt game of geocaching where we augmented the activity to make it a parallel experience over distance. We selected geocaching as our focal activity for a number of reasons. First, geocaching includes walking or hiking, which are activities with relatively low physical thresholds where people often converse during the activity. Thus, it is a social activity. Second, geocaching includes navigation and looking for specific items. This requires individual efforts and can also include tightly coupled collaboration. Thus, geocaching contains acts that would be found in other outdoor activities like sightseeing or those involving wayfinding. Third, geocaching can be done in a variety of areas. In urban settings, video is being used in a public area with the risk of privacy concerns. This generalizes to future settings where one may be able to easily record or broadcast public scenes through wearable devices.

In our study, two people geocached in different locations where each hunted for his/her own geocaches but could see the other person's view and converse via an audio link. Thus, people could help each other out as needed, or simply 'be together' while doing the activity. The goal of our study was to understand how the audio and video links supported the activity, the technical or social challenges that existed, and the broader implications of using video streaming in public settings. Our results show that video streaming supported navigation tasks in 'shared geocaching' but it was challenging to use the video feed for fine-grained

CHI 2014, April 26–May 1, 2014, Toronto, Ontario, Canada.

ACM 978-1-4503-2473-1/14/04..$15.00.
http://dx.doi.org/10.1145/2556288.2557198

searching activities. We also found our technology probe created a 'micro' shared experience between two people where they were somewhat detached from the rest of the environment around them. Most participants saw this as a positive experience; however, it did create safety concerns. Video streaming in public areas was generally seen as being acceptable, yet this was often based on assumptions of what was permitted in an area. Given these results, designers should consider appropriate feedback mechanisms, remote user disembodiment, and asymmetric participation.

RELATED WORK

Video Chat with Family and Friends

Video chat is a technology that has rapidly proliferated in usage in the home for connecting family and friends over distance and many find it extremely valuable for maintaining relationships and feeling close to one another [1,13,22]. Studies have uncovered varied ways family members use existing video chat systems including sharing conversations as well as more detailed activities and shared experiences [4,13]. For example, grandparents and grandchildren share play times together [13], couples connect their homes to virtually "live together" [22], teenagers do homework together, [5] and children share playtime together [34]. Most closely related to our study, O'Hara et al. [26] conducted a study of mobile video telephony that showed that people used mobile video chat in public places (such as while commuting on public transit) to talk with friends or family. In these situations, privacy challenges emerged when bystanders could potentially see the video display or when they were being captured on video. Mobile devices were also found to be awkward to hold for long video calls.

Video Chat Prototypes

We also see new uses of video chat with research prototypes that present 'always-on' portals [15], shared desktop or table spaces for interaction [33], and video embedded tangible objects like storybooks [27]. More specific to our focus, there are also video chat prototypes for sharing *mobile* experiences. For example, Peek-A-Boo [21] supported a video link between a smartphone and an in-home picture frame with the goal of sharing outdoor activities (e.g., child soccer games) with a grandparent at home. Experiences2Go [12] also provided a live-video feed between a mobile device and an in-home display. A study showed that adults like to converse during shared activities. While both Peek-A-Boo and Experiences2Go offer experiences similar to our design goals, in both cases, only one person is mobile and only one person is performing the outdoor activity. Our work explores how *both* parties participate in the experience, in parallel, together.

There are also systems that focus on video records or the production of video from mobile settings. For example, Caleido provided multiple users with a means to collaboratively collect and share video of events [9]. The Mobile Vision Mixer allows film directors to view and combine multiple mobile video streams [10].

Commercial video chat systems such as Google+ Hangouts and Skype are available on mobile devices and can be used to share the types of outdoor activities that we are investigating. Yet we have not seen published studies of how people utilize these technologies in an outdoor context. The closest known activity is the online documented use of Google+ Hangouts for "Virtual Photo Walks" [31] where a person shares video of an experience with people who are unable to leave their home (e.g., on bed-rest). Again, our research focuses on parallel experiences.

Designing for Shared Physical Activities

Researchers have also explored how technology can encourage shared physical activities with others. Consolvo et al. [8] conducted a study of a shared step counting system and found that people valued social support and encouragement from friends. Mueller et al. [20] designed a shared soccer game over video for distance-separated friends. People enjoyed the social atmosphere of playing with a remote person. Stanley et al. [29] designed a GPS-based game where parents created walking routes for their children to follow at a later point; thus, the focus was on asynchronous and not synchronous shared experiences.

O'Brien and Mueller [24] explored social jogging and found that a key problem was finding a jogging partner with the same pace and same start location. They also learned that most people liked to converse while jogging rather than compete with a running partner. People jog with others so they are motivated to run faster, have more fun, and actually go on a jog. Following this study, they designed the Jogging Over a Distance prototype [18,19] that allows two joggers who are geographically separated to jog together. The technology transmits spatial audio to provide a sense of the remote jogging partner's location (same pace, ahead, behind). We build on this research by exploring video's role in parallel experiences, in addition to audio.

Geocaching

Geocaching is a GPS-based treasure hunt where players search for hidden containers that include a logbook to sign one's initials. Forestry studies have highlighted the motivations people have for geocaching [7] and the need for preserving the environment while still allowing people to geocache [6]. Kelley [16] describes how geocaching has moved from forests and parks to everyday urban centers. This creates a paradigm shift for the activity and means it can now easily interweave its way into one's everyday activities. O'Hara's [25] study elaborates on the motivations that people have for geocaching and include giving purpose to walks, improving profile statistics, challenging oneself, and participating and competing with others. Geocaching is also described as a shared social activity where groups of people find and hide geocaches for others [25]. Neustaedter et al. [23] elaborate on this to illustrate the role of community in geocaching where players create and maintain the game long term.

TECHNOLOGY PROBE

To explore 'shared geocaching' over distance, we created a technology probe shown in Figure 1 that consisted of existing commercial software and hardware. It included a wearable mobile video camera that captured the wearer's field of vision by being attached to an article of clothing such as a hat or a pair of glasses. We used a Looxie 2 camera and an ordinary pair of sunglasses (glasses for evening usage) to prototype the experience. Using a Bluetooth connection and a specially designed smartphone application (by Looxie), the camera transmitted live streaming video to a local smartphone. By leveraging the smartphone's mobile Internet connection, the application broadcasted the video to a remote user's smartphone at 640 x 480 resolution and 24 fps, in the best case. At times, this resolution was algorithmically reduced if network bandwidth became constrained. The camera also captured and transmitted audio to the remote person, so the users could talk to one another throughout the experience. Both parties could send and receive video simultaneously to establish a symmetrical exchange where each could view the other's field of vision.

We modified a wearable runner's armband to hold a smartphone that showed the remote user's video (Figure 1, right). This freed up the users' hands to hold a GPS device (for geocaching) if they wanted to. It also allowed them to look periodically at the remote user's video by looking at his or her arm. This contrasts a head-mounted display (e.g., smartphone attached to a helmet, or augmented-reality glasses), as we wanted to make video selectively available to users. Thus, they could choose when to look at the remote user's video feed. This also meant that the video feed did not obscure a person's normal vision.

Even though it was crude looking, the technology probe sufficed for exploring the experience that we were interested in without investing in large development efforts. This is a critical goal for technology probes [17].

STUDY METHODOLOGY

We conducted a study to explore how our technology probe would be used for 'shared geocaching' over distance. The goal of our study was to understand how the audio and video links supported the activity and what technical or social challenges existed, such as privacy concerns.

Participants and Recruitment

We recruited sixteen people in total for our study—eight pairs of friends or family members—via advertisements on online geocaching forums and within our university community. 10 of 16 participants were between 20 and 30 years old, two were between 40 and 50 years, and four were between 50 and 60; thus, our participants generally represented a young demographic. Occupations included pharmacy technician, special education teacher, journalist, videographer, retail salesperson, and students. Eleven participants frequently participated in outdoor activities and ten said that they often went on hikes or walks with friends. All but one participant was familiar with the concept of geocaching, though ten had never found any geocaches. Three people had found between one and four geocaches, one had found more than ten, one had found over 500, and another had found over 1,000 geocaches. Thus, overall, our participants were mostly novice or beginner geocachers with the addition of two highly experienced geocachers.

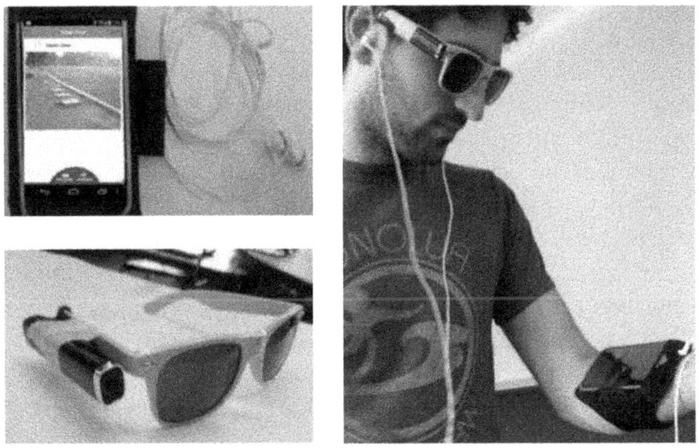

Figure 1: The 'shared geocaching' technology probe.

Given this, our study focuses predominantly on the reaction and experiences of participants to the technology probe and the idea of participating in a parallel experience with video streaming. Thus, we do not report on the broader implications of 'shared geocaching' in terms of the culture and community associated with geocaching and how 'acceptable' community members may find the activity. There are a great number of questions that existing geocachers could have about how to conduct 'shared geocaching' according to the implicit rules of the game. For example, if a person finds a remote geocache with someone, are they 'allowed' to record the find even though they did not actually physically find the cache in person? Our study does not address these types of questions or explore the broader cultural questions about 'shared geocaching' as this would require a different study than the one we conducted. However, we feel this would make for very interesting future work in the area.

Method

Our study method consisted of several stages:

1. Initial Survey – We first conducted written surveys with each participant to gather demographics and obtain background information on how they normally participated in outdoor activities like walking, hiking, or geocaching, if at all, and how this included, or did not, family members or friends. The survey took ~15 minutes to complete.

2. Shared Geocaching – Participants then walked around an area adjacent to our university campus and were told that they should separate and collectively try to find two geocaches each within an hour time period. The area contained five geocaches that we told participants about within a one kilometer (0.6 mile) radius. The area contained a large shopping mall, parking lot, and an urban park with sidewalks and trees. This meant participants were usually separated by a distance of 100-300 meters, though buildings, trees, and other structures visually separated these areas to create the feeling of a more distant connection. Geocaches ranged in size from 'micro' (a film canister) to 'regular' (a small Tupperware container). They also varied in difficulty. For example, an easy geocache was hidden in a stump underneath some tree bark. A difficult geocache blended in to the environment by being hidden behind a false electrical cover on a parking lot post.

Participants used our technology probe and were told they could use any additional devices or applications that they normally geocached with. We also provided participants with paper printouts of maps showing the location of each geocache along with the information found on each cache's web page. We did this so that all participants would have access to the same basic cache information regardless of whether they brought additional devices or applications.

In this study stage, we were interested in seeing when and how audio and video were used and, if any, what challenges or interesting social situations participants experienced. We imagined that participants would mutually help each other as they hunted for their own geocaches. We also anticipated they would engage in casual conversation about other activities, their surroundings, etc. Alternatively, we could have tried to create nearly identical geocaches in two locations so people could have the exact same shared experience. However, we felt this was largely impractical and not likely to occur more broadly in geocaching. We also purposely restricted the study to geocaches within a walking distance as opposed to ones requiring participants to drive with a vehicle. This would have created a very different type of shared experience and we encourage future studies to investigate this area.

3. Final Interview – After completing the geocaching activity, participants were separately interviewed about their overall thoughts on the experience. We asked them to give us a step-by-step account of the activity, and we also asked them questions about how they made use of the audio and video links and how they interacted with their partner. Thus, we received feedback and descriptions of the activity and the overall experience by all participants individually where responses were not biased by what a partner might have said. At times, participants even commented on the activities of their partner and perceived annoyances.

Data Collection & Analysis

All interviews were audio-recorded and handwritten notes were kept. We analyzed our interview transcriptions and notes using thematic analysis to understand the main and recurring themes in our data. We purposely did not go with the participants to observe them while they participated in the activity because we wanted them to feel as though the only person they were doing the activity with was the remote partner. Going with them to observe could have easily confounded this sense of 'togetherness.' This meant, however, that our data analysis relied on retrospective verbal accounts. We also did not record the video or audio that was streamed through the probe for the same reasons.

Next we present our results based on the themes that emerged in our analysis. First, we outline general reactions to the idea of 'shared geocaching' and how the probe was used. Second, we explain the environmental factors and pragmatics that affected the general usage of the technology. Third, we describe the idea of a 'micro' shared experience within a broader public context. This relates to the role of audio and video, distractions, and exclusions. Fourth, we outline findings on safety. And, fifth, we outline the privacy and social challenges participants faced as a result of the activity and technology.

GEOCACHING OVER DISTANCE

Overall, nearly all participants enjoyed participating in 'shared geocaching' with their partner over distance. Participants expressed the same sentiments that are typical with geocaching: they enjoyed doing a physical activity with someone else, they liked being outdoors, they enjoyed the challenge of searching for geocaches, and they liked the novelty of the technology.

"It was more fun. It was more of a social experience rather than being by yourself. In terms of, even when you geocache with other people, you're finding the same one. Here you have more options, because if you don't find one, you can help someone else find theirs." (P7)

In general, experienced geocachers described the experience as being 'not as good as' geocaching with someone in person but a reasonable proxy if one's partner lived far away.

"It was a different experience...I kept wishing I was there to help him instead of just seeing him and trying to talk him through it. I usually geocache with someone else. And the two of us together, talking through it, looking together, is to me a better idea." (P3)

Some participants struggled with finding geocaches and only found one or two, while others found four of the five geocaches in our study set. Searching success was often based on one's prior experience with geocaching.

As one would expect, not everyone liked the experience. One participant without any geocaching experience felt 'shared geocaching' was not very appealing. Some became frustrated when they could not find particular caches, but this also a common problem with geocaching in general.

Participants told us that they talked nearly continuously over the audio feed, which was said to be the most valuable part of the experience. Conversations focused on discussions of geocaching, the 'new' technology being used, what participants saw around them, as well as casual talk typical amongst friends. Video was used to show the environment around the participants in general. For example, participants commented on how they showed each other funny things they saw, homeless people they passed by, attractive bystanders, etc. Video was also used to show aspects of the environment that were more specific to geocaching (e.g., landmarks, likely hiding locations, etc).

Navigation vs. Searching

Geocaching typically involves two activities: 1) orienting oneself geographically and navigating to a specific area; and, 2) performing a fine-grained search within a specific location for a geocache container (e.g., a Tupperware container, magnetic keyholder, a film or pill canister). Participants described the technology probe as working especially well for navigating to a geocache's general area. This was because the resolution of the video lent itself most naturally to seeing scenery and a location's general environment, rather than specific attributes. For example, one couple described how they shared a GPS device to find the geocaches. In this instance, the partner with the GPS device directed the other partner by looking at both her GPS device and his video feed to see where he was located.

"[My partner] was able to find her way and I was able to help her by looking at the phone. So I was able to see where she was that way. I could recognize markers outside. So when she was moving her head, looking around, I could see what she was looking at, and I could see a sign for [the store] and I knew exactly where she was and I told her to go right." (P6)

On the other hand, it was often difficult to help remote users with fine-grained container searching once they reached a geocache's general area because the resolution of the streamed video was not high enough to show specific environmental details that might reveal where a geocache container was hidden. Fine-grained searching also required viewing the area at certain angles and distances, which was often difficult for participants to frame with the head-mounted camera.

"I couldn't help [him] find his [geocache] because I had no sense of what he was looking at. He thought he found it...but I think it was a power box the city put there. I looked at his screen to see. I had no sense of orientation. The camera was crooked. The shot was too tight." (P2)

"This way there was a disconnect because you can't be physically right there moving things and helping. And that was frustrating. And what I could see was limited. He was looking down a lot. So I couldn't locate him space." (P3)

In some instances, participants helped with fine-grained searching by pointing out general areas that their partners could look in, but, again, they were unable to help with more detailed searching. Similarly, participants also talked about showing each other the geocache containers that they found so that the less experienced geocachers would know what style of containers to look for.

"The video actually did help where [my wife] helped me with orientation with where the caches might be." (P4)

"[My partner] corrected me and told me I should be in the buggy area. So he's telling me...I looked again, there was a hint of 'black', and I didn't see anything black. He said, 'look up', and I looked up, and there it was." (P8)

"We were talking and seeing where each other were. I was able to see where he was and what he was looking at. He was looking at a log. I tried to get him to look in it. And when I found mine, I showed him so he knew what he was looking for." (P12)

All partner sets tended to use a leader-follower paradigm when geocaching: one person, often the more experienced geocacher, would help out the less experienced person. This caused geocaching conversations and video viewing to focus most often on the less experienced geocacher.

'MICRO' SHARED EXPERIENCES

All participants expressed a strong sense of a 'shared experience' with their partners. What was most interesting about this was that the description of the shared experience was very intimately tied with each participant's partner, despite the experience and activity occurring within the broader context of the public setting that included bystanders. We refer to this as a 'micro' shared experience in the sense that the experience was a microcosm within the larger set of activities and events occurring in the setting where participants engaged in 'shared geocaching'. This is because participants had a very strong sense that they were participating in an activity with only one other person, as opposed to the larger backdrop of people coming and going around them. In this context, participants talked about the audio as creating a very personal link to their remote partner. That is, the audio link provided the strongest sense of connection to one's partner. Video was seen as an additional benefit on top of the audio and added to the sense of a close, intimate experience by providing remote viewers with the view as seen by their partners (a view one typically does not get).

Distraction

Participants were often so engaged in the experience with their partner that they became distracted from the other happenings around them because they were so engaged with talking to and seeing what their partner was doing. This was despite the selective availability of the video (e.g., choosing when to look at one's arm to see the video).

"He's like the voice inside my head. Because with the earphones on you kinda shut out the other noises around you. It's interesting because I'm hearing what he's hearing. It's kinda weird that the stuff I'm hearing might not relate to what I'm seeing. You need to get used to that. Eventually I took out one ear so I could actually hear what's going on around me." (P1)

"Um...I'd say I might have focused too much on trying to see what he was doing rather than doing what I was doing. I may have ignored some of my surroundings." (P2)

Because participants became so immersed in the connection they shared with their partner, at times the activity of 'shared geocaching' became unsafe and participants had to explicitly remember to pay attention to their settings in order to stay out of harm's way.

"I could hear her...so I was paying more attention to her than I was to my own task...I was paying so much attention to the screen that I forgot I was in area with moving cars. So I had to pay a little attention to ...you know, I was in a parking lot with moving vehicles." (P6)

"At first we found that we were watching the screens way too much. When we were walking and one of us came up to a street it would be like, okay, we have to stop watching the screen and focus on crossing the street now." (P11)

Participants often found it difficult to completely focus on both settings—the connection with their partner and their own surroundings—at the same. Both required a large degree of effort in order to follow what was happening.

In addition to this, two participants told us that sometimes they did not like to be always sharing the experience with their partners. For example, one participant preferred to spend some 'individual time' to find her geocache and did not want her partner to bother her:

"He kept busy looking at mine though. He kept saying 'you're walking the wrong way'. I vaguely know where it is so I kept walking and he kept looking at my screen. I found it distracting and told him to mind his own business." (P5)

Another person related the experience to 'living life through a camera lens' where a person is overly focused on a camera and not seeing the world through her own eyes:

"When you're on vacation, and you take a video of something scenic. I do it, and I hate it. Why not just look at it? The video link could take away from certain experiences. Especially with nature and outdoor beauty." (P8)

Appearance and Visibility

Participants also commented on the effects of wearing a 'new' type of technology in a public setting. They felt that the wearable camera made it easy to notice them or get extra attention in a public setting as did the crudeness of the prototype. Many participants described getting looks from other people in the general public resulting from the prototype as well as the ongoing conversations that they were having with their partners. This tended to not bother most people because they felt the looks were associated with being a part of something 'new,' which they were experiencing with their partner, not alone.

"I got a few strange looks from people because I'm walking and talking but you see that more these days anyway. I feel the camera might have looked weird to some people but I didn't notice it." (P3)

Concerns were also explicitly tempered because participants were participating in the activity with someone else who could relate to their feelings about the experience and even see the remote person's situation as it occurred.

"...she was walking through the mall and she said people were looking at her, and I was able to look at the screen and see that people were staring at her." (P7)

As one might expect, not everyone was comfortable with the additional public attention because of the technology probe. A small number of participants expressed concerns about feeling self-conscious because of it. Here the shared experience of participating with someone else was not enough to overcome apprehension.

"Except when I was in the mall...I felt a bit self conscious...I felt like everyone was looking at me. I think people thought it was more weird at first because people could hear me talking to somebody, and then they would look up and see the glasses and be like 'Oh, she's doing something strange.' Especially when it got dark, because the red light stood out a little bit." (P12)

Exclusion

Participants commented that sometimes the experience moved away from being intimate with their partner and this explicitly occurred when the partner began interacting with a member of the general public. For some participants, this 'ruined' the experience because they no longer felt the close connection with their partner. For example, one husband described how he felt completely 'left out' and even spiteful when his wife started talking with a person in the street and asking for directions:

"Then I could overhear [my wife] talking to people in the street asking for directions. And I said well wait a minute, I should be helping you because we're supposed to be collaborating. [I felt disconnected] because now [my wife's] talking to other people. And I know what it's like when you're on the phone and you're talking to people next to you and you've got a voice in your ear..." (P6)

The challenge with the above scenario is that the husband had no way to interact with other people at the remote location. Instead, his interactions were solely with his partner. Moreover, other people at the remote location did not even know that he was a part of the activity because he had no live presence or embodiment next to his partner.

SAFETY

Some participants completed the study during the evening when it was darker and explained that they felt safer because of the video feed. Thus, the video streaming made participants more comfortable to carry on the activity at times during the day when they may not have normally been out alone.

"I liked being able to see where he was what he was doing because I didn't like walking in that parking lot by myself...so knowing someone else could see what I was seeing and what was going on was a nice feeling." (P12)

We also found that safety *issues* can also arise because of the technology. Thus, it does not always mitigate problems; sometimes it creates them. In one instance, a participant ended up in a verbal altercation with a homeless man. The participant was talking to his partner via the headset, and the man passing by thought he was talking to him. The homeless man began shouting at the participant. Luckily he calmed down when he realized that the participant was actually talking to a remote person. Again, in this situation, the participant was thankful that a remote person could see what was occurring on the video feed.

In another instance, the technology probe created a potentially risky situation, as perceived by the participant who felt others might think he was engaging in criminal activity because of the visible wearable technology. This went beyond normal concerns that geocachers often express about being noticed by others (non-cachers).

"People started looking at me a little bit funny. Shoppers, in the parking lot. I assumed they thought I was maybe scoping out cars, like a possible break-in or something. This may be a high-crime area, I'm not sure. I was mindful of that." (P6)

PRIVACY

After their experience, we asked participants if they had any privacy concerns or if they felt that bystanders in the public would have any concerns with them using the technology. We also asked them about any privacy sensitive situations.

Streaming Video in a Public Setting

Participants tended to not think about the privacy of others in the general public without us prompting them. When asked specifically about it, most felt that it was okay to use the technology probe and provided a variety of reasons.

First, participants talked about the difference between streaming video and recording video. Most participants felt that the privacy of others was not being compromised because the video was not being recorded. Streaming video was seen as ephemeral whereas video recording was considered much more permanent and privacy intrusive.

"If you're holding up a camera, it looks like you're actively filming someone. If you have a tiny little camera strapped to your head, and you've synced two devices so you can talk...it doesn't feel like you're actively filming people. It just feels like a private communication between two people. If someone walked by with a head-mounted camera...if they're talking to someone else, I'm not worried about them publishing it because it looks like they're just showing it to someone else in real time." (P11)

Participants did not comment on the lack of feedback within the prototype that, if it existed, would provide bystanders with an understanding that the device was only streaming video and not recording it. There was a common assumption that others would simply know that the device was only streaming and not recording even without such feedback from the device.

Second, participants talked about video streaming being used in a public place and cameras being 'everywhere' already. For example, when asked if she worried about the privacy of others, one participant said:

"No. They're in public...if you're in public you're putting yourself in a spot to be recorded. You're subject to your picture getting taken." (P2)

Some participants described laws that were said to permit photo and video capture in public places without the explicit consent of those being captured. Because of such policies, these participants felt that the technology probe was no different than existing videography and photography activities. Similarly, one participant was a professional photographer/videographer who often filmed live events like weddings and skateboarding competitions. He said he did not have any privacy concerns for other people because he was already very comfortable filming strangers in public because of his profession.

The study also revealed that the notion of what is public vs. private is often obscured. At one point, the shopping mall's security team alerted us that 'filming' was not allowed on mall property (in this case, a plaza outside of stores). Thus, despite it appearing to be a public location, the mall was actually considered to be private property with its own rules for video capture.

Three participants told us they did not feel comfortable streaming video of bystanders while they participated in the study. One person talked about being 'eyed' by security and feeling like she should conceal what she was doing and move along before they hassled her.

"People notice it. People see that I'm recording because of the red light. It kind of worries me getting from place to place. People could see this. So I'm a bit more cautious when I'm pointing it at them. It's like...I'm just gonna go on my way. I'm worried for them because it's not my intention to record them all." (P1)

In one case, privacy became an actual issue between two partners during the study. After initially leaving to find their first geocaches, one participant stopped at the mall bathroom to use the facilities before heading outside. This activity was accidentally broadcast to his partner.

Self-Censorship

While we had told participants that video was only being streamed to their partner, at times participants were not sure if this was actually the case. This was partially a result of the software we used: the Looxcie software application shows a series of public video broadcasts on its home screen, which participants saw when starting the application in the study. These could falsely cause users to think that all streams are set to be publicly available online; in contrast, we had set up each device to only stream between the two participants' devices. Despite this, people still expressed concerns and would sometimes self-censor what they said.

"I just kinda wondered, so you're streaming, now who can see the stream? That was what I was wondering. I think about, okay, so I have to be careful what I say to [my partner]. Just in general. I wasn't overly concerned because it was a study." (P8)

"I think I thought about what I said a bit more in case someone else could hear it. Maybe made less snarky comments to [my partner]." (P12)

This reveals that people still feel video may somehow be broadcasting their call more broadly despite the settings they choose.

ENVIRONMENTAL AND PRAGMATIC FACTORS

We also found a variety of environmental and pragmatic factors that affected the ways in which participants engaged in the activity and experienced the technology. These relate mostly to usability. First, the technology probe was affected by weather conditions such as rain and sun. Participants who participated in the rain talked about how the glasses would get wet, which would obscure their vision. Similarly, they talked about how the armband holding the smartphone would get wet and make it difficult to see the video display. Those who participated on sunny days complained about glare from the sun on the smartphone case as well as issues of shade when near buildings or trees.

Second, participants sometimes saw the technology probe as being bulky and awkward. The activity of geocaching involves feeling around and touching various surfaces in order to find the hidden geocache container. This was sometimes difficult especially if a person tried to use the hand that contained the armband.

Third, some participants faced pragmatic challenges from wearing the probe's glasses. For example, one participant wore a turban and struggled to get the glasses and camera on his head in a comfortable manner.

Lastly, at times participants experienced video or audio lag. This ranged from a couple of seconds to upwards of fifteen seconds. When it occurred, audio lag tended to be more detrimental to the experience than video lag. In cases when audio began to lag, conversations became completely disrupted. Yet when video lagged, participants could easily wait to see the video 'catch up'.

DISCUSSION AND CONCLUSIONS

Our study has described the experiences of participants in using video streaming as part of 'shared geocaching' over distance. Here we focus on discussing the broader and more complex challenges that should be carefully considered when supporting parallel experiences through video streaming in public settings.

Navigation vs. Fine-Grained Searching

First, we see that 'shared geocaching' and our technology probe worked reasonably well for shared navigation to areas containing geocaches, where the remote participant could see the area and help the other person navigate. This suggests that activities beyond geocaching that contain general wayfinding, navigation, and discussion about locations would similarly benefit from a setup like we had. This might include activities like walking, hiking, or tourist sightseeing.

Yet when it came to more fine-grained tasks, the video stream was not as useful. This related to resolution issues, but we also feel it relates to one's viewpoint and who is in control of that viewpoint. For example, participants commented on the challenges of not knowing where their partner was looking or not understanding the camera's orientation. When it comes to video chat technologies, people are very used to seeing a view of others that shows their face and background. However, in contrast, they are much less used to seeing a first person view, which can be confusing without broader experience and exposure to such views. This type of remote view is also most likely continually moving while one is mobile and walking. This means that the control of what is seen is in the hands of the remote person and not the viewer.

Overall, this suggests that activities that require more fine-grained control and specific views of an area may not immediately benefit from setups like our technology probe, unless the viewer has more options of controlling what is seen. This might include situations like sightseeing if a person wants to show a remote friend a specific aspect of a building. It could also occur in 'shared shopping' situations if a person is trying to show various items in a store over video chat. Potential solutions include having cameras capture a larger, panoramic view of an area, where remote viewers can choose what portion of the view they get to see with the ability to zoom in to such regions. This may also alleviate potential issues with 'bouncing' video images because of movement.

'Micro' Shared Experiences

Our technology probe was also especially beneficial for creating an intimate shared experience with one's remote partner. We described this as a 'micro' shared experience because of its placement within the broader context of happenings around the participants' activities (e.g., bystanders and their activities). Yet this too created some challenges.

First, participants could easily become distracted from the 'real world' because of the experiencing they were sharing with their remote partner. This can create safety issues.

Second, they may also want to be able to 'escape' the shared experience for short time periods to 'do their own thing' without interruption from a remote partner. Both of these issues suggest that selective availability of a video and/or audio feed is important. It also reveals that remote partners may experience a situation differently—one may want to talk and one may not. We had assumed that 'always-on' video and audio would be desired by participants throughout the activity, yet our study revealed that this may not be the case. Together, this highlights the importance of supporting asymmetrical experiences and being able to easily move into and out of contact with the remote person while not detracting from the close intimacy that was highly valued by many of our participants. Research on media spaces in the workplace similarly points to the value of asymmetrical experiences [32].

Third, we also found that when a person interacts with someone else at his or her location in the 'real world' the intimacy of the experience with one's remote partner breaks down. This can be disconcerting and even emotionally distressing for the person 'left out.' We feel this arises because the remote participants have only a minimal representation or embodiment at the remote location, e.g., a small video feed on a smartphone. People at the remote location cannot easily see them and nor are they able to easily interact with them. This suggests new opportunities for designing for remote embodiments, if one wants to create an experience where interactions with other people in the surrounding environment are possible.

These findings also reveal that 'shared geocaching' and other similar activities likely work best in a paired situation. Engaging in parallel experiences with two people at a single location while another person is remote would certainly isolate the remote participant and create feelings of presence disparity (previously defined for workplace and classroom settings [30]). Similarly, having more than two people participate in a parallel experience where all are in different locations would also create large challenges in understanding whose video to look at and when.

Video Streaming in Public Settings

More generally, our study also explored the use of video streaming in a variety of public settings, e.g., a mall, parking lot, an adjacent plaza, and an urban park. None of our participants commented on privacy issues as it related to audio streaming, likely because of the prevalence and accepted understanding of using mobile phones in public settings. Despite knowledge of potential issues, most participants did not feel there were problems with streaming video from these locations. This was because the camera was streaming and not recording, or people felt local laws allowed them to stream video without consequence. Yet there are clearly issues.

First, the camera we used did not provide feedback that differentiated streaming from recording, which is clearly a design limitation. If they noticed the camera, bystanders had no understanding of whether they were being captured or streamed, and, if streamed, who they were being streamed to. The remote viewer was completely disembodied in the physical space of his or her partner [1]. These observations clearly suggest design opportunities for feedback mechanisms and remote embodiment.

Second, only one of our participants actually knew what the local laws were about capturing video in a public setting. The rest of our participants were operating under an assumption that it was okay without any real knowledge. Related to this, we also learned that locations are not always clear-cut in terms of what is private and what is public space. Shopping malls may feel like public places to people, yet they are actually private property and may come with their own distinct set of rules. Thus, there is easily a disconnect between the perception of a place and the actual rules that govern it. The design implications of how to address this are less clear, though it points to important considerations for video streaming technologies.

Third, we also recognize that if one were to design privacy-preservation solutions for situations such as video streaming in public settings, the paradigm of such solutions would need to be different than traditional privacy-preservation techniques for video communication systems. Historically, research on privacy in media spaces has looked at obfuscation techniques to mask what is being shown while still presenting some degree of information [3]. In workplace and home settings, this might mean 'blurring' out a person's image or their background. Yet in the case of public settings, the reverse needs to happen. Instead of masking out the person using the video (because she is likely behind the camera lens), privacy preservation strategies will need to think about masking out particular aspects of the user's view, be it other people or parts of the environment.

Applications and Future Work

We can imagine that these themes and implications might generalize to a number of applications beyond geocaching. Given the similarity between geocaching and activities like walking, hiking, and sightseeing, we believe this research could closely inform the design and evaluation of mobile-to-mobile video streaming for other outdoor recreational activities. Our findings may also extend to more diverse domains like search-and-rescue or jobsite inspection. However, this would need to be verified with further study. It would likely be the case that the importance of the themes we discovered would vary from application to application. For example, in a life-or-death scenario like search-and-rescue, safety issues would likely be crucial while privacy issues would be much less important. We believe the issues we have raised around privacy, safety, navigation, and 'micro' shared experience can act as lenses of investigation for this future work.

Limitations

We recognize that, overall, our demographic was relatively young and this may have an effect on our results in terms of people's acceptance of video streaming in public settings. That said, we did not see any obvious differences in opinions and usage between our younger and older participants. Nonetheless, future work should explore the different perceptions of video streaming in public settings with broader demographic samples. Our research also focuses on the participants' overall high-level experience of shared geocaching. Because we did not observe participants in the field, we were unable to obtain observation data that might have provided an objective perspective on the activity. We believe our interview method provided sufficient insight into the participants' experiences, but future researchers may want to find a way to observe or record participants' activities in the field. This kind of observation could illustrate things like how long or how often participants utilize the video feed.

ACKNOWLEDGMENTS

We thank NSERC and the GRAND NCE for funding this research.

REFERENCES

1. Ames, M. G., Go, J., Kaye, J. J., & Spasojevic, M. Making love in the network closet: the benefits and work of family videochat, Proc. CSCW, ACM Press (2010).

2. Bellotti, V. Design for Privacy in Multimedia Computing and Communications Environments, in *Technology and Privacy: The New Landscape*, MIT Press (1998) 63-98.
3. Boyle, M., Neustaedter, C., and Greenberg, S. Privacy Factors in Video-based Media Spaces, *Media Space: 20+ Years of Mediated Life*, Springer (2009).
4. Brubaker, J., Venolia, G., and Tang, J. Focusing on Shared Experiences: Moving Beyond the Camera in Video Communication, *Proc. DIS,* ACM Press (2012).
5. Buhler, T., Neustaedter, C., and Hillman, S. How and Why Teenagers Use Video Chat, *Proc. CSCW,* (2012).
6. Chavez, D.J., Courtright, R., and Schneider, I. Over the River and through the Woods, *Parks & Recreation,* 39, 4 (2004), 68-72.
7. Chavez, D.J., Schneider, I., and Powell, T. The Social Psychology of a Technology Driven Outdoor Trend: Geocaching in the USA, *Proc. HICSS 2004*, ACM Press (2004).
8. Consolvo, S., Everitt, K., Smith, I., Landay, J. A. Design Requirements for Technologies that Encourage Physical Activity, *Proc. CHI*, ACM Press (2006), 457-466.
9. de Sá, M., Shamma, D.A., Churchill, E.F. Live mobile collaboration for video production: design, guidelines, and requirements, Personal and Ubiquitous Computing, Springer (2013).
10. Engström, A., Zoric, G., Juhlin O., and Toussi, R. The mobile vision mixer: a mobile network based live video broadcasting system in your mobile phone, Proc. Mobile and Ubiquitous Multimedia (MUM '12).
11. Inkpen, K., Du, H., Roseway, A., Hoff, A., and Johns, P. Video Kids: Augmenting Close Friendships with Asynchronous Video Conversations in VideoPal, *Proc. CHI,* ACM Press (2012).
12. Inkpen, K., Taylor, B., Junuzovic, S., Tang, J., and Venolia, G. Experiences2Go: Sharing Kids' Activities Outside the Home with Remote Family Members, *Proc. CSCW,* ACM Press (2013).
13. Judge, T.K., and Neustaedter, C., Sharing Conversations and Sharing Life: Video Conferencing in the Home, *Proc. of CHI,* ACM Press (2010).
14. Judge, T.K., Neustaedter, C. and Kurtz, A., The Family Window: The Design and Evaluation of a Domestic Media Space. *Proc. CHI*, ACM Press (2010).
15. Judge, T.K., Neustaedter, C., Harrison, S., and Blose, A., The Family Portals: Connecting Families Through a Multifamily Media Space. *Proc. ACM CHI*, (2011).
16. Kelley, M.A. *Local Treasures: Geocaching across America.* Santa Fe: Center for American Places (2006).
17. Hutchinson, H., Mackay, W., Westerlund, B., Bederson, B., Druin, A., Plaisant, C., Beaudouin-Lafon, M., Conversy, S., Evans, H., Hansen, H., Roussel, N., Eiderbäck, B. Technology probes: Inspiring design for and with families, *Proc. CHI,* ACM Press (2003), 17-24.
18. Mueller, F., O'Brien, S., and Thorogood, A. Jogging over a Distance, *Proc. CHI,* ACM Press (2007).
19. Mueller, F., Vetere, F., Gibbs, M., Edge, D., Agamonlis, S., and Sheridan, J. Jogging over a Distance Between Europe and Australia, *Proc. UIST,* ACM Press (2010), 189-198.
20. Mueller, F., Agamanolis, S., and Picard, R., Exertion interfaces: sports over a distance for social bonding and fun, *Proc. CHI,* ACM Press (2003), 561-568.
21. Neustaedter, C. and Judge, T. Peek-A-Boo: The Design of a Mobile Family Media Space, *Video Proc. Ubicomp*, Springer (2010).
22. Neustaedter, C., and Greenberg, S., Intimacy in Long-Distance Relationships over Video Chat, *Proc. CHI,* ACM Press (2012).
23. Neustaedter, C., Tang, A., and Judge. T, The Role of Community and Groupware in Geocache Creation and Maintenance, *Proc. CHI 2010,* ACM Press (2010).
24. O'Brien, S., and Mueller, F. Jogging the Distance, *Proc. CHI,* ACM Press (2007).
25. O'Hara, K. Understanding Geocaching Practices and Motivations, *Proc. CHI 2008,* ACM Press (2008).
26. O'Hara, K., Black, A., Lipson, M. Everyday Practices with Mobile Video Telephony, *Proc. CHI*, ACM Press (2006), 871-880.
27. Raffle, H., Ballagas, R., Revelle, G., Horii, H., Follmer, S., Go, J., Reardon, E., Mori, K., Kaye, J., and Spasojevic, M. Family story play: reading with children, *Proc. CHI,* ACM Press (2010).
28. Salovaara, A., Johnson, M., Toiskallio, K., Tiitta, S., and Turpeinen, M. Playmakers in Multiplayer Game Communities, *Proc. ACE 2005*, ACM Press (2005).
29. Stanley, K., Livingston, I., Bandurka, A., Kapiszka, R., Mandryk, R. (2010) PiNiZoRo: A GPS-based Exercise Game for Families, *Proc. Future Play,* (2010), 276-279.
30. Tang, A., Neustaedter, C., and Greenberg, S. Embodiments in Mixed Presence Groupware, *British HCI,* ACM Press (2006).
31. Virtual Photo Walks, www.virtualphotowalks.org
32. Voida, A., Voida, S., Greenberg, S., and He, H. A. Asymmetry in media spaces, *Proc. CSCW,* (2008).
33. Yarosh, S., Cuzzort, S., Mueller, H., and Abowd, G.D., Developing a Media Space for Remote Synchronous Parent-Child Interaction, *Proc IDC*, ACM Press (2009).
34. Yarosh, S., Inkpen, K., and Brush, A.J., Video Playdate: Toward Free Play Across Distance, *Proc. CHI,* ACM Press (2010).

A Gaze-preserving Situated Multiview Telepresence System

Ye Pan, Anthony Steed
Department of Computer Science
University College London, UK
y.pan, a.steed@cs.ucl.ac.uk

ABSTRACT
Gaze, attention, and eye contact are important aspects of face to face communication, but some subtleties can be lost in videoconferencing because participants look at a single planar image of the remote user. We propose a low-cost cylindrical videoconferencing system that preserves gaze direction by providing perspective-correct images for multiple viewpoints around a conference table. We accomplish this by using an array of cameras to capture a remote person, and an array of projectors to present the camera images onto a cylindrical screen. The cylindrical screen reflects each image to a narrow viewing zone. The use of such a situated display allows participants to see the remote person from multiple viewing directions. We compare our system to three alternative display configurations. We demonstrate the effectiveness of our system by showing it allows multiple participants to simultaneously tell where the remote person is placing their gaze.

Author Keywords
Non-planar displays; camera arrays; gaze

ACM Classification Keywords
H.4.3 Communications Applications: Computer conferencing, teleconferencing, and videoconferencing

INTRODUCTION
When a group of people communicate face to face, numerous cues of attention, eye contact, and gaze direction provide important additional channels of information, such as attention targets, conversational turn-taking indicators [1]. However, those non-verbal cues can be lost in traditional teleconferencing systems [9].

A variety of systems have been developed to support gaze awareness in group video conferencing, though the majority use a 2D planar display [4]. We propose to use a cylindrical display which provides the same angle of view from all directions. We further propose to use a camera array to surround the remote person horizontally, capturing unique and perspective-correct videos for each potential observer's viewing direction (see Figure 1(a) to Figure 1(d)). A projector array is arranged in the same manner as the camera array around

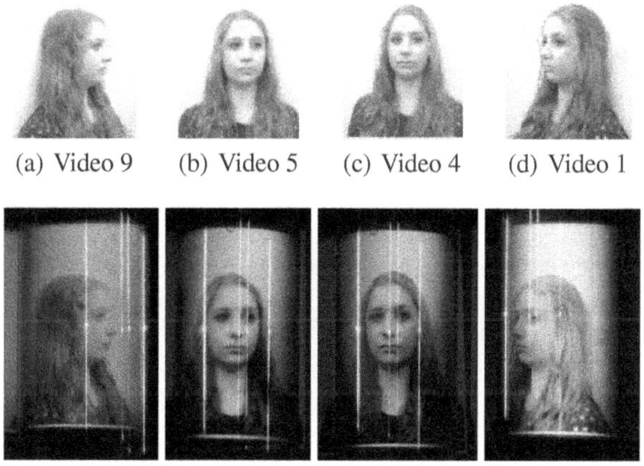

(a) Video 9 (b) Video 5 (c) Video 4 (d) Video 1

(e) View 9 (f) View 5 (g) View 4 (h) View 1

Figure 1. The remote person is gazing at target 5. The top row is four videos simultaneously captured from four different cameras. The bottom row is four photos of the same display from four different perspectives. See Figure 2 for camera, target and viewpoint numbers.

the cylindrical display, which allows each observer to see different views simultaneously (see Figure 1(e) to Figure 1(h)).

We evaluate the effectiveness of our system by measuring the ability of observers to accurately judge which target the remote person is gazing at. We run an experiment to demonstrate that our system can convey gaze relatively accurately, especially for observers viewing from off-center angles. This demonstration and results thus motivate the further study of novel display configurations and the supporting camera and networking infrastructure for them.

BACKGROUND
Many systems have achieved accurate reproduction of gaze direction in group video conferencing, including MAJIC [5], Hydra [10], GAZE-2 [11], Animatronic shader lamps avatars [3] and 3-d live [8]. These systems support correct gaze direction when used with one participant per site. Several current multiview display systems use a single display and a filter method or a lenticular separation method to produce different views. These methods divide the resolution of a display among multiple views so that each view has only N/K pixels, where N is the pixels of the full display and K is the number of views. MultiView [4] supports K full-resolution views. However, those planar displays are visible from the front only. Current situated displays, such as, TeleHuman [2] and SphereAvatar [6], are viewable from 360°. These systems achieved maintaining accurate gaze by providing a perspective correct image via a single user's head

CHI'14, April 26–May 1, 2014, Toronto, Canada.
Copyright © 2014 ACM 978-1-4503-2473-1/14/04...$15.00.
http://dx.doi.org/10.1145/2556288.2557320

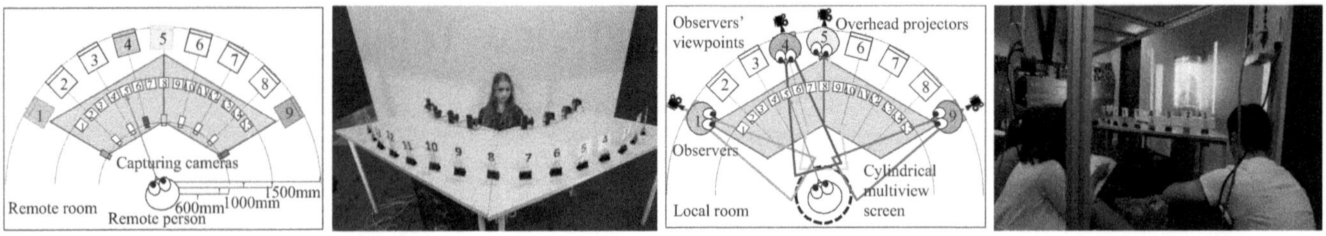

(a) Remote room schematic layout (b) Photo of the remote person (c) Local room schematic layout (d) Photo taken behind observer 1

Figure 2. Experiment setup: In the remote room, a camera array is used to capture unique and correct perspectives of the remote person gazing at the target 5. In the local room, a cylindrical multiview display is used to allow each observer to view their respective perspectives simultaneously. One of observers seating in viewpoint 1, only sees the video captured by camera 1.

position tracking. Eventually only a mono or stereo image is presented on the display, thus they are currently developed for a single observer. We propose a very low-cost telepresence system that combines the features of both multiview displays and situated displays discussed above.

SYSTEM DESIGN

The goal of our system is to allow multiple *observers* to perceive the gaze of a *remote person* accurately. That is observers can each see a unique and perspective-correct image from their viewing directions simultaneously. Each camera is linked to the corresponding projector to stream real-time video using TCP. The cylindrical screen ensures that each projected image will only be seen by an observer who is in the viewing zone for that projector. Also, using available off-the-shelf components allows our system to be built at a low cost. The cost for a three person multiview display would be approximately $1000, for a nine person multiview display would be approximately $2920.

Semicircular camera array construction

In the remote room, nine PlayStation® Eye USB digital cameras are vertically mounted on an angled table at radius of 600mm every 15°, as illustrated in Figure 2(a) and Figure 2(b). We manually adjust the cameras to look at the point above the center of the angled table. We then use Camera Calibration Toolbox for Matlab® to locate the cameras' positions and orientations accurately. The accurate positions and orientations of the cameras are used in the arrangement of projectors, so that accurate projecting of video can be done. The cameras are set to the 56° field of view setting. The cameras capture at 30 Hz at 640×480 pixel resolution. We arrange each camera vertically in order to make full use of the pixel resolution to represent the remote person's head.

Cylindrical multiview screen design

In the local room, the cylindrical screen is located at the center of an angled table which is the same size as the one in the remote room. We designed a cylindrical screen 32 cm in diameter and 70cm in height. The size is small enough to situate almost anywhere in a room. This display is visible from all directions, whereas flat displays are only visible from the front. The radius of curvature of the screen is similar to a real convex face to avoid the TV-screen-turn effect [1]. Using a cylindrical screen surface significantly simplifies projecting correct vertical perspective to observers at different heights and distances from the display.

The screen's main function is to reflect the image produced by a projector only to an observer in a very specific viewing zone. The idea of creating multiview screen for video conferencing is proposed by Nguyen et al. [4], where the screen's optics carefully retro reflects the light in the direction of the projector but diffuses it vertically, allowing viewers to see the image from any positions above or below the projector. Our screen consists of a retroreflective layer around the cylinder, with a one-dimensional diffuser layer 6mm above. Experimentation was conducted with different retroreflective materials, leading to the decision to use "white number plate reflective" from ORALITE® ($10), because it has a strong retroreflective characteristic, minimal reflective properties and good diffusive properties to reduce glare effects. A 1D lenslets-based lenticular sheet is used as the one-dimensional diffuser. The lines of the lenticular sheet placed horizontally to provide vertical diffusion. A 6mm or more physical spacing between retroreflective layer and lenticular sheet allows the light to mix vertically. The smooth side of the lenticular sheet is facing the observes and projectors. The 40 lenticules per inch (LPI) sheet with 49° viewing angle from Pacur® ($30) is chosen for two reasons: the thin thickness (0.838mm) of this sheet allows it easily to wrap around the cylinder; we only require a modest amount of vertical diffusion. More diffusion would hurt the brightness of the image.

Semicircular projector arrays construction

Nine projectors and observer viewpoints were set around the half annular table with a radius of 1500mm at every 15° which exactly line up with each camera in the remote room as depicted in Figure 2(c) and Figure 2(d). We vertically mounted each projector at a height of 1800mm, allowing an observer to sit under a projector. We use Projector-Camera Calibration Toolbox® to align the projectors' positions and orientations accurately. Each projector projecting a unique image on the part of the cylinder at the same horizontal level, but there are some overlap between images that projected by different projectors. The cylindrical multiview screen controls diffusion and produces relatively narrow viewing zones above, below, and slightly to the sides of a light source. Therefore, a observer sitting under the bottom of a projector sees only the image from that projector. We used NEC® NP110 projectors with resolutions of 800×600 pixels.

EXPERIMENT

The purpose of the experiment was to demonstrate that our cylinder multiview system can better represent the remote person's gaze for multiple observers. We measured the effectiveness of the displays by measuring the ability of multiple observers to accurately judge which target the remote person was gazing at.

We compared four display conditions. *Cylinder multiview multi-video* condition was our system discussed above, which could support correct viewing for multiple viewpoints around a conference table (see Figure 3(a)). *Cylinder multiview single-video* condition was identical to the cylinder multiview multi-video condition, except that only the center camera was used for capturing the remote person (see Figure 3(b)). All projectors project this video, instead of projecting unique perspective-correct videos. Thus, observers would perceive the gaze direction as if they were standing straight in front. This condition should show the benefit of using camera array. *Cylinder diffuse single-video* condition used a curved diffuse white projection screen. Only the center camera and projector were used (see Figure 3(c)). This condition mimicked TeleHuman [2], which developed for a single user; other users can view the display but will see a distorted view. *Flat diffuse single-video* condition used a conventional 2D flat screen, instead of 3D cylinder surface. This condition mimicked the commonly found Mona Lisa gaze effect, which occurs when 3D objects are rendered in 2D, causing the gaze perception of all in a room to be the same (see Figure 3(d)). Image quality remained the same in all conditions. We expect that viewers in cylinder multiview single-video condition and flat diffuse single-video condition will see much more incorrect targets compared to those in cylinder multiview multi-video condition. We further expect the cylinder diffuse single condition to lie between these two in performance, as the 3D cylindrical surface eliminates Mona Lisa gaze effect but viewers only could see part of head in some extreme viewpoints.

We explored four observers' viewpoints (1, 4, 5 & 9). We included viewpoint 5 where the observer at the center position as a benchmark; viewpoint 1 and 9 where observers sat at two extreme viewing angles; and viewpoint 4 where the observe sat right next to observer 5. In the cylinder multiview multi-video condition, we expect a similar level of error for observer perceiving targets at all viewpoints. For the other three display conditions, we expect the level of error will increase symmetrically as the viewpoint diverges horizontally from the central position.

Method

Participants

48 participants, students at University College London, were recruited to take part as observers in our user study. All participants had normal or corrected to normal eye sight. One further participant was an remote person recorded on video.

Apparatus and materials

We video-recorded the remote persons' head movements (see Figure 2(a)). The remote person sat at the center position of the table and his or her head is captured by 4 cameras simultaneously. The remote person listened to an audio

(a) (b) (c) (d)

Figure 3. Photos of display conditions taken from viewpoint 1: when the remote person gazing at the target 10, observers perceive different targets in four display conditions.

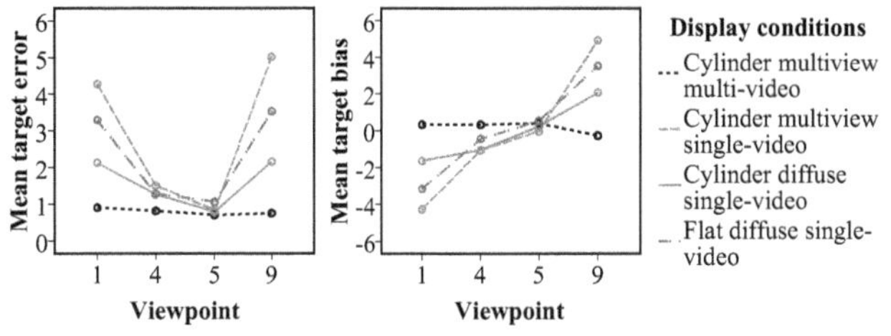

(a) Mean target error (b) Mean target bias

Figure 4. The mean target error and mean target bias for each display conditions and viewpoints.

recording that instructed to turn his or her head to look at the targets. A new target was given every 10 seconds. The targets were randomly ordered, each one was gazed at only once, amounting to 15 targets in the audio instruction and thus in the recorded videos. One set of 4 videos were generated.

Procedure

12 groups of four were used for testing, and each group experienced one of four different display conditions with each observer sat at one of the four viewpoints (see Figure 2(c)). Each observer was given a sheet of paper with an empty grid of 15 squares. The video of the remote person reoriented to a new target card every 10 seconds. At the same time an audio prompt to the observers instructed them that this was a new target. Then, observers would then judge which target (1-15) the remote person was gazing at and then write this in the relevant grid square. The experiment took about 5 minutes. Participants received chocolates as compensation.

Result

The primary measurement in our results was the level of error in perceiving targets. We defined target error (ϵ_i) to be the absolute value of difference between the observer's perceived target number (t_{oi}) and the actual target number (t_{ai}): $\epsilon_i = |t_{oi} - t_{ai}|$. Figure 4(a) shows the target error at the four viewpoints in four display conditions. The line of the cylinder multiview multi-video condition shows that it achieved the lowest mean target error. The means were very similar across the four viewpoints, indicating that the viewpoint had little impact in this display conditions. At the extreme viewpoints (1 and 9), the means were significantly below that of the other three display conditions. In addition, the graph shows that the central viewpoint had the lowest mean target error, where four display conditions all had perspective-correct video; the mean target error increased symmetrically as the viewpoint diverges from the central position for cylinder multiview single-video condition, cylinder diffuse single-video condition and flat diffuse single-video condition. This is expected as when the observer did not sit in viewpoint 5, those display conditions still used the video from camera 5.

A 4 display conditions × 4 viewpoints × 15 target positions mixed design ANOVA was conducted on the target error, with display condition and viewpoints as two between-subjects factors and target positions as a within-subjects factor. Mean target error differed significantly across the four display conditions, $F(3,32) = 32.167, p < .001$. Tukey post-hoc tests revealed significant mean differences between each of the display conditions. The cylinder multiview multi-video condition ($M = .800, 95\%\ CI\ [.473, 1.127]$) gave significantly lower mean target error than the cylinder diffuse single-video condition ($M = 1.589, 95\%\ CI\ [1.262, 1.916]), p = .008$, the cylinder multiview single-video condition ($M = 2.911, 95\%\ CI\ [2.584, 3.238]), p < .001$, and the flat diffuse single-video condition ($M = 2.294, 95\%\ CI\ [1.968, 2.621]), p < .001$. This supports the primary hypothesis. Results also revealed a significant main effect of viewpoints, $F(3,32) = 39.448, p < .001$. Tukey post-hoc comparisons indicated the mean target error at viewpoint 5 ($M = .856, 95\%\ CI\ [.529, 1.182]$) is significantly lower than viewpoint 1 ($M = 2.65, 95\%\ CI\ [2.323, 2.977]), p < .001$ and viewpoint 9 ($M = 2.867, 95\%\ CI\ [2.54, 3.194]), p < .001$, which supports the second hypothesis; however, it did not significantly differ from viewpoint 4 ($M = 1.222, 95\%\ CI\ [.895, 1.549]), p > .05$, which is expected as the seat position only slightly diverges from the front. The mean target error at viewpoint 1 did not significantly differ from viewpoint 9, $p > .05$, which is also expected as the viewing angles of viewpoint 1 and 9 are equal only opposite in direction. The display conditions × viewpoints interaction was significant, $F(9,32) = 7.277, p < .001$, indicating that mean target error due to viewpoints were different in four display conditions.

We further investigated whether there was leftward bias or rightward bias in perceiving targets in different display conditions. We defined target bias (β_i) to be the difference between the observer's perceived target number (t_{oi}) and the actual target number (t_{ai}): $\beta_i = t_{oi} - t_{ai}$. Figure 4(b) shows the target bias at four viewpoints in four display conditions. Positive values indicated leftward biases whereas negative values indicated rightward bias. For the cylinder multiview multi-video condition, the mean target bias did not change substantially across different viewpoints. This further supports the hypothesis. By contrast, for the other three display conditions, the biases depended on the observers' viewpoints. For the flat diffuse single-video condition, the biases of four viewpoint in this study nicely fit in the previous work [7] that is the mean target bias varies linearly according to seat position. The graph also shows that the bias of cylinder diffuse single-video condition is less than flat diffuse single-video condition. This parallels the previous finding [1] that biases occur differently while observing convex, flat and concave surfaces.

CONCLUSION

We presented a novel display system for video conferencing. The highlights of this system are as follows. Firstly, the cylindrical display offers a 360° view whereas flat displays are only visible from the front. Secondly by using a camera array, a projector array and a multiview screen, we are able to transmit the remote person to multiple observers gathered around the cylindrical display, maintaining accurate cues of gaze direction. A similar cylindrical multiview display could also use a very dense projector array covering 360°, thus supporting a large number of viewpoints from any directions without introducing crosstalk and reducing resolution. Our current system is used for asymmetric conversations, such as a teaching scenario. Systems using similar principles could be configured to support symmetric conversations, by arranging camera arrays that are denser but further from the users. As cameras and projectors are now becoming very cheap, the low cost and ease of setup make this an interesting platform for next generation video conferencing.

REFERENCES

1. Anstis, S. M., Mayhew, J. W., and Morley, T. The perception of where a face or television'portrait'is looking. *The American journal of psychology* (1969).
2. Kim, K., Bolton, J., Girouard, A., Cooperstock, J., and Vertegaal, R. Telehuman: effects of 3d perspective on gaze and pose estimation with a life-size cylindrical telepresence pod. In *SIGCHI*, ACM (2012), 2531–2540.
3. Lincoln, P., Welch, G., Nashel, A., Ilie, A., and Fuchs, H. Animatronic shader lamps avatars. *VR* (2011).
4. Nguyen, D., and Canny, J. Multiview: spatially faithful group video conferencing. In *SIGCHI* (2005), 799–808.
5. Okada, K., Maeda, F., Ichikawaa, Y., and Matsushita, Y. Multiparty videoconferencing at virtual social distance: Majic design. In *CSCW* (1994), 385–393.
6. Oyekoya, O., Steptoe, W., and Steed, A. Sphereavatar: A situated display to represent a remote collaborator. In *SIGCHI* (Austin, Texas, USA, 2012), 2551–2560.
7. Pan, Y., and Steed, A. Preserving gaze direction in teleconferencing using a camera array and a spherical display. In *3DTV-CON*, IEEE (2012), 1–4.
8. Prince, S., Cheok, A. D., Farbiz, F., Williamson, T., Johnson, N., Billinghurst, M., and Kato, H. 3-d live: real time interaction for mixed reality. In *CSCW* (2002).
9. Schreer, O., Kauff, P., and Sikora, T. *3D videocommunication*. Wiley Online Library, 2005.
10. Sellen, A., Buxton, B., and Arnott, J. Using spatial cues to improve videoconferencing. In *SIGCHI* (Monterey, California, USA, 1992), 651–652.
11. Vertegaal, R., Weevers, I., Sohn, C., and Cheung, C. Gaze-2: conveying eye contact in group video conferencing using eye-controlled camera direction. In *SIGCHI* (Ft. Lauderdale, Florida, USA, 2003), 521–528.

OneSpace: Shared Visual Scenes for Active Free Play

Maayan Cohen[1,2] **Kody Dillman**[2] **Haley MacLeod**[3] **Seth Hunter**[4] **Anthony Tang**[2]

[1]Ontario College of Art and Design [2]University of Calgary [3]Indiana University [4]MIT Media Lab

mc11om@student.ocadu.ca {kody.dillman | tonyt}@ucalgary.ca hemacleo@indiana.edu hunters@mit.edu

ABSTRACT

Children engage in free play for emotional, physical and social development; researchers have explored supporting free play between physically remote playmates using videoconferencing tools. We show that the configuration of the video conferencing setup affects play. Specifically, we show that a shared visual scene configuration promotes fundamentally active forms of engaged, co-operative play.

INTRODUCTION

Many early psychologists emphasized the importance of physical and social play in early childhood development [7,10]—both for the development of practical motor skills, and cognitive and social reasoning skills. Yet play is frequently mediated through video game technology, where technology is used to bridge the distance between physically remote playmates (e.g. [3,4,11-13]). Using video-based technology to support free play has recently become of interest (e.g. [13,14]). Much of this work concerns sharing activities [3], or artefacts such as books (e.g. [11]) or a surface (e.g. [13])—much along the lines of Montessori's notion of "prepared materials" to help structure and focus interaction [7]. In contrast, our interest has been to engage children in more active forms of free play—where children can actively explore space, and devise rules for interaction with a remote participant.

Our approach is based on the idea that for children, *play* is not strictly limited to toys in a "play area"; instead that a child's body, and his/her interaction with his environment functions as the play space [7]. Thus, our interest is in allowing the child and his/her entire environment to be the subject of play, along with the play partner. As illustrated in Figure 1, where a mother and child play "paddycake", OneSpace (see [6] for technical details) is a video conferencing tool that merges the video feeds of two remote sites into a single shared visual scene (like [3,4,8]). Consequently, the visual scene, inhabited by the child *with* his/her partner, becomes a shared play area.

CHI 2014, Apr 26 - May 01 2014, Toronto, ON, Canada
ACM 978-1-4503-2473-1/14/04.
http://dx.doi.org/10.1145/2556288.2557117

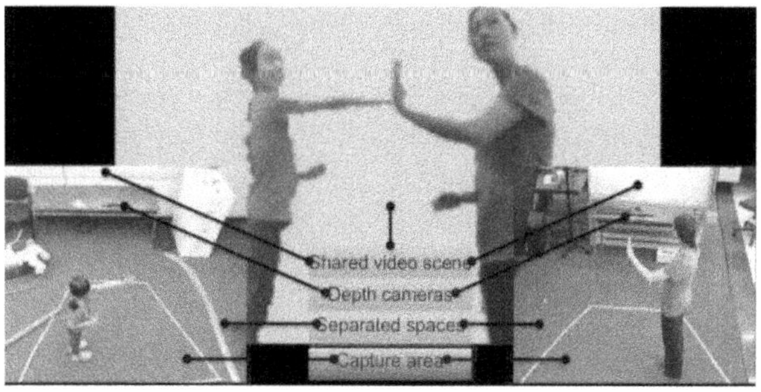

Figure 1. Illustration of OneSpace configuration.

We evaluated OneSpace as a tool to support play between 14 participants (two child-child pairs, and five child-parent pairs), comparing it to a conventional video conferencing configuration. Our findings demonstrate that the OneSpace configuration produces an entirely different "flavour" of interaction—one whose nature is fundamentally physical, and with high levels of engagement (as opposed to a "show-and-tell" and "pretend" interaction as in [12]).

VIDEO WITH CHILDREN: OBSERVATIONS

Several prior authors have explored the use of video conferencing tools with children. While an extensive review is beyond the scope of this note, we synthesize findings from prior work relevant to our purposes here.

Mental model & visibility. Children have a difficult time understanding "visibility" in conventional video conferencing. In real life, if I can see grandpa, he can see me; however, this is not necessarily the case in video conferencing: while I may see his face on screen, I may not be visible to the camera on my side [12,13]. *Managing attention*. Some prototypes have introduced multiple displays—perhaps one on a play space, and one on the person's face (e.g. [12,13])—and while this helps to focus activity to certain screens, it means that a remote partner is sometimes "looking at the wrong screen" (e.g. when I show you something, I want you to see it, rather than look at my face). *"Person space is play space"*. Yarosh et al. explore a "rug play area" condition, where the rug was captured and projected to a remote rug. The children co-opted both the projected rug and the image of the remote person's body into their play, suggesting that a person's body as an object (in addition to their facial reactions) contribute to play. *Field of play*. Size of the capture area is important—likely, if we capture and present more of a person's body and environment, we would expect to see increased physical activity. For example, art installations (e.g. [5]) typically capture the entire body, whereas conventional videoconferencing focuses on capturing the face.

The OneSpace configuration was designed to address these challenges [6]. Drawing on early work [2,8], we merge two remote spaces, placing participants in a shared visual scene, where their entire bodies (and toys) are represented. The system is implemented using commodity depth-cameras, which allows us to address the "who's in front" problem of earlier green-screen approaches (e.g. [8]). It simplifies issues of visibility, and reduces the number of screens that are important to pay attention to. Most related to our work is WaaZaam, which allows people to personalize/customize the environment and gesturally transform themselves [4].

OBSERVATIONAL STUDY

How does the OneSpace video configuration change the nature of interaction between remote parties? We conducted an observational study where we compared free play between the OneSpace configuration, and a more conventional configuration (akin to Skype). Our goal was to understand the nature of free play in these mediated environments, in terms of the kinds of play (play types), the nature of engagement between the participants, and the level of physical activity participants would engage in. We were interested in whether OneSpace offered alternative ways for movement and play with the physical body.

Characterizing Play and Interaction. To support our efforts, we rely on previous work studying play types and engagement. While many schemes exist for describing play types, we adapted Bronson's scheme to comprise six types of play activity among children [1]: active; make believe; manipulative; creative; learning; object play. As a measure of engagement between participants, we rely on Parten's articulation, where each level describes the level of engagement (or involvement) for a child with regard to the play of another [9]: unoccupied; solitary; onlooker; parallel; associative; cooperative. For each scale, we also categorized "transitions" between activities. While most researchers aim to design systems that really engage children (i.e. at cooperative levels of engagement), our intention was just to study whether there would be differences between the configurations.

Participants. Table 1 shows ages and sex of the 14 people we recruited (two child-child, and five child-parent pairs). We selected only children between 6 and 10 years.

Design & Method. We employed a simple within-subjects design with two conditions: OneSpace configuration and conventional configuration. Participants were recruited as pairs (who knew each other), and after minimal warm-up (5-10 minutes of collocated play) were separated into two independent spaces. They were then asked to play with each of the two configurations (at least 10 minute sessions each, though some groups played longer), where presentation order was counterbalanced across groups. To illustrate each system, children stood within a marked trapezoid, and were told "When you stand here, your partner can see you." We provided participants with a range of toys (about two to three for each of Bronson's play types, e.g. stuffed animals, masks, books, drawing materials, large lego, etc.), and when they were separated, given roughly equivalent sets of toys to play with. We then interviewed the participants.

Group	P1 (sex-age)	P2
G1	M-9	M-10
G2	M-8	M-8
G3	M-6	M-Dad
G4	F-9	F-Mom
G5	F-8	F-Mom
G6	M-6	F-Mom
G7	M-6	M-Dad

Measures & Analysis. We captured video data (three angles) during sessions, recorded audio of interviews, and collected field notes. The video data was coded according to both Bronson's types of play framework, and Parton's engagement framework at a sampling interval of 5s, with the dominant play type/engagement level coded. One rater coded all the video, while a second rater coded two groups' data to ensure reliability (Cohen's κ=0.75 for 7 types of play; Cohen's κ=0.65 for 6 engagement levels).

FINDINGS

Play in the two configurations was different in terms of depth of engagement, and overall type of play. Even though the quality of the video in OneSpace was poorer (image quality and framerate), we saw many activities in OneSpace that were impossible in the conventional condition.

Engagement. The OneSpace setup seemed to encourage a more engaged co-operative and organized play, where both participants would take on an active role in structuring the play with one another. Since participants' actions would have visual consequences in the shared video scene, this would tend to stimulate additional discussion and action. Figure 2 provides an illustrative example of G3, where the child and the father have set up a scene where the blocks (set up by the father) are now being virtually destroyed by the child's dinosaur. The father stands out of the "visible" area, and responds to the child's movements by taking apart various parts of the tower. Here, both the father's and son's actions in their independent physical spaces is entirely

Figure 2. The boy is using a dinosaur to destroy a Lego tower his father built. The father stands outside the capture area and takes pieces off to complete this illusion.

guided by the merged video scene—their interactions are mutually relating to one another. This kind of interaction between body, physicality, and action was extremely common in the OneSpace condition (e.g. Figure 1).

In contrast, as illustrated in Table 2, the conventional configuration exhibited fairly high levels of parallel and associative play. Particularly striking was that while participants *began* playing with one another, they would usually disengage with one another: their play devolving into parallel or associative play—where their interactions were strictly mundane conversation, unrelated to the "play" taking place (i.e. individuals' play did not influence the other's play). This was particularly striking in our parent-child pairs, since parents were actively trying to engage their child. As a fairly instructive example, in G7, a child sat to draw a picture, while his father did the same. This continued for five minutes, and while the father initiated some small talk, neither looking up during the activity. Parten's phrasing of Associative Play really resonates with our observations here—in our child-parent participant groups, when the child "disengaged" in joint activity, the parent would try to strike up conversation with the child.

Play Type. The type of play also varied substantially between the two conditions, with more active play in OneSpace compared to make-believe being the main driver in the conventional configuration (Table 3). The nature and affordances of these video configurations have a strong impact on the style of play that participants choose. Figure 3 provides an illustrative account of an active and learning episode from the OneSpace condition. Here, the child is playing with a hulahoop. Her mother tries to join in, but has lost her hulahooping skills. The child then begins instructing her mother on how to properly hulahoop by standing next to and in front of her mother, demonstrating the correct motion for her mother to mimic.

Active (and physical) play was characteristic of play that we observed in OneSpace—participants (particularly the children) generally moved about the scene far more. For instance, groups played "tag" in OneSpace, or would run from one side of the shared scene to the other, and so forth. Figure 1 illustrates a pair playing "paddycake," while others would also play fight, miming punches and kicks, and feigning injury. This active play went beyond merely moving one's limbs around—indeed, our coding revealed that participants physically moved around far more (i.e. took steps) in the OneSpace condition. What is striking about these physical activities is that it seemed representative of the same physical activity one would expect of children in collocated scenarios. Of course, how they would "touch" one another in OneSpace and watch one another was different, but the character of the movement was natural.

Figure 3. The daughter teaches/demonstrates the hulahoop motion for her mother to mimic.

Perhaps because the conventional configuration enforces the separation of space, participants playing across the sites *needed* to engage in make believe to feel closer. As an illustrative example, G4 decided to play through a fashion show together, dressing up dolls in various costumes and creating a narrative between the characters. The physical separation between the spaces is extremely evident in these instances—the only real bridge between these spaces is the conversation to create a shared imaginary domain, and a video link that shows the facial reactions of one's partner.

Affordances of the Configurations. The OneSpace configuration seems to afford physical activity by virtue of the shared visual space that encompasses the entirety of both participants' bodies. The fact that both shared the same visual space means they are, in a sense, competing for the visual stage. Because the system handles this by respecting their "depth relationship" (i.e. whoever is closer to the camera is displayed), one could easily "upstage" or "take over" the scene by simply moving closer over to the other person, and closer to the camera. Recognizing this seemed to spark instances of playfulness, where participants would take turns trying to upstage one another. One common behavior was that participants would sometimes hide from view *in the scene*—this meant hiding from the camera (i.e. going out of view), but also sometimes hiding behind one another, and integrating this into their play. G5 used this technique to make a four-armed mosquito, where the child pretended to be the mother's arms by standing "in front of" her mother, but flapping her arms around. In this way, their bodies became objects of play in this shared space. The shared representation also allowed participants to use the space to gesture and point at body parts and objects in what would otherwise be only the remote space (e.g. Figure 3).

	Trans.	Solitary	Onlooker	Parallel	Associative	Cooperative
OneSpace	146	1	52	66	145	411
Conventional	91	4	55	132	361	194

Table 2. Engagement levels on 5s intervals across groups. Scheme adapted from [10].

	Trans.	Active	Make-believe	Manipulative	Creative	Learning	Object
OneSpace	150	477	110	16	7	34	27
Conventional	91	222	228	83	97	16	41

Table 3. Play types on 5s intervals across groups. Scheme adapted from [1].

In contrast, the conventional configuration seems to afford more solitude among participants. Even though the captured video space (i.e. the entire body) is the same, we saw substantially less "active" play. Instead, a lot of play centered on activities that each could engage in by themselves, and instances of "show and tell" where one would ask the other to look at something on their side.

Attention & Visibility. Children did seem to understand in the OneSpace condition what could be seen—they would regularly play with their partners in the video scene. Yet, we still observed instances in the OneSpace condition where children would ask, "Can you see me?" when they were in/out of the frame, though this seemed to occur markedly less than in the conventional configuration. There, we observed far more instances of the parents (for instance) coaching the child, "Why don't you back up so I can see you all the way? [G3]" Of interest is that for children, it was clear that the details presented by the video scene really mattered. In one instance, a child asked, "What are you looking at […] it doesn't look like you are [looking at me] [G4]," even though the parent was looking at the screen. Here, the child had noticed that the eye gaze of the parent was incorrect (due to camera positioning). In this case, the parent explained to the child how cameras worked, etc. Similarly, one pair discounted OneSpace entirely, citing its poor, blocky resolution and low framerate as reasons why they would simply not use it.

DISCUSSION & CONCLUSION

OneSpace's design builds on considerable prior work, not only in the research space [2,4,8,12], but also in the artistic space (e.g. [5]), where artists have long recognized the role of bodies—not only as subjects, but also as objects. Our application of these ideas to the domain of child freeplay is a natural extension of this, recognizing that children also consider their bodies and environments as objects of play.

Although the size of our subject pool is small, we believe the results to be generally representative. Like Yarosh et al. [12], we found that in conventional setups, children engaged in make-believe/pretend play; in our OneSpace configuration, which was related to the rug condition in [12], there was a lot more active/movement play. The differences in the quality of the play and the type of engagement between OneSpace and conventional video conferencing was immediately striking—not only to us, but to at least some of participants, one who noted: "Before [in OneSpace] we felt really close; now using Skype, it feels like we're really really (*sic*) far apart. [G4]"

It seems clear that the problem of managing attention and understanding visibility remains in OneSpace. While it does address attention across two disjoint displays, the subtleties and details of interaction (particularly eye gaze) are meaningful and powerful cues to children. This is perhaps unsurprising, since this age group is learning to read and respond appropriately to non-verbal social cues.

One concern with generalizability of these results is the novelty effect. Our lab-based study design did not allow us to address this effect; however, none of our children had ever had experience with video conferencing (i.e. not even a conventional setup). In future work, we will conduct long-term deployments of OneSpace into participant homes. We will also explore digital entities such as costumes or objects (to augment physical ones) in the shared play space.

This work contributes to the ongoing discussion in the research community about how to provide playful environments to connect children at a distance. Rather than focusing on a shared activity [3,11] or play surface [12,13], we focused here on giving children a visual representation that shows themselves with a playmate. Based on our study, we suggest two major lessons for future work in this space: first, for children, the body is actually a "play area" and that this should be an area of exploration, and second, creating a shared space environment for remote play can lead to a more active and physical play—thus forcing us to ask questions about what closeness and separation actually mean to people that inhabit these spaces.

REFERENCES

1. Bronson, M. B. (1995) The Right Stuff for Children Birth to 8: Selecting Play Materials to Support Development. National Association for the Education.
2. Cullinan, C. & Agamanolis, S. (2002). Reflexion: a responsive virtual mirror. In Ext Abs of UIST 2002.
3. Follmer, S., et al. (2010). Video play: playful interactions in video conferencing for long-distance families with young children. In Proc IDC 2010, 49-58.
4. Hunter, S., et al. (2014). WaaZam! Supporting creative play at a distance in customized video environments. In Proc CHI 2014.
5. Krueger, M. (1983). Artificial Reality. Addison-Wesley.
6. Ledo, D. et al. (2013). OneSpace: shared depth-corrected video interaction. In CHI EA 2013, 997-1002.
7. Montessori, M. (1995). The Absorbent Mind. Henry Holt and Company: New York.
8. Morikawa, O., and Maesako, T. (1998). HyperMirror: toward pleasant-to-use video mediated communication system. In Proc CSCW 1998, 149-158.
9. Parten, M. (1932). Social participation among preschool children. J. of Abnormal and Soc. Psyc. 28 (3): 136–147.
10. Piaget, J. (1926). The Language and Thought of the Child. Harcourt, Brace & Company, Inc., NY, USA.
11. Raffle, H., Revelle, G., et al. (2011). Hello, is grandma there? let's read! StoryVisit: family video chat and connected e-books. In Proc CHI 2011, 1195-1204.
12. Yarosh, S., Inkpen, K. M., and Brush, A. J. (2010). Video playdate: toward free play across distance. In Proc CHI 2010, 1251-1260.
13. Yarosh, S., Tang, A., et al. (2013). "Almost touching": parent-child remote communication using the sharetable system. In Proc CSCW 2013, 181-192.

i-dentity: Innominate Movement Representation as Engaging Game Element

Jayden Garner[1], Gavin Wood[2], Sebastiaan Pijnappel[1], Martin Murer[3], Florian 'Floyd' Mueller[1]

[1]Exertion Games Lab
RMIT University
Melbourne, Australia
{ jayden, sebastiaan, floyd }
@exertiongameslab.org

[2]Culture Lab
Newcastle University
Newcastle, UK
g.wood2@newcastle.ac.uk

[3]ICT&S Center
University of Salzburg
Austria
martin.murer@sbg.ac.at

ABSTRACT

Movement-based digital games typically make it clear whose movement representation belongs to which player. In contrast, we argue that selectively concealing whose movement controls which representation can facilitate engaging play experiences. We call this "innominate movement representation" and explore this opportunity through our game "i-dentity", where players have to guess who makes everyone's controller light up based on his/her movements. Our work reveals five dimensions for the design of innominate movement representation: concealing the association between movement and representation; number of represented movements; number of players with representations; location of representation in relation to the body and technical attributes of representation. We also present five strategies for how innominate movement representation can be embedded into a play experience. With our work we hope to expand the range of digital movement games.

Author Keywords

Movement representation; ambiguity; digital play; game design; engagement; social play; entertainment

ACM Classification Keywords

H.5.2 [Information interfaces and presentation]: User Interfaces – Interaction Styles

INTRODUCTION

HCI designers often use unconventional approaches that turn interactive entertainment and interaction design on its head to enable the creation of new and unexpected play experiences, such as uncomfortable, intense and exertion interactions [4, 20, 22]. Strategies to achieve such experiences include creating ambiguity rather than offering clarity [10], withholding information to provoke interpretation [28] and deliberately engineering discomfort to provoke physical effort [21]. In this paper, we explore another unconventional strategy focused on digital play experiences: innominate movement representation. By this we mean a strategy in digital games where the design deliberately conceals whose movement representation belongs to which player.

Fig. 1. Playing i-dentity

Movement-based computer games generally utilize digital representations of players' movements, for example, most Nintendo Wii, Sony Move and Microsoft Kinect games feature digital representations of players' movements on the screen, often achieved through avatars. We notice existing digital games often make the association between movement and avatar obvious, so that players know whose movements control which avatar. This is congruent with established game design and HCI principles that teach that feedback to player actions should be clear and non-confusing [6]. In contrast, we propose that game designers can deliberately make associations between movement and representation unclear - in particular selectively conceal - in order to utilize it as a game element for engaging play experiences.

We created a game called i-dentity (Fig. 1) to explore this opportunity. By analysing our design as well as observations of gameplay and feedback from players, we gained insights on the role of innominate movement representation on peoples' play experiences. In result, we make the following contributions:

- We articulate five dimensions that span a possibility space for designers to think about when designing games that aim to utilize innominate movement representation.
- We present five practical design strategies to support the development of innominate movement games.

CHI 2014, April 26–May 1, 2014, Toronto, Ontario, Canada.

ACM 978-1-4503-2473-1/14/04...$15.00.
http://dx.doi.org/10.1145/2556288.2557257

With this work, we hope to extend the range of digital movement games, furthering the associated engaging experiences for players and ultimately the field of digital games.

RELATED WORK

Research on digital games that engage with innominate or more broadly concealed data associated with players is sparse yet valuable. In Fish 'n' Steps [17] for example, a representation of a fish grows larger when 'fed' by a corresponding player's physical activity. The system innominates all players' movement data so as to hide whose represented fish belongs to which player. The system conceals this association to ensure the data associated with each player remains private, so others cannot work out who has performed less physical activity than others. This shows how systems can be designed to conceal data associated with players, in particular in regards to movement, in order to affect the player's experience. However, we still do not yet know how concealing data associated with players can be used to facilitate engaging digital play.

There are several examples of games that conceal player associations in the non-digital realm that have inspired our work. Many role-playing, card and board games conceal the player's association to a particular fantasy role, such as Werewolf, Celebrity Heads and Battleship [32, 5, 3]. Salen and Zimmerman [27] describe the engaging social drama that emerges in Mafia, where engagement results from the ambiguity around the unknown player associations with specific roles. The ambiguity and uncertainty that is featured in these games, such as the bluffing that occurs in Poker, builds tension and engagement between players thanks to the concealed associations [27]. These non-digital games show how ambiguity as a result of concealing player associations can facilitate engaging play, which we took onboard with our design. However, there is still a lack of understanding about how this ambiguity could be utilized when designing games that conceal player associations to digital representations.

We found that most existing games that conceal a player's association with a representation rely on game rules rather than it being a direct result of the player's actions (for example see [17]). This inspired us to explore an alternative approach where the players' actions determine the extent to which their associations to representations are made unclear. Whereas prior games have mostly either concealed or revealed associated data, we aim to explore "selectively concealing", where the division between an association being either concealed or revealed becomes blurred. This introduces a sense of ambiguity within the game's design.

There are many interactive designs that explore the practical use of ambiguity to engage people with technological systems (e.g. [11, 15]). While conveying ambiguous information is traditionally regarded as a problem in the design of usable systems, Gaver et al.'s work [10] shows how incorporating ambiguity into the design of interactive systems can have intriguing, mysterious, and delightful outcomes: for example the ambiguity of using indirect sensor mappings of embodied interaction (e.g. [1]), unconventional mappings for reflection on the unexpected (e.g. [26]), or exploring the interpretive space of embodied and situated aspects of interaction that results in physical play facilitating discovery (e.g. [31]). Thus, we were inspired to extend the notion of ambiguous interaction design to the practice of movement representation to explore whether having an unclear relationship between movement and representation can facilitate engaging play experiences. In particular, we explore ambiguity as a result of having selectively concealed player associations to movement representations.

We learned from the new games movement [8] that we should explore the novel opportunities for play that digital technology can enable. We are inspired by its advocates such as Bernard DeKoven [16], who suggests that designers should renew their interest in play by reconsidering old playground games and explore how we play together. JS Joust [34] is an example inspired by this thinking that shows how digital elements can enhance a play experience by retaining non-digital elements of collaboration, light-hearted playfulness and face-to-face interaction. Technology support for such types of physical play experiences is mostly minimal, with an often-increased reliance on player judgement (e.g. [19]). We consider these non-digital elements important to our design for how selectively concealing digital representation can enable new opportunities for engaging play. However, we believe that selectively concealing whose movements are represented is not something that has previously been considered by designers of digital games.

In this paper, we look at how to design games where the player's actions can selectively conceal player associations to representations. In particular, we focus on movement representation and call it "innominate movement representation". We start to develop this understanding by designing and consequently studying player experiences with a game that uses innominate movement representation.

USING INNOMINATE MOVEMENT REPRESENTATION AS A DIGITAL GAME ELEMENT

We now introduce a game that we designed, called "i-dentity", as a practical example of innominate movement representation. It is played with only a set of Sony Move controllers [24] and no screen.

I-DENTITY

i-dentity is a collaborative movement-based game involving four players that benefits from being played in front of an audience. Players assume the role of an interrogator or one of three spies. The three spies each hold a Move controller, with one Move controller randomly selected by the game to represent the spies' leader. The leader's movements illuminate all three of the spies' controllers, while the spies' movements are ignored. Vibration feedback is discretely sent to the leader's controller to let them know their role in the game. A leader's role is only known amongst the spies.

The interrogator, whose goal is to identify the spies' leader, conducts or asks the spies to perform movements. For example, during playtests we have observed commands such as asking the group to jump up and down, they could be asked to "pretend they had just been shot", or to play air guitar. However, the interrogator can only address the spies together, as a group (so the interrogator cannot say "only the person in the middle should jump"). While the leader moves his/her controller in response to acting out a command, all the spies' lights turn on (Fig. 2). When the leader is stationary the lights go out. The spies copy their movements in an attempt to innominate the representation so the interrogator cannot work out whose movement controls the light (Fig. 3).

Fig. 2. Interrogator asks the spies to stand on one leg to figure out who the leader is.

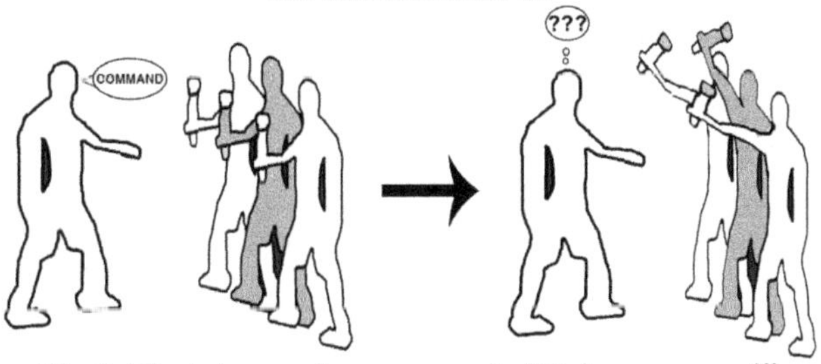

Fig. 3. The interrogator commands, "Raise your arm!" The leader and his/her spies coordinate their movements so it is difficult for the interrogator to identify whose movements light up all controllers.

The game continues until the interrogator believes she/he knows the identity of the spies' leader. At this stage, the interrogator points towards the leader. This player then waves their controller; if all spies' controllers illuminate, the interrogator wins and he/she switches roles with the leader, otherwise the leader and the spies win. Players often agreed to impose a limit upon the amount of commands that could be asked before requiring the interrogator to select a leader. This occurs during an "exposition" [4] stage before a game begins, where players negotiate specifics of the rules, such as how many and what types of commands the interrogator is allowed to use.

Implementation

The players' Sony Move controllers are connected to a computer via Bluetooth. When the leader moves, all controllers light up with the same color. Controller orientation determines the light's color. Speed, measured from accelerometer and gyroscope sensor values, determines level of illumination, with fast movements resulting in brighter colors.

Design Process

We began designing i-dentity at the CHI "Game Jam" workshop [9]. The game jam development environment emphasized collaboration as well as rapid and experimental design of physical digital games. As part of the event, the developers observed 20 players' experiences of playing i-dentity as part of the design process. A total of 8 playtesting sessions took place at various stages of development beyond the Game Jam. We also conducted a more formal study, which we report next.

STUDY

This section discusses details of our study, which aimed to gain insight into play experiences with i-dentity.

Participants

25 participants played i-dentity at play sessions. 12 of these participants were interviewed. 8 rounds were played at each venue, at a total of 4 venues, with each venue having between 5-7 participants. Overall, this meant the game was played 32 times during our study.

Procedure

A playtesting session lasted around 30 minutes. At the end of a game, participants switched roles with people who had not yet played a particular role. We ensured everyone played every role in the game, so that all players could reflect on these roles during the interviews. Our encouragement to play every role is obviously not present in non-study contexts; however, we believe the benefit of having everyone play each role gave us the advantage of a diverse range of feedback.

Data gathering and analysis

Three different data sources were used to understand participants' play experiences:

- We took notes of our observations.
- We recorded video footage of play. The primary author then went through the videos, looking for what tactics players engaged in, what movements people performed, examining their social interactions including facial expressions and body language.
- We conducted semi-structured group interviews at the conclusion of the play session. We encouraged participants to discuss, reflect on and give feedback on their play experience. We also video-recorded these interviews. They were analyzed alongside the recordings of the participants during play.

Firstly, the primary author watched all video recordings of people playing i-dentity. The author took notes while watching the gameplay recordings 3 times as suggested by grounded theory [30]. Secondly, the author watched the video recordings of the interviews 3 times. Again, the author took notes. Finally, the author went back and

Fig. 4: a,b,c. People had a fun, engaging and enjoyable experience with i-dentity.

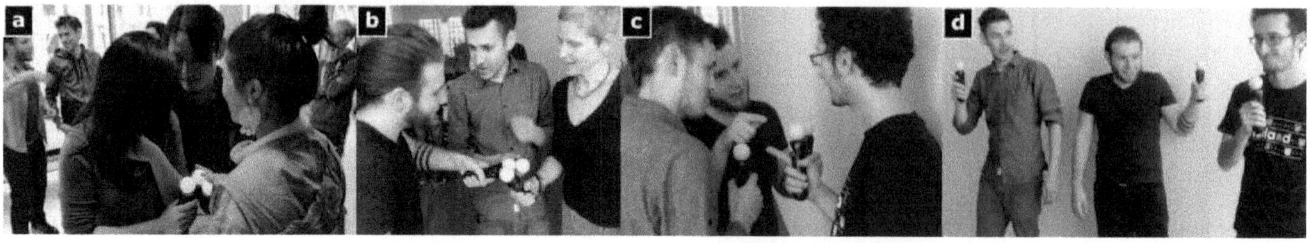

Fig. 5: a,b,c,d. People playing the role of spy collaborated with other spies.

watched the video recordings of people playing to check with notes taken during the interview recordings. After each stage of this process, the primary author gathered with the other authors to discuss the notes taken. At these meetings, interim analysis results were presented and debated. This helped to develop and refine findings. We used an open-ended process of rapid reflection [23] to discuss ideas and concepts that had emerged. The findings emerging from the data were extensively questioned, debated and discussed.

The resulting higher-level concepts were discussed amongst the group and then presented to 10 games researchers to gather feedback. The outcome was subsequently checked with 8 of the study participants (those who where available, so a selection bias might have occurred), refined and reviewed again by the authors.

FINDINGS

We now discuss the findings of our study. We begin by describing reactions to the game.

[F1] i-dentity is a compelling game experience

Participants found playing i-dentity to be a fun, enjoyable and engaging experience, replying with positive responses, such as:

> *P1: It was awesome.*

> *P6: It was fun both to move, be in front of each other and try and compete with each other.*

Participants would often verbally express their enjoyment while playing together and our observations of body language further support the occurrence of a sense of enjoyment from the game, with smiles and intrigued glances often displayed (Fig. 1, 4a, 4b, 4c, 6c).

[F2] Innominate gameplay can stimulate verbal communication amongst the players

Participants on both sides verbally communicated with each other, aiding each other by giving advice or suggestions:

[Interrogator with audience]	[Group of spies]
P9: Who's moving?	*P6: I want them to think it's you.*
P10: I would say P8.	*P11: Ready? 1, 2, 3!*
P7: Yeah, me also.	*P8: Let's do this!*

Participants enjoyed this opportunity for verbal communication:

> *P1: I liked the game because it encourages, um, discussion amongst the players, cause I feel there's like this dynamic that emerges between the players who have the PlayStation Move controllers and the people who are trying to guess, I feel like both sides would try to deceive each other and trying to trick each other, um, I like that the game allows for that to happen!*

> *P3: Communication was another reason why it was fun.*

[F3] Innominate gameplay can cause players to conceal verbal communication from other players

The two groups of players (spies & leader and interrogator & audience) would often separate to discuss strategies amongst themselves (Fig. 5a, 5b, 5c, 6b). Interestingly, people deliberately concealed these discussions from the other side, despite not being required to do so.

[F4] Ambiguity of the innominate gameplay can be engaging

Participants appreciated the sense of ambiguity that emerged from the innominate gameplay:

> *P1: I like the ambiguity of when you're not sure if people are actually trying to help, or if they are [the leader].*

> *P3: Yeah, it was like 'I think it's P1 but it's not him', and he knows it's not but he tried to convince other people.*

> *P5: But he could also be telling the truth, he wants his team to win so he's trying to help. I like the ambiguity as well.*

> *P6: It was most fun when it was hard to figure out, when we didn't know what was going on.*

Furthermore, players enjoyed how the spies often used body language to heighten the ambiguity of their relationship to the representation.

[F5] Body language was used to deceive others

A tactic often used by the leader was to try to deceive the interrogator and audience to make them believe they were not the leader (Fig. 5d):

Fig. 6: a,b,c. Interrogators using people from the audience to help them.

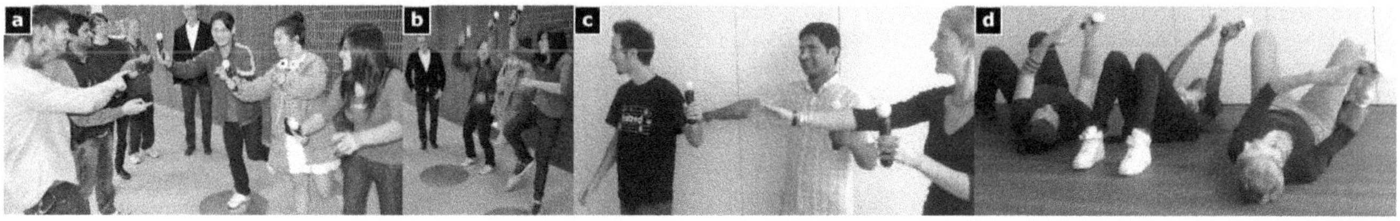

Fig. 7: a,b,c,d. People enjoyed the physical challenge resulting from the innominate gameplay.

> *P3: We think its not a person, right, so we were like, okay it's not you, we will just focus on someone else.*
>
> *P6: We did that to you [points toward P1] and you were trying to pretend like it was you, right, and you tried to get back on the suspicion list.*

[F6] Trying to conceal movement representation can lead to engaging performances

Participants enjoyed the physical challenge of concealing movement representation, which led to enjoyment with the associated physical performances:

> *P3: It was interesting that I didn't like so much getting commands as I did executing it together as a group performing. You know, you get commands and do things that I ask you but at the same time try to do it as good as you can so they don't get anything out of it.*
>
> *P4: The funny movements were like a key part, with another person asking for a funny movement, and the other person trying to do that [...] that was a lot of fun; the choreography was like dancing.*

Participants playing the role of spy enjoyed the sense of connection they seemed to share with other people's movements:

> *P1: What's so beautiful about the game is, when your teammates notice that you're moving and know you're going to give away yourself, and then they start going as well to copy you. I really like that.*

Spectators would often express their enjoyment together, with grunts, smiles, laughter and intrigued glances being shared while watching the game unfold (Fig. 1, 4a). We noticed spectators would often laugh when people performed silly or hilarious movements, such as hopping on one leg or performing dance moves (Fig. 1, 7a, 7b, 7d). These reactions suggest that enjoyment can emerge from people's engagement with concealed movement representation, both when performing and observing.

[F7] The innominate gameplay motivated spectators to collaborate

The interrogator often talked to audience members to get them involved. Rather than standing back and observing the movements being staged, we noticed spectators would often share conversations with one another and become involved in gameplay by advising the interrogator on who they think is the leader, or suggesting challenging movements that would help to reveal the leader (Fig. 6a). The interrogator often utilized the spectators by tasking them to assist, focusing their attention on observing the performance of a particular spy. The interrogator would often gather with spectators to discuss whom to select as potential leader, while also concealing this discussion from the spies (Fig. 6b). This suggests the involvement of others was important in helping them make a more informed decision.

[F8] Participants enjoyed using different strategies and play styles to reveal the association of representation

Participants liked how the game accommodated multiple strategies and play styles:

> *P3: I liked that you had, like, different strategies, right, so there's not like one particular way of playing, there are multiple ways of playing. By being, um, the person, the identity, being it and the other side as well.*
>
> *P1: I like that the rules are negotiated between all the players so that it fits everyone's play style.*
>
> *P3: I liked to find the flaws in the rules; try and make it impossible for the others to figure out.*
>
> *P6: Yeah, you tried to break the game. [Shared laughs]*

We observed players experimented with a range of tactics, such as deciding to have a spy look more suspicious then the other spies (Fig. 5d), or positioning spies so it was difficult for them to see each other (Fig. 7c). Participants found that confusing the spies with multiple commands at once could help get someone to move out of sync:

> *P2: [Point to the] ceiling, then point your controller down. Now, please. Look at the ceiling, look at the ceiling. [Group looks up] And now jump. [Group jumps] Look at the ceiling. Now move a little bit, with the control – P4 is already moving! [Interrogator and audience laughs]*

[F9] Triggering accidental movements was used to reveal the association of representation

An interrogator often tried to provoke accidental movements that could not be controlled by the spies, for example getting them to laugh:

P5: I think you [the interrogator] got onto something when you made us laugh, I think that I always thought well it's going to be the deliberate movements, but it would actually be the accidental movements [that revealed the leader]. [...] So once we got onto something as personal as a laugh, it was beyond choreography.

P2: Exactly what I was scared about - laughing, you know cause laughing was the only way that I can [hand shaking motion] ha-ha, laughing was impossible for me to avoid.

P6: If you're laughing, then make sure everyone moves.

P1: They would get you holding your hand up for 2 minutes, and your whole arm aches.

P3: They would abuse you to actually do a workout there.

P6: Yeah, that was quite a good one to do, just make them hold their hand up until they wobble.

[F10] Access to movement representation can be part of the game's challenge
The interrogator did not seem to have many problems in retaining focus on both movement and representation at once. However, we did notice two instances when an interrogator found it difficult to see all of the lights at once. Sometimes this occurred when a spy faced an opposing direction to an interrogator, as their body blocked the interrogator's access to their light unless they physically moved around the space. Other times, a strategy a spy used against the interrogator was to restrict access to their light: a spy would physically concealed access to their light by covering the sensor with one of their hands, or holding their controller behind their back so that it could not be seen. This suggests that while the close proximity of physical and digital made it relatively easy to focus on movement, this also resulted in times where it was challenging to see how a spy interacted with their controller.

[F11] Using technical characteristics of the movement representations was a strategy to reveal association
We noticed a strategy the interrogator often used was to spin the spies around in a circle. Interestingly, the interrogator most often did not move around with the spies while doing so. This suggests the type of display used had an affect on how difficult it was for people to access the representation; in our case the Move controller lights made it easy for people to see the representation from where they were standing, except for times when other bodies obscured their view. This was a popular tactic people enjoyed.

[F12] Manipulating representation response time is an option to adjust the game's challenge, however can also cause confusion
The Move controller generally provided a near-instant response to represent movement. However, there were a few times when the response would slow down during the game. This mostly occurred when there were a large number of movements being performed at once. This was due to the Bluetooth connection. When this happened, the players became confused, which suggests they expected an instant response, and that not providing this instant response had a negative impact on their experience.

DIMENSIONS FOR THE DESIGN OF GAMES USING INNOMINATE MOVEMENT REPRESENTATION
We use our findings as well as our design experience of i-dentity to derive five dimensions for designing games using innominate movement representation. We use these dimensions to highlight a range of possibilities for the design of new games in this space.

DIMENSION 1: CONCEALING THE ASSOCIATION BETWEEN MOVEMENT AND REPRESENTATION
Our first dimension looks at the extent to which the game design facilitates concealing movement associations to representations. The two poles of this dimension are made up of the system concealing player associations to representations on one end and the player's movements concealing these representation associations on the other. While most movement-based systems are designed using a direct mapping of the players' movements to digital representations, i-dentity extends the notion of ambiguous design to show how this mapping can be purposely obscured to facilitate an engaging play experience. This rather unconventional method of mapping input to output reminds us of Rogers et al.'s Snark system [26] that uses ambient technologies to explore the concept of the unexpected to foster reflection. Similarly, Gaver et al.'s work on ambiguous design [10] suggests benefits of employing ambiguity in mappings between input and output when designing interactive systems, with an example being Antle et al.'s whole-body system [1], which deploys ambiguous design through indirect mappings of embodied interaction. We extend this thinking to game design and showed with i-dentity some benefits to having movements conceal associations between movement and representation, as it stimulated verbal communication (F2, F3), collaboration (F7) and engaged players through body language (F4, F5) and physical performance (F6).

Dimension 1.1: Concealed by system
The system could determine how and when associations to representations are concealed. In i-dentity, the system assists the players to conceal the association by copying the light functionality across to the other controllers. Alternatively, systems could be designed to ensure player associations to representations remain concealed to encourage thoughtful reflection of physical activity [17], however this may limit opportunities for strategic gameplay.

Dimension 1.2: Concealed by movements
In i-dentity the players with controllers can selectively conceal the represented player. Other players could not interpret whose movement was represented while the group retained synchrony with one another's movements. This approach can engage players via ambiguity and strategic gameplay (F3, F4, F5, F9, F10).

DIMENSION 2: NUMBER OF REPRESENTED MOVEMENTS

Our second dimension looks at the extent to which designers adjust the number of represented vs. non-represented movements. The two poles of this dimension are made up of either having one player's movement represented on one end or having multiple players' movements represented on the other. Although we opted for a single player's sensed movement representation to be copied across to other players' controllers (Fig. 8), designs could alternatively represent all players and just be unclear as to who is controlling which representation. Prior work has shown how multiplayer movement-based games use interactive technology to enable rich social play [14] and this can occur by giving players shared control of one representation (e.g. [13]). We now describe different options designers have for mapping input to output by having either one movement representation or multiple movements represented.

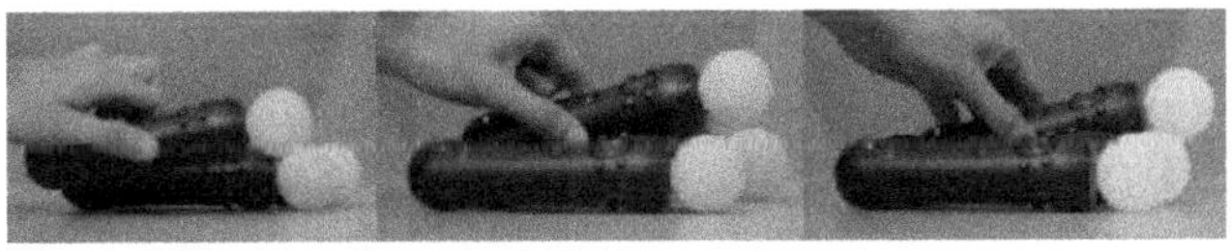

Fig. 8. We had only one of the controllers sensing movement.

Dimension 2.1: One movement represented

Designers could have one player whose movements are represented. In i-dentity, one player's movement representation was duplicated multiple times across to the others' sensors.

Dimension 2.2: Multiple movements represented

Designers could have two or more players' movements represented. For example, there could be many players whose movements are all represented differently, with everyone else being required to move together at the same time to selectively conceal who controls which representation.

DIMENSION 3: NUMBER OF PLAYERS WITH REPRESENTATIONS

Our third dimension concerns the number of players with representations. The two poles of this dimension are made up of either a large or small group of represented players. In i-dentity we had one small group of three players with controllers. A larger group expands the scope of possibilities for movements that could be represented. This means a person is less able to observe all the movements at once. Designers can accommodate more players by breaking up the players into multiple groups. In our case we decided a single group of three was an appropriate group size for the small number of participants so that it would challenge those observing without becoming too overwhelming. Alternatively, networked games such as SpyParty [29] and Assassin's Creed 3 [2] show how designers can combine player-controlled avatars with computer-controlled non-player characters (NPC's) and challenge the players to complete objectives while remaining inconspicuous to other players and NPC's.

Dimension 3.1: Larger group of players

By adding more players, this expands the scope of possibilities for represented movement. More players would take longer for a person to work out the represented from non-represented players. Players may become overwhelmed by all the possibilities that they resort to random guessing.

Dimension 3.2: Smaller group of players

Fewer players with representations limit the scope of possibilities for represented movement. In i-dentity a small group meant players had to be careful with their movements, as a represented or non-represented player was more likely to be spotted if they moved out of sync.

Dimension 3.3: Multiple groups of players

Designers could break up the players into multiple groups who then take turns to perform movements. This can be a good option for designers to manage a larger number of players, rather than having a single group so large it impacts observers' ability to interpret all of the movements.

DIMENSION 4: LOCATION OF REPRESENTATION IN RELATION TO THE BODY

Our fourth dimension considers the notions of proxemics [12], embodiment with tangible interfaces [7] and the effect of technology-mediated performative interactions on a spectator experience [25]. These help to describe the extent to which players are represented in relation to their bodies. In our case an embodied digital interface facilitated engaging physical performance (F6). Designers should consider where representations are in relation to a player's body, as these can affect people's ability to interpret differences between movement and representation. On one end of the pole of this dimension the representation is away from the moving bodies, as seen in many movement-based games such as Wii Sports [33]: the avatar is usually 2-3 meters away from the moving body. On the other end, designers representing movement can place this representation on the body, as seen in i-dentity and JS Joust [34]. To describe design options along this dimension, we borrow from two distinct proxemics interaction spaces based on distance of technology to people in physical space: Public and Personal Interaction Space [18].

Dimension 4.1: Away from bodies (Public Interaction Space)

There is a physical disparity between movement and representation when screens are positioned away from bodies. This can affect the ability of players to focus on both movement and representation at the same time. Designers could use this effect if they would like to challenge players by requiring them to quickly shift attention between movement and representation. However, having developed an earlier version of i-dentity with a separate screen (the Move controllers only sensed movement - no lights were used – while all innominate data was displayed on a shared laptop screen), we identified having a large physical disparity can demand players to switch from representation to movement and back to an extent where it distracted from the innominate representation challenge itself [9].

Dimension 4.2: With bodies (Personal Interaction Space)

In i-dentity, screens (the controller's light) are combined with movements (i.e. the player holds the screen) to orchestrate people's focus towards the players' movements. The small disparity between movement and representation allowed focusing on the gameplay challenge. However, there was still some physical disparity: the distance between hand and the Move's light is about 10cm, allowing for a small wrist movement to result in a larger (i.e. more visible) controller movement. We can envision games where representations are even closer to their origin, for example by utilizing displays that are directly attached to the body, enabled by technological advances such as display tattoos. In i-dentity, the emphasis on the players' bodies appeared to facilitate engagement through their body language (F4, F5), which stimulated discussion (F2, F3). However, such a body focus may cause self-consciousness issues for some players, although we didn't encounter this during our study.

DIMENSION 5: TECHNICAL ATTRIBUTES OF REPRESENTATION

Our final dimension is concerned with the extent to which technical attributes of representation have an affect on the level of challenge presented by the innominate gameplay. In particular, we found that designers should consider the impact of visual fidelity, response time, display characteristics and non-visual representation. Advanced sensing technology such as motion capture is capable of detecting subtle changes in movement. This can produce highly accurate visual representations of movement and games often strive for realism. In contrast, in i-dentity, we reduced the fidelity of representation so as to increase the innominate gameplay challenge. We therefore confirmed that using low fidelity representations could engage players with other players' movements [9]. Movement-based games typically provide near-instant feedback in response to movement; in our case we found a significant delay in response to have negative impacts (F12). When representing movement on screens, designers should also consider how display characteristics could affect the extent to which people are able to access the representation (F11).

Dimension 5.1: Visual fidelity

In most Kinect games, a player's avatar quite accurately mimics a player's movements in virtual space. These games often aim to engage high visual fidelity, in part through enhanced representations that aim to represent even the subtlest movements (fuelled by technical advancements such as the successor Kinect One). In contrast, i-dentity used low fidelity representation to make it harder to discern differences between movement and representation.

Dimension 5.2: Response time

Designers can choose to have technology respond quickly to movement to make it easier for those observing to match movement with representation. Alternatively, designers can manipulate the response time as a measure to increase the challenge, for example for more experienced players.

Dimension 5.3: Display characteristics

Designers should consider the type of representation display used, paying attention to size, viewing angle and brightness characteristics to make the display more or less accessible. For example, playing i-dentity with mobile phone displays instead of the Move controller would make it harder for an audience to access the representation, as the representation would not be viewable at all angles and beyond close proximity. In i-dentity we used the almost 360 degree Move controller lights, which made it relatively easy for people to access the representation (F11).

Dimension 5.4: Non-visual representation

Designers could choose to not visually represent movement, or combine visual with non-visual representation. We did not explore this much, however, we found that a non-visual representation could be useful even when it does not have a direct effect on the innominate representation challenge: our vibration feedback let a player know their role as the leader without the others' knowing. This caused concealed discussion prior to the game (F3).

STRATEGIES FOR IMPLEMENTING INNOMINATE MOVEMENT REPRESENTATION

We now provide a set of design strategies that we derived from our study of using innominate movement representation to facilitate an engaging play experience. While the above design dimensions provide a framework for thinking about digital games using innominate movement representation informed by our experiences with i-dentity, the following strategies complement those dimensions by offering practical lessons from our study on how to build better digital games in this design space.

Number of represented movements

Have only one player's movement represented

In i-dentity, we gave all players a controller, however only one of those had their movement represented. Having more than one player be represented would give people a greater chance of correctly guessing someone who was represented. To accommodate a larger group of people, designers could experiment with having multiple leaders be represented (D2), or multiple groups (D3). However, in our case we decided to limit this so there was only ever one leader; we found having more leaders would make the game too complex and confusing for audiences. Having one player's movement represented can also simplify implementation: for example, we can imagine a game of i-dentity with 100 players, where only one player needs to be sensed.

Technical attributes of representation

Provide a quick response to movement (response time)

In i-dentity, the technology represented a player's movement with near-instant response. Any delay in the technology's response time between movement and representation made it more challenging for those observing (F12). People used this quick response to their advantage to provoke accidental movements, which often proved to be an effective strategy (F9), we therefore recommend to designers to provide a quick response time.

Use a low fidelity representation (fidelity)
Most digital games represent movement with relatively high fidelity. In contrast, i-dentity uses a low fidelity representation. There is only one 'pixel' that represents movement: the light at the end of the controller. We believe it can be important for designers implementing innominate movement representation to consider how the level of fidelity in the representation affects the ability for people to discern the differences between a person's movement and the representation. We originally experimented with more high fidelity representations (a graph representing movement displayed on a laptop) [9]: it appeared this made it more challenging for others to uncover the actions responsible for the representation. In contrast, in the final i-dentity implementation, players appreciated the challenge presented by the low fidelity representation, as it caused engagement with the ambiguity of innominate gameplay (F4, F5) facilitating assistance from an audience (F2, F3).

Use a display that is highly accessible to others (display characteristics)
In i-dentity, people could see the representation even if they were a far distance away (F11). Unlike most conventional displays that place a restriction on where to stand in order to see the representation, the Move controller's light has an almost 360 degree viewing angle, which enabled audiences to stand almost anywhere and still be able to see each representation. This was welcomed, as it drew a crowd (F7) and facilitated engagement with physical performance (F6).

Location of representation in relation to the body

Give a player control across multiple representations
Games typically have player actions only represented on one screen. In i-dentity, the represented player was given the ability to control multiple screens all situated within a close proximity to one another. This meant observers had to spread their attention across all of the movements and screens. Designers should be mindful about how the physical distance screens are from one another affect a person's ability to balance representation and movement awareness, as having them further apart could made it more difficult for observers to keep attention on all of them at once (D4).

EXTENDING THE APPLICATION OF INNOMINATE MOVEMENT REPRESENTATION IN GAME DESIGN

We now articulate how the idea of innominate movement representation may be used to inform the design of a whole range of novel play experiences beyond i-dentity. We sat down and envisioned a number of different application domains, then described why innominate movement representations could be beneficial to the game's design.

Extending innominate representations through shared avatar control to facilitate social play

We see an opportunity for movement-based systems to explore having innominate representations when multiple players are given shared control of a virtual avatar on a single public display. For instance, we can envision a 4-player Kinect game in which players have to quickly identify who controls which limb of an avatar in the game. Like i-dentity, this game uses innominate movement representations, yet engages different technology (Kinect) with representations on a shared screen as well as different sensed body action (every person controls a different limb) (D2.2).

Using innominate representations to foster awareness of physical activity while addressing privacy concerns

Innominate movement representations in public settings could be used to inspire more thoughtful reflection on people's physical activity by keeping personal data private yet accessible to others, inspired by the Fish 'n' Steps system [17]: for instance, we can envision a 1000-player game where every player in a village wears a Fitbit pedometer that measures step-count. The goal is to identify which family does the most steps in a month displayed on a large public outdoor display (D5.3) that shows each family's step-count, but does not show which data belongs to which family (D1.1). This game also uses innominate movement representation, while again engaging different technology (Fitbits) with team representations of a different body action (steps) involving a much larger player count (D3.1) than i-dentity.

Extending innominate gameplay through orientation of bodies in relation to a screen as engaging element

Proxemic interactions [18] suggest design opportunities when using sensing technologies to influence how players are oriented in relation to one another. Building on this, we can envision a 2 to 4-player Kinect game where players assume the role of leader or 1-3 followers. A leader stands closest to the Kinect and tries to avoid colliding with falling obstacles represented on a screen. Followers stand in a line behind the leader and try to avoid being detected by the Kinect by moving their bodies with the leader (D1.2). Only the leader's movements are represented by the system as an avatar on the screen (D2.1). Rather than using movement to conceal roles from other players, our innominate mechanic has followers move in sync so the system's Kinect camera does not sense their movements, with no face-to-face play due to the screen's location away from bodies (D4.1).

Extending innominate interaction design with alternative input methods while facilitating knowledge of own and another's body

Although our work focuses on movement representation, the notion of innominate game mechanic can extend to encompass alternate forms of sensed input, such as button presses, heart rate data, touch-screen or voice input. Game controllers could combine motion data with sensors that measure, for example, breathing data and have an avatar respond differently to each input. We can envision a group of 2 players each with these controllers: the first player's movement data is mapped to the avatar's movement direction and speed attributes while the second player's breathing direction and force controls attacks on enemies. The game uses our innominate mechanic as players synchronize their interactions to conceal from others who controls what from the other team, facilitating collaborative engagement with a combination of input methods.

In sum, these proposed concepts (ranging from very similar to i-dentity to rather different) aim to demonstrate that the idea of our innominate mechanic can be generalizable to a wide range of games and we believe it has much potential that is yet to be explored.

CONCLUSION

In this paper, we introduced innominate movement representation as an unconventional form of digital play to facilitate engaging experiences. We implemented i-dentity, a game using innominate movement representation as a novel game element, where players selectively conceal whose representation belongs to whom. We reported on our findings, which show that innominate movement representation can facilitate an engaging play experience.

We also contributed a design space for games that use innominate movement representation. We articulated ways how designers can think about innominate movement representation through five design dimensions. We also presented game designers with a set of practical strategies for implementing innominate movement representation. We hope that our work contributes to game design research and practice by providing insights into how innominate representation can be leveraged in future designs of movement-based games.

ACKNOWLEDGEMENTS

We thank the organizers of the CHI'13 Game Jam workshop and the attendees for their valuable feedback.

REFERENCES

1. Antle, A.N., Corness, G., and Bevans, A. Springboard: Designing Image Schema Based Embodied Interaction for an Abstract Domain. In *D. England, ed., Whole Body Interaction*. Springer London, 2011, 7–18.
2. *Assassin's Creed*. http://assassinscreed.ubi.com/
3. *Battleship*.http://en.wikipedia.org/wiki/Battleship_(game)
4. Benford, S., Greenhalgh, C., Giannachi, G., Walker, B., Marshall, J. and Rodden, T. 2012. Uncomfortable interactions. *Proc. ACM CHI '12* (2012), 2005–2014.
5. *Celebrity*. http://onlinetoys.com.au/celebrity-head.html
6. Crawford, C. *Chris Crawford on Interactive Storytelling*. New Riders Games. 2004.
7. Dourish, P. 2004. *Where The Action Is: The Foundations Of Embodied Interaction*. MIT Press.
8. Fluegelman, A. ed. 1976. *New Games Book*. Headlands.
9. Garner, J., Wood, G., Pijnappel, S., Murer, M., and Mueller, F. 2013. Combining moving bodies with digital elements: design space between players and screens. *Proc. Interactive Entertainment 2013*, ACM, 17:1–17:10.
10. Gaver, W., Beaver, J. and Benford, S. Ambiguity as a resource for design. *ACM CHI '03* (2003), 233–240.
11. Gaver, W. and Dunne, A. Projected realities: conceptual design for cultural effect. *ACM CHI '99* (1999), 600–607.
12. Hall, E.T. 1966. *The hidden dimension*. Doubleday.
13. Huggard, A., De Mel, A., Garner, J., Toprak, C., Chatham, A.D. and Mueller, F. 2013. Musical embrace: facilitating engaging play experiences through social awkwardness. *ACM CHI '13 EA* (2013), 3067–3070.
14. Isbister, K. Enabling Social Play: A Framework for Design and Evaluation. R. Bernhaupt, ed., In *Evaluating User Experience in Games*. Springer London 2010,11–22.
15. Koleva, B., Taylor, I., Benford, S., Fraser, M., Greenhalgh, C., Schnädelbach, H., vom Lehn, D., Heath, C., Row-Farr, J. and Adams, M. Orchestrating a Mixed Reality Performance. *Proc. ACM CHI'01* (2001), 38-45.
16. Koven, B.D. 1978. *The well-played game: a player's philosophy*. Anchor Press.
17. Lin, J.J., Mamykina, L., Lindtner, S., Delajoux, G. and Strub, H.B. Fish'n'Steps: encouraging physical activity with an interactive computer game. *Proceedings of Ubicomp* (2006), 261–278.
18. Marquardt, N. and Greenberg, S. 2012. Informing the Design of Proxemic Interactions. In *IEEE Pervasive Computing. 11, 2* (Apr. 2012), 14–23.
19. Márquez Segura, E., Waern, A., Moen, J. and Johansson, C. 2013. The design space of body games: technological, physical, and social design. *CHI '13* (2013), 3365–3374.
20. Marshall, J. and Benford, S. 2011. Using fast interaction to create intense experiences. *ACM CHI '11*, 1255–1264.
21. Mueller, F., Agamanolis, S., Vetere, F. and Gibbs, M. 2009. Brute force interactions: leveraging intense physical actions in gaming. *Proc. OZCHI 2009*, 57–64.
22. Mueller, F., Edge, D., Vetere, F., Gibbs, M.R., Agamanolis, S., Bongers, B. and Sheridan, J.G. 2011. Designing sports: a framework for exertion games. *Proc. ACM CHI '11* (2011), 2651–2660.
23. Pedell, S., Graham, C., Kjeldskov, J. and Davies, J. Mobile Evaluation: What the MetaData and the Data Told Us. *Proc. OZCHI 2003*, 96-105
24. PS Move. http://us.playstation.com/ps3/playstation-move/
25. Reeves, S., Benford, S., O'Malley, C. and Fraser, M. 2005. Designing the spectator experience. *Proc. ACM CHI '05* (2005), 741–750.
26. Rogers, Y., Scaife, M., Harris, E., et al. Things Aren't What They Seem to Be: Innovation Through Technology Inspiration. *Proc. ACM DIS '02* (2002), 373–378.
27. Salen, K. and Zimmerman, E. 2003. *Rules of Play: Game Design Fundamentals*. The MIT Press.
28. Sengers, P. and Gaver, B. Staying open to interpretation: engaging multiple meanings in design and evaluation. *Proc. ACM DIS '06* (2006), 99–108.
29. *SpyParty*. http://spyparty.com/
30. Strauss, A. and Corbin, J.M. *Basics of Qualitative Research: Techniques and Procedures for Developing Grounded Theory*. SAGE, 1998.
31. Wakkary, R., Hatala, M., Lovell, R. and Droumeva, M. 2005. An Ambient Intelligence Platform for Physical Play. *Proceedings of the 13th Annual ACM International Conference on Multimedia*, 2005, 764–773.
32. *Werewolf*. http://www.eblong.com/zarf/werewolf.html
33. *Wii Sports*. http://wiisports.com/
34. Wilson, D. (2012). *Designing for the Pleasures of Disputation -or- How to make friends by trying to kick them!* PhD Dissertation, IT University of Copenhagen.

Movement-Based Game Guidelines

Florian 'Floyd' Mueller
Exertion Games Lab
RMIT University
Melbourne, Australia
floyd@exertiongameslab.org

Katherine Isbister
New York University
2 Metrotech Center
Brooklyn NY 11201, USA
katherine.isbister@nyu.edu

ABSTRACT
Movement-based digital games are becoming increasingly popular, yet there is limited comprehensive guidance on how to design these games. We present a set of guidelines for movement-based game design that has emerged from our research-based game development practice. These guidelines have been examined and refined by 14 movement-based game design experts with experience in the academic, independent and commercial game development domains. We contextualize the guidelines using current findings about movement-based game and interaction design, taken from both published research papers and game design venues. Our primary contribution is a body of generative intermediate-level knowledge in the design research tradition that is readily accessible and actionable for the design of future movement-based games.

Author Keywords
Movement-based games; whole-body interaction; play; digital games; exertion

ACM Classification Keywords
H.5.2. [Information Interfaces and Presentation]: User Interfaces - Miscellaneous.

INTRODUCTION
There has been a recent increase in the number of movement-based games, i.e. digital games in which gross-motor bodily input influences the game's outcome [31]. This trend has been fueled by advances in sensor technology, incorporated in game console systems (e.g. Microsoft Kinect, Nintendo Wii and Sony Playstation Move), but also in mobile phones that can sense limb and body movement. Researching these games is important, as they can offer mental, social and physical health benefits [15, 17, 24] as well as entertainment opportunities [3], but also expand the design space for digital games [30, 31].

ACM 978-1-4503-2473-1/14/04...$15.00.
http://dx.doi.org/10.1145/2556288.2557163

Movement-based games align with a larger trend in HCI around embodied interactions [10] that put the body in the center of the interactive experience. However, proponents of this trend have lamented that there is a limited understanding of how to design such experiences [1, 19, 31]. Researchers have pointed out that there has been progress on higher-level theory in the form of frameworks and abstract concepts [31]. However, what is still missing is intermediate-level knowledge in the design research tradition [13, 18, 47] that designers can use in their practice for creating these systems [19].

Such design knowledge could help game designers avoid previously identified pitfalls. It could also provide them with a structured approach to engage with movement-based game design, as well as opportunities to learn from other people's experiences. All this will result in higher quality games, advancing the field, and consequently supporting players in profiting from the benefits associated with playing movement-based games.

In this paper, we present intermediate-level knowledge in the form of practical guidelines for the design of movement-based games. These guidelines have emerged from our combined 20 years of research-based game design practice and engagement with the movement-based game field. The guidelines have been examined and refined by 14 movement-based academic, independent and commercial game design experts. The result is a readily accessible and actionable body of generative intermediate-level knowledge for the design of future movement-based games. We also present insights from our approach of generalizing practical guidance from design-research practice and surfacing associated tacit knowledge [35] from expert designers.

GUIDANCE FOR GAME DESIGNERS
Academic papers often aim to provide designers with abstract frameworks that can then be applicable to game design (for example see [3, 4]). Less theoretical guidance

for game designers often comes in the form of books that offer a set of lenses through which to examine one's practice [12, 38]. Recently, alternative formats have emerged that aim to narrow the gap between theoretical frameworks and the design practice, most often in the form of design cards [33, 37]. Evidence suggests that these practice-oriented approaches can indeed support the creative process [19].

Most of this practical guidance, however, focuses on interactive systems in general or games in particular, but not on movement-based games. Prior works argue that designing movement-based games is different than designing button-press games [31]. There have been attempts to highlight the challenges and opportunities for designers of these games [15, 43]. However, they either focus on abstract frameworks [29, 31] or emphasize individual aspects of movement-based gaming experiences, such as health benefits [5], affective responses [6, 24] or social benefits [28]. What is missing is a comprehensive understanding of how to design these movement-based games, presented in a format that matches the practice-based focus of the game design field. In response, we present a set of guidelines for movement-based games.

OUR APPROACH TOWARDS DEVELOPING THE GUIDELINES

We developed the guidelines through the following process.

Reflection on academic work and achievement

First, we reflected on existing literature on the topic of movement-based game design as well as on our own prior work, which includes 20 years of combined experience in this field. This body of work includes several award-winning games, including games winning and being shortlisted at venues such as Indiecade, Mindtrek, the European Innovative Games Award and the Fun and Games Award. Our games have also been exhibited at international game festivals (Freeplay, Indiecade East, etc.), and international conferences (CHI Interactivity, Fun and Games, DiGRA, etc.). We also reflected on our teaching on movement-based games. In total we taught 6 classes and 5 workshops and game jams on this topic. Lastly, we visited each other's labs to gain insight into our design and teaching practices around movement-based games.

Analyzing notes

We then compiled the generated notes, looking for overarching themes and commonalities. We worked on these notes individually before we discussed them together, which was an iterative process over 2 years of ongoing conversations. This included discussions face-to-face, where we used our bodies not only to play games we had at hand, but also to mime games that we knew about to articulate our arguments. These discussions continued online when we were back at our respective labs, where such bodily discussions were much harder. This experience reminded us of the challenge to communicate guidelines about movement-based games without having people move; in response, we decided to incorporate many examples that we suggest readers should play (if available) while using the guidelines.

Website and feedback from the labs

We believed the best way to reach our target audience was to make the guidelines available online in a manner similar to other design guidelines (such as [2, 16]). We created a website and showed it to our lab members to get feedback on both content and presentation, asking them first for verbal feedback in a group setting, then individually. We took notes during both rounds of feedback and presented the findings again to the group members.

Feedback from experts

After the compilation of the guidelines, we sought feedback from movement-based game design experts to refine our findings, and ultimately, to substantiate our claim that these guidelines can be perceived as useful by game designers.

Participants

We recruited 14 movement-based game design experts from our network, including a) commercial designers and user researchers, as commercial practitioners probably develop the largest volume of movement-based games today, b) independent game designers, as they are able to explore novel game design ideas without the marketing constraints of corporations, and c) teachers and researchers, as we were also looking for feedback from an academic perspective. All have experience designing movement-based games and/or have supervised and taught designers of movement-based games. All have extensive experience in this young field; one practitioner was keen to point out that he was *"in this field from the very beginning"*.

Here is a breakdown of the backgrounds of interviewees:

Commercial:

- Design lead, Dance Central 3; designer, Dance Central 2 at Harmonix.
- User research lead, Dance Central and Kinectimals at Microsoft Game Studios.
- User researcher, Just Dance, the Michael Jackson Experience, Your Shape and Fitness Evolved at Ubisoft.
- User researcher, Sony's Eyetoy games, Singstar and Sports Champions at Sony.

Indie:

- Co-director of the Come Out and Play Festival; instructor of the Big Games class at the Interactive Technology Program at New York University; creator of many commissioned games.
- Director of Indiecade East; designer of Recurse, a commissioned movement-based game that is also released on the iPad.
- Creator of Indiecade finalist game Hit Me; Eyebeam fellow; instructor of Beyond the Joystick.

- Curator of physical game exhibitions including Street Level; game educator and co-founder of Kokoromi game collective.

Academia:

- PhD student in game design, Co-founder of w00t play festival, member of Copenhagen Game Collective.
- Associate professor in a design faculty, artist with many award-winning movement-based installations.
- PhD student in game design, co-director of indie game collective, curator of games arcades and exhibitions.
- Associate professor in a design faculty, coach of many student design projects involving tangible and movement-based play.
- PhD Student in Games and Motivation, Game Jam organizer Games4Health Jam, Game Jam CHI.
- Recently finished PhD on dance game interfaces, currently a game designer for Microsoft Studios.

Procedure

We asked the experts to examine the guidelines in their own time and reflect on them. Several experts took notes during this process that they brought to the interview, which we conducted either in person or via Skype. We asked for general feedback on the guidelines, such as whether they thought we had forgotten any, whether we could delete some, etc. We then went through the guidelines one by one, seeking specific feedback. Based on the experts' insights, we refined the guidelines, and emailed the refined version back to them to gather final feedback as to whether we were successful in implementing their suggestions. We pointed out that we aimed for a consensus approach, and were not able to implement every suggestion, as some were contradicting each other while others were too time consuming to implement.

Data Collection and Analysis

We interviewed participants individually for approximately one hour each. We recorded the session and also took notes. The interviews were almost evenly split among the authors. We each took notes on the recorded interviews that we did not attend. We compared notes and coded them, looking for repeating themes. We used these to refine the guidelines before sending them back to our experts for final feedback. The results are available at movementgameguidelines.org.

GUIDELINES

We now present 10 guidelines. We see these as a starting point tackling key concerns. It is of course possible to generate more detailed and refined guidelines, for example considering particular player target groups, game types and game genres. Other existing categorizations of movement-based games (for example see [32, 45]) might help in identifying further guidelines for more specific game types. Our guidelines aim to capture a range of games and players while providing concrete advice, i.e. we were aiming to be broad while also specific. By proposing guidelines we engage a constant balancing act between being too specific and too general, a challenge expressed previously in work on design patterns [9] - design patterns were one of our inspirations as they have previously been used to articulate best practices in game design [8]. Engaging in this balancing act has distinct advantages and potential pitfalls for researchers, such as the guidelines being useful for a wide range of game ideas, yet not engaging enough for practitioners to use. Our aim was to hit the "sweet spot" between being too broad (and therefore not applicable and useful for practitioners) and too specific (and therefore resulting in guidance that practitioners do not read) based on our over 20 years experience.

Structure

The guidelines are grouped into three categories. Each guideline has a short heading to make it easy to remember, phrased in language we hope appeals to game designers, followed by 2-3 sentences that explain the guideline in more detail. We also included example games that illustrate each guideline in practice and a set of strategies to help designers apply the guideline. The final part offers advice on what designers should and should not do. Many of these advices come from our teaching practice, and were further refined by our experts. Due to space constraints of this paper, we abbreviated many of the guidelines (full guidelines are available online) and limited the amount of example games presented. We also added more scholarly context to each guideline.

GUIDELINES: MOVEMENT REQUIRES SPECIAL FEEDBACK

Embrace ambiguity

Instead of fighting the ambiguity of movement, embrace it.

Ambiguity in movement-based games arises from the fact that no two movements are the same, and most sensor data is messy. Trying to force precision may only frustrate the player, and make the limitations of the sensor obvious in a very un-fun way. So instead of trying to remove this ambiguity, work with it: players enjoy surfing uncertainty and trying to figure out optimal strategies in a somewhat messy system.

Figure 1: Pixel Motion

Pixel Motion (Fig. 1)'s movement sensor is a surveillance camera that picks up overall motion flow patterns instead of tracking individuals. This allows for a group interaction with a 'more the merrier' feel to it. Anyone in the camera's field of view can join in 'wiping' pixels off the video feed by moving around within the play space. The lack of system coupling with individuals means that people watching feel more free to jump in and interact, which helps everyone succeed. The game takes advantage of the sensor ambiguity to encourage group play.

Strategies for Designers

- Get to know the limits of your sensors, and use these limits as a design resource.
- Construct the player's actions in a way that gives room for sensor error without drawing attention to it.
- Avoid game mechanics that require precise control.

DOs and DON'Ts

DO use the ambiguity of movement and sensor data to enhance the game.
DON'T use buttons during the early development phase (even if it seems easier), as you will miss the opportunities arising from dealing with ambiguity.

Additional references (not in guideline)

HCI research has previously highlighted the potential of ambiguity to contribute to an engaging experience by giving the user opportunities to "fill the gaps" [14]. We draw on this idea and remind designers that movement is inherently ambiguous due to the many degrees of freedom inherent in movement. This, combined with the fact that most movement-sensor data is far from precise [4], makes for experiences filled with ambiguity. Designers can try to reduce this ambiguity, for example reducing complex movement to simple gestures [5] or refining sensor capabilities (such as done with the Wii MotionPlus); however, we encourage engagement with ambiguity as a resource for design as well [14, 43].

Celebrate movement articulation

Celebrate how well players articulate movement, and the joy of movement, by giving feedback on movement quality moment-to-moment.

In button-press games players get feedback if and when they press a button. With movement-based games, it is not just if and when, but also how movement is performed. Also, you are not always performing movements to achieve an outcome. Sometimes movement can be enjoyable on its own (whereas pressing a button is not usually a noteworthy pleasure for the player). Therefore celebrate the joy of movement and its articulation by providing players with feedback on the quality of their movement. This feedback has to be instantaneous, so that players can improve their movement articulation moment-by-moment.

Example: Dance Central 2 celebrates movement articulation with bright smooth streaks on-screen when the quality of a dance move is "flawless" compared to the dance instructor.

Strategies for Designers

- You need not judge articulation, you can just provide feedback by highlighting players' articulation to allow them to reflect on and learn from it by themselves.

DO's and DON'Ts

DO provide feedback *if* and *when* movement occurred, but also on *how*.
DON'T worry about judging the *how*, players can figure it out themselves as long as they get feedback.

Additional references (not in guideline)

Research on affect in games demonstrates that certain movements facilitate positive emotional effects [7, 20, 24, 46]. For example, raising your arms after a successful game action can add to the experience. However, there is still much to be explored about how variations in movement qualities affect players' enjoyment and wellbeing [22], and it is clear from designers' reports (e.g. [21, 43]) that conscious and creative variation in movement is interesting and enjoyable for players. Thus we recommend that game designers nurture players' articulation of movement to promote positive affective responses and heightened enjoyment of the movement experience.

Consider movement's cognitive load

Moving can demand a lot of mental attention, creating high 'cognitive load', especially when learning new moves. Don't overload players with too much feedback.

Developing movement skill requires not only bodily, but also cognitive attention, with is a limited resource. Initially, players need to focus on learning a new movement (so focus the feedback on this). Once they are better at the movement, they can devote more attention to more complex and nuanced forms of feedback. For example, the first time you try to pat your head and rub your belly at the same time, you probably cannot do much else, but when you get better at it, you can probably also carry on a conversation.

Example: Dance Central 3 provides multiple layers of feedback to players. Beginners can focus their limited attention on imitating the avatars. More advanced players can use the diagrams and score details to refine their moves.

Strategies for Designers

- Start by providing feedback on the movement itself, without too much worrying about scores, multipliers etc.
- Provide several forms of feedback, but do not require players to engage all of them: better to let players choose which ones to engage based on their cognitive abilities, and shift their attention as mastery grows.

DOs and DON'Ts

DO reduce cognitive complexity during movement: for example, if your player can usually remember 3 rules, as soon as she/he moves, she/he will only remember 1.
DON'T forget once players learn new movements, they may need to re-learn old ones as they integrate new skills.

Additional references (not in guideline)
Even button-press games require considerable cognitive effort, because of their interactive nature [42]. Learning new movements requires a great deal of concentration and focus, which can compete with the attention needed to parse feedback [41]. For this reason, we suggest that movement game designers take into account the additional learning and cognitive load demanded from the player when designing feedback systems.

Focus on the body

Focus on the body, not just the screen, when designing player feedback.

In movement-based games, the body is a major focus of attention: audiences enjoy watching moving bodies, and players listen to their own bodies via proprioception. Do not distract players from this focus on the body by drawing too much attention to the screen.

Figure 2: i-dentity

The game i-dentity (Fig. 2), in which players hold a Sony Move controller each, have to find out whose movement is sensed while moving in sync, and whose controller lights up simply at the same time, focuses on the players' bodies, not a screen (there is no screen).

Strategies for Designers

- Think past screen-based feedback. You can use audio and haptics, as well as other players to offer feedback.

DOs and DON'Ts
DO start imagining your game without a screen.
DON'T forget that for players who feel self conscious or reluctant to move, diverting attention away from the body might be beneficial to reduce the barrier to play.

Additional references (not in guideline)
The body is at the center of the interaction in movement-based games [31], yet many current games focus on what is happening on the screen rather than the body. Some indie developers have critiqued the prevailing reliance of current game design on screen focus. Indie examples [44] help to show this is a missed opportunity to positively contribute to the play experience, for example by turning any bodily movement into a spectacle that attracts audiences [39].

GUIDELINES: MOVEMENT LEADS TO BODILY CHALLENGES

Intend fatigue

If you use fatigue as a game challenge, make it intentional rather than incidental.

Movement results in fatigue. On the one hand, it can be a welcomed challenge for players if they have to manage this fatigue (for example in endurance sports), on the other hand, fatigue can negatively affect engagement. Therefore, intend fatigue when using it as a game challenge, but avoid it when it is not part of the game.

Figure 3: Hanging off a Bar

In Hanging off a Bar (Fig. 3) fatigue is intentional: the challenge for the player is to hang onto the bar as long as possible, the only opportunities for recovery are rafts to jump onto when they pass by.

Strategies for Designers

- Minimize chances of fatigue by creating short game cycles.
- Minimize chances of fatigue by varying movements.
- Distract players from fatigue, e.g. through music.

DOs and DON'Ts
DO use the management of fatigue as a game mechanic.
DON'T assume players know how to manage fatigue, support them in figuring it out.

Additional references (not in guideline)
Research highlights that managing fatigue can be an engaging game mechanic [31]. Of course, not all movement-based games need to engage this game mechanic—for example a party game designer may avoid fatiguing players. Yet designers should remember that movement can fatigue players, and if this fatigue is not managed and is not contributing to the game, it can distract from the experience [15].

Exploit risk

Exploit physical risk sensibly.

Movement, especially in everyday indoor environments, has an inherent sense of risk associated with it: there is risk of injury, risk of breaking furniture, risk of hitting another person. However, with risk also comes a sense of thrill, which can contribute positively to the game experience.

Figure 4: JS Joust

In JS Joust (Fig. 4), players try to jostle each other's Move Controller out of perfect level position. The risk of jostling the other player's body as well adds thrill to the experience.

Strategies for Designers

- Make players aware they are engaging in risky activity.
- Consider the environment when exploiting physical risk.
- Let players' movements interfere with each other to facilitate body contact, which has physical risk associated with it.

DOs and DON'Ts

DO put the player's safety first.
DON'T assume players will be fully aware of any emerging physical risks, as they might be distracted by engaging play.

Additional references (not in guideline)

HCI research has previously highlighted the potential for risk to positively contribute to the interactive experience [26, 31], as people might experience "feelings of thrill [arising] from a combination of fearful anticipation, followed by an extreme physical sensation, and then the euphoria of relief at having survived" [3].

Map imaginatively

Map movements in imaginative ways.

The computer allows mapping movements in many imaginative ways, in particular in ways that are not possible in real life, offering players fantasy-fuelled opportunities they do not have otherwise. Mapping does not need to be literal or slavishly true-to-life.

Wii Tennis maps every simple up-down arm movement into a successful tennis serve, fuelling the player's fantasy of being a successful and accomplished tennis player.

Strategies for Designers

- Map movement in a non-linear fashion, for example in a tennis fantasy game a weak forehand movement results in a strong hit.
- Add additional virtual movement to mapped movement.
- Engage "avateering": make the player's movements look better than they really are.

DOs and DON'Ts

DO engage your creativity in the mapping process.
DON'T use this guideline if you want to simulate a real-world sports experience, such as designing a golf simulator.

Additional references (not in guideline)

Prior research has highlighted that playing movement-based sports games is not the same as engaging in the equivalent sports activities [17]. This guideline reminds game designers that this is rightfully so, as most movement games are not intended to be highly accurate simulations of a real-world physical activity. If we only focus on simulations, we miss an opportunity to engage players' fantasy, one of the key reasons why people play digital games [27].

Highlight rhythm

Help players identify rhythm in their movements.

Movement is rhythmic: the head bopping when dancing, footsteps when walking, even when playing tennis there is a rhythm to the arm swinging back and subsequent follow-through. Movement can be rhythmic on an individual action level (tennis swing), but also the overall movement experience often follows a rhythm of high and low-intensity actions. Movement becomes easier with a beat, so support players in identifying a rhythm to their movements.

Figure 5: Mary Mack 5000

Mary Mack 5000 (Fig. 5) is a technologically-enhanced twist on the classic schoolyard hand clapping game, highlighting the rhythm in movement through the clapping that results from players having their movement in sync.

Strategies for Designers

- Play music for players to help them identify a beat.
- Visualize previous and upcoming movements so players can identify a rhythm in their movements.
- Think of haptics not only as a feedback mechanism for action, but also as a rhythm aid.
- Use other players to help a player identify a rhythm in his/her movements.

DOs and DON'Ts

DO see movement in games not just as a string of independent actions, but as a sequence of rhythmic actions that, with a beat, get easier.

DON'T forget that engaging competitive gameplay can emerge when allowing players to try to throw their opponents off their beat.

Additional references (not in guideline)

Research has previously highlighted the key role rhythm plays when it comes to movement, for example, in sports science, the use of rhythm through music can enhance performance and enjoyment of physical activity [25]. Movement can be enriched by adding music; however, this guideline also reminds designers that movement itself often has a beat to it, and by highlighting this through appropriate feedback, the movement experience can be enhanced [34].

Support self-expression

Support players in expressing themselves using their bodies.

We communicate a lot about ourselves in how we move. Thus playing a movement-based game is always a form of self-expression, especially with other people around us. Take advantage of this to increase fun for players.

In Guitar Hero, lifting the guitar activates "rock-star mode", motivated by the opportunity to earn more points. Guitarists lift their guitars to show off, not to play better. So building this movement into gameplay enhances a person's ability to show off and create a spectacle.

Strategies for Designers

- Allow players to perform different kinds of movements to achieve the same outcome.
- Encourage players to try out these different movements.
- Celebrate self-expression by showing players the result of their self-expression, for example in forms of photos of their movements as trophies.
- Offer opportunities for secondary performances - movements that do not contribute directly to the goal of the game - such as lifting the guitar in Guitar Hero.

DOs and DON'Ts

DO see movement as a form of self-expression that can make your game more fun.

DON'T forget self-expression is not only concerned with the player, but also with other players and any audience.

Additional references (not in guideline)

Movement is not only a form of game input, but also supports people in their self-expression, for example the showy lifting of the guitar in Guitar Hero [7]. In particular, secondary performance or "gestural excess" [40], that is movement that does not directly contribute to the outcome of the game, can allow players to express themselves, which contributes positively to the experience [7, 21]. Good design creates opportunities for self-expression to occur through game mechanics such as the in-game reward opportunities when lifting the guitar to "show off". However, games that aim for specific movements, such as rehabilitation games, should probably limit support for self-expression in order to promote consistent movement.

Facilitate social fun

Facilitate social fun by making movement a social experience.

Moving with others is fun. Movement is typically visible to others and easily becomes a performance, whether we intend it or not. Therefore, design for multi-player, including other players and an audience.

Figure 6: Yamove!

Yamove! (Fig. 6) is a b-boy style dance battle game. Players compete in pairs, aiming for high intensity, in-synch, diverse dance routines. Each player wears an iOS device strapped to the forearm. The game is hosted by an MC and scoring is based on accelerometer data from the devices. Yamove illustrates that a game can facilitate social fun for players, moderators, and spectators alike.

Strategies for Designers

- If you plan to design both multi-player and single-player modes for your game, consider starting with multi-player.
- Make the game a spectacle: encourage movements that are, by nature, a spectacle others enjoy watching.
- Turn bystanders into players: allow the audience to easily join the game.
- Make the game easy to learn by observing, so that spectators figure out what is going on quickly and want to try.

DOs and DON'Ts

DO engage other players and audiences by turning the movement into a performance.

DON'T forget that movement in spaces where others do not know that there is a game going on, such as public spaces, might create socially awkward situations.

Additional references (not in guideline)

The inclusion of movement (in contrast to playing the same game with button-presses) can change the character of the experience from playing to win to playing to socialize [28]. This is a result of the positive affect resulting from body movement [20, 28] as well as the performative character of movement that can draw audiences [39]. We found in our teaching practice that it is easier to design for multiplayer first, then single player second when it comes to movement-based games. This contrasts common game design practice, where development tools often suggest starting with single player first, as multiplayer is more difficult to implement.

FEEDBACK FROM THE EXPERTS

During the interviews, our experts expressed delight about the guidelines: *"This is great." "This is super useful."*

Fulfilling need

The experts confirmed that the guidelines fulfill a need that is timely: *"It's great that someone is finally doing this." "We would have loved that when we did [commercial title]."* They pointed out that the guidelines reminded them of their experiences when playtesting their movement-based games as part of their design processes: *"This absolutely confirmed with what we found in our playtests."*

Usefulness for experts

Experts also commented on how some guidelines were not very useful for their own practice, as they were *"following them anyhow."* Also, they pointed out that they follow some of the guidelines *"intuitively"* already. However, they found these guidelines still useful for teaching and supervision, to articulate design decisions and as a form of checklist (see below).

Teaching and coaching

The experts expressed that the guidelines will be useful for their teaching (all academics except the PhD students and 3 developers teach). They said the guidelines would help them structure class content and communicate key aspects of movement-based game design. Industry experts said the guidelines would be useful for them when coaching less experienced staff and supervising teams. They also said they would use the guidelines as a checklist to see if they have considered the key aspects during a design process.

Providing a language

The industry experts were especially thankful that the guidelines provided them with a language for the design choices they make during their practice, allowing them to communicate to others: *"This could have helped me when I was previously trying to argue for a design decision with the marketing department."*

Inspirational

Our experts were particularly excited about guidelines they usually do not consider in their practice, described them as *"inspirational"*: *"I really like this 'Intend Fatigue', I had not thought about this one before."* Another is *"Engage Risk"*, something industry experts had not previously considered: *"That's interesting that you say that this is not just something to avoid, but can be a positive thing."*

CHANGES AFTER EXPERT FEEDBACK

The experts welcomed the guidelines. However, they also pointed out aspects to improve about individual guidelines, many of these were concerned with clarification, sentence flow or the need for additional examples. We do not go into detail about these here. However, there was more general feedback we received that helped us to refine the guidelines overall and might aid others when aiming to generate guidelines based on expert feedback.

More examples

All experts wanted more examples for each guideline, underscoring the usefulness of a portfolio of examples in presenting results of design research [13].

Open to interpretation

Initially, we tried to articulate the guidelines in a very precise manner, carefully crafting the language so that each one of them was very clear. Further precision in the language was asked for by one of the academic experts. However, all other experts welcomed language that was more open to interpretation (without being vague or ambiguous), as it allowed them to use the guideline as a suggestion that they were able to apply to their specific practice and design cases, rather than being confronted with a command to be followed.

Rules are for breaking

Seven experts pointed out that they had either themselves created or observed games in which at least one of the guidelines was not followed, yet resulted in engaging gameplay. As such, they were concerned that others might follow the guidelines too strictly. In response, we added a sentence on the front page: *"The guidelines are like rules in any creative field: of course you can also break them, but first, you need to know them before you can break them."*

LIMITATIONS

Games-focus rather than play-focus

We focused on movement-based games, rather than movement-based play. We see games as more formal, with rules and goals [36], and play as a larger design space that encompasses games. We began with the smaller design space, but we find movement-based play a fascinating area, in particular in light of the movement-based play that emerged in the 1970's under the term "New Game Movement" [11] that we believe holds tremendous potential when thought of in combination with digital technology.

Location-based games

The personal experience of both ourselves and our experts steered our thinking towards games played in living rooms, arts venues and conference exhibits. We note that emerging location-based games, played over large areas, are also movement-based. We acknowledge that there is not much specific guidance for these types of games in our guidelines. However, we believe some of our guidelines (in particular Intend Fatigue, Consider Movement's Cognitive Load and Exploit Risk) are easily applicable to these location-based games, suggesting that our work might also be useful when designing these kinds of games.

Evidence of utility of guidelines

We acknowledge that it would be ideal to observe use of the guidelines in practice. Our prior work led to design guidance that supported the ideation process [33]; we believe this work may also be useful in such scenarios.

FUTURE WORK

We plan on releasing the guidelines to the public, and tracking usage based on website hits. We also plan to conduct follow-up interviews with our experts as to whether they have used the guidelines in their practice. This will help us better understand how the guidelines work in practice, and provide insights about how they need to be developed further. We anticipate the need to periodically revisit the guidelines and examples. Movement technologies continue to evolve, and canonical examples of excellent movement games continue to appear.

CONCLUSIONS

We presented a set of guidelines for movement-based game design that have emerged from our research-based game development practice. These guidelines have been examined and refined by 14 movement-based game designers with experience in academic, independent and commercial game design domains. Their positive feedback suggests that our process of engaging in design practice ourselves, analyzing and reflecting on existing games, and getting feedback from lab members and experts, can lead to practical guidelines that practitioners appreciate. The fact that the experts said they use some of the recommendations in the guidelines in their current practice and that the underlying findings match their experience suggests that we created guidelines with applicability beyond our own practice. By making the guidelines publicly available in both a paper and online format we hope we are able to reach out to both academics and practitioners, furthering the practical potential of these guidelines.

We believe our approach of directly engaging with multiple accomplished design practitioners significantly strengthened the end result in terms of both clarity and applicability. This supports the notion that researchers should not only deliver results to practitioners, but also actively engage them in the knowledge production process (e.g. [23]). Just as we as HCI researchers value and prioritize engaging end users in evaluating experiences we design, we should also value and prioritize engaging expert practitioners in the evaluation of the usefulness of the tools for design our research generates. In our particular field of game design, the boundaries between what researchers, commercial game developers and independent game designers do are overlapping more and more, and we believe everyone can benefit from sharing work in progress and reflections about practice.

We encourage other HCI researchers to incorporate design practitioners in the development of practical guidelines in order to make conceptual thinking readily applicable to the target design community. In return, we urge practitioners to support researchers when creating these guidelines (as our experts did) in order to advance the development of knowledge. If we work together in this way, we can take better advantage of the strengths and knowledge of both communities to advance the field as a whole.

ACKNOWLEDGEMENTS

We thank all the experts and our lab members. Florian 'Floyd' Mueller is the recipient of an Australian Research Council Fellowship (DP110101304).

REFERENCES

1. Antle, A.N. Embodied child computer interaction: why embodiment matters. *ACM Interactions, March+April.* (2009), 27-30
2. Apple. iOS Human Interface Guidelines, 2013. https://developer.apple.com/library/ios/documentation/UserExperience/Conceptual/MobileHIG/UEBestPractices/UEBestPractices.html#//apple_ref/doc/uid/TP40006556-CH20-SW1.
3. Benford, S., Greenhalgh, C., Giannachi, G., Walker, B., Marshall, J. and Rodden, T., Uncomfortable interactions. In *Proc. CHI 2012*, ACM Press (2012), 2005-2014.
4. Benford, S., Schnädelbach, H., Koleva, B., Anastasi, R., Greenhalgh, C., Rodden, T., Green, J., Ghali, A., Pridmore, T. and Gaver, B. Expected, sensed, and desired: A framework for designing sensing-based interaction. *ACM Transactions on Computer-Human Interaction (TOCHI)*, *12* (1). (2005), 3-30.
5. Berkovsky, S., Coombe, M., Freyne, J., Bhandari, D. and Baghaei, N., Physical activity motivating games: virtual rewards for real activity. In *Proc. CHI 2010,* ACM Press (2010), 243-252.
6. Bianchi-Berthouze, N. Understanding the role of body movement in player engagement. *Human-Computer Interaction*, *28* (1). (2013), 40-75.
7. Bianchi-Berthouze, N., Kim, W. and Patel, D. Does Body Movement Engage You More in Digital Game Play? and Why? In Paiva, A., Prada, R. and Picard, R. eds. *Affective Computing and Intelligent Interaction*, Springer Berlin / Heidelberg, 2007, 102-113.
8. Björk, S. and Holopainen, J.A. *Patterns in game design.* Charles River Media, 2005.
9. Borchers, J.O. A pattern approach to interaction design. *AI & SOCIETY*, *15* (4). (2001), 359-376.
10. Dourish, P. *Where the Action Is: The Foundations of Embodied Interaction.* MIT Press, 2001.
11. Fluegelman, A. *The new games book.* Main Street Books, 1976.

12. Fullerton, T., Swain, C. and Hoffman, S. *Game Design Workshop*. Morgan Kaufmann, 2004.
13. Gaver, W., What should we expect from research through design? *CHI 2012*, ACM Press, 937-946.
14. Gaver, W.W., Beaver, J. and Benford, S., Ambiguity as a resource for design. *CHI 2013*, ACM Press, 233-240.
15. Gerling, K., Livingston, I., Nacke, L. and Mandryk, R., Full-body motion-based game interaction for older adults. *CHI 2012,* ACM Press (2012), 1873-1882.
16. Grammenos, D. Game Over! http://www.ics.forth.gr/hci/ua-games/game-over/.
17. Graves, L., Stratton, G., Ridgers, N.D. and Cable, N.T. Comparison of energy expenditure in adolescents when playing new generation and sedentary computer games: cross sectional study. *BMJ*, *335* (7633). (2007), 1282-1284.
18. Höök, K. and Löwgren, J. Strong concepts: Intermediate-level knowledge in interaction design research. *ACM Trans. Comput.-Hum. Interact.*, *19* (3). (2012), 1-18.
19. Hornecker, E., Creative idea exploration within the structure of a guiding framework: the card brainstorming game. *TEI 2010*, ACM Press, 101-108.
20. Isbister, K. Emotion and motion: games as inspiration for shaping the future of interface. *interactions*, *18* (5). (2011), 24-27.
21. Isbister, K., How to stop being a buzzkill: designing yamove!, a mobile tech mash-up to truly augment social play. *MobileHCI 2012*, ACM Press (2012), 1-4.
22. Isbister, K. and DiMauro, C. Waggling the form baton: Analyzing body-movement-based design patterns in Nintendo Wii games, toward innovation of new possibilities for social and emotional experience. in *Whole Body Interaction*, Springer, 2011, 63-73.
23. Isbister, K., Flanagan, M. and Hash, C., Designing games for learning: insights from conversations with designers. *CHI 2010,* ACM Press, 2041-2044.
24. Isbister, K., Schwekendiek, U. and Frye, J., Wriggle: an exploration of emotional and social effects of movement. *Ext. Abstracts CHI 2011,* ACM, 1885-1890.
25. Karageorghis, C. and Priest, D.-L. Music in Sport and Exercise : An Update on Research and Application. *The Sport Journal*, *11* (3). (2008).
26. Klemmer, S. and Hartmann, B., How Bodies Matter: Five Themes for Interaction Design. In *Proc. DIS 2006*, ACM Press (2006), 140-149.
27. Lazzaro, N. 4 Fun Keys: Testing Emotions and Player Experiences. in *Game Usability: Advice from the Experts for Advancing the Player Experience*, Morgan Kaufmann, San Francisco, CA, 2008.
28. Lindley, S.E., Le Couteur, J. and Berthouze, N.L., Stirring up experience through movement in game play: effects on engagement and social behaviour. In *Proc. CHI 2008*, ACM Press (2008), 511-514.
29. Loke, L., Larssen, A., Robertson, T. and Edwards, J. Understanding movement for interaction design: frameworks and approaches. *Personal and Ubiquitous Computing, 11* (8 Special Issue Movement-Based Interaction). (2007), 691-701.
30. Mueller, F., Agamanolis, S. and Picard, R., Exertion Interfaces: Sports over a Distance for Social Bonding and Fun. *CHI 2003,* ACM Press, 561-568.
31. Mueller, F., Edge, D., Vetere, F., Gibbs, M.R., Agamanolis, S., Bongers, B. and Sheridan, J.G., Designing Sports: A Framework for Exertion Games. In *Proc. CHI 2011*, ACM Press (2011), 2651-2660.
32. Mueller, F., Gibbs, M. and Vetere, F., Taxonomy of Exertion Games. *OzCHI 2008*, ACM Press, 263-266.
33. Mueller, F., Gibbs, M.R., Vetere, F. and Edge, D., Supporting the creative game design process with Exertion Cards. In *Proc. CHI 2014,* ACM Press (2014).
34. Park, T., Lee, U., Lee, B., Lee, H., Son, S., Song, S. and Song, J., ExerSync: facilitating interpersonal synchrony in social exergames. *CSCW 2013*, ACM Press, 409-422.
35. Polanyi, M. and Sen, A. *The tacit dimension*. Peter Smith Gloucester, MA, 1983.
36. Salen, K. and Zimmerman, E. *Rules of Play: Game Design Fundamentals*. MIT Press, 2003.
37. Schell, J. The Art of Game Design - The Cards. http://artofgamedesign.com/cards/.
38. Schell, J. *The Art of Game Design: A book of lenses*. Morgan Kaufmann, 2008.
39. Sheridan, J. and Bryan-Kinns, N. Designing for Performative Tangible Interaction. *International J. of Arts and Technology*, *1* (3/4). (2008), 288-308.
40. Simon, B. Wii are out of control: Bodies, game screens and the production of gestural excess. *Loading... 3* (4). (2009).
41. Spelmezan, D., Jacobs, M., Hilgers, A. and Borchers, J., Tactile motion instructions for physical activities. In *Proc. CHI 2009,* ACM Press (2009), 2243-2252.
42. Sweller, J. Cognitive load theory, learning difficulty, and instructional design. *Learning and instruction*, *4* (4). (1994), 295-312.
43. Waern, A., Marques-Segura, E., Moen, J. and Johansson, C., The Design Space of Body Games: Technological; Physical; and Social Design. In *Proc. CHI 2013*, ACM Press (2013), 3365-3374.
44. Wilson, D. Designing for the Pleasures of Disputation - or- How to make friends by trying to kick them!, PhD thesis, IT University of Copenhagen, 2012.
45. Yim, J. and Graham, T.C.N., Using games to increase exercise motivation. In *Proc. Future Play 2007*, ACM Press (2007), 166-173.
46. Zangouei, F., Gashti, M.A.B., Höök, K., Tijs, T., de Vries, G.-J. and Westerink, J., How to stay in the emotional rollercoaster: lessons learnt from designing EmRoll. *NordiCHI 2010*, ACM Press (2010), 571-580.
47. Zimmerman, J., Forlizzi, J. and Evenson, S., Research through design as a method for interaction design research in HCI. *CHI 2007,* ACM Press (2007), 493-502.

Effects of Skill Balancing for Physical Abilities on Player Performance, Experience and Self-Esteem in Exergames

Kathrin M. Gerling[1], Matthew Miller[1], Regan L. Mandryk[1], Max Birk[1], Jan Smeddinck[2]
[1]University of Saskatchewan, Saskatoon, SK, CA, firstname.lastname@usask.ca
[2]University of Bremen, Germany, smeddinck@tzi.de

ABSTRACT

Game balancing can help players with different skill levels play multiplayer games together; however, little is known about how the balancing approach affects performance, experience, and self-esteem–especially when differences in player strength result from given abilities, rather than learned skill. We explore three balancing approaches in a dance game and show that the explicit approach commonly used in commercial games reduces self-esteem and feelings of relatedness in dyads, whereas hidden balancing improves self-esteem and reduces score differential without affecting game outcome. We apply our results in a second study with dyads where one player had a mobility disability and used a wheelchair. By making motion-based games accessible for people with different physical abilities, and by enabling people with mobility disabilities to compete on a par with able-bodied peers, we show how to provide empowering experiences through enjoyable games that have the potential to increase physical activity and self-esteem.

Author Keywords

Motion-based games, balancing, exergames, player experience, physical abilities.

ACM Classification Keywords

K.8.0 [Personal Computing]: General - Games.

INTRODUCTION

Many computer and video games include the element of competition between multiple players. Competition is optimal when the outcome is uncertain because the players are well matched, complicating multiplayer games where players have different skill levels. Commercial games provide balancing options so that people with different skill levels can compete, including asymmetric driver and gunner roles in Mario Kart: Double Dash, 'rubber banding' in Mario Kart, and bullet magnetism in the Halo series.

Previous research has supported game balancing. In particular, Bateman et al. [2] showed that the reduced score differential of balanced competitions increased the fun that assisted players experienced, while not changing the fun that non-assisted players had. However, these results derive from a genre (target shooting) where assistance was hidden from players. There are many genres where balancing cannot be hidden. For example, in symmetric performance games like the Guitar Hero or the Dance Central series, competition is balanced by having players explicitly select different difficulty levels. Thus players are aware that assistance is provided to one player in terms of reduced difficulty. How players respond to explicit balancing is an open question; however, the work by Bateman et al. [2] gives some insight. In their study, the majority of assisted players felt that assisting a player is unfair because the win does not reflect actual ability, the win does not count if it was actually due to computer assistance, and the scores would be meaningless. These results suggest that if weaker players win through assistance known to both players, the experience may not be positive.

Balancing competition in games is further complicated when the relative strength of the players is a matter of innate ability, rather than skill acquired through practice. For example, dominating a competition based on practiced skills (e.g., professional golfer trounces amateur friend) does not carry the same stigma as dominating a competition based on given traits (e.g., 6-foot man crushes 5-foot man in one-on-one basketball) or ability (e.g., able-bodied child routs child with mobility impairment in race). The reason for the disparity in player strength (e.g., due to skill, ability, age, fitness level) may differentially affect how players feel about games that balance competition by providing assistance to weaker players. This is important because the effects of providing assistance to players of different abilities may not only affect play experiences, but may also affect how the player feels about themselves – *empowering players through balancing assistance is desirable*, whereas, *harming players' self-esteem is not.*

To explore balancing strategies in multiplayer games, we studied the effects of balancing symmetric competition in a motion-based game. We focus on symmetric competition to explore explicit versus hidden balancing approaches and on motion-based games to explore balancing in dyads with a range of game skills and physical abilities. In Study 1, we explore the effects of 4 balancing approaches (input, time, score, and no balancing) on performance, experience, and self-esteem in a custom-built dance game. We also compare physical play to play with a gamepad to see whether differences arose when disparity in player strength was

CHI 2014, April 26 - May 01 2014, Toronto, ON, Canada
Copyright 2014 ACM 978-1-4503-2473-1/14/04...$15.00.
http://dx.doi.org/10.1145/2556288.2556963

more related to physical ability than game skill. In Study 2, we explored balancing for dyads with vastly different physical abilities–comprised of dyads where one player was able-bodied and the other used a wheelchair. Based on results from Study 1, we adapted our game to use a combined balancing approach so that the able-bodied players used the dance mat, whereas the participants in wheelchairs played by moving around with the wheelchair.

Results of our studies show that: 1) explicit input balancing, similar to the approach used in commercial games, reduced feelings of self-esteem in both the weaker and stronger players, and resulted in lower relatedness between the pairs; 2) hidden time balancing best balanced score differential, but did not change the game outcome (i.e., stronger player still won more often), and also improved self-esteem for both players; 3) weaker players felt less guilty competing against their partner when using the motion-based controls than the sedentary controls, where disadvantage was more related to skill than physical ability; 4) people who use wheelchairs performed well in the game and enjoyed competing in a motion-based game against their able-bodied friends; and 5) the able-bodied competitors were concerned about ensuring a level playing field, which is possible by tuning the balancing parameters in our game.

Balancing motion-based exergames is an important step toward engaging people with different skills and abilities in physically-challenging play, which can reduce sedentary behaviour and benefit health. By making motion-based games accessible for people with different physical abilities, we can provide enjoyable games with the benefit of increasing physical activity. More importantly, by enabling joint motion-based play using hidden balancing, we can help increase self-esteem by providing empowering experiences for players.

RELATED WORK

Defining Skills and Abilities

Skills generally refer to a set of learned abilities to perform a task. In the physical context, Merriam-Webster defines skills as "dexterity or coordination especially in the execution of learned physical tasks"[1]. In contrast, abilities are referred to as "the quality or state of being able"[2], emphasizing that certain abilities are given, and not acquired through practice. Thus, individual performance depends on the basic ability to participate, e.g., ability to run, and on the acquired skills, e.g., dribble a soccer ball.

Physical Competence and Self-Concept

Cairney et al. show that physical activity can improve well-being [5], but positive effects can be lost in competitive settings. On a basic level, perceived physical competence influences whether people enjoy physical activity, and follow through with physical activity in adulthood [5], but can depend on comparisons to peers. This may lead to negative self-perception, despite increased objective performance [16]. These findings are supported by research by Goni et al. on sport in schools [9], showing that sports have a positive impact on students' self-concepts, but that balanced competition leads to greater improvements. If perceived and objective relative physical skill and ability in sport influences an individual's self-concepts, we must explore whether these effects prevail in video games that require physical activity, and which balancing strategies can be applied to ensure a positive player experience.

Balancing Skills and Abilities in Sports and Games

In sport, balancing is often applied to improve competition between players with different abilities (physical, cognitive) or skill to compete. Handicapping is an approach that determines the outcome based on a combination of the player's performance and their skill level or physical ability, and is used with both able-bodied players (e.g., in golf [22]) and people with disabilities (e.g., the system of the Paralympic Games [12], where athletes with disabilities are classified based on the kind and severity of disability, and scoring parameters are adjusted). Likewise, balancing has been applied in video games to support player of varying skill. The most common way of adjusting games to the skills and abilities of the players are different levels of difficulty settings, based on predefined difficulty parameters, determined via extensive testing. However, such difficulty levels frequently prove too coarse. *Dynamic difficulty adjustments* (DDA) can foster more personalized and subtle balancing. In DDA, adjustments to the gameplay variables happen in real time based on the player's performance [1]. The physical nature of motion-based games adds another level of complexity to balancing: Sinclair et al. show that games do not only have to account for different skill levels of players in relation to mastering in-game challenges, but also in relation to their physical skills and abilities [20].

Balancing Multiplayer Experiences

In addition to player balancing to adapt in-game challenges to the skill level of an individual player, balancing has been applied in multiplayer settings to account for differences in skills and abilities between players, a process that affects the aspect of perceived fairness. Strategies for multiplayer game balancing summarized by Bateman et al. include asymmetric roles, matchmaking, and individual difficulty adjustment [2]. The authors examined aim assist techniques to balance shooting-gallery games played in a co-located setting using the Nintendo Wii Remote [2]. Their results show that players generally accept skill balancing in group settings, and that the player experience of less skilled players can be improved by providing assistance. Multiplayer game balancing in exertion-based games is complicated by the need to consider both player skill and fitness. Although the game in [2] was played with a motion-

[1] http://www.merriam-webster.com/dictionary/skills
[2] http://www.merriam-webster.com/dictionary/ability

based controller, the physical effort of pointing input does not compare to that required by many exergames. Different approaches for balancing exertion games have emerged in literature: The game Life is a Village [23] implements asymmetric player roles (cycling on a recumbent bike and using the Nintendo Wii Remote for gestural input), whereas Heart Burn [21] uses difference from target heart rates to balance for people with difference fitness levels. Likewise, Mueller et al. [15] demonstrated that heart rate balancing contributes to player experience in a remote jogging application, because it allows players to focus on their own fitness levels while still engaging with another person.

We present a game that is played with sedentary or motion-based controls in either unbalanced or balanced settings to examine player performance, experience, and self-esteem.

A SYSTEM TO STUDY PLAYER BALANCING IN MOTION-BASED GAMES

To study the effects of balancing in motion-based play, we implemented a dancing game similar to Dance Dance Revolution – a popular motion-based game [11] – that is playable by able-bodied persons (using dance mats) and persons with mobility disabilities (wheelchair input). We chose this game for two reasons. First, the game draws much of its appeal from symmetric player roles where competing players are required to complete similar challenges; therefore, it is interesting to study balancing. Second, performance in the game is determined by a combination of the player's level of coordination and their physical ability; therefore it is interesting for balancing a broad range of intra-dyad differences in skill and ability.

Gameplay

The gameplay consists of performing steps synchronously to the beat of a song. There are four different types of steps: up, down, left, and right. The game uses arrows that point in the direction of the steps to indicate which steps the user has to perform. The arrows appear at the top of the screen and move downward. A stationary set of targets (one for each type of step) is displayed near the bottom of the screen. The player aims to perform the move indicated by each arrow at the moment when the arrow is in line with the target. The player is awarded points based on how close the arrow was to the target at the moment they performed the indicated step. For the two-player competitive mode, the screen is divided in half, with each half having its own set of targets and arrows. We included dance music similar to the music used in commercially available dance games.

Game Input

The game was implemented in C# using Microsoft XNA Game Studio 4.0 and the Microsoft Kinect SDK alongside the KINECT^{Wheels} toolkit [7] for wheelchair input.

The game includes input modes for motion-based (dance mat or wheelchair) and sedentary (game pad) play.

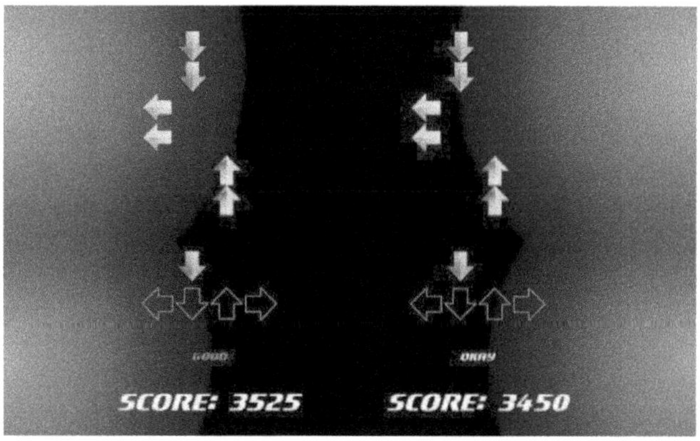

Figure 1. Screen of the two-player dancing game we created.

Dance Mat. The dance mat is a 1 square meter pad, divided into a 3-by-3 grid (see Figure 2). Players stand in the center cell of the grid, and perform steps by stepping on cells with their feet. The cell in front of the player corresponds to up arrows, the cell behind the player corresponds to down arrows, and the cells to the left and to the right of the player indicate left and right arrows, respectively.

Game Pad. The sedentary input mode uses the four action buttons (arranged in a diamond pattern) on a standard game controller. Players press the top button to perform an up-step, the lower button to perform a down-step, and the left and right buttons to perform left- and right-steps.

Wheelchair. The wheelchair mode emulates the dancing approach of the dance mat version, by requiring players to move around with the wheelchair. The player performs an up-step by moving the wheelchair forward, a down-step by moving backward, and left and right steps by turning the wheelchair to the left and right, respectively. Wheelchair movements are captured by a Microsoft Kinect sensor.

Balancing Parameters and Approaches

We implemented three balancing approaches that varied in perceptibility and interaction with game's mechanics and adapted parameters addressing game accessibility guidelines by Yuan et al. [24]. Each balancing approach varies features three game parameters. (1) *Step count*. Each step is associated with a specific time in the song at which it must be performed and coincides with a beat. Nine step charts were created for each song – the first step chart contains a large number of steps, and each successive chart removes a constant number of steps from the previous chart. (2) *Hit interval*. Steps must coincide with the moment when the arrow hits the stationary target. The timing window around this moment can be adjusted, giving players more or less time to obtain full points for performing the correct move. (3) *Score multiplier*. The number of points awarded for steps of varying quality can be changed to increase or decrease the final score. By varying these parameters, we created three balancing approaches.

Input Balancing. Input balancing uses a different step chart for each player. In order to account for score discrepancies resulting from fewer total steps, the score multiplier is also adjusted so that both players have an equal chance of obtaining the same score. Hit intervals are kept constant. Input balancing is visible to players because the interface displays fewer falling arrows for one player.

Time Balancing. Time balancing adjusts the hit interval for each player. Step count and score multiplier are kept constant. There are four possible results: input is too late and will not be scored, it is rather late and players will receive "okay" as feedback, it is slightly late and will be rated as "good", it is right on time and can be classified as "perfect". In the time balancing condition, we extended the time interval during which input would be recognized as "perfect" to give the weaker player an advantage, but we did not adapt the overall interval during which input was recognized. Time balancing is most hidden from players.

Score Balancing. Score balancing sets individual score multipliers for each player. Step count and hit interval are kept constant. Balancing is hidden from players in the sense that in-game challenge appears to be similar. However, it may become apparent when players compare their scores.

STUDY 1: BALANCING FOR ABLE-BODIED PLAYERS

In the first study, we examined the effectiveness of the balancing approaches, and explored how player balancing affected player experience, self-esteem, and relatedness.

Balancing Conditions

In addition to the input, time, and score balancing approaches described previously, we also included a control condition, i.e., no balancing, and a sedentary condition, i.e., no balancing, played with a game pad.

Participants and Procedure

The experiment was conducted in a university laboratory; the game was presented on a 42 inch flat-screen. 34 students (24 female, mean age=25.24 years, SD=4.79) participated in the study. 58.7% of the participants indicated that they play games at least a few times per month; 47% were experienced with the gamepad, 55% with a dance mat. Dyads were composed of friends and acquaintances.

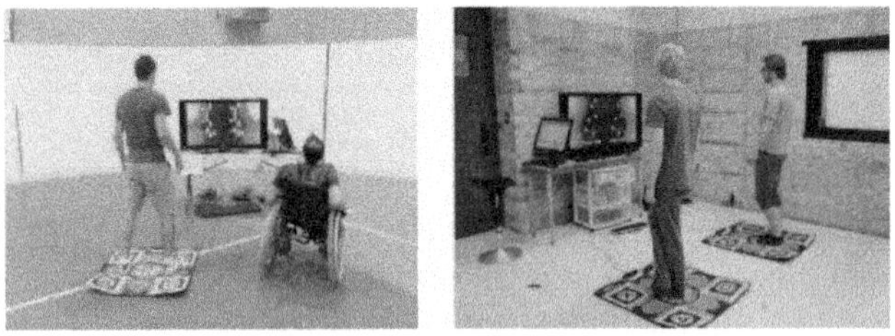

Figure 2. Study setup for able-bodied players and players in wheelchairs (left) and able-bodied dyads (right).

After providing informed consent, one participant completed an introductory questionnaire about their current affective state, while the other participant completed an ability pretest in a separate room. They then switched roles. The ability pretest was comprised of a training song followed by an assessment sequence of increasing difficulty and speed, and was scored by the number of completed moves. The score differential between the two players that resulted from this ability test determined the amount of balancing applied in the main part of the experiment. In addition, the score differential was used to set group values for step count in the control condition. Participants were not informed about their performance relative to their partner. During the main part of the experiment, participants played the game together in each of the five balancing conditions. Each condition was comprised of three songs (consistent across conditions and participating dyads) resulting in six minutes of play per condition. The order of presentation of the motion-based conditions was balanced using a Latin square. The sedentary condition was presented first for half of the participants and last for the other half, to avoid switching controllers multiple times during the experiment. After each condition the participants completed questionnaires assessing their affective state, experience with the game, their self-esteem, and their perception of the balancing techniques. At the end of the experiment, participants completed a demographic questionnaire, which included questions about sex, age, and game experience.

Measures

We collected dependent measures using in-game logging and validated scales. Cronbach's-α for all constructs by conditions was acceptable (α>.693), except for relatedness in score balancing which was unacceptable (α>.392).

Performance Logging. The system logged a variety of performance measures. In our analysis, we discuss the following values: *step count*, i.e., the number of correct steps players made during gameplay, and the information on the *overall score*, i.e., the points a player achieved regardless of their step count. Overall score is used to determine the winner of the game.

Player Experience Measures. We collected a variety of measures to assess player experience. These are all validated scales that are common for assessing play experience (e.g., [3, 19]). Please see [3] for details on the scales used. We assessed emotional valence using the 5-point Positive Affect Negative Affect Schedule (PANAS) [25]. To deconstruct player experience into its underlying constructs, we employed the 5-point Player Experience of Need Satisfaction Scale (PENS) [19], which assesses five constructs: *Competence*, *Autonomy*, *Relatedness*, *Immersion*, and *Intuitive Control*.

Player Self-Perception. To assess self-esteem after play we used the Rosenberg Self-Esteem Scale (RSE) [17], which has been used in games user research before [13]. In the RSE participants are asked to rate on their agreement on ten statements using a 4-point scale ranging from 1 (strongly disagree) to 4 (strongly agree), e.g., "On the whole, I am satisfied with myself".

Data Analyses

We categorized each member of the dyad as either the weaker or stronger player, depending on his or her ability pretest score. Player experience data were analyzed per player using RM-ANOVA with balance type (input, score, time, control) as the within-subjects factor and player strength (weaker, stronger) as a between-subjects factor; performance data were analyzed per group using RM-ANOVA with balance type as the within-subjects factor. All parametric tests were performed after validating the data for assumptions of ANOVA use. Degrees of freedom were corrected using the Huynh-Feldt method, if the assumption of sphericity was not satisfied. Pairwise comparisons used the Bonferroni method. Perception data were analyzed with non-parametric tests (as described in the results section) separately for the weaker and stronger players. Significance was set at α=0.05. The sedentary condition was analyzed separately.

Results

We present results for performance, player experience and then player perceptions of game balancing.

Table 1. Means (SD) for player experience and performance data by player strength. ***Values are in thousands of points***

	Weaker Players				
	Input	Score	Time	Unbalanced	Sedentary
	mean *(SD)*	mean *(SD)*	mean *(SD)*	mean *(SD)*	mean *(SD)*
Self-Esteem	29.88(2.83)	32.76(3.61)	31.76(3.93)	31.18(4.93)	30.35(4.43)
Competence	3.41(0.79)	3.49(0.94)	3.65(0.84)	3.55(0.93)	3.59(0.86)
Autonomy	3.04(0.85)	3.02(0.92)	2.96(0.89)	2.76(0.96)	3.18(0.57)
Relatedness	3.25(0.86)	3.33(0.63)	3.27(0.6)	3.25(0.66)	3.27(0.58)
Immersion	2.85(0.9)	2.91(0.88)	2.84(0.86)	2.84(0.91)	2.96(0.67)
Control	3.59(0.89)	3.71(0.83)	3.63(0.87)	3.65(0.98)	3.39(0.81)
Neg. Affect	1.35(0.37)	1.42(0.45)	1.46(0.46)	1.44(0.46)	1.63(0.53)
Pos. Affect	3.35(0.77)	3.46(0.73)	3.19(0.87)	3.19(0.93)	3.22(0.66)
Score* (m)	11.6(2.5)	12.2(2.8)	9.7(3.1)	7.7(3.3)	10.1(2.5)
Hits (m)	106.7 (36.5)	111.7 (37.7)	118.9 (32.3)	109.1 (37.4)	139.7 (20.8)
	Stronger Player				
Self-Esteem	29.94(4.15)	31(5.92)	31.71(5.68)	31.76(6.13)	32(4.46)
Competence	3.67(0.79)	3.78(0.68)	3.82(0.71)	3.88(0.6)	4.14(0.5)
Autonomy	3.27(0.86)	3.33(0.75)	3.35(0.79)	3.31(0.78)	3.35(0.84)
Relatedness	3.27(0.78)	3.61(0.62)	3.43(0.72)	3.45(0.73)	3.45(0.7)
Immersion	3.19(0.69)	3.05(0.69)	3.06(0.72)	3.09(0.78)	3.05(0.82)
Control	3.73(0.71)	3.84(0.59)	3.94(0.6)	3.98(0.64)	4.06(0.79)
Neg. Affect	1.31(0.32)	1.38(0.46)	1.21(0.24)	1.42(0.57)	1.18(0.2)
Pos. Affect	3.03(0.94)	3.02(0.85)	3.14(0.86)	3.28(0.86)	3.19(0.89)
Score* (m)	12.6(2.5)	11.8(2.5)	11.0(2.8)	9.1(3.6)	11.5(1.8)
Hits (m)	132.3(41.8)	118.8(34.2)	123.4(30.8)	119.6(34.7)	150.2(10.6)

Performance and Outcome

Did balancing approach affect performance? A RM-ANOVA on the score differential (calculated as the difference between the sum of each player's scores over the three songs in a single balancing condition) and the step count differential (calculated in a similar fashion for step count) revealed that balancing type changed both score differential ($F_{1.94, 31.11}$=4.50, p=.020, η^2=.22) and step count differential ($F_{1.69,27.1}$=11.61, p≈.000, η^2=.42). Pairwise comparisons show that input balancing – which balanced the number of arrows given to participants – yielded a greater step count differential than the other three approaches (score, p=.012; time, p=.009; control, p=.018). In terms of the resulting score differential, time balancing resulted in a lower score differential than input (p=.011) or score (p=.033) balancing. There were no other differences.

Did the balancing approach change the outcome (win/lose)? We counted the number of songs won by each player for each balancing type (range: 0-3). A Friedman test showed that the number of songs won by the weaker player was different across the balancing types (χ^2_3=16.7, p=.001). Pairwise Wilcoxon tests showed that a greater number of games were won by the weaker player with score balancing (30/51) than input (15/51, p=.002), time (17/51, p=.008), or no balancing (14/51, p=.008).

As Figure 3 shows, compared to the control (no balancing), the time balancing resulted in more wins by the weaker player (more blue bars), but closer games (more lower bars), however, the score approach resulted in many wins by the weaker player with the weaker player greatly outscoring the stronger.

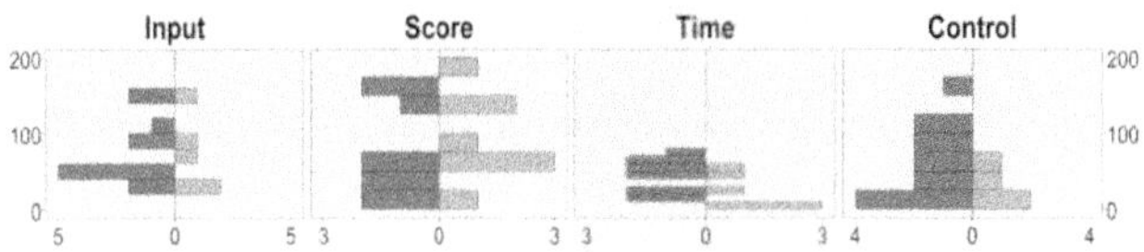

Figure 3. Histograms for score differential (y-axis x10^2). Green bars are wins by weaker player; blue bars are wins by stronger players. Lower bars show a smaller score differential and higher bars show a higher score differential

Player Self-Esteem

Did balancing type affect post-play self-esteem? There was a main effect of balance type on self-esteem ($F_{3,96}$=9.10, p≈.000, η^2=.22). Pairwise comparisons showed that input balancing resulted in lower ratings of self-esteem than score (p≈.000), time (p=.001), or no (p=.018) balancing. However, a significant interaction with player strength ($F_{3,96}$=2.87, p=.040, η^2=.08) revealed that the input approach resulted in lower self-esteem than score (p≈.000) or time (p=.021) approaches for weaker players but only the time (p=.036) approach for stronger players (see Table 1).

Player Experience

Did balance approach affect the player experience? There was a main effect on relatedness ($F_{3,96}$=2.70, p=.050, η^2=.08). Pairwise tests showed that score balancing resulted in slightly higher relatedness than input balancing, although this comparison failed to reach statistical significance (Bonferroni-corrected p=.052). There were no other significant main effects of balance type or player strength.

There was a significant balance type by player strength interaction on increase in positive affect ($F_{3,96}$=4.10, p=.009, η^2=.11) showing that score balancing resulted in a bigger increase in positive affect than time balancing for weaker players (p=.037), but not stronger players (p≈1.00).

Player Perception of Balancing

Was balancing perceived? We asked players to report after each balancing condition on whether or not one of the players had been given assistance (for frequencies see Table 2). In general, players assumed that balancing had not been applied. Chi-squared tests show that this position was significant for weaker players for score balancing and no balancing and for stronger players in time balancing.

Table 2. Frequencies per balancing type. Grey rows: choice that balancing was *not* applied (/17). White rows: choice of who was stronger player (me, no difference, my partner; /17).

	Input			Score			Time			Control		
	N	χ^2	*p*	*N*	χ^2	*p*	*N*	χ^2	*p*	*N*	χ^2	*p*
Weaker	12	2.88	.090	13	4.77	.029	12	2.88	.090	14	7.12	.008
Stronger	11	1.47	.225	10	0.53	.467	14	7.12	.008	12	2.88	.090
Weaker	2,2,13	14.2	.001	4,5,8	1.53	.465	3,4,10	5.06	.080	2,2,12	12.5	.002
Stronger	12,0,5	2.88	.090	6,6,5	1.53	.943	8,5,4	1.53	.465	13,1,3	14.6	.001

How did players perceive their relative performance? After each balancing condition, we asked players to choose who was the stronger player: themselves, their partner, or neither. Chi-squared tests showed that weaker players thought their partner was stronger when input balancing or no balancing was used. Stronger players thought that they were the better player with no balancing (see Table 2).

How did players feel about beating or losing to their partner? We asked players to rate their agreement with the statement "I tried my best to beat the other player" and Competing against the other person made me feel guilty". Friedman tests showed no differences in both questions for either the weaker or stronger players (see Table 3). Interview results show that players were comfortable competing against their friends. When reflecting upon situations in which they would feel uncomfortable winning and consider letting another person win, many players referred to young children, a player group with largely different abilities. Additionally, player statements suggest that dyads usually were aware of each other's physical abilities, and had expectations of who would win a game.

Table 3. Means (SD) for agreement on a 5-point scale (1=strongly disagree, 5=strongly agree), and Friedman tests.

		Input	Score	Time	Control	Friedman
Tried Best	Weaker	3.8 (.73)	3.7 (.92)	3.8 (1.1)	3.6 (1.0)	χ^2=3.00, p=.392
	Stronger	3.7 (.77)	3.7 (.92)	4.0 (.61)	3.8 (.88)	χ^2=3.84, p=.279
Feel Guilty	Weaker	1.9 (.86)	1.7 (.69)	1.8 (.81)	1.6 (.62)	χ^2=3.44, p=.329
	Stronger	2.1 (.75)	1.8 (.64)	1.8 (.75)	2.1 (1.2)	χ^2=2.35, p=.503

Results for Balancing the Sedentary Game

Performance. The ability pretest was based on the motion-based version of the game, so we first looked to see whether there were performance differences between the control and sedentary conditions. Paired-samples t-tests showed no difference in the score differential (t_{16}=1.46, p=.886) or number of songs won by the weaker player (t_{16}=0, p=1.00).

Self-Esteem and Player Experience. We conducted a RM-ANOVA on all experience measures with player strength as a between-subjects factor. There was no effect of controller ($F_{1,32}$=0.15, p=.697), or interaction of controller and player strength ($F_{1,32}$=0.50, p=.484) on self-esteem. There was an interaction of controller and player strength on negative affect increase ($F_{1,32}$=7.5, p=.010, η^2=.19), showing that the weaker players had negative affect drop more in the motion-based condition than the sedentary condition, whereas the stronger players displayed the opposite pattern. There were no other differences.

Perception of Balancing. When asked to report on whether assistance was provided to a player, weaker players chose 'no' a significant percentage of the time in both the control (14/17, χ^2_1=7.12, p=.008) and sedentary (14/17, χ^2_1=7.12, p=.008) conditions, whereas stronger players chose 'no' more in the sedentary (16/17, χ^2_1=13.2, p=.000) condition, but not significantly so in the control (12/17, χ^2_1=2.9, p=.090) condition. When asked to report on who was the stronger player, weaker players chose their partner significantly more in both (control: 12/17, sedentary: 11/17) conditions, and stronger players chose themselves significantly more in both (control: 13/17, sedentary: 13/17) conditions. Chi-squared tests show that these choices are all significant (all p<0.029). When asked to report on whether they tried their best to beat the other player, controller made no difference in the ratings for weaker (χ^2=1.6, p=.107) or stronger (χ^2=0.5, p=.603) players. When asked to report on whether they felt guilty competing against the other player, controller made no difference for the stronger players (χ^2=0.9, p=.366); however, weaker players felt less guilty in the motion-based game (mean=1.59, SD=0.62) than in the sedentary game (mean=2.06, SD=0.66) (χ^2=2.3, p=.021).

Summary for Sedentary Interaction

The use of motion-based or sedentary controls made little difference to how balancing affected play. It is interesting that weaker players felt less guilty competing against their partner when using the motion-based controls (where they were at a disadvantage) than the sedentary controls (where any disadvantage was not related to physical ability).

Summary of Findings for Study 1

Our experiment showed a variety of differences between the balancing approaches. **Input balancing** best balanced step count, which is not surprising because fewer arrows were presented, thus it was more likely that the arrows would be hit. However, input balancing was a visible approach, making the difference in ability between the participants explicit, and it negatively affected the weaker participants' feelings of self-esteem and of their own performance compared to their partner's. This visible approach also negatively affected the stronger player in terms of reduced self-esteem and the dyad in general in terms of reduced feelings of relatedness (note that Cronbach's-α for score balancing relatedness was low). **Time balancing** best balanced the score differential (i.e., brought the score closest), but did not result in more games actually won by the weaker player. This was the least visible method and least perceived by stronger players. Time balancing also had good effects on self-esteem for both the weaker and stronger players. **Score balancing** resulted in more games won by the weaker player; however, score balancing may have overbalanced the game in that it not only resulted in more games won by the weaker player, but also the highest score differential, where the weaker player often outscored the stronger player. This resulted in higher self-esteem and higher positive affect for the weaker player, likely due in part to the fact that score balancing was the least perceived balancing approach for weaker players.

In Study 1, the players had different physical abilities in terms of fitness and ability to interact with the game; however, these differences were not drastic. Both participants were generally healthy individuals able to participate in the game. Had one member of the dyad been physically unfit due to injury, health, or general wellness, the effects of balancing may have been different. To investigate the situation where two members of a dyad playing an exergame have vastly different physical abilities, we conducted a second study where one member of the dyad had a mobility disability and was using a wheelchair.

STUDY 2: BALANCING ABLE-BODIED PLAYERS AND PLAYERS WITH MOBILITY DISABILITIES

In the second study, we investigate whether motion-based games can be balanced in a way that provides an enjoyable experience for people with extreme differences in physical ability. Based on the findings from Study 1, we created a new version of our game that combines the hidden balancing strategies (time balancing and score balancing).

Participants, Procedure, and Methods

This study was conducted in conjunction with the Canadian Paraplegic Association's wheelchair relay, an annual family sports event. Four dyads of people using wheelchairs and an able-bodied friend (mean age=34, 5 male) participated. All play video games; 4 had dance mat experience. After providing informed consent (one dyad consented to use only their interview data), participants completed a questionnaire about their affective state and self-esteem, followed by the ability pretest. Participants then played two songs in the game using the combined balancing approach, followed by a post-play questionnaire. Observations and interviews provided qualitative data. Measures were the same as in Study 1, except that emotion was assessed using the shorter Self Assessment Manikin (SAM) [4].

Results

Because of the small number of participants, we do not make statistical comparisons between the groups.

Playability

Was the game suitable for people using wheelchairs? Yes. Players using wheelchairs scored between 5662 and 8163 points per song. Observations suggested that wheelchair game controls were intuitive. We observed a wide range of interaction styles, with some players moving the wheelchair in a slow, careful way, and others trying to keep up with the pacing of the game. Feedback suggests that the type of assistive device may have influenced the way players interacted, *"if I had my sports wheelchair, I would just have to move my arms for the side turns."* (G1).

Are there performance differences between persons using wheelchairs and able-bodied players? Although players using wheelchairs were able to participate, their able-bodied opponent generally outscored them. We compared results to the mean score (10600) from Study 1. One-sample t-tests show that players using a wheelchair had a lower score (mean=7061, SE=737, t_2=4.80, p=.041) than the able-bodied participants in Study 1, but the scores for able-bodied players show no differences (mean=10292, SE=2324, t_2=0.13, p=.907). In one pair, the players scored the same number of points in the pre-test, so no balancing was applied.

Player Experience

Are there any differences in the experience of persons using wheelchairs and able-bodied players? We performed one-sample t-tests separately for able-bodied players and participants using wheelchairs against the neutral rating for PENS data (3), see Figure 4. The results yield no significant differences for able-bodied players, but wheelchair users showed heightened satisfaction of autonomy (t_2=8, p=.008), relatedness (t_2=3.464, p=.037), enjoyment (t_2=8.5, p=.007), and competence (mean=4.0, t not computed because SD=0). This is supported by statements showing that players enjoyed how the game integrated the wheelchair, with one stating that *"it is nice to see my wheelchair in the game instead of being an object that stands between me and the world"* (G2, person using wheelchair).

How did players feel about competing against a person with different physical abilities? Player feedback on competing against a person with radically different abilities suggests that balanced competition is not only beneficial for the experience of the player with a mobility disability, but also affects the able-bodied participant. Players using wheelchairs generally did not seem to mind losing to the able-bodied person, stating that *"[Competing against an able-bodied person is] fine, doesn't really bother me cause it was fun so it was cool beans"* (G2, person in wheelchair), and that *"I didn't care if I was losing or winning, I never played the game before"* (G4, person using wheelchair). In contrast, only one able-bodied person stated that she felt *"comfortable competing with a person in a wheelchair."* (G1, able-bodied person). Other able-bodied participants were concerned about the fairness of competition: *"I don't think it is fair. We don't seem to be on an equal playing*

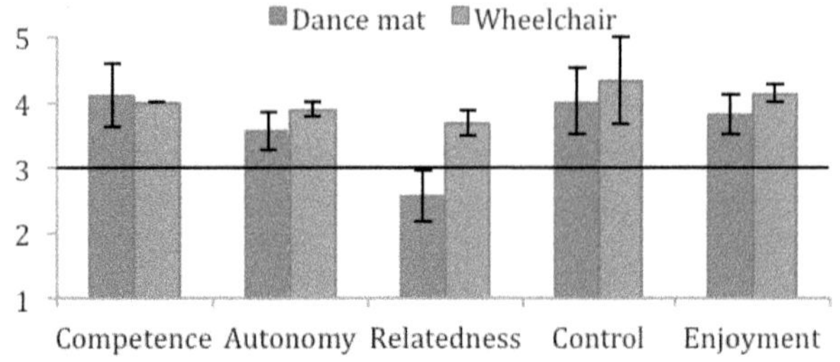

Figure 4. Mean (±SE) scores for Study 2 by input device. The line represents a neutral response.

field." (G4, able-bodied person), and the impact of their physical abilities, claiming that they *"felt bad that [the player using the wheelchair] did such a good job and I still beat him"* (G2, able-bodied person). This reinforces comments from Study 1 where participants mentioned that beating certain groups of people that differed radically in ability (e.g., young children) would not be acceptable. The expected level of physical abilities plays a role in the experience of the stronger participant; however, it is likely that an experienced player who uses a wheelchair could be stronger than their able-bodied opponent using a dance mat.

Interestingly, one able-bodied participant (G4) who claimed that she felt uncomfortable winning against her partner in the motion-based game pointed out that competition would be *"completely fair if we were playing on a hand-held"*, suggesting that skill differences as a result of practice are acceptable, but differences in physical abilities as a result of a disability that lead to different in-game scores are not. Finally, one participant pointed out that she had lower expectations of winning, stating that she *"didn't expect to do really well, he's an athlete"* (G3, person using wheelchair). In addition, she noted that she'd been more competitive with another person in wheelchair, saying that if she *"was competing with someone else in a chair, I may have felt bad losing"*, suggesting that she does not perceive an able-bodied person a contender she could beat.

Summary of Findings for Study 2

Our game was accessible to people using wheelchairs, and they enjoyed playing. Experience ratings and feedback show that people using wheelchairs enjoy the integration of their assistive device into the game. However, performance differences within dyads show that balancing needs to be increased to bridge score gaps. Although players using wheelchairs did not mind losing to the able-bodied player, able-bodied persons felt uncomfortable beating a person with a disability; therefore, balancing is not only important to empower the weaker player, but also to improve the experience of the stronger player.

DISCUSSION

The work presented in this paper investigates balancing strategies for co-located motion-based games with a focus on the effects of player performance, experience, and self-esteem. In Study 1, we showed differences in player experience depending on whether the balancing strategies were explicit or hidden; in Study 2, we included people with mobility disabilities in competition, and outlined how player experience is affected by extreme differences in player abilities. In this section, we discuss our findings in the context of game design, we tie them back to findings from sports psychology, and we outline how they can be applied to design better motion-based game experiences for able-bodied people and people using wheelchairs.

Effective Balancing for Motion-Based Video Games

In this section we discuss our findings with a focus on balancing strategies for co-located motion-based games.

Choosing Suitable Balancing Approaches

Results of our study suggest that explicit input balancing – the kind of balancing commonly applied in commercially available dance games such as *Dance Dance Revolution* or *Dance Central* – poses the biggest risk in terms of player experience because it is clearly visible to both players. In contrast, hidden strategies offer the opportunity of subtly mitigating skill differences between players. Our work shows that score balancing is a suitable means of closing extreme performance gaps between players, whereas time balancing can be applied to reduce smaller differences and to account for the impact of asymmetric physical input (e.g., if one player uses a wheelchair).

Accommodating Extreme Ability Differences

Large score gaps in Study 2–despite the combined balancing approach–suggest that optimization is necessary to enable people with extreme ability difference to compete. Our observations showed that the characteristics of wheelchairs led to differences in input difficulty, causing some in-game sequences to be easier for the able-bodied player than for the player using the wheelchair (e.g., moving from a side turn into a forward motion). To optimize our approach, it is necessary to consider difficulty levels of input sequences as balancing factor: By adapting transitions between movements in a way that is suitable for players using wheelchairs (e.g., giving more time between turns), it can be adapted to their needs without affecting the game experience of able-bodied players.

The Effects of Player Differences in Skills and Abilities in Co-Located Motion-Based Games

In this section, we discuss the effects of skills, abilities and balancing on player experience and self-esteem.

Explaining the Effects of Balancing on Player Experience

The results of our studies suggest that balancing strategies for co-located motion-based games do not only affect the in-game performance of the weaker player, but extend into the experience of both members of the dyad. Locus of control theory [18] suggests that the attribution of failure and success plays a major role in how people perceive themselves. In the context of game balancing, this means that adaptation should allow players to attribute their performance to the relationship between task difficulty and their own ability. This is difficult if players are aware of game balancing: with explicit balancing, the visibility of the adaptation is likely to hinder the attribution of game success to the weaker player's abilities. Likewise, if difficulty is drastically lowered in hidden balancing scenarios, weaker players might attribute a win to a source outside of their control. At the same time, the stronger player can attribute a loss to the software support of the weaker player. If the stronger player is able to beat a supported player, additional challenge might increase the value of a win, while also introducing guilt. Our results also show that the weaker player has a negative experience when aware of assistance, yet unable to beat the stronger player. Hindering the stronger player introduces a similar problem by allowing for outcome attribution to his or her lowered ability.

Explaining the Effects of Balancing on Self Esteem

The results of Study 1 suggest that players are aware of skill differences between themselves and the other player, that they have an intuitive understanding of their own physical abilities, and that they are able to perceive game balancing under certain circumstances. People constantly compare themselves with others to estimate their own abilities in a social context [14]. The effect of balancing mechanisms is intertwined with the process of social comparison by artificially equalizing skill differences and making an initial estimate meaningless. In Study 1, self-esteem is conceptualized as a state variable, and measured depending on balancing approach. The underlying assumption is that people update themselves in comparison with a self-standard: if actual performance differs too much from expected performance, self-esteem and well-being are threatened. This explains how balancing mechanisms affect self-esteem and player experience of interdependent dyads by narrowing a natural gap of ability.

Understanding the Effects of Perceived Ability Differences

Our results show that perceived differences in player abilities and expectations regarding player performance play a role in the experience of both weaker and stronger players. This is particularly interesting in the context of balancing dyads with extreme ability differences. When comparing Study 1 and Study 2, there seems to be a shift in player expectations and experience: Our results suggest that persons with disabilities have lower expectations regarding their performance, leading to a positive experience even when losing. Able-bodied players perceive the same ability differences, and report negative emotions despite winning against the person using a wheelchair. We believe that this difference in the evaluation of the outcome of competition may be caused by the extreme difference in abilities and general perceptions of persons with disabilities: if, in the eyes of the able-bodied person, the player using the wheelchair never had a chance of winning, this reduces the value of their victory and may induce feelings of guilt.

Ability Differences and the Risk of Overbalancing

The previous sections have addressed the effects of balancing on player experience and self-esteem, and how perceived ability differences affect competition if performance gaps cannot be closed in a suitable way. However, designers also need to consider the risk of overbalancing. If games are overbalanced and give a large advantage to the weaker player, this may affect the player experience of the stronger participant (as demonstrated by results for score balancing in Study 1). Interestingly, this is in line with discussions related to the participation of persons with disabilities in sports tournaments directed towards able-bodied participants, where some athletes claimed that certain assistive devices lead to an unfair advantage [6]. This suggests that balancing intensity needs to be adapted carefully to strike an acceptable balance between enabling the weaker player to win while allowing the stronger player to experience in-game competence. From a cognitive perspective, it is important that the gap closed by adaptation is reasonable and accepted by both players; only then it is possible for players to develop positive relationships and have rewarding experiences.

LIMITATIONS AND FUTURE WORK

There are several limitations and opportunities for future work. To study the long-term effects of ability differences and balancing strategies on player experience – particularly when able-bodied persons and persons with disabilities compete against each other – a longitudinal study would be necessary. Additionally, participants in Study 1 were asked to bring a friend. In a follow-up, it would be interesting to control for the kind of relationship to investigate the effect, e.g., if romantic partners or parents and children play together. Studying a broader range of able-bodied players and players using wheelchairs would provide insights into how physical abilities affect competition and experience. Studying the effects of disabilities beyond the use of manual wheelchairs would be valuable, e.g., whether users of power wheelchairs could play the game, either in a motion-based or in a sedentary setting using the joystick of their wheelchair as input device. Finally, there are aspects related to the impact of player performance on player experience that have not yet been explored. For instance, facing challenges (e.g., competing with a stronger opponent) may at first result in negative affect, but release a strong positive influence once the challenge is overcome. Such time-dynamics are very hard to predict but might play an important role and have not yet been investigated.

CONCLUSION

Developing suitable balancing strategies for co-located motion-based games is an important step to mitigate negative effects of player performance on player experience and self-esteem, enabling players of different abilities to engage in playful competition. In this paper, we demonstrate the effects of explicit and hidden balancing strategies, and we provide insights into the application of balancing strategies to bridge extreme ability gaps between players. By keeping motion-based game controls accessible for persons with different levels of physical abilities – including people with wheelchairs – co-located motion-based games can be a means of motivating physical activity among broad audiences. Additionally, such games may have other benefits: joint play between able-bodied persons and persons with disabilities can help provide empowering experiences for both players, and contribute to the development of inclusive motion-based games.

ACKNOWLEDGMENTS

We thank the Canadian Paraplegic Association for supporting our research, and the participants for their contribution during the evaluation phase. We thank all of our CHI reviewers for their helpful comments and NSERC and the GRAND NCE for funding.

REFERENCES

1. Adams, E. *Fundamentals of Game Design*. Berkeley: New Riders, 2010.
2. Bateman, S., Mandryk, R.L., Stach, T., and Gutwin, C. Target Assistance for Subtly Balancing Competitive Play. In: *Proc. of CHI 2011*, ACM (2011), 2355-2364.
3. Birk, M. & Mandryk, R.L. Control Your Game-Self: Effects of Controller Type on Enjoyment, Motivation, and Personality in Game. In: *Proc. of CHI 2013*, ACM (2013), 685-694.
4. Bradley, M.M. and Lang, P.J. Measuring emotion: the self assessment manikin and the semantic differential. *Journal of Behavior Therapy and Experimental Psychiatry* 25, 1 (1994), 49–59.
5. Cairney, J., Kwan, M.Y.W., Veldhuizen, S., Hay, J., Bray, S.R., and Faught, B.E. Gender, perceived competence and the enjoyment of physical education in children: a longitudinal examination. *Int Journal of Behavioral Nutrition and Physical Activity* 9, 26 (2012).
6. Epstein, D. Fair or foul? Experts split over whether Pistorius has advantage. Available at http://sportsillustra ted.cnn.com/2012/olympics/2012/writers/david_epstein/ 08/03/oscar-pistorius-london-olympics/index.html, last access: 10/09/13.
7. Gerling, K.M., Kalyn, M.R., and Mandryk, R.L. KINECTWheels: Wheelchair-Accessible Motion-Based Game Interaction. In: *EA of CHI 2013*, ACM (2013).
8. Gerling, K.M., Mandryk, R.L., and Kalyn, M.R. Wheelchair-Based Game Design for Older Adults. In: *Proc. of ASSETS 2013*, ACM (2013).
9. Goni, A. and Zulaika, L. Relationships Between Physical Education Classes and the Enhancement of Fifth Grade Pupils' Self-Concept. *Perceptual and Motor Skills* 91, (2000), 246-250.
10. Hernandez, H.A., Ye, Z., Graham, T.C.N., Fehlings, D., and Switzer, L. Designing Action-based Exergames for Children with Cerebral Palsy. *Proc. of CHI 2013*, ACM (2013).
11. Höysniemi, J. International Survey on the Dance Dance Revolution Game. *Comp in Entertainment* 4, 2 (2006).
12. IPC. *Paralympic Classification*. Available at http://www.paralympic.org/Classification/Introduction/, last access: 21/08/2013.
13. Jung, Y., Li, K. J., Janissa, N. S., Gladys, W. L. C., & Lee, K. M. Games for a better life: effects of playing Wii games on the well-being of seniors in a long-term care facility. In: *Proc. of IE '09,* (2009), 5.
14. Leary, M. R., Tambor, E. S., Terdal, S. K., & Downs, D. L. Self-esteem as an interpersonal monitor: The sociometer hypothesis. *Journal of personality and social psychology* 68, 3 (1995), 518.
15. Mueller, F., Vetere, F., Gibbs, M.R., Edge, D., Agamanolis, S., Sheridan, J.G., and Heer, J. Balancing Exertion Experiences. *Proc. of CHI 2012*, ACM (2012).
16. Ninot, G., Billard, J., and Delignières, D. Effects of integrated or segregated sport participation on the physical self for adolescents with intellectual disabilities. *Journal of Intellectual Disability Research* 49, 9 (2005), 682-689.
17. Rosenberg, M. (1965). *Society and the adolescent self-image*. Princeton, NJ: Princeton University Press.
18. Rotter, J. B. (1975). Some problems and misconceptions related to the construct of internal versus external control of reinforcement. *Journal of consulting and clinical psychology* 43, 1 (1975), 56.
19. Ryan, R. M., Rigby, C. S., Przybylski, A. K. Motivational pull of video games: A self-determination theory approach. *Motivation and Emotion* 30, (2006).
20. Sinclair, J., Hingston, P., and Masek, M. Exergame development using the dual flow model. In: *Proc. of IE '09*, ACM (2009).
21. Stach, T., Graham, N., Yim, J., and Rhodes, R.E. Heart Rate Control of Exercise Video Games. In: *Proc. of GI 2009*, ACM (2009), 125-132.
22. Swartz, T.B. A New Handicapping System for Golf. *Journal of Quantitative Analysis in Sports* 5, 2 (2009).
23. Yim, J. and Graham, T.C.N. Using Games to Increase Exercise Motivation. *Proc. of FuturePlay 2007*, ACM (2007), 166-173.
24. Yuan, B., Folmer, E., Harris Jr., F.C. Game Accessibility: a Survey. *Univ Access Inf Soc* 10, 1 (2011), 81-100.
25. Watson, D., & Clark, L. A. *The PANAS-X: Manual for the positive and negative affect schedule-Expanded Form*. Iowa City: University of Iowa (1994).

Supporting the Creative Game Design Process with Exertion Cards

Florian 'Floyd' Mueller[1] **Martin R. Gibbs**[2] **Frank Vetere**[2] **Darren Edge**[3]
[1]Exertion Games Lab, RMIT University, Melbourne, Australia
[2]Computing & Information Systems, University of Melbourne, Melbourne, Australia
[3]Microsoft Research, Beijing, China
floyd@exertiongameslab.org, {martin.gibbs, f.vetere}unimelb.edu.au, darren.edge@microsoft.com

ABSTRACT
Advances in sensing technologies have led to research into exertion games that support physically effortful experiences. Despite the existence of theoretical frameworks that can be used to analyze such exertion experiences, there are few tools to support the hands-on practice of exertion game design. To address this, we present a set of design cards based on the "Exertion Framework", grounded in our experience of creating exertion games for over a decade. We present results demonstrating the value and utility of these Exertion Cards based on our studies of their use in three workshops held over seven sessions with 134 design students and experts. We also articulate lessons learned from transforming a theoretical framework into a design tool that aims to support designers in their practice.

Author Keywords
Exergame; whole-body interaction; exertion interface; creative process; design cards; workshops; game design

ACM Classification Keywords
H.5.2. [Information Interfaces and Presentation]: User Interfaces - Miscellaneous.

INTRODUCTION
There has been a recent trend in HCI that places the human body at the center of the user experience, fostering "exertion"-based interactions that require intense physical effort from users [18]. Computer games currently provide a growing range of exertion systems, with the Microsoft Kinect, Nintendo Wii and Sony Move, along with virtual reality exercise bikes [16], mobile games fueled by exercise [5, 14] and our own systems [17, 18, 20, 21] populating a design space that highlights the potential of such mediated exertion experiences. Researching these games is important, as they can offer mental and social benefits, as well as benefits to physical health [13]. Research has previously highlighted a limited theoretical understanding of these exertion experiences [7, 9]. In response, we developed the "Exertion Framework" [19] – a systematic conceptual understanding of the ways in which the body engages in exertion experiences as well as the ways in which interactive technologies can support such experiences.

However, our Exertion Framework, like so many other HCI frameworks [11], can be criticized for not offering "step-by-step guidance" for designers and hence not lending itself to support the designer's creative process [11]. We agree with Hornecker when she says that "frameworks tend to be systematic and abstract, which makes them hard to use in creative practice" [11], and the Exertion Framework can probably also be characterized by this abstract nature. Despite frameworks offering designers the ability to reason and justify design decisions, the gap between theoretical frameworks and the practical design process has long been an issue for HCI and a source of frustration for many practice-based design researchers [1, 6, 12]. Recent research has investigated how to close this gap in order to support design researchers [1, 11], with one suggested way being to turn the framework under investigation into a design tool [11]. In particular, Hornecker proposes to transform the abstract themes of a framework into colloquial questions to which designers can relate [11]. These questions are then framed in a card-based format and introduced to the design process in order to offer guidance from the themes of the framework. As evidence for the utility of this approach, she demonstrated the transformation of a tangible framework into design cards and used them in a series of workshops with positive outcomes in the form of novel design ideas [11].

We utilized a very similar approach to transform our abstract framework into a useful design tool. We opted to lean on this prior work as the conditions are comparable: the author, like us, devised her own framework, which is

CHI 2014, April 26–May 1, 2014, Toronto, Ontario, Canada.

http://dx.doi.org/10.1145/2556288.2557272

based on an embodied approach to interaction design [11], very similar to our investigations into exertion. Furthermore, both her and our work is targeted at designers of interactive technology.

More generally, our research builds on previous work on design cards and associated workshops [2, 8, 10, 15, 23]. Physical cards used to facilitate design activities have previously been shown to function as orienting devices, providing structure to the creative sessions and supporting progression from the initial starting point [11]. The physicality of the cards can help make arguments tangible during discussions, supporting focus and helping create common ground [4]. Furthermore, design cards support focus shifts, as they can be spread out and distributed amongst participants [10]. Previous research on the use of design cards for game design has also been shown to facilitate the ideation process [8, 15]. We built on this prior work and transformed the Exertion Framework into a set of design cards. As a result, our work is the first that presents design cards specific to exertion games. Our work is also the first that explicitly encourages a consideration of trade-offs among the dimensions articulated with the design cards, extending the notion of trade-off-driven design from Cognitive Dimensions (for example see [3]) to design cards. Lastly, we also examined how these design cards supported the ideation process in three workshops held over seven sessions with 134 participants. With this, we are able to provide details on the use of individual cards and insights on each card's role in the design process as well as detailed challenges when designing with cards, extending prior design card work that mostly offers a coarse view on people's experiences with using the broad themes articulated by a range of cards. With this approach, we aim to offer designers of future cards structured guidance on the design of each individual card.

THE EXERTION FRAMEWORK

The Exertion Framework [19] consists of four lenses through which exertion can be examined. These lenses, conceptualized as concentric, onion-like layers, offer different perspectives through which to examine a set of themes, or "things to think about". The lenses are: The Responding Body (how the body's internal state changes over time as a result of exertion, e.g. heart rate), the Moving Body (how body parts are muscularly repositioned relative to one another), the Sensing Body (how the body is sensing and experiencing the world) and the Relating Body (how bodies and people relate to one another). These four lenses provide different perspectives on each of six cross-cutting exertion themes: uncertainty of exertion; awareness of exertion; expression of exertion; rhythm of exertion; risk of exertion; and understanding of exertion [19].

Turning the framework into design cards

Prior work presented the usefulness of transforming a framework into design cards, but does not describe a process of how to turn a framework into design cards [11]. We therefore constructed our own process, but we were guided by her examples as well as our own experiences of using the framework in our practice of designing exertion games for over a decade. The goal was to turn the framework's themes into colloquial, provocative questions whose purpose is to promote creative design thinking.

We also added a "dimension" to each question, which highlights that interactive qualities are not simply present or absent, but can vary in their degree from *a little* to *a lot*. For example, "uncertainty of exertion" can be supported "a little" or "a lot". Furthermore, a dimension highlights also that choosing to keep a theme at a minimum (e.g. by preventing it from occurring) is also a design decision that can have merit.

We now describe the process we created to turn the themes of the Exertion Framework into design cards. This process is not the only way to turn themes into cards, nor has it been validated beyond our own work. Nevertheless, we structure it via groupings that we believe might be useful for others when orienting themselves to a similar task. With this approach, we aim to extend prior work on design cards that often tends to focus on the design of theory *as* cards (for example see [11]) by providing one of the first attempts to detail the transformation of design theory *into* cards. Our process consisted of the following five stages:

Establish target boundaries

We began by establishing target boundaries, in particular, we decided to aim for a relatively small number of cards (ultimately 14) in order to minimize the chances of designers feeling overwhelmed.

Scrutinize framework

We looked at the themes of the Exertion Framework, and picked one aspect of each that related to one particular layer of the body lens. For example, for "rhythm of exertion", we selected the "Relating Body". Furthermore, we also picked each lens individually to support the analysis of technology augmentation. For example, we transformed the "Responding Body" into a question about (measuring) effort.

Reduce items

In order to reach our target boundary, we focused on questions we felt could challenge game designers. This resulted in 14 questions.

Visualize

We wrote the questions on index cards and gave each design card a short and descriptive title. We also selected two pictures to represent examples of either end of the dimension. We used images that offered easy entry points into the topic while at the same time not implying any specific use. Next, we assigned a positive example to each end of the dimension to provoke the reader to consider divergent possibilities, so that a reader might ponder: "If I support a lot of this, I will foster experience X, but if I support a little, I will foster experience Y" (where Y is not simply the absence of X). For three cards, we opted to provide additional details to clarify what it would mean for participants if they would choose the middle of a dimension that has no obvious medium value: for example, we highlighted that medium intensity can mean that intensity in movement might not be interpreted by the system, but could be communicated to another person.

Incorporate feedback

After having generated all cards, we discussed the results extensively with senior researchers who gave feedback on how to improve the cards' wording and their presentation. Based on this feedback, we refined the associated examples and the card layouts several times. In addition, we discussed the cards with two fellow researchers in order to verify that the descriptions on the cards were understood even if we were not explaining them.

The cards were color coded with four different colors, one for each lens of the framework (Fig. 1). The centerpiece of each card was the question that came out of the transformation process above. These questions were meant to work on a more pragmatic level than the theoretical concepts [11]. We aimed to make the questions easily accessible in order to support the creative process rather than requiring a deep understanding of the framework. The challenge was to find a balance between abstract concepts and inspiring questions, without falling into the trap of presenting rules that suggested they needed to be followed [11]. The aim was to create questions that designers use as thought-provoking suggestions to guide their creative process. The cards are available at exertiongameslab.org.

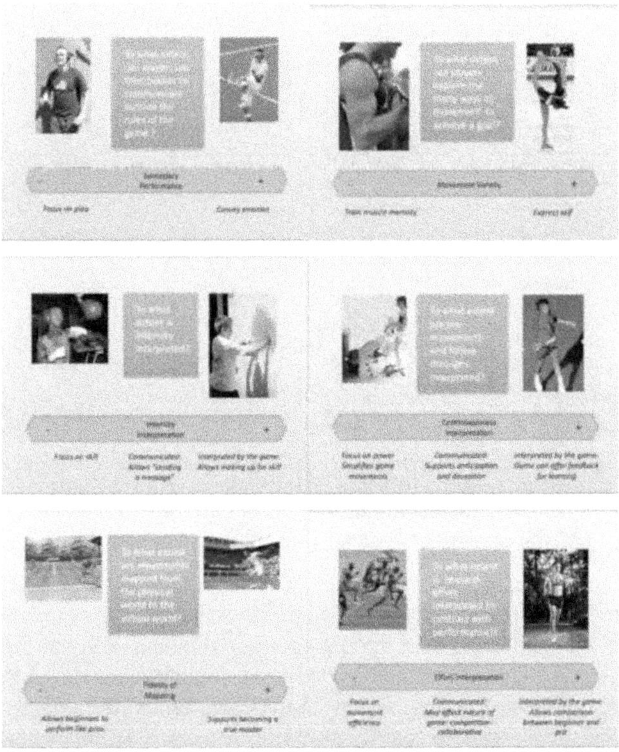

Figure 1. The Exertion Cards based on the Exertion Framework

WORKSHOPS

We decided to study the use of the design cards in workshops with designers to see how they could be incorporated into the creative design process. The purpose of this study was to demonstrate the value and utility of the design cards in designers' practice, which in turn would strengthen the argument for the usefulness of the framework. Evaluating the design cards in short (3h) workshops is of course not the same as a designer's day-to-day practice. However, previous work has also utilized workshops [8, 11, 15], suggesting that they might be a way to approximate design practice. Furthermore, a workshop with team-based design exercises is similar to the teamwork environment to which designers are often exposed. Lastly, workshops provide a tight, time-constrained format for creative teamwork, which we found similar to the environments we have encountered in our own practice.

The Workshops

We conducted three workshops, with two of them conducted over multiple sessions to accommodate large participant numbers. Workshop A and B were repeated twice and four times respectively (Table 1). The workshops were carried out across three sites, with sessions adapted to the different contexts, number of participants and room layouts. Each participant attended one session only.

Workshop	Participants (in sessions)		Context, Duration	
A x 2	**14** (8,6)	Designers & researchers from two technology companies	Conference room	3 h
B x 4	**55** (14,14, 13,14)	Design students	Design studio	3 h
C x 1	**65** (65)	Digital game design students	Classroom	3 h
Total	**134**			

Table 1. Three workshops across seven sessions with 134 participants in total.

Structure of the workshops

The three workshops had different constraints and opportunities but all shared the same structure around the cards (Fig. 2). The participants were invited with the premise they would learn about designing exertion games, and as an exercise they were asked to come up with an exertion game idea. We began each workshop by defining the term exertion game ("a digital game that requires physical effort from players" [19]). We then showed video examples of exertion games before explaining the design challenge. The goal of the workshops was for each team to design an exertion game. We did not want to confine the scope of the workshop too much, so participants could make the content applicable to their respective design practices. For example, the design students could work on a game idea that they might want to develop further in their classes.

Figure 2. Participants discussing a particular design card

Participants

In Workshop A, the 14 participants were volunteers from Microsoft Research in Beijing, China (Microsoft Research was working on the Kinect at the time). The participants' backgrounds ranged from Computer Science to HCI and Design, which is representative of the target group of the design cards. The second session was conducted in the same company, but for this session, half of the participants came from Nokia Research's team that was interested in supporting their customers' play desires. In Workshop B, 55 design students took part across four sessions that were conducted in a design studio in Australia. In workshop C, 65 students from a game design course in Australia participated in a classroom setting. This setting was less adaptable to group work, but participants were free to roam during the workshop.

Figure 3. The participants placed how they used the cards on a dimension from "a little" to "a lot". The card on the bottom indicated that it was "not useful"

Task

Each workshop lasted 3 hours. The participants were asked to form teams of around 5 people. Most sessions had teams of 4-5 members, with the remaining participants (due to the total amount of participants) forming smaller teams down to 2 members. The challenge was to design an exertion game. The goal was to come up with an original idea that participants were asked to present to their peers at the end of the workshop. Each team was asked to write down or sketch out any game ideas they might have. They were free to explore if and how the design dimensions could support them in their creative process. Once a team decided on a final design, and there was time due to the other teams still working, they were asked to mark on a large sheet of paper which design dimensions (if any) they used and how. We suggested they align the cards along a spectrum from positive to negative, with neutral in the middle. For example, if the group decided to incorporate "a lot" of "integrated communication", they attached the card to the "+" side of the paper, if they decided to include only "a little", they attached it to the "–" side. Participants were also encouraged to discard cards if they did not think they were useful for their particular task (Fig. 3).

Feedback

After the exercise, the participants were interviewed and their answers recorded. The posters they used to present their ideas and any other supporting materials they developed were also captured. Due to the size of workshop C, not all participants had a chance to provide feedback; as a result, those participants were also given the opportunity to post any comments on a dedicated website. Participants of all workshops were also given a questionnaire at the end that asked them about each card, including how useful they thought it was. Furthermore, participants were asked what their favorite card was and why. This question was designed to reveal how cards could be made most applicable to their design practice.

Data collection

We captured video for the entire participant group for each workshop. After each design exercise, the participants were interviewed per team, and their answers were video recorded per team and notes were taken. The final presentations of each team were videotaped, and any sketch and note materials were photographed. The comments on the website were captured and analyzed, as were the questionnaires. We were also interested if and how participants used the cards beyond the workshop, and therefore interviewed the participants of the workshop C two months after their workshop. 75 participants of the original workshop were available for this group interview.

Data analysis

We initiated the analysis by reading and watching all the material. Then we started the coding of the data, guided by the processes suggested by Strauss and Corbin [25]. We began by looking for all relevant mentions of design cards. This meant identifying instances that described if and how design cards were used. We also looked for any other instances that related to the cards and any themes from the framework. This included looking for evidence that pointed to the use of the cards in a way that sparked new ideas or changed existing ones. In addition, the data from the questionnaires was analyzed and visualized using a spreadsheet program. In session 2 of the first workshop we accidentally did not include the contention cards in the questionnaire. As a result, we did not generate graph plots of these two cards from the questionnaire data.

Figure 4. Skip to the Beat: augmented jump rope promoting multi-player skipping to music beats.

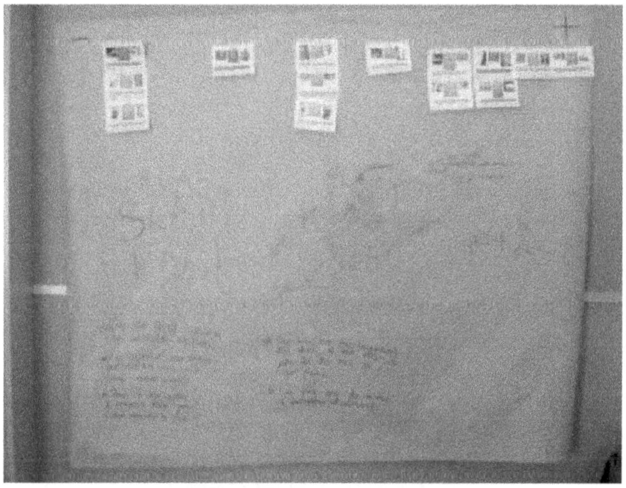

Figure 5. Virtual Slam Ball: 2-player slam ball experience with sensors in gloves and trampoline

Figure 6. Dodge ball: augmented gym that tracks and throws balls for larger group exertion experiences

RESULTS

First, we present a few of the ideas participants came up with during the sessions in order to suggest that the workshops led to creative ideas. The pictures are photographs of the posters presented, with design cards attached by participants according to their use (Fig. 4, 5, 6). Next, we will elaborate on the role of the cards on the creative process that led to these ideas.

Perceived usefulness of cards

The data from the questionnaires suggests that participants agreed with the statement that each card was useful for their design task. In particular, a majority of participants either agreed or strongly agreed to this statement in the questionnaire (Fig. 7).

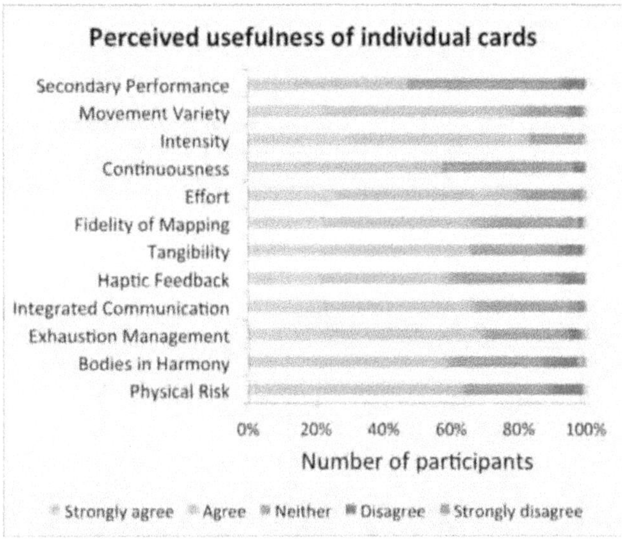

Figure 7. Likert-scale results on how useful participants found each card

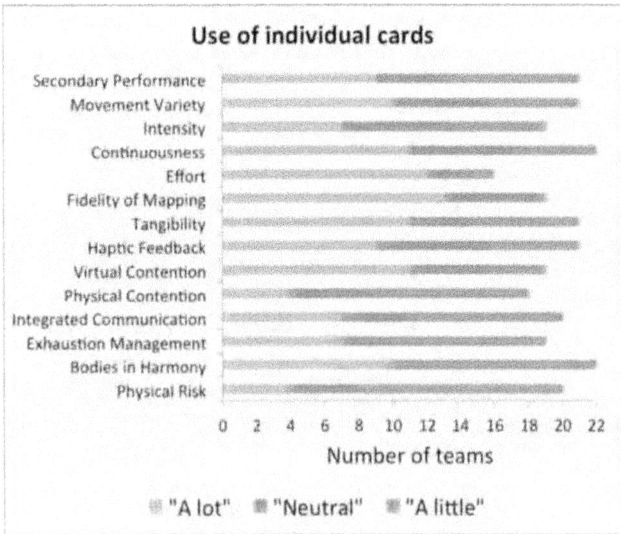

Figure 8. The placement of the cards in terms of use.

Use of individual cards

The next figures display how participants' teams used the cards for their particular design task. A typical placement of the design cards can be seen in Fig. 3. When asked to place their cards on a dimension from "a little" to "a lot" in response to how they used a particular card, the following data resulted (Fig. 8).

Participants were also asked to note or discard the cards they did not find useful (see Fig. 9). There was no card that all teams found "not useful"; this suggests that every card was useful for at least one team. Out of 22 teams who placed their cards, six teams (the highest number) found "effort interpretation" not useful.

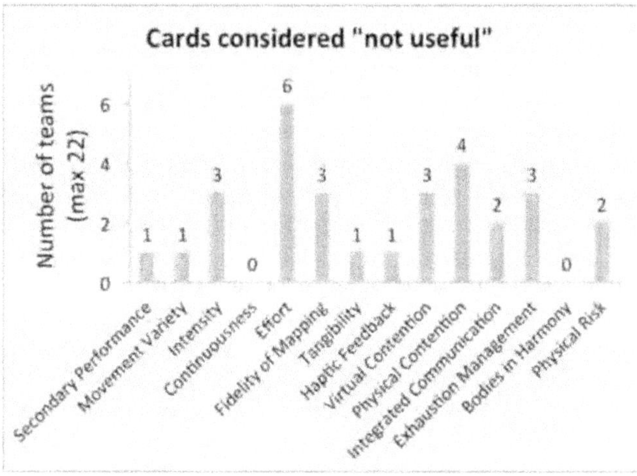

Figure 9. Cards not placed on the dimension

The majority of teams found only one to two cards not useful. The highest number of cards one team did not consider of value was 9 (see Fig. 10).

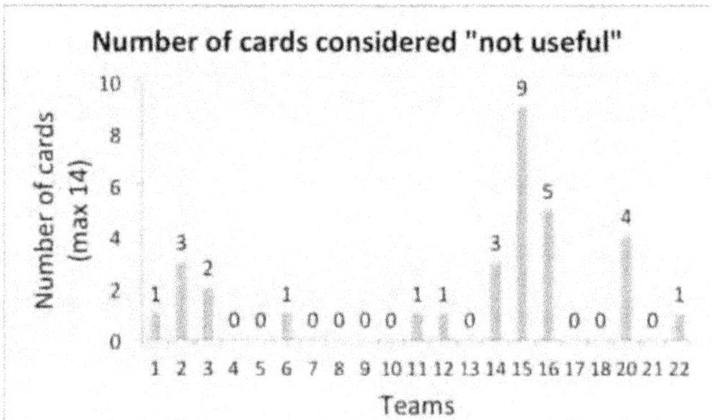

Figure 10. The amount of cards not placed on the dimension.

Role of cards

The participants were also asked at the end of the workshop what role the cards played in their design process. The data show that the cards had multiple roles. When combining "Strongly agree" and "Agree", the following list emerges with the top answer listed first. The individual composition can be seen in fig. 11.

1. The cards helped me to improve my ideas
2. I found the cards useful for generating ideas
3. The cards helped my team to focus
4. The cards helped me to articulate my ideas
5. The cards helped my team to come to a consensus/agree on items we discussed
6. I had ideas I would not have had without the cards

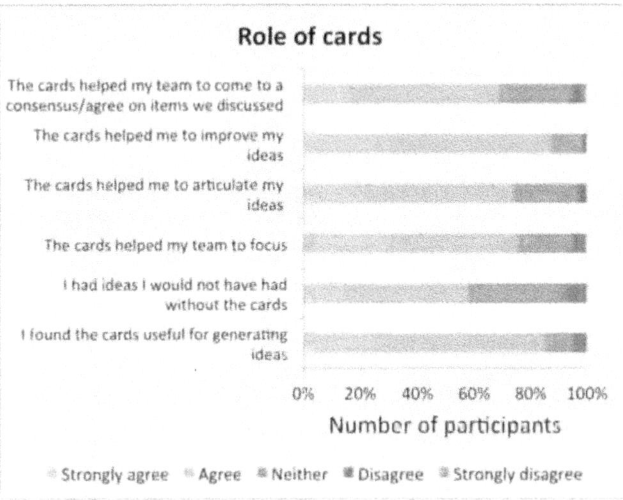

Figure 11. How participants assessed the role of cards

Through a freeform field, the questionnaire gave participants the option to note any additional roles they thought the cards played. 59 participants thought the cards had additional roles. By structuring them based on logical closeness, we derived three major additional roles. The cards helped participants to fine-tune their ideas, offered guidance for the design process, and supported expanding participants' horizons.

Cards helped fine-tune ideas

Twelve participants stated that an additional use of the cards was to fine-tune their ideas. They expressed that the cards supported them in making their idea more concrete and explicitly focused on the experience they wanted to create. A common statement was: *"The cards helped refine our ideas."*

Cards offered guidance

Six participants found that the cards offered them some guidance as a group on how to proceed with the design task: *"They are good guidelines/building blocks." "It gave our group clear direction and order, something that we sometimes lack."* The cards provided a *"framework for analysis."*

Cards expanded horizons

A strong theme was also that the cards helped to expand participants' horizon: *"It enabled our group to consider areas that we normally would not consider, like synchronization."* This resonates with another statement that appeared repeatedly: participants appreciated that the cards helped them to consider *"all aspects"* of the game, reminding them of perspectives that they otherwise might have overlooked: *"[The cards helped] generating and incorporating ideas that weren't thought of before."*

Danger of card reliance

One participant was critical in his/her comment, saying that the cards have the potential to overcomplicate the process: *"They gave a broader outlook of possibilities, however not necessarily 'better' ideas. In perspective of 'easy fun'/'hard fun' stuff, some cards may overcomplicate games for a particular audience."*

Additional results

The data coming from the video recordings and freeform fields provided additional insights detailed below.

Offering guidance

The cards offered guidance to the creative process. The participants called the design dimensions an *"easy to understand guideline for starting and refining games."* Others found that the cards helped them identify aspects of their design they had overlooked so far, further strengthening the view of the cards as a guide: *"I think the dimensions for exertion games work really well to help guide the design of a game. While our group discussed each card in reference to our game I found the dimensions helped us to work out what our game might be lacking, and what could be added to improve it."* Some participants saw the cards as tools that not only guided existing ideas, but also helped generate new ones: *"The flashcards are very useful for people such as myself, because I can never come up with an idea on the spot. The dimensions are perfect for producing further ideas to elaborate on as well as a guide."* In this sense, people used it as a tool: *"the idea of game design [is now] a whole lot deeper. Like most I found the design dimension cards to be a useful tool in improving a game."*

One participant praised the potential of the cards for industry and academia alike: *"I think that as a tool, not only to be used by game companies but also for teaching, the design dimensions are really great."* Another participant noted how the design dimensions will be useful as a guide for future games and how they will be used in his/her practice: *"I found the design dimension cards to be a useful guideline. [...] I will be referring to it from time to time, in order to analyze the quality of our next game."*

The cards offered the participants a more efficient way to reach their goals when compared to their existing methods. They praised how they generated results much quicker when using the design dimensions: *"I found the dimensions really helpful, by being aware of the elements that are in games, it makes it so much easier, faster and most likely better to come up with new games and improve existing ones. I found dimensions jump-started my thoughts in a way, that most cards got me thinking of new ideas and/or ways to improve them and got me thinking about different aspects of games that I had not considered before and now seem integral." "We obtained a lot of fresh ideas and faster than any other method I know myself. But to say that we would have never gotten these ideas without them is another thing, I think it's a time factor more than a possibility factor."*

Shifting processes

The cards helped the participants to see how they could approach the creative task in a different way. They described the use of the cards *"as an eye opener"*, helping to *"view design in a different way"*, as *"the idea of dimensions helps me think."*

One participant explained how the cards helped the group *"to rediscover what it is specifically that we want out of our game. It has given us a ground, or a foundation, from which we can mold and develop our concept"*. By having a clear goal, participants found it easier to assess their ideas: *"They're a really useful and clear way of looking at our games for refining and moving beyond 'What can we add to our game?' to 'What could we add to our game to emphasize or draw out more of a certain quality our game has or needs?'"*

Factorizing tasks

The cards helped some participants break down the creative process into individual elements that were easier to handle. Firstly, the cards enabled them to identify that there are several elements that make a successful game: *"[it made me] realize that so many factors can affect the game and make it different."*

Secondly, the cards helped participants to identify these different elements. In other words, the cards supported them in breaking down the task into individual factors: *"I did like the break down of the categories." "Say you have a job to do [...] The dimensions would help you define the different aspects of the game and what kind of rules and gameplay to include."*

Equipped with these factors, many participants felt empowered to make strategic decisions during the design task: *"What made [altering the game] easier was that the cards gave definable characteristics of exertion games, so rather than thinking 'how do I make it more physical?' we could pin point several aspects of the game and the 'player experience', and alter one factor, rather than trying to pull something new out of thin air and risk changing everything."*

Weighing up options

The cards allowed some participants to assign a qualitative weight to certain aspects of their designs: *"The cards were really helpful in figuring out where our game's strong points are, or more importantly where they are not."* Being able to weigh up certain elements gave many participants the confidence to focus on specifics, which they used to identify which aspects to improve first: *"It makes us know what we need to do for improving our game." "I found the cards to be incredibly helpful, especially in regards to tweaking some flaws in our game idea."*

Focusing the aim

The cards helped some participants focus on the main aim; creating an engaging game. *"This sort of thing is great for someone like me who tends to get caught up in what they're focusing on and slowly becoming more and more tunnel visioned."* The cards helped them to stay true to the original goal of making an engaging game by diverting them from any distractions such as attention to technical implementation too early: *"I believe the dimensions were a great way of allowing us designers to refocus on the essence of the game; the approach to 'fun' if you will. [Without the cards] we tend to concentrate too much on technology and implementation, and less on how the player(s) are enjoying the game. "*

DISCUSSION

We now discuss the individual findings in detail, relating them back to the cards and the framework. In summary, by-and-large, the cards were found to be useful in the creative design process.

Usefulness

The majority of participants considered all cards useful in their design task. They found the cards useful as a whole, and most participants did not differ much in their assessment of individual cards. The following sections discuss how participants used the cards during the design process.

All cards were useful

Participants used many cards "a lot" or "a little" as indicated by the placement task, and found only a few not useful for their particular design process. No single card was considered "not useful" by all teams, suggesting that each card had found a use in the workshops. This indicates that teams found the cards useful. As expected, not all cards were useful for all design processes, but participants found more cards useful than not useful. "Effort interpretation" and possibly "physical contention" were the cards that received the most (although still modest) count of "not useful", suggesting that in future iterations of the cards, these cards should be refined first.

What cards were useful for

Participants confirmed that the cards were useful for idea generation, idea improvement and articulation. The cards also offered a language to discuss certain aspects of the design, and supported teams in focusing their efforts. In addition to these anticipated roles, the participants also expressed that the cards helped them to fine-tune existing ideas, and helped them to be more concise in their efforts. The participants also appreciated the cards as a guide and found their role in the creative process valuable in terms of goal development, efficiency and effectiveness. In sum, the cards offered a structure for the design process that often expanded their range of ideas.

Such an assessment of the roles of the cards is similar to previous findings [11]. The data suggest that the design cards do not fulfill an isolated role in the design process, but can rather serve multiple roles and complement other methods, depending on the way participants see fit for them.

The cards also helped (re-)focus participants' aim towards the "bigger picture" of creating an engaging game, and diverted them from getting bogged down in details too early. The cards were simultaneously able to support the identification of individual elements (such as technical implementation details) while highlighting the bigger picture (such as the desired play experience). So while the cards supported a micro-level view on the task at hand, they also brought a macro-level to the participants' attention.

Challenges when working with cards

The study also revealed that turning conceptual frameworks into practical design guides it not an easy undertaking. Participants valued the benefits the cards can provide, however, it was important for them that the tool does not get in the way of the creative process. For example, some participants criticized that the wording of the design dimensions was sometimes difficult to interpret, and that some cards were too similar to others. In particular, a few participants expressed difficulty in understanding the meaning of some cards, noting that the study was undertaken within different cultural contexts and with participants who had different first languages: *"I found myself rereading some cards because I found them slightly hard to work out."* When cards were difficult to comprehend, participants' focus shifted from the creative process to interpreting the cards, reducing the benefits of the cards. Future revisions of the cards should refine the wording and images for easier comprehension. Another solution could be to reduce the number of cards, although many participants were generally in favor of the amount of cards: *"The amount of cards were just right to grab just about every aspect of a game"*.

Supplementing other methods

As mentioned in prior work [11], the cards are not a method: the designers still have to sort the cards themselves and find out in which order (if any) they apply them (and which cards to discard). The purpose is to facilitate but not restrict the creative process. However, some participants expected more directive guidance from the cards. This may have been due to two reasons: a) participants wanted a method as they felt this could enhance their creative process; and/or b) participants expected a method from the instructions given and were disappointed that they did not receive one.

LIMITATIONS

As with any investigation that aims to combine theory with practice, there are limitations that are shaped by both theoretical and practical concerns. One limitation of the work is that it was us who presented the design cards during the workshops, adding potentially our own personal bias. However, two of the sessions in workshop B were run by other interaction designers. Although they were instructed by us, this suggests that the design cards can be used in other settings where we are not the main facilitator, indicating that the knowledge lies in the design cards, not in the person presenting them.

A further limitation of the work is that we did not attempt to evaluate the quality of the ideas generated. We find assessing the quality of creative work challenging, we therefore opted to focus on how the design cards facilitated the creative process, rather than on judging the quality of the generated ideas. To hint at the creative contribution the participants made in the workshops we included a snapshot of some of the ideas in the form of the posters generated that suggest that the design cards can indeed facilitate creative ideas. On the other hand, we acknowledge that assessing the quality of the ideas (for example through processes such as suggested by [24]) might add weight to the argument of the usefulness of the design cards.

Furthermore, comparing the results from our workshops is limited by the fact that our participants had different expertise levels, consisting of both researchers and students. However, this approach allowed us to examine the use of the cards across a range of early career to more senior designers.

Lastly, another limitation was the use of a questionnaire. Questionnaires can only paint a limited picture of a complex phenomenon, such as the design task investigated in this study. However, we wanted to give all participants the opportunity to provide feedback, and considering the number of participants in some of the workshops, a questionnaire seemed a practical tool to achieve this. In order to minimize the limitations of questionnaires [22], we always looked for confirming statements for each questionnaire entry in the interview data.

CONCLUSION

The exertion design cards were considered useful by participants in design workshops for the creative task of designing an exertion game. The participants expressed that the cards, which were derived from the Exertion Framework, supported them in their task, suggesting the utility of the design cards and in turn the usefulness of the framework. The cards achieved this by, for example, helping the participants break-down the task into individual elements. This resulted in participants realizing that they might have overlooked an important aspect if they had not used a specific card.

This work therefore extends prior research by providing further evidence to the value of transforming frameworks into design tools. In particular, this work makes a contribution by presenting the Exertion Cards as well as a description of the process that lead to them based on the Exertion Framework. Furthermore, this work makes a contribution by demonstrating the utility of the design cards by adding empirical evidence that the design cards can positively affect the design process of exertion games: the participants found that the design cards covered (almost) the entire spectrum of themes they found valuable for their practice, and considered the amount of cards appropriate. This adds weight to the argument that the framework consists of the major themes relevant for exertion games.

In sum, the study demonstrated the Exertion Framework in action through a set of design cards. The data collected from a range of workshops with an extensive number of participants indicates that the design cards can support the creative process of designing exertion games.

ACKNOWLEDGEMENTS

We thank Bert Bongers and team, Microsoft Research and Nokia in Beijing. Florian 'Floyd' Mueller is the recipient of an Australian Research Council Fellowship (110101304).

REFERENCES

1. Antle, A.N. Embodied child computer interaction: why embodiment matters. *ACM Interactions, March+April.* (2009), 27-30.
2. Belman, J., Flanagan, M. and Nissenbaum, H. Instructional Methods and Curricula for "Values Conscious Design". *Loading... 3* (4). (2009).
3. Blackwell, A. and Green, J. Notational systems - the Cognitive Dimensions of Notations framework. in Carroll, J.M. ed. *HCI Models, Theories and Frameworks: Toward a multidisciplinary science*, Morgan Kaufmann, 2003, 103-134.
4. Brandt, E. and Messeter, J., Facilitating collaboration through design games. In *Proc. Participatory design: Artful integration: interweaving media, materials and practices-Volume 1*, (2004), ACM, 121-131.
5. Consolvo, S., Everitt, K., Smith, I. and Landay, J.A., Design requirements for technologies that encourage physical activity. In *Proc. CHI 2006*, ACM Press (2006), 457-466.
6. Dan R. Olsen, J., Evaluating user interface systems research. In *Proc. UIST*, ACM Press (2007), 251-258.
7. de Kort, Y.A.W. and IJsselsteijn, W.A. People, places, and play: player experience in a socio-spatial context. *Computers in Entertainment (CIE)*, *6* (2). (2008).
8. Flanagan, M., Nissenbaum, H., Belman, J. and Diamond, J., A method for discovering values in digital games. In *Proc. DiGRA 2007*, (2007).
9. Fogtmann, M.H., Fritsch, J. and Kortbek, K.J., Kinesthetic Interaction - Revealing the Bodily Potential in Interaction Design. In *Proc. OZCHI 2008*, ACM Press (2008).
10. Halskov, K. and Dalsgaard, P., Inspiration card workshops. In *Proc. DIS 2006*, ACM Press (2006), 2-11.
11. Hornecker, E., Creative idea exploration within the structure of a guiding framework: the card brainstorming game. In *Proc. TEI 2010*, ACM Press (2010), 101-108.
12. Landay, J.A. I give up on CHI/UIST, 2009. http://dubfuture.blogspot.com/2009/11/i-give-up-on-chiuist.html.
13. Lanningham-Foster, L., Jensen, T.B., Foster, R.C., Redmond, A.B., Walker, B.A., Heinz, D. and Levine, J.A. Energy Expenditure of Sedentary Screen Time Compared With Active Screen Time for Children. *Pediatrics*, *118* (6). (2006), 1831-1835.
14. Lin, J., Mamykina, L., Lindtner, S., Delajoux, G. and Strub, H., Fish'n'Steps: Encouraging Physical Activity with an Interactive Computer Game. In *Proc. UbiComp 2006*, ACM Press (2006), 261-278.
15. Lucero, A. and Arrasvuori, J., PLEX Cards: a source of inspiration when designing for playfulness. In *Proc. Fun and Games 2010*, ACM Press(2010), 28-37.
16. Mokka, S., Väätänen, A., Heinilä, J. and Välkkynen, P., Fitness computer game with a bodily user interface. In *Proc. Entertainment Computing*, 2003, 1-3.
17. Mueller, F., Agamanolis, S., Gibbs, M. and Vetere, F., Remote Impact: Shadowboxing over a Distance. In *Proc. CHI 2009*, ACM Press (2009), 3531-3532.
18. Mueller, F., Agamanolis, S. and Picard, R., Exertion Interfaces: Sports over a Distance for Social Bonding and Fun. In *SIGCHI conference on Human factors in computing systems*, 2003,ACM, 561-568.
19. Mueller, F., Edge, D., Vetere, F., Gibbs, M.R., Agamanolis, S., Bongers, B. and Sheridan, J.G., Designing Sports: A Framework for Exertion Games. In *Proc. CHI 2011*, ACM Press (2011), 2651-2660.
20. Mueller, F., Gibbs, M. and Vetere, F., Design Influence on Social Play in Distributed Exertion Games. In *Proc. CHI 2009*, ACM Press (2009), 1539-1548.
21. Mueller, F., Vetere, F., Gibbs, M.R., Edge, D., Agamanolis, S. and Sheridan, J.G., Jogging over a distance between Europe and Australia. In *Proc. UIST 2010*, ACM Press (2010), 189-198.
22. Neuman, W.L. *Social Research Methods*. Pearson Education, USA, 2006.
23. Schell, J. The Art of Game Design - The Cards. http://artofgamedesign.com/cards/.
24. Shah, J.J., Smith, S.M., Vargas-Hernandez, N., Gerkens, D.R. and Wulan, M., Empirical studies of design ideation: Alignment of design experiments with lab experiments. in *ASME Design Theory & Methods Conference*, (2003), 2-6.
25. Strauss, A. and Corbin, J. *Basics of Qualitative Research: Techniques and Procedures for Developing Grounded Theory*. SAGE Publications, Thousand Oaks, CA, USA, 1998.

WADE: Simplified GUI Add-on Development for Third-party Software

Xiaojun Meng[1], Shengdong Zhao[1], Yongfeng Huang[1], Zhongyuan Zhang[1], James R. Eagan[2], Ramanathan Subramanian[3]

[1]NUS-HCI Lab, National University of Singapore, [2]Télécom ParisTech & CNRS LTCI UMR 5141, [3]ADSC, University of Illinois at Urbana-Champaign

[1]{xiaojun,zhaosd}@comp.nus.edu.sg, [1]xgjonathan@gmail.com, [1]zhang_zhongyuan@nus.edu.sg
[2]james.eagan@telecom-paristech.fr, [3]subramanian.r@adsc.com.sg

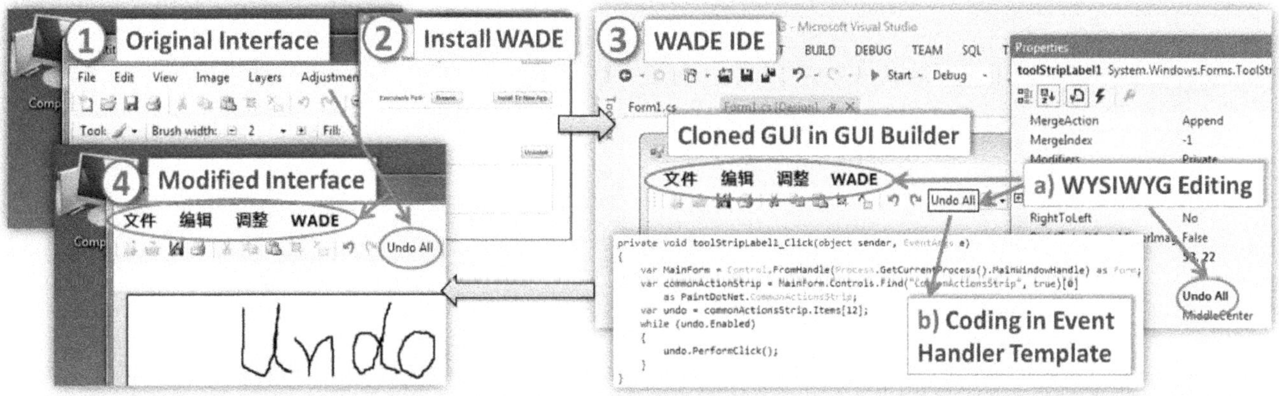

Figure 1: WADE overview: 1) Kevin wants to make the following modifications to the original Paint.NET interface i) change menu labels from English to Chinese, ii) remove unused menus and icons, and iii) add a new "undo all" function. To this end, he 2) Installs WADE in Paint.NET, 3) Clones the Paint.NET GUI into the GUI builder of a WADE-supported IDE. Then, he (a) modifies the GUI using a WYSIWYG editor, and (b) writes code associated with the "undo all" widget via the event handler template. 4) All the above changes are compiled to an add-on that can be installed into Paint.NET for easy and convenient future use.

ABSTRACT

We present the WADE Integrated Development Environment (IDE), which simplifies the modification of the interface and functionality of existing third-party software without access to source code. WADE clones the Graphical User Interface (GUI) of a host program through dynamic-link library (DLL) injection in order to enable (1) WYSIWYG modification of the GUI and (2) the modification of software functionality. We compare WADE with an alternative state-of-the-art runtime toolkit overloading approach in a user-study, finding that WADE significantly simplifies the task of GUI-based add-on development.

CHI 2014, April 26–May 1, 2014, Toronto, ON, Canada.

http://dx.doi.org/10.1145/2556288.2557349

Author Keywords

WADE; GUI; Add-on Integration; WYSIWYG; IDE

ACM Classification Keywords

H.5.2. Information Interfaces and Presentation: User Interfaces

General Terms

Human Factors

INTRODUCTION

Software rarely fulfills the needs of all users all the time [7, 12]. Mindful of the need to make software adaptable to individual needs, developers typically allow for software customization by providing:

- Capabilities for reconfiguring existing features and functions to suit personal taste (*e.g.*, via preferences panes or dot files), or
- Software architecture for incorporating add-ons (*e.g.*, using plugins, scripts and/or extensions) to enhance/modify the behavior of the original application.

While these approaches can provide users with a great deal of control, every approach necessitates additional effort from the software developers to explicitly provide customization support at the software development stage. For example, plugins, scripting interfaces and extensions require the developer to provide and maintain an external API to their software, which may potentially require maintaining an additional and separate interface to internal functionality.

Owing to the above issues, many software developers do not provide support for add-ons. Even when they do, such support is often limited [1]. To address this limitation, much research has focused on approaches that enable third-party developers to modify the interface or behavior of existing applications *without access to source code* or to *an external API*. These approaches typically work by either: 1) operating on the surface-level of the interface, intercepting input events and output pixels before they are delivered to the application (*e.g.*, Prefab [2, 3], Façade [14]), or 2) integrating with the toolkit to gain access to the internal program structures (*e.g.*, Scotty [4], SubArctic [5]). For convenience, we call the former as *surface-based approaches* and the latter as *toolkit-based deep approaches*.

Surface-based approaches allow modifications to GUI elements without access to the internal structure of an application. For example, Façade allows for reconfiguring GUI elements via a simple drag and drop interface [14]. However, such approaches are limited by their ability to infer the structure and functionality of the interface because they do not have access to the internal program objects or their semantics. *E.g.*, adding new functionality or modifying the behavior of a GUI widget is difficult to accomplish using surface-based approaches [4].

This limitation can be overcome to some extent by toolkit-based deep approaches such as Scotty [4] or SubArctic [5], which operate below the surface of the program to reveal the underlying program logic and functionalities. This allows them to alter the system's appearance and behaviors beyond the surface level. However, toolkit-based deep approaches can be challenging to use. They require a thorough understanding of the relevant parts of the system in order to realize the desired behavior. Even for experienced developers, much effort is needed to make relatively simple modifications to third party software.

Therefore, there exists a trade-off between generalizability, ease of use, and power (the ability to perform deeper modifications). While all previous approaches have their advantages, additional solutions are still needed to better balance the power and ease of use for runtime modification of third-party software.

In this paper, we propose WADE, a simplified and WSYWYG Add-on Development Environment that can ease the task of modifying GUI-based functions in existing software with or without source code, while still enabling developers to make deep changes to the software behavior. To achieve this, WADE injects a dynamically-linked library (DLL) into the host program to retrieve the GUI hierarchy of the host program. It then clones the interface in the IDE so that properties of GUI elements can be directly modified. Furthermore, WADE provides scaffolding to directly associate event handlers to existing widgets, so that enhancing/modifying software behavior becomes simpler.

Figure 1 shows an example add-on development scenario using WADE. Currently, WADE supports add-on development using both the open source SharpDevelop 4.2 and the Microsoft Visual Studio 2012 Ultimate IDEs for *Windows Form* applications on the Windows XP and Windows 7 platforms.

We conducted an experiment to compare WADE with a Scotty-like toolkit-based deep approach for modifying third party applications. Our results show that users subjectively found WADE much easier to use, and were objectively able to develop GUI-based modifications 2.4 times faster than the alternative approach on average. To summarize, the contributions of this work are:

- We present the WADE prototype along with its software architecture as an integrated solution for significantly facilitating add-on creation for third party software without source code.
- The WADE IDE provides scaffolding for code-based GUI modification through template generation, thereby enabling robust implementation of the complex boilerplate associated with runtime modification.
- We present the results of an empirical comparison between WADE and the state-of-the-art Scotty approach for modifying software [4], which shows that WADE is significantly faster for GUI modifications.

RELATED WORK

As previously mentioned, surface-based adaptation [2, 3, 14, 15] and toolkit-based subsurface modification [4, 5, 16] are the two main approaches that support third-party application modifications without access to the software's source code. As a comprehensive review of the different variants of these two approaches has already been discussed in Eagan *et al.* [4], we now highlight those works most relevant to WADE.

Surface-level modification

Surface-level modifications do not require any support by the application developer. Instead, they operate on the interface that is presented to the user and the input events he or she provides. For example, Yeh *et al.*'s Sikuli scripting environment [17] allows users to write scripts that reference screenshots of particular controls, to refer to existing application elements.

Stuerzlinger *et al.*'s UI Façades [14] intercept individual widgets as they interact with the window server. This allows a developer to easily replace them at the window server level with an alternate implementation, such as by regrouping together widgets from different applications or replacing a radio button with a pop-down menu. Dixon and Fogarty's Prefab [2] examines pixels as they are drawn on the screen to infer which parts correspond to which widgets.

It then allows the interception and replacement of these pixels to change the output of a particular interface. Combined with input redirection, Prefab can enable alternate software functionality.

However, all of these solutions are limited by their ability to infer the structure and functionality of the interface. They do not have direct access to internal program objects or their semantics. As a result, it is typically challenging for such approaches to make modifications that alter both GUI elements and their underlying program logic. Such limitations can be overcome to some extent by toolkit-based deep modification approaches.

Toolkit-based deep modification

Edwards *et al.*'s SubArctic toolkit [5] extends Java's AWT to provide explicit hooks that allow third-party developers to add new UI modifications. These hooks provide specific support for extensibility, allowing a third-party developer to add new functionality to existing applications built with the SubArctic toolkit, without explicit software support. However, UI modifications are only feasible for applications built using the SubArctic toolkit. For other types of applications, such modifications become infeasible.

Eagan *et al.*'s Scotty [4] uses injection to perform runtime toolkit overloading, in which an existing toolkit is altered specifically to provide explicit support for modifications. It provides a *meta*-toolkit for developers to modify existing third-party applications. Third-party developers must, however, explicitly *inspect* and *make sense of* the existing application before eventually applying acquired knowledge in a separate coding environment [6, 9]. This process can be complex, creating barriers that limit such modifications to experienced and dedicated programmers.

USING WADE

Our goal with WADE was to create an interface that unifies the various tasks and tools involved in creating third-party program modifications. In contrast to Scotty, where *sense-making* and *coding* are independent, WADE integrates the two phases into a single environment, making software modification more user-friendly and practicable even to novice programmers.

A third-party developer can use WADE to make a variety of modifications to an application, such as a) basic property changes to a GUI's widgets, b) altering actions associated with interface elements, and c) adding entirely new functionalities. We demonstrate the utility of WADE through the following scenarios. All scenarios have been implemented using WADE.

Language localization and template creation

Kevin has created a diary template for Notepad.NET and wants to share it with his Russian friend Ivanov, who is not comfortable with English. Unfortunately, Notepad.NET does not currently have a Russian translation, so Kevin loads the WADE property editor add-on into Notepad.NET. In the property editor, he systematically changes each

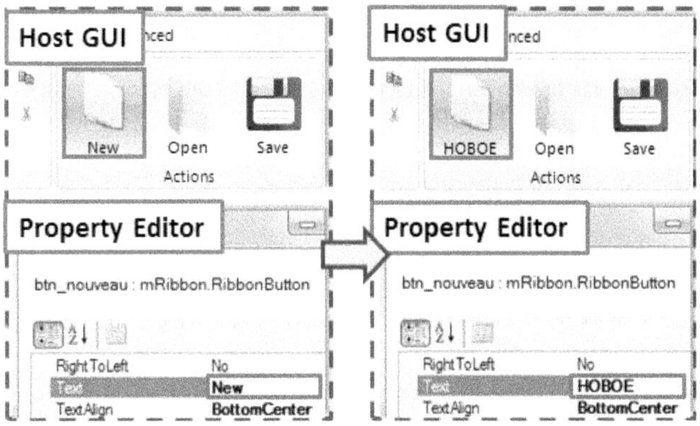

Figure 2: Changing the label of the program from English to Russian using WADE's property editor. The user first selects the GUI widget (the *New* button), and types its Russian name in the text field of the property editor. Changes to the text are immediately reflected in the host GUI.

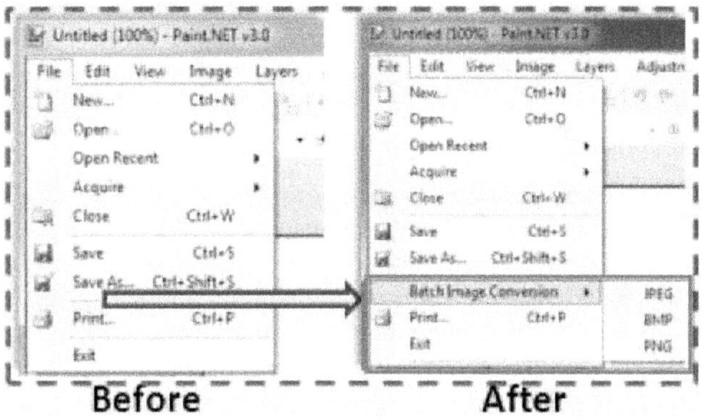

Figure 3: Using WADE, one can easily add an external service to the host program. The utility enabling batch image conversion to JPEG, BMP and PNG is added to Paint.NET by linking to the ImageMagick graphic library.

widget's label to its Russian translation, as shown in Figure 2. He then exports those changes to a new add-on component that Ivanov can load into his English copy.

Kevin then decides to add a toolbar button as a shortcut to the new diary template he has created. While the property editor can alter properties of existing widgets, it cannot add new widgets. Kevin loads the WADE IDE and chooses the **Clone GUI** command to clone the Notepad.NET interface into a new project. Using the WADE add-on that Kevin already loaded into Notepad.NET for translation, the clone command walks the interface hierarchy and serializes it to the WADE IDE. In the WADE IDE's GUI builder, Kevin then adds a new toolbar button for the diary. He then uses WADE to generate an event handler template, into which he writes the code to load his new diary template.

Link to external function call

Lee took a lot of photos in RAW format on her recent trip to Toronto and wants to convert them to JPEGs so that she can open them in Paint.NET. Unfortunately, Paint.NET does not have a batch conversion interface. There is a command-line tool that offers that capability, but she can never remember the right incantation to make it work. She clones Paint.NET's interface into WADE and adds a new **Batch Conversion** menu (Figure 3). She then uses WADE's event handler template to invoke the appropriate actions using the command line library, compiles the add-on and installs it into Paint.NET.

Discussion

The above scenarios illustrate some of the different kinds of third-party program modifications that WADE supports. In the first example, Kevin is able to provide a translation for a third-party interface for his friend Ivanov, just by using WADE's property editor add-on for existing programs. For more complex modifications to the interface, such as when Lee adds batch conversion support to Paint.NET, it is necessary to write some code for the new functionality. Here, WADE provides a) support to clone the existing interface into a new project and b) scaffolding to help Lee write her event handlers. The only code she needs to write is the code specifically related to her functionality, which she can then integrate into the cloned GUI hierarchy using WADE's GUI editor. We present the detailed implementation in the following sections.

Comparison with previous approaches

Other tools provide similar kinds of third-party program modification. Façade [14] enables the user to easily simplify an interface by removing and regrouping widgets. However, it does not support changing labels, font styles, background images, *etc.*

Prefab uses a localization example similar to Kevin's scenario in order to show the power of pixel-based approaches. However, Prefab can only access pixels but not the text, and must therefore apply a character recognition process to extract associated text strings. In contrast, WADE retrieves the original label text directly from the host application's internal structure.

The remaining modifications require deep access to the program's internal structures. As such, surface approaches such as Façade and Prefab cannot pierce through the surface to decipher these structures.

Toolkit-based subsurface approaches, such as Scotty, can accomplish all the tasks above, but do not provide the scaffolding and support of an IDE that WADE does. In order to perform language localization, for example, a developer must inspect the UI hierarchy and associate program objects to identify widgets and corresponding labels, before writing the appropriate code from scratch to change the labels to another language. WADE, on the other hand, simplifies this process by presenting a unified environment and scaffolding for many of these changes. We now describe how WADE facilitates software modifications using the GUI builder.

WADE IDE FOR ADD-ON DEVELOPMENT

While the details of developing add-ons for third-party software without source code can be complex, the basic idea involves two important aspects. First, third-party applications may not come with a pre-designed add-on architecture. Therefore, an environment should be designed in which the host application can manage and communicate with add-ons created and integrated with it at a later time. Second, because the application source code is not available, the IDE must facilitate understanding of the host application's internal structure and provide tools to support the creation of add-ons.

Injecting WADE add-on manager to host application

To achieve the first goal, WADE adopts an approach similar to Scotty's, by injecting an add-on manager into the host application's process space. While Scotty is designed to work on the Mac OS X Cocoa platform, WADE is developed for *Windows Form* applications on the Windows operating system. WADE uses the registry key binding technique to insert compiled code, in the form of a Dynamic Linked Library (DLLs), into the host application at runtime. Once loaded, the injected DLL can use the *CreateRemoteThread* method to create threads that run in the virtual address space of the host processor. This allows it to serve as an add-on manager to load and register any compiled add-ons (also in the form of DLLs) within the host application [13].

Supporting third-party add-on development

However, simply enabling external add-ons to be integrated with the host application is not enough. In order to create meaningful add-ons, a third-party programmer must make sense of an existing application, and apply that knowledge to the development of any new functionality.

Scotty provides various tools including a hierarchy browser, an object inspector, a widget picker, and an interactive interpreter (Python) to support sense-making in the *Cocoa* environment [4]. While none of the individual tools may be too difficult to use, they only provide partial answers. Knowing how and where to get the different pieces of information, and discovering how to combine them effectively to obtain a high level picture, are both tedious and challenging. Therefore, typically, only experienced programmers are able to use Scotty-like approaches.

In order to reduce the knowledge barrier involved in integrating the different tasks mentioned above, we introduce an IDE specifically for third-party add-on development. An IDE is a software application that provides comprehensive facilities to computer programmers for software development. It is designed to maximize programmer productivity by providing tightly-knit components for authoring, modifying, compiling, deploying and debugging software with similar user interfaces. The IDE, therefore, is more user-friendly and powerful as compared to multiple distinct tools provided by Scotty.

Modern IDEs often come with an integrated GUI builder (also known as GUI editor), which simplifies GUI creation by allowing the designer to arrange widgets using a drag-

and-drop WYSIWYG editor. As today's user interfaces are commonly programmed using an event-driven architecture, GUI builders also simplify creation of event-driven code, by supporting code that connects widgets with the incoming (input) and outgoing (drawing) events that trigger functions providing the application logic.

Integrating WADE with the IDE and GUI builder

However, integrating an IDE with a GUI builder into the third party add-on development process is no simple task. GUI builders in existing IDEs are designed to facilitate the creation of new interfaces from scratch, rather than to modify existing interfaces. In addition, existing GUI builders tend to assume that source code associated with the GUI components will be available. In our case, however, that crucial piece of information is missing.

In order to enable the WADE GUI builder to modify GUI components and their associated program logic for a third-party application, the following steps are needed:

1) Extract the GUI hierarchy information from the host application.
2) Send this information to the GUI builder inside of an IDE.
3) In the IDE, convert this information into a format that can be displayed as GUI widgets in the GUI builder, so programmers can manipulate them in a WYSIWYG fashion.
4) Analyze and compile the changes made by the programmer into an add-on that can correctly modify the appearance and behavior of the host application at runtime.

Before elaborating on the implementation process, we will first define a few terms.

GUI frameworks typically organize widgets into a tree. The root tree has sub-trees that represent windows and their associated widgets.

We term the root tree of the host application as *host GUI hierarchy*, which contains many *host widget sub-trees*. Each *host widget sub-tree* represents a window that has a hierarchy of *host widgets*.

We replicate the *host GUI hierarchy* inside the IDE's GUI builder. The replicated copy is called the *cloned GUI hierarchy*, which consists of many *cloned widget sub-trees*. Each *cloned widget sub-tree* has many *cloned widgets*.

The relationship between these terms is illustrated in the left and right panels of Figure 4. We now describe in more detail the steps involved in using WADE to modify GUI components and associated program logic for a third-party applications.

Step 1: Extract GUI hierarchy information

We overload the *Injected Add-on Manager* to perform several additional steps beyond basic add-on management. In order to gain access to all of the widgets in the host GUI

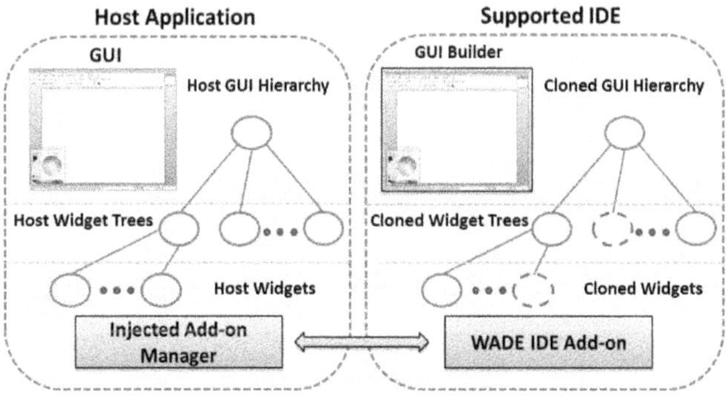

Figure 4: WADE components: the *Injected Add-on Manager* (left panel) inside the host application manages add-ons and communicates the GUI information with a compatible IDE via the *WADE IDE Add-on* component (right panel). The *WADE IDE Add-on* then clones the host application's GUI in the IDE's GUI Builder to allow WYSWYG modification of the original UI. The changes made in IDE can then be compiled into a third-party add-on to alter the appearance and behavior of the host application.

hierarchy, the Injected Add-on Manager walks each of these trees to extract its structure and to identify the properties (*e.g.*, name, size, location, label, etc.) of each widget in the hierarchy. We use the System.Windows.Forms.Control class in .NET, whose controls property exposes a collection of all of these child controls. Through this component, we can access the structure and properties of an entire application's existing interface.

In addition, the *Injected Add-on Manager* constructs a *component dictionary* of all the widgets of the unmodified *host GUI hierarchy* by using the *name* and *address* of each widget as a (key, value) pair in the dictionary. This information is saved as a reference point so that any potential changes made by a third-party programmer using the IDE can later be discovered.

Step 2: Send information to the GUI builder

The *Injected Add-on Manager* then serializes the extracted properties of each *host widget* via the *WADE IDE Add-on* to the IDE. For most widgets, information such as name, size, location, text, *etc.* are directly sent through a basic text stream. For widgets with background images or complex structures, such information is first saved as cache files in image or XML format before being transferred over.

Step 3: Convert and present GUI information in GUI builder

After receiving complete GUI information from the *Injected Add-on Manager*, the *WADE IDE Add-on* then constructs a project with the same UI properties as extracted from the original program. With the extracted UI information, the *WADE IDE Add-on* clones the existing interface into a new project in the IDE. In our current WADE implementation, we have integrated the *WADE IDE Add-on* with SharpDevelop 4.2 and Microsoft Visual Studio 2012 Ultimate to provide code and GUI builder support. The *WADE IDE Add-on* uses the serialized information to replicate the *host GUI hierarchy* on the canvas of the supported IDE's GUI builder.

Step 4: Analyze and apply changes
Third-party add-on developers can then modify the *cloned GUI hierarchy* in a WYSIWYG fashion. This modified *cloned GUI hierarchy* and its associated program behavior is compiled into an add-on (in a DLL) that can be loaded into the host application by the *Injected Add-on Manager*.

Using the earlier constructed *component dictionary*, the *Injected Add-on Manager* can then examine the modified *cloned GUI hierarchy* inside the add-on and apply the changes to the *host GUI hierarchy* as described by the following simplified algorithm:

1) *make all widgets in the host GUI hierarchy invisible*
2) *for each cloned widget tree in the cloned GUI hierarchy:*
3) *perform a breadth-first walk through all the cloned widgets, and for each cloned widget:*
4) *try to find its corresponding host widget by looking up in the component dictionary using the widget name as the key*
5) *if a corresponding host widget is found:*
6) *iterate through the properties (including event handlers) of the cloned widget and set them to those of the host widget, and make it visible*
7) *if a corresponding host widget cannot be found:*
8) *add this cloned widget to the parent of the corresponding host widget in the host GUI hierarchy, and make it visible*

Using this algorithm, WADE can apply a third-party programmer's changes in the *cloned* GUI hierarchy to the GUI hierarchy of the *host* application. These changes include adding or deleting a widget, modifying the properties of a widget, or adding or modifying the event handlers of a widget.

Adding widgets is handled in the 7th and 8th statements of the algorithm. When the *Injected Add-on Manager* finds a *cloned widget* not in the *component dictionary*, it knows it is a new widget and adds it accordingly to the *host GUI hierarchy*.

Deleting widgets is implicitly handled by initially setting all *host widgets* to be invisible (1st statement in algorithm), and only making visible those found in the *cloned GUI hierarchy*. The deleted widgets therefore will remain invisible after this process, and will appear to the user as if they had been deleted from the host application. We choose to hide the widget instead of deleting it because removing a widget at runtime may be risky. As a widget may have unknown runtime dependencies, permanently removing it may cause the application to crash. Thus, we choose a safer approach to achieve a similar effect.

Property modification of a widget is also handled in a simple yet effective fashion in the 5th and 6th statements of the algorithm. The number of widgets in the host GUI hierarchy is typically not exhaustive. So, instead of expending effort to explicitly detect individual changes, we simply reset all properties of all host widgets to the properties of their corresponding cloned widgets, regardless of whether the cloned widget has been modified or not.

Event handler modifications are also implicitly handled during the property resetting process because the .NET framework treats event handlers as part of the properties of a widget. Changing and associating new program logic with *host widgets* can be effectively applied without much additional effort beyond implementing the desired functionality.

As such, we successfully integrate the GUI builder and a number of IDE features into the third-party software add-on development process.

While WADE demonstrates a promising step towards addressing the power and ease of use trade-off for runtime modifications, it is important to note that WADE is not without limitations.

Interface dynamics
WADE enables the user to perform WYSIWYG modification of the GUI hierarchy only to the initial application state. Many interfaces, however, are dynamic and rely on runtime code that may alter the interface from how it appeared at the moment it was imported into WADE (i.e., dynamic widgets). Since the content of a widget can change at runtime, content modification through the GUI editor may not be applied back to the original application. Changes to the application may also conflict with the modifications implemented in WADE, possibly leading to unstable modifications that may not behave as expected.

However, certain interface dynamics can still be addressed using the WADE approach. For example, if dynamic widgets are initialized only once upon program invocation, it may still be possible to apply modifications using a monitoring program that knows when to take action after initialization.

Custom widgets
Another limitation of WADE is that the current implementation provides limited support for modification of custom widgets. Custom widgets often have derived custom properties and behaviors that are not recognizable by the GUI builder; they therefore cannot be properly displayed in the IDE.

However, not all custom widgets are unrecognizable. Custom widgets that derive from a standard, known widget will be treated as the base widget. The GUI editor can thus handle the inherited properties, but will be ignorant of any derivative behavior and properties.

Overall, developers are advised to first get familiar with the application behavior to clearly identify customization and runtime interface dynamics before using WADE to perform runtime modifications.

Security implications

Overloading at runtime can cause problems if the replacement method violates any of the assumptions in the original application's design. It is thus recommended to practice careful and defensive programming to avoid breaking the original application logic [4].

However, as compared to toolkit modification approaches, WADE diminishes the risk of breaking the host application. In existing approaches, all modifications involve writing arbitrary code. With WADE's property editors and templates, the surface footprint of this code is diminished, and supported modifications can use known clean implementations. Writing additional code will remain risky as in Scotty and other toolkit approaches, but certain common modifications are now much safer.

USER STUDY

In order to assess the usefulness of WADE, we performed a user study. In terms of purpose and capabilities, WADE is most similar to Scotty [4]. Other alternatives, while having their own advantages, are less comparable to WADE in terms of the functionality provided or applicability. For example, surface-based approaches such as Façade and Prefab lack the ability penetrate underneath the surface; SubArtic requires use of the SubArtic toolkit to begin with.

While we expected WADE to significantly simplify add-on development as compared to Scotty, a primary objective of the user-study was to quantify the speed-up obtained with WADE over Scotty while modifying third-party software, and identify those WADE characteristics responsible for the speed-up. To this end, we performed a controlled experiment to assess and compare the strengths and limitations of the Scotty and WADE approaches.

Participants

Eight participants (7 males, 1 female) ranging from 21 to 32 years old ($\mu = 25.5$, $\sigma = 3.34$) participated in this study. All participants were experienced computer users and programmers.

Apparatus

The experiment was conducted using a DELL Optiplex 990 Desktop computer running on the Windows XP operating system, with 4 GB RAM and Intel Core i7-2600-3.40 GHz CPU. A Dell E2211H monitor, a USB optical mouse and a standard keyboard were used as the input/output devices. The Paint.NET interface to be modified is implemented in C# using Microsoft Visual Studio.

As Scotty was developed for the Cocoa framework in Mac OS whereas WADE runs on the .NET framework in Windows, we created a Scotty-like development environment (Scotty simulator) to support user tasks on Windows using the following tools:

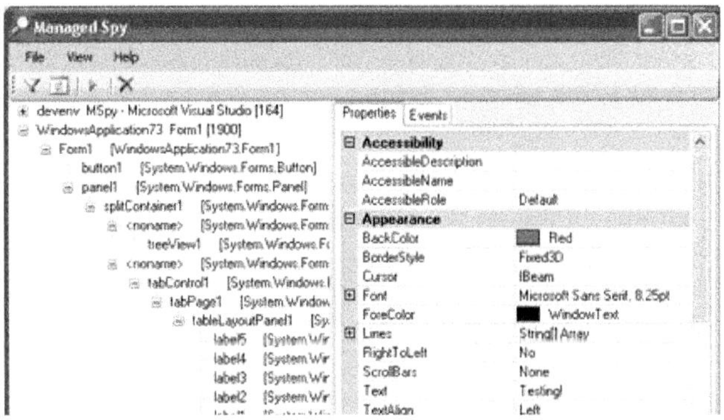

Figure 5. Screenshot of the ManagedSpy tool.

Runtime add-on manager: a tool that enables a compiled add-on to be installed onto an existing program at runtime.

ManagedSpy: a Microsoft utility program that allows developers to spy on an application's GUI at runtime. Figure 5 presents a screen-shot of the program which allows a user to discover the names, types, and properties of the host application's GUI components at runtime. The ManagedSpy serves a similar functionality to the hierarchy browser, widget picker, and object observer tools offered in the Scotty environment. For WADE, we provided the add-on manager and the WADE IDE based on SharpDevelop 4.2 with GUI builder as previously described.

Task and Training

Before the actual experiment, each participant was given a tutorial demonstration and three practice tasks similar to the experimental tasks to familiarize him/herself with the use of the Scotty simulator and WADE. For each approach, we provided a manual with the information necessary for the users to complete the tasks.

The manual for the Scotty-like approach included step-by-step instructions for (i) accessing the GUI window and child widgets, (ii) changing widget properties using the information retrieved by ManagedSpy, (iii) coding snippets to hide items, (iv) coding snippets to add new widgets, and (v) using the add-on manager to insert DLLs back to the host application. The WADE manual included instructions on how to (i) trigger commands to inject the add-on manager DLL, (ii) clone the host application, (iii) write GUI modifications to a DLL and (iv) re-inject this DLL back to the host program.

Note that the instructions we provided made code-based modifications (as with the Scotty simulator) much easier, because in real world scenarios, the methodology for achieving GUI modifications is not obvious and must be figured out in a trial and error fashion. However, to facilitate participants' completion of the tasks, we provided all the requisite information in the user manual.

The tasks to be completed using (a) our Scotty simulator and (b) WADE in the experiment are described below:

- **Personalized reconfiguration**: In the first task, users were required to rename two menu items, hide three menu items, change the font size and style of the main menu bar, and change the representational picture for a widget.
- **Adding functionality via add-ons**: For the second task, users were required to add a new button called "Undo all" on the icon bar (as in Figure 1). Once the "Undo all" button is clicked, it would undo all user modifications for a particular session.

Experimental Design

We used a within-participants design in which all participants were asked to perform all tasks using both approaches. Participants were randomly assigned to two groups of four participants each. Half of the participants performed the two tasks with the Scotty simulator first, followed by WADE, while the other half performed the two tasks in the reverse order. Each participant performed the entire experiment in one sitting lasting 1-2 hours, with optional breaks between tasks.

In summary, the design was as follows (excluding practice tasks): 8 subjects × 2 coding approaches (Scotty-simulator vs. WADE) × 2 tasks (GUI reconfiguration, add-on development) = 32 tasks in total. Comparative factors were time spent on the tasks, whether or not the task was successful, and participants' subjective preferences in their post-experiment questionnaire.

Results

The user-study results confirmed that software modification is much easier with WADE than with Scotty.

Accuracy: Seven participants finished all tasks, while one participant only finished the first task using both approaches. Therefore, from the task completion point of view, there was no difference between the two approaches.

However, there was a difference in the number of attempts it took for participants to finish each task. An *attempt* denotes each instance a participant believed the task was complete, and tried to execute the modifications he/she had made. Errors in program execution, therefore, resulted in multiple attempts. On average, participants required 1.13 attempts to complete a task using WADE, and 1.75 attempts with the Scotty-like approach. A paired *t*-test comparison between the two approaches revealed that this difference is marginally significant ($t_7 = 4.07$, $p = .083$). This result suggests that users are likely to commit fewer mistakes during interface modification using WADE than Scotty.

Time to task completion: We then conducted a 2x2 repeated measures ANOVA on the task-completion times with the approach type (WADE/Scotty) and task type (reconfiguration/add-on integration) as the relevant factors. Figure 6 presents the results. As expected, we found a significant main effect of the approach used ($F_{1,7} = 31.41$, $p<0.01$) on the task-completion time, which implies that on average, users completed the two tasks significantly (about 2.4 times) faster using WADE (264.4 s) than with the Scotty-simulator (639 s).

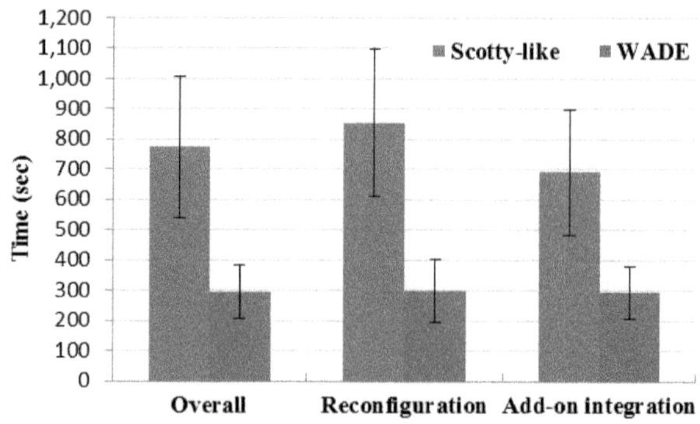

Figure 6: Comparison of task completion times for WADE and Scotty.

Qualitative comparison: After the experiment, participants were asked to rate various aspects of the two approaches on a 5-point Likert scale. In all, they answered four questions concerning *usefulness* (how useful was the software modification tool?), *user productivity* (how much did this tool improve your productivity?), *learnability* (how easy was it to learn the steps involved in this approach?) and *overall satisfaction*. WADE received a minimum average score of 4.75 on all counts. On the other hand, the Scotty-like approach received a highest score of 3.25 for *usefulness*, and a lowest score of 2.25 on *user productivity*.

Discussion

Factors contributing to WADE's performance advantage

Results of the user study clearly demonstrate the advantages of using WADE's integrated approach for reconfiguration and add-on development tasks. The performance gain with WADE arose due to a number of factors as enumerated below.

1) The WYSIWIG GUI editor allows participants to more directly interact with and manipulate widgets and their properties. This consequently saves time and effort required to look up the GUI widget hierarchy for appropriate names and properties before applying any changes, as indicated by our participants: "*WADE enables direct manipulation which is easy, faster and intuitive. (P1, P5)*".

2) Fewer task completion attempts using WADE can be attributed to the fact that direct interface manipulation essentially involves *recognition* of widgets and their properties, while coding relies on *sense making* and *recall.* It is easier to make mistakes using the pure coding approach, as indicated by the higher average number of attempts mentioned earlier.

3) Although coding is necessary to add/modify GUI functionality, the WADE IDE provides scaffolding in the form of event handler templates to aid the development

process. "*The event handler template makes coding easier*" (*P1*).

4) In the Scotty-like approach, the sense-making process and coding for the add-ons are separate tasks handled using different tools and applications, causing additional overhead both cognitively, in terms of remembering and linking the information, as well as physically, in terms of operating and interacting with multiple, different tools. In WADE, the IDE provides an integrated environment for coding, which can reduce the time spent on managing and interpreting the code. As indicated by P4: "*Switching back and forth between ManagedSpy and IDE is tedious and frustrating*".

5) Finally, as all necessary instructions required for modifying UI components using the Scotty simulator, typically unavailable in the real world, were provided to users, latency involved in discovering the correct modification commands is not accounted for in this study. Therefore, one can expect WADE to enable an even larger performance gain over toolkit-based deep approaches such as Scotty in real-world scenarios.

In summary, the advantages of WADE over Scotty-like approaches are (1) Direct and easy location-cum-manipulation of target widgets due to the WYSIWYG editor; (2) Fewer chances of committing errors during interface modification as the UI modification process is simplified by the WADE IDE; (3) Scaffolding provided by WADE for incorporating add-ons, in the form of event handlers, enables easier and faster addition/modification of functionality; (4) Facilitation provided by the IDE significantly reduces switching time between different applications and tools; (5) Less search time required to find the correct statements to manipulate GUI properties.

While the user study conclusions are not surprising, as WYSIWYG GUI editing is easier than explicit code hacking, it demonstrates that an IDE greatly simplifies UI modification as compared to a Scotty-like approach even for relatively experienced programmers. All of our participants mentioned that they are less likely to use the Scotty simulator for implementing third-party add-ons. On the other hand, WADE significantly lowers the knowledge barrier for developing third-party GUI add-ons. Six out of eight participants indicated that they would use WADE to write add-ons for third-party software.

Limits of the GUI builder metaphor

While many of the modifications were easier to perform using a GUI builder, participants also found it less convenient when dealing with repetitive or looping tasks. For example, if a participant is asked to change 6 out of 7 labels to a different font type, it is easier to use a loop than manually perform the changes multiple times. The GUI metaphor delivers important benefits to learnability, memorability, and error prevention, but it can be inefficient for frequent users [8]. In such cases, a command language may be preferred as it allows simpler programming of similar and repetitive tasks, but at the cost of requiring the user to learn command names and syntax, putting more demands on the user's memory and increasing the chance of errors. Combining both approaches may mitigate this trade-off. For example, Inky [8] allows for sloppy command input and provides rich visual feedback to reduce the cost on user's memory, making it less error-prone. Sikuli [17], on the other hand, enables inclusion of visual images in the command to make it easier and more intuitive to refer to graphical elements. To some extent, WADE follows the same approach by introducing the GUI builder into Scotty's command line programming environment to improve the ease of use and robustness of the third party add-on development. However, our user study has revealed that there is room for improvement to better combine the advantages of the GUI builder and command line programming to further improve the efficiency and ease of use of third party add-on development.

EXTENSION TO OTHER FRAMEWORKS & PLATFORMS

Although WADE is currently only implemented for the *Windows Forms* framework, its approach can be generalized to most other frameworks and platforms.

In general, the WADE approach involves the following three framework-dependent steps:

1) Create an injected add-on manager that can enter the runtime process to manage add-ons, retrieve the GUI hierarchy information, and apply changes back to the host application.

2) Identify a suitable IDE that has GUI builder support and allows add-on integration.

3) Implement an add-on for the IDE that can import the GUI hierarchy from the host application, display it in the GUI builder, and compile the changes to a DLL add-on.

Choosing runtime code intervention method

The key to step 1 is runtime code observation and intervention. On Windows, we use DLL injection. (A solution for Mac OS X is described in [4].) While there are several ways to achieve DLL injection in Windows, we present two primary methods below: a) registry key-based injection and b) system hook-based injection [14].

Registry key-based injection works by adding a new DLL to a registry AppInit key. In Windows Vista and Windows 7, this feature is disabled by default, but can be achieved through code signing. Whenever a new application loads, the DLL will be loaded into the same process as well.

System hook-based injection works by using a separate background monitoring application that detects new programs and uses methods such as SetWindowsHookEx. While more cumbersome and complex, this approach injects the DLL at the deeper thread level and can be used by all versions of Windows.

Choosing which method to use depends on the frameworks used. Some (*e.g.*, Windows Forms) allow modification of the UI thread in the process level. Other frameworks (*e.g.*, QT [11]) do not allow such modifications; therefore, thread level intervention becomes necessary. Once the appropriate runtime code observation and intervention method is identified for a particular framework and platform, the remaining effort mostly concerns the work of writing the injected add-on manager for the framework.

Identifying IDEs with GUI builder and add-on support

The second step is to choose a suitable IDE that supports GUI editing for add-on development. To shorten the development time, it is recommended that an existing IDE be chosen for a particular framework to work.

As WYSIWYG GUI editing becomes more popular, it is not difficult to identify such IDEs for many of the modern frameworks. For example, in the Java platform, NetBeans and Eclipse are two such IDEs; Qt Creator [10] is an example that satisfies these requirements for the popular Qt framework; XCode is an IDE that is suitable for the Mac OS Cocoa framework. We implemented the WADE prototype for both the Visual Studio and Sharp Develop IDEs.

Developing an add-on for importing and presenting GUI

Once a suitable IDE is identified, the steps mentioned in the implementation section can be followed to create an add-on that can import and present the host GUI hierarchy in the IDE's GUI builder. The exact process of implementing add-ons may be complex and depends on the details of the particular environment. However, it is technically feasible and the approach we have proposed in the implementation section can serve as a useful guideline for the development process.

CONCLUSIONS AND FUTURE WORK

The WADE IDE is shown to be useful for realizing a variety of GUI-based modifications in existing software. The presented user study confirms that while these modifications are achievable employing alternative approaches, WADE significantly lowers the requisite knowledge and effort barriers. Future work involves extending the current implementation to other OS platforms, widening WADE support to handle custom and dynamic widgets, and potentially enabling debugging capabilities inside the WADE IDE for add-on development.

ACKNOWLEDGMENT

We thank the AC and anonymous reviewers for their constructive comments and feedback. We thank members of the NUS-HCI Lab for their support. This research is supported by National University of Singapore Academic Research Fund WBS R-252-000-414-101 and by A*STAR, Singapore, under the Human Sixth Sense Program (HSSP) grant.

REFERENCES

1. Besacier, G., and Vernier, F. Toward user interface virtualization: legacy applications and innovative interaction systems. In EICS, 157–166, 2009.
2. Dixon, M., and Fogarty, J. Prefab: implementing advanced behaviors using pixel-based reverse engineering of interface structure. In CHI, 1525-1534, 2010.
3. Dixon, M., Leventhal, D., and Fogarty, J. Content and hierarchy in pixel-based methods for reverse engineering interface structure. In CHI, 969–978, 2011.
4. Eagan, J.R., Beaudouin-Lafon, M., and Mackay, W. E. Cracking the cocoa nut: user interface programming at runtime. In UIST, 225–234, 2011.
5. Edwards, W. K., Hudson, S. E., Marinacci, J., Rodenstein, R., Rodriguez, T., and Smith, I. Systematic output modification in a 2d user interface toolkit. In UIST, 151–158, 1997.
6. Grigoreanu, V., Burnett, M., Wiedenbeck, S., Cao, J., Rector, K., and Kwan, I. End-user debugging strategies: A sensemaking perspective. In TOCHI, 19(1):5:1–5:28, May 2012.
7. Mackay, W.E. Triggers and barriers to customizing software. In CHI, 153–160, 1991.
8. Miller, R.C., Chou, V.H., Bernstein, M., Little, G., Kleek. M.V., Karger, D., and schraefel. M. 2008. Inky: a sloppy command line for the web with rich visual feedback. In UIST (2008), 131-140.
9. Pirolli, P. and Card, S. The sense-making process and leverage points for analyst technology as identified through cognitive task analysis. In ICIA, 2005.
10. Qt Creator. http://gitorious.org/qt-creator/qt-creator
11. Qt framework. http://qt-project.org/
12. Robinson, M. Design for unanticipated use. In ECSCW, 187–202, 1993.
13. Shewmaker, J. Analyzing DLL Injection, http://www.bluenotch.com/files/Shewmaker-DLL-Injection.pdf.
14. Stuerzlinger, W., Chapuis, O., Phillips, D., and Roussel, N. User Interface Facades: Towards Fully Adaptable User Interfaces. In UIST, 309–318, 2006.
15. Tan, D.S., Meyers, B., and Czerwinski, M. Wincuts: manipulating arbitrary window regions for more effective use of screen space. In CHI extended abstracts, 1525-1528, 2004.
16. WineHQ. http://www.winehq.org/.
17. Yeh, T., Chang, T., and Miller, R. Sikuli: using gui screenshots for search and automation. In UIST (2003), 183-192, 20

Pixel-Based Methods for Widget State and Style in a Runtime Implementation of Sliding Widgets

Morgan Dixon[1], Gierad Laput[1,2], James Fogarty[1]

[1] Computer Science & Engineering
DUB Group, University of Washington
{mdixon,jfogarty}@cs.washington.edu

[2] Human-Computer Interaction Institute
Carnegie Mellon University
gierad.laput@cs.cmu.edu

ABSTRACT

Pixel-based methods offer unique potential for modifying existing interfaces independent of their underlying implementation. Prior work has demonstrated a variety of modifications to existing interfaces, including accessibility enhancements, interface language translation, testing frameworks, and interaction techniques. But pixel-based methods have also been limited in their understanding of the interface and therefore the complexity of modifications they can support. This work examines deeper pixel-level understanding of widgets and the resulting capabilities of pixel-based runtime enhancements. Specifically, we present three new sets of methods: methods for pixel-based modeling of widgets in multiple states, methods for managing the combinatorial complexity that arises in creating a multitude of runtime enhancements, and methods for styling runtime enhancements to preserve consistency with the design of an existing interface. We validate our methods through an implementation of Moscovich et al.'s Sliding Widgets, a novel runtime enhancement that could not have been implemented with prior pixel-based methods.

Author Keywords

Pixel-based runtime modification; Prefab; Sliding Widgets; hybrid touch and mouse interaction; real-world interfaces.

ACM Classification Keywords

H.5.2. [Information interfaces and presentation]: User Interfaces;

INTRODUCTION

Pixel-based methods for runtime interface modification offer great potential for democratizing interaction. Because all graphical interfaces ultimately consist of pixels, these methods enable modifying applications without their source code and independent of their underlying toolkit implementation. Pixel-based systems have demonstrated a wide variety of promising enhancements to existing interfaces, including contextual and video-based tutorials [2,31,43], automated visualization retargeting [33], improved window managers [39], interface testing frameworks [7], ink annotation overlays [29], systems for exploring document workflow histories [17], and web content retargeting [22].

Despite the promise of pixel-based systems, they have been limited to relatively simple overlays that primarily point at or highlight existing elements. At least two key challenges have limited prior enhancements: (1) modeling a widget's *behavior*, and (2) capturing an interface's *style*. Structured support for these two tasks would enable more advanced modifications to a variety of existing interfaces.

Although current systems support the interpretation of pixels in an individual screen capture, the behavior of widgets in an interface is difficult to model because many potential enhancements require an understanding of how an interface changes across multiple frames (e.g., if a checkbox becomes checked, if a slider thumb has moved). In addition to monitoring these changes, more advanced enhancements also require manipulating the interface (e.g., sending click events to set a checkbox, dragging a slider). As a result, developers are faced with implementing their own complex frame-to-frame analysis of interfaces together with low-level input redirection mechanisms.

Capturing an interface's style is important because many runtime modifications do not fully alter the appearance of an existing interface, but instead directly overlay new elements onto the interface. Therefore it is important that these enhancements are styled to preserve consistency with

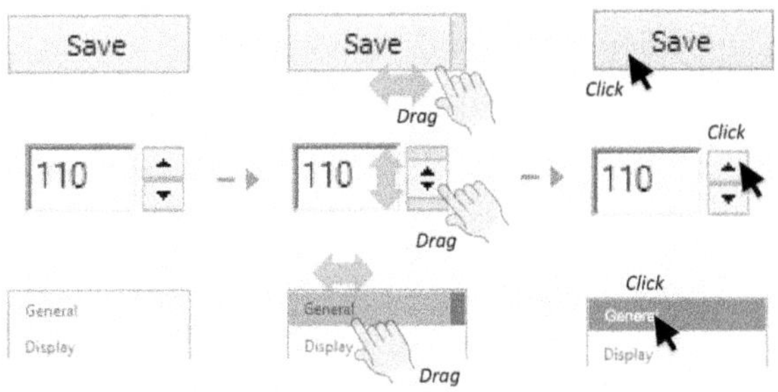

Figure 1: We present new pixel-based methods for modifying existing interfaces at runtime, and we use our methods to explore Moscovich et al.'s Sliding Widgets in real-world interfaces. We overlay Sliding Widgets throughout Microsoft Windows 8, replacing standard mouse-based elements to improve interaction with hybrid touch-and-mouse devices.

CHI 2014, April 26 - May 01 2014, Toronto, ON, Canada.

http://dx.doi.org/10.1145/2556288.2556979

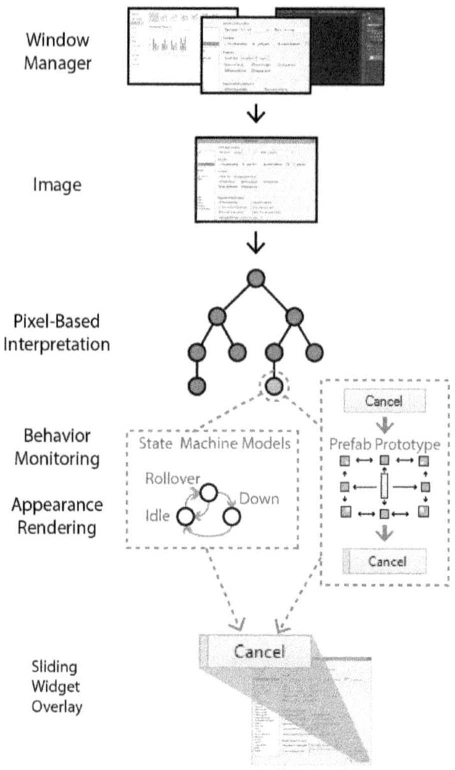

Figure 2: We build upon Prefab's methods for pixel-based identification of interface elements. Identified elements are replaced by overlaying a corresponding Sliding Widget. The original widget is then modeled and manipulated using state machine models. Finally, we style the appearance of overlaid Sliding Widgets by mapping elements of pixel-level appearance from Prefab's prototypes of the original interface.

the existing interface. Without proper support for capturing style, enhancements are likely to be jarring and unusable.

This paper addresses these limitations with novel methods for modeling the state and capturing style of individual widgets. Specifically, we build upon Prefab's pixel-based methods for interpreting interfaces [8,9,10,11]. We first introduce methods for real-time modeling of widgets in multiple states. We then describe methods for linking an original widget's state into the representation needed by a new surface enhancement. Finally, we introduce style mappers and show how they can be used to render entirely new widgets in an existing interface while maintaining a style that is consistent with the original design. We focus on these widget-level methods because they serve as building blocks for complex enhancements to entire interfaces.

We contextualize these contributions in an implementation of Moscovich et al.'s Sliding Widgets, touch widgets activated by sliding a moveable element [24]. Our implementation dynamically overlays Sliding Widgets on mouse-based interface elements throughout Microsoft Windows 8. For example, Figure 1 and our associated video present screenshots of our implementation in a variety of popular interfaces, including Microsoft Word 2013, Adobe Reader, Gmail in the Google Chrome Browser, and Windows Explorer. We replace elements in these applications using various types of Sliding Widgets, including Sliding Buttons, Sliding Spinners, Sliding Toggles, and Sliding Dropdown Menus. Sliding Widgets are well beyond the capabilities of prior pixel-based systems, and the implementation in this work informs and validates the design of our new methods.

In addition to validating our methods, we choose to implement Sliding Widgets in the context of existing interfaces because the implementation could directly benefit an emerging set of *hybrid* devices that support both touch and mouse input. Examples of these devices are shown in our associated video. Unfortunately, graphical interfaces for hybrid devices are either difficult to use or expensive to produce. This is because developers either: (1) provide standard mouse-based interfaces with small and densely arranged targets, or (2) implement an entire alternate interface optimized for touch. We therefore explore the approach of dynamically replacing existing mouse-based elements with touch controls. This approach can improve interaction with hybrid devices without the burden of designing and implementing two entire alternate interfaces.

Figure 2 overviews our system. We first query the window manager for images of windows, and then interpret their elements using Prefab's pixel-based methods [9,10,11]. Specifically, we use Prefab to recover an interface hierarchy containing a node for each interface element (e.g., a leaf for a text label, an inner node with children for a button and any interior content). We walk this tree to determine what elements to replace, and then we overlay our Sliding Widget. To maintain a style consistent with the source interface, our overlay renders each Sliding Widget using elements of the pixel-level appearance, as captured by Prefab's prototypes. This process modifies a single frame captured from an interface, and so we repeat this many times per second, synchronizing each Sliding Widget with its underlying widget. Specifically, we use state models to monitor and manipulate underlying widgets. Transitions in a state model cause the Sliding Widget to update its appearance and behavior, and interaction with a Sliding Widget generates input manipulating the underlying widget.

The specific contributions of our work include:

- Methods for pixel-based modeling of widgets in multiple states. Specifically, we introduce *abstract state models* for describing how to interpret and manipulate categories of widgets. Abstract models are then parameterized with pixel-level data specifying the appearance of a specific widget in each of the modeled states.
- Methods for managing the combinatorial complexity that arises in creating a multitude of runtime enhancements that can apply to a multitude of widgets. Specifically, we show how runtime enhancement can be framed in the Model-View-Controller pattern, and we introduce *linkers* for specifying how a particular runtime enhancement relates to a particular abstract state model.

- Methods for styling runtime enhancements to preserve consistency with the design of an existing interface. Specifically, we introduce *mappers* that use pixel-level elements of an interface's appearance to style runtime enhancements to match that interface.
- An implementation of Sliding Widgets as a runtime pixel-based enhancement that can be applied to existing interfaces. This validates our new pixel-based methods and also unearths implications for the design of Sliding Widgets and future pixel-based runtime enhancements.

RELATED WORK

Surface-Level Runtime Modification. Runtime modification has broad applications in accelerating innovation and facilitating adoption. In prior work, Edwards et al. [13] and Olsen et al. [28] modify interfaces by replacing the toolkit drawing object and intercepting commands (e.g., draw_line, draw_string). They update interfaces with new functionality, such as search and bookmark widgets. More recent examples include application mash-ups [14,18,36], re-authoring desktop applications for mobile interfaces [25,26], and automating repetitious interactions [5,23].

Traditional approaches to runtime modification are based in accessibility APIs [36] or injecting into an interface's underlying toolkit [12,13,28]. Accessibility APIs expose interface state, but are frequently incomplete because application developers fail to implement the API. For example, Hurst et al. found 25% of widgets are completely missing from the accessibility API [21]. Injection techniques attempt to gain full access to an interface by inserting custom logic via the toolkit or other runtime system. However, injection must be carefully crafted for each interface and underlying toolkit, making it difficult to apply to general-purpose whole-desktop enhancements like the Sliding Widgets we pursue here. Perhaps most importantly, both methods expose widget models, not necessarily their on-screen view (e.g., the pixel-level appearance of a slider thumb is intentionally encapsulated). But understanding pixel-level appearance is a requirement for many potential enhancements. For example, we use the pixel-level appearance of existing widgets to style Sliding Widgets to match the interface.

Pixel-Based Methods. Pixel-based methods do not require cooperation from an application's original developers and also overcome the fragmentation of interfaces and toolkits. Applications expose pixels as normal, and their raw pixels are then used as a foundation for additional functionality. Researchers have explored a variety of low-level abstractions to enable a range of pixel-based runtime modifications. Classic work by Zettlemoyer et al. [44,45] examined widget identification in IBOTS and VisMap for interface agents and programming by example [32,34]. St. Amant et al. [35] developed Segman for cognitive modeling applications. Olsen et al.'s [29] ScreenCrayons link interactive ink annotations to arbitrary screen elements. Tan et al.'s [37] WinCuts interactively subdivides windows via a copy-paste metaphor. Yeh et al.'s Sikuli [42] uses template matching and voting based on invariant local features to identify targets in interface scripting and testing applications. Dixon et al.'s Prefab [9,10,11] demonstrates real-time modification using input and output redirection together with pixel-based reverse engineering of interface content and structure. They also demonstrate rudimentary pixel-based strategies for rendering interface overlays [11]. Our current work is informed by this prior research, contributing to pixel-based methods and demonstrating deep implementation of Sliding Widgets.

The strengths and limitations of pixel-based methods versus application introspection motivate hybrid strategies that combine the two approaches. For example, Chang et al. [6] explored several synergies in PAX, including use of Sikuli to obtain paths to elements in the accessibility API, pixel-level analyses to locate screen-rendered text, and the use of Sikuli to find elements in portions of the screen where the accessibility API's representation is incomplete. We focus on core pixel-based methods required for state and style, and future work could extend these to hybrid approaches if needed for more complex or niche interfaces.

Our work presents the first general-purpose pixel-based methods for modeling widgets in multiple states. Prior work explores basic solutions for monitoring interface changes, but these methods are tailored to the goals of a specific enhancement. The most sophisticated example is Banovic et al.'s Waken, a system for reverse engineering and augmenting video tutorials [2]. Their system observes changes in an interface via lightweight frame differencing, and uses these observations to identify widgets. In contrast, our abstract state models are capable of capturing any transition in a widget's appearance, and they can also invoke transitions in a widget's state. These capabilities enable advanced runtime enhancements, moving beyond the identification of widget occurrences in a frame.

This paper combines the development of new pixel-based methods with an examination of an interaction technique in the context of real-world interfaces. This combination parallels the work of Dixon al. in their implementation of a general-purpose target-aware pointing enhancement [8]. They validate novel pixel-based methods in the context of an implementation of Grossman and Balakrishnan's Bubble Cursor, an area cursor that dynamically expands to always capture the nearest target [16]. Like our Sliding Widgets implementation, their cursor functions across the desktop, providing an opportunity to examine its behavior in real-world interfaces. In contrast, the Bubble Cursor only requires the context of a single frame to interpret targets, and it does not require deep knowledge of an element's style to render its overlay. Our Sliding Widgets require this complex modeling, and we therefore advance the state-of-the-art in pixel-based methods with new support for modeling widgets in multiple states and for styling new widgets to be consistent with existing interfaces.

Improving Touch Interaction. A fundamental challenge in touch-based interaction is addressing the fat finger problem, the ambiguity caused when a finger touches multiple targets. Our implementation of Moscovich et al.'s Sliding Widgets is exemplary of a large body of techniques that also explore the problem (e.g., see [24] for an enumeration of many techniques). Few of these techniques were specifically designed for hybrid touch and mouse devices, but many have explored touch support for legacy interfaces. These include techniques designed to overcome the occlusion of the target and selection point, such as [3,38,40,41]. Other techniques address the ambiguity caused by reducing a touch's contact area down to a single selection point, such as Pointing by Zooming and Rubbing [1,4,30]. Although these techniques offer great potential, many of them remain difficult to evaluate and deploy in the context of real interfaces, due to the difficulty of modifying existing interfaces at runtime. Thus our new pixel-based methods offer the opportunity to better understand and deploy techniques like these, helping researchers bridge the gap from the lab to the field.

IDENTIFYING AND INTERPRETING ELEMENTS

We interpret interfaces using Prefab's pixel-based methods for reverse engineering interface structure [9,10,11]. Specifically, we use Prefab Layers and Prefab Annotations to identify an interface hierarchy and then recover Sliding Widget metadata for nodes in that hierarchy.

Prefab Layers structure pixel interpretation as a series of tree transformations. The root corresponds to the processed image, and each identified interface element is added as a node in the tree. Each transformation might add new elements, tag elements with metadata, or remove elements. Transformation code is organized into layers, which can be grouped into chains. An interface is then interpreted by executing a layer chain: the raw image is passed into the first layer, then the output of each layer is passed into the next. Developers reuse and compose existing functionality by concatenating layer chains.

Prefab Annotations support robust annotation of interface elements with metadata that has been inferred, provided by a developer, or collected from end-users of pixel-based enhancements. More concretely, an annotation stores metadata to be applied to a node in a recovered hierarchy. For example, Figure 2's green node has been annotated with metadata indicating it should be replaced with a Sliding Button. Collections of annotations are stored in libraries that layers use to inform their interpretation logic.

Figure 3 shows the resulting layers implemented for our enhancement along with their accompanying annotation libraries. The black layers and libraries are Prefab's existing methods for identifying interface hierarchy. We implement the layers shown in red, and populate the red annotation libraries with data specific to Sliding Widgets. The next two subsections first present Prefab's existing layers and annotations and then describe our layers and annotations.

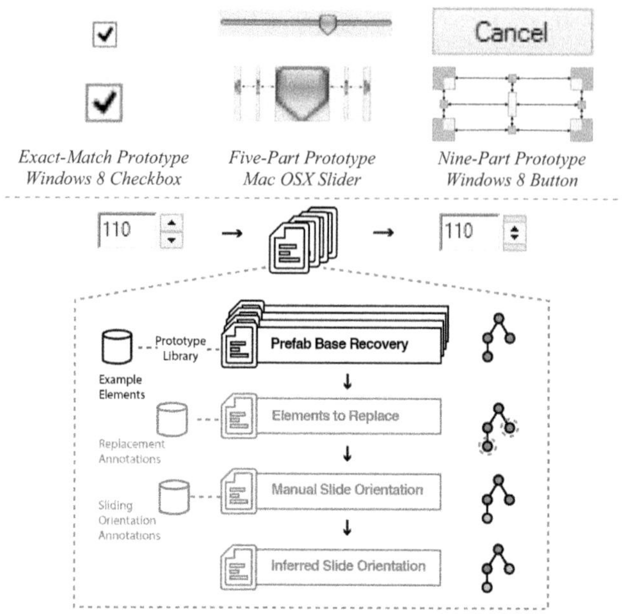

Figure 3: Prefab uses examples of interface elements to generalize prototypes of the appearance of families of widgets. Building from a library of these prototypes, we interpret which elements to replace with Sliding Widgets as well as their sliding orientation. Our novel methods are shown in red, while Prefab's existing methods are in black.

Identifying Interface Hierarchy with Prefab

Prefab's identification layers use annotation libraries containing images of example elements (e.g., an image annotated to identify a region containing a button). The layers then extract a library of *prototypes* generalized from these annotations (e.g., generalizing the example button to describe all buttons of the same type). A prototype describes an arrangement of pixels, and the layers use two high-level strategies to identify elements based on prototypes: (1) exactly matching prototype pixels against an image, or (2) modeling prototype background and then differencing pixels in an image to identify foreground interface elements. Prototype parts can be features (defined as exact patches of pixels) or regions (defined as methods for painting areas of variable size, such as gradients or repeating patterns). The top of Figure 3 illustrates three prototypes selected to show a range of complexity.

The simplest are exact-match prototypes, which consist of a single feature exactly matching the pixels of an example. These do not generalize, but many interface elements also do not vary in appearance (e.g., checkboxes, icons, radio buttons). For example, the left prototype in Figure 3 identifies all standard checked Windows 8 checkboxes.

A more complex *slider* prototype uses multiple parts to account for the variable length of the slider and the variable thumb position. Five parts characterize the slider's thumb, the left and right ends of the trough, and a repeating trough pattern on either side of the thumb. The middle prototype in Figure 3 was generalized from the illustrated example and identifies all standard Mac OS X sliders.

A *nine-part* prototype adds the ability to model background and use runtime pixel differencing to identify unpredictable foreground elements. For example, the prototype at the right of Figure 3 identifies all Windows 8 default buttons and any text or icons painted over their gradient background. It was generalized from the illustrated example button. Nine-part prototypes are first identified by matching their four corners and four edges. Prefab then uses the interior content region to identify elements painted over the background. Discussion of content regions, including how Prefab generalizes a background from examples that include foreground elements, is available in [11].

Interpreting Replacement and Sliding Widget Direction

We have described how Prefab identifies a hierarchy of elements, but any hierarchy is by itself insufficient for most applications. In our case, Sliding Widgets requires metadata indicating (1) which elements should be replaced and (2) the direction in which a replacement Sliding Widget should slide. To obtain these, we combine automated interpretation of Prefab's recovered hierarchy with social annotations, wherein people interactively correct erroneous behavior. Interfaces are procedurally generated, so their pixel-level appearance rarely changes. Familiar interfaces will therefore be thoroughly annotated and "just work". But our combination of automatic interpretation and social annotations allows end-users or designers to interactively correct newly-released or niche interfaces.

For manual annotation, any node can be tagged with a type of Sliding Widget to replace it (e.g., *sliding button*, *sliding dropdown menu*). Nodes can be explicitly tagged *do not replace*, or can be implicitly unavailable for replacement due to replacement of an ancestor. For sliding direction, elements can be tagged *left*, *right*, *up*, *down*, or a diagonal direction (e.g., *down right*). Finally, for multi-function Sliding Widgets such as the spinner replacement in Figure 3, we allow *horizontal* and *vertical* tags. We store tags using support provided by Prefab Annotations, and tag nodes using two layers. Specifically, for each annotation we store a path descriptor based on properties of an element, its location in the hierarchy, and its ancestors. At runtime the layer retrieves annotations by matching against each node's path. Thus, the first layer tags the set of nodes annotated with replacement metadata, and the second specifies the direction for those nodes.

Social annotation can be sufficient in a broad deployment that leverages social mechanisms, but can be expedited by even minimal automation. We currently include a layer that automatically tags nodes with a sliding direction. This layer iterates over elements marked for replacement and assigns directions in a rotating clockwise manner. We ignore elements in dense layouts, and leave widgets in sparse layouts with a default *left* or *horizontal* direction. Finally, the layer ignores any element with a direction assigned by the preceding exact-match layer, thus allowing end-users or designers to manually override the default. Our later section on Examining Sliding Widgets presents examples of interfaces where it is desirable to override sliding direction due to unexpected usability issues in real-world interfaces.

MODELING AND LINKING WIDGET STATES

The previous section describes how Prefab interprets elements within a static frame. Because our methods modify interfaces at runtime, defining the behavior of Sliding Widgets requires monitoring an interface many frames per second and then programmatically redirecting input to manipulate that interface. For example, when a person activates a Sliding Widget by moving its thumb, the system must send a click to the underlying original element. And if that button or any other widget then becomes disabled in response to the interaction, the Sliding Widgets should mirror this change in their behavior and appearance.

The solution to these challenges comes from the insight that a change in appearance of an interface element corresponds to an underlying change in widget state. We therefore model widget dynamics using finite state machines. Although a widget may not be explicitly implemented with an internal state machine, the event-driven nature of interfaces means such a state machine is generally implicit (i.e., widgets exist in some state and change that state in response to interaction events). State machines offer an explicit model of the dynamics of interface elements, which we use to provide *getters* and *setters* for monitoring and manipulating widgets. Specifically, getters allow enhancements to subscribe to events fired when there is a traversal across one or more edges (e.g., signifying rollovers, clicks, drags). Setters can prepackage logic that sends input to an element, transitioning it to a new state.

The critical challenge in modeling state machines is that there are both: (1) a wide variety of existing widgets to be translated into Sliding Widgets, and (2) several types of Sliding Widgets, each requiring a different mapping. A naïve approach would therefore create a combinatorial explosion translating each widget to each Sliding Widget. We instead decouple parts of the translation using an approach similar to a Model-View-Controller pattern. A *state model* is the model, a Sliding Widget or other enhancement the view, and a *linker* the controller that synchronizes state models of the original interface with the representations used in a pixel-based enhancement. Figure 4 illustrates this decomposition.

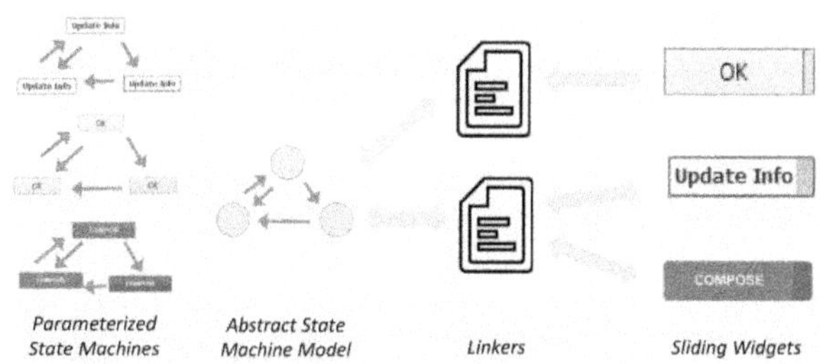

Figure 4: Abstract State Models and Linkers decouple the logic of translating widgets to Sliding Widgets, thus avoiding the combinatorial explosion of direct translation.

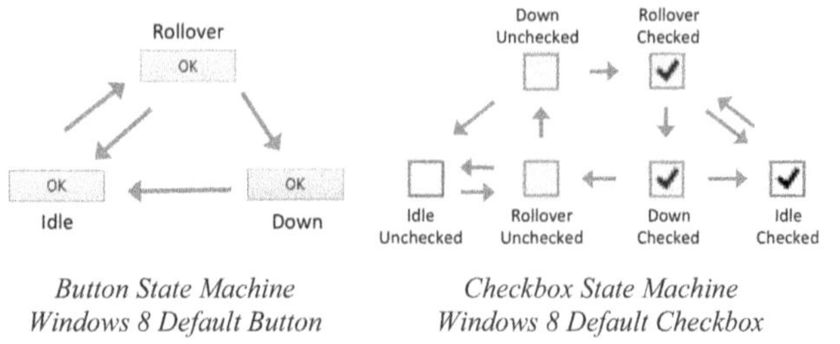

Figure 5: Abstract State Models are parameterized with prototypes describing the appearance of a widget. These two state models are parameterized with prototypes generated from Windows 8 Default Buttons and Checkboxes.

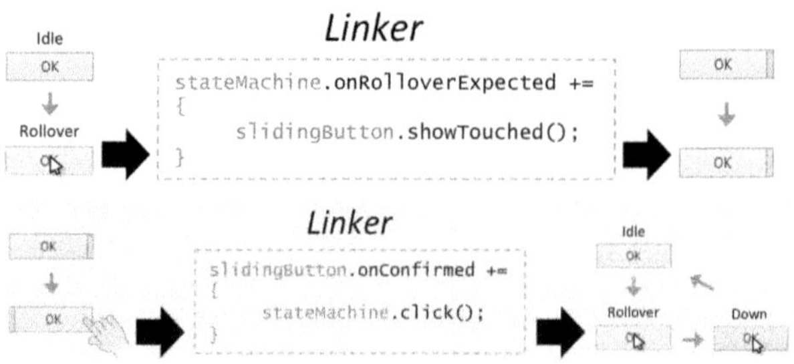

Figure 6: Linkers synchronize state models and Sliding Widgets. These two snippets are from a linker that synchronizes Sliding Buttons with mouse-based buttons.

Abstract State Models

An abstract state model is defined as a combination of states and transitions describing the behavior of a class of widgets. This state model is then parameterized with prototypes describing the appearance of a particular widget in each of the states. For example, Figure 5 presents two state models parameterized to represent behavior for the Windows 8 default button and checkbox. The same models could be parameterized with different prototypes to represent different buttons or checkboxes.

Abstract state models build on Prefab's rudimentary support for observing a transition from one prototype to another [10]. Each transition is defined by a prototype that initiates the transition, a prototype that triggers the transition, and a set of constraints. At runtime, Prefab checks for transitions that are in progress and could be triggered subject to their constraints. After given the option to trigger, these transitions are then given the option to expire (i.e., removed from the set in progress). Finally, the current frame is examined for prototypes that initiate new transitions, which are added to the set in progress.

An abstract state model composes multiple transitions, each defining an edge between two states. States are then parameterized by providing the specific prototypes used in each transition. There are several potential approaches to parameterizing a state model, including interactive authoring tools or more automated methods that passively observe interaction with interfaces, choose among possible state models, and populate each state. We currently use an authoring tool, leaving integration of more advanced methods for future work. Importantly, our methods separate modeling of state machines from recognition of widget appearance, allowing development of abstract models that can be used across a variety of concrete widgets.

At runtime our system maintains a set of parameterized state models that are potentially in progress. This set is populated using the active transitions monitored by Prefab. The triggering of a transition invokes a traversal across the corresponding edge in a state model. When a transition expires, its state model is given the option to expire, denoting a widget is no longer present in the interface. Abstract state models include setters for transitioning between states via manipulation of the interface. Specifically, the setter logic executes input events necessary for traversing edges in a state model. For example, the state model in Figure 5 packages a "click" function that sends mouse down and up events to the source application. This code is defined in the abstract state model, requiring only a single definition for any widgets that share this behavior.

Linkers

A state model defines the dynamics of an element, but those dynamics also need to be related to a Sliding Widget. We therefore provide *linkers*. Specifically, a linker (1) listens for edge traversals in a state machine and updates the Sliding Widget accordingly, and (2) listens for interaction events fired in a Sliding Widget and updates the state model. A single linker can be implemented for an abstract state model paired with a class of Sliding Widgets. For example, Figure 6 illustrates a linker that connects a button abstract state model to a Sliding Button, highlighting the flow of events passed between them.

Upon observing an interaction with a Sliding Widget, a linker can induce arbitrarily complex state machine manipulations. For example, our linker in Figure 6 executes a range of actions depending on the observed Sliding Button interaction. The simplest case is when a user touches down on a Sliding Button and the linker induces a mouse rollover, traversing a single edge in the state machine. In contrast, confirming activation of a Sliding Button induces multiple edge traversals. The linker sends a click to the underlying button, which transitions it first to the state machine's pressed state and then back to the rollover state. Importantly, the separation of a linker from the Sliding Widget allows designers to create Sliding Widgets without a need to implement complex input redirection logic.

Although a state model can be manipulated by sending input events to the source interface, its state does not change until the underlying element's appearance changes. The length of this delay depends on time it takes to process input, and could be problematic for Sliding Widgets or other enhancements that want to provide instant visual feedback after an interaction. To address this problem, each active state model maintains pointers to two states: the *current* state and the *expected* state. The expected state reflects the state to which the machine is expected to traverse, but has not yet visualized. When a state model is manipulated via a setter, it first sets its expected state and then sends input to the underlying widget. A state model also fires an event when its expected state changes (e.g., `onRolloverExpected` in Figure 6), allowing a linker to provide instant updates to the Sliding Widget.

MAPPING WIDGET APPEARANCE

We have presented methods for modeling existing widgets, but there is also a challenge in styling the appearance of the runtime enhancement. Because our Sliding Widgets overlay existing interfaces, it is important that they maintain a style that is consistent with the underlying interface.

We address this problem with *mappers*, which automatically style Sliding Widgets consistent with their underlying original interface. In our solution, we first separate Sliding Widget style from content as in Hudson and Smith [19]. We also use customizable parts as in Hudson and Tanaka [20]. We then use mappers to translate Prefab prototype parts to the Sliding Widget parts. Prototypes model the pixel-level appearance of existing elements, and so we extend their usage from identification to also informing the rendering of new widgets.

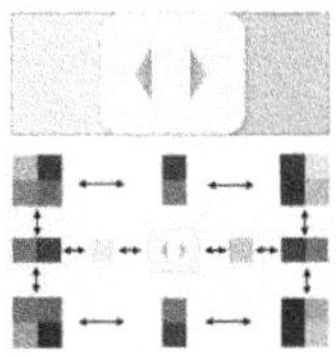

Decomposition of a Sliding Widget into customizable parts is straightforward. Parts render fixed bitmaps or repeating patterns, such as simple repeating colors or more complex gradients. The pixels used in these parts are parameterized to define a specific appearance. Here a Sliding Button is decomposed into eleven parts, each parameterized with a simple appearance. Four bitmaps define the corners of the slider, four patterns the edges, two patterns the left and right troughs behind the thumb, and a single bitmap for the thumb itself. We use similar but more complex models to render other Sliding Widgets, such as the Sliding Spinners and Sliding Dropdown Menus in Figure 1.

Designers can leverage these decompositions to manually style Sliding Widgets, but our mappers expedite this process with methods for styling Sliding Widgets consistent with their underlying original interface. Mappers can be designed for reuse among many prototypes or for a specific prototype. They accept source prototypes and output Sliding Widgets with their parts parameterized based on those prototypes. The following examples illustrate three mappers currently in our framework: basic one-part mappers, nine-part mappers, and multi-prototype mappers.

One-part mappers translate one-part prototypes into Sliding Widgets. An example we have implemented uses two colors extracted from the prototype to define chrome in a Sliding Button. Specifically, we render the corners and edges of the Sliding Widget using the darkest color in the prototype. We then render the trough by extracting the lightest color in the prototype and creating a gradient from the darkest color to the lightest color. The above example shows this one-part mapper applied to a save button.

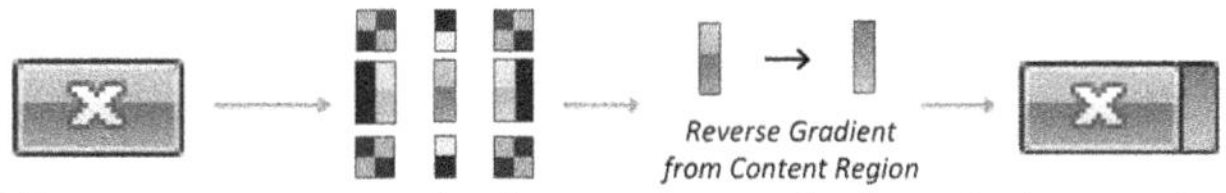

Nine-part mappers obtain more complex renderings using Prefab's nine-part prototypes. This is an example nine-part mapper that translates the appearance of a Windows 8 close button. It maps the corners and edges of the button prototype to the Sliding Widget thumb. It then obtains a recessed look by painting the trough using a reverse of the gradient obtained from the prototype content region.

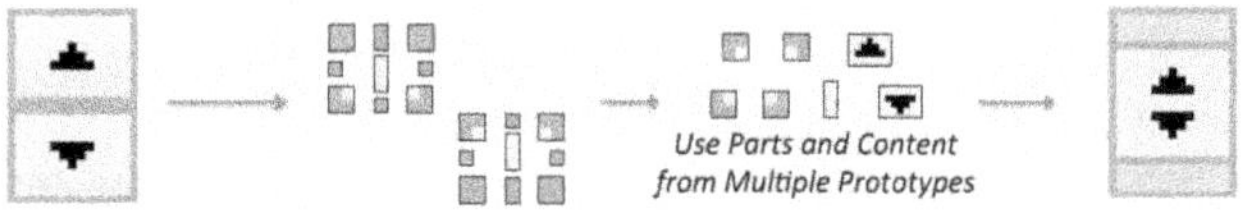

The previous two examples use parts from a single prototype to parameterize the appearance of a sliding widget. It is also possible to perform more complex mappings using multiple prototypes. Here we show an example multi-prototype mapper where we map from prototypes that define the two arrows of a spinner. The content regions of those prototypes provide the up and down arrows, which are mapped into the thumb of the slider. Our associated video shows additional Sliding Widgets created using multi-prototype mappers, including a Sliding Checkbox created from two one-part prototypes that describe the appearance of a Windows 8 checkbox in its checked and unchecked states.

EXAMINING SLIDING WIDGETS IN THE WILD

Sliding Widgets and other techniques addressing the fat finger problem are often designed, discussed, and evaluated using fields of abstract widgets or other limited testbeds. Because our implementation provides the ability to deploy Sliding Widgets, we sought to determine what insights we could gain from examining them in real-world interfaces. Our findings identify three challenges: (1) the challenge of supporting both area and point cursors within the same interface, (2) limitations of sliding in complex interfaces, and (3) limitations of replacing individual widgets.

Challenges with Supporting Area and Point Cursors

A major challenge is defining Sliding Widgets that work within the same interface as mouse-based widgets. Consider the spinner shown in the bottom-center of Figure 7, which illustrates a common scenario where a spinner controls the contents of an adjacent textbox. The spinner can be replaced with a Sliding Widget, but it then becomes difficult to manipulate the textbox directly. This is because Sliding Widgets leverage the entire contact area of touch input, but the touch here also overlaps the text field for which area cursor input is undefined. Sliding Widgets can resolve this ambiguity by alternating their orientation for disambiguation among other adjacent Sliding Widgets, but this strategy does not resolve the scenario where a touch area overlaps both a Sliding Widget and an element designed only for point-cursor interaction.

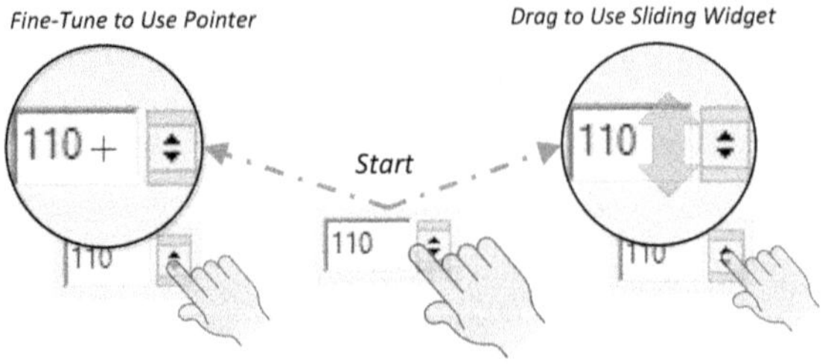

Figure 7: We modify Vogel and Baudisch's Shift [38], employing pointing when the user fine-tunes and contact area-based touches when the user drags.

Sliding Widgets were unusable without the ability to disambiguate between pointing and sliding, so we developed a strategy for gracefully degrading from a contact area to a standard point cursor. More concretely, when a person touches a point-cursor element, we pass the standard touch point to the underlying interface (typically computed as the contact area centroid). However, when a person touches a Sliding Widget, our overlay will send the entire contact area to the widget. In dense layouts, we employ an enhanced implementation of Vogel and Baudisch's Shift to enable fine cursor adjustment [38]. After a touch event, Shift creates a callout showing a copy of the occluded screen area and places it in a non-occluded location. Shift was designed for point-cursor interaction, so we extend it to support area cursor input. Our goal is to make it possible to swiftly activate a Sliding Widget without eliminating precise control of a pointer. Thus, the core challenge in this task is to separate fine-tuning input from the dragging needed to activate a Sliding Widget.

Figure 7 storyboards our solution for disambiguating elements in dense layouts. When a user dwells over an element, we present a callout showing the occluded screen area. We then distinguish fine-tuning from dragging using a threshold on input velocity. Specifically, slow movements below the threshold are categorized as fine-tuning, and fast movements are treated as drags. Fine-tuning moves the position of a point cursor over mouse-based targets, and for any Sliding Widgets under the point cursor it sends touch down events. Alternatively, dragging only manipulates Sliding Widgets. The drag moves a Sliding Widget's thumb in the direction of the drag, allowing activation while hiding that input from any other point-cursor targets.

Limitations of Sliding in Complex Interfaces

Sliding Widgets use the metaphor of real-world sliding manipulations, but it is unclear how this applies to certain

elements. One example is in hierarchical widgets, where an interactive element contains an interactive child element. In this screenshot of a panel in Adobe Photoshop, each row is clickable (to select a layer) along with its inner buttons (to toggle layer visibility). Unfortunately, this has no clear Sliding Widget analog. Sliding Widgets could potentially be nested in a larger Sliding Button, but this would be awkward when sliding either the outer or inner widgets.

We also found limitations of the sliding metaphor in the context of groups of related elements. Moscovich et al. demonstrate the promising feature of Sliding Widgets where a list of elements is selected in a single stroke. Our associated video also demonstrates an example of this interaction in the context of a Skype dialog. However, in most real interfaces where multiple elements are frequently toggled together, developers provide a "select all" toggle. In other cases, elements tend to be unrelated or infrequently toggled, leaving single stroke interactions undesirable.

We believe this problem is largely due to conflicts between Sliding Widget behavior and the intentional design of interfaces for point cursors. More concretely, it may be possible to redesign an entire interface to exploit the advantages of single-stroke sliding interactions, but only at the obvious cost of needing to overhaul much of the design. Dixon et al. raised a similar tension between target-aware pointing and existing pointing-based interfaces [8], so perhaps this problem surfaces a larger conflict present in designing surface-level modifications to existing designs.

Limitations of Individual Widget Replacement

Our implementation mostly replaces individual elements with individual Sliding Widgets. However, this approach can introduce conflicts when multiple widgets are related.

We partially anticipated this in our implementation of a Sliding Spinner. A naïve implementation would replace each button in the spinner with a Sliding Button and alternate their direction to help with disambiguation. However, this can conflict with a person's expectations of the interface if the chosen sliding direction is different than the semantic direction of the spinner. For example, the spinner in Figure 1 adjusts the numerical value in its textbox, and sliding horizontally may seem less appropriate than sliding vertically. The problem is magnified if the arrows from the original spinner are mapped into the appearance of the Sliding Widget. We addressed this problem with the Sliding Spinner that understand the relation between the two buttons and behaves appropriately.

While our strategy for grouping multiple related widgets works for spinners, the strategy is much more difficult to implement for larger collections of related widgets. For example, consider this enhanced Windows 8 Calculator interface. It includes a typical grid

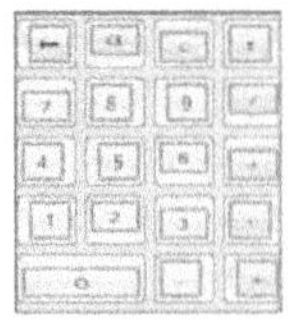

of buttons, but replacing each individual button yields an interface that is jarring and difficult to use. The calculator's original layout is relatively dense, so it seems useful to alternate sliding directions. But then a person has to carefully inspect each button to understand how to slide it. Instead, the entire panel of buttons should be replaced with a Sliding Widgets optimized for these types of grid layouts.

This problem suggests that a more global understanding of interface layout is necessary for replacing some elements. One possible strategy is to employ a mechanism similar to

Nichols et al.'s Smart Templates for replacing entire groups of controls [27]. This technique uses parameterized templates to specify when different conventions might be applied. Our approach to replacing spinner widgets can be seen as an initial example of this, but we imagine there is an opportunity to extend this idea to more sophisticated templates capturing a variety of conventions and semantics.

DISCUSSION AND CONCLUSION

Although we describe our pixel-based methods in the context of implementing Sliding Widgets, our modeling of state and our approaches to styling widgets using prototype parts can enable and inform a variety of future enhancements. For example, other enhancements can directly re-use our state models. An enhancement to support crossing-based widgets on hybrid pen and mouse devices could use our same state models, implement new linkers relating their crossing widgets to our models, and style their widgets using our techniques. Even more complex enhancements might go beyond replacing individual widgets, using our models to drive entire new interfaces automatically generated by a system like Supple [15].

We described how our state models provide getters and setters for widget state, encapsulating low-level details required for monitoring and manipulating widgets. These turned out to be additionally beneficial because they provide an API that is similar to the API of the underlying toolkit itself. For example, our checkbox state model provides a familiar `getChecked()` method, which hides details of what states and prototypes the model uses to represent the checkbox. We believe that there is a rich opportunity for future work that investigates a more general set of *semantic views* that encapsulate pixel-based methods. The goal of these views would be to provide developers of pixel-based enhancements with a higher-level toolkit that is more similar to existing interface toolkits. For example, a `getLabel()` method on a semantic view of a button would manage the details of obtaining the button's prototype, recovering its content, and processing those pixels to recover its text.

Our linkers automatically map Sliding Widget interactions into a sequence of mouse events to manipulate the underlying interface element. Current windowing systems are not designed to support this type of behavior. In particular, the overlay and the underlying enhancement must share the same input stream, which requires blocking input from one or the other during different stages of an interaction. This limitation also makes it difficult to support simultaneous manipulation of elements (e.g., Moscovich et al. suggest using an area cursor to drag two sliders at the same time). Deeper exploration of new input management frameworks is an opportunity for future work. For example, a framework might provide multiple input streams, separating live input from redirected input.

We implemented several basic linkers for synchronizing Sliding Widgets and state machines in most interfaces, but we imagine developers will extend these or create more sophisticated linkers tailored for specific applications. As one motivation, our example linker maps touches to mouse rollovers, thus making it possible to view tooltips or other rollover responses in existing interfaces. But Moscovich et al. also demonstrated more complex responses to touch events with their action-preview-on-touch behaviors [24]. In their design, touching a button displays a preview of the action it will perform if activated. Future work might therefore examine linkers that execute these previews by monitoring and manipulating multiple state models. Importantly, our Model-View-Controller pattern for separating linkers from state models and Sliding Widgets makes it possible to define custom behaviors without modifying state model or Sliding Widget code.

Our application is the first practical general-purpose implementation of Sliding Widgets. There is nearly always a fundamental gap between the knowledge that can be gained in lab studies versus the implications of this knowledge for real-world contexts, and we believe this work narrows the gap for Sliding Widgets. We are exploring the best way to deploy our application on Windows 8 hybrid devices to further bridge the gap from the lab to the field. We also envision tools accompanying the deployment where developers can gather logged usage data to provide insight into real-world challenges (e.g., testing alternative designs, visualizing problems reported by end-users of pixel-based enhancements). Our hope is to help catalyze interaction research in escaping the lab, putting it into the hands of end-users who stand to benefit from the field's rich innovation.

ACKNOWLEDGEMENTS

We thank Scott E. Hudson and Daniel S. Weld for advice, discussion, and thoughts that helped shape this research. This work was supported in part by the National Science Foundation under award IIS-1053868.

REFERENCES

1. Albinsson, P.-A. and Zhai, S. High Precision Touch Screen Interaction. *CHI 2003*, 105–112.
2. Banovic, N., Grossman, T., Matejka, J., and Fitzmaurice, G. Waken: Reverse Engineering Usage Information and Interface Structure from Software Videos. *UIST 2012*, 83–92.
3. Baudisch, P. and Chu, G. Back-of-Device Interaction Allows Creating Very Small Touch Devices. *CHI 2009*, 1923–1932.
4. Benko, H., Wilson, A.D., and Baudisch, P. Precise Selection Techniques for Multi-Touch Screens. *CHI 2006*, 1263–1272.
5. Bolin, M., Webber, M., Rha, P., Wilson, T., and Miller, R.C. Automation and Customization of Rendered Web Pages. *UIST 2005*, 163–172.
6. Chang, T.-H., Yeh, T., and Miller, R. Associating the Visual Representation of User Interfaces with Their Internal Structures and Metadata. *UIST 2011*, 245–254.
7. Chang, T.-H., Yeh, T., and Miller, R.C. GUI Testing Using Computer Vision. *CHI 2010*, 1535–1544.

8. Dixon, M., Fogarty, J., and Wobbrock, J. A General-Purpose Target-Aware Pointing Enhancement Using Pixel-Level Analysis of Graphical Interfaces. *CHI 2012*, 3167–3176.

9. Dixon, M. and Fogarty, J. Prefab Layers and Prefab Annotations: Extensible Pixel-Based Interpretation of Graphical Interfaces. *In Preparation.*

10. Dixon, M. and Fogarty, J. Prefab : Implementing Advanced Behaviors Using Pixel-Based Reverse Engineering of Interface Structure. *CHI 2010*, 1525–1534.

11. Dixon, M., Leventhal, D., and Fogarty, J. Content and Hierarchy in Pixel-Based Methods for Reverse Engineering Interface Structure. *CHI 2011*, 969–978.

12. Eagan, J.R., Beaudouin-Lafon, M., and Mackay, W.E. Cracking the Cocoa Nut: User Interface Programming at Runtime. *UIST 2011*, 225–234.

13. Edwards, W.K., Hudson, S.E., Marinacci, J., Rodenstein, R., Rodriguez, T., and Smith, I. Systematic Output Modification in a 2D User Interface Toolkit. *UIST 1997*, 151–158.

14. Fujima, J., Lunzer, A., Hornbæk, K., and Tanaka, Y. Clip, Connect, Clone: Combining Application Elements to Build Custom Interfaces for Information Access. *UIST 2004*, 175.

15. Gajos, K.Z., Wobbrock, J.O., and Weld, D.S. Automatically Generating User Interfaces Adapted To Users' Motor and Vision Capabilities. *UIST 2007*, 231–240.

16. Grossman, T. and Balakrishnan, R. The Bubble Cursor : Enhancing Target Acquisition by Dynamic Resizing of the Cursor's Activation Area. *CHI 2005*, 281–290.

17. Grossman, T., Matejka, J., and Fitzmaurice, G. Chronicle: Capture, Exploration, and Playback of Document Workflow Histories. *UIST 2010*, 143–152.

18. Hartmann, B., Wu, L., Collins, K., and Klemmer, S.R. Programming by a Sample: Rapidly Creating Web Applications with d.mix. *UIST 2007*, 241–250.

19. Hudson, S.E. and Smith, I. Supporting Dynamic Downloadable Appearances in an Extensible User Interface Toolkit. *UIST 1997*, 159–168.

20. Hudson, S.E. and Tanaka, K. Providing Visually Rich Resizable Images for User Interface Components. *UIST 2000*, 227–235.

21. Hurst, A., Hudson, S.E., and Mankoff, J. Automatically Identifying Targets Users Interact with During Real World Tasks. *IUI 2010*, 11–20.

22. Kumar, R., Talton, J.O., Ahmad, S., and Klemmer, S.R. Bricolage : Example-Based Retargeting for Web Design. *CHI 2011*, 2197–2206.

23. Little, G., Lau, T.A., Cypher, A., Lin, J., Haber, E.M., and Kandogan, E. Koala: Capture, Share, Automate, Personalize Business Processes on the Web. *CHI 2007*, 943–952.

24. Moscovich, T. Contact Area Interaction with Sliding Widgets. *UIST*, (2009), 13–22.

25. Nichols, J., Hua, Z., and Barton, J. Highlight: A System for Creating and Deploying Mobile Web Applications. *UIST 2008*, 249–258.

26. Nichols, J. and Lau, T. Mobilization by Demonstration: Using Traces to Re-author Existing Web Sites. *IUI 2008*, 149–160.

27. Nichols, J., Myers, B. a., and Litwack, K. Improving Automatic Interface Generation with Smart Templates. *IUI 2004*, 286–288.

28. Olsen, D.R., Hudson, S.E., Verratti, T., Heiner, J.M., and Phelps, M. Implementing Interface Attachments Based on Surface Representations. *CHI 1999*, 191–198.

29. Olsen, D.R., Taufer, T., and Fails, J.A. ScreenCrayons: Annotating Anything. *UIST 2004*, 165–174.

30. Olwal, A., Feiner, S., and Heyman, S. Rubbing and Tapping for Precise and Rapid Selection on Touch-Screen Displays. *CHI 2008*, 295–304.

31. Pongnumkul, S., Dontcheva, M., Li, W., Wang, J., Bourdev, L., Avidan, S., and Cohen, M.F. Pause-and-Play: Automatically Linking Screencast Video Tutorials with Applications. *UIST 2011*, 135–144.

32. Potter, R. Triggers: Guiding Automation with Pixels to Achieve Data Access. *A. Cypher, eds. MIT Press.*

33. Savva, M., Kong, N., Chhajta, A., Fei-fei, L., Agrawala, M., and Heer, J. ReVision : Automated Classification , Analysis and Redesign of Chart Images. *UIST 2011*, 393–402.

34. St Amant, R., Lieberman, H., and Potter, R. Visual Generalization in Programming by Example. *Communications of the ACM 43*, 3 (2000), 107–114.

35. St Amant, R., Riedl, R., Ritter, F.E., and Reifers, A. Image Processing in Cognitive Models with SegMan. *HCII 2005.*

36. Stuerzlinger, W., Chapuis, O., Phillips, D., and Roussel, N. User Interface Façades: Towards Fully Adaptable User Interfaces. *UIST 2006*, 309–318.

37. Tan, D.S., Meyers, B., and Czerwinski, M. WinCuts : Manipulating Arbitrary Window Regions for More Effective Use of Screen Space. *CHI 2004*, 1525–1528.

38. Vogel, D. and Baudisch, P. Shift : A Technique for Operating Pen-Based Interfaces Using Touch. *CHI 2007*, 657–666.

39. Waldner, M., Steinberger, M., Grasset, R., and Schmalstieg, D. Importance-Driven Compositing Window Management: *CHI 2011*, 959–968.

40. Weldon, J. and Shneidermanss, B. Improving the Accuracy of Touch Screens: An Experimental Evaluation of Three Strategies. *CHI 1988*, 27–32.

41. Wigdor, D., Forlines, C., Baudisch, P., Barnwell, J., and Shen, C. LucidTouch : A See-Through Mobile Device. *CHI 2007*, 269–278.

42. Yeh, T., Chang, T.-H., and Miller, R.C. Sikuli: Using GUI Screenshots for Search and Automation. *UIST 2009*, 183–194.

43. Yeh, T., Chang, T.-H., Xie, B., Walsh, G., Watkins, I., Wongsuphasawat, K., Huang, M., Davis, L.S., and Bederson, B.B. Creating Contextual Help for GUIs Using Screenshots. *UIST 2011*, 145–154.

44. Zettlemoyer, L.S. and St. Amant, R. A Visual Medium for Programmatic Control of Interactive Applications. *CHI 1999*, 199–206.

45. Zettlemoyer, L.S., Amant, R.S., and Dulberg, M.S. IBOTS : Agent Control Through the User Interface. *IUI 1999.*

The Usability of CommandMaps in Realistic Tasks

Joey Scarr[†], Andy Cockburn[†], Carl Gutwin[‡], Andrea Bunt[*], Jared Cechanowicz[‡]
[†]Computer Science, University of Canterbury, Christchurch, New Zealand
[‡]Computer Science, University of Saskatchewan, Saskatoon, Canada
[*]Computer Science, University of Manitoba, Winnipeg, Canada
{joey,andy}@cosc.canterbury.ac.nz, gutwin@cs.usask.ca, bunt@cs.umanitoba.ca

ABSTRACT
CommandMaps are a promising interface technique that flattens command hierarchies and exploits human spatial memory to provide rapid access to commands. CommandMaps have performed favorably in constrained cued-selection studies, but have not yet been tested in the context of real tasks. In this paper we present two real-world implementations of CommandMaps: one for Microsoft Word and one for an image editing program called Pinta. We use these as our experimental platforms in two studies. In the first, we show that CommandMaps demonstrate performance and subjective advantages in a realistic task. In the second, we observe naturalistic use of CommandMaps over the course of a week, and gather qualitative data from interviews, questionnaires, and conversations. Our results provide substantial insight into users' reactions to CommandMaps, showing that they are positively received by users and allowing us to provide concrete recommendations to designers regarding when and how they should be implemented in real applications.

Author Keywords
CommandMaps; spatial memory; hierarchies; real tasks.

ACM Classification Keywords
H.5.2 [User Interfaces]: Interaction Styles.

INTRODUCTION
The CommandMap, introduced by Scarr et al. [23], is a full-screen interface intended to replace hierarchical menus and toolbars (Figure 1). When displayed by pressing a command key or clicking a dedicated button, a CommandMap uses the whole screen to display functionality, flattening the command hierarchy and exploiting users' strong ability to remember item locations in spatial layouts. These properties theoretically enable expert CommandMap users to reach a high level of performance. Furthermore, since they are based on visual, point-and-click interaction, they require little training and allow users to maintain a predominantly 'see and point versus learn and remember' modality of interaction that assists novice users [24]. However, there are also risks to the CommandMap approach: for example, the complexity of the full-screen UI may deter novice users, and the workspace occlusion caused by the CommandMap's modal presentation may disrupt the user's workflow.

Scarr et al. validated the CommandMap design in a series of command selection experiments. In brief, their results demonstrated that once users were familiar with the CommandMap layout and interaction mechanics, they could access commands more quickly than when using traditional menus or the Microsoft Office Ribbon user interface. These are promising and important findings, showing that CommandMaps have the *potential* to improve performance in the frequent and basic task of selecting commands. However, there are many factors influencing UI success in the real world that were not present in these lab studies; consequently, there are several further research questions that need to be answered before CommandMaps can be deployed with confidence in real-world software.

The fundamental question motivating this research is "*Do CommandMaps work in the real world?*" From a methodological perspective, this is a critical question to answer, especially when proposing an interface mechanism that changes the basic method for presenting and accessing commands. The importance of addressing this question is accentuated by the many previous HCI studies that have demonstrated divergence between results obtained in the lab and in the field, with lab studies typically generating stronger, more positive findings [5, 8, 20]. Further, the importance of triangulating results through complementary methods is well known in the behavioral and social sciences [17], including HCI [14].

More specifically, this paper comprises an attempt to answer the following research questions:

Q1) *Do CommandMaps demonstrate performance and subjective advantages in real tasks?* Real tasks, such as document formatting or image editing, have many characteristics that were not present in previous studies. For example, an individual command selection usually forms a small step of a larger task, which may also include content creation activities such as typing or drawing. If CommandMaps somehow interfere with the other cognitive and physical activities involved in task completion, then these drawbacks may outweigh the benefits.

CHI 2014, April 26–May 1, 2014, Toronto, Ontario, Canada.

ACM 978-1-4503-2473-1/14/04...$15.00.
http://dx.doi.org/10.1145/2556288.2556976

Q2) *How do users respond when first using CommandMaps?* Scarr et al.'s previous studies showed that users without item location knowledge were not adversely affected by CommandMaps, but participants were allowed time to become familiar with the interface first. Therefore, the issue of users' initial 'out of the box' experience, both in terms of performance and subjective impressions, requires further examination.

Q3) *How do performance and subjective impressions change in real tasks as users gain experience?* While previous studies have shown that performance and subjective preferences favor CommandMaps after condensed periods of command selection, the progression from novice to expert over a realistic period of time (e.g., a week) has not been studied.

Q4) *Do CommandMaps generalize to multiple application contexts?* In order to recommend the use of CommandMaps in the real world, we need to know whether they are successful in different application genres (such as word processing and image editing), and whether there are characteristics of different applications that make CommandMaps more or less useful.

Q5) *What usability issues arise with CommandMaps in real-world use?* By observing real use, we can identify usability issues and improve their design.

In order to answer these questions, we examine the use of CommandMaps in realistic tasks. We first present two implementations that modify real-world software systems to use CommandMaps – Figure 1 shows these systems, based on Microsoft Word and the open-source painting and photo editing application 'Pinta'. These implementations serve as our experimental platforms in two studies.

The first study, addressing **Q1**, examines how users complete moderately realistic word processing tasks when using the Microsoft Word CommandMap. For baseline comparison, we also examined an equivalent task when using an unaltered version of Microsoft Word 2007. Results show that the CommandMap was at least as fast or faster than the unaltered Ribbon UI (depending on the amount of tab switching required), and was strongly preferred.

The second study, addressing **Q2-5**, focuses on user opinions, and the evolution of those opinions, during the first week of interaction with CommandMaps. Participants interacted with a CommandMap and the standard interface in both Microsoft Word and Pinta. They were given realistic tasks to complete; they were invited to complete them in any way they saw fit; and they repeated the tasks every day for a week. Observations of use, interviews, and questionnaires gave us a rich pool of data, from which we determined the following key results: 1) many participants, even those highly familiar with the standard Word interface, preferred the CommandMap after using it for a week; 2) novice users found the CommandMap useful for gaining an overview of the interface; 3) performance increased at about the same rate as standard interfaces; 4) CommandMaps were most effective in replacing interfaces with deep menu hierarchies; and 5) there are several specific opportunities to improve CommandMaps' usability (described later in the paper).

This work makes three primary contributions. First, we present two real-world implementations of CommandMaps in very different application domains (word processing and graphics editing). Second, our studies provide clear and compelling evidence that CommandMaps are a usable and learnable interface alternative that provides higher performance, reduced search times, and higher approval ratings from most users. Our studies, combined with the laboratory work that has been done previously, strongly indicates that UI designers should adopt the CommandMap idea and its foundational principles of flattened command hierarchies, spatial memory, and fast access. Finally, the results of our second study allow us to recommend design alterations to CommandMaps, as well as providing concrete advice regarding when and how designers should consider implementing them in real-world applications.

RELATED WORK

Building a credible body of empirical evidence in support of the CommandMap design is a critical motivator for this work. In our treatment of previous work, therefore, we first consider the importance of validating an experimental hypothesis using multiple research methods. Second, we perform a review of systems similar to CommandMaps and discuss the experimental evidence available for each.

Experimental Triangulation

In the design of any research question, there exists a tension between the goals of internal and external validity. Mackenzie [15] discusses this trade-off, noting that strong empirical results often require a narrow research question (e.g., "does Technique A provide faster selection time than Technique B after one hour of use?"), while striving for external validity leads to broad, less easily testable questions ("is Technique A better than Technique B?"). While the former approach produces replicable empirical data, it can often fail to answer the broader question of whether a technique will be successful in the real world. McGrath [17] asserts that "it is only by accumulating evidence, over studies done so that they involve different – complementary – methodological strengths and weaknesses that we can begin to consider the evidence as credible, as probably true, as a body of empirically-based knowledge."

Mackay and Fayard [14] concur that "it is simply not possible to use a single study that addresses all the possible threats to validity", and argue that the solution is triangulation, or "using more than one research approach to address the same question" (p. 231). The importance of using more than one research approach to answer the same question is highlighted by several case studies in HCI (see [5, 8, 20]). In these examples, initial laboratory studies provided positive results, but later field studies revealed usability issues only present in real-world conditions.

a) The standard version of Word. b) The default state of CM-Word. c) CM-Word with CommandMap visible.

d) The standard version of Pinta. e) The default state of CM-Pinta. f) CM-Pinta with CommandMap visible.

Figure 1. Standard (left) and CommandMap (middle, right) versions of Word and Pinta.

Parallel Menus and Full-Screen Command Layouts

One way of supporting rapid, point-and-click selection of items in a graphical user interface is to present items in a flat, spatially stable structure. Interfaces such as these support rapid selection by leveraging two complementary facets of performance. The first is human memory for item locations, which develops automatically as a by-product of interaction [11] and facilitates extremely quick item revisitation over time [6, 19, 23]. We refer the reader to Scarr et al. [22] for a review of spatial memory. The second is that when item locations are known, flat hierarchies allow optimal retrieval time (i.e., flat structures allow users to point directly to the target, as opposed to having to navigate through a hierarchical control structure) [2]. Spatially stable, full-screen 2D layouts have been investigated in several application domains, including bookmark browsing [21] and document navigation [3], with results showing strong performance benefits for revisitation in each case.

Scarr et al. [23] presented the CommandMap as a spatially-stable interaction technique that used flat hierarchies to provide quick access to commands. They validated their prototype system using highly repetitive command selection tasks, showing that expert users were able to perform faster command selections compared to menus and the Microsoft Office Ribbon. Gutwin and Cockburn's earlier ListMap design [6] showed similar advantages for experts, but reduced performance for novices (which they attributed to visual search difficulties in the constrained interface space).

Selection time benefits of parallel command menus have also been demonstrated by Hochheiser and Shneiderman [9], whose experiment showed that simultaneous menus on websites provided advantages for "experienced users performing complex tasks" compared to hierarchical menus. Malacria et al. [16] proposed a related method using menu parallelization to display hotkey bindings in their ExposeHK system, although it was not evaluated.

To date, research on parallelized command menus such as CommandMaps is promising but limited. In particular, while the previous CommandMap studies provide compelling evidence in favor of their use, the studies were performed with cued-selection tasks, which omit many of the subtleties and usability issues involved with completing tasks in the real world.

A COMMANDMAP FOR MICROSOFT WORD

Our implementation of the Microsoft Word CommandMap is based on Scarr et al.'s original prototype, with some adjustments (Figure 1b,c). The prototype displayed no commands until a command key was pressed, at which point all of the commands were displayed in parallel, overlaying the document. We modified this design for Microsoft Word CommandMap so that the *Home* tab was continually displayed at the top of the window (see Figure 1b). We had two main reasons for this: first, it provides convenient visual access to the most frequently used commands; and second, it provides a visual focus of attention for displaying a tip for novice CommandMap users that instructs them on how to access other commands. This tip takes the form of a dropdown tab with the label "More commands... <Ctrl>" (see top-left of Figure 1b). When the "More commands" tab is clicked, or when the <Ctrl> key is held, the CommandMap is displayed, making all commands from all tabs available at once by pointing and clicking (see Figure 1c). Releasing the <Ctrl> key without making a selection cancels the command and hides the CommandMap. Selecting a command completes the command and hides the CommandMap.

Implementation and Design

The CommandMap is implemented as a plug-in for Microsoft Word 2007. To assist replication or further development, the plug-in is available at www.cosc.canterbury.ac.nz/research/RG/HCI/HCIlab/. The plug-in uses an open-source, third-party Ribbon control (officeribbon.codeplex.com/) to mimic the look and feel of the original Word 2007 Ribbon. The visual appearance of controls is replicated using the original Word 2007 icons. When the CommandMap is displayed, either by holding <Ctrl> or by clicking the on-screen drop-down button, the CommandMap appears as a borderless overlay at 95% opacity on top of the main Word window. It displays tabs in a vertical arrangement below the already-visible Home tab. Interaction with the controls in the CommandMap works the same way as the Ribbon: clicking an item invokes its corresponding command using the Word Object Model.

Although the plug-in provides good coverage of Microsoft Word's interface capabilities in a fluid and convincing user interface, certain features of Word were difficult or impossible to replicate using the plug-in approach. For example, contextual tabs, which are only visible in certain editing contexts (such as when a table or image is selected), still appear in the topmost Ribbon, as do the tabs of other Word plug-ins, such as EndNote. "Galleries" of pre-defined content (such as the WordArt, Symbol and Equation menus) were also excluded, due to the significant amount of engineering required to replicate them.

A COMMANDMAP FOR PINTA

To explore the application and use of CommandMaps in a domain other than word processing, we also designed and implemented a CommandMap for an image editing application. We chose an image editing application because content creation and editing of images is predominantly mouse-based, which is substantially different to the keyboard creation and editing actions when word processing. We selected Pinta, a version of Paint.NET, as the base application because its C# codebase is open source. The adapted version of Pinta replaces its menus with a CommandMap, requiring various interface adaptations to the CommandMap concept, as described below.

Implementation and Design

Pinta is implemented in C#, using the .NET Framework. We forked the code and built a CommandMap-based version, as shown in Figure 1d-f.

Image editing programs such as Pinta typically have toolbars, as well as various palettes (such as Tools, Colors, Layers, and History) that are docked around the edge of the screen. This raises the design question: *when converting an application's interface to a CommandMap, what subset of controls should the CommandMap contain?*

User interface palettes are often used to provide convenient ready-to-hand access to related controls, thus obviating the need for the user to navigate through menu structures for those controls. Palettes, therefore, serve a related function to CommandMaps, although for much smaller command subsets. Therefore, in our version of Pinta, we left the always-visible palettes and toolbars as-is, and included only the menu-based commands in our CommandMap. One exception was the Tools palette, which we moved into the CommandMap to encourage our study participants to use the CommandMap more often.

STUDY ONE

In this study, our goal was to answer **Q1**: *do CommandMaps demonstrate performance and subjective advantages in real tasks?* We therefore compared user performance and subjective assessments for a word processing task when executed using the unmodified version of Microsoft Word and when using it with our CommandMap plug-in installed. Participants were given written instructions describing the formatting of a document. The tasks involved elements of text selection, command execution and typing. Each participant completed the tasks using both versions of Microsoft Word.

Participants and Apparatus

Ten paid participants (7 male, 3 female; aged 18-34 years) were recruited from a local university. All were familiar with Microsoft Word 2007, using it for a mean of 15.6 hours/week, and none had seen a CommandMap UI before.

The experiment was performed on a quad-core Windows 7 machine with Microsoft Word 2007 installed. Participants used a 23″ monitor running at 1920×1080 resolution, and a standard keyboard and mouse.

Procedure

Participants first completed a demographics questionnaire. They then completed two experimental tasks ('Task One' and 'Task Two', see Table 1), with one performed using the CommandMap and the other using the standard Word Ribbon. The order of CommandMap and standard Ribbon interfaces was counterbalanced between participants. To familiarize the participant with both the upcoming interface and the commands used in the upcoming task, a brief practice task (not timed) was performed immediately prior to both Task One and Task Two. Participants timed themselves by clicking on-screen Start and Stop buttons before and after each task, and were instructed to complete tasks as quickly and accurately as possible.

In order to measure initial impressions of the CommandMap and analyze whether opinions changed after actual use, we administered a Likert-scale questionnaire (Table 2) immediately after participants were first shown the CommandMap, as well as an equivalent one after participants had completed a task with it. Participants also completed an unweighted NASA-TLX [7] survey after using each interface (Table 3) and gave written comments.

Tasks

With each interface, participants performed a practice task followed by a timed task. The nature of the task and the instructions were nearly identical between the practice task and the following experimental task, with the only difference being that the practice task was performed on a smaller document requiring fewer changes. Tasks One and Two were always performed in the order One, then Two (although, to repeat, the interface order was counterbalanced between them). Each task involved 25 change review subtasks, followed by 14 annotation subtasks (see Table 1 for a summary).

Task One operations	**Task Two operations**
Select text Click *Accept Change* (automatically moves to next change) Go back and re-select accepted text Click *Strikethrough*	Select text Click *Reject Change* (automatically moves to next change) Go back and re-select rejected text Click *Superscript*
25 repetitions	**25 repetitions**
Select paragraph Click *Word Count* Memorize number of words Close *Word Count* dialog Click *Insert Footnote* Type word count into footnote	Select paragraph Click *Word Count* Memorize number of words Close *Word Count* dialog Click *Insert Comment* Type word count into comment
14 repetitions	**14 repetitions**

Table 1. The operations required for each task in Study One.

To minimize learning effects, the tasks were designed to be isomorphic, but not identical (Word Count was the only command used in both). As Study One is primarily concerned with performance issues and initial impressions, the experimental tasks are designed to focus on the key difference between the user interfaces – their methods of command selection. We note, however, that command-heavy usage is not always unrealistic: for example, Lafreniere et al.'s study of application use [13] showed single sessions that contained up to 1489 separate command invocations. Study Two, reported later, examines less constrained experimental tasks.

Design

Our experimental analysis was structured as a 2×2 mixed design ANOVA, with within-subjects factor *Interface* (*standard*, *commandmap*) and between-subjects factor *Task Pairing* (*cm-first*, *standard-first*). We included Task Pairing as a factor in our analysis to check for any asymmetric skill transfer effects, which might stem from one of the interfaces in Task 1 serving as better preparation for the second interface in Task 2. Our primary dependent variable was task completion time; we also analyzed TLX responses for each condition, and responses to the Likert-scale questionnaires before and after use of the CommandMap.

Hypotheses

Previous studies of CommandMaps examined command selection time in response to a stimulus that identified the target command. In this experiment, the stimuli for command selections are placed into a more realistic interaction context, where selections are made to enact actual changes to the document. This difference could potentially influence experimental results for CommandMaps, for at least two reasons. First, in making a series of changes to a document, participants are likely to be expending some of their cognitive resources on activities such as remembering their location within the document – this may decrease the advantage of using a CommandMap, which relies on spatial memory. Second, using the CommandMap involves a substantial display context switch, with the CommandMap temporarily obscuring the work surface. This may interrupt the user's higher-level task flow, including their memory of their location in the document, how far through the task they were, or what they were supposed to do next. However, the same risks apply to standard user interfaces – for example, a user searching through tabs in the Ribbon to find a command may be just as likely to lose task flow. We therefore hypothesized that the previously observed benefits for CommandMaps would continue to hold. Our formal hypotheses were:

H1. Subjects will complete tasks more quickly with the CommandMap than with the standard interface.

H2. Subjects will prefer CommandMap to the standard UI.

In addition, we planned an exploratory comparison between the Likert-scale questionnaire measures before and after CommandMap use (Table 2), in order to quantify whether users' initial impressions of CommandMaps changed.

Results

Task time

A two-way ANOVA on task time showed a significant main effect of *Interface* ($F_{1,8} = 31.6$, $p < 0.001$, $\eta^2 = 0.8$), with *commandmap* (mean 366s) significantly faster than *standard* (mean 453s). There was also a significant interaction effect between *Interface* and *Task Pairing* ($F_{1,8} = 17.0$, $p = 0.03$). Figure 2 depicts the nature of this interaction effect, suggesting that while *commandmap* was faster overall, the benefit was more pronounced for Task 1 than Task 2. Participant comments suggested that Task 2 may have been easier with the Ribbon interface than Task 1, with one noting that Task 2 required fewer tab switches (the sequence [Word Count, Insert Comment] requires a tab switch while [Word Count, Footnote] does not, leading to 78 tab switches in Task One compared to 50 in Task Two). Previous research [23] has also shown that user performance with the Ribbon is highly dependent on the number of tab switches involved. Examining performance on each task individually using between-subjects analyses, we find a significant effect of *Interface* in Task 1 ($F_{1,8} = 5.5$, $p = 0.046$), but none in Task 2 ($F_{1,8} = 1.1$, $p = 0.3$). We therefore partially accept **H1**. An alternative explanation of

Question (1 = Disagree, 5 = Agree)	Before CM use [mean (s.d.)]	After CM use [mean (s.d.)]	Wilcoxon z	Sig (p)
Q: It will be/was easy to find controls in the full-screen interface.	3.8 (0.6)	4.0 (0.7)	0.7	0.2
Q: I will be/was able to remember the locations of controls in the full-screen interface.	**3.5 (0.9)**	**4.4 (0.7)**	**2.3**	**0.01**
Q: The full-screen interface is/was visually overwhelming.	3.2 (0.9)	2.9 (1.0)	0.8	0.2
Q: I will be/was able to interact quickly with the full-screen interface.	**3.5 (1.0)**	**4.4 (0.8)**	**2.5**	**0.01**
Q: I would be discouraged from using software with this kind of interface in the future.	2.0 (0.9)	1.6 (0.8)	1.6	0.05

Table 2. Likert-scale questions and responses before and after CommandMap use in Study One. Significant differences in bold.

the interaction is that asymmetric skill transfer occurred – although it might be argued that the CommandMap was particularly good preparation for the Normal user interface in Task 2 (explaining the larger improvement across Tasks One and Two with Normal than with CommandMaps), the previous explanation seems more compelling. Further, even if the explanation of asymmetric skill transfer is correct, then this would suggest a further and unexpected benefit of CommandMaps in helping users learn standard interfaces.

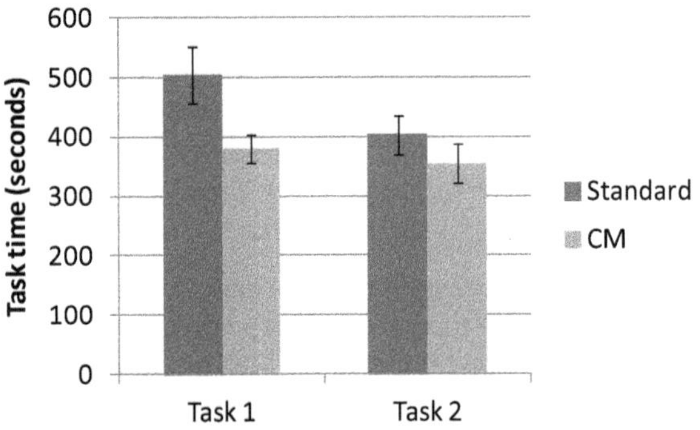

Figure 2. Mean task times in Study One. Error bars ±1 s.e.m.

Subjective responses

NASA-TLX responses (Table 3) showed that participants found CommandMaps to be less physically demanding, less temporally demanding, easier to use and less frustrating than the standard interface. Subject preferences were also in favour of CommandMaps, with nine out of ten users preferring CommandMaps and one preferring the standard interface ($\chi^2 = 4.9$, $p = 0.03$); we therefore accept **H2**.

	Standard		CommandMap		Wilcoxon z	Sig
Mental demand	2.8	(0.9)	2.6	(1.0)	0.4	0.34
Physical demand	**3.2**	**(1.1)**	**1.9**	**(0.9)**	**2.2**	**0.01**
Temporal demand	**3.1**	**(1.1)**	**2.2**	**(0.6)**	**1.9**	**0.03**
Success	4.2	(0.4)	4.3	(0.5)	0.0	0.5
Hard work	**3.2**	**(1.2)**	**2.1**	**(0.9)**	**1.9**	**0.03**
Frustration	**2.5**	**(1.4)**	**1.6**	**(0.8)**	**1.8**	**0.04**

Table 3. Mean (st. dev.) NASA-TLX values (1=low, 5=high). Rows in bold indicate significant differences.

Results for the CommandMap questionnaire indicated that participants' opinions of the CommandMap improved after they were given the opportunity to use it. In particular, participants underestimated their ability to remember control locations and interact quickly with the CommandMap (Table 2). This result was reinforced by subjects' comments, for example: *"at first glance I thought that the interface was too busy to find items. But later I found that I could remember icons exactly without the need to look for them. I could use the interface when I pushed <Ctrl> so the interface was not on the screen all the time and it was easy to push or release the <Ctrl> button."* There was also a marginal effect ($p = 0.05$) in the change of response to the question *I would be discouraged from using software with this kind of interface in the future*. Initially, the responses expressed disagreement (mean 2.0, s.d. 0.9); and after using the system their level of disagreement was stronger (mean 1.6, s.d. 0.8). There was no change in perceived ease of finding controls, or the degree to which the interface was seen as visually overwhelming.

STUDY TWO

Study One showed that user performance and subjective preferences for CommandMaps exceeds that of the standard interfaces when executing repetitive tasks that are interwoven with realistic activities on a document. This extends prior results showing that command selection time (without any associated task) is reduced with CommandMaps. In Study Two, we move our investigation further toward real-world use, adding the following elements of realism.

Different application contexts. CommandMaps are designed to be a general technique, so our second study examines both word-processing (Microsoft Word) and painting (Pinta) applications.

Realistic learning curve. Previous CommandMap studies have all used highly repetitive selections of a small number of commands within short duration experiments. Study Two, in contrast, examines a week of daily skill development in a more realistic task. Further, to gain better insight into novice interaction (and unlike prior studies), no explicit initial training was given.

Less-repetitive tasks. Unlike previous studies, most of the commands used in Study Two were executed only once per task, and there was a wider range of commands. Furthermore, the tasks were designed to intersperse typing and drawing activities between command selections.

Open-ended tasks. Study One gave participants a specific set of instructions, relieving the participant from the need to expend cognitive resources on issues such as task strategy; in Study Two, in contrast, participants were simply given a target document or image and asked to reproduce it.

Participants and Apparatus

Twelve paid participants (10 male, 2 female; aged 21-34 years) were recruited from a local university. None had

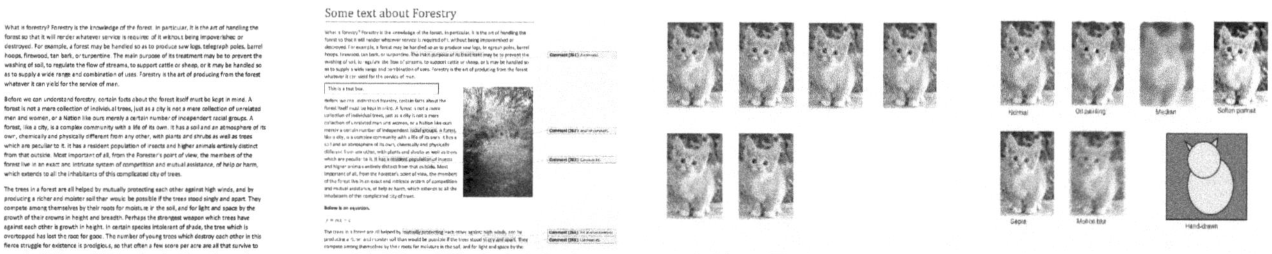

a) Word Task 1 (before) b) Word Task 1 (after) c) Pinta Task 1 (before) d) Pinta Task 1 (after)

Figure 3. Initial and target states for two of the tasks in Study Two.

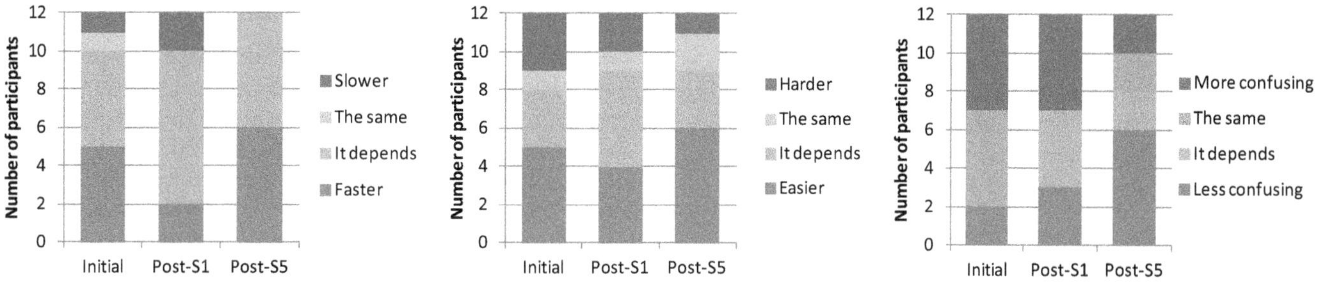

a) Faster/slower b) Easier/harder c) More/less confusing

Figure 4. Participants' opinions before the experiment, after Session One, and after Session Five, on whether CommandMaps are faster or slower, easier or harder to use, and more or less confusing than the standard interfaces.

been involved in Study One, nor had any previously seen a CommandMap. Apparatus was the same as Study One.

Procedure

Participants were assigned four tasks to complete on each of five successive days. Two tasks were completed using Word, and two using Pinta. One of the tasks with each application was performed using the CommandMap version of the software, and the other task was completed using the application's standard interface. To facilitate rigor in the analysis of skill development over the week, the experimental task with each interface was held constant for each of the five days. All participants completed the two tasks with each application in the same order, but the order of the applications and of their versions (standard and CommandMap) was counterbalanced between participants. Each of the four tasks took 5-10 minutes to complete.

For each Word task, participants were provided with an on-screen document containing text, as well as a printout of the intended formatting (see Figure 3). In the Pinta tasks, participants were given an initial image and had to apply filters and use drawing tools to replicate a target state shown on a printout. Participants were instructed to complete tasks in any way they wished, and to click 'Start' and 'Stop' buttons at the beginning and end of the task.

Participants completed a demographics questionnaire before the experiment, and filled out NASA-TLX [7] worksheets after each task. We gave additional questionnaires probing opinions of CommandMaps at the beginning and end of the first day (Session One) and at the end of Session Five. The participants were interviewed after completing all tasks on the fifth day. All sessions were videotaped.

Results

Study Two was intended to answer research questions **Q2** to **Q5**. We therefore present our results in terms of those questions, drawing on quantitative performance and preference measures as well as qualitative data from the video transcripts, questionnaires and post-study interviews.

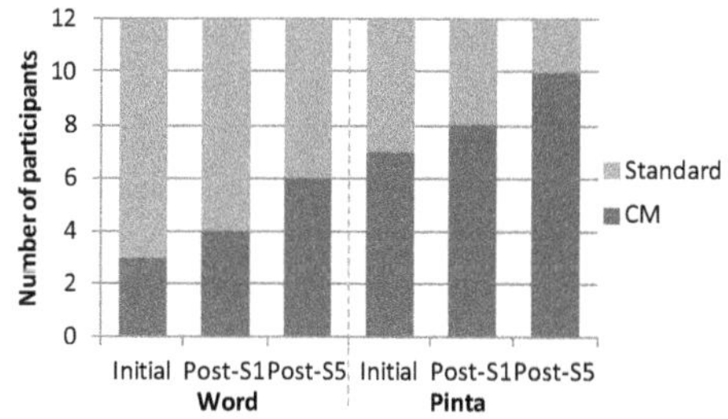

Figure 5. Participants' interface preferences for Word and Pinta throughout Study Two.

Q2.How do users respond when first using CommandMaps?
Initial reactions to the Word and Pinta CommandMaps were mixed (see Figures 4 and 5, leftmost bars). One participant expected the CommandMap to slow his performance, but almost all others thought they would be faster at least some of the time. Measures of anticipated ease of use and confusion were less favorable, with three users anticipating the CommandMap to be harder than the normal interface, and five users rating it as initially more confusing. Eight participants commented that when they first saw the CommandMap, they found it overwhelming; but all of those participants said that their initial impression changed after only one or two five-minute sessions. For example, P3 said *"when I first pulled it up, it was like 'whoa'... but then you quickly figure out the categories and then it's pretty quick."* As seen in Figure 5, most participants initially

preferred the normal interface for Word, though six participants explicitly mentioned that the main factor in their decision was their existing familiarity with the Word interface. In comparison, with Pinta – an application that participants were less familiar with – the majority of participants (7/12) initially preferred the CommandMap.

Despite initial impressions, six participants commented in interviews that CommandMaps would be most advantageous for new users, since they provide an overview of an application's functionality. P1 thought that the main advantage of CommandMaps was *"getting to know the commands that are in a new application quickly"*, and P4 stated that *"one of the advantages is showing options that you maybe might not have known about"*. P1 indicated that he would recommend the interface to his mother, a novice Word user: *"I'd say 'just hold the Ctrl key and look, and you'll find it in there.' And that would help her, I think."*

Two participants also commented that they were able to transfer their existing spatial knowledge of the Ribbon to the Word CommandMap: P8 stated that *"I could apply my existing knowledge to the layout of the CM, so I knew what section it was under and roughly how far along it was."*

Q3. Do performance and subjective impressions change…?
As expected, performance improved throughout the week in all four interfaces (Figure 6). We conducted 2×5 ANOVAs on the Word and Pinta data for within-subjects factors *Interface* (*standard*, *commandmap*) and *Session* (*1 – 5*). As Figure 6 suggests, there was no effect of *Interface*, which is unsurprising given the relatively free-form method.

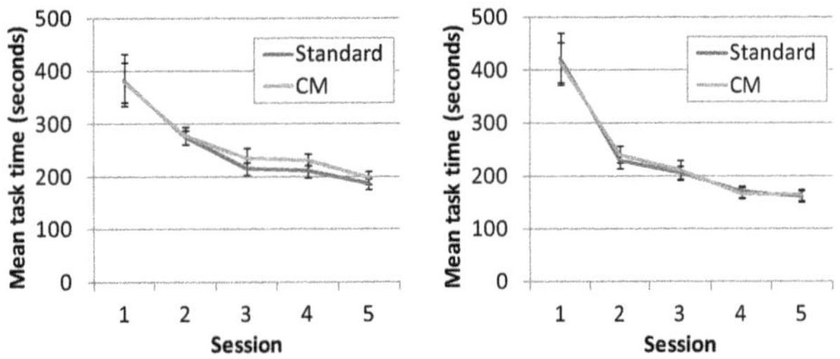

a) Word **b) Pinta**

Figure 6. Mean task times for each session in Study Two.

Subjective impressions of the CommandMaps improved through the week (Figures 4 and 5). By the end of the week, 10/12 participants preferred CommandMaps for Pinta (χ^2 = 4.1, p = 0.04), but preferences were evenly split for Word. Interview comments showed that several participants initially thought the CommandMap would be difficult to use, but changed their minds after trying it. Five participants mentioned that they liked the Pinta CommandMap because it removed submenus: *"once you get to know it, it's really fast. Like if you know the blur button is going to be here (points), it's basically Ctrl and then move your mouse and it's almost instantaneous, instead of going through the submenus."* Two participants also liked the full-screen workspace with CommandMaps.

Q4. Are CMs successful in multiple application contexts?
Figure 5 shows that CommandMap preferences were stronger in Pinta than Word, with familiarity with Word's Ribbon being mentioned by six participants in explaining their preferences. The two participants who maintained a preference for Pinta stated that its menu hierarchy made it easier to find commands compared to the CommandMap's parallelized layout. The perceived advantages of CommandMaps were the speed of accessing commands (five participants), not having to scroll through Ribbon tabs (one participant), and the ability to see an overview of all commands in the application (six participants).

Q5. What usability issues do CommandMaps encounter?
Seven participants mentioned that they had problems using the Control key to activate the CommandMap. In particular, the CommandMap would briefly appear when issuing hotkey shortcuts: *"Once I finish a sentence, I automatically save. It's nothing I even think about, and [the CommandMap] flickers on screen."* Three participants also noted that they would prefer the activation key to act as a toggle, rather than needing to hold it for continual display.

Nine participants mentioned that item layout was critical to both interfaces' success, with three stating that the Word Ribbon categories were poorly named. Four indicated that the Pinta CommandMap needed an improved layout, and P3 suggested placing category labels on the left-hand side of the CommandMap to improve category identification. Several participants disliked having Pinta's toolbox in the CommandMap: P5 said that *"when you're rapidly changing between different tools, I don't think CommandMaps are useful… I think you should be able to determine based on frequency which commands should be in a CommandMap and which should be permanently available"*.

Prior to the study we were concerned that the modal appearance of the CommandMap, hiding nearly the entire view of the work surface, might disorient users and interfere with their task flow. However, apart from flicker when using keyboard shortcuts, only two participants mentioned this as an issue. Five participants explicitly said it was not a problem, with several mentioning that it was better than the standard interface; P8 said *"I think it was more effective,"* P4 said *"with Word, you have to go to a different tab, and go back and do something, which can be a bit disorienting… whereas with this it's always the same thing,"* and P12 said *"You were kind of still looking in the same place as well, because it's right in the middle of the screen. I found I didn't lose track of where I was, whereas if I went back to the menu and had to go back down again I'd find that more distracting"*. The semi-opaque CommandMap display also received positive comments: P3 said *"I liked with the Pinta one, it was kind of transparent, so you could push Ctrl and still see what's underneath."*

DISCUSSION

To recap, Study One demonstrated that CommandMaps have performance advantages over standard interfaces in a task that involved interweaving command invocation with actions on the work surface. Study Two analyzed the evolution of CommandMap perceptions over a week, with positive results: 7/12 participants immediately preferred the Pinta CommandMap to traditional interface controls, and 10/12 preferred it after five days of use; and half preferred the Word CommandMap to the highly refined and familiar Ribbon interface after just a few sessions of use.

Overcoming initial reactions

We believe that commercial developers should consider deploying CommandMaps. However, the key cause for concern in doing so is that users may have a negative initial reaction to the substantially changed command layout. Participant comments lend some support to this: eight of the 12 Study Two participants made some sort of reference to an initial impression of visual overload (though this dissipated after a few minutes of use). However, this concern is one that is often encountered when a vendor wishes to improve the user's experience through interface revisions [10]. Primary tools for overcoming such concerns are advertising and consumer education. CommandMaps can also be designed to maximize knowledge transfer from existing interfaces. For example, our Word CommandMap maintained item layout within each category group, and the display of the Home tab was identical across the CommandMap and traditional interface.

Design issues and improvements

CommandMap invocation

In our systems, the CommandMap was displayed by pressing the Control key, which caused minor usability problems for several of our participants, particularly when issuing keyboard shortcuts. Re-purposing a less-frequently used key such as Alt as the activation key would reduce the incidence of overloaded interface actions. An attractive supplemental method for activating the CommandMap is to use a dedicated button on a mouse, which would allow for unimanual interaction. Many mice support configurable buttons, and repurposing one of these for CommandMap activation would be a natural choice, particularly if CommandMaps were widely deployed.

CommandMap hotkeys

Pursuing the opposite idea to including CommandMap invocation on the mouse, there are interesting possibilities in moving CommandMap item selection onto the keyboard. Recent studies demonstrated the effectiveness of ExposeHK [16], which overlays visual controls with their hotkeys when a modifier key is pressed. CommandMaps would allow all hotkeys for the interface to be browsed at once, possibly with the CommandMap invoked by pressing Ctrl, and the hotkey overlay by additionally pressing Alt. Command selection could then be completed either by clicking as normal with the mouse, or by pressing the associated hotkey. This should also improve the learnability of hotkeys over the Ribbon, by allowing hotkey browsing without to the need to first move the cursor over the target.

In what situations are CommandMaps most useful?

CommandMaps provide two primary advantages over traditional methods for organizing commands in graphical user interfaces, such as menus and ribbons. First, they help novice or intermediate users gain an overview of an application's functionality. Second, they increase the efficiency of expert users who have learned item locations. We therefore advocate for the use of CommandMaps in any situation where the command set is small enough to fit everything on-screen at once.

In applications with extremely large command sets (such as Autodesk Maya or 3ds Max), providing a CommandMap containing all of the functionality of an application may be infeasible. In these circumstances, there are other ways in which a CommandMap could be used to improve performance. First, it could provide a broad top-level hierarchy to the command set, similar to Maya's Hotbox [12]. Second, it could be provided as a shortcut interface, allowing the user to customize the CommandMap with the tools they most frequently use. Alternatively, it could contain a subset of the controls most frequently needed by novice users, providing access to a basic overview of the application's functionality.

Lessons for menu design

Several studies of menu selection time with hierarchies of different breadth and depth have shown that selection times can follow a U-shape with depth, suggesting that menus should be broad, but not too broad [18]. However, the success of CommandMaps suggests that selection times can be reduced by making the hierarchy as broad as possible, reducing hierarchy depth to a single level. The combined results of this paper and [23] support Cockburn and Gutwin's [2] assertion that when users know item locations or can predict them based on some structure (e.g., alphabetical ordering or semantic categories), performance is optimized by flat command structures; studies such as [18] showed different results because they used random command arrangements and did not allow users enough time to develop item location memory. We refer the reader to [2] for a more complete analysis of menu layout studies.

More generally, these studies support the idea that spatial memory should be prioritized over visual search when optimizing control layouts. Current cognitive theory [4] shows that visual search is the primary location mechanism for novice users, and that retrieval from spatial memory is used when available. However, spatial memory develops rapidly [4, 11, 23] and as a consequence, users spend more of their lifetime with a software product retrieving locations from memory rather than searching for them. The interested reader should refer to [22] for more information on the theoretical aspects of spatial memory in HCI.

Another surprising outcome of Study Two was that users did not consider the modal nature of the CommandMap to be an impediment to use. This implies that with careful design (i.e. using translucency and a quasi-modal activation key), future interfaces can successfully use a modal separation between content and interface controls to allow more screen real estate to be devoted to both.

Supporting future implementations

A field study of CommandMaps is the next logical step in this project. However, in order to study their use 'in the wild', the technique would ideally be integrated with widely used software. Our experiences with developing a CommandMap version of Word suggest that achieving this integration can be difficult due to the lack of extensibility and support for modification in many commercial applications. For example, the Word Object Model API provided access to limited functionality, prohibiting our complete replication of the original Ribbon interface. Pinta, in contrast, was much easier to extend, but its small user base would limit the value of its use in a field study. In order to provide support in future for CommandMaps and similar HCI research, it would be useful if UI toolkits allowed manipulation of control and panel locations, as well as providing better support for programmatically accessing interface functionality. Metisse [1] is one example of a partial workaround created by the research community, though it only works on the X window system.

CONCLUSION

The CommandMap is a user interface command selection technique that makes all, or nearly all, commands available to the user in a single display that is overlaid on the workspace when a modifier key is pressed. A previous study demonstrated the potential of CommandMaps by showing that the time to acquire a CommandMap item in response to a cued stimulus is faster than with menus or ribbons. However, critical unanswered questions remained regarding their practicality. To examine issues affecting the use of CommandMaps in realistic tasks, we implemented two real-world versions of CommandMaps for Microsoft Word and Pinta. Our first study showed advantages of CommandMaps over the Ribbon in tasks that involved interleaved access to the workspace and the CommandMap. Our second study showed how users' perceptions of CommandMaps rapidly evolve over the first week of use, as well as highlighting their advantages and opportunities for improvement. In future work, we will study how best to arrange commands in full-screen interfaces, and develop further CommandMap systems for use in field studies.

REFERENCES

1. Chapuis, O. and Roussel, N. Metisse is not a 3D desktop! in *UIST '05*, ACM, NY, USA, 2005, 13-22.
2. Cockburn, A. and Gutwin, C. A Predictive Model of Human Performance with Scrolling and Hierarchical Lists. *Hum.-Comp. Interaction 24*, 3 (2009), 273-314.
3. Cockburn, A., Gutwin, C. and Alexander, J. Faster Document Navigation with Space-Filling Thumbnails. in *Proc. CHI '06*, ACM Press, (2006), 1-10.
4. Cockburn, A., Gutwin, C. and Greenberg, S. A Predictive Model of Menu Performance. in *Proc. CHI '07*, ACM Press, (2007), 627-636.
5. Duh, H.B.-L., Tan, G.C.B. and Chen, V.H.-h. Usability evaluation for mobile device: a comparison of laboratory and field tests. in *MobileHCI '06*, 181-186.
6. Gutwin, C. and Cockburn, A. Improving List Revistation with ListMaps. in *Proc. AVI '06*, 396-403.
7. Hart, S. and Staveland, L. Development of NASA-TLX. in *Human Mental Workload*, 1988, 139-183.
8. Hertzum, M. User testing in industry: A case study of laboratory, workshop, and field tests. in *User interfaces for all. Proc. 5. ERCIM workshop*, (1999), 59-72.
9. Hochheiser, H. and Shneiderman, B. Performance Benefits of Simultaneous Over Sequential Menus. *IJHCI 12*, 2 (2000), 173-192.
10. Kabay, M.E. A discussion of the Microsoft office fluent user interface. *Ubiquity 2008*, March (2008), 1-4.
11. Kaptelinin, V. Item Recognition in Menu Selection: The Effect of Practice. in *InterCHI '93*, 183-184.
12. Kurtenbach, G., Fitzmaurice, G.W., Owen, R.N. and Baudel, T. The Hotbox: efficient access to a large number of menu-items. in *CHI '99*, ACM, 231-237.
13. Lafreniere, B., Bunt, A., Whissell, J.S., Clarke, C.L.A. and Terry, M. Characterizing large-scale use of a direct manipulation application in the wild. in *GI 2010*, 11-18.
14. Mackay, W.E. and Fayard, A.-L. HCI, natural science and design: a framework for triangulation across disciplines. in *DIS '97*, ACM, Amsterdam, 223-234.
15. MacKenzie, I.S. *HCI: An Empirical Research Perspective*. Elsevier Science, 2012.
16. Malacria, S., Bailly, G., Harrison, J., Cockburn, A. and Gutwin, C. Promoting hotkey use through rehearsal with ExposeHK. in *CHI '13*, ACM, Paris, 573-582.
17. McGrath, J. Methodology Matters: Doing Research in the Behavioral and Social Sciences. in *Readings in Hum.-Comp. Interaction: Towards the Year 2000*, 1995.
18. Miller, D. The depth/breadth tradeoff in hierarchical computer menus. in *Proc. HFES*, (1981), 296-300.
19. Newell, A. and Rosenbloom, P.S. Mechanisms of Skill Acquisition and the Law of Practice. in Anderson, J. ed. *Cog. Skills & Acquisition*, Erlbaum, 1981, 1-55.
20. Nielsen, C.M., Overgaard, M., Pedersen, M.B., Stage, J. and Stenild, S. It's worth the hassle!: the added value of evaluating the usability of mobile systems in the field. in *NordiCHI '06*, ACM, Oslo, Norway, 2006, 272-280.
21. Robertson, G., Czerwinski, M., Larson, K., Robbins, D., Thiel, D. and van Dantzich, M. Data Mountain. In *UIST '98*, (1998), 153-162.
22. Scarr, J., Cockburn, A. and Gutwin, C. Supporting and exploiting spatial memory in user interfaces. *Foundations and Trends® in HCI 6*, 1 (2013), 1-84.
23. Scarr, J., Cockburn, A., Gutwin, C. and Bunt, A. Improving command selection with CommandMaps. in *CHI '12*, ACM, Austin, Texas, USA, 2012, 257-266.
24. Shneiderman, B. Direct Manipulation: A Step Beyond Programming Languages (excerpt). in *Readings in HCI: A Multidisciplinary Approach*, 1987, 461-467.

Novice Use of a Predictive Human Performance Modeling Tool to Produce UI Recommendations

Kyung Wha Hong and Robert St. Amant
Department of Computer Science
North Carolina State University, Raleigh, NC 27603
khong@ncsu.edu, stamant@ncsu.edu

ABSTRACT
This note describes two studies of the use of a performance modeling tool, CogTool, for making recommendations to improve a user interface. The first study replicates findings by Bonnie John [7]: the rates at which novice modelers made correct recommendations (88.1%) and supported them (68.2%) are close to the values in John's study (91.7% and 75.1%, respectively). A follow-on study of novice modelers on the same task without CogTool produced significantly lower values. CogTool improves the UI design recommendations made by novices.

Author Keywords
CogTool; usability analysis; interface design.

ACM Classification Keywords
H.5.2 User Interfaces: Evaluation/methodology.

General Terms
Human Factors; Design.

INTRODUCTION
CogTool [6] is a cognitive modeling tool for HCI; it predicts human performance for storyboarded user interfaces. In the past few years it has been applied in real-world software development projects to good effect [1].

John [7] reports a study in 2011 of 100 novice modelers who used CogTool to produce recommendations for improving two Web sites. Modelers show significant consistency in their results, and the majority of their recommendations are well supported with quantitative justifications based on CogTool models. These results are important: modeling tools are typically viewed as helpful mainly to expert modelers in understanding user performance; John demonstrates that CogTool can be easily learned and applied by those new to modeling and relatively new to interface design.

This note describes a replication of John's study. Wilson et al. [8] advocate for replication in HCI, to ensure that past results generalize, to check assumptions about prior work, and to build new findings on solid ground. The first contribution of this note is the finding that John's results generalize beyond the sample of novice modelers at CMU, taught to use CogTool by one of its developers. Novice modelers at a different university, taught by an instructor with light experience using CogTool, produced and justified design recommendations for improving a specific user interface with similar accuracy and consistency. The implication is that learning of CogTool can scale, knowledge we believe is important for shaping future generations of HCI practitioners in the classroom.

CHI 2014, April 26 - May 01 2014, Toronto, ON, Canada
Copyright 2014 ACM 978-1-4503-2473-1/14/04...$15.00.
http://dx.doi.org/10.1145/2556288.2556972

CogTool shares the goals of other task modeling techniques for HCI (e.g., the Keystroke Level Model [2]), but we are aware of no empirical comparison between CogTool and these techniques for making design recommendations. A second contribution is a follow-on study in which novice modelers, without knowledge of CogTool but with the same exposure as in Study 1 to the KLM and other techniques, recommended improvements to the same user interface. Relatively large differences in performance were observed. In the remainder of this note we describe the two studies and discuss their implications.

METHOD
Undergraduate computer science students in an HCI course participated in the studies. The course is a conventional survey of topics in HCI, using *The Resonant Interface* [4] as the textbook. At the time of each study, modeling topics in class had covered Fitts' Law, KLM, GOMS, and modeling for HCI in general (three 1.25-hour lectures in all). Students (hereafter "modelers") submitted models as part of a homework assignment, worth 5% of their course grade.

In both studies, modelers were given an explicit task to perform on a Web site, as shown in Figure 1. We chose a simple task comparable to John's for interpretability of our

1. Visit the Web page http://www.amazon.com. (If you are automatically logged into your Amazon account, log out, then reload the page.)
2. Click in the Search text box.
3. Type "kinect" (without quotation marks) in the Search text box, and press return.
4. Click on the top link that is shown in the search results; for me this is "Kinect Sensor with Kinect Adventures and Gunstringer Token Code."
5. Click on the Add to Cart button on the right.

Figure 1. Task instructions given to novice modelers

Determine three potential improvements to the usability of the Web site, for this task, based on the information in the visualization. For each of your improvements,

1. Give a short phrase that identifies the improvement.
2. Optional: If the phrase doesn't entirely specify what the change to the Web site should be, explain it in more detail.
3. Give a screenshot of the visualization, annotated to show how the improvement would change performance (e.g., a circle around some pattern).
4. In words, summarize the pattern you've identified in the visualization.
5. Give the time savings, in seconds and milliseconds, that your improvement would produce.

Figure 2. Modeling instructions given to novice modelers

findings. If our results did not match, we would have an additional explanatory factor for the differences. Our interest is in the generalizability of CogTool across populations of users; we must leave generalization to more complex tasks for future work.

Modelers were also given instructions for building a model for the task and making three recommendations for improving the interface. Additional instructions, elided here, directed modelers to carry out the task by hand first, to be as specific as possible in their recommendations, and to remember that (a) the goal was to model expert behavior and (b) not all potential changes, such as reducing visual clutter or changing the color scheme, would plausibly improve expert behavior, and such changes were not amenable to analysis using the techniques the modelers were to rely on.

Figure 2 gives the modeling instructions for Study 1: modelers were to build their models in CogTool and support their recommendations with annotations of a CogTool timeline visualization. Study 1 replicates John's as follows: the participants were new to modeling and CogTool, they were given a step-by-step description of a task, and they completed their modeling and recommendation activities within one week. The instructions were equivalent to John's, though more explicit in describing the required structure for submissions. There were differences. The participants were all computer science majors rather than HCI majors with a mix of backgrounds, and they were asked to analyze a different Web site from the ones used by John. The introduction to CogTool, including a demonstration, took an additional half hour of class time. The introduction was given by someone not on the CogTool development team, and unlike John's study no hands-on working session followed during which questions could be answered. (A few procedural questions were answered via email.) Otherwise Study 1 was as close to John's as practicable.

When we attribute performance to a specific influence—here, CogTool—we must ask about performance in its absence. We thus conducted a follow-on study one semester later in the same course. The conditions in Study 2 were the same as in Study 1, except that the modeling task was given to students *before* the introduction of CogTool. (They used CogTool later in the course for their project work.) The modeling instructions for Study 2 gave more generic guidelines, without mention of CogTool: *Base your structured description on the material in Chapter 7 and our discussion in class: the Model Human Processor, with its visual, motor, and cognitive capabilities; the Keystroke Level Model; various GOMS techniques.* Modelers worked without specialized tools, mostly relying on Fitts' Law and KLM. Aside from the use of CogTool, Study 1 and Study 2 are effectively identical, with respect to the task and the background of the participants.

STUDY 1: RECOMMENDATIONS WITH COGTOOL

In Study 1, 53 modelers submitted recommendations. Two submissions were produced without using CogTool and are not included in our analysis. Of the remaining 51, two modelers provided only two recommendations rather than three, giving 151 recommendations in all.

Two evaluators independently created categorizations over the aggregate set of recommendations.[1] The evaluators then worked together to agree on a specific category for each recommendation. As shown in Figure 3, the most common recommendations were to place an additional "Add to cart" button beside each product and to make targets for mouse clicks larger or to place them closer together.

Following John, the recommendations were judged with respect to being "correct" (whether they would reduce the predicted duration of the task) and "well supported" (by reference to a visualization produced by CogTool). The evaluators judged 68.2% of the recommendations correct and well supported (c+ws), below John's 75.1%. An additional 19.9% were correct but "vague or inarticulately argued," in most cases because the explanation did not refer to the model (cf. John's 16.6%). The remainder were incorrect. In total, 88.1% of the recommendations were judged to be correct, if not necessarily well supported (cf. 91.7%).

Figure 3 shows all of the correct and well-supported recommendations given by modelers; no others were identified. All but one modeler (98%; cf. John's 100%) gave at least one correct recommendation. 42 of the 51 gave at least one correct *and* well-supported recommendation (82%; cf. John's 96%—possibly due to the abbreviated instructions for CogTool in Study 1). Fourteen modelers gave one or more incorrect recommendations (27%; cf. John's 21%).

[1] Our emphasis is not on the categorization of novice design recommendations, but we note the challenge of consistent categorization of usability improvements based on textual descriptions and CogTool visualizations, working without an *a priori* set. The two evaluators (with both research and practical experience in HCI and usability) differed in the number and assignment of categories they identified, due to ambiguities or combinations of categories in the modelers' descriptions. There was initial agreement on 74% of the recommendations, with Kappa = 0.693.

	Study 1, with CogTool				Study 2, without CogTool			
Recommendation	*# Modelers*	*(%)*	*Median*	*IQR*	*# Modelers*	*(%)*	*Median*	*IQR*
"Add to cart" button for each product	25	(49%)	1.93	0.22	18	(12%)	2.33	1.30
Closer/larger targets	22	(43%)	0.18	0.35	8	(5%)	0.70	0.86
Incremental search, per-keystroke updates	17	(33%)	1.67	0.72	10	(7%)	0.75	1.83
Autofocus in search box	15	(29%)	2.54	1.25	20	(13%)	1.64	1.23
"I feel lucky" button	4	(8%)	1.89	1.00	5	(3%)	2.01	2.38
Keyboard navigation versus mouse clicks	4	(8%)	0.57	3.40	3	(2%)	0.93	3.57
Search autocomplete	4	(8%)	0.70	0.55	2	(1%)	0.26	0.28

Figure 3. Correct and well-supported recommendations, with median and interquartile range of time savings in seconds.

These represent poorer performance than John's numbers, but most measures are surprisingly close.

Figure 3 also shows the median duration and interquartile range of the time savings calculated by the modelers, per category of recommendation. The total time for the task is more than ten seconds, and most of the recommendations would each save half a second or more. We find it notable that novice modelers can justify recommendations for improving a professionally designed interface in wide use.

Variability in estimates of time savings (in the IQR column) is inevitable, due to the coarseness of categorization. For example, changing the size or location of a target icon can reduce duration, but how much depends on the new size or location; *Search autocomplete* and *Incremental search* can reduce typing time, but the reduction depends on how many keystrokes are saved. Some but not all modelers modified their models for these two design changes; others estimated the savings by subtracting some number of keystrokes. The latter approach appeared to be common, but it will not always produce accurate results. *Incremental search* savings are inflated because most modelers did not include the required shift of visual attention to a dynamically changing set of products. Even for more straightforward recommendations, such as *Autofocus in search box*, modelers differed in whether the *Think* operator should be included in the savings. As long as the recommendation was correct and the annotation included the relevant cognitive/visual/motor components of the task, it was considered well supported.

One category of interest not included in Figure 3 is *Remove extraneous content*. Many modelers observed that removing clutter could improve performance by allowing for target elements to be closer together (leading to a *Closer/larger targets* categorization), but other modelers recommended reducing clutter based on incorrect arguments (e.g., that experts are distracted by a cluttered visual display, or that thinking time is spent processing screen information not included in a model). These were considered incorrect.

In general, incorrect recommendations were of two types: within the scope of the task but not likely to improve an expert user's performance (e.g., removing ads or changing button colors—8% of all recommendations); or out of scope, without regard for expertise (e.g., providing more results to scroll through—4% of all recommendations).

We evaluated the consistency of the recommendations with the Any-Two Agreement (A2A) statistic [5]. A2A is the number of common problems found by two modelers, divided by the total number of problems found by those two modelers, averaged over all modelers. John's A2A value of 34% puts her study above 9 of the 12 studies in Hertzum and Jacobsen's survey [5]; our A2A value of 30% is above 8. Study 1 adds evidence to the view that CogTool may reduce the evaluator effect by providing a model-based grounding for recommendations [7].

Two weeks after the completion of the modeling exercise a brief, informal survey was given. 47 modelers submitted free-form text answers to questions about their use of CogTool. (The survey was anonymous to allow the question, *Did you follow the instructions?*; all respondents answered yes.) The most informative answers were to the question, *Describe in a few sentences how CogTool fit into the process of your making recommendations for design improvements.* John has demonstrated that novice modelers can produce useful results with CogTool; our survey provides initial clues about how they integrate modeling into their analysis, as well as how CogTool improves the process.

Our informal analysis of the responses showed three categories of interest. The most common answer, from 26 modelers (51%), described using CogTool to identify appropriate areas for design changes. "I would use CogTool to see which areas of an application take the longest for a user to move through." "I looked at the model that CogTool presented and looked for areas where there were actions canceling each other out, such as moving a hand to the mouse and then back... and tried to understand how to eliminate some of those steps." Most then described using CogTool to justify their recommendations in quantitative terms.

Nine modelers (18%) also mentioned making comparisons between models, to evaluate the differences between interface designs. "I then looked at side-by-side comparisons... to see where differences existed."

Thirteen modelers (25%) only mentioned using CogTool to validate design decisions they had thought of on their own: "It helped give me proof that my suggestions would actually help by providing estimated times." .

	Study 1		Study 2	
Performance	c%	*c + ws*%	c%	*c + ws*%
$k = 3$	69%	49%	40%	28%
$k \geq 2$	94%	73%	62%	48%
$k \geq 1$	98%	82%	88%	54%

Figure 4. Study 1 versus Study 2 performance per modeler as tail distribution functions: *c*% shows the percent of modelers giving *k* or more correct recommendations, *c + ws*% *k* or more correct and well-supported recommendations.

STUDY 2: COMPARATIVE ANALYSIS

For Study 2, in which modelers did not use CogTool, 50 modelers submitted 150 recommendations in total. The same evaluators followed the same procedure as in Study 1 to categorize recommendations, except using references to the modeling techniques above rather than to CogTool in their evaluation. Figure 3 shows that the correct and well-supported recommendations in Study 2 are comparable to those of Study 1 in the numerical distribution of categories and estimates of time savings. But the totals were considerably lower. In Study 1, 88% of recommendations were correct, versus 63% in Study 2; for correct and well-supported recommendations the values were 68% and 43%.

Figure 4 shows the tail distributions for the count of correct/well-supported recommendations, aggregated over modelers; that is, 35/51 or 69% of modelers in Study 1 gave three correct recommendations, and so forth. A complete statistical analysis is beyond the scope of this note, but a two-sample Kolmogorov-Smirnov exact test shows a significant difference between Study 1 and Study 2: $D = 0.321$, $p < 0.01$. (Treating the counts as continuous data, we can ask about the difference between the mean number of correct recommendations per modeler, 2.6 in Study 1 versus 1.9 in Study 2: $t(99) = 3.97$, $p < 0.01$.) Analysis of correct and well-supported recommendations shows the same result. In other words, performance in these studies is not determined purely by the task and the background knowledge of modelers; use of CogTool is a significant factor.

A2A in Study 2 is 20%. The drop from 30% in Study 1 is not unexpected, given the greater variation in modeling procedures. No new correct and well-supported recommendations were identified, but there was a wider range of incorrect recommendations. These fell into the same general classes as in Study 1: changes affecting performance outside the scope of the task (e.g., multiple item selection or filtering capabilities—11% of all recommendations), and not focusing on expert users as specified in the instructions (25% of all recommendations). The latter is not surprising. In an HCI survey course, the clearest illustrations of usability issues are often based on the challenges that novice users face in complex interfaces; CogTool currently targets expert users. The former category of incorrect recommendations is more surprising, though not in retrospect. CogTool also appears to help novice modelers remain aware of the boundaries of a specific task when attempting to improve user performance by changing the UI design.

CONCLUSION

John's experience teaching CogTool to HCI majors at CMU extends to computer science majors at a different university (without a formal HCI program), and detailed knowledge of CogTool is not needed for adequate instruction. This is promising news for practical modeling, recognized by some of the novice modelers: "I would never have thought about these areas taking up users' time, so CogTool did help..."

Existing research provides limited information about how modeling can best be integrated into interface design tasks (e.g., [1, 3]), but the strategies used in Study 1 are among those typically recommended by experienced HCI modelers. Notably, the novices were able to find effective ways to use CogTool without explicit guidance, to produce correct, well-supported recommendations.

Study 2 indicates that CogTool is a decisive factor in helping novice modelers produce good design recommendations—it was not because the task was too easy. With CogTool, recommendations were much more often correct and well supported, and the proportion of modelers who made such recommendations was higher. CogTool appears to help novice modelers to focus their recommendations on those relevant to a specific class of users, within the boundaries of specified tasks. Further exploration of how and why, as well as implications for professional UI development, remain for future work.

REFERENCES

1. Bellamy, R., John, B. E., Kogan, S. Deploying CogTool: Integrating quantitative usability assessment into real-world software development. In *Proc. ICSE*, ACM (2011), 691-700.
2. Card, S. K., Moran, T. P., & Newell, A. The keystroke-level model for user performance time with interactive systems. *CACM 23*, 7 (1980), 396-410.
3. Couix, S., and Burkhardt, J.-M. Task descriptions using academic oriented modelling languages: A survey of actual practices across the SIGCHI community. In *LNCS (HCI–INTERACT)*, 6948, Springer (2011), 555-570.
4. Heim, S. *The Resonant Interface: HCI Foundations for Interaction Design*, Addison Wesley, 2007.
5. Hertzum, M., and Jacobsen, N.E. The evaluator effect: A chilling fact about usability evaluation methods. *IJHCI 13*, 4 (2001), 421-443.
6. John, B. E., Prevas, K., Salvucci, D., and Koedinger, K. Predictive human performance modeling made easy. In *Proc. CHI*, ACM (2004), 455-462.
7. John, B. E. Using predictive human performance models to inspire and support UI design recommendations. In *Proc. CHI*, ACM (2011), 983-986.
8. Wilson, M.L., Mackay, W., Chi, E., Bernstein, M., Russell, D., and Thimbleby, H. RepliCHI-CHI should be replicating and validating results more: Discuss. In *Ext. Abstracts CHI*, ACM (2011), 463-46.

On the Selection of 2D Objects Using External Labeling

Jan Balata, Ladislav Cmolik, and Zdenek Mikovec
Department of Computer Graphics and Interaction, Faculty of Electrical Engineering
Czech Technical University in Prague, Prague, Czech Republic
balatjan@fel.cvut.cz, cmolikl@fel.cvut.cz, xmikovec@fel.cvut.cz

ABSTRACT
We present an external labeling laid over small and/or overlapping 2D objects as an efficient representation for their selection. The approximation of objects with points allows us to transform the labeling problem to graph layout problem, which we solve by means of force-based algorithm. The input parameters allow us to influence the resulting layout of label boxes (e.g. to adapt their distance for imprecise input devices). In a study with 15 participants two implementations of our algorithm were compared against labeling method, where all label boxes share the same offset from corresponding objects. The results of the study show that implementation using a special functionality (temporary freezing of the label box position recalculation) was 14% faster with a comparable accuracy. The subjective evaluation revealed that the implementation with temporary freezing is perceived as most comfortable, fastest and most accurate. The implementation without temporary freezing showed much higher error rate and cannot be recommended.

Author Keywords
Object selection; external labeling; visualization; user study.

ACM Classification Keywords
H.5.2. [Information Interfaces and Presentation]: User Interfaces – Graphical user interfaces; Interaction styles

INTRODUCTION
In this paper we deal with the problem of selection of moving 2D objects in the screen space with given resolution. In general, when displaying objects on the screen, the size of objects' selection areas should follow guidelines [10] to ensure that the objects can be easily pointed with a pointing device (e.g. mouse cursor, touch input). The more imprecise the pointing device is, the bigger the size of selection area needs to be. However, in situations where the guidelines for the size of selection areas cannot be met it might be hard to point the desired object with a pointing device. This holds especially when many small objects are close to each other and/or certain objects are overlapping. The overlapping of objects makes visual identification of the desired object even harder.

CHI 2014, April 26–May 1, 2014, Toronto, Ontario, Canada.
Copyright © 2014 ACM 978-1-4503-2473-1/14/04..$15.00.
http://dx.doi.org/10.1145/2556288.2557288

We have identified this problem during the work on the graphical user interface (GUI) for operation of Unmanned Aerial Vehicles (UAV). UAV is a small robotic plane or helicopter without human pilot that autonomously fulfills high level commands of the operator [12]. The primary task of the operator is to control many UAVs from the ground using our GUI of UAV control center prototype. The execution of such missions is often time critical and the low level of cognitive load is fundamental for fast and precise selection and assignment of the mission tasks to the particular UAV(s). In fact, the operator solves two complex tasks: visual search of the desired UAV, and pointing of the UAV with a pointing device as fast and accurate as possible. According to our pre-study the visual search task is the dominant one (84% of total time on average). The UAVs are displayed as small 2D objects overlaid over the map. The selection of UAVs becomes complicated due to their movement, proximity and/or overlapping. Other scenarios can be a real-time control of larger group of agents in multi-agent systems (transport of people in city, simulation of ecosystem) and tracking objects on the map.

In this paper, we separate the selection from the presented 2D objects. We introduce a selection space into which we put a handler for each object and deform the space to meet the guidelines for the size of selection areas of the handlers. We overlay the presented 2D objects with the deformed selection space. To establish the connection between the handlers and the 2D objects we join each handler with a corresponding object with a straight line. In this way we create an external labeling of the objects.

The external labeling should exhibit a number of criteria [7], which deal with the positions of label boxes (handlers), anchors (points approximating the objects), and leader lines (lines connecting anchors with label boxes). In our implementation we consider the following criteria: Leader lines do not cross. Anchors are not too near to each other. Leader lines are as short as possible so label boxes are near to the corresponding objects. Label boxes are not too near to each other. Label boxes do not overlap anchors. Movement of label boxes is temporally coherent.

We propose a hypothesis that an external labeling which exhibits these criteria (see Figure 1(b)) is an effective representation for selection of small and/or overlapping 2D objects. We test the hypothesis on a scenario where the operator selects UAVs, small moving and often overlapping objects. As the visual search and pointing are inseparable we test both tasks. Note that the visual search is the dominant task.

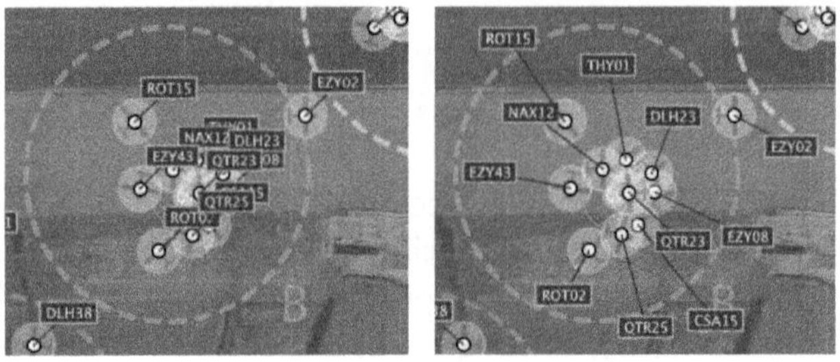

Figure 1. ***Fixed*** **mode (a) and** ***Dynamic/LabelFreeze*** **mode (b).**

RELATED WORK

The problem we are solving is to find such positions of label boxes (for given anchors) that do not occlude the objects (approximated by anchors) or the remaining label boxes. An approach to this problem where the user specifies a circular focus containing the anchors and the label boxes are placed outside of this focus was introduced by Fekete and Plaisant [2]. Bertini et al. [1] improved the approach for areas with high and/or uneven density of anchors and Fink et al. [3] improved the approach by preventing leader lines from crossing, allowing curved leader lines, and clustering the anchors in areas with high density and providing a detailed view of the clusters on demand. All approaches above are designed for selection of static targets and their extension to the selection of moving targets is nontrivial.

As Stein and Décoret [11] we utilize the whole free screen area to place the label boxes. Inspired by work of Götzelmann et al. [5] we transform the labeling problem to the graph layout problem and use the force-based algorithms [4, 9] to solve it. In the area of moving targets selection our work is related to time freezing [6] and static proxies of moving targets [8].

EXTERNAL LABELING ALGORITHM

In our GUI the UAVs are small objects and therefore it is possible to approximate each UAV with a 2D point, anchor $\vec{a}_i$, in the center of its bounding box. Each label box is also approximated with a 2D point, endpoint $\vec{e}_i$, in the center of each label box. In our case all label boxes have similar size. Our algorithm operates with the anchors and endpoints. The labeling problem is solved in each frame as the position of anchors (UAVs) changes in time. The algorithm is as follows:

1) For each endpoint calculate the applied force $\vec{F}$.
2) Move each endpoint according to the applied force $\vec{F}$.
3) If there is the movement of endpoints or maximum number of iterations is not reached go to Step 1.

Our preliminary study showed that temporal coherence is crucial for efficiency of visual search and pointing. The limited number of iterations provides better temporal coherence and limits distracting fast movements of endpoints (label boxes), but at the price of leader lines crossing.

To calculate forces applied on the endpoints we construct graph $G(V, E)$. The set of nodes V contains the anchors and endpoints of the leader lines. The set of edges E contains two types of edges. The first type represents the attractive force between the nodes (representing 2D points) and the other one represents the repulsive force between the nodes. We model the attractive force $\vec{F}_a$ between points $\vec{p}_i$ and $\vec{p}_j$ as a spring according to Hooke's law

$$\vec{F}_a(w_a, \vec{p}_i, \vec{p}_j) = w_a(\vec{p}_j - \vec{p}_i) \quad (1)$$

We consider the spring relaxed when $\vec{p}_i = \vec{p}_j$. Thus, $\vec{p}_j - \vec{p}_i$ is a dilatation of the spring and w_a is the spring constant which we use as weight to influence the attractive force. We model the repulsive force $\vec{F}_r$ between points $\vec{p}_i$ and $\vec{p}_j$ as an interaction of charged particles according to Coulomb's law

$$\vec{F}_r(w_r, \vec{p}_i, \vec{p}_j) = \overbrace{k_e \cdot q_i \cdot q_j}^{w_r} \frac{\hat{v}_{ji}}{|\vec{v}_{ji}|^2} \quad (2)$$

where $\vec{v}_{ji} = \vec{p}_i - \vec{p}_j, |\vec{v}_{ji}|$ is a length of $\vec{v}_{ji}$, $\hat{v}_{ji}$ is a unit vector in direction of $\vec{v}_{ji}$, and w_r is a positive weight used to influence the repulsive force. In the equation, the weight w_r substitute the positive Coulomb's constant k_e multiplied by the negative charges q_i and q_j of the endpoints.

The edges in the graph are constructed according to the criteria for anchors and label boxes:

Anchor distance. As we cannot move the positions of anchors (UAVs), we omit this criterion.

Leader line length. We create an attractive edge between each anchor a_i and its associated endpoint e_i. Thus, the leader lines will be as short as possible and the label boxes will be near to the associated objects. The force used is $\vec{F}_1 = \vec{F}_a(w_1, \vec{e}_i, \vec{a}_i)$ and is influenced by the weight w_1.

Endpoint distance. We create a repulsive edge between each endpoint and all other endpoints to ensure that the endpoints are not too near to each other. The repulsive force applied on the endpoint $\vec{e}_i$ is $\vec{F}_2 = \sum_{j=1, j\neq i}^{n} \vec{F}_r(w_2, \vec{e}_i, \vec{e}_j)$ where n is the number of endpoints. The force is influenced by the weight w_2.

Anchor label box distance. We create a repulsive edge between each endpoint and all anchors to ensure that the label boxes do not overlap UAVs. The repulsive force applied on the endpoint $\vec{e}_i$ is $\vec{F}_3 = \sum_{j=1}^{n} \vec{F}_r(w_3, \vec{e}_i, \vec{a}_j)$ where n is the number of anchors. The force is influenced by the weight w_3.

Temporal coherence. We apply three additional attractive forces to improve the temporal coherence of endpoints. The first force, influenced by the weight w_4, is attracting an endpoint to its projection in the direction of its associated UAV. The second force, influenced by the weight w_5, is attracting the endpoint to its previous position. The last force, influenced by the weight w_6, is attracting all endpoints.

The total force $\vec{F}$ applied on the endpoint $\vec{e}_i$ is $\vec{F} = \sum_{i=1}^{6} \vec{F}_i$. The weights $w_i, i = 1 \ldots 6$ are used to fine tune the behavior of the algorithm. We use $w_1 = 0.27$, $w_2 = 1200$, $w_3 = 395$, $w_4 = 0.86$, $w_5 = 0.83$, and $w_6 = 0.27$. An example of labeling produced with these weights is in Figure 1(b). To see

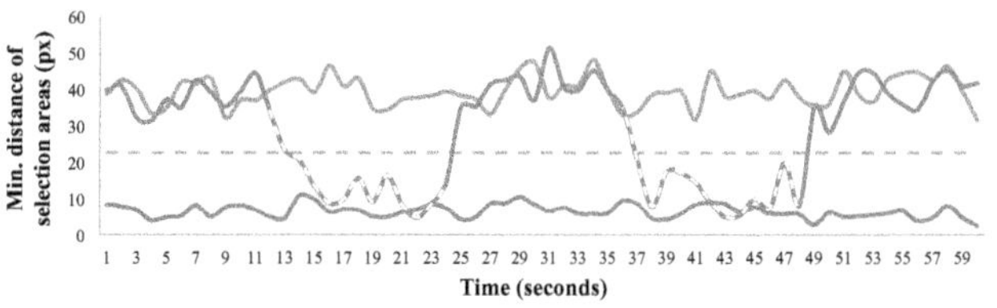

Figure 2. The minimum distance of selection areas of label boxes for *Dynamic* labeling mode (blue), *LabelFreeze* mode (red) with Ctrl key pressed (dashed red), and *Fixed* mode (green). The recommended distance of the selection areas for mouse is depicted as gray dashed line.

the interaction with the UAVs please look at the accompanied video. The external labeling algorithm using these weights ensures that the minimum distance of selection areas is always bigger than the recommended distance for mouse, see Figure 2. We define the minimum distance as a shortest distance between all pairs of endpoints and the recommended distance as a diameter of circle circumscribed to the selection area of recommended size [10].

The external labeling algorithm was implemented in *Dynamic* and *LabelFreeze* labeling modes. Unlike *Dynamic* mode, *LabelFreeze* mode gives an operator the ability to temporarily turn off the calculation of label box positions by pressing and holding Ctrl key. Then the mutual position of label boxes and anchors gets frozen and label boxes move with their associated anchors, until the Ctrl key is released. This should result in more predictable movements of label boxes while Ctrl key is pressed, but at the price of not fulfilling the recommended distance of selection areas (see Figure 2).

For evaluation purposes we implemented an external labeling method where all label boxes share the same static offset from the anchors, called *Fixed* mode (see Figure 1(a)). Due to the similar size of label boxes and UAVs the overlapping of the label boxes will be comparable. The *Fixed* mode does not fulfill the recommended minimum distance, see Figure 2. Our assumption is that this will make the selection of UAVs more difficult.

Our aim was to research if the measured speed of selection of UAVs (in UAVs per minute) is higher for our labeling method (*Dynamic, LabelFreeze* modes) than for *Fixed* mode.

EVALUATION

Participants. Fifteen participants (7 females) were recruited from our university. All were daily users of computers. They ranged from 26 to 67 years ($mean = 40.1, SD = 13.8$).

Apparatus. The hardware consisted of a standard PC computer with a 22 inches LCD display (resolution 1680×1050 pixels), a PC keyboard and optical mouse with 2 buttons. There were 30 UAVs whose movement was simulated based on a real UAV behavior to ensure the same conditions for all participants. The prototype of the UAV control center used in the experiment was developed in Java. We added name into each label box to be able to formulate selection tasks during the evaluation. The UAVs are selected by clicking either on the UAV or on the label box. The software recorded timestamps for each mouse click and distinguished between the click on the UAV itself, on the label box, and on the background. Usage of Ctrl key was also recorded. Two buttons were created in the GUI for starting and ending each experiment task.

Procedure. The experiment was performed in a usability lab dedicated for execution of user tests. Before the experiment was started the participants adjusted the position of the display and the mouse to feel comfortable. The experimenter explained the GUI, three labeling modes and the tasks. The experiment began with a training session. The participants were asked to accomplish two tasks for each labeling mode two times. The first task was to select 10 UAVs with a particular name in given order. The other one, more complex task consisted of three subtasks: 1) the selection of all UAVs with names starting with a specific prefix and moving on routes passing through a given area; 2) the selection of all UAVs with names ending with a specific suffix and moving on rounded routes; 3) the selection all UAVs with names starting with another specific prefix and moving on routes passing through another area. The intention was to simulate use-cases where the operator is asked to select the UAVs not only by their names, but also by other attributes. Each participant performed this training two times (105 UAVs selected, duration 30-40 minutes). The goal was to let the participants get familiar with the operation of the UAV control center, get used to the experiment procedure and to minimize any learning effects. The training session was followed by the test with the same two tasks for each labeling mode but with different UAVs to select. For each task there was prepared one set of UAVs for all three labeling modes (but with different names, to avoid the possibility to remember position of UAVs) to ensure the same conditions.

The participants were asked to proceed as quickly and accurately as possible. Between each task they were allowed to take short breaks. Each participant selected 72 UAVs and the test lasted 15-20 minutes. The participants were interacting with the mouse by means of moving cursor and performing left mouse button single click. For *LabelFreeze* mode participants could use Ctrl key on the PC keyboard to activate the freeze functionality.

After the data collection, the participants were asked on demographic data and completed a questionnaire investigating their subjective judgment about the level of comfort, speed and support for minimizing misclicks of each labeling mode (Likert scale 1-5 was used).

Design. The experiment was one factor (with three levels) within-subject design. The independent variable was the labeling mode. The order of labeling modes was counterbalanced using a Latin square. The total amount of UAVs to select (excluding training) was 15 participants $\times$ 3 labeling modes $\times$ 24 UAVs/mode = 1080 UAVs. The main measures were speed, calculated as a number of UAVs selected per minute, and error rate, calculated as a portion of misclicks in proportion to all clicks performed by the participant. Misclicks were defined as either clicking the background or a wrong UAV. For statistical analysis repeated measures ANOVA was used.

RESULTS AND DISCUSSION

Speed. There was a significant difference in speed between the labeling modes ($F_{2,24} = 7.38, p < .005$). The average speed for *Fixed* mode was 7.4 UAV/minute, for *Dynamic* 8.8 UAV/minute and for *LabelFreeze* 8.4 UAV/minute. A post hoc Scheffé test revealed significant differences between the *Fixed-Dynamic* and *Fixed-LabelFreeze* pairings ($p < .05$). There was no significant difference between *Dynamic* and *LabelFreeze* modes. The group effect was not detected.

Error Rate. The effect of labeling mode on error rate was significant ($F_{2,24} = 5.93, p < .01$). The average error rate for *Fixed* mode was 4.2%, for *Dynamic* 11.4% and for *LabelFreeze* 5.6%. A post hoc Scheffé test revealed significant differences between the *Fixed-Dynamic* and *Dynamic-LabelFreeze* pairings ($p < .05$). There was no significant difference between *Fixed* and *LabelFreeze* modes. The group effect was not detected.

Subjective Evaluation. We also asked the participants about the level of comfort, speed and error rate of each labeling mode. The average subjective rating of the error rate for each mode is as follows: 3.53 for *Fixed* mode, 3.07 for *Dynamic* mode, and 1.93 for *LabelFreeze* mode. The average subjective rating of comfort was: 3.93 for *Fixed* mode, 2.2 for *Dynamic* mode, and 1.67 for *LabelFreeze* mode. The average subjective rating of speed was: 3.87 for *Fixed* mode, 2.4 for *Dynamic* mode, and 1.93 for *LabelFreeze* mode.

There were significant differences between the labeling modes in all three measures (comfort: $F_{2,24} = 43.59, p < .0001$; speed: $F_{2,24} = 23.09, p < .0001$; error rate: $F_{2,24} = 9.72, p < .001$). A post hoc Scheffé test revealed significant differences between *Fixed-Dynamic* and *Fixed-LabelFreeze* pairings in comfort ($p < .0001$) and speed ($p < .0005$), but not between *Dynamic-LabelFreeze* pairing. *Dynamic* and *LabelFreeze* modes were perceived as more comfortable than *Fixed* mode. There were significant differences between *Fixed-LabelFreeze* and *Dynamic-LabelFreeze* pairings in error rate ($p < .05$), but not between *Fixed-Dynamic* pairing. *LabelFreeze* mode was perceived as producing fewer errors than *Dynamic* or *Fixed*. The group effect was not detected.

These results indicate that our labeling methods (*Dynamic* and *LabelFreeze* mode) are faster than *Fixed* mode in visual search and pointing tasks. However, *Dynamic* mode leads to much higher error rate (2.7× higher) than *Fixed* mode, what is caused by the unpredictable movement of label boxes. *LabelFreeze* mode, which makes the label boxes movement more predictable, reduces the error rate significantly (2× lower than *Dynamic* mode) to the same level as *Fixed* mode, while preserving the same speed as *Dynamic* mode. The reason why *LabelFreeze* mode is not significantly faster than *Dynamic* mode can be that the time of the pointing task is very small in comparison to the time of visual search. From subjective perspective *LabelFreeze* and *Dynamic* modes were perceived as more comfortable and faster than *Fixed* mode. *LabelFreeze* mode was moreover perceived as producing minimum errors in comparison to other two modes. According to high error rate *Dynamic* mode cannot be recommended as a promising solution.

CONCLUSION

We presented two external labeling methods with fixed anchors and floating label boxes called *Dynamic* and *LabelFreeze*. *LabelFreeze* mode showed up as an effective representation for selection of small and/or overlapping 2D objects. It is 14% faster than *Fixed* mode, it has similar error rate (objective measures) as *Fixed* mode, and is subjectively perceived as more comfortable and faster than *Fixed* mode. The study showed that *Dynamic* mode suffers from more than 2× higher error rate than *LabelFreeze* or *Fixed* mode.

ACKNOWLEDGMENTS

This research has been supported by the Technology Agency of the Czech Republic under the research program TE01020415 (V3C – Visual Computing Competence Center).

REFERENCES

1. Bertini, E., Rigamonti, M., and Lalanne, D. Extended excentric labeling. *Computer Graphics Forum 28*, 3 (2009), 927–934.
2. Fekete, J.-D., and Plaisant, C. Excentric labeling: Dynamic neighborhood labeling for data visualization. In *CHI '99*, ACM (1999), 512–519.
3. Fink, M., Haunert, J.-H., Schulz, A., Spoerhase, J., and Wolff, A. Algorithms for labeling focus regions. *Visualization and Computer Graphics, IEEE Trans. on 18*, 12 (2012), 2583–2592.
4. Fruchterman, T. M. J., and Reingold, E. M. Graph drawing by force-directed placement. *Software Practice & Experience 21*, 11 (1991), 1129–1164.
5. Götzelmann, T., Hartmann, K., and Strothotte, T. Agent-based annotation of interactive 3D vis.s. In *SG '06*, vol. 4073/2006 of *LNCS* (2006), 24–35.
6. Hajri, A., Fels, S., Miller, G., and Ilich, M. Moving target selection in 2d graphical user interfaces. In *INTERACT 2011*, vol. 6947 of *LNCS* (2011), 141–161.
7. Hartmann, K., Götzelmann, T., Ali, K., and Strothotte, T. Metrics for functional and aesth. label layouts. In *SG '05*, vol. 3638/2005 of *LNCS* (2005), 115–126.
8. Hasan, K., Grossman, T., and Irani, P. Comet and target ghost: Techniques for selecting moving targets. In *CHI '11*, ACM (2011), 839–848.
9. Kamada, T., and Kawai, S. An algorithm for drawing general undirected graphs. *Inf. Proc. Letters 31*, 1 (1989), 7–15.
10. Microsoft. Design Guidlines: Mouse and Pointers. Available at: msdn.microsoft.com/library/windows/desktop/bb545459.aspx.
11. Stein, T., and Décoret, X. Dynamic label placement for improved interactive exploration. In *NPAR '08* (2008), 15–21.
12. Vokrinek, J., Novak, P., and Komenda, A. Ground tactical mission support by multi-agent control of UAV operations. In *HoloMAS '11* (2011), 225–234.

Real-time Feedback for Improving Medication Taking

Matthew L. Lee
Philips Research North America
Briarcliff Manor, NY, USA
matthew.lee@philips.com

Anind K. Dey
HCI Institute, Carnegie Mellon University
Pittsburgh, PA, USA
anind@cs.cmu.edu

ABSTRACT
Medication taking is a self-regulatory process that requires individuals to self-monitor their medication taking behaviors, but this can be difficult because medication taking is such a mundane, unremarkable behavior. Ubiquitous sensing systems have the potential to sense everyday behaviors and provide the objective feedback necessary for self-regulation of medication taking. We describe an unobtrusive sensing system consisting of a sensor-augmented pillbox and an ambient display that provides near real-time visual feedback about how well medications are being taken. In contrast to other systems that focus on reminding before medication taking, our approach uses feedback *after* medication taking to allow the individual to develop their own routines through self-regulation. We evaluated this system in the homes of older adults in a 10-month deployment. Feedback helped improve the consistency of medication-taking behaviors as well as increased ratings of self-efficacy. However, the improved performance did not persist after the feedback display was removed, because individuals had integrated the feedback display into their routines to support their self-awareness, identify mistakes, guide the timing of medication taking, and provide a sense of security that they are taking their medications well. Finally, we reflect on design considerations for feedback systems to support the process of self-regulation of everyday behaviors.

Author Keywords
Medication adherence, sensors, feedback, behavior change, self-efficacy, ambient display, self-regulation

ACM Classification Keywords
H.5.m. Information interfaces and presentation (e.g., HCI): Miscellaneous.

INTRODUCTION
Over two-thirds of people over the age of 60 take four or more medications on a daily basis, and those with multiple chronic conditions take nine or more daily medications [6]. However, former U.S. surgeon general C. Everett Koop famously quipped, "*Drugs don't work in patients who don't take them.*" Approximately 20-50% of patients do not take at least 80% of their prescribed medications [13]. Improving medication adherence can lead to improved health outcomes and decreased health care costs [19].

CHI 2014, April 26 - May 01 2014, Toronto, ON, Canada

ACM 978-1-4503-2473-1/14/04...$15.00.
http://dx.doi.org/10.1145/2556288.2557210

Medication *non*-adherence comes in two forms: intentional (*e.g.*, due to inconvenience or fear of side effects) and unintentional (*e.g.*, due to being forgetful or careless). Much attention has been devoted to interventions to reduce intentional non-adherence by motivating individuals using complex programs involving education, individual attention from a clinician, counseling, and rewards [13]. However, unintentional non-adherence due to forgetfulness or carelessness is still pervasive, with 70% of a large sample of people with chronic diseases reporting instances of unintentional non-adherence [10].

Reminder systems such as MEMS [28] and CAMP [17] can provide alerts for medication taking. However, they can interfere with the individual's routines, do not reinforce the individual to self-initiate, and may undermine the individual's autonomy, an important mediator for medication taking [26]. Thus, there is a need for interventions for individuals already motivated to take their medications that do not adversely affect their autonomy.

Motivated individuals engage in self-regulation to adhere to their medication regimen by setting goals, actively pursuing these goals, and checking their progress or attainment of their goals [18]. Individuals must have feedback about their behaviors to compare their current behavior and their goal behavior and make adjustments to be more consistent. However, reflecting on medication taking is difficult because it is such an uninteresting, routine task performed every day. As a result, mentally tracking and self-reporting of medication adherence tends to be inaccurate [11].

Technologies such as sensors and ambient displays embedded in the home can provide the objective feedback necessary for engaging in self-regulation. These solutions can sense how the individual performs their medication taking and provide information about missed, late, or incorrectly taken medications. The information can also be delivered in a timely and locationally appropriate context that actually allows the individual to compare their current performance with their desired performance and adjust to perform better.

In this paper, we investigate how providing real-time sensor-based feedback about medication taking affects how consistently individuals take their medications. We describe a sensing and feedback system consisting of 1) a sensor-augmented pillbox that objectively monitors the individual's medication taking behavior and 2) an in-home ambient display that provides visual feedback about how well medications were taken for the current day. We deployed this system in the homes of older adults who take multiple daily medications in a longitudinal study for 10 months to examine the effect of feedback on medication taking behavior over time.

We demonstrate how the addition of a real-time feedback display helped individuals improve the promptness, correctness, and reduce the variability of their medication taking, when compared to their own baseline without the feedback display, and when compared to a control group who did not receive the real-time feedback display. The sensor-based feedback about successes and failures in medication taking also improved ratings of self-efficacy. In the next section, we describe related work before introducing the system, deployment study, and results.

RELATED WORK

Medication adherence review studies [12,13] show that clinical interventions with the largest effect sizes involve dosage simplification or combinations of counseling, reminders, follow up, supervised self-monitoring, and feedback. To avoid unintentional non-adherence due to carelessness or forgetfulness (a common issue for both older adults or busy younger adults) [10], motivated individuals need to be equipped with the skills to carry out their intention to take their medications.

One way to provide external assistance for medication taking is to use reminders. For example, a weekly phone call from a nurse can improve adherence rates [9]. Simple reminders like the GlowCap [28] as well as intelligent, context-aware reminders [11] based on multiple sensors around the home can also improve adherence rates. However reminders can be intrusive or heavy-handed, particularly for individuals who believe they take their medications well and do not need a reminder [20]. Reminders also do not fit well into the self-regulation process used to adopt a new behavior because they do not provide feedback for refining the behavior. Another approach for providing assistance for medication taking is to transform it from being a burdensome task to a social or entertaining task using a mobile game [23] with other medication takers. Our approach aims to be more lightweight, supporting the patient's autonomy without imposing a predefined routine for medication taking. We unobtrusively collect and present objective behavioral information to empower individuals to self-initiate their medication taking *on their own* using their natural process of self-regulation.

Self-Regulation Theory [2] provides a framework to understand the process of how individuals use contextual information to make decisions and follow through on intentions for behavior change. According to Self-Regulation Theory, human behavior is "regulated by the continual exercise of self-influence" [2]. To engage in self-regulation, individuals must 1) self-monitor their own behaviors and determinants of these behaviors, 2) make judgments about their behaviors with respect to personal standards, and 3) effectively self-reinforce their behaviors. Within this framework, feedback systems are well suited to help individuals self-monitor their behaviors more objectively and more easily than previously possible and to deliver this information in a way that allows them to draw comparisons with their goal behaviors.

Medication adherence is a self-regulatory process, where the individual sets a mental goal to take their medications, attempts to take their medications consistently, self-monitors how consistent they have been, and self-regulates their attitudes and behaviors to reach their adherence goal. Moreover, goal setting [16], a technique explored in other technologies for behavior change (*e.g.*, [5]), also facilitates the process of behavior change. In particular, frequent feedback about achieving sub-goals can make the sub-goals feel more tangible and also shows progress towards the larger overall goal.

An individual who experiences success in reaching a sub-goal such as taking his morning medications correctly today may also increase his self-efficacy [1], the feeling of confidence that he can perform his medication taking well despite obstacles such as being busy or forgetful. High self-efficacy is predictive of better performance, as long as the individual has the feedback to recognize his successes and failures and adjust accordingly to improve his medication-taking performance.

Feedback to the individual in clinical studies has usually involved manual self-recording of medication taking with diaries and have been combined with other interventions with limited success [13]. In the HCI domain, automated behavioral feedback has been useful in other behaviors that depend on self-regulation, such as performing physical activity [4,15], reducing resource consumption [7] and maintaining self-awareness [14]. In our work, we also use an approach for unobtrusively and objectively sensing medication-taking behavior that does not require the individual to do anything differently. We reflect their behaviors back to the individual with an in-home ambient display to determine whether the feedback helps individuals improve the consistency of their medication taking. This reflection approach follows a tradition of using ambient displays [4, 25] that afford informational feedback at a quick glance to facilitate behavior change.

RESEARCH QUESTIONS

In this paper, we set out to answer the following questions:

1. How does real-time feedback help individuals improve the consistency of their medication-taking behaviors?
2. How does real-time feedback affect self-efficacy for medication taking?

3. How do medication-taking behaviors change when removing real-time feedback after long-term use?

To answer these questions, we designed, built, and deployed a system for sensing and providing near real-time feedback for medication taking and evaluated this system using a 10-month longitudinal study to identify the effects of feedback on medication-taking behaviors.

SENSING AND FEEDBACK SYSTEM

To track medication taking unobtrusively, we designed and built a custom pillbox sensor. Commercial MEMS trackers like the Vitality GlowCap [28] were not used in this study because participants used weekly pillboxes (not pill bottles) in their medication taking routines. GlowCaps also uses reminders instead of providing real-time feedback for self-regulation. Instead, we augmented a 7-day pillbox [Figure 2] commonly found in drug stores with 1) a 3-axis accelerometer to track when the pillbox is picked up and 2) spring switches on the doors to track when the doors are opened and 3) custom circuitry with PICAXE microcontrollers and a XBee wireless modem. The design of the pillbox was similar to approaches used by Fishkin [8] and Hayes [11], but was wireless and more easily integrated into the user's routines. The pillbox sensor transmitted its data to a laptop in the participant's home using a ZigBee-wireless network. The laptop uploaded data periodically to a remote server where the sensor data was processed to identify and assess episodes of medication taking. A pill-taking episode consists of opening the correct pillbox door and inverting the pillbox to pour out the pills. While it is true that the sensor cannot actually detect whether the individual has swallowed the pills, the sensor can still capture the important step of remembering when and which pills to take to avoid *unintentional* non-adherence. The pillbox battery lasted between 4 to 6 weeks before needing to be replaced by a researcher.

The sensor-augmented pillbox was one sensor in a suite of sensors in the *dwellSense* system deployed in participants' homes which comprised other sensors to track Instrumental Activities of Daily Living, including motion/seat sensors, a sensor to track phone misdials, and an augmented coffee maker to track the routine, cognitively-demanding task of making coffee. In this paper, we focus only on medication taking because it is a widely recognized problem.

Near real-time feedback about medication taking was presented on a tablet display placed in the home of the individual. The display used a 10" Samsung Galaxy Tab running a custom application that shows a dashboard view [Figure 1] of how well the individual carried out her medication taking, phone use, and coffee making so far for the current day. The top row shows the status of medication taking for the morning and evening episodes including the time of day, which pillbox doors they opened, and whether they were taken on time, late, or not at all. We asked each individual 1) what time of day they normally take their morning and evening pills and 2) what time of day they

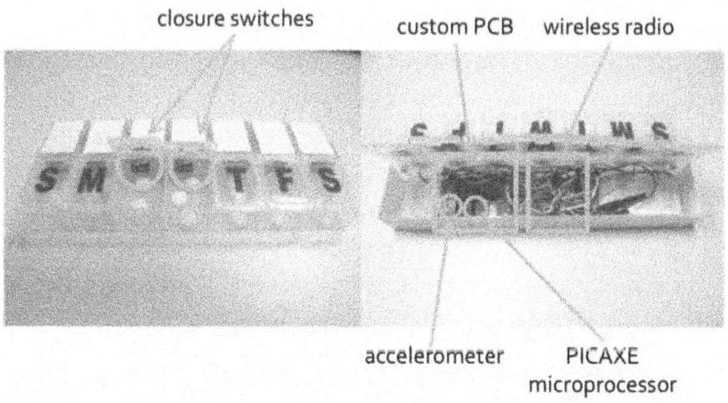

Figure 2. Sensor-augmented pillbox unobtrusively monitored medication taking over 10 months.

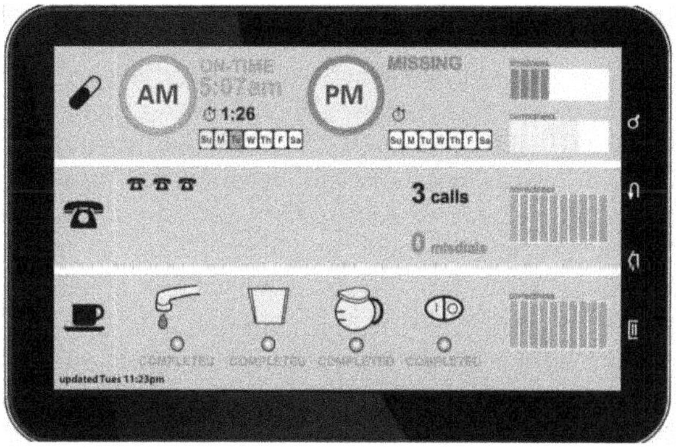

Figure 1. An in-home tablet-based display shows feedback about how well individuals carry out their medication-taking, phone use, and coffee making. It shows information about what time meds were taken, whether it was on-time, late or missing, what pillbox doors were opened, and a glanceable visual rating (right) for the promptness and correctness of medication taking.

would consider it to be late but still acceptable to take their pills. Users typically set the "late time" to be at least three hours after their normal pill taking time.

The status for the AM and PM medication taking episodes would light up in green with the text "ON-TIME" if pills were taken *before* the user-defined late time. The status changes to red with the text "MISSING" if the pills were not taken by the user-defined late time. The display changes to yellow with the text "LATE" if they took their pills *after* the late time. The bars on the right show a glanceable rating for promptness and correctness (opening the correct pillbox door to match the current day). The promptness bar shows all 10 bars if both AM and PM episodes are taken on-time, only 7 bars if either episodes are late, and at most 5 bars if either episodes are missing. The correctness bar shows all 10 bars if only the correct door was opened in both episodes, 7 bars if an extra door was opened, and at most 5 bars if the correct door was not opened. The display updates itself approximately once every 30 minutes to prevent displayed values from oscillating too quickly as tasks were being performed, which could be perceived as distracting or confusing. At the end of the day while the individual was asleep, the values of the display were automatically re-initialized, so users would see only the activity reports for the current day. Aside from pressing the "back" button that showed the report from the previous day, the display required no other user input and acted as an always-on ambient display. All other features on the tablet were disabled. The visual design of the display was pilot-tested with three older adults for two weeks and was revised based on user feedback before the subsequent deployment.

DEPLOYMENT STUDY

Participants were recruited from a local senior apartment building for people over 55 years old. The inclusion criteria included individuals who took multiple medications (pills) daily and were living alone. From 34 who expressed interest in the study, 12 older adults (9 female, 3 male) were willing to use the pillbox sensor and were enrolled in the study. The sample's age range was 52 to 83 (mean of 67.5) years. Each had multiple chronic conditions (averaging 2.5 conditions), such as diabetes, arthritis, hypertension, and COPD. All participants initially reported that they were taking their medications consistently every day. Thus, none felt they needed assistance to improve their medication taking but still had the overall goal to take their medications consistently. Participants were given a $30 grocery gift card each month for participating in the study. The gift card was not tied to their medication-taking performance.

Each individual was assigned randomly to either the feedback group or control group. Both groups had their medication taking monitored with the sensor-augmented pillbox. The six participants in the *feedback group* received the tablet display that showed real-time feedback on their task performance. The remaining six participants were assigned to the *control group* and never received the tablet display. There were no statistically significant differences ($p > 0.10$) in age, number of chronic conditions, and gender between the two groups as measured by Student's t-tests.

Deployment

To capture the impact of real-time feedback on medication-taking behaviors, the pillbox sensor was installed in the homes of the participants for 10 months. According to their existing routine, participants kept the pillbox either in the living room, kitchen, bedroom, or bathroom. A researcher visited on average once or twice a month to check on the sensors, replace batteries, and administer questionnaires throughout the study.

Months 1 and 2 of the study formed the baseline period for both the control and feedback groups in which no feedback was presented to participants. The feedback group received the tablet display in the beginning of month 3, providing them with real-time feedback on their medication taking. Each member of this group chose to keep the display in the living room where they spent most of their time. We provided an instruction guide on how to read the display, walked through the display with the participant, and tested the participant's comprehension of the data values before completing the visit. We did not prescribe exactly how often and when the participant should look at the display, but recommended that the participant look at the display whenever they wanted to, with suggested examples including before or after their medication-taking time. We also emphasized that the point of the study was NOT that they *should* take their medications any differently unless that was something they wanted to do for themselves. In fact, the researchers directed the participant's attention to reporting any errors they may see in the display, for example when the display did not match their behavior.

After 6 months of deployment (end of month 8), the display was removed from the homes of the feedback group. The pillbox sensors continued to track their medication taking behaviors for 2 months following the removal of the tablet.

The control group never received the tablet display. Instead, at the end of the month 4, the control group received a paper printout showing when they had taken their medications during the months 3 and 4 of the study. We presented this limited, one-time feedback to ensure that both groups would be familiar with the type of data being collected by the pillbox sensor. Thus, both groups knew exactly how their behaviors were being monitored.

At the end of month 10, all the sensors were removed from the participants' homes. Once a month over the entire study period, researchers used verbal questionnaires to assess each participant's self-efficacy in medication taking.

Measures

We consider the effect of real-time feedback on the consistency of medication-taking behaviors as captured by the sensor data, and self-efficacy to take medications as captured by verbal questionnaires.

Measures of Medication-taking Consistency

We consider the following important features of medication taking for our analysis: *adherence*, *correctness*, *promptness*, and the *variance in the time of day* the pills were taken.

Medication *adherence* characterizes how often pills are taken and is calculated as a percentage by summing all the pill-taking instances when the individual has taken their pills and dividing the sum by the prescribed number of instances in a given time period.

Correctness characterizes whether the individual took the pills assigned for that particular day. A pill-taking instance was considered correct if the individual opened up the pillbox door that matched the current day of the week. Users could open up any other doors *in addition to* the door that matched the current day and the instance would still be considered correct because it is likely they took the correct pill after realizing they opened the wrong door(s).

It is recommended to take medications (*e.g.*, for managing blood pressure [27]) at the proper time to ensure a steady level of medication in the body, so we consider two measures of timeliness: *promptness* and *variance*.

Promptness characterizes whether the pills are taken before the user-specified time-of-day threshold for late pills. We asked each participant to specify a time of day that they considered later than they normally would take their morning and evening pills. The rate of promptness was calculated as a percentage by summing the number of pill-taking instances before the late time and dividing it by the total number of instances taken over a given period of time.

Variance in the time of day measures how the time of day that medications were taken varied from one day to another. *Lower* variance is better because it spreads out the dosages more evenly and ensures that the level of medication in the individual's system remains more consistent from day to day. The variance was calculated by converting the time of day to a decimal number between 0 and 24 and then taking the variance of the numeric times over a given time period.

Measure of Self-Efficacy

To measure the individual's self-efficacy in taking medications over time, once every month a researcher verbally administered the Self-Efficacy for Appropriate Medication Use Scale (SEAMS), a validated 13 item questionnaire [24]. Each item in the questionnaire presented a potentially challenging situation (such as encountering side effects, having a busy day, or taking pills multiple times a day) and had the respondent rate their confidence as "Not Confident", "Somewhat Confident", and "Very Confident" in these situations.

RESULTS

Based on 5,785 episodes of medication taking by 12 older adults over 10 months, we investigate how real-time feedback affects medication-taking behaviors and self-efficacy. Participant P04 (control group) withdrew from the study after month 5 because he moved out of his apartment. During the initial 2 months (the baseline period) before any intervention, the groups were equivalent and had no significant differences in measures of medication-taking adherence (p=0.649), promptness (p=0.610), correctness (p=0.804), variance in the time of day taken (p=0.714), or ratings of self-efficacy (p=0.614) as measured by t-tests.

Participants with the display reported that they looked at the display at least once or twice a day, with most reporting they looked at it periodically throughout the day because "it was there." Participants found the display to be relatively easy to interpret, with the exception of the [Su M T W Th F Sa] correctness display for each episode. They initially interpreted it as showing their progress for the current week, when in fact, it shows which doors were opened for today's AM or PM episode. After a researcher clarified it, participants understood the correctness display.

Data Analysis Procedure

For the analysis of behavior change, we focus on whether the real-time feedback display had an effect, as compared to both the control group's behavior and also the feedback group's own baseline (to account for individual differences). The rate of adherence, rate of promptness, rate of correctness, and variance in the time of day were calculated for each month for a repeated-measures analysis.

The first 2 months represent a Baseline phase where both groups received no intervention and provides each individual's baseline level of performance. In the subsequent 6 months, called the Display phase, the feedback group had the feedback tablet display in their homes. All analyses were performed using a one-way ANOVA repeated-measures design and the Huynh-Feldt correction when data variables did not satisfy conditions of sphericity (as determined by a significant effect with Mauchly's test). The results report the significance of the interaction effect between group and phase, that is, whether the feedback group improved in performance while the control group stayed the same.

Real-time feedback improves medication-taking behaviors

The introduction of the feedback display resulted in significant improvements in promptness, correctness, and time of day variance for the feedback group. Adherence increased but the change was not statistically significant. Effect sizes were calculated using the following equation for pre/post with control designs: $d = (\Delta\mu_f - \Delta\mu_c)/\sigma$, where $\Delta\mu_f = \mu_{f2} - \mu_{f1}$; $\Delta\mu_c = \mu_{c2} - \mu_{c1}$; μ_{f1}, μ_{f2}=mean of feedback group in baseline and display periods respectively; μ_{c1}, μ_{c2}=mean of control group in baseline and display periods respectively; σ=pooled stdev at baseline [21].

Adherence

The feedback group improved in their adherence rate increasing from 94.5% in the baseline phase to 98.4% in the feedback phase (Figure 3, Left). The control group remained relatively unchanged, going from 93.7% to 92.1%. The interaction between group and phase was not statistically significant ($F[1,67]=2.33, p=0.131$). Participants started off highly adherent (averaging > 90%) and with the display, reached a level that neared perfect adherence (100%), the upper bound for a ceiling effect. In fact, all six participants with the feedback display had at least one two-week streak of never missing a dose, something not previously achieved. The lack of statistical significance may be due to this ceiling effect. Further, Cohen's effect size value ($d = 1.05$) suggests a high practical significance.

Promptness

The promptness rate of the feedback group also significantly improved from 75.1% to 90.8% after the introduction of the feedback display, while the control group stayed relatively unchanged, going from 78.8% to 75.4% ($F[1,67]=11.40$, $p=0.0012$) (Figure 3, Center) Cohen's effect size value (d =1.30) suggests a high practical significance.

Correctness

The correctness rate of the feedback group significantly increased from 94.9% to 99.2% for the feedback group after they received the feedback display while the control group remained unchanged (95.1% to 95.0%). The interaction

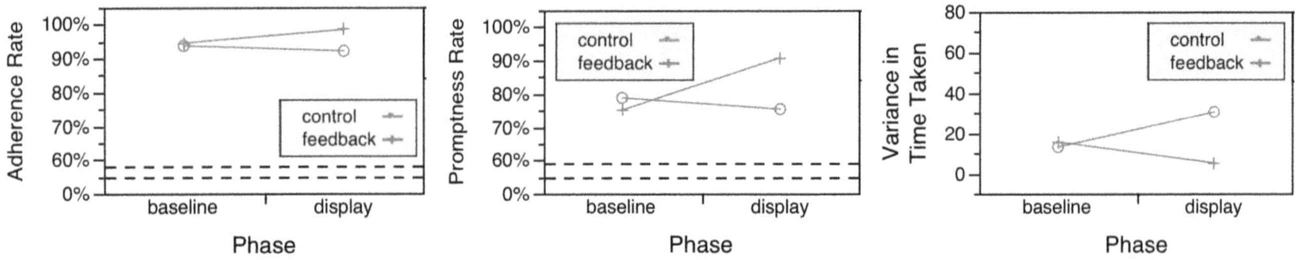

Figure 3. (Left) The feedback group improved in their adherence rate with the feedback display, but this difference was not statistically significant (p=0.131), possibly due to a ceiling effect. (Center) Promptness rates significantly increased in the feedback group while the control group did not change significantly (p=0.0012). (Right) The feedback group significantly decreased in the variance in the time of day pills were taken (p<0.0001) whereas the control group increased in the variance (which likely resulted from settling into the study).

effect between group and phase was statistically significant (F[1,67]=4.18, p=0.0448). Cohen's effect size value (d = 0.95) suggests a high practical significance.

Variance in the time of day

The variance in the time of day medications were taken (Figure 3, Right) also significantly decreased from 15.5 to 5.0 in the feedback group but increased for the control group from 13.07 to 30.47. The interaction effect between group and phase was statistically significant (F[1,66]=17.33, p<0.0001). Cohen's effect size value (d = -2.67) suggests a high practical significance. The feedback display helped the feedback group to take their medications closer to the same time of day from one day to the next. For example, the week before he received the feedback display, participant P2 took his pills at 8:18, 9:41, 6:08, 10:11, 7:16, 11:45, and 8:09am. The first week with the display, P2 took his pills most consistently around 7am, at 7:10, 6:58, 5:30, 7:30, 7:08, 7:05, and 6:55am. Interestingly, the control group *increased* in the variance in the time of day during this period. This can likely be attributed to participants feeling more relaxed about having their medications recorded, as they entered months 3 and 4 without feedback, and being less conscientious about taking their medications at the same time of day everyday. Thus, the feedback display seems to help maintain the level of vigilance on the consistency of medication taking rather than letting it extinguish after the initial boost from being monitored.

Qualitative improvements in medication-taking behaviors

Interviews with participants reveal that individuals used the display to remind themselves to take their medications. However, unlike reminder systems, the informational feedback from the display also enabled participants to self-regulate their medication taking behavior by 1) increasing their awareness, 2) identifying errors, and 3) confirming their memory, which helped them maintain their behavior. We describe these actions in the following paragraphs.

The process of self-regulation requires individuals to develop strategies that help overcome the obstacles to perform the target behavior. Individuals used the feedback display as a visual *reminder* for their medication taking. Even though participants reported that they took their medications very consistently, they all mentioned at least a few instances when they had forgotten and happened to glance at the display, which reminded them to take their medications. P01 said, "*I look up and I see 'Oh! I didn't take my evening pills', so it's a nice reminder, it's not a nasty kind of thing, you know.*" In this case, P01 saw that the evening pill status was still gray and not yet been filled in, not some alert or visually salient change in the display. It should be noted that the feedback display did NOT show time-triggered reminders for on-time medication taking because it only updated after the individual took their medications or after the predefined late time. Even though automatically changing the status to "MISSING" after the late time can act as a trigger, the data show that participants increased both in the rate of adherence and in the rate of promptness, indicating that they mostly took their pills before the status changing to "MISSING" could act as a reminder. Nonetheless, individuals appropriated the presence of the display as a visual reminder to assist them in taking their medications.

In addition to reminding, real-time feedback also provided the individual with key information to self-regulate. One of the most common themes emerging from the interviews was about how the display provided individuals with a sense of *awareness* of their medication taking behaviors and habits that they had not previously realized, which is necessary for self-regulation. P01 remarked, "*You know, [the display] tells me what I have done or what I haven't done. The time to take my pills would be varied. I would get them in me but the times are varied.*" P05 said, "*It always tells you what time you get your medication then in the meanwhile sometimes it tells you when you have missed your medication. That way, it's good.*"

Self-regulation requires feedback about when the behavior was performed in error or inadequately to reach a sub-goal. Individuals need feedback to direct their attention to differences between their current behavior and their goal behavior. The feedback display helped individuals to *identify errors* in their medication-taking behavior such as opening the wrong door on the pillbox and taking another day's pills, as remarked by P02 who said, "*[The display] lets you know if am I making mistake, like if I open another door one day and it came up [on the display].*" The timeliness of the feedback was also important because it highlighted errors earlier than when refilling the pillbox at the end of the week. For example, P10 said, "*Before, if I made a mistake and forgot it, I might not notice until the end of the week or something. [With the display] you notice it, you see it right away.*"

The feedback display also helped individuals to not only identify errors but also *confirm correct behaviors*. P02 said he made looking at the display part of his daily routine, "*I find myself [checking the display] every day, to make sure I was on time or make sure I was right or make sure I did thing I was supposed to.*" P06 reported that it was her habit to take her pills and then look at the screen to see when it would register her pill taking, "*I would take my pills and few minutes later I'm looking at [the display] to see how long it takes for the light up.*" Both P06 and P02 developed such strong habits to check the display to confirm their behavior that even after it was removed, they reported they still glanced over to where the display used to be.

Real-time feedback improves qualitative self-efficacy

Self-efficacy is one of the main modifiable determinants of behavior change [1]. One way to increase self-efficacy is to experience successes in performing a behavior, which can, in turn, motivate the individual to carry out the same behavior successfully again. The feedback from the tablet display can provide a signal that the medications were successfully taken promptly and correctly, which can increase self-efficacy and reinforce more consistent medication-taking behaviors.

Real-time feedback had no quantitative effect on self-efficacy

Responses to each of the 13 items in the SEAMS questionnaire were assigned a value of 1 for "Not Confident", 2 for "Somewhat Confident", and 3 for "Very Confident". The values were summed up across all 13 items, for a possible total self-efficacy score of 39.

At baseline, before any intervention was introduced, participants rated themselves with very high self-efficacy, with an overall average of 33.75. This high score indicates that participants were quite confident in their abilities to overcome challenges when taking their medications.

The introduction of the feedback display did not have a significant effect on medication-taking self-efficacy. The feedback group remained relatively unchanged, going from an average self-efficacy score of 34.41 to 34.86 with the display, as did the control group, going from 33.1 to 32.1. A repeated-measures ANOVA showed no significant interaction effect between group and phase ($F[1,34]=0.406$, $p=0.528$).

These results can be interpreted in two ways: the first being that feedback had no effect on self-efficacy, the second being that our measure of self-efficacy was not sensitive enough to detect the subtle change in self-efficacy. The latter interpretation is reasonable given that our sample may have reached a ceiling effect for the SEAMS instrument, as most of them gave the highest confidence ratings to 8 (a majority) of the 13 items. A finer-grained scale may have been able to measure an effect.

Real-time feedback qualitatively improved self-efficacy

To overcome the ceiling effect of the instrument, we conducted a follow-up interview and asked participants to compare their feelings of self-efficacy before they received the feedback display and their feelings with the display. For each of the 13 scenarios in the SEAMS questionnaire, we asked, "*With the help of the display, do you feel more confident, less confident, or no difference about taking their medications.*" If the response was "more confident" or "less confident", we asked the participant to rate the degree of how much more/less confident on a scale of 1 to 5, with 1 being "just a little" and 5 being "very much".

Of the 6 participants in the feedback group, we only could reach 5 of them for the follow-up interview because P09 was unavailable due to a family matter. None said the display made them feel less confident, only 1 participant (P01) reported that the display did not change her confidence level in any of the items, and the remaining 4 all reported that the display helped them feel *more* confident in their medication taking in at least one of the SEAMS scenarios. These 4 participants each reported it helped them feel more confident (average degree: 3.75) in taking their medication in scenario #6 ("when no one reminds you to take your medicine"). 3 of these participants also thought the feedback display helped them feel more confident in scenario #1 ("when you need to take several different medications per day") (average degree: 4.33) and scenario #8 ("when your normal routine gets messed up") (average degree: 4.0).

Removing Real-Time Feedback

In this section, we investigate whether the feedback display had a lasting effect after it was removed. After 6 months with the display (the Display phase), the feedback display was removed from the homes of the feedback group. The sensor-augmented pillbox continued to track medication taking behaviors for another 2 months, which we label the Follow_up phase. We compare the medication-taking behaviors during these 2 phases. Measures of behavior were averaged for each month in these phases and a repeated-measures one-way ANOVA was used to find differences after the display was removed. Two control group participants were excluded from the analysis because Follow_up data was lost due a laptop disk failure (P07) and a move to another apartment (P04).

Even though real-time feedback supported a higher level of performance in the medication-taking task, the analysis revealed that the improved level of performance was *not* sustained after the real-time feedback was removed. Without the display, individuals significantly decreased their medication adherence (from 98.4% to 96.2%, $F[1,41]=5.86$, $p=0.0201$), promptness (from 90.8% to

83.6%, F[1,41]=5.8, p=0.0208), and correctness (from 99.2% to 97.1%, F[1,41]=7.08, p=0.011). There was also a marginally significant increase in the variance of the time of day medications were taken (from 5.03 to 9.82 hours F[1,41]=3.34, p=0.075). Post-hoc comparisons using the Tukey HSD test indicated the mean rates for adherence, promptness, and correctness were not significantly different (p>0.05) from the rates in the Baseline phase before participants received the display. In other words, once the feedback display was removed, individuals dropped in performance to a level slightly (but not statistically significantly) above their baseline performance level. In the control group, none of the corresponding measures of adherence (F[1,26]=1.96, p=0.174), promptness (F[1,26]=4.07, p=0.0545), correctness (F[1,26]=0.676, p=0.419), and variance (F[1,26]=0.424, p=0.521) experienced statistically significantly changes in this period, as would be expected.

DISCUSSION

Improving medication taking, like many health behaviors, is not often accomplished simply by an act of will. Adopting health behaviors requires a process that involves interplay among the individual's motivation, goals, and feedback to carry out their intentions. Feedback can play a role in helping individuals self-monitor and self-regulate.

Using Real-time Feedback to Self-Regulate Behavior

One of the research questions in this study is how feedback affects an individual's medication-taking behaviors. The results demonstrate that near real-time sensor-based feedback about medication taking behaviors presented in an ambient in-home display enabled individuals to self-monitor their medication taking more consistently. As a result, those who received the feedback display took their prescribed doses significantly more promptly (before a user-defined "late time"), selected the right pills to take slightly more often, and took them significantly more consistently at the same time of day across multiple days. Real-time feedback allowed participants to self-regulate their medication taking by 1) increasing their awareness, 2) identifying errors, and 3) confirming their memory, which helped them improve their behavior.

Another important research question we addressed in this study was about what happens after individuals are cut off from feedback after using it for a relatively long period (in our case, 6 months). The results demonstrate that the gains in performance mostly disappeared after the feedback display was removed from their home. Previous studies of self-monitoring [22] have shown that the boost in performance associated with manual self-recording usually diminishes once the individual stops self-monitoring, perhaps due to the effort and attention required for manual self-monitoring. In contrast, our approach used automated self-monitoring with sensors that require minimal effort by the user. The results show our automatic approach had a similar drop off after the feedback was removed. This indicates that the ongoing feedback itself (and not the effort of self-recording behaviors) was instrumental for boosting performance. Participants reported they had integrated the ambient feedback display into their daily routines and continued to use it for self-regulation by checking the display multiple times to see whether they took their pills earlier in the day, to identify errors, and also to confirm that their earlier medication taking had registered in the system. Without the frequent, immediate feedback from the display, individuals did not see progress on how well they were achieving the daily sub-goals of taking their medications well and were not able to self-regulate their medication-taking behaviors as well.

Supporting Self-Efficacy with Feedback

Regular feedback about successes and failures in medication taking supported a qualitative increase in self-efficacy for medication taking. Even though the SEAMS questionnaire used for measuring self-efficacy was not able to detect a quantitative increase in self-efficacy due to a ceiling effect, individuals reported in interviews that the feedback display was instrumental in helping them feel more confident in taking their medications independently, when no one was available to remind them, when they had to take multiple medications in a day, and even when their daily schedule may be non-routine.

According to Social Cognitive Theory (SCT), high self-efficacy is one of the most powerful predictors of behavior change, even more powerful than demographics, personal/ environmental factors, and barriers [3]. One of the main mechanisms for building self-efficacy is successfully reaching a goal (or sub-goal) by performing the target behavior. Individuals reported that it made them feel good when they saw the status on the screen light up green, indicating that they took their medications promptly and correctly. It is also interesting to note that the display also provided negative feedback about missed or late pills. SCT predicts that self-efficacy can decrease if individuals encounter failures in performing the task. However, if individuals have the means to adjust their environment or strategies to avoid future failures, then confidence will not necessarily be eroded [1]. With our approach of providing feedback almost immediately, individuals could be made aware of a mistake, recall the circumstances from earlier in the day or yesterday that led to the mistake, and develop a strategy to avoid making the mistake again. Our study demonstrates that even individuals with high self-efficacy could (and did) improve their medication-taking behaviors even further with the addition of feedback. The results reinforce the need for behavior change interventions to support self-awareness in addition to self-efficacy. Ubiquitous sensing and feedback technologies are well-suited to provide the data necessary for self-awareness.

Design Considerations for Feedback Systems

The results of this paper indicate that 1) feedback from a ubiquitous sensing system is useful for supporting self-regulation and behavior change in medication taking and 2) medication taking is an ongoing behavior that requires continued feedback beyond six months to maintain consistency in the behavior. Many other ongoing behaviors like maintaining physical activity or managing diet may also require continued feedback to sustain improvements in behaviors. Thus, it is important for designers of ubiquitous sensing systems that use feedback for behavior change, to consider how these systems can be deployed and used over the long-term to sustain behavior improvement. In evaluating dwellSense, the sensing and feedback system described in this paper, we suggest future systems to minimize the burden of sensing on the user and rely on either unobtrusive sensing or input willingly reported by the user over a long period of time. For example, the pillbox sensor used in this study was purposely designed to be used exactly as a normal pillbox, so individuals did not have to change their routines for the system to monitor their natural behaviors. An even more integrated example that similarly requires little additional demand on the user is the Proteus Digital Health Feedback System [29] that senses physiological parameters through an ingestible sensor.

We also suggest embedded feedback in a way that is easily visible and easily integrated into the individual's routines. The ambient tablet display we used in this study was always on and situated rather prominently in the user's living room where they spend most of their time. Users could not help but glance at it once in a while. As a result, glancing at it became part of their routine to support and confirm their medication taking. We speculate that if we required the user to walk up to the tablet and request a report to get feedback that they would not have viewed the feedback very often, if at all, particularly because most felt they did not need "help" in taking their medications.

The ambient (rather than highly interactive) display also affords a sense of security. Many individuals may balk at the idea of using a system to assist or persuade them in performing behaviors perceived to be simple like medication taking. However, participants in our study commonly looked at the screen just to check how they were doing and this made them feel secure, even though most did not believe they needed the feedback display to take their medications well. Technologies that monitor and provide feedback while preserving the individual's autonomy can be presented to users to support a feeling of security rather than solely as assistive technology.

Knowing when and how often to provide feedback is also an important design consideration for feedback systems. The timing of the feedback may be related to the type of behaviors the system is trying to support. Providing longer-term logs of their behaviors can provide a better view of trends in the data to indicate larger problems or good performance. However, frequent behaviors like medication taking require frequent, actionable feedback that helps users recall the reason for their mistake while it is fresh in their mind, so feedback should be provided before the next repetition of the activity (*e.g.,* this evening's medication taking) displaces the previous instance from memory.

Finally, automated feedback systems should be considered as one tool within a larger holistic coaching strategy that addresses the many factors that lead to behavior change. Lowly activated, passive individuals may need their beliefs about medication taking first addressed through education, whereas more highly activated and motivated individuals would likely benefit more from the real-time feedback systems to adopt and maintain a desire behavior.

LIMITATIONS & FUTURE WORK

The study examined how real-time feedback deployed into actual homes of users over a long term affected their medication-taking behaviors. One of the limitations of this study was the relatively small sample size, with a total of 12 participants, equally divided between the intervention group and control group. However, the experiment was structured with two points of comparison: an individual's own baseline (the first 2 months without intervention), and with the control group, which makes it less likely for significant effects to result from unaccounted personal factors. Similar to [23], we encountered ceiling effects due to our sample being highly adherent and reporting high efficacy at baseline. As a result, improvements in medication-taking behaviors, though often statistically significant, were somewhat small in absolute magnitude. However, effect tests indicate that the magnitudes of improvements were approximately one standard deviation, which suggests a fairly substantial increase. Self-regulation theory predicts that highlighting the discrepancy between the current and goal state can increase motivation. Feedback will show a larger discrepancy for low adherers than high adherers, which can motivate lower adherers even more, assuming they have the skills and self-efficacy to improve (via coaching, achieving success, social support, *etc*). In future work, we will validate this prediction without ceiling effects. Another limitation was that the control group was not a strictly no-intervention group. They received a chart showing 2 months of their medication-taking behaviors so that they could understand the type of data being collected. It is possible that seeing this chart may have reinforced their existing performance level, but it is more likely this one-time feedback had no significant lasting effect on their performance. In future work, we will investigate how less frequent reflection on longer-term data can impact self-awareness and behaviors.

CONCLUSION

Medication adherence is a self-regulatory process that requires an active process of self-monitoring and adjustments to perform medication taking consistently over time. Systems that sense and reflect back behavioral information can provide feedback for this self-regulatory process. This paper demonstrated such a system that captured medication-taking behaviors with an unobtrusive sensor-augmented pillbox and presented real-time feedback about the task on an in-home ambient display. This system enabled individuals to take their medications more frequently, promptly, and correctly, but these improvements diminished almost immediately without continued feedback. Feedback about when they took their medications earlier in the day enabled individuals to 1) increase their awareness, 2) identify errors sooner, and 3) confirm their memory which helped to increase their self-efficacy, sustain their performance, and preserve their autonomy without resorting to disruptive reminders. Our approach of understanding the particular self-regulatory process of the target behavior and designing a system that senses and displays timely behavioral information to close the feedback loop necessary for self-regulation, can also be applied in other behavioral domains such as improving physical activity, eating habits, and resource consumption.

ACKNOWLEDGEMENTS
This work was supported by the Robert Wood Johnson Foundation Project HealthDesign Grant RWJ67167 and National Science Foundation ERC Grant EEEC-0540865.

REFERENCES

1. Bandura, A. Self-efficacy: toward a unifying theory of behavioral change. Psychological review 84, 2 (1977), 191.
2. Bandura, A. Social cognitive theory of self-regulation. Organizational behavior and human decision processes 50, 2 (1991), 248–287.
3. Brus, H., Van de Laar, M., Taal, E., Rasker, J., and Wiegman, O. Determinants of compliance with medication in patients with rheumatoid arthritis. Patient Education and Counseling 36, 1 (1999), 57–64.
4. Consolvo, S., Klasnja, P., McDonald, D.W., et al. Flowers or a robot army?: encouraging awareness & activity with personal, mobile displays. In *Proc. Ubicomp 2008*, ACM (2008), 54–63.
5. Consolvo, S., McDonald, D.W., and Landay, J.A. Theory-driven design strategies for technologies that support behavior change in everyday life. In *Proc. CHI 2009*, ACM (2009), 405–414.
6. Elliott, R.A. Problems with medication use in the elderly: an Australian perspective. Journal of Pharmacy Practice and Research 36, 1 (2006), 58.
7. Erickson, T., et al. The dubuque water portal: evaluation of the uptake, use and impact of residential water consumption feedback. In *Proc CHI 2012*, ACM (2012), 675–684.
8. Fishkin, K.P., Wang, M., and Borriello, G. A ubiquitous system for medication monitoring. In *Proc. Pervasive 2004*.
9. Friedman, R.H., et al. A Telecommunications System for Monitoring and Counseling Patients With Hypertension. Am J Hypertension 9, 4 (1996), 285–292.
10. Gadkari, A.S. and McHorney, C.A. Unintentional non-adherence to chronic prescription medications. BMC Health Services Research 12, 1 (2012), 98.
11. Hayes, T.L., Cobbinah, K., Dishongh, T., et al. A study of medication-taking and unobtrusive, intelligent reminding. Telemedicine and e-Health 15, 8 (2009), 770–776.
12. Haynes, R.B., Ackloo, E., Sahota, N., McDonald, H. P., & Yao, X. Interventions for enhancing medication adherence. Cochrane database syst Rev, 2, 2 (2008), 11.
13. Kripalani, S. Interventions to Enhance Medication Adherence in Chronic Medical Conditions. Archives of Internal Medicine 167, 6 (2007), 540.
14. Lee, M.L. and Dey, A.K. Reflecting on pills and phone use: supporting awareness of functional abilities for older adults. In *Proc. CHI 2011*, ACM (2011), 2095–2104.
15. Li, I. Personal informatics & context: Using context to reveal factors that affect behavior. J. Ambient Intell. Smart Environ. 4, 1 (2012), 71–72.
16. Locke, E.A. and Latham, G.P. A theory of goal setting & task performance. Prentice-Hall, Inc, 1990.
17. Lundell, J. et al., Continuous activity monitoring and intelligent contextual prompting to improve medication adherence. In Proc. EMBS, IEEE (2007), pp. 6286–6289.
18. Maes, S. and Karoly, P. Self-Regulation Assessment and Intervention in Physical Health and Illness: A Review. Applied Psychology 54, 2 (2005), 267–299.
19. McDonnell, P.J. and Jacobs, M.R. Hospital admissions resulting from preventable adverse drug reactions. The Annals of pharmacotherapy 36, 9 (2002), 1331–1336.
20. McGee-Lennon, M.R., Wolters, M.K., and Brewster, S. User-centred multimodal reminders for assistive living. In *Proc. CHI 2011*, ACM (2011), 2105–2114.
21. Morris, S.B. Estimating effect sizes from pretest-posttest-control group designs. Organizational Research Methods, 11, 2, (2008), 364-386.
22. Nelson, R.O. and Hayes, S.C. Theoretical Explanations for Reactivity in Self-Monitoring. Behavior Modification 5, 1 (1981), 3–14.
23. De Oliveira, R., Cherubini, M., and Oliver, N. MoviPill: improving medication compliance for elders using a mobile persuasive social game. In *Proc. Ubicomp 2010*. ACM (2010), 251–260.
24. Risser, J., Jacobson, T.A., and Kripalani, S. Development and psychometric evaluation of the Self-efficacy for Appropriate Medication Use Scale (SEAMS) in low-literacy patients with chronic disease. Journal of nursing measurement 15, 3 (2007), 203–219.
25. Rogers, Y., Hazlewood, W.R., Marshall, P., Dalton, N., and Hertrich, S. Ambient influence: can twinkly lights lure and abstract representations trigger behavioral change? In *Proc. Ubicomp 2010*, ACM (2010), 261–270.
26. Williams, G., Rodin, G., Ryan, R., Grolnick, W. and Deci, E. Autonomous regulation and long-term medication adherence in adult outpatients. *Health Psychology*, 17, 3 (1998), 269.
27. Zhu, L.L., Zhou, Q., Yan, X.F., Zeng, S. Optimal time to take once-daily oral medications in clinical practice. International Journal of Clinical Practice, 62 (2008), 1560.
28. http://www.vitality.net/glowcaps.html.
29. http://proteusdigitalhealth.com/.

Don't Forget Your Pill! Designing Effective Medication Reminder Apps That Support Users' Daily Routines

Katarzyna Stawarz
UCL Interaction Centre
Gower Street
London, WC1E 6BT, UK
k.stawarz@cs.ucl.ac.uk

Anna L Cox
UCL Interaction Centre
Gower Street
London, WC1E 6BT, UK
anna.cox@ucl.ac.uk

Ann Blandford
UCL Interaction Centre
Gower Street
London, WC1E 6BT, UK
a.blandford@ucl.ac.uk

ABSTRACT
Despite the fact that a third of all cases of unintentional medication non-adherence are caused by simple forgetfulness, the majority of interventions neglect this issue. Even though patients have access to smartphone applications ("apps") designed to help them remember medication, neither their quality nor effectiveness has been evaluated yet. We report the findings of a functionality review of 229 medication reminder apps and a thematic analysis of their 1,012 user reviews. Our research highlights the gap between the theory and practice: while the literature shows that many medication regimens are habitual in nature and the presence of daily routines supports remembering, existing apps rely on timer-based reminders. To address this disparity, we present design requirements for building medication reminders that support the routine aspect of medication-taking and its individual nature, and demonstrate how they could be implemented to move from passive alerts to a smarter memory and routine assistant.

Author Keywords
Smartphone apps; medication reminders; forgetfulness; habits; routines

ACM Classification Keywords
H.5.m. Information interfaces and presentation (e.g., HCI): Miscellaneous. H.5.2 User Interfaces: User-centered design.

INTRODUCTION
Medication non-adherence reduces the effectiveness of a treatment and imposes a financial burden on health care systems [23, 47]: in the USA alone, the estimated cost of non-adherence reaches $100 billion each year, including the cost of 10% of hospital and 23% of nursing home admissions [45]. The majority of adherence interventions developed to address this issue focus on intentional non-adherence and their aim is to educate people and change their attitudes and beliefs [18]. However, even motivated people can forget: forgetfulness accounts for 30% of cases of unintentional non-adherence [43] and around one million unwanted pregnancies each year are the result of non-adherence [37] and irregular use of the contraceptive pill ("the Pill"), with forgetfulness as one of the main causes [25, 41]. And yet, interventions explicitly addressing forgetfulness, especially for preventative therapies such as oral contraception, are not only few and far between, but also tend to focus on reminders alerting people to take their medication at a specified time [18, 46]. This focus on timed alerts disregards the fact that time-based tasks are more difficult to remember than tasks related to routine actions [34] and many medication regimens are habitual tasks that could be easily incorporated into a daily routine, which in itself also supports remembering.

CHI 2014, April 26 - May 01 2014, Toronto, ON, Canada

ACM 978-1-4503-2473-1/14/04...$15.00.
http://dx.doi.org/10.1145/2556288.2557079

The routine support could be provided by technology. With the increasing popularity of smartphones, people now have access to thousands of health-related applications ("apps") [27] that could help them remember their medication. Even though in recent years a few app reviews have been published (e.g. [10, 31, 33, 38]), to date, medication reminder apps have not been reviewed or evaluated by academic researchers, and as a result their effectiveness or the extent to which they meet users' needs are not known.

Our paper makes two main contributions and presents a new direction in research that could be exploited to support medication-taking. Firstly, we review the functionality of smartphone medication reminder apps and highlight the weaknesses of apps that take a "one size fits all" approach and support remembering by providing simple, timer-based reminders. Secondly, we propose a set of design requirements for building reminder apps that take into account the habitual nature of medication regimens. To demonstrate the feasibility of this approach, we illustrate these requirements with a use case scenario that describes how apps supporting medication routines could be implemented. We argue that by taking advantage of the habitual nature of many medication regimens and by incorporating routine support in addition to timer-based reminders, technology could be more effective in supporting the user and reducing unintentional medication non-adherence.

REMEMBERING MEDICATION

Remembering to take medication is a prospective memory task and as such it relies on a set of cognitive processes responsible for completing actions at some point in the future [13]. There are two main types of prospective memory tasks: time-based tasks that need to be completed at a specified time (e.g. take medication at 9:00) or after a set period of time has elapsed (e.g. take antibiotics every 8 hours); and event-based tasks, where the task is linked to an existing event and the environment in which it takes place, e.g. taking medication with breakfast. Depending on individual circumstances, a medication regimen can be classified as either of these tasks.

All prospective memory tasks rely on cues, which can be internal (e.g. thoughts), external (reminders, notes, etc.) or paired with an event that triggers the task ("conjunction reminders") [20]. External and conjunction reminders are the most effective as they provide more cues [13, 30]. As a result, event-based tasks support memory more effectively than time-based tasks: they are easier to remember and the presence of a routine guides behavior and provides more contextual cues, increasing the adherence to a medical treatment [34] and supporting habit formation [5].

Habits & Routines

Habits are an effect of gradual learning of patterns of behavior and associations between the task or its features and the environment (e.g. location), especially when actions are regularly and frequently performed in a sequence [1, 49]. To be turned into a habit, a task should be simple [16, 28], be associated with an existing routine task [16, 34] and provide positive reinforcement [16, 28]. It also needs to be repeated enough times to become a routine behavior [1, 29].

As medications often need to be taken regularly and within a particular period of time, many regimens are *de facto* habitual tasks – patients learn to associate their medications with a specific time of day, location or event. According to the Medication Adherence Model [24], such patterned behavior is an important part of medication-taking, as it is personalized, unique for each individual and reflects their lifestyle and daily activities. As a result, timing (e.g. breakfast time) and the location (e.g. kitchen) are key elements of a routine, and make it more memorable, meaningful and reliable [24]. For example, the act of eating breakfast in the kitchen initially serves as a cue to take the medication and, with time, transforms the behavior into a habitual action. However, while routines can make repetitive tasks easier through the creation of automatic actions, they can also be dangerous when the task requires deliberation [36]. The automaticity of a behavior combined with disruptions to the routine increase the likelihood of omission and repetition errors [3, 12], which should be taken into account when designing a technology that utilizes routines.

Routines & Remembering The Pill

To better understand the role routines play in supporting habitual medication regimens, we conducted an online survey that explored women's strategies for remembering oral contraception. Preliminary results illustrate the impact of routines and technology on remembering the Pill regimen.

The survey was advertised on popular social networks, online forums and among students and university staff, and resulted in 971 complete responses. Possibly due to the nature of advertising channels, 76% of respondents were women aged 18-25 years old. The results showed that nearly half of the respondents reported completely missing the Pill at least once during the month preceding the survey, and during the same period 75% took it later than they should. When asked how they remembered the Pill, 61% said it was a part of their daily routine. It does not come as a surprise then that the most common causes of forgetting were changes in the daily routine (54%), being busy or distracted (47%), and simple forgetfulness (46%). Yet, women who relied on their daily routines forgot less often: in the routine group (N=589) 41% of women completely forgot the Pill at least once in the past month and 69% were late, compared to 56% and 86% respectively among those who did not mention daily routines (N=382). Chi-square tests for independence indicated significant ($p < .001$) associations between fewer forgetting incidents and the presence of routines, which is in line with the literature.

Only 25% of women mentioned using some sort of technology as a reminder, predominantly their cellphone's alarm clock. Dedicated medication reminder apps were used by 5% (N=45) of women, which came as a surprise given the age range of the majority of respondents and the fact that 66% of 16-24 year olds in the UK own a smartphone and are likely to download apps [32]. A quarter of women who used technology to support their memory also said that the Pill-taking was a part of their routine, which indicates that cellphones might have been used as a backup reminder.

Our preliminary findings show that women rely mainly on routines and this strategy increases their adherence. They also tend not to use technology, despite the fact that cellphones are ubiquitous and have capabilities to provide reminders and support routines. This suggests that users either do not see the need to use medication reminder apps or that apps in their current form are not fit for purpose. The following sections investigate this issue in more detail.

MOBILE REMINDERS

According to the latest statistics, 92% of UK adults own a cellphone and 39% own a smartphone [32]. The ubiquity of mobile devices, combined with their personal nature [44] and their functionality, such as text messaging, apps, or Internet access, make cellphones an effective platform for delivering health interventions [15, 26, 50]. Among cellphone-based interventions aimed at supporting remembering, text message reminders are the most widely used.

Text Messages

Text messages (SMS or short message service) have been used as reminders in several health interventions (e.g. [7, 14, 21]). For example, Hou *et al.* [21] evaluated the impact of SMS reminders on adherence to oral contraception. For three months, at a time chosen before the trial, 82 participants received a daily SMS reminder to take the Pill. The results showed that despite the daily reminders, the intervention did not improve adherence compared to the control group. Moreover, women who ended the trial with an excellent adherence record had felt at the beginning of the study that they would not need SMS reminders, which suggests that they either already used their own reminders or relied on a routine.

The study also shows that text messages are not flexible enough: they are simple timer-based reminders that require immediate attention. As each SMS was sent only once, women were not able to postpone the reminder if they could not take the Pill immediately, which suggests that smartphone apps with reminders that can be 'snoozed' might be better suited as a memory support tool.

Smartphone Apps

Smartphone users have easy access to thousands of health-related mobile apps [27]. Even though several reviews of health apps have been conducted, medication reminders have not been assessed to date. For example, a review of the top 500 medical apps available in Italian app stores conducted in 2012 [31] identifies 58 "health diaries", which includes "medication scheduling apps". However, no further information about these apps is provided. Another review from 2013 [10] describes over 160 medication adherence apps available for different types of smartphones, and although medication reminders were included, the focus was on intentional non-adherence and evaluating the apps from a pharmacist's perspective. Despite the fact that the effectiveness of the apps had not been formally evaluated at the time and their relevance to users' needs had not been assessed, authors concluded that these apps have potential to help with medication regimens.

Rather than evaluating existing apps, some researchers have proposed their own solutions. For example, Silva *et al.* [39] designed a medication reminder app that allowed users to enter multiple medications, showed due times and taking instructions, and highlighted overdue doses. The app did not differ much from commercial apps, and since its focus was on reminders, routine support was not available. However, the authors created a set of functional requirements that address a number of accessibility issues, including automated reminders with different modalities (visual and auditory alerts) and the snooze option to prevent missing doses, which could be considered when designing a reminder system that takes routines into the account.

De Oliveira *et al.* [11] took a different approach: to help people develop routines, they designed an app that encouraged continuous use by adding a competitive element to medication-taking. Users were awarded adherence scores, which were then shared with their peers and displayed on a leader board. The game did not provide reminders and users had to remember by themselves, although the focus was on winning the game and taking the medication at a specific time rather than simply taking it every day. As a result, routines were not sufficiently well defined and users needed their own timer-based reminders.

Nevertheless, the approach taken by De Oliveira *et al.* shows that medication reminders do not need to focus on timer-based alerts and that reminder apps could support routines. Below we present two studies we conducted to investigate how commercial apps available for smartphones prevent forgetting and whether they support daily routines.

STUDY I: APPS FUNCTIONALITY REVIEW

As interventions tend to focus on timer-based reminders and our study showed that women who take the Pill tend not to use medication reminder apps despite their wide availability, we wanted to explore this issue in more detail. We conducted a review of existing apps to understand what functionality they offer, how they support memory, whether approaches other than timer-based reminders are available and to what extent the apps support routine behavior.

Method

As Apple and Android devices accounted for 86% of new smartphones purchased in 2012 [30], apps available in the UK versions of Apple iTunes Store [2] and Google Play [17] were included in the analysis. Free and paid apps, and full and limited ("lite") versions were included in the review and counted separately, as they offered different functionality. Similarly, apps available in both stores were treated as separate apps, as due to operating system differences their functionality and types of alerts differed. As the focus of the study was on smartphone medication reminders, apps for tablets, generic reminders and other health support apps were excluded.

Prior to the main analysis, a list of popular features was prepared based on the first 25 apps found in each store after searching for "medication reminder". Identified features were grouped into categories and used later to aid data collection. "Medication reminder", "pill reminder", "contraception reminder" and "birth control reminder" were used as search keywords to ensure a wide range of medication reminders was covered. Details of each app, including its name, user rating, number of user reviews, and the presence of feature categories identified during the initial analysis were recorded. Features not fitting into the predefined categories were also noted and later grouped to create additional categories.

In total, 229 medication reminder apps met the inclusion criteria (123 for iPhones and 106 for Android-based smartphones, including 15 available for both platforms). Among them, 86% were generic medication reminder apps and 14% supported a specific regimen, mainly contraception (25 apps). Their functionality is summarized in Figure 1 and described in more detail in the next section.

Reminder Apps Functionality

As expected, nearly all (97%) of identified apps offered timer-based reminders. Eight apps either did not have them listed on their description page or did not provide them due to version limitations. Most reminder apps (83%) supported multiple medications, and only contraception reminders and lite versions were often limited to a single daily dose. A third of apps (33%) imposed limitations on alert scheduling, e.g. by allowing only one alert per medication per day or not supporting time intervals such as alerts every X hours or X days. Surprisingly, only 39 apps (17%) offered an option to postpone a reminder ("snooze").

Some apps provided additional personalization features: customizable alerts allowing users to select different types of notifications such as pop-up messages, status updates or flashing lights (18%); customizable sounds (39%); and an option to add medication pictures to help with recall (21%). Over a third of apps (38%) allowed users to check their medication and regimen history, and export the data (7%) or email it to others (18%). In some cases (7%) users were able to add and track medication taken "as needed", e.g. painkillers, which were also included in their medication log. Six per cent of apps automatically tracked missed and late doses, highlighting them in the history report, and 5% offered statistics and charts describing usage trends, adherence rates and sometimes even treatment costs. In addition, 11% of apps, mainly contraception reminders, provided password protection, and 8% offered an option to back up the data or synchronize it with other devices.

Many apps offered additional features that aimed to support memory: refill reminders (26%); user notes and a calendar view with medication times (26%); a database with medication information e.g. dosage and side effects (14%); or an option to alert other people about missed doses (8%). Less frequent options included time zone support to ensure medication is taken at the right time when travelling (10 apps); smart silencing, to ensure alerts do not go off when user is asleep or during a Pill-free week in oral contraception regimens (seven apps); the ability to track mood and side effects after taking each dose (eight apps); and an overdosing protection with alerts informing when a daily limit of a medication (mainly taken "as needed") has been reached (five apps). More complex apps also stored user's health information, e.g. their allergies or blood type (11% of apps) or health care provider and pharmacy details (16%), and provided treatment cost estimates and discount codes for medications (3%). Doctor's appointment reminders were also available in 18 apps.

Only four apps (2%) provided options supporting habit formation and regular medication-taking. One encouraged continuous use by allowing users to take care of a tree [42], while the other three rewarded users with points that either could be compared or shared with friends, or redeemed into vouchers for other apps.

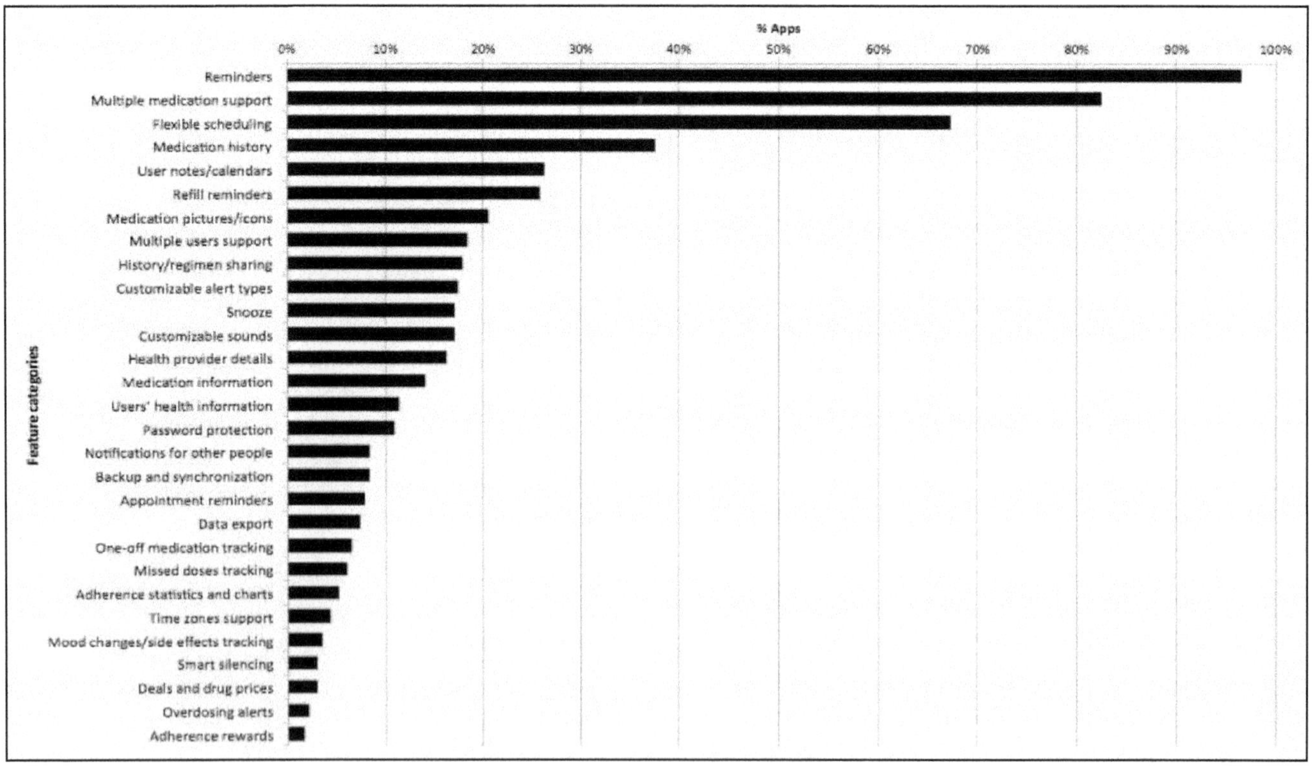

Figure 1. Functionality offered by smartphone reminder apps (N=229)

Types of Reminder Apps

As medication reminder apps provided functionality of varying complexity, based on their features they were grouped into three main categories:

- *Simple medication reminders (SMR)*. Apps offering basic functions supporting prospective memory, such as alerts, flexible scheduling, customizable alert types and sounds, snooze, etc.
- *Advanced medication reminders (AMR)*. Apps providing options that support both prospective and retrospective memory, such as time zone support, overdosing protection, medication pictures, user notes, late doses tracking, medication log, smart silencing, etc.
- *Medication management apps (MMA)*. AMR apps that also help to manage health and medication regimens. As some of them support multiple user accounts, they can be further split into *personal medication management apps* and *family medication management apps*. They allow users to store their health information, doctor's contact details, provide appointment reminders, etc.

Conclusions

Regardless of the type, complexity or functionality offered, all apps focus on timer-based reminders: their main purpose is to remind users about medication at a specific time. As a snooze option is rarely available and alerts cannot be postponed, users are expected to react immediately so that the reminder is not forgotten [9]. The apps seem to be designed to encourage users to rely on them, even though over-reliance on external cues can be associated with increased number of omission errors [12]. Despite the fact that medication-taking is a habitual task, functions that explicitly support the creation of routines are not available.

In essence, many apps (especially SMR) are nothing more than SMS alerts or alarm clocks packaged as medication reminders and could be easily replaced by a smartphone's default functionality with no loss to the user. Moreover, since all cellphone alarm clocks allow users to postpone the reminders, in many cases they may be a better option. AMR expand the alarm clock's functionality by allowing users to check later whether a medication was taken. Their options such as time zone support and smart silencing help to manage medication-taking in situations when the routine changes. MMA, the most advanced group, provide the same functionality as AMR and add treatment support and health monitoring, although the unique features they offer do not support remembering or habit formation in any way. In addition, local health care providers may not always support automatic refills or accept automatic emails with medication history from the app.

Our results highlight disparities between the medication reminder apps' functionality and prospective memory and habit literature. Even though research suggests that routines are key in supporting medication-taking, these apps focus on timer-based reminders, neglecting the habitual nature of medication regimens. They do, however, offer functions that could guard users against the dangers of a routine. For example, some AMR and MMA allow users to view their medication history to check whether a dose was taken. They also provide features such as time zone support or smart silencing that help in situations when a routine changes. In our next study we investigate how useful users find these and other features, and to what extent medication reminder apps meet their needs.

STUDY II: APPS REVIEWS' ANALYSIS

Method

Forty apps out of 229 identified in Study I were selected for the analysis, representing the most reviewed 10 apps in each category (MMA were divided into personal medication management apps and family medication management apps to ensure an equal coverage of apps with varying complexity and available functionality). For each app, 50 reviews were recorded; if an app had fewer than 50 reviews, all available reviews were noted. Only apps from Google Play were reviewed as, due to technical limitations, it was not possible to copy comments from the iTunes App Store application.

During the data collection phase, all reviews were sorted by "Helpfulness" to ensure a mix of positive, negative, new and old reviews was included. Each review was classified in terms of its general sentiment (positive, negative, neutral) and its type (general praise, complaints, comments on functionality, feature requests, other). Codes describing the content were added to each review by the first author and discussed later with the second, although we did not collect a measure of inter-rater reliability, which is typical of many textbook methods [40]. Thematic analysis [6] was used to make sense of the data.

Types of User Reviews

In total, 1,012 reviews were collected. Based on the overall sentiment and the content of a review, user comments were divided into two main groups: general comments presenting users' attitudes towards the apps, and comments mentioning specific functionality. Over a half of the reviews (595 or 59%) fell into the latter category, and these reviews were further divided into descriptions of existing functionality (42% of reviews) and "feature requests" (17%), in which users demanded specific changes or wished certain options were available. The remaining 417 reviews (41%) were general praise comments (e.g. "So far it's worked like a charm!"), complaints (2%; e.g. "Really unhelpful app"), or other miscellaneous comments (1%). As online ratings tend to be skewed towards the extremes and users predominantly post positive reviews [8, 22], comments not mentioning functionality were excluded from the analysis.

User Preferences

Even though feature requests, positive functionality reviews and negative functionality reviews were analyzed separately, the results of all three analyses showed that the most important features and characteristics of a medication reminder app were reliable reminders, customization, good usability and positive user experience.

As medication routines are unique for individuals, reliable and customizable alerts were the most important feature. The customization was especially important for users on complex (multiple medications or multiple doses per day) or irregular regimens (e.g. an oral contraception regimen with Pill-free weeks).

> *"I have one med I take every 3 days, this app had no problem letting me schedule that, other apps did!"* – Review #737

In general, users expected the apps to offer functions that help them with their regimen. Due to their limited functionality, many SMR were seen as lacking and not useful.

> *"Uninstalling. Seems to do nothing more than what I can get my alarm to do. In fact, my alarm is better as I can snooze it if I'm not around my medicine at the moment."* – Review #392

Users appreciated the role of back-up reminders in situations when their routine changed and liked alerts that were visible until they took their medication.

> *"I only take one medication, but on days where my routine changes, I often forget to take it. This app has definitely been extremely helpful. No more non-compliance for me!"* – Review #380

> *"Love this app! I like how the pill icon stays in* [the] *bar until you confirm you took the pill. Never miss my meds!"* – Review #143

Customizable apps also allowed users to select relevant, meaningful and discreet alerts that not only helped them remember and provided notifications appropriate for a given situation, but also protected their privacy.

> *"It's useful and doesn't just flash a message across my screen in an embarrassing way."* – Review #318

Because of the issues with stability, apps were often seen as unreliable. Users frequently complained that apps would sometimes stop working, lost data and the alert schedule after software updates or froze their smartphone. Smaller incidents such as alerts that occasionally did not work or confusing functionality also reduced users' trust.

Conclusions

Results show that functions desired and liked by users tend to be those that support remembering and to some extent could support the individual nature of daily routines: reminders, flexible scheduling, and customization. These are also features mentioned by Silva *et al.* [39] on their requirements list. Reminders in all their forms (timer-based reminders, additional alerts, snooze) help users to take medication on time and guard them against changes in the routine. The ability to customize and schedule alerts in a flexible way could help to adjust them to an existing routine. However, while all these features have the potential to support unique daily routines, they have not been explicitly designed to do so, nor are they able to facilitate the creation of new routines.

DISCUSSION

Both studies show that despite the number of options and varying levels of complexity offered by medication reminder apps, they predominantly focus on the provision of timer-based reminders. In many cases these reminders offer very little benefit to users and as the snooze option is often not available, they do not differ much from SMS reminders or simple alarm clocks available on cellphones. In addition, with only 18% of apps providing customizable alerts, they take a "one size fits all" approach and disregard the fact that medication routines are personalized and unique to each individual; simple timer-based reminders are not able to support them well enough. To be effective, these reminders should combine different modalities, including subtle status bar notifications [4], and allow users to select alert types that suit their needs depending on their capabilities and social context [48].

Currently available medication reminder apps neglect the habitual nature of medication regimens, even though smartphone apps have capabilities to support habit formation and many behavior change apps already do so, e.g. those encouraging physical activity by providing regular feedback [35]. And yet, commercial medication reminder apps do not try to replicate or adapt this approach. Instead, they teach users to rely on technology that is often unreliable and can easily break. As a result, while users acknowledge the role of routines in medication-taking (see for example Review #380 earlier), they do not consider these apps to be a tool that could help them create or maintain daily routines. Users do not see the lack of routine support as a problem, nor do they ask for it in their feature requests, which suggests that they might not be consciously aware of the importance of habitual behavior in supporting medication-taking or they do not expect that technology could address its routine aspect. After all, timer-based reminders are all that is available and all they know.

However, despite their weaknesses, smartphone apps have the potential to successfully support the creation of sustainable habits and to provide additional reminders when needed. Features provided by some AMR and MMA could support daily routines: personalized alerts matching a complex regimen could be incorporated into an existing routine and serve as back-up reminders. Similarly, some apps already offer functions, often in the form of a medication log, that help to establish whether a medication was taken. While such a log in itself does not actively support remembering, it can reduce omission and repetition errors.

The design of medication reminder apps could be modified to shift the focus from timer-based reminders to a smart routine support. Based on the prospective memory and habit literature and our research findings, we present design requirements for building medication reminder apps that take into account the habitual and personal nature of many regimens, utilize the benefits of a routine behavior, and guard against the dangers of the automaticity it brings.

DESIGN REQUIREMENTS

To effectively support medication-taking and be a reliable system that supports individuals and their habitual behavior, a reminder app should (i) help to create a new routine, (ii) allow users to set up and customize back-up notifications for situations when the routine is disrupted, and (iii) provide a way to check whether a medication has been taken. We now describe each requirement in more detail.

1. Routine Creation

As associating a new task with an existing routine helps to build a new habit [16, 34], the app should suggest pairing medication-taking with an existing routine. This could be done explicitly by asking the user to specify their existing routine or providing a list of examples to choose from; or implicitly by simply letting them know that people in general find it easier to remember their medication when they take it right after a regular task, e.g. eating breakfast or brushing their teeth. As users' preference for customization highlighted in Study II emphasizes the fact that they want to be in control and that routines are unique for each individual, the routine creation should take that into the account and allow them to select a routine event that best fits their schedule and their needs. They should also be able to modify the settings when their daily routine changes.

2. Back-Up Notifications

Back-up notifications guard against changes in the routine and remind users about their medication if their circumstances change. As users value customization and flexible alert schedule, they should be able to control when and how they are notified. They should also be able to snooze their notifications if they are not able to respond immediately. The mechanisms behind back-up notifications could be simple and based on the app usage patterns (as demonstrated later in the Use Case Scenario), or more complex, taking full advantage of smartphones' capabilities, e.g. the app could combine location data with usage trends and provide smarter, context-aware back-up notifications. It could also make use of the user's calendar to anticipate future routine changes.

However, there is a danger that users who are used to timer-based reminders might start using back-up notifications as primary alerts. Thus, these notifications should be subtle or indirect, and designed in a way that will prevent them from becoming the main reminder.

3. Post-Completion Check

The reliance on routines introduces the dangers of automatic behavior and increases chances of omission and repetition errors [3, 12] as users may not remember if they completed the task already. Therefore, users should be able to check whether a dose has been taken. Medication logs in existing apps already provide this option. A back-up notification could also serve as a post-completion check feature: as long as the notification is visible, users know they still have not taken their medication (see Review #143 earlier).

Use Case Scenario

The following scenario describes the use of a hypothetical app based on these design requirements. We use oral contraception as an example of a typical habitual regimen.

Ms. Smith is prescribed contraceptive pills that need to be taken every day at the same time. She downloads and installs the app, and on the welcome screen is asked to enter the details of her regimen. Ms. Smith enters one dose per day and indicates that she wants to take it at 8 every morning. The app then informs her that combining medication-taking with an existing routine supports remembering and, based on the regimen details she entered, suggests she takes the Pill after one of typical morning routine events such as brushing the teeth or eating breakfast (Figure 2a). *Ms. Smith then selects the option that matches her routine: taking the Pill after eating breakfast. Next, she is told that back-up reminders will pop-up approximately an hour after her specified time and that she is able to change the type of the alert. After setting up the app, she puts the blister pack into her bag to have it at hand the next time she needs to take the Pill.*

The next morning, about 30 minutes before the specified time, a subtle message shows up on her smartphone's notification bar, reminding her to take the medication after breakfast, which further reinforces the association between the medication-taking and the daily routine. About an hour later, another, a more prominent notification shows up, asking whether she took her Pill earlier. Ms. Smith can select 'Not yet' or 'I did!' (Figure 2b).

The app registered frequent 'Not yet' responses and after a week asks Ms. Smith if the time of the day is working for her. Ms. Smith has been really busy lately, and as a result she had modified her usual routine and had been buying breakfast on her way to work. If not for the back-up notifications, she would have missed the Pill a couple of times. The app now suggests selecting a new routine, e.g. taking the Pill after brushing her teeth (Figure 2c).

After Ms. Smith selects the new routine, the app starts monitoring the responses again. If the 'I did!' responses are consistent, after three months the app asks how useful the early morning alert is. As Ms. Smith stopped paying atten-

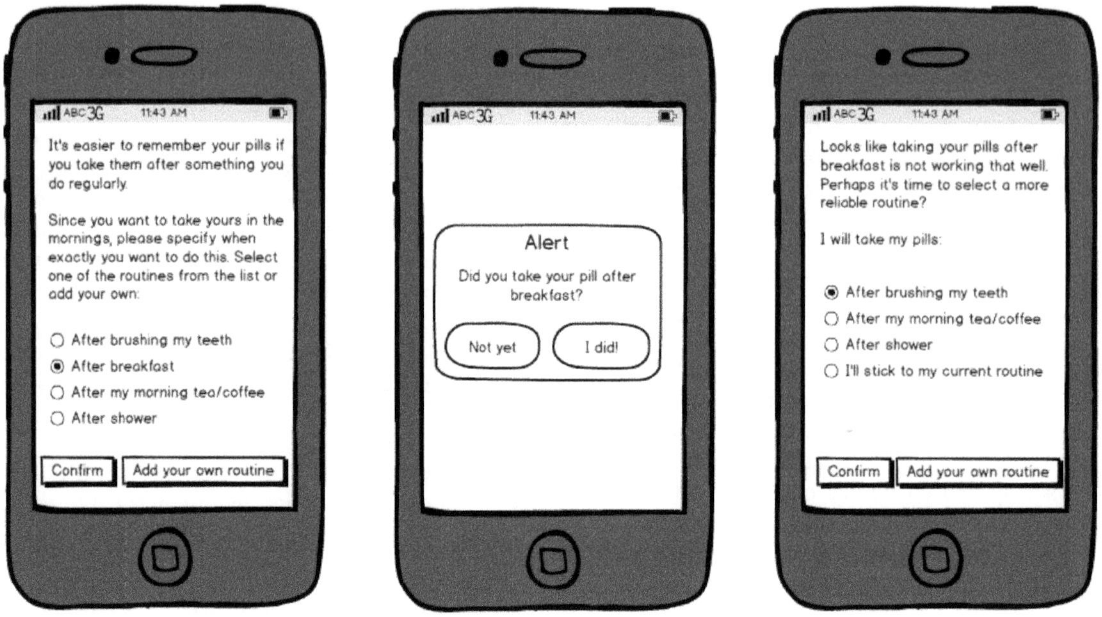

Figure 2. Sketches of a hypothetical app supporting routines. From the left: (a) setting up a new routine, (b) an example of a back-up notification, (c) adjusting the routine to user's behavior

tion to the alert, she indicates that she does not need it. The app then disables the alert and now provides only back-up notifications.

CONCLUSIONS

Forgetfulness is a major, albeit largely neglected, aspect of unintentional medication non-adherence. Even though it can have grave consequences, the adherence research tends to prioritize education and changing attitudes and beliefs over addressing forgetfulness, despite the fact that even motivated people forget.

Due to increasing popularity of smartphones, people have access to a wide range of health apps, including medication reminders aiming to support their memory. The studies we have presented are the first to evaluate medication reminder apps and to highlight weaknesses of timer-based alerts around which these apps are designed. They are also the first to investigate how technology could exploit the habitual nature of many medication regimens to reduce unintentional non-adherence. While the importance of daily routines has already been acknowledged in the treatment for chronic conditions (e.g. [19]), they were only a part of a wider intervention. In the context of preventative therapies, and oral contraception in particular, there are no studies focusing on remembering strategies selected by users themselves or on technology that supports them.

Despite the fact that the habit and prospective memory literature show clear benefits of combining medication-taking with accompanying routine events [16, 24, 34], our studies show that medication reminder apps available for the most popular smartphones do not support the routine aspect of medication regimens, even though they have capabilities to do so, and they often neglect the personal and unique nature of daily routines. To address this disparity between the theory and practice, and to show how the functionality of reminder apps could be extended to provide an explicit routine support and to match users' behavior, we presented a set of design requirements for building smart medication reminder apps. We illustrated them with a use case scenario, which is just one example of many ways in which the elements of a "routine-friendly" medication reminder app could work together to provide a smarter and personalized memory support. At this point the scenario and the app example are a concept that has not yet been fully evaluated. However, they already highlight the difference in approach between a routine-friendly user-centered medication support app and a "one size fits all" app that relies on timer-based reminders. Instead of passively reminding users to take their medication at a specified time, the app could be seen as an assistant that helps them achieve their goal and guides them towards developing a new behavior. The focus shifts from simple reminders that users learn to rely on completely, to a smart assistive technology that helps users to create their own personalized routines and intervenes when these routines are disrupted.

While this approach is best suited to support single dose long-term regimens such as oral contraception, it could be adapted to more complex regimens or even applied beyond medication adherence interventions. Remembering multiple daily doses requires multiple relevant trigger events to support the routine and identifying them might be difficult, especially when the doses have to be evenly spaced. However, understanding patients' daily routines could make it easier to tailor the regimen to their needs and to identify relevant trigger events, which then could be suggested by the technology. Such smart routine support could also benefit other health-related behavior change interventions that rely on the creation of new habits, such as promoting healthy eating or regular exercises.

Even though more research is needed to understand how explicit the smart assistance should be and how best to implement each component, our example already demonstrates that this new approach is feasible. Current smartphones have capabilities to meet the three requirements defined above and to move from the simplest possible solution, i.e. a timer-based alert, to a more sophisticated technology that takes into account users' behavior and the unique nature of their daily routines. Our research shows that functionality of existing medication reminder apps could be expanded to incorporate the support for personalized daily routines, to add non-intrusive back-up notifications, and to allow post-completion checks. We also demonstrate that by embracing daily routines and the habitual nature of medication regimens, smartphone apps have a real potential to reduce medication non-adherence.

ACKNOWLEDGEMENTS

Research funded by the UK EPSRC grant [EP/G059063/1] CHI+MED: Multidisciplinary Computer-Human Interaction research for the design and safe use of interactive medical devices. We would like to thank Dr. Chris Vincent and Dr. Duncan Brumby for their valuable feedback on an early draft of the paper.

REFERENCES

1. Aarts, H., & Dijksterhuis, A. Habits as knowledge structures: Automaticity in Goal-Directed Behaviour. *Journal of Personality and Social Psychology*, 78, 1 (2000), 53–63.
2. Apple Inc. *iTunes Store.* http://www.apple.com/itunes/
3. Bargh, J. A. The four horsemen of automaticity: awareness, intention, efficiency, and control in social cognition. In R. S. Wyer & T. K. Srull (Eds.), *Handbook of social cognition: Vol I basic processes*. Lawrence Erlbaum Associates (1994), 1–40.
4. Bentley, F. and Tollmar, K. The Power of Mobile Notifications to Increase Wellbeing Logging Behavior, *Proc. CHI '13*, ACM Press (2013), 1095–109.
5. Bickmore, T., Mauer, D., Crespo, F., & Brown, T. Persuasion, task interruption and health regimen adherence. *Persuasive Technology*, (2007), 1–11.
6. Braun, V., & Clarke, V. Using thematic analysis in psychology. *Qualitative Research in Psychology*, 3, 2 (2006), 77–101.
7. Castaño, P. M., & Martínez, R. A. Harnessing technology for adolescent health promotion. *Adolescent Medicine: State of the Art Reviews*, 18, 2 (2007), XIII, 400–406.
8. Chevalier, J. A., & Mayzlin, D. *The effect of word of mouth on sales: Online book reviews*, No. w10148 (2003), National Bureau of Economic Research.
9. Cramer, J. A. Overview of Methods to Measure and Enhance Patient Compliance. In J. A. Cramer & B. Spilker (Eds.), *Patient compliance in medical practice and clinical trials*. Raven Press (1991), 3–10.
10. Dayer, L., Heldenbrand, S., Anderson, P., Gubbins, P. O., and Martin, B. C. Smart- phone medication adherence apps: Potential benefits to patients and providers. *Journal of the American Pharmacists Association*, 53, 2 (2013), 172–181.
11. De Oliveira, R., Cherubini, M., & Oliver, N. MoviPill: Improving medication compliance for elders using a mobile persuasive social game. *Proc. UBICOMP'10*. ACM Press (2010), 251–260.
12. Einstein, G. O., McDaniel, M. A., Smith, R. E., and Shaw, P. Habitual Prospective Memory and Aging: Remembering Intentions and Forgetting Actions. *Psychological Science*, 9, 4 (1998), 284– 288.
13. Ellis, J. Prospective memory or the realization of delayed intentions: A conceptual framework for research. In M. Brandimonte, G. O. Einstein, & M. A. McDaniel (Eds.), *Prospective memory: Theory and applications*. Lawrence Erlbaum Associates (1996), 1–22.
14. Fairhurst, K., & Sheikh, A. Texting appointment reminders to repeated non-attenders in primary care: randomized controlled study. *Quality & Safety in Health Care*, 17, 5 (2008), 373–376.
15. Fjeldsoe, B. S., Marshall, A. L., & Miller, Y. D. Behavior change interventions delivered by mobile telephone short-message service. *American Journal of Preventive Medicine*, 36, 2 (2009), 165–173.
16. Fogg, B. J. *Tiny Habits*. http://tinyhabits.com/
17. Google. *Google Play*. https://play.google.com/store
18. Haynes, R. B., Ackloo, E., Sahota, N., McDonald, H. P., Yao, X. Interventions for enhancing medication adherence. *Cochrane database of systematic reviews*, CD000011 (2008).
19. Haynes, R. B., Gibson, E., Hackett, B., Sackett, D., Taylor, D. W., Roberts, R., & Johnson, A. Improvement of medication compliance in uncontrolled hypertension. *The Lancet*, 307, 7972 (1976), 1265-1268.
20. Henry, J. D. J., Rendell, P. P. G., Phillips, L. H. L., Dunlop, L., & Kliegel, M. Prospective memory reminders: A laboratory investigation of initiation source and age effects. *The Quarterly Journal of Experimental Psychology*, 65, 7 (2012), 1274–1287.
21. Hou, M., Murwitz, S., Kavanagh, E., Fortin, J., and Goldberg, A. Using Daily Text-Message Reminders to Improve Adherence with Oral Contraceptives: A

Randomized Controlled Trial. *Obstetrics & Gynecology*, 3, 116 (2010), 633–640.

22. Hu, N., Pavlou, P. A., and Zhang, J. Can online reviews reveal a product's true quality? *Proc. EC'06.* ACM Press (2006), 324–330.

23. Hughes, D. A., Bagust, A., Haycox, A., and Walley, T. O. M. The impact of non-compliance on the cost-effectiveness of pharmaceuticals: a review of the literature. *Health Economics*, 10, May (2001), 601–615.

24. Johnson, M. J. The Medication Adherence Model: A Guide for Assessing Medication Taking. *Research and Theory for Nursing Practice*, 16, 3 (2002), 179–192.

25. Jones, R. K., Darroch, J. E., and Henshaw, S. K. Contraceptive Use Among U.S. Women Having Abortions in 2000-2001. *Perspectives on Sexual and Reproductive Health*, 34, 6 (2002), 294– 303.

26. Klasnja, P., & Pratt, W. Healthcare in the pocket: mapping the space of mobile-phone health interventions. *Journal of Biomedical Informatics*, 45, 1 (2012), 184–198.

27. Laird, S. (2012). *How smartphones are changing healthcare.* Retrieved 11/07/2013, from http://mashable.com/2012/09/26/smartphones-health-care-infographic/

28. Lally, P., & Gardner, B. Promoting habit formation. *Health Psychology Review*, 7, supl (2011), 1–22.

29. Lally, P., van Jaarsveld, C. H. M., Potts, H. W. W., and Wardle, J. How are habits formed: Modeling habit formation in the real world. *European Journal of Social Psychology*, 40, 6 (2010), 998–1009.

30. Maylor, E. A. Age and prospective memory. The Quarterly Journal of Experimental Psychology, 42, 3 (1990), 471–493.

31. Obiodu, V., & Obiodu, E. An Empirical Review of the Top 500 Medical Apps in a European Android Market. *Journal of Mobile Technology in Medicine*, 1, 4 (2012), 22–37.

32. Ofcom. *Communications Market Report* (2012) http://stakeholders.ofcom.org.uk/binaries/research/cmr/cmr12/CMR_UK_2012.pdf

33. O'Neill, S., & Brady, R. R. W. Colorectal smartphone apps: opportunities and risks. *Colorectal Disease*, 14, 9 (2012), e530–e534.

34. Park, D. C., & Kidder, D. P. Prospective memory and medication adherence. In M. Brandimonte, G. O. Einstein, & M. A. McDaniel (Eds.), *Prospective memory: Theory and applications.* Lawrence Erlbaum Associates (1996), 369–390.

35. Rabin, C. & Bock, B., Desired Features of Smartphone Applications Promoting Physical Activity, *Telemedicine and e-Health*, 17, 10 (2011), 801– 803.

36. Reach, G. Role of habit in adherence to medical treatment. *Diabetic Medicine*, 22, 4 (2005), 415–420.

37. Rosenberg, M. J., & Waugh, M. S. Causes and consequences of oral contraceptive non-compliance. *American Journal of Obstetrics and Gynecology*, 180, 2 Pt 2 (1999), 276–279.

38. Rosser, B. A., & Eccleston, C. Smartphone applications for pain management. *Journal of Telemedicine and Telecare*, 17, 6 (2011), 308–312.

39. Silva, J. M., Mouttham, A., and El Saddik, A. UbiMeds: a mobile application to improve accessibility and support medication adherence. *Proc. MSIADU'09.* ACM Press (2009), 71–78.

40. Smith, J. A. *Qualitative psychology: a practical guide to research methods*, London, Sage, (2003).

41. Smith, J., Oakley, D. Why Do Women Miss Oral Contraceptive Pills? An Analysis of Women's Self-Described Reasons for Missed Pills, *Journal of Midwifery & Women's Health*, 50, 5 (2010), 380–385.

42. Thryve. *Foster - Pill Reminder.* https://itunes.apple.com/gb/app/foster-pill-reminder/id554168976?mt=8

43. Unni, E. J., & Farris, K. B. Unintentional non-adherence and belief in medicines in older adults. *Patient education and counseling*, 83, 2 (2011), 265–268.

44. Ventä, L., Isomursu, M., Ahtinen, A., and Ramiah, S. "My Phone is a Part of My Soul" – How People Bond with Their Mobile Phones. *Proc. UBICOMM'08*, IEEE (2008), 311–317.

45. Vermeire, E., Hearnshaw, H, Van Royen, P., and Denekens, J. Patient adherence to treatment: three decades of research. A comprehensive review. *Journal of clinical pharmacy and therapeutics*, 26, 5 (2001), 331–342.

46. Vervolet, M., Linn, A. J., van Weert, J. C. M., de Bakker, D. H., Bouvy, M. L., and van Dijk, L., The effectiveness of interventions using electronic reminders to improve adherence to chronic medication: a systematic review of the literature, *Journal of the American Medical Informatics Association: JAMIA*, 19, 5 (2012), 696–704.

47. WHO. *Adherence to long-term therapies: Evidence for action.* World Health Organization (2003).

48. Williamson, J. R., McGee-Lennon, M., and Brewster, S. Designing multimodal reminders for the home. *Proc. ICMI'12.* ACM Press (2012), 445–448.

49. Wood, W., & Neal, D. T. A new look at habits and the habit-goal interface. *Psychological Review*, 114, 4 (2007), 843–8.

50. Yun, T. and Arriaga, R. I. A Text Message a Day Keeps the Pulmonologist Away, *Proc. CHI '13*, ACM Press (2013), 1769–1778.

@BabySteps: Design and Evaluation of a System for using Twitter for Tracking Children's Developmental Milestones

Hyewon Suh, John R. Porter, Alexis Hiniker, Julie A. Kientz
Human Centered Design and Engineering
University of Washington
{hyewon25, jrporter, alexisr, jkientz}@uw.edu

ABSTRACT
The tracking of developmental milestones in young children is an important public health goal for ensuring early detection and treatment for developmental delay. While numerous paper-based and web-based solutions are available for tracking milestones, many busy parents often forget to enter information on a regular basis. To help address this need, we have developed an interactive system called @BabySteps for allowing parents who use Twitter to track and respond to tweets about developmental milestones using a special hashtag syntax. Parent responses are parsed automatically and written into a central database that can be accessed via the web. We deployed @BabySteps with 14 parents over a 3-week period and found that parents were able to learn how to use the system to track their children's progress, with some using it to communicate with other parents. The study helped to identify a number of ways to improve the approach, including simplifying the hashtag syntax, allowing for private responses via direct messaging, and improving the social component. We provide a discussion of lessons learned and suggestions for the design of interactive public health systems.

Author Keywords
Children; health; microblogging; Twitter; social media; data capture; memories; parents; public health.

ACM Classification Keywords
H.5.m. Information interfaces and presentation (e.g., HCI): Miscellaneous.

INTRODUCTION
The tracking of developmental progress in young children is one of the key ways of ensuring the early detection of developmental delay. Typically, the earlier these children are diagnosed, the sooner treatment can begin, which can greatly improve outcomes for these children [7]. One current approach for screening for developmental progress is to ask parents a series of questions about their children's abilities in areas such as gross motor, communication, and problem solving. For example, "does your baby say two syllable sounds, such as 'da da' or 'ga ga'?" or "can your child walk up stairs while holding onto a railing?" Standardized screening questionnaires administered by doctors and public health clinics may consist of many of these questions periodically. One popular screener tool, the Ages and Stages Questionnaire (ASQ), consists of 22 questionnaires with 30 questions each across the child's first five years [19]. The screener can either be conducted via paper or through a website, and is usually administered at Well Child Visits with the child's pediatrician. There are some limitations to using milestone questionnaires for screening, such as child variability or the potential for parent anxiety. However, they are currently the most effective method for screening according to the American Academy of Pediatrics [4].

CHI 2014, April 26 - May 01 2014, Toronto, ON, Canada

ACM 978-1-4503-2473-1/14/04...$15.00.
http://dx.doi.org/10.1145/2556288.2557386

The problem with paper-based or even web-based screener surveys is that it is often difficult to ensure that parents complete each survey, especially since there are more screener questionnaires than scheduled Well Child Visits during the first 5 years of a child's life. In addition, when parents answer questions in a single sitting, they may not have the opportunity to try each activity with their child if the question asks about an activity that does not always occur. Also, busy parents often just forget to keep track of milestones using both paper and web-based systems [12]. Tools that can help prompt parents to answer questions at more regular intervals can possibly result in more complete and accurate responses and better parent involvement and awareness of their child's activities. The CHI community has recently begun developing such software (e.g., [11]).

There are limitations with standalone software applications in that they require the parent to remember to open the application to answer questions. Even with proactive notifications or email reminders, parents may still not engage as easily and as often as they might otherwise. In addition, because these tools are intended to be used over a long period (e.g., up to 5 years), they require methods to maintain parent engagement. To help address some of these limitations, one solution is to design and develop tools to help parents answer questions using technology with which they are already familiar and engaged with, such as mobile phones or social media. A recent study [16] suggests that integrating a health intervention into social sites that people already visit can increase adherence. Although parents are often too busy to remember to complete baby books or other manual tracking systems [11], they are already using social networking systems to share information on their children [15]. Inspired by earlier studies, our first approach has been to develop a tool to automatically prompt parents via Twitter to respond to questionnaires about their child, which can be stored in a centralized database.

In our system, @BabySteps, we use a specified syntax of hashtags to allow parents to respond to age-appropriate milestone questionnaires automatically tweeted by accounts based on a child's birth month. A script then uses the Twitter API to read parent responses and write them to a database. The child's developmental progress can be viewed via a companion website we have developed. We conducted a 3-week feasibility study of @BabySteps with 14 parents of children aged 2 months to 2 years. Parents responded to milestone prompts via Twitter and then could access a website to review their child's progress. The study explored how the specialized syntax could be used to create an interactive public health system and encourage parents to continue engagement. The results of the study helped identify areas for improvement and implications for the design of public health applications using Twitter or other social media. The main contributions of this work are the design and development of a novel system for using Twitter to track developmental progress in young children and a study understanding how these types of systems are accepted by users, which leads to design considerations.

RELATED WORK

@BabySteps builds upon previous work on supporting the needs of parents with young children and leveraging technologies and social media for health and safety.

Designing for the Health of Young Children

Designing interactive technologies to support the health and wellbeing of young children and their families has been a growing area of interest in the field of human-computer interaction. A workshop called "Motherhood and HCI" was held at CHI last year, showing an increase in interest in supporting parents and the health issues of their children. D'Alessandro & Dosa [2] describe how information technology can be empowering to parents and children, and thus there is great motivation to use it to support their health.

The motivation and design of @BabySteps was inspired directly by a formative study on designing for tracking developmental progress in young children [12] and the subsequent Baby Steps software application [11]. We extend this work by developing and studying a Twitter-based application that can link into a website component modeled after the software application. Similar applications have tracked other aspects of health of young children. The ENSURE system developed by Park et al. [18] looked at how interactions with a child's pediatrician can be supported through interactive technologies, such as tracking temperature or medications. Tang et al. [21] developed a mobile application called Estrellita for observing premature infants' daily living activities (such as feeding and diaper changes), prompting parents to do exercises at home, and reminders of upcoming appointments. VisiBabble is a tool for monitoring emerging speech in young children [5], whereas Child's Play uses sensor-enabled toys to monitor children's development [24]. Similar commercial applications, such as Trixie Tracker [22] and LENA [15] also allow for parents to track information about feeding and diapers and tracking language respectively. While these applications all have the goal of tracking information about young children, including their development, @BabySteps is the first application we are aware of to use Twitter in an interactive format.

Interactive Technologies & Social Media

In recent years, public health outreach efforts have benefited greatly from the large-scale communication afforded by SMS messaging. With the rising prevalence of prepaid mobile plans, public health campaigns integrating SMS are able to communicate with populations who have traditionally been difficult to reach as a result of scale, geographic dispersal, limited technology use, or other concerns. For example, beginning in 2003, the telecommunication company MTN began sending out mass quarterly informational SMS messages to all of its subscribers in Nigeria in an effort to promote HIV/AIDS awareness [23]. Similar projects like the outreach campaign from Hoefman & Apunyu in Uganda used two-way communication, interspersing 'quiz' and survey questions amongst informational messages to which recipients could respond [8].

Juxtaposing this sort of 'blanket' approach to SMS outreach regarding a ubiquitous health concern, similar programs have more recently been implemented to target more specific populations. Jordan et al.'s Text4baby system used an opt-in model, wherein expectant mothers signed up for the service via an initial SMS, after which they received three informational SMS messages per week about their pregnancy and related health concerns [10]. By using an opt-in model where users provide relevant personal information during an initial phase of interactivity, it is possible to tailor outgoing content specifically for the recipient. In the case of Text4baby, provision of the user's due date enabled sending of time-appropriate information based on pregnancy trimester. Woolford et al. used a more complex approach in their development of an SMS system to encourage adherence to a weight management program among obese adolescents; a detailed initial survey was used to tailor the set of potential messages a user might receive to optimally appeal to their values, motivations, and goals [25].

Meanwhile, the Internet and social networking platforms have facilitated numerous different efforts related to health and wellness. Numerous online communities and information hubs have been developed to provide direct and indirect counseling and psychotherapeutic aid to those in need [1]. De Choudhury et al. developed a system which could assess the public tweets of women to predict with some confidence those most likely to undergo significant postpartum emotional or behavior change [3]. While this work demonstrated that health data of this type could be gathered on a large scale via social media, it is limited in the nature of the data available to it. Although psychological analyses of this sort can be based on sentiment gleaned from any user-authored text, more specific health information is unlikely to spontaneously appear in social media at all, let alone in workable form. For that reason, it is necessary for the user to be made aware of not only the nature of the desired content, but also the form.

While the latter might seem a massive obstacle given the freeform nature of social media postings, recent work has shown that Twitter in particular has a great deal of promise. The Tweak the Tweet project has demonstrated on an ongoing basis that, even in dynamic and high-stakes contexts, populations of Twitter users could be made to quickly adopt an efficient standardized syntax for the sharing of specific pieces of information, such as needs and availabilities during crisis events [20].

When considering the landscape of these outreach and coordination systems, a useful way to classify them is according to two distinct dimensions: the engagement level of the end user or users, and the communicative relationship being encouraged or supported. Figure 1 marks the position of some of the aforementioned major systems on these dimensions. Its horizontal axis represents relationship and direction of information flow, ranging from a one-to-many model where a single agent outwardly communicates with a large population, to a many-to-one model in which the constituents of a population channel a large amount of information towards a single agent; the midpoint can be seen as either one-to-one or many-to-many, as these relationships are functionally similar in this context. The vertical axis denotes engagement level and ranges from passive to interactive.

Viewing the existing work through this lens, the relative

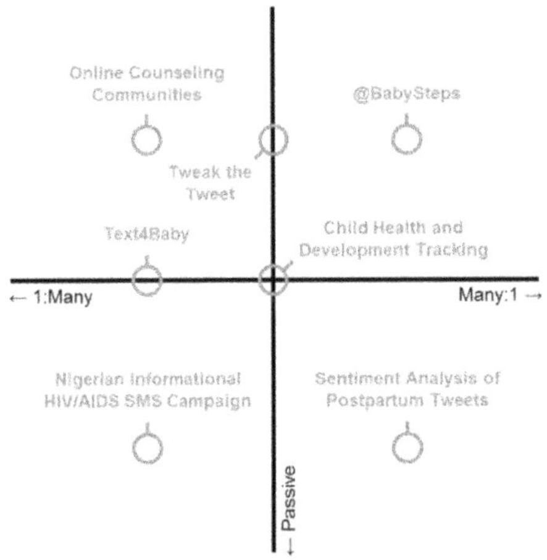

Figure 1: Space of interactive technology for public health

emptiness of the upper right quadrant suggests the untapped potential of a system that seeks to *interactively* relate to users on a *many-to-one* basis – that is, a system that explicitly solicits a population to provide it with specific information. @BabySteps seeks to occupy this region and test its viability.

@BABYSTEPS SYSTEM DESIGN

In this section, we describe the design and implementation details for @BabySteps. The Twitter-based system was designed to be a component of a larger suite of tools for allowing parents to respond to milestone question prompts, which also includes a website and a mobile text messaging system. A centralized database stores all of the parent information and responses. The design of @BabySteps was based on a series of formative studies ([6,9,12]), with additional input from a study on the use of social networking by mothers of young children [16].

Functionality and Usage

To use the @BabySteps system, users first register in our system with their name, email address, and Twitter handle. For each of their children, they provide a name, gender, and date of birth. If a user is uncomfortable with their child's real first name being used in public communications, they are able to provide a pseudonym that can be used instead. After registration, a user follows the main Baby Steps Twitter account (@BabyStepsUW), which is used to send out announcements and study information to all participants and is manually operated by the research team. They also follow a Twitter account associated with their child's birth month, and if applicable, grant permission for it to follow them back. So, for example, a user with a child born in August 2011 would follow @BabyStepsAug11.

At regular intervals, this latter account sends out tweets asking age-appropriate milestone questions about the child's development. Each of these tweets contains a unique closing hashtag that we refer to as a milestone ID (see Figure 2 for an example).

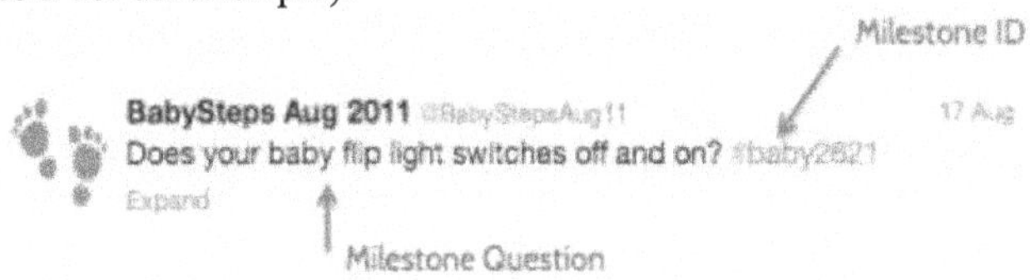

Figure 2: Exemplary milestone question tweet

Users respond to these questions either publicly by posting to their timeline or privately via direct message to the account that originally posted the question. In either case, the user's response must contain a minimum of two specific elements: 1) the milestone ID hashtag from the prompt they are responding to and 2) their response to the question in the form of a hashtag – either *#yes*, *#sometimes*, or *#no / #notyet* (these two are handled identically). For users who have multiple children registered in our system, they must additionally include the relevant child's first name or pseudonym as a hashtag. Beyond these required elements, users are free to include any other free text or additional hashtags in their tweet as well. This allows them to naturally include their response in an unassuming tweet that makes sense to their own followers, should they choose to do so.

If all required pieces are included, such as in Figure 3, their response to the milestone will be logged in our database.

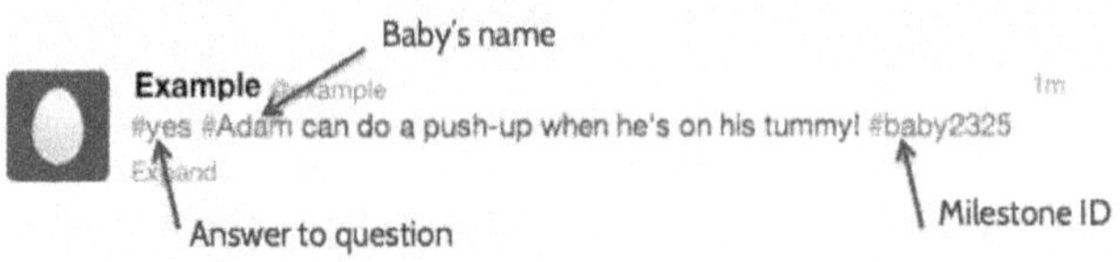

Figure 3: Exemplary response from users

Some milestones have figures that go along with them, such as showing a close up of a child doing a pincer grasp. We uploaded figures to pic.twitter.com and included a link in the prompt for relevant milestones. In addition to specific responses to our prompts, users are also able to create a free-form "memory" about their child by including the hashtag *#babymemory* in a tweet (e.g., #Billy visited the zoo today! #babymemory). When doing so, the remainder of the text in the tweet will be included as a memory on their child's Baby Steps timeline on the companion website. Also, because there are only 30 milestones in a 2-3 month period, we had static tips and activities that were tweeted on regular basis, such as advice about vaccinations and ideas for activities that encourage development. Tips and activities used the #tips and #activity hashtags respectively.

Twitter System Implementation

The Twitter system was developed in Python, and consists of a series of scripts which run on the server that also houses the website. MySQLdb, a Python MySQL connector module, is used to interface with a centralized database shared across different pieces of the Baby Steps suite. Twitter interaction is achieved by making calls to Twitter's REST API v1.1. @BabySteps uses a collection of automated Twitter accounts, each of which have authorized full read/write access to our registered Python application. These accounts are each named with a given month and year combination, e.g. @BabyStepsAug11, @BabyStepsNov12. Generally speaking, our system can be broken into two general pieces: the "push" component and the "pull" component. Their basic operation is described as follows.

Push Component

Three times per day, during normal daytime hours in our local time zone, this component of our system is executed via a cron job. It iterates through each of the authorized month-specific accounts sequentially. For each account, we identify the integer ID of the last milestone question that was tweeted out. This ID is then incremented, and the next milestone in the sequence is checked in the database. Each milestone has an age range for when it is appropriate to be asked. The age implied by the month and year in the Twitter account's handle is then compared against this range. If the new milestone is age-appropriate, it is sent out as a new tweet, with the hashtag *#baby[ID]* appended to the end, where [ID] is the milestone's integer ID. If all relevant milestones for the age bracket have been exhausted, the system sends out a random age-appropriate activity or tip.

Pull Component

This script executes every half-hour around the clock and also iterates through our accounts sequentially. It begins by identifying the unique Twitter-assigned ID of the last incoming tweet that was received. All public tweets from the users followed by and following this account, as well as all direct messages, created since this last check ID are then collected for processing. From the raw text of each individual tweet, the set of hashtags are extracted. To identify milestone responses, we look for tweets whose hashtag sets contain the minimum set of required elements outlined previously. If all required components are present, the user's response to the milestone prompt is recorded in our database. Alternately, if the tweet contains the hashtag *#babymemory*, the tag is stripped from the raw text, and the remainder is inserted into the user's log of baby memories. In either case, the entry is time stamped according to when the user tweet was originally authored.

Companion Website

In addition to the Twitter-based system, Baby Steps also had a companion website where participants could log on to edit milestone responses, view a timeline of their child's progress and memories, and see an assessment of their child's progress based on their responses (e.g., whether they are on track developmentally or if they should get in touch with a doctor for additional assessment). The website also had a frequently asked questions page with information on how to use the system and a resources page that had contact information for public health resources to encourage parents to get in touch with their doctor if there is any concern about their child's development. The eventual goal of the Baby Steps work is to have our state's public health department conduct follow-up phone calls with parents based on their response to milestone prompts, but this system is not yet in place. Thus, the website served as an intermediary for parents to understand their child's progress.

DEPLOYMENT STUDY DESIGN

To test the feasibility of the @BabySteps system design, understand the usability of our hashtag syntax, and to gauge the acceptability of using Twitter for sharing a child's milestone progress, we conducted a real world deployment study with parents of young children. We conducted a qualitative, exploratory study, as Klasnja et al. have argued is the best first step for evaluating novel health systems [13] along with some quantitative data logging. This section includes the details of the study design and the participants we recruited.

Study Procedure

Before deploying @BabySteps, we sent out a pre-study survey asking participants about their demographics, Twitter usage, and parenting practices. With this information, we manually registered our participants in our system.

Stage 1: Two Weeks of @BabySteps Usage on Twitter

Because our Twitter system required use of special syntax in tweet responses, we sent out Twitter instructions to participants before Baby Steps' monthly accounts started tweeting out. On the instruction page, there was information about how to use the three hashtags and information about how to follow the Baby Steps main account and monthly accounts. Also, because we acknowledge that privacy can be of concern to parents, we encouraged our participants to check their account's privacy settings. We also did not limit the form of response – it could be a reply to our tweet, a new tweet, a re-tweet, or a direct message. That way, participants have the ultimate say in what they want to share publicly vs. privately. Then, for two weeks, each monthly account tweeted out developmental milestones, a set of functional skills or tasks that most children can do at a certain age range. Based on their observation, participants responded 'Yes', 'Sometimes', 'Not Yet / No' accordingly. Occasionally, both the main account and monthly accounts sent out reminders for syntax and study-related announcements, as inspired by Tweak the Tweet [20].

Stage 2: One Week of @BabySteps plus Website Usage

After participants used @BabySteps and responded for two weeks, we made the Baby Steps companion website available for parents to view their child's progress based on milestones they answered via Twitter. The goal of this study was not to test the website itself, although participants were welcome to provide feedback on the system's design. For this study, the script only parsed tweets which used the right syntax. Due to this, not all of the participants' Twitter responses were successfully recorded on the website. However, because the progress report may not accurately show child developmental progress until all 30 milestones are answered for a certain age range, we notified participants about this fact and encouraged them to answer any milestones that they have missed via the website before reviewing the progress report. To reduce any unnecessary parental stress, we explained in recruitment materials that development is variable with a wide range of what is typical as children grow in different areas at different rates. Participants had approximately one week to use our website before we deployed a post-study survey, though they were free to use the website indefinitely after our study completed. We did not open up the site initially since we wanted to study how parents used Twitter for responding to milestone prompts before they had a chance to answer questions via the website. The post-study survey included questions about the frequency of tweets, the ease of learning the hashtag system, any concerns about sharing child developmental information publicly, and open-ended questions about how to improve the design of @BabySteps.

Participants

As the main body of our study occurred in Twitter, we recruited our participants via Twitter. The research team tweeted a short study description and a link to a screener survey to their personal accounts and asked for people to retweet. Some followers re-tweeted or to forwarded it to a relevant person, with the majority of participants coming from a re-tweet by a person with nearly 20,000 followers (who also enrolled in our study as P5). The screener survey asked if they were parents of a baby between 2 months and 2 years, the number of children in the household, their experience with Twitter, and optional demographic information. We received 72 responses to the screener survey. Of those that responded to the screener, we sent invitations to approximately 40 participants to recruit a large, diverse set. Of the invitations sent, a total of 19 parents ended up consenting, completing the pre-study, and enrolling in the

Table 1: Participant details

ID	Age	Gender	# of children	Years Using Twitter	# of Twitter accounts	# Followed	% Personal acquaintance	# of Followers	% Personal acquaintance	Protected tweets	Twitter Frequency	Baby's Initial Age(s) in months	Baby's Gender(s)
P1	25 - 30	F	1	> 3 years	1	329	30-50%	226	< 10%	No	Several per day	21	F
P2	25 - 30	F	2	> 3 years	1	772	< 10%	329	< 10%	No	Several per day	4, 24	F, F
P3	25 - 30	M	1	> 3 years	3+	402	50-70%	602	30-50%	No	Several per day	12	M
P4	25 - 30	F	1	> 3 years	2	5	> 70%	5	> 70%	Yes	Once per 2 weeks	13	F
P5	25 - 30	F	1	> 3 years	1	8,169	< 10%	19,736	< 10%	No	Several per day	13	M
P6	31 - 40	F	2	1 - 3 years	2	175	< 10%	235	< 10%	No	Several per day	8	F
P7	31 - 40	F	1	> 3 years	2	577	< 10%	1598	< 10%	No	Several per day	22	M
P8	31 - 40	F	2	1 - 3 years	1	277	< 10%	214	< 10%	No	Several per day	16	F
P9	31 - 40	F	5	> 3 years	1	385	30-50%	269	30-50%	No	Several per day	5, 5	F, M
P10	31 - 40	F	1	1 - 3 years	1	150	< 10%	80	< 10%	No	Several per day	16	M
P11	31 - 40	F	2	1 - 3 years	1	305	10-30%	68	> 70%	Yes	Once per day	13	M
P12	31 - 40	F	1	> 3 years	1	795	< 10%	364	< 10%	Yes	Several per day	10	F
P13	31 - 40	F	2	> 3 years	3+	~900	10-30%	~4,000	10-30%	No	Several per day	22	M
P14	31 - 40	F	2	1 - 3 years	2	~100	10-30%	50	50-70%	No	Several per day	20	F

study. During the course of the study, one decided to withdraw because of concerns over sharing tweets about her child publicly on Twitter, and two people never sent tweets to @BabySteps and thus dropped out. Two participants replied to via Twitter to milestone posts, but did not respond to our post-study survey (P1 and P7). Overall, we have @BabySteps usage data from 14 participants and 12 responses from the post-study survey (see Table 1).

The participants were a mix of demographics from all over the United States, though most were younger as they had young children. Since we recruited via Twitter, most of our participants had good experience with it. Six participants had multiple Twitter accounts and nine participants have used Twitter more than 3 years. All participants currently record information in varying ways about their child, and many often bring notes to doctors. However, lack of time and forgetting to record were the most common difficulties they face in keeping records regularly, which makes them ideal candidates for @BabySteps. Two participants (P2 and P9) used @BabySteps with their two children, with P9 having fraternal twins. All participants consented via the web and received a $20 Amazon.com gift card as a token of appreciation. See Table 1 for participant details.

RESULTS

We here report findings from the @BabySteps deployment study on how participants used our system, learned the predefined syntax, reacted to privacy issues, interacted with one another, used the website in complement to Twitter, and their overall reaction to the system.

Overall Tweeting Activity

For this study, Baby Steps set up twelve accounts including the main Baby Steps account. Over the three weeks, each account associated with a baby's birth month tweeted out age-appropriated milestone questions as well as useful parenting tips (#tip) and activities (#activity) that parents can try with their children. A total of 670 tweets were sent (5 from the main account) averaging approximately 60.5 tweets among eleven monthly accounts (average 2.88 tweets per day). The composition of those 60.5 tweets was 42.1 milestone questions, 8.1 tips, 8.4 activities, and 1.9 study-related announcements (e.g. reminders to use predefined hashtags, functionalities, etc.). Depending upon the age range, there could be slight difference in the number of milestone questions, tips, and activities. In response to our tweets, 14 participants made 319 milestone responses (22.3 per participant, see Table 2).

We also wanted to know what participants thought about the frequency and timing of tweets made by Baby Steps. In this study, an average of 2.88 tweets were sent out at random times per day, rather than tweeting at set intervals, to be more noticeable by participants checking Twitter at any time of the day. Eight participants thought this frequency was just right, while four thought it was too often. However, when it came to tweeting each tweets at different times, we received mixed opinions.

P6: *"(...) whenever I checked twitter I usually would see at least one tweet from baby steps, which I really liked."*

P12: *[in response to how to improve system] "Sending out the tweets at designated times every day (or even repeating them) so I would know to expect them."*

Our system was designed to tweet parenting tips and activities after all milestone questions for an age group had been exhausted. One participant expressed that she would prefer if the system sends out them in parallel.

P5: *"The ideal frequency would be a balance of the milestones with the tips. Some days were just tips. Others were just milestones. It seemed unbalanced, hard to predict, irregular."*

From our pre-study survey, we found out that all participants had their own ways of recording child development and are currently keeping records of it. The most common difficulties they face are lack of time and forgetting to record. As Twitter has a "Favorite" feature, some participants used it to save some of our tweets for later.

P5: *"Because I checked the Twitter when [my baby] was asleep or not with me, and it was a milestone activity I hadn't tried yet with him. I wanted to wait until I could try it, and sometimes favorited the milestone so I'd remember to.*

Table 2: Overall usage by the 14 participants in our study. The sparklines to the right are meant to give an overview of activity over 3 weeks. P5 started the study later than others.

ID	Total Tweets	Avg. per Day	Tweet Frequency by Time
P1	6	0.3	
P2	9	0.4	
P3	31	1.3	
P4	28	1.2	
P5	22	1.0	
P6	10	0.4	
P7	25	1.1	
P8	14	0.6	
P9	26	1.1	
P10	47	2.0	
P11	26	1.1	
P12	23	1.0	
P13	12	0.5	
P14	33	1.4	
Avg.	22.3	1	

It was more common to favorite #tip or #activities rather than milestone questions, but overall favoriting was low.

Using Twitter Syntax

For our system to correctly recognize and store user responses, we required three hashtags (in any order) to be included in each milestone response: 1) answer to the milestone question, 2) baby's name or pseudonym, and 3) milestone ID. Hashtags are very common on Twitter, however, they are generally created by users organically. We thought it might be new for participants to be required to include specific hashtags for a certain purpose and might need some training. Thus, we sent out instructions (via a website link) and occasional reminder tweets about the syntax. As a result, among 319 milestone responses, 198 (62%) were correctly formatted and 121 (38%) were missing some parts.

There were a few cases (8 tweets) where the response had different answers (e.g. maybe, rarely don't know, not sure, etc.) instead of the given answer options (yes/sometimes/no/notyet) but the majority of errors came from missing the # sign before answers to the question or a missing milestone ID. For example:

- @BabyStepsAug12 #baby2464 yes. Can turn pages himself **[missing # before 'yes']**
- @BabyStepsDec12 #yes so cute! **[missing milestone ID]**

Because of reminder tweets, most of the participants learned the correct syntax over time, but some participants expressed difficulties following the rules.

P2: *"It [Syntax] was good but a little complicated - would have been nice to not have to do a hashtag for all responses, as that doesn't seem like a typical way to use hashtags. As in, you would never normally do a hashtag in front of 'yes' or 'no'. I had to keep going back to the email with instructions to remember what format you wanted the responses in."*

The most preferred method of responding to milestone questions was via the Twitter mobile phone or tablet application (54% of all responses), which made it more difficult to follow the syntax. Approximately 28% of the posts were via the Twitter website, and another 11% were either via a special app like TweetDeck or TweetBot for iOS and an additional 7% were of unknown origin (due to being direct messages). Four participants reported they used only the mobile phone application, whereas there was only one participant who solely used the Twitter website.

P11: *"It was difficult to remember to use the correct syntax, period, but probably a bit harder on the phone."*

P9: *"Using it from mobile, I had to remember the correct hashtag (ex. #baby1234) because it was not visible when I was typing. This would not be the case with Twitter on the web, but I most often use my phone to tweet."*

There was one interesting case of the participant who was responding to milestone tweets for her two 5-month old twins. She responded to the milestone prompt for both children within the same tweet (@BabyStepsMar13 #yes #baby2325 #babyname1 #babyname2). Our system could not handle this syntax, so this was not parsed correctly. She eventually split up the tweets into separate ones for each.

Tweeting in Public

Twitter, unless the user explicitly chooses to go private, is placed in the public domain and whatever the user tweets will be broadcasted to the world at large.

Privacy

As the main body of the study occurs on Twitter, privacy issues naturally came to the surface. Some participants expressed that they were completely fine with sharing child developmental progress on Twitter.

P13: *"I don't mind publicly responding. I already do a lot of public responses, and tweets about my children. Response did not affect my preference."*

P12: *"My account is private but I don't mind responding publicly. My child is meeting milestones as expected. Even if she weren't I wouldn't mind responding publicly."*

However, not everyone agrees on that. In fact, one of the participants withdrew from the study because she did not feel confortable in sending tweets with her baby's developmental information, even though her timeline is protected. She expressed that although her account is protected and private, she was concerned about tweeting negative answers to milestone questions. Also, P5, who responded via Direct Message (DM), expressed a similar privacy concern before consenting. After the study, she added her reasons for responding via DM rather than public tweets and frustration she had gone through because of her choice.

P5: *"I prefer to respond privately, because a public message is a) incomprehensible to anyone viewing my public timeline and b) runs the risk of giving peering strangers more information about my baby than I care to give."*

P10: *"I didn't use DM b/c I thought it was too complicated on my phone. (...) I responded publicly b/c it was easier on my phone. But I didn't put a lot of identifying info. Just yes, no, etc."*

Too Much Baby Talk?

In addition to and/or aside from privacy and security concerns, some parents have expressed their conscientiousness in posting too many baby stories on Twitter, which was a concern raised in Morris's study of mothers and social networking use [16]. There was also a fear of overshare, which might lead to unfollowing [14]. People with this kind of concern may also choose to answer via Direct Message.

P4: *" I feel like most people don't want to see me tweeting about my child's development -- I try not to inundate people with pictures on fb (just instagram), so I would feel the same on twitter."*

P6: *"I did not know DM was an option but I would have preferred it. I did not want to tweet publicly multiple times in a row about my baby's development. It seemed a little spammy."*

Social Interactions

Because the study was relatively short-term and the number of participants was small, opportunities for social interaction were limited. However, as the nature of Twitter is as a social networking service, we were interested whether participants ever interacted with each other. Among the eleven monthly accounts we had, three had multiple participants – two with two participants and one with three participants. We received several testimonies of interaction, from one following the other to a brief conversation between the two.

P5: *"I saw who else was following the @babystepsjul12 and followed those who seemed interesting."*

P10: *"I conversed with a woman on twitter who was also following the same BabySteps birth month account. We talked about enjoying the study."*

In addition, P14 showed her desire to interact with parents with a baby born in the same month. Future studies will include more participants to study this social dynamic at a larger scale.

P14: *"I think I might have been the only person in my group so it wasn't as interactive as I would have hoped.*

Twitter and Website Integration

After responding to milestone questions via Twitter for two weeks, participants were introduced to the Baby Steps website. They could view their child's developmental progress based on their responses via Twitter and were able to answer additional milestone questions, add photos, share a timeline of their child's progress, get useful resource information, etc. Although testing the Baby Steps website was not the main goal of this study, because users had a week to explore, we received quite amount of feedback that it served well as a companion of @BabySteps and they complement each other.

P6: *"I love it! So well structured. And I love that I can use it to put in milestones that I missed on twitter."*

Despite it not being a popular feature from @BabySteps, keeping sentimental records of a child with #babymemory and checking it on the website received positive feedback.

P12: *"I liked that I could record #babymemory bits to check back on later."*

However, because the system only parsed and recorded the tweets with correct syntax for this study, not all of participant responses were recorded on the website, which caused frustration to some participants.

P4: *"It didn't actually pull in the responses that I had posted to twitter -- it only recorded three of the responses, and I had responded to all the questions"*

P11: *"None of my responses are there because I messed up the syntax."*

Overall Feedback

In the post-study survey, we asked participants about their general perceptions and suggestions for improvement or new features. Most participants had a positive reaction to @BabySteps and the website. Nine out of twelve participants who completed survey said that they want to continue to use both @BabySteps and website after the end of the study. They also said that they would like to recommend our system to friends. For the most part, many favored that the system identified informed tasks and developments that baby should be doing.

P4: *"It was really nice to learn about how her development is potentially matching up with where she should be. "*

P8: *"It encouraged me to try some things with my daughter (like letting her feed herself with a spoon) which I hadn't thought to do yet."*

Also, some participants appreciated how @BabySteps made them more aware of their child's development and grateful for their child meeting development progress on time.

P6: *"I loved that it reminded me about the less obvious milestones she was achieving."*

P3: *"I think some of the development that happened we just took for granted... so getting to keep track of it showed that our kid was developing at a pace."*

Ratings in a 5-point Likert scale (5 being the positive answer) revealed that participants think our system can be helpful to both first time parents ($M = 4.25$, $SD = 0.87$) and parents with multiple children ($M = 4.17$, $SD = 1.03$).

P9: *"I can see how the tips and activities could be useful, especially for a 1st time mom."*

P13: *"Used it for my second child, and enjoyed re-learning about various milestones I had experience with my older child >3 years ago."*

It turned out that we had a pediatrician among our participants. She revealed it in the post-study survey. Her motivation for participating was because she recalled that remembering the developmental milestones was difficult during her training. She gave great comments about our system.

P12: *"Full disclosure - I'm a pediatrician... You have created a fantastic tool for tracking and for guidance for parents on how their child is doing developmentally. I would love to be able to use this in my own practice. (...) This is an objective way to track milestones. I love it and I hope I get to continue using it! I've been using a blog that is open to only family to track milestones and post pictures - this is even better for milestone tracking. Thank you so very much!"*

DISCUSSION

Overall, we believe the deployment study showed that the @BabySteps system was successful in achieving its initial goals. In the end, all participants were able to learn the syntax and successfully respond to milestone messages. For most participants, the system kept them engaged over the course of the study, and we received positive feedback on the overall use and idea of the system.

Despite the initial success of our system design in our first trial of it, we believe there are a number of actions we can take to improve the usability and overall acceptability of @BabySteps. For example, our original design had enforced each participant to include 2-3 three different hashtags within their responses to milestone prompts. This included the response (#yes, #sometimes, or #no/#notyet), the baby milestone ID (e.g., #baby2343), and if there was more than one child registered in the system, the child's name or pseudonym (e.g., #sally or #daughter). However, because participants sometimes forgot the hashtag on the response, it would be easy to modify the system to allow for answers to not require the hashtag. In addition, we could allow participants to omit the baby milestone hashtag if they reply directly to the message, since the Twitter API allows us to identify which tweets are in reply to another message. This would alleviate some of the difficulty of having to copy the hashtag, especially when using a mobile device. Finally, we could simplify the baby code slightly. We chose 4 digit codes initially, thinking they would be more distinct, but because there are only about 660 unique milestones across the entire 5 years of a child's life, we could number the milestones between #baby1 and #baby660 to shorten what the participant has to remember. These changes may prevent more user error and allow for flexibility, though it may still be necessary to be strict in the event of multiple children (like the case with P9, who tried to combine a tweet for her two twins).

In addition to simplifying the hashtag system, we believe there are additional improvements we can make to the system itself that could help participants in the beginning to learn the syntax and to also account for human error, typos, etc. The Tweak the Tweet application [20] had similar issues with having participants tweet using the right hashtags as well, which is why we had reminder tweets about the syntax. We believe adding to our script the capability of sending automated replies in the event that the user sends an improperly formatted tweet would help with correcting errors sooner. We believe these should be via direct message (DM). For example, if the user tweeted "@BabyStepsNov12 #yes, my daughter can kick a ball," we could send a DM back that says "Thanks! However, we cannot process your request due to: missing child name hashtag (#sally), missing milestone id hashtag (#baby234)."

In addition, although we did not encounter this in the short duration of our study, it is possible that a person could learn about @BabySteps via someone they follow and wish to start using the system, which we hope will happen to help broaden the reach of our system's design. However, if they are not registered with our system, their replies cannot be processed. Thus, we could send an automated message to anyone who sends us a message inviting them to register on the Baby Steps companion website.

Using Twitter for a public health application is also not without its challenges, which would be useful for others interested in working in this space. First, the 140-character limit and the need to allow for additional characters for replies was somewhat challenging. The system we built and the milestone content was inspired by the Ages and Stages Questionnaire [19]. However, due to the 140-character limit, we could not use the exact wording of the milestone questions, which in some cases were as long as 300-400 characters. Because the ASQ is a validated tool, this likely would break validation and may not be as reliable as the original. There is a similar issue with other public health campaigns that have used SMS messaging and have run into 160 character limits, and thus there are public health organizations that are working on shortened, validated messages for this format. This could be one solution to this issue, but may take some time and cooperation from the original sources of the content. Second, because Twitter remains in the public domain, privacy can be a critical issue. We cannot expect all of our users to have a strong level of media literacy. Therefore, it is important for us not only to inform them about the risk in advance, but also to give them options that they can choose to control privacy. Our future work is exploring alternatives to Twitter to track milestones, so for those who are not comfortable with using this method, they have several other options.

There is also a question on how frequent postings should be to avoid overload, missing milestones, and also keep the parent engaged without forgetting the syntax. There is currently not much guidance on how often to send messages, and we believe it is likely dependent on the health domain (e.g., it is possible parents may be willing to receive more milestone messages than they would reminders about quitting smoking). Although most of the participants in our study believed that the three milestones per day frequency was just right, there were a few who believed it was too many, or they would like to see milestones balanced more with the tips and activity suggestions. We believe additional studies are necessary to determine this correct balance.

Finally, one last issue is the need for having the companion website. It would be ideal if the system could reside entirely on Twitter, but for developmental milestone tracking, it is not enough to just collect responses from parents. We also needed to prompt them to communicate that information with their doctor and follow up as necessary. Although the eventual use case for Baby Steps is to have our state's public health system monitor parent responses in the database and directly follow up with participants based on the results, this system is not yet in place. Thus, we had to have the website where participants can log in, see all of their responses, print out the results to bring with them to the doctor, and find local resources on who to contact if they are concerned about their child's development. There may be other health applications where this may not be needed, since the tweet itself could direct them to resources.

CONCLUSIONS & FUTURE WORK

We presented the design and implementation details of @BabySteps, a system for using Twitter to create an interactive public health system for recording children's developmental milestone progress. We conducted a 3-week deployment study to understand the feasibility of such a system. Our system was successful in teaching participants to use the proper syntax to reply to tweets, we had engagement with participants over the course of the study, and we received a number of positive comments about the system's design. Our study revealed several issues in how we can improve these types of systems. This research has two primary contributions: 1) the design and development of a novel system for using Twitter as an interactive public health platform and 2) the results of the deployment study demonstrating its feasibility. The findings from our study have implications for designing such systems and can inform others of lessons learned in using Twitter for this purpose.

We believe there are a number of opportunities for future work. This system and study has just scratched the surface for what is possible with using Twitter as an interactive public health platform that can shift the flow of information from many to a single source. We plan to conduct a study experimenting with the frequency of Tweets to determine the right balance to maintain engagement but avoid fatigue. We will also conduct a longer-term study of @BabySteps to determine whether this approach can maintain engagement over the long term and improve self-efficacy and patient activation, as well as understand how parents prefer to respond to and share milestone information when compared to just a website or other mediums, such as text messaging.

ACKNOWLEDGMENTS

We wish to thank Chun-Ku Lin, Sean Munson, Kiley Sobel, Li-Tien Ou, Robert Racadio, Mira Shah, Yuna Shim, Yi-Chen Sung, and Xiaotong Yang for their assistance with this research. This research was funded by National Science Foundation grant #0952623. The University of Washington's Institutional Review Board approved all research.

REFERENCES

1. Barak, A., Hen, L., Boniel-Nissim, M., & Shapira, N. A. (2008). A comprehensive review and a meta-analysis of the effectiveness of internet-based psychotherapeutic interventions. *JTHS*, 26(2-4), 109-160.
2. D'Alessandro, D. M., & Dosa, N. P. (2001). Empowering children and families with information technology. *JAMA Pediatrics*, 155(10), 1131.
3. De Choudhury, M., Counts, S., & Horvitz, E. (2013). Predicting postpartum changes in emotion and behavior via social media. *CHI 2013*, pp. 3267-3276.
4. Duby, J. C., et al. (2006). Identifying infants and young children with developmental disorders in the medical home: An algorithm for developmental surveillance and screening. *Pediatrics*, 118(1), 405-420.
5. Fell, H., Cress, C., MacAuslan, J., & Ferrier, L. (2003). visiBabble for reinforcement of early vocalization. *ASSETS 2003*, pp. 161-168.
6. Foucault, B.E. Designing Technology for Growing Families. *Technology@Intel Magazine*. 2005.
7. Guralnick, M. J., & Bricker, D. (1987). *The effectiveness of early intervention for children with cognitive and general developmental delays*. Academic Press.
8. Hoefman, B., & Apunyu, B. (2010). Using SMS for HIV/AIDS education and to expand the use of HIV testing and counseling services at the AIDS Information Centre (AIC) Uganda. *M4D 2010*.
9. Jeong, H. Y., et al. (2008). Opportunities to support parents in managing their children's health. *CHI 2008 Extended Abstracts*, pp. 3225-3230.
10. Jordan, E. T., et al. (2011). Text4Baby. *Nursing for Women's Health*, 15(3), 206-212.
11. Kientz, J. A., Arriaga, R. I., & Abowd, G. D. (2009). Baby steps: evaluation of a system to support record-keeping for parents of young children. *CHI 2009*, pp. 1713-1722.
12. Kientz, J. A., et al. (2007). Grow and know: understanding record-keeping needs for tracking the development of young children. *CHI 2007*, pp. 1351-1360.
13. Klasnja, P., Consolvo, S., & Pratt, W. (2011). How to evaluate technologies for health behavior change in HCI research. *CHI 2011*, pp. 3063-3072.
14. Kwak, H., Chun, H., & Moon, S. (2011). Fragile online relationship: a first look at unfollow dynamics in twitter. *CHI 2011*, pp. 1091-1100.
15. LENA. Retrieved Sept. 18, 2013 from http://www.lenababy.com
16. Morris, M.R. (2014) Social Networking Site Use by Mothers of Young Children. *CSCW 2014*.
17. Munson, S. A., et al. (2010). Happier Together: Integrating a Wellness Application Into a Social Network Site, *Persuasive 2010*.
18. Park, S., Jeong, H., & Zimmerman, J. (2008). ENSURE: Support for Parents in Managing their Children's Health. *Design and Emotion*.
19. Squires, J., & Bricker, D. (2009). *Ages & Stages Questionnaires®*. Baltimore, Maryland, 257-182.
20. Starbird, K., & Palen, L. (2011). Voluntweeters: Self-organizing by digital volunteers in times of crisis. *CHI 2011*, pp. 1071-1080.
21. Tang, K. P., et al. (2012). Designing a mobile health tool for preterm infant wellness. *Pervasive Health 2012*, pp. 232-235.
22. Trixie Tracker Software. Retrieved Sept. 18, 2013 from http://www.trixietracker.com
23. Victoria Udoh. Nigeria: MTN to Broadcast Anti-Aids Messages. (September 2003). Retrieved Sept. 18, 2013 from http://allafrica.com/stories/200309260162.html
24. Westeyn, T. L., et al. (2012). Monitoring children's developmental progress using augmented toys and activity recognition. *PUC*,16(2), 169-191.
25. Woolford, S. J., et al. (2010). Tailored mobile phone text messages as an adjunct to obesity treatment for adolescents. *JTT*, 16(8), 458-461.

DoDo Game, a Color Vision Deficiency Screening Test for Young Children

Linh-Chi Nguyen[1], Ellen Yi-Luen Do[1], Audrey Chia[2], Yuan Wang[1], Henry Been-Lirn Duh[1]

[1] Keio-NUS CUTE Center, Interactive & Digital Media Institute,National University of Singapore
{idmnlc, ellendo}@nus.edu.sg

[2]Singapore National Eye Centre
11 Third Hospital Avenue Singapore 168751
Audrey.Chia.W.L@snec.com.sg

ABSTRACT

This paper presents "DoDo's Catching Adventure," a new color vision deficient screening test for young children. Early detection of color blindness among children is useful for parents and teachers to better understand children's needs, to overcome difficulties in learning, and for life and career planning. Unfortunately, current color screening tests are not designed for young children; most require more advanced verbal or cognitive skills. DoDo game has taken a new approach by embedding game elements into a color vision screening test. A user study conducted at Singapore National Eye Centre on twenty-eight children, identified fourteen as Red-Green deficient subjects as did by Ishihara screening test, showed that DoDo was adequately effective in identifying Red-Green color vision deficiency and comparable to two current gold standard colorblind tests, Ishihara and D15.

Author Keywords

Digital game, color deficiency test, children game

ACM Classification Keywords

H.5.2 User Interfaces, K.8.0 Games

General Terms

Colorblind, children game

INTRODUCTION

Digital games are developed for entertainment and education but rarely for clinical screening. Current standard color vision deficient tests are not attractive, nor child-friendly to sufficiently engage children at their verbal knowledge and color perception level. Children often find computer and videogames engaging for their interaction experience with fun elements. Very young children often enjoy playing games on computers and handheld mobile devices [14]. However, none of the validated color vision test for children is in the form of a digital game. We believe using screen based digital game technology can provide a powerful and efficient clinical tool to help detect color vision deficiency in children. This paper introduced a digital game specifically designed as a new color vision deficiency test kit for young children aged two and a half to six years old.

CHI 2014, April 26–May 1, 2014, Toronto, Ontario, Canada.

ACM 978-1-4503-2473-1/14/04...$15.00.
http:/dx.doi.org/10.1145/2556488.2557334

NEED OF COLORBLIND TEST FOR YOUNG CHILDREN

Congenital color vision deficiency affects 5% to 10% of males and 0.4% to 0.5% of female population [11]. In its most common form, X-linked Red-Green color blindness, either the photo-pigment of the green or red cone is absent, and the photo-pigment response of the green cones is shifted towards that of the red cones (deuteranomaly) or vice versa (protanomaly). Yellow-Blue color blindness (tritanopia and tritanomaly), rod and blue-cone monochromaly exist but are extremely rare [1].

As children with in-born (or congenital) color defects have never experienced the full color experience, they may not even be aware of their deficit. Pragmatically, children with Red-Green color blindness have difficulty in differentiating colors with variable mix of red and green. This may cause confusion as color-based learning is often used during early education. Currently, no treatment exists for congenital color vision defects. However, diagnosis of these defects early in life may help children adjust better to tasks at school, avoid dangerous situation in everyday living caused by color vision deficiency, and may help parents understand their child's limitations in future career choice[12].

LIMITATIONS OF CURRENT COLOR VISION DEFICIENCY TEST

Commonly used tests in clinical practice today include isochromatic plates, arrangement tests, anomaloscopes, and lantern tests. Each category has unique attributes that make it suitable for a particular clinical situation. Clinicians are trained on the requirements for administering and grading each test type. Factors such as the quality of the illuminant and the size of the field of view are important elements in setting up a proper color vision laboratory [12].

The Ishihara test is currently the most widely used screening test for detection of congenital Red-Green color deficiency [2]. After which color defects are better defined and classified using other tests such as the Farnsworth-Munsell D15 test [3]. Non-verbal or numeral-illiterate children, however, are unable to perform the Ishihara test. There are some paper-based color tests designed for children, such as the H-R-R Test for children and Color Vision Test. However, they are still not as effective as the Ishihara test, and involve tasks that may not be appealing to children [4,5,9,11,13]. There have been attempts to present color vision on computers, but the designs are often not child-friendly [9,15]. Embedding color vision tests in a digital game may be a viable means to detect various forms of color deficiencies even in persons without verbal or reading skills, and with short-attention spans [8].

THE GAME DESIGN

DoDo game is available for computer and tablet application. In this game, players are asked to tap the screen to pick an object (e.g., a butterfly, a lady bug, an owl, or a fish) with similar color profiles. With a tablet computer, young children could easily touch the images and play the games. The DoDo game includes 4 sub-games designed to test for Yellow–Blue and Red-Green color deficiency, total color blindness, and to classify between deuteranopia and protanopia (Figure 1).

Figure 1: DoDo game's main layout on a tablet computer

In its current form, each sub-game consists of six quick stages where each participant is asked to pick 1 object out of 4 objects that looks the most similar in color to the sample object. The extended level (level 2) of sub-game 3 for Red-Green deficiencies asks participants to pick one object out of six objects. In this level 2 of sub-game 3, we added two more color-blind's choice objects to increase the difficulty level for color deficient subjects (Figure 2).

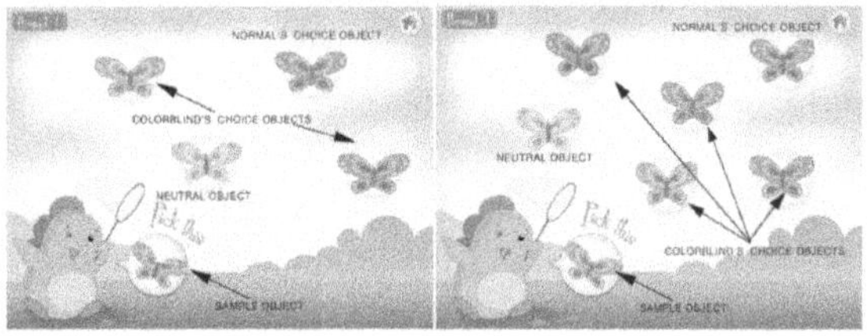

Figure 2: Sub-games 3 Level 1 (left) and Level 2 (right) layout with annotation of object groups

There are four groups of objects in each game: a sample object, normal vision's choice objects, color-blind's choice objects and neutral objects. Table 1 shows example objects of these four groups. In the start of each sub-game, the blinking sample object (e.g., a butterfly) appears in a talk bubble next to the DoDo character with the "Pick This" text and audio. Then four groups of objects appear on the screen for the kid to pick the most similar one. Based on his/her color vision the kid will pick either normal vision's choice objects or color-blind's choice objects or neutral objects. Figure 2 shows sub-game 3 with butterfly characters and Table 1 shows the four object groups for sub-game 3.

The game's win-lose condition is independent on whether the participants have color deficiencies. The player would be prompted to play the game again if his/her choices are the content neutral objects as this reveals the player does not fully understand the rules of the game or is being uncooperative. Otherwise, the player always wins the game. In the end of the game the screen always displays the message "You Win!" This is designed intentionally to not discourage color deficient children. Parents or clinicians can click on the information icon located on the top right of the screen to access the color deficiency test result.

Design method

The design of the DoDo game is based on the assumption that differences in hue and saturation of objects would direct subjects with color deficiency to group objects differently than those with normal vision. A Red-Green color deficient person will see the hue of objects 1,2,3 of Figure 3 are alike, hence they will pick objects of similar saturation (e.g., object #3). A normal vision person will pick objects with similar hue (e.g., object #1).

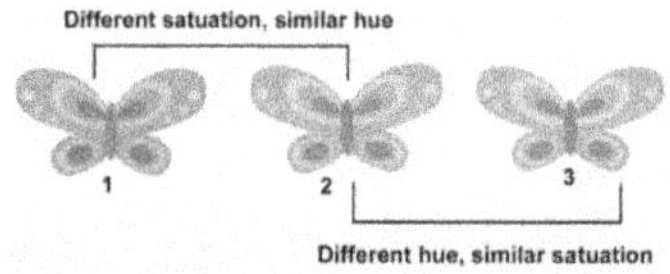

Figure 3: DoDo game design concept

The color design was adopted from Ishihara PC based version with isocromatic data for Red–Green color deficiency established by Lakowski for the 10th edition [9]. Vischeck color deficiency vision simulation was used to simulate the color rendering of objects to color deficiency vision for color-blind's choice objects [7].

	Sample object	Normal vision's choice	Colorblind's choice		Neutral Object
Objects' color in normal vision	R1	R2	G1	G2	
Objects' color in Deutan vision					
Objects' color in Protan vision					

Table 1: Objects in Sub-game 3 (level 1). The color deficiency vision objects simulated by Vischeck.

Due to Gestalt principles, such as the law of similarity in visual perception, we tend to group similar objects together. Similarity could be defined by shape, color, size or brightness [16]. When a colorblind individual cannot distinguish the hue of objects since they look alike, they can only notice the difference of object's saturation and brightness. The key of DoDo game design is to compensate the low resolution in the recognition of hues as the colorblind individual tends to be more sensitive to the differences in saturation [10]. An individual with normal vision can hardly notice the difference of saturation of R1 and R2 object and naturally choose R2 when asked to pick an object similar toR1 (Table 1). For Red-Green deficient individual, all R1, R2, G1, G2 have similar hue. The person will naturally choose rather G1 or G2, depending on the type of Red-Green color deficiency and is unlikely to choose R2 when asked to pick an object similar to R1. Table 1 demonstrates objects in Sub-game 3 (Level 1) viewed by a Deutan and a Protan, using Vischeck computer simulation. The other 3 sub-games are designed based on the same background framework.

USER STUDY

All the tests were conducted under good indoor lighting in a clinical environment with both eyes tested simultaneously. The study was supervised by optometrists at Singapore National Eye Centre. In the Ishihara test, participants are required to recognize and read numbers from plate 1 to 17 presented within the test book (Ishihara 24 plates Edition, year 1998). Each plate contains circle dots of different colors forming a target number that would be invisible to a person with color deficiency but visible to a normal vision person, or the other way around. In Farnsworth D15 Panel test, participants were asked to arrange sixteen color caps in correct order in a rainbow order. The IPad version of DoDo game was used in this study. The screen's brightness was kept balanced as the default setting (auto brightness). Twenty–eight subjects (N=28, Mean Age = 10.83, 1 Female) participated in the study. Fourteen of them are Red-Green color deficiencies, detected by Ishihara test before. The control group is consisted of fourteen normal color vision participants. The average playtime of DoDo game is 3.12 minutes to finish four sub-games.

The ideal color vision test will reliably detect, categorize and grade the severity of the protan, deutan and tritan color vision deficiencies. Currently, the two gold standard tests, Ishihara and the D15, are the most used color vision test in optometry clinics [6]. Clinicians at Singapore National Eye Centre suggested using them to compare DoDo game's effectiveness on Red-Green color deficiency detection. Yellow-Blue color deficiency (tritan) is extremely rare so we were not able to recruit participants at this current stage. Ishihara test has a very high sensitivity and specificity for the detection of protan and deutan deficiencies though it has no tritan plates, makes very little indication of severity, and classification plates are not very reliable [2, 6]. The Farnsworth D15 test (D15) is used worldwide to select applicants for employment in occupations that require good color vision. People with normal vision or slight color deficiency will pass the D15 test and people with significant color deficiency will fail [6]. Although DoDo game was designed for young children aged two and a half to six years old, current clinical practice does not ask children at that age to do colorblind tests at hospitals, therefore, no color-blind participants younger than 6 would be available for recruitment. This user study recruited 6-17 years old participants so that gold standard Ishihara and D15 tests can be used to evaluate the game's reliability. The implication of using this older participant group is that we can't claim the generalizability of the originally intended target group. However, the study validated that DoDo game produced comparable results with gold standard tests.

Sensitivity and specificity

Ishihara, D15 and DoDo Game all have 1.00 of sensitivity In DoDo game, fourteen controls picked right objects without mistake. Sub-game 2 result shows none of the subjects are tritan as expected. Along with Sub-games 3, and 1 (total color blindness), sub-game 4 (Deutan/Protan classification) are also able to reflect abnormal choices of Red-Green deficient subjects. DoDo's Red-Green deficiency result is based on the number of mistake out of eighteen choices of sub-game 1, sub-game 3 and sub-game 4. The sub-game 3 contains two levels, therefore we grouped the result into two groups: DoDo 1 (game with sub-game 3 level 1) and DoDo 2 (game with sub-game 3 level 2)(Table 2).

DoDo game successfully detected ten significant Red-Green deficient subjects who are detected by both Ishihara and the D15. For four borderline subjects who failed Ishihara test and passed D15, DoDo has a mixed result. Clinicians actually found this interesting. Subject #19 who passed D15 also passed both DoDo 1 and DoDo 2 with no mistake. Subject #26 passed DoDo 1 with two mistakes out of eighteen choices and failed DoDo 2 with four mistakes out of eighteen choices. DoDo 1 suggested that subject #20, #24, #26 who passed D15 are mild Red-Green deficiencies (Table 2).

	Red-Green Deficiencies (by Ishihara) 14 subjects		
	Fail D15 (Significated Red-Green Deficiencies) **10 subjects**	**Pass D15** (Normal or Slight deficiencies) **4 subjects** (#19, #20, #24, #26)	
DoDo 1 –Sub game 1,3(Level1) & 4	**Fail DoDo** (Red-Green Deficiencies) **10 subjects**	**Fail DoDo** (Mild) **2 subjects** (#20,#24)	**Pass DoDo 2 subjects** (#19, #26)
DoDo 2- Sub game 1,3(Level 2) & 4	**Fail DoDo** (Red-Green Deficiencies) **10 subjects**	**Fail DoDo** (Mild) **3 subjects** (#20,#24,#26)	**Pass DoDo 1 subject** (#19)

Table 2: Red-Green Deficiencies test data summary

Classification

The sub-game 4 are designed to classify protanopia and deuteranopia. DoDo game suggests that a subject who picked Purple owls more than Red owls is a Deutan and the other way around is a Protan. Subjects who have picked Purple owls and Red owls equally or picked mostly Grey owls were unable to be classified.

Ishihara test's protan/deutan classification plates are more effective for Deutans than for Protans while D15 classification is considered to be more reliable than Ishihara test [6] therefore we focused on the comparison between the results of D15 and DoDo game. Four subjects #19, #20, #24, #26 were detected as normal/slight deficiencies in both the D15 and DoDo game. These subjects were unable to classify on sub-game 4 designed to classify protanopia and deuteranopia. Both tests also cannot classify subject #15. DoDo game and D15 have the same result for seven Deutan and one Protan subjects. The only difference is subject #21 who is classified as a Protan by DoDo game but as a Deutan by D15 (Table 3).

	Deutan	Protan	Not able to classify
	11 (#2 #5, #6,#15, #17, #19, #21, #22, #23, #24, #26)	**0**	
D15	**8** (#5, #6, #17, #18, #21, #22, #23, #27),	**1** (#2)	**5** (#19, #20, #24, #26, #15)
	7 (#5, #6, #17, #18, #22, #23, #27)	**2** (#2, #21)	

Table 3: Protan and Deutan classification- data summary

DoDo's criteria, grading for severity and weakness

Both Ishihara and D15 do not provide a clear grading and give little indications of severity based on the numbers of mistakes. DoDo game also does not provide detailed and clear grading system. The game allows normal color vision participants to make no more than 1 mistake in each sub-game and no more than 3 in total out of the 3 sub-games (Sub-game 1, 3 and 4) to detect Red-Green Colorblind. For Yellow-Blue, normal vision user is allowed to make only 1 mistake in each sub-game and no more than 2 in total out of the 2 sub-games (Sub-game 1 and 2).The percentage to distinguish between mild and strong color deficient is more than 50%. Therefore in Red-Green color deficient detection, if the ratio is from 10/18 errors and above, the participant will be a strong color deficient. The group falls between 4-9/18 errors is slight/mild color deficient.

CONCLUSION

The paper shows the potential of the DoDo game as a new clinical tool for color vision screening test. DoDo's sensitivity and specificity is compatible with the two gold standard tests Ishihara and D15. It can be the better choice for color vision screening for children. More importantly, the user study has strengthened our understanding and helped fine-tuning the design elements to better detect color vision deficiency and provided a better grading for severity. Optometrists who help supervised the study suggested that DoDo game could be used in color vision tests with more difficult tasks for adults. In future work we would test this game with a larger population of young children. The idea of the DoDo game has illustrated a new approach for digital game design to help screen children at pediatric clinics or at home. The same technique of using digital games in tablet computers may be applicable for other types of vision tests for children as well.

ACKNOWLEDGMENTS

This research is supported by the Singapore National Research Foundation under its International Research Center Keio-NUS CUTE Center @ Singapore Funding Initiative and administered by the IDM Program Office. Thanks Dr. Weiquan Lu for helping in data analysis.

REFERENCES

1. Birch, J. Diagnosis of defective color vision. Oxford : Butterworth-Heinemann, 2001.
2. Birch, J. Efficiency of the Ishihara test for identifying red-green color vision deficiency. *Ophthalmic Physiol Opt 17*, 5 (1997), 403–8.
3. Birch, J. Use of the Farnsworth—Munsell 100-Hue test in the examination of congenital color vision defects, Ophthalmic and Physiological Optics, Wiley Online Library, 1998.
4. Choi, S.Y., Hwang, J.M. Ishihara test in 3- to 6-year-old children, *Jpn J Ophthalmol 53* 5 (2009), 455-7
5. Cotter S.A., Lee, French A.L. Evaluation of a new color vision test: 'Color Vision Testing Made Easy. *Optom Vis Sci 76* (1999), 631–6.
6. Dain, S.J.Clinical colour vision tests, *Clin Exp Optom 87* 4-5 (2004), 276-293
7. Dougherty, B., Wade, A. Vischeck simulates colour-blind vision. http://www.vischeck.com
8. Grammenos, D., Savidis, A., Stephanidis, C. Designing universally accessible games. *Comput Entertain 7*, 1 (2009), 1-29.
9. Hoffmann, A., Menozzi, M. Applying the Ishihara test to a PC-based screening system, *Displays 20* 1 (1998), 39-47
10. Kohei, M. Color Universal Design (CUD) - How to make figures and presentations that are friendly to Colorblind people. http://jfly.iam.u-tokyo.ac.jp/color/#see
11. Ling, B.Y., Dain, S.J. Color vision in children and the Lanthony New Color Test. *Visual Neuroscience 25* (2008), 441-444.
12. Melamud, A., Hagstrom, S., Traboulsi, E. I., Color vision testing, *Ophthalmic Genetics 25* 3 (2004), 159–187.
13. Neitz, M., Neitz, J. A new mass screening test for color-vision deficiencies in children, Color Research & Application, Special Issue: In *Proc of the International Color Vision Society 26* S1 (2001), 239-249.
14. NPD Group. Among American kids ages 2-17, 82 percent report that are gamers. Press Release (Dec 2) Port Washington, New York, 2009.
15. Pardo, P.J. PeÂrez, A.L., Suero, A.L. A new color vision test in a PC-based screening system, *Displays 21* 5 (2002), 203-6
16. Soegaard, M. Gestalt principles of form perception. www.interaction-design.org/encyclopedia/gestalt_principles_of_form_perception.html

The Influence of Emotion on Number Entry Errors

Paul Cairns
University of York
York Y010 5GH
paul.cairns@york.ac.uk

Pratyush Pandab
University of York
York Y010 5GH
pratyush.pp@gmail.com

Christopher Power
University of York
York Y010 5GH
christopher.power@york.ac.uk

ABSTRACT
Given the proliferation of devices like infusion pumps in hospitals, number entry and in particular number entry error is an emerging important concern in HCI. There are clearly design features that could greatly improve accuracy in entering numbers but the context of the task could also play an important role. In particular, the emotional state of a person is known to strongly influence their response to a difficult situation and hence the errors that they make. In this paper, we consider the impact of the emotional state of the user on the accuracy with which people enter numbers. Our experiment shows that participants who are in a more positive emotional state are more accurate. The effect is small but could be very important when considering the potentially highly-charged emotional contexts where many healthcare devices are used.

Author Keywords
Number entry; human error; affect; healthcare

ACM Classification Keywords
H.5.m. Information interfaces and presentation (e.g., HCI): Miscellaneous.

NUMBER ENTRY ERROR
Number entry is a ubiquitous daily task for many people whether it is needed to use a PIN for a cash card or data entry as part of a job. Given human nature, errors are inevitable from time to time and in many situations, and they are usually little more than an inconvenience. But in the medical context, an incorrect number entered into a drug delivery device can have serious consequences, potentially the death of the patient. For example, a baby in intensive care died after a nurse mistakenly gave it 10 times the dose of calcium it needed. To add to the tragedy, the nurse also later took her own life despite this being the only serious medical mistake that she ever made [1]. Indeed, a large proportion of adverse drug events are believed to be due to numerical errors. [15].

Naturally, this has become an important topic for research into solutions, such as, in the interface design of the devices used [11], in the underlying software of the devices [14] and alterations to the task to include redundancy [18]. What has been harder to look at is the context in which the devices are used. There is evidence that how the devices are used varies enormously within the different medical domains [17]. However, capturing sufficiently many errors with the contextual richness of a functioning hospital environment remains elusive. Here, we therefore focus on aspects of the context that may be reliably manipulated in the more controlled setting of an experimental study. In particular, affective state has been shown to be an important factor in understanding how people react in safety-critical situations as discussed below but this has not been investigated at all, to the best of our knowledge, in the context of number entry error. Therefore, because healthcare can be a particularly emotive environment, we conducted an experiment manipulating the affective state of participants to investigate if, in principle, it may influence the rate at which people make number entry errors.

CHI 2014, April 26–May 1, 2014, Toronto, Ontario, Canada.

http://dx.doi.org/10.1145/2556288.2557065

EMOTION AND ERROR
Emotion is an integral part of human rational behaviour [3]. It is aroused by external events, and reactions or responses are directed towards these events. From a psychologist's point of view, emotion points to a domain of phenomena of feelings, behaviours and bodily reactions [4]. Affect is most usually considered to be a two-dimensional construct [5] with the typical dimensions used being valence, that is whether the emotional state is positive or negative, and the degree of arousal associated with the emotion. So a highly aroused negative state corresponds to anger whereas a low aroused positive state would be something like contentment.

Emotional state is known to influence people's thinking. Common findings suggest that negative emotions make people avoid the task that produces negative emotions and impairs the processing efficiency in a cognitive task [3]. Similarly, Ashby et al. [2], reports that positive affect is associated with flexibility in reasoning, greater creativity in problem solving and seeking out variety. As a consequence, the affective state of people is able to influence their interactions with digital devices. For instance Aula and Surakka [3] showed that synthetic positive feedback improved the speed with which people completed simple arithmetic tasks over either neutral or negative feedback. Klein et al. [9] also showed that, in a game which provoked frustration, if the system gave the appearance of acknowledging the frustration, then participants were subsequently willing to play the game for longer.

When it comes to human error, it is recognized that how people make errors and respond to errors, particularly in safety critical environments, is substantially influenced by their affective state. For example, Causse et al. [6] demonstrated in a controlled study that negative emotional states can provoke plan continuation errors in pilots, meaning they are more likely to continue acting even when available evidence indicates they should stop. Similarly, Jeon et al. [7] demonstrated that there are behaviour changes when a driver is in different emotional states such as anger and fear, even when those states share the same emotional valence. It is also the case that negative emotions can have positive impacts, with Peters et al. [12] showing that a state of worry is a good predictor as to whether people will take precautions to avoid error. However, when it comes to the small-scale tasks, such as number entry, relatively little is known.

EXPERIMENT

The aim of the experiment is to see whether the affective state of users is a possible influence in the number entry errors that they make. The specific hypothesis here is that people who are in a negative affective state will make more errors than those in a more positive affective state. The level of arousal is not considered here, partly because it is difficult to manipulate but also because there are ethical concerns with putting someone into a highly aroused negative state (ie making them very angry). In order to conduct error studies with a lab-based experiment, it is necessary to provoke an observable error rate and this has implications for the ecological validity of the work as will be discussed.

Design

This was a between-participants design to avoid learning effects and the possibility of the experimental manipulation having effects in more than one condition. The independent variable is the affective state of the participant. A standard way to influence affect is the use of the International Affective Picture System (IAPS) [10]. This is a database of images that have been validated for inducing different levels of affect in both the valence and arousal dimensions. Each image has a standardised score on each dimension between 1 and 9, with 5 indicating neither positive nor negative valence. The intention was to use positive valence images to induce positive affect and negative valence images to induce negative affect. However, the negative valence images are, not surprisingly, somewhat disturbing being images of mutilation, injuries and people in distress and some of the positive valence images have erotic content. Therefore, to avoid unduly stressing participants or making them feel awkward, images were selected first for content and the very negative valence images were avoided. This made the conditions asymmetric about the neutral rating: images in the negative valence condition were rated between 2 and 4, whereas in the positive condition they were rated above 7. One exception is an image of a member of the skinhead subculture which has a mean valence of 1.64 for women. The IAPS is separately scored for men and women but we deliberately chose images that had similar affective valences for both sexes and our analysis did not distinguish between men and women as this has not been previously observed as a potential factor in number entry errors.

The dependent variable is the number of errors made. Currently the extent and variety of number entry error is only just emerging, e.g. [16], so error here is treated simply as a person entering a number different from the number they were required to enter. They were able to correct errors they noticed in the course of entering a number using a backspace key. Also, to check the experimental manipulation, participants were asked to complete the Self-Assessment Manikin for affect [5]. This was converted to a number on the same scale as the IAPS measure of valence, from 1 to 9.

Participants

Twenty-eight participants, 14 in each condition, were recruited to the study by opportunity sample. All were students from The University of York at either Undergraduate or Masters level. The participants' ages ranged from 20 to 30 with a median age of 23. There were 20 women and 8 men.

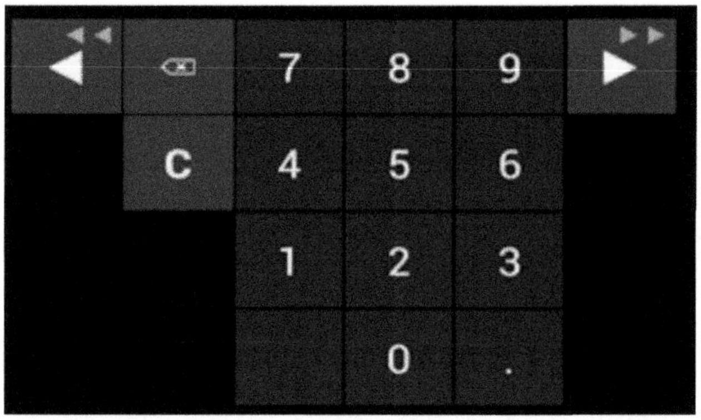

Figure 1. The number pad interface used in the experiment (the arrow keys are not used in this study).

Materials

Two applications were used in the study. The first was a Microsoft PowerPoint presentation which was set up to display 24 images of either negative or positive valence depending on the experimental condition. In order to encourage participants to properly look at and consider the images, after seeing each image, participants were asked to rate how that image made them feel on a paper copy of the SAM affective valence scale.

The second application was Microsoft Excel which was used to randomly generate numbers and display them at seven second intervals. Both PowerPoint and Excel were displayed on a 14.1 inch laptop.

Participants had to enter the displayed number into a tablet, a Google Nexus running Android 4.2, using a number pad touch interface to simulate using a keypad that might be found on a typical medical device, see figure 1. The 'C' key was used to confirm the number entered. Normally, 'C' indicates Clear the display and this was a potential source of confusion but after training, no such confusion was seen in the data.

The time limit of 7sec was used partly based on being a feasible time in which to enter a number of 6 or 7 digits as found in a pilot study but also to apply pressure to participants. Error rates in such studies can be very low [13] so some further manipulation, such as time pressure, is needed in order to make sure there are sufficiently many errors to allow a useful analysis.

Procedure

The participants were welcomed and told about the purposes of the experiment before signing the informed consent form. They were then briefed on the use of the SAM scale based on the briefing given in [10] and given a chance to try it on some example images. They were also shown how to use the number pad on the tablet.

When they were ready, participants were shown the 24 images for their particular experimental condition and asked to rate each one as they went along. After completing this, they moved on to the number entry task. They were instructed not to lift the tablet from the table and to use one finger to enter the number – this was to remove one potential source of variation between participants. They were given 51 randomly generated numbers to enter. Data was automatically collected through the number pad application.

Results

The 28 participants entered 1428 numbers in total and made 240 errors, or approximately 16.8%. Thus participants made a mean number of 8.6 errors (SD = 2.64), ranging from 4 to 15. As hoped with the experimental manipulation, a Mann-Whitney showed significant difference between the SAM ratings for the positive valence images (M = 6.87, SD = 0.53) and the negative valence (M = 3.69, SD = 0.45) conditions, $W(14,14) = 196, p < 0.001$.

Participants in the positive valence condition made a mean number of 7.4 (SD = 1.65) errors, while for the negative valence stimuli the mean number of errors was 9.7 (SD = 3.00), see also Figure 2. A Mann-Whitney also showed this to be significant, $W(14,14) = 55$, $p = 0.046$.

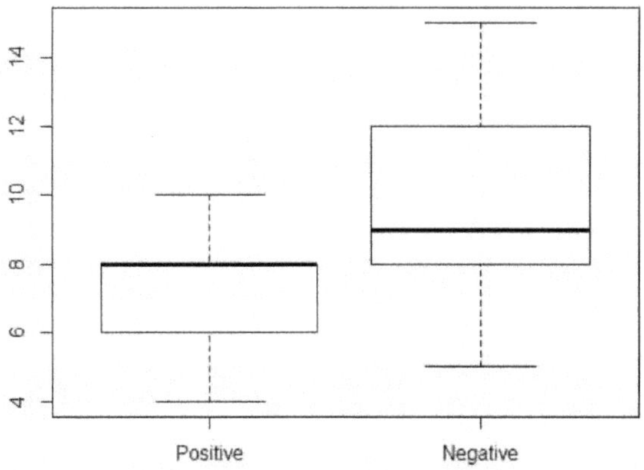

Figure 2. Boxplot of number of errors per participant against experimental condition.

DISCUSSION

As intended, the participants were able to appropriately attribute the expected valence to IAPS images. This suggests that the images were influencing the affective state of the participants and the experimental manipulation had worked. As a consequence, there was a significant effect of the affective state of the participants on the number of errors that they made.

The overall error rate is quite high. The error rate seen in number entry studies varies very much depending on the experimental tasks from between 2% [13] to 30% where the task is very challenging [16]. This suggests that the time pressure component made this into a somewhat challenging task, with an overall error rate of 16.8%, but this is not an unrealistic situation. In many health related situations, staff may find themselves trying to do tasks quickly either for the immediate well-being of the patient or because of the pressures of the job. What the limited time also does is prevent the possibility of a speed/accuracy trade-off. The participants in the positive valence condition cannot be more accurate because they took more time.

There are several issues of ecological validity which were compromises we felt necessary in order to be able to see if, in principle, affective state could influence number entry errors. Participants were required to enter many long numbers in quick succession. This is not how number entry is usually performed, at least not in the healthcare domain that motivates this work. However, without such techniques it is difficult to establish an appreciable error rate that could test the hypothesis. Number pads are also not the only style of interface seen in healthcare nor are they used exclusively with one-finger nor are they usual touchscreens. However, both the style of interface and style of typing are sources of variability in any such experiment and we chose to control rather than manipulate them in this early investigation. Touchscreens are a pragmatic tool for setting up experimental interfaces. It is hard to produce a physical replica of real devices suitable for experiments of this sort and, actually, with the proliferation of touch screen devices, it may be that touchscreens do become more common in healthcare.

IAPS is also not a realistic reflection of how emotional state is induced in people. What the experimental manipulation does demonstrate though is that mere exposure to affective images is enough to influence performance on safety-critical tasks. In healthcare, not only do staff see distressing *real* situations, they may be actively involved in working with such situations. It may be important to manage staff's response to not only the most stressful situations resulting in PTSD [8], but also more generally emotive situations to reduce errors when treating patients.

Further work would of course be need to overcome the ecological limitations of the current work and see the effect across a range of number entry tasks on a variety of interfaces. We also have plans to work on number entry in a hospital setting and so have the opportunity to engage nurses as participants in our work and to better understand the richer context in which they work, particularly with regards to management of their affective state.

CONCLUSIONS

Motivated by the safety-critical nature of number-entry in the healthcare domain, this paper has described an experiment supporting that, in principle, users in a more negative affective state are more likely to make number entry errors. Though only in early stages, this work does provide evidence that the affective state of device users is an important consideration to address and manage when trying to reduce number-entry errors and could have important consequences for patient safety.

REFERENCES

1. Aleccia, J. (2011) Nurse's suicide highlights twin tragedy of medical errors. *NBCNews.com,* 27th June, 2011. http://www.nbcnews.com/id/43529641
2. Ashby, F. G., Isen, A., Turken, A., A neuropsychological theory of positive affect and its influence on cognition. *Psychological Review, 106,* 3 (1999), 529-550
3. Aula, A. and Surakka , V. Auditory emotional feedback facilitates human-computer interaction, *People and Computers*, (2002) 337–350
4. Barrett, L., Haviland-Jones, J. and Lewis, M. (Eds.), *Handbook of Emotions*, Third. Guilford Publications, 2008.
5. Bradley M. M. and Lang, P. J. Measuring emotion: the self-assessment manikin and the semantic differential, *J. of behavior therapy and experimental psychiatry*, *25,* 1 (1994), 49–59.
6. Causse, M., Dehais, F., Péran, P., Sabatini, U. and Pastor, J. The effects of emotion on pilot decision-making: A neuroergonomic approach to aviation safety. Transportation Research Part C: Emerging Technologies, 33, 0 (2013), 272-281.
7. Jeon, M., Yim, J-B. and Walker, B. An angry driver is not the same as a fearful driver: effects of specific negative emotions on risk perception, driving performance, and workload. In *Proc of AutomotiveUI '11*, ACM, New York, NY, USA (2011), 137-142.
8. Kim, S. H., Schneider, S, Bevans, M.. Kravitz, L., Mermier, C., Qualls, C. and Burge, M. PTSD Symptom Reduction With Mindfulness-Based Stretching and Deep Breathing Exercise: Randomized Controlled Clinical Trial of Efficacy, J. of Clinical Endocrinology & Metabolism, May, (2013), online.
9. Klein, J., Moon, Y. and Picard, R. W. This computer responds to frustration: theory, design and results. *Interacting with Computers, 14* (2002), 119-140.
10. Lang, P. J. and Bradley, M. M. International affective picture system (IAPS): Technical manual and affective ratings. Technical Report, 2001.
11. Oladimeji, P., Thimbleby, H. and A. Cox Number entry interfaces and their effects on error detection,"*Proc. Interact 2011*, (2011), 178–185
12. Peters, E., Slovic, P., Hibbard, J. H., & Tusler, M. Why worry? Worry, risk perceptions, and willingness to act to reduce medical errors. *Health Psychology, 25*, 2 (2006), 144.
13. Soboczenski, F., Cairns, P., Cox, A. Increasing accuracy by decreasing presentation quality in transcription tasks. *Proc. Interact 2013*, Springer LNCS 8118 (2013) 380-394.
14. Thimbleby, H. and Cairns, P. Reducing number entry errors: solving a widespread, serious problem, *J. of the Royal Society Interface*, *7* (2010), 1429–1439.
15. Vicente, K. J., Kada-Bekhaled, K., Hillel, G., Cassano, A. and Orser, B. A. Programming errors contribute to death from patient-controlled analgesia: case report and estimate of probability. *Canadian. J. of Anesthesiology, 50* (2003), 328-332.
16. Wiseman, S., Cairns, P. and Cox, A. A taxonomy of number entry error, *Proc. BCS HCI* (2011), 187–196.
17. Wiseman, S. E. M., Cox, A. L., Brumby, D. P. Designing Devices With the Task in Mind: Which Numbers Are Really Used in Hospitals? *Human Factors, 55*, 1 (2013a), 61-74.
18. Wiseman, S., Cox, A. L., Brumby, D. P., Gould, S. J. J., O Carroll, S. Using checksums to detect number entry error. *Proc. ACM CHI 2013*, (2013 b) 2403-2406.
19. Zhang, J., Patel, V. L., Johnson, T. R. and Shortliffe, E. H. A cognitive taxonomy of medical errors, *J. of Biomedical Informatics*, *37*, 3 (2004), 193–20

Both Complete and Correct? Multi-Objective Optimization of Touchscreen Keyboard

Xiaojun Bi **Tom Ouyang** **Shumin Zhai**
Google Inc.
Mountain View, CA, USA
xjunbi@gmail.com ouyang@google.com zhai@acm.org

ABSTRACT
Correcting erroneous input (i.e., correction) and completing a word based on partial input (i.e., completion) are two important "smart" capabilities of a modern intelligent touchscreen keyboard. However little is known whether these two capabilities are conflicting or compatible with each other in the keyboard parameter tuning. Applying computational optimization methods, this work explores the optimality issues related to them. The work demonstrates that it is possible to simultaneously optimize a keyboard algorithm for both correction and completion. The keyboard simultaneously optimized for both introduces no compromise to correction and only a slight compromise to completion when compared to the keyboards exclusively optimized for one objective. Our research also demonstrates the effectiveness of the proposed optimization method in keyboard algorithm design, which is based on the Pareto multi-objective optimization and the Metropolis algorithm. For the development and test datasets used in our experiments, computational optimization improved the correction accuracy rate by 8.3% and completion power by 17.7%.

Author Keywords
Smart touch screen keyboard; mobile; intelligent user interfaces; keyboard algorithm; optimization; correction; completion; text input

ACM Classification Keywords
H.5.m. Information interfaces and presentation (e.g., HCI): Miscellaneous.

INTRODUCTION
Text entry is one of the most basic, common and important tasks on touchscreen devices (e.g., smartphones and tablets). A survey reported by time.com [22] shows that the top three most common activities on smartphones are texting, emailing, and chatting on social networks: all of them involve intensive text input. According a study from Nielsen [20], a teenager on average sends over 3,000 messages per month, or more than six texts per waking hour.

CHI 2014, April 26–May 1, 2014, Toronto, Ontario, Canada.
ACM 978-1-4503-2473-1/14/04.
http://dx.doi.org/10.1145/2556288.2557414

Despite its popularity and importance, touchscreen text entry is inherently error-prone and challenging, because of the imprecision of finger touch and the small key size. To improve the efficiency of text entry, modern "smart" keyboards are becoming intelligent: they are able to correct user's erroneous input (i.e., correction) and complete a word based on partial input (i.e., completion). For example, the Google keyboard on Android corrects "thaml" to "thank", and completes the word "computer" after a user types "comput" (Figure 1).

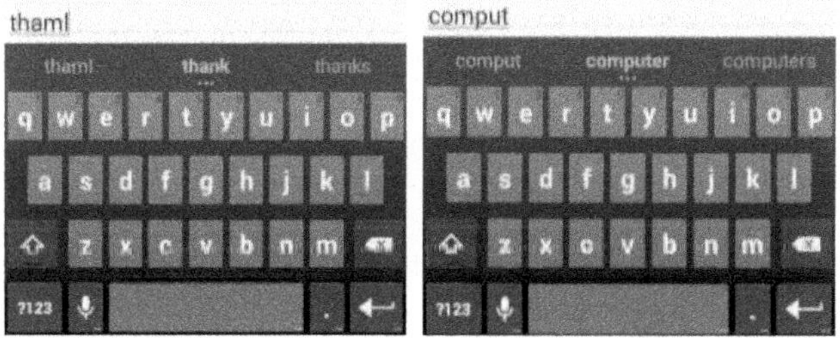

Figure 1. Examples of correction and completion on the Google keyboard. Left: "thaml" is corrected to "thank". Right: "comput" is completed to "computer". The corrected/completed words are displayed in the middle of the suggestion bar. A user enters the word by selecting it from the suggestion bar, or pressing the space bar.

Both correction and completion take advantage of the information regularities in a language, matching users' input signals against words from a lexicon. However, they cast the language regularities for different purposes. Correction uses the language regularities for correcting errors due to the imprecision of the finger touch or spelling errors such as inserting /omitting /substituting /transposing letters, while completion uses the language regularities for predicting unfinished letters based on partial (either correct or erroneous) input to offer keystroke savings.

Correction and completion are different, although related, aspects of modern text input systems. In some cases, these two capabilities might conflict with each other. For example, given the input string "knowl", a strong correction algorithm might treat it as a letter substitution error and suggest "known", while a strong completion algorithm might be in favor of suggesting "knowledge" to save 4 more keystrokes. To effectively correct errors and also maximize potential keystroke savings, the keyboard algorithm needs to strike a balance between correction and completion.

A large amount of research [16, 8, 10] has been conducted to improve the qualities of touch screen keyboard algorithms. However, most of the previous research focused on correction. Completion has received little attention in the recent research literature. Furthermore, the relationship between these two capabilities remains unknown. We do not even know whether it is possible to design a keyboard algorithm performing well for both, given the potential conflict between them.

In this paper, we propose a technique based on the Metropolis optimization algorithm and Pareto multi-objective optimization to simultaneously improve the correction and completion capabilities of a keyboard algorithm, and investigated their relationship. We conceptualize the keyboard algorithm design as a multi-objective optimization problem, with the two optimization objectives 1) correction (measured in word score to be defined later) and 2) completion (measured in keystroke saving ratio).

Our investigation shows that correction and completion have only a minor conflict in the optimization space. The algorithm simultaneously optimized for both performs equally well with the algorithm exclusively optimized for correction in correcting input, and has only a minor loss in the completion capability (1.5% difference in keystroke saving ratio) compared with the keyboard exclusively optimized for completion.

Our research demonstrates that the proposed technique is effective in improving a keyboard's correction and completion capabilities. One of the optimized keyboard algorithms (P_{W+S}) improves the performance by 8.3% in correction and 17.7% in completion over the keyboard before the optimization ($P_{Baseline}$).

RELATED WORK

Improving Correction

A sizeable amount of research has been conducted to improve the keyboard error correction ability. Goodman et al. [12] proposed combing a language model with a key press model to select the most probable key sequence other than the key sequence dictated by strict key boundaries. Kristensson and Zhai [16] invented an "elastic" keyboard, which viewed the hit points as a geometric pattern. The pattern was matched against patterns formed by the letter key center positions of legitimate words in a lexicon. The evaluation showed that the keyboard was capable of correcting words even if the user missed all the intended keys, as long as the user's tapping pattern is close enough to the intended word. Findlater and Wobbrock [8] proposed improving ten-finger touchscreen typing through adaptation. By adapting the underlying key-press classification model, the keyboard improved the typing speed compared to a control condition with no personalization. Kane, Wobbrock, and Harniss et al. [14] developed *TrueKeys*, combining models of word frequency, keyboard layout and tying error patterns to correct typing mistakes. Goel, Findlater and Wobbrock [10] developed the WalkType keyboard which leveraged a mobile device's built-in accelerometer to compensate for extraneous movement while walking. Goel, Jansen, and Mandel et al. [11] proposed reducing the text entry error rates by leveraging information about a user's hand posture. Yin, Ouyang, Partridge, and Zhai [24] further proposed adapting the keyboard underlying spatial model to factors including input hand postures, individuals, and target key positions. With a hierarchical spatial backoff model, the adaptation was capable of reducing the language-model-independent error rate by 13.2%.

Improving Completion

In contrast to correction, improving the completion capability on a touchscreen keyboard has received little attention in the recent HCI research literature. Instead, some related work can be found in earlier research focused on users with motor impairments. Word prediction is a major component in computer-based augmentative and alternative communication (AAC) systems to help people with disabilities communicate in the areas of speech, writing, and computer applications. Keystroke savings provided by several commercial word prediction systems [13] have been measured in the range of 35- 47%. Koester and Levin [15] further developed a model to simulate users' word entry time during the word prediction use.

Although word completion has received limited attention from academic research, it has been playing a major role in commercial products. The majority of present touchscreen keyboards such as Android, iPhone, Windows phone keyboards provide completion to various degrees.

Keyboard Optimization

Optimization has been widely adopted as an approach to improve the keyboard performance, though the previous work mostly focuses on optimizing the keyboard layout.

As early as 1986, Getstow et al [9] used a simple greedy algorithm to optimize a keyboard for motor-impaired users. MacKenzie and Zhang [19] manually optimized their "OPTI" layout. Zhai, Hunter and Smith [25, 26] introduced the Metropolis keyboard and later ATOMIK using the Metropolis randomized optimization technique. All these were layouts optimized to improve the speed of stylus/one finger text entry for a single language. Bi, Smith and Zhai [5] optimized the touch screen keyboard layout for five languages: English, Spanish, French, German, and Chinese at the same time. The optimized layout has minor performance drop compared to the layout exclusively optimized for one language. Bi, Smith and Zhai [4] also explored optimizing the layout while maintaining a certain level of familiarity with Qwerty layout. Their work led to the Quasi-Qwerty layout, which minimized the finger/stylus travel distance and each key was at most one-key away from its original position on the Qwerty layout. Dunlop and Levine [6] later introduced the tap interpretation clarity as the third measure, conducting multidimensional Pareto optimization for speed, familiarity and improved spell checking. Their research was the first in the keyboard literature to apply Pareto optimization and led to a triple optimized keyboard layout. Oulasvirta, Reichel and Li et al. [21] extended the layout optimization to a split keyboard for two-thumb typing. The optimized KALQ layout minimizes the thumb travel distance and maximizes the alternation between thumbs.

THE KEYBOARD ALGORITHM

Text entry on touch keyboards can be viewed as an encoding and decoding processes: the user encodes the intend word w into a series of touch points $(s_1, s_2, s_3 \dots s_n)$, and the keyboard algorithm acts as the decoder, retrieving w from the spatial signals.

At an abstract level, the decoder selects a word w_i from the keyboard's lexicon and calculates its probability of being the intended word based on the information from the following three sources:

1) The proximities of letters in w_i to the touch points $(s_1, s_2, s_3 \dots s_n)$

2) The prior probability of w_i from a language model.

3) The possibilities of spelling errors (e.g., inserting/omitting/transposing/substituting letters).

Pruning out the improbable ones, a list of the most probable words is then ranked and suggested to the user.

While many modern keyboard algorithms may work similarly at this abstract level, the actual implementations of industrial modern keyboards may be rather complex and vary across products. Since most of the commercial keyboard algorithms are not published, it is impossible to develop a general model representing all of them. Fortunately, we could conduct the present research on open source keyboards.

The Baseline Keyboard

We developed a keyboard, referred as $P_{Baseline}$ hereafter, based on the latest version (Android 4.3_r3) of the Android Open Source Project (AOSP) Keyboard [1] which is open-sourced and broadly deployed in Android mobile devices.

$P_{Baseline}$ shared the similar algorithm as the AOSP keyboard which can be read and analyzed by any researcher or developer. In brief, it worked as follows. The lexicon composed of around 170,000 words was stored in a trie data structure. As the algorithm received spatial signals $(s_1, s_2, s_3 \dots s_n)$, it traversed the trie and calculated the probabilities for nodes storing words, based on the aforementioned three sources.

A critical part of the algorithm is to calculate the probabilities of word candidates by weighting information from three sources. Same as the AOSP keyboard, the weights of different sources are controlled by 21 parameters illustrated and explained in Table 1. These parameters are pertinent to the performance of $P_{Baseline}$. Altering them adjust the relative weights of information from different sources, leading to different correction and completion capabilities. For example, reducing the cost of un-typed letters (i.e., lowering COST_LOOKAHEAD) would make the keyboard in favor of suggesting long words, but it might be detrimental to the correction ability. $P_{Baseline}$ is implemented based on the AOSP keyboard, and the parameters in $P_{Baseline}$ shared the same values as those in the AOSP keyboard, which serves as the baseline condition in the current research.

MEASURING CORRECTION AND COMPLETION

Typical laboratory-based studies demand intensive labor and time to evaluate keyboards and may still lack the necessary sensitivity to reliably detect important differences amid large variations in text, tasks, habits, and other individual differences. Bi, Azenkot, Partridge and Zhai [3] proposed using *remulation* – replaying previously recorded data from the same group from the same experiment in real time simulation – as an automatic approach to evaluate keyboard algorithms. We adopt a similar approach in the present research: we evaluated a keyboard algorithm against previously recorded user data to measure its performance. Unlike the *Octopus* tool [3] which evaluated keyboards on devices, we simulated the keyboard algorithm and ran tests on a workstation. Octopus evaluates keyboards in a "black box" fashion without access to their algorithms and source code. The off-device approach in this work is limited to the keyboards whose algorithm and source code are accessible, but is much faster than Octopus.

Datasets

We first ran studies to collect data for optimization and testing. The data collection studies were similar to those in Azenkot and Zhai [2], and Bi et al. [3]. To avoid data collection's dependencies and limitations on keyboard algorithms, a Wizard of Oz keyboard was used in the study (Figure 2), which provided users with only asterisks as feedback when they were entering text.

Each participant entered the same set of 50 phrases randomly chosen from the MacKenzie and Soukoreff's phrase set [10]. All touch events were logged. Participants were asked to enter text "as naturally and as fast as possible." The first 10 phrases for each user were considered a warm-up and excluded in the dataset. A Galaxy Nexus phone was used throughout the study, and

Parameter	Current Value	Description
DISTANCE_WEIGHT_LENGTH	0.132	Weight for the length of a word
PROXIMITY_COST	0.086	Weights for the distances between touch points and the corresponding letters in a word
FIRST_PROXIMITY_COST	0.104	
OMISSION_COST	0.458	Weights for omission errors
OMISSION_COST_SAME_CHAR	0.491	
OMISSION_COST_FIRST_CHAR	0.582	
INSERTION_COST	0.730	Weights for insertion errors
INSERTION_COST_SAME_CHAR	0.586	
INSERTION_COST_FIRST_CHAR	0.623	
TRANSPOSITION_COST	0.516	Weights for transposition errors
SPACE_SUBSTITUTION_COST	0.319	Weights for space substitution errors
ADDITIONAL_PROXIMITY_COST	0.380	Weights for the distances between touch points and the corresponding letters in a word
SUBSTITUTION_COST	0.403	Weights for substitution errors
COST_NEW_WORD	0.042	Weights for starting a new word
COST_SECOND_OR_LATER_WORD_FIRST_CHAR_UPPERCASE	0.25	Weights for capitalized words
DISTANCE_WEIGHT_LANGUAGE	1.123	Weight for language model
COST_FIRST_LOOKAHEAD	0.545	Weight for un-typed letters in a word
COST_LOOKAHEAD	0.073	
HAS_PROXIMITY_TERMINAL_COST	0.105	Weights for terminal nodes
HAS_EDIT_CORRECTION_TERMINAL_COST	0.038	
HAS_MULTI_WORD_TERMINAL_COST	0.444	

Table 1. Parameters for calculating the probability of a word candidate in the P_{base} and AOSP keyboard algorithms. They control the weight of information from different sources. These values were from "scoring_params.cpp" in the AOSP source tree [1] (Android 4.3 on Sep. 16, 2013).

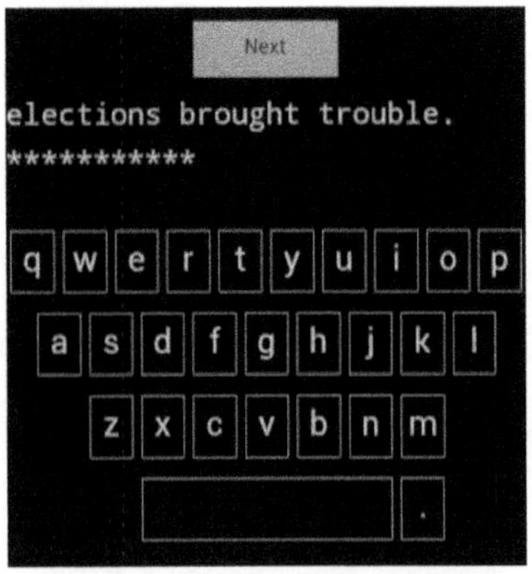

Figure 2. The WOZ keyboard for data collection, which was designed to capture fundamental text entry behaviors.

the keyboard was equal to the stock Android keyboard in dimensions.

We conducted two studies. The first one was to collect data for the algorithm parameter optimization (referred as the development dataset), and the second one was for testing (referred as the test dataset). In the first study, we recruited 40 participants. The average age was 32 (the youngest was 18 and the oldest was 59). Five were left-handed. They were allowed to freely choose text entry hand postures. Twenty-four users entered text with two thumbs, 4 with one thumb, and 12 with the index finger. It included 1,597 phrases in total.

In the second study, we recruited 24 participants, with ages between 20 and 30. All were right handed. They all entered text with index fingers. This data set included 960 phrases in total.

The keyboard algorithm's correction and completion capabilities were evaluated using the collected data. Current touchscreen keyboards perform word-level correction: they correct or complete a word after a word terminator such as a space or punctuation is entered. Therefore, the collected data was segmented into words in evaluation. After the segmentation, the development dataset included 7,106 words, and the test dataset had 6,323 words.

Correction

Correction is measured in *word score*, which reflects the percentage of correctly recognized words out of the total test words. The word score (W) is defined as:

$$W = \frac{\text{the number of correctly recognized words}}{\text{the number of words in test}} \times 100\% \quad \text{Eq. 1}$$

Completion

Completion is measured in keystroke saving ratio (S). Given a data set with n test words, S is defined as:

$$S = \left(1 - \frac{\sum_{i=0}^{n} S_{min}(w_i)}{\sum_{i=0}^{n} S_{max}(w_i)}\right) \times 100\% \quad \text{Eq.2}$$

$S_{max}(w_i)$ is the maximum number of keystrokes for entering a word w_i. In the worst scenario where the keyboard fails to complete w_i, the user needs to enter all the letters of w_i and presses the space bar to enter it. Therefore,

$$S_{max}(w_i) = \text{length of } w_i + 1 \quad \text{Eq. 3}$$

$S_{min}(w_i)$ is the minimum number of keystrokes needed to enter w_i. Assuming that users fully take advantage of the completion capability, w_i will be picked as soon as it is suggested on the suggestion bar. Therefore, $S_{min}(w_i)$ is the least number of keystrokes needed to bring w_i on the suggestion bar plus one more keystroke for selection. The number of the slots on the suggestion bar may vary across keyboards. The keyboard used in this work provides three suggestion slots, the same as the AOSP keyboard.

Note that the measure defined above is the maximum savings offered to a user by the keyboard algorithm. If and how often the user takes them depends on the UI design, the user's preference and bias in motor, visual and cognitive effort trade-offs which are separate research topics.

OPTIMIZING KEYBOARD ALGORITHM FOR CORRECTION AND COMPLETION

In this section, we introduce a method for optimizing a keyboard algorithm for correction and completion, and apply it to $P_{baseline}$. In brief, we conceptualize the keyboard algorithm design as a multi-objective optimization problem with two objectives 1) correction and 2) completion. For $P_{baseline}$ particularly, it is equivalent to optimizing the 21 parameters in Table 1 for these two objectives.

To solve a multi-objective optimization problem, a simple approach is to convert the multiple objectives into one objective function, where each objective is a component in a weighted sum. However, the challenge of this approach is choosing an appropriate weight for each objective. Also, this method returns only one solution, which might not be the most desirable solution.

Instead of returning a single solution, we performed a Pareto optimization [7], which returns a set of Pareto optimal solutions. A solution is called Pareto optimal or non-dominated, if neither of the objective functions can be improved in value without degrading the other. A solution that is not Pareto optimal is dominated: there is a Pareto optimal solution which is better than it in at least one of the criteria and no worse in the other. Analyzing the Pareto optimal solutions reveals the trade-off between multiple objectives. Additionally, the Pareto set provided a range of optimal solutions, allowing keyboard designers and developers to pick the desirable one according to their preferences.

We adopted the Metropolis optimization algorithm [25] to search for the Pareto set. The process was composed of multiple sub processes. Each sub process started from a random set of the 21 parameters in the range [0, 5], the estimated range of the parameter values based on the analysis of the algorithm. The sub process then optimized the 21 parameters for the objective function (Eq. 4) based on the collected development dataset:

$$Z = \alpha W + (1 - \alpha)S \quad \text{Eq. 4}$$

which is a sum of word score (W) and keystroke saving ratio (S) with a weight α ($0 \leq \alpha \leq 1$). α was randomized at the beginning of each sub process and remained unchanged during the sub process. α changed across sub processes. Our purpose was to ensure that the Pareto set covered a broad range of Pareto optimal solutions.

In each iteration of a sub process, the 21 parameters moved in a random direction with a fixed step length (0.01). We then evaluated the keyboard algorithm with the new parameters against the development dataset according to the objective function (Eq. 4). Whether the new set of parameters and search direction were kept was determined by the Metropolis function:

$$W(O \rightarrow N) = \begin{cases} e^{\frac{\Delta Z}{kT}} \; if \; \Delta Z < 0 \\ 1 \quad if \Delta Z \geq 0 \end{cases} \quad \text{Eq. 5}$$

$W(O \rightarrow N)$ was the probability of changing from the parameter set O (old) to the parameter set N (new); $\Delta Z = Z_{new} - Z_{old}$, where Z_{new}, and Z_{old} were values of objective functions (Eq. 4) for the new and old set of parameters respectively; k was a coefficient; T was "temperature", which can be interactively adjusted.

This optimization algorithm used a simulated annealing method. The search did not always move toward a higher value of objective function. It occasionally allowed moves with negative objective function value changes to be able to climb out of a local minimum.

After each iteration, the new solution was compared with the solutions in the Pareto set. If the new solution dominated at least one solution in the Pareto set, it would be added to the set and the solutions dominated by the new solution would be discarded.

After 1000 iterations, the sub process restarted with another random set of parameters and a random α for the objective function Eq. 4. We ensured that there was at least one sub process for each of the following three weights: $\alpha = 0, 0.5,$ and 1. The optimization led to a Pareto set of 101 Pareto optimal solutions after 100 sub processes with 100,000 iterations in total, which constituted a Pareto frontier illustrated in Figure 3.

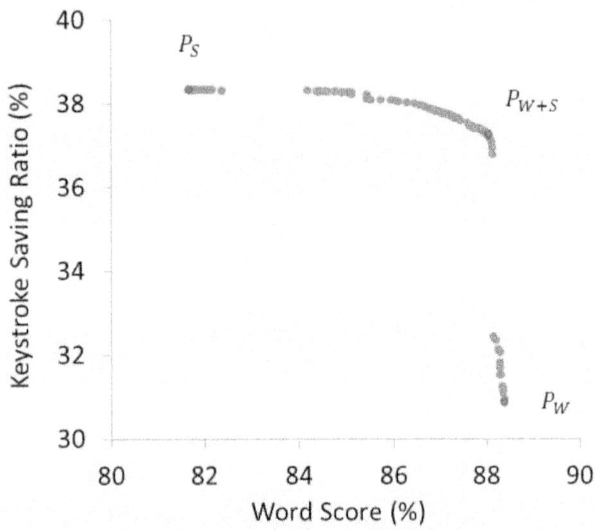

Figure 3. The Pareto frontier of the multi-objective optimization. The three red dots were solutions with the most word score (P_w), the most keystroke savings (P_S), and the highest $0.5W + 0.5S$ (P_{W+S}) respectively.

The Pareto frontier shows that the Pareto optimal solutions distribute in a small region, with keystroke saving ratio ranging from 30% to 38% and word score ranging from 81% to 88%. As shown in Figure 3, the Pareto frontier forms a short, convex, L-shaped curve, indicating that correction and completion have little conflict with each other and the algorithm can be simultaneously optimized for both with minor loss to each. Among the 101 Pareto optimal solutions, we are particularly interested in three solutions, illustrated in red dots in Figure 3:

1) The solution with the highest word score (W), denoted by P_w. It is the solution exclusively optimized for correction.
2) The solution with the highest keystroke saving ratio (S), denoted by P_S. It is the solution exclusively optimized for completion.
3) The solution with highest $0.5W + 0.5S$, denoted by P_{W+S}. It is the solution optimized for both correction and completion, with 50% weight for each objective.

P_w and P_S reveal the highest correction and completion capabilities a keyboard can reach, while P_{W+S} is the most balanced solution with equal weights for correction and completion. The parameter sets, correction and completion capabilities for P_w, P_S and P_{W+S} are reported in Table 2.

The optimization results showed the default parameter set taken from the AOSP keyboard in Android 4.3 (Sep. 16, 2013) was sub-optimal in both correction and completion according to the criteria and the development dataset used in this study P_w, P_S, and P_{W+S} all improve the word score and keystroke saving ratio by at least 10% over $P_{Baseline}$.

It is more illuminating to compare the three Pareto optimal solutions P_w, P_S, and P_{W+S}, since they are all optimized under identical conditions with the same dataset. Table 2 shows that P_{W+S} is close to P_S in keystroke saving ratio, and close to P_w in word score. It indicates simultaneously optimizing for both objectives causes only minor performance degradation for each objective. These results were later verified with the separate test dataset.

Parameters moved in various directions after the optimization. For such a complex optimization problem with 21 free parameters, it was difficult to precisely explain why each parameter moved in such a direction after the optimization. However, we observed some distinct patterns of parameter value changes, which partially explain the performance differences across keyboards.

For examples, the parameters pertinent to the cost of proximity of touch points to letters (i.e., PROXIMITY_COST, FIRST_PROXIMITY_COST) decreased substantially from $P_{Baseline}$ to P_w, P_S, and P_{W+S}, indicating that the optimized algorithms tend to be more tolerant to errors in spatial signals. The cost of untyped letters in a word (i.e., COST_FIRST_LOOKAHEAD) also decreased, indicating that the optimized algorithms were more likely to predict untyped letters as the user's intention, especially after typing the first letter, to save keystrokes.

EVALUTING KEYBOARD ALGORITHMS

To test the external validity of the optimization results, we evaluate the keyboard algorithms before and after the optimization using the test dataset, which was collected from 24 users not participating in the development dataset collection.

Correction

Word Score. We first analyzed the word scores for different keyboards. An ANOVA showed that the keyboard algorithm had a significant main effect on word score ($F_{3,69} = 58.379$, $p < 0.001$). The mean (SD) scores were 82.7% (9.1%) for $P_{Baseline}$, 91.0% (4.9%) for P_{W+S}, and 86.9% (7.9%) for P_S, and 91.2%(4.6%) for P_w. Pairwise mean comparison showed the differences were significant for each pair ($p < 0.001$) except for P_w vs. P_{W+S}. ($p = 0.509$). Figure 4 also shows the mean (SD) word score per word length. As shown, P_w, and P_{W+S} performed almost equally well across all word lengths. The biggest gap between these

	$P_{Baseline}$	P_w	P_S	P_{W+S}
Word Score	**77.5%**	**88.4%**	**81.7%**	**88.0%**
Keystroke Saving Ratio	**20%**	**30.9%**	**38.3%**	**37.3%**
Parameters				
DISTANCE_WEIGHT_LENGTH	0.132	0.052	0.412	0.172
PROXIMITY_COST	0.086	0	0	0
FIRST_PROXIMITY_COST	0.104	0.01	0.08	0.05
OMISSION_COST	0.458	0.048	0.458	0.108
OMISSION_COST_SAME_CHAR	0.491	1.371	0.991	0.951
OMISSION_COST_FIRST_CHAR	0.582	0.092	0.582	0.382
INSERTION_COST	0.730	1.17	1.13	0.740
INSERTION_COST_SAME_CHAR	0.586	0.01	0.08	0
INSERTION_COST_FIRST_CHAR	0.623	0.753	0.613	0.583
TRANSPOSITION_COST	0.516	0.576	0.436	0.436
SPACE_SUBSTITUTION_COST	0.319	0.22	0.210	0.06
ADDITIONAL_PROXIMITY_COST	0.380	1.20	1.08	1.06
SUBSTITUTION_COST	0.403	1.603	1.143	1.143
COST_NEW_WORD	0.042	0.12	0.02	0.332
COST_SECOND_OR_LATER_WORD_FIRST_CHAR_UPPERCASE	0.25	0.69	0.370	0.09
DISTANCE_WEIGHT_LANGUAGE	1.123	1.783	1.463	1.573
COST_FIRST_LOOKAHEAD	0.545	0.053	0	0.095
COST_LOOKAHEAD	0.073	0.08	0	0
HAS_PROXIMITY_TERMINAL_COST	0.105	0.20	0.11	0.04
HAS_EDIT_CORRECTION_TERMINAL_COST	0.038	1.098	1.418	0.998
HAS_MULTI_WORD_TERMINAL_COST	0.444	1.434	0.994	1.224

Table 2. Word Scores, Keystroke Saving Ratios and Parameters for the algorithm before ($P_{Baseline}$), and after (P_{W+S}, P_w, P_S) the optimization. The blue indicates the parameters decreased and red means the values increased after the optimization.

two keyboards was for words with 7+ characters: the word score of P_W was 1.5% higher. Both P_W, and P_{W+S} performed better than $P_{Baseline}$ and P_S across all word lengths, especially for words with 5 or more letters. The word scores for P_W, and P_{W+S} were at least 14% (absolute) higher than $P_{Baseline}$ and 6% higher than P_S.

Ratio of Error Reduction. In addition to word score, we also examined the keyboard's capability of correcting users' erroneous input strings, which is measured in *Ratio of Error Reduction (RER)* [3]. RER is defined as:

$$RER = \frac{E_{literal} - E_{transcribed}}{E_{literal}} \times 100\% \quad \text{Eq. 6}$$

$E_{literal}$ is the error rate of the literal text, which reflects a user's uncorrected keyboard output. The literal text is generated from the closest key labels on the keyboard to users' actual touch points. This is a naïve key-detection algorithm that offers no error correction, and literally transcribes the user's touch points. Since the test data set was segmented into words, $E_{literal}$ is measured as:

$$E_{literal} = \frac{\text{number of incorrect words in the literal text}}{\text{number of tatal words}} \quad \text{Eq. 7}$$

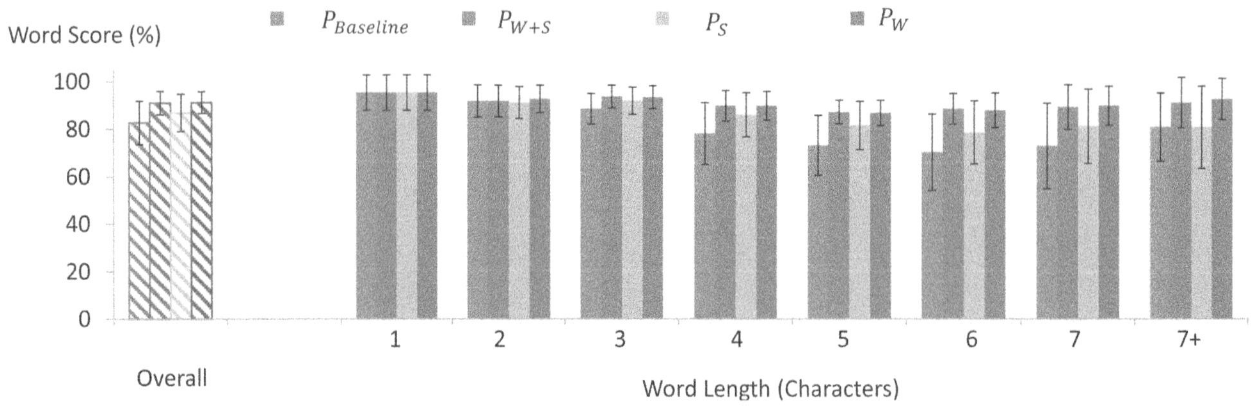

Figure 4. Mean (SD) word scores across 24 participants for $P_{Baseline}$, P_{W+S}, P_S, and P_w. The striped bars show overall results and solid bars show results per word length.

$E_{transcribed}$ is the error rate of the transcribed text, the output of a keyboard. It is defined as:

$$E_{transcribed} = 1 - \text{word score} \quad \text{Eq. 8}$$

Note that RER is applicable only when $E_{literal} > 0$.

The analysis showed that $E_{literal}$ is 28.8%. The RERs were 40.9% for $P_{Baseline}$, 70.0% for P_{W+S}, 54.5% for P_S and 70.4% for P_w. P_{W+S} was close to P_w in correcting users' input errors. Both of them corrected 30% more errors than $P_{Baseline}$, and 15% more than P_S.

Table 3 shows examples of correction for different keyboards.

Literal	Intended	$P_{Baseline}$	P_S	P_w and P_{W+S}
agsim	again	agsim	agsim	again
popilariry	popularity	popular	popularity	popularity
quivj	quick	quivj	quivj	quick

Table 3. Correction examples for keyboards. Words in red are erroneous literal text or incorrect corrections.

Completion

We examined the keystroke saving ratio for different keyboards. An ANOVA showed a significant main effect of keyboard on keystroke saving ratio ($F_{3,69} = 7531, p < 0.001$). The mean (SD) keystroke saving ratios were 18.5% (1.0%) for $P_{Baseline}$, 36.2% (9.8%) for P_{W+S}, and 37.7% (1.2%) for P_S, and 30.3%(1.2%) for P_W. Pairwise mean comparison showed that the differences were significant between every two conditions ($p < 0.005$).

Figure 5 also shows the mean(SD) keystroke saving ratio per word length. The keystroke saving ratio for P_S was slightly higher than P_{W+S}, but the difference between them was small. The biggest difference was for words with 7 characters, where the keystroke saving ratio of P_S was 3% higher than that of P_{W+S}. Both P_{W+S} and P_S saved more keystrokes than $P_{Baseline}$ and P_W, especially for words with 5 or more characters: P_{W+S} and P_S saved more than 20% keystrokes than $P_{Baseline}$, and 7% more than P_W for these words. Table 4 showed examples of keystroke savings for these keyboards.

$P_{Baseline}$	P_{W+S}	P_S	P_W
provide	**prov**ide	**prov**ide	**prov**ide
favorite	**fav**orite	**fav**orite	**fav**orite
watch	**watc**h	**watc**h	**watc**h

Table 4. Examples of completion for different keyboards Letters predicted by a keyboard are illustrated in gray and typed letters are in bold black.

Dataset-Independent Keystroke Saving Ratio. The keystroke saving ratios illustrated in Figure 5 were calculated based on the test dataset collected from a prior user study. In addition, we estimated keystroke saving ratios based on an assumption of perfect input: each touch point was placed on the center of the intended key. This method separated the effect of a particular data set, and also simulated the behaviors of one type of users who type extremely carefully and accurately. Such results were complementary to the results in Figure 5, which simulated the behavior of experts who usually typed ahead and always trusted keyboards' correction and completion capabilities.

Assuming perfect input, the keystroke saving ratios were 20.9% for $P_{Baseline}$, 37.9% for P_{W+S}, 39.9% for P_S, and 32.5% for P_W, based on the same set of words in the test data set. They were approximately 2% higher than the corresponding values estimated from the test data set. The results also echoed the finding shown in Figure 5: P_{W+S} and P_S were close in keystroke saving, and both of them were considerably better than $P_{Baseline}$ and P_W.

Discussion

Correction and completion have only a minor conflict. The algorithm simultaneously optimized for two objectives (i.e., P_{W+S}) performs almost equally well with the algorithms optimized for one objective only (i.e., P_w and P_S), in the corresponding measure. The word score of P_{W+S} has no significant difference from that of P_w: both of them are able

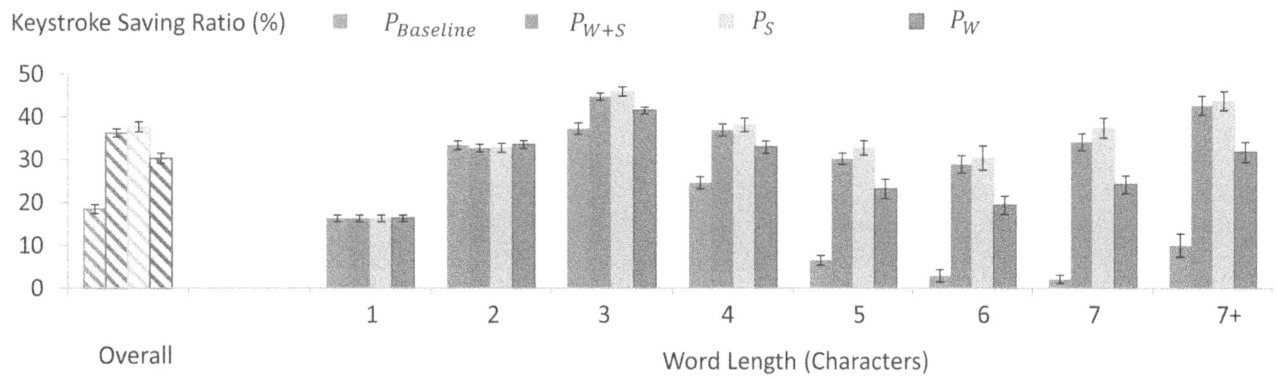

Figure 5. Mean (SD) keystroke saving ratios across 24participnts for $P_{Baseline}$, P_{W+S}, P_S and P_W. The striped bars show overall results and solid bars show results per word length.

to correctly recognize around 91% of the words. P_S is slightly better than P_{W+S} in completion (1.5% higher), but at the cost of having a significantly lower word score (4.1% lower).

This finding suggests that it is possible to simultaneously optimize a keyboard algorithm for both correction and completion at the same time, with little compromise compared to the specialized models that are optimized for only one objective.

Pareto optimization improves a keyboard's correction and completion capabilities. The results (Figure 4) shows that P_{W+S} improves the word score by 8.3%, and keystroke saving ratio by 17.7% over $P_{Baseline}$ based on the test dataset, echoing the findings from the development dataset (Figure 5). These results indicate that the proposed method based on the Pareto optimization and the Metropolis algorithm is an effective approach of improving keyboard algorithm quality.

The improvements are more pronounced for long words. P_{W+S} improves the word score by 14% and the keystroke saving by 20% for words with 5 or more letters, over $P_{Baseline}$. P_{W+S} is also more effective than $P_{Baseline}$ in correcting users' input errors: it reduces users' input error by 70% while $P_{Baseline}$ only reduces input error by 40.9%.

LIMITATIONS AND FUTURE WORK

The datasets used this paper were collected in a Wizard of Oz setting, and covered a vocabulary of common English words. As a result, the optimal values for the parameters may change as the usage environment and/or vocabulary become more diverse We plan to further expand this work to larger and more diverse data sets, both from lab studies and long-term longitudinal studies.

We employed a remulation-based approach [3] to evaluate keyboard algorithms, which measured the correction and completion power a keyboard algorithm can offer, but did not evaluate the entire user experience of a touchscreen keyboard. How and to what degree a user can take advantage of a keyboard's correction and completion power depends on the UI design, users' preferences and bias in motor, visual and cognitive effort trade-offs, However, based on the success of popular mobile and for example CJK (Chinese, Japanese, Korean) text input methods, it is safe to say both correction and completion are desirable features. One question was whether completion be done without significant loss of correction power for the user, which this work is focused on.

The same proposed Pareto optimization process may be applicable for various keyboard algorithms. Due to the limited scope one paper can cover and the accessibility of the keyboard algorithms, we only applied it to a variant of the AOSP keyboard. It would be interesting to apply it to other keyboards, to examine the shape of the Pareto frontiers, and to investigate the improvements it can bring.

CONCLUSIONS

Although correction and completion are featured in almost all modern touchscreen keyboards, their relationship has not been studied in the research literature. The present work explores the optimality issues of them, resulting in the following contributions.

First, the work suggests that correction and completion have only a minor conflict with each other. It is possible to optimize a keyboard algorithm for both at the same time, with no compromise to correction, and only a minor compromise to completion. Before this investigation, it was unknown whether this would be possible because one could imagine that optimizing for one objective would come at a large cost for the other.

Second, we demonstrated the effectiveness of applying a Pareto optimization method based on the Metropolis algorithm to improve the correction and completion of a keyboard algorithm. Our investigation based on an variant of AOSP keyboard showed that a keyboard after the optimization (i.e., P_{W+S}) improved the word score by 8.3% and keystroke saving ratio by 17.7% over the keyboard before the optimization (i.e., $P_{Baseline}$) . The methods developed in this work can be applied to other keyboards with minor modifications.

REFERENCES

1. Android Open Source Project http://source.android.com/
2. Azenkot, S. and Zhai, S. (2012). Touch Behavior with Different Postures on Soft Smart Phone Keyboards. *Proc. of MobileHCI'12*. 251-260.
3. Bi, X., Azenkot, S., Partridge, K., Zhai, S. (2013) Octopus: Evaluating Touchscreen Keyboard Correction and Recognition Algorithms via *Remulation, Proc. of CHI'13*, 543 – 552.
4. Bi, X., Smith, B., Zhai. S. (2010) Quasi-Qwerty Soft Keyboard Optimization , *Proc. of CHI'10*, 283~286.
5. Bi, X., Smith, B., Zhai. S. (2012) Multilingual Touchscreen Keyboard Design and Optimization. *Human-Computer Interaction* , Volume 27, Issue 4, 352-382.
6. Dunlop, M. and Levine, J. (2012) Multidimensional pareto optimization of touchscreen keyboards for speed, familiarity and improved spell checking. *Proc. of CHI'12*, 2669-2678.
7. Matthias Ehrgott (2005). *Multicriteria Optimization. Birkhäuser*. ISBN 978-3-540-21398-7.
8. Findlater, L., and Wobbrock, J.O. (2012). Personalized input: improving ten-finger touchscreen typing through automatic adaptation. *Proc. of CHI '12*. 815-824.
9. Getschow, C. O., Rosen, M. J., and Goodenough-Trepagnier, C. (1986). A systematic approach to design a minimum distance alphabetical keyboard. *Proc. of RESNA (Rehabilitation Engineering Society of North America) 9th Annual Conference*, 396-398.
10. Goel, M., Findlater, L. and Wobbrock, J. (2012) WalkType: using accelerometer data to accomodate situational impairments in mobile touch screen text entry. In *Proc. of CHI '12*. 2687-2696.
11. Goel, M., Jansen, A., Mandel, T., Patel, S., and Wobbrock. J. (2013) ContextType: using hand posture information to improve mobile touch screen text entry. *Proc. of CHI '13*, 2795-2798.
12. Goodman, J., Venolia, G., Steury, K., and Parker, C. (2002). Language modeling for soft keyboards. *Proc. of AAAI '02*, 419-424.
13. Higginbotham, J. (1992) Evaluation of keystroke savings across five assistive communication technologies *Augmentative and Alternative Communication* Vol. 8, No. 4 , 258-272.
14. Kane, K. S, Wobbrock, J., Harniss, M., and Johnson, K. (2008) TrueKeys: identifying and correcting typing errors for people with motor impairments. *Proc. of IUI'08*, 349-352.
15. Koester, H. H., Levine, S. P. (1994) Modeling the speed of text entry with a word prediction interface, *IEEE Transactions on Rehabilitation Engineering*, Volume: 2 Issue: 3 177 – 187.
16. Kristensson, P-O., Zhai, S. (2005) Relaxing Stylus Typing Precision by Geometric Pattern Matching. *Proc. IUI'05*, 151–158,
17. MacKenzie, I. S., and Soukoreff, R. W. (2003). Phrase sets for evaluating text entry techniques. *Proc. of CHI EA '03*, 754-755.
18. MacKenzie, I. S., and Tanaka-Ishii, K. (Eds.). (2007). *Text Entry Systems: Mobility, Accessibility, Universality*: Morgan Kaufmann Publishers.
19. MacKenzie, I. S., and Zhang, S. X. (1999) The design and evaluation of a high-performance soft keyboard. *Proc. of CHI '99*, 25-31.
20. Nielsen. nielsen.com/us/en/newswire/2010/u-s-teen-mobile-report-calling-yesterday-texting-today-using-apps-tomorrow.html
21. Oulasvirta, A., Reichel, A., Li, W., Zhang, Y., Bachnynskyi, M., Vertanen, K. and Kristensson, P.O. (2013) Improving two-thumb text entry on touchscreen devices. *Proc of CHI*. 2765 – 2774.
22. Time.com techland.time.com/2011/07/21/study-fewer-than-50-of-smartphone-users-make-calls/
23. Wobbrock, J.O. (2007). Measures of text entry performance. Chapter 3 in I.S. MacKenzie and K. Tanaka-Ishii (eds.), Text Entry Systems: Mobility, Accessibility, Universality. San Francisco: Morgan Kaufmann, pp. 47-74.
24. Yin, Y., Ouyang, T., Partridge, K., and Zhai, S. (2013) Making touchscreen keyboards adaptive to keys, hand postures, and individuals: a hierarchical spatial backoff model approach. *Proc. of CHI '13*. 2775-2784.
25. Zhai, S., Hunter, M., & Smith, B. A. (2000). The Metropolis Keyboard - an exploration of quantitative techniques for virtual keyboard design. *Proc. of UIST'00*. 119-218.
26. Zhai, S., Hunter, M., & Smith, B. A. (2002). Performance optimization of virtual keyboards. Human-Computer Interaction, 17(2,3), 89-129.

Uncertain Text Entry on Mobile Devices

Daryl Weir[1], **Henning Pohl**[2], **Simon Rogers**[1], **Keith Vertanen**[3], **Per Ola Kristensson**[4]
[1]University of Glasgow, UK, [2]University of Hannover, Germany,
[3]Montana Tech, Montana, USA, [4]University of St Andrews, UK
darylw@dcs.gla.ac.uk, henning.pohl@hci.uni-hannover.de, simon.rogers@glasgow.ac.uk,
kvertanen@mtech.edu, pok@st-andrews.ac.uk

ABSTRACT
Users often struggle to enter text accurately on touchscreen keyboards. To address this, we present a flexible decoder for touchscreen text entry that combines probabilistic touch models with a language model. We investigate two different touch models. The first touch model is based on a Gaussian Process regression approach and implicitly models the inherent uncertainty of the touching process. The second touch model allows users to explicitly control the uncertainty via touch pressure. Using the first model we show that the character error rate can be reduced by up to 7% over a baseline method, and by up to 1.3% over a leading commercial keyboard. Using the second model we demonstrate that providing users with control over input certainty reduces the amount of text users have to correct manually and increases the text entry rate.

Author Keywords
Mobile text entry; keyboard error correction

ACM Classification Keywords
H.5.2 [Information Interfaces and Presentation]: User Interfaces—*Input devices and strategies, Interaction styles*

INTRODUCTION
Touchscreen keyboard input is inherently *uncertain*. This uncertainty stems from a number of sources. When trying to press a key, users often touch a location offset from their intended target—this is the well known *Fat Finger Problem* [32]. Further, users might be unsure about the spelling of some words, leading to incorrect input. Finally, touch sensor readings also introduce a degree of uncertainty.

There is a growing body of research on using probabilistic techniques to model this uncertainty in order to improve the performance of touch interactions. For text entry, there are two primary approaches. The first is offset modelling, which aims to predict the intended touch target given the recorded touch location. Weir et al. [37] used a Gaussian Process (GP) regression approach to predict the distributions over possible touch locations. Goodman et al. [9], Kristensson and Vertanen

CHI 2014, April 26–May 01, 2014, Toronto, ON, Canada.

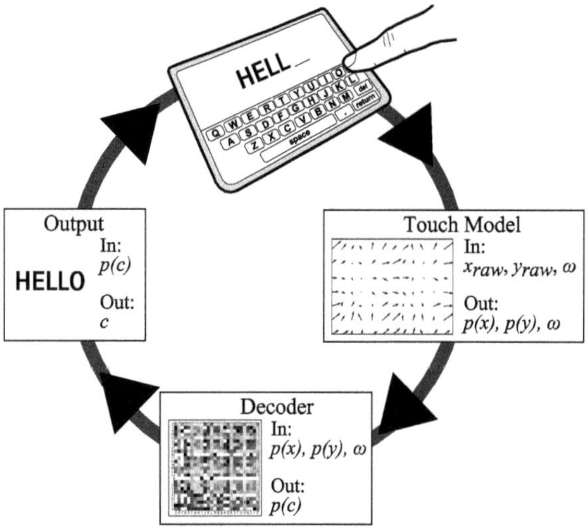

Figure 1. We present an autocorrect method for typing on a pressure-sensitive touchscreen. Given a touch location (x_{raw}, y_{raw}) and a touch pressure (ω), a touch model assigns probabilities to keys while a language model assigns probabilities to possible words. A decoder algorithm combines these to make a prediction on the entered text. Pressure information can be used to control the text correction behavior.

[17] and Bi and Zhai [2] used information about the location of on-screen targets to obtain the probability that a given touch was meant for a given target. The second approach is language modelling, using statistical properties of text to obtain the most likely interpretation of a stream of key presses. For example, Goodman et al. [9] showed that it was possible to reduce error rates by a factor of 1.67 to 1.87.

We present a flexible decoder that combines state-of-the-art probabilistic touch models with a long-span language model (Figure 1). Our decoder searches for the most likely text given the uncertainty of the tap locations, possible missing key presses, and possible extra key presses. Using our decoder we have tested a variety of correction strategies, such as whether the decoder is free to change previous characters.

We consider two touch models representing different approaches to modelling and controlling touch uncertainty. The first is GPType, which uses a GP to model user specific touch offsets and their variance in different areas of the screen. The GP is based on training data and hidden from the user. Thus GPType represents an *implicit* uncertainty model, mirroring existing autocorrection techniques in commercial devices.

In our second system, ForceType, we allow users to explicitly control the level of uncertainity in their input via pressure information. This gives users control over the relative influence of the language model (LM) and allows them to handle situations where typical correction systems might fail. For example, when typing words not found in the training corpus of the LMs, mixing languages, or using slang words, text may be autocorrected to something unintended. Using existing systems, users have to take action to revert to the entered text. While users can be casual and allow their phones to correct their mistakes for most text, they can elevate their level of control for phrases where they feel the autocorrection algorithm may go astray.

RELATED WORK

Text Entry Correction Approaches

Several on-screen keyboard correction methods have been explored in the literature [16]. Goodman et al. [9] were the first to combine a language model and a touch model to increase accuracy on soft keyboards. They determined the best key sequence for a touch sequence by maximizing the likelihood, significantly reducing error rates. Kristensson and Zhai [20] presented an alternative approach that used pattern matching to identify the words that most likely corresponded to users' tap sequences. Gunawardana et al. [10] presented an approach with dynamic key-target resizing which defined a minimum target size, preventing key targets from shrinking too much. Rudchenko et al. [29], with their *Text Text Revolution* game, showed that per-user touch models and personalized key-target resizing can further improve typing accuracy. Kristensson and Zhai [19] presented the gesture keyboard *Shark²*, which combined a shorthand writing system with a language model. Goel et al. [8] showed how accelerometer data can be used to correct typing errors resulting from inaccuracies due to walking.

Offset Modelling

On any touchscreen device, the location a user touches and the location the user *intended* to touch are offset. This has been studied as a perception problem based on how users target things hidden by their fingers [14]. This is also caused in part by the softness of the finger causing a large touch area—the so-called *Fat Finger Problem* [32].

A body of research exists based on modelling and correcting touch offsets. For example, Henze et al. [11] collected millions of touches in an Android typing game and modelled offsets using polynomials to improve text entry accuracy. Weir et al. [37] demonstrated offset modelling using a GP regression model, and in particular showed the importance of user specificity in offset models. Bi and Zhai [1] extend Fitts' law to finger touch using a dual Gaussian distribution approach. Bi and Zhai [2] further extend this to handle target selection on a touchscreen using their *Bayesian touch criterion*, demonstrating a significant increase in accuracy.

Pressure Input

Pressure has been used in interactive systems for a wide range of applications. Ramos et al. [26]'s *pressure widgets*, showed how stylus pressure can be used in selection tasks and how many pressure levels can be discriminated. *Force Gestures* by Heo et al. [12] augmented tapping and dragging operations with pressure to extend the available gesture set. A more general investigation of pressure-based interaction was done by Stewart et al. [34] who looked at how holding a device influences target acquisition times.

There is some work on combining typing with pressure data. For keypads, McCallum et al. [23] showed how pressure-based disambiguation allows faster text entry than multi-tap. Shi et al. [31] showed that using a fisheye function for pressure-based selection reduces error rates. Brewster and Hughes [3] used pressure to allow the selection of letter case when typing. Clarkson et al. [5] presented a way of marking messages as urgent when typed more forcefully which is similar to our approach of giving more weight to more forceful typing. In *One-press control* [6], pressure is used to create a new set of modifier keys. *TypeRight* [13] is a physical keyboard that prevents errors by increasing the resistance of keys for out of vocabulary (OOV) words.

Autonomy Handover

The ForceType system presented in this paper allows users to influence how much control they want to give to autocorrection. Flemish et al. [7] referred to this concept as the *H-metaphor* and liken it to riding a horse where people can 'loosen or tighten the reins' to vary their level of control. Williamson [38] looked at interactions as a control process, where the level of uncertainty influences how much control is exerted and what kind of feedback has to be provided. Uncertain input for GUIs has been investigated by Schwarz et al. [30], who tried to enable vague input handling for standard widgets. Pohl and Murray Smith [25] frame the change of control as a *casual interaction continuum*, where users themselves choose how much they want to engage, allowing them to refrain from tight control when close interaction with their device is frowned upon socially.

THE GPTYPE SYSTEM

GPType is a correction system consisting of three parts: (1) a LM which assigns probabilities to sequences of text, (2) a touch model, which assigns probabilities to each key on a keyboard given a touch location, and (3) a decoder which combines the LM and touch model probabilities and decodes what the user was trying to type.

Language Model

We adapted a language model that has previously been used for a thumb-typing touchscreen keyboard [24]. The Twitter-based language model was trained based on 778M tweets sent between 12/2010 and 6/2012. Duplicate tweets, retweets, and non-English-language tweets were eliminated via a language-identification module [21] (with a confidence of 95%). Based on a tweet's source string we removed all tweets that did not originate from a mobile device. Tweets were split into sentences and we only kept sentences where all words existed in a list of 330K words drawn from Wiktionary, Webster's dictionary, the CMU pronouncing dictionary, and GNU aspell. The final dataset consisted of 94.6 M sentences, 626 M words, and 2.56 G characters.

The language model was built using the SRILM toolkit using a vocabulary of A-Z, space, apostrophe, comma, period, exclamation point and question mark. The character-based 7-gram language model was smoothed using Witten-Bell and no count cutoffs. The model was then entropy-pruned to reduce the memory footprint in anticipation of using the model on a mobile device. The final model had 225 K n-grams and a compressed disk size of 2.0 MB.

Touch Model

To generate input probabilities for the decoder, we use GP regression to model each user's touch offset function. GPs are flexible, non-parametric statistical tools commonly used for regression and classification. Given 2D touch locations $\mathbf{s} = (x, y)$, the GP learns a function which maps to the offsets (Δ_x, Δ_y). The GP is defined in terms of its mean function $\mu(\mathbf{s})$, which we choose to be zero since in the absence of data we wish to predict no offset, and its covariance function $C(\mathbf{s}_n, \mathbf{s}_m)$, which defines how similar the n-th and m-th outputs should be given the corresponding inputs. A full treatment of GP regression and classification is given in [27], and an example of using a GP for touch offset modelling can be found in [37].

Following Weir et al.[37], we choose a linear combination of a linear and a Gaussian covariance function:

$$C(\mathbf{s}_n, \mathbf{s}_m) = a\mathbf{s}_n^T\mathbf{s}_m + (1-a)\exp\left\{-\gamma||\mathbf{s}_n - \mathbf{s}_m||_2^2\right\},$$

where a controls the relative influence of the terms, and γ is the scale parameter of the Gaussian function.

The advantage of the GP over a parametric method such as a polynomial (used in e.g. [11]) is that the prediction is a distribution over possible offset values. For text entry, we use this to obtain probabilities over the different keys on the keyboard for a given touch. The probability of a given key is found by integrating the density function of the predictive Gaussian over the rectangular area of the key. In practice this is not possible analytically, so we approximate the probability by sampling from the Gaussian, counting which keys the samples fall into, and then normalising these counts to obtain probabilities.

The sizes of the predictive Gaussians, and consequently the probabilities produced by the model, are learned from training data. Thus, in areas of the screen where the offsets are more variable, the Gaussians are larger and the probabilities more diffuse. This gives the language model more latitude to correct inputs in these areas. The GP models the uncertainty in the touch interaction and uses information about that uncertainty to make predictions. This is an advantage over other probabilistic approaches, such as that proposed by Bi and Zhai [2], which model the touch uncertainty with fixed parameters for all users. The tradeoff is that users must provide calibration touches before using the system.

Decoder

We created a decoder which searches for the most probable character sequence given a sequence of taps. Each "tap" is in reality a probability distribution over every keyboard character. These tap distributions were set according to the GP tap model as well as the ForceType model.

As we will describe shortly, we explored four different correction strategies in our interface. Each strategy involved changing how much of the tap sequence the decoder was allowed to change. To facilitate this, the decoder allows some taps to be marked as fixed. Fixed taps served as language model context, but were not eligible for change during the decoder's search.

The decoder searches in the space of all possible character sequences for the non-fixed taps in an observed sequence. During this search, a tap would most likely generate the actual key hit. But the decoder also allows substitution with all other possible keys according to the provided tap distribution.

Our decoder allows an observed tap to be deleted without generating a character. Similarly, it explores inserting all possible characters without consuming an observation. Both insertion and deletion hypotheses incur a configurable penalty.

During its search, the decoder makes use of a character language model. As each output character is generated, we combine the tap probability with the probability of the character given the language model by taking a weighted product. The relative contribution of the tap distribution and the language model is controlled by a configurable scale factor.

The search over all possible character sequences is exponential in the length of the sequence. Pruning is thus critical to ensure real-time performance. During its search, any hypothesis that becomes less probable then the current best answer is pruned. Additionally, we employed beam width pruning. In beam width pruning, the decoder tracks the best hypothesis found thus far for each position in the tap sequence. Hypotheses that are too improbable (i.e. outside the beam width) compared to the best one at a particular position are pruned. By varying the beam width, we can control the speed accuracy tradeoff during recognition. The free parameters of the decoder were optimized with respect to the data we used to learn the GP probabilities.

STUDY 1: GP AND CORRECTION STRATEGIES

In order to build our text correction system, we required training data. This data came in two parts: (1) training points for the GP offset model, and (2) typing data to which we could apply various correction strategies to identify the optimal technique. This section details the procedure conducted to collect this data and the details of the resulting model.

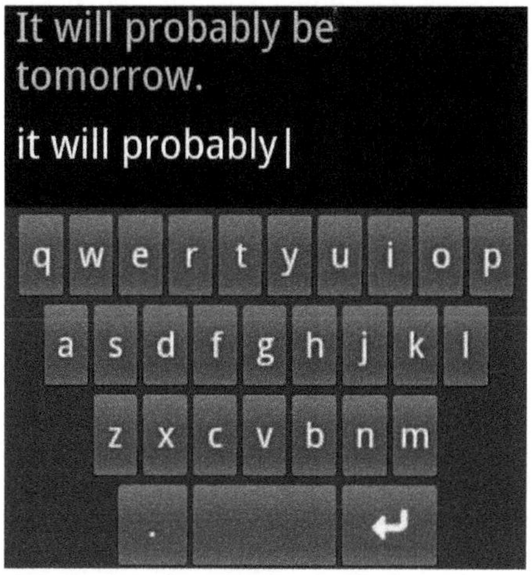

Figure 2. A screenshot of our logging application. The target phrase, the currently entered text and our simplified keyboard are shown.

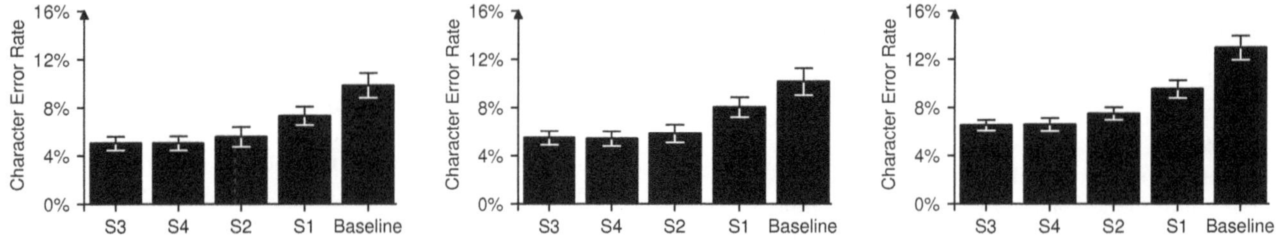

(a) Sitting (b) Standing (c) Walking

Figure 3. Character error rates after applying our four different correction strategies to the typing data gathered in our model building study, separated by mobility condition (Study 1). Plots show mean and standard error across all participants. The baseline method represents the literal keys touched.

We built our models based on data collected from 10 participants (4 female) who volunteered for three 45 minute sessions. Participants ranged in age from 19–31 (mean = 25.4, sd = 4.25). All participants were smartphone owners, and rated themselves as intermediate to expert users of touchscreen devices. At the end of the data collection period, participants were paid £10 for their time.

To collect training data for the GP, we built a custom keyboard running on a *Samsung Galaxy SII* smartphone, with Android version 4.0. The keyboard had a simplified layout consisting only of the alphabetic keys, space bar, period and an enter key. Participants were asked to press a sequence of keys until 10 presses were logged for each key. When a key was pressed, the keyboard logged the time and touch location, as well as the location of the center of the requested key. Touches which were more than 3 key widths from the intended key were filtered out, as these were deemed likely to be mistakes. Participants repeated this process in three mobility conditions: sitting, standing, and walking. We chose not to use a pace setter for the walking condition, instead asking participants to move at whatever speed they were comfortable walking and typing. Participants walked in a set path, and their laps were timed so that walking speed could be determined. We trained our GPs offline using MATLAB. The covariance function parameters were optimised on a user specific basis using 10-fold cross validation to find the model which minimised the RMS error between the offset touch locations and the centers of the target keys. The implicit assumption that users target the key center is without loss of generality—if in truth they target some other feature, the offsets would simply be shifted.

Each participant also provided typing data. We used phrases from the Enron Mobile Email dataset [36] as stimuli. This phrase set consists of phrases drawn from genuine mobile emails and has been shown to result in similar text entry performance as the MacKenzie and Soukoreff [22] phrase set [18]. We filtered out any phrases containing characters not on our keyboard, and then removed sentences with fewer than 4 or more than 10 words. This left a set of 427 phrases. Participants were shown a random subset of these and asked to type them as quickly and accurately as possible using our custom keyboard. As there was no backspace key, participants had to leave any mistakes uncorrected. This was done so that we could evaluate the quality of our model's corrections on the text as entered. During each of the three sessions, participants typed for 10 minutes in each mobility condition. The order of mobility conditions was counterbalanced across both participant and session. Participants were instructed to hold the phone in two hands and type with their thumbs. The stream of touches for each typing session was passed through the best GP for that participant to obtain offset touch locations and key press probabilities. These probabilities were then passed through the decoder to obtain the corrected sentences. We evaluated four correction strategies:

S1 Single-Key Correction—for each key press, we input the letter with the highest combined LM/GP probability, holding all previously entered characters fixed.

S2 Modifiable Context Correction—as S1, except that the decoder is also free to change previously entered letters.

S3 Word Correction—when the user types a word delimiter (space or period), the system uses the LM and GP to identify the most likely word, holding previously entered words as fixed context.

S4 Single-Key + Word Correction—combination of S1 & S3.

We measured performance in terms of the character error rate (CER) after correction, averaged across all phrases and all users for a given mobility condition. CER is the number of characters that need to be inserted, substituted, or deleted in order to transform the corrected text into the reference text, divided by the number of characters in the reference text. For each correction strategy, we also tested a range of values for the cost and maximum number of insertions and deletions, the beam width of the decoder's search, and the relative scaling of the probabilities from the LM and GP.

Our results are summarised in Figure 3. These plots show the mean CER achieved for each correction strategy, along with the baseline error between the characters as typed and the stimuli.

In general, we found that S3 and S4 were the optimal correction strategies — there was no significant difference between them for any mobility. S2 was slightly worse than either of these. In theory S2 represents the most thorough search, since at each new tap the system is allowed to change all previous letters. In practice, multiple such corrections can introduce insertion or deletion errors which accumulate over time, leading to the increased error rate seen here. S1 is the worst of the correction schemes, since it is only able to fix cases where the wrong key was hit, and cannot correct transposition errors

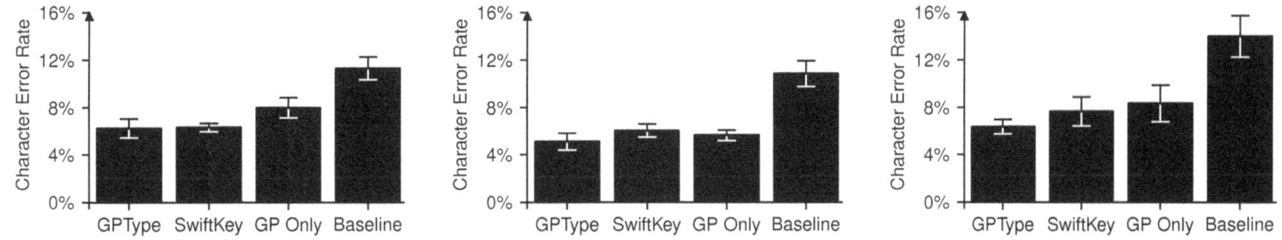

(a) Sitting (b) Standing (c) Walking

Figure 4. Character error rates for the two keyboards we evaluated, separated by mobility condition (Study 2). Plots show mean and standard error across all participants. The baseline method represents the literal keys touched, while GP Only shows the keys hit after the mean GP offset is applied.

such as typing 'teh' in place of 'the'.

The observed error rates were not significantly different between the sitting and standing mobility conditions, but the error rates for the walking condition were significantly higher (paired t-test, $p < 0.05$). The lowest error rates obtained using the optimal correction strategies were 5.02% for sitting, 5.47% for standing, and 6.5% for walking.

STUDY 2: COMPARISON WITH SWIFTKEY

We evaluated our best correction system in a study. The goal of this study was to determine whether the benefits shown in our offline simulations were reflected in a live typing task. We also wanted to assess how our system compared to an existing commercial soft keyboard. For this we chose SwiftKey[1], a popular Android keyboard which also uses language modelling to perform intelligent correction.

We ported the GP, LM and decoder to Android and adapted our custom keyboard from the model building study. We used S3 as our correction style, since it was as good at correcting as S4 and required fewer LM searches. We used 5 examples of a user's touch per key to train the GP, rather than the 10 used in model building, in order to prevent input from slowing down due to large matrix operations.

Participants

We recruited a further 10 participants (3 female) to take part in this evaluation. Ages ranged from 18–28 (mean = 22.4, sd = 4.22). 8 participants were smartphone owners and considered themselves expert users. The other 2 did not own smartphones and had little experience using touch screen devices. No participant in this study took part in the previous study. Participants were paid £10 for their time.

Apparatus

Participants typed using our custom logging application, again running on a Samsung Galaxy SII. This smartphone has a 4.3 inch screen with a 480 × 800 pixel resolution. A screenshot is shown in Figure 2. The stimulus phrase appears at the top of the screen, and the text entered by the participant is shown below. The time remaining in the current typing task is shown in the upper right. Visually, this application was identical to the one used in the model building study. The backspace key in the logging app was disabled, as we wanted to evaluate the quality of the corrections made by our system without participants manually backspacing to correct errors.

As mentioned above, we also collected typing data using the SwiftKey keyboard. The keys on our custom keyboard have the same size and layout as those in SwiftKey, so the two logging interfaces were very similar. As SwiftKey is a third party product, it was not possible to disable the backspace key and so participants were instructed not to use it and accept any corrections from the keyboard.

Procedure

The procedure for the study consisted of three sessions. In the first session, participants provided calibration data for the GP in each of the three mobility conditions. This was collected in the same way as in the model building study. Afterwards, participants typed for five minutes, while seated, on each of the two study keyboards to familiarise themselves with the layouts. As in Study 1, participants typed phrases from the Enron Mobile Email set [36]. In each of the other two sessions, participants performed 10 minutes of typing in each mobility condition. They used GPType in one session, and SwiftKey in the other. All tasks were carried out in a meeting room, with a clear path marked for walking.

Design

Our study was a within-subjects 2x3 factorial design with factors: Keyboard (levels: GPType, SwiftKey) and Mobility (levels: Sitting, Standing, Walking). The presentation order of the keyboards was counterbalanced across participants, and the order of mobility conditions was partially counterbalanced across participants and between sessions. A full counterbalancing was impossible with 3 levels and 20 sessions.

Results

We measure performance of the corrections produced by each keyboard in terms of CER between the corrected text and the stimulus phrase. Our results are summarised in Figure 4, which shows the mean and standard error across all participants, separated by mobility condition. The baseline is the CER between the keys hit by the participant's touches and the stimulus phrase. Also shown is a *GP Only* condition, in which we apply the mean offset from the GP to the user's touch and see which key was hit by the resulting touch. The GP Only condition does not use the decoder or LM.

Both keyboards offer a significant improvement over the baseline in all mobility conditions (paired t-test, $p < 0.05$). The

[1] http://www.swiftkey.net

CER reduction over the baseline for GPType was 4.9% for sitting, 5% for standing, and 7.6% for walking. Further, GPType offers a small but significant improvement over SwiftKey in the standing and walking mobility conditions (approximately 1% reduced CER for the standing condition and 1.3% for walking). No significant difference between the keyboards was observed in the sitting condition. This is likely an effect of the participants' touch offsets becoming more pronounced when standing or moving. Interestingly, the standing condition had the lowest CER for both baseline and the evaluated keyboards. It is unclear why this should be the case.

Also of interest is the fact that the GP Only condition is significantly better than the baseline. This indicates that both the offset modelling and the decoding play a role in producing the observed reduction in error rate. By computing the mean touch offset, many substitution errors can be corrected. The decoder can then decrease the error rate further by fixing transposition errors and performing insertions or deletions.

We also measured participants' text entry rates for both keyboards. However, we saw no significant difference between GPType and SwiftKey. This is perhaps to be expected, given that the physical layout of the keyboards was the same and that backspace was disabled, so the observed entry rates do not subsume manual error correction.

THE AUTOCORRECT TRAP

So far we have explored a novel approach of error correction for touchscreen keyboards. Current touchscreen keyboards use a wide range of other autocorrection techniques (e.g., adaptive but clamped target resizing [10]). These techniques, as well as our GPType method presented here, implicitly model uncertainty: the user has little influence on the way autocorrection works. In any such system, users might be able to reject a proposed correction, delete a character and retype with autocorrection switched off, or select the corrected word and pick from the originally typed version, or other suggestions. While this theoretically allows users to control text correction according to their needs, there are still widespread frustrations and situations where text prediction falls short. When typing unknown words, using regional dialects, or mixing languages, autocorrection is often not flexible enough.

We thus propose giving users control over how their phones correct text. Empowering users to vary the level of error correction per word allows users to fall back to automatic error correction for phrases they deem correctable while being able to tighten the reins during phrases they feel their phones cannot handle. This assumes that users have a sense of whether a phrase is hard for the text prediction on their phone or not. To get an idea of how the capabilities of auto-correction are viewed by users, we conducted a study.

We designed a questionnaire listing 20 phrases of varying levels of difficulty—some consisting only of common English words and others with proper nouns, slang, and/or words or phrases borrowed from other languages (e.g., *summa cum laude*). Participants were recruited using mailing lists and social media. For each phrase, participants were asked to rate on a 5-point Likert scale whether they thought autocorrect would change it or not when entered on a smartphone.

We received 28 responses (8 female, ages 17–44, mean = 29.0, sd = 7.5) to the questionnaire. Asked to rate their English language skills, 86% of participants rated themselves as functionally native speakers. The rest of the participants still rated themselves at a near native level.

To establish a ground truth on whether our phrases would be autocorrected or not, we entered them into three smartphones—an iPhone 5 running iOS 6.1, an LG E700 running Windows Phone 7.5, and a Samsung Galaxy S3 Mini using the SwiftKey keyboard on Android 4.1. We noted for each phone which phrases were autocorrected. In cases of disagreement, where some phones corrected and others did not, we used majority voting to produce a singe binary value for each phrase. Next, we split the user ratings for corrected and uncorrected phrases and produced histograms showing the counts for each rating. By normalising these histograms we obtain discrete probability distributions over the ratings for the two groups of phrases. Our results are shown in Figure 5. For phrases which would actually be autocorrected, the most probable rating is 1 (certain correction) and the least probable is 5 (no correction). The monotonic decrease across the other ratings shows a clear trend, indicating our respondents had a good sense of phrases that would be autocorrected.

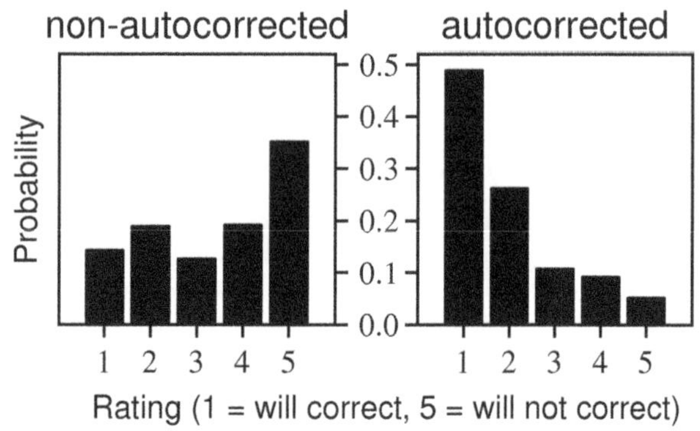

Figure 5. For a set of 20 phrases, we asked 28 people whether they thought their phone's autocorrect would change it when entered, or leave it unchanged. Participants gave a rating between 1 (will definitely be changed) to 5 (will definitely not be changed). We classified each phrase by testing it for autocorrection on several different phones. This figure shows the probability of each point on the rating scale for both classes (changed and unchanged).

For phrases that were not corrected, the trend is less pronounced. The most likely rating is for no correction and there is a remarkably high probability that users rate these uncorrectable sentences as certain or near certain corrections. In essence, users overestimate how likely autocorrect systems are to take action. This is not necessarily an issue—if a user takes action to prevent autocorrection when none would have occurred, there is no difference to their final input. These results motivate the need for a system with finer control over automatic error correction behaviour. The distributions over ratings are significantly different (Wilcoxon test, $p \ll 0.01$) for the two groups of phrases. This suggests that users have a functional mental model of the way autocorrect operates and would be able to identify situations where preventing autocorrection is desirable.

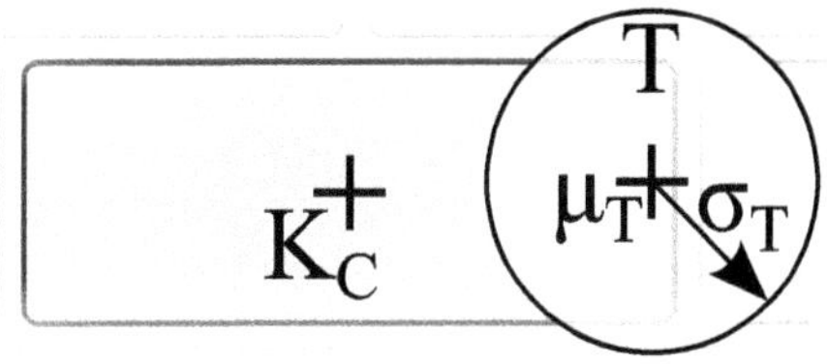

Figure 6. The touch model used by our correction system ForceType. For each key K, we evaluate the likelihood of its centre K_C under a Gaussian on the touch point μ_T. The standard deviation σ_T is controlled by pressure. Higher pressure causes a narrower distribution.

FORCETYPE: PRESSURE AS CERTAINTY

Given that users already have a mental model of which words are likely to be autocorrected, we desire an input modality which enables them to express certainty about words they do not want corrected. In essence, we wish to allow users to negotiate control between themselves and the language model. For normal typing, the autocorrect functions as it does on current phones, but when the user suspects the word they are entering is unknown to the phone's dictionary they can smoothly limit the autocorrect behaviour. We choose pressure as the factor to control this negotiation. When the user wishes to indicate certainty, they simply press harder on the keys. Srinivasan and Chen [33] have shown pressure to be controllable by users and the idea of pressing hard for a different input behaviour is simple to grasp.

Other research has considered negotiated uncertainty through user input. Rogers et al. [28] use the height of the finger above the screen as a proxy for uncertainty when browsing a map. However, although 'hover' input of this form is now being introduced on commercial phones, such as the *Samsung Galaxy S4*, it is not an appropriate choice for a typing application. Subramanian et al. [35] showed that users display unintentional drift when varying hover height, so controlling uncertainty via this modality may be suboptimal—hence our choice of the pressure modality.

Correction Model

We use the same language model and decoding algorithm as for GPType, but rather than generating key press probabilities from a GP we use a pressure dependent touch model. The likelihood of a key given a touch is computed as a Gaussian with a standard deviation that changes dependent on the pressure. In particular, we take the standard deviation as: $\sigma_T = C/\omega_T$, where C is a constant and ω_T is the pressure for touch T. Thus for high pressure touches the variance is small and the probability mass is concentrated in the pressed key, whereas for lower pressure touches the probability mass is spread over the keyboard, allowing correction to take place. The touch model is illustrated in Figure 6.

The constant C needs to be calibrated appropriately. We chose a value such that the distribution for a 'typical' touch had a standard deviation equal to half a key width. To determine what defined 'typical', we asked 10 participants to repeatedly write *the quick brown fox jumps over the lazy dog*, an English pangram, on our input device, a pressure sensitive touch pad called the ForcePad (more information on this hardware is given in the next section). This was done without presenting any feedback about what was typed, and in the absence of any correction scheme. This provided us with pressure information for typing with every key on the keyboard. From a histogram of the logged pressure information, it was the clear the data were not normally distributed and had high positive skew. We chose to fit a gamma distribution to the data. Next, from the 2333 collected datapoints we removed 144 outliers (>2 sd away from the mean — these were primarily points where the hardware reached its upper sensing limit). We then refitted a gamma distribution to the remaining data. The mean of this distribution was $168.28\,\mathrm{g/cm^2}$ (sd = $106.20\,\mathrm{g/cm^2}$). We then chose C such that the Gaussian distribution for a touch with this mean pressure had a standard deviation equal to half a key width.

STUDY 3: FORCETYPE EVALUATION

We conducted a user study to determine the effects of pressure-based scaling of text correction. We hypothesize that:

H1 Pressure-adaptive error correction requires fewer word corrections by the user than constant-scale text correction.

H2 Users are faster when typing words unknown to the error correction algorithm when utilising pressure adaptation.

To test these hypotheses, we had participants type a series of phrases in two conditions: with and without pressure adaptation. For the latter, we use the same correction model but rather than adapting the variance of the touch Gaussian based on pressure, we used a fixed value, chosen such that the standard deviation was equal to one key width. This corresponds to the standard deviation in the pressure sensitive model when the touch has mean pressure and approximates the behaviour of autocorrect on modern smartphones.

We used a between-subjects design for the study, so that each participant used only one correction model. This decision was made due to the difficulty of having a participant learn the pressure sensitive model and then asking them to "type normally" for the other condition. The conditions could thus not be properly counterbalanced in a within-subjects design.

In order to assess the impact of using the model on the text entry speed for the pressure group, the phrase set used needs to contain both *correctable* phrases, containing only words known to the correction model, and *uncorrectable* phrases, containing at least one word unknown to the model. The former should not require pressure typing invocations if the user has a good understanding of the language model behavior, while the latter set will require one or more invocations.

Participants

We recruited 16 participants (5 female, age 21–39, mean = 25.69, sd = 4.48), where all but three were smartphone owners. On average, participants had over 3 years of smartphone experience. On a 1–5 scale (1 = beginner, 5 = functionally native), participants rated their English language skills at 3.06. Each participant was randomly assigned to one of the two conditions—text entry with pressure-adaptive autocorrect and text entry without. After the experiment, participants were given a small non-monetary gratuity.

Apparatus

For pressure sensing and finger tracking we use a *Synaptics ForcePad* sensor. The device weights 526 g and measures $14.2 \times 12.2 \times 1.1$ cm. The touch-sensitive area covers 10.9×6.9 cm on the device's surface. The sensor's diagonal thus is 12.9cm—within roughly 6% of a *Samsung Galaxy S III's* 12.19cm. Overall, the Forcepad is slightly larger but considerably heavier (an S III only weighs 133 g) than current mobile devices. However, it does provide a comparable experience when holding the device in landscape mode and typing. Thus, we feel confident the Forcepad is a valid placeholder device for evaluating how future mobile devices incorporating pressure sensing touch could be used.

The ForcePad provides capacitive tracking with pressure information for up to 5 fingers. Force readings are provided with 6 bit resolution at 67 Hz. We take the maximum value in the last 10 frames as the pressure value for a touch. The force sensitivity of the ForcePad made us choose this device instead of for example approaches using accelerometers to infer typing pressure [15]. Such approaches are typically limited or inaccurate, and in the first instance we wanted accurate values to assess how users controlled the system. However, we consider an exploration of using these techniques to bring ForceType to modern smartphones as an important avenue for future work.

Figure 7. Modified Synaptics ForcePad used in the *ForceType* system.

The ForcePad is an input-only device and cannot display visual feedback or instructions directly on its surface. Using an external monitor for feedback, however, would not allow us to evaluate normal typing behaviour. We thus modified the ForcePad by attaching a 132×32 px LCD to the device on which we can display three lines of text in a medium-sized font. The LCD was glued to the top of the ForcePad increasing the overall weight to 651 g without impeding hands holding the device. The modified device is shown in Figure 7. An Arduino is used for control and allows the connected PC to set display content via the serial port. This combination of ForcePad and LCD enables us to simulate future mobile devices with pressure-sensitive touch. One limitation of this hardware is there is no visual feedback on corrections before they happen—this is another reason that exploring pressure proxies on current smartphones is a focus for future work.

To simulate an onscreen keyboard, we glued a keyboard overlay on the ForcePad. We used a modified version of the iOS landscape keyboard with all buttons triggering mode switches removed (so as not to confuse participants). The glued-on keyboard does not introduce new haptic cues and thus provides an experience comparable to current smartphone keyboards.

Procedure

We used a subset of the English *NUS SMS Corpus* (version 2012.04.30) as phrase set [4]. This dataset contains 41537 text messages, sent primarily by users in Singapore, India, and the USA. Text messages often contain slang and shorthand, making them a good example of the a text where autocorrect fails. However, not all messages are equally appropriate for our evaluation and we removed all messages that:

- are shorter than 15 or longer than 50 characters
- contain any character not in the set given by the ISO basic latin alphabet plus the space and period characters
- are shorter than three words
- contain unknown one-letter words

This filtering leaves us with set of 5733 phrases. Our main concern is our requirement for unknown words in the messages—words that can not be found in a standard dictionary known to a language model. To determine such unknown words, we make use of the built-in Android `en-us` dictionary. We now split our phrase set into two parts:

correctable phrases Phrases that only contain words found in the dictionary ($n = 1272$).

uncorrectable phrases Phrases that contain at least one word not found in the dictionary ($n = 4461$).

For every participant, 20 correctable and 20 uncorrectable phrases were picked at random. While phrases were chosen randomly, a post-hoc analysis showed that there was no significant difference across users in the number of OOV words per sentence ($p > 0.4$). Participants were not provided with an indication whether a phrase was correctable or not.

At the beginning of the study, we gave participants the chance to familiarise themselves with our prototype. Participants then had to complete 40 trials. In each trial, they were shown the complete phrase on a screen in front of them and then had to copy that phrase. During text input, the phrase (clipped to the display size) was shown alongside the response text on the device. We asked participants to copy the phrases accurately—if they noticed a mistake, whether from a language model correction or their own typing, they were instructed to correct it. After using backspace to delete part of a word, autocorrect was disabled until the next word. This is equivalent to the behaviour on phones and prevents infinite correction loops. Participants had to submit each phrase with the return key.

Results

One participant was excluded from the analysis, as the touch offsets were so large the touches rarely hit the correct key.

Errors

As our performance measure, we use Active Correction Rate (ACR), defined as the proportion of words which the user has to actively correct by backspacing and retyping. This is a similar approach to Hoffman et al. [13], where they looked at the number of times backspace needed to be pressed. If **H1** is accepted, we should see a decrease in ACR since users can use pressure to prevent autocorrection of non-standard words. We chose this metric over CER, since in this study users were able to manually change unwanted corrections. In GPType, corrections made by the system could not be changed, since

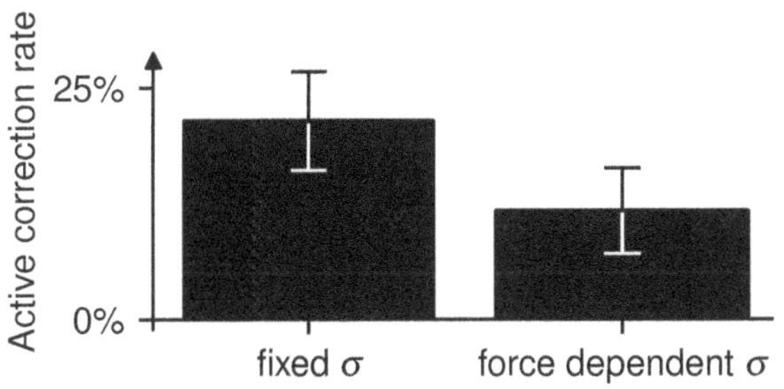

Figure 8. ForceType requires significantly fewer active corrections from users when entering text. Required corrections dropped by ≈ 10 percentage points. Errors bars are 1 sd.

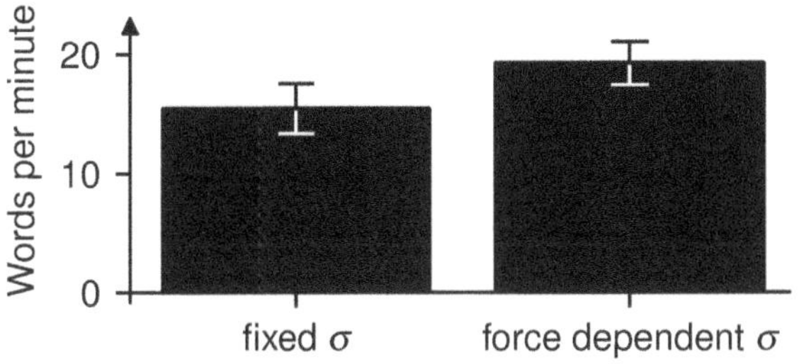

Figure 9. ForceType enabled users to enter phrases $> 20\%$ faster. A significant increase over the baseline. Errors bars are 1 sd.

we evaluated the quality of the corrections, not the ability of users to control the system. Our choice is supported by the results—the mean CERs for the two study groups were not significantly different ($\sim 3\%$ in each case).

Figure 8 shows the ACR. Using pressure adaptation, the average user had an ACR of 10.86%, compared to a value of 19.48% for users without pressure adaptation. This is a significant decrease compared to the baseline condition (independent two-sample t-test: $t_{12} = -3.48, p < 0.005$). We can thus reject the null hypothesis and accept **H1**.

The ACR values for both groups are quite high. Since the phrases are from an SMS corpus, many of the words are not found in common English. Unfamiliarity with the form factor of our apparatus may also have increased ACR.

Entry Rate

Entry rate was measured using words per minute (WPM), with a word being defined as five consecutive characters, including spaces. With pressure adaptation active, users typed 19.23 WPM, while without they only typed 15.42 WPM (Figure 9). This is a significant increase in typing speed (independent two-sample t-test: $t_{12} = 3.5002, p < 0.005$). We can reject the null hypothesis and also accept **H2**.

We also looked at the impact of uncorrectable phrases on typing speed. A small drop in speed could be expected, as users have to invest more mental effort in processing those phrases. We saw WPM go down by 3.97 (ForceType) and 2.61 (baseline). Both changes are significant ($p < 0.05$), while the difference between the two changes is not ($p > 0.13$). Thus, ForceType and the control are both equally affected by uncorrectable phrases, resulting in a small performance drop. Overall, ForceType resulted in a faster text entry rate.

DISCUSSION

The goal of our work was to show the advantages of combining a probabilistic touch model with a language model and decoding algorithm to increase text entry accuracy. With GPType, we used a touch offset model to correct for systematic errors in a user's touches and then compute probabilities over keys. This successfully reduced character error rates in a real typing task to a level comparable with a leading commercial product. Indeed, when users were standing or walking our system was slightly better than the commercial keyboard.

Our second system, ForceType, tackled cases where traditional autocorrect systems failed. By allowing users to convey certainty in their input using pressure, autocorrect can be dynamically turned off to allow entry of words not in standard word lists, such as acronyms or words from local dialects. ForceType was successful in increasing typing speed and reducing the number of cases where users had to manually correct their entered text.

These two systems represent different approaches to the uncertainty inherent in text entry. In GPType, we model this uncertainty in a manner that is hidden from users, allowing the system to account for and correct many commonplace errors. In ForceType, the uncertainty is *explicitly* controlled by the user, allowing finer control over the system when the user can anticipate undesired autocorrection behaviour.

It is likely that neither of these approaches is strictly better than the other. In future work, it would be interesting to combine offset modelling with explicit pressure control and see if input accuracy can be further increased.

CONCLUSIONS

Text entry is a ubiquitous activity on modern mobile devices, but continues to present challenges. The process is naturally very uncertain, both because of physical effects (e.g. the Fat Finger Problem) and due to uncertainty of intent—existing correction systems often assume users are trying to type words known to a dictionary, but this is certainly not always the case. In this paper we have presented two systems that improve the text entry experience by combining a state-of-the-art decoder and LM with a model capturing individual users' physical uncertainty (GPType) and an input system that allows users to explicitly control uncertainty (ForceType).

Evaluating GPType, we showed competitive reductions in character error rate for real typing tasks, without reducing the text entry rate. GPType reduced the character error rate by 4.9% over the baseline for sitting, 5% for standing, and 7.6% for walking users. Further, GPType obtained an average 1% decrease in CER over SwiftKey, a leading commercial keyboard, for standing and a 1.3% decrease for walking users.

Evaluating ForceType, we showed that users could successfully prevent autocorrection of words they did not want to be changed by varying their input pressure as they typed, resulting in faster overall text entry rates.

ACKNOWLEDGMENTS

This research was supported by Scottish Informatics and Computer Science Alliance (SICSA).

REFERENCES

1. Bi, X., Li, Y., and Zhai, S. FFitts Law: Modeling Finger Touch with Fitts' Law. *Proc. CHI '13*. 1363–1372.
2. Bi, X. and Zhai, S. Bayesian Touch - A Statistical Criterion of Target Selection with Finger Touch. *Proc. UIST '13*. 51–60.
3. Brewster, S.A. and Hughes, M. Pressure-Based Text Entry for Mobile Devices. *Proc. MobileHCI '09*. 9:1–9:4.
4. Chen, T. and Kan, M.Y. Creating a Live, Public Short Message Service Corpus: the NUS SMS Corpus. *Language Resources and Evaluation*, 2012:1–37.
5. Clarkson, E.C., Patel, S.N., Pierce, J.S., and Abowd, G.D. Exploring Continuous Pressure Input for Mobile Phones. Tech. Rep. GIT-GVU-06-20, Georgia Tech, 2006.
6. de Jong, S., Kirkali, D., Schraffenberger, H., Jillissen, J., de Rooij, A., and Terpstra, A. One-Press Control: A Tactile Input Method for Pressure-Sensitive Computer Keyboards. *Proc. CHI EA '10*. 4261–4266.
7. Flemish, F.O., Adams, C.A., Conway, S.R., Goodrich, K.H., Palmer, M.T., and Schutte, P.C. The H-Metaphor as a Guideline for Vehicle Automation and Interaction. Tech. Rep. TM-2003-212672, NASA, 2003.
8. Goel, M., Findlater, L., and Wobbrock, J. WalkType: Using Accelerometer Data to Accomodate Situational Impairments in Mobile Touch Screen Text Entry. *Proc. CHI '12*. 2687–2696.
9. Goodman, J., Venolia, G., Steury, K., and Parker, C. Language Modeling for Soft Keyboards. *Proc. AAAI 2002*. 419–424.
10. Gunawardana, A., Paek, T., and Meek, C. Usability Guided Key-Target Resizing for Soft Keyboards. *Proc. IUI '10*. 111–118.
11. Henze, N., Rukzio, E., and Boll, S. Observational and Experimental Investigation of Typing Behaviour Using Virtual Keyboards for Mobile Devices. *Proc. CHI '12*. 2659–2668.
12. Heo, S. and Lee, G. Force Gestures: Augmenting Touch Screen Gestures with Normal and Tangential Forces. *Proc. UIST '11*. 621–626.
13. Hoffmann, A., Spelmezan, D., and Borchers, J. TypeRight: A Keyboard with Tactile Error Prevention. *Proc. CHI '09*. 2265–2268.
14. Holz, C. and Baudisch, P. The Generalized Perceived Input Point Model and How to Double Touch Accuracy by Extracting Fingerprints. *Proc. CHI '10*. 581–590.
15. Iwasaki, K., Miyaki, T., and Rekimoto, J. Expressive Typing: A New Way to Sense Typing Pressure and Its Applications. *Proc. CHI EA '09*. 4369–4374.
16. Kristensson, P.O. Five Challenges for Intelligent Text Entry Methods. *AI Magazine*, 30(4), 2009:85–94.
17. Kristensson, P.O. and Vertanen, K. Asynchronous Multimodal Text Entry using Speech and Gesture Keyboards. *Proc. Interspeech 2011*. 581–584.
18. Kristensson, P.O. and Vertanen, K. Performance Comparisons of Phrase Sets and Presentation Styles for Text Entry Evaluations. *Proc. IUI '12*. 29–32.
19. Kristensson, P.O. and Zhai, S. SHARK^2: A Large Vocabulary Shorthand Writing System for Pen-Based Computers. *Proc. UIST '04*. 43–52.
20. Kristensson, P.O. and Zhai, S. Relaxing Stylus Typing Precision by Geometric Pattern Matching. *Proc. IUI '05*. 151–158.
21. Lui, M. and Baldwin, T. langid.py: An Off-the-shelf Language Identification Tool. *Proceedings of the ACL 2012 System Demonstrations*. 25–30.
22. MacKenzie, I.S. and Soukoreff, R.W. Phrase Sets for Evaluating Text Entry Techniques. *Proc. CHI EA '03*. 754–755.
23. McCallum, D.C., Mak, E., Irani, P., and Subramanian, S. PressureText: Pressure Input for Mobile Phone Text Entry. *Proc. CHI EA '09*. 4519–4524.
24. Oulasvirta, A., Reichel, A., Li, W., Zhang, Y., Bachynskzi, M., Vertanen, K., and Kristensson, P.O. Improving Two-Thumb Text Entry on Touchscreen Devices. *Proc. CHI '13*. 2765–2774.
25. Pohl, H. and Murray-Smith, R. Focused and Casual Interactions: Allowing Users to Vary Their Level of Engagement. *Proc. CHI'13*. 2223–2232.
26. Ramos, G., Boulos, M., and Balakrishnan, R. Pressure Widgets. *Proc. CHI '04*. 487–494.
27. Rasmussen, C.E. and Williams, C.K.I. *Gaussian Processes for Machine Learning*. The MIT Press, 2005.
28. Rogers, S., Williamson, J., Stewart, C., and Murray-Smith, R. FingerCloud: Uncertainty and Autonomy Handover in Capacitive Sensing. *Proc. CHI '10*. 577–580.
29. Rudchenko, D., Paek, T., and Badger, E. Text Text Revolution: A Game That Improves Text Entry on Mobile Touchscreen Keyboards. *Proc. Pervasive '11*. 206–213.
30. Schwarz, J., Hudson, S., Mankoff, J., and Wilson, A.D. A Framework for Robust and Flexible Handling of Inputs with Uncertainty. *Proc. UIST '10*. 47–56.
31. Shi, K., Irani, P., Gustafson, S., and Subramanian, S. PressureFish : A Method to Improve Control of Discrete Pressure-based Input. *Proc. CHI '08*. 1295–1298.
32. Siek, K.A., Rogers, Y., and Connelly, K.H. Fat Finger Worries: How Older and Younger Users Physically Interact with PDAs. *Proc. INTERACT'05*. 267–280.
33. Srinivasan, M.A. and Chen, J.s. Human Performance in Controlling Normal Forces of Contact with Rigid Objects. *Proc. ASME'93*, vol. 49. 119–125.
34. Stewart, C., Rohs, M., Kratz, S., and Essl, G. Characteristics of Pressure-Based Input for Mobile Devices. *Proc. CHI '10*. 801–810.
35. Subramanian, S., Aliakseyeu, D., and Lucero, A. Multi-layer Interaction for Digital Tables. *Proc. UIST '06*. 269–272.
36. Vertanen, K. and Kristensson, P.O. A Versatile Dataset for Text Entry Evaluations Based on Genuine Mobile Emails. *Proc. MobileHCI '11*. 295–298.
37. Weir, D., Rogers, S., Murray-Smith, R., and Löchtefeld, M. A User-Specific Machine Learning Approach for Improving Touch Accuracy on Mobile Devices. *Proc. UIST '12*. 465–476.
38. Williamson, J. *Continuous Uncertain Interaction*. PhD thesis, University of Glasgow, 2006.

Mobile Attachment - Causes and Consequences for Emotional Bonding with Mobile Phones

Alexander Meschtscherjakov, David Wilfinger, Manfred Tscheligi
ICT&S Center, University of Salzburg
Sigmund-Haffner-Gasse 18, 5020 Salzburg, Austria
{alexander.meschtscherjakov, david.wilfinger, manfred.tscheligi}@sbg.ac.at

ABSTRACT
This paper addresses the phenomenon of emotional attachments to mobile phones. We introduce the term "mobile attachment" and define it as a bond between a person's self and a mobile phone that varies in strength. Based on a critical reflection of interdisciplinary literature, a conceptual mobile attachment model is developed. Within this model causes, consequences, and influencing factors of mobile attachment are exposed and elaborated. We argue that mobile attachment emerges when the mobile phone becomes part of the user's self concept. The link between the user and their mobile phone may be fostered when it empowers, enriches, or gratifies the user's self. Attachment causes lead to "design space determinants" that enable user experience designers to design for mobile attachment. Attachment consequences may be operationalized for user experience evaluation.

Author Keywords
Emotional attachment; mobile phones; user experience.

ACM Classification Keywords
H.5.m. Information Interfaces and Presentation (e.g. HCI): Miscellaneous

INTRODUCTION
"[The mobile phone is] *a device that is truly a personal technology, helping people to feel safer, less lonely, more human.*" [10]. In 2013, the number of mobile-cellular subscriptions (6.8 billion) has almost reached global population[1]. For most of mobile phone users, their phones have become an indispensable and, sometimes, beloved part of their everyday life. Some need it to be constantly available, for others its their linkage to relatives and friends. Yet, for others it is a status symbol or an expression of their personality.

[1]http://www.itu.int/en/ITU-D/Statistics/Documents/facts/ICTFactsFigures2013-e.pdf

CHI 2014, April 26 – May 01 2014, Toronto, ON, Canada.
Copyright 2014 ACM 978-1-4503-2473-1/14/04...$15.00.
http://dx.doi.org/10.1145/2556288.2557295

Regardless of the reasons behind ownership mobile phones led to a fundamental transformation of people's perception of the self and the world. Various studies have investigated a user's emotional attachment to mobile phones in different disciplines (e.g., [27], [28], [12]). People even built attachment to virtual possessions, such as SMS message archives [20]. Consumer research has been focusing on brand attachment and its effect on marketing (e.g., [22], [15]), whereas the design community has investigated product attachment and its influence on product design (e.g., [25], [19]). User experience (UX) research has suggested that UX and emotional attachment are related concepts [17] and that emotional attachment to a product increases when it is incorporated into the user's life [12]. Nonetheless, a proper definition of people's attachment to mobile phones and a model describing it's causes and consequences is missing.

This paper presents a definition and as well as a conceptual model of *mobile attachment*. Both were developed based on a critical reflection on interdisciplinary attachment literature. Thus, this model derives from theory and targets application to phones and other mobile devices in a future step. The model describes causes, consequences, and influencing factors of mobile attachment. It contributes to the field of UX research by providing a model that can be used by UX designers to design for mobile attachment and UX researchers to evaluate mobile attachment. Thus, it contributes to the emerging field of experience-oriented design of technology [8]. In the following chapter, a reflection on attachment research from various disciplines is given. We then present our mobile attachment definition, followed by the introduction and discussion of the conceptual mobile attachment model. Finally, we conclude how the model may be used by UX researcher to design for mobile attachment and evaluate it.

BACKGROUND
In this chapter we present attachment research from psychology, consumer research, design and HCI. These theories and models serve as a basis for the development of the conceptual mobile attachment model.

Attachment Theory and the Extended Self
Attachment theory has its origin in psychology and addresses the bonding a child has to its caregiver. It originates in the work of John Bowlby [3] and is a psychological and evolutionary theory that provides an explanatory model for understanding interpersonal relationships between human beings.

Bowlby proposes that human infants are born with a set of attachment behaviors, such as proximity maintenance and separation distress. Based on Bowlby's pioneering work other forms of emotional attachment have been investigated. For example, Csikszentmihalyi et al. [5] report that objects play an important role in people's definition of who they are and who they wish to become. Belk [2] investigated the relationship between possessions and the sense of self and introduced the concept of *the extended self*. Belk states that external objects may be viewed as part of oneself, when one is able to control them and serve as reminders and confirmers of one's identity. Objects in our possessions may literally extend the self, as when a tool allows us to do things of which we would otherwise be incapable. They serve as an enhancement of the personal power. Possessions may be convenient means of storing memories and feelings providing a sense of who we are as a link to our past or serve as a symbol of who we are or to which group we belong. Here we want to stress that Bowlby's attachment theory is not equal to our interpretation of mobile attachment but it bears some similarities important to be researched.

Material Possession Attachment and Brand Attachment

Research in consumer behavior focuses on attachment to consumer products [26]. Kleine et al. [15] define *material possession attachment* as a multifaceted property of the relationship between an individual and a specific material object that has been decommodified and singularized through person-object interaction. Since mobile phones can be seen as one category of material possessions, it can be argued that mobile attachment is a special case of material possession attachment. Marketing research has investigated the relationship between consumers and brands. *Brand attachment* is the strength of the cognitive and affective bond connecting the brand with the self [22]. Since there is a strong connection between the mobile phone and the brand (e.g., iPhone and Apple) brand attachment and mobile attachment are related to each other.

Product Attachment and Designing for the Self

The design community has defined *product attachment* as "the strength of the emotional bond a consumer experiences with a specific product" [25]. Three implications of this definition can be derived. First, it suggests that a strong tie exists between the consumer and the product. Second, it implies that the product triggers emotions within the consumer. Third, experiencing attachment to products is a matter of degree [15]. Schifferstein et al. [24] proposed a conceptual model of consumer-product attachment. Based on Greenwald's [7] four facets of the self (*the diffuse self*, *the private self*, *the public self*, and *the collective self*), they state that different product meanings emerge from these facets. The four resulting determinants of product attachment (enjoyment, individual autonomy, group affiliation, and life vision) reveal the different ways in which products support the owner's self. Mugge [19] states that people develop attachment to products that convey a special meaning to them. She proposes four product meanings as possible determinants of product attachment to ordinary durables: self-expression, group affiliation, memories, and pleasure.

Zimmerman's [29] approach *designing for the self* focuses on the question "How to design products with the goal of helping people become the person they desire to be through their interaction with these products?". Thereby, he differentiates between role enhancement and role transition. Role enhancement refers to the design of products that help people move closer to their idealized sense of self, while role transition specifies the design of products that support the process of discovering and inventing yourself in a new role. Odom et al. [21] investigated the value of virtual possessions and how people form attachments to these immaterial things.

Emotional Attachment in UX Research

Law et al. [17] have suggested that there is a relation between UX and emotional attachment. Above that, they highlighted the difference between UX and brand experience. In their view brand experience is broader than UX including not only interaction with the branded products, but interaction with the company, all its products, and services. Mobile phones are almost always strongly related with the manufacturer and therefore brand experience plays an decisive role in the user experience with mobile phones. Imagine the close connection between an iPhone and Apple. The mobile phone and the provided services (e.g., telephone, SMS) are closely related to each other. Mobile attachment is often targeted towards the mobile phone but equally towards the emotional goals the mobile phone enables and therefore towards the provided services [27].

Karapanos et al. [12] investigated the temporality of UX (i.e., how the quality of users' experience develops over time) empirically. They propose a conceptual model of temporality of experience consisting of three consecutive UX phases (orientation, incorporation, and identification) and correspondent "forces" (increasing familiarity, functional dependency, and emotional attachment). They state that emotional attachment evolves in the last of these three UX phases when the product becomes a personal object participating in private and social contexts. Emotional attachment is connected to the type of product. Mobile phones connect user to loved ones, allows adaptation, and is always nearby communicating self-identity.

Vincent [27] argued that the attachment to mobile phones rises out of the omnipresence and capabilities of mobile phones in society today. Odom et al. [20] have researched how teenagers form attachment to their virtual possessions including archived SMS messages. Wehmeyer [28] uses the term "user-device attachment" to describe the relationship between users and their mobile phone. He proposes three dimensions of user-device attachment: symbolism, aesthetics, and perceived necessity.

MOBILE ATTACHMENT DEFINITION

These studies shows that attachment has been investigated in various disciplines. Nevertheless, from a UX perspective neither a common definition, nor a conceptual model, which identifies causes for mobile attachment, exist. Based on the related literature we will now provide a definition of mobile attachment.

Bowlby [4] has defined attachment as "an emotion-laden target-specific bond between two persons". Park [22] applies this definition to brands and defines brand attachment as "the strength of the cognitive and emotional bond connecting the brand with the self". Schifferstein et al. [25] defines the degree of consumer-product attachment as "the strength of the emotional bond a consumer experiences with a product". Based on a critical reflection of these definitions it can be concluded that attachment is both an emotional and cognitive bond between a person and an attachment object. Consequently, we define "mobile attachment" as follows:

Mobile attachment is a cognitive and emotional target-specific bond connecting a person's self and a mobile phone that is dynamic over time and varies in strength.

Thus, attachment is a psychological state of mind in which a strong cognitive and affective bond connects the mobile phone with an individual in such a way that the mobile phone is assumed to be an extension of the self and, therefore, becomes part of the self-concept. It is in agreement with Karapanos et al. [12] who state that emotional attachment to products evolves when the product is capable of expressing one's self. This definition has five implications:

1. The attachment object (mobile phone) includes the device itself (hardware), the operating software, and the applications that run on the mobile phone (software), the services that are provided by hard- and software, and the content that is stored within the mobile phone. It forms with specific mobile phones, not with brands or product categories.
2. It implies the existence of a connectedness between the individual's self and the mobile phone. This relationship reflects the extend to which the mobile phone is linked to the self.
3. It suggests that the mobile phone triggers both cognitive and emotional responses within the user. Positive thoughts and feelings are emerging automatically within the user.
4. It is not a binary property (i.e., either one is attached or is not attached) but varies in strength. If a user experiences a strong mobile attachment, the particular mobile phone becomes irreplaceable. The weaker it gets, the easier it is for the user to replace it. The strength of the attachment is dependent on the degree of the mobile-self connectedness. In its strongest form, the mobile phone can be experienced as an extension of the self.
5. It evolves over time and is dynamic in nature. The development of attachment results from repeated interactions between the individual and the attachment object over time. These interactions start when the user becomes aware of the mobile phone for the fist time (e.g., through advertisement), take place when the user handles the mobile phone for the fist time (e.g., when unpacking the mobile phone) and proceed through possession rituals like using, displaying, cleaning, discussing, and personalizing. Karapanos et al. [12] state that after an orientation and incorporation phase people become emotionally attached to their phones when they have reached the identification phase.

CONCEPTUAL MOBILE ATTACHMENT MODEL

Based on the definition of mobile attachment, we present a conceptual model of mobile attachment. For the formation of the model we took Park's [22] causes-and-consequences model of brand attachment. We adapted it for mobile phones and included a critical reflection of related literature from different disciplines. The model specifies causes for the emergence of mobile attachment, factors that influence this attachment, and resulting behavioral consequences for the individual who is attached to his or her mobile phone.

Figure 1 (on the next page) illustrates the conceptual mobile attachment model in detail. Mobile attachment is fostered by various causes. These causes provide a linkage between the mobile phone and the self via different routes. Based on these device-self linkage routes design space determinants have been elaborated. A possible mobile attachment is influenced by a variety of factors. These factors are regarded as user, device or environment related. Finally, the existence of mobile attachment leads to different mobile attachment consequences. These consequences are be the deliberate investment of limited or self-image resources. Simultaneously, a variety of other behavioral and emotional responses occur. The observable consequences can be used to measure mobile attachment. In the following sections we will describe and discuss the model in detail.

MOBILE ATTACHMENT CAUSES

Mobile attachment implicates a kind of mobile-self connectedness. Mobile attachment emerge when the user appreciates their mobile phone and the role it plays in achieving certain goals. The device becomes meaningful and significant. The mobile phone becomes connected to the self when it is perceived as part of the user's self concept. Mobile attachment exist when the mobile phone and the self are interlinked (i.e., it is perceived as part of the user's self concept). This link between the device and the user's self is fostered via different routes.

Analogous to to Park's [22] distinction of causes for brand attachment we argue that there are at least three device-self linkage routes. Mobile phones contribute to the self-concept when they have the capability for *empowerment*, *enrichment* and *gratification* of the self. First, the mobile phone becomes linked to the self by offering utilitarian meaning leading to an empowerment of the self. Second, the mobile phone offers a symbolic meaning, when enriching the self by representing one's self. Third, the mobile phone is connected to the self by providing hedonic meaning and, thereby, gratifying the self by offering aesthetic pleasure.

The enrichment of the self again has different dimensions. Temporally, a distinction between the past self, and the present and future self (cf. [22]). The mobile phone enriches the past self by providing memories and enrich the present and future self by protecting and enhancing the user's self concept. In addition, we suggest to differentiate between the the private, the public, and the collective self. The private self reflects the self-image a person conceives, the public self reflects the affiliation of the self with a group or the differentiation from others, and the collective self symbolizes a rather

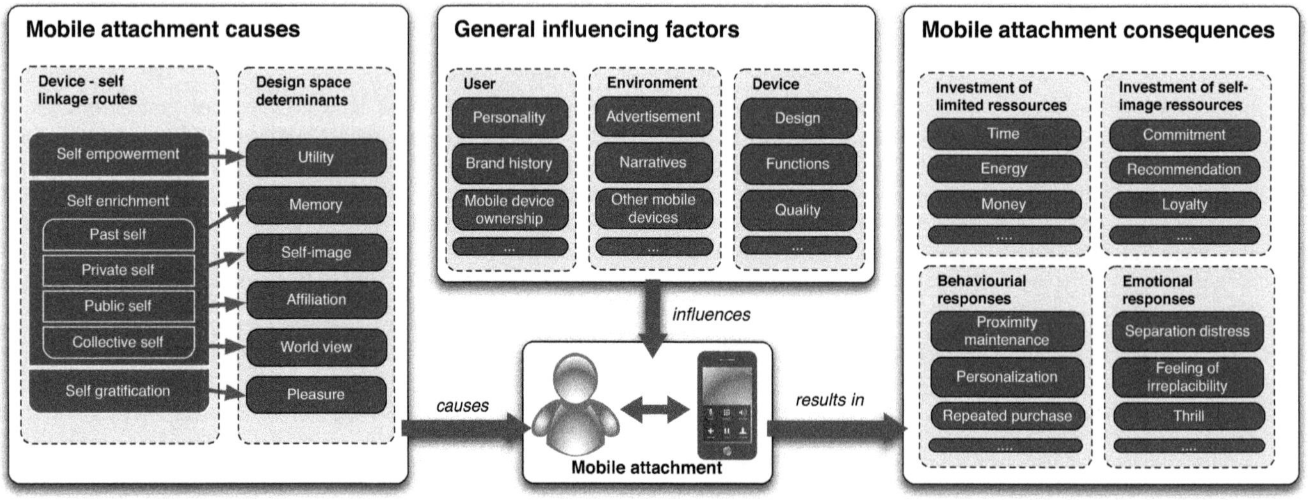

Figure 1. Conceptual mobile attachment model consisting of causes, general influencing factors, and consequences.

abstract idea or world view. This distinction is motivated by Greenwald's [7] facets of the self-schema: the diffuse self, the private self, the public self, and the collective self.

Each of the proposed routes are seen as a different determinant within a mobile phone design space. These determinants assign specific meanings of the mobile phone for the owner's self concept. In reality the mentioned reasons are not mutually exclusive; meaning that any or all combinations of causes can foster strong mobile attachment. The more links a mobile phone provides to the self and the more intense these links are, the stronger the mobile attachment becomes. In the following, the different device-self linkage routes and design space determinants will be discussed in detail.

Self Empowerment

Strong mobile attachment can occur when a mobile phone creates an efficacious and capable self, empowering owners to achieve mastery goals. If a mobile phone enables the user to exert control over his or her environment in order to reach desired goals and avoid undesired ones, it may be regarded as part of the self and, therefore, mobile attachment emerges. In its strongest form, mobile phones is seen as an extension of the self. Since the mobile phone in this case provides mainly utilitarian functions, the resulting design space determinant is labeled "utility".

The utilitarian meaning of a product serving as a necessary condition for emotional attachment is a matter of discussion in scientific literature (e.g., [19]). For example, Schifferstein et al. [24] claim that product utility is not a necessary condition for consumer product attachment. They argue that people hang on to products to which they are attached even when these products are broken or do not work properly. In their opinion, the fact that a product fulfills its primary utilitarian function (e.g., a clock shows the correct time) does not contribute to the degree of product attachment. Nevertheless, they admit that in cases where a product performs better than the average (e.g., is extremely easy to use) may foster attachment. In case of mobile attachment, we claim that it is very unlikely that a person still experiences a strong attachment to his or her mobile phone when it no longer works properly. Additionally, it can be argued that, above all, mobile phones offer possibilities without which many people could not imagine a fulfilled life.

Due to the role of mobile phones in modern society, the situation for these kind of objects is slightly different. Even if people do not feel attached to a specific mobile phone, they often experience a special relation to services provided by their mobile phones which, again, enables the owner to live a modern life. It is a fact that mobile phones have become an integral part of many peoples lives. Following these arguments it can be assumed that even people who do not feel a special bond to their own mobile phone, but agree that they need a mobile phone to live a fulfilled life, experience a (weak) form of mobile attachment. In this case people feel attached to the services and possibilities the mobile phone provides, rather than to the mobile phone itself. Nevertheless, the specific mobile phone is the carrier of the desired functionalities. A loss of the mobile phone may lead to distress until a new mobile phone substitutes the old one. This argumentation is supported by Belk [2] in his concept of the extended self. It suggests that material possessions can help us to define ourselves, when they serve as an enhancement of personal power, allowing us to do things of which we would otherwise be incapable. In the special case of mobile phones, Wehmeyer [28] includes the dimension perceived necessity in his user-device attachment construct. He argues that the ubiquity of the mobile communication device develops into a necessity for users both in business and private spheres.

If mobile phones can be regarded as part of the user's extended self by providing services without which the user cannot live a fulfilled life, then they can be seen as attachment objects, even though the mobile phone itself is replaceable by any other similar mobile phone. This view is also reflected in the way mobile phones are called in various languages. For example, the Finnish term for mobile phones is *kännykkä*, which literally means an extension of the hand. In German mobile phones are labeled *Handy*[2], which characterize the mobile phone as something that can be carried by hand.

In summary, it can be argued that a mobile phone can be regarded as part of the self-concept by empowering the self through its utilitarian functions and, therefore, utility serves as a determinant for mobile attachment. Utility alone may not be sufficient enough to foster strong mobile attachment, but it might increase the degree of mobile attachment.

Self Enrichment

Another contributor to a strong mobile attachment is when the mobile phone enriches the self by providing symbolic functions. The important role of symbolism for attachment is reflected in various literature. Park [22] argue that brands offer symbolic meaning, enriching the self by representing one's past, present, and future self. Belk [2] states that an object may support the desired identity, symbolizing who one is or to which group one belongs, as well as by providing an autobiographical function. Schifferstein et al. [24] argue that that people become attached to objects, when they support the private self, the public, and the collective self. Mugge [19] proposed self-expression, group affiliation, and memories as symbolic determinants of product attachment. Wehmeyer [28] claims that symbolism is an important factor for user-device attachment.

In general, two perspectives on the symbolic function of the attachment object can be identified. Park et al. [22] distinguish especially between temporal aspects (i.e., past self, present self, and future self), whereas Schifferstein et al. [24] distinguish between different self concepts (i.e., diffuse self, private self, public self, and collective self). For the conceptual model of mobile attachment, both temporal dimensions as well as the distinction between different self concepts are used to describe different aspects of how a mobile phone can enrich the self through its symbolic function. We argue that the following four symbolic functions are important routes to how mobile phones can enrich the self. The *past self* is enriched by the mobile phone, when it serves as a *reminder* of one's identity. The *private self* is enriched by means of a mobile phone, when it helps creating a person's identity by reflecting a *self-image*. The *public self* is enriched when the mobile phone represents a group *affiliation* and serves as a status symbol. The *collective self* is enriched, when the mobile phone symbolizes a *world view*.

Past Self Enrichment

Mobile phones can enrich the self by symbolically representing one's past self. The mobile phone may provide an autobiographical meaning by evoking memories of the past and by linking the present self to the past. For example, the mobile phone could serve as a reminder of the pleasant feeling of unpacking it for the first time. Another example is, when the mobile phone was a present from a cherished person or was obtained in a special context. The resulting design space determinant is labeled "memory".

In literature, past self enrichment through objects that remind oneself of the past are proposed by various authors as possible causes for emotional attachment. Mugge [19] introduced memories as one possible determinant for product attachment. She argues that products may remind a person of people, events, or places that are important to him or her and, therefore, help to maintain a sense of the past, which is assumed to be essential to define one's identity. Belk [2] argues that possessions may provide a link to an individual's past and, therefore, gained a symbolic meaning. Kleine et al. [15] names autobiographical and story-telling values as possible causes of possession attachment. The former marking life events and, therefore, contributing to define the self, the latter helping to tell personal stories of self-discovery, growth, and achievement.

Private Self Enrichment

Mobile phones can take on symbolic meaning representing one's private self. In this case the mobile phone has a self-definitional purpose. It serves as an expression of one's identity and represents how the owner sees himself or herself. It embodies how the owner wants to be. For example, an individual who rates himself or herself as a modern person may favor a modern mobile phone. People who see themselves as fashion-conscious prefer a fashionable mobile phone emphasizing appearance. Other people may define themselves as environmental friendly and choose mobile phones which are assumed to be produced in a sustainable way. Such mobile phones provide a link to individual's ideal self by representing their values and beliefs. Inimitable mobile phones may also serve as a symbol of uniqueness and individuality. This could be achieved through personalization. Since the mobile phone in this case symbolizes the image of oneself it the resulting design space determinant is "self-image".

Related research has highlighted the importance of the self defining purpose of products for the emergence of emotional attachment. Mugge [19] used the term self-expression to entitle the related determinant for product attachment. According to her, self-expression originates in the person's desire to differentiate oneself from others and to express his or her identity. This could be achieved by acquiring, displaying, and using products. Schifferstein et al. [24] suggest the determinant individual autonomy as a driver of attachment. They argue that products to which we become attached should reflect our identity and express individual autonomy supporting the private self. Csikszentmihalyi et al. [5] argue that objects may be used for achievement of selfhood based on conscious reflection and emotionally significant possessions may reflect and influence a person's growth

Public Self Enrichment

The mobile phone may serve as a status symbol underlining that the owner is part or not part of a specific group and, therefore, enriching the public self. This determinant stems from the people's need to be connected, associated, and involved with others [19]. For example, the newest BlackBerry mobile phones may be only allocated to managers within a company, whereas other employees 'only' get 'normal' mobile phones. These circumstances trigger mobile attachment within those

[2]The German word for hand is *Hand*.

who are equipped with BlackBerry phones. People who are not in this group feel the desire also to be rewarded with a BlackBerry. In the case of teenagers, the particular brand, color, size, logo, and ring tone of the mobile phone may define to what group an individual belongs. In these cases, the mobile phone itself symbolizes important persons or a whole group, because they enhance that part of the self that needs to feel connected. The resulting design space determinant is labeled as "affiliation".

In literature the affiliation value of cherished objects have been recognized broadly. Mugge [19] include group affiliation into her determinant set for product attachment. She argues that products that support group affiliation define to which group a person belongs and, therefore, symbolize desirable connections to family members, friends or social groups. Schifferstein et al. [24] claim that the public self 's aim is to look for approval of others resulting in a group affiliation meaning of the product. Additionally, it is related to Jordan's [11] socio-pleasure notion, which involves emotions that arise based on the relationships with others. Kleine et al. [15] name affiliation value as a possible facilitator for possession attachment. Mugge [19] mentions that, although the determinant group affiliation (i.e., affiliation) seems to oppose the determinant self-expression (i.e.,self-image), they can actually co-exist. On one hand, people are seeking for autonomy trying to establish and maintain a unique identity. On the other hand, they are seeking for affiliation to maintain interpersonal connections that also define the self.

Collective Self Enrichment

Mobile phones may enrich the self by symbolically representing one's collective self. Schifferstein et al. [24] state that "the collective self searches for approval from a reference group. After internalizing the norms of a reference group, people strive to conform to these norms." They name the inhabitants of a country, a subculture, or an ethnic minority as examples. The objects do not refer to specific people within the reference group, but symbolize an idea or a philosophy of life. In the case of mobile attachment, the mobile phone symbolizes a specific world view. For example, people who disagree with Apple's restrictive policy (e.g., Apps on iPhones are only available via the Apple's App Store) may refuse buy an Apple product due to this policy. They might strive for an alternative mobile phone (e.g., open-source based smartphone such as an Android mobile phone) in order to have the same functionality without Apple's restrictions. In this case the mobile phone symbolizes a general attitude towards life the corresponding design space determinant is labeled "world view".

In literature Schifferstein et al. [24] primarily utilize the collective self to derive the determinant life vision for consumer-product attachment. They additionally argue that the collective self and Jordan's [11] ideo-pleasure, which include values like tastes, moral values, or personal aspirations are related. The enrichment of the collective self bares some similarities to both private self enrichment and public self enrichment. Compared to the former, the enrichment of the collective self does not necessarily represent oneself (e.g., how somebody perceives oneself) but a philosophy. Compared to the latter, the collective self does not symbolize the relationship to individuals (e.g., members of a peer group) but rather an idea. Nevertheless, in reality, mobile phones can enrich the self through any or all three routes.

Self Gratification

A mobile phone may be emotionally important for the owner when it provides gratification through its hedonic properties (e.g., [22]). In this case, it supports the diffuse self [24]. It might please the owner through any combination of sensorial pleasures experienced during interaction. The mobile phone's overall visual appearance (e.g., form, color, background image) pleases the owner whenever he or she looks at it. Its tactile characteristics (e.g., material, surface texture, temperature) gratify the owner whenever he or she touches the mobile phone. Its auditory properties (e.g, ringtones, alarm sound, stored music) delight the owner whenever he or she listens to it. The familiarity of interacting with a well-known mobile phone enjoys the user. Mobile phones with such qualities may elicit positive emotions within the owner making him or her a happier person. Strong mobile attachment, thus, evolves through aesthetic and hedonic characteristics of a mobile phone that evoke sensory gratification for the self [22]. The derived design space determinant is called "pleasure".

Various authors propose self gratification through pleasure as a determinant for attachment. Mugge [19] recommends pleasure as a possible determinant for product attachment. Schifferstein et al. [24] propose enjoyment as a determinant of consumer-product attachment. Following their argumentation, the diffuse self, physio-pleasure, and visceral design share the involvement of sensory gratification. Wehmeyer [28] names aesthetics as a determinant for user-device attachment.

MOBILE ATTACHMENT INFLUENCING FACTORS

The second part of the conceptual model are various factors which may influence the emergence of mobile attachment (see Figure 1). These *general influencing factors* are characteristics which exist *independently* from the existence of mobile attachment. Nevertheless, they may influence the emergence of mobile attachment in one or another way. We used Huuskonens [9] categorization of mobile UX research. It includes the categories *user*, *environment*, and *mobile device*. These areas are not mutually independent from each other but overlap in some areas. In the following, essential examples for each area are provided.

User

The first area which have an impact on the emergence of mobile attachment are the users themselves. Personality related, cultural or demographical aspects may have an influence on mobile attachment. They may include the person's attachment styles [3] or the tendency of a person being extraverted or introverted, sensing or intuitive, intellectual or emotional person. Some people admit the existence of an emotional bond between them and their mobile phones, whereas others categorically refuse having any kind of emotions to inanimate objects.

Additionally, different types of purchase behavior influence mobile attachment. For example, people who see themselves as early adopters may develop mobile attachment easier than late followers, since they often seek individuality. Regarding the influence of cultural aspects, related research suggest that in Asia the relationship with mobile phones is very intimate. Mobile phones in Asia may be seen as spiritual phones [13]. Concerning demographical aspects age seems to be an influencing factor for mobile attachment. Various studies highlight the importance of mobile phones in life of teenagers indicating that particularly in young people mobile attachment arises (e.g., [21]). Taking gender into account, Geser [6] reports that "more women than men have assimilated the mobile phone as a central component of their personal existence: by integrating it into their lifestyle or by becoming so dependent on it that life without it has become unimaginable."

Other factors which can influence mobile attachment are the user's brand history (i.e., the user's experiences with a specific brand) or the user's mobile phone ownership (i.e., the user's experiences with other mobile phones over time). For instance, Khong and Song [14] have proposed that computer experience and capability are two antecedent variables of users' emotional response to IT products usage. It has been shown that user's emotional experiences with products and their remembered experiences change over time. Especially in the early stages of use, users tend to overestimate their positive emotions whereas the importance of usability increased over time [16].

Environment

Another area influencing mobile attachment is the environment in which the user is perceiving the mobile phone. In this context, the environment includes all factors which are not directly related to the user or the mobile phone. As an example it includes mobile phone advertisements, which often do not only promote the outstanding performance and usability of a product but also sell a life style. They draw a picture that owning the praised mobile phone brings pleasure and status and, therefore, influences the public opinion of a mobile phone. The public opinion again is important for the mobile phone to serve as a status symbol. Advertisements for products and transported messages contribute a lot to the success of these products.

Another influencing factor for mobile attachment are narratives or recommendation of colleagues, friends, or family members. For example, if all members of a clique own a certain type of mobile phone it is more likely to become part of the group when one also own the same type of mobile phone. This is especially true if the mobile phone offers services only available on this type of mobile phone. As an example, the popular game Ingress is only working on Android mobile devices. Thus, mobile attachment to this specific type of mobile phone is fostered. Other mobile phones on the market also influences mobile attachment. Since almost everyday newer and 'better' mobile phones are presented a once stylish mobile phone might be outdated rather soon and mobile attachment decreases.

Device

Finally, the characteristics of the mobile device itself influence mobile attachment. This includes the design of the mobile phone, the provided functions and applications, as well as the quality of used materials and supplied services. From a hardware perspective, the visual, tactile, and acoustical properties of the device influence mobile attachment. This includes qualities like the device's dimension, its texture, materials used, colors, input modalities, layout and position of various elements, sensors, speech quality, battery life time, storage size, and possibilities to personalize the mobile phone. From a software perspective, the visual design, as well as the interaction design, may foster mobile attachment. This again includes size, shape, and colors of elements, the underlying operating system, the possibility to install third party apps, and the possibility to personalize visual and acoustical elements. Also, the provided services may influence mobile attachment as the success of SMS has shown.

In general, all possible design decisions have the potential to influence mobile attachment. The more these design decisions support the design space determinants proposed above, the more likely mobile attachment emerges.

MOBILE ATTACHMENT CONSEQUENCES

The third part of the conceptual model are possible *mobile attachment consequences* (see Figure 1). If a person is emotionally attached to his or her mobile phone, a variety of behavioral and emotional consequences can be observed. When mobile attachment is strong, the device typically means a lot to the owner and consequently the person will experience emotional loss if that device is lost [24]. Therefore, these consequences serve as an indicator for the degree of mobile attachment.

Based on related work of attachment theory [3], consumer research [22] and product attachment [24], four conceptually different but yet related areas of possible mobile attachment consequences are introduced: the investment of limited resources, the investment of self-image resources, behavioral responses, as well as cognitive and emotional responses. Again, these areas are not mutually independent from each other but influence each other. The following sections provide examples for each area. Similar to the last section on influencing factors for mobile attachment, a completed list of consequences is not the focus of this paper.

Investment of Limited Resources

Regarding brand attachment, Park et al. [22] argues that the strength of the emotional bond connecting the brand and the self engenders the effect that the brand become self-relevant, impacting one's readiness to allocate discrete and self-image resources to the brand. Discrete resources include time, energy, and money.

In the case of mobile phones, this means that a strong mobile attachment leads to behaviors like the personalization of the mobile phone. This includes investing time and money to alter the appearance and functionality of the mobile phone to better fit one's personality. Examples are the decoration of the mobile phone, changing background images, assigning shortcuts, install selected applications, entering personal information, assigning different ringtones to different contacts, and involvement in mobile phone communities. This includes participating in blogs and spending time to make the device unique.

Investment of Self-image Resources

The investment of self-image resources refer to psychological resources for the sake of the mobile phone including self-pride and self-esteem. By publicly displaying, defending, advocating, or promoting the mobile phone, the owner is willing to face the risk of social rejection. The more resources the individual is willing to risk, the stronger the mobile attachment is likely to be.

If the mobile phone is seen as an extension of the self, attacks or criticism against the mobile phone are interpreted as a personal threat [22]. A person who is attached to his or her mobile phone is likely to demonstrate commitment to the cherished mobile phone, recommend this phone to friends, and show loyalty to publicly defend it. In these cases the borders between mobile attachment to a specimen and brand attachment are fluent.

Behavioral Responses

Previous research on mother-child attachment has identified different indicators of attachment [1]. Regarding behavioral responses, proximity maintenance seems to be a main consequence of mobile attachment. People who take their mobile phone with them wherever they go (e.g., holiday, bed) are more likely emotionally attached than those people who do not seek constant proximity to their mobile phones. Another behavioral response of people who are attached to their mobile phones is the level of mobile phone personalization. The more the user personalizes their mobile phone to fit their personal needs, the stronger mobile attachment is.

Additional evidence for the existence of mobile attachment is when the user repeatedly purchases the same mobile phone. This might be the case when the mobile phone is irretrievably lost or damaged beyond repair. A strongly attached person would purchase an exact replica mobile phone and personalize it in a way that it exactly matches the lost one. In these cases the difference between mobile attachment and other forms of product attachment (e.g., the attachment to a memorabilia) become evident. The mobile phone specimen often completely looses its value, when it does not work anymore.

Cognitive and Emotional Responses

Park et al. [22] argue that an emotional attachment to brands automatically elicits cognitive and affective responses within the customer. Such emotional responses are also an indicator for the existence of mobile attachment. Ainsworth's [1] presents indicators of attachment in the realm of mother-child attachment. Among the other indicators, separation distress seems to be the main indicator for mobile attachment. This point of view is supported by removing mobile phones from students during school hours as a form of punishment, when the student has not switched off the mobile phone during lessons. Since the mobile phone itself is regarded as a special object belonging to the private sphere of students, recently the mobile phone itself is not confiscated but the SIM card. At the end of the school day the SIM card is then returned to the student.

Vincent et al. [27] have shown that people felt strong negative and positive emotions towards their mobile phones. On one hand, they reported that people felt panic when being separated from their mobile phone. On the other hand, people felt thrill about the novelty of a new mobile phone. Such thrills may be regarded as emotional responses of mobile attachment. Finally, Schifferstein et al. [24] propose a close relationship between irreplaceability and product attachment. Therefore, a feeling of irreplaceability can be regarded as direct consequences of mobile attachment.

CONTRIBUTIONS FOR UX RESEARCH

This paper contributes to the field of UX research in three ways. First, the definition and model can be used in a theoretical way to understand the relationship between the concept of user experience and emotional attachment. Second, it provides design space determinants which can be useful for designers to design for mobile attachment. Third, it can serve as the basis for an evaluation framework of mobile attachment.

Theoretical contributions

There is a close relation ship between UX and emotional attachment, but most UX experts (rather) dissent that UX and emotional attachment are identical [17]. The presented definition and model add to sharpen the understanding of the differences between these two concepts. First, UX always present when a user interacts with a device whereas emotional attachment evolves over time [12]. Even a single withdrawal of money at an ATM engenders a certain experience within the user, although it is very unlikely that an emotional attachment targeted at the ATM within the user evolves in this short interaction period. Therefore emotional attachment can be assumed to be a subset of UX sharing similarities with – what Roto calls – the "overall UX" [23]. Second, people have user experience with a multitude of systems, whereas they usually experience strong attachment only with a few objects, if at all. Third, although UX is said to be subjectively dealing with hedonic qualities and particularly the positive outcomes of technology use [8] it also covers non emotional interactions as well as emotionally negative experiences.

Design contributions

In order to design for attachment, we first have to understand how the emotional relationships between the user and the mobile phone is formed. The developed design space determinants may be fruitful for designers to understand mobile attachment. Based on the model mobile attachment may be fostered when the designer succeeds in linking the mobile phone and the users self concept. This is achieved through self empowerment, self enrichment, and self gratification. The designer can address the following design space determinants:

Design for Utility The mobile phone should be treated as a utilitarian extension of the self. Reliability and trust should be an important design goal. Since attachment evolves over time long-term usability has to be achieved by the designer.

Design for Memory The mobile phone should provided an autobiographical meaning to the owner. This may be achieved when it serves as a container for memories or is related to pleasurable memories of past experiences. E.g., the out-of-the-box experience could be designed to evoke pleasure and pride.

Design for Self-Image To enrich the private self, mobile phone should be able to reflect the owner's identity or help to define the self. This could be achieved by either representing the owner's self perception or by symbolizing the owner's desired identity. Designers should facilitate personalization and foster individuality of mobile phones.

Design for Affiliation Attachment arises when the mobile phone is seen as a status symbol. Thus, the design of mobile phones should foster group affiliation and status. E.g., by providing features only for a specific group of users or through the possibility of personalization.

Design for World View The mobile phone should be designed to represent a world view (i.e. the fundamental cognitive orientation of an individual including values and ethics). E.g., the mobile phone is designed for sustainable people consisting only of sustainable elements or the device might be designed following the open source paradigm.

Design for Pleasure Designers can influence mobile attachment by stimulating the experience of pleasure from a mobile phone. E.g., through an aesthetic design, the use of valuable materials or joyful applications. Lee at al. [18] propose to incorporate hidden interfaces into the design of mobile phones in order to foster pleasure and mobile attachment.

Evaluation contributions

Finally, the identified attachment consequences can serve as a basis for an evaluation framework of mobile attachment. These consequences can be seen as indicators of the existence andy the degree of mobile attachment. The investment of limited resources such as time, energy and money may indicate that the user is attached to the mobile phone. Also the investment of self-image resources such as publicly displaying, defending, advocating, or promoting the mobile phone signifies a bound between the user and their mobile phone. These indicators can be observed in the filed or revealed in content analysis of various sources (e.g., online blogs). Behavioral responses such as proximity maintenance, personalization, and repeated purchase of mobile phones may be gathered through observations or through interviews. Emotional responses such as thrill can be revealed by observing unboxing. Separation distress could be revealed by performing breaching experiments (e.g., taking away the mobile phone for some time).

CONCLUSION AND FUTURE WORK

This paper presents a definition of mobile attachment and conceptual mobile attachment model. We claim that mobile attachment is fostered by various causes which provide a link between the mobile phone and the self via different routes. We have outlined how independent factors have an influence on mobile attachment. Finally, the existence of mobile attachment leads to different mobile attachment consequences. The mobile attachment definition and model was developed based on a critical reflection on interdisciplinary attachment literature. Here we want to mention that the model is primarily suited for the western usage of mobile device. The way that property is perceived may differ in different parts of the world.

We also want to highlight that we see a close link between attachment to the physical device itself and the brand including the software platform ecosystem (especially in the case of the most prominent example of the iPhone). We argue that device attachment and brand attachment overlap and the attachment to a mobile device specimen may be transferred to a newer version of the same brand. Nevertheless, it is the artifact, which embodies the attachment and when an, for example, iPhone user looses his beloved object he might experience loss and pain. Thus, it is this specimen to which the owner is emotionally attached. But the cause for the attachment (in the case of Apple Fanboys, often the "public self enrichment") changes abruptly when there is a new iPhone on the market. In this case, the old iPhone is no longer a status symbol and, therefore, looses its attractiveness. Attachment to the specimen diminishes and is likely to be replaced by the attachment to the new iPhone.

As future work we see above all a validation of the presented model by means of empirical studies. We are aiming at providing examples how particular mobile phones relates to our model. Another trajectory for research is a in depth analysis of the similarities and differences between brand attachment and mobile attachment—especially in case of the iPhone. The presented model is rather broad and future research will be needed to developed an enhance mobile attachment model.

ACKNOWLEDGMENTS

The financial support by the Federal Ministry of Economy, Family and Youth, the National Foundation for Research, Technology and Development is gratefully acknowledged (Christian Doppler Laboratory for "Contextual Interfaces").

REFERENCES

1. Ainsworth, M. D. S., Blehar, M. C., and ans Sally Wall, E. W. *Patterns of attachment: a psychological study of the strange situation*. Lawrence Erlbaum Associates, Hilsdale, New Jersey, USA, 1978.
2. Belk, R. W. Possessions and the Extended Self. *Journal of Consumer Research: An Interdisciplinary Quarterly 15*, 2 (1988), 139–68.
3. Bowlby, J. *Attachment and loss, Vol. 1: Attachment*. Basic Books, New York, 1969.
4. Bowlby, J. *The Making and Breaking of Affectional Bonds*. Tavistock, London, 1979.
5. Csikszentmihalyi, M., and Rochberg-Halton, E. *The Meaning of Things, Domestic Symbols and the Self*. Cambridge University Press, New York, NY, USA, 1981.

6. Geser, H. Are girls (even) more addicted? Some gender patterns of cell phone usage. *Sociology in Switzerland: Sociology of the Mobile Phone. Online Publications* (June 2006).

7. Greenwald, A. G. A social-cognitive account of the self's development. In *Self, ego, and identity: Integrative approaches*, D. K. Lapsley and F. C. Power, Eds. Springer-Verlag, New York, 1988, 30–42.

8. Hassenzahl, M., Heidecker, S., Eckoldt, K., Diefenbach, S., and Hillmann, U. All you need is love: Current strategies of mediating intimate relationships through technology. *ACM Trans. Comput.-Hum. Interact. 19*, 4 (Dec. 2012), 30:1–30:19.

9. Huuskonen, P. Interaction Through Non-interaction: Context Awareness and Distributed Applications. Keynote speech at Applied Spoken Language Interaction in Distributed Environments (ASIDE2005), November 10-11 2005.

10. Jones, M., and Marsden, G. *Mobile Interaction Design*. John Wiley & Sons, West Sussex, UK, February 2006.

11. Jordan, P. W. *Designing Pleasurable Products: An Introduction to the New Human Factors*. Taylor and Francis Ltd, Philadelphia, PA, USA, 2000.

12. Karapanos, E., Zimmerman, J., Forlizzi, J., and Martens, J.-B. User experience over time: an initial framework. In *CHI '09: Proceedings of the 27th international conference on Human factors in computing systems*, ACM (New York, NY, USA, 2009), 729–738.

13. Katz, J. E., and Suygiyama, S. Mobile phones as fashion statements: The co-creation of mobile communication's public meaning. In *Mobile Communication and the Re-negotiation of the Social Sphere*, R. Ling and P. E. Pedersen, Eds., CSCW. Springer-Verlag, London, UK, 2005.

14. Khong, P. W., and Song, J. P. Exploring user's emotional relationships with it products: a structural equation model. In *DPPI '03: Proceedings of the 2003 international conference on Designing pleasurable products and interfaces*, ACM (New York, NY, USA, 2003), 45–50.

15. Kleine, S. S., and Baker, S. M. An Integrative Review of Material Possession Attachment. *Academy of Marketing Science Review 2004*, 1 (2004), 1–35.

16. Kujala, S., and Miron-Shatz, T. Emotions, experiences and usability in real-life mobile phone use. In *Proceedings of the SIGCHI Conference on Human Factors in Computing Systems*, CHI '13, ACM (New York, NY, USA, 2013), 1061–1070.

17. Law, E. L.-C., Roto, V., Hassenzahl, M., Vermeeren, A. P., and Kort, J. Understanding, scoping and defining user experience: a survey approach. In *CHI '09: Proceedings of the 27th international conference on Human factors in computing systems*, ACM (New York, NY, USA, 2009), 719–728.

18. Lee, M.-H., Kim, D.-H., Kim, H.-J., and Nam, T.-J. Understanding impacts of hidden interfaces on mobile phone user experience. In *Proceedings of the 7th Nordic Conference on Human-Computer Interaction: Making Sense Through Design*, NordiCHI '12, ACM (New York, NY, USA, 2012), 45–48.

19. Mugge, R. *Emotional Bonding with Products: Investigating Product Attachment from a Design Perspective*. VDM Verlag, Saarbrücken, Germany, 2008.

20. Odom, W., Zimmerman, J., and Forlizzi, J. Teenagers and their virtual possessions: design opportunities and issues. In *Proceedings of the SIGCHI Conference on Human Factors in Computing Systems*, CHI '11, ACM (New York, NY, USA, 2011), 1491–1500.

21. Odom, W., Zimmerman, J., Forlizzi, J., López Higuera, A., Marchitto, M., Cañas, J., Lim, Y.-k., Nam, T.-J., Lee, M.-H., Lee, Y., Kim, D.-j., Row, Y.-k., Seok, J., Sohn, B., and Moore, H. Fragmentation and transition: understanding perceptions of virtual possessions among young adults in spain, south korea and the united states. In *Proceedings of the SIGCHI Conference on Human Factors in Computing Systems*, CHI '13, ACM (New York, NY, USA, 2013), 1833–1842.

22. Park, C. W., MacInnis, D. J., and Priester, J. R. Beyond Attitudes: Attachment and Consumer Behavior. *Seoul National Journal 12*, 2 (2006), 3–36.

23. Roto, V. User Experience from Product Creation Perspective. In *Proceedings of the COST294-MAUSE affiliated workshop: Towards a UX Manifesto*, E. Law, A. Vermeeren, M. Hassenzahl, and M. Blythe, Eds. (Lancaster, UK, 2007), 31–34.

24. Schifferstein, H. N., and Zwartkruis-Pelgrim, E. P. Consumer-Product Attachment: Measurement and Design Implications. *International Journal of Design 2*, 3 (2008), 1–13.

25. Schifferstein, H. N. J., Mugge, R., and Hekkert, P. Designing consumer-product attachment. In *Design and Emotion*, D. McDonagh, P. Hekkert, J. van Erp, and D. Gyi, Eds. CRC Press, London, UK, 2003, 378–383.

26. Schultz, S. E., Kleine, R. E., and Kernan, J. B. "These are a few of my favourite thing" toward an explication of attachment as a consumer behavior construct. *Advances in Consumer Research 16* (1989), 359–366.

27. Vincent, J. Emotional attachment and mobile phones. In *Thumb Culture: The Meaning Of Mobile Phones For Society*, G. P. Bertschi S., Ed. Transcript Verlag/Transaction US, Bielefeld, Germany, 2006.

28. Wehmeyer, K. User-device attachment scale development and initial test. *Int. J. Mob. Commun. 6*, 3 (2008), 280–295.

29. Zimmerman, J. Designing for the self: making products that help people become the person they desire to be. In *CHI '09: Proceedings of the 27th international conference on Human factors in computing systems*, ACM (New York, NY, USA, 2009), 395–404.

Hooked on Smartphones: An Exploratory Study on Smartphone Overuse among College Students

Uichin Lee, Joonwon Lee, Minsam Ko, Changhun Lee[†], Yuhwan Kim[§], Subin Yang
Koji Yatani[‡], Gahgene Gweon, Kyong-Mee Chung[♯], Junehwa Song[§]
Knowledge Service Engineering Department, KAIST, [†]Web Science and Technology Division, KAIST
[‡]Microsoft Research Asia, [§]Computer Science Department, KAIST
[♯]Department of Psychology, Yeonsei University
{uclee, joonwonlee, msko, changhun, yuhwan, subin.yang, ggweon, junesong}@kaist.ac.kr
[‡]koji@microsoft.com [♯]kmchung@yonsei.ac.kr

ABSTRACT
The negative aspects of smartphone overuse on young adults, such as sleep deprivation and attention deficits, are being increasingly recognized recently. This emerging issue motivated us to analyze the usage patterns related to smartphone overuse. We investigate smartphone usage for 95 college students using surveys, logged data, and interviews. We first divide the participants into risk and non-risk groups based on self-reported rating scale for smartphone overuse. We then analyze the usage data to identify between-group usage differences, which ranged from the overall usage patterns to app-specific usage patterns. Compared with the non-risk group, our results show that the risk group has longer usage time per day and different diurnal usage patterns. Also, the risk group users are more susceptible to push notifications, and tend to consume more online content. We characterize the overall relationship between usage features and smartphone overuse using analytic modeling and provide detailed illustrations of problematic usage behaviors based on interview data.

Author Keywords
Smartphone Overuse; Measurement

ACM Classification Keywords
H.5.m. Information Interfaces and Presentation (e.g. HCI): Miscellaneous

INTRODUCTION
The popularity of smartphones has been increasing rapidly in recent years. In most of developed countries, the rate of smartphone adoption exceeded 50% in the first half of 2012 [2]. Thus, smartphones have now become an integral part of the daily lives of many individuals. However, negative aspects of their use have emerged, such as the disruption of social interactions. In addition, researchers have found close relationship between their overuse and poor mental health (e.g., sleep deprivation and attention deficits) [24]. Interactive characteristics of smartphones contain inducing and reinforcing features that promote excessive usage behaviors [17, 10]. For example, Oulasvirta et al. [25] have demonstrated that frequently checking dynamic content (e.g., updates from online social networks) on mobile devices weakens self-regulation, which may lead to smartphone overuse [17, 10].

Researchers have tried to identify the problematic usage patterns that are related with smartphone overuse [5, 16], mainly through self-reported scale which are subjective and prone to recall errors [27]. Thus far, relatively little information is known about how smartphone overuse is reflected in the actual use of smartphones. In this paper, we investigate the college students as a focusing lens on emerging technological issues. Smartphones are used widely by college students. In the first half of 2012, the smartphone adoption rates in the UK and South Korea were 72% and 86%, respectively [2]. Moreover, college students are considered to be vulnerable to technology overuse because of their developmental dynamics and relative independence from social roles and expectations [14].

We collected actual smartphone usage data from 95 college students (over 50,000 hours of usage data) and performed an exploratory data analysis along with the smartphone addiction psychometric scale [15]. Our smartphone usage logger allowed for unobtrusive monitoring that has minimal impacts on user behavior [27]. Participants were divided into two groups based on rating score: a risk group (whose scores indicated a potential for smartphone overuse) and a non-risk group. We examined the differences in the usage patterns of the two groups by comparing various usage features, which were extracted from the dataset (e.g., overall usage and content-specific usage). These usage differences were validated by analytic modeling, and also corroborated by the findings from our interviews.

We identified several usage patterns that were closely related to smartphone overuse. The risk group spent more time on smartphone use per day (risk group: 253.0 min *vs.* non-risk group: 207.0 min) compared with the non-risk group,

CHI 2014, April 26–May 1, 2014, Toronto, Ontario, Canada.

ACM 978-1-4503-2473-1/14/04 ...$15.00.
http://dx.doi.org/10.1145/2556288.2557366

and there were also diurnal usage differences (greater usage in the morning and evening). The usage sessions that were initiated by the push notifications were longer for the risk group, which demonstrated that notifications acted as external cues related to problematic usage patterns. The risk group consumed significantly more online content that can provide instant gratifications (e.g., pastimes, entertainment, and information seeking).

These findings were supported by the results of our analytic modeling and the analysis of our interview data. Regression analysis showed that the key components of smartphone overuse, such as interference, withdrawal, and tolerance, were closely related to usage features. In addition, we used machine learning techniques to test the predictive power of the usage features and found that smartphone overuse could be classified accurately based on these features with an F-score of 0.87. The interview results provided more detailed examples of problematic usage behavior, such as limited self-control when consuming online content (e.g., aimlessly following web/Facebook links while in bed). Our key findings support the existing theories related to technological addictions [11, 17, 10]. In particular, repeated consumption of online content may lead to addictive behaviors, and problematic behaviors depend mainly on specific functions rather than the volume of usage.

BACKGROUND AND RELATED WORK

Technological Addiction and Smartphone Overuse

Technological addictions are defined as behavioral (non-chemical) addictions, where interactive components of computer devices can have inducing and reinforcing features that may promote addictive tendencies (e.g., tolerance, withdrawal, interference, and relapse) [11]. Despite recent clinical and scientific evidence, however, there is a lack of agreement on the existence of technological addictions. According to Morahan-Martin's report [22], some researchers argue that the pathological use of technology services is driven by attempts to avoid the underlying mental or social problems. Others contend that technology is merely a medium for service delivery, and that obsessive use is related to specific services such as gambling and games. These arguments are debatable, but an awareness of technological addictions is growing in scientific communities. The Diagnostic and Statistical Manual of Mental Disorders, Fifth Edition (DSM-5), which was released in May 2013 by the American Psychiatric Association (APA), officially recognized behavioral addictions for the first time and recommended further research into existing technological addictions for later inclusion [1].

Prior studies have identified contributing factors that make digital media, such as the Internet and cell phones, attractive and often addictive [11, 17, 10]. Digital media provide easy and convenient ways of accessing a large amount of online content (e.g., music, news, and games) and maintaining social relationships. Such access gives instant gratifications to users (e.g., interpersonal utility, pastimes, information seeking, and entertainment), in turn reinforcing continuous usage of it [17, 10]. This concept is known as operant conditioning, which is one of the fundamental learning theories in behavioral psychology [21]. Excessive usage may follow subsequently, possibly due to deficient self-regulation or maladaptive thinking [11, 18, 17, 10].

Previous studies of Internet addiction showed that excessive use of online communication and games occurs often, which is related to various psychological factors, including social anxiety, depression, impulsivity, self-esteem/identity deficits, and situational stress during life changing events [23, 28, 19]. Similarly, excessive usage has also been studied in the context of mobile phone use [5, 13]. Carbonell et al. [5] reported that the excessive use of mobile phones by teenagers is attributable to text-messaging and mobile games. Hwang et al. [13] showed that it is also related with various psychological factors such as social anxiety, depression, and impulsivity. In contrast to previous studies [5, 13], we perform an exploratory data analysis of real usage datasets to uncover the usage features related to smartphone overuse, and validate the differences between usage patterns using analytic modeling and analysis of interview data.

Smartphone Usage Studies

Cui and Roto [6] found that the main use of smartphones was task-oriented with goals of information seeking, communications, online transactions, and managing personal information. In an observational study of smartphone usage on the Stanford campus, Ames [3] showed that the availability of always-on connectivity meant that the students had to exhibit the techno-social practices of balancing their extended networks with the immediate surroundings and to limit the negative impacts of smartphone usage (e.g., social pressure, and multi-tasking). Harmon and Mazmanian [12] identified two themes of smartphone use that are reflected in commercials, where one theme recommends the deep integration of smartphones in daily life, and the other urges people toward disintegration. Oulasvirta et al. [25] reported that the use of mobile devices may lead to the development of a checking habit that involves brief and frequent content consumption (e.g., checking emails and Facebook updates).

A few studies have characterized how users access their mobile devices during their everyday lives. For example, Falaki et al. [8] studied the usage patterns of Android and Windows Mobile phones by analyzing user interactions, app use, network traffic, and energy consumption. Despite the differences in the objectives and frequencies of smartphone use, they found that there were similarities in the fine-grained usage patterns of users (e.g., the session time distribution). Böhmer et al. [4] analyzed a large-scale, global dataset primarily from the US and Europe. They found that users typically spent almost one hour per day on smartphones, and that the average session duration was less than one minute. Their study also indicated the different time dependencies for app usage. For example, news apps were accessed most frequently in the morning, whereas communication apps (email and SMS) were used throughout the day. Although earlier studies [8, 4] provided general overviews of smartphone usage, they did not investigate the usage patterns related to smartphone overuse. By contrast, our study examines the similarities and differences between the smartphone usage among users with overuse risks and those without.

HCI Research into Addictive Behavior

Addiction-related studies have been increasing recently in the HCI community. A major goal of these studies is to explore the main factors to develop effective addiction intervention mechanisms. Seay and Kraut [26] showed that self-regulation is critical for controlling online gaming behaviors, and they considered how it can be incorporated into the game designs to prevent addictive behaviors. Another direction is to design new computing services or to simply use existing services to mitigate problematic use and assist traditional treatments. Wang et al. [29] built a smartphone-based system for tracking sobriety after patients left a rehabilitation center and for communicating relevant information to fellow patients and counselors. Yarosh [30] performed an observational study on the role of technology in alcoholism recovery. Our study attempts to identify the usage patterns related to smartphone overuse and to provide several guidelines to facilitate the design of intervention software.

METHODOLOGY

Participants

We investigated the smartphone usage behaviors of undergraduate students at a large university in Korea during the fall semester of 2012. We selected this homogeneous user population to help improve the internal validity of this study. This is a common practice in psychological studies [5, 28]. Selecting college students as the study groups is also beneficial because the smartphone adoption rate among young adults is very high [2]. In addition, they are vulnerable to technology overuse due to their developmental dynamics (e.g., identity formation) and relative independence from social roles and expectations [14]. We recruited students in 2012 during the time period between the mid-term and final exams in order to avoid the influence of exams affecting our study. Ninety-five students participated in the experiment for at least two weeks. The average age of the participants was 20.6 years (SD 1.7); and 67 (i.e., 70.5%) were male. Data were collected for an average of 26.8 days (SD 9.5). All of the participants were compensated for their participation with a gift that was equivalent to $20.

Smartphone Usage Logging

We developed the *SmartLogger* software to log a variety of application events (active/inactive apps, touch and text input events, web browsing URLs, and notification events), system events (power on/off and screen on/off/unlock), and phone events (calls and SMS). SmartLogger operates as an Android accessibility service. After an accessibility service has been enabled in the system settings, it runs automatically in the background.

Our approach can be considered as an unobtrusive method because the participants were generally unaware that they were being observed, which meant that their usage behavior was not affected by the data collection process [27]. We examined whether there were any significant differences in the daily usage levels during the experimental period (excluding the data obtained on the day of installation). We found that there were statistically significant differences only in the first two days compared with the remainder of the first week, and there were

F1	*"My school grades (or work productivity) dropped due to excessive smartphone use."* *"People often complained about excessive smartphone use."*
F2	*"Using a smartphone is more enjoyable than spending time with my family or friends."* *"When I cannot use my smartphone, I feel like I have lost the entire world."*
F3	*"It would be distressing if I am not allowed to use my smartphone."* *"I become restless and nervous when smartphone use is impeded."*
F4	*"Even when I think I should stop, I continue to use my smartphone."* *"Spending a lot of time on my smartphone has become a habit."*

Table 1. Illustration of Smartphone Addiction Proneness Scale (its subfactors include F1: Interference, F2: Virtual World, F3: Withdrawal, and F4: Tolerance)

no significant changes subsequently. Therefore, we excluded the data recorded during the first two days of participation from the subsequent analysis.

User Surveys and Interviews

Before initiating the data collection process, we administered surveys to acquire demographic data and measure the level of smartphone overuse. We used the *Smartphone Addiction Proneness Scale for Adults* [15], which is an established scale for smartphone overuse. The scale comprises 15 four-point Likert-scale questions (see the examples in Table 1), which measure four factors associated with addictive behaviors (interference, virtual world, withdrawal, and tolerance). The scale was designed to classify users into three groups (i.e., high-risk, at-risk, and normal user groups) [15]. In our study, we divided the participants into two groups: i.e., high/at-risk (total score ≥ 40 or F1: interference score ≥ 14) and non-risk (the remaining participants). This decision was based on the fact that the sample size would have been too small for subsequent analyses otherwise ($< 3\%$ as the threshold used to separate the high-risk group was set at 2 SD above the mean in the scale). Figure 1 shows the distribution of the participants based on the F1 (interference) score and the total score. The risk and non-risk groups comprised 36 and 59 participants, respectively.

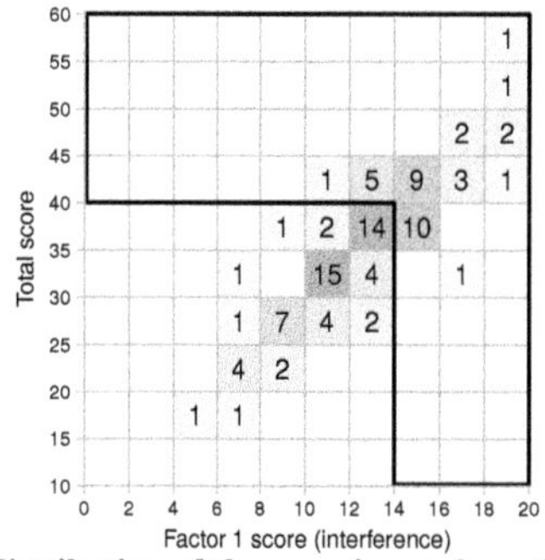

Figure 1. Score distribution of the experimental participants (high/at-risk groups: factor 1 score $\geq$ 14 or total score $\geq$ 40, non-risk group: remaining participants)

After the data collection process, we performed additional surveys and interviews to supplement the results from our quantitative data analysis and to characterize problematic usage behaviors. In the exit-surveys, we explored the usage of mobile instant messaging and its negative impacts. In addition, we selected seven participants (four risk and three non-risk) to participate in semi-structured interviews, where our selection criterion required that their average smartphone usage per day exceed four hours. We aimed to enhance our understanding of the usage characteristics determined in the quantitative analysis and to identify more detailed themes related to problematic usage behaviors. All of the interviews were transcribed and open coding was performed to facilitate content analysis.

Data Analysis Model

Active smartphone usage can be represented based on a series of sessions, as shown in Figure 2. A session was defined as the time between turning on and off events of the screen.

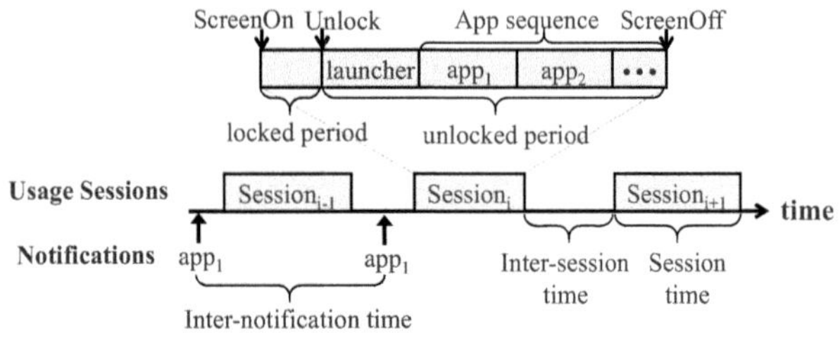

Figure 2. Usage data analysis model

During a typical session, a participant first unlocked the phone and then operated a series of apps; we excluded launcher usage in between apps. Several types of events, such as notifications and battery charging, could switch on the screen automatically. In our analysis, we filtered out the events that did not elicit further user interactions (i.e., screen unlocking). Users may have apps that provided notification messages (e.g., for new chats and emails). In Android, an icon appears in the notification area, and users can open the notification drawer to check the details and interact with their apps. For app-specific usage analysis, we designed simplified categories based on existing app categories from app stores and a previous study [4].

OVERALL DIFFERENCES IN USAGE PATTERNS

We analyzed the aggregated usage, session-level usage, and temporal usage patterns to identify differences in the specific usage levels of the risk and non-risk groups. The overall usage results are presented in Figure 3 and Figure 4.

Aggregated Usage: For a given day, the daily usage time was defined as the sum of all the session times. We calculated the mean daily usage time for each participant. There was a significant difference in the daily usage time, where the risk group (253.0 min, SD: 90.9, $p = .011$, Cohen's $d = 0.54$) had a longer average smartphone usage period than the non-risk group (207.4 min, SD: 77.2). We also measured how often the participants interacted with their smartphones by calculating the mean session frequency per day and the mean inter-session duration (i.e., the interval between two consecutive sessions), but there were no significant differences. The risk group had a slightly higher mean session frequency (risk: 111.5 *vs.* non-risk: 100.1, $p = .146$, Cohen's $d = 0.31$) and a shorter mean inter-session time (risk: 729.1 s *vs.* 816.6 s, $p = .216$, Cohen's $d = 0.26$), but the differences were not significant.

Session-level Usage: We also investigated whether the usage patterns within a session differed between the groups. We

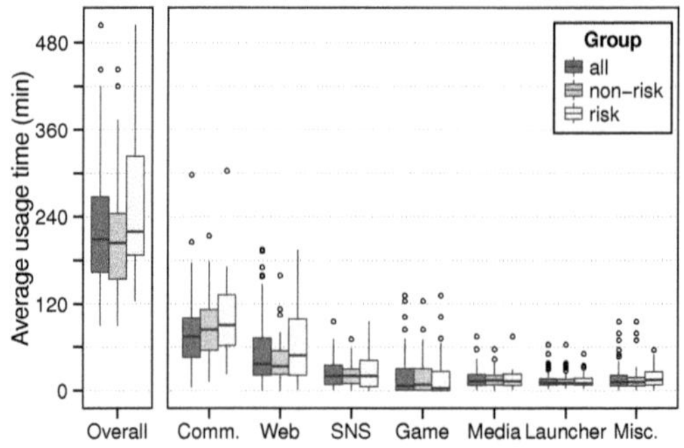

Figure 3. Usage amount: overall and app-specific results

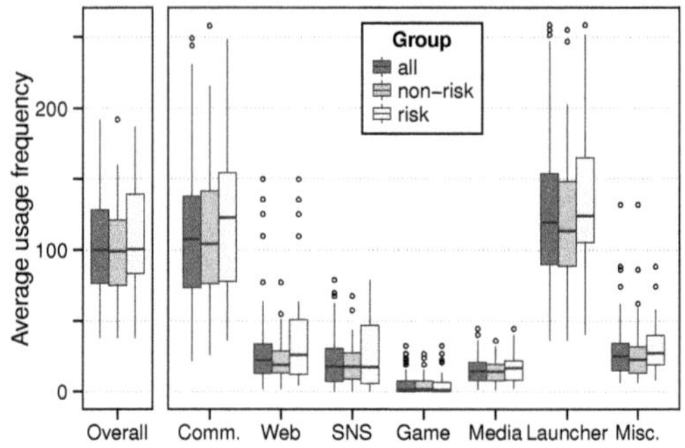

Figure 4. Usage frequency: overall and app-specific results

inspected the number of apps used during each session. We assumed that a session comprised a sequence of n apps used, $\{a_1, a_2, \cdots, a_n\}$ where a_k denotes the name of the kth used app, and the sequence length was simply given as n. Our results indicated that the sequence length was slightly longer for the risk group, but the difference was not significant (risk: 3.53 *vs.* non-risk: 3.16, $p = .072$, Cohen's $d = 0.43$).

We examined the app usage patterns of the risk group in order to determine whether the patterns were skewed. We checked the number of unique apps used during the experiment, but there was no significant difference (risk: 66.1 *vs.* non-risk: 65.5, $p = .885$, Cohen's $d = 0.03$). We used the entropy metric to measure the degree of usage for the top-k apps. For a given user, the entropy value was calculated based on the usage time distribution for the top-k apps using $-\sum_{i=1,k} p(i) \log p(i)$, where $p(i)$ is the relative usage time of the ith app. Entropy has the following property. The lower the entropy, the higher the level of focus on certain apps. For example, if a person only uses a single app, the entropy becomes zero. If she spends an equal amount of time on every app, the entropy is maximized.

Given that most participants frequently used a small number of apps, we examined the number of top-k apps using $k = 5$, 10, and 50, and we then calculated the entropy values. There was a significant difference in the top-5 app usage ($p = .046$, Cohen's $d = 0.42$), which showed that the top-5 usage patterns of the risk group were highly skewed. We performed unpaired t-tests (two-tailed) of the usage levels for the k-th ranked apps and found that the risk group spent more time interacting with the first ranked apps and on the second ranked apps (primarily KakaoTalk, Facebook, and browsers). The mean usage times of the first-ranked apps were 97.8 min and 69.9 min ($p = .003$,

Agg. Usage	Non-Risk [95% CI]	Risk [95% CI]	T	P	d
Usage time (m)	207.4 [187.3, 227.5]	253.0 [222.3, 283.8]	2.61	.011	0.54
Usage freq	100.1 [91.5, 108.6]	111.5 [97.2, 125.9]	1.47	.146	0.31
Session Usage	Non-Risk [95% CI]	Risk [95% CI]	T	P	d
Session time (s)	129.9 [115.6, 144.1]	157.6 [123.6, 191.6]	1.53	.134	0.36
Inter-ses. time (s)	816.6 [726.9, 906.4]	729.1 [623.7, 835.5]	1.25	.216	0.26
# unique apps	65.5 [60.0, 70.1]	66.1 [60.1, 72.1]	0.15	.885	0.03
Sequence len.	3.16 [2.9, 3.3]	3.53 [3.2,3.9]	1.84	.072	0.42
Agg. seq. len	204.2 [181.7, 226.6]	235.2 [204.4, 265.9]	1.66	.099	0.35
Top-5 entropy	1.96 [1.9, 2.0]	1.85 [1.7,1.9]	2.02	.046	0.42
Top-10 entropy	2.53 [2.5, 2.6]	2.40 [2.3, 2.5]	1.74	.085	0.36
#1 app time (m)	69.9 [60.6,79.0]	97.8 [81.5, 114.2]	3.02	.003	0.66
#1 app freq	115.4 [105.1,125.5]	134.7 [119.0,150.6]	2.18	.031	0.46
#2 app time (m)	37.2 [32.5, 42.6]	47.4 [38.4, 56.4]	1.93	.060	0.43
#2 app freq	70.3 [62.4, 78.1]	85.3 [70.2, 100.4]	1.78	.080	0.41

Table 2. Two-sample t-test results of the aggregated usage (two-tailed)

Cohen's $d = 0.66$), and the mean usage times for the second-ranked apps were 47.4 min and 37.5 min ($p = .058$, Cohen's $d = 0.43$), for the risk and non-risk groups, respectively.

Diurnal Usage: We hypothesized that the risk group would have different diurnal patterns compared with the non-risk group because they used smartphones for longer periods of time. We divided each day into four blocks; i.e., night: [0, 6), morning: [6, 12), afternoon: [12, 18), and evening [18, 24). We performed unpaired t-tests (one-tailed) of the usage levels with Bonferroni correction. Figure 5 shows that the risk group used their smartphones for significantly more time in the morning ($p = .022$, Cohen's $d = 0.53$) and evening ($p = .038$, Cohen's $d = 0.49$). Comparisons of the mean session durations across time blocks revealed that our participants had longer usage sessions during the morning and night blocks; e.g., morning *vs.* afternoon ($p = .004$, Cohen's $d = 0.43$) (detailed information can be found in the Appendix).

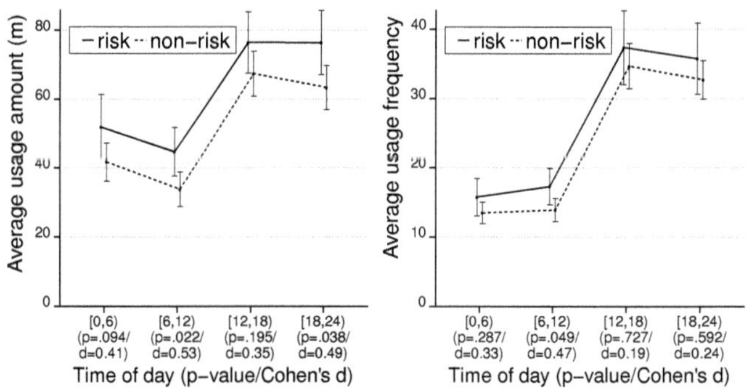

Figure 5. Overall diurnal usage time and frequency (mean value with 95% confidence interval, p-value/Cohen's d)

Summary of Findings: Our results showed that the risk group used their smartphones for more time than the non-risk group (risk: 253.0 min *vs.* non-risk: 207.0 min). The risk group users tended to use smartphones more frequently and to engage in longer usage sessions. Their app usage was highly skewed toward a small number of frequently used apps. In particular, significant differences were found in the usage amount/frequency of the first ranked apps. In addition, diurnal usage differences were observed, where the risk group used their smartphones for more time during the morning/evening than the non-risk group. Despite these usage differences, there was no significant difference in the number of unique apps used (risk: 66.1 *vs.* non-risk: 65.5).

Comm. Usage	Non-Risk [95% CI]	Risk [95% CI]	T	P	d
Usage time (m)	87.1 [75.8, 98.3]	98.8 [80.0, 118.6]	1.15	.257	0.24
Usage freq	112.5 [100.7, 124.2]	126.3 [107.4, 145.2]	1.32	.189	0.28
Voice time (m)	12.0 [9.4, 14.6]	14.5 [8.9, 20.0]	0.83	.411	0.20
Voice freq	6.2 [5.4, 7.0]	5.8 [4.6, 7.0]	0.51	.610	0.11
SMS time (m)	2.7 [2.1, 3.3]	4.4 [2.4, 6.4]	1.64	.108	0.41
SMS freq	6.9 [5.8, 8.0]	9.5 [6.7, 12.2]	1.75	.086	0.42
MIM time (m)	65.8 [56.1, 75.6]	75.6 [58.8, 92.3]	1.08	.281	0.23
MIM freq	76.9 [66.6, 87.2]	91.2 [73.9, 108.5]	1.53	.130	0.32
Inter-MIM time (m)	25.6 [19.8, 31.4]	21.0 [16.2, 25.8]	1.21	.228	0.23
Inter-MIM noti (m)	9.5 [4.9, 14.0]	6.9 [3.8, 10.0]	0.94	.351	0.17
MIM noti freq	378.5 [227.1, 529.8]	451.8 [449.1, 454.7]	0.64	.353	0.16
Web Usage	Non-Risk [95% CI]	Risk [95% CI]	T	P	d
Usage time (m)	41.1 [33.6, 48.6]	67.1 [48.4, 85.9]	2.60	.012	0.61
Usage freq	22.3 [18.7, 26.0]	38.5 [25.7, 51.3]	2.47	.018	0.61
Inter-web time (m)	81.0 [68.4, 93.5]	71.4 [53.3, 89.4]	0.90	.370	0.19

Table 3. Two-sample t-test results of category-specific usage (two-tailed)

CATEGORY-SPECIFIC USAGE PATTERNS

Our results revealed differences in aggregated usage between the risk and non-risk groups. In this section, we investigate these usage differences in detail by considering two of the most popular app categories: communications and web browsing. The overall results are presented in Table 3.

Communication App Use

Mobile Instant Messaging Usage: Figure 6 shows the usage times for different communication channels. Mobile instant messaging (MIM) dominated the overall communication usage, followed by voice calls, SMS, and emails. Because of the dominance of MIM usage, our analysis was focused on KakaoTalk, which is the most widely used MIM service in Korea. All of our participants, except one, used KakaoTalk on a daily basis.

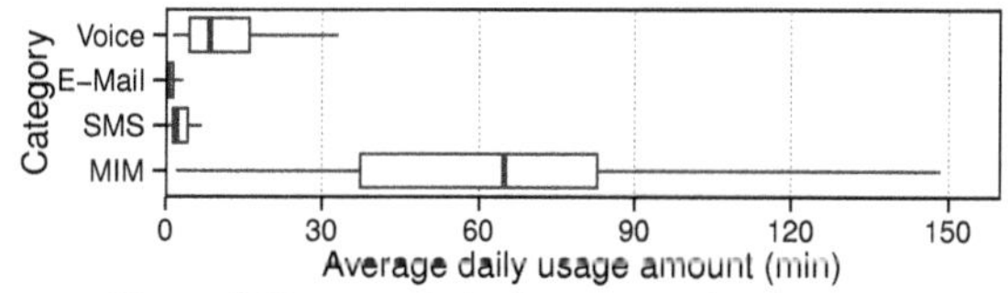

Figure 6. Usage statistics for communication apps

We calculated the mean daily usage time and frequency for KakaoTalk. The results showed that the risk group tended to use KakaoTalk slightly longer (risk: 75.6 min *vs.* non-risk: 65.8 min) and more frequently (risk: 91.2 *vs.* non-risk: 76.9), but significant differences were not found (see Table 3). To examine the KakaoTalk usage process more closely, we calculated the inter-app time (i.e., the time between consecutive KakaoTalk uses) and compared the mean inter-app time for the groups. The risk group had a slightly shorter mean inter-app time, but there was no significant difference (risk: 21.0 min *vs.* non-risk: 25.6 min; $p = .228$, Cohen's $d = 0.23$). We also calculated the inter-notification time (i.e., the time interval between two consecutive new notification arrivals). In Android, if a new message arrives when KakaoTalk is not an active app (hidden in the background or off-screen), an arrival event is placed into the notification drawer and a vibration or sound alert is generated. The inter-notification time was short (median = 26.6 s), but there was no significant difference (risk: 6.87 min *vs.* non-risk: 9.46 min; $p = .351$, Cohen's $d = 0.17$). Additionally, the number of notifications

		Externally Cued					Internally Cued					Total
		Kakao	FB	Email	Voice	Total	Kakao	FB	Email	Voice	Total	
Total num. sessions per day	Risk	38.9	5.4	0.5	6.0	76.7	*11.2	2.9	0.1	0.7	25.1	101.3
	Non-Risk	32.0	4.7	0.5	5.1	68.5	*7.2	1.7	0.1	1.2	18.8	89.0
Total app seq. length per day	Risk	*88.7	16.6	1.8	11.5	*199.6	14.9	4.5	0.1	1.3	36.2	235.2
	Non-Risk	*63.9	13.3	1.5	10.2	*164.6	11.2	2.6	0.2	2.4	31.6	204.2
Total session duration per day (s)	Risk	*4978.9	1084.7	112.0	305.8	*11910.7	540.5	272.0	1.4	14.3	1585.8	*13525.8
	Non-Risk	*3661.5	1010.0	112.3	251.8	*9645.8	385.4	134.2	10.2	36.6	1179.4	*11006.8
Per session duration (s)	Risk	170.1	233.9	209.6	58.8	390.4	55.3	69.5	3.0	31.0	64.3	335.5
	Non-Risk	164.6	263.2	170.8	57.6	348.4	64.7	70.1	30.7	24.9	70.6	314.2
App seq. length per session	Risk	2.6	3.2	2.9	2.1		1.4	1.4	0.2	2.0		
	Non-Risk	2.6	3.1	3.8	2.6		1.8	1.3	0.9	2.3		

Table 4. Usage differences in external and internal sessions (* $p < .05$)

per day was quite high, but the difference was not significant (risk: 451.8 *vs.* non-risk: 378.5; $p = .353$, Cohen's $d = 0.16$).

Notifications as External Cues for Usage: Smartphone usage can be triggered by external cues (e.g., incoming calls and messages), or internal cues (e.g., outbound calls/messages and web searches). In studies of technological addictions, external cues are regarded as a potential trigger of problematic usage behavior [18, 17, 10]. Given that our participants received a large number of notification alerts (more than 400 notifications; 90% of them from KakaoTalk), we investigated whether there were any usage differences among the externally cued sessions. We defined a session as externally-cued (or simply an external session) if any notifications from the apps that were used in the session have arrived during the time interval between that session and the preceding session (see Figure 7). Otherwise, sessions were treated as internal sessions.

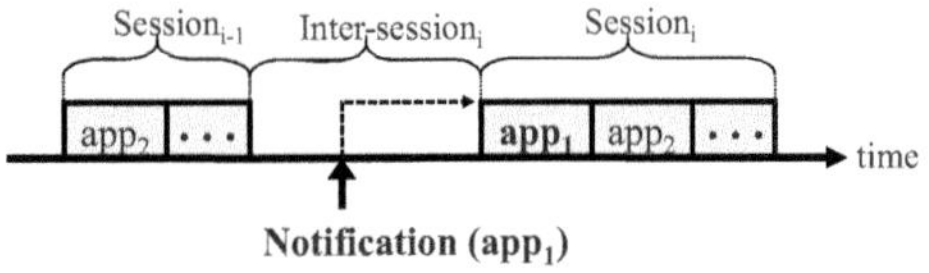

Figure 7. Illustration of an external session

Our data showed that the majority of sessions were external (79%). We further divided the external sessions based on the first app that was used in the respective session. For example, if an external session began with KakaoTalk, we referred to it as a KakaoTalk cued session. We considered KakaoTalk, Facebook, Email, and Voice Call as the first apps in external sessions because most notifications came from these apps.

For the external sessions, we found significant differences in the mean usage time per day ($p = .037$, Cohen's $d = 0.44$) and in the aggregated sequence length of the usage sessions per day ($p = .033$, Cohen's $d = 0.45$) (see Table 4). However, the number of sessions did not differ significantly ($p = .192$, Cohen's $d = 0.28$). We found no significant differences in these features of internal sessions. We examined the external sessions based on the first app (i.e., into KakaoTalk, Facebook, and Voice call cued sessions), and found significant usage differences only for KakaoTalk cued sessions with respect to the mean usage time per day ($p = .030$, Cohen's $d = 0.50$) and the aggregated sequence length of usage sessions per day ($p = .029$, Cohen's $d = 0.50$).

Summary of Findings: Our participants mainly used MIMs for mobile communications, and the usage was over 60 minutes per day. Each participant typically received more than 400 notifications per day on average and 90% of these notifications were from MIMs. There were no significant differences in the overall MIM usage, but MIM use tended to be longer (with the effect size of > 0.2) for the risk group and more frequent than the non-risk group, which was also supported by our diurnal usage analysis results (see Appendix). After dividing smartphone usage into internally-cued and externally-cued sessions, we found that 79% of the usage was external usage (e.g., MIM and Facebook). We found that the usage time of MIM-initiated sessions was significantly greater for the risk group compared with the non-risk group. This result confirms that MIM notifications act as external cues for smartphone usage and they can be considered to be a cause of problematic smartphone usage.

Web Browsing App Use

Usage Pattern Analysis: There were significant differences in the usage of web browsing apps between the groups (see Table 3). The daily usage times for the risk and non-risk groups were 67.14 min (SD: 55.25) and 41.14 min (SD: 28.87), respectively. Similarly, the daily usage frequencies for the risk and non-risk groups were 38.50 (SD: 37.77) and 22.30 (SD: 13.96), respectively. In addition, we compared the inter-app times of web browsers for the two groups. The risk group showed a shorter mean inter-app time: risk: 71.4 min (SD: 53.3) *vs.* non-risk: 80.9 min, (SD: 48.2), but the difference was not significant.

Content Consumption Pattern Analysis: We also compared the content consumption patterns of the risk and non-risk groups. We only considered the participants who used the default web browser, which allowed us to record their URL histories. As a result, there were 24 participants from the non-risk group, and 18 from the risk group. For each participant, we extracted the top ten frequently visited web sites and calculated their average usage frequencies per day. We aggregated these statistics within each group, and the results are presented in Table 5. We classified each domain name manually using the following categories: online communities, web portals (e.g., Naver and Yahoo!), news, web searches, entertainment (e.g., webtoons and movies), school web sites, and miscellaneous sites. Unequal-variance t-tests (one-tailed) showed significant differences in web portal usage ($p = .049$, Cohen's $d = 0.60$) and web search usage ($p = .013$, Cohen's $d = 0.75$). Web portals, such as Naver, Daum and Nate, are the top three web portals in Korea as a whole.

	Community	Portal	News	Search	Entertainment	School	Misc.	Total
Risk (SD)	43.7(101.7)	8.9 (14.8)	19.0 (59.2)	9.6 (9.2)	0.6 (0.8)	2.4 (3.8)	14.3 (11.3)	99.5 (130.6)
95% CI	[9.3, 78.1]	[3.9, 13.9]	[1.0, 39.1]	[6.5, 12.7]	[0.3, 0.8]	[1.1, 3.7]	[10.5, 18.1]	[55.3, 143.7]
Non-Risk (SD)	7.5 (13.2)	2.7 (3.1)	1.0 (1.4)	4.0 (5.3)	1.6 (3.6)	1.5 (2.1)	7.6 (11.6)	24.8(28.6)
95% CI	[4.0, 10.9]	[1.9, 3.5]	[0.6, 1.3]	[2.6, 5.3]	[0.4, 2.8]	[1.0, 2.1]	[4.6, 10.6]	[17.3, 32.2]
P (d)	.076 (0.53)	.049 (0.60)	.107 (0.46)	.013 (0.75)	.125 (0.42)	.189 (0.30)	.034 (0.57)	.014 (0.79)

Table 5. Distribution of the visit frequency on each category by the risk and non-risk groups

These web portals have similar content and functionalities, such as web search, news, trending issues, and links to other portal services. The risk group tended to check the portal pages for information updates more often (8.9 *vs.* 2.7 visits per day on average), and to search for information needs more frequently (9.6 *vs.* 3.9 visits per day on average) compared with the non-risk group. Detailed usage analysis of the Naver search queries showed that the risk group participants searched for trending issues (i.e., top search keywords) more often than the non-risk group participants.

We found that five participants who visited these sites to an excessive degree all belonged to the risk group. Three of these visited specific community sites 414.0, 166.3, and 96.7 times per day on average, respectively. Two other participants in the risk group visited news pages an average of 250.8 and 55.8 times per day, respectively. The most popular online communities among our participants included Todayhumor (sharing jokes, as on 9gag), Ruliweb (sharing game and animation information), and Ppomppu (shopping and discount information). These sites were visited primarily for the purpose of sharing user-generated content. We uncovered a unique usage pattern based on a detailed analysis of the URLs visited by our participants. Community web sites typically have a number of topical boards, and the participants would visit each separate board to check for new posts. Existing sites display new posts on a daily basis, but heavy web users checked these sites very frequently throughout the day, thereby exhibiting this pattern of checking for new information.

Summary of Findings: Compared with the non-risk group, our results showed that the risk group browsed the web more often and they tended to search for content updates more frequently (e.g., visiting web portals, and checking trending issues). Moreover, a few of the risk group participants searched for and consumed online content in an excessive manner and they exhibited unique surfing patterns while searching for this content.

ANALYTIC MODELING OF USAGE BEHAVIOR

Our results revealed quantitative differences in the usage patterns of the risk and non-risk groups. However, these results did not indicate how the usage features were associated with the key factors of smartphone overuse and how the usage features can be used to predict the potential for smartphone overuse. Thus, we perform analytic modeling of the usage behavior using multiple regression and machine learning.

Regression Analysis

The key factors (or symptoms) in the Smartphone Addiction Proneness Scale include interferences with work/personal activities (interference), virtual world orientation (virtual), emotional alterations such as anxiety and irritation if smartphone use is impeded (withdrawal), and habituated usage

	Total	Inter.	Virtu.	Withd.	Toler.
Model Summary					
Adjusted R^2	.12**	.14**	.07*	.07*	0.14**
F	6.25	5.05	6.83	6.84	7.76
Standardized β					
Usage freq	.26**			.26**	
Top 1 app time		.30**			
6-12 usage time			.26**		
Web usage time	.21**				.31**
# ext. sessions					.23**
Ext. MIM agg. seq. len.		.48**			

*p<0.05, **p<0.01

Table 6. Regression analysis results

without reducing the level of usage (tolerance) [15]. Because of our limited sample size for regression analysis, we selected a set of representative features that characterized the general usage behaviors, including overall usage features (usage time/frequency, top-1 app usage time/frequency, top-5 app entropy, and usage time in 6-12/18-24 blocks) and category-specific usage features (MIM usage time/frequency, Web usage time/frequency, MIM/Web usage time in 6-12/18-24 blocks, external MIM session frequency, and aggregated MIM external session length/time).

Table 6 summarizes the regression results. Overall, the usage time and frequency were closely related with smartphone overuse. Given that the usage of instant messaging was dominant, we hypothesized that its usage may play a critical role in problematic usage behaviors. Incoming MIM messages acted as external usage cues for smartphone use. The participants who experienced more interference tended to have longer session sequence lengths of MIM initiated sessions. Moreover, web usage and external cues were related to the tolerance factor; i.e., consuming online content that provides gratifications causes people to continue to use smartphones. These observations agree with the well-known theories of technological addictions [11, 17, 10]. Repeated content consumption (message exchanges, and web content) forms a habitual usage pattern, which may lead to addictive behaviors. External cues further reinforce this behavior.

Classification Analysis

We used machine learning algorithms to test the feasibility of the risk-group classification. During model training, we considered all of the features explored in the previous sections. For each feature, we considered the following basic statistics: mean, median, SD, and soft min/max (mean$\pm$2SD). We used the classification models in Weka v3.6 such as Decision Tree (DT), Naive Bayes (NB), and Support Vector Machine (SVM). We reduced the number of features using the Information Gain filter and Rank-based search algorithms. To determine the importance of the feature categories, we tested the performance using different category combinations (see Table 7). The general set contained the general usage features, such as the usage time/frequency, top-k entropies, and

Feature set	Acc. (%)	Pre.	Rec.	F-score	Classifier
All	81.05	.816	.811	.813	DT
General	72.63	.723	.726	.724	DT
Category	87.37	.874	.874	.874	DT
Temporal	78.95	.792	.789	.790	DT
ExtCue	64.21	.622	.642	.632	NB
ExcludeGeneral	85.26	.863	.853	.858	DT
ExcludeCategory	80.00	.806	.800	.803	NB
ExcludeTemporal	77.89	.782	.779	.780	DT
ExcludeExtCue	81.05	.816	.811	.813	DT

Table 7. Classification Results

sequence length. The temporal set included the diurnal usage features for aggregated usage and category-specific usage. The category set included the category-level usage features (no temporal aspects). The external set included all of the usage features for the external sessions. The models were evaluated based on a 10-fold cross validation. The dataset was divided into 10 roughly equal subsets. One subset was left out for validation, and the remaining subsets were used for training. The average performance of the classifiers were estimated by repeating this process for each subset.

Table 7 shows the best accuracy, precision, recall, and F-score values. We obtained the best performance when the category set was used with DT (F-score = 0.87). The ranked features in the best model included the web usage time (mean, SD, median), SNS usage time (SD), SNS usage frequency (soft max, median), inter-MIM time (median), and inter-browser time (mean, SD, soft max). By contrast, the performance was lower when all of the features were employed, where the ranked features included four general features, four category features, and two diurnal features. In addition, we examined the predictive power of each feature set. The performance of the general and temporal feature sets did not differ substantially, although the external feature set had the poorest performance. To measure the performance gain for each feature set, we trained the classifiers by excluding each set. As shown in the table, removing the category feature set resulted in a significant performance drop, which demonstrated its importance for classification. Moreover, the general features had negative effects on the overall performance.

In summary, we found that investigating various category-specific usage patterns was of critical importance, and our classification model allowed us to accurately classify whether a person belonged to the risk group. The current study focused mainly on communications and web browsing, but our feature selection results indicated the importance of other features. Thus, other categories such as social networking and mobile games may be explored in our future research.

PROBLEMATIC USAGE BEHAVIOR

We perform a content analysis of the interview/survey data to corroborate the earlier findings and to better characterize problematic usage behaviors.

Overall Usage Behavior

Our participants used smartphones for various purposes, which ranged from managing personal information and building social relationships, to passing the time and managing moods. Here, the seven participants who participated in the interviews are referred to using R (for the risk group) and N (for the non-risk group) followed by a number. Participants commented: *"In general, I use it to check news and updates. I can easily satisfy all of my curiosities with smartphones."* (N1); *"When I have nothing to do like waiting for someone, or if I feel bored during a class, I check Facebook."* (R1). The temporal usage patterns were closely related to the typical school lifestyle. Students have more free time in the morning (fewer classes), late at night (going to sleep), and over the weekends (no classes). During the day, smartphone usage was frequent and brief, as explained by N3: *"I frequently check my smartphone if there are new messages or alarms. I check it in every 5 to 20 minutes. I don't use it for a long time unless I play a game."* In general, our participants concurred that smartphone usage tended to last longer during the night, in the morning, or at the weekend (e.g., for relaxing and checking). For example, N1 stated: *"Unless I'm really tired, I always check my smartphone before going to bed. When I get up, I check my smartphone. Lots of updates [like Facebook] happen overnight."*

Frequent Interferences

We asked the participants an open-ended question to determine whether instant messaging interfered with their daily lives (in an exit-survey after the data collection process). The data showed that 92% experienced interference in various situations. One participant complained about a loss of attention and stated that: *"I sometimes lose track of a lecture due to KakaoTalk."* Similarly, another participant mentioned, *"I have to focus, but I check KakaoTalk in almost every 5 minutes."* Sleep patterns were disturbed, and one participant reflected, *"I sometimes chat before going to bed, and it makes me to stay up until late. Also, I was woken up by silly messages from my friends, who asked for game time via KakaoTalk."* Social activities were also interrupted often. One participant commented, *"When I'm dating or hanging out with friends, KakaoTalk messages make me feel nervous. I have had experiences where KakaoTalk disrupted ongoing conversations."* As demonstrated earlier, after receiving external cues, the risk group spent more time for using their smartphones. External cues disrupted the users' attention, and they may have experienced greater attention loss as their session durations became longer. Thus, the degree of interferences attributable to instant messaging was probably greater for the risk group than the non-risk group.

Habitual Usage and Limited Self-Control

The risk group expressed difficulty in regulating their smartphone use. They felt more compelled to check their smartphone: *"I keep paying attention, because I feel like new messages may have arrived."* (R1). Moreover, the risk group participants were less conscious of their smartphone use: *"I don't have any thoughts when using my smartphone. ... At that moment, [I'm] without any sense of time."* (R1). R2 reported an experience of excessive usage: *"It's not like I plan to use my smartphone, but I just turn on my smartphone unconsciously. I once used my smartphone to wake myself up in the morning. I got up at 9AM, but it turned out it was already 11AM."* R3 even claimed that smartphone usage is not problematic at all, by stating: *"I'm not a person who is likely to be addicted to something. I sometimes feel that I use my smartphone too much, but only very occasionally."*

The content consumption behavior of the risk group was less structured than that of the non-risk group, particularly when online content was consumed. In general, the risk group participants had difficulties in explaining the details of their content consumption behavior. R1 mentioned: *"I check articles in online communities in the morning, and I keep checking whether there are any updates. ... If one community does not have any updates, I visit other communities to check for updates."* R4 commented about Facebook usage: *"For example if there are no updates in Facebook, I check out a new person or keep following pages to seek for new content."* This behavior sometimes disturbed their sleep patterns. R4 acknowledged: *"I use my smartphone before going to bed, but in the end spend too much time; about one to two hours. There is always something new because I can dig in deeply. I don't sleep well because of this. After about two hours, I sometimes fall asleep even though I didn't think of stopping."*

By contrast, usage behavior was self-regulated in the non-risk group although they were also heavy users: *"I use my smartphone for about 20 minutes before going to bed. I take care of messages piled up in KakaoTalk, and check Facebook, and webtoon updates at 11:30 PM. After checking that, I'm done!"* (N1). N3 commented: *"I feel like Facebook is part of my daily task. I use Everytown [a game] when I feel drowsy after a meal, but not to fall asleep because it makes me feel lazy. I use Joara [an online novel app] when I have time to pass. I mostly use my smartphone, when I really don't feel like studying for an exam, when I have done all the work and there is nothing to do, and when I'm waiting for my friends, and I have some time to wait."*

DISCUSSION AND CONCLUSION

Our exploratory data analysis determined the usage patterns related to smartphone overuse. We found that the risk group spent longer time engaged in smartphone usage than the non-risk group. The number of apps used was similar, but the risk group exhibited a highly skewed usage pattern with respect to a few frequently used apps. In addition, there were significant diurnal usage differences, where the risk group used smartphones for longer periods in the morning and evening. Overall, our participants mainly used their smartphones for communications. MIM was the most frequently used app, followed by voice calls, SMS, and emails. They received a large number of MIM notifications per day (> 400). We found that the risk group spent more time on MIM-triggered sessions. This result serves as evidence that MIM notifications act as external cues that can lead to excessive smartphone usage. Another major component of smartphone usage was consuming various types of online content that provide instant gratifications (e.g., pastimes, entertainment, and information seeking). The risk group users spent more time on the web consuming these types of online content.

According to our analysis, the overall difference in the usage times between the risk/non-risk groups was not very high (< 50 minutes). In previous studies of technological addictions, however, researchers reported that the excessive and problematic usage depends mainly on function rather than the usage amount [11, 17]. For example, repeated usage for mood adjustment purposes (e.g., relieving boredom, stress, or depression) may form habitual usage and lead to addictive behaviors [11, 17, 10]. Our regression results demonstrated that smartphone overuse is closely related to the content consumption function of smartphones. Our interview results also provided detailed evidence of addictive usage behaviors. The risk group showed limited self-control, particularly when consuming online content (e.g., aimlessly following web/Facebook links while in bed). These findings provide new insights into previous research on scale development and problematic usage behaviors [16, 5, 13].

Understanding smartphone usage patterns has been an active area of research [8, 4, 25]. Our work supplements previous measurement studies [8, 4, 25] by reporting recent smartphone usage patterns (e.g., mobile instant messaging)—detailed information can be found in the Appendix—and by investigating problematic usage behaviors, which are emerging social issues associated with technology overuse. We observed significant changes in usage behaviors compared with the usage statistics based on the earlier datasets collected in 2009 [8] and 2010 [4]. We hypothesize that the much longer usage duration (224.7 min *vs.* 59.2 min [4]) may be attributable to the participant demographics, as well as the network effect of smartphones and MIM. Moreover, our research extends the study of Oulasvirta et al. [25] by examining real usage patterns from the perspective of smartphone overuse, and we demonstrated the importance of externally-cued usage behavior.

Our study provides new insights into the usage practices related to mobile communications [20, 3, 12]. We studied the latest trends for MIM use. As we reported, its usage is prevalent, and it can be indicative of overuse risks (e.g., causing negative impacts on an individual's personal and social activities). Thus, our results help to understand the impacts of semi-synchronous communication channels such as MIM, on the social expectations related to constant connectivity [3] and interruption management practices [20].

The use of computing technology for promoting health and sustainable behaviors has been of great interest to the HCI community [9]. In addition, addiction-related research has been increasing recently [26, 29, 30]. Our study on usage analysis and automatic behavior assessment may be useful when designing mobile software that can moderate excessive use (e.g., visualizing usage information, and utilizing social support), or it could facilitate the design of intelligent parental controls (e.g., addressing a child's smartphone overuse). We consider that designing and evaluating intervention software may be an interesting avenue for future HCI research [7]. Our research may provide a foundation for such research.

Similar to any cross-sectional and single-site study, the generalizability of this research may be limited by the characteristics of our participants. However, an earlier analysis partly affirmed the generalizability of this research [8]; i.e., fine-grained usage features such as the session time distribution exhibited consistent patterns across the datasets collected from different sites. We suggest that further exploratory and confirmatory studies might consider different sites, demographics, mobile devices/platforms, and cultural backgrounds. The present analysis could be extended by investigating additional contextual factors (e.g., location and activity), and content categories (e.g., social networking and mobile games).

ACKNOWLEDGEMENTS

This research was supported in part by the MSIP, Korea, and Microsoft Research, under the IT/SW Creative research program supervised by the NIPA (National IT Industry Promotion Agency) (NIPA-2013-ITAH0503130110270001000100100), by the IT R&D program of MSIP/KEIT [10041313, UX-oriented Mobile SW Platform], and by the National Research Foundation of Korea (NRF) grant funded by the Korea government (MSIP) (No. 2011-0018120, 2012R1A1A1008858). We thank the anonymous reviewers for their many useful comments and suggestions, which helped improve the paper.

REFERENCES

1. DSM-5. `http://www.dsm5.org/`.
2. The Mobile Consumer: A Global Snapshot, The Nielsen Company, Feb. 2013.
3. Ames, M. G. Managing Mobile Multitasking: The Culture of iPhones on Stanford Campus. In *CSCW* (2013).
4. Böhmer, M., Hecht, B., Schöning, J., Krüger, A., and Bauer, G. Falling Asleep with Angry Birds, Facebook and Kindle: A Large Scale Study on Mobile Application Usage. In *MobileHCI* (2011).
5. Carbonell, X., Chamarro, A., Griffiths, M., Oberst, U., Cladellas, R., and Talarn, A. Problematic Internet and Cell Phone Use in Spanish Teenagers and Young Students. *Anales de Psicologia* (2012).
6. Cui, Y., and Roto, V. How People Use the Web on Mobile Devices. In *WWW* (2008).
7. de Abreu, C. N., and Góes, D. S. *Psychotherapy for Internet Addiction*. Internet Addiction, John Wiley & Sons, Inc., 2011.
8. Falaki, H., Mahajan, R.and Kandula, S., Lymberopoulos, D., Govindan, R., and Estrin, D. Diversity in Smartphone Usage. In *MobiSys* (2010).
9. Fogg, B. J. *Persuasive Technology: Using Computers to Change What We Think and Do*. Morgan Kaufmann, 2002.
10. Greenfield, D. *The Addictive Properties of Internet Usage*. Internet Addiction, John Wiley & Sons, Inc., 2011.
11. Griffiths, M. D. Technological Addictions. *Clinical Psychology Forum* (1995).
12. Harmon, E., and Mazmanian, M. Stories of the Smartphone in Everyday Discourse: Conflict, Tension & Instability. In *CHI* (2013).
13. Hwang, K. H., Yoo, Y. S., and Cho, O. H. Smartphone Overuse and Upper Extremity Pain, Anxiety, Depression, and Interpersonal Relationships among College Students. *The Journal of the Korea Contents Association* (2012).
14. Kandell, J. J. Internet Addiction on Campus: The Vulnerability of College Students. *CyberPsychology & Behavior* (1998).
15. Kim, D., Jung, Y., Lee, J., Kim, M., Lee, Y., Kang, E., Keum, C., and Nam, J. Development of Smartphone Addiction Proneness Scale for Adults: Self-Report. *The Korean Journal of Counseling* (2012).
16. Koo, H. Y. Development of a Cell Phone Addiction Scale for Korean Adolescents. *J Korean Acad Nurs* (2009).
17. LaRose, R. *Use and Gratifications of Internet Addiction*. Internet Addiction, John Wiley & Sons, Inc., 2011.
18. LaRose, R., Lin, C. A., and Eastin, M. S. Unregulated Internet Usage: Addiction, Habit, or Deficient Self-Regulation? *Media Psychology* (2003).
19. Leung, L. Stressful Life Events, Motives for Internet Use, and Social Support among Digital Kids. *CyberPsychology & Behavior* (2007).
20. Levine, L. E., Waite, B. M., and Bowman, L. L. Mobile Media Use, Multitasking and Distractibility. *IJCBPL* (2012).
21. Miltenberger, R. G. *Behavior Modification: Principles and Procedures*. Cengage Learning, 2011.
22. Morahan-Martin, J. Internet Abuse: Addiction? Disorder? Symptom? Alternative Explanations? *Social Science Computer Review* (2005).
23. Morahan-Martin, J., and Schumacher, P. Loneliness and Social Uses of the Internet. *Computers in Human Behavior* (2003).
24. Murdock, K. K. Texting While Stressed: Implications for Students' Burnout, Sleep, and Well-Being. *Psychology of Popular Media Culture* (2013).
25. Oulasvirta, A., Rattenbury, T., Ma, L., and Raita, E. Habits Make Smartphone Use More Pervasive. *Personal Ubiquitous Computing* (2012).
26. Seay, A. F., and Kraut, R. E. Project Massive: Self-regulation and Problematic Use of Online Gaming. In *CHI* (2007).
27. Tossell, C. C., Kortum, P., Shepard, C. W., Rahmati, A., and Zhong, L. Getting Real: A Naturalistic Methodology for Using Smartphones to Collect Mediated Communications. *Advances in Human-Computer Interaction* (2012).
28. van den Eijnden, R. J., Meerkerk, G.-J., Vermulst, A. A., Spijkerman, R., and Engels, R. C. M. E. Online Communication, Compulsive Internet Use, and Psychosocial Well-Being Among Adolescents: A Longitudinal Study. *Developmental Psychology 44* (2008), 655–665.
29. Wang, K.-C., Hong, M.-T., Kao, C. H.-L., Lin, A. C., Wang, C.-A., You, C.-W., Pan, C.-H., Huang, M.-C., Liang, C.-M., and Chu, H.-H. A Phone-based Support System to Assist Alcohol Recovery. In *CHI EA* (2013).
30. Yarosh, S. Shifting Dynamics or Breaking Sacred Traditions?: the Role of Technology in Twelve-step Fellowships. In *CHI* (2013).

Broken Display = Broken Interface? The Impact of Display Damage on Smartphone Interaction

Florian Schaub,* Julian Seifert, Frank Honold, Michael Müller, Enrico Rukzio, Michael Weber
Institute of Media Informatics
Ulm University
89069 Ulm, Germany
fschaub@cs.cmu.edu, firstname.lastname@uni-ulm.de

ABSTRACT
This paper is the first to assess the impact of touchscreen damage on smartphone interaction. We gathered a dataset consisting of 95 closeup images of damaged smartphones and extensive information about a device's usage history, damage severity, and impact on use. 88% of our participants continued to use their damaged smartphone for at least three months; 32% plan to use it for another year or more, mainly due to high repair and replacement costs. From the dataset, we identified three categories of damaged smartphone displays. Reading and text input were most affected. Further interviews (n=11) revealed that users adapt to damage with diverse coping strategies, closely tailored to specific interaction issues. In total, we identified 23 different strategies. Based on our results, we proposed guidelines for interaction design in order to provide a positive user experience when display damage occurs.

Author Keywords
Smartphone; mobile interaction; broken display; display damage; user experience.

ACM Classification Keywords
H.5.2 Information Interfaces and Presentation (e.g. HCI): User Interfaces; K.8.2 Personal Computing: Hardware.

INTRODUCTION
Current smartphones are mainly operated via touchscreens that cover a large part of the device's front panel. The large display area of smartphones increases the risk of damage to the display when the phone is dropped. In two recent surveys with UK owners of damaged mobile phones (n=2,579), a mobile insurance company found that 37% of devices suffered damage in the first three months of use [3] and that 23% of iPhone owners (n=2,471) have a smartphone with a broken display, with 31% not planning to get it repaired [4]. Many smartphone owners continue to use their smartphone after it got damaged. We found that the main reason for continued use are high repair and replacement costs. Current smartphones require replacement of the complete display unit, which costs 150–250 USD depending on the model.

*Florian Schaub conducted this work while at Ulm University. He is now affiliated with the School of Computer Science at Carnegie Mellon University.

CHI 2014, April 26–May 1, 2014, Toronto, ON, Canada.
Copyright © 2014 ACM 978-1-4503-2473-1/14/04..$15.00.
http://dx.doi.org/10.1145/2556288.2557067

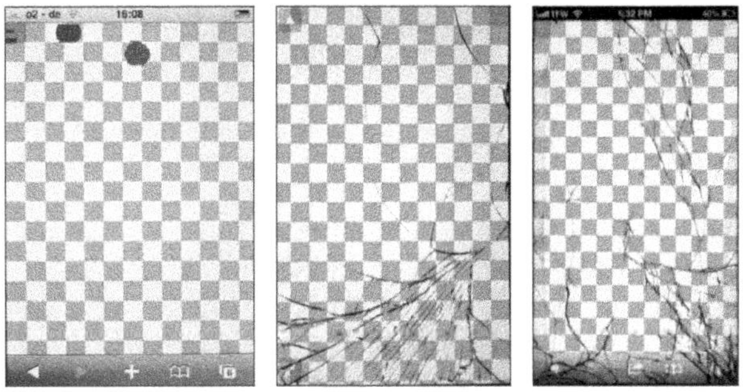

(a) minor damage (b) medium damage (c) severe damage

Figure 1. Representative examples of damaged smartphone displays from the identified display damage categories. The checkerboard pattern facilitated image rectification and damage identification.

Considering the combination of visual output and touch input on the display, as well as the visual nature of smartphone software and apps, display damage likely impacts the user's interaction with the smartphone. Scratches, cracks, and screen faults deteriorate the user experience by occluding parts of the displayed content or impairing touch input.

In this work, we assessed the impact of damaged displays on smartphone interaction and how users cope with the damage. Our results can help interaction designers in supporting the growing group of smartphone owners that use a smartphone with a damaged display. Towards this goal, we performed an explorative analysis, resulting in the following contributions.

We conducted an online survey and an Amazon Mechanical Turk (MTurk) study with owners of damaged smartphones. The resulting dataset consists of 95 closeup images of damaged smartphones and extensive information about the devices' usage history, severity and cause of the damage, impact on use, and reasons for continued use. We conducted a structured image analysis, including manual damage annotation. With cluster analysis, we identified three categories of damaged smartphone displays. Figure 1 shows representative examples of those categories. The complete damaged display dataset, including analysis data, is made available alongside this paper to foster further research in this area.[1]

In addition, we conducted interviews with owners of damaged smartphones recruited from the online survey (n=11), to gain deeper insights into reasons for continued use and implications of damage on smartphone interaction. Our participants reported 23 different coping strategies, often tailored to individual interaction issues.

Based on our quantitative and qualitative results, we propose interaction design strategies that can support many of those coping strategies already at design time, or facilitate adaptation of interfaces when damage occurs.

RELATED WORK

Not much prior work has considered the implications of hardware damage on user interaction, particularly not the case of users that continue to engage with damaged devices and their interfaces for longer periods of time. However, damage has been studied as a concept. Ikemiya and Rosner [15] define damage as a malfunction or degradation of an artifact, either caused through user engagement or not. Hence, damage is related to *wear*, i.e., the degradation of an artifact over time due to use. Motivations for keeping or discarding personal items can be highly complex [16]. Yet, Huang and Truong present clear insights on when and why people switch to a new mobile phone [14]. The majority of their study participants switched devices when offered a new one with contract renewal or a new contract. About a quarter of their participants switched because their mobile phone broke; another quarter reported they had their phones repaired in the past.

Designing for and Coping with Damage

Damage of artifacts can be addressed with protective measures at design time and during use, as well as reactive measures after damage occurred. One radical approach that embraces the change and transience of artifacts by damage are ephemeral interfaces [9]. Such interfaces are specifically designed for very fast degradation rather than lasting use, e.g., a display created by falling water or interaction handles provided by soap bubbles. Interaction with an ephemeral interface often carries an imminent risk of destroying it [9].

Rosner et al. give examples on how anticipation of potential damage during the design phase of physical artifacts can improve their longevity [18, 15]. For instance, by covering a ceramic plate with a silicon layer, the plate can retain its utility and structure if it shatters. Our proposed interaction design strategies follow a similar goal by considering the impact of potential damage already during app design. Huang and Truong caution to also consider an artifact's expected time of use during its design [14]. For instance, a short-lived artifact may not require durable casing.

The notion of relative obsolescence as discussed by Cooper [7], provides further insights why and when artifacts are being replaced. He distinguishes three types of obsolescence: psychological obsolescence driven by a reduced attractiveness and user satisfaction; technological obsolescence related to changes in functionality, quality, or effectiveness; and economical obsolescence pertaining to value reduction and excess repair costs relative to replacement. Planned obsolescence [6] assumes that manufactures already design products towards obsolescence in order to increase product sales. For instance, designing mobile devices with built-in batteries that cannot be replaced by users on their own. However, our own results indicate that high prices for new smartphones trump perceived obsolescence for many smartphone owners, who continue to use even severely damaged devices.

Accessibility Support and Interaction Alternatives

While little research focused on interaction with damaged devices, a large body of work exists on accessibility support. Such mechanisms could potentially also assist users of damaged smartphones in coping with interaction impairments caused by device damage. Current smartphones offer speech input to control certain features (e.g., Siri [2] or Google Now [11]). Apple's iOS devices further support on-screen emulation of hardware buttons and voice overs for visually impaired users [1]. Recent smartphones, like Samsung's Galaxy S4, support touch-less interaction above the display (*air gestures*) or gaze interaction. Eyes-free interaction without use of the display has also been proposed [22]. Other proposals for alternative mobile device input include scratching [12] or tapping on the phone [13, 17], as well as stomping with the foot [21].

To the best of our knowledge, no work has been conducted that focused on the impact and effects of damaged displays on smartphone interaction or interfaces of mobile devices in general. We are the first to explore and investigate how damage of smartphone displays affects interaction and use.

DISPLAY DAMAGE OF SMARTPHONES

We analyzed smartphone display damage based on a dataset collected through online surveys. In the following, we outline how the data was obtained and analyzed, and discuss respective results.

Survey Methodology

To gain insights on how smartphone displays get damaged, to what degree, and how different types of damage affect interaction, we conducted an online survey with owners of damaged smartphones. Based on the findings of Ross et al. [19], we opted for a MTurk study addressing potential participants from the United States, Europe, and India in order to elicit responses from different cultural and economic backgrounds. In addition, an online version of the survey was widely advertised at multiple schools and universities.

Participants had to provide a photo of their damaged smartphone displaying a given checkerboard pattern, as shown in Figures 1 and 3(a)), in order to ensure high visibility of damage. In initial experiments, the selected green-white pattern proved most suitable for different types of display damage. Each participant also completed multiple questions on phone usage and personal background. The checkerboard pattern

[1]The broken interface dataset is available online under a Creative Commons license: `http://uni-ulm.de/broken-interfaces`

further served as an authenticity check, as bogus pictures not showing the pattern could be removed easily. Furthermore, participants that took the effort of taking and uploading a photo are likely also inclined towards answering the questions accurately. After rigorously rejecting submissions that did not meet our requirements, we are confident that images and data in our dataset are genuine.

Broken Interface Dataset

In total, we received 260 submissions through MTurk and the online survey. 165 of these submissions were discarded as they did not meet the requirements for the photo of the damaged smartphone, e.g., the smartphone display was not turned on or did not show the website with our checkerboard pattern. The resulting dataset includes 95 entries, each consisting of a photo and extensive information on the pictured device's usage history, its damage, and how the damage affects smartphone use. We made our dataset freely available online.[1]

Demographics

Images and information in our dataset were provided by participants from 9 countries, mainly from the United States (50.5%), Germany (32.6%), and India (6%). They were aged 14 to 54 years ($\bar{x}$=M=26, σ=6.7); 39% of them female, 49% male, 12% did not specify a gender. Participants reported a large variety of main occupations, such as students, teachers, or developers. The majority (22.1%) reported a low income (500-1.500 USD/month), 20% a very low income (under 500 USD/month), 15.8% were in the range of 1.500-2.500 USD per month, while 26.3% provided no income information.

Smartphone devices and usage

The dataset contains smartphones from ten manufacturers. The majority were devices from Apple (35.8%), followed by Samsung (30.5%) and HTC (16.8%). A majority of the devices used Android (57.9%), followed by iOS (35.8%). 54.7% of the participants reported that they bought their smartphones without a contract. 17.8% paid a subsidized price or received it free as part of a mobile plan. 22.1% indicated that the smartphone was a gift and 2.1% indicated that it was given to them by their employer. 4.2% obtained a phone through other ways, e.g. using a used phone from a friend.

As to be expected, participants reported to use their smartphones mainly for messaging (e.g., via WhatsApp, SMS, or email), phone calls, and media consumption. Web browsing, personal information management (e.g., calendars, contacts), camera functionalities, as well as gaming were also commonly reported smartphone applications. 83% reported to use their smartphone exclusively for personal use. 16% reported to use it for both, personal and business reasons. Only one participant used the phone only for business. This rather small percentage of business related usage is most likely related to the sample of participants in our online survey.

Results: Reported Degree of Damage

In the online survey, participants rated the damage of different aspects on a five-point scale ranging from *no damage* to *completely broken*. Figure 2 shows the answer frequencies, note that multiple components may be affected per device.

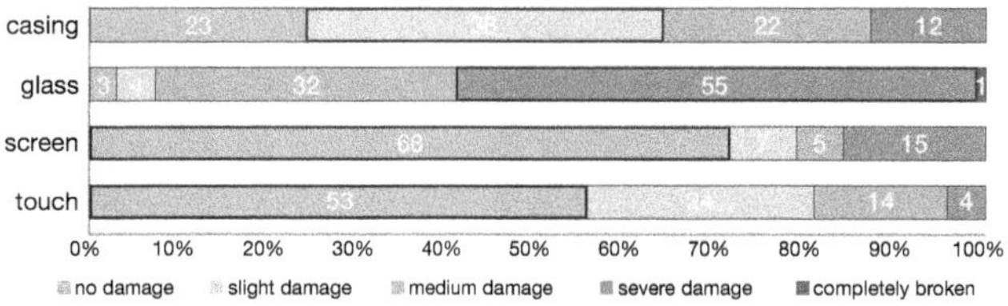

Figure 2. Damage rating frequencies for different components (n=95).

Display *glass* was damaged in most cases, with a median rating of severe damage. For the LCD *screen*, 15.8% reported a severe damage. Concerning *touch*, 4.2% reported severe and 14.7% reported medium damage.

The damage did usually not change after it occurred (72.6%). It deteriorated over time in 24.2% of the cases. Only 3.2% experienced irregular damage of functionality.

Analysis of Damaged Display Images

As mentioned before, participants not only rated damage, but also provided a photo of the damaged device, displaying a checkerboard pattern we provided as a website. The checkerboard pattern served multiple purposes: it provided a consistent background to make glass and screen damage visible, it provided information about the scale of the damage and a reference for color correction.

We performed a structured analysis of all images in the dataset to objectively quantify the damage of smartphone displays. Hereby, we focused on visible damage to the display (*glass*, *screen*) as we were mainly interested in interaction issues with the smartphone software. *Touch* damage was also not considered in image analysis, as it was not visible.

All images were pre-processed to account for differences between submitted photos in terms of illumination, as well as position and size of the damaged smartphone in the image. Images were first de-skewed and rectified based on the checkerboard pattern in order to obtain a rectangular view of the smartphone display. We further normalized colors with an automatic white balancing filter and cropped images to the display area, as shown in Figure 3(a).

In experiments, automated detection of different types of damage showed insufficient reliability. For instance, edge detection would not only detect actual cracks in the glass, but also the web browser address bar, visible on some photos, or reflections on the display. Hence, we employed a manual approach to reliably annotate different types of damage in the pre-processed images. We embedded the image in a Scalable Vector Graphics (SVG) file. Visible damage was then traced by hand with a digital drawing tablet (see Fig. 3(b) & (c)). We followed an iterative approach in the annotation to consistently annotate different types of damage. First, we browsed all original photos to gain an overview of occurring damage types, such as cracks or scratches. Afterwards, we annotated images with the initially identified damage types, extending the set of damage types whenever a new type was encountered. Each damage type was drawn on to a dedicated layer in the SVG to support detailed analysis. Subsequently, annotation results were cross-validated against the original photos.

(a) (b) (c) (d)

Figure 3. The image analysis process included (a) pre-processing the phone image and (b) manual tracing of visible damage. (c) The resulting damage annotation was used for further analysis and (d) to obtain a topology of visible (*colored*) and occluded areas (*black*).

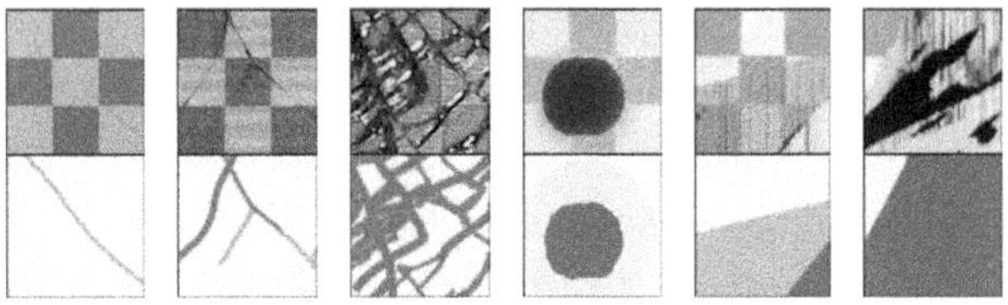

(a) scratch (b) crack (c) spider web (d) color issue (e) grayout (f) blackout

Figure 4. Identified damage types with original photo (*top*) and annotation (*bottom*): (a)–(c) glass issues and (d)–(f) screen issues.

The identified damage types can be categorized as either *glass issues* or *screen issues*. Based on severity, we distinguished glass issues as *scratches*, *cracks*, and *spider webs*, which are marked in shades of red (see Fig. 4(a)–(c)); screen issues as *color issues*, *grayouts*, and *blackouts*, which are marked in shades of blue (see Fig. 4(d)–(f)). Grayouts are areas with partial occlusion, whereas blackouts denote areas with full occlusion, typically caused by screen backlight failure.

Based on the damage annotation, we determined the percentage of visible, intact display areas, as well as damaged and occluded display areas. We further quantified the number of disjunct partitions of a display, separated by cracks or other damage types. In Matlab, we used morphological functions to close small areas and gaps in the damage annotation and sorted resulting areas based on their pixel size. Figure 3(d)) shows an example of the resulting topology of visible (*colored*) and occluded areas (*black*).

Results: Categories of Smartphone Display Damage

Figure 5 shows the distribution of damaged and occluded display areas resulting from the analysis of the damage annotation (cf. Fig. 3(c)). In general, damage (including all damage types shown in Figure 4) covered a low percentage of the display. For 92.6% of the analyzed smartphones, less than 20% of the display was occluded or damaged.

However, displays are partitioned by damage into multiple visible areas, as shown in Figure 3(d). To analyze this data and to assess whether categories can be identified, we employed a two-step approach in cluster analysis. First hierarchical clustering was used to estimate the number of existing clusters. Analyzing the distance between the resulting clusters revealed three main categories and one outlier with a fully damaged display (image 46693-88 in dataset, see also Fig. 6 on the left). Representative examples for the categories are shown in Figure 1. Subsequently, we used k-means clustering to determine cluster members.

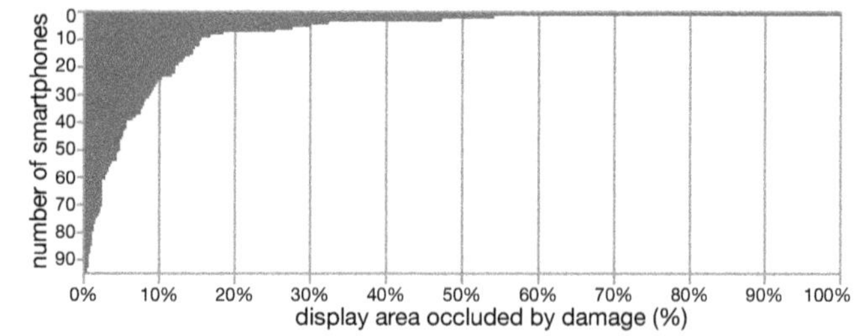

Figure 5. Distribution of damaged and occluded display areas (n=95).

The *minor display damage* category contained 45.3% of the analyzed cases. In this category, the sum of the three largest visible areas covered 93.1% of the overall display area on average (min=77.3%; max=99.9%). The category *medium display damage* contained 15.8% of all cases. Only 62.5% of the display area were included in the three largest visible areas on average (min=45.8%; max=73.9%). The remaining 37.9% were classified as *severe display damage*. In this category, the three largest visible areas contained less than 35.3% of the display on average (M=17.9%; min=7.2%). There is a considerable drop between the medium and severe damage categories in terms of visible area, as shown in Figure 6. Cases in the severe display damage category exhibited extensive spider webs and many scratches and cracks spanning the whole display, with only small unpartitioned areas remaining. The damaged display shown in Figure 3 falls into this category. Devices at the lower end of the medium category also exhibited spider webs but those did not cover the whole display. Thus, the largest visible areas tended to be bigger.

With the visual damage annotation approach, non-visible damages of touch input could not be quantified. Hence, we tested for correlation (using Spearman rank correlation) between visible display damage (percentage of three largest visible display areas) and the subjective rating of touch input damage (cf. Fig. 2). We did not find a correlation between subjectively rated touch input damage (on a five-point scale) and the size of the visible display area (r=-.131; p=.21). Yet, reducing the subjective rating of touch input damage to a binary scale (i.e., touch damage existing or not) revealed a significant correlation (r=-.273; p=.007). This indicates that display damage and touch input issues are likely connected. Although touch input issues of varying severity occur across all three identified display damage categories, as shown in Figure 6. In the severe display damage category, there is a notable concentration of slight and medium self-reported touch damage. However, there are also multiple cases with minor visible display damage but medium to severe touch damage. Thus, while severe display damage appears to co-occur with the presence of touch damage, touch issues may also occur without extensive visible display damage.

LIVING WITH THE DAMAGE

The online survey also inquired about the participants' experiences of living with a damaged smartphone. In addition, we

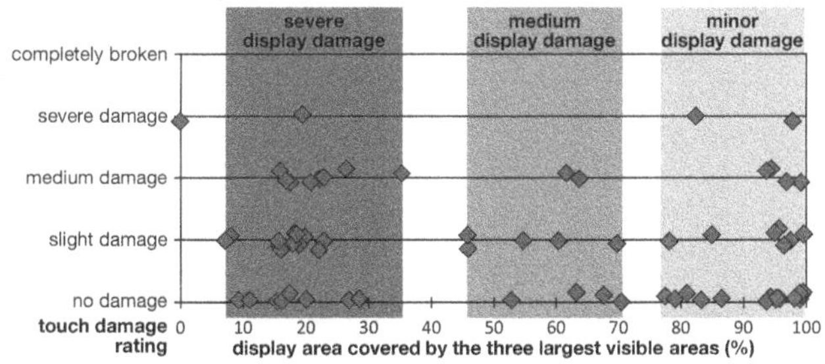

Figure 6. Distribution of touch damage in relation to visible display area and respective display damage categories (n=95).

conducted interviews with eleven owners of damaged smartphones to gain more differentiated insights.

Results: Survey Responses

Participants of the online survey indicated how damage affected different applications and activities, as well as how long and why they continued to use the damaged phone.

Impact of damage on smartphone use

Participants were asked to rate the impact of their smartphone damage on application categories and activities (same categories as for smartphone use above). Figure 7 shows results for the four most impacted application categories, as well as the least affected category.

Reading was most impacted by damage, particularly in the medium (*mode*=5, *M*=4) and severe damage categories (*mode*=*M*=3). The non-parametric Kruskal-Wallis test indicated no significant differences between groups. The effect on *text input*, which was also rated the most important aspect of smartphone use, varied significantly between groups (Kruskal-Wallis: $H(2)=8.87$, $p<.05$). While minor and medium display damage had a small impact on text input (both *mode*=*M*=2), severe damage had a higher impact (*mode*=*M*=3). Post-hoc analysis (Mann-Whitney U with Bonferroni correction) shows that the difference between minor and severe damage was significant (U=485, $p<.0167$, r=-.33). *Gaming* also exhibited significant differences between groups ($H(2)=9.68$, $p<.01$). Compared to minor damage (*mode*=1, *M*=2), damage impact was rated significantly higher in the medium (*mode*=5, *M*=3; U=518, $p<.0167$, r=-.29) and severe damage categories (*mode*=4, *M*=3, U=188.5, $p<.0167$, r=-.32). The impact on *media use*, i.e., playback of photos, music or videos, was also rated highest in the medium damage category (*mode*=4, *M*=3), but differences were not significant. Across groups, *phone calls* were least impaired by display damage. The mode for all three groups was a rating of no effect (1), with a marginally higher impact in the medium and severe display damage categories (both *M*=2), but no significant differences between groups.

Notable in Figure 7 is that the third quartiles are higher in the medium damage group than the severe damage group for the four most affected categories. A potential explanation is that smartphones with medium damage are continued to be used more actively than those with severe damage. This is corroborated by the fact that phones with medium damage were

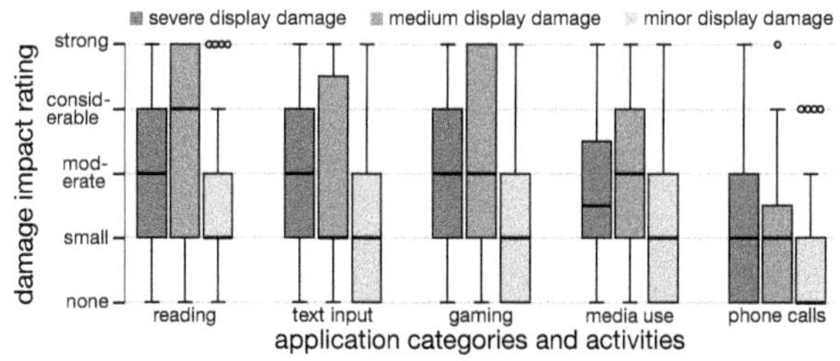

Figure 7. Perceived impact of damage on phone usage (n=94).

used for longer (*months*) after the damage occurred (*mode*=2, *M*=4) than severely damaged phones (*mode*=1, *M*=3).

Continued use of damaged smartphone

Of the 95 participants, 97.9% continued to use their device after it got damaged; 82.1% still used it when completing our survey. On average, a damaged smartphone was used for 5.1 months (σ=5.3, *M*=4). However, 8 participants (8.4%) were already using their damaged smartphone for 1 year or longer; 3 years in the most extreme case. Furthermore, 85.3% planned to continue using the damaged smartphone. While one third (35.8%) planned to use the damaged phone for 3 months or less, another third (32.1%) planned to use it for at least another year or longer. These numbers align with the frequency of switching phones. The majority (49.5%) switched their smartphone every two years, which corresponds to typical mobile plans in many countries. 18.9% specifically indicated they switched smartphones when offered a new one by their provider, which conforms to Huang and Truong's results [14]. Non-periodic reasons for switching smartphones were damage (24.2%), release of a new model (15.8%), and lack of functionality or performance (3.2%).

67 participants (70.5%) did not plan to get their damaged phone repaired. The main stated reason was high repair costs (*n*=61), followed by being able to live with the damage (*n*=48), new phones being too expensive (*n*=43), and waiting for the release of a new model (*n*=22). The main stated reasons for abandoning a damaged phone were impaired visibility of display content (*n*=11), important functionality being broken (*n*=10), or risk of injury from broken glass (*n*=8).

Interviews

The survey results indicate that display damage mainly impacts visual output and touch input. Despite that, most displays are not repaired, mainly due to financial reasons, and are continued to be used for prolonged periods of time. We conducted interviews with owners of damaged smartphones to elicit specific interaction issues that arise in daily use and coping strategies that users developed to deal with them.

Interview Methodology

Interviewees were recruited from participants of the online survey (except MTurk workers). The 11 semi-structured interviews consisted of 17 open questions. They were conducted either at our lab (8) or via online video chat (3). Interviews were video-recorded to capture interaction with damaged devices. Participants received 10 Euro as compensation.

	age / gender	*user group*	*importance*	*display damage*
P1	47 / female	mobile utilizer	moderate	severe
P2	25 / female	mobile utilizer	moderate	minor
P3	22 / female	mobile utilizer	important	minor
P4	27 / female	mobile utilizer	important	severe
P5	32 / male	social communicator	moderate	severe
P6	25 / female	social communicator	high	medium
P7	19 / female	social communicator	high	minor
P8	25 / male	social communicator	high	minor
P9	26 / male	social communicator	high	minor
P10	27 / male	social communicator	body extension	minor
P11	26 / male	social communicator	body extension	severe

Table 1. Interview participants and their characteristics.

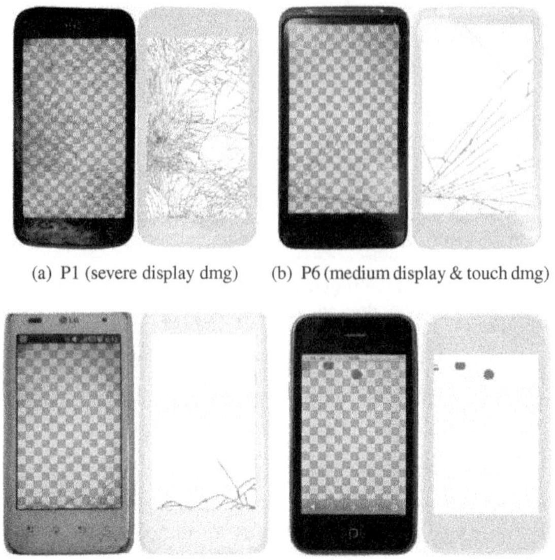

(a) P1 (severe display dmg) (b) P6 (medium display & touch dmg)

(c) P7 (minor display dmg) (d) P10 (minor display dmg (screen))

Figure 8. Examples of damaged phones from interview participants with photo (*left*) and annotated damage (dmg) (*right*).

We employed grounded theory [8] with iterative coding for qualitative analysis. First, three of the authors independently coded the same two interviews. Based on these results, a joint consolidated set of coding categories was developed, which was further refined through a second iteration. Inter-rater reliability was verified with a randomly selected interview (P2), before the remaining interviews were coded separately. Fleiss' Kappa [10] showed substantial agreement between the three raters (κ=.64). The coded data was then analyzed with affinity diagramming to identify concepts and insights.

Participant categories and phone damage

The 11 interviewees (6 female, 5 male) came from different German cities, had mainly an academic background (student or researcher), and used smartphones for 1.5–7 years (M=3). We categorized them into two groups, as shown in Table 1, based on the importance of their smartphones to them. *Mobile utilizers* appreciated the mobility and utility of smartphones, but placed less emphasis on social networking or communication with peers. *Social communicators* used their phone primarily to stay in touch via messaging, social networks, and gaming apps. They appreciated mobile Internet access and reachability, but did not talk much on the phone. Almost all rated the importance of their phones higher than mobile utilizers, seeing it as highly important for staying in touch with peers. P10 and P11 described their phone as a *"body extension."* P11 characterized it as a *"permanent social link"* and *"competence extension."* All mobile utilizers were female in our sample; social communicators dominantly male.

Almost all of the participants' phones suffered damage from a fall, either because the phone slipped out of the hand (6) or a pocket (4). P6 and P7 reported that their phones slipped out of their pants' back pocket while in the restroom. P1 dropped the phone in a parking lot without noticing it, and assumed that a car drove over it before she found it (see Fig. 8(a)). P11's phone was damaged while inside a bag. In 9 cases, only the phone's display glass was broken (*minor* to *severe*). P6 also experienced broken glass (*medium*), but the upper part of her display also became unresponsive to touch after a while (see Fig. 8(b)). P10's phone suffered only screen damage (blackouts in two spots, see Fig. 8(d)), with glass and touch being intact (*minor*). The distribution of minor (55%), medium (10%), and severe display damage (36%) in Table 1 roughly corresponds to the display damage distribution in the overall dataset (45.3%, 15.8%, 37.9%).

Results: Reasons for Continued Use

Many participants continued to use the damaged device because it was still usable with minor constraints (4), or because the damage was deemed too insignificant to justify replacement or repair (5). What degree of damage was perceived as still usable varied considerably, ranging from minor glass (P2, P8) or screen damage (P10) to medium (P6) and severe display damage (P1). However, P1 and P6 planned to replace their phones soon. The threshold for replacing a phone was quite high in both groups. Acceptability of damage was mainly traded off against financial considerations. 5 participants were not willing to pay full price for a new phone. 3 expected to receive a new phone through renewal of their mobile plan. P8 usually bought a new phone every 1.5 years and planned to keep the current phone for another 6 months. P6 continued to use the damaged phone, because she did not like the phones available in her price range.

7 participants thought repairing the phone was too expensive, which corresponds to our online survey results. While 5 participants did not consider repair, others looked into getting it repaired (P1, P2, P5) or self-repair (P8). However, only P4 had the phone repaired at the time of the interview (after 4 months) and P11 had bought a new phone (after 2 months). In general, repair costs were considered too close to the purchase price: *"repair costs 170 Euro, the phone cost 300 Euro. What should I do?"* (P1); *"repair would also cost 200 Euro, I would rather buy a new one then"* (P2). While this suggests economical obsolescence, the high price of a new phone did not lead to replacement [7]. For repair, P6 was also skeptical about placing a new display in the old casing, and P1 feared further malfunction. P2 and P5 knew that high repair costs were caused by combined glass-display units and wished that the glass was easier to replace.

4 participants stated that the damage did not change their perception of the phone manufacturer, and would not influence purchase decisions. However, P11 switched to a different manufacturer after breaking two phones from the same manufacturer. Interestingly, P4, P6, P7, and P9 perceived their phones as more robust, because they were still usable despite the damage. This increased trust in the manufacturer of their phone (P6, P7, P9), but also decreased trust in other manufacturers (P4, P6, P9). For instance, P6 stated *"[...] you see even more broken iPhones. I think those are even easier to break."*

Results: Interaction Issues

Reported interaction issues can be categorized as *viewing/output issues* and *touch/input issues*. Viewing issues are caused by glass and screen damage. Their severity depends on the location, extent, and opacity of the damage. Scratches had a negligible impact on most applications (P2, P3, P7, P8), although reading can be slightly impaired by fine cracks (P2). In line with our survey results, reading was reported to be most affected by damage. P4 stated that reading was *"awkward"*, because the damage was in the display's center. Spider webs made reading particularly difficult, as the display provided only a tessellated view of the text with cracks partially covering words and characters, thus, requiring to *"look between the cracks"* (P1), see Fig. 9(a). Characters are easily confused (P6 mentioned *O/Q* and *r/f* mix ups, cf. Fig. 9(c)) and text passages might have to be guessed (P11). P6 noted that reading issues also impact typing, as typed text can be occluded, resulting in a lack of feedback.

Damage impact can further depend on device orientation. P10 reported hardly any issues in portrait mode (see Fig. 8(d)), but noticeable effects in landscape mode. The dark spots would only cover the browser's address bar in portrait mode, but be in the middle of the text in landscape mode. When using Twitter in landscape mode, the dark spots would either only cover avatars or also be in the middle of text. As a consequence, P10 reported being conscious about the more awkward landscape orientation and having a viewing field reduced to the area between the two spots, with the area below only being used for *"a bit of preview"* (see Fig. 9(d)). Glass and screen damage further impact apps that rely on display content being read by other machines, e.g., displayed barcodes being scanned as entry or bus tickets (P6).

Regarding input, display cracks create a tactile sensation, which is particularly noticeable for swipe gestures (P5). Advanced degradation of the glass surface is also a potential source for injury, as demonstrated by P1 (see Fig. 9(b)), who stated that one *"has to be careful when typing."*

Damage of input-related hardware had the strongest impact on interaction. P3 reported a defect proximity sensor that caused her to accidentally mute calls with her cheek, and a sporadically defective home button (*"it's annoying, if you can't get out of the apps anymore"*). P6 experienced the most severe input issues, after the top part of her display became unresponsive. As a consequence, UI elements located at the top of the screen could not be activated anymore. For instance, the Android notification bar could not be pulled down; the browser address bar and the search field in the app store could also not be activated anymore. Mails could not be sent, and multiple games became unusable, because the buttons to skip ads were placed at the top.

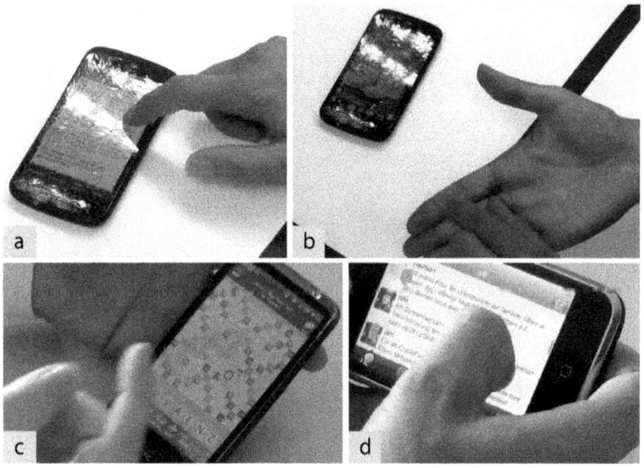

Figure 9. Examples of interaction issues: (a) P1 positioned text between cracks; (b) P1 caught glass splinters on her finger from touching the display; (c) P6 moved characters around in a Scrabble game to enhance readability; and (d) P10 positioned text between two damage spots.

Results: Coping strategies

Participants developed coping strategies to adapt to their phone's damage. In total, our 11 interviewees reported 23 different coping strategies, listed in Table 2.

Preventive strategies aimed to prevent further deterioration (4), e.g., by placing a protective film on the display (S1). P10 considered purchasing an outdoor phone (S2).

Viewing strategies addressed output issues. Most participants (5) used scrolling to move text and UI elements around damaged display areas (S3), cf. Figure 9(a) & (d). 3 participants with severe damage and 1 with minor damage stated that their perception had adapted so that they hardly noticed the damage anymore (S4). P2, P5, and P10 focused on a smaller part of the screen, typically the largest visible area (S5). Rotating the device (S6) and zooming (S7) also helped to position content in intact display areas. P5 noted that cracks were less visible on darker backgrounds, while P10's reflective screen made blackout spots almost see-through in direct sunlight (S8). Hiding or expanding UI elements, such as the virtual keyboard or menu bars, were also used to move content into viewable display areas (S9, S10), e.g., P11 would hide the keyboard to expand the visible area. When viewing a WhatsApp conversation, P6 clicked immediately into the text field in order to show the keyboard and move the message text up into less damaged display parts. P6 would also hold the phone at different angles to recognize text (S11) or just guess based on context (S12). P10 initially massaged the screen to stall spread of blackouts (S13), which eventually grew to their current size (cf. Fig. 8(d)).

Touch and input strategies are concerned with direct contact with the damage. P1, P6, and P7 used or considered protection films to smooth interaction and prevent injury (S14). P1 and P6 also tried to type and click carefully (S15). P11

	Strategy	*Category*	*Freq.*
S1	adding protection film to stall display degradation	preventive	4
S2	possibly buying durable outdoor phone	preventive	1
S3	scrolling	viewing	5
S4	ignoring the damage (perceptual adaptation)	viewing	4
S5	using only reduced viewing field	viewing	3
S6	rotating the device	viewing	3
S7	zooming	viewing	2
S8	adjusting brightness or color theme	viewing	2
S9	hiding UI components (browser bar/keyboard)	viewing	1
S10	expanding UI components (browser bar/keyboard)	viewing	1
S11	adjusting viewing angle	viewing	1
S12	guessing based on context	viewing	1
S13	massaging screen to stall blackouts	viewing	1
S14	adding protection film for smoother interaction	touch	3
S15	touching carefully to avoid injury	touch	2
S16	rotating phone to avoid touching broken glass	touch	1
S17	increased/repeated pressing of hardware buttons	touch	1
S18	using other apps	touch	1
S19	using hands-free telephony	calling	2
S20	using call forwarding to second phone	calling	1
S21	emulating hardware buttons with software	interaction	1
S22	leveraging alternative interaction methods	interaction	1
S23	moving social group to other app(s)	interaction	1

Table 2. Coping strategies employed by interview participants to deal with damage (n=11).

avoided landscape mode as the thumb would rest on broken glass (S16). P3 would press faulty hardware buttons repeatedly or used two fingers to increase pressure (S17). P6 switched to other apps, because certain apps had UI elements only in the touch-damaged area (S18). Surprisingly, no participant rearranged icons on the home screen to make them more accessible. Even P6 did not move icons from the top part of the screen, because *"they can still be activated by clicking them on their very bottom"*. This suggests that customization with widgets and home screen arrangements is rather a tool for personalization [5] than a coping mechanism.

Calling strategies served to make phone calls with minimal phone contact. P1 and P3 made calls in speaker mode to avoid holding the damaged phone against their face (S19). Later on, P1 automatically forwarded calls to an older feature phone in order to take calls more conveniently (S20).

Interaction strategies enabled users to perform activities with alternative means. P6 added the *settings* icon to her home screen to compensate for defective volume controls (S21). P6 also used alternative interaction paths to cope with partially defective touch input (S22). Because the address bar in the browser could not be clicked, she opened a new tab via the context menu, which would directly select the address bar. In the contacts list, the top entry could not be selected, thus she read the number from the contact preview and typed it manually to place a call. Because she could not send emails with her mail app anymore, she used the Web interface of her email provider, which allowed to *"track and scroll the display [in the browser]."* However, this process was perceived as too cumbersome. P6 engaged in multiple social gaming apps to keep in touch with friends. One game became unusable due to a *next* button located at the top of the screen. Another game had a similar setup but allowed to reach the main menu by pressing back. Thus, she actively persuaded her friends to only play the second game (S23): *"I told them all: 'Guys, no more playing WordBlitz, only Razzle."'*

Limitations

Our interview participants all had an academic background, either being students or researchers, coming from different German universities. In our sample population, we only identified mobile utilizers and social communicators as explicit groups. With higher diversity more user categories might emerge that may also exhibit additional or different coping strategies. More users affected by touch damage would be of particular interest, as P3 and P6 exhibited rich and elaborate coping strategies to compensate for partial touch damage. While the list of named coping strategies may not be exhaustive, it highlights the diversity of strategies and the adaptability of users. The interviews also made apparent that seemingly innocuous design decisions, such as the placement of a *next* button to skip ads can have a large impact when interaction is impaired by damage.

SUPPORTING INTERACTION WITH BROKEN DISPLAYS

Our survey and interview results show that the majority of participants continued to use a damaged phone (98%); 88% for at least three months. 32% plan to use it for another year or more. Repair costs are deemed too high by most, regardless of the degree of damage. Yet, new smartphones are also deemed too expensive to justify unplanned purchases. Only if the damage becomes intolerable, e.g., when touch input is strongly affected, damaged phones are actively replaced.

Users adapt to their phone damage with diverse coping strategies, closely tailored to their individual interaction issues. Many of these strategies can already be supported at design time of smartphones and mobile applications. Supporting those strategies would not only provide a positive user experience in the face of display damage, but may also prevent affected users from switching to different apps or platforms, potentially moving their social group with them. Next, we propose respective design guidelines for manufacturers and interaction designers that potentially lessen the impact of display damage on interaction.

Support scrolling and device rotation

The frequently named coping strategies scrolling (S3) and rotating the device (S6) can be actively supported. Scrolling up and down enables users to position screen content and text in less damaged display areas. Inertial scrolling (or rubber-band scrolling) further supports this coping strategy by allowing to move slightly *beyond* the beginning and end of a screen. Allowing to move screen content also slightly to the left or right (2D inertial scrolling) makes it easier to recognize text occluded by damage (S11, S12). The inertia, i.e., how far content can be moved to the sides, should be configurable to enable users to adapt it to the extent of their display's damage. While inertial scrolling is commonly provided by UI widgets, app designers could also integrate it in apps that tend to have non-scrollable screens, such as games.

Switching between portrait and landscape mode changes the perceived visual impact of damage, because different UI elements may be occluded. Apps could also use different layouts for portrait and landscape modes in order to offer the ability to gain access to previously occluded screen content and functionality. Thus, app designers should strive to provide, both, portrait and landscape layouts, whenever possible.

Facilitate layout and theme customization

Coping strategies that rely on expanding and hiding UI elements (S9, S10), such as the keyboard or status bars, indicate a need for flexible UI concepts. Affected users should be able to customize the layout of an app to better suit their needs — damage related or not. For instance, rearranging status bars or soft buttons would have allowed P6 to move essential components to screen areas still responsive to touch. Thus, customization does not only facilitate personalization but can also reduce the impact of potential display damage.

Darker colors make it easier for affected users to ignore glass cracks (S4), because reduction of screen brightness coincides with a reduction of light reflected by cracks. Operating systems and apps could support this by providing different themes to choose from. Some smartphones (e.g., Nokia Lumia 920) already provide sunlight readability modes, which adapt screen contrast and color dynamically. Similar modes could be created to make display damage less noticeable.

Provide alternative interaction paths

By providing multiple alternative interaction paths, utility of an app can be maintained even if the primary intended interaction paths have been rendered unusable by damage (S22). Relying on a single exclusive interaction path may render the whole application unusable, which poses the risk of not only losing the affected users, but their social sphere as well (S23). Alternative interaction paths can often be provided without much additional effort. For P6, the ability to press the *back* button to skip an in-game ad rather than having to use the app's *next* button made all the difference. Similarly, providing redundant options in context menus can suffice as interaction alternatives. Another approach could be to allow to change the function of hardware buttons, such as volume controls, on the system level to sequentially tab through UI elements, e.g., in order to select the browser's address bar for text entry. A short press could mean tab, a long press could act as a trigger. A further option is to provide additional input and output modalities, such as projected UIs [20] or gaze-based interaction [22], to compensate display and touch damage.

Detect and adapt to damage

An avenue for further research is the detection of drops and resulting damage with integrated sensors. Accelerometers could recognize drops as free fall and a sudden stop. A gyroscope could determine whether the device hit the ground with an edge, corner, the front, or the back. Such sensor information could be combined with empirical damage models to estimate whether damage occurred and to what extent, which could also benefit manufacturers to adapt their design.

Accelerometer peaks can also be used to detect taps on the device [17], in oder to determine when intended taps were not sensed properly, e.g., when the display is tapped repeatedly (S17). Over a period of time, this should allow to determine in which display areas touch input is impaired. Smartphones could then either adapt system aspects to detected damage or suggest suitable coping strategies to improve continued use.

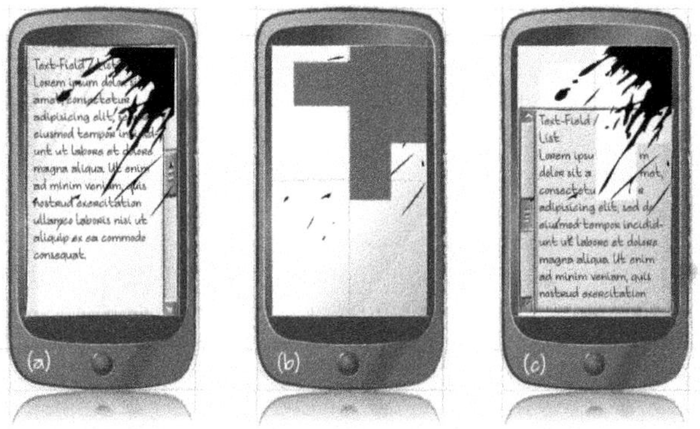

Figure 10. Adaptive content rendering example: (a) A text area is partially occluded by display damage. (b) The user marks the damaged area on a grid (*red*). (c) An adaptive text renderer floats the text around the damaged area (*green*) and moves the scroll indicator to the left. In this scenario, the upper-left corner can also not be used anymore (*yellow*).

Provide adaptive content representation

Named interaction issues were dominated by viewing and reading impairments caused by occlusion of content. By offering user control over how content is presented, readability could be enhanced, e.g., by allowing to change font size or family (S11, S12) or by not only supporting zooming for websites, maps, and images, but also for app content (S7).

A potentially useful approach could be adaptive text and content rendering. Display areas highly occluded by damage could either be automatically detected, as proposed before, or manually marked by the user, if touch input is intact. As a result, the phone would be aware of areas with major damage and could adapt content rendering and representation, accordingly, e.g., by excluding parts from rendering or rearranging UI components. Figure 10 shows a simplified example of how this approach might work. Further research is required to assess the potential of such an approach and the impact on readability and user experience, as well as to develop suitable adaptive rendering mechanisms.

CONCLUSIONS

In this work, we have shown that display damage has indeed a large impact on smartphone interaction. Our broken interface dataset is a rich resource on display damage in the wild, including detailed images of damaged phones, information about the damage severity, how damage occurred, as well as the impact of the damage on prolonged use. Participants' damage assessment in combination with image analysis and manual damage annotation showed that three categories of visible display damage can be distinguished (*minor*, *medium*, *severe*), with a considerable gap between the latter two. While touch issues occur across categories, we identified a positive correlation between those categories and the reported presence of touch damage. We provided our damaged display dataset[1] to the CHI community to foster more research on the impact of damage on user interaction.

Our semi-structured interviews revealed that the severity of damage has a stronger impact on interaction than the type of use or assigned importance of the phone. Both survey and interview results indicate that even heavily damaged smartphones are continued to be used for multiple months; phones with less severe damage potentially for years. Main reasons for continued use are high repair or replacement costs, which are balanced against the severity of the damage. Reported interaction issues are dominated by viewing issues due to visible display damage. However, when touch input issues emerged, they were typically more severe. Through our 11 interviews, we collected over 20 coping strategies. Those strategies highlight the adaptability of users, if provided with flexibility in how to interact with their smartphones and apps.

A valuable insight for application developers is the indication that not catering for potential display damage may not only cause affected users but their whole social group to abandon an app, as reported by interviewee P6 (strategy S23). Based on our results, we discussed strategies for interaction designers to cater for potential damage. The proposed strategies support many of the reported coping strategies, and most of them can be readily considered in application design without major effort. Conceptual strategies, such as damage-aware adaptive content rendering and sensor-based damage detection, require further investigation to assess their potential and overcome associated challenges.

ACKNOWLEDGMENTS

Parts of this work have been conducted within the Emmy Noether research group *Mobile Interaction with Pervasive User Interfaces* funded by the German Research Foundation. The authors would like to thank Jens Nickels for help with damage annotation, Alexander de Luca for extensive feedback on an earlier draft, and the anonymous reviewers for their feedback.

REFERENCES

1. Apple Inc. iOS accessibility, 2013 (last accessed 2013/09/18). `http://www.apple.com/accessibility/ios/`.
2. Apple Inc. Use your voice to do even more with Siri, 2013 (last accessed 2013/09/18). `http://www.apple.com/ios/siri/`.
3. Big Idea Media Ltd. Most broken mobiles damaged within first 3 months of owning, 2013 (last accessed 2013/09/18). `http://www.mobileinsurance.co.uk/Information/Blog/1017-/Most-Broken-Mobiles-Damaged-Within-First-3-Months-of-Owning`.
4. Big Idea Media Ltd. Quarter of iphone owners using handset with broken screen - mobile insurance blog, 2013 (last accessed 2013/09/18). `http://www.mobileinsurance.co.uk/Information/Blog/1004-/Quarter-of-iPhone-Owners-Using-Handset-with-Broken-Screen`.
5. Böhmer, M., and Krüger, A. A study on icon arrangement by smartphone users. In *CHI '13*, ACM (2013), 2137–2146.
6. Bulow, J. An economic theory of planned obsolescence. *Quarterly Journal of Economics 101*, 4 (1986), 729–749.
7. Cooper, T. Inadequate life? evidence of consumer attitudes to product obsolescence. *Journal of Consumer Policy 27*, 4 (2004), 421–449.
8. Corbin, J., and Strauss, A. *Basics of Qualitative Research: Techniques and Procedures for Developing Grounded Theory*, 3rd ed. SAGE Pub., 2008.
9. Döring, T., Sylvester, A., and Schmidt, A. A design space for ephemeral user interfaces. In *TEI '13*, ACM (2013), 75–82.
10. Fleiss, J. L. Measuring nominal scale agreement among many raters. *Psychol. Bulletin 76*, 5 (1971), 378–382.
11. Google Inc. Google now, 2013 (last accessed 2013/09/18). `http://www.google.com/now/`.
12. Harrison, C., and Hudson, S. E. Scratch input: creating large, inexpensive, unpowered and mobile finger input surfaces. In *UIST '08*, ACM (2008), 205–208.
13. Heo, S., and Lee, G. Forcetap: extending the input vocabulary of mobile touch screens by adding tap gestures. In *MobileHCI '11*, ACM (2011), 113–122.
14. Huang, E. M., and Truong, K. N. Breaking the disposable technology paradigm: opportunities for sustainable interaction design for mobile phones. In *CHI '08*, ACM (2008), 323–332.
15. Ikemiya, M., and Rosner, D. Broken probes: toward the design of worn media. *Personal and Ubiquitous Computing (online)* (2013), 1–13.
16. Odom, W., Pierce, J., Stolterman, E., and Blevis, E. Understanding why we preserve some things and discard others in the context of interaction design. In *CHI '09*, ACM (2009), 1053–1062.
17. Ronkainen, S., Häkkilä, J., Kaleva, S., Colley, A., and Linjama, J. Tap input as an embedded interaction method for mobile devices. In *TEI '07*, ACM (2007), 263–270.
18. Rosner, D. K., Ikemiya, M., Kim, D., and Koch, K. Designing with traces. In *CHI '13*, ACM (2013), 1649–1658.
19. Ross, J., Irani, L., Silberman, M. S., Zaldivar, A., and Tomlinson, B. Who are the crowdworkers?: shifting demographics in mechanical turk. In *CHI EA '10*, ACM (2010), 2863–2872.
20. Rukzio, E., Holleis, P., and Gellersen, H. Personal projectors for pervasive computing. *IEEE Pervasive Computing 11*, 2 (2012), 30–37.
21. Scott, J., Dearman, D., Yatani, K., and Truong, K. N. Sensing foot gestures from the pocket. In *UIST '10*, ACM (2010), 199–208.
22. Yi, B., Cao, X., Fjeld, M., and Zhao, S. Exploring user motivations for eyes-free interaction on mobile devices. In *CHI '12*, ACM (2012), 2789–2792.

Leakiness and Creepiness in App Space: Perceptions of Privacy and Mobile App Use

Irina Shklovski[1], Scott D. Mainwaring[2], Halla Hrund Skúladóttir[1] and Höskuldur Borgthorsson[1]

[1]ITU Copenhagen
Rued Langgaards Vej 7
2300 Copenhagen, S. Denmark
irsh@itu.dk, {hallahsk,hoskborg}@gmail.com

[2]Unaffiliated
Portland, Oregon, USA
scottmainwaring@gmail.com

ABSTRACT

Mobile devices are playing an increasingly intimate role in everyday life. However, users can be surprised when informed of the data collection and distribution activities of apps they install. We report on two studies of smartphone users in western European countries, in which users were confronted with app behaviors and their reactions assessed. Users felt their personal space had been violated in "creepy" ways. Using Altman's notions of personal space and territoriality, and Nissenbaum's theory of contextual integrity, we account for these emotional reactions and suggest that they point to important underlying issues, even when users continue using apps they find creepy.

Author Keywords

Mobile devices; data privacy; bodily integrity; learned helplessness; creepiness;

ACM Classification Keywords

H.5.m. Information interfaces and presentation (e.g., HCI): Miscellaneous.

INTRODUCTION

"*I feel like I am constantly tracked either on my phone or on my computer, at stores, etc. I feel like this is a part of daily life now*" – Survey, USA

What does it mean to "feel" like you are constantly tracked by unseen and largely unknown entities? In the quote above who was doing the tracking was not named and for most of our respondents through the interviews and the survey they remained unknown, largely abstract entities that somehow collect personal, sometimes even intimate information. With the rise of personal computing in the 1980s and especially of the world-wide web in the 1990s and 2000s, and the movement of computers out of offices and into homes, computing became understood as technology of mass consumption and marketing, raising new questions about consumer tracking (especially via web cookies) and targeting [24]. Mass data collection is becoming "designed in" to everyday life [36] as we increasingly rely on technologies capable of monitoring, storing and distributing information about us. Occasionally data collection by governments, organizations, corporations or even small application developers comes to light causing a public outcry [39]. Yet much of the tracking and data collection does not necessarily happen with insidious goals, but is a result of businesses attempting to deliver personalized services and advertising more effectively [40]. Despite potentially positive outcomes of this kind of tracking, the public response remains negative often because people simply find it *creepy*. At the same time, people continue to use the technologies and applications implicated in data collection even as they express outrage over such activities. This is typically seen as an expression of the "privacy paradox" where intentions and behaviors around information disclosure often radically differ [2,32,40].

Over the last decade, especially since the launch of the first app store by Apple in 2008, computing has moved out of the home and into our pockets, purses, hands, and even bedsides, bringing with it a new wave of concerns, increasingly framed in terms of "creepiness." We will define *creepy* more carefully later on in the paper but we note here that we use this term to denote an emotional response to a sense of wrongness that is difficult to clearly articulate. We argue that the notion of creepiness is a concept worth unpacking, and by way of example analyze a corpus of data recently collected from smartphone app users in a number of western countries using perspectives of bodily integrity, personal space and territoriality [3,30,31,34].

From this analysis a different notion of "users" emerges. Listening closely and empathically to our study participants, more than seeing them just as decision-making agents, we began to identify them as people[1] caught up in a

CHI 2014, April 26 - May 01 2014, Toronto, ON, Canada
Copyright 2014 ACM 978-1-4503-2473-1/14/04...$15.00.
http://dx.doi.org/10.1145/2556288.2557421.

[1] For the purposes of this paper, when we say "people" we are referring to fairly affluent consumers in developed Western countries. Questions of personal space and privacy are clearly culturally dependent, and from, e.g., Chinese or Global South perspectives smartphones may have very different meanings.

bind over the limits of their personal space: On the one hand, smartphones felt like intimate zones and extensions of their bodies. On the other hand, in order to empower themselves through this boundary-enlarging technology, they felt they had to accept the possibility of unknown, foreign access into this zone of expanded intimacy. Reframing the "privacy paradox" in these terms opens different opportunities and responsibilities for technology development and policy design.

SMARTPHONES AS EXTENSIONS OF THE SELF

Ubiquitous, nearly infinitely personalizable and most often individually owned at least in the Western world, mobile phones have variously been discussed as deeply personal extensions of the self [26,29] or even organic parts of the self [23,33]. As mobile technologies developed and become domesticated, smartphones have moved from an expensive curiosity to a commodity deeply integrated into their users' everyday lives. The functions these devices perform are not just about practical problem solving, escapist entertainment or convenient extensions of sociability, but also about projecting and constructing the self [12].

Like our homes, smartphones are implicated in the way of being and deeply embedded in the life experience. Yet in HCI research aesthetic or emotional experiences are less of a concern than the serious business of sociability, friendship, collaboration and getting ahead in life. Finding a particular experience "creepy" is a kind of emotional experience, but it can also serve as an indication of a disjuncture between the way developers and users experience and interpret functions or applications. Much of the discussion of discomfort or feelings of creepiness in the course of technology use in HCI has been conflated with user privacy concerns of data access and security. We use two theoretical frameworks familiar to HCI researchers for thinking about privacy, but extend the conversation to consider how creepiness might be conceptualized in this context.

Altman's notions of personal space and territoriality

Irwin Altman's theory of privacy regulation has been discussed in prior work [34]. Altman conceptualizes privacy as a process through which people attempt to achieve a desired privacy level in any situation in life by selectively adjusting access to themselves through controlling information they disclose or receive [3]. In other words, people keep secrets and manage themselves and their secrets through ongoing acts of revealing and concealment [30]. Altman conceptualized privacy as one of the four key concepts central to the study of environment and social behavior: privacy, personal space, territoriality and crowding. Altman explains personal space and territorial behavior as mechanisms people use in the service of privacy goals to regulate interpersonal boundaries and environmental factors.

Personal space is typically conceptualized as a "boundary around a person, intrusion into which is often uncomfortable and generally not permitted" [3]. Intrusions or invasions of personal space represent privacy violations and can result in a variety of responses from feelings of anxiety to actions designed to increase distance and reduce interaction.

Territorial behavior is another type of a social regulation mechanism. Altman argues that just like animals are territorial about their feeding or mating areas, people also regard certain places and objects as their personal or primary territories. A primary territory usually refers to an area, a place or an object that fulfills certain needs or motives and where ownership is clearly conveyed through some form of personalization. Entry into another person's primary territory is typically done with permission only and trespassing is considered an invasion that can elicit intense emotional responses and physical action [3].

Several researchers have explored user decisions to allow physical access to their smartphones and personal data, showing that people regard their phone as highly private and are reluctant to share it with others, expressing discomfort even when sharing it with close friends [16,17]. Research has also shown that smartphone users are surprised and feel violated when they find out that applications are accessing data on their smartphones ostensibly without their knowledge [10,25]. In other words they feel that this data access breaches their privacy norms and should be done with their informed consent, the same reaction people show when their primary territory is breached.

Increased computerization affects individuals and society as a whole as it brings increased imbalance in power between individuals and large institutions. In the case of smartphones, the power balance between the smartphone user and the application developers is quite uneven. The user has few means of safeguarding his territory and often she is unaware of the encroachment. Her options include shifting the desired level of privacy towards the actual level; a common approach used when repeated attempts to regulate privacy have failed.

Nissenbaum's contextual integrity model

Helen Nissenbaum's theory of contextual integrity complements Altman's notions of personal space by calling attention to context-dependent social norms and regulated information flows [31]. Even from within the most private, personal space, people never interact with information in the abstract, but always as it is embedded in a particular social context. Nissenbaum defines contexts as "structured social settings characterized by canonical activities, roles, relationships, power structures, norms (or rules), and internal values (goals, ends, purposes)" [31]. Smartphones may be extensions of personal space, in Altman's terms, but through them people participate in a variety of quite different contexts. These may indeed vary on an app-by-app basis: what is socially legitimate information sharing for a health app might include highly sensitive information about one's body and behaviors, whereas what it is socially legitimate for a game like Fruit Ninja to share, while difficult to precisely define and probably not yet worked out by its many stakeholders, is sure to be much less sensitive.

Contextual integrity is maintained if information flows according to contextual norms. However, digital technologies make it easy to disregard such norms either through ignorance or intentionally [4]. That a digital system is respecting contextual integrity may be difficult and expensive to attain, often beyond the capabilities of any particular individual. However, individuals can sometimes (and dramatically) detect when a breach of norms has occurred when they see that information they consider off limits with respect to the context in which it was given is being used in ways antithetical to its socially sanctioned expectations.

What are we feeling when we are creeped out?

Encountering a violation of contextual integrity of one's information can result in a range of emotional responses, though it may not necessarily lead to outward action to alleviate the problem. One can be outraged, exasperated, horrified, even cynically bemused. Along with or in addition to these, people often describe their discomfort by referencing the word "creepy".

Collins English dictionary defines *creepy* as "having or causing a sensation of repulsion, horror, or fear, as of creatures crawling on the skin" [8]. The reference to creepy-crawlies on the skin grounds this experience in a certain kind of fundamental, embodied boundary violation, in Altman's terms. In Nissenbaum's terms, creepy information flows often involve realizations that personal secrets have been, or could be, revealed to those who have not been explicitly granted access to them. "Creepy" does not necessarily signal that the end result (contextually appropriate advertisement for example) is not beneficial to the user, but to a kind of dual violation of deeply held expectations not just of "contextual integrity" in terms of respecting social norms, but "personal zone integrity" in terms of control over sensitive boundaries.

TRACKING AND DATA LEAKAGE

Discussions of information disclosure practices via mobile phones have been extensive though mostly focused on location-based services and interpersonal information disclosure [22,28]. Researchers have turned their attention to smartphone app data distribution, often termed "data leakage" to third parties without direct owner notification only recently [25]. Ostensibly, users give permission for smartphone applications to access their use data and to utilize it for a range of purposes when they press "agree" on the End User License Agreement (EULA) screen in the process of installing a smartphone application. Despite this, revelations of data distribution by many common applications to third party advertisers have resulted in expressions of concern and discomfort by smartphone users [9,10,19,25].

Where does the data go?

In a survey of 5000 mobile users reported by Think Insights, 82% of the participants claimed to notice ads on their smartphones and 49% had taken action based on those ads[2]. Advertising in applications has a substantial effect on users and their purchase patterns. The global mobile advertising market was valued around 5.3 billion dollars in the year 2012 illustrating just how valuable it is for advertisers to have access to user patterns and personal data [14]. Ad libraries and analytic companies buy the data that smartphone apps collect, analyzing and aggregating user data to build a profile for targeted advertising.

Imagine a smartphone owner who has on her phone a typical flashlight application like the High-Powered Flashlight from iHandy inc., and a simple one-player game application like Fruit Ninja from Halfbrick Studios. Both apps require access to the phone number and device ID, the remote number if a call is active and which other applications are used on the device. Additionally the flashlight app has access to precise location, hardware controls and system tools that enable it to change system configuration and display settings. The Fruit Ninja app also requires access to the list of accounts known by the device. The information these apps collect is sold to several third parties, one of which is Flurry, a big ad and analytics company that according to its website prides itself on taking in two terabytes of data from 2.8 billion app sessions per day [11]. Flurry buys data from both these apps and can build a profile of a user that includes information about what type of phone she has, what applications she uses and how frequently, what accounts she has on her phone, which numbers she calls (which can link to other consumer profiles in the Flurry database) and precise location of the phone which, if logged with timestamps, gives an accurate estimate of where she lives, works and travels. By properly aggregating this information the company gets a detailed profile of her as a consumer, information that is worth money.

Smartphone users' response to tracking and data collection as well as the willingness to share data with others varies but users are invariably surprised at the extent of data leakage on their phones [5,22,25]. Although many are willing to share data with developers in the right context, particularly when the type of information collected and its purpose is made clear, it is difficult to justify why gaming applications that are about fruit slicing or sling shooting birds would need the user's location, phone number or information about other running apps. The user in the example above has given her permission for the Flashlight and Fruit Ninja apps to collect and distribute her information at the point of installation when she clicked through the End User License Agreement (EULA). Yet smartphone users often have little

[2] Think Insights by Google reporting on a study conducted by Ipsos OTX. Retrieved from http://goo.gl/SRTh4

understanding of which permissions they consent to and what these mean. Moreover, studies show that most users simply ignore permissions completely [9,10]. People ignore EULAs for various reasons, for example warning fatigue [10], lack of motivation [15], or an overriding desire to install the app where reading the EULA is seen as a cost without a clear benefit [25].

"Data leakage" at one level appears to be a misnomer — the data flows the app is enabling are most likely not accidental oversights or unintended consequences, but central to the business model the makes the app possible in the first place. "Intended data distribution" would seem more apt a term and this is how tracking is often included in EULA. However, upon closer inspection, calling this *leakage* captures an important aspect of the consequences of installing the app: if the user conceptualized her personal space as having integrity, and a more-or-less controllable border, from her perspective the app makes this border "leaky", and intentionally so.

While ensuring readability and usability of EULA is important, here we consider why people continue to use apps even when they know these apps reveal personal data to advertisers. We also discuss why it is important to consider these issues both at the individual level and in the broader social context. The studies we present consider what it means to loose control over access to the self to unknown third parties with few concrete or obvious consequences. Why does it matter that third-party advertisers can gain access to certain types of personal information via smartphones? How do people react to finding this out and what might they be willing to do about it?

STUDYING ATTITUDES TOWARD DATA LEAKAGE

We conducted two studies investigating how smartphone users feel about data access on their phones. The first study was a qualitative investigation conducted in two countries in order to assess whether smartphone users may be willing to change their behavior once they have been informed about tracking and data leakage. We exposed our participants to data leakage to see if they made changes in their user patterns when informed of potential privacy breaches. In the second study we conducted a survey on an international opportunity sample where we explored how data privacy sentiments might affect smartphone users when choosing and downloading applications. Furthermore we explored how important it was for our participants to maintain their privacy while using applications on smartphones.

Study 1 — Interviews

In February 2013 we conducted 13 semi-structured interviews in two countries: 6 in Iceland 7 in Denmark. We recruited users from our own personal networks and by advertising on Facebook. The prerequisite was that our users owned and used Android smartphones and were between 25 and 60 years of age. Our sample consisted of 8 men and 5 women, and the age distribution was between 27 and 55 years with a mean of 33,5.

We chose to use the Android OS as our research platform because the system presents the user with the permission screen each time she downloads an application. Our participants then would have encountered the terms of use more often than an iOS smartphone user.

The interviews were conducted in English, Danish or Icelandic depending on participant preference and lasted 40-70 minutes each. We started with general questions regarding smartphones and applications and then asked participants to think aloud while demonstrating how they usually go about accessing the Google Play Store on their mobile phones and downloading an application of their choosing. After our participants downloaded an app, we moved on to questions regarding attitudes and beliefs about data privacy. We also asked users what they think their apps do with the data they access, to get insight into participants' mental models of data security on smartphones.

In the second half of the interview we introduced some of the most common permission statements found on popular apps in Google Play and discussed what they mean. We also showed them a website that allows users to scan apps, and asked users to download an app in Google Play that scans permissions and analytic libraries connected to apps currently located on the user's mobile phone[3]. Finally, we asked participants to download and try out a popular game on Google Play, Fruit Ninja, then explained its main functions and discussed the permissions our users had accepted before downloading the app to their mobile devices.

Three weeks after the initial interviews we sent our participants a follow-up questionnaire where we asked them questions regarding their use patterns and conducted a follow up interview via email or phone. All interviews were transcribed and coded. We used an iterative analysis process of open and thematic coding throughout the data collection process. This allowed us to test emergent themes in follow up interviews.

Study 2 — Survey

In March and April of 2013 we deployed a survey to gain a better understanding of privacy sentiments of smartphone users more broadly. We obtained an opportunity sample by recruiting via our own networks on Facebook and by sending participation requests to university student mailing lists in Iceland and Denmark. A total of 272 respondents answered our survey and 187 completed it (116 women and 71 men). Although this was an opportunity sample it was quite diverse. The majority of participants were between the

---

[3] In our study we used http://privacyscore.com/mobilescan and Addons Detector by denper available from the Google Play store http://goo.gl/TM9g2

ages of 25 and 44 (81%) although participants ranged in age from 18 to 74. Over 60% were highly educated (graduate degree) and approximately 13% had less than a bachelor degree. Most of the respondents lived in Denmark (43%), Iceland (20%), USA (20%) and Sweden (10%). However, the sample included participants from 12 countries. Although slightly over half of our respondents were veteran smartphone users (51%), having used a smartphone for over 2 years, 18% were new to the smartphone world, having used the device for less than a year.

We measured attitudes toward app stores, personalized advertising and general sentiment toward data collection by businesses as well as the general level of concern about threats to personal privacy. We also developed a set of questions focused specifically on attitudes towards data collection and management by smartphone apps.

In order to measure attitudes toward data collection by mobile applications respondents were randomly presented with either Fruit Ninja game app or Flashlight app with the developer description of the app. Below the description we listed permissions that the app requires the user to agree to before downloading and asked respondents to indicate which they felt permissions were appropriate or inappropriate given the functionality of the app.

On the next page we explained which ad-libraries and analytics companies received the data the apps collected from the mobile phones and added the explanation these companies generally give for how this data is utilized. We followed up with questions regarding awareness about data collection and distribution in mobile applications and whether participants read the EULA prior to downloading apps. The final question of the survey was free response, asking users to share how they felt about data distribution to third parties in general. Due to space constraints all survey instruments are available upon request.

Nearly 50% (89 of 187) of participants that had completed the survey responded to this question and we coded these responses using an iterative coding process by moving from an initial open coding through axial and thematic coding to distill thematic categories. Where necessary, quotes presented in this paper were translated from Icelandic or Danish. Quotes and excerpts are marked Interview or Survey to indicate the source and Country to indicate location of the respondent.

FINDINGS

In broad strokes, many of our findings confirmed other studies of attitudes toward mobile phone data leakage and privacy. Similar to the findings in [7] our interview participants became more concerned with data leakage as a kind of privacy violation throughout the interview. Similar to findings in [25] they also indicated that these privacy concerns were often overridden by other factors when they made decisions about whether to install a particular application. As in [9,10,17] our participants had strong opinions on what data they considered sensitive (emails, images and messages) and substantial misconceptions about what data applications they used were accessing on their mobile phone, as has been noted by [10,25].

Just like the participants in [10] and [15] our interviewees ignored the EULA when they were asked to install an application of their own choosing from the app store during the interview. Yet they had typically expressed concern about their privacy in the prior portion of the interview, discussing privacy implications of smartphone application data leakage. When asked why they had ignored the EULA two explanations dominated similar to those described in [9,18,25]. First, they had never had any real negative consequences from data collection. Second, the desire to have the application trumped any concerns for data collection, which was explained away as "the way things are."

"*Yes, I used to think about it, but I decided to stop it. I know I am agreeing to this (data collection). If I really want the app, I take my chances.*" – interview, Denmark

Other researchers have argued that it is important to redesign the EULA to help users be more aware of what is going on in their smartphones [25,41]. In the final portion of the interview, participants were asked to install Fruit Ninja and researchers walked them through the EULA explaining all permissions requested by the application. Similar to [25], this exercise revealed a mismatch between the interviewees' mental models of what Fruit Ninja might reasonably request in order to function and the kind of data it actually requested. That is, they expected the data collected via the app to be contextually appropriate to a single-player game of slicing fruit. Not surprisingly, this mismatch caused participants significant discomfort similar to [9,24]:

"*I feel deceived, I had no idea it was this systematic*" – interview, Iceland

During the follow-up interview three weeks later our participants said they wanted to be more cautious and were trying to pay attention to what they were downloading and installing on their mobile phones. More than half (7 of 13) had deleted an application although in most cases it was Fruit Ninja:

"*I deleted Fruit Ninja because it was gathering a lot of information, although it might also be the case with other apps on the phone I don't want to delete them, I simply enjoy them too much.*" – interview, Iceland

This was to be expected as it was not their choice to download Fruit Ninja and the majority of our participants did not have prior experience with this app. Even though participants were not willing to trade personal data for useless applications they accepted the possibility that other more "meaningful" applications might be doing the same thing. Although some approached their smartphones with more caution they admitted they had not changed their practices very much:

"I just get the applications I want, I had forgotten all about this data gathering stuff." – interview, Denmark

Similar to findings in [15] and in slight contradiction to [18] the extensive explanations and demonstrations of what can be done to monitor privacy more closely, installation of detector applications on participants' phones and introductions of trackers websites, our participants did not use these tools, or looked for new ones, because they regarded it as a waste of time:

"I will never waste my time reading privacy policies, my time is simply too valuable. To some extent I just have to accept this." – interview, Iceland

The survey findings followed a similar pattern. Our participants were generally aware of data collection and distribution to third parties and believed that more data was collected than necessary. Nevertheless, few respondents restricted mobile data while using their phones. Indeed, 78% had data turned on continuously with 56% saying they use data a lot. Similar to findings in [10] nearly 57% said they had deleted an app and roughly 62% had aborted the installation process of an application because of privacy concerns.

Overall survey respondents were concerned about information disclosure to businesses (mean=2.29, sd=.487, range 0-3 where 3=high concern) and reported moderate levels of concern regarding threats to personal privacy (mean=2.01, sd=.466, range 0-3 where 3=high concern). Participants were also quite concerned about smartphone integrity and their privacy in regards to that, which manifested in low scores on our scale of how trusting smartphone users were toward the integrity of app stores and app developers (mean=1.23, sd=.65, range 0-3 where 3=highly trusting).

Beyond the Privacy Paradox

Results from both studies clearly illustrated what is commonly called a privacy paradox where our participants expressed concerns about data leakage, but their actions suggested otherwise. In both studies participants expressed a desire for greater transparency and control over information disclosure. Where none of this is particularly surprising, we were struck by the fact that sentiments expressed by survey participants about data collection and smartphone usage seemed to fall into three broad categories (see Table 1). We then explored more closely the sentiments expressed by both survey and interview study participants about data leakage and why they said they continued to use their phones the way they did. Our findings suggest that the notion of "privacy paradox" that is often used to explain these findings may obscure complex dynamics around technology use and data disclosure.

Tracking is understandable

Although the vast majority of responses in interviews and survey expressed significant distaste for tracking and third party data collection activities, some felt that there are legitimate reasons for data collection:

"I see the purpose of collecting data for improving the application behavior e.g. Amazon book suggestions, but I do not approve the selling of my data to third parties, especially when I am not getting a share of the revenue!" – survey, location undisclosed.

After all, people did want personalization of services, although they tended to identify these activities with expected, and thus contextually appropriate data usage. Others pointed to the typical business model of smartphone application and other online businesses, as they understood it:

"I understand that this information is a revenue stream for free apps - but I believe it has gone too far" – survey, USA

Theme	Code	N
Tracking is understandable	Collecting data is OK	1
	Developers need it	6
The concerned and the outraged	Should be illegal	8
	Users need to be informed / more control	7
Dejected acceptance and compliance	Nothing is free	6
	The user has to comply	14
Tracking is Disturbing/Creepy		50
Unconcerned "I do not care"		2

Table 1: Thematic coding of qualitative data from the survey (total N=89, some statements were coded in more than one category)

The reality of the information economy is such that in the course of mundane interactions with everyday technologies users move smoothly between consumption of services and production of content that is in turn monetized by service providers. This kind of information economy turns all data produced by consumers into commodities that are either fed back to the consumer through improved services and personalization or sold elsewhere. Many of our participants understood this dynamic quite well:

"I understand the appeal from the developer's perspective -- being able to collect large amounts of data about users could be crucial to targeted ads and later versions of an app." – survey, USA

Alongside this understanding, most expressed concern for the amount of tracking and qualified their statements to caution about the run-away train of the scale of data collection. Many participants said they didn't care if advertisers had data about their application usage or how many times they played a game on their phone during work hours. Yet a vague concern for how this data might eventually be used and interpreted remained:

"*I'm ok with them collecting some information about me, but it is a slippery slope and the developer should only engage in the activity if they are willing to accept the consequences and responsibility of handling it properly.*" – survey, USA

Most of our participants called for greater transparency, regardless of whether they approved of data collection or not. Identifying what kind of data is collected, where it is delivered and how it might be used is no small task and most of the time it is impossible. Even the most technically savvy smartphone users often do not conceptualize quite the extent of data leakage.

The concerned and the outraged

In most cases, news of data leakage elicited expressions of mild discomfort and references to creepiness:

"*I think it's creepy and makes me think about all the apps I have on my phone. I use flashlight very often and I find it disturbing that it can collect personal information off my phone*" – survey, Iceland

In several cases, however participants expressed significant outrage. When asked why, in all cases they explained they had not expected data collection to be quite so rampant, but perhaps the level of outrage was associated with the kinds of potential outcomes they envisioned:

"*This is completely ridiculous, I would not invite people into my closet, this is way out of line. No I don't find it appropriate to give up personal information in exchange for this game and that they don't need more approval than they apparently do.*" – interview, Denmark

If we conceive of smartphones as extensions of the self then the owners expect informed consent prior to entry into these personal territories. In the quote above, the interviewee equates the smartphone to a closed personal space (a closet) — entry into which would require high levels of intimacy and trust. People react to these breaches in different ways. Some uninstalled the offending application immediately, while others called for some sort of regulation:

"*No such data collection and/or distribution should be permitted.*" – survey, Denmark

Curiously, only a few of our participants were able to articulate who it was that they expected to act as a gatekeeper for data collection and tracking. Several noted that this was the function of the app stores. Most, however, appealed to some sort of vague general policies or even laws that "ought to be in place." Many also called for greater transparency. After all, much of what goes on with user-produced data, whether it is content on Google or data leaked by the Flashlight application on Android, is shrouded in mystery:

"*There should be much stronger regulations against third-party data collection and people should be better informed about this risk of third-party data collection*" – survey, Iceland.

Where the general sentiment here was that the practice of data collection and tracking should be somehow limited or stopped, only the very few actively limited their own app usage. Although many called for greater transparency, few admitted to reading the EULA before installing applications of their choice. In the vast majority of cases the same participants expressed another sentiment, that of compliance in the face of constant demands on data.

Dejected acceptance and compliance

Taking care of private information on smartphones takes effort; reading the EULA, scanning the phone and monitoring application updates which often involve increased numbers of permissions. Some of our participants stated that in order to use their smartphone they had to cave in and accept data collection. After all, what's the harm anyway?

"*I don't know what can really be done [about data collection] because then you have to stop using the smartphone as a smartphone.*" – interview, Denmark

Others said that they had never experienced anything negative and therefore had lowered their threshold of privacy concerns. It has become a part of their expectations and the more that this continues to happen the more they will expect it.

"*This is just how these things develop and this will only get worse, we can not change it. But I don't see how I can be personally affected by them knowing stuff about me.*" – interview, Denmark

Although people are willing to trade their personal data for a benefit their reaction is often not one of dismissal of privacy concerns but one of discomfort from the loss of control they feel. To some extent people want the option to be included in the negotiations, not to be robbed of their data.

"*There is not much you can do about this. If you want the app you just have to accept this. Otherwise you are not using the phone the way it was intended.*" – interview, Iceland

Our participants continued with their habits after being exposed to the data leakage, saying that it is 'good enough'. Nine of the 13 interviewees told us that although the information they learned from us did not result in them changing how they used their phones, they didn't quite feel as comfortable about it anymore.

"*The attitude has changed but the usage has not, I just feel a lot more uncomfortable using my phone*" – interview, Denmark

The level of resignation was striking in most of these responses. More often than not, the explanation for why our participants didn't spend the time to read the EULA, overlooked that some of their favorite applications leak data and ignored the assortment of tools available for limiting data leakage of this kind was one of helpless compliance:

"*It's unsettling and not ok, but I feel very powerless against it.*" – survey, Denmark.

Although we might expect people to exhibit high levels of concern for their privacy, how can we expect them to act on these concerns if they are convinced that there is not much they can really do? According to Altman [3] such lack of recourse can result in adjustments to the desired privacy level towards actual privacy level. People do so when they feel that they have no boundary control options to fend off repeated encroachments. After all maybe we are not looking at a privacy paradox. What we are seeing is a certain shift in norms and tensions between what our participants want, increased control and transparency and what they realize they can get. This is where our participants exhibit a pragmatic attitude and choose the benefits of owning and using a smartphone without limitations over the cost that comes with guarding their personal data from overprivileged applications. Smartphone users do not want to uninstall all of their overprivileged applications. They accept that this is payment for getting something for "free", and they feel at ease with paying for it as long as nothing negative happens, or as one respondent phrased it:

"*I believe the adage: "When you think you're getting a free lunch; you're actually being served to someone else." It's a trade-off for free entertainment.*" – survey, USA

From privacy paradox to learned helplessness

Altman notes that repeated invasion into a primary territory can have serious consequences to a person's self-identity and inability to regulate access can in the long run cause a lack of self-esteem [3]. Invading a person's privacy is paramount to taking control of a person's life away from that person which can seriously affect an individual's autonomy and dignity [30]. According to Altman "it is a loss of control to others that is serious, not so much the mere exposure of information" [3]. Repeated invasions into a persons' privacy and a conviction that there is no recourse can result in learned helplessness [23,30], when people stop responding to invasions even when presented with ways to defend themselves. Learned helplessness was originally identified in an experiment where a dog was put in an inescapable situation, as it was experiencing electric shock. Shortly thereafter, it was put into a different kennel where it could stop the shocks by performing a simple action. The dog did not attempt to evade the shocks; it just remained seated and stoically endured electric shocks, while the dogs in the control group quickly learned how to avoid the shocks [37].

The conception of learned helplessness was subsequently developed into a theory of helplessness and personal control [1], applied to a variety of situations and identified as a significant factor in mental health. Learned helplessness typically happens when people come to believe that a situation is unchangeable or inescapable and will often construct reasons for why this is so even if solutions become available later on. Consider the following statements:

"*I silently accept it. When you make me think about it, I kind of don't like it, but have probably forgotten all about it next time I download an app.*" – survey, Denmark

"*It seems like a necessary evil at this point. Because it is so ubiquitous, I think that it's likely that this sort of thing will never go away.*" – survey, USA

In both cases there is an implicit agreement that the respondent has no way of affecting the situation and must accept it if they are to be able to go on. The implication here is that perhaps there are other explanations for what has been termed the privacy paradox [36], beyond decision-making conundrums and situational constraints.

DISCUSSION

When informed of information sharing practices of certain apps on their smartphone, our research participants for the most part expressed dismay, even outrage — but then proceeded with business as usual when it came to using their smartphones. To the directed advertising industry, this can be seen as good news, suggesting that consumers may protest information sharing but deep down do not really care enough to actually alter their behavior.

We take from our findings a different message: that at this stage in the smartphone era, many people are essentially creeped out (or, if they knew, would be creeped out) by the information sharing behaviors of the apps with which they have outfitted this extension of their personal space and primary territory. They may have formally agreed to it, and are able to rationalize their use of such apps when asked; and they may prefer to put the creepiness out of their minds in order to enjoy their moments of interacting with the apps; but this foundation of creepiness undermines and makes precarious the standing of the smartphone as part of daily life. From a business perspective, our finding is that any business model that depends on taking personal data from smartphone users without first establishing a solid basis for the level of emotional trust this entails is ripe for disruption.

We do not see the solution to these privacy issues in improving EULAs and in making informed consent more robust. Given that privacy concerns are generally rooted in complex social configurations, such approaches would seem to depend on people predicting that something might go badly and mitigating information flows on the front end. The reality is, however, that people have great difficulty predicting such outcomes because in fact there are far too many variables to consider - and the vast majority of times the negative consequences are the result of "not thinking" ahead. From a policy perspective then, the EULA hardly qualifies as informed consent for this sort of data distribution to third parties. Instead, our analysis suggests that designers of apps and their data sharing policies need to confront the nature of creepiness head on. For this, we need a practical theory of creepiness, its varieties, and its temporalities (e.g., does creepiness fade over time with familiarity, and if so, what replaces it?). This paper is a first step in this direction but much more work needs to be done.

We also need apps that behave, and can be seen to behave, in ways that respect the user's personal space and the integrity of the context of use, much better than they currently do. Apps like High-Powered Flashlight or Fruit Ninja present themselves as simple, even trivial consumer products or services; people expect them to be simply fun ways of outfitting their personal space (in the form of the app space on their phone). Their creepiness lies in the realization that they *are more than they seem* – they are actually conduits for personal information to "leak" (intentionally) out of my personal space, indeed, out of myself. Upon discovering their underlying information gathering and dispersing nature, I suddenly find that I am actually sharing my personal space with unknown, and unruly entities that I did not really invite in, regardless of the EULA.

Telling people, in rational terms, that apps have this nature — of extending me beyond my personal space, and of allowing outside influences in — is likely not enough. Perhaps we (technologists) need to find ways to make people *feel* apps' active, connective nature in some visceral way. So far, the only *visceral* way people feel these sensations of discomfort and personal zone invasion/boundary collapse is what gets termed *creepy*. Are there more positive, visceral, affective responses that we could design for? Or can apps become effectively transparent in this regard — rather than a EULA, their design itself communicating a sense of access/thrill/risk (of both upside, and downside).

Altman posited negative psychological consequences if the person whose privacy is repeatedly violated is unable to regain control and to successfully manage access to the self [3]. From our data, we are not able to demonstrate that there are long-term negative consequences for consumers (e.g., encouraging lower commitments to personal privacy or placing creepy aspects of their personal environments out of sight and out of mind). But we suspect there are, perhaps through mechanisms that create and sustain bio-neurological stress, the harmful health consequences of which are increasingly being documented. We also acknowledge that creepy experiences may not always be negative and unwanted, as recent HCI research into "uncomfortable user experience" has begun to explore [6].

CONCLUSION

An analysis such as ours into negative emotional and moral reactions to smartphone app experience can be considered an exercise about values in design [13,20]. As our interview and survey respondents were able to articulate, their values and the values implicit in the design and behavior of certain smartphone apps were not well aligned [21].

From a values in design perspective, what is at stake here is the kind of future we want to live in, beyond just how we wish people would use apps and what kind of responsibility we wish they could take for their own data. The issue of designing the kinds of sharing and disclosure applications is in part hitting the right balance between what can be seen and what can be kept secret, between control and automaticity. In part it is also about pushing changes in the norms around information sharing — we are fumbling with the now norms rather than looking to the where these norms might move as a result of technologies we are developing.

Cultural norms change over time, subject to a great many short- and long-term forces, technical, economic, social, and legal. Acceptable entertainment app behavior in 2013 will likely be different than in 2023. This will not eliminate creepy experiences, but will change the conditions under which they are encountered. Nor does the inevitability of cultural change diminish the need for responsible, value-sensitive design.

ACKNOWLEDGMENTS

This work was supported in part by the Intel Science and Technology Center for Social Computing. Big thanks to Jason Hong and his graduate students for providing support and advice in the initial stages of this work. We are indebted to all our respondents for their generous participation.

REFERENCES

1. Abramson, L., Seligman, M. & Teasdale, J. (1978) Learned helplessness in humans: critique and reformulation. *Journal of abnormal psychology*, 87, 1, 49-74.
2. Acquisti, A., & Grossklags, J. (2005). Privacy and Rationality in Individual Decision Making. *IEEE Security and Privacy*, 26-33.
3. Altman, I. (1975). *The Environment and Social Behavior*. Belmont, California, USA: Wadsworth Publishing company, Inc.
4. Barkhuus, L. The mismeasurement of privacy: using contextual integrity to reconsider privacy in HCI. In *Proceedings of CHI 2012* (Austin, Texas, 2012). ACM
5. Barkhuus, L., & Polichar, V. E. (2011). Empowerment through seamfulness: smart phones in everyday life. *Personal and Ubiquitous Computing*, 629-639.
6. Benford, S., Greenhalgh, C., Giannachi, G., Walker, B., Marshall, J., & Rodden, T. (2013). Uncomfortable user experience. *Communications of the ACM, 56*(9), 66-73.
7. Braunstein, A., Granka, L., & Staddon, J. (2011). Indirect content privacy surveys: measuring privacy without asking about it. *SOUPS '11*. NY, USA: ACM.
8. *Collins English dictionary*. HarperCollins Publishers, City, 2009.
9. Felt, A., Egelman, S., & Wagner, D. (2012). I've got 99 problems, but vibration ain't one: A survey of smartphone users' concerns. *SPSM '12* (pp. 33-44) NY: ACM.

10. Felt, A., Ha, E., Egelman, S., Haney, A., Chin, E., & Wagner, D. (2012). Android Permissions: User Attention, Comprehension & Behavior. *SOUPS '12* NY: ACM
11. Flurry. (2013). Retrieved April 12, 2013, from Big Data: http://www.flurry.com/big-data.html
12. Fortunati, L. (2001). The mobile phone: an identity on the move. In *Personal & Ubiquitous Computing*: Springer-Verlag London.
13. Friedman, B. (1997) *Human values and the design of computer technology*. CSLI Publications, Stanford, CA.
14. Futuresight. (2011). Retrieved from User perspectives on mobile privacy: http://goo.gl/9sgZXR
15. Good, N., Dhamija, R., Grossklags, J., Thaw, D., Aronowitz, S., Mulligan, D., et al. (2005). Stopping spyware at the gate: a user study of privacy, notice and spyware. *SOUPS '05* (pp. 43-52). NY: ACM
16. Häkkilä, J. & Chatfield, C. 'It's like if you opened someone else's letter': user perceived privacy and social practices with SMS communication. *Proceedings of MobileHCI* (Salzburg, Austria, 2005). ACM
17. Karlson, A., Brush, A. J. & Schechter, S. Can I borrow your phone?: understanding concerns when sharing mobile phones. In *Proceedings of CHI 2009* (Boston, MA, 2009). ACM
18. Kelley, P., Consolvo, S., Cranor, L., Jung, J., Sadeh, N., & Wetherall, D. (2012). A conundrum of permissions: installing applications on an android smartphone. In *Proceedings of FCDS12* (pp. 68-79). Berlin: Springer-Verlag, Heidelberg
19. Kelley, P., Cranor, F., & Sadeh, N. (2013). Privacy as part of the app decision-making process. In *Proceedings of CHI 13* (pp. 3393-3402). NY: ACM.
20. Knobel, C. & Bowker, G. (2011) Values in design. *Communicatinos of the ACM*, 54, 7, 26-28.
21. Le Dantec, C., Poole, E. & Wyche, S. Values as lived experience: evolving value sensitive design in support of value discovery. *Proceedings of CHI 2009* (Boston, MA, 2009). ACM
22. Lederer, S., Mankoff, J., & Dey, A. (2003). Who wants to know what when? Privacy preference determinants in ubiquitous computing. *CHI EA '03*. NY: ACM.
23. Lenhart, A., Ling, R., Campbell, S., & Purcell. K. Teens and Mobile Phones. *Pew Internet and American Life Project*. (2010).
24. Lin, D., & Loui, M. (1998). Taking the byte out of cookies: Privacy, consent and the Web. *Computers and Society*, 28 (1), 39–51.
25. Lin, J., Sadeh, N., Amini, S., Lindqvist, J., Hong, J., & Zhang, J. (2012). Expectation and purpose: understanding users' mental models of mobile app privacy through crowdsourcing. *UbiComp '12* (pp. 501-510). NY: ACM.
26. Ling, R. (2008). *New tech, new ties: How mobile communication is reshaping social cohesion*. Cambridge, MA: MIT.
27. Maier, S., & Seligman, M. (1976). Learned helplessness: Theory and evidence. *Journal of Experimental Psychology: General, 105*(1), 3-46.
28. Muslukhov, I., Boshmaf, Y., Kuo, C., Lester, J., & Beznosov, K. (2012). Understanding users' requirements for data protection in smartphones. In *ICDE Workshops, 2012*. Washington, DC, USA.
29. Nafus, D. & Tracey, K. (2002) Mobile phone consumption & concepts of personhood. In J. Katz & M. Aakhus (Ed). *Perpetual contact: Mobile communication, private talk, public performance*. University Press, Cambridge
30. Nippert-Eng, C. E. (2010). *Islands of privacy*. Chicago ; London: The University of Chicago Press.
31. Nissenbaum, H. F. (2010) *Privacy in context: Technology, policy, and the integrity of social life*. Stanford Law Books, Stanford, CA.
32. Norberg, P., Horne, D. & Horne, D. The privacy paradox: Personal information disclosure intentions versus behaviors. *Journal of Consumer Affairs* 41, 1 (2007), 100–127.
33. Oksman, V. & Rautiainen, P. (2003) "Perhaps it is a Body Part": How the Mobile Phone Became an Organic Part of the Everyday Lives of Finnish Children and Teenagers. In J. E. Katz (Ed). *Machines that become us: The social context of personal communication technology*. Transaction Publishers, New Brunswick, N.J
34. Palen, L. & Dourish, P. Unpacking "privacy" for a networked world. In *Proceedings of the CHI 2003* (Ft. Lauderdale, FL, 2003). ACM
35. Peterson, C., Maier, S., & Seligman, M. (1993). *Learned helplessness: A theory for the age of personal control*. NY: Oxford University Press.
36. Rose, N. (1999) Powers of Freedom: Reframing Politica l Thought, NY: Cambridge University Press
37. Seligman, M. E. (1972) Learned Helplessness. *Annual Review of Medicine*, 23, 1, 407-412
38. Sundar, S., Kang, H., Wu, M., Go, E., & Zhang, B. (2013). Unlocking the privacy paradox: do cognitive heuristics hold the key? In *CHI '13 Extended Abstracts*, Paris, France: ACM
39. Vijayan, J. Flashlight app vendor settles with FTC over privacy violations. *Computerworld.com*, IDG Network, Dec 6, 2013, http://goo.gl/OJ7P8P
40. Xu, H., Luo, X., Carroll, J., & Rosson, M. (2011). The personalization privacy paradox: An exploratory study of decision-making process for location-aware marketing. *Decision Support Systems, 51*(1), 42-52
41. Zhou, Y., Zhang, X., Jiang, X., & Freeh, W. (2011). Taming information-stealing smartphone applications (on Android). *TRUST'11* (pp. 93-107), Heidelberg: Springer-Verlag.
42. Zafeiropoulou, A., Millard, D., Webber, C., & O'Hara, K. (2013). Unpicking the privacy paradox: can structuration theory help to explain location-based privacy decisions? *WebSci*, Paris, France.

Personalisation and Privacy in Future Pervasive Display Networks

Nigel Davies[1], **Marc Langheinrich**[2], **Sarah Clinch**[1], **Ivan Elhart**[2], **Adrian Friday**[1], **Thomas Kubitza** [1,3] **and Bholanathsingh Surajbali**[1]

[1]Sch. of Computing & Comms.
Lancaster University
Lancaster, England

[2]University of Lugano (USI)
Via G. Buffi 13
Lugano, Switzerland

[3]University of Stuttgart
Pfaffenwaldring 5a
Stuttgart, Germany

ABSTRACT

There is increasing interest in using digital signage to deliver highly personalised content. However, display personalisation presents a number of architectural design challenges – in particular, how best to provide personalisation without unduly compromising viewers' privacy. While previous research has focused on understanding specific elements of the overall vision, our work presents details of the first significant attempt at a system that integrates future pervasive display networks and mobile devices to support display personalisation. We describe a series of usage models and design goals for display personalisation and then present Tacita, a system that supports these models and goals. Our architecture includes mobile, display and cloud-based elements and provides comprehensive personalisation features while preventing the creation of user profiles within the display infrastructure, thus helping to preserve users' privacy. An initial evaluation of our prototype implementation of the architecture is also included and demonstrates the viability of the Tacita approach.

Author Keywords

Digital signage; personalisation; privacy; architecture.

ACM Classification Keywords

H.1.2 User/Machine Systems: Human factors.

INTRODUCTION

Large digital displays are commonplace in shopping centres, city streets and other public spaces. Traditionally such displays have acted as a simple broadcast medium with content "pushed" to passers-by with no regard for viewer preferences. However, recent advances in video-based sign analytics[1] mean that display owners are now able to personalise content based on factors such as the age and gender of those in front of the display. This move towards personalised content in the signage industry precisely mirrors the shift towards personalised content that has occurred in the Web.

[1]e.g. Intel® AIM (`https://aimsuite.intel.com/`)

CHI 2014, April 26–May 01 2014, Toronto, ON, Canada

`http://dx.doi.org/10.1145/2556288.2557287`

Whilst personalisation is often motivated by advertising, within the digital signage domain it offers the opportunity to transform the medium by adding value for viewers who have previously been shown to avoid or ignore digital displays [17]. In everyday life many of us are familiar with the desire to personalise displays around us; perhaps to change the channel in a sports bar, highlight relevant flight details at an airport, see navigation signs in our own language, or simply ensure that advertising content is more relevant. Personalisation of displays offers the potential to transform digital signage from a simple broadcast medium to an interactive system that responds to the needs and preferences of viewers.

Personalised public displays are not a new idea, and a range of usage models have been proposed. Weiser's classic ubicomp article describes the work of Theimer and Nichols [23] who created a public display that "attunes its public information to the people reading it". More recently, researchers have created prototypes in which mobile users can ask displays to show personalised information such as maps, public transit timetables and daily menus from local lunch spots [5] or express their allegiance to local soccer teams [12]. Similarly, appropriating displays, e.g., as an external display to supplement a user's mobile device has also been proposed to support medical experts [3].

In all of the above works, the proposed approaches rely on users passing identity information (either explicitly or implicitly) to the displays that they wish to personalise. What is still missing, is a *comprehensive* system architecture designed to support display personalisation without unduly compromising user privacy, i.e. without allowing a display network to track and profile individual viewers. Our work builds on demonstrations of such a system shown at HotMobile 2012 and Mobisys 2012 [14] and is, we believe the first significant attempt to describe such an architecture in detail.

In this paper, we identify a set of usage models for personalisation of displays and highlight key privacy concerns. We present an approach for designing privacy-aware display personalisation that avoids the creation of profiles within the display infrastructure and demonstrate its viability through a sample implementation and evaluation.

PERSONALISTION USAGE MODELS

We identify three distinct usage models for display personalisation. The most well-known form is *walk-by personalisation* in which viewers passing by a single display see content that is relevant to them (as exemplified in the 2002 film Minority

Report in which the characters are subject to personalised adverts as they journey across the city). However, at least two others forms of personalisation exist.

In *longitudinal personalisation* users may express a preference to see personalised content and this is realised as an overall shift in the programming for a given geographic area such as a campus or shopping mall – typically over an extended period of time. The aim of such a usage model is not to try and ensure that any given display shows content for a specific user, but to try to ensure that, within a geographic region, the content viewers see is more representative of their interests than would be possible without personalisation. In practical terms this might mean, for example, that the content shown on the displays at a university campus automatically changes during vacation time or that content in a shopping mall adjusts during weekends or school holidays. Finally, in *active personalisation* users (inter-)actively engage with a display system to control personalised applications on a nearby display, e.g. to extend a mobile phone display for better viewing of complex data.

PRIVACY AND PERSONALISATION ISSUES

Within the context of personalisable public display networks there are a number of broad areas of privacy concern: disclosure through location tracking; disclosure through the display of inappropriate or revealing content; and disclosure through interaction with the display infrastructure.

Location Disclosure

For any system that involves connected mobile devices there is a risk that a user's location can be tracked through a range of techniques such as Bluetooth sightings, self-reported position information in the context of location-based services, or tracking by the wireless provider. Emerging features such as NFC-enabled devices may give rise to further opportunities for location tracking.

The problem of location tracking is not peculiar to public display networks and has been extensively studied (e.g. [2, 7]). We do not attempt to develop further solutions in this space. Rather we consider it sufficient to ensure that our approach does not provide any further ways for a user's location to be tracked. Thus, the aim of our approach is that the widespread deployment of a personalisable public display network does not provide any new location privacy threats for mobile users – despite providing more relevant information on displays.

Personalised Content Disclosure

The second area of concern is information disclosure through the display of inappropriate or revealing information. For example, if a public display provides personalised adverts based on recent shopping patterns (a commonly envisaged scenario) then it may be possible for bystanders to gain insights into a person's shopping activities simply by observing the adverts that are shown when that user is in front of a display.

A number of authors have suggested building "privacy" interfaces for information shown on a public display, often involving a wearable or handheld device that allows users to "outsource" sensitive parts of the presented information (e.g., [20]) to a more private interface. While we discuss these approaches in more detail in our related work section, much of the phenomenon surrounding the idea of disclosing personal information in public is actually a social issue, rather than a technical one. A few years ago most people would have balked at the idea of discussing sensitive business and personal matters in front of an audience of dozens of strangers – today it is hard to escape the large number of often-intimate mobile phone conversations conducted loudly in packed suburban trains. Goffman's work "Behavior in Public Places," describes our ability for "civil inattention," which, e.g., prompts us not to openly stare or eavesdrop in public [10]. Clearly, mobile phones are continuously challenging our ability to ignore certain conversations, yet even if pervasive displays would allow people to show intimate calendar entries or directly route potentially embarrassing emails to them, we expect to see civil inattention regulate much of our social environments' reaction.

This is not to say that the public use of personalisable displays may not lead to embarrassing situations. However, in our work we focus on applications that are designed to display desired, non-embarrassing information only, such as personalised tourist information, news, and adverts. We do not consider more intimate display scenarios (e.g. the display of emails or calendar entries) and note that the protection of private information shown in public is outside the scope of our work.

Use of Display Infrastructure

Our main area of privacy concern is information disclosure that can occur as a result of deploying or using a display infrastructure that supports personalised content and display appropriation by mobile users. If personalised information is displayed to users based on the detection of their presence (for example using Bluetooth) then there are obvious privacy implications. First, users would need to leave their mobile devices in discoverable mode – thus opening them up to tracking and observations by third parties. Second, even in the absence of any malicious third parties, users would still be disclosing significant personal information (including their location and application preferences) to components of the display infrastructure. For example, to support personalised travel information the display system might want to identify the viewer, their location (i.e., in front of a known display) and their wish to make use of a particular application (including parameters). More general personalisation, e.g. by ensuring displays show appropriate adverts, would require even more information disclosure.

It is the tension between the desire to provide personalised services and the need to protect personal information that lies at the heart of the challenges of privacy preservation in systems that combine mobile devices and pervasive display networks. In this work we focus on addressing this third concern by *limiting disclosure of personally identifiable information (i.e., profiles) to the interactive display infrastructure.* Our approach ensures that we can achieve personalisation without having to share any personally identifiable information with the (typically untrusted) display network.

DESIGN GOALS

In developing a system architecture we aimed to build on the vision of previous research and our own multi-year experiences [9] of developing display applications, to create a comprehensive solution that addressed the following design goals:

1. **Multiple usage models:** Existing display personalisation systems typically target a single usage model in which viewers passing by a single display see content that is relevant to them (walk-by personalisation). Our aim is to design a system that supports walk-by, longitudinal and active personalisation.
2. **Multiple presence models:** The different personalisation models have varied requirements in terms of positional accuracy, and are likely to require different location technologies and/or presence models. Moreover, existing research has shown that using a single mechanism such as Bluetooth for detecting proximity to displays does not work well in all situations [5]. We therefore wish to support a range of different technologies and models.
3. **Viewer Privacy:** Our main aim is to design a system that enables display personalisation while limiting disclosure of personally identifiable information (i.e. profiles) to the display infrastructure. We do not attempt to address location tracking happening outside the signage system (see Krumm [13] for an overview of options), but we do provide suggestions on content display privacy.
4. **Signage System Integration:** There is a large installed base of signage systems. Any system to support personalisation should integrate with a range of these systems and have a low barrier to adoption for the creator of new signage systems. Demands on the display system for additional hardware or software should be kept to a minimum. In addition, the system should be able to scale to many displays, users and applications.

ARCHITECTURE

Overview

Our architecture consists of four distinct components: *mobile clients* that run on viewer's smart phones and issues personalisation requests on a viewer's behalf; *public displays* that the viewer wishes to influence in order that they show appropriate content; *cloud-based applications* that supply this content; and, *map providers* that supply mobile clients with information on how to personalise displays in their area.

To highlight how the system works we provide a brief walkthrough as shown in Fig. 1. In the first interaction step, the mobile client receives an announcement of the personalisation capabilities of a nearby display, either directly from individual displays or, more likely, from known map providers (1). In Step 2, the user selects sets of applications that they wish to use for personalisation (3). As the user moves (Step 3), their mobile client monitors for entry into the trigger zone of a display that supports one of the user's applications. At this point the mobile client makes a request to the user's cloud-based applications informing them of entry into the trigger zone of a particular display (4). The applications process these requests

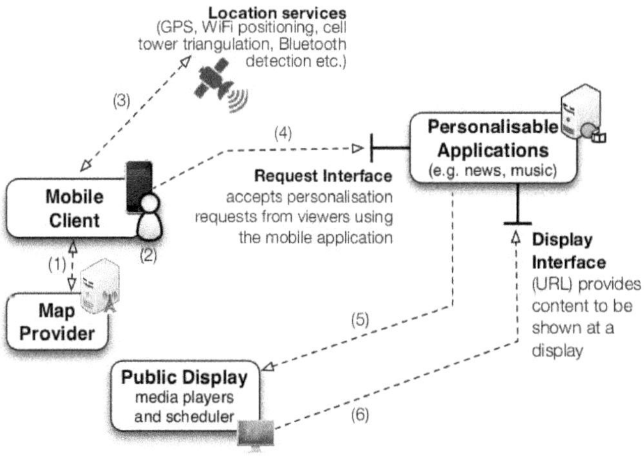

Figure 1. Architecture and System Walkthrough.

and can then request screen real-estate from the associated display (5), the display then fetches the content from the application (6) and renders it. While the user remains in the trigger zone, the client sends keep-alive messages to the applications. When the user leaves the trigger zone the requests time out and the personalisation ends.

Communications and Trust Relationships

The first key design decision underpinning our architecture is to support personalisation by having *displays announce their capabilities for personalisation to mobile devices* – rather than having mobile devices broadcast preferences or tracking of personal identifiers. Our approach is in contrast to most existing research in the area that has relied on users either explicitly broadcasting preferences or requests (e.g. [5]) or by being "observed" by displays (e.g. in [19]).

Our display announcements tell mobile users which applications a display supports and specify the geographic scope associated with the display, i.e. the area within which mobile users should request personalised content for the display.

This is our second key design decision, *to decouple the statement of geographic scope from any specific networking technology*. In most previous systems proximity has been supported implicitly through the use of low-range wireless communications such as Bluetooth. In practice attempting to define appropriate trigger zones using RF propagation is fraught with problems. Encoding an explicit description of geographic scope provides two important benefits. Firstly, we can offer a much more flexible means of specifying when a user should trigger the personalisation of a display. This is important as it allows, e.g., *trigger zones* to be specified that cause personalisation in advance of a user being able to see a display – providing time for the infrastructure to affect the personalisation. The second benefit is that by explicitly including scope information we enable announcements to be collected and cached in the form of maps of displays and their characteristics.

Our approach is inherently designed to provide a basic level of scalability and user privacy – by default mobile viewers leave no trace in the system and are not observable by the infrastructure. Even regular users of the system can enter a physical space and leave no trace if they do not wish to interact with the system at that point in time. However, viewers that do wish to influence content on displays must indicate this – raising an obvious point at which privacy may be compromised. Thus, our third decision is that users should indicate their desire for content to be customised or for space on a display to be appropriated directly to the (typically cloud-based) applications that produce the content for the display concerned and not to the display itself. *In our architecture there is no need for direct communication between viewers and displays.* This removes the need for viewers to have any form of trust relationship with displays that they encounter in their travels – all user interactions are with the applications that they have explicitly selected and with which we can assume they have established trust relationships. This approach also helps signage operators maintain network security as they need not support access from arbitrary clients.

Our trust assumptions are thus as follows: we assume users trust the providers of applications for which they have signed up (e.g. Google or Facebook). We assume users do not necessarily trust the providers of displays (or more generally: users don't trust arbitrary third parties they encounter in the wild). Finally, we assume that bona-fide display owners can establish trust relationships with bona-fide cloud-based applications that will provide displays with content. For example, Starbucks could choose to trust personalised content being supplied by the BBC. Note that we do not require users to trust any given application with all of their data and there is no need for continuous location tracking – rather when they wish to have an application customise a display for them then at that point users must disclose information to the application in question. Once a viewer has informed an application that they wish to have specific content on a given display, the application communicates directly with the display to schedule the content onto the display.

One area of potential concern regarding these assumptions is that by transferring our focus of trust from displays to cloud-based applications it becomes necessary for a viewer at a display to disclose to the cloud-based applications both their preferences (though not necessarily their identity) and the display to be personalised. Of course this information needs to be supplied regardless of whether the user communicates directly with the cloud (our architecture) or via the display (conventional systems). The critical point is that in our case the amount of information captured is limited to that which the user chooses to share with the application: users control when the cloud application is contacted and only share information with the application when they are near a display that supports the chosen form of personalisation. Should a user choose to unsubscribe from a cloud application then no further data can be collected by that application. Moreover, there is no leakage between applications – the personalisation requests a user sends to e.g. the BBC are not linked to the requests they may send to other cloud services such as Facebook or Google. If required, standard web anonymisation techniques can also be employed to hide the identity of user devices connecting to cloud-services. In contrast, existing personalisation architectures that rely on users broadcasting their preferences to displays require that users share their personalisation profiles with every display they encounter and, through the process of establishing communication, leave an identifiable trace of their presence at the display.

In summary, our approach removes the possibility of display networks building up profiles of users and makes it unlikely that any single cloud-based provider would be able to gain a "big brother" overview of a users personalisation requests.

Capability Announcements

Our approach relies on reversing the existing trend for viewers to broadcast their identity or preferences; instead we require displays to announce their capabilities. Capability announcements contain: a display URI, the geographic scope of the display, a list of applications (and associated parameters) that the display supports and, finally, any additional data relevant to the display. The display URI is passed by the viewer to applications that they wish to access in order to identify the display that they wish to customise and the geographic scope provides a method for mobile clients to determine whether they are co-located with the display.

A difficulty lies in determining an appropriate model of location that works effectively in all display environments. In our prototype we use a simple model in which each display is assigned a geographic scope defined in terms of a circle sector. Each circle sector is defined as a centre point (using Latitude and Longitude), radius, and start and end angles. We believe this approach provides a reasonable compromise between an overly simple model of a circular triggering zone centred around a display (which fails to capture, for example, the fact that most displays are not visible from behind) and a complex model in which displays can be associated with multiple 3D trigger zones. Mobile devices can calculate their containment within the sector using a combination of any location technology and simple processing.

Capability announcements also provide details of supported applications in terms of resolvable URIs rather than directly accessible URLs. This discourages client software from simply "blindly" following links that a display broadcasts – clients must instead have already formed trust relationships with entities (e.g. applications or app-stores) that can resolve these URIs to appropriate application addresses. In addition to URIs for applications, capability announcements can also include details of any constraints on how the application can be used or parameters that can be passed to the application.

Finally, capability announcements can also support a small amount of additional data about the display. This can be used by the display for a wide range of purposes and may or may not be processed by client software. For example, while non-personalisable displays need not broadcast a capability announcement they could choose to do so in order to provide clients with additional data on content being displayed when a viewer passes by.

Distributing Announcements

Because capability announcements contain explicit geographic scoping information, mobile devices can obtain these announcements though a range of mechanisms rather than having to rely on a specific wireless technology to provide an implicit (and often inaccurate) scope. Apart from having displays broadcast their capabilities directly (e.g. via short-range wireless), announcements may also be collected into *display maps* that contain details of collections of displays and their capabilities. If display capabilities change relatively slowly, these maps can be cached and distributed to mobile devices using a wide range of channels. This removes the need for displays to have specific support for broadcasting capabilities - they may instead rely on their capabilities being listed in display maps available from well-known repositories which we term *map providers*.

Presence Tokens

While decoupling capability announcements from physical proximity offers significant flexibility, there are many situations in which applications do wish to verify that users are actually close to a physical display and thus it is appropriate to respond to their requests. The aim is to avoid, for example, a user sitting at home deliberately manipulating a display in a public space.

In our architecture, a display can verify a viewer's location through the use of *presence tokens*. Presence tokens are temporary numeric identifiers, typically pseudo-random numbers, that a display updates periodically (e.g. every few minutes). Presence tokens may be combined with capability advertisements or transmitted via a separate (short-range) channel, such as Bluetooth, a dynamic NFC tag, Infrared, or a number or QR-code shown on-screen.

A client wishing to demonstrate its proximity to a particular display simply submits the presence token it just received to an application. Applications can compare such tokens with a dynamic list from the individual display. If the submitted token does not appear on the list of recent tokens used, the application may treat the request as not genuine and ignore it. Displays can also request that applications pass on the tokens so that the display can independently verify presence. Note that in most cases the use of presence tokens is transparent to the user – they will only need to manually enter a presence token if the display does not support any form of short-range communications and but does require confirmation of user presence.

It may not be obvious, but in many practical cases presence tokens will not be necessary. Mass manipulation of public displays will often be made infeasible by virtue of each user generally having to register with the cloud-based applications they are issuing requests to. Such applications could trivially detect one of its users requesting local data simultaneously (or within seconds of each other) on many displays and prevent this. Applications may also charge a (small) fee for each use or have user-based quotas, thus making mass manipulation a costly endeavour. Many displays will therefore not require any sort of additional hardware (e.g. Bluetooth) to support local dissemination of proximity tokens. Indeed, in many cases display owners may not even care whether viewers are actually close to the display and fully leave it up to applications to detect malicious behaviour – especially if the display is charging the application owner for access to screen real-estate.

We should emphasise at this point that our presence mechanism is not designed to provide high levels of confidence in verifying presence. For example, the system could be circumvented by a user that places a mobile device close to a display and uses this device to relay out the presence tokens. However, we believe that in practice this type of attack will be relatively unlikely and that our approach represents a reasonable trade-off between cost and benefit.

Application Requests

In our system, cloud based applications receive requests from mobile devices to personalise specific displays. In addition to parameters passed to support personalisation, applications may require the mobile to present authentication credentials to validate the request. If an application decides to act upon the request it can prepare appropriate content for the target display. Displays and applications can use a mixed-initiative model for content exchange: while applications may contact displays and explicitly request screen estate for their content, displays may also offer pieces of screen real estate to individual applications for scheduling on a regular basis. In this latter case personalisation can be used to dynamically ensure content for pre-scheduled slots is relevant to viewers.

It is important to stress that applications may choose to carry out significant aggregation and anonymization of user requests. For example, user requests may simply be used to weight the applications internal content selection processes, or multiple requests may be combined to provide composite output. This allows a display to potentially handle a large number of concurrent user requests.

Displays

In our system displays are responsible for rendering content. In practice of course applications may interact with proxies representing multiple physical screens. Displays are free to implement a range of scheduling algorithms that dictate how they interleave scheduled content and user requests. For example, they may choose to preempt scheduled content for user items, or they may choose to show both simultaneously by dividing the screen.

PROTOTYPE

To validate our architecture we have created a prototype consisting of a fully functioning Android mobile client, several web applications capable of delivering personalised information, and the key components of the Tacita architecture required to deliver this service on a public display infrastructure. The system has been tested in the context of an experimental digital signage system consisting of approximately 25 large LCD displays in prominent public spaces across a university campus and has been demonstrated at a number of venues.

Android Mobile Client

Our mobile client allows users to control the personalisation of public displays. The central function of the client is to maintain a list of applications to which the user is subscribed and then, using its knowledge of displays and their capabilities, to trigger applications when the user is within range of a given display.

Figure 2. Mobile UI. (a) Main screen. (b) Display Application detailed view. (c) Available screens for chosen application.

Users can view a list of available applications and select those that they wish to enable [Fig. 2(a)]. For each enabled application the user can also set any parameters required by the application (e.g. search terms or location of interest), these are passed to the cloud-based application as required [Fig. 2(b)]. A map of nearby public displays that support the selected display application can also be shown, highlighting the user's own position and the areas around the displays that trigger an application request when entered [Fig. 2(c)]. The mobile client can decide to trigger a personalisation request in two ways: implicitly based on location sensed by the mobile device or explicitly by users scanning a QR-code provided by the display. In the latter case, in addition to the display URI, a volatile presence token is encoded in the code and sent as a parameter to the requested applications.

Display Player Component

We have created two examples of player components: a web-based player that only requires a browser run in kiosk mode, and a stand-alone Python-based player that supports extended features such as content pre-fetching. Both support the rendering of collections of arbitrary content such as images and videos, along with the ability to invoke and render remote web applications.

Our prototype uses a simple scheduling model in which user-requested content has a higher priority than scheduled content. Requests from multiple applications triggered by different users near the same display are handled by tiling the screen into equally sized rectangular parts. Whilst this approach is clearly limited by display size, viewing distance and number of viewers, it offers a simple model for handling small numbers of simultaneous users. Not all concurrency support must be provided within the display node – when multiple users make requests to the same application, the application itself may be able to aggregate these requests into a single page prior to display.

Applications

We have created a series of applications to demonstrate the potential of the our approach. These include personalised news and weather, a world clock (see below), a personalisable jukebox and a remote desktop client that enables users to connect to a remote virtual machine (similar to the follow-me desktop application in [1]).

Our applications are built using a common design pattern and support two distinct interfaces: (1) a *Request Interface* (RI) that allows mobile devices to submit requests for a display to be personalised, and (2) a *Display Interface* (DI) that is accessed by public displays and that presents application content in a format suited to the known resolution of the display.

For example, in the clock application the RI receives requests from the mobile client that include a user identifier (optional, illustrates how services can support user identification or authentication), an identifier for the display upon which the time should be shown and the location of interest (e.g. 'Seattle, WA, USA'). The clock application resolves the textual names into appropriate locations and timezones that are then passed to a set of HTML5 widgets[2] which are then arranged for subsequent presentation on the public display.

Figure 3. Use of the Prototype Clock Application

Through the DI, the clock application provides displays with a feed of times for a range of locations. The application uses three sources of information to determine which locations to display information for: the display's own location (i.e. the local time for the display), any user-generated time requests, and a number of randomly-generated requests. The application supplies to the display a page that comprises the local time plus two other times [Fig. 3]. At the display it is possible to identify the local time, but the user-generated and randomly-generated requests are indistinguishable. This is an example of how applications can support "plausible deniability," i.e. helping viewers hide the fact that they are responsible for specific content.

EXPERIMENTS

Performance Measurements

It many cases it is important that personalisation of public displays can be achieved in a timely fashion. In the most demanding use case of walk-by personalisation there is only a

[2]http://www.clocklink.com/

small time window in which it makes sense to display information directed to a specific user. In Tacita the elapsed time from the moment a mobile client enters a display's triggering area to the moment the display changes can be divided into 3 components:

1. The time it takes a mobile client to detect that it is within a display's triggering range and to determine which applications to contact.
2. The time taken for a mobile device to make a request to an application though a GPRS/3G or WiFi connection.
3. The time taken by an application to recognise the user request and to initiate a corresponding change at the display.

The first component varies with the update frequency of the location technology. We measure GPS, WiFi, and Bluetooth sightings, both in combination and alone. In each case we used the best available update rate available (~1 second for GPS, ~5 seconds for Bluetooth and variable for WiFi). We acknowledge that continuous, fast, sample rates are not a practical solution within the constrains of a mobile device: in future work this rate may be dynamically altered based on factors such as the usage model desired or previous readings and the display configuration retrieved from the map provider (e.g. increasing the sampling rate when a user enters an area densely populated with displays).

We instrumented our system to measure the remaining two components (Tab. 1). Our set-up is atypical in the sense that the application and display are located within the same campus network. Our prototype uses a player-component that polls a Web server every 3 seconds for changes to the page, rather than using a persistent connection. Using a persistent connection would result in a significant decrease in step (3) which is currently dominated by the polling interval. Almost half the total delay is due to the latency of the 3G communication between the mobile device and the application server.

	Mean [s]	Median [s]	σ [s]
2) Mobile to App server	1.96	1.70	0.99
3) App server to Display	2.35	2.22	0.19
Sum	**4.31**	**4.13**	1.01

Table 1. Propagation times of a display foreground request calculated from 20 measurements

Tab. 1 raises the question of the minimal triggering radius required to ensure a display changes when a viewer passes by. Assuming an average walking pace of 1.39 metres per second (~3 miles per hour) and our measured propagation times (mean values) the theoretical minimum radius around a display for our prototype is 7.39 ± 1.64 metres.

Practical Tests

Overview

We have access to a large-scale campus deployment of public displays. In order to understand how Tacita performs in practical situations we deployed the system on two representative displays and conducted a series of walk-by tests to determine the extent to which Tacita could support effective personalisation. Our objective was not to provide a comprehensive performance evaluation – the "in-the-wild" nature of our experiments mean that numerous factors affect performance (e.g. display configuration, network and location technology availability, mobile device and user characteristics), rather we wished to capture figures to provide insight into how Tacita performs in a specific real-world deployment.

Site Selection

For the trials we selected two locations typical of a public display deployment. Location A [Fig. 4(a)] is a display mounted in a glass fronted foyer facing a large plaza. Location B [Fig. (b)] features two screens mounted in a busy thoroughfare on the ground floor of a building.

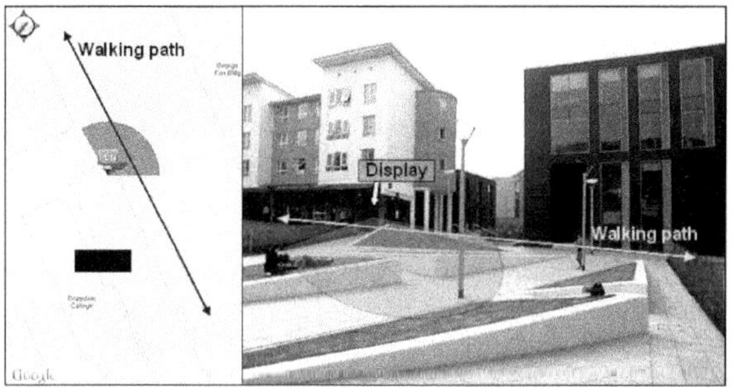

(a) Location A: (left) map view and triggering sector, (right) situation photo.

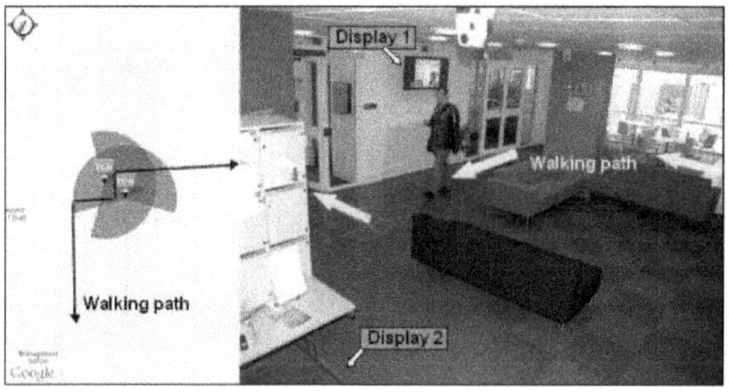

(b) Location B: (left) map view and triggering sector, (right) situation photo.

Figure 4. Our two trial locations.

Methodology

For each location we initially selected a default geographic scope (triggering radius) of 15m and set the angles to reflect a best-guess at the appropriate trigger zone. This correlated well to the viewing area in location A but was substantially larger than the viewing area in location B. For each location we then selected two of the most common walking paths that went past the display. Each path started well outside the triggering zone, passed by the display, and continued on beyond the trigger zone. The mobile client was set to request a specific content item, 10 seconds in duration, when the user was within the trigger zone. If the user was still within the zone at the end of the content item then the content was reshown.

We then conducted a series of walking tests following these paths and using GPS, Wifi and Bluetooth, first in isolation and then together, to determine viewer location relative to the display. One researcher acted as a potential viewer and followed the prescribed paths. A second researcher recorded the time the viewer entered and left the potential viewing area for the display (note that the viewing area is distinct from the triggering zone) and the time the content appeared and disappeared from the display. We then increased the angle of the sector by 30 degrees and the size of the trigger zone from 15m to 24m and repeated the walking tests. This size increase of 9m corresponds to the time taken to trigger content according to our lab-based measurements.

Three walking tests were performed for each path, location, radius and sensing technique, resulting in a total of 84 walks along the paths (Bluetooth is independent of the map triggering sectors, reducing the number of experiments).

Results

From the timings we calculate two measures of the effectiveness of our system, i.e. *content exposure* and *content accuracy*. Content exposure is the percentage of time that the content was shown on the display while the viewer was within range and characterises the effectiveness of the system at showing content to the viewer. Content accuracy is the percentage of time that the content could have been seen by the viewer relative to the total amount of time that the content was shown. For example, a system that continuously showed a single content item for a target user irrespective of whether they were present would have a high content exposure but low accuracy.

	Bluetooth	*Trigger Zone*	GPS	Wifi	All
Loc. A	0.21/0.34	*15m*	0.2/0.26	0.0/0.0	0.38/0.35
		24m	0.25/0.16	0.83/0.44	0.89/0.64
Loc. B	0.58/0.51	*15m*	0.01/0.01	0.35/0.5	0.74/0.63
		24m	0.64/0.65	0.53/0.54	0.98/0.26

Table 2. Mean exposure/accuracy analysis for each deployment and location technology.

Tab. 2 shows the results of our experiments. In almost all cases Tacita was able to achieve non-zero exposure – i.e. the system was able to show personalised content that could be seen by the intended recipient as they passed by. Reasonable accuracy was also achieved – in the best cases an average of 65% of the time that the content was on the screen the intended viewer was also within the viewing area of the screen. In all cases, the use of a combination of location technologies provided for better results than the use of any single location technology on its own. This is particularly noticeable in the case of Locaction A (15m) where individually none of the technologies provided a high level of exposure.

As expected, increasing the size of the trigger zone increases exposure – intuitively this is obvious as it increases the likelihood of having the content on the screen before the viewer leaves the viewing area. Increasing the size of the trigger zone might also be expected to reduce accuracy. However, our measurements show this is not always the case. We attribute this to the fact that by increasing the size of the trigger zone we increase the probability that the content will start to be shown when the viewer has recently entered the viewing area. In most cases this means that the content will finish shortly after the viewer leaves the zone (recall that content is of a fixed duration). For smaller trigger zones there is an increased probability that the content will appear just as the viewer is leaving the viewing area – negatively impacting both the exposure and accuracy. We believe that showing content for a fixed minimum duration is an important feature of a signage system – without this constraint it may appear to viewers as though content appears and disappears almost at random before they have time to finish viewing it. This is particularly the case for viewers of the signage system who are not actively personalising the display – for this type of viewer the results should still be an aesthetically pleasing set of outputs.

Overall we are encouraged by the results of our measurements in the field. They show that for two representative displays in a real-world testbed we can personalise content in response to a viewer's presence (i.e. exposure is > 0) while maintaining accuracy levels in excess of 50%.

ANALYSIS: DESIGN GOALS REVISITED

Multiple usage models

We have shown through the creation of multiple different types of application that our system can support a range of personalisation scenarios. The news, weather and clock applications are all designed to support walk-by personalisation in which the user is hoping to see this content when they pass by the display. In contrast, the remote desktop application provides an example of active personalisation is which the user wishes to engage with a specific application and is triggering this on a display. Finally, the music player application provides an example of longitudinal personalisation in which the preferences of users in a space are reflected over time.

Multiple presence models

There are two distinct elements of presence detection. Our prototype has shown how we can use multiple different technologies to detect presence in order to trigger display adaption. For most of our applications we do not require any validation of the user's position - in other words it is possible for a user to "spoof" their location. However, we are able to use QR codes as a simple presence token and it is possible for cloud applications to verify presence by checking that an appropriate QR code has been scanned. More work is required to demonstrate the use of short-range wireless technologies as an alternative form of presence token distribution.

Viewer Privacy

Our current implementation provides a first step towards preserving privacy – routing display requests through applications not only hides the user's identity from the displays in the environment, but also provides an opportunity for applications to aggregate data requests or introduce random content to help offer viewers plausible deniability. However, further improvements are possible. Since each personalisation request to an application always includes a display location, an application provider could track every service invocation in order to obtain movement data.

To counter this, the introduction of a user proxy could allow application requests to pass through a trusted entity running on the user's own hardware. This entity could make generic requests for application content on behalf of the user and then forward the resulting output to a display for scheduling. Proxies could use network anonymization techniques to hide their identity from displays – however, they might still need to authenticate the user with the application server. Whilst this method may prevent applications from tracking movement, it also prevents request aggregation and so reduces deniability gains made this way. This also offers no protection against a collusion attack in which displays and applications can use timing information to track requests. Moreover, the cost of implementing such a system might not be economically viable and seems excessive given typical consumer trust models and the nature of the application domain. A much more reasonable solution would instead be a regulative approach that would legally require application providers to not record movement data from their users, or only use it to improve the application service itself, assuming prior customer consent.

Signage System Integration

Our architecture enables personalisation to be added to existing signage systems without (in most cases) requiring any changes to the underlying hardware and software. In particular, if a signage system is able to display content from one or more applications in real-time then it is possible for personalisation to be provided with no changes to the signage system at all. Generally most signage systems support this type of web-based content and displays can typically be controlled individually or in groups. The capabilities of the displays could be specified statically, with an unchanging presence token, and this information disseminated to potential viewers using existing distribution channels (recall that it is not critical from where mobile users obtain display capability announcements).

All communication with viewers comes through the applications themselves which adjust the content appropriately. The scheduling, presentation and management components of the display system do not require any modifications. To enforce presence for personalisation, presence tokens would need to be generated. Such tokens could (with additional hardware) be transferred over short-range communications (e.g. Bluetooth) but hardware changes could easily be avoided by transmitting the presence token through a software-generated QR code shown alongside content on the public display. This ability to provide personalisation without necessitating significant changes to the installed signage base is an important characteristic of our architecture.

In order to make personalisation requests of display applications, our implementation requires users to run a custom application on their mobile device. This application accesses the user's location, obtains appropriate capability announcements and makes personalisation requests. As an alternative, this functionality could be provided by a third party, e.g. through the use of an appropriate cloud-based location service. All processing can then be carried out within the cloud and additional mobile software is no longer required. However, the user must then have a trust relationship with a location sharing provider, allowing it to query for local displays on their behalf.

Finally, we note that our system may need to integrate with *interactive applications*. In the case in which interaction occurs using technologies such as touch or gesture recognition on the display itself Tacita can be used as normal – with requests from the mobile client triggering the display of the relevant interactive content and interaction with the sign being channeled back to the web application using the same mechanisms as any other interactive web page. However, Tacita provides an interesting alternative interaction point, i.e. the mobile device. In the current implementation the mobile client provides an interface that enables the user to specify configuration parameters for each display application. It would be relatively straightforward to add to the mobile client a user interface for each application. This interface could then propagate user commands to the cloud-based application that could, in-turn, control the display. This approach also offers the possibility for the mobile to be used to enter sensitive information and for multiple people to control the application in parallel.

RELATED WORK

A number of projects have explored display personalisation. FLUMP [8], personalised display content (e.g. unread mail messages) to passers-by identified using an Active Badge system – a similar IR device was used in McCarthy's GroupCast and UniCast [16]. Villar et al. [22] used a custom-built wireless device worn around the neck (called Pendle) to broadcast a user's interest into the environment. Roecker [18] similarly used RFID readers installed at displays to read out user profiles from body-worn RFID tags. InstantPlaces [11], e-Campus [5] and BlueTone [6] allowed viewers to take control of the display using Bluetooth.

In each of these systems a single networking technology was employed and users explicitly broadcasted content or preferences to the display, potentially revealing personal data to both the infrastructure and other passers-by. Strohbach et al. [21] addressed this issue by using Bluetooth pings to contact only registered devices, avoiding the need for broadcast communication. In Tacita, displays have their location and personalisation capabilities registered in a public directory, which mobile clients can then anonymously target through an app proxy.

The idea of using infrastructure-based broadcasts to improve user privacy is not new. Langheinrich [15] proposed pawS, a beacon approach to disseminate data collection and processing within a smart environment. To the best of our knowledge, however, our work is the first to carry this into the domain of public displays and to provide a comprehensive architecture for personalisation.

Similar to the trigger zones in Tacita, AT&T Cambridge's classic "Sentient Computing" project [1] used a *spatial monitor* to detect when a user would be close to a display. Trigger zones in Tacita are typically larger and use a much simpler containment model, due to the lower precision of the employed location technologies (GPS or WiFi-based) and the faster movement speeds typically found in transit zones such as hallways.

Previous work has also suggested the use of personal mobile devices as private "co-displays" to display sensitive information that has been blurred on a larger public display [20] whilst others have used aggregation to protect individual privacy [4]. In our work, we specifically focus on scenarios that involve non-sensitive information (i.e. suitable for public display) and thus assume that plausible deniability (as provided, e.g. by aggregation) is sufficient to protect the actual interests of users. However, we can also directly support co-display solutions, as the architecture supports the tight coupling of display content and a user's mobile phone.

CONCLUSIONS

We believe that future public display networks will make extensive use of personalisation to tailor their output to match the interests and needs of mobile users. Indeed, it is difficult to envisage a future in which public displays remain "dumb" broadcast channels, instead of following the clear trend towards personalised experiences seen in the Web.

In this paper we have made three contributions. Firstly, we have described in detail the first system architecture that integrates display networks and mobile devices into an interactive signage network while addressing a wide range of design goals. The proposed architecture supports multiple personalisation models and can be integrated with existing signage systems. It enables personalisation while preserving viewer privacy and capitalises on user's existing trust relationships. Secondly, we have reported on a prototype and a series of experiments in a practical setting that explored whether our approach can be used to effectively personalise displays in the most demanding usage model, i.e. walk-by personalisation. Finally, we have contributed a design pattern for display applications and guidelines for establishing trigger zones around displays that can be used by future designers and developers of personalised display networks.

ACKNOWLEDGEMENTS

The authors acknowledge the financial support of the Future and Emerging Technologies (FET) programme within the 7th Framework Programme for Research of the European Commission, under FET-Open grant number: 244011 (PD-NET).

REFERENCES

1. Addlesee, M., Curwen, R., Hodges, S., Newman, J., Steggles, P., Ward, A., and Hopper, A. Implementing a sentient computing system. *Computer 34*, 8 (Aug. 2001), 50–56.
2. Beresford, A., and Stajano, F. Location privacy in pervasive computing. *Pervasive Computing 2*, 1 (2003).
3. Clinch, S., Harkes, J., Friday, A., Davies, N., and Satyanarayanan, M. How close is close enough? understanding the role of cloudlets in supporting display appropriation by mobile users. In *PerCom* (2012).
4. Cox, D., Kindratenko, V., and Pointer, D. Intellibadge : Towards providing location-aware value-added services at academic conferences. In *UbiComp* (2003).
5. Davies, N., Friday, A., Newman, P., Rutlidge, S., and Storz, O. Using bluetooth device names to support interaction in smart environments. In *Mobisys* (2009).
6. Dearman, D., and Truong, K. BlueTone: A framework for interacting with public displays using dual-tone multi-frequency through bluetooth. In *UbiComp* (2009).
7. Duckham, M., and Kulik, L. A formal model of obfuscation and negotiation for location privacy. In *Pervasive* (2005).
8. Finney, J., Wade, S., Davies, N., and Friday, A. Flump: The FLexible Ubiquitous Monitor Project. In *Cabernet Radicals Workshop* (1996).
9. Friday, A., Davies, N., and Efstratiou, C. Reflections on long-term experiments with public displays. *Computer, IEEE 45*, 5 (2012).
10. Goffman, E. *Behavior in Public Places*. Glencoe, 1963.
11. José, R., Otero, N., Izadi, S., and Harper, R. Instant Places: Using Bluetooth for situated interaction in public displays. *Pervasive Computing 7* (2008).
12. José, R., Pinto, H., Silva, B., and Melro, A. Instant places: Using pins and posters as paradigms for content publication for situated displays. *Computer Graphics and Applications, IEEE* (2013).
13. Krumm, J. A survey of computational location privacy. *Personal Ubiquitous Computing 13*, 6 (2009).
14. Kubitza, T., Clinch, S., Davies, N., and Langheinrich, M. Using mobile devices to personalize pervasive displays. *ACM SIGMOBILE Mobile Computing and Communications Review 16*, 4 (October 2012), 26–27.
15. Langheinrich, M. A privacy awareness system for ubiquitous computing environments. In *UbiComp* (2002).
16. McCarthy, J. F. Using public displays to create conversation opportunities. In *Public, Community and Situated Displays (Workshop at CSCW 2002)* (2002).
17. Müller, J., Wilmsmann, D., Exeler, J., Buzeck, M., Schmidt, A., Jay, T., and Krüger, A. Display blindness: The effect of expectations on attention towards digital signage. In *Pervasive* (2009).
18. Roecker, C. Providing personalized privacy support in public places. In *3rd Conf. on Privacy, Security, and Trust* (2005).
19. Sharifi, M., Payne, T., and David, E. Public display advertising based on bluetooth device presence. In *MIRW* (2006).
20. Shoemaker, G. B. D., and Inkpen, K. M. Single display privacyware: Augmenting public displays with private information. In *CHI* (2001).
21. Strohbach, M., Kovacs, E., and Martin, M. Towards pervasively adapting display networks. In *1st International Workshop on Pervasive Advertising (at Pervasive)* (2009).
22. Villar, N., Schmidt, A., Kortuem, G., and Gellersen, H.-W. Interacting with proactive public displays. *Computers & Graphics 27*, 6 (2003).
23. Weiser, M. The Computer for the 21st Century. *Scientific American 265*, 3 (1991).

A Field Trial of Privacy Nudges for Facebook

Yang Wang,[‡] Pedro Giovanni Leon,[*] Alessandro Acquisti,[*]
Lorrie Faith Cranor,[*] Alain Forget,[*] and Norman Sadeh[*]

[‡]Syracuse University
ywang@syr.edu

[*]Carnegie Mellon University
{pedrogln, acquisti, lorrie, aforget, sadeh}@cmu.edu

ABSTRACT

Anecdotal evidence and scholarly research have shown that Internet users may regret some of their online disclosures. To help individuals avoid such regrets, we designed two modifications to the Facebook web interface that nudge users to consider the content and audience of their online disclosures more carefully. We implemented and evaluated these two nudges in a 6-week field trial with 28 Facebook users. We analyzed participants' interactions with the nudges, the content of their posts, and opinions collected through surveys. We found that reminders about the audience of posts can prevent unintended disclosures without major burden; however, introducing a time delay before publishing users' posts can be perceived as both beneficial and annoying. On balance, some participants found the nudges helpful while others found them unnecessary or overly intrusive. We discuss implications and challenges for designing and evaluating systems to assist users with online disclosures.

Author Keywords

Behavioral bias; Online disclosure; Social media; Facebook; Nudge; Privacy; Regret; Soft-paternalism

ACM Classification Keywords

H.5.m Information Interfaces and Presentation (e.g., HCI): Miscellaneous

INTRODUCTION

Online social networks such as Facebook are designed to encourage sharing, facilitating the seamless and immediate broadcasting of all kinds of information. While sharing information through social networks generally benefits users, seemingly innocuous disclosures can lead to substantial negative consequences. Lack of awareness of the potential audience, posting while in highly emotional states, and hasty disclosures have been shown to lead social media users to experience regret [28]. Research in the fields of psychology, behavioral economics, and behavioral decision making has uncovered cognitive and behavioral biases that affect decision making. These biases are systematic deviations from what traditional economists call rational decisions. Furthermore, when limited resources (e.g., time or information) are available to make a decision, human beings often rely on heuristics or shortcuts. These biases and heuristics have been shown to impact privacy decisions [1, 4, 5] and privacy blunders in social media are vivid examples of the hurdles users face.

Behavioral economists have proposed the use of soft paternalistic interventions to help people overcome behavioral biases that affect decision making. These interventions are designed to "nudge" (instead of force) people towards behaviors that have been shown to be publicly desired, but difficult to follow, without limiting people's autonomy [24]. Acquisti has proposed to use soft paternalistic interventions to improve security and privacy decisions [2]. We refer to soft-paternalistic mechanisms that nudge people towards more thoughtful and informed privacy-related decisions as *privacy nudges*.

Inspired by the literature on behavioral decision research and nudging, as well as by our prior work on regrettable Facebook behavior [28], we investigated the impact of Facebook privacy nudges. In this paper, we describe the design and evaluation of mechanisms that nudge Facebook users to consider more carefully the content and context of their online disclosures through visual cues and time delays. We developed a platform that enables us to deploy nudges and evaluate them with users in longitudinal field trials.

We conducted an exploratory 6-week field trial with 28 Facebook users. Our goal was to gain an understanding of how users perceive and interact with the features of our nudges. We analyzed both quantitative and qualitative data about participants' interactions with the nudges, the content of their posts, as well as their opinions collected through a final survey. We found that reminders about the audience of posts can prevent unintended disclosures without major burden; however, introducing a delay before publishing users' posts can be perceived as both beneficial and annoying. While many participants found the nudges helpful, others found them unnecessary or overly intrusive, suggesting that nudges may not be appropriate for everyone.

Our work makes two contributions. First, we developed an experimental platform that modifies Facebook's interface and collects users' behavioral data to operationalize and evaluate the concept of Facebook privacy nudges. Second, we identified key aspects worth considering when designing and evaluating a privacy nudging system.

CHI 2014, Apr 26 – May 01 2014, Toronto, ON, Canada
ACM 978-1-4503-2473-1/14/04.
http://dx.doi.org/10.1145/2556288.2557413

BACKGROUND AND RELATED WORK

Our work was inspired by scholarly research on problematic disclosures on social media, cognitive and behavioral biases, privacy decision making, and nudging.

Potential for Regret

Offline, people are naturally good at tailoring comments, gestures, and actions to specific audiences [14]. However, online (and in particular on social media such as Facebook), users tend to communicate with many groups (e.g., friends, co-workers) simultaneously, and as a result encounter difficulties in adapting messages for different audiences. Thus, shared content is often visible across groups, leading to a phenomenon called "context collapse" [21]. These issues are exacerbated by the fact that even experienced users have difficulties with Facebook privacy settings [3, 20]. Hence, a variety of dynamics lead to regrettable Facebook posts. Content is sometimes viewable by unintended audiences and users create posts "in the heat of the moment," which can lead to unintended disclosure and regret [28]. Unintended disclosures can lead to a range of consequences, including stalking, identity theft, blackmail [15], and reputation damage [9].

Biases, Heuristics, and Privacy Decision Making

Behavioral biases and heuristics can lead to systematic errors in decision making [26]. While, biases and heuristics have been studied in many contexts, here we focus on those that are closely related to our nudges. Bounded rationality forces individuals to rely on heuristics to simplify the choices available; however, sometimes choices with the best outcomes may be inadvertently discarded [22]. The economic effects of asymmetric information, which limits rational decision making, has been studied in the market of used cars [6]. Nearly half a century later, problems of bounded rationality and incomplete information are alive in social media.

Bounded rationality and asymmetric information prevent individuals from anticipating the audience for their posts. While it is easier for users to think in terms of broad audiences (e.g., friends, friends of friends, public), more granular groupings (e.g., parents, neighbors, church) can help mitigate unintended disclosures. Similarly, as Facebook comments inherit the audience of the original status update, it may be impossible for the person commenting to determine the audience of his or her comment—an example of asymmetric information. In fact, recent research by Bernstein et al. found that Facebook users "consistently underestimate their audience size for their posts, guessing that their audience is just 27% of its true size" [7]. As a result, Facebook users often post content that can be viewed by an unintended audience, which may lead to regret [28]. One of the nudges we present here attempts to mitigate problematic online disclosures associated with bounded rationality and asymmetric information.

Another relevant bias is known as hyperbolic time discounting, the fact that individuals use variable and inconsistent discount rates over time and often assign higher utility to present choices than to future ones [18]. For instance, people tend to procrastinate because they over-estimate the enjoyment of not doing work now and under-estimate the future consequences of delaying work [13]. In the privacy domain, Acquisti has shown that people often trade their personal information for immediate gratification [1]. The work on dual process theory is also relevant. For instance, Kahneman posits the existence of two processing systems in our brains: intuition (System I) and reasoning (System II). Intuition tends to be fast, automatic, and rely on heuristics, while reasoning is slower and involves more conscious judgement [17]. Our prior work on regrets found evidence of impulsive behavior, often driven by highly emotional states [28]. The second nudge we present was designed to mitigate problematic disclosures potentially due to hyperbolic time discounting and impulsive behavior.

Soft-paternalism and Privacy Nudges

Soft paternalistic interventions attempt to help individuals by mitigating behavioral biases (or, in some cases, exploiting them) to achieve the outcomes that better align with users' preferences. Thaler and Sunstein popularized the idea of nudging. They defined a nudge as "any aspect of the choice architecture that alters people's behavior in a predictable way without forbidding any options or significantly changing their economic incentives" [25]. Acquisti described the role of hyperbolic discounting and immediate gratification in the so-called privacy calculus [1]. He further proposed that nudges could be used to influence privacy decision-making in a manner that decreases users' regret [2].

Although not explicitly referred to as nudging, researchers in the fields of HCI and Persuasive Technology have explored mechanisms to assist users with privacy and security decision making. Forget et al. built a system to nudge users to create stronger passwords [12]. Ur et al. showed that certain password meter designs may encourage users to create stronger passwords [27]. Wilson et al. studied the effect of predetermined privacy profiles to assist users with location sharing disclosures [30]. Choe et al. investigated the impact of the "framing" heuristic (i.e., people would prefer alternatives that are framed as gains over those framed as loses, even when the two alternatives are equivalent) in the context of mobile apps selection; and found that the framing effect had minimal impact on participants' trust perceptions [10]. A recent longitudinal Facebook study highlighted how profoundly Facebook interface changes can impact users' information sharing — indicating a potential for Facebook privacy nudges [23].

Several mechanisms have also been proposed to improve privacy decision making for social media. For example, Fang et al. described a wizard that creates sharing categories automatically [11]. Lipford et al. examined interfaces for online social network privacy controls, comparing expandable grids to visual policies [19]. Besmer et al. built a tool that allows Facebook users to negotiate about photo tagging [8]. Unlike these mechanisms, our approach aims to proactively nudge users away from posting potentially regrettable content.

PRIVACY NUDGE DESIGN

Our study focused on two types of nudges: one that reminds users about the audience for their post, and one that encourages users to pause and think before posting. In line with the concept of soft paternalism, neither of these nudges limits users' ability to disclose information, or affects the trade-offs associated with their disclosures. Instead, both nudges provide contextual clues intended to assist users in making better informed information-disclosure decisions. The nudge designs were improved based on two pilot studies conducted in April and July of 2012, respectively. We conducted a third pilot study in February 2013 to confirm that our experimental platform was stable enough to use in a field trial.

Audience Nudge

Inspired by the literature on bounded rationality and asymmetric information, the audience nudge aims to help Facebook users anticipate the audience for their posts.

This nudge initially included only the message: "these [number] people can see this post" based on the privacy setting of the post. However, after testing this feature in the first pilot study, we realized that participants did not find the intervention particularly useful, because the intervention message hardly varied over time — users often use the same privacy setting for their posts, and thus the message stayed the same.

In order to make the nudge more dynamic and salient, we considered using visual, rather than merely textual, cues. We designed a profile picture feature that displays five profile pictures, randomly selected from the pool of people who can view the post, based on that post's current privacy setting. This feature was inspired by Jenni and Loewenstein's work on the "identifiable victim effect," which finds individuals are willing to expend more resources on identifiable than unidentified victims [16]. In our context, the profile pictures provide some form of identifiability to both familiar contacts such as family members, close friends, and co-workers, as well as unfamiliar acquaintances or strangers, prompting Facebook users to think about who should see their posts.

We then combined both features (textual and visual information) into one "audience nudge," shown at the top of Figure 1. The nudge addresses two complementary aspects of audience perception: specific members of the audience, and the size of that audience. The pool of profile pictures and the audience size were determined by the privacy setting of the post. Our nudge implementation was able to detect and work with complex privacy settings of status updates such as "friends except certain people or groups" and "friends of friends." However, given the restrictions imposed by Facebook, the nudge cannot always precisely measure the audience size. In such cases, the message would provide qualitative rather than quantitative information, e.g., "These people, your friends, AND FRIENDS OF YOUR FRIENDS can see your post."

Timer Nudge

The timer nudge was inspired by literature on hyperbolic time discounting and dual process theory. It was designed to encourage users to pause and think (i.e., switch from System I to System II) before posting. It introduced a visual delay of 20 seconds after a user clicked the "post" button before publishing the submitted post. During the countdown, the user could cancel this post; otherwise the post was made automatically at the end of the countdown.

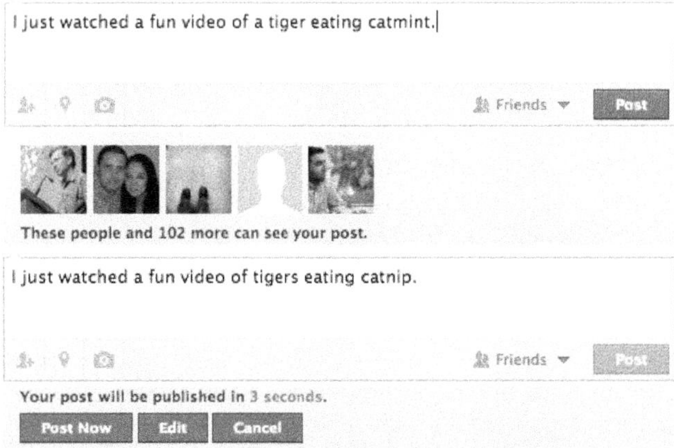

Figure 1. Audience+timer nudge. As the user types a post, five profile photos are displayed, selected randomly from people who will be able to see this post (top). After the user clicks "Post," a countdown timer appears and delays the post for ten seconds (bottom). During the count-down period users could edit or cancel the post, click a button to go ahead and post immediately, or do nothing and when the count-down expires the post will be made automatically.

In the first pilot, participants found this nudge interesting, but also suggested reducing the time delay as well as allowing users to bypass the delay or edit the post. Accordingly, we reduced the delay to 10 seconds and added three links: "post now," "edit," and "cancel."

"Audience+Timer" Nudge

In the second pilot study, we tested the audience and timer nudges. Participants of this pilot study found both the picture and timer nudges somewhat helpful. However, some participants did not realize that the *post now, edit* and *cancel* links could be clicked [29]. To address this issue, we changed the design of these links to buttons that mimicked the Facebook look-and-feel. Furthermore, to create an improved Facebook privacy nudge, we combined the best aspects of two nudges we previously tested during the pilot into a single, new "audience+timer" nudge (Figure 1).

We built an experimental platform to both implement the nudge on Facebook and monitor how users interact with it. The platform consisted of a Facebook application to access users' Facebook data and a Chrome browser plugin to insert the nudge interface seamlessly into the Facebook interface.

In the second pilot study, we encountered a few technical issues. First, our nudges were not always shown. Second, our system did not reliably log users' Facebook behavior and interactions with the nudges. We discovered that both issues were partly due to significant changes introduced by Facebook after deploying our system. The lack of reliable behavioral logs prevented us from doing any quantitative analysis of the nudges [29]. We fixed these issues and implemented reliable logging of system events (e.g., display the nudge UI) and user behavior (e.g., click cancel). We then tested the updated system in the third pilot study. We identified some minor technical issues (e.g., Facebook pages loaded more slowly than usual, and some participants were unable to comment on certain public pages), but otherwise the system appeared stable and was able to log events reliably. We fixed these minor issues before the 6-week field trial. However, Facebook continued to make changes during our field trial and the comment problem reoccured.

STUDY METHODOLOGY

To evaluate the "audience+timer" nudge, we conducted a 6-week field trial with 28 Facebook users during April and May, 2013. We posted study ads on the Craigslist pages of the 12 most populated US cities as well as Syracuse and Pittsburgh. The ads directed prospective participants to a screening survey. The survey invited respondents to participate in the study if they met the following criteria: active adult US Facebook users who posted or commented at least once per day on average; native English speakers who posted in English and used Chrome, primarily, to access Facebook (because our platform was implemented for Chrome).

Study participants were required to install a Chrome plugin and an associated Facebook application. The 6-week field trial was divided into two phases. During the first three weeks (the *control period*) data collection took place without nudging interventions. At the end of the control period we asked participants to complete a mid-term survey to allow us to better understand participants' Facebook behavior during this period. We asked about unusual events, whether posts had caught the attention of unexpected audiences, and any regrets since the start of the study. During the remaining three weeks (the *treatment period*), in addition to data collection, all 28 participants were also shown our nudges. At the end of the treatment period, we asked participants to complete a final survey about their Facebook experiences during this period and their opinions of our nudges.

Participants were compensated with a $10 Amazon gift card for each week of participation and a $10 bonus for study completion. The study received IRB approvals at both Syracuse University and Carnegie Mellon University.

Since our nudges were highly dependent on the Facebook platform, we had to keep up with Facebook's frequent and unpredictable interface changes. To maintain our system during the 6-week study, we spent about an hour every day testing our system with all Facebook features it might interact with. We also had a programmer on standby to update the system if we found any issues. Despite these efforts, the system still encountered two technical problems during the six-week study. First, some participants were intermittently unable to post comments. This problem occurred most frequently for comments on public Facebook pages (e.g. for a company or celebrity). Second, participants experienced slow performance caused by our Chrome browser plugin.

RESULTS

In this section we present the study results. We first describe participants' demographics and their posting frequency during the study. We then report participants' interactions with our nudges and changes to privacy settings made while our nudges were active. Finally, we present a detailed participant-level analysis looking into whether and how our nudges impacted each of our study participants.

ID	Gender	Age	Days Control	Days Treat.	Status updates Control	Status updates Treat.	Comments Control	Comments Treat.
P1	F	49	18	22	1	0	171	68
P2	F	31	18	22	2	9	14	17
P3	F	28	18	22	2	5	57	158
P4	M	27	20	20	35	16	69	16
P5	F	30	18	22	20	24	31	50
P6	M	31	18	22	223	244	396	176
P7	F	45	19	21	45	87	822	950
P8	F	44	19	21	17	17	45	55
P9	F	39	18	22	1	7	14	18
P10	F	20	18	22	32	47	363	386
P11	M	23	18	22	5	9	52	27
P12	M	36	18	22	3	0	235	53
P13	F	50	18	22	1	3	14	15
P14	F	20	18	22	22	41	60	21
P15	F	23	18	22	4	17	4	12
P16	F	32	18	22	7	16	65	102
P17	M	28	21	21	2	5	144	17
P18	F	45	21	21	13	6	22	2
P19	F	19	21	21	86	37	290	132
P20	M	51	21	21	3	6	45	34
P21	F	28	21	21	34	33	77	48
P22	F	23	21	21	1	2	14	4
P23	F	27	21	21	10	7	34	42
P24	F	26	19	22	10	6	26	8
P25	M	27	19	22	4	1	3	3
P26	M	21	19	22	4	10	7	31
P27	F	22	19	22	20	1	46	11
P28	M	49	19	22	30	1	126	1
	Min	19	18	20	1	0	3	1
	Max	51	21	22	223	244	822	950

Table 1. Summary of participants' demographics and number of status updates and comments made during the control and treatment periods.

Demographics and Facebook Posting Activities

Our participants included 19 females and 9 males between the ages of 19 and 51 (M=32, SD=10) from 16 U.S. states. All of them reported being active Facebook users, posting status updates or comments daily. Twelve (43%) self-reported having posted something on Facebook that they later regretted. Our participants came from a variety of occupations including medical staff, engineers, students, managers, teachers, homemakers, retired, and unemployed. Two had completed high school and the rest had at least some college education.

Table 1 summarizes participants' demographics, and the number of status updates and comments made during the control and treatment periods. We use a combination of one letter and one number to refer to each participant. As shown in Table 1, there is a large variability in the frequency of posting across participants. Overall, there is no obvious difference in posting frequency between the control and treatment periods. While our nudges might have impacted posting frequency, we cannot attribute those changes exclusively to the nudge. For example, participants explained that they had posted with unusual frequency, during both the control and treatment periods, due to factors such as vacations, illness, or new jobs. Thus, we do not use posting frequency to evaluate the impacts of our nudges.

Interactions with Nudges

There are many ways a participant could interact with our nudges. We focused on four types of interactions with our nudges: hovering over profile pictures displayed by the audience nudge, and clicking *post now*, *edit*, and *cancel* buttons displayed by the timer nudge.

Hovering Over Profile Pictures

When a user hovers over the five profile pictures displayed by the audience nudge, the corresponding Facebook user's profile name appears. Twenty-four out of 28 participants hovered over profile pictures at least 3 times, and half of them did that throughout the treatment period, suggesting that most participants saw the pictures and interacted with them. However, participants only rarely clicked *edit* or *cancel* or changed the privacy setting after hovering over a profile picture. This suggests that participants were interested in identifying the people shown in the profile pictures, but generally did not feel the need to exclude them from seeing their posts.

Clicking Post Now

In the timer nudge, users could either wait for the post to be submitted automatically after the 10-second delay, or click the *post now*, *edit*, or *cancel* buttons. Twenty-four and 26 participants clicked *post now* at least once for status updates and comments, respectively. Participants clicked *post now* more often for status updates (64%) than comments (25%).

Clicking Edit

Participants used the *edit* button less than *post now,* but when they clicked *edit*, they did it more for comments (4.7%) than for status updates (1.7%). Eighteen participants clicked *edit* for comments, while only five participants did that for status updates. Seven participants clicked *edit* only once, while another 11 participants clicked it at least three times.

We also found that participants used the *edit* button in different manners. Clicking *edit* did not necessarily result in a different post, since in many cases the final post was not modified, suggesting that participants were using the *edit* feature to stop the timer and review their posts. A handful of participants ended up canceling their posts after clicking *edit*. Some participants used the *edit* option to correct typos, slightly rephrase, or complement their posts with additional information, while others made major changes to their original posts.

Clicking Cancel

We logged only seven cancellations for status updates (1.0%) and 15 for comments (0.6%) from eight participants. In some cases, participants refrained from submitting their post altogether, while in other situations they started a new rephrased post. In a few cases, as detailed in the per-participant analysis that follows, participants seemed to cancel potentially sensitive posts.

Privacy Settings Changes

Inline settings allow Facebook users to specify the audience for their status updates. Facebook users can select from a set of predefined groups (e.g., only me, friends, friends of friends, and public), create groups (e.g., high school classmates, co-workers, neighbors), and customize the setting to

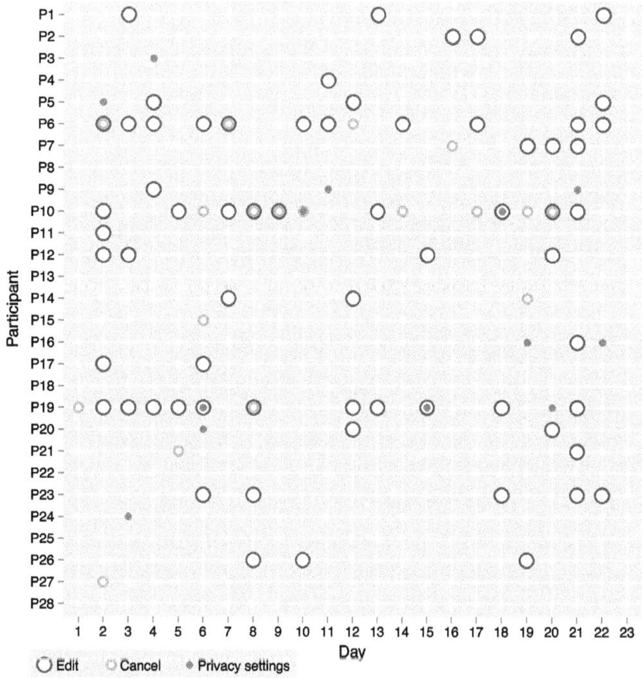

Figure 2. The days on which each participant clicked edit or cancel, or changed their privacy settings during the treatment period. The blue and green circles denote a participant who clicked edit or cancel at least once on that day, respectively. The red dot denotes a participant who has changed the inline privacy setting at least once on that day.

include or exclude specific people or groups. The setting remains the default for future status updates until it is modified again. The privacy setting of a comment inherits the setting from the corresponding status update. We expected that our nudges would help participants to more carefully select privacy settings for their status updates.

Six and eight participants modified their inline privacy settings during the control (number of changes per user: M=.6, SD=1.8) and treatment (M=.5, SD=.9) periods, respectively. Some of them changed the privacy settings both during the control and treatment periods, suggesting that our nudges were not necessarily associated with those changes. However, four participants changed their inline privacy settings only during the treatment period. In one of these cases a participant made his privacy settings more restrictive after hovering over a profile picture.

Interactions Over Time

To investigate novelty and habituation effects, we analyzed the temporal distribution of interactions with our nudges. Figure 2 shows the days on which participants clicked the edit and cancel buttons or made changes to their privacy settings during the treatment period. While there were six participants who did not exhibit any of these interactions and four who only interacted in the first few days, the majority of participants paid attention to and interacted with our nudges throughout the treatment period.

Participant-Level Analysis

To investigate the impact of our nudges on each participant, we analyzed each participant's interactions with our nudges as well as their survey responses. This allows us to understand why some participants liked the nudges and found them useful while others did not, and also helps us tease apart the impact of the audience and timer nudges. We categorized each participant into one of five descriptive groups defined by two dimensions: participants' attitudes and participants' level of interaction with our nudges.

Frequent Interactions and Positive Attitude

This group includes four participants (P4, P10, P20 and P23) who made extensive use of our nudges, and believed that at least one of the nudges could be helpful for themselves or others. These interactions include clicking the *cancel* or *edit* buttons and hovering over profile pictures.

P4 said, "I didn't post more or less, but I did post more cautiously. The constant reminder of who would be seeing my post was kind of an eye opener." He reported having used the time delay "to correct grammatical errors or statuses that looked 'off.'" We found that while he often clicked the *post now* button, for a few posts he waited several seconds before clicking it, yet for others did not click it. He clicked *edit* for several comments, for example, he changed "long out" for "sign out" when writing about logging off of Facebook. He also hovered over pictures for many posts. For instance, after looking at the pictures, he checked the privacy setting without any change before posting, "I just started selling gold in the RMAH...I got a few auctions sold beforehand... :(" He told us that the nudges made him "a bit more aware. Especially the first day. That was almost the 'Oh wow' moment when I realized that more people could see my posts than I thought about." He also suggested that the nudges "should be default for all users."

P10 found the time delay helpful because it helped her avoid "getting into fights on Facebook because you have to stop and think." Despite experiencing some technical issues, her overall opinion was positive. She summarized, "I generally made better decisions." She normally clicked *post now* within 3 seconds, but later on she waited longer for a few of her posts. Besides, she clicked *cancel* for a few posts and then posted edited versions. For example, she canceled the status update, "not excited about still being sick wtf" and then posted, "not excited about still being sick after spending all afternoon in bed not doing my paper or having fun."

P20 canceled and edited a few posts. For example, he clicked *edit* and then ended up not posting: "Traded your Z in for that? :P." He also changed the privacy setting from public to only me after hovering over the profiles pictures shown when posting, "I've been nice up to this point, but the guy has to go! Eating all the bird seed. Where's my bebe gun?" In the final survey he said, "I think I was careful of what I said."

P23 found both nudges helpful. She explained, "I did like knowing when posts were going to be made public (like if a friend's wall is not protected to only their friends, etc.)" and elaborated, "I was going to respond to something snarky... I cancelled it because the application informed me that the entire internet could see my post." She also found the timer nudge helpful when she posted on other people's walls because it prevented her from "entering a discussion ... on someone's wall who posts religious or other annoying stuff all the time." However, she said she "was annoyed when I was using it to post to my own wall or to my close friends wall - those are not when I need the reminder." This suggests she might have preferred a nudge she could customize to fit her needs. Despite some technical glitches that prevented her from posting some comments, P23 had a positive opinion of the nudges overall because "It made me think twice about what I posted and who might see it." Our log data also show that she often hovered over the audience profile pictures and used the *edit* button to make minor changes to her posts.

Limited Interactions and Positive Attitude

Ten participants who had few interactions with our nudges stated that they thought at least one of the nudges could be useful for them or others (P8, P9, P11, P12, P15, P18, P21, P24, P25, and P26). For instance, P8 did not consider our nudges helpful to her, but said they could benefit "young people who are more likely to fly off the handle." She explained, "I didn't benefit, but trouble makers and kids would since it's an extra step and not just post and go-it may make someone think twice before posting hurtful comments." This participant used the friends privacy setting for all her posts and often clicked *post now* within 2 seconds. While she hovered over some profile pictures, she did not perceive any benefit from them since, "just wanna hit post and be done, not mess around with the delay or figure out who may or may not see it since I have my privacy settings the way I want them." Nonetheless, she did edit some of her posts when she caught spelling or grammar errors.

While our logs show that P9 hovered over profile pictures, she reported not seeing any profile pictures. She based her opinion on the timer nudge and said she did not benefit much, but "it would be good for someone with a short temper." She said the nudge might be useful, "if I'd made a spelling error or tagged the wrong person." She clicked *post now* within 3 seconds on all her status updates and mostly used the friends privacy setting. In one case where she changed her privacy setting, she selected her Farmville friends group and explicitly excluded two friends before posting a Farmville-related request. She once clicked *edit* for a comment, but ended up reposting the same comment.

P11 reported that the profile pictures "helped me shape some of my posts." He further reported having canceled some posts because "I didn't want other people to think I'm stupid." However, he also expressed that, "the countdown timer annoys me a bit." He clicked *post now* within 2 seconds for all his status updates. Overall, he felt the nudge "made me think about what I was going to say."

P12 did not post any status updates during the treatment period and he used the public privacy setting for all his status updates during the control period. He clicked *post now* for most of his comments within 3 seconds and did not hover over pictures or click the *cancel* button. However, he clicked *edit* five times for his comments, two of which he ended up not posting, and three of which were reposted without changes. He concluded, the nudges are "not really for me, but I can see how it could be useful for others."

P24 found the audience nudge useful: "I think seeing all of the profile pictures made me rethink what I was going to post if it was slightly offensive or using curse words." However, the only interactions she had with ours nudges were hovering over pictures a few times. In the treatment period, she did change her privacy setting to exclude three friends when she posted, "So I bought a Rick Pitino Makers bottle for $50 and turned around and sold it for $180, lol..." Overall, she thought the nudge "made very little impact."

Limited Interactions and Negative Attitude

Three participants (P7, P14, and P22) neither interacted with our nudges, nor liked them. P7 was an active user who made over a thousand posts during the treatment period. She thought clicking *post now* was necessary to send her posts, which frustrated her. She explained, "I found it to be a pain because some of my posts I just like to post and go." She often clicked *post now* within a few seconds. Furthermore, while she hovered over profile pictures for about one third of her status updates, it did not seem to have any effect on what she posted as most of her status updates were public posts related to products, coupons, and promotions.

P14 also disliked the nudges. She did not click any buttons or hover over profile pictures when posting status updates. She clicked *post now* for three comments, and all were within three seconds. She also canceled one comment because "I was impatient!!" She explained, "I could see how the timer and the profile pictures would be beneficial but I just thought it was annoying."

P22 also did not like the nudges or interact with them. She only made six posts during the treatment period. She remembered seeing our nudges, but said that she did not pay attention to them. Our logs confirmed that she had no interaction with our nudges. When asked if there was any situation where the nudge negatively affected her, she replied, "for me, I don't care, so every time." She also seemed to post on Facebook just to get paid for participating in our study, posting the comment: "i'm only commenting on stuff b/c im being paid to by some app to spy on me and if i dont do enough social stuff they'll stop letting me do it."

Frequent Interactions and Negative Attitude

Seven participants did not like our nudges, but had extensive interactions with them (P2, P3, P6, P16, P17, P19, and P27). P2 experienced technical problems with our nudges and strongly disliked the timer. She complained, "the delayed posting thing which I HATE... makes posting harder." She believed that the timer is "not needed" and she did not "need anyone editing or censoring me." Although she indicated that she preferred the profile pictures over timer, she based her negative opinions on the timer. She explained, "I try to not put anything too embarrassing or horrible. I didn't mind that you were watching or anyone. I say what I want or feel," adding that, "there is no way to protect people from posting embarrassing or life impacting information online while mad or upset or whatever. It's human nature to be stupid sometimes." She often clicked the *post now* button when commenting, sometimes waiting several seconds before doing it and sometimes clicking it right away. For example, she waited 3 seconds before clicking *post now* for the comment: "David's burrito defeated him. It was HUGE," but waited 8 seconds for: "Off subject but the worst my arm pits have felt was during laser hair removal...Most painful area so far." She also clicked *edit* a few times without changing any comments, suggesting that she was using the *edit* option to take a second look at her comments. She also clicked *edit* to change one of her comments from "Or its like saying it transcends life. Negative Nelly aka Autumz..." to "Or its like saying it transcends life. I guess we all know your glass is half empty."

P6 hovered over profile pictures and clicked the *cancel* and *edit* buttons a few times. In addition, he often clicked *post now*, sometimes waiting a few seconds and sometimes clicking it right away. An active user, he made more than 400 posts during the treatment period. He thought that the plugin "made posting slightly more frustrating, but did not affect output." He explained that he was annoyed by "the fact I had to keep re-confirming that I wanted to post something I was sure about posting." This was another participant who thought that clicking *post now* was necessary to send his posts and did not realize that after the 10 seconds delay, his posts would be automatically posted.

P19 was another participant who frequently interacted with the nudges but did not like them. She said, "I didn't care about this feature at all, it did not affect my facebook usage at all, I just ignored it, like most people would." She also complained about encountering technical issues with the timer nudge. Interestingly, she acknowledged that she often regrets her posts, but said she solves the problem by just deleting them: "I almost always post things that I wish I wouldn't have, then I just delete them and the problem is solved." But, in some cases damage may have already been done before deleting a post. P19 did not seem to be concerned about this, and thus did not find utility in the nudges. While she disliked the nudge idea, she hovered over the audience nudge profile pictures 10 times, clicked *cancel* for a status update and a comment, clicked *edit* for 21 comments, and made two privacy setting changes during the treatment period. Most of her edits were minor rewording of the posts. For one lengthy status update about love and betrayal she changed the privacy setting to exclude one particular friend before she started typing her post, suggesting that she had a clear idea of her intended audience before she posted. Overall, the nudges did not seem to help her avoid making potentially controversial posts, but did give her a chance to make minor edits of her posts.

Indifferent

Four participants expressed indifference about the nudges (P1, P5, P13, and P28). They either did not receive enough exposure to the nudges to form an informed opinion or simply expressed a neutral opinion even after having interacted with the nudges. Lack of exposure was due to participants posting less frequently or using different browsers or devices to post.

P1 reported having seen profile pictures and using the time delay to review her posts. She did not post any status update during the treatment period and often clicked *post now* within 3 seconds for her comments. She hovered over pictures before making several comments and clicked *edit* twice to correct typos. She was among those participants who had problems posting some of their comments which likely affected her overall opinion of the nudges. Although she used the nudges while posting and mentioned that the nudge could be useful "in case you are commenting on the wrong post," she was also not impressed and "could take it or leave it."

P5 neither expressed a positive nor a negative opinion and her behavioral data did not show any relevant interactions with the nudge as she only clicked *post now* right away. Similarly, P13 often clicked *post now* right away and did not have other interaction with the nudges. She explained, "In most cases I changed the time to posting to now so I didn't have to wait, I also didn't have to edit my posts because I wasn't saying anything I didn't want anyone to see." P28 hardly noticed the nudge as he only posted one status update and one comment using the plugin during the treatment period.

DISCUSSION

The goal of our nudging interventions was to help users be more thoughtful when posting on Facebook, in order to reduce the potential for posting status updates or comments they might later regret. Consistent with the tenets of soft paternalism, we designed our nudges to encourage users to think about the audience and content of their posts without limiting their ability to post on Facebook. Here, we discuss participants' perceptions of our nudges and the challenges of conducting longitudinal field trials. We also offer recommendations for designing and testing nudges.

Varied Perceptions

Participants varied in how they perceived the general nudging idea and the two specific nudge features (audience and timer). Some participants were positive about the nudging intervention, e.g., P26 said "i like the plugin and think it is a great idea, i would love using this as the final product." In contrast, others had negative opinions. For example, P2 disliked the timer nudge because she did not "need anyone editing or censoring me."

We found that how participants use Facebook often played a role in their perceptions of our nudges. Generally, we found that those who use Facebook to post personal thoughts perceived the nudges as more beneficial than those who use it to broadcast news articles and other public information. On the other hand, those who use it for commercial or money making purposes (e.g. to share information about products and coupons) had negative opinions. We also found that those participants who had prior experience adjusting privacy settings and seemed to be careful about what they posted recognized the benefits of the nudges, but believed they did not need them.

Nudging toward Audience Awareness

The profile picture feature of the nudge was designed to remind Facebook users of the prospective audience for their posts. We found that most participants paid attention to and interacted with the profile pictures and several valued this feature, stating that it made them think about whether there post might offend someone.

Profile pictures were accompanied by a an indication of the number of people who could potentially see a post. Some participants said they found this information helpful, especially when posting comments on friends' posts.

In this study, we bundled the profile pictures and audience size information together. Further work is needed to determine their effectiveness in isolation.

None of the participants complained about the profile pictures, as they were less intrusive than the countdown timer. Users can ignore them, as some of our participants did, and go about their posting as usual. We found that most participants hovered over the profile pictures, and anecdotes from the final survey suggest that some of the participants benefited from having seen profile pictures. For example, one participant reported having decided not to post something after seeing the profile pictures. We also observed a participant change to a more restrictive privacy setting after hovering over a profile picture. This suggests that profile pictures can assist users in making better privacy decisions, but sometimes their effect can be subtle or difficult to measure.

Nudging with A Countdown Timer

The countdown timer was designed to encourage participants to stop and reflect on the content of their posts in order to avoid regrettable, "heat of the moment" posts. Participants were quite divided in their views. Some participants found the countdown timer valuable for giving them a chance to review their posts "a little more carefully" and "catch misspelled words or grammar errors." On the other hand, some participants voiced frustration about what they perceived as a requirement to take an extra step or wait 10 seconds to complete their posts.

We observed that the nudge was successful in helping some participants reconsider their posts. It had an additional benefit of helping users catch typos and other minor errors in their posts. A number of participants rephrased or even canceled their posts during the delay. However, this benefit came at the cost of delaying every post. The timer countdown was both the most liked and disliked nudge feature we implemented.

For the most part, participants were not as concerned about their posts being delayed for 10 seconds as they were about having to wait 10 seconds before they could move on to something else. In reality there was no need for them to watch the countdown, but some participants seemed unwilling to trust that their post would get posted after 10 seconds and others thought they *had* to click *post now*. Our timer nudge seemed to leave some participants feeling uneasy and afraid to move on until their massage got posted. We could design an interface where the post would appear on the user's screen as if it had been posted (perhaps by posting it to "only me") while the timer is counting down. Even though the nudge would still have the same functionality, a change in the visual display might make it more acceptable.

The idea of delays may be applied in other scenarios where people may benefit from some extra time to think about their actions. However, since the time delay interrupts primary tasks (in this case Facebook posting), it should be used selectively and with caution. Future research should explore other ways to slow people down and encourage them to think about their actions, as well as ways to introduce time delays more selectively.

Challenges and Limitations

Conducting our investigation as a longitudinal field trial allowed us to investigate the impact of our nudges under real life conditions, but that made our study more challenging to run and resulted in a number of limitations.

One source of limitations stemmed from implementation challenges. Since Facebook changes its interface frequently and unpredictably, we had to constantly monitor, test, and adapt our code to keep up with those changes. Despite this concerted effort, our nudges malfunctioned a few times during our field trials. For instance, some participants experienced some of their comments not being posted. In addition, since our nudge was not an integral part of the Facebook platform, we had to work around the Facebook UI to embed the nudge features. We also had to add logging functionality to capture all possible user-driven events. However, this extra logging slowed down our nudges and indirectly affected some participants' Facebook experience. These technical challenges made it difficult to run our field trial for an extended period of time. In addition, some participants disliked our nudges primarily because of these issues.

As with any research involving observation of participant behavior, one methodological concern is the Hawthorn effect: participants may change their behavior simply because they are in a study. To mitigate this we minimized our interactions with participants once the study began. In the mid-term survey, we explicitly asked them whether their posting behavior had changed. Some participants noted posting with different frequencies due to various reasons, but un-related to our study. Several participants also reported in the final survey that they thought our nudges were introduced by Facebook rather than us.

External factors beyond our control and observation likely affected participants' posting behavior, making it difficult to determine causality. Similarly, measuring the effectiveness of our nudges in preventing regret is also challenging because generally only a small fraction of the posts made by users may lead to regret, and arguably even fewer lead to the short-term regret we may detect in this study. In addition, it is often difficult to measure the effect of a nudge; users may not react to them in a noticeable way, or the reaction might be gradual.

While our combination of different nudge features might increase the chance that we detect some effect of our nudges, it makes it difficult for us to isolate the effects of individual nudge features or account for interactions between features.

Implications for Designing and Testing Privacy Nudges

We identified a set of key aspects to consider when designing and evaluating privacy nudges. First, designers should consider the intrusiveness of the nudges. We found that our less-intrusive audience nudge was better received by users than our more-intrusive timer nudge. On the other hand, we observed more direct benefits from the timer nudge. It would be useful to investigate whether the timer nudge could be improved by making it less visually intrusive — for example, showing a user's post actually posted but visible to "only me" until the end of the countdown.

Second, designers should keep in mind that some users will dislike the sense of being watched. Designers should look for ways to nudge people without making them feel that a new "big brother" is watching. In our second pilot study users disliked being judged by a nudge that provided subjective feedback on the sentiment of the users' posts [29]. The nudges we tested in this study, on the other hand, were not perceived as judgmental by participants.

Third, designers should consider the extent to which they should allow users to control or customize a nudge. In our system, we did not give users any ability to control the nudges except for the *post now* button that allowed them to skip the time delay. Some users wanted to be able to turn off the nudges or personalize them according to their needs and preferences. Controls could allow users to configure nudges such that they are enabled only under certain circumstances, such as at specific times, when certain people can see their posts, or when they type certain sensitive words.

Fourth, it is critical that the nudges function properly and do not interfere with the usability and reliability of the system in which they are embedded. Our nudges suffered from technical glitches that decreased their perceived value for some participants. However, without help from Facebook, we found it difficult to improve the reliability of our system.

Lastly, but importantly, nudges are difficult to evaluate both quantitatively and precisely when they are designed to impact behaviors that may occur only occasionally, or that may be hard to observe. And yet, when it comes to privacy, it could be precisely occasional, rare behaviors that end up causing the most damage — for example, a spur-of-the-moment status update that leaves a long and painful trail of unintended consequences. Collecting enough measurable, quantitative data to compute aggregate results from a small sample of users is difficult under such circumstances. Unless it is feasible to study a large number of users, an evaluation strategy including qualitative participant-level analysis is likely to provide more informative results than a quantitative analysis.

CONCLUSIONS

While the field study we presented in this paper should be considered exploratory, our results suggest that privacy nudges have the potential to be a powerful mechanism to assist users in avoiding unintended disclosures. Although our findings come from a Facebook case study, the principles underlying the privacy nudges we tested may be extended to similar services such as Twitter or to other types of services such as e-commerce, location sharing, and smart phone applications.

ACKNOWLEDGEMENTS

We thank Jeff Dyer, Colleen Eagan, Emily Forney, Eric Balebako, Yao Li, and members of the Privacy Nudge group at Carnegie Mellon for their help; CHI reviewers for their feedback; and our participants for their insights. This paper is based upon work supported by the IWT SBO Project on Security and Privacy for Online Social Networks (SPION), the NSF Grant CNS-1012763 (Nudging Users Towards Privacy), and a Google Focused Research Award on Privacy Nudges.

REFERENCES

1. A. Acquisti. Privacy in electronic commerce and the economics of immediate gratification. In *Electronic commerce*, pages 21–29. ACM, 2004.
2. A. Acquisti. Nudging privacy: The behavioral economics of personal information. *IEEE Security and Privacy*, 7(6):82–85, 2009.
3. A. Acquisti and R. Gross. Imagined communities: Awareness, information sharing, and privacy on the facebook. In *PETS*, pages 36–58. Springer, 2006.
4. A. Acquisti and J. Grossklags. Privacy and rationality in individual decision making. *Security & Privacy, IEEE*, 3(1):26–33, 2005.
5. I. Adjerid, A. Acquisti, L. Brandimarte, and G. Loewenstein. Sleights of privacy: Framing, disclosures, and the limits of transparency. In *SOUPS*, pages 9:1–9:11. ACM, 2013.
6. G. A. Akerlof. The market for "lemons": Quality uncertainty and the market mechanism. *The quarterly journal of economics*, pages 488–500, 1970.
7. M. S. Bernstein, E. Bakshy, M. Burke, and B. Karrer. Quantifying the invisible audience in social networks. In *SIGCHI*, pages 21–30. ACM, 2013.
8. A. Besmer and H. Lipford. Tagged photos: concerns, perceptions, and protections. In *Proc. CHI Ext. Abs.*, pages 4585–4590, 2009.
9. d. boyd and N. Ellison. Social network sites: Definition, history, and scholarship. *J. of Computer-Mediated Commun.*, 13(1), 2007.
10. E. Choe, J. Jung, B. Lee, and K. Fisher. Nudging people away from privacy-invasive mobile apps through visual framing. In *INTERACT*, pages 74–91. Springer Berlin Heidelberg, 2013.
11. L. Fang and K. LeFevre. Privacy wizards for social networking sites. In *WWW*, pages 351–360. ACM, 2010.
12. A. Forget, S. Chiasson, P. C. van Oorschot, and R. Biddle. Improving text passwords through persuasion. In *SOUPS*, page 112. ACM, 2008.
13. S. Frederick, G. Loewenstein, and O. T. Time discounting and time preference: A critical review. *J. of Econ. Lit.*, 40(2):351 – 401, 2002.
14. E. Goffman. The presentation of self in everyday life. 1959. *Garden City, NY*, 2002.
15. R. Gross and A. Acquisti. Information revelation and privacy in online social networks. In *WPES*, pages 71–80, 2005.
16. K. E. Jenni and G. Loewenstein. Explaining the identifiable victim effect. *Journal of Risk and Uncertainty*, 14(3):235–257, 1997.
17. D. Kahneman. A perspective on judgment and choice: Mapping bounded rationality. *American psychologist*, pages 697–720, 2003.
18. D. Laibson. Golden eggs and hyperbolic discounting. *The Quarterly J. of Econ.*, 112(2):443–478, May 1997.
19. H. R. Lipford, J. Watson, M. Whitney, N. Carolina, H. Lipford, K. Froiland, and R. W. Reeder. Visual vs . Compact : A Comparison of Privacy Policy Interfaces. *Interfaces*, pages 1111–1114, 2010.
20. M. Madejski, M. Johnson, and S. M. Bellovin. The failure of online social network privacy settings. Technical report, Columbia University, 2011.
21. A. Marwick and d. boyd. I tweet honestly, i tweet passionately: Twitter users, context collapse, and the imagined audience. *New Media & Society*, 13(1):114, 2011.
22. H. A. Simon. A behavioral model of rational choice. *The Quarterly J. of Econ.*, 69(1):99–118, Feb. 1955.
23. F. Stutzman, R. Gross, and A. Acquisti. Silent listeners: The evolution of privacy and disclosure on facebook. *J. of Privacy and Confidentiality*, 4(2), Mar. 2013.
24. R. H. Thaler and C. R. Sunstein. Libertarian paternalism. *Am. Econ. Rev.*, 93(2):175–179, 2003.
25. R. H. Thaler and C. R. Sunstein. *Nudge: Improving Decisions About Health, Wealth, and Happiness*. Yale University Press, 1 edition, Apr. 2008.
26. A. Tversky and D. Kahneman. Judgment under uncertainty: Heuristics and biases. *science*, 185(4157):1124–1131, 1974.
27. B. Ur, P. Kelley, S. Komanduri, J. Lee, M. Maass, M. Mazurek, T. Passaro, R. Shay, T. Vidas, L. Bauer, N. Christin, and L. Cranor. How does your password measure up? the effect of strength meters on password creation. In *Proc. USENIX Security*, 2012.
28. Y. Wang, S. Komanduri, P. G. Leon, G. Norcie, A. Acquisti, and L. F. Cranor. "I regretted the minute I pressed share": A qualitative study of regrets on facebook. In *SOUPS*, 2011.
29. Y. Wang, P. G. Leon, K. Scott, X. Chen, A. Acquisti, L. F. Cranor, and N. Sadeh. Privacy nudges for social media: An exploratory facebook study. *PSOSM*, 2013.
30. S. Wilson, J. Cranshaw, N. Sadeh, A. Acquisti, L. F. Cranor, J. Springfield, S. Y. Jeong, and A. Balasubramanian. Privacy manipulation and acclimation in a location sharing application. In *UbiComp*, pages 549–558. ACM, 2013.

In Situ with Bystanders of Augmented Reality Glasses: Perspectives on Recording and Privacy-Mediating Technologies

Tamara Denning
Computer Science & Engineering
University of Washington
tdenning@cs.washington.edu

Zakariya Dehlawi
Information School
University of Washington
zaxim@uw.edu

Tadayoshi Kohno
Computer Science & Engineering
University of Washington
yoshi@cs.washington.edu

ABSTRACT
Augmented reality (AR) devices are poised to enter the market. It is unclear how the properties of these devices will affect individuals' privacy. In this study, we investigate the privacy perspectives of individuals when they are bystanders around AR devices. We conducted 12 field sessions in cafés and interviewed 31 bystanders regarding their reactions to a co-located AR device. Participants were predominantly split between having indifferent and negative reactions to the device. Participants who expressed that AR devices change the bystander experience attributed this difference to subtleness, ease of recording, and the technology's lack of prevalence. Additionally, participants surfaced a variety of factors that make recording more or less acceptable, including what they are doing when the recording is being taken. Participants expressed interest in being asked permission before being recorded and in recording-blocking devices. We use the interview results to guide an exploration of design directions for privacy-mediating technologies.

Author Keywords
Augmented reality; wearable camera; privacy; surveillance.

ACM Classification Keywords
K.4.0 [**Computers And Society**]: General.

INTRODUCTION
Audiovisual recording is pervasive in public spaces. This recording takes place predominantly via two classes of devices: handheld devices such as camera phones, and infrastructure devices such as closed-circuit television (CCTV). These two recording paradigms can be characterized and contrasted via axes such as mobility, recording cues, typical recording duration, content ownership, and intended usage.

CHI 2014, April 26 - May 01 2014, Toronto, ON, Canada

ACM 978-1-4503-2473-1/14/04...$15.00.
http://dx.doi.org/10.1145/2556288.2557352

A new form factor for recording hardware—glasses-style augmented reality (AR) devices—is poised to become more common. If commercialization attempts (e.g., [14, 24, 33]) succeed in creating a market for these types of devices, there could be a massive increase in the number of people using wearable cameras. This class of device shares characteristics with both camera phones and CCTVs; however, the result is a unique amalgamation of properties. For example, AR-style glasses—unlike camera phones—are well-suited for periodic, continuous, and low effort audiovisual recording. In contrast to CCTVs, AR glasses are mobile and controlled by individuals.

While research has been conducted on the relationship between recording and privacy, most prior work focuses on the current dominant form factors. There is a need for more research into how wearable and glasses-style devices differ from other classes of cameras. Moreover, these cameras have not yet achieved significant market penetration. As a result, we have the opportunity to study how perceptions and usage patterns change over the adoption of a new technology.

In this study we consider the perspectives of bystanders of AR glasses. In particular, we consider their perceptions of how and why these devices might impact their privacy. Bystanders are particularly relevant for study: they are the largest stakeholder group. We have the opportunity to explore technology designs that can mitigate bystander concerns.

In this paper we report on our in-situ approach to investigating bystander perspectives on AR-style recording. We wore a mock AR device in cafés around a city over the course of 12 field sessions. During these sessions, we conducted semi-structured interviews with 31 individuals on their reactions to the co-located device. Our analysis of interview data surfaces: (a) reasons why participants do or do not consider AR glasses to change the bystander experience; and (b) factors that contribute to participants not wanting to be recorded. Additionally, we explore participant thoughts on permission and blocking technologies for recording. We use the interview results to explore design axes for recording technologies that respect bystander privacy. With this research, we hope to help make the adoption of AR technologies smoother and more considerate to a larger group of stakeholders.

RELATED WORK

Infrastructure Recording Technologies

Early research on media spaces—such as by Adams [2] or Bellotti and Sellen [6]—explores the privacy issues that result from an environment instrumented with recording capabilities. This research is particularly transferable to CCTVs, but also has some transferability to AR privacy issues for bystanders.

More recently, Nguyen et al. [25] interviewed participants to explore their feelings about CCTV recording. They interpreted their results largely via Smith's Concern for Information Privacy model [30]; this model breaks privacy concerns into the dimensions of collection, improper access, unauthorized secondary use, and errors.

Massimi et al. [23] use the Day Reconstruction Method [19] to interview participants about the recording technologies that they encounter in their daily lives. Their results have a heavy focus on infrastructure-style CCTV cameras rather than on individuals' mobile cameras.

Friedman et al. conduct an in-depth analysis of interviews with bystanders to a camera installation recording a public fountain area [12]. The authors investigate underlying issues and interviewee justifications. For example, participants viewed the installation to be less acceptable if the footage was streamed to a remote location.

Mobile Recording Technologies

Steve Mann (e.g., [3]) and Thad Starner (e.g., [32]) have bodies of work on AR technologies. More topically, they have both worn AR devices for extended periods of time and in public. They have anecdotally reported their experiences wearing AR devices. For example, in 2012 Mann reported that he was assaulted by a staff member in a Paris McDonald's due to his use of EyeTap [19].

Nguyen et al. conducted a study with many parallels to our own [26]. They also wished to investigate bystander reactions to a wearable camera. However, the camera in question was one primarily positioned as an assistive device for users with memory or vision impairment. The stated purpose potentially affects bystander reactions to the device. The study collected data via paratyping (see below).

Methodologies

Paratyping (e.g., [1, 18]) is a methodology for collecting in-situ feedback from bystanders via situated experience prototyping. With this technique, participants are recruited to act as proxies for the researchers. Participants carry short surveys and distribute them to bystanders with whom they interact. The surveys, which are returned by mail, probe bystander reactions to ubiquitous technologies in the context of their recent interactions. These bystanders can optionally be contacted for follow-up interviews.

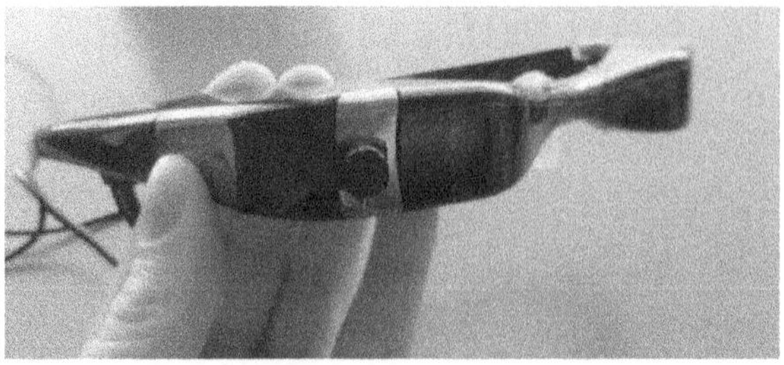

Figure 1. A photo of the mockup device worn during field sessions. The device is a Myvu Crystal Personal Media Viewer with an attached (non-functioning) camera.

Choe et al. investigate participant attitudes to sensors in the home via sensor proxies [11]. Participants placed repackaged motion sensor lights in locations around the home. Light activation served to probe participants to record reactions to the hypothetical sensors in study diaries.

Mancini et al. explore reactions to hypothetical technologies via a video prototyping methodology they call ContraVision [20]. In particular, they present a video that portrays the technology in a positive light together with a video that portrays the technology in a negative light.

METHOD

Field Sessions and Interview Protocol

Each field session was conducted using two researchers: a researcher wearing a mock AR device and a researcher conducting interviews. The AR mockup consisted of a pair of media glasses—the Myvu Crystal Personal Media Viewer—and an attached, non-functioning camera (see Figure 1); see the Methodology Discussion for the reasoning behind our decision not to record. Field sessions proceeded as follows: the interviewing researcher would enter the café, order food or drinks, and take a seat. The researcher wearing the mockup device would then enter the café, order, and sit down to work. Patrons that had obvious reactions to the AR device, were likely to have noticed the AR device, or were pertinent for theoretical sampling (e.g., were accompanied by children) were approached for an interview. The interviews were semi-structured and based around the following questions:

1. *Did you notice the glasses that (s)he's wearing? What about them did you notice?*
2. *Have you heard about those kinds of glasses? What have you heard?*
3. *Did you know that those kinds of glasses have electronics and a display attached?*
4. *Did you know that you can record video with those kinds of glasses?*

5. *Why do you think someone would want to wear those kinds of glasses?*
6. *Do you think recording with those glasses is similar or different to recording with a cell phone? Why?*
7. *How do you feel about being around someone who is wearing those kinds of glasses? Why?*
8. *Would you want someone with those kinds of glasses to ask your permission before recording a video?*
9. *Would you be willing to wear something that would block someone from being able to record you?*

The progression of increasing specificity in the questions was arranged to probe participants on the more general topics in a non-leading way.

The protocol served as a guide for the interview; questions were modified or discarded based on the flow of the conversation and any time constraints set by the participants. Interviews were not recorded: the interviewing researcher took interview notes and both researchers made observation notes. The researchers—one male and one female—took turns wearing the AR mockup and conducting interviews. Our human subjects Institutional Review Board reviewed and approved the study protocol.

Methodology Discussion

Our investigative methodology has both benefits and drawbacks. We deploy (non-recording) AR-style glasses into real environments and give participants a chance to observe them before they are interviewed. During interviews, participant responses are grounded by the presence of the device in the environment. Moreover, because we approach individuals "in the wild," we are potentially able to interview people who do not respond to research recruitment ads.

We found cafés to be suitable settings for a number of reasons: they are publicly accessible; they have a reasonable throughput of traffic; they are settings where researchers can position themselves for extended periods of time; and they are environments in which it is plausible to approach individuals for an interview. Moreover, within a single city—and even within a neighborhood—the character of a café and its clientele can vary greatly. Different cafés attract different demographics and subcultures. At various times, cafés draw people engaged in a variety of activities: socializing, eating, reading, meeting, working alone, studying in groups, or playing games.

As mentioned, this investigative methodology has some drawbacks. We chose not to record interviews. This was done both to make the process less daunting to participants and to facilitate soliciting perspectives from individuals who might object to the idea of being recorded. Although the interviewer took notes during and after the interview, the pace of the interview and the need to engage with participants inevitably means that these notes are not as complete as a full transcript. Additionally, we attempt to be respectful of potential participants and their time. The interviewer chose to approach only those individuals who seemed like they could be interrupted; this meant, for example, that individuals focused on their laptops and groups in deep conversation were excluded.

Data Collection

A total of 12 field sessions were held in 8 different cafés over the course of 3½ months in spring and summer 2013, and ranged in duration from 20-90 minutes each. The field sessions were performed at different times of day and on different days of the week, including weekends. At the end of an observation session, individuals or groups were solicited for interviews. If a group was approached, everyone in the group was included in the interview. These 12 field sessions yielded 23 interview sessions with 31 participants. The participants (M=18; F=13) represented a variety of age groups (18–22=8; 23–25=5; 26–34=3; 35–44=6; 45–54=3; 55–64=5; 75+=1). The researchers approached 4 additional individuals who subsequently declined to be interviewed.

Coding

The codes for the data analysis were developed via an iterative process. After nearly half the interviews were collected, two of the researchers independently went through the interviews and created an initial set of codes. Following this, the researchers met to discuss the similarities and differences in their initial set of codes and agreed on a codebook. The researchers then used the codebook to code interview data segments via consensus. When appropriate, nested codes and multiple codes were applied to a single segment of interview data. As additional interviews were performed, the researchers reexamined existing codes and made modifications as necessary to the codebook, going back and recoding previously coded interviews. This iterative process was repeated until all interviews were coded and the final codebook was created. All interview responses were coded, regardless of whether or not the interview was truncated.

INTERVIEW EXCERPTS: PARTICIPANT SNAPSHOTS

The next section (Results) presents interview results and analysis; however, before we focus on subcomponents of the interviews, we convey a sense of the interviews as a whole. We present below excerpts from three interview sessions. The participants reflect different positions along the spectrum of reactions and different levels of familiarity with AR technologies. The interviews also focus on different underlying themes.

Interview J: The Evolution of Social Norms

Participant J (a 23-year-old unemployed philosophy student and reader/writer), described himself as interested in technology, but did not consider himself a techie. *"I'm straddled between the prehistoric and the modern."* He was familiar with Google Glass, but did not *"think that their quality was high enough to break into the market yet."*

J was definitely aware that these kinds of devices can record: *"I would be surprised if their cameras aren't always on...It would make them easier to interact with, like the Kinect for the XBox One. Plus, how else would you fuel the tinfoil hat conspiracy theorists?"* On the topic of how he felt about being recorded by such glasses, he said, *"If I got drunk and puked on a friend, I wouldn't want that out there, but it shouldn't affect my ability to get elected to public office...There are things that we don't want in the public, but it won't be harmful, especially in the future...But, in the interim, people do lose their jobs over Facebook posts."*

When asked if there are spaces where we shouldn't record, he replied, *"The extreme example is the bathroom or the bedroom. But it's only a matter of socialization. Right now it's not civilized to record in the bathroom. But consider the [Ancient] Greeks. They didn't use to work out in the nude, until they realized that it was better. So they accepted that."*

Interviews E & F: Technology and Isolation

Participant E (a 55-year-old female teacher) and Participant F (a 57-year-old male engineer) were interviewed together. E described herself as having *"limited knowledge"* of AR devices, but then proceeded to express an appreciable understanding of the concept. *"A screen comes over the eye,"* she demonstrated, holding up her smartphone to her face, *"and you don't need a computer; you just cloud WiFi it."* She was aware that the glasses could take pictures and recordings: *"It seems creepy because they can take pictures surreptitiously. You can go around and take pictures,"* again, she illustrated by using her hand, *"hot girls [click], hot girls [click]."*

While discussing how they would feel about being bystanders to such a device, F chimes in, *"If I really researched privacy issues, I would be more bothered, since it's probably worse than we know—almost certainly worse than we know...I don't think the ethical questions have caught up with the technology."*

E explained, *"I teach young people—18 to 30—and they would probably get the device because it's the cool new thing. It doesn't appeal to me. I can't think of a reason to use them. Technology portrays itself as creating community, but instead it destroys community."* F added, *"People's attention spans have been brought down to sound bites."*

In response to being asked, both E and F expressed an interest in having AR users ask their permission before taking recordings, but E said, *"I don't think there's an actual etiquette for that...or any etiquette for devices in general."* When asked if they would be interested in technology that would allow them to block themselves from being recorded, both E and F were interested, but F added, *"We probably wouldn't need to...Once you get to a certain age—over 50—we are invisible anyway."* E stated, *"In the future technology will let you remove people from videos. 'I only want to see hot chicks; get rid of people over 25.'"*

Interviews V & W: Context and Content Ownership

Pariticipant V (a 20-year-old female dance major) and Participant W (a 21-year-old female dance major) were interviewed together. V had heard of Google Glass, but neither she nor W knew that they could take photos and recordings. W exclaimed, *"Wow, like Spy Kids. It's real! [laughter]"*

When asked if recording with these types of glasses is similar or different to recording with a cell phone, they expressed that it was different. V said, *"It's more obvious with a cell phone. It's like, 'I'm recording something.' With the glasses, it's like, 'Are you recording my conversation?' I don't know. Does it blink?"*

She would find being around an AR device *"a little unsettling—but not too unsettling."* W elaborated a bit more: *"I'm a dancer, so if I saw a video camera coming down the street I'd probably jump in front of it. [laughs] But if I saw someone coming into a performance—or a movie theatre, I guess—that would be a problem. But if they're just recording our conversation, it isn't that interesting."* Upon being asked about a potential interest in blocking technologies, V explained, *"I'm a broke college student. If it bothered me, I'd approach them. If it got to be an issue—like for working in the theatre—if a lot of people started coming in with these devices I'd probably tell my boss to get one to stop all the recording. That's actually pretty smart."*

RESULTS

In this section we present our analysis of interview data. When specific analysis codes appear in the text they are indicated by a bold font. This is a qualitative study that is primarily intended to explore relevant issues. As a result, participant counts should be taken as a rough indicator of our population rather than an absolute measure.

Bystander Reactions

At the beginning of each interview, we asked the participant whether or not they had noticed the second researcher's AR glasses. Many of the participants (11/31) had not made any particular note of the glasses (**Noticed Glasses: No**), despite the bias in our sampling methods (see Method section).

As we proceeded with the interview, participants expressed a range of reactions regarding the idea of being a bystander to an AR recording device. As part of our analysis, we coded these sentiments as **AR Bystander: Positive**, **AR Bystander: Negative**, or **AR Bystander: Indifferent**.

Participants were split in their reactions, but they primarily either reacted indifferently (16/31) or negatively (12/31) to AR recording; only one participant had a positive reaction. Also notably, some of the participants (6/31) expressed more than one type of sentiment, highlighting the fact that people can have conflicting or complex reactions.

The Familiar: Legality and the Public Stage

When participants offered reasons why recording with an AR device is acceptable or makes no substantive difference to their experience as a bystander, they primarily did so in the context of comparisons with existing technologies. When we probed them, 10 participants indicated that they view AR recording as similar to cell phone recording (**Cell Phone Comparison: Similar**). Some participants volunteered comparisons to other existing camera technologies. For example, 5 participants specifically commented on the preexisting prevalence of CCTV cameras (**CCTV Comparison**). A few participants made comparisons to other recording technologies, such as the GoPro wearable camera (**Camera Comparison**).

In general, participants rhetorically used these comparisons in one of two ways: to indicate that AR technologies make no difference in the legal landscape, or to indicate that AR technologies make no difference in their expectation of being recorded. For example, Participant N (a 21-year-old male game designer) indicated that he cannot legally stop someone from taking his picture, regardless of device type. Participant AC (a 64-year-old male video producer) is in the Screen Actors Guild; he indicated that no one is allowed to capture his image without written permission.

Multiple participants expressed that—between cell phones, CCTVs, and other cameras—they already expect to be recorded whenever they are in public. Not all participants seemed pleased or indifferent about that fact; however, the introduction of AR technologies did not affect their expectations of being recorded. Below are three participant quotes (paraphrased from transcript notes) that illustrate viewpoints along this spectrum:

- Participant L (a 48-year-old female IT manager and informatics student): *I'm fully aware that I'm being photographed all the time. Look at the tracking activities of the police in Boston* [referencing the 2013 Boston Marathon bombing]. *That was "fantastic," in the literal sense of the word, not necessarily the positive sense.*
- Participant B (a 39-year-old female lawyer): *People are aware that there are a lot of CCTVs around—there's not a street corner in Seattle that's not recorded. It's a bit Big Brother, but we accept it as a society, and it's not like you're in a house.*
- Participant K (a 50+-year-old male who described his occupation as spiritual): *I am consciously sharing just by being present. If I didn't want to be seen I would lock myself up and never go out.*

Several participants focused on the concept of appearing in public. This viewpoint is reminiscent of Goffman's theory of the presentation of self in everyday life. In this theory, he describes our interactions as times when we are performing: we are scrutinized by others, and dynamically adapt to their reactions. At other times, we do not wish to be seen, and hide away "backstage" [13].

The Foreign: Subtleness and (Lack of) Prevalence

When probed on the topic, 8 participants indicated that recording with an AR technology is different than recording with a cell phone (**Cell Phone Comparison: Different**). Elaborations on these answers surfaced some reasons why participants regarded these technologies as creating a different experience for the bystander.

Over half (16/31) of the participants—including Participant V quoted in the Interview Excerpts section—raised the fact that AR glasses are potentially a more subtle form of recording than other form factors (**Subtleness**). Participants indicated that bystanders consequently may not be aware that they are being recorded. This concept of subtleness is somewhat intertwined with the fact that it is relatively easy to initiate a recording (**Ease of Recording**)—an issue that was articulated by 5 participants.

Some participants (8/31) gave another reason why bystanders might not expect to be recorded by AR glasses: the technology's current lack of prevalence (**AR Prevalence**). They indicated that the scarcity of AR devices meant that people would not expect glasses to be recording. In some cases, as in the quote below, the participant explicitly indicated that this expectation would change as the technology becomes more common:

> Participant I (a 43-year-old male working in science): *It's slightly more clandestine, but if it gets popular people would be clued in.*

Perspectives on Recording: Who, What, When, Where, Why, and How

Throughout the course of the interviews, participants expressed a number of factors that affected their feelings towards being recorded. For some participants, these factors described why they prefer not to be recorded. Other participants mentioned factors that affect the circumstances in which it is or is not acceptable to be recorded. While some of these issues have been surfaced in prior work (see Related Work section), we show that they arise again: in a different time and place and with a different technology. We present these factors below in approximate order of their prevalence in interview data.

Place

The majority of participants indicated that **Place** plays a role in whether or not it is acceptable to make recordings. This discussion was predominantly in the context of recording in "public" versus "private." Some of the participants, however, articulated particular places or types of places in which one should not record. Some of these places were unacceptable by virtue of **Social Norms** (bathrooms, bedrooms, in others' homes). Other locations were described as off-limits owing to existing camera policies (locker rooms, theatres, government buildings, gun stores, some cafés and bars). Participants V and W discuss this issue in their interview (see Interview Excerpts).

Bystander Behavior and Sharing Context

Participants indicated that the acceptability of being recorded was somewhat dependent upon what they were doing at the time (**Bystander Behavior**). For example, one participant did not want an AR user to "shoulder surf" her at the ATM. The majority of the references, however, were in the context of impression management. Again in the context of Goffman [13], we might describe people's behavior as an interactive performance tailored to a particular audience. When this performance is taken out of context, undesirable or unanticipated consequences can follow. As a result, sharing images or videos online—or the context in which they are shared—affects bystander feelings regarding being recorded (**Sharing Context**). Participant J (see Interview Excerpts) gives one example of how bystander behavior and sharing can have negative consequences; most participant examples were similar. Participant R (a 35-54 male who works in a mix of entertainment and technology), on the other hand, provides an example where his behavior is not the issue in question, but the sharing context still is: someone else could "superimpose" his recording over a porn film. While this scenario may seem unlikely, it has parallels to media reuse for satirical or damaging purposes.

Perception of Recorder

Participants judged whether or not they minded being recorded based upon their evaluation of the AR user (**Perception of Recorder**). A contextual evaluation is illustrated by the following quote, paraphrased from interview transcripts:

> Participant M (a 60+-year-old male retired marine biologist): *I look over at him, I size him up, and if he doesn't look like a pervert—if he just looks like Joe Schmuck—it's not a problem.*

Participants also indicated that the gender of the person wearing the glasses affected their perception of the device.

Other participants expressed evaluating the AR user based upon his or her perceived role; for example, some participants trusted individuals and distrusted corporate and governmental organizations, while other participants had the opposite reaction:

- Participant O (a 32-year-old female dancer, catechist, and graduate student): *Well, he's—I guess he could be from the government or a large corporation—he's an individual, and I feel like that's fairly benign, and I trust that he's not going to do anything too bad with it.*
- Participant L (a 48-year-old female IT manager and informatics student) is concerned about individuals recording, since they are not held to the same moral and ethical bounds as law enforcement.

Identification

Participants articulated concerns about being recorded by AR technologies based on the idea that they—or others—might be identified in the resulting images or videos (**Identification**). Several participants provided further context regarding their concerns:

- Participant A (a 42-year-old female working in customer service) is a foster parent and is concerned that her foster children might be identified in footage.
- Participant Q (a 35-54 male who works in a mix of entertainment and technology) is concerned that he might be tagged in a video alongside a person of interest or a criminal element, resulting in "guilt by association."
- Participant AE (a 43-year-old female who works in social services) is concerned that victims of domestic violence might be identified online, facilitating abusive ex-partners "coming after them."

Vexation

A few of the participants indicated that they would object to being recorded only if it presented an interruption or an irritation (**Vexation**)—if the AR user was "up in their space" (Participant B, 39-year-old female lawyer) or "disturbing" them (Participant G, 22-year-old male retail worker going to school for graphic design).

Exploring Consent and Control

One of our interview questions probed whether or not participants would want someone to ask them before recording them with AR glasses. The follow-up question asked participants if they would be interested in a device that could block others from recording them. These questions were intended to: (a) surface relevant underlying issues; and (b) explore whether or not a technological mechanism supporting notification, consent (e.g., [4, 8, 29]), or blocking (e.g., [28]) would be of interest to participants.

Permission

Most of the participants (17/31) expressed that they would prefer for someone to ask their permission before recording them with AR glasses (**Permission: Yes**). 7 of them would prefer not be asked or expressed indifference (**Permission: No / Don't Care**). 7 of the responses were uncodable due to ambiguity, truncated interview, or omission (**Permission: Uncodable**). Responses were frequently accompanied with caveats. For example, some participants expressed that they would wish to be asked, but that it is not practical for the AR user to do so (**User Feasibility**). Other participants

Design Axes for Privacy-Mediating Technologies

Push		Pull
Proactive		Reactive
Opt-in		Opt-out
Recording-time		Sharing-time
Compliance-dependent		Compliance-independent
Enforced		Suggested
Place-based	Proximity-based	Identity-based
User-based	Bystander-based	Third-party
Technical	Physical	Social

Figure 2. A breakdown of potential design axes for privacy-mediating technologies. See the Design Considerations section for further discussion.

wished to be asked, but expressed a sense of **Helplessness** regarding their ability to enact their preferences.

For many participants, whether or not they would want their permission sought was dependent upon whether or not they were the focus of the recording (**Focus of Recording**).

Blocking

12 of the participants expressed an interest in a device that would allow them to block others from recording them (**Blocking: Yes**). 6 of the participants were not interested in such a device (**Blocking: No**). 13 participants' responses were uncodable due to interview truncation, omission, or ambiguity (**Blocking: Uncodable**). Participants variously expressed that their interest was dependent upon:

- The cost of the device in question;
- Whether or not they would have to wear the device (versus installing an app on their phone);
- Device size;
- Effort involved in using the device; and
- The prevalence of AR recording devices (for some participants, a prevalence of AR devices would encourage them to use a blocking technology, while for others it was the opposite).

Some participants expressed an interest not particularly for the purpose of blocking AR recording, but for the ability to use them on recording technologies in general:

> Participant O (a 32-year-old female dancer, catechist, and graduate student): *ABSOLUTELY.* [emphasis in transcription] *Not so much for the glasses—I trust the average Joe—but for the cameras everywhere else.*

DESIGN CONSIDERATIONS

The themes that emerge from our results suggest a number of design considerations, both for AR technologies themselves and for companion technologies in the recording ecosystem. We discuss them in the following subsections and ground them with research references.

Figure 2 presents a set of axes by which to characterize or explore the design space of privacy-mediating technologies; these axes provide a framework with which to consider the following discussions. Illustrative references to the axes are included using an italic font.

Offsetting Subtleness and Negotiating Permission

As noted by participants, one of the key ways that AR technologies are different from other technologies is the subtleness of the recording experience for bystanders. Additionally, participants expressed an interest in being asked permission or being able to block recordings. We explore mechanisms for notification, blocking, and permission below.

Physical Measures

Subtleness may be partially offset by visual or aural cues to bystanders that a recording is taking place. Unfortunately, this method runs the risk of being bypassed by malware (e.g., [9]) or by non-compliant devices. Alternatively, devices could be designed such that their cameras may be physically blocked by switches or shutters.

Technical Measures

The possibility of push-pull interactions leads to an array of potential notification and permission mechanisms. For example, an AR device could push notifications to nearby cell phones that a recording is taking place (*push, user-based*). Such a notification could include information about where the recording might be posted. The AR device could solicit privacy preferences from bystanders' devices (*pull, proximity-based*). Alternatively, bystander cell phones could choose to broadcast their owners' privacy preferences (e.g., [4, 8]). Continuing with this example, the AR user might choose to respect the preferences of bystanders and keep a recording private (*social, suggested*). The system could also support sending automated notifications to bystanders if relevant photos or videos are posted (*sharing-time*). One way to support these interactions would be to rely upon messages exchanged while the devices are co-located (*proactive*). Alternatively, the system could cryptographically support sending notifications after the fact while still supporting all parties' anonymity (e.g., [22]).

At the other end of the spectrum, privacy preferences could be technically enforced rather than suggested (*compliance-dependent, enforced*). For example, a system could guarantee that all bystanders have the ability to take down a recording at any time in the future (e.g., [15]). Similarly, some individuals—including some of our participants—may have interest in a technology which actively blocks cameras' ability to record them, with or without the operator's cooperation (*bystander-based, compliance-independent*, e.g., [28]).

A discussion of recording preferences and blocking naturally segues to ethical, philosophical, and legal discussions about the ownership of space, the rights of an AR user, and the ownership of content. Many spaces where recording devices are used are privately owned. As such, the owners or event managers might wish to enforce their own policies (*place-based*, e.g., [5]). On the other hand, such a mechanism has the ability to limit individuals' ability to capture and express material. An individual might want to—or have the moral or legal right to—record for a variety of purposes, including: the creation of digital memories for informational or emotional purposes, self-protection, journalism, or social justice. Another question arises once a recording is created: who has ownership over the data? Although there are exceptions, the current model in social media networks is that the content is owned and managed by the uploader. This can create tensions between the media owner and any subjects in the content. Subjects can manually or automatically ask the owner to untag, restrict access to, or remove the content (*suggested, reactive*, e.g., [7]); however, this does not necessarily circumvent social conflict. Further afield are models for collaborative management of media content (e.g., [31]).

Place as a Social Construct

Previous research has found that the acceptability of recording varies by location, and this study is no exception. Participants indicated that spaces such as homes, locker rooms, and theatres require special treatment. Location and space have definite social and societal meaning, and we do not dispute that there is value in supporting space-based restrictions on recording.

We suggest, however, that designers and technologists consider the broader view of place, rather than space. We use the word "place" to encompass the social characteristics of a space as situated in time and space [16]. For example, an auditorium is a type of space which can at different times host a children's play, an Alcoholics Anonymous meeting, or a burlesque show; each of these events constitutes a different place and has different accompanying social expectations.

While it may be more difficult to form automated decisions based on a social context than on physical location, it is also a more meaningful distinction. Devices could attempt to gather such context based on co-located individuals, online listings, physical artifacts in the environment, or even the user's calendar entries. For example, calendar invites or event locations could include recording policies. Even further afield, AR devices which have "prior knowledge" about a given event space's recording policies could broadcast that knowledge to surrounding devices.

Identification Mitigation

Several participants expressed discomfort with the idea of being recorded on the basis that it facilitates identification. In some cases, participants gave reasons why identification could lead to negative consequences, including bodily harm. Below we explore some potential ways to mitigate this concern.

Individuals might choose to wear opt-out markers (e.g., [29]) if they do not wish to be recorded. Conversely, they could wear opt-in markers if they do not mind being recorded (*opt-in, compliance-based*). However, outside of specific, structured environments, this strategy is most likely unrealistic.

Counterintuitively, if AR devices could rely upon facial recognition to identify everyone in an image, they could then use that information to blur or obfuscate individuals who have previously expressed or registered that they do not want to be recorded (*opt-out, proactive*). It should be noted, however, that this avenue puts the responsibility of registering on the bystander. Moreover, this approach potentially leaks as much private information as it protects. At the other end of the spectrum, facial recognition of acquaintances could be utilized to anonymize everyone who is not an acquaintance, thereby protecting bystanders.

The above approaches could be used to suggest to AR users that they avoid sharing media with sensitive identifications (*identity-based, suggested*). These approaches could also enforce recording deletion or obfuscation (*enforced, compliance-dependent*). As previously discussed, preventing or altering recordings raises questions of the AR user's rights to aesthetic and accurate memories—not to mention the implications regarding legal evidence (e.g., [10]).

Further afield, bystanders or social media platforms could run independent "watchdog" software (*third-party, reactive*). These agents could review media where the bystander might appear based on metadata such as time and place (e.g., [17]). This approach would allow bystanders to monitor their appearances in public data without relying upon ecosystems or interoperating protocols (*bystander-based, compliance-independent*).

DISCUSSION

The interviews took place in cafés in Seattle: a city with multiple universities and a concentration of technology companies. We expect that general bystander perspectives regarding recording will shift by city, region, and country. Moreover, while cafés are a rich source for study, they do not capture the full scope of human behaviors. This methodology could be extended to a variety of location types with pertinent theoretical properties, such as: power dynamics (e.g., workplace); specific population types (e.g., playground); disheveled appearances (e.g., gyms); or casual atmosphere (e.g., bars).

In our study, we investigate how individuals perceive AR-style recording in comparison to other classes of recording devices. Participants were split as to whether or not AR devices create a substantively new bystander experience; those who found it different cited subtleness, ease of recording, and the current lack of prevalence as the relevant factors. The scarcity of AR devices is not an inherent property of the technology; however, it can contribute to whether or not an individual expects to be recorded. It remains to be seen whether these factors continue to be perceived as relevant as the novelty of the technology fades.

People frequently: (a) are unable to adequately assess their reactions to a technology before they encounter it—an obstacle which we attempt to lessen with our interview methodology (see Methodology Discussion); (b) change their perceptions with repeated exposure to the technology; or (c) change their views as they become active users of the technology (e.g., [27]). Data gathered now may or may not reflect how individuals will perceive AR recording in the future; either way, it can be used to characterize the adoption of an emerging technology.

Participants expressed interest in the possibility of being asked permission and being able to block recording devices; however, they expressed concerns regarding feasibility and convenience. These factors suggest that privacy-mediating technologies are a space that merit further research. We discuss a range of such technologies in our Design Considerations section. Furthermore, we characterize the systems by supplying axes for design directions (e.g., *proactive* vs. *reactive*, *enforced* vs. *suggested*, *technical* vs. *physical* vs. *social*). The investigation of such technologies is timely: the nascence of AR technologies can potentially be used to bootstrap the inclusion of privacy-mediating measures. The utility of such measures and the utility of characterizing axes extend beyond AR devices to new classes of emerging technologies.

CONCLUSIONS

Glasses-style AR devices are starting to enter the commercial marketplace. The recording capabilities of these devices have the potential to increase the frequency with which bystanders are recorded in publicly accessible locations. While there has been much controversy in the media surrounding these technologies, little is known about how the general populace perceives such devices.

We sought to help address this knowledge gap with an in-situ qualitative study: we wore a glasses-style AR mockup in cafés and conducted semi-structured interviews with café patrons. Subsequent analysis yielded a variety of information: for example, participants described AR recording as different from other types of recording due to its subtleness and the current scarcity of AR devices. Participants also surfaced factors that make recording less acceptable. For instance, their reactions to recording can be affected by their perception of the AR user and whether or not they can be identified in the recording. Many participants expressed interest in being asked permission or being able to block recording devices; however, they were concerned about the logistics of such capabilities.

We use our interview results to guide a discussion on design considerations for privacy-mediating technologies. Additionally, we contextualize the technical directions with a number of potential design axes (e.g., *push* vs. *pull*, *sharing-time* vs. *recording-time*, *place-based* vs. *proximity-based* vs. *identity-based*).

The fact that AR technologies are nascent affords opportunities to the research community. Since these devices are not yet common, we can study how perceptions and usage develop throughout their adoption. Moreover, we have the opportunity to explore privacy-mediating mechanisms; the user experience for AR devices has not yet become standardized. Our hope is that findings from this and similar studies will help emerging technologies such as AR devices respect the priorities of all stakeholders.

ACKNOWLEDGMENTS

We thank the participants and the study locations for their time. We thank David Molnar for the loan of his equipment. We thank Eun Kyoung Choe, Karen Fisher, Jaeyeon Jung, Julie Kientz, Adam Lerner, David Molnar, Alex Moshchuk, Oriana Riva, Franziska Roesner, Helen Wang, and Information School students for their input. We thank the Pervasive Computing Intel Science and Technology Center. We thank Security Innovation.

REFERENCES

1. Abowd, G.D., Hayes, G.R., Iachello, G., Kientz, J.A., Patel, S.N., Stevens, M.M., and Truong, K.N. Prototypes and Paratypes: Designing Mobile and Ubiquitous Computing Applications. *IEEE Pervasive Computing 4*, 4 (2005).
2. Adams, A. Multimedia Information Changes the Whole Privacy Ballgame. In *Proc. Computers, Freedom and Privacy 2000*.

3. Bailey, J. and Kerr, I. Seizing Control?: The Experience Capture Experiments of Ringley & Mann. *Ethics and Information Technology 9*, 2 (2007).

4. Barhm, M.S., Qwasmi, N., Qureshi, F.Z., and el-Khatib, K. Negotiating Privacy Preferences in Video Surveillance Systems. In *Proc. Modern Approaches in Applied Intelligence 2011.*

5. Bell, M. and Lovich, V. US Patent: 8254902 - Apparatus and Methods for Enforcement of Policies Upon a Wireless Device. 2012.

6. Bellotti, V. and Sellen, A. Design for Privacy in Ubiquitous Computing Environments. In *Proc. CSCW 1993.*

7. Besmer, A. and Lipford, H.R. Moving Beyond Untagging: Photo Privacy in a Tagged World. In *Proc. CHI 2010.*

8. Brassil, J. Technical Challenges in Location-Aware Video Surveillance Privacy. In *Protecting Privacy in Video Surveillance*, 2009.

9. Brocker, M. and Checkoway, S. iSeeYou: Disabling the MacBook Webcam Indicator LED. Department of Computer Science, John Hopkins University. Technical Report 13-02. 2013.

10. Cheng, W.C., Golubchik, L., and Kay, D.G. Total Recall: Are Privacy Changes Inevitable? In *Proc. CARPE 2004.*

11. Choe, E.K., Consolvo, S., Jung, J., Harrison, B., Patel, S.N., and Kientz, J.A. Investigating Receptiveness to Sensing and Inference in the Home Using Sensor Proxies. In *Proc. UbiComp 2012.*

12. Friedman, B., Kahn, P. H., Jr., Hagman, J., Severson, R. L., and Gill, B. The Watcher and the Watched: Social Judgments about Privacy in a Public Place. *Human-Computer Interaction 21*, 2006.

13. Goffman, E. The Presentation of Self. *Life as Theater: A Dramaturgical Sourcebook (2nd ed.)*, 2006.

14. Google. Glass. http://www.google.com/glass/.

15. Halderman, J.A., Waters, B. and Felten, E. W. Privacy Management for Portable Recording Devices. In *Proc. WPES 2004.*

16. Harrison, S. and Dourish, P. Re-Place-ing Space: The Roles of Place and Space in Collaborative Systems. In *Proc. CSCW 1996.*

17. Henne, B. Szongott, C. and Smith, M. SnapMe if You Can: Privacy Threats of Other Peoples' Geo-Tagged Media and What We Can Do About It. In *Proc. WiSec 2013.*

18. Iachello, G., Truong, K.N., Abowd, G.D., Hayes, G.R. and Stevens, M. Prototyping and Sampling Experience to Evaluate Ubiquitous Computing Privacy in the Real World. In *Proc. CHI 2006.*

19. Kahneman, D., Krueger, A.B., Schkade, D.A., Schwarz, N., and Stone, A.A. A Survey Method for Characterizing Daily Life Experience: The Day Reconstruction Method. *Science 306*, 5702 (2004).

20. Mancini, C., Rogers, Y., Bandara, A.K., Coe, T., Jedrzejczyk, L., Joinson, A.N., Price, B.A., Thomas, K., and Nuseibeh, B. Contravision: Exploring Users' Reactions to Futuristic Technology. In *Proc. CHI 2010.*

21. Mann, S. and Ferenbok, J. New Media and the Power Politics of Sousveillance in a Surveillance-Dominated World. *Surveillance & Society 11*, 1/2 (2013).

22. Manweiler, J., Scudellari, R., Cancio, Z., and Cox, L.P. We Saw Each Other on the Subway: Secure, Anonymous Proximity-Based Missed Connections. In *Proc. HotMobile 2009.*

23. Massimi, M., Truong, K. N., Dearman, D., and Hayes, G. R. Understanding Recording Technologies in Everyday Life. *IEEE Pervasive Computing 9*, 3 (2010).

24. Meta. SpaceGlasses. https://www.spaceglasses.com/.

25. Nguyen, D.H., Bedford, A., Bretana, A.G., and Hayes, G.R. Situating the Concern for Information Privacy Through an Empirical Study of Responses to Video Recording. In *Proc. CHI 2011.*

26. Nguyen, D. H., Marcu, G., Hayes, G. R., Truong, K. N., Scott, J., Langheinrich, M., and Roduner, C. Encountering SenseCam: Personal Recording Technologies in Everyday Life. In *Proc. Ubicomp 2009.*

27. Palen, L., Salzman, M., and Youngs, E. Going Wireless: Behavior & Practice of New Mobile Phone Users. In *Proc. CSCW 2000.*

28. Patel, S.N., Summet, J.W., and Truong, K.N. BlindSpot: Creating Capture-Resistant Spaces. In *Protecting Privacy in Video Surveillance*, 2009.

29. Schiff, J., Meingast, M., Mulligan, D.K., Sastry, S., and Goldberg, K. Respectful Cameras: Detecting Visual Markers in Real-Time to Address Privacy Concerns. In *Protecting Privacy in Video Surveillance*, 2009.

30. Smith, H.J., Milberg, S.J., and Burke, S.J. Information Privacy: Measuring Individuals' Concerns about Organizational Practices. *MIS Quarterly 20*, 2 (1996).

31. Squicciarini, A.C., Xu, H., and Zhang, X. CoPE: Enabling Collaborative Privacy Management in Online Social Networks. *J. Am. Soc. Inf. Sci. Technol. 62*, 3 (2011).

32. Starner, T., Mann, S., Rhodes, B., et al. *Augmented Reality Through Wearable Computing*, 1997.

33. Technical Illusions. CastAR. http://www.kickstarter.com/projects/technicalillusions/castar-the-most-versatile-ar-and-vr-system.

Listening to the Forest and its Curators: Lessons Learnt from a Bioacoustic Smartphone Application Deployment

Stuart Moran[1], Nadia Pantidi[1], Tom Rodden[1], Alan Chamberlain[1], Chloe Griffiths[2], Davide Zilli[3], Geoff Merrett[3] and Alex Rogers[3]

[1]Mixed Reality Lab, University of Nottingham, UK, {firstname.lastname}@nottingham.ac.uk

[2]Located Knowledge Lab, Wales, UK, C.Griffiths@LocatedKnowledgeLab.org

[3]Electronics and Computer Science, University of Southampton, UK, {dz2v07;gvm;acr}@ecs.soton.ac.uk

ABSTRACT

Our natural environment is complex and sensitive, and is home to a number of species on the verge of extinction. Surveying is one approach to their preservation, and can be supported by technology. This paper presents the deployment of a smartphone-based citizen science biodiversity application. Our findings from interviews with members of the biodiversity community revealed a tension between the technology and their established working practices. From our experience, we present a series of general guidelines for those designing citizen science apps.

Author Keywords

Bioacoustics; biodiversity; citizen science; community practices; mobile; participatory sensing; tradition; tension.

ACM Classification Keywords

H.5.2 [Information Interfaces and Presentation]: User Interfaces - Interaction styles

INTRODUCTION

Debates concerning our environment often center on the threat people pose to the biological diversity of our planet. A raft of national and global initiatives has emerged to highlight the importance of biodiversity and the threat posed by the extinction of species. A critical part of many of these initiatives centers on gathering detailed information about the diversity of our natural world and the status of the variety of species involved. Initiatives such as the IUCN red list (www.iucnredlist.org) maintain a detailed record of species under threat. Core to this is the undertaking of surveys of our natural world to capture evidence of species and to understand the nature of the particular population. The scale involved in capturing the biological diversity of our planet is vast. The need to capture information about species is becoming ever more critical given the rate with which natural habitats are disappearing. This is particularly important as environmentalists need evidence to inform environmental policies and to argue for programmes of intervention.

The scale of the task at hand and its societal importance makes biodiversity a natural candidate to exploit the growing trend of citizen science. Initiatives such as Galaxy Zoo (www.galaxyzoo.org) or Folding @ home (http://folding.stanford.edu/) have utilized digital technologies to recruit volunteers from the general public to tackle critical scientific challenges. Volunteers have been provided access through a growing number of internet tools to catalogue galaxies, transcribe handwritten texts and help in the folding of protein structures. The increasingly ubiquitous nature of smartphones that offer sophisticated sensing capabilities has opened up the possibility of moving these volunteer citizen scientists out of the home and into the field allowing the general population to be engaged in undertaking the species surveys so critical to biodiversity and consequently conservation.

This paper presents the development and deployment of a smartphone-based citizen science biodiversity application. The application seeks to recruit members of the general public to find evidence of a rare cicada in the UK that might already be extinct. The challenge of finding evidence for the cicada is that its distinctive chirp is at a frequency that is only just audible to the human ear. However, it is within the range of the microphones in most smartphones. Hence, it is possible to record, process and detect a cicada's song directly on the phone; with location determined by the GPS.

We discuss findings from a set of studies that involved interviews with employed biodiversity professionals and volunteer amateur naturalists as well as observations of a biodiversity event where the app was launched to the general public. In addition to commenting upon the application itself, our studies highlight the distinctive challenges that emerge as citizen science goes mobile and engages with scientific endeavors in the field. Although offering considerable potential advantages in terms of scale and engagement with the public, the turn to citizen science in biodiversity also raises tension in terms of the nature of the scientific endeavor, and its current culture and practices. We elaborate some of these key tensions and suggest a

CHI 2014, April 26–May 1, 2014, Toronto, Ontario, Canada.
Copyright ©ACM 978-1-4503-2473-1/14/04...$15.00.
http://dx.doi.org/10.1145/2556288.2557022

number of general guidelines for those involved in the development of citizen science applications.

BACKGROUND

While citizen science is a relatively new term, the tradition of public participation and collaboration in scientific research goes back centuries. Indeed much of this has focused on capturing information about the natural world. The National Audubon Society's Christmas Bird Count (http://birds.audubon.org/christmas-bird-count) was established in 1900, and continues even today, with amateur and professional bird watchers joining forces in cataloguing bird species. There are instances of recording even earlier than this, as during the 17th century farmers, hunters, clergymen and other members of the public actively contributed in collecting and classifying various nature datasets for research purposes [3,18].

Today, citizen science has been able to take advantage of internet based technologies. Citizen scientists work remotely on large-scale data sets that are increasingly becoming a key feature of scientific investigation in the natural sciences. For example, Galaxy Zoo engaged the public in examining images of galaxies and classifying their basic characteristics. While the bat detective project (www.batdetective.org) asks volunteers to identify potential bat calls in audio surveys collected by researchers. Other projects have gamified aspects of such classifying tasks to make them more appealing to a wider audience, motivating and educating the public involved in the project [1]. Web-based communities have also been formed to support socialising and sharing between citizen scientists such as eBird [24] and Key To Nature [17].

Advancements in mobile and ubiquitous technologies have allowed a move away from domestic desktop interaction, and enabled people to contribute valuable new datasets by engaging with their environment *in-situ*. Participatory sensing approaches enable people equipped with sensors or their own mobile devices to collect information from their environment as part of their everyday activities and interpret it within context [5,6]. Environmental impact has been a particular focus for participatory sensing with the general public tracking and measuring climate change and pollution [2,8,19].

Existing work in participatory sensing for sustainability has shown positive results in making people more aware of, and actively engaged with, their environment. It has also shown the importance of the *in-situ* experience and how it can contribute to the interpretation of the collected data [6,12,20]. Education has also played an important role, with environment-visiting based work such as Ambient Wood [21], Ubigreen [11] and e-Science in schools [23] using mobile devices/sensors to educate participants about the environment. These systems emphasize managed groups [4] openly exploring, and reflecting on the physical space [13,21]. In distinct contrast, Citizen Science has emphasized using an anonymous crowd to survey/analyze data. Work related to this has revealed a number of challenges in terms of privacy, storage, dissemination and interpretation of the data. Paxton and Benford [20] stress the "*complex balance between the various needs, limitations and the preferences of both the users and the sensing tools*" and how this can affect both the experience of the user as well as the quality of the data interpretation. In considering this, along with the capabilities of mobile phones today, we can see that participatory sensing lends itself to the field of biodiversity monitoring, in terms of supporting the recording and classification of species.

Bioacoustic Participatory Sensing

One of the main benefits in the use of mobile phones for biodiversity is in the use of their microphones as a sensor [14]. In many respects this can serve as an ideal tool for species surveying. As would be expected, acoustic sensors typically focus on species with *recordable* and *predictable* vocalizations, such as amphibians, insects and birds [26]. With an ongoing trend in the increased adoption of smartphones by the public, there is a move toward utilizing the onboard microphone for recording purposes. There are already projects which make use of microphones, such as CrowdSense@Place [7] for the classification of places based on sound and NoiseTube [16] for assessing noise pollution. Much of this work relies on server-side post processing of the recordings using software such as the Extensible Bioacoustic Tool (XBAT) [10]. Equally, with the computational power available on smartphones, there exist possibilities for localised classification of acoustics. This type of automatic detection for surveying has been described as the '*ultimate*' smartphone application [15], and as a paradigm shift for many ecologists [26]. In the following section we describe a smartphone application that seeks to bring about such a shift.

CICADA HUNT MOBILE APPLICATION

The New Forest cicada (*Cicadetta montana s. str.*) is the only cicada native to the UK. The prevalence of the species is currently in question as the last *unconfirmed* sighting of the cicada was in 2000. Along with a general decline in the species there are three problems, which make surveying for the cicada particularly challenging for professionals.

1) The New Forest cicada lives underground for seven to eight years as a larva, before emerging and taking on its adult form for just four to six weeks between May and July. Unlike periodical cicada, its emergence is not synchronized, and thus, this significantly decreases the number of cicadas present during the already small and tight timeframe.
2) The size of the New Forest is approximately 600km^2, making it impossible for a small number of experts to effectively cover the area during the few sunny days when the males sing.
3) The cicada sings at a frequency of 13-14kHz, which is at the limits of hearing for most adults. This makes

one of the primary means of in situ identification of insects by experts unusable (i.e. listening).

These difficulties in coverage, detection and a narrow season motivated the surveyors to explore the possibilities of a technological solution. Through a series of meetings with core stakeholders (expert entomologists and members of the New Forest National Park Authority), the use of participatory sensing was agreed upon as a viable and effective technological medium for promoting and assisting in the survey of the cicada; particularly given the untapped ~13 million day-visits per year to the New Forest National Park.

Design and Development

The pervasiveness of smartphone ownership underpins their appeal as a participatory sensing tool in the forest setting. Furthermore, through trials it was found that the microphone in a typical smartphone was sensitive enough to pick up the frequency of the cicada. To assist in the process of acoustic classification, an algorithm was developed to accurately distinguish and specifically detect the New Forest cicada [27]. Given the onboard computational power available on smart phones, it was also possible to run the (typically server side) classification algorithm locally on the device in real time. This classifier is based on a hidden Markov model, which is fed the ratio of two key frequencies extracted through the Goertzel algorithm as a single feature vector (for more details see [27]). It was trained using recordings from Slovenia where the same species of cicada is still abundant. The classifier also has the potential to detect common species of Orthoptera, including: wood cricket, Roesel's bush cricket and a field grasshopper.

An interesting constraint during the design of the app was the difficulty in trialling it in-situ. For this reason, a number of circuit board 'electronic cicadas' were developed to emit a constant acoustic square wave between 15kHz–18kHz to imitate the cicada's song. These were used during preliminary field trials of the application which were subsequently used to iteratively inform the design of the mobile application.

The final design (called 'Cicada Hunt') included a sonogram, which was used to visualise the algorithm, taking inspiration from the popular music application Shazam (www.shazam.com) and drawing on a user's likely familiarity with it. The sonogram was thus visualised in a circular way, as opposed to the more commonly found horizontal format. The sonogram displayed the real-time fluctuations relating to the audio's frequency and amplitude. This detail was not only intended to act as a means of education for users about frequency and sound, but also to speak to professionals who frequently make use of sonograms. Interaction with the application was designed to be as simple and lightweight as possible, in order to serve

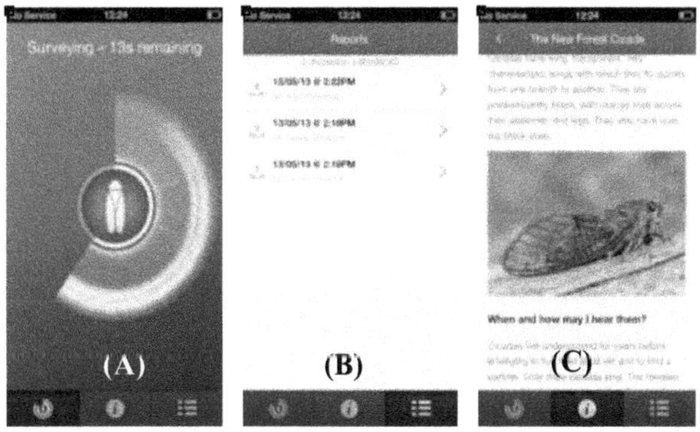

Figure 1 'Cicada Hunt' mobile phone application

many different types of users. To use the app, users press the cicada icon (see Figure 1 (A)) to start a survey, which records and analyses the next 30 seconds of audio in the environment.

If a cicada is detected, the users are informed and a report consisting of the location, time, and audio, is uploaded to a server. In the case of a negative record, a report is also being sent with the location, date and time but without any sound file. Users can review the record of their sent reports on the app (see Figure 1 (B)) and can also access information about the app itself (instructions, project), the cicada species and habitat, and the New Forest National Park in general (see Figure 1 (C)). Access to all users' records is provided through a password protected dashboard on the project's website.

A typical feature of a participatory sensing application is the use of a map to indicate where surveys have been conducted. This can help with motivating surveyors to fill in the recording gaps on the map and also to create a sense of community. However, during pre-development discussion with the stakeholders, this was not perceived as a desirable feature as it was anticipated that it might encourage users to wander off the tracks and venture deep into the forest (to fill the gaps). This is a particular problem, as the cicada and ground nesting bird seasons coincide. For this reason, this feature was consciously excluded from the application.

Deployment and Use

The application was launched on both the iOS app store and the Android Google play store during May 2013 (search for 'Cicada Hunt'). This was intended to coincide with the emergence of the cicadas. The app was promoted through significant news press coverage and with a launch event during a Bioblitz. Over a period of 3 months, more than 4,000 surveys were conducted, and 1,500 unique downloads to phones; unfortunately no cicada was found. The top ten users accounted for almost ¼ of all surveys, suggesting a key group of power users (see Figure 2). While these usage statistics provide some indication of the level of use of the app, they say little about who used it and what the issues involved in using the app might be.

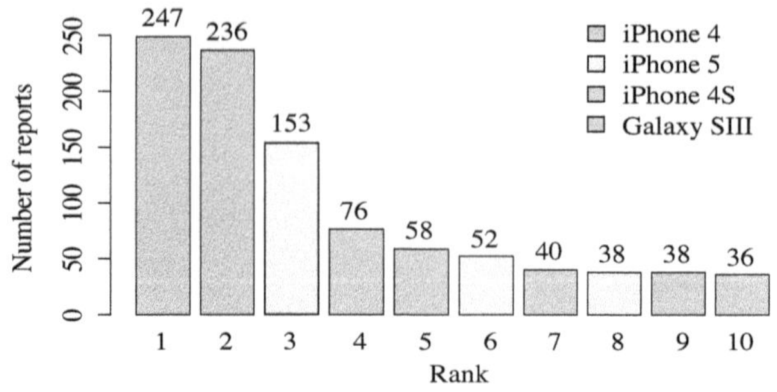

Figure 2 Top ten anonymous power users and their devices

Method

In order to build a richer picture of app use, we carried out a number of in-depth interviews with a range of employed biodiversity professionals and volunteer amateur naturalists. Participants were selected based on the types of biodiversity activities they engage with. We focused on those that carry out surveying, store and manage data, and make strategic decisions regarding forest management. Participants were approached through the New Forest National Park Authority (NFNPA) and local surveying groups in Hampshire and Sherwood. Interviews were carried out at locations where participants conduct their activities (i.e. during the bioblitz, at the New Forest National Park Authority and at the Sherwood Forest Trust). A total of 15 participants were interviewed (~1 hour), with 8 male and 7 female, aged between 23-72. Interviews were conducted over a 3 month period. Participants are grouped by role and location:

1) Forest Managers, NFPA [**FM1**, **FM2**, **FM3**]
2) Ecologists, NFPA [**E1**, **E2**, **E3**, **E4**]
3) Biological Data Managers, NFPA [**D1**, **D2**, **D3**]
4) Community Managers, Sherwood [**CM1**, **CM2**]
5) Rangers, Sherwood [**R1**, **R2**]
6) Ecologist, Ceredigion [**E5**]

Ecologists and rangers are active fieldworkers who directly conduct surveys of the environment. They carry out similar curation-based tasks, but each specialises in a particular species including: birds, bats, lizards, dragonflies and pond life. The remaining roles are typically adopted by ecologists later on in their careers. For example, biological data managers who receive the data from surveys, storing the information in databases and managing how it is shared internally or across local authorities. Forest and community managers focus on strategic decisions related to cultural and natural heritage, landscape and habitat preservation, and public engagement activities. During the interviews, our focus was the utility of a citizen science approach to the scientists involved, how the application was received by domain experts (professionals and amateurs) and how it might be used for surveying and educating the public. Interviews were transcribed in full, and an inductive thematic analysis was carried out. The data was iteratively coded at a low level, and grouped together to reveal themes.

The interview results were augmented with a number of short participant-observation studies during a public biodiversity event in the New Forest (Bioblitz). Bioblitzes are outdoor events where members of the public meet-up with professional naturalists to intensively survey as many species as possible over a 24 hour period. The aim is to both engage the public with nature and collect genuine survey data. Approximately 60 people, mainly young families and older amateur naturalists, took part during the event. The event was held in an open field in the New Forest, with pop-up stalls providing different nature related activities for children and for signing up to organised surveys. We observed a number of these intensive surveys over the 24 hours including: moth, bat, plant, bird, seashore and pond surveys (see Figure 3). Each event saw small groups (up to 10) guided by a professional naturalist, conducting real surveys of the species over a few hours. This gave us the opportunity to better understand some of the existing practices of surveying, but to also examine how they are used to engage members of the public. The cicada app was also officially launched to the public during the event from a stall which provided free Wi-Fi. This gave us the opportunity to observe and discuss the use of the application in-situ.

Through the interviews and the actual deployment of the cicada mobile application the tension between engaging and inviting citizens to the forest, and protecting the habitat of the species under consideration came to the fore. This tension underpinned the previous decision to exclude the map style interface traditionally associated with participatory sensing approaches. As we began to unpack this, we found that the app was surfacing critical issues about the use of citizen science for biodiversity. However, before we consider these issues in detail, it is worth understanding the nature of the biodiversity community.

THE BIODIVERSITY COMMUNITY

The biodiversity community includes both biodiversity professionals and amateur naturalists who play an active role in the work of the community. Biodiversity professionals are involved as part of their job with the natural environment. Their daily work entails a variety of activities depending on their specific role but, in general, they engage with monitoring and preserving natural habitats and the species that are part of those. Some of them might be forest rangers; others might be ecologists, scientists (entomologists, botanists etc) or heritage specialists. Most of them share their time between being out in the field observing and collecting information about species, and deskwork analysing that information, creating reports and disseminating them for purposes of planning, policy making and educating.

Amateur naturalist is a term used by the biodiversity professionals to describe members of the general public that engage in species surveys and other biodiversity activities.

Figure 3 Bio Blitz in the New Forest National Park

Amateur naturalists self identify with the term and distinguish themselves from the professionals despite the fact that sometimes they are just as knowledgeable as a result of their long-term engagement with species recording. Very often, they are locals, residents near a park area that work closely with the county recorders in regular, organized group surveys or people who just record things on their own while walking the dog.

The biodiversity community, both professionals and amateur naturalists, share an affinity and sense of wonder for the natural environment that motivates them to engage with its preservation. In many cases this seems to have been instilled in them from a young age. Many of the professionals that we interviewed vividly described memories of their childhood with family walks in the forest and the excitement of seeing and getting to know more about the species:

"From an early age with my parents and they instilled that kind of... the wonder of nature and the world is such a diverse place and people are so diverse [...] and they take it for granted. To understand it is just beautiful and it changes, day to day, season to season [...] you always learn something new no matter where you went." CM1

Protecting the natural environment is of utmost importance for this community. Biodiversity professionals identified two activities as vital in achieving that: conducting surveys and educating the public; in particular children. Instilling a love of nature, biodiversity and its preservation in the younger generations is of great importance for all professional and amateur naturalists:

"I'm in to what I do because of my dad. You know, a natural interest from a young age. I went out with him and I fell in love with nature, but a lot of kids these days don't have that [...] you need to get them while they're young to kind of nurture that interest and that passion." R1

"If I have enthused, you know, 5 kids really into it, really excited, for me that makes my job worthwhile." R2

Survey as a Tool of Data Collection

The emotional attachment to their work is also reflected in the professionals' view of surveys and the tools used for surveying. Despite the advances and availability of technology in this digital era, professionals tend to conduct

Figure 4 Amateur naturalists surveying species on paper

surveys using pen and paper, and ID books (see Figure 4). Several reported using a camera or audio recorder and a GPS to define location, but equally admitted to avoiding using digital devices when possible as they lack the romanticism of the old ways. Pointing at a smartphone, one of our participants said:

"There is nothing romantic about this, you can see the records but you cannot feel them as you would with the ones in your nature diary." E1

In the same context, another referred to the feel of their field guide:

"You have your field guide that you have had for years and you know, you kinda know the pages because of the way you have twisted them? It's things like that isn't it?" R2

Amateur naturalists conduct surveys in the same way, often with even less digital support unless this is done in the context of a joint organized survey with the professionals. After a survey is complete, the collected records usually have to be transferred into a digital form so that they can be disseminated, checked and archived in county and national databases, and planning, management and policy making offices or other relevant organizations. Not only is this process tedious, but it is also clear that people are not particularly inclined to share data:

"You suspect there's an awful lot of useful data out there, but some people umm don't like sharing it [...] it's easy for them to put in a note book and then it's more hard work and perhaps not so much what they want to do is to then get those records into the biological record centres." E2

"[Another heritage group] been surveying for 40 odd years, and they've got a fantastic database but they won't let us see it." D3

Checking the work of volunteers

Accessing, disseminating and checking survey records is also challenging with respect to the volunteers. Biodiversity professionals and amateur naturalists both stressed a distinct lack of consistency among the recordings of volunteers:

"When you get some data in, from some people that will be very meticulous, to the letter and ya know [...] and then you get really sketchy data, and to try to put the two lots of data together... was

quite difficult, so I think maybe the apps might help a little more uniformity and that data reduction." E3

This fuels a general suspicion of data collected by volunteers and the extent to which it can be used for biodiversity purposes:

"There needs to be some clear scientific vetting, to say that that is a confirmed record or a possible record, so we have certainty over the presence or not of a species." CM1

This is obviously highly problematic and while standardizing data collection techniques (including the use of digital entry systems) and intensive training sessions can address these issues, the concern remains about not knowing who has done the survey:

"It could be anyone. I think the thing is when you're dealing with individuals, people are going to each do things to a greater or lesser level." E3

However, recruiting volunteers willing to be trained makes a challenging task even more difficult: *"finding groups that want to come out and do surveys is a challenge in itself"* (CM1) which often results in compromising with less accurate data or more verification work from the professionals' part.

In addition to providing data, surveys are also increasingly used as a means of public engagement. Recruiting the general public to participate in surveys is as much about enthusing them and promoting awareness about particular habitats and species as it is about scaling data collection.

Surveys as a Tool of Engagement

As mentioned earlier, getting the public engaged with and enthused by the natural environment as well as educating them on the dangers it is facing and how these can be addressed is a significant part of biodiversity conservation. To increase the numbers of survey volunteers and nurture a long-term engagement, day-long or weekend events are organized where professionals, amateur naturalists and the general public get together to learn and conduct species surveys. Social media is also starting to become more popular in supporting the organizing and publicizing of these and other biodiversity activities.

Scepticism for the use of the digital *in capturing data* was evident when biodiversity professionals and amateur naturalists spoke about doing surveys. However, this is replaced by enthusiasm when the digital serves as a *means of engagement*. Digital technology is seen as a way to entice and engage new (in particular young) people into the tradition of nature conservation and surveying:

"The younger generation do everything digitally don't they?" E5

"It is like social media [...] I don't mind some aspects of it, but some of it I would rather do without, but unfortunately it is a very powerful tool for interacting with large audiences [...] things will move on, gradually technology, people's aspirations and interests, and we will be left behind." R1

Still, concerns remain about the extent to which social media is used and what this might mean in terms of people's experience of the natural world.

"I do think that we need to be careful that we use it as a means to an end, rather than an end itself. So social media is great, but if we have everybody sitting at home just looking at pictures of the New Forest, then I think that's not right, to properly love something, to get a connection with something, then we do have to try and realise that umm firsthand experience [...] ya know going and seeing a tree or witnessing butterflies in a meadow, those are the important things." FM1

Several still see technology engagement and the engagement with the natural environment as clashing; the latter should be about *being in nature* and *being with each other in nature*. Discussion on the use of the app brought this into sharp contrast:

"Personally I don't really like it as much as you physically going out there having a natural interaction, but I think unfortunately given the fact that time has moved on, technology has moved on, it is the 21st century now, things have changed, you do need some other approach if you want to appeal to new people." R1

"People have said things about umm being in wild places being an escape from technology, and an escape from always being in communication with people and that they feel technology stands between people somehow as a barrier between people." E5

Having presented the ways in which biodiversity professionals and amateur naturalists view public involvement and the role of the survey, it is clear that the turn to digitally mediated citizen science might raise a number of issues for this community. In the following section we discuss their reactions to the cicada app.

OLD PRACTICES AND NEW TOOLS

With a more grounded understanding of the existing motivations, practices and traditions of expert users, we can now explore and better appreciate the ways in which the cicada application was received during the deployment and follow-up interviews. As the Cicada Hunt application moved from its initial design to a deployed real world application it brought into focus the underlying sensitivities within the community and the tensions surrounding the involvement of the public in biodiversity surveys.

Disturbing the Forest

As the Cicada Hunt application was deployed, the distinct nature of the environment emerged as a critical issue. The environment itself is a fragile entity which needs preservation as much as the cicada does; indeed the two are interdependent. As the nature of the interaction with the environment became clearer, so did concerns about the possibility that untrained citizens using the app might disturb or interfere with the habitats:

"I suppose the danger with the app is that you are actively encouraging people on to sensitive habitats, which might not be visited in the normal course of their visit." FM1

This issue was particularly significant given the open and rather accessible nature of the environment itself:

"The New Forest is in this special situation because it's open access throughout and [...] people can penetrate quite deeply into areas which are reasonably tranquil and undisturbed. Now they have the perfect right to do that, so there's no real way you could stop them even if you wanted to." FM1

As well as offering a potential benefit, the Cicada Hunt app was seen by biodiversity professionals and amateur naturalists as offering both a positive promise and a significant threat. Many were torn between sharing their passion for the environment and the potential impact the app might have:

"The concern I have, a lot of people have, is the sheer number of visitors who come to the forest, but my personal feeling is if people come to the forest because they want to observe, study, enjoy the wildlife, that's great." FM2

As well as the potential for physical damage, the concern focused on the extent to which the experience of visiting the new forest would alter:

"On one hand, it would be really exciting if loads of people do it, but on the other hand someone else might be oh god there's thousands of people wandering around with their phones, and that might cause disturbance." E2

Managing How the Forest is Shared

The concern surrounding physical impact was matched by concerns about the digital sharing of information about the forest. Many felt that over-sharing of information and 'knowing too much' about what is in the forest can also cause damage. Reactions drew upon previous systems and stories of the use of other biodiversity apps to illustrate the potential damage to the forest:

"There Is a lot more advantages to the apps than there are disadvantages [...] there are positive things, it is just that occasionally they can be used for the wrong purpose [...] I suppose with the iSpot thing, you take a photo of a flower and you upload it, you don't really think about it do you, until someone goes and digs it up (laughs) [...] it is a shame but unfortunately there are people out there, abusers, it's just about sensitivity." R1

Sharing detailed information was viewed as important when recording data about rare and sensitive species. However, people were concerned in some instances that public sharing of this information may result in the capture or killing of dwindling species:

"They had this very rare fern and they publicized it and collectors came in and collected the fern and it lost its AAA status." R2

"If you show people where sand lizards are on a site then people will go and collect them [...] so there's quite a kind of concern of how the data collected will be made available to people." E4

Some of these even focused on the public's negative reactions to specific species, requiring particular discretion about the publicity of information:

"There's a lot of sensitivity with the public availability of data with adders because that can be a sort of contentious issue, some people don't like knowing that there are adders around because they are concerned, mis-placed concerns in my opinion [...] if someone could find where all the adders were hibernating, they might go there and kill them, which has happened before." E4

The need to control dissemination about the environment engendered a strong sense of ownership of finds and data. This was further amplified by the need to keep data for either publication or exploitation:

"There is a delay because it is quite often [...] we will want to keep that information because we were to publish it in a scientific report, so there is often a time lag between me releasing that information before I have written the paper." E1

Coordinating Activities in the Forest

The forest is also viewed as a managed physical resource that is subject to a range of surveys for different purposes. The need to think how these different activities are coordinated led to a further concern on how public endeavours might interfere with ongoing surveys.

"The other side of sensitivity is because umm I think others are doing surveys, ya know the physical ground survey for the cicada [...] it would just be sods law if umm they'd found a new, ya know a suitable habitat they were just doing, and suddenly yeah just lots of people going through it and disturbing it." E2

"I know this study is out now, actually going in tandem with [...] a parallel scientific contract being led by the forestry commission to look in certain areas where they think they've found, and you wouldn't want [...] any conflict between those. What you want is to, umm, complement." FM1

Automating the Citizen Scientist

Another set of issues focused on the automatic classification of the cicada as part of the app. As people trialled the app, the level of involvement of the person holding the sensor was debated. Many saw the benefits of the automation as simplifying the process. The emphasis on the app as a treasure hunt was seen as a good way to engage the general public with surveying:

"Something that is automatic can be fun, that you can, it is almost like a game really [...] it can give you the confidence if you are starting out [...] to say 'I heard' or 'I saw' and what certainty that you can put to that." R2

The automation was also viewed as a reasonable way to standardize the data collection process without having to train volunteers, offering the opportunity to ease recruitment tensions:

"There are elements of training in my job. It is not as much as it should be, and it is not to high enough standards that I think you can totally guarantee you know someone using the field guide. I

think that is the bit that the app provides, that extra insurance of the quality of the records." CM1

"This automated collection of where the person is, when they've done that, where the record is [...] it cuts out possibly what might be barrier to somebody taking part in the survey." E2

"If people could go out and survey using some technology which would mean they don't have to have like an incredibly detailed knowledge [...] I think that can be quite an empowering thing." E4

The ability to capture sound at a distance was also appealing with respect to interaction with the species:

"The fact that you don't have to physically find something is good from a sort of non-invasive view." CM1

Although some viewed the automation positively, concerns were raised about the impact on learning and loss of skill. This is an important consideration, given the role of surveys in educating people about biodiversity:

"There could be an element of laziness, that, you know, not gonna take it any further, that you just rely on the app to identify it for you, rather than drilling down into it." CM1

"It makes it more accessible for everybody as a hobby [...] cause for me that is the only way really that you start to learn, cause you hear a sound and it finds it automatically... I don't think you learn quite as much, it is not like experiential learning." R2

Many of these concerns echoed the issues of personal attachment to the environment and the drive to share enthusiasm for the environment with the public:

"that would be good, that would be very useful... maybe too useful, maybe it takes all the excitement out of pouring through your text books and looking through various possibilities." FM2

"I've found sort of learning those songs for myself to be a really life-enhancing thing ya know, I can now go for a walk and it feels like I'm kind of experiencing nature in another dimension as well, not only the things I can see but the things I can hear as well." E4

Validation of Results

The importance of verification became an area of scepticism for some experts with respect to the cicada app. They argued that while Cicada Hunt may be automated, there still remains a need to have a human expert verify any app-confirmed detection of a cicada. They also felt that the application may help narrow down the search for the cicada, but it cannot (yet) replace a human expert's identification:

"If the app was to find something, then there would need to be some follow up, you wouldn't just say 'yeah that's fine' and walk away." D1

"You're still always going to need an expert with the skills to identify it [...] you can't just send a whole load of people out with this app and say 'yep, we've found it here, here and here'. It's got to have someone still to go out and check." D2

"I wouldn't want to just rely on [the app] because there's always an exception to any rule isn't there?" E5

Dealing with Disappointment

The framing of the app as a Cicada Hunt also raised comments. Due to its rarity, it was always highly unlikely that users were going to detect the species. This meant that users were likely to experience a significant number of consecutive 'fail' results. This can de-motivate public users, particularly given the effort required to visit and walk around the forest compared to other desktop based crowd sourcing systems:

"To get a report that says nothing found, it just leaves... it could leave people feeling a little cold and empty." CM1

"It's highly likely you're not going to find something. That will put people off, you know there's only so many times 'I still haven't found one', 'I still haven't found one', before you'll just give up." E5

The challenge is how to develop a system that enhances the users' experiences and encourages them to persist.

DISCUSSION

Cicada Hunt wishes to harness the potential of citizen science and participatory sensing to re-discover and protect a rare species. However, as the application was deployed and grew in use, significant issues surfaced surrounding the use of citizen science approaches to tackling biodiversity. In particular, a rather fundamental tension emerged where it became clear that because of its fragility and rarity the species was both supported and endangered by the use of the application. Biodiversity professionals and amateur naturalists recognized the potential of the technology but were concerned about the need to create a balance between widespread searching and the need to educate and protect:

"It is that constant battle though isn't it? It's like, how do you inspire people [...] you've got this amazing plant or amazing species that is here but then it's at the risk of people abusing it, so you can't share nature with people. It's that, do we share it or do we keep it secret? Which a lot of people do keep sites secret, but then a lot of people will never get that advantage to experience something pretty, ya know, amazing biodiversity wise, so it is that kind of weighing it up, where is the line?" CM2

"You want to make it available so you can have interactions shared as experiences and there are places where the people would have that experience but at the same time you don't want it because it is sensitive and it is an endangered species." R1

Other participatory sensing projects have faced a number of challenges with respect to the situated nature of the activity [5,20] yet the cicada application reveals one more. Unlike the sensing of polluted air or traffic patterns, the very sensing of the cicada can contribute to, instead of resolving, the problem that created the need for participatory sensing in the first place. It can also endanger other species in the forest that might be rare. The fragility of the cicada and its habitat creates a new challenge for participatory sensing and citizen science that emerges as a result of the nature of the science. The use of citizen science within biodiversity requires us to collect data in *fragile environments,* about *endangered species* and alongside a community of users who have *established practices* to achieve the same goal.

Our core contribution lies with explicating how use of the crowd plays out in practice when surveying endangered species in a fragile environment. We reflect on this with three lessons learnt that arise from citizen science for biodiversity.

The Danger of Scale: Citizen Science traditionally recruits large anonymous crowds to work online to aid scientists. Such open ended large scale recruitment of inexperienced participants becomes problematic when surveying involves visiting fragile habitats at risk from footfall and direct engagement.

The Need to Curate the Crowd: The challenge is how to curate the crowd both *physically* and *digitally* to protect the environment. Visiting experiences (e.g. [21]) often encourage open inspection of natural settings, but this was a point to be avoided in our case requiring a physical curation of crowd activities. Citizen science emphasizes sharing information with others. However, in fragile environments, controlling information disclosure is often a priority for the curators suggesting the need for digital curation of the crowd.

Recognition of Emotional Engagement: This community has a deep emotional connection with nature and a detachment from technology is cited as an important aspect of this. Consequently, engagement with nature through technology is met with skepticism. This raises a cautionary note for cases where the digital mediates engagement with nature or where digital data collection is foregrounded; and suggests the need for a more mindful and situated approach to the design of technology that understands the broader socio-political framing of environmental issues [9].

To assist designers of this class of biodiversity citizen science application, we propose a series of guidelines in light of the above lessons.

(1) Curating through Technology: A tension exists between recruiting the public to survey and protecting fragile environments. To address this, systems might support physical curation by proactively responding to footfall by guiding users via GPS to protect fragile zones and segmenting areas to allow different forms of surveys to coexist based on the experience of the surveyors.

(2) Managing Disclosure: The sensitive nature of survey results requires disclosure to be carefully managed. The types of data shared and with whom should be carefully considered in order to better protect the environment. This focus on digital curation extends beyond existing approaches to Citizen Science which tend to emphasise open-ended sharing.

(3) Reframing the Survey: There is a need to frame Citizen Science in a way that is considerate to fragile environments. We suggest including interactions with the crowd *before*, *during* and *after* the survey. *Before,* the crowd might be taught about the environment and how to proceed when in it. *During* data collection, the crowd can be proactively managed with feedback on their movement and the environment. *After* the crowd has experienced the forest, the collected data should be managed accordingly to protect the environment.

(4) Promoting Discussion: Citizen Science offers the opportunity to promote discussion and reflection on broader environmental and sustainability issues [4]. This may take the form of social media [25] or even build upon the use of narratives in pervasive sensing systems (e.g. [22]).

CONCLUSION

Cicada Hunt aimed to educate and engage members of the public in assisting the re-discovery and conservation of an endangered species simply by performing short audio surveys with their mobiles phones while visiting the New Forest. The in situ deployment illustrated a number of issues that are critical to how such applications can be both beneficial and problematic to the preservation of species and the environment in general, which highlights the need to reconsider their design and potentially the role of citizens altogether. What is involved in using technological devices within a physically sensitive context or in educating the general public to the standards of the professionals arises as the critical debate for biodiversity citizen sensing applications. This calls for a closer coupling between the tradition of biodiversity surveying, educating citizens and the design of such technologies with respect to the fragility of our environment.

REFERENCES

1. Von Ahn, L. Games with a purpose. *Computer 39*, 6 (2006), 92–94.
2. Aoki, P.M., Honicky, R.J., Mainwaring, A., et al. A vehicle for research: Using street sweepers to explore the landscape of environmental community action. *Proceedings of SIGCHI Conference on Human Factors in Computing Systems*, ACM (2009), 375–384.
3. Brenna, B. Clergymen abiding in the fields: The making of the naturalist observer in eighteenth-century norwegian natural history. *Science in Context 24*, 2 (2011), 143–66.
4. Brynjarsdottir, H., Håkansson, M., Pierce, J., Baumer, E., DiSalvo, C., and Sengers, P. Sustainably unpersuaded: how persuasion narrows our vision of sustainability. *Proceedings of the SIGCHI Conference on Human Factors in Computing Systems*, ACM (2012), 947–956.
5. Burke, J., Estrin, D., Hansen, M., et al. Participatory sensing. *First Workshop on World-Sensor-Web: Mobile Device Centric Sensory Networks and Applications in*

conjunction with ACM Conference on Embedded Networked Sensor Systems, ACM (2006), 117–134.

6. Chamberlain, A., Paxton, M., Glover, K., et al. Understanding the design of mass participatory pervasive computing systems for environmental campaigns. *Personal and Ubiquitous Computing In Press*, (2014).
7. Chon, Y., Lane, N., Li, F., Cha, H., and Zhao, F. Automatically characterizing places with opportunistic crowdsensing using smartphones. *Proceedings of the International Conference on Ubiquitous Computing*, ACM (2012), 481–490.
8. Cuff, D., Hansen, M., and King, J. Urban sensing: Out of the woods. *Comm. of the ACM 51*, 3 (2008), 24–33.
9. DiSalvo, C., Sengers, P., and Brynjarsdóttir, H. Mapping the landscape of sustainable HCI. *Proceedings of the SIGCHI Conference on Human Factors in Computing Systems*, ACM (2010), 1975–1984.
10. Figueroa, H. and Robbins, M. XBAT: An open-source extensible platform for bioacoustic research and monitoring. *Proceedings of the International Expert Meeting on IT-based Detection of Bioacoustical Patterns*, (2007), 143–155.
11. Froehlich, J., Dillahunt, T., Klasnja, P., et al. UbiGreen: investigating a mobile tool for tracking and supporting green transportation habits. *Proceedings of the SIGCHI Conference on Human Factors in Computing Systems*, ACM (2009), 1043–1052.
12. Jacobs, R., Benford, S., Selby, M., Golembewski, M., Price, D., and Giannach, G. A conversation between trees: What data feels like in the forest. *Proceedings of the SIGCHI Conference on Human Factors in Computing Systems*, ACM (2013), 129–138.
13. Kuznetsov, S., Odom, W., Pierce, J., and Paulos, E. Nurturing natural sensors. *Proceedings of the international conference on Ubiquitous computing*, ACM (2011), 227–236.
14. Lane, N. D., Miluzzo, E., Lu, H., Peebles, D., Choudhury, T., & Campbell, A.T. A survey of mobile phone sensing. *Communications Magazine, IEEE 48*, 9 (2010), 140–150.
15. Law, C., Roe, P., and Zhang, J. Using mobile technology and augmented reality to increase data reliability for environmental assessment. *Proceedings of the Australian Computer-Human Interaction Conference*, ACM (2012), 327–330.
16. Maisonneuve, N., Stevens, M., and Ochab, B. Participatory noise pollution monitoring using mobile phones. *Information Polity 15*, 1 (2010), 51–71.
17. Martellos, S. and Nimis, P. KeyToNature: Teaching and learning biodiversity: Dryades, the Italian experience. *Proceedings of the International Association for the Scientific Knowledge International Conference "Teaching and Learning,"* (2008), 863–868.
18. Miller-Rushing, A., Primack, R., and R. Bonney. The history of public participation in ecological research. *Frontiers in Ecology and the Environment 10*, 6 (2012), 285–290.
19. Paulos, E., Honicky, R., and Goodman, E. Sensing atmosphere. *Proceedings of the International Workshop on Sensing on Everyday Mobile Phones in Support of Participatory Research in conjunction with the 5th International Conference on Embedded Networked Sensor System (SenSys)*, ACM (2007).
20. Paxton, M. and Benford, S. Experiences of participatory sensing in the wild. *Proceedings of the International Conference on Ubiquitous Computing*, ACM (2009), 265–274.
21. Rogers, Y., Price, S., Fitzpatrick, G., et al. Ambient wood: designing new forms of digital augmentation for learning outdoors. *Proceedings of the Conference on Interaction design and children*, ACM (2004), 3–10.
22. Rowland, D., Porter, D., Gibson, M., et al. Sequential art for science and CHI. *Extended Abstracts on Human Factors in Computing Systems*, ACM (2010), 2651–2660.
23. Ryokai, K., Oehlberg, L., Manoochehri, M., and Alice Agogino. GreenHat: exploring the natural environment through experts' perspectives. *Proceedings of the SIGCHI Conference on Human Factors in Computing Systems*, ACM (2011), 2149–2152.
24. Sullivan, B., Wood, C., Iliff, M., Bonney, R., Fink, D., and Kelling, S. eBird: A citizen-based bird observation network in the biological sciences. *Biological Conservation 142*, 10 (2009), 2282–2292.
25. Willett, W., Aoki, P., Kumar, N., Subramanian, S., and Woodruff, A. Common sense community: scaffolding mobile sensing and analysis for novice users. *Proceedings of the 8th international conference on Pervasive Computing*, Springer (2010), 301–318.
26. Wimmer, J., Towsey, M., Planitz, B., Williamson, I., and Roe, P. Analysing environmental acoustic data through collaboration and automation. *Future Generation Computer Systems 29*, 2 (2013), 560–568.
27. Zilli, D., Parson, O., Merrett, G., and Rogers, A. A hidden Markov model-based acoustic cicada detector for crowdsourced smartphone biodiversity monitoring. *Proceedings of the International Joint Conference on Artificial Intelligence*, (2013).

Making Public Things: How HCI Design Can Express Matters of Concern

Carl DiSalvo, Thomas Lodato, Tom Jenkins
Georgia Institute of Technology
Atlanta, GA, USA, 30308
cdisalvo | thomas.lodato | tom.jenkins @gatech.edu

Jonathan Lukens
University of Tennessee
Knoxville, TN, USA, 37996
jon@infopollen.net

Tanyoung Kim
Nokia
Sunnyvale, CA, USA, 94086
tanyoung.kim@nokia.com

ABSTRACT
Science studies scholar Bruno Latour suggests that contemporary democracy is shifting from "matters of fact" to "matters of concern": contentious conditions entwined with everyday life. What is the role of human-computer interaction (HCI) design in this shift? In this paper we draw from five design projects to explore how design can express matters of concern by communicating the factors and consequences of issues. In the process, we consider the role of design in contributing to the formation of publics and discuss an emerging orientation to publics in HCI design.

Author Keywords
Design; Matters of Concern, Publics; Public Design

ACM Classification Keywords
H.5.m. Information interfaces and presentation (e.g., HCI): Miscellaneous.

INTRODUCTION
In the 2005 exhibition *Making Things Public: Atmospheres of Democracy,* science studies scholar Bruno Latour and artist/curator Peter Weibel explored the ways artists and designers construct systems that express and enact current social conditions and imagined futures [33]. A mammoth book, with over 100 essays from social scientists and theorists, accompanied the exhibition. Taken together, the book and exhibition document a constellation of thoughts and cultural production that wrestle with contemporary democracy. What is common across the projects and essays is that they all seem to be probing the question: *How does one "do" democracy in the 21st century?*

CHI 2014, April 26 - May 01 2014, Toronto, ON, Canada
Copyright 2014 ACM 978-1-4503-2473-1/14/04...$15.00.
http://dx.doi.org/10.1145/2556288.2557359.

In answering this question, four entwined themes are important [17]. The first is that contemporary democracy is *object-oriented*: it occurs through the stuff we make. The second is that contemporary democracy is about *matters of concern*: contentious issues and their consequences. Third, *things* are the association of objects and matters of concern: when the stuff we make is experienced in light of the contentious issues and the consequences surrounding that stuff, we are living in what Latour refers to as a kind of "dingpolitik." Fourth and finally, these things can function to organize *publics*: groups committed to addressing an issue. Understanding a bit about these terms sheds light on the significance of the exhibition title. The phrase "Making Things Public" is shorthand for exploring the interplay of objects and issues, and how socio-cultural situations are disputed through collective endeavors.

Design is implicit in this endeavor of "Making Things Public." The "things" Latour refers to and the ways they are "made public" do not come about by accident. They arise through traceable processes where choices have been made. For the exhibition, Latour and Weibel selected projects they interpreted as working to express matters of concern. To an extent, design is taken for granted in the exhibition, as the images, artifacts, and systems are presented with minimal interpretation. There is little inquiry into *how* these objects *do* politics or express matters of concern. But as design researchers, this question of "how" is precisely what interests us: How can products and processes of design function to express matters of concern?

In this paper we explore some of the ways human computer interaction (HCI) design can function to express matters of concern. We do this through a reflexive analysis of five design projects. Each of these projects highlights different design tactics used to identify and communicate the multiple factors of an issue. Taken together, they provide a set of descriptive examples and generative themes for HCI researchers and practitioners. Before discussing the projects individually, we present the concepts of "matters of concern" and "design things". Then, after presenting the design projects, we explore the relation between the endeavor of expressing matters of concern and recent work in HCI concerning publics.

MATTERS OF CONCERN AND DESIGN THINGS

What is the difference between "matters of fact" and "matters of concern" and why is this of significance to HCI? Matters of fact are conditions considered as objective data, separate from political conditions. Matters of concern, in contrast, are perceived situations and their consequences; they are subjective experiences that constitute political conditions. The distinctions between objective data and subjective experience are not absolute; they are constructed. Recognition of this process of construction and how it affects knowledge and politics is one of the distinguishing qualities between matters of fact and matters of concern. Consider climate change as an example. Treated as a matter of fact, we can record various environmental conditions, compare and contrast these data, construct computational models with some level of assumed veracity, deliberate possible causes, and courses of action. Treated as a matter of concern climate change includes all of that *plus* the lived experience and near-future effects of rising tides and fluctuating weather pattern, publically debated in the value-charged and politicized forums of technology, economics, and religion.

Acting effectively in a democracy, requires engaging with topics as matters of concern—with the lived qualities of political conditions. This does not mean abandoning rationality. But it does means placing the experiential, the affective and the desired alongside the presumed objective.[6,23,24,33] Moreover, it requires recognition of the constructed quality of categories that characterize political conditions, and the development of tactics for troubling those categories and intervening in those conditions such that they become better known and able to be acted upon.

What is the role of objects in addressing matter of concern? Within politics, objects are typically not included in the debate themselves. In contrast, for an increasing number of social scientists and theorists [6,23,32], this exclusion is a problem. In their view, objects already participate in political debates. Objects often function as expressions of matters of concern, encapsulating aspects of an issue to make them accessible to a broader public.[17,23] In *Design Things* [3], Binder, De Michelis, Ehn, Jacucci, Linde, and Wagner picks up on Latour's work and extend it into design. One of the many contributions of this scholarship is the distinction between design projects and design things. The former are closed systems with clear and definable goals and timeframes. The latter are not. They explain that design things are relational expressions that draw together humans and non-humans, resources and passions, in order to make issues manifest. Put another way, we might say that design things are shorthand for design that does the work of expressing matters of concern.

Within HCI, the use of design to express matters of concern resonates with reflective [8,28], critical [9,10] and speculative design [14]. It also suggests a shift in the orientation of HCI, toward a more publicly facing practice. As HCI expands into social arenas and contested subjects such as sustainability, healthcare, and international development, HCI scholars and practitioners must understand the capacity of design work in these arenas. Certainly building working systems is important. However if we take the ideas of matters of concern and object-oriented democracy seriously, HCI has to extend beyond the planning and building of working systems—it has to engage with issues.

DESIGN CASES

How design things function to express matters of concern is the fundamental question of our research. Over the past five years we have taken a research-through-design approach [12,34] to this question—crafting design things to reflexively [14,8,28] examine this approach to contemporary democracy. In what follows we present five projects and discuss how each attempts to express matters of concern.

Smog is Democratic

Smog is Democratic was a media installation commissioned as part of the exhibition "Consequential Matters," at the museum of the Centers for Disease Control and Prevention. The purpose of the installation was to explore the issues of scientific representation, particularly with regard to pollution. We sought to design a series of visualizations that combined the lived qualities of particulate matter with common forms of technical representation of pollution. To that end, the media designs that were constructed for the installation were not intended to establish or prove facts. Rather, the designs were interpretive and expressive, with the goal of considering how a range of sources and measurements of particulate matter might be aesthetically rendered in order to generate reflection.

The title of the installation, "Smog is Democratic" is taken from the sociologist Urlich Beck [2]. While some have argued that the claim "smog is democratic" is not accurate because the effects of environmental damage are unevenly distributed—in cases of environmental racism, for example—we find the phrase compelling and appropriate, for it communicates that the air around us is both shared and contested.

In working to express air pollution as a matter of concern, we began by considering how the sources and measurements of particulate matter might be displayed in order to generate reflection and debate. Often the role of visualization as a technique is to clarify a scene. Instead, as a deliberate design choice, data was used to obscure—to render the scene *less* visible. The intention was both to confound expectations of what visualization does and also express the nature of the object under examination—particulate matter in the air actually can inhibit visibility.

The data visualizations were based on air quality, smog,

Figure 1. ***Distribution in Time 1: Particulate Matter* (still image taken from video)**

and particulate matter data from 2008, maintained by the Environmental Protection Division of the Georgia Department of Natural Resources. This database records both predicted and observed smog alerts as well as daily ratings of the air quality index. In each visualization, the data are used differently.

For example, in *Distribution Over Time 1: Smog Alert Days Over Air Quality Index 2008 (Observed),* a large format digital print approximately 40" by 20", the image is divided into 366 equal vertical slices, one for each day of 2008. In the bottom half of the image, the slices are distorted relatively according to the observed Air Quality Index for each corresponding date. In the top half of the image, slices that correspond to each observed smog alert have been removed (obscured by a semi-transparent soot gray). Similarly, in "*Distribution In Time 1: Particulate Matter 2008*" (see Figure 1) particulate matter data are used to generate the disruptions of the images in a video loop of a fly over of the city of Atlanta. The distortion in that video loop has been modified according to the 2008 fine particulate matter data from a local monitoring site. Each frame of the video corresponds to one hour of data. The loop was displayed on a large monitor in the center of the exhibition and ran continuously.

In addition to these two visualizations, "Smog is Democratic" included a third visualization which was presented as a large format poster, as well as a reading area filled with books and periodicals about particulate matter from the CDC library, and an area displaying photographs of twenty-five sources of particulate matter. Titled "Do You See What I See?", the twenty-five photographs revealed common sources of local particulate matter including road dust, mold, dead skin, hair, fabric, and engine exhaust.

Through these media formats, and the installation as a whole, we sought to frame particulate matter as *both* a lived experience and an objective entity. As a topic, particulate matter brings together multiple themes in contemporary society: our concern with pollution, the relationship between urban living and hygiene, and the desire to produce techniques of measurement against the threat of the unseen. Rather than resolving any tension between these themes, the design of the visualization was intended to collectively express their intermingling. The location of the installation within the Centers for Disease Control and Prevention—one of the institutions charged with assessing and communicating public health risks—added to the reflexivity of project. Whereas some would normally expect only the most rigorous of data driven displays in this locale, what was presented was an array of designs that freely combined the objective and subjective.

Pollen Calendar and Map

Like *Smog Is Democratic* the *Pollen Calendar and Map* sought to combine lived qualities of pollution with common forms of technical representation, but it added in the capacity for interactivity between people and social media.

The city of Atlanta, Georgia, has one of the highest annual pollen counts of any city in the United States. Every spring, pollen blankets the city. Pollen counts are orders of magnitude greater than the threshold set for a "High" pollen count by the National Allergy Bureau. These numbers are reported daily on dedicated websites and other media channels. The numbers report the facts of the daily pollen count and signal the dramatic nature of pollen in the city, but they fail to express the experience of living with pollen.

The process of measuring pollen count is laborious and expensive. Every day, an expert must use sophisticated equipment to collect and tally microscopic spores from the previous 24 hours. Because of the exhaustive nature of measurement, pollen counts are collected for large geographic areas only—at city or regional scale. These measures may be useful for tracking wide trends, but their value is limited when applied to the variation between neighborhoods, as distribution and interaction with pollen is affected by conditions like tree cover, landscaping, wind patterns, architecture, and infrastructure.

In response to these common methods and forms of pollen counting and reporting we designed two tools: the *Pollen Calendars* and the *Pollen Map*. These design of these tools was motivated by two principles: 1) to emphasize local details over macro-scale abstractions and 2) to emphasize the anecdotal expression of pollen over the generic reporting of facts. As with other participatory sensing projects around environmental and urban contexts [16], we sought to provide users an opportunity to interpret their own sensing schemes, allowing them to use their own experiences in helping construct how information might create meaningful dialogues around issues. As with *Smog is Democratic*, these design principles inverted the common methods and forms of counting pollen and reporting a simple data point. Instead, we sought to design a sensing system that emphasizes the material qualities and lived experience of data in the world.

Pollen Calendars

Pollen Calendars are meant to provide a way for individuals to enact their own localized pollen measurements in a manner that calls attention to the materiality of pollen. The Pollen Calendars are analog sensing platforms constructed from vacuum-formed plastic. Each calendar is approximately 30cm by 20cm, and has 31 recessed wells and laser-cut labels that provide markers for the days of the week. A sheet of clear acetate is affixed over the calendar and a flap is cut into it over each plastic well, allowing it to be opened and closed. Each well is lined with petroleum jelly. Pollen adheres to the jelly when the well is opened and exposed to air.

To be used, the *Pollen Calendars* are hung outside. Each morning, users lift an acetate flap to open another well to collect pollen for that day. The following morning, that flap is closed off with a bit of tape, and the next well exposed. Given the size of many forms of pollen and the density of the pollen fall in Atlanta, the collection of pollen in each individual well is at times visible. Under conditions when the pollen fall is both heavy and volatile, it is possible to visibly detect variations in collection over time—the wells create a natural sensor for pollen fall.

At the end of the month, the calendars are scanned. Using a simple Photoshop macro, an image of each well in the month is extracted. These images can be analyzed using a variety of software tools, or more simply compared side by side or sequenced together to generate an abstract slideshow of collected pollen for that particular location. These images can also be tagged with a location and date and manually added to the *Pollen Map*.

The Pollen Map

The *Pollen Map* provides a way for individuals to view and compare the aggregate experience of pollen in different localities. The pollen data reported is drawn from social media, and as such, provides a more personal and interpretive expression of the experience of pollen. Specifically, the *Pollen Map* is an online digital map integrated with user-generated text and images. A script searches Twitter and Flickr for geo-located content with relevant keywords and tags (such as 'pollen,' 'allergies,' etc.). This content is scraped and stored in the *Pollen Map* database. In addition, users can choose to tag tweets with the hashtag #pollenATL, adding the contents of those tweets, including username, timestamp, texts and images, to the Pollen Map database.

With the *Pollen Map*, users can navigate the text and images as they are sorted by time and location. To try to build a relationship with existing metrics, the map's timeline can be "scrubbed" through and that day's pollen count is displayed beneath the map. As people share pollen related content through Twitter or Flickr, that content is automatically aggregated and placed on the map. Through this process, users of the Pollen Map can view mostly personal reactions to or reflections on the pollen fall, ranging from exclamations of disgust to pleas for alternative allergy remedies to humorous remarks. In addition, users of the map view photos that document the visible effects of pollen at a given moment.

We can speak individually of our own experience with pollen, but the *Pollen Map* provides a platform for aggregating and sharing a collective experience. As this data accretes over time—images of pollen in situ, quips about streets turned yellow, vivid complaints about coughs and dreary eyes—the map becomes and ever-richer representation of the lived-experience with pollen. Moreover, the *Pollen Map* has an enduring quality to it—functioning as both an expression of the localized experience in the here and now, and also an archive, as users navigate backwards in time to previously posted and captured social expressions.

The *Pollen Map*, *Pollen Calendar* and *Smog is Democratic* share qualities and tactics. These include the use of visualizations, integration of documentary photography as a form of expressive visual evidence, and an attentiveness to the materiality of the matter of concern. This attentiveness to materiality signals a more general appreciation of the particular. This is significant because matters of concern are not generic affairs. They are distinguished by the factors that constitute them. To express them requires a commitment to the particularities of the situation. In these cases, the particularities are material entities and their qualities, and in order to make the matter of concern accessible, what is necessary is to place the particularities of the situation front and center in the designed thing.

The Political Grid

The *Political Grid* project is a Twitter-based website where people respond to the tweets of politicians running for office. The site was launched for the 2012 United States presidential election and followed the tweets of the two leading candidates, Barack Obama and Mitt Romney (@BarackObama and @MittRomney). Upon registering at the website, users view the tweets side by side and then can choose to "vote" on any tweet based on two standards—how much she *agrees* with the idea expressed in the tweet, and how *important* it is to her. Each vote is cast along a scale, and then placed in a corresponding location on a grid (one axis being I Care / I Don't Care, the other axis I Agree / I Don't Agree). Once the user votes on a given tweet they can see the results of others' vote on that same tweet, and across all of the tweets for a particular candidate. They can also compare the candidates side by side. Finally, the interface provides a simple word cloud that expresses the prevalence of terms within the tweets for each candidate (See Figure 2).

Building upon current trends in visualization, using *Political Grid* provides opportunities for reflection through visualization [15] at multiple levels. This occurs first at the

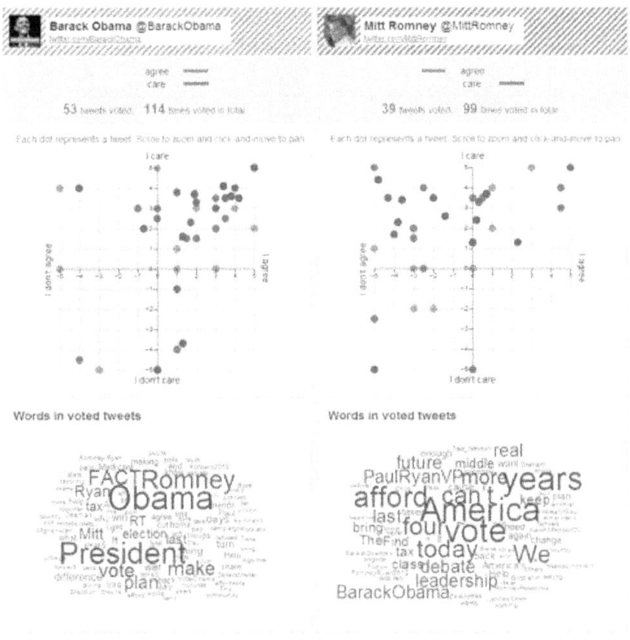

Figure 2. ***Political Grid*** **(screen capture)**

individual scale, as a user can examine her political preference and the voting results of each tweet or voice in a greater detail. At a broader level, among the collective of *Political Grid* users, one can compare votes, word frequency of tweets, and the temporal trends of voting. Standard rhetorical strategies emerge: for instance, that Mr. Obama tends to tweet his own name and the word "President" but that Mr. Romney avoids mention of the president by name. One can also see how each individual candidate is generally perceived through the clustering of tweet votes and their comparison between candidates.

But what is perhaps most significant in the project is the choice of the categories for voting. These are not categories concerned with the veracity of the tweet, nor even their persuasiveness. Rather, these are categories concerned with the *affective orientation* of the user towards the statement(s) of a given politician.

What the design of the *Political Grid* attempts to do, then, is draw attention to affective aspects of contemporary politics through familiar channel of social media and relatively simply visual forms. This purposeful and direct engagement with affective orientation is in contrast to much of the common treatment of politics in interaction design that strives for rational deliberation [18] or in HCI to mitigate the expression of "extreme" opinions [25]. This approach emphasizes the affective character of politics and argues that it is imperative to acknowledge and allow for the affect in political discourse and decision-making. Rather than displacing the affective quality of politics, *Political Grid* puts it front and center.

Finally, a notable quality of *Political Grid* is that the interaction on the site does not simply end with voting. Because the data that accrues over time is saved and remains available—like the *Pollen Map*—it can function as a historical repository, in this case of political affect. This repository reflects the changing (or unchanging) perspectives of individual users, candidates, and the collective field of participations, enabling multiple avenues for data analysis and reflexivity. One can imagine the use of the system over an extended period of time, capturing and charting the changing affective sentiments of publics.

In thinking about the transition from matters of fact to matters of concern, *Smog is Democratic*, the *Pollen Calendars* and *Pollen Maps*, and *Political Grid* all contain what one would commonly consider facts—numerical datum. Indeed, all the projects rely upon data for their representational forms. Working to express matters of concern, then, is not a reactionary or naïve rejection or manipulation of data. Nor is it predicated on maintaining rigid distinctions between the so-called subjective and objectives qualities of a condition. Rather, what each of these projects attempts to do is call attention to the interplay between the counted and perceived. This interplay, this messiness in the construction of facts and issues is well-known and well-articulated by scholars in many fields of the social sciences and humanities [16,21,22,32]. The challenge and opportunity for designers is to make this messiness accessible in experiential form.

Growbot Garden

The preceding projects shared similarities in structure—all involved data visualization, and to varying degrees, interaction with those visualizations. The following examples shift toward participatory design. The designed forms include workshops and hackathons, the experiential and material props made for those events, and the concepts and prototypes that emerged through co-design.

The *GrowBot Garden* project was a design research project reflecting trends in HCI around sustainability, DIY, and participatory design [3,11,27,30,31]. The central objective was to enable participants with no prior knowledge of robotics and sensing technologies to imagine how these technologies might be designed to better facilitate their practices and enact their desires and values. This required developing scaffolding activities that would enable informed speculation. The project took the form of a variety of workshops and extended participation in an arts festival.

While we were able to use and extend some previously developed tools with our participant, the novel subject matter of robotics and sensing combined with the culture and practices of small-scale local agriculture required the development of new activities for learning, discovery, and invention and a series of specific, deliberate design decisions regarding to the workshops' structure.

The full-day workshops provide a concrete example of the extended engagement between the design research team and the workshops' participants. At the first *GrowBot Garden* workshop, twenty-two people attended and participated in the daylong event, along with nine researchers. Participants ranged from laypeople interested in growing technologies to farmers, gardeners, cheese-makers, community organizers, and other food-producing stakeholders. Additionally, a student studying soil science and two students of industrial design attended the event as participants. The gender split among the participants was approximately equal, with a few more women than men. Approximately half of the participants were between 20 and 35, with the other half ranging from 35 to 60.

The workshop began with a short presentation on the current state of the art of robotics. We structured our visual survey of contemporary robotics as a dynamic conversation—participants were encouraged to speak out throughout the conversation, to openly make commentary, ask questions, and to chat among themselves and with us in real-time to the images being projected. After the overview presentation, participants engaged in an exercise in which they created a physical model of their farm on a small rectangle of cardboard using craft supplies. Taking turns, the participants stood up to describe their model and their growing practices. We chose this tactic to ground the conversation in the practices of farming, to highlight the participants' intrinsic knowledge, and to provide a material basis for imagining robotics in their environs.

Next, we presented a series of learning stations designed to inform participants about the basic capabilities of robotic systems. The stations were designed to be easy to understand and demonstrate sensing technology in a simple and straightforward manner. For example, at one station, a computer with a webcam was used to demonstrate the basics of computer vision and sensing. Using a simple program written in Processing, participants could select a specific color from the webcam feed, effectively isolating a single color range from the feed. To make this demonstration relevant to growers and farmers, the station was stocked with a bowl of fruit to demonstrate how the technology could easily be used to identify the differences between apples, oranges, and bananas.

The afternoon was devoted to brainstorming, prototyping, and discussion of the prototypes. Immediately after lunch, participants were asked to self-organize into groups for the afternoon activity, which we informed them would be about inventing new applications of robotic and sensing technologies for small-scale agriculture. Each group delivered a their application concept as both a drawing and as a physical model.

After the brainstorming session, participants were given a quick overview of available prototyping materials. To support a range of skills, interests, and expressive styles, we had selected a wide range of materials for prototyping including cardboard, modeling clay, plastic toy farm animals, tractors, trucks and other farming vehicles, toy and hobby robots, circuit boards salvaged from computers, older mobile phones, and craft supplies such as felt and wire. These items were displayed along two tables and a shelving unit, in a way that mirrored the lunch buffet: as an aesthetic collection of goods for their use and enjoyment. In addition to these materials, tools such as wire cutters and screwdrivers were provided, and a table was used as a dedicated hot glue station.

Figure 3. Prototype from *GrowBot Garden*

After approximately two hours we stopped prototyping, and the groups presented their concept drawings and models. Each group was asked to first identify the issue that was being addressed by their designs and then explain how the prototype would address that issue.

Eight prototypes were made and these fell into three categories of farming tasks or activities: irrigation/watering, mowing, and pest control (see Figure 3). The pest control prototypes most clearly engage in matters of concern. Many of the participants were organic farmers and did not use pesticides, a practice that adds difficulty to dealing with bugs. Also, as some of our participants pointed out, some insects can be beneficial to the production of plants. According to one group, in an ideal world, a farm robot would be able to distinguish between the wanted and unwanted insects, and act accordingly. This idea materialized as the BugBot prototype, which was designed as a roving robot that utilized fabric sails to brush insects off of leaves. It included a computer vision system that could distinguish between different kids of insects. When appropriate, the prototype could retract its sails so as not to disturb helpful bugs. A related concept addressed pest control by distributing organic pest repellant through a rover. This concept did not entail any fundamental new technology or activity, but rather the application of technologies currently used to assist in the use of pesticides to instead assist in the use of pesticide alternatives. A third example, the Bio-Rover, was notable for the way the group envisioned the role of the robot. This robot was to be outfitted with a series of sensors that would collect information about pests throughout the farm environment. Rather than taking direct action against the pests, the robot would return the information to the farmer, who would then make decisions and take action regarding the pests detected.

These prototypes are expressions of matters of concern for small-scale farmers. Each prototype encapsulates a set of conditions for the farmer, communicating perspectives on how technology might address those conditions in ways that align with the farmer's values and practices. In selecting conditions, participant-designers are bundling problematic relationships —both materially and conceptually. These objects are then arguments: arguments for new sets of conditions where these formerly problematic conditions are eliminated through their intersection with designed objects.

Food Data Hack

Food Data Hack was a one-day hackathon on the topic of local food systems. Specifically, *Food Data Hack* focused on the relationships between access to food, land use and zoning, and urban agriculture within the Atlanta, GA metropolitan area. The goal of the event was to form small working groups around subtopics related to these issues. These groups were tasked with developing means to address particular opportunities or gaps, with potential actions taking the form of concept sketches for artifacts, services, systems, and strategies.

During the planning phase, we invited the heads of two organizations, Atlanta Community Food Bank (ACFB), and Atlanta Local Food Initiative (ALFI), as well as a representative of the Office of the Mayor, to brainstorm the theme for the event. During this conversation, the group identified land use and zoning as a contemporary issue for urban agricultural efforts within metro Atlanta, especially with regards to populations with low access to local agriculture and healthful foods.

The *Food Data Hack* began with a short breakfast where attendees conversed. While this may seem inconsequential, these casual moments are important because they allow attendees to listen and interact more openly. We deliberately invited a variety of people from what we perceived as non-overlapping communities: designers, developers, agricultural entrepreneurs, community organizers, local policymakers, and NGO representatives. These groups brought different perspectives to the issues *Food Data Hack* was designed to address.

After breakfast, we briefly explained the overall purpose and theme of *Food Data Hack*. The representatives from ACFB and ALFI further framed the day's activities with presentations. This introductory session closed by asking attendees to self-select subtopics. Six subgroups emerged, each around particular issues. For example, one group formed around building an application for mapping under- or un-utilized lands. This group was comprised of a visual artist, two local growers, and an application developer. A second group formed around the topics of fostering urban farm volunteers. This group was comprised of application developers, service designers, volunteer coordinators, and local growers. A third group coalesced around rethinking zoning policy and was comprised of an academic computer scientist, an agricultural entrepreneur, a technology researcher, and a representative from City of Atlanta Office of Sustainability.

Over the course of the day, all the groups discussed, brainstormed, and diagrammed ideas. Unlike a typical hackathon, we emphasized the early designing and planning phases by having materials available to produce conceptual work such as paper storyboards and wireframes rather than the production of code. The groups presented their developed ideas twice over the course of the day. These presentations included low fidelity materials, such as hand sketches and sticky notes.

Food Data Hack exhibits several key components of expressing matters of concern. While the issues around *Food Data Hack* can be generalizable and found in different cities, the pre-event brainstorming and event introduction grounded the topic as a local matter of concern within the city of Atlanta, engaging particular, situated materials, relations, constraints, and opportunities. In a similar way, the curation of attendees provided a way to scope and scale the event's impact. As designers of the *Food Data Hack* event, we brought together people, their perspectives, and their broader organizational commitments as a way of articulating what is relevant. These perspectives and commitments defined the matter of concern as existing in the relationship between technologists, designers, policymakers, growers, entrepreneurs, and officials.

Like many participatory design projects, The *GrowBot Garden* project and *Food Data Hack* expand design beyond the activities of professional designers and actively enroll others in the design process. However in projects such as these, the design activities shift from contributing to the production of functional systems to participating in the production of experiential structures, activities, and props to support a collective speculation. This is a new mode of community-based participatory design [26]. In this participatory design, the primary design task is one of developing support structures to undergird collective inquiry into matters of concern. The designer becomes a facilitator, using her knowledge of design methods and processes to create the conditions for collective articulation of matters of concern.

DISCUSSSION: ARTICULATING ISSUES, GIVING FORM TO PROBLEMATIC SITUATIONS, AND PUBLICS

Each of the preceding "design things" attempts to express matters of concern: they convey lived experience, perceived consequences and desired futures. One way that products and processes of design work to express matters of concern is by articulating issues and giving form to problematic situations. This leads us to a notion of a public orientation in design—an orientation explicitly concerned with contributing to the construction of publics.

In his book *The Public and its Problems,* American philosopher John Dewey characterizes a "public" as a distinctive social organization, formed to address the conditions or consequences of a problematic situation or issue [5]. For Dewey, there is not a singular public, but rather a multitude of publics that form, take action, and dissolve. The problematic situations or issues that give rise to a public do not need to be political. They can be, and often are, formed around lived experience—for instance, the experience of living with pollen. What characterizes these problematic situations or issues is that they are moments "where instinctive or habitual responses of the human organism to the environment are inadequate for the continuation of ongoing activity in pursuit of the fulfillment of needs and desires." [13]

We may experience these situations individually, but for a public to coalesce around a respective issue, those issues have to be articulated so that they can also be collectively considered. To articulate an issue or give form to a problematic situation is to identify and communicate the connections between the qualities and factors of a condition and its consequences. What design adds to this endeavor is an experiential quality. *Smog is Democratic, Pollen Calendar* and *Pollen Map* employ design to articulate issues of air quality and situations of pollution/pollen in an experiential manner. By focusing on pluralistic methods of displaying different sources, quantity, and distribution of particulate matter data, *Smog is Democratic* expressed the ubiquity and longevity of particulate matter as an ongoing part of the lived experience of Atlantans. The smog data was used to "blanket" the image of the city—distorting the view of the visualizations for all. *Pollen Calendar* and *Pollen Map* achieve similar ends through different means. In designing an object that democratizes the recording and sharing of pollen data, both the calendar and the map encourage users to interact with a matter of concern in a visceral way. This interaction re-contextualizes the practice pollen data collection, measurement and recording, removing it from the realm of experts only, and re-casting it as a shared endeavor.

Without articulation, problematic situations and issues may remain muddled, unnoticed, or inaccessible. But design events and activities of prototyping can function as a means of articulation. At the *GrowBot Garden* and *Food Data Hack* events, participants came together to collectively communicate factors affecting small-scale agriculture and food systems. In *GrowBot Garden,* the participants manifested issues through their prototypes, demonstrating how ag-tech design currently does not, but might in the future, align with their practices, e.g., those of pest management. By coalescing the interests and metaphors of a computer scientist, an entrepreneur, a technology researcher, and a government policymaker at the *Food Data Hack* event, the group discovered that one of the impediments to local food systems was a different kind of code: zoning policy.

Such efforts to articulate issues and give form to problematic situations are, we argue, part and parcel of an emerging orientation in design toward publics. This does not necessarily signal a new category of design, but it does suggest shifting purposes and priorities.

A Public Orientation in HCI

The relationship between publics and issues has received significant attention at the intersection of Science and Technology Studies (STS), Design, and HCI. For example, Noortje Marres has explored how technologies such as smart meters and eco-homes cohere publics concerned with sustainability [23]. Her research provides insight into the role of devices and systems in expressing an issue and providing objects with which to "materially participate" in that issue [23]. Similarly, within design studies DiSalvo has explored how speculative and critical design might contribute to the construction of Deweyan publics through the articulation of issues [6].

Within HCI, Le Dantec has explored design and publics through a series of projects and papers [19,20]. This work demonstrates the applicability of publics as a conceptual frame for describing and analyzing community-based HCI research as it unfolds across multiple contexts. Lindtner has further extended the discourse on publics in HCI by using the work of Michael Warner [32] his theories of counter-publics to produce a novel interpretation of media sharing collectives [22]. Throughout this scholarship the concepts of publics and the articulation of issues have, primarily, operated as *analytic frames.* They can also function as *generative devices* for initiating and guiding design activity. Moves toward this can be found in the recent participatory design scholarship [3,4,11,26,29,].

Increasingly, when we "do" HCI we are acting in fraught contexts such as sustainability, healthcare, or development. In some situations, it may not be clear what the appropriate role for HCI design is, or even whether design is the appropriate response to a condition at all [1]. A public orientation takes a step back from the common design imperatives of providing solutions or initiating change. Adopting a public orientation in HCI sets the articulation of issues and giving form to problematic situations as the primary design objective—the purpose of design becomes to identify the qualities and factors of a condition and make those qualities, factors and their relations experientially accessible.

Although this orientation may seem simple or obvious, we argue it is a meaningful shift in the purpose of design, with implications for practice and criticism. From this orientation, the basis for assessment and judgment is not whether an issue or situation resolved through design. Rather the basis for assessment and judgment is whether we now have a better recognition and understanding of the contours of the issue or situation.

We began this paper with the question *How can design products and processes function to express matters of concern*? Drawing from the examples and with these ideas of articulating issues, giving form to problematic situations, and contributing to the construction of publics, we can begin to identify particular tactics and strategies.

For the practicing designer, a key task is to **provide scaffolding or infrastructure** to support articulation and form-giving toward the construction of publics [3,4,6,11]. This scaffolding is meant to support an active process of coming to know through experience the qualities and factors of a condition. This scaffolding can take any material or interactional form depending upon the format of the design object. For instance, this might include activities within a workshop or tools for reflective use. It could also be material mediating the designed object itself, explaining its context or production. For example, documents from the Centers for Disease Control and Prevention library were gathered and presented as part of *Smog is Democratic* to provide background on pollution monitoring and representation.

The effect of a public design orientation is that **artifacts, systems, and events function to expose and re-imagine constraints and parameters surrounding issues and problematic situations.** With the *Pollen Calendars* and the *Pollen Map* these systems were designed to re-imagine what processes and technologies might constitute environmental sensing and monitoring. If we expand the data of environmental sensing and monitoring to include hyper-localized, coarse, and anecdotal reporting, how might our desires for and expectations of future systems and processes change?

Through these activities of re-imagination, **designers and participants are engaging in prototyping new social, economic, and political arrangements**. With *GrowBot Garden*, for instance, modeling a process in which small-scale famers become actively engaged in the conceptualization and specification of agricultural technologies that support their values and practices was more important than any particular model of a robot or potential feature.. This prototyping of new social, economic, and political arrangements was even more pronounced in *Food Data Hack,* which explicitly sought to foster new working relations between stakeholders that might lead to innovations in the use of data to support small-scale agriculture.

Through this process, objects take on particular roles too: **objects become arguments for alternate situations in which the problematic condition which give rise to publics have been reconfigured.** The models created in the *GrowBot Garden* project are perhaps the best examples: they demonstrate a possible future in which robotic products *do exist* that serve the values and value-driven practices of the participants. The objects materially advance an argument that if small-scale farmers and other relevant stakeholders are included in the design process, and their practices are taken into account, appropriate and compelling technologies for small-scale agriculture could be invented.

CONCLUSION

In this paper we have explored the ways design might work to express matters of concern across a variety of formats, including media design, visualizations, workshops, and hackathons. Certainly our examples are not exhaustive. They merely begin to highlight some of the ways that we might use design to encapsulate and communicate the experiential qualities of matters of concern. More work is needed to better describe, evaluate and critique these methods and forms.

Fundamental to the activity of expressing matters of concern is the articulation of issues and giving form to problematic situations, with the consideration that such articulation and form giving might contribute to the construction of publics. Inspired by this idea we propose the term "public design" to characterize this work.

Public design is not meant to be new genre of design, such as speculative or critical design [9,10,14] or reflective design [8,28]. Rather, we consider it as an orientation in design applicable across genres. That is, one could imagine a given speculative, critical, or reflective design as being more or less oriented toward the construction of publics. This orientation can serve both analytic and generative purposes. Analytically, one could assess the extent to which a given design operates to identify the qualities and factors of a condition and make those qualities, factors and their relations experientially accessible. Generatively, one could set the design task as that of creating experiential scaffolds or infrastructure for coming to know the qualities and factors of a condition. As a term, then, public design can be used to encapsulate a collection of design tactics and strategies, applicable to a variety of practices and genres.

Expressing matters of concern requires new approaches to design and HCI and sets new purposes and expectations for the field. But why trouble with this? By way of conclusion it is worthwhile to revisit the question that seemed to motivate *Making Things Public* [33]: how does one "do" democracy in the 21st century? That question also seems present throughout many domains of HCI and its numerous sub-fields. There is no single answer to that question. However, we believe that one approach, as a starting point, is to use HCI design as a means to make known the qualities and factors that comprise contemporary social conditions.

ACKNOWLEDGMENTS

These projects would not have been possible without the help of Beth Schechter, Thomas Barnwell, Laura Fries, Amanda Meng, and Sarah Fox. Their work helped us think through this topic. This work is supported in part by the Intel Science and Technology Center for Social Computing.

REFERENCES

1. Baumer, E. and M. Six Silberman. When the implication is not to design (technology). In *Proc CHI 2011*, ACM Press (2011), 2271-2274.
2. Beck, U. *Risk Society: Towards a New Modernity*. Sage, London, 1992.
3. Binder, T., De Michelis, G., Ehn, P., Jacucci, G., Linde, P., Wagner, I. *Design Things,* MIT Press, Cambridge, MA, 2012.
4. Björgvinsson, E, Ehn, P, and P. A, Hillgren. Participatory Design and "Democratizing Innovation". In *Proc PDC 2010*. ACM Press (2010), 41-50.
5. Dewey, J. *The Public and its Problems*. Swallow Press, Chicago, 1954.
6. DiSalvo, C. Design and the Construction of Publics. *Design Issues 25*, 1 (2009), 48–63.
7. DiSalvo, C. *Adversarial Design*. MIT Press, Cambridge, MA, 2012.
8. Dourish, P., Finlay, J., Sengers, P., and P Wright. Reflective HCI: towards a critical technical practice. *CHI '04 extended abstracts on Human factors in computing systems*, ACM (2004), 1727–1728.
9. Dunne, A. and Raby, F. *Design Noir: The Secret Life of Electronic Objects*. Birkhäuser, Berlin, 2001.
10. Dunne, A. *Hertzian Tales: Electronic Products, Aesthetic Experience, and Critical Design*. MIT Press: Cambridge, MA, 2006.
11. Ehn, P. Participation in design things. In *Proc. PDC 2008*, ACM Press (2008), 92–101.
12. Fallman, D. Design-oriented Human-Computer Interaction. In *Proc CHI 2003*, ACM Press (2003),225-232.
13. Feld, R. "John Dewey," Internet Encyclopedia of Philosophy. July 14, 2005. (Accessed Sept 17, 2013)
14. Gaver, G. 2012. What should we expect from research through design?. In *Proc CHI 2012*, ACM Press (2012). AC Press, 937-946.
15. Kim, T. and C. DiSalvo. Speculative Visualization: A New Rhetoric for Communicating Public Concerns. In *Proc DRS 2010,* Design Research Society (2010), n.p.
16. Kuznetsov, S. and E. Paulos, Participatory Sensing in Public Spaces: Activating Urban Surfaces with Sensor Probes. *Proc DIS 2010,* ACM Press (2010), 21–30.
17. Latour, B. "From Realpolitik to Dingpolitik." In *Making Things Public: Atmospheres of Democracy*, Weibel, P. and B. Latour, eds. MIT Press: Cambridge MA (2005), 14-44.
18. Lausen, Marcia. *Design for democracy: Ballot and election design*. University of Chicago Press, 2008.
19. Le Dantec, C. 2012. Participation and Publics: Supporting Community Engagement. In *Proc CHI 2012*, ACM Press (2012), 1351-1360
20. Le Dantec, C. A. J. E. Christensen, M. Bailey, R. G. Farrell, J. B. Ellis, C. M. Danis, W. A. Kellogg, and W. K. Edwards. A tale of Two Publics: Democratizing design at the margins. In *Proc DIS 2010,* ACM Press (2010), 11-20.
21. Lindtner, S., and D. Li. "Created in China: The Makings of China's Hackerspace Community." *interactions* 19.6 (2012): 18-22.
22. Lindtner, S., J. Chen, G. R. Hayes, and P. Dourish. 2011. Towards a Framework of Publics: Re-Encountering Media sharing and its User. *ACM Trans. Comput.-Hum. Interact.* 18, 2, Article 5 (July 2011).
23. Marres, N. *Material participation: Technology, the Environment and Everyday Publics*. Palgrave Macmillan, New York, 2012.
24. Martin, A. and M. Lynch, M. (2009). Counting things and people: The practices and politics of counting. *Social Problems*, *56*(2): 243-266.
25. Munson, S. and P. Resnick. 2010. Presenting Diverse Political Opinions: How and How much. In *Proc CHI 2010,* ACM Press (2010), 1457-1466.
26. Olander, S, Lenskjold, T, Yndigegn, S, and M. Foverskov. 2011. Mobilizing for Community Building and Everyday Innovation. *interactions* 18, 4: 28-32.
27. Paulos, E. 2013. The Rise of the Expert Amateur: DIY Culture and the Evolution of Computer Science. *SIGPLAN Not.* 48, 4 (March 2013): 153-154.
28. Sengers, P., Boehner, K., David, S., and "Jofish" Kaye, Reflective Design. In *Proc 4th Decennial Conference on Critical Computing* ACM Press (2005), 49–58.
29. Seravalli, A. 2012. Infrastructuring for opening production, from participatory design to participatory making?. In *Proc PDC 2012*, ACM Press (2102), 53-56.
30. Tanenbaum, J., Williams, A. Desjardins, A. and K. Tanenbaum. Democratizing Technology: Pleasure, Utility and Expressiveness in DIY and Maker Practice. In *Proc CHI 2013*, ACM Press (2013) 2603-2612.
31. Wang, T. and J. 'Jofish' Kaye. 2011. Inventive leisure practices: understanding hacking communities as sites of sharing and innovation. In *CHI '11 Extended Abstracts*, ACM Press (2011), 263-272.
32. Warner, M. *Publics and Counterpublics.* Zone Books, MIT Press, Cambridge, MA, 2001.
33. Weibel, P. and B. Latour, eds. *Making Things Public: Atmospheres of Democracy* MIT Press, Cambridge, MA, 2005.
34. Zimmerman, J., Forlizzi, J. and Evenson, S. 2007. Research through Design as a Method for Interaction Design esearch in HCI. In *Proc CHI 2007,* ACM Press (2007), 493-502

Just Awful Enough – The Functional Dysfunction of the Something Awful Forums

Jessica Pater, Yacin Nadji, Elizabeth D. Mynatt, and Amy Bruckman
College of Computing
Georgia Institute of Technology
Atlanta, GA 30322 USA
{pater, yacin}@gatech.edu, {mynatt, asb}@cc.gatech.edu

ABSTRACT
The Something Awful Forums (SAF) is an online community comprised of a loosely connected federation of forums, united in a distinctive brand of humor with a focus on the quality of member contributions. In this case study we find that the site has sustained success while deviating from common conventions and norms of online communities. Humor and the quality of content contributed by SAF members foster practices that seem counterintuitive to the development of a stable and thriving community. In this case study we show how design decisions are contextual and inter-dependent and together these heuristics create a different kind of online third place that challenges common practices.

Author Keywords
online community; design; case study; third place

ACM Classification Keywords
H.5.3 Group and Organization Interfaces

INTRODUCTION

"We here on the Something Awful Forums are very elitist and strict assholes. We pride ourselves on running one of the most entertaining and troll-free forums on the Internet" (SAF Welcome Message)

The Something Awful Forums (SAF) is a loosely connected federation of forums that support a variety of user interests. As we show, there exists an undercurrent of humor coupled with a focus on meaningful community contributions that offers cohesion and connectedness to a "group of goons" that often deviates from common online community standards and practices.

There are numerous examples of scholarship discerning the practices behind successful online communities [4]. There have been compelling analyses of online communities like Wikipedia [3], Reddit [1], and Facebook [5], that examine the strength of social ties within the platform, the impact of trolling, and the influences of the platform on community behavior. One of the unifying threads in these studies is that the platforms serve as a *third place* for their members, a space outside of work or home where individuals find broader ways to meaningfully connect [15]. Successful online communities typically employ common practices: help users quickly learn community norms [10]; remove barriers for new users [3]; have a clear and sustainable code of conduct [8]; utilize technical and social mechanisms to combat deviant behavior [2]; and present a consistent, predictable, and controllable user experience [6].

This paper presents a case study of the SAF. While the basic site features and activities of the SAF are consistent with typical discussion sites, the site's policies and social norms are unusual. This study was designed to understand a community that has found sustained success even when deviating from common conventions and norms of online communities. SAF has been consistently active since 1999 and has sustained a community of over 181,000 paying users (as of September 2013). Through interviewing SAF members and analyzing site content and member guidelines, we describe several ways in which SAF challenges conventional practice (*abuse of newbies, amplification of boundary pushers, public humiliation, banning being boring, and lack of internal consistency of moderation*) and two unifying themes (*humor and meaningful contributions of users*). We will discuss how these deviations actually work to strengthen connectedness and culture across the community. Our study of SAF is an example of how supporting unifying concepts like humor and high quality contributions in an online community can create cohesion in what one might assume to be disorder.

WHAT IS SOMETHING AWFUL?

Richard "Lowtax" Kyanka created SAF as an online community rooted in the idea that dialogue should matter and bad behavior, as long as it is funny, is welcomed. SAF is a pay-to-play space, charging a one-time fee for participation. This fee is described on the site as a "filter to keep the environment troll-free." Users can pay additional fees to give them an ad-free experience, search the website, access the archives, upload pictures, and report questionable behavior.

SAF is comprised of 31 separate forums or gathering spaces which house an additional 32 sub-forums. Sample forum topics include: gaming, crafting, automotive repair, pop culture, politics, and FYAD - a general forum which stands for "Fuck Yourself and Die" and the only place on the site where flame wars and trolling are tolerated. Each forum and sub forum has its own code of conduct that may differ from the general site's code of conduct. Punishments are common within the SAF and are classified as probations (brief loss of posting), bans (users can buy an unbanning.), and perma-bans (users cannot pay for a new account or re-register).

METHODS

The goal of this case study is to provide an example of a sustained and successful online community where the community has deviated from common practices and norms. We used multiple qualitative approaches, consisting of content analysis of forum and sub forum codes of conduct, semi-structured interviews with users, and participant observation. We conducted interviews with eight community members: four general users, three moderators and one administrator. Each interview lasted approximately one hour and took place through text, audio, and video communication platforms. We designed the interviews to focus on how participants got started in the SAF, what they contribute to the community, their perceptions of the site behavior and moderation, and how their participation has changed overtime. Two researchers conducted the interviews and collectively spent over 60 hours lurking within the site in an attempt to understand the cultural norms within the community.

We also conducted a thematic content analysis of 45 codes of conduct in SAF. There is one global code of conduct for SAF. In addition to this global code of conduct, there are 44 sub-forum codes of conduct within the 63 sub-forums that members must adhere to during their time in the community.

DEVIATIONS FROM THE EXPECTED

The SAF has several deviations from common online community practice that make it an interesting subject for further review. We describe five areas where SAF deviates from common practices (*abuse of newbies, amplification of boundary pushers, public humiliation, banning being boring, and lack of internal consistency of moderation*) and two unifying themes (*humor and meaningful contributions of users*).

Abuse of the Newbie

New users are essential for a thriving community – they help grow the user base as well as replace the normal attrition of departing current members. Logically, there is an incentive for communities to welcome these new users as well as help them navigate from the periphery of the community to more constructive membership roles through a quicker new user process [10].

New SAF users have an atypical experience. The SAF takes a more humorous and irreverent approach to the cultural acclimation of new users. Figure 1 below is an example of such approach. When a new user signs up, unless they spend an additional $5 for a custom profile picture or gif, they receive the "stupid newbie" profile picture.

Figure 1. Standard new member avatar

New members are also more susceptible to violating community standards and getting probated or banned. In the general conduct section of the global community rules, lurking is the first activity that is brought up and is highly recommended to the new user because of the benefits to both the user and the community [13]. Members are told not to regurgitate content on the site and to only post if "what they have to say is funny, informative, or interesting on any level." For a new member, this prescription is daunting. This barrier is further compounded by access to the rich history of the site. The SAclopeida serves as the external memory of the site – a community maintained collection of their shared experiences, history and lore. New users are expected to have internalized SAclopedia and all codes of conduct, and lurked within the forums before submitting a single post.

"You should definitely look into SAclopedia. This is where the community documents our history. You can definitely tell when a newer member posts and hasn't spent anytime looking around there. As mods that's where we exercise the ability to be an asshole and teach them a lesson - usually through a short probation." (P8)

Raising barriers to entry is a common practice used to encourage commitment to the community [16]. Compared to other online communities, these barriers to entry might seem extreme yet were not an issue for the participants we interviewed: For example, one of our participants (P3) spent over 10 months lurking before posting.

Amplification of the boundary pushers

Research shows that one method to maintain cohesion within an online community is to punish or regulate users who push the boundaries of the site rules [7]. In the global code of conduct for SAF, there is evidence of the site developers and administration setting up loose parameters that allow for the boundaries to be malleable [10].

"Offensive terms or "hate speech" may or may not be bannable based on the context of the sentence...[T]his rule is 100% subjective and based on the mod reading the post." (SAF Rules)

"Flames and insults do not constitute harassment." (SAF Rules)

In a more traditional forum, these behaviors would be deemed unacceptable and would warrant a punishment to the offender. In SAF, these boundary-pushing activities are celebrated and codified within the code of conduct. The idea that rule breakers are given a platform for their activities was further supported through community activity observations by one of the interview participants.

"I don't think 'Fuck Yourself and Die (FYAD)' forum users troll in other forums SA in as an attempt to get a ban or probation, they do it to fuck with other forum members for comedy's sake. It used to be a common catchphrase in the Forums that [when users were trolling] 'FYAD was leaking' back before catchphrases were bannable offenses." (P4)

By giving the users a public platform to push the boundaries, users are celebrated and rewarded for their efforts. On the SAF homepage, humorous articles are presented, which often deal with provocative subjects being discussed in the community. That "[SAF] actually find authors for [our] front-page-articles from the more active and popular forum members" (P8) is a testament to members being rewarded for embodying these behaviors.

Public Humiliation

A common practice in an online community is to make the moderation of behavior a private action, not an event for a public stage, but between the user and the site moderator(s) [7]. There are several reasons for this approach, primarily to spare the user the humiliation of being reprimanded in front of their peers.

PROBATION	9/16/13 03:28pm	You make pretty bad posts for...anything, really. User loses posting privileges for 6 hours.	*Moderator Name*

Figure 2. Excerpt from Leper's Colony

SAF takes a different approach. The moderation of behavior takes place in a public forum called the Leper's Colony, another humorous design feature. Figure 2 is an example post taken from the Leper's Colony. The hyperlink on the type of ban takes you to the offensive post so the community can be entertained by the transgressions that took place. While it may seem harsh to degrade members in such a public manner, SAF members often view bans and probations as entertainment.

It's fun to see why they're banned...[s]ome of my favorite threads are people slowly falling apart, resulting in a ban or such. We all like to watch other people burn..[I] think that is the common bond that ties most SA people together...[a]t least most old-time SA people. (P5)

The thematic analysis of the codes of conduct revealed that over half (54%) of the 34 forum codes of conduct incorporated some form of public humiliation, mostly associated with the moderation system. Several codes of conduct find ways to both humiliate based on actions taken by users as well as attack potential attributes of those users.

"If you create some bullshit thread like 'SELLING MY LOVE!' you're probably an idiot and you will be banned for being a goddamn moron" (The SAF Mart Forum Rules)

Banning the Boring

Something Awful is a unique environment where finding the boundaries for what is considered "shitposting" and what is considered valuable contributions can be a daunting task, especially for new users. This challenge is reinforced via the message a user receives when posting a comment in any of the forums (see Figure 3).

Figure 3. Forum post pop-up window

Between lurking in the community and reading the codes of conduct, long-time users often tend to implicitly know where the boundaries are for quality as it relates to posting in the community.

"There is sorta a line – you can be fucked up to a point. It is hard to articulate, but you know it when you see it." (P3)

Another interesting concept within SAF is the high volume of moderator effort focused on low-content community contributions as opposed to contributions that are offensive or inflammatory. Previous research shows that under-contribution is a problem for online communities [13].

"No low-content or no-content posts. Posts that add nothing to the thread will be probated. Humor is content, horrible attempts at humor probably aren't." (Discuss and Debate forum)

By heavily penalizing the low content posts, SAF has created a culture that focuses on the quality of the content that keeps members engaged with the community. Over the course of a week we analyzed the moderator rationales for 471 punishments in the Leper's Colony and found that 51.8% reflected actions associated with boring content, including lack of content and improper grammar[1]. Below are examples of these rationales:

- A post this useless deserves a reward!
- There's no thread to talk about that because it's the stupidest fucking thing I've ever seen anyone say. Go live on Tumblr where morons like you congregate.

[1] A second coder coded 20% of the posts with 88.6% inter-rater reliability.

- The only thing set low is your posting standards. Please take a day and suck less when you get back. Gracias.

Lack of internal consistency of moderation

Another interesting component of SAF is the lack of internal consistency of the guiding rules. In many instances, there is an explicit statement that the moderators don't care if it seems unfair:

"Decisions do not have to be fair. If a moderator thinks you are being a dick, you will be banned, regardless of whether you broke a specific rule." (Inspect Your Gadgets Forum)

Some moderators talk about not wanting to have written rules and just seeing what works for them as a sub-community.

There may be other rules in the future, but to be honest I'd prefer it if this were it. I'd like for people to extend this philosophy to reporting people as well. If you want a fairly relaxed forum maybe go easy on the trigger unless something is really a problem."(Rapidly Growing Deaf Forum Rules)

Four of the total sixty-three forums had no written code of conduct or no pointer that the global code of conduct still applies. The community doesn't seem to see this lack of consistency as a problem as seen with other research [12]. They see this ambiguity as an extension of being a part of the community – knowing where there are inconsistencies and either trying to exploit them for a humorous attempt

DISCUSSION

Consider these rules of thumb:

- Erect high barriers of participation for new members.
- Treat new members as inferior.
- Publicly shame members not only for being inappropriate, but also for being boring.
- Deliberately leave standards for conduct unclear.

Intuitively, the above practices don't make a lot of sense. It's amusing to imagine other online sites adopting them. For example, can you imagine Facebook or Twitter management publicly shaming someone for a boring status update or tweet? Surprisingly, SAF has incorporated these heuristics and have maintained an active and diverse community since 1999.

The broader lesson is that design decisions are contextual. Decisions are also inter-dependent—together these heuristics create a different kind of online third place. This short case study contributes insights into how an unusual kind of site is constructed, which opens up intriguing questions about what other genres of online community could be created with different social norms grounded in different design decisions. The HCI community could benefit from further exploring the contextual basis of online community design decisions.

REFERENCES

1. Bergstrom, K. "Don't feed the troll": Shutting down debate about community expectations on Reddit.com. *First Monday*, 16, 1, (2011).
2. Bruckman, A., Danis, C., Lampe, C., Sternberg, J., & Waldron, C. Managing Deviant Behavior in Online Communities. Proceedings of CHI 2006, ACM Press (2006), 21-24.
3. Bryant, S., Forte, A., & Bruckman, A. Becoming Wikipedian: Transformation of Participation. In a Collaborative Online Encyclopedia. Proceedings of GROUP 2005, ACM Press (2005), 1-10.
4. Ellison, B & boyd, d. Sociality Through Social Network Sites. In *The Oxford Handbook of Internet Studies,* Dutton, w., Ed. Oxford University Press, Oxford, (2013), 151-172.
5. Gilbert, E. & Karahalios, K. Predicting Tie Strength with Social Media. In Proceedings of CHI 2009, ACM Press (2009), 211-220.
6. Gurzick, D. & Lutters, W. Towards a Design Theory for Online Communities. Proceedings of DESRIST 2009, ACM Press (2009).
7. Kiesler, S., Kraut, R., Resnick, P. & Kittur, A. Regulating Behavior in Online Communities. In *Building Successful Online Communities.* Kraut, R. Resnick, P. Eds. MIT Press (2012), 125-278.
8. Kim, A. *Community Building on the Web: Secret Strategies for Successful Online Communities.* Berkeley, CA: Peachpit Press, (2000).
9. Kollock, P., Design Principles for Online Communities. *PC Update*, 15, 5, (1998), 58-60.
10. Lampe, C., & Johnston, E. Follow the (slash)dot: Effects of Feedback on New Members in an Online Community. Proceedings of GROUP 2009, ACM Press (2009), 209-218.
11. Lave, J. and Wenger, E. Situated Learning: Legitimate Peripheral Participation. Cambridge University Press: Cambridge, UK, (1991).
12. Lazar, J., and J. Preece. Social Considerations in Online Communities: Usability, Sociability, and Success Factors. In *Cognition in the Digital World*, Oostendorp, H., Ed. Lawrence Erlbaum Associates, New Jersey, (2003).
13. Ling et. al., Using Social Psychology to Motivate Contributions to Online Communities. *Journal of Computer-Mediated Communication*, 10, 4, (2005).
14. Nonnecke B., & Preece, J., Lurker Demographics: Counting the Silent, Proceedings of CHI 2000. ACM Press (2000), 73-80.
15. Oldenberg, R. *The Great Good Place.* Marlowe & Company: New York, (1999)
16. Ren, Y, Kruat, R.E. & Kiesler, S. Encouraging commitment in online communities. In *Building Successful Online Communities.* Kraut, R. Resnick, P. Eds. MIT Press (2012), 77-124.

Everyday Ideation: All of My Ideas Are On Pinterest

Rhema Linder
Interface Ecology Lab
Texas A&M University
College Station, Texas
rhema@ecologylab.net

Clair Snodgrass
Interface Ecology Lab
Texas A&M University
College Station, Texas
clair@ecologylab.net

Andruid Kerne
Interface Ecology Lab
Texas A&M University
College Station, Texas
andruid@ecologylab.net

ABSTRACT
We develop new understanding of how people engage in digital curation. We interview twenty users of Pinterest, a social curation platform. We find that through collecting, organizing, and sharing image bookmarks, users engage in processes of *everyday ideation*. That is, they use digital found objects as creative resources to develop ideas for shaping their lives. Curators assemble information into new contexts, forming and sharing ideas with practical and emotional value. We investigate cognitive and social aspects of creativity that affect the digital curation practices of everyday ideation. We derive implications for the design of curation environments that support information-based ideation.

Author Keywords
information-based ideation; creativity; pinterest; curation; everyday design

ACM Classification Keywords
H.5.m. Information interfaces and presentation (e.g., HCI): Miscellaneous.; H.5.3. Group and Organization Interfaces: Asynchronous interaction - Web-based interaction.; K.4.2. Computers and society: Social Issues.

INTRODUCTION
We develop new understanding of how people engage in digital curation with social media to support ideation in ordinary life. Through a grounded theory investigation of Pinterest, we find that digital curators perceive themselves to be finding and keeping information to form ideas. Social and interactive aspects of digital curation platforms shape the experience of and its role in everyday activities and design.

A growing number of increasingly popular platforms support *digital curation*: collecting, organizing, and sharing content from the Web [27]. Curation is a creative activity [26] that employs qualitative human reasoning to gather and organize items into collections, creating value beyond the sum of each asset [16]. Exercising creativity, such as by curating, fills a deep human need associated with health, well being, self-esteem [18], learning, and self-actualization [5]. Personally encountering new facts, concepts, and ideas progressively increases one's potential for realizing creativity: from mundane to more eminent manifestations. Ideation is the creative process of generating ideas and exploring possibilities.

CHI 2014, April 26 - May 01 2014, Toronto, ON, Canada

ACM 978-1-4503-2473-1/14/04$15.00.
http://dx.doi.org/10.1145/2556288.2557273

People commonly gather, analyze, and manipulate objects in the home in response to needs through iterative processes. In the concept of *everyday design*, a critique of creative industries, everyday people engaged in the same activities as designers [25, 14]. Artifacts and actions serve as resources for addressing and streamlining life's situations and constraints.

Curation affords gathering and organizing information. Kerne et al. define *information-based ideation* (IBI) as human activities involving information in which new ideas are generated and developed [11]. IBI activities encompass a broad range of open-ended tasks such as redecorating a room, picking a thesis topic, and inventing new technologies. As people engage in IBI, they search for, find, organize, compile, and collect information, creating a curation product. The present research shows how Pinterest users engage in everyday forms of information-based ideation.

After conducting semi-structured interviews and analysis of digital curation in social media via Pinterest, we discovered IBI phenomena. We found that Pinterest boards are used as digital media of everyday design. Tens of millions of people use Pinterest [21] to collect Pins. Pins are based on clippings [11], i.e., images with short text snippets that effectively represent ideas within webpages and enable refinding. Pins (Figure 2) cover many topics [8], including recipes, photography, tutorials, and health and beauty advice. We report on a significant use of Pinterest where users gather Pins as *ideas* in meaningful and valuable ways, arranging them into boards which become design objects.

By *everyday ideation*, we mean ongoing processes in which curators look for, find, organize, and return to meaningful information as a means of provoking and forming ideas that address practical and emotional needs. These curators are informal designers that work with digital representations of information as design objects. Our contribution establishes that gathering and shaping ideas is a significant activity of digital curators, who function as *everyday ideators*.

We connect findings from creativity, design, personal information management, social psychology, and prior studies of Pinterest. We present our approach to qualitative data gathering and analysis. We derive four interrelated categories of phenomena: *Conceptualization*, *Social Interaction*, *Identity*,

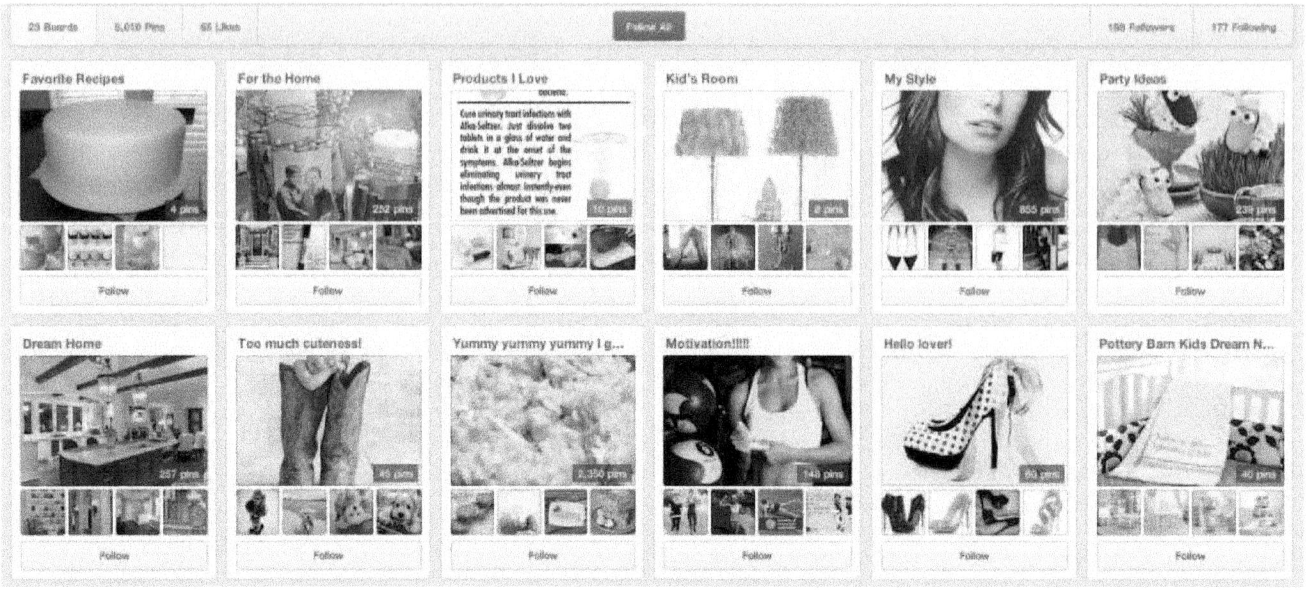

Figure 1. A selection of P9's 23 boards she uses to ideate and Keep Found Things Found. She says, *I do a lot, like, for the home: renovating or decorating ideas, I have kid's room stuff for my daughter, I have a lot of fashion, hair and beauty for myself, party ideas for little parties for my daughter . . . my dream home . . . food, . . . exercise, one just for shoes, . . . travel . . . and parenting tips. . . . This is where all of my ideas are. I don't have them anywhere else at all.*

and *Pinterest Every Day*. We conclude by discussing findings and developing implications of design.

RELATED WORK

To help formulate theory explaining observed ideation phenomena in Pinterest, we connect concepts from a range of interrelated research. We identify curation as an inherently creative activity. Because Pins can serve as bookmarks, we relate activities on Pinterest to Personal Information Management and media of curation. As emerging curation platforms increasingly employ feeds and sharing, we describe potential effects of social influence on both creativity and influence.

Creativity and Curation

In this work, we report on findings about *everyday* ideation. Kaufman et al. defines four kinds of creativity. In this model, kinds of creativity range from the everyday (little-c or mini-c) to eminent at the societal scale (Pro-c or big-C). Further, engaging in learning and synthesis can transition everyday forms of creativity into more eminent ones [10]. Exercising creativity increases self-esteem [18], and helps one learn and self-actualize [5]. The present research is based in mini-c and little-c forms of creativity. Participants reported using Pinterest to learn and combine.

Digital curation is a creative activity that requires human reasoning to collect and organize items into a meaningful whole [26]. The result is a collection of items with value beyond the sum of the assets [16]. Kerne et al. analyze media of curation at two levels: the medium of elements of curation (e.g. Pins) and the medium of their assemblage (e.g. boards) [11]. Webb et al. [26] develop a model of the curation process: people alternate focus among organizing, reflection, and interpretation. Wolf et al. link curation to learning through collecting, organizing, retelling, publishing, and interpretation [27].

Prior researchers have defined visual media for elements of curation. Teevan et al. found that for search and revisitation tasks, visual snippets, i.e., images with text overlaid, better summarize web pages than text or image representations alone [24]. *Rich bookmarks* go further, directly enhancing image clippings with structured metadata, in addition to affording revisitation [26]. Pins constitute rich bookmarks by enhancing an image clipping with title, source URL, creational context (user and board), and sometimes with additional metadata. The present research addresses how the role of the medium of Pins as elements of design contribute to their perception in social contexts.

Everyday Design

Wakkari and Maestri develop a concept of *everyday design* in which people commonly function as designers to address life's needs [25]. They broaden the definition of "designer" beyond professionals in creative industries, potentially to all people. Maestri and Wakkary describe how families develop solutions as they make adjustments over time [14]. They describe phenomena of *appropriation*, i.e., remaking an artifact by placing it into a new context and thereby personalizing it. This corresponds to Kerne et al's finding of Pins as digital found objects and elements of curation [11]. We see everyday design on Pinterest on two levels: (1) ideators gather and appropriate Pins as "ideas", (2) boards function as media of everyday design. We present data showing how people use boards for pragmatic and emotional reasons, such as entertainment, comfort, and life planning.

Personal Information Management

Jones et al. performed an extended workplace study, investigating practices of Personal Information Management (PIM) for keeping track of URLs and content via browsers, email, and handwritten sticky notes [9]. Their functional analysis

Figure 2. P9's board, entitled *Hello Lover* is "Just about shoes." Its title refers to a recurring line in the series *Sex In the City* where the main character exclaims over expensive designer shoes. Placing shoes in this context changes their social significance.

develops aspects of effective bookmarking strategy: portability, persistence, ease of access, ease of maintenance, and ease of sharing. Jones et al. title their work with an insightful question, "Once found, what then? [9]" The present research looks deeply into personal experiences of meaning and value in ongoing collections to answer their question anew.

Lindley et al. interviewed seventeen participants to investigate PIM on websites for personal archive, e.g., Flickr, Gmail, and Pinterest [12]. They identify five types of content, including collections that are curated online (e.g. Pinterest), and "content for consumption" and "content for the moment" (e.g. Twitter). We observed phenomena of development over time as well as daily planning on Pinterest. The present research focuses on PIM in which users engage in ideation.

Social Psychology and Creativity

Amabile takes a social psychology approach, modeling creativity as a function of three components: expertise, creative thinking skills, and motivation [1, 2]. She distinguishes between intrinsic and extrinsic motivation. Intrinsic motivation originates from within the individual, e.g. curiosity, drive to solve a problem, or enjoyment from performing creative tasks. Extrinsic evaluations, such as being penalized for missing deadlines, are detrimental to creativity. Amabile compared the performance of students writing silly essays under two conditions: expecting evaluation of content, and expecting to self-rate their mood [22]. Students who were told their content would not be judged produced more creative essays. Likewise, our participants do not feel judged or watched as they Pin. This positively impacts creative self-efficacy.

In some circumstances, however, extrinsic motivation can foster creativity. For example, when a consequence is perceived as bonus rather than a penalty, creativity may be positively impacted. The repin mechanism works as a consequential bonus to Pinterest users. It does not create a sense of impending evaluation.

Cialdini develops the principle of *social proof*, which states that one way people reason about expected behavior is to observe the actions of those around them. For example, children who were frightened of dogs were shown a video of a boy playing with a puppy. Four days later, sixty-seven percent of them voluntarily climbed into a pen with a dog. The effects of social proof are most powerful when the subject sees the other person as similar. When a person sees that someone like them can do something, they expect to be able to do the same thing [6]. On Pinterest, we argue that continued exposure to diverse content pinned by others perceived as 'like me' to a user encourages them to approach unfamiliar interests and try new things.

Pinterest

Pinterest's medium of elements is the Pin, and its medium of assemblage is the board. Users curate content by *pinning* from the Web, and *repinning*: using others' Pins. They may originally add a Pin by entering a URL, clicking a "Pin Me" button from a website, clicking a bookmarklet that enters the current URL for them, or uploading a picture directly. Alternatively, repinning, which accounts for four out of five Pins [21], enables users to copy any Pin they see to their own boards, while retaining attribution.

Pins can also be "liked" and commented on. To store and organize pins, users curate content into *boards* (See Figures 1 and 2). Pinterest supports a variety of ways to follow, browse, and find Pins. A user can search, browse categories, and view popular content and streams of Pins from boards s/he follows. Pinterest supports a variety of ways to follow, browse, and find Pins. Pins are visualized in a flow layout that places them contiguously into columns.

Gilbert et al. [7] collected a detailed algorithmic sampling of Pins from around the world. After analyzing a large sample, they found eighty percent of Pinterest users are female and twenty percent are male. They also compared comments on Pins to tweets on Twitter. Rather than using statistics, we investigate Pinterest qualitatively.

Hall et al. categorized activities on Pinterest as collecting, discovering, collaborating, and publishing. They investigated both professional and personal Pinterest activities, describing Pins as boundary objects with ranges of interpretation [28]. We explore how Pins and boards are conceptualized, attain practical and emotional value, and support everyday ideation.

METHODOLOGY

We conducted a qualitative study to investigate the perspectives of Pinterest users through experiential data. We engaged in a grounded theory methodology, building theory in a constant comparative process of data collection and analysis [23]. The goal of our study was to develop a better understanding of how and why people curate digitally.

Organizing Phone Interviews via Mechanical Turk

We conducted twenty telephone interviews with Pinterest users that we organized via Mechanical Turk. Mechanical Turk allows individuals or businesses to post small jobs, called "HITs", (Human Intelligence Tasks) that Turk workers may browse and complete for monetary compensation [15].

Name	Age	Sex	Occupation	Hrs
P1*	31	f	teacher	2
P2	54	f	IT project manager	5
P3	23	f	photography studio manager	6
P4	27	f	not employed	2
P5	27	f	part-time admin	3
P6	30	f	equestrian facility	7
P7	25	f	bartender	3
P8	23	f	shift manager at a restaurant	10
P9*	32	f	works as a personal banker	9
P10	29	f	doctors assistant	1
P11	27	f	mother	9
P12	55	f	works as a lab technician	5
P13	33	f	freelance transcription	5
P14	45	f	playground supervisor	5
P15*	32	f	secretary and mother	10
P16*	27	f	parental consultant	6
P17*	66	f	grandmother	6
P18	25	m	works as an artist manager	13
P19*	36	f	math teacher	8
P20	25	m	works in sales	4

Table 1. Table of participants, name, age, gender, occupation, and the number of reported hours of spent on Pinterest per week. Asterisks indicate we were able to collect curation products.

Turk workers are usually offered jobs that are menial and pay in amounts lower than a dollar.

Our HITs contained instructions to call a phone number for a fifteen to thirty minute interview. A Pinterest user called from ten to forty minutes after a HIT was posted. Speaking with participants directly removed the need to perform data validation. We conducted each interview, later fully transcribing it for analysis. To vet very casual users of Pinterest, we asked that workers only take the HIT if they had collected at least 100 Pins. To make calls inexpensive for participants, we restricted the HIT to workers within the United States. To lower chances of receiving spam workers, we only accepted workers with an acceptance rate at least ninety percent.

We interviewed eighteen women and two men, echoing Pinterest [21] and Mechanical Turk [17] demographics. One participant used Pinterest solely for professional reasons (P18). A few used Pinterest for both work and personal collections. The majority solely used Pinterest non-professionally. In this way, our data addresses everyday users and their experiences. Participants were diverse (see Table 1). They reported using Pinterest between one and thirteen hours per week.

Data Collection and Analysis Process

We conducted semi-structured interviews, allowing the researcher to focus on questions most relevant to each participant. This allowed the subjects to discuss at any length what they saw as most important. We organized the interview guide questions by topic, and then from the most basic, broad questions to more specific, higher level ones. This hierarchy encouraged the participant to think critically about their own actions, and gave them time and a basis for articulating their thoughts and feelings on a topic. This process often led to the participant naturally going on to answer questions that had not yet been asked. Ultimately, our interview process gave the study flexibility, allowing each participant to independently highlight information and phenomena unique to their individual experiences using Pinterest.

After each interview, brief observational notes were recorded. After every five interviews, researchers convened to discuss the data and iteratively revise the interview guide. This iterative process helped us to ask clearer, more specific questions to pursue emerging phenomena. For example, instead of, "What do your boards mean to you?" We began to ask, "What makes your boards valuable to you?" This wording elicited less confusion and deeper responses from participants. The interview guide contained twenty-one questions in the first draft, and sixty-seven questions by the final five interviews. Interviews ran from eleven to forty-five minutes long, depending on the participant.

After a majority of the interviews were complete, two researchers independently open coded the transcriptions, noting themes that were interesting or persistent. Coding in this context refers the analytic processes through which data are fractured, conceptualized, and integrated to form theory [23].

We developed over thirty codes initially. We compared notes and codes, finished the interview and transcription process completely, and grouped codes and phenomena into categories. Four main categories of data were established. The researchers then selectively coded using these categories. This process gave us experiential insight into the motivations and behaviors of Pinterest users.

Adding Artifacts

After interviewing participants, we wanted to see the boards they made so that we could connect interview transcripts with artifacts participants created. We used Mechanical Turk's API to send an email inviting our participants to perform a HIT to this end. Seven of the twenty responded. For each of these participants, we collected a PDF snapshot of their boards and user page as seen from a web browser. The artifacts provided complementary visual context to our analysis.

RESULTS AND ANALYSIS

We present our analysis derived through open and selective coding, which form the basis of our theory.

Conceptualization

Our participants appropriate information from the Web into Pins as resources for ideation, conceptualizing them as ideas that serve particular purposes in situated contexts. In Amabile's model, creative production is maximized when creative thinking skills, motivation, and expertise are high. Participants reported being motivated by Pins (see Figure 2). Pins link to information resources, such as tutorials, which can support users' increasing their expertise. We found that participants apply information-based ideation and creative thinking skills in seeking, collecting, analyzing, and testing ideas from Pins.

Pins Are Ideas

In answering questions about Pinterest, our participants use the word *idea* to describe Pins they collected. They use the words "Pins", "things", and "ideas", along with concrete nouns, interchangeably. The overwhelming majority, eighteen out of twenty participants, referred to looking for or collecting Pins as "ideas". Gilbert et al. provide statistical evidence that the word "idea" plays a key role in distinguishing comments on Pins from tweets on Twitter [7]. We interpret this to mean that forming and presenting ideas is essential to how everyday ideators use Pinterest as a social medium of curation. We found that Pins support engagement in ideation by providing rich representations of many "different" ideas.

> P11: I like that [Pinterest] has different *ideas* ...[for making] crafty things for your house.

> P12: I'd much rather do Pinterest [than watch TV], because there's so many different *ideas* out there to look at.

Pins enable ideation, revealing previously unknown concepts and approaches. Everyday ideators use Pinterest to be inspired, not only by newfound ideas, but also by others engaged in everyday design in unexpected ways.

> P7: [Pinterest] has a lot of ideas that I wouldn't think of on my own and they're really neat, and that you can just try just around the house. ... [There are] a lot of creative things that you can find on there.

> P11: Pinterest is a direct field to what you want in certain crafts...I can type in "wreath", "homemade wreath", and it directs me tons of different ideas for wreaths, where if I go on the internet, I'm going to have to search through fifty million things.

People also think of and treat Pins like things. When talking about their boards, they do not say that they have pictures of things, but use diction consistent with owning corporeal collections. Similarly, they show each other pins from phones and other devices directly, as if they were objects.

Pins Are Flexible
Pins and boards span a wide range of topics. Our participants appropriate Pins for many aspects of their lives.

> P4: There's a few [boards] that are for recipes: various types, one for alcoholic drinks, one for non-alcoholic drinks, one for vegetarian foods, one for just dinner ideas, a dessert one, I've got a Dr. Who board and one that's just cats, one that's just cake, like some design ones... and then lots of crafting ones.

Pins are used as a digital shorthand, connecting products or tutorials to the common to-do list.

> P17: I redid my closet, in the hallway ...I got the idea from Pinterest and I used it to plan out like what I was gonna buy and what I needed for that project.

> P4: I pin things ... that I plan to do in the future.

Everyday ideators curate Pins to suit personal means of emotional fulfillment, including entertainment or comfort.

> P4: I just, I really like cats and if I'm ever, in, like, a bad mood, pictures of cats being ridiculous kinda cheer me up.

Pinterest users curate Pins for both personally practical and emotional reasons, planning for life's current and future needs.

More Than Pictures
Because Pins link to web pages, they are used as a visual medium for bookmarks. Many participants reported being frustrated with Pins that do not link properly to source pages. An example would be a user a intending to buy a product represented by a Pin, but it is sold out or was made with a temporary link. Mis-linked Pins are sufficiently common that a website P5 mentioned, thehunt.com, rewards those that find substitute or original product links that correspond to images.

> P12: I wanted to collect recipes off the internet, and rather than bookmarking them, I just wanted an easier place to put them to get easier access to them.

> P17: If [a Pin] looks pretty, then that will make me go to the blog to investigate it.

The medium of Pins as rich bookmarks, combining images with links and metadata, enhances how people experience them. As our participants appropriate information from the Web, they situate them into a board with personal context. Ultimately, Pins as elements of curation are flexible and serve many purposes in fulfilling emotional and practical needs through ideation.

Social Interaction
Comments on Pinterest are rare, usually occurring among friends and family. Social actions mostly go unnoticed, removing inhibitions typically experienced when authoring social media. Though Pinterest does not support direct messaging, participants use alternate digital media and face-to-face communication to talk about Pins and boards. Ironically, despite the myriad of repinning, users perceive Pinterest as a solitary space for collecting ideas. They see other social media, such as Facebook, as spaces for conversation, e.g. self-promotion.

Commenting on Pins
Our participants rarely comment on Pins. Seven said they had never commented on Pinterest, despite long-term use. P19 uses Pinterest 8 hours a week, but has never commented:

> P19: Um, not really no. I didn't even realize we could [comment on Pins] until I saw somebody else comment on one, but I've never commented on one.

When participants did comment, the Pin was usually authored by a friend or family member.

> P7: Sometimes, [I comment on Pins], if I like it and if it's somebody I know.

While Pins display the attribution of who pinned and repinned them, our participants report that they pay little attention to the Pin authors, unless it is a friend or family member.

> P18: I mainly focus on the Pins themselves, the ideas. It doesn't really matter who the person is. Are they really famous or not, or somebody that's pinned something that I've liked before? It doesn't really matter.

> P8: I don't [pay attention to the Pin author] because a good idea is a good idea either way.

Despite the public nature of boards, Pinterest users do not feel scrutinized as they pin. They are more interested in the Pins themselves than where they came from, or who found them. This contributes to the feeling of anonymity in Pinterest users, which serves to dampen the kind of extrinsic motivation that is detrimental to creativity.

Pinterest allows a user to make up to three "secret" boards that can be only be seen by the creator. Four participants report having secret boards. Secret boards may contain ideas for health, life goals, or Christmas presents.

> P11: [My secret boards are] like diet stuff I put in one board; and, then, when my daughter's birthday [was coming up] I didn't really want other people to see what I was going to do for it, so I put that in the board as well. ... There's certain things I don't really need everyone else to know, that I'm on a diet or just, I feel, that's just something I keep private in my life.

Comparing Sociality In Other Networks

We asked participants to compare aspects of using Pinterest to other social media platforms they use, such as Facebook, Twitter, and Instagram.

The social actions of pinning or repinning are generally publicly visible. Yet, Pinterest users do not feel watched or judged. Forte et al. [28] compare the semi-anonymous feeling of using Pinterest to walking unnoticed through a busy marketplace. Participants enjoy the feeling of separateness afforded by Pinterest. It creates a sense of personal space.

> P13: On Facebook and Twitter, I felt a little more connection with the people posting, so comments would be a little more personal. But with Pinterest ... I don't really feel personally connected with people. Which makes me like it more, actually. Yeah, I actually prefer to be a little separate from people. ... It makes me not feel as involved, which means that it doesn't take as much of my energy.

> P12: It seems more private in Pinterest than it is in Facebook, because it feels like Pinterest is just for me. ... [On] Facebook everyone else is seeing everything, I guess some people are seeing it [on Pinterest], but they don't know me, I guess.

Because users feel that they have a separate space, they are not pressured by extrinsic judgments on the quality of their Pins and repins. According to Amabile's model [2], this avoids "killing creativity".

Participants contrast this sense of uninvolved sociality with social networks, which users sometimes grow tired of, causing them to take breaks or even delete their accounts altogether [4]. Other social networks are seen as venues for self promotion. Pinterest is seen as space for sharing things and ideas, with few social constraints.

> P10: [With Pinterest], it's like "Let me share this cool thing I found with you", but not like, "Oh look at me." ... Facebook is more for family and friends more, to keep in touch ... Pinterest is more like sharing ideas.

> P9: I just haven't seen the negativity on Pinterest that has been on Facebook... I know they're not gonna make mean comments or tell me I'm stupid... I don't think a lot of people even comment on stuff. They just repin it.

Our participants report that getting a "repin", when a Pinterest user Pins something from another's board, is a minor, yet positive, social interaction. The repin is not expected, but it is a welcome occurrence.

> P8: It makes me feel like I've got a good idea that somebody else wants to use.

> P2: Oh it's a compliment. Um, not only is it nice to know that someone shares my interests, it also feels like someone complimented you. It makes me smile every time I see that someone repinned it. ... Like someone patting you on the back is what I think of.

The repin produces extrinsic motivation which encourages creativity because it is an unanticipated bonus. Repins provide encouragement without making users feel obligated to engage in further social interaction.

Identity

We find that Pinterest affords exploring and shaping identity. We asked participants, "Who do you pin for?" They consistently report that they pin for themselves, and sometimes for their families as well.

Identity can be understood through sets of personal attributes, such as interest, skills, and beliefs [20]. Our participants use boards to express interests and motivate personal change. As they revisit collections over time, they sometimes reflect on how their sense of self has changed.

Pins accrue intrinsic value as users develop new tastes, hone skills, and become motivated. Boards attain an irreplaceable quality as everyday ideators integrate them into their lives, making them very valuable. Repeated exposure to others' Pins constitutes tacit social proof, making new goals and personally untested ideas appear achievable.

Discovering Tastes and Interests

Participants used curation as a means to discover and articulate tastes and interests. P14 uses curation on Pinterest to learn about herself and discover her tastes over time.

> P14: I ... thought ... if I collect enough of these pins, I would be able to get a visual [sense] of my style. Like something would emerge, like a common theme or something that would help me understand myself more.

P4 uses Pinterest to broaden her interests.

> P4: I think I've expanded the types of recipes and everything that I try ... I can bake bread better. I make lotion and soap now!

Personal Value

As Pinterest users acquire Pins, they feel their boards accrue intrinsic and practical value.

> P20: [Pinterest is] almost like a record book, for me, so it has almost more of an intrinsic value than ... putting a status update on Facebook ... that no one really cares about. [Pinterest has] an emotional value ... It gives me kind of a archive to hold on to things that I think are important.

Personal attachment to boards increases with their size and use, seen in P9's response to the question, "What would you do or what alternative would you turn to if Pinterest shut down?"

> P9: I've got 3,600 Pins so far... I would just die, especially my recipes ... I don't know what I would do.

Social Proof

In Cialdini's concept of social proof [6], people observe the actions of others to help them understand what is socially acceptable and personally achievable. This effect is most pronounced when observed actions are performed by people perceived as similar. A user will sometimes sense that another is "like them" because the other user curates Pins that are relevant to their interests or similar to their own tastes. Common situations, such as birthday or dinner parties make ideas and tutorials on Pins seem personally achievable.

> P5: I didn't even know how to cook or, how to do the simplest meals. [Pinterest] gives me step by step [instructions], and I see other people trying it. Then, I'm like, "Okay this isn't that hard." ... I've seen people [on Pinterest], like, I should be their friend because they have all the same stuff as me.

> P11: My daughter's first birthday was last Wednesday, so I used it to plan her first birthday party. ... I typed in "Mickey Mouse Clubhouse" [to Pinterest search] and I got different ideas from different people that have had birthday parties... from decorating, food ideas, on crafting ideas, so I took everything off of Pinterest, basically.

Pinterest Every Day

Our participants replaced prior entertainment habits with Pinterest, in part because they believe it uplifts their lives. They see Pinterest as a better use of time compared to other forms of entertainment, such as watching television. From spare moments to hour-long sessions, users are constantly growing boards, looking for new ideas.

We asked participants to describe a typical Pinterest session. We found that those who spend less time on Pinterest each week tend to use it in bursts during in-between time, especially on a mobile device or tablet. Those who used Pinterest five or more hours a week replaced or augmented other entertainment habits with sustained sessions, in which they use Pinterest for an hour or more. P2 uses Pinterest as part of her daily routine, comparing it to the habitual act of reading the newspaper. Because Pinterest is accessible on many devices, such as mobile phones, participants such as P10 can use Pinterest in short bursts that last only a few minutes, several times throughout the day.

> P2: Growing up, we'd always have the newspaper, right, and that's what you read in the morning and go get your breakfast. And now I have a laptop instead ... Part of the news is Pinterest.

> P10: [I use Pinterest] whenever I have a few minutes here and there, a lot of times I'll be on my phone. Or if I'm on my laptop I'll go on. But it varies it could be morning, it could be late at night. Just whenever I have spare time.

Participants made quick decisions on whether or not to repin, reporting that they take fewer than five seconds to determine. They experience excitement when they encounter Pins worthy of collecting.

> P20: Usually I just go on kind of just for visual stimulation, ... but I don't go on with the intent of finding a specific pin or specific content.

> P19: If it's funny, ... and if I think it's gonna be useful, ... how it looks, how easy it is to understand, [If] I can look at and get right away, or ... If I don't have time to do it right then, I'll pin it so I can look at it later.

Our participants used Pinterest on a daily basis, growing curations over time. We observed two kinds of seeking behavior: (1) casual browsing with no particular goal in mind, such as with P10, and (2) responding to a specific IBI task, such finding a new hairstyle.

> P10: I log in like just once a day and ... I kinda just go through things and pin them if I like them. ... I don't have the time to go through because there's so many like sites I'm on and other things I need to take care of.

> P13: I'm usually browsing for particular things. I'll be like I might be looking for like a new hair product, or a new hairstyle. ... I don't have a lot of time so I just stay focused.

We asked participants, "Have you ever finished a board?" All users responded that they had never finished a board. Curation on Pinterest is an ongoing process.

> P9: Finished a board? ... Is there like a limit to how many pins we can have? Because I mean, I didn't know if you could limit one out or not. ... There's always more ideas that you can pin.

In daily use of Pinterest, our participants grew boards to address the needs of life, both practically and emotionally. Boards are constantly altered by Pinterest users in ongoing processes that become entwined with everyday life.

DISCUSSION

We discuss how everyday ideators use boards as a medium for design, curating for different purposes. Pins, once appropriated into boards, function as uniquely contextualized found objects. The meaning and utility of these found objects change as people exercise creativity and invoke their ideas. Social perceptions of Pinterest help motivate everyday ideators, increasing their expertise and creativity.

Everyday Ideation

Pinterest users engage in everyday processes in which they look for, find, organize, and return to meaningful information as a means of provoking and forming ideas that address both practical and emotional needs. They see Pins as ideas, assembling them into boards with specific purposes. Through pinning and repinning, they curate personally meaningful archives, engaging in self-directed information-based ideation. While everyday designers manipulate furniture and objects in the home to support daily routines and activity, these everyday ideators grow boards which function as design media of curation.

Pinterest users often have an information-based ideation task in mind, such as P17's trip to Italy with her daughter, or her plans for weekly meals and entertainment for her friends and family. P17 makes weekly meal plans on Pinterest, and each week, she adds Pins to a temporary board for meal planning. After she tries a recipe, she moves the Pin into either her "Tried It Loved It" or "Tried It Wouldn't Make It Again" board. In this way, P17 curates a reusable repository for responding to her life's needs.

As social online curation platforms grow, more people use them for everyday ideation. People appropriate information to address life's needs, and use curation to plan, motivate, and expand their interests. The phenomena of everyday ideation we observed on Pinterest are a product of general human needs, the affordances of the Pins / boards conjunction as a medium of curation, and the Pinterest platform's support for social interaction.

Appropriation Into Pins as Found Objects

Through the act of choosing a Pin and placing it into a board, a user changes its context and purpose, transforming an image clipping into a *found object*. Duchamp introduced *Fountain* as a found object under the alias, "R. Mutt", by placing a urinal in an art exhibit [13]. He appropriated the urinal, creating new significance and meaning by changing its context and function. The creative act of finding, choosing, and placing an object or Pin into a new context changes its meaning and function.

As Pinterest users curate Pins, they appropriate them to suit their own personal needs and taste. Personal context determines a Pin's purpose and meaning. For example, P17's Italy board contains a Pin of a "salted rose" pastry. In a dessert or food board, the salted rose would not have locational significance, but P17's board maps out activities for P17 and her daughter's trip to Italy. The salted rose pastry Pin in this context carries additional meaning as a planned activity involving Italian culture. Fitness and life planning boards similarly appropriate and recontextualize Pins.

To Duchamp, changing the place and title of a found object has the potential to transform its useful significance [13]. In this same way, a board's title transforms its Pins' meanings. P13 collects shoes in her board "Hello Lover," referencing a recurring line in the television series *Sex in the City*; the main character, Carrie Bradshaw, has a strong affinity for designer shoes. This reference possesses cultural connotations of wealth, sexiness, and style. Pinterest users apply cultural references to board titles to add meaning and personality.

Motivational boards exemplify the appropriation of heterogeneous found objects. P9's board, entitled "Motivation!!!!!", includes 144 diverse Pins, including an image of a bowl full of yogurt, fruit, and nuts, and pictures of women exercising on the beach. Again, Pins are transformed and accrete meaning through the context of a board. "Motivation!!!!!" integrates the practical function of providing tips to become healthier with visual reminders of the ideal self. It serves as a source of personal strength. Similarly, while the cats P4 curated come from a variety of sources with different original purposes, the context of her board uses them to provide her with comfort and entertainment. When P4 is in a bad mood, she uses her cat board to help feel better. This curation serves her as a useful and meaningful assemblage of found objects.

The Purposes of Pins

Pins are flexible. Everyday ideators appropriate information, pinning and repinning with particular purposes. Purposes we encountered include: motivation, planning, ideation, goal-setting, to increase expertise, to comfort, to entertain, and to self-actualize.

P5's recipe board motivates her to try new things. P11 collected ideas to plan her daughter's birthday party. P13 uses a secret board to set longterm life goals. P12 has increased her crocheting and cooking expertise. P4's cat board entertains and comforts her. P14 uses Pinterest to self-actualize, expressing and developing her style and interests in the pursuit of "learning about herself".

The purpose and meaning of Pins and boards may change over time. Consider P17's trip to Italy with her daughter. When she started the board, she had the practical purpose of planning her trip. After her trip, she did not delete her board because it still held value; its meaning evolved to represent memories of her vacation. When she goes on another trip, she can reuse Pins. For example, one of the Pins on the Italy board includes a comprehensive checklist of items to bring on international vacations. When P17 needs this Pin again, it will be easily accessible. In this situation, the board becomes practical again, while still retaining its emotional significance. Similarly, many kinds of boards evolve in meaning as context and needs change. For example, food, vacation, and wedding boards may become more meaningful after the events they were created for have passed.

When users take ideas from Pins and invoke them, such as following craft guides or traveling to planned destinations, Pins become more meaningful. P17's board *Try It Loved It* contains one hundred Pins, mostly recipes. This personalized archive is a system she uses to plan meals. Pins' accrue what P20 calls "intrinsic value" serving both as a record and a reusable system.

A Social Medium For Not Killing Creativity

In Amabile's model [2], motivation and expertise are key for creative production. Pinterest's medium of curation affects motivation by providing a sense of unevaluated workspace, the opportunity for a bonus validation, and a culture of positive feedback. Everyday ideators' expertise broadens through repeated exposure and social proof.

Pinterest provides a sense of unevaluated workspace. In curating, our participants ironically felt nearly anonymous. Users feel free to work on Pinterest without judgement, in contrast to social networks like Facebook and Twitter. To P12, everyone sees everything on Facebook, but "it feels like Pinterest is just for me." Pinterest users see boards as works in progress rather than finished ones. This sense of virtual solitude averts the extrinsic evaluation that can kill creativity.

At the same time, pinning creates the potential for a repin, which acts as a motivational bonus. To have a Pin repined provides outside validation of one's ideas. From P2's perspective, the repin serves as a compliment because another person shares her interest. P2 compares this to a pat on the back. Comments on Pinterest, while rare, are also overwhelmingly positive.

Our participants used Pinterest to increase their expertise, and often felt other users were similar to them. Participants reported seeing many "different" ideas from others with whom they share common interest. They are constantly exposed to ideas from users they follow and Pins others have collected. The effects of social proof strongly influence a person's perception, making unfamiliar activities seem achievable. In trying new things, people gain skills and expertise, key components of creativity.

IMPLICATIONS FOR DESIGN

We develop implications for design of social media of curation that support everyday ideation, addressing the representation of media of curation and the level of sociality of shared workspaces.

Curation Media: Assemblage of Image Clippings

Represent elements of curation with image clippings. Enable them to be visually assembled. This will support expression, decision making, and juxtaposition as scaffolding for ideation.

Pins, Pinterest's elemental medium of curation, are image clippings that function as rich bookmarks [26]. Pins possess visceral and informational value. For most participants, a Pin's image is most important. Images convey implicit information that is immediately understandable. Our participants enjoyed looking at and collecting images they consider beautiful and inspiring. For example, P4's looks at her collection of cat images to feel better.

The visual semantic nature of Pins helps users choose and evaluate their metadata. Our participants prefer Pins that catch their eye, are easily understandable, or are in a particular style. In searching Pinterest or browsing large boards, they evaluate many Pins. Participants reported taking fewer than five seconds to decide to pin. They rely on fast visual cognition when choosing and refinding. Metadata affords exploration of the source page, board, or original pinner.

Boards show Pins together, visually assembling the elements of curation into rich juxtapositions. Combining content in different ways stimulates the generation of new understanding and ideas [11]. P14 uses boards as a basis for reflection. As she curates, she *looks* for emergent themes that build and express a sense of her style. Baddeley has established the role of human capabilities involving visual cognition and integration, beyond cognition of text [3]. By invoking visual, textual, and integrative human cognitive capabilities, the medium of boards of Pins provides scaffolding for ideation. The medium affords everyday ideation in ways that textual entries and individual element views cannot.

New contexts are created by assembling digital found objects as Pins into boards. P9's "Hello Lover" (Figure 2) board develops layers of cultural context through image clippings, metadata, and assemblage. The medium of boards of Pins also contributes to social context. They build social proof, making unfamiliar activities, such as making soap, seem achievable, because people "like me" perform them.

Support Lightweight Collaboration

Create spaces for lightweight social engagement and collaboration that simultaneously enable independent work and access to others' ideas. Pinterest users pin for themselves. They rarely comment on Pinterest. Users report that Pinterest avoids negative external evaluation, which Amabile showed is detrimental to creativity [2]. P13 reported that it takes less "energy to Pin" than to post on Facebook, because she experiences Pinterest as "her own" space.

Ironically, despite users reporting that they experience Pinterest as a separate space, four out of five Pins are repins [21], copied from another user's board. Anyone may curate a public Pin into their own board, constituting a lightweight form of collaboration.

As participants' Pins were repinned, they felt encouraged, but not obligated to further engage socially. Pinterest notifies the owner when someone repins. This reinforcement encourages engagement through pinning, without an onus for follow-up social action. While 7 of our participants had never commented directly on a Pin, they frequently repin.

Prior experiments in brainstorming in Engineering Design show that restricting overt communication, e.g. textual or verbal interaction, generates more ideas in groups [19]. In C-Sketch, a technique for collaboratively generating ideas, people communicate visually, without textual or verbal communication during ideation. To begin the technique, a person starts a sketch. Next, s/he passes it to a group member to continue sketching. This is repeated until ideas converge. C-Sketch supports individual ideation to increase creative production. Pinterest users also communicate visually. They assemble Pins into new contexts, combining ideas. Because P17's Italy board contains many repins, it constitutes a lightweight collaboration among many Pinterest users. These collaborators only needed the medium of the Pin and social affordance of the repin. Create spaces where lightweight collaboration is supported, but overt communication is not required, to foster everyday ideation.

CONCLUSION

We formulated the notion of everyday ideation, in which people engage in popular curation activities as a means of generating ideas, which they see as enriching their lives. We developed a new understanding of how social media of digital curation can support everyday ideation. Using grounded theory, we discovered that everyday ideators use Pinterest to gather information and form ideas through the medium of Pins. Boards constitute a medium for assemblage of Pins to support planning, goal setting, comfort, entertainment, gains in expertise, and self-actualization. By appropriating Pins and information from others, people use boards as lightweight social contexts in which they juxtapose and recontextualize found objects, supporting information-based ideation.

As a social and collaborative platform, Pinterest fosters creativity with "just for me" workspaces, which remove fear of evaluation, while enabling positive feedback. At the same time, social proof effects from constant exposure to others' Pins encourage users to expand their expertise and interests. Everyday ideators create new meaning in ongoing processes of appropriating information in response to personal needs, shaping ideas through media of curation into systems that improve their lives.

ACKNOWLEDGMENTS

This work is funded through NSF Grant IIS 0747428.

REFERENCES

1. Amabile, T. *The social psychology of creativity*. Springer series in social psychology. Springer-Verlag, 1983.
2. Amabile, T. M. How to Kill Creativity. *Harvard Business Review 76*, 5 (Sept. 1998).
3. Baddeley, A. The episodic buffer: a new component of working memory? *Trends in cognitive sciences 4*, 11 (2000), 417–423.
4. Baumer, E. P., Adams, P., Khovanskaya, V. D., Liao, T. C., Smith, M. E., Schwanda Sosik, V., and Williams, K. Limiting, leaving, and (re)lapsing: an exploration of facebook non-use practices and experiences. In *In Proc. CHI*, ACM (2013).
5. Burleson, W. Developing creativity, motivation, and self-actualization with learning systems. *International Journal of Human-Computer Studies 63*, 4 (2005).
6. Cialdini, R. *Influence*. HarperCollins, 2009.
7. Gilbert, E., Bakhshi, S., Chang, S., and Terveen, L. "i need to try this": A statistical overview of pinterest. In *In Proc. CHI*, ACM (2013).
8. Hall, C. Exploring social curation. *D-Lib Magazine 18*, 11/12 (2012).
9. Jones, W., Dumais, S., and Bruce, H. Once found, what then? a study of "keeping" behaviors in the personal use of web information. *In Proc. American Society for Information Science and Technology 39*, 1 (2002).
10. Kaufman, J. C., and Beghetto, R. A. Beyond big and little: The four c model of creativity. *Review of General Psychology 13*, 1 (2009), 1.
11. Kerne, A., Webb, A. M., Smith, S., Linder, R., Lupfer, N., Qu, Y., Moeller, J., and Damaraju, S. Evaluating information-based ideation with creativity measures of curation products. *In Review. ACM Transactions*.
12. Lindley, S. E., Marshall, C. C., Banks, R., Sellen, A., and Regan, T. Rethinking the web as a personal archive. In *In Proc. WWW* (2013).
13. Lippard, L. *Dadas on Art*. Prentice Hall, 1972.
14. Maestri, L., and Wakkary, R. Understanding repair as a creative process of everyday design. In *Creativity and Cognition*, ACM (2011).
15. Mason, W., and Suri, S. Conducting behavioral research on amazon's mechanical turk. *Behavior research methods 44*, 1 (2012).
16. Rosenbaum, S. *Curation Nation: How to Win in a World Where Consumers are Creators*. McGraw-Hill, 2011.
17. Ross, J., Irani, L., Silberman, M., Zaldivar, A., and Tomlinson, B. Who are the crowdworkers?: shifting demographics in mechanical turk. In *In Proc. CHI*, ACM (2010).
18. Schmid, T. *Promoting health through creativity: for professionals in health, arts and education*. Wiley, 2006.
19. Shah, J. J., Vargas-Hernandez, N., Summers, J. D., and Kulkarni, S. Collaborative sketching (c-sketch)—an idea generation technique for engineering design. *Journal of Creative Behavior 35*, 3 (2001).
20. Shoemaker, D. *Personal Identity and Ethics: A Brief Introduction*. Broadview guides to philosophy. Broadview Press, 2008.
21. Smith, C. 22 amazing pinterest stats. http://expandedramblings.com/index.php/pinterest-stats/ 09, 13.
22. Sternberg, R. *Handbook of Creativity*. Cambridge University Press, 1999.
23. Strauss, A., and Corbin, J. *Basics of Qualitative Research: Techniques and Procedures for Developing Grounded Theory*. SAGE Publications, 1998.
24. Teevan, J., Cutrell, E., Fisher, D., Drucker, S. M., Ramos, G., André, P., and Hu, C. Visual snippets: summarizing web pages for search and revisitation. In *In Proc. SIGCHI*, ACM (2009).
25. Wakkary, R., and Maestri, L. The resourcefulness of everyday design. In *ACM C&C* (2007).
26. Webb, A. M., Linder, R., Kerne, A., Lupfer, N., Qu, Y., Poffenberger, B., and Revia, C. Promoting reflection and interpretation in education: Curating rich bookmarks as information composition. In *ACM C&C* (2013).
27. Wolff, A., and Mulholland, P. Curation, curation, curation. In *Proceedings of the 3rd Narrative and Hypertext Workshop*, ACM (2013).
28. Zarro, M., Hall, C., and Forte, A. Wedding dresses and wanted criminals: Pinterest. com as an infrastructure for repository building. In *Proc. AAAI Conf. on Weblogs and Social Media* (2013).

Understanding User Adaptation Strategies for the Launching of Facebook Timeline

Pamela Wisniewski
The Pennsylvania State University
University Park, PA 16802
pam@pamspam.com

Heng Xu
The Pennsylvania State University
University Park, PA 16802
hxu@ist.psu.edu

Yunan Chen
University of California, Irvine
Irvine, CA 92697
yunanc@ics.uci.edu

ABSTRACT
This paper applies coping theory to understand user adaptation strategies to major interface changes on Social Networking Sites (SNSs). Specifically, we qualitatively examine 1,149 user comments posted to the Facebook's official Timeline blog in order to get a large and unobtrusive sample of real Facebook users' perceptions about the launch of Timeline. Our data suggests a high level of stress associated with the transition to the new interface introduced by Timeline. We also found evidence which suggests that increasing users' perceptions of control over major interface changes may help facilitate user adaptation to these changes. This study offers valuable insights to SNSs for mitigating user stress and facilitating successful adaptation during major interface changes.

Author Keywords
Facebook Timeline; User Adaptation; Change; Stress; Coping; Privacy

ACM Classification Keywords
H.5.m. Information interfaces and presentation (e.g., HCI): Miscellaneous; K.4.1 Public Policy Issues: Privacy.

INTRODUCTION
At Facebook's September 2011 annual conference "F8," Mark Zuckerberg unveiled Facebook's new interface, "Timeline," as a "new way to express who you are" [5]. However, the rollout of Timeline was not the first time that Facebook made major interface changes. New Facebook features have been introduced consistently and frequently, such as the App Platform (2007), "New" Facebook (2008), "Like" button (2009), "New" Profile (2010), and most recently Graph Search (2013) [7]. These new features allow Facebook users to connect with more people and share more information than ever before [7].

CHI 2014, April 26 - May 01 2014, Toronto, ON, Canada
Copyright 2014 ACM 978-1-4503-2473-1/14/04…$15.00.
http://dx.doi.org/10.1145/2556288.2557363

Yet, the launch of Timeline was unique for a few different reasons. First, Timeline drastically changed how Facebook users used Facebook. Now, instead of one's Wall being a place to share and connect with friends, Timeline was meant to be a searchable, personal archive for historical life events [5]. Second, Timeline was one of the most controversial Facebook interface changes of all time. Sodahead conducted a survey of over 1,000 Facebook users and 86% of their respondents declared that they wanted Facebook to rollback Timeline [14]. A possible reason for the momentous backlash against Timeline was that so many major interface changes were rolled out in one release. In addition to changes specific to Timeline, Facebook also included additional changes in this release; they added a News Ticker that posted friends' Facebook activities using a real time, scrolling sidebar [9]; changed the sort order for the News Feed [9]; and modified other features, such as the chat interface [12].

Given these unique characteristics, we use the launch of Facebook Timeline as a case to examine how existing social networking site (SNS) users adapt to major interface changes within an established SNS environment. Past research has primarily focused on the initial adoption [3], subsequent use [10], and non-use of SNSs [1]. Very little research has studied how existing users respond to major SNS interface changes. To fill this gap, we study how Facebook users respond to the launching of Facebook Timeline. In particular, we examined 1,149 comments posted to the Facebook's official Timeline Blog between September 2011 and April 2012. We use coping theory [11] to understand users' perceptions and observed a significant amount of stress associated with the switch to Facebook Timeline. We describe why this stress occurred and how Facebook users coped in order to reduce stress. We conclude with suggestions for how SNSs could mitigate user stress and facilitate user adaptation to major interface changes in the future.

BACKGROUND

User Adaptation
User adaptation is defined as "the cognitive and behavioral efforts performed by users to cope with significant information technology events that occur" [2]. Most of the work that has focused on user adaptation to new technologies has been contextualized within organizational settings. For example, Beaudry and Pinsonneault applied

coping theory [11] to the introduction of new information technologies within companies [2]. However, organizations often have goals, policies, and culture that influence the adaptation process. In contrast, SNS websites are communities designed mainly for personal use and end user goals are more likely driven by the individual and influenced by one's social circles. This distinct difference makes adapting technologies in social media settings an interesting, new area of study. Yet, very few studies have examined user adaptation to technological changes within the context of social media. Previous research has highlighted Facebook users' reactions to new features, such as New Profile [17] and Friendship Pages [13]. However, these studies focused solely on the privacy concerns users perceived with these interface changes instead of the broader context of user adaptation to the changes themselves. To our knowledge, our research is one of the first to apply coping theory [11] to examine how users react to major interface changes within SNSs.

Conceptual Framework

Lazarus and Folkman's seminal work on *Stress, Appraisal, and Coping* [11] is one of the most widely accepted theories of the coping process [2]. Because their theory deals directly with how individuals cope with stress caused by environmental changes, we felt that it was an appropriate and relevant theory in which to frame our analysis. **Figure 1** highlights the main tenets of coping theory [11]. ***Stress*** is defined as a relationship between a ***person*** and the ***environment*** that is perceived to be taxing, exceeding of one's resources, or detrimental to one's well-being [11]. ***Change*** within the environment is one key source of stress because it requires the individual to adapt to that new environment [11].

When a change occurs within one's environment, an individual asks him or herself, "*How does this change affect me?*" This assessment is called a ***primary appraisal*** of the situation, which can be positive, stressful, or irrelevant [11]. A ***positive*** appraisal is construed as a benefit for the individual while an ***irrelevant*** appraisal means that the individual is indifferent to the change [11]. ***Stress appraisals*** occur when individuals believe that the change negatively affects them; stress appraisals can be further classified into sub-categories: 1) ***loss or harm*** denotes that the individual has already sustained some damages; 2) ***threats*** are anticipated harm or loss that may occur in the future; and 3) ***challenges*** acknowledge the potential for growth or opportunity due to the change [11].

If an individual perceives a change as stressful, the next question they ask themselves is, "*What can I do about this change?*" This cognitive thought process is called a ***secondary appraisal*** [11]. Generally, there are two types of secondary appraisals: Individuals who perceive that they have ***high levels of control*** believe that they possess the necessary resources to address the change in the environment and reduce stress. In contrast, ***low perceived control*** is associated with individuals who believe that there is little or nothing that they can do about the change.

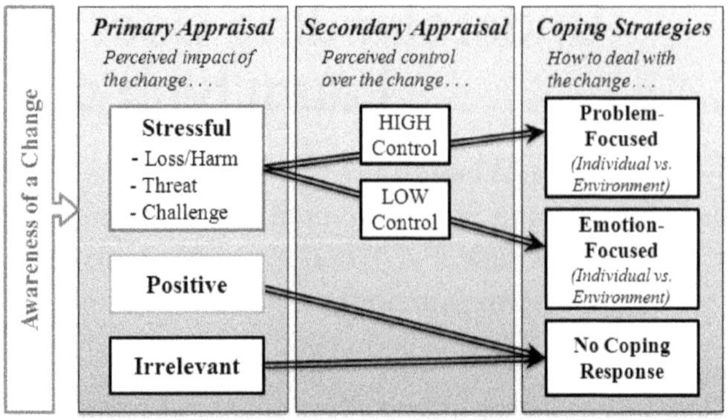

Figure 1: Conceptualization of Coping Theory

Coping strategies are cognitive and behavioral efforts an individual takes to reduce stress caused by environmental change [11]. They can either be emotion-focused or problem-focused. ***Emotion-focused*** coping mechanisms focus on an individual's internal emotional regulation as a means to adapting to environmental change. Coping strategies tend to be emotion-focused when individuals perceive a low level of control over the environment [11]. ***Problem-focused*** coping strategies tend to be action-based and externally focused on trying to find ways to change the environment to suit the individual's needs. Therefore, coping strategies are essentially means of negotiating an equilibrium between the ***individual*** and the ***environment*** as to reduce stress [11]. We use coping theory, as defined above, to better understand how Facebook users appraised and coped with the transition to Facebook Timeline.

Facebook Timeline

Timeline became publicly available as an opt-in feature to Facebook users on December 15, 2011 [5]. On May 21, 2012, Timeline became a mandatory upgrade for all users [4]. Facebook gave users a 7-day grace period so that they could remove, hide, or customize the visibility of old posts before they went live on Timeline [6]. Some of the main changes bundled into the launch of Timeline included [6]:

- Ability for users and friends to access past posts by date, as opposed to having to scroll through a reverse chronological list of historical posts
- Ability for users to add content anywhere on the Timeline of posts (life events, photos, etc.)
- Ability to highlight certain life events across the new two-column layout
- Inline privacy controls to remove, customize visibility, or hide anything on the Timeline
- Groupings of profile information at the top of a user's Timeline (photos, likes, apps, etc.) and a cover photo
- An activity log that allows users to view and share all of their Facebook activities (posts, likes, etc.)

Prior to the launch of Timeline, Facebook released an official Timeline blog [5] to introduce various new features. This blog also allowed users to ask questions and share their opinions about Timeline via comments. The blog was first launched on September 22, 2011, and the last user comment posted to the blog, before user commenting was deactivated, was on April 2, 2012 [5].

METHODOLOGY

Data Collection and Sampling

On April 19, 2012, we manually collected the first 100 pages of Facebook user comments that were posted on the Facebook Timeline Blog [5]. Since commenting ceased on April 2, 2012, we were able to sample from the full set of 4,439 user comments that were ever posted to this blog. The most popular Facebook user comments (based on number of Likes) were posted first and in descending order of Likes, along with all direct replies to those comments. Therefore, we collected a total of 84 of the most popular original comments and 1,065 comments that replied to this set of 84 most popular comments. Our final dataset for analysis contained 1,149 comments from a total of 676 unique Facebook users. Based on names and profile pictures, our sample consisted of 288 females and 369 males, with the remaining users unidentifiable by gender. Comments suggested that users ranged from technology novices to experts. The average number of comments made per user was 1.7 with a standard deviation of 1.89 comments. The most frequent commenter posted a total of 21 times. We discarded 191 comments from our data set due to lack of relevance. These comments either lacked sufficient context or consisted of flaming wars or spam.

Qualitative Coding

We based our qualitative coding schema on coping theory [11]. Therefore, we coded based on the following theoretical constructs: Primary Appraisal (Positive, Stressful, Irrelevant); Stressful Type (Harm/Loss, Threat, Challenge); Reason (Open coded); Secondary Appraisal (Low-Control, High-Control); Coping Type (Problem-Focused, Emotion-Focused); Coping Focus (User, Environment); and Coping Strategy (Open coded). In cases where comments contained multiple codes for one category (e.g. multiple coping strategies), we double counted these comments across the codes. Also, additional codes emerged as we applied coping theory to the unique context of user adaptation to Facebook Timeline.

After the primary researcher developed a standard code book using coping theory, she then trained two other coders. The comments were divided equally among the three coders. As new codes emerged, the three coders defined and shared their new codes with the other coders in order to ensure consistency. We calculated a metric for inter-rater reliability (IRR) by having all three coders code a subset of 100 comments; the secondary coders' levels of agreement with the primary coder were 95% and 83%. The combined IRR for all three coders was 81%. After all the data were coded, the primary researcher reviewed all of the codes and resolved any conflicts by collaborating with the secondary coders. Data coding and analysis were performed using Microsoft Excel® data filters, pivot tables, and graphs.

RESULTS

Primary Appraisal: *How does this change affect me?*

Individuals cognitively assess how changes in the environment personally affect them; such an assessment is called a primary appraisal [11]. A total of 752 comments (78%) contained a primary appraisal about how Facebook users perceived the impact of Timeline. Of the primary appraisals, 64% represented stress appraisals, 20% positive appraisals, and 16% suggested that the change was irrelevant to the Facebook user. We will address each type of primary appraisal in descending order of emergence in our data set. We first discuss stress appraisals (Loss/Harm - 54%, Threats - 25%, and Challenges - 21%), followed by positive appraisals and irrelevant appraisals.

Stress Appraisals: Loss/Harm

In coping theory, loss or harm denotes that the individual has already sustained some damages [11]. Even though coping theory groups loss and harm in the same category, we found a distinct difference between loss and harm in our data. In our research context, loss tended to result from the feeling that something a Facebook user once had has been taken away. Harm, on the other hand, was a direct negative consequence that was associated with Timeline. Loss represented approximately 53% of primary stress appraisals while actual harm was less than 1% of all stress appraisals. Harm most commonly resulted from unintentional privacy breaches. For example, one user shared that her homosexual friend "*has come out to the world when he didn't want to,*" because of Timeline.

Since loss represented over half of all stress appraisals, we focused on analyzing why Facebook users perceived stress due to a sense of loss. The top five reasons Facebook users expressed a sense of loss included loss of familiarity (29%), control (25%), intended use (18.5%), simplicity (17%), and user satisfaction (10.5%), respectively.

Loss of familiarity was the strongest lament of Facebook users who posted on the Timeline blog. Thirty percent of loss appraisal comments just wanted Facebook to bring the "old" Facebook back. These Facebook users generally were opposed to change and expressed a sense of loss because the new interface simply was not the old one that they were used to. This sentiment is summed up by the first commenter's post that received 3,412 Likes:

"shut the eff up and bring the old facebook back," Harmoni, Comment #1, 3412 Likes

Loss of control was the second highest reason for loss appraisals. These Facebook users were often upset that Facebook did not give them the choice to opt-in or opt-out of Timeline. These users tended to believe that, as Facebook's users, they should have the final say before Facebook releases new changes:

"I don't mind change...but I'd like the option to change it back if I don't like it...shouldn't FB at least give us options instead of forcing it on us?" Deanne, Comment #723, 321 Likes

Loss of intended use surfaced as the main stressor in 18.5% of the loss appraisals. A number of comments reflected user frustration that Facebook had completely changed how the site was meant to be used. Many users saw Facebook as a place to share and connect with their friends, and they were uncomfortable that Timeline changed that purpose by making it a personal archive for old posts:

"I agree with you this totally sucks!!! Now we need to find a social page because our old social page has become a virtual diary/scrapbook." Kathy, Comment #681

Other Facebook users were upset that features that they had in "old" Facebook were taken away or, in some cases, new features that they did not want were added. Interestingly enough, however, most of these posts tended to have very little to do with the main changes attributed to Timeline itself. Instead, these complaints were about additional interface changes that were bundled together with Timeline. Facebook users often did not know the conceptual difference between these features and Timeline. For example, numerous complaints surfaced about the sort order of one's News Feed, the addition of the News Ticker (a.k.a. "*stalker bar*"), and the new chat interface:

"It's been three months but i still hate this new facebook specially the news feed & ticker!!!!" Asif, Comment #223

Loss of simplicity was another type of loss appraisals. These users were stressed because Facebook no longer seemed to have the simple interface that they used to be able to easily navigate. They felt that the new Facebook was too complex and cumbersome:

"Why can't you guys just leave Facebook the way it was... People loved it simple and now with all this new stuff your just pushing people towards other sites..." Jacob, Comment #898, 92 Likes

Loss of user satisfaction was the final reason Facebook users gave for making a loss appraisal. Some comments specifically criticized the new look and feel of Timeline while others expressed a more generalized dislike:

"i know how to use it. im just not enjoying it," Dustin, Comment #736, 8 Likes

Stress Appraisals: Threats
Threats are anticipated harm or loss that may occur in the future [11]. Twenty-five percent of stress appraisals were made because Facebook users perceived Timeline as an imminent threat to their personal **privacy**. We observed that ***intrusiveness***, or concern over invasions into one's life [15], was the top privacy threat. "Jay" was the most frequent blog commenter, and he had developed quite a following of Facebook users who agreed with him that Timeline promoted stalking and that Facebook was trying to push an agenda for the erosion of personal privacy:

"This sounds like it's tailor made for stalking," Jay, Comment #274, 1,873 Likes

Facebook users also felt threatened by the new ***aggregation*** [15] of their personal information into one place. This was especially true for how Timeline displayed personal profile information at the top of one's profile:

"Plus seriously, like look when we comment look beside our names? U can see our location, [what] schools we go to an where we work, just little things like that suck! really come on, its not as safe i hate it," Christina, Comment #92

Other Facebook users were concerned about the increased ***accessibility*** [15] to their personal information:

"There are some people who're trying to make a change in their lives and move on from the past. This new Timeline stuff isn't helping. you're only opening your past to the public. I wouldn't be complaining if they could have some privacy settings on this but not even one? Really? You're gonna let the whole world access your past like that?" Tony, Comment #218

While this user was misinformed about how the new privacy settings actually worked, he was accurate in his assessment that the new design threatened personal privacy by increasing the potential longevity of past posts. Even though Timeline did not actually change what information could be accessed, they did make past posts more accessible by allowing users to search for past posts by year.

Stress Appraisals: Challenges
Challenges are stress appraisals that acknowledge the potential for future opportunities after certain difficulties have been overcome [11]. Challenges represented about 21% of the stress appraisals. These comments reiterated that the change to Timeline was indeed stressful. However, they did so with the glint of a silver lining and hope that, in time, Timeline would prove to be a positive change.

The learning curve associated with the interface changes introduced with Timeline represented 60% of the challenge appraisals. In many cases, Facebook users were well aware that they would have to learn the new Facebook privacy settings in order to protect themselves from Timeline's enhanced capabilities for accessing someone's past posts:

"u decide what is seen on ur timeline ... a lot of privacy settings has been [added], every single part of your timeline can be protected ..." Amy, Comment #456

However, many Facebook users acknowledged that using the new privacy settings was not a trivial task:

"I am in a huge learning curve "The Facebook Blog" videos are re-running in my head, I am searching for [a way] to [toggle] for all these new changes over and over in my dreams and night mares, I will survive..." Sandra, Comment #174

Adapting to change (31%) was the second most discussed type of challenge. "Zac" was the first one to reply to Harmoni's "shut the eff up," comment, and he received even more likes than the original poster:

"the old facebook was the new facebook once. the world changes, get used to it," Zac, Comment #2, 4,599 Likes

Quite a few replies tagged Zac directly, agreeing with his post. These Facebook users tended to take an evolutionary viewpoint where they accepted that Facebook had to change in order to improve. This viewpoint was in direct antithesis to the loss, stress appraisals that generally felt that change was bad. These users often acknowledged the considerable amount of stress that comes with learning how to adapt to change, but they believed it was worth the efforts.

Positive Appraisals

Twenty percent of Facebook comments suggested that the change to Timeline was a positive event. Interestingly, the most common reason (29%) for this positive primary appraisal was that these users believed Timeline actually increased their level of privacy control:

"facebook timeline has better security on privacy. even every item on your profile info can be set one by one," – Day, Comment #522

Other common reasons for positive appraisals included seeing Timeline as a privilege (19%), preferring the new interface (18%), believing that innovation is necessary for Facebook's survival (16%), liking the new organization of the website (11%), and being able to share more effectively with friends (7%).

Irrelevant Appraisals

Sixteen percent of Facebook users believed that the change to Timeline was irrelevant to them and other users. For the most part, these Facebook users were directly responding to others' stressful appraisals of Timeline as a privacy threat. The majority (83%) of these comments argued that the change did not matter because Timeline did not share any information that SNS users had not already shared in past. They argued that Timeline had no effect on privacy because it was the individuals' personal responsibility (just like before) to make good decisions about what they chose to disclose or not disclose on Facebook.

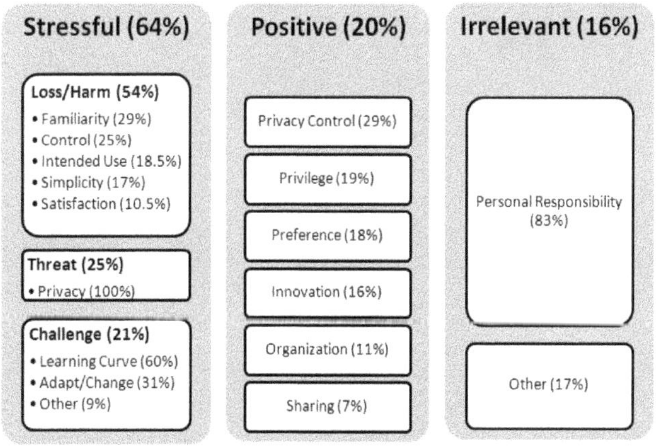

Figure 2: Summary of Primary Appraisals

"Well, you can choose what to include and what not to include. It's the same as always. Not to be the devil's advocate, but all the information doesn't pop up on Facebook by magic; it's there because you obviously chose to share it." Angela, Comment #360

Figure 2 summarizes the full set of primary appraisals within our data set and the reasoning behind each. It is clear from this analysis that users' assessments of Timeline varied drastically and, at times, were contradictory of one another. This highlights how primary appraisals were based on individual user's perceptions of Timeline, not necessarily based on the actual interface changes that were made.

Secondary Appraisal: *What can I do about it?*

Secondary appraisals of what can be done about a stressful situation are characterized with high or low levels of control over the situation [11]. We found both types of secondary appraisals in our data set. The majority (57%) of comments tended to reflect low levels of control. These users felt that they had little or no voice when it came to Facebook interface changes:

"Facebook is FREE! You do not 'own' it. It's a service provided to you for free. YOU do not have the right to make any demands." Trish, Comment #127

In contrast, 43% of the comments reflected high levels of perceived control. These comments tended to be more positive about the changes:

"The timeline sounds great eh! :) What an awesome way to keep track of EVERYTHING that YOU want to SHARE :)," Jamie, Comment #59, 5 Likes

Figure 3 depicts the overall relationship between primary and secondary appraisals in our data set. This graph is based on 642 comments that were coded with both a primary and secondary appraisal. It shows the percent of comments that depicted either high or low perceived control (secondary appraisals) for each type of primary appraisal. Irrelevant and positive appraisals tended to be accompanied

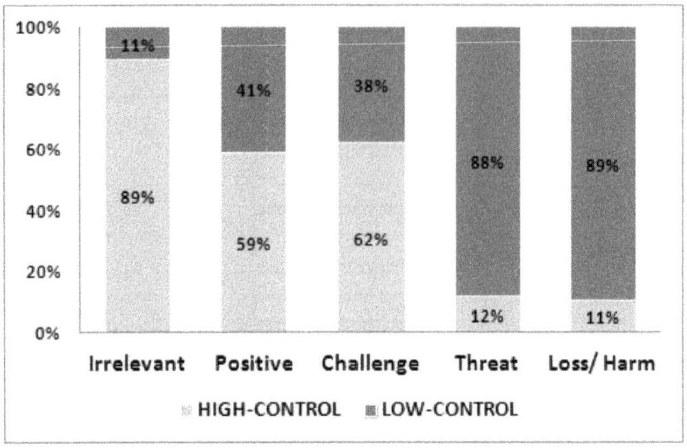

Figure 3: Primary versus Secondary Appraisals

with higher levels of perceived control. Loss/harm and threat stress appraisals tended to be associated with lower levels of perceived control. However, when individuals perceive a challenge, they tended to have higher levels of perceived control than the other types of stress appraisals. This finding is consistent with coping theory, which defines a challenge as a stressful situation that has the potential for positive outcomes and tends to be associated with higher levels of control [11]. Overall, Facebook users who perceived lower levels of control over the transition to Timeline tended to be more stressed.

Coping Strategies

Primary appraisals of what is "at stake" and secondary appraisals of perceived control work together to determine the amount of stress imposed on an individual. Individuals must decide how they are going to cope in order to reduce this stress [11]. Coping strategies can vary along two dimensions: First, they can be either ***problem-focused*** or ***emotion-focused***. Second, coping strategies can be an attempt to alter either the ***environment*** or the individual [11], in this case, the ***user***. We coded a total of 848 coping strategies within 753 comments. **Figure 4** depicts the coping strategies that emerged in our data set, as they varied along these two dimensions. Based on our analysis, user adaptation strategies tended to be slightly more problem-focused (51%) than emotionally-focused (49%). Users focused more on trying to change the environment (64%), as opposed to trying to change themselves (36%). The following sections will go into more details about the four profiles of coping strategies.

Emotion-Environment Focused Coping

Complaints about Facebook Timeline were, by far, the most prevalent (33%) coping strategy that we observed in our data set. Facebook users overwhelmingly used the blog to voice their displeasure over the launch of Timeline:

"Facebook, you're not near as smart as you think you are...Everything you do to try to simplify things only complicates things more. Every attempt you make to

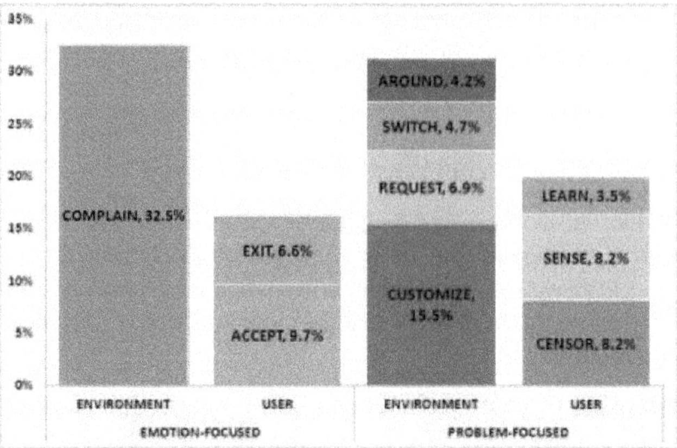

Figure 4: Coping Strategies

improve things inevitably ends up in a HUGE step backwards..." Declan, Comment #903, 76 Likes

While some of the complaints were civil, many of them became irate:

"FUCKBOOK !!!I HATE.." Wulan, Comment #1066

Even though it seemed like some users perceived a high level of control over Facebook, this tended to be an illusionary sense of control that only served to frustrate them further when they realized that Facebook was taking away rights that the user believed that they were entitled. These Facebook users had a strong sense that they were the user community (not the products) of Facebook. Therefore, Facebook would fail without their continued use and customer loyalty:

"they have PLENTY of obligations to us. we are the customers! remember how myspace died??? dont think our opinion doesnt matter." Taliesin, Comment #121

In general, complaints were emotionally charged criticisms directed at Facebook. These comments showed users' stress and frustration to both Facebook and other users.

Emotion-User Focused Coping

Another coping option was to alter the way users felt internally about the transition to Timeline (17%). In these cases, users often felt a low sense of control over the situation and were resigned that they could not change Facebook Timeline. Therefore, they had only two available coping strategies: To accept it or to leave.

Accepting Timeline by adapting to the change was either accompanied with an evolutionary view of change as necessary for survival (in this case innovation) or associated with a sense of resignation due to lack of control:

"change is inevitable and its going to happen so lets stop bitching about something we get completely free," Brandon, Comment #1,050, 20 Likes

Exiting Facebook to avoid transitioning to Timeline was another emotion-focused coping strategy. A number of Facebook comments took the standpoint that if someone did not like the Timeline changes, they should just leave. Simply leaving Facebook without going elsewhere would require the user to give up social networking altogether. Therefore, suggesting that another user should leave, go back to Myspace, or build their own SNS if they did not like Facebook, represented a definite lack of control and somewhat of a deliberate irony. These Facebook users often pointed out that Facebook was a free service. If users were not happy with it, they should just leave:

"You signed up to the site and agreed to it's terms and conditions of it allowing you to use it's site. Please see the deactivate button." Kiki, Comment #75, 3 Likes

Problem-Environment Focused Coping

A number of comments (32%) suggested that users felt that they had high levels of control which they translated into action in order to gain mastery over Facebook. They did this through customizing the interface (16%), making requests (7%), threatening to switch SNSs (5%), and working around Timeline features (4%).

Customizing the new interface by using built in settings was one way that users adapted to Timeline. To some extent, the customizations served to disable new features that users did not like:

"yall are stupid, you can [disable] certain features as always, stop hating," Christopher, Comment #498

However, in other cases, Facebook users started to experiment with the various settings and realized that the Timeline interface was highly customizable to their needs:

"I am finding that I can choose whom to share certain info with -- which is comforting to me. For example, my friends don't really like playing games and are tired of seeing all the game activity on my wall/profile. I can restrict my "game playing" to just my game players..." Melody, Comment #633

Requests were slightly different than complaints because these comments suggested specific things Facebook could do to address users' stress levels. In most cases, these requests were desperate pleas or angry demands to go back to the old Facebook:

"PLZ change fb back :(," Jordan, Comment #942, 51 Likes

However, some of the requests were more constructive solutions for how Facebook could have better handled the transition to Timeline:

"realistically speaking, alot of ppl out there are not technically inclined. their brains are not wired for techy stuff. i think FACEBOOK should provide options available on the site that allows ppl to conform their page to their level." Dawn, Comment #815

Threatening to switch to other SNSs, such as Google+, was another way of solving the problem. These users realized that they were not dependent on Facebook as their only option for socializing online. A total of 80 comments compared Facebook to other SNS websites. Seventy-two percent of the comments about Google+ saw it as a viable substitute and preferred interface over Timeline:

"TODAY FACEBOOK WILL END,, GOOGLE+ WILL START , AND A NEW ERA HAS BEGUN HAHAHA LOL .. GOOGLE+ IS VERY SIMPLE TO USE," Vinci, Comment #139

However, 28% of comments suggested that Timeline was Facebook's response to Google+, which they were not fond of:

"I HATE THE NEW FACEBOOK LAYOUT !!!! ALL FEATURE JUST SAME AS GOOGLE+... SHAME ON FACEBOOK," Wulan, Comment #57

Almost all the comments about Myspace were negative, warning to Facebook to not make the same mistakes:

"YOUR MAKING SHIT TOO PUBLIC AND LAME MYSPACE WANNA BE. NOTICE MYSPACE ISn't POPULAR ANYMORE WONDER WHY?" Brittany, Comment #956, 18 Likes

A few comments also compared Facebook to other social networking alternatives, such as Twitter, Diaspora, Clicks, and Multiply. These Facebook users realized that they had options other than Facebook, which gave them a higher sense of control over how they social networked.

Workarounds allowed users who were unsatisfied with the built-in capabilities of Timeline ways to override aspects of the interface. Many of the workarounds were focused at getting rid of Timeline altogether. A number of browser extensions were developed and posted to the blog in order to modify the Timeline interface. For example, a link to a Facebook page called "Get Old face book[1]" was posted at least 15 times. It pointed Facebook users to a website called "Timeline Remove.[2]" Other browser extensions included "Social Fixer[3]" and "FB Purity[4]." While the main goal of these extensions was to remove Timeline, some of them also provided users with higher levels of control over the Facebook interface:

"by using the BFB (Better Facebook) [extension] that Matt made. It let's u take away and add almost w/e u want. So ur FB looks how YOU want it to! It's pretty awesome!!!" Jessica, Comment #931

In summary, these Facebook comments took a problem-focused approach toward changing Facebook in a way that would reduce stress about Timeline. In cases where Facebook users could not change Facebook directly, they found other SNS alternatives.

---

[1] https://www.facebook.com/0ldfaceb00k
[2] http://www.timelineremove.net/
[3] http://betterfacebook.net/
[4] http://www.fbpurity.com/disable-facebook-timeline.htm

Problem-User Focused Coping

Some comments (20%) suggested coping strategies that were problem-focused but focused on the user, instead of the environment. These comments reflected a high level of perceived control because users felt that it was just a matter of taking the problem into their own hands. These coping strategies included self-censorship (8%), using common sense (8%), and learning about Timeline (4%).

One of the main blog threads was started by a Facebook user who was particularly stressed when she realized that Facebook had posted the entire trail she had run while using the Nike app:

"It might as well say "if anyone wants to mug me, I'll be walking alone through Central Park at 1:00 am, just east of the great lawn."" Amber, Comment #275, 472 Likes

However, she received a torrent (over 100) replies that suggested ways that she could cope with this potential privacy threat. **Self-censorship** was one of the main ways that other Facebook users suggested. These Facebook users felt that it was the individual's responsibility to simply not post private information to Facebook:

"They can only steal what you put out. If you don't want your "friends" to know where you ran, don't post it..." Emily, Comment #278, 31 Likes

Using common sense was another coping strategy for interacting with others through Facebook. For instance, Facebook users frequently suggested to others that if they were going to share personal information, that they not friend people that they did not trust:

"So don't add people you don't know? ... Who the hell stalks their close friends?" Kiki, Comment #735, 8 Likes

Learning about the Timeline interface changes before making judgments about it was one positive way users could cope with the change. Some users were annoyed by people who were complaining about Timeline and emphasized that they should attempt to learn about the new interface before they whined about it:

"has anyone even sat down & done some reading [about] the new features?? Too dumb maybe??" Josephine, Comment #733, 49 Likes

A few Facebook users acknowledged the importance of personally learning about Timeline before passing judgment. Yet, one older user pointed out that learning to adapt to the new interface was somewhat of a challenge:

"I'm still learning the new system,,,,a [little] harder for me being old and all after reading a lot of these post have learned so much..." Tina, Comment #803

In summary, these coping strategies focused on the personal responsibility of users who had a high level of perceived control over how they adapted to Timeline.

DISCUSSION

Perceived Control and User Appraisals

As shown in **Figure 3**, there was a clear relationship between primary and secondary appraisals: Users who perceive higher levels of control tend to assess major interface changes more favorably than those who feel that they lack control. Hearkening back to coping theory, if an individual feels helpless in dealing with a stressful situation, the amount of stress can be great. Lazarus and Folkman further clarify that primary appraisals do not necessarily precede secondary appraisals [11]. Therefore, while we cannot confirm a causal relationship between primary and secondary appraisals in respect to Timeline adaptation, we can note a strong correlation between higher levels of perceived control and more positive appraisals of Timeline. An implication of this finding is that empowering SNS users with control could potentially increase users' positive response to major interface changes.

Perceived Control and User Adaptation

Earlier, ***user adaptation*** was defined as the efforts put forth to successfully cope with technological change within one's environment [2]. In our case, we examined SNS users' transition to Facebook Timeline. Coping theory defines ***adaptive coping*** strategies as efforts that lead to positive outcomes, such as life satisfaction/morale and higher functioning at work and socially [11]. For our purposes, adaptive coping would result in successful adaptation to Timeline. In contrast, ***maladaptive coping*** is defined as counterproductive, often reducing short-term stress at the expense of increased long-term stress [8, 11]. Therefore, we consider any coping strategies that prolong or negate the successful transition to Timeline as maladaptive. For example, Baumer at al. suggest that leaving Facebook may give some users a sense of empowerment, but leaving may also cause strain on one's relationships [1]. Similarly, self-censorship could be considered a type of social withdrawal that negates social networking with friends. Past research suggests that self-censorship within SNSs can lead to a sense of regret due to loss of authentic self [16].

Learning how to use Timeline, customizing it to meet one's needs, using common sense, making requests for changes, and ultimately accepting Timeline are the coping strategies from our data that could be construed as successful user adaptation to Timeline. Complaining, self-censoring, quitting Facebook, switching to another SNS, and using workarounds can be considered maladaptive coping because they may increase emotional distress and/or reduce the long-term, potential benefits of Timeline. Given this logic, approximately 67% of all coping strategies for stress appraisals that we observed could arguably be considered maladaptive (**Figure 5**). From this figure, we see that high levels of perceived control were often associated with adaptive coping strategies while low control was associated with maladaptive coping strategies. Users' desires to exert influence on how Facebook launched Timeline, but the

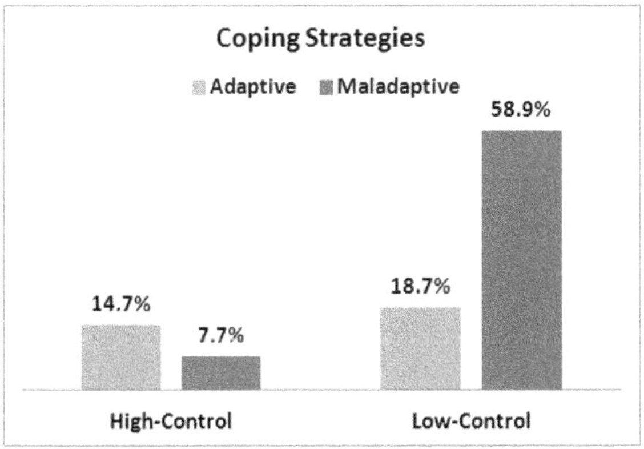

Figure 5: Adaptive versus Maladaptive Coping

inability to do so, tended to result in high levels of stress, often leading to emotionally charged, maladaptive coping responses. Thus, increasing SNS users' control perceptions could potentially facilitate users' successful adaptive coping to interface changes. For instance, when users were given the option to beta test Timeline, many were eager adopters. These users felt like they had more control, so they challenged themselves to learn all of the new features and customize the interface to meet their needs. Yet, many users became outraged when they found out that Timeline would become mandatory. These users were more emotionally reactive and spent their time protesting the change instead of embracing it. The opt-in strategy may have increased Facebook users' perceived levels of control and contributed to more positive appraisals and adaptive coping strategies. **Figure 6** summarizes our high-level findings regarding user adaptation to Facebook Timeline. We applied coping theory to create this framework of user adaptation to major interface changes. We saw a consistent pattern between high levels of perceived control and users' adaptive coping to Timeline. Therefore, users' perception of control is a key factor in SNS user adaptation and needs to be examined further in future research.

Collaborative Coping

Our application of coping theory to user comments posted to the Timeline blog is unique because users were not coping individually; *they were coping together*. Coping theory suggests that the introduction of new information or feedback from others provides individuals with an opportunity to reappraise changes in the environment [11]. Past SNS research also highlights the importance of peer influence, finding that Facebook users who knew someone who had deactivated their account were three times more likely to deactivate their own Facebook accounts [1]. In our case, approximately 11% of the coping strategy comments posted to the Facebook blog urged users to either leave Facebook or switch to another SNS. Furthermore, users had no feedback from Facebook as a company, so they could only rely on new information (valid or invalid) from other users. In some cases, this created a bandwagon effect where extreme opinions became even more polarized and fairly deconstructive as users engaged in heated arguments. In

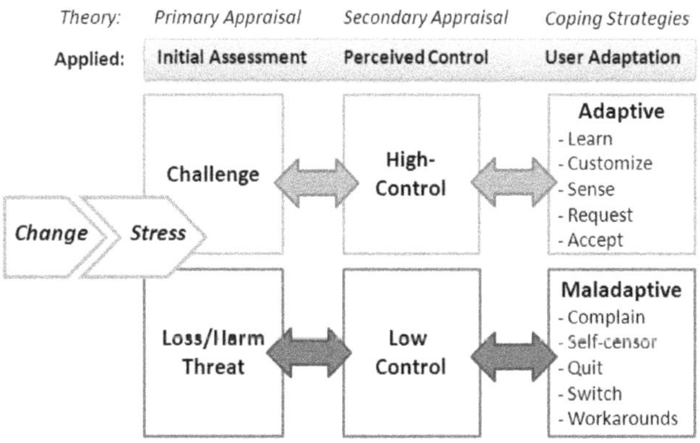

Figure 6: Framework of User Adaptation as an application of Coping Theory

instances like these, introducing a Facebook moderator may have helped deescalate some conflicts. Alternatively, in a smaller number of cases, Facebook users turned to other users as external resources [11] for understanding and adapting to Timeline. They asked questions about how to customize the new interface to meet their needs, such as adjusting privacy settings. Therefore, it may be beneficial in future releases for Facebook to assign facilitators who could also answer questions, correct misinformation, and give users the perception that their voices were being heard.

Implications for Practice

Direct implications for SNS designers are to proactively assess how interface-induced changes may affect end users and to embed appropriate options into the design and deployment process. A key point is that major interface changes induce psychological stress as well as technology-related stress. Our findings suggest that increasing users' perceived control over major interface changes may help facilitate users' adaptive coping strategies to these changes. Our work demonstrates the need for SNS designers to understand how users appraise a major interface change and highlights the importance of providing users with adequate control options so that they can successfully enact adaptive coping to the interface change. These design options may include, for example, communicating additional information about the new interface, so that users have a better understanding of its consequences; providing user choices through opt-in or opt-out mechanisms; providing better privacy control features; refraining from removing existing functionality; and facilitating communication among users for collaborative coping.

Limitations and Future Research

Our analysis was based on comments posted to the Facebook Timeline blog. Our methodology allowed us to unobtrusively analyze a diverse and large qualitative data set and capture users' in-situ reactions about the launch of Timeline, providing first-hand insights for understanding users' perceptions. However, there are some inherent weaknesses associated with this approach. First, commenting was deactivated prior to Timeline becoming mandatory for all users. Therefore, our analysis is largely based on users' reactions to the impending launch of Timeline, though some users had already transitioned (willingly or unwillingly). Second, comments posted to the blog may reflect strong and extreme opinions that are not representative of the typical Facebook user. Finally, this dataset is inadequate for providing us with deep insights regarding users' longitudinal behaviors; we did not confirm if users actually executed their stated coping strategies. In order to fill this gap in our research, we plan to do a follow-up study in which we send a follow-up survey via a private Facebook message to the 676 Facebook users that were captured in this data set. We believe that this follow-up study will give us further insights as to the long-term effects of major interface changes on SNS users.

CONCLUSION

This research demonstrates the need for HCI researchers and SNS service providers to understand how major interface changes are perceived by SNS users and to maintain user satisfaction by facilitating adaptive user coping during these times of change. While this research constitutes a step toward a better understanding of user adaptation in SNS, it raises questions that need to be addressed in future research. We hope that the ideas and preliminary results put forth in this paper will stimulate research on user adaptation in SNS, which remains a relatively unexplored area in our field.

ACKNOWLEDGEMENTS

The authors are very grateful to the AC and anonymous reviewers for their constructive comments and to Charlise Harris and Saijing Zheng for their assistance on this project. This research was partially supported by the U.S. National Science Foundation under grant CNS-0953749. Part of the work of Heng Xu was done while working at the National Science Foundation. Any opinion, findings, and conclusions or recommendations expressed in this material are those of the authors and do not necessarily reflect the views of the National Science Foundation.

REFERENCES

1. Baumer, E., Adams, P., Khovanskaya, V., Liao, T., Smith, M., Sosik, V. S. and Williams, K. Limiting, Leaving, and (re)Lapsing: An Exploratoration of Facebook Non-Use Practices and Experiences. In *Proc. Conference on Human Factors in Computing Systems* (2013).
2. Beaudry, A. and Pinsonneault, A. Understanding User Responses to Information Technology: A Coping Model of User Adaptation. *MIS Quarterly*, *29*, 3 (2005), 493-524.
3. boyd, D. Friends, friendsters, and myspace top 8: Writing community into being on social network sites. *First Monday*, *11*, 2 (2006).
4. DeNinno, N. *Facebook Timeline Mandatory Date Set for May 21*. 2012, http://www.ibtimes.com/facebook-timeline-mandatory-date-set-may-21-final-rollout-coming-next-week-report-698346.
5. Facebook. *The Facebook Blog*. 2011, https://blog.facebook.com/blog.php?post=10150408488962131.
6. Facebook. *Introducing Timeline: Tell your life story with a new kind of profile*. 2011, https://www.facebook.com/about/timeline.
7. Facebook. *Timeline*. 2013, http://newsroom.fb.com/Timeline.
8. Horney, K. *Our Inner Conflicts: A Constructive Theory of Neurosis*. W W Norton & Company Inc, New York, 1945.
9. Kincaid, J. *Facebook News Feed Gets Smarter - And the Ticker Makes Its Big Debut*. 2011, http://techcrunch.com/2011/09/20/facebook-news-feed-gets-smarter%E2%80%94%C2%A0and-the-ticker-makes-its-big-debut/.
10. Lampe, C., Ellison, N. B. and Steinfield, C. Changes in use and perception of facebook. In *Proc. Proceedings of the 2008 ACM conference on Computer supported cooperative work* (2008), 721-730.
11. Lazarus, R. S. and Folkman, S. *Stress, Appraisal, and Coping*. Springer Publishing Company, New York, 1984.
12. Perez, S. *Rolls Out Changes to Chat, Other Experiments, Leads to Problems*. 2011, http://techcrunch.com/2011/08/11/facebook-rolls-out-changes-to-chat-other-experiments-leads-to-problems/.
13. Shi, P., Xu, H. and Chen, Y. Using contextual integrity to examine interpersonal information boundary on social network sites. In *Proc. Proceedings of the SIGCHI Conference on Human Factors in Computing Systems*, ACM (2013), 35-38.
14. SodaHead. *Public Opinion Rejects Facebook's Changes*. 2011, http://www.sodahead.com/united-states/public-opinion-rejects-facebooks-changes-infographic/question-2175115/.
15. Solove, D. J. A Taxonomy of Privacy. *University of Pennsylvania Law Review*, *154*, 3 (2003).
16. Wisniewski, P., Lipford, H. and Wilson, D. Fighting for My Space: Coping Mechanisms for SNS Boundary Regulation. In *Proc. Conference on Human Factors in Computing Systems* (2012).
17. Zheng, S., Shi, P., Xu, H. and Zhang, C. Launching the new profile on facebook: understanding the triggers and outcomes of users' privacy concerns. In *Proc. Proceedings of the 5th international conference on Trust and Trustworthy Computing*, Springer-Verlag (2012), 325-339.

Curation through Use: Understanding the Personal Value of Social Media

Xuan Zhao[1, 2] and Siân Lindley[1]
[1]Microsoft Research
21 Station Road, Cambridge, CB1 2FB, UK
[2]University of Michigan
105 South State St., Ann Arbor, MI 48109, USA
xuanzhao@umich.edu; sianl@microsoft.com

ABSTRACT
Content generation on social network sites has been considered mainly from the perspective of individuals interacting with social network contacts. Yet research has also pointed to the potential for social media to become a meaningful personal archive over time. The aim of this paper is to consider how social media, over time and across sites, forms part of the wider digital archiving space for individuals. Our findings, from a qualitative study of 14 social media users, highlight how although some sites are more associated with 'keepable' social media than others, even those are not seen as archives in the usual sense of the word. We show how this perception is bound up with five contradictions, which center on social media as *curated*, as a *reliable* repository of *meaningful* content, as readily *encountered* and as having the potential to present content as a compelling *narrative*. We conclude by highlighting opportunities for design relating to curation through use and what this implies for personal digital archives, which are known to present difficulties in terms of curation and re-finding.

Author Keywords
Personal information management; archive; exhibition.

ACM Classification Keywords
H.5.m. Information interfaces and presentation (e.g., HCI): Miscellaneous.

INTRODUCTION
Content generation on social network sites has been considered mainly from the perspective of networking, with researchers emphasizing interaction via social media as a performance of identity and a means of maintaining relationships. Site features such as newsfeeds and notifications, along with emerging social conventions that emphasize 'nowness' [11] result in an environment in which users focus on the 'present' [23] and avoid posting old content, which will surface 'out of time' [11]. Yet this content does, of course, persist, and because of this social network sites accumulate content including status updates, pictures and videos. Thus, social network sites have also been positioned as hosting 'virtual possessions' [22], which become more personally meaningful over time [32], and which form part of a wider space in which online content in itself can be considered an archive [17].

CHI 2014, April 26 - May 01 2014, Toronto, ON, Canada

http://dx.doi.org/10.1145/2556288.2557291

However, the fact that social media persists by default (there is no option to 'keep' social media – it is simply *there*) poses challenges to maintaining a collection that is meaningful and that can be held in what is, after all, a public space. Hogan [12] positions social media as an enduring 'exhibition' of personal data, and recent work around deletion [e.g. 28, 29] highlights the problem of keeping social media on display. Content that does not fit the way one wishes to present oneself must be removed. This concern with audience and self-presentation contrasts with the curation work that underpins more personal archives. For example, material possessions can be hidden away in 'deep storage' [15], and virtual possessions become buried in nested folders on laptops and hard drives [26]. These possessions are rarely encountered by their owners, let alone by others, and so the curation work that underpins them can entail a focus on what one wants to keep rather than what one wishes to share.

In this paper, we explore whether social media has archival value, given that it is curated as an exhibition rather than as something to be kept in the long-term. We consider whether new opportunities for design open up if social network sites are positioned as comprising an archive of sorts, rather than content that is ephemeral [11] and trivial [17]. As pointed out by Good, research is needed to identify "social media users' self-archiving habits, desires, abilities and awareness online" [8, p. 570].

To explore this further, we undertook a qualitative study in which 14 participants were asked to create digital keepsakes using their social media content. While participants did not typically view social media sites as repositories in the usual sense of word, their practices nevertheless resonate with certain aspects of personal information management. Social media generated for particular audiences results in a landscape of content across social media sites, with some (especially Facebook) hosting content viewed as personally meaningful. Our findings indicate that social media is *curated* and is considered a *reliable* place to store *meaningful* content. Furthermore, it is easily *encountered* and has the potential to present content as a compelling *narrative*. We draw implications for design relating to the notion of curation through use, and the bridging of online and offline archival spaces. We build on this to consider what opportunities lie in drawing together social media and personal digital archives.

RELATED WORK

Before describing the study in more depth, we provide an overview of related research. We focus on prior work in which social media is positioned firstly, as a means of connecting with others, and secondly, as a virtual possession.

Research on why people use social network sites, and what they get out of them, often highlights values such as social connection and social surveillance [13, 3, 14]. In this network-centric view, social media is conceptualized as a tool to facilitate tailored and purposeful identity performance [e.g. 5, 16], in which user activities are shaped by different audiences present in online [1, 18] and faceted [6] networks.

This concern for audience, however, is dynamic. Recognizing that social media sites do not only facilitate interaction in the moment, but also present an aggregated history of interactions (e.g. via the Facebook Timeline), recent research suggests that identity performance in social media should no longer be considered simply as a snapshot in time, but something to be revisited, re-evaluated, and that is subject to changes in audience and relationships that unfold in the long-term. For example, Hogan [12] points out that social media, once generated, become an exhibit that is encountered by different audiences and in different contexts. Performance of self is not an ephemeral act, but an enduring act. He emphasizes the system's role as 'curator' of this exhibition; algorithms mediate the audience's experience of social media. However, it is clear that users also play a role in curating these exhibitions. For example, recent research on deletion of social media highlights users' on-going curation work, work that is triggered especially due to changing circumstances, such as relationship breakdowns, and which can occur long after the moment of upload [28, 29, 32].

This conceptualization of social media as enduring exhibition highlights a form of curation work that is quite different to that underpinning personal archives, but this is not to say that social media does not have personal archival value. Research has shown that social network sites are host to meaningful content that might be considered a form of 'virtual possession' [22], which can support reminiscing [24] and reflection [30, 33]. In line with this view, recent work by Zhao *et al.* [32] shows that as social media content becomes older, its value to the user shifts from supporting the performance of identity to something that is more personal. Their participants were less concerned with whether content would be viewed by others after a certain point, focusing instead on whether the content would have personal value. Lindley *et al.* [17] have also suggested that online repositories such as Flickr, together with social media sites, blogs and webmail accounts, work in concert to form an online archive of sorts, although in this account the potential for social media to comprise a good deal of trivial content is also highlighted.

The above suggests that social media could have archival value for the self, but also highlights the complexity here. Social media has been described as both meaningful and trivial, being generated for the maintenance of a social network, but also potentially accruing personal value over time. Furthermore, it is well known that people already struggle with the task of managing their digital content. Digital archiving is subject to many difficulties: special content is mixed in with the mundane; digital content in general is sorted, organised and encountered only infrequently [26]; and users find it surprisingly difficult to locate even their favourite photos [31] or other cherished digital mementos [27]. It is possible that positioning social media as another form of personal digital archive may only add to this melee. In this paper, we begin to explore opportunities for design in this space. Can social media, which is principally curated as an exhibition and means of sharing, be re-considered as a meaningful personal archive? And if social media, and the web more generally, can be considered an online archive of sorts [17], what does this suggest for archives that are located more privately, but that may suffer from problems of organization, curation and a lack of revisitation?

RESEARCH AIMS

The aim of this study is to consider more carefully whether social media has value as an archive, both in itself, within and across sites, and as part of a wider array of virtual possessions. We do this through an activity designed to encourage participants to reflect more closely on the value of content hosted on various social network sites, by making a 'keepsake' out of social media. This positions social media as something that one might wish to keep rather than share. We interpret our findings in the context of digital archiving.

METHOD

Participants

14 participants completed the study. They were 9 women and 5 men, with an age range of 20-53 years (M=29, SD=8.83). Most were in their 20s, however, we deliberately included two people in their forties and fifties as we expected they might show different attitudes towards and practices in using social media. All participants were living in and around a city in the south-east of England, although eight nationalities were represented. The social media tools participants frequently used include Facebook, Twitter, Instagram, Snapchat, Pinterest, Vine and LinkedIn. Participants were given a £30 gift voucher to thank them for their participation.

We recruited social media users through university email lists and Facebook posts. Participants were screened via a survey, through which we collected demographic information and details of frequently used social media tools. In order to have a diverse sample of people who use different social media platforms, but also share some common experiences, we sought to recruit Facebook users who were also active users of other social media sites.

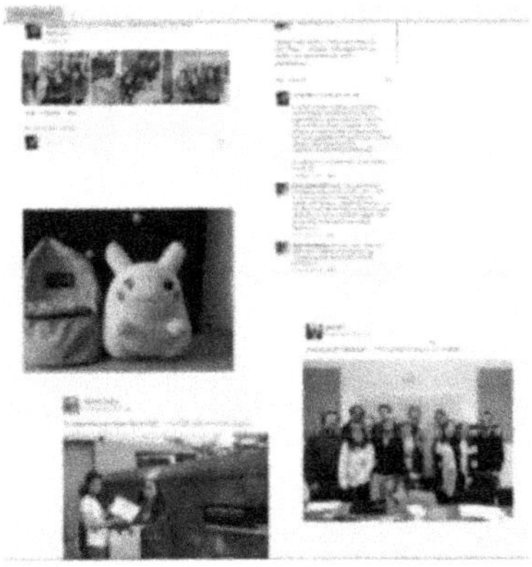

Figure 1. Anonymized example of a digital 'keepsake' produced by a participant.

Interviews and Activity

Participants were invited to our research lab for a 60-minute in-depth interview about their experiences with different social media tools, and how they perceive the social media that is produced through these platforms. The first 15 minutes of the interview focused on reasons for using different social media tools, the nature of social media that persists on these platforms, and how social media archives are perceived as different or similar to personal archives stored either online or on personal devices. Following this, participants were asked to browse content from their various social media profiles and make a digital 'keepsake', by capturing online content (for example, pictures, status updates, comments, etc.) that they would like to keep. They organized this content in a way that was meaningful to them using OneNote 2013, a free-form screen clipping and note taking tool (see Figure 1 for an example). The activity was designed as a way of encouraging participants to react to and reflect upon their social media archives, with a particular focus on the value of the social media that persists there, and was inspired by a study bc Pctrclli *et al.* [25], in which participants captured 'future memories' by making time capsules. Participants spent 15 minutes alone to focus on making their keepsakes before continuing the activity with the researcher present. The keepsakes as well as the social network sites that were used in their making grounded the remainder of the interview.

Analysis

The interviews were audio- and video-recorded, and screengrabs were taken of the keepsakes produced by the participants. Our analysis focuses on the interviews rather than the keepsakes, as these were primarily intended to serve as prompts for discussion. Interviews were fully transcribed and analyzed for emergent themes using grounded theory techniques [7]. In initial data analyses, open codes were developed and assigned; these were then iterated and the relationships between them explored through axial coding. Axial codes include: management strategies for different social media tools; the nature of social media; and sentiment around losing content. Five high-level themes were then identified; these are curation, meaningfulness, encounterability, reliability, and narrative. The first author developed the coding scheme. Both authors read all transcripts and discussed and reached consensus with regard to coding at each iteration of the analysis.

FINDINGS

We introduce our findings by describing firstly, how participants responded to the activity of making a keepsake, and secondly, how they viewed the value of social media across different sites. We then present the five overarching themes that emerged in the analysis.

Making a Digital Keepsake

The process of making a digital keepsake out of social media led participants to reflect on both the experience of making and the value of the social media they came across. We focus on the latter in more depth in the following section, as it is nuanced, but reactions to the activity in general were positive. The process was described as similar to *"a story you are writing"* (P2) or to the curation of an old photo album, and was engaged in as a meaningful activity:

"It's brilliant. I definitely haven't been down this bit of my Facebook for a long time. There were loads of comments and stuff that I didn't know were on there as well, which is good... it just makes me laugh." (P10)

Participants tended to organize their keepsakes either around major life events (e.g. having a baby, getting engaged, moving to a new location, getting a new job) or around significant relationships (e.g. family, close friends, romantic relationships), and selected content accordingly:

"I think it would still be centered largely on big events... Other than that, I guess, more mundane parts of life, I probably wouldn't [include them]." (P1)

"My idea is to create my multiple identities, academic life, me as a friend, my life as a wife probably, and my life as a daughter." (P14)

Photos formed a substantial part of the keepsakes, in line with more traditional ideas of photo albums, collages and scrapbooks. They were described as *"the best thing you can do to try to recall a memory"* (P1). Yet other content was also included, such as status updates, conversations, and even URLs that had been posted. The social metadata (e.g. comments and likes) that accompanied such content online was also typically included in the snipped version; indeed, some participants described that the value of such content was to be found in the conversations that augmented it:

"Because I really liked this link, I liked the conversation that I had with my friends, I liked what I've said and I don't often do this, you see I don't often share links but... I like the story that was relevant to the link that was one of my memories about something." (P5)

Even though Facebook was only one amongst a range of social media sites used by our participants, and we encouraged them to reflect on content spread across different platforms when building their keepsakes, Facebook was in most cases the go-to site during the activity. Next, we consider why this was so.

The Value of Social Media across Sites

Facebook was often the first port of call when building a keepsake, despite it being only one of many social media sites used by the participants. The predominance of photos used by participants may partly account for this, as most had photos hosted on Facebook. However, participants also described the existence of a 'higher bar' for posting content to Facebook, which made it more probable that social media worth keeping would be found there. This seemed bound up with two properties of social media: its expected audience and its expiry rate. These are not mutually exclusive, but together influence expectations around the value of social media and how this is maintained over time.

Expected audience

Consistent with work that explores social media as a means of maintaining relationships, we found different social network sites were associated with different audiences. For example, for our participants, Twitter was mostly associated with peers and people with shared interests but who are not real-life contacts, whereas tools like Snapchat were mainly used with small and specific groups of friends. Facebook tended to be associated with the most diverse audiences, mainly family and friends, but also contacts from different spheres of life. This broad audience encompasses parents, extended family and ex-boyfriends, and was often described as having built up over time as the Facebook network had expanded. The diversification of network composition, from an initial group of *"college friends"*, meant that participants perceived a need to be more careful in posting content on Facebook:

"On Twitter it's about a TV show or it's about where I am going, whereas on Facebook I don't like to update it so often but [only for] something I want a lot of people to know about...like graduation." (P3)

In addition to writing fewer silly and mundane updates, the nature of interactions via Facebook had also changed. Wall conversations were noted as having declined, with the emphasis now being on the sharing of personal content:

"*When I got Facebook originally like when it was still for university only... you had a much smaller number of friends, you know, it was more of a personal thing, like you could just write on somebody's wall...It's funny as time progressed I found it became less of a 'I'm going to write on this person's wall' or whatever, and it became more of this push-out model, like publishing your own content."* (P4)

However, this is not to say that such interactions no longer exist. Instead, they had shifted to sites like Twitter and Snapchat:

"I have become more selective of what I post (on Facebook) as I get older, and that might be because of the introduction of Twitter. All the stuff that I used to post on Facebook when I was younger, like going out tonight duh duh duh, I do that on Twitter now." (P3)

Content expiry rate

As noted in prior research [11, 32], content on social network sites falls out of currency fairly rapidly, after which commenting on or otherwise interacting with it becomes unexpected and goes against social conventions. Participants in this study noted how this rate of expiry differs across sites:

"It expires. I mean you tweet and like 20 minutes later it's not on your feed, anyone's feed anymore... Whereas on Facebook, it's like one week or so... It kind of sticks on your profile on Facebook..." (P6)

This 'stickiness' is sociotechnical. The *"deluge of information"* (P4) on Twitter meant that tweets were perceived as expiring more quickly, and of course this is self-reinforcing. *"Less meaningful discussions or ... more meaningless things"* (P4) could be posted to Twitter, whereas the higher bar for posting to Facebook meant that less content was there, and so it expired more slowly. Tools like Snapchat, whereby expiry is built in, inevitably facilitated the generation of playful content.

Bound up with this are the ways in which different social media sites offer ways of encountering content that is due to, or has already, expired. Facebook especially was felt to offer more scope for looking back at content, through the Timeline on the profile page but also via photo albums and features such as 'See Friendship', which filter content by relationship. Nevertheless, it was not considered typical to look back at the Facebook Timeline, unless in the context of making a new Facebook 'friend'.

As shown, the combination of a diverse audience and a relatively slow expiry rate (when compared with other social media) led participants to perceive a higher threshold for posting content to Facebook in particular. Indeed, some participants selectively synched content to the site from other social networks, such as Instagram and Twitter. For these participants, Facebook became a kind of *"hub"* (P1), representing the *"best"* and *"most selective"* of their social media content. However, Facebook was not necessarily interpreted as a repository of meaningful content, nor as something to be kept in the long-term. In the following section, we consider why this was so, through five contradictions in our participants' attitudes to social media.

Social Network Sites as Personal Archives?

Consistent with much prior work on social media and identity management, participants described the primary purpose of social media as to support interactions with others at the moment of posting. Social network sites were seen as a tool to support communication in the moment, rather than a place for storing data. Of course, this emphasis on content being for consumption by others meant that participants self-censored and avoided topics that might be considered controversial by their network:

"I don't know, I quite often try and put myself into other people's shoes and think okay if I was them and I saw that I had posted this on Facebook what would I think?" (P8)

This audience-centered perception of social media contrasts with a typical understand of archives, which are usually thought to be places to *"put stuff there just for me"* (P10).

"[I post the photo] just to share it with my friends... if I just want to keep it I can just keep it on my phone then people wouldn't see it... " (P3)

However, social network sites were used in ways that could be considered as similar to archives. They were *curated* repositories of *meaningful* content, and were noted as *reliable* data stores (sometimes more so than personal devices). Furthermore, they were said to be *encountered* more frequently, and to provide a better *narrative* of the past, than archives held on personal devices. Thus, our findings comprise quite nuanced views with regards to how our participants viewed the long-term value of social media. In the following, we look to these five factors.

Social media is beyond curation / social media is curated

The first theme explores the notion of curation. Social media sites were not generally seen as curated repositories of content. Indeed, some participants commented that social network sites were simply *"beyond curation"*; they contained content generated by too many people, they contained too much trivial content, and they went too far back in time to be manageable.

However, participants did also recognize that simply through using the sites, they were undertaking a form of curation. As noted above, Facebook was a site with a surprisingly high bar for posting content, and participants who used Instagram highlighted that it too resulted in a collection of images that had been carefully selected and edited. These sites comprised a collection that offered an alternative archive to that stored on computers and phones. Indeed, offline archives did not receive the same level of attention as their online counterparts, the motivation to curate being highlighted as social:

"Why do you put photos in a [printed] photo album, because that takes time and effort doesn't it? And that [sharing on Facebook] is for sharing with an audience." (P3)

Thus, participants spent time when presenting photos online, selecting a subset of *"the best"* photos to upload to Facebook, creating albums (something that was often not done with photos stored on laptops and phones), *"adding interesting captions"* (P13), and on Instagram, *"adding filters to make it prettier"* (P6). This was done with a view to presenting content that others would appreciate, whilst also avoiding overloading them with content:

"There's obviously a lot of stuff that isn't on there from that age, but it must've been my favorite bits from when I was at that age." (P12)

Furthermore, these sites used in combination were interpreted as offering different ways of looking at content, each with unique advantages. P5 describes how Instagram provided a nicer view of her year than Facebook, where holidays were over-represented because photo albums were made to represent them. On Instagram, a quick overview of her year, featuring few duplicates, could be found:

"Because [on Instagram] they are single pictures and it's like a single picture that represents a moment or a single picture from a certain week or a holiday, rather than a whole album, like visually you can see a kind of mosaic, a collage of time of just one photo, you don't have to go into each album." (P5)

She goes on to describe how these different social media collections work together, demonstrating how sites work in concert with offline archives in enabling her to manage and revisit her photo collection:

"There is the collection of absolutely everything which is on my computer, there is the collection of everything which is the best of everything on Facebook, and then there is an even smaller one [on Instagram], which is this nice grid view."

For a minority, social media sites were explicitly curated after posting, as a means of changing the view of the past presented. For example, one participant curated the Facebook Timeline following the breakdown of a relationship, saying that he didn't wish to come across content associated with it in the future, and another edited what was shown on the Timeline when it was first introduced, as it made visible too much content she did not wish to be so easily accessible on her profile page. This part of our findings corresponds well with previous deletion studies that highlight the tension between present and past self-presentation needs [cf. 29, 32]. However, for others, curation was a systematic and ongoing pursuit, aimed at removing content deemed to be no longer 'current' or 'relevant', such as links, conversations or status updates that had expired. This activity was bound up with self-presentation and personal branding:

"Because it was just something I wanted to share with my friends... after a time period I decided to delete it because it is not the actual thing, it is not a current thing (any more)." (P2)

Therefore, although social media is posted in line with a particular expectation of what an audience would be interested in, with its initial value being *social*, the curated collection has *personal* value. As P5 summarizes, *"I'm curating for the public, but I am also curating for the self"*.

Social media is trivial / social media is worth keeping

The second theme deals with where participants perceived value in their social media. This was complex; some social media had evident personal value, some was seen as obviously trivial, but even trivial content could be reinterpreted as meaningful after a period of time.

Nevertheless, most of our participants agreed that the value of social media was often compromised by the fact that it encompasses a breadth of content, ranging from favorite photos and records of important events, to comments and URLs of little relevance, to content that not only had been forgotten about, but that triggered no memories when encountered. This aggregation of large amounts of content made it difficult to find that which is meaningful and of interest, and this was confounded further by the presence of other people's content, mixed in with one's own:

"I think the thing is that Facebook is full of a lot of crap as well... so you look at it and say if somebody's not very good at curating their Facebook they'll post like a million photos of you and some of them are rubbish." (P5)

Yet, amongst the trivia lies content about key events. For some participants social media was seen as part of their history; for example P8 had been using the site since she was 14 years old, and P2 noted how the main events in her life were detailed on the site:

"All the big parts (of my life), you know, something I want to share with all my family and friends are on Facebook. Something that's huge for me, like I don't know, my degree or something like that. Not every day life really." (P2)

Often these key events would be represented by a photo (*"If it was really important, I would have a picture [on Facebook]"* – P5), although other types of content, such as comments, were also noted as having value by some:

"I haven't got a very close family... a lot of them I don't have their phone numbers but I have them on Facebook. When I got my degree and stuff like that they had congratulations on there, and I would be quite upset if I lost that..." (P6)

However, photos were highlighted as the media type most likely to be of value. Participants generally felt that the "*things that are important to me is pictures, photography, just pictures"* (P9). Comments were generally seen as *"of secondary importance to the photo"* (P5) and conversations on the wall, despite being unique to the site, were often deemed trivial, perhaps because they are closest to the 'tool-like' and ephemeral aspects of social media use: *"I guess most of the conversations with people [on the site] could be lost"* (P6).

On the other hand, even trivial social media could become valued later: *"... Something will happen to me, like you meet somebody whether it's whatever a significant other or like just a good friend or something, you're not going to know whether that first meeting, like the first picture that you had with them was like actually going to mean something to you in a while or not."* (P4)

In summary, social media comprises a record of key events that are of personal value, which is compromised by the presence of trivial exchanges and other people's poorly curated content. However, even small communications can become valuable over time.

Social media is a duplicate/ social media is the go-to place

The third theme relates to how personal content is encountered. Participants often compared the archival value of social media in relation to other archives, especially those on laptops and mobile phones. Most participants believed that the content most important to them comprised photos that were also held elsewhere, for example on the phones or cameras they had used to take the photos (see also [17]). Thus, social media sites were seen as comprising lower resolution duplicates of content held in other archives:

"I've never taken a picture directly from the Facebook [app]. No. It's just because Facebook is the base for my communication, so it is ALSO there." (P9)

Because of this, social media sites did not host as much content as these other repositories and were not considered as *"complete"* (P9) archives. However, some participants did think that Facebook in particular gave a fair representation of occasions they would like to remember:

"It's definitely not a biography, maybe not 100%, but it could be, why not? In the end I have all important events there, when my friends come and visit me, when I was doing something somewhere, when I visited China... they are all very important to me and they are all here since 2008." (P12)

The fact that social media sites contained less content was even beneficial in some sense. As already noted, Facebook was seen as a *"curated exhibition"* (P14), and consequently as more selective than other, private, archives. This had the result that the site was, for some, a *"go-to album"* used over and above other repositories:

"When you take photos, there are too many photos and we just select the best to put on Facebook... I don't even look back my computer, for photos, but just look at the albums on Facebook." (P13)

"Because it's ordered, it's been selected, and it's been updated in a way that it has meanings and you may want to go back again and look at it. It has more opportunities to be looked at again." (P14)

However, despite the finding that social media produced an archive that was more frequently encountered, participants were resistant to the idea of disposing of the complete offline collection. They preferred to keep everything, even if this would produce difficulties in managing and revisiting content:

"It's probably gonna be enough with only the information on Facebook... and I'm not gonna look at 5000 pictures in my computer ever again – but you feel if I lose all the pictures it would be really horrible." (P12)

This resonates with previous work on digital archiving [31], but it raises an important question that we shall return to in the discussion: as increasing amounts of social media are generated, how can we help users navigate these spaces, as well as their personal digital archives, if they are uncomfortable with the notion of deletion [9, 19]?

Social media is insecure / social media is safe

The fourth theme relates to the perceived reliability of social media sites. This highlights another set of contradictions, in that participants perceived social media sites as both more insecure and more powerful and safe than offline archives. On the one hand, social media sites were seen as transitory, unlikely to withstand the face of technological innovation:

"I see Facebook as very ephemeral. I don't see it as a repository... It's just a tool. I mean have you ever seen the old floppy disks?" (P7)

Furthermore, and in line with prior research [21], content on social media sites was associated with a weak sense of control:

"I think the [offline] digital content allows you to hold on to the idea that you own this stuff and it's yours and you have control over it [...] this gives you a sense of ownership that Facebook doesn't give." (P14)

Yet this attitude was transformed in the circumstance of data loss, and for some participants (the younger ones especially) this seemed to be developing into a more general shift. Some participants deleted content from their phones after posting it to Facebook, as a means of freeing up memory on their own devices, and others stored hidden files on their timeline, re-appropriating the site as a means of reliable cloud storage. And of course, social media also offers a way to build shared albums, functionality seen as supporting file-sharing. Most surprisingly though, some participants expressed the view that Facebook was more reliable than personal devices such as laptops and phones. Again, this opinion was expressed by the younger participants in the study, who had experienced sufficient problems with losing devices or having them fail to see social media as comparatively safe:

"...Because I cannot store a lot of photos on my phone and my laptop is pretty dead, so to be able to like store them and then look back at them [on Facebook]... they are always going to be there." (P3)

Social media tells a story / an inauthentic history

The final theme relates to narrative, and how social media supports the creation of stories but also can inhibit this through content that is inauthentic to the past. Facebook in particular offered compelling ways of revisiting past content:

"I guess it's the way it's presented, you know? Like when you graduate, it's like a big banner and she's graduated. She's got a new job." (P6)

Some features, such as See Friendship, provide a way of pulling together disjointed social media when revisiting it, creating a narrative from a number of smaller pieces.

"At some point I looked at the friendship between my husband and I, it was very cool because I was able to see pictures and comments and status we have shared since 2009, that's why I look at it in a story-telling way... not only I can see our pictures at the honeymoon or our wedding, but I can read the comments he used to put up on my wall when we were dating." (P14)

However, participants noted that some features of social media sites produced a version of the past that was not authentic. Lists of friends and profile pages were both highlighted as comprising content that could not really be revisited as they had been at a particular moment in time, and changes to profile pictures which were propagated through the site also had the result that content was not preserved accurately:

"Well it's not... because the profile picture has changed. That has changed. So it's not what exactly as I put it up... and how I put it up [when I look back]. I mean that's probably why I wouldn't see it as a repository." (P7)

A final observation here relates to how participants attempted to preserve aspects of the past when revisiting it, rather than altering old content through new interactions. As noted, prior work points to social norms that deem it inappropriate to surface social media 'out of time' [11]. Here we see that doing so may be permitted so long as the content is reinterpreted in relation to the present, while the original artifact is preserved. P12 described how she and her friends capture screengrabs of old content to discuss on Facebook. This allows them to shift the discussion from the original photo to the photo plus its metadata. Furthermore, the redefinition of the artifact under discussion means that the original object is kept intact, and social norms are maintained:

"[Taking a screenshot of a Facebook content] is like separating it from the original, so taking a picture of what we were before and attach a whole new message to it would make it – so like when you are in a museum kind of thing like you have old documents and stuff that you keep, so it would just make it like a different joke if you see what I mean?" (P12)

This final theme highlights how additional sense-making around significant relationships, major life events or even 'expired' content plus its metadata can alter perceptions of social media from the seemingly trivial to meaningful stories. This type of behavior was also evident when making the keepsake, where content that is relevant to a story becomes valued through its aggregation.

DISCUSSION

Our aims for this study were to explore whether social media has value as an archive, given that it is principally understood as an exhibition [12], and to consider whether it can support personal archiving more generally, given the complexities of managing digital content. Our findings suggest that, while social media sites are not really viewed as repositories of valued content, they nevertheless form an archive of sorts, one that is different to but could complement more traditional notions of file stores such as folders of photos and the camera rolls on mobile phones. The content found online is not the 'complete' collection that is found on one's computer, but it does represent a medley that is more selective, easier to browse, and encountered more often.

In this discussion, we develop these ideas further. We firstly consider what the use of social media in concert with other file stores suggests for the design of digital archives, and whether the curation work done in exhibiting social media to an audience can be translated to a personal, offline, archive. We then consider what implications our findings have for the creation of narratives on social network sites themselves.

Design for Digital Archives

Curation through use

In line with previous work [17], participants in this study used different social media sites for different purposes, and so understood them to host different types of content, some about friendship and family, some about the user's professional life, some about beautiful photography, and so on. These sites, alongside personal archives stored on their own devices, form a complex repository that suggests different implications for the design of archiving tools to prior work. Our findings demonstrate that the organization and management of personal content is integrated with its generation for different sites and audiences: in this sense, *curation is inherent to use*. Selective uploading, the formation of photo albums, and the addition of annotation and filters is often simply part of the process of using a social network site.

These findings emphasize that users as well as systems [cf. 12] are curators of social media, as conceptualized as an enduring exhibition. But they also resonate with Kirk and Sellen's [15] analysis of home archiving. Kirk and Sellen's focus on cherished objects leads them to highlight three types of storage in the home: objects on display; objects stored for functional use; and objects placed in deep storage. These different types of storage support different values, for example, objects on display support ready reminiscence; objects in functional storage enable the honoring of others through their use; and objects in deep storage support 'forgetting', in that one may wish to avoid encountering something, but feel uncomfortable getting rid of it. If we consider a photo album uploaded to Facebook to be on display, and photos on an external hard drive to be in deep storage, we can begin to unpack how these different digital spaces support different values in the same way that different places in the home do.

Like physical objects, photos on display, or that have been exhibited in an online space, seem to support ready reminiscence. Our findings suggest that Facebook and Instagram photos in particular were more frequently encountered than those saved offline, and this is in line with research that suggests photos archives are rarely revisited [31]. Furthermore, the fact that these sites are associated with different audiences, and with different thresholds for posting, means that users have a sense of where to look to re-find meaningful content. Again, this is something that users are known to struggle with when dealing with digital archives [26]. The notion of curation through use, at a time when digital photos are abundant and frequently cited as becoming unmanageable, is a value that should not be underestimated.

Safekeeping and forgetting

A finding that was somewhat unexpected, however, was that users would view social media sites to be reliable repositories. Of course this was not the case for all of our participants, and issues relating to a lack of sense of ownership arose here as they have done in prior work [21]. However, some of our participants were beginning to see social media sites as the locale where their content was most likely to persist, and this was especially the case for younger users. This obviously raises challenges, notwithstanding what would happen in the face of data loss or accounts being shut down. Returning to Kirk and Sellen's [15] storage types, social media cannot be put into deep storage, an action that is necessary if an archival space is to be multi-faceted and persist over time. We saw clear examples of this limitation in our data, whereby deletion of online content would be done for a range of reasons, from hiding from an audience to hiding from oneself, or 'forgetting', as Kirk and Sellen describe it. If one wishes to forget, there is only one option on a social media site, and that is to delete. The feature 'to hide' on Facebook means hiding from others, not hiding from oneself. Yet it is quite possible that the participant who had broken up with his girlfriend would have preferred some other option to the rather blunt 'delete' to deal with content relating to her (see also [28]). If social media sites represent 'objects on display', being able to take objects 'off' display and selectively download them or make them invisible to oneself, whilst supporting safekeeping, seems desirable.

This suggests the value of a design space around bridging online and offline spaces, and being able to translate the curation work done in exhibiting content online to an offline, private space. For example, if users find it difficult to manage their digital photo collections, but undertake a form of curation when they choose which photos to upload to the internet, it may be worth reflecting this in offline collections as well. If an operating system could indicate which photos are on Facebook and the tags associated with it, this could support users in navigating offline, higher resolution, versions of those same photos in an offline (and private) space. Further, it could indicate which photos the user might want to back up elsewhere, and may even support 'forgetting'. For example, photos that are deleted from Facebook could also be suppressed offline, by being hidden in features such as the random slideshows of photos that run on personal devices.

Of course, it is important to acknowledge that, while there may be benefits in reflecting the curation work done through using social media sites offline, the translation is unlikely to be perfect. Curation for exhibition is different to curation for archiving, and while the former may provide a starting point for the latter, it cannot provide a complete solution. It is worth noting also that both repositories have their limitations. Just as is the case with personal digital archives, users of social media sites can struggle to marshal out important and meaningful things in the increasing volume of content. The abundance of social media meant that participants encountered difficulties when looking back and making sense of it. Supporting users in filtering this content, or transforming it into a more compelling narrative, is the final point we wish to explore in this discussion.

Building Personal Narratives from Social Media

Bamberg and Georgakopoulou [2] argue that 'small stories', including tellings of on-going, future, hypothetical, and shared events, are used by people in everyday, mundane situations to create a sense of who they are. While their focus is on synchronous conversation, social media content, as captured through individuals' day-to-day interactions with their network, can similarly be considered instances of the talked-about that have a role to play in identity work. Page [23] has argued that social network users are adept at creating narratives out of the small stories they post on social network sites, and in this study we see how certain site features, such as See Friendship, as well as the activity of building a keepsake in itself, can be used to produce larger narratives. However, in order to make these narratives compelling, small stories need further selection, filtering, and sense-making.

It was notable that support for this sense-making was largely lacking on social network sites. See Friendship was the exception here, but features such as the Facebook Timeline, which are intended to produce 'the story of your life', tended to comprise too much trivial and mixed content to live up to this claim. It has been argued that time is 'configured' rather than simply reproduced in the formation of narratives about the past; the past is drawn on selectively when forming life stories [e.g. 4]. We suggest that social media sites could offer a greater range of actions that could be used in the formation of these narratives. One possibility would be to give users the option to privately 'favorite' photos; actions such as download or print that indicate preference might also be capitalized upon here. These favorites could be used as anchors to other related content, supporting sense-making and the creation of a framework for browsing when revisiting past content. Finally, and returning to the observation that users seem more motivated to 'curate' their content if reaching out to an audience than if simply keeping it for themselves, we suggest the possibility of supporting the formation of new narratives through interaction and sharing with others. For example, this could be accomplished by shifting the 'unit' in social media sites from a single piece of content to content plus metadata, or even to a collage of multiple pieces of content. This could encourage users to draw social media together in meaningful ways, and to potentially resurface it 'out of time', without breaking social norms, as one of our participants did through the use of screengrabs. If social media sites could capitalize on connections between old and new conversations about the same content, this could also facilitate the browsing and formation of new narratives.

CONCLUSION

Findings from our qualitative study suggest that, while social media sites are not explicitly viewed as archives, they nevertheless form a repository that could complement personal file stores. Social media is curated through use, and thus comprises a collection that is selective, organized, and annotated. It is more encountered than content in private archives, and so supports ready reminiscing. And it can be more reliable than private archives; for those who have had the experience of losing their own devices or have had them fail, social media can become the back-up. However, the concept of social media sites as archival is limited by the presence of data considered trivial and tensions over ownership and authenticity. We conclude by highlighting the possibilities for bridging social media and personal archives as a potential way forward. Personal archives could benefit from being imbued with some of the curation that is inherent to social media use; reflecting which content has been uploaded, and to where, could offer a novel way of filtering the higher resolution photos stored on a personal computer. Conversely, social media sites could benefit from a richer grammar of action [cf. 10], allowing users to place content in deep storage or otherwise 'keep' it. Identifying meaningful social media through such actions, for example by picking up on what has been printed or downloaded, could offer a more natural way of structuring reflective sense-making on social network sites. In conclusion, unpacking the personal value of social media may mean pulling online and offline archives together, so that actions in one are echoed across the other.

ACKNOWLEDGMENTS

We thank our participants and members of the SDS group at MSR Cambridge. This research was undertaken while the first author was an intern at Microsoft Research.

REFERENCES

1. Baym, N and boyd, d. Socially mediated publicness: An introduction. *Journal of Broadcasting and Electronic Media 56*, (2012), 320-329.

2. Bamberg, M. and Georgakopoulou, A. Small stories as a new perspective in narrative and identity analysis. *Text & Talk 28*, (2008), 377-396.
3. Burke, M., Kraut, R. and Marlow, C. Social capital on Facebook: Differentiating uses and users. In *Proc. CHI 2011*, (2011), 571–580.
4. Carr, D. *Time, Narrative and History*. Indiana University Press, Bloomington, 1986.
5. Ellison, N., Heino, R. and Gibbs, J. Managing impressions online: Self-presentation processes in the online dating environment. *Journal of Computer-Mediated Communication 11*, 2 (2006), 415-441.
6. Farnham, S. and Churchill, E. Faceted identity, faceted lives: Social and technical issues with being yourself online. In *Proc. CSCW 2011*, (2011), 359-368.
7. Glaser, B. and Strauss, A. *The Discovery of Grounded Theory: Strategies for Qualitative Research*. Aldine Publishing Company, Chicago, 1967.
8. Good, K. D. From scrapbook to Facebook: A history of personal media assemblage and archives. *New Media & Society 15*, 4 (2013), 557-573.
9. Gulotta, R., Odom, W., Forlizzi, J. and Faste, H. Digital artifacts as legacy: Exploring the lifespan and value of digital data. In *Proc. CHI 2013*, (2013), 1813-1822.
10. Harper, R., *et al.* What is a file? In *Proc. CSCW 2013*, (2013), 1125-1136.
11. Harper, R., Whitworth, E. and Page, R. Fixity: Identity, time and durée on Facebook. In *Proc. IR 13.0*, (2012).
12. Hogan, B. The presentation of self in the age of social media: Distinguishing performances and exhibitions online. *Bulletin of Science, Technology & Society 30*, (2010), 377–386.
13. Joinson, A. 'Looking at', 'looking up' or 'keeping up with' people?: Motives and use of Facebook. In *Proc. CHI 2008*, (2008), 1027-1036.
14. Karnik, M., Oakley, I., Venkatanathan, J., Spiliotopoulos, T. and Nisi, V. Uses & gratifications of a Facebook media sharing group. In *Proc. CSCW 2013*, (2013), 821-826.
15. Kirk, D. and Sellen, A. On human remains: Values and practice in the home archiving of cherished objects. *ACM Trans. Comput.-Hum. Interact. 17*, 3 (2010), 10.
16. Krämer, N.C. and Winter, S. Impression management 2.0. The relationship of self-esteem, extraversion, self-efficacy, and self-presentation within social networking sites. *Journal of Media Psychology 20*, (2008), 106–116.
17. Lindley, S., Marshall, C.C., Banks, R., Sellen, A. and Regan, T. Rethinking the web as a personal archive. In *Proc. WWW 2013*, (2013), 749-760.
18. Litt, E. Knock, knock. Who's there? The imagined audience. *Journal of Broadcasting and Electronic Media 56*, (2012), 330-345.
19. Mayer-Schönberger, V. *Delete: The Virtue of Forgetting in the Digital Age*. Princeton University Press, Princeton, 2009.
20. Marshall, C., McCown, F. and Nelson, M. L. Evaluating personal archiving strategies for internet-based information. In *Proc. Archiving 2007*, (2007), 151–56.
21. Odom, W. Sellen, A., Harper, R. and Thereska, E. Lost in translation: Understanding the possession of digital things in the cloud. In *Proc. CHI 2012*, (2012), 781-790.
22. Odom, W., Zimmerman, J. and Forlizzi, J. Teenagers and their virtual possessions: Design opportunities and issues. In *Proc. CHI 2011*, (2011), 1491–1500.
23. Page, R. Re-examining narrativity: Small stories in status updates, *Text & Talk 30*, (2010), 423-444.
24. Peesapati, S.T., Schwanda, V., Schultz, J., Lepage, M., Jeong, S. and Cosley, D. Pensieve: Supporting everyday reminiscence. In *Proc. CHI 2010*, (2010), 2027–2036.
25. Petrelli, D., van den Hoven, E. and Whittaker, S. Making history: Intentional capture of future memories. In *Proc. CHI 2009*, (2009), 1723-1732.
26. Petrelli, D. and Whittaker, S. Family memories in the home: Contrasting physical and digital mementos. *Pers. Ubiquit. Comput. 14*, (2010), 153-169.
27. Petrelli, D., Whittaker, S. and Brockmeier, J. AutoTopography: what can physical mementos tell us about digital memories? In *Proc. CHI 2008*, (2008), 53-62.
28. Sas, C. and Whittaker, S. Design for forgetting: Disposing of digital possessions after a breakup. In *Proc. CHI 2013*, (2013), 1823-1832.
29. Sleeper. M., Cranshaw, J., Kelly, B., Ur, A., Acquisti, L. and Cranor, N. 'I read my Twitter the next morning and was astonished'. A conversational perspective on Twitter regrets. In *Proc. CHI 2013*, (2013), 3277-3286.
30. Sosik, V.S., Zhao, X. and Cosley, D. See Friendship, sort of: How conversation and digital traces might support reflection on friendships. In *Proc. CSCW 2012*, (2012), 1145-1154.
31. Whittaker, S., Bergman, O. and Clough, P. Easy on that trigger dad: A study of long term family photo retrieval. *Pers. Ubiquit. Comput. 14*, (2010), 31-43.
32. Zhao, X., Salehi, N., Naranjit, S., Alwaalan, S. Voida, S. and Cosley, D. The many faces of Facebook: Experiencing social media as performance, exhibition, and personal archive. In *Proc. CHI 2013*, (2013), 1-10.
33. Zhao, X., Sosik, V.S. and Cosley, D. It's complicated: How romantic partners use Facebook. In *Proc. CHI 2012*, (2012), 771–780.

Together Alone: Motivations for Live-Tweeting a Television Series

Steven Schirra, Huan Sun, Frank Bentley
MIT Comparative Media Studies
Cambridge, MA USA
{schirra, sunhuan, bentley}@mit.edu

ABSTRACT
In this paper, we explore motivations for live-tweeting across a season of a television show. Using the third season of *Downton Abbey* as a case study, we followed 2,234 live-tweeters from the show's premiere episode to its finale, finding that nearly a third of users returned each week to tweet. Semi-structured interviews with 11 diverse live-tweeters revealed that the decision to live-tweet is dependent upon a variety of personal considerations and social conventions forming around this emerging TV viewing practice. This includes the desire to feel connected to a larger community that is interested in the show. Participants actively sought to protect the user experience of others by following good live-tweeting "etiquette," including limiting their number of posts and censoring content that might spoil the show for others. Over time, live-tweeting helped users build and maintain a network of fellow *Downton Abbey* viewers with shared interests.

Author Keywords
Live-tweeting; annotation; user research; social television; second screen; Twitter

ACM Classification Keywords
H.5.m. Information interfaces and presentation (e.g., HCI): Miscellaneous.

INTRODUCTION
The use of Twitter during live television viewing has become an increasingly common practice. Using second screen devices such as laptops and mobile phones, viewers collectively annotate and provide commentary for their favorite programs in real time, often using show-specific tags and keywords. For fans, the act of "live-tweeting"—the real-time annotation and discussion of television shows on Twitter—can provide an instant, online forum for connecting with others watching the same show, making TV viewing an even more social experience.

This emerging practice has also caught the interest of television networks and advertisers. At a time when many viewers either DVR or download television programs to watch at their convenience (and fast-forward through commercials), encouraging live viewing practices such as live-tweeting has become a priority for the television industry. In the realm of social television, Twitter activity has become a standard for measuring the real-time impact of television shows. Networks also routinely display an official hashtag at the beginning of each show to encourage live-tweeting. The Nielsen Company, the lead TV audience measurement firm in the United States, has created the "Nielsen Twitter TV Rating," set to debut in late 2013.[1]

As live-tweeting and television become more interconnected, understanding the user motivations behind this practice can lead to better social television experiences. Much of the previous work on television live-tweeting has focused on the quantitative study of television events, such as presidential debates [16, 17], or single television episodes within a series [8, 11, 16]. In this mixed-methods study, we expand upon existing research by looking at live-tweeting behavior related to a serial drama whose story unfolds across multiple episodes. In particular, in order to guide the design of future social television systems, we sought to understand what motivates viewers to live-tweet and why they continue to participate in this online activity throughout the season. We were also interested in how people balanced watching the show and tweeting as well as exploring browsing versus posting behaviors.

Using the PBS serial drama *Downton Abbey* as a case study, we identified a sample of 2,234 users who live-tweeted the show's highly publicized third season premiere and studied their activity across subsequent episodes. We wanted to understand the extent to which this activity was sustained beyond the novelty of the first episode, especially in light of other popular television shows airing at the same time. In addition, semi-structured interviews were completed with 11 diverse live-tweeters that focused on the motivations behind their *Downton Abbey* live-tweeting activity. This research suggests that live-tweeting is a complex social process with its own set of emerging conventions and practices. Understanding these conventions has wide implications for the development of television programming and second screen applications.

CHI 2014, April 26 - May 01 2014, Toronto, ON, Canada
Copyright 2014 ACM 978-1-4503-2473-1/14/04···$15.00.
http://dx.doi.org/10.1145/2556288.2557070

[1] http://www.nielsen.com/us/en/press-room/2012/nielsen-and-twitter-establish-social-tv-rating.html

PREVIOUS WORK

Earlier research on social TV focused on the design and study of companion systems meant to enhance viewers' social connections with friends and family. Rather than focusing on asynchronous, online discussions about TV, these systems connected viewers together during live broadcasts. For example, AmigoTV offered viewers a suite of social tools for viewing television with friends, such as voice chatting and on-screen animated emoticons [4]. Another system, Social TV 2, combined lightweight messaging with a physical device to signal when others with the system were watching television, allowing users to coordinate viewing together at a distance [6]. While these systems did not enjoy widespread adoption, viewers continue to tap into real-time audio and video tools offered by programs such as Skype and Google Hangouts to watch television with friends at a distance [9].

In the case of FriendFeeds, Basapur et al. [1] developed a second-screen application to encourage the sharing of related content about a show amongst already-existing small groups of friends.

The popularity of microblogging services such as Twitter has shifted much of the discussion about social TV toward second-screen applications that allow large groups of viewers to collectively annotate a television show as it airs. Twitter allows for more open conversations among interested viewers beyond friend groups. Huang et al. [7] found that users tag content on Twitter to participate in conversational "micro-memes"—time-sensitive, ad hoc discussions around a topic. Conversational tagging is particularly relevant to television live-tweeting, as using show-specific hashtags helps categorize a particular tweet while also providing a window into wider conversations with friends and strangers about a television show.

Live-tweeting itself has been studied in previous work from a variety of perspectives. Using social network analysis, Doughty et al. [5] studied how users converse on Twitter during different types of television shows (reality TV and a current events show). They found that entertainment-oriented shows exhibited less reciprocity in Twitter mentions than the current events show. Conversation about entertainment shows was more focused on discussions with celebrity Twitter accounts, while discussions around the current events show occurred among smaller, connected groups of friends.

Researchers have also looked at aggregate live-tweeting data to help them understand how television events unfold. Shamma et al. [16] studied Twitter use during the 2008 presidential debates, finding that the structure of live-tweeting activity can be used to predict the structure of media content. In addition, they found that tweeters did not tweet to summarize or discuss the content of the debate, but instead posted their immediate reactions and evaluated the debaters' performance.

Relatedly, Lochrie and Coulton [8] conducted a quantitative study around the reality TV show *X-Factor*, finding that, unlike with previous work studying debates, in which tweets rarely correlated with the specific topics being discussed by politicians, live-tweets related to this entertainment show significantly correlated to the content of the program. The authors speculate that the visuality of entertainment programming is more conducive to second-screen interactions.

Several qualitative studies have analyzed the types of content live-tweeters post about television. Wohn and Na [18] analyzed the content of tweets posted about both a political speech and a reality television show. Categorizing the tweets in an AEIO matrix—attention, emotion, information, opinion—they found that the content of live-tweets correlated strongly with the television show content. They also observed a rise in tweeting activity during commercial breaks.

In study of live-tweeting around the show *Glee* by McPherson at al. [11], viewers discussed live-tweeting as a way to feel connected to a wider audience of viewers, a feeling also expressed by viewers in our study of *Downton Abbey*. A content analysis of *Glee* tweets showed that the two most common tweet categories were providing play-by-plays of the action unfolding on the screen, and making comments about their enjoyment of the episode or the show in general. While McPherson et al collected data from multiple episodes, they did not look at temporal activity throughout the season or motivations to continue tweeting from week to week.

Previous work on Twitter and television focuses almost exclusively on the content of Tweets, however we are interested in the context of Twitter use and specifically on user motivations for live-tweeting and understanding emerging practices. Our work reveals users' motivations to live-tweet throughout the season and is informed by a wide array of considerations, both personal and social.

DOWNTON ABBEY

Downton Abbey is a period drama set in post-Edwardian England, following the lives of an aristocratic family and its large staff of servants. The show's third season aired for seven episodes in the United States between January and February 2013 on the Public Broadcasting Service (PBS), a non-profit television network. This show provides an interesting social television case study for several reasons. First, the show was the subject of much critical acclaim, thus making its return to television a highly anticipated television event. This provided an opportunity to see how live-tweeting activity about the show changed after a widely publicized first episode of the season.

In addition, *Downton Abbey's* third season had aired the previous year in the United Kingdom, meaning that some American viewers in our study had already watched the entire season in advance of its United States debut.

Interestingly, for some viewers, knowing the plot twists in advance seemed to enhance their social television experience, allowing them to compare the reactions of UK and American audiences.

As a show broadcast on a public television station, *Downton Abbey* is presented in the United States without commercial interruptions, meaning that viewers who wish to live-tweet during the show must manage their television viewing with their second screen use. The show's lack of commercials led to many discussions in our qualitative study about live-tweeting and distractions.

Lastly, while many for-profit networks strategically shift airing dates or times for new episodes of their most popular shows in light of television events such as the Super Bowl or major awards shows, PBS did not make such schedule adjustments. Therefore, *Downton Abbey* aired consistently each week on Sunday nights beginning at 9 p.m. EST (8 p.m. CST) from January 6 through February 17, including going up directly against the Super Bowl and Grammy Awards.

Using *Downton Abbey* as our case study, we sought to explore the following research questions: 1) What motivates viewers to live-tweet throughout a season of a television show? 2) Is this motivation affected by social settings, or only by personal feelings? and 3) What do Twitter users perceive as acceptable live-tweeting behavior, and how do these emerging norms inform their live-tweeting practices?

METHODS

To obtain our initial sample of live-tweeters for our study, we ran a TweeQL [10] query for the keywords "`downton abbey`" and "`downtonabbey`" during *Downton Abbey*'s first episode. This program queries the Twitter Search API to return, for example, tweets that mention the show's name, tweets containing the #downtonabbey hashtag, or tweets mentioning the official @DowntonAbbey Twitter account.

We began our data collection 30 minutes before the show began, and ended 45 minutes after it ended, allowing time to capture both anticipatory tweets and post-show discussions. In total, our query returned 26,540 tweets from the Twitter Streaming API from 13,828 unique users. Following previous work [11], we eliminated users from our sample who tweeted only once about the show, leaving a sample of 3,805 unique live-tweeters.

After *Downton Abbey*'s complete third season had aired, we refined this sample further, downloading Twitter profile data for each user, as well each user's complete Twitter timeline posted between the show's premiere and its finale. We removed users from our sample who had not self-identified as living in the Eastern or Central Time Zones (n=1,304), users whose accounts were subsequently deleted or set to private (n=165), and users whose complete Twitter timelines could not be obtained due to Twitter Search API limitations (n=102). This final sample of 2,234 users and their corpus of tweets was used in our initial analysis.

Twitter Timelines

To analyze this larger corpus of Twitter data, we divided user timelines into segments corresponding to the times *Downton Abbey* aired on PBS, allowing extra time before (30 mins) and after (45 mins) to capture related conversations that happened outside the show's airing window.

In total, these segments contained 100,186 tweets. We compared each tweet against a list of 81 show-specific keywords (e.g. names of characters, actors, and production staff, locations and settings, etc.) compiled by a researcher intimately familiar with the show, revealing 40,304 *Downton Abbey*-related tweets (40.23% of all tweets during these intervals).

We validated this process by having one of the authors manually code a random sample of 400 tweets for relevance to *Downton Abbey*. The computer-coded tweets matched the human-coded tweets in 95.5% of cases (Cohen's kappa = 0.901), demonstrating a high level of agreement.

Recruitment

To recruit participants for our qualitative study, we randomly selected users from our sample and analyzed their Twitter use during the times *Downton Abbey* appeared on television. Using this information, we constructed an initial recruitment list of 33 users who had varying Tweeting habits. The features we considered in this selection process included number of shows tweeted, frequency of tweets, and number of retweets and mentions.

These users were contacted through one of the authors' personal Twitter accounts. An initial tweet informed participants that the researcher was studying Twitter use and *Downton Abbey*. Users who expressed interest were sent a link to an informational website where they could access information about the research project and sign up for an interview. Participants were offered a $10 gift certificate for completing the interview.

Interestingly, this method of recruitment resulted in a high yield of interested interviewees. Of the initial 33 participants contacted, 15 requested more information on the study, and 11 (33%) signed-up for an interview. The final 11 participants were diverse in terms of age (19–50, mean age of 34), gender (3 male, 8 female) and occupation (e.g. college student, librarian, administrative assistant). As an exploratory study, we did not attempt to characterize the entire audience of viewers or tweeters, but instead sought to speak with viewers who had a range of experiences with live-tweeting. The final 11 participants completed a semi-structured interview with a researcher via phone or Skype, which lasted about 30 minutes.

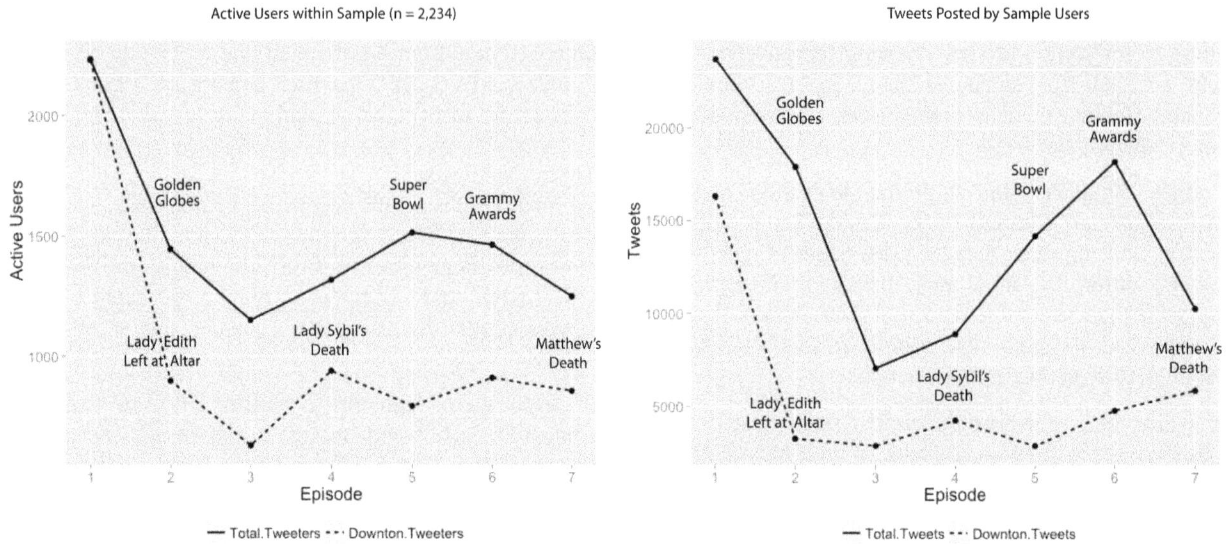

Figure 1: Graphs of overall and *Downton Abbey*-related Twitter activity for users within our sample, showing active users (left) and total tweets posted (right). The top bold line represents all activity by users in the sample, whereas the dotted line represents activity related to *Downton Abbey*. Major competing programs airing during the same broadcast window as *Downton Abbey* displayed above chart.

Interviews

Participants were asked generally about their television and social media habits, and then more targeted questions about their use of Twitter during *Downton Abbey*. In addition to explaining their reasoning behind posting particular *Downton Abbey* tweets from their timelines, participants were asked questions relating to their tweeting conventions (e.g. use of @mentions, RTs), their relationships with other live-tweeters, and how they managed second screen use with live television viewing. These interviews were audio recorded and transcribed.

With this qualitative data, our team conducted a team-based grounded theory analysis described by Metcalf and Harboe [12]. Using this method, we "extracted observations and behavioral descriptions from the data, identified patterns in the items, and named and described those patterns" [12]. One researcher analyzed the interview transcripts and identified the items for analysis, which were diverse quotes from our participants. These items were then organized by all co-authors through the method described above. Each theme discussed below has support from multiple diverse participants.

USER ACTIVITY ACROSS THE SERIES

Our analysis of Twitter user timelines revealed that many users from our sample returned to tweet about *Downton Abbey* in subsequent episodes (see Figure 1). The amount of activity devoted to *Downton Abbey* is at times surprising, given that the show aired in the same broadcast window as several highly popular television programs such as the Golden Globes and the Super Bowl. (The Super Bowl, for example, attracted 108.7 million viewers and was the subject of 26.1 million tweets.[2])

In the weeks following *Downton Abbey*'s premiere, the number of active Twitter users from our sample ranged from 51–65% each week. Looking at those who posted about *Downton Abbey* during its airing window, 28–40% of users posted about the show during a given episode.

The frequency of tweets per user was significantly higher during the premiere than in subsequent episodes, which speaks to the season premiere's status as a more "tweetable" television event than subsequent episodes.

Plotting the volume of tweet activity over the course of each episode shows notable spikes in activity at some of the show's tensest and most surprising moments. Figure 2 (below) displays the user activity for two episodes in season three of *Downton Abbey*. Episode four in particular contained several scenes relating to the dramatic death of one of the show's characters, and the viewer reaction to this event is apparent within the timeline. Our interviews with live-tweeters confirmed that this was one of the season's most "have-to-tweet-about" moments.

FINDINGS

Analysis of the qualitative data from our interviews with live-tweeters revealed that live-tweeting is a complex social process in which users make many considerations about their post content and frequency of tweeting. In this paper we discuss six major themes from our analysis that help

[2] http://www.nielsen.com/us/en/newswire/2013/super-bowl-xlvii-draws-108-7-million-viewers-26-1-tweets.html

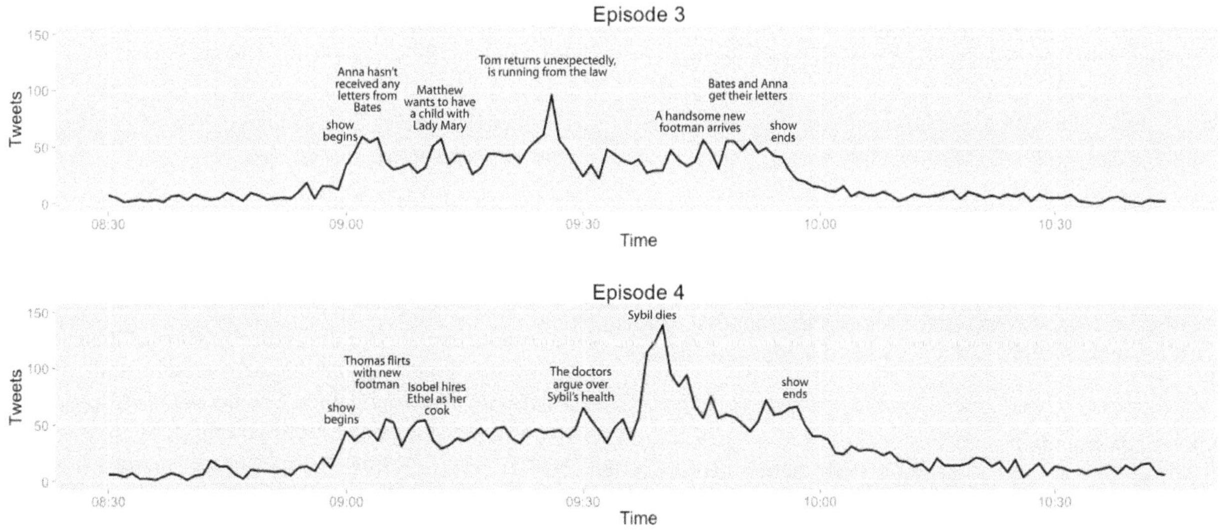

Figure 2: Time plots of tweet activity (tweets per minute) for episodes three and four of *Downton Abbey*. Annotations describe the on-screen action associated with the spikes in user activity. Episode four contains a notable increase in activity during the dramatic death of a character.

build a broader understanding of this emerging television practice: personal benefits, etiquette, triggers, attention management, and impacts on friendships and ratings.

Live-Tweeting "Triggers"

In general, participants noted that twists in the plot or story arc were the most obvious "have-to-tweet" moments. As interviewees described them, their reasons for live-tweeting fell into three broad categories.

Sadness/Grief

Many participants mentioned that feelings of grief and sadness prompted them to post tweets about the show. They attributed this to the emotional connections they had made with the characters throughout the series. In particular, the unexpected deaths of two main characters caused many users both to tweet and seek out others' tweets. P1 said: "Sybil's death, that was probably the most, you know, need to tweet about moment of the last season. Um, that's because it was so, you know, sudden and shocking that you sort of want to interact with other people about it and see what their feelings about it were." P8 mentioned similar feelings: "Obviously like the huge, crazy death of Matthew Crawley in the finale, and the death of the sister Sybil, that was something I tweeted about."

Interestingly, in cases where users had watched the show online in advance of its United States TV premiere, these major plot twists created the opposite effect—participants decided *not* to post to their Twitter timelines. Instead, they focused on reading others' reactions. P3 said:

"At the very end, you know, I knew Matthew was going to die ... so I was already starting to tear up. I think that the particular scene where Matthew is holding the baby and Mary's lying there and they are all in their glory and it all looks so wonderful ... when I knew my timeline would explode with people being upset and with the anger and, I didn't tweet anything because I just wanted to just see what people were going to do or say."

During the death scenes, P2 also focused on reading her Twitter timeline to see if others were experiencing the same kind of grief she felt months earlier: "Since I had watched [previously] in December, literally I had gone through the grief on my own, because I couldn't really say anything to everybody, because I didn't want it to be a spoiler. I had to see [the Twitter reactions] because—it was like so many months later. Because when I was watching it, nobody else was watching it."

Television viewers can develop attachments the show's characters over the course of a series, making startling events such as character deaths particularly shocking and saddening. In our study, participants turned to Twitter not only as a means to share their own sadness and grief, but also to view and understand the reactions of others.

Humor

Comedic moments in the show were also mentioned by participants as a main inspiration for their tweets and retweets. For P7, tweeting about *Downton Abbey*'s humor helped provide contrast to the serious plot lines of the show: "I think anything really comedic I would tweet about. Because it is such a dark show sometimes. You really kind of need to cling to those comedic aspects, so I would try to tweet about those."

In particular, the pithy, one-line insults delivered by the character Violet Crawley were at the center of many conversations. P8 noted, "For me I expected when I first started to watch it that it [Downton] was going to be very dry, but I think the most tweetable moments and the ones that, you know, pop up the most online and in conversation the next day with my friends would always be one-liners." Several participants mentioned that they often retweeted postings from Downton Abbey parody accounts that captured the show's most humorous lines.

Humor was also expressed by making light of the characters' unfortunate moments. As P11 recalled, "When Edith got left at the altar, there were lots of funny comments. Bless her little heart." These types of tweets were described by several interviewees as "snarky" and "sarcastic," making light of the very serious moments in the show.

Character Development

A third reason for live-tweeting dealt with issues of character development. In general, these types of tweets were posted when participants noticed long-term changes in a character's actions or ambitions. For example, P8 noted, "I definitely posted and saw a lot of people who I follow post about the development of the character of Tom who was Sybil's husband who became the widower turned new father, you know, dealing with everything." P9 tweeted when she considered a character's current actions in light of the character's tragic past: "[I tweeted because Edith was] kind of stepping forward and moving on from all the pain she's been through in the season. That's basically what I was thinking. Instead of just sitting around and waiting, she just went out and tried to seize a couple of things on her own."

Sometimes, these tweets are not directed toward the show's characters, but instead at the show's producers. P6 posted a tweet because he was upset that a plotline between two characters had turned stale: "[I tweeted because] I thought that [Downton] was spending too much time on if Matthew was going to give the money to the house, and Mary was getting all upset about it, and to me they were spending too much time on it, and it looked like they needed to get a baby or do something else."

This category of tweets is not simply based on an immediate response to the action on the television screen, but also incorporates a viewer's deeper knowledge of the characters spanning several episodes, or the entire series.

Personal Benefits of Live-Tweeting

Users in our study described an array of personal benefits they gained from live-tweeting. In general, tweeting while watching television gave participants a sense of connectedness with a broader audience.

Feeling part of a wider phenomenon

Most participants articulated a sense of feeling part of a larger phenomenon that included not only their circle of friends, but others across the country sharing in the same television experience. As P1 explained, the difference between watching *Downton Abbey* with and without Twitter is "sort of like the difference between watching a movie at home on a DVD and watching the movie in a movie theater ... Like when you go to a movie theater and you feel like you're part of an experience because there are other people sharing it with you."

P3 described live-tweeting *Downton Abbey* as participation in a larger "process," and several other interviewees mentioned the excitement of feeling a part of an "interactive" television viewing experience.

According to P4, building a following of other interested viewers is something that happens slowly, and only through consistent Tweeting habits. She noted, "Twitter seems to be one of those things, the more you do it, the more people see what you say. And the more hashtags and mentions you put in, the more likely it is that people will see what you've written." Like other participants in our study, P4 is motivated to continue tweeting about particular shows to help augment and maintain her Twitter audience.

Not feeling alone

Eight of our interviewees discussed live-tweeting as a viewing practice that allows them socialize with others, especially when they are watching television alone. In some instances, this is because friends and spouses have different television interests. P3 says she turns to Twitter because her husband does not share her interest in British television shows: "Since [me and my husband's] TV habits are so different, in a sense by using social media I'm sort of getting that same experience, but with strangers."

P2 finds the live-tweeting community comforting when she has no one around to talk to. "If I can't say it to anyone else around me, I'll just put it up on the Internet. Someone will read it, someone will agree with me at some point. I'm not alone. It's just a reassurance that I'm not alone."

Affirming personal opinions

Many participants used the live-tweeting community as a way to affirm their own personal thoughts about the events in the show. In particular, interviewees expressed satisfaction in knowing that others agreed with their observations about *Downton Abbey*. P9 said, "It was kind of interesting because I found out a couple people were thinking the same things I was thinking during the show."

For P6, finding that others share his thoughts about the show helps create feelings of a shared experience: "It's just that everybody's watching the same thing that you're watching, and so, and then reading their tweets you can tell that they're having the same thoughts that you do, and it's just, that's what I get out of it, that's what makes it fun."

Live-Tweeting Etiquette

In discussing their own live-tweeting practices, many of our participants in turn described what they considered an emerging set of best practices for Twitter and TV.

Avoiding "Overtweeting"

Many interviewees described feeling concerned about the amount of live-tweets they posted to their Twitter timelines. In fact, P11 even created a separate Twitter account for live-tweeting: "A lot of people follow me on my regular Twitter that really don't care ... what I have to say about television."

P1 explains that there should be a "balance" in the amount of tweets one posts about a particular show. On his own Twitter timeline, he notes that some members he follows "go on these tweeting and retweeting rampages ... where they'll post 10 tweets in 30 seconds, and then rewet every tweet that's possibly related to what they tweeted about. It just becomes too much."

P6 also mentioned his frustration with live-tweeters who make too many posts. Instead of "redoing the whole entire show" on their Twitter feeds, he says live-tweeters should instead post "specific lines that make your mind melt. The quips characters say. Those make good tweets." He tries to limit his own tweeting to those he finds particularly meaningful or humorous.

For P3, her excessive tweeting about television led to a disagreement with a family member. She recalled: "My sister-in-law once said to me, 'I started following you on Twitter, but you live-tweet all these dang shows and you fill up my timeline, and so I unfollowed you.' I was like, Okay, whatever." P3 says despite this complaint, she will not change her tweeting habits, because "If you don't want to see [my live tweets], then don't follow me."

Signaling Intention to Live-Tweet

Some participants try to mitigate any negative impacts their live-tweeting might have on their relationships with followers. Three participants mentioned "signaling" their intention to live-tweet on their timelines before a show begins. This alerted like-minded followers that they were watching the show, while also serving as a "disclaimer," according to P11, that "I am going to yammer about TV shows."

Avoiding "Spoiler" Tweets

Because live-tweeters recognize that not all of their followers watch *Downton Abbey* during its live broadcast, many participants in our study developed ways of posting about major plot twists in the show without spoiling the show for others. P11 says this is especially important because she has Twitter followers in California, where the show is broadcast several hours later.

Most participants use demonstrative pronouns as a way to mask the specifics of the scenes they are live-tweeting. P5 says she makes comments such as, "'I can't believe he just said that,' or, 'What is this ridiculous situation?' You know, things that other people watching will understand, but it's not going to be evident to anybody who doesn't know what's going on what's going on."

P8 avoids putting any of his live-tweets in "black and white terms" so his tweets about *Downton Abbey* can be overlooked by followers who are not currently tuned into the show.

Despite many participants' efforts to avoid posting spoilers themselves by avoiding social media sites if they miss a television episode, several have had key plot points spoiled by others. For P5, *Downton Abbey* was spoiled when a local coffee shop tweeted about the death of a character several days after its broadcast. She said, "I sent them a grumpy tweet back, saying, Hey, not all of us have seen that yet. It was the week that Sybil died." After the spoiler was revealed, P5 decided to stop watching the show.

P8 notes that many tabloids rush to publish spoilers: "People magazine will tweet, 'She might have been jilted at the alter, but Edith looked beautiful! ... I'm like, Oh my god, I can't believe that. I'm not home now, I can't watch this." P2 had a similar experience with friends posting spoilers on her Twitter timeline: "I was like, damn it, I have to watch it. I closed my computer and I went and watched [the show] live ... I turned off Twitter and I turned off my phone and I watched it—in peace."

Live-Tweeting Live—or Not at All

Several participants discussed the fact that live-tweeting is only meaningful to audiences at the time the show is airing on television. As P8 summarized, "When somebody's tweeting about something days later, that's terrible. It looks like Twitter pollution," adding that users should "live-tweet it or don't tweet it at all."

P5 noted that she is hesitant to live-tweet about the television shows she's watching since she does not "watch a lot of TV that's happening." She felt that thoughts she had after the show had aired were "not relevant to tweet about."

Managing Social TV Activity

Tweeting as a Distraction

Managing second screens with television viewing is an ongoing challenge for live-tweeters. In a show such as *Downton Abbey* with no commercial breaks, viewers must strategically time their tweeting with the action unfolding on the screen. P7 mentioned that "it's a bummer that the show doesn't have commercials, because I would definitely tweet more."

For some participants, live-tweeting is no different than other everyday distractions. As P5 notes, "I'm pretty distractible, so [tweeting] doesn't really matter. If it's not that, it's the cat, or the cracks on the ceiling, or some noise. The show is only going to keep a certain percentage of my attention anyway."

However, most of our interviewees could recall moments where live-tweeting caused them to miss an important moment in the show. P3 said that tweeting has changed her TV viewing experience: "You can miss things, you don't concentrate as well because you're doing two things at once. Your brain is engaged in something visual and then your brain is engaged in, you know, writing what you're thinking and feeling."

Our participations mentioned several strategies for managing their live-tweeting and television viewing. P11 waits "until a slow part in the story" or pauses the show to send her tweets. When P6 and P9 feel like tweeting is distracting them from important scenes in the show, they put away their second screens and focus only on the show.

If viewers do miss parts of the show due to live-tweeting, P7 says the stakes are low due to the availability of many TV shows online: "I feel like the process of recording your reactions to the show at the time outweigh the fact that you might miss one or two lines. And then if you really do miss it, you can always watch it later, like online the next day."

A Social TV Ecosystem

While Twitter is the most prevalent social media service for the live-annotation of television shows, many participants noted that their social television viewing experience unfolds across a variety of services and platforms. In particular, participants noted that when they communicate with family and close friends about television, they often switch from Twitter to less public methods of communication.

Three participants often send text messages to friends and relatives while watching television shows. P7 explained that, compared to Twitter, text messages deliver social television content to friends on a "more personal level." P11 texts "quite a bit" while watching TV because "not everybody cares" what she has to say about the show.

P9 recalled connecting with her cousin through Skype so she could remotely watch a television show on a premium cable channel. "We talked while the show was on [on Skype]. They were watching from their house, and I was on Skype talking to them. It was fun."

When considering their interactions with the wider viewing audiences, participants mentioned GetGlue as another social television platform they had used or had seen others use. P1 describes GetGlue as "sort of like FourSquare for media" where fans can "check into" their favorite shows and interact with other viewers.

Most interviewees mentioned Facebook as an "occasional" source for social television commentary; however, several participants discussed the differences between Facebook and Twitter that makes Facebook less conducive for social television. P11 said that Facebook postings "make more of a lasting statement" than Twitter postings, which are "more of a short-term response."

P3 says she often gets annoyed when her friends inappropriately try to use Facebook to make live commentary about television shows: "[Live-tweeting] is not what Facebook is about, and it kills me if I just have to get on Facebook when there's a football game going on … I just wanted to go, People, live-tweeting the game is on Twitter, not on Facebook. I don't need to see your updates every minute while you're watching the game."

Strengthening Real-Life Friendships

While many live-tweeting interactions experienced by participants were with online-only friends or strangers, live-tweeting also provided an opportunity to strengthen existing real-life friendships, as has been observed in previous work on messaging while watching videos together [15], and even create new online friends who are watching the same show. However, for our participants, Twitter added a layer of serendipity to the discovery of shared television interests.

P7 learned that one of her college friends was interested in *Downton Abbey* after he favorited several of her tweets:

"My friend Seth, I didn't even know he liked Downton Abbey, and then he started like, favoriting my tweets. And I was like, You like Downton Abbey! So the next time I saw him, I was like, My Downton friend! And he's like, Ahhh! And so we all were like really excited that we knew, because we didn't know about that. And so tweeting about that kind of helps people know, Oh this person likes that too, which is kind of a cool thing about Twitter."

Several participants noted that their live-tweets became later topics of conversation among their real-life friends. According to P11, "Usually [friends will say in real life], 'That was really funny,' or 'I agree completely,' or 'Did that catch you off guard?' I'm usually not scared to talk about television with people. For me, it's always a good groundbreaker, conversation wise."

In P3's case, her live-tweeting has led to the creation of several new, real-life friendships: "We live like 90 minutes away from each other and we meet up and we see British films and we have lunch." She added, "It's fascinating to me because I don't think [making these new friends] would have happened without Twitter."

Influencing Ratings

When asked whether they thought the production staff of *Downton Abbey* had seen any of their live-tweets, none of the participants thought this was likely. However, they still thought that television networks and television producers monitored live-tweets. This led them to feel as though their tweets had an impact on a show's chances for renewal.

According to most interviewees, the strength of a show's Twitter community can serve as a public display of its success—or failure. As P8 recalled: "I've noticed that whenever a show that I've watched that inevitably gets canceled gets canceled, usually it's something that I'm not reading a lot about on Twitter, and if I do check the hashtag or the official Twitter account, the activity will be very, very low. There won't be a lot of replies, there won't be a lot of people tweeting about watching or enjoying it."

Participants also perceived live-tweeting to be a way for viewers to help increase a show's viewership. P3 wondered whether the live-tweeting community had contributed to the "explosion of popularity" of *Downton Abbey* throughout season three.

P7 views Twitter as more than just a platform for fans to converse about television. He has seen Twitter users mobilize to help shows on the brink of cancelation, coordinating their tweets to create Twitter trending topics and bringing wider visibility to the show.

In this sense, live-tweeters are motivated by a desire to help their favorite shows succeed, and see live-tweeting as a form of material participation in the shows they enjoy.

DISCUSSION

As a social media service in which most content is public and easily collected, Twitter has proven popular among researchers. Taken together, the analysis of this data has helped "open a surprising window into the moods, thoughts and activities of society at large" [14]. However most of the existing research has focused on what can be learned from the tweets themselves. Our research goes beyond this work to explore what cannot be found in the content itself through in-depth interviews about current practices.

In the realm of social television, large-scale studies of tweeting behavior have revealed key findings about the behavior of television audiences, and have also provided new sets of tools for the real-time analysis of viewer sentiment and engagement. Despite the abundance of such quantitative research, few studies have focused on what motivates individual Twitter users to live-tweet, and how live-tweeting fits within their everyday television viewing practices. In this study, we have attempted to look at these big questions surrounding live-tweeting on a small scale.

One key finding from this research is that television viewers are particularly motivated to live-tweet when viewing television alone, either due to viewers having different tastes in television than their friends and spouses or participants living alone. The live-tweeting community, then, allowed viewers to still feel that they were watching the show with others. Interestingly, these feelings of connectedness with others were still experienced by live-tweeters even if no one acknowledged their tweets.

In her book "Alone Together," Turkle [17] argues that communication on SNS provides hollow, inauthentic communication that distracts from in-person interactions. However, in our study, we observed Twitter having the opposite effect, particularly in contexts where participants' spouses or housemates did not have an interest in the show. Live-tweeting helped strengthen existing friendships or form new ones while conversing about the television content, even though participants were physically alone.

While some small-scale systems that help connect close friends who are watching television have been created (e.g. [1, 13]), there is a much larger design space for making people feel together with a larger audience while watching content and experiencing reactions to key events in the show together.

Our study aligns with previous research showing that shocking or surprising moments in the show did prompt viewers to tweet [11, 18]. However, when discussing their reasoning for posting particular messages, participants rarely thought of their tweets as a simple reaction to what was happening on the screen. Character development in particular relies upon the viewer's long-term knowledge of the show's plot and characters and implies that future systems should help users to see a series as a whole and not just a set of disconnected episodes and characters.

Though few viewers in our qualitative study posted live-tweets each week throughout the series, most reported that their Twitter use itself was more regular. Even if they did not post tweets for a particular episode, participants still watched others' reactions on Twitter on their computers and phones. In some instances, viewers were more interested in reading others' thoughts about a plot development than posting their own. This suggests that posting tweets is not necessarily a live-tweeter's first instinct at interesting moments in an episode, and that a lack of tweeting activity does not necessarily translate to a lack of interest. Future models of viewer engagement should consider the importance of *listening* as a form of participation [3] in the realm of social television. This was particularly visible in the current study as viewers described their interest in reading the reactions of others in the show's tensest moments, rather than rushing to post their own content.

We have also uncovered how Twitter content related to a television show can prompt off-network behavior, such as talking about a show in person with a friend who was previously not known to watch the particular show that they tweeted about. The ability for Tweets and other forms of television-based presence to inspire communication is a rich area for future system development.

As a relatively new television viewing practice, the live-tweeting community is still in the process of developing a collective understanding of etiquette and best practices. As Baym [2] notes, "Community norms of practice are displayed, reinforced, negotiated and taught through members' shared behaviors," which develop and evolve over time. To some degree, viewers' live-tweeting practices are constrained by considerations within their own social networks. Fear of spoiling the show or excessively tweeting can provide limitations for how often one live-tweets and what the content of those tweets will be. In fact, live-tweeters may deliberately mask the show-specific content in their tweets, which has wider implications on the wide-scale collection and analysis of live-tweeting data. Therefore attempts to objectively quantify engagement based on volume of tweets may not reflect viewer's accurate experiences with the show.

CONCLUSION

In this research we have discussed an array of personal and social considerations that inform users' decisions of when to live-tweet—and why. Live-tweeting can help viewers feel connected to a large online viewing audience, while also helping to strengthen social bonds with real-life friends, providing a context for conversation around shared interests. Looking at user timelines across the entire season showed that many viewers continued live-tweeting about *Downton Abbey* in the weeks following the much-anticipated first episode. However, our qualitative study suggests that posting activity alone may serve as a weak indicator of engagement with others during a television show, since many social activities, such as interacting with friends face-to-face or using other media after seeing a Tweet are not visible on Twitter.

Live-tweeting presents an interesting domain for further research, in that it presents a context in which participants actively seek to protect the user experience of others. This research suggests that, while a desire to live-tweet can indeed be triggered by immediate reactions to the events unfolding on the television screen, oftentimes viewers developed their live-tweets by carefully considering the show's plot and characters over the course of many episodes or seasons. This shows that live-tweeters balance a desire for immediacy and relevancy in their tweets with a thoughtful consideration of tweet content.

This paper describes a set of motivations and practices around live-tweeting; however, we must consider that these practices may be specific to the *Downton Abbey* viewing audience. Future work should study live-tweeters around a variety of television genres, as different habits may become visible. Nonetheless, this work illustrates the constellation of social and personal motivations and benefits to live-tweeting, highlighting important considerations for the design of new social television systems.

ACKNOWLEDGMENTS

We would like to thank our participants for their time and valuable insights, the MIT Comparative Media Studies department for funding this work, and the members of the Social Media Collective at MSR for their feedback on early versions of this work.

REFERENCES

1. Basapur, S., Mandalia, H., Chaysinh, S., Lee, Y., Venkitaraman, N., and Metcalf, C. 2012. Fanfeeds: Evaluation of Socially Generated Information feed on Second Screen as a TV Show Companion. In *Proc. EuroITV '12*. ACM, 87-96.
2. Baym, N. K. *Personal connections in the digital age*. Polity, New York, 2010.
3. Crawford, K. 2009. Following you: Disciplines of listening in social media. *Continuum: Journal of Media & Cultural Studies*, 23 (4), 525-535.
4. Coppens, T., Trappeniers, L., & Godon, M. 2004. AmigoTV: towards a social TV experience. In *Proc. iEuroITV '04*.
5. Doughty, M. Rowland, D. and Lawson, S. 2012. Who is on your sofa?: TV audience communities and second screening social networks. In *Proc. EuroiTV '12*. ACM, New York, NY, 79-86.
6. Harboe, G., Metcalf, C. J., Bentley, F., Tullio, J., Massey, N., & Romano, G. 2008. Ambient social tv: drawing people into a shared experience. In *Proc. CHI '08*, ACM, 1-10.
7. Huang, J., Thornton, K. M., and Efthimiadis, E.M. 2010. Conversational tagging in twitter. In *Proc. Hypertext and Hypermedia*. ACM, New York, NY, USA, 173-178.
8. Lochrie M. and Coulton P. 2012. Sharing the viewing experience through second screens. *In Proc. EuroiTV '12*. ACM, New York, NY, 199-202.
9. Macaranas, A., Venolia, G., Inkpen, K., & Tang, J. 2013. Sharing Experiences over Video: Watching Video Programs Together at a Distance. *In Proc. INTERACT '13*.
10. Marcus, A., Bernstein, M. S., Badar, O., Karger, D. R., Madden, S., & Miller, R. C. 2011. *Tweets as data: demonstration of TweeQL and Twitinfo. In Proc. ACM SIGMOD '11*, ACM, 1259-1262.
11. McPherson, K., Huotari, K., Cheng, F., Humphrey, D., Cheshire, C., & Brooks, A. L. 2012. Glitter: a mixed-methods study of twitter use during glee broadcasts. In *Proc. CSCW '12*, ACM, 167-170.
12. Metcalf C. and Harboe G. 2006. Sunday is Family Day. Ethnographic Praxis in Industry Conference Proceedings, 49–65.
13. Metcalf, C., Harboe, G., Tullio, J., Massey, N., Romano, G., Huang, E. M., and Bentley, F. 2008. Examining presence and lightweight messaging in a social television experience. *ACM TOMCCAP*, 4 (4), 27-43.
14. Savage, N. 2011. Twitter as a medium and message. *Commun. ACM*, 54, 18–20.
15. Shamma, D. A., and Liu, Y. Zync with Me: Synchronized Sharing of Video through Instant Messaging. In *Social Interactive Television: Immersive Shared Experiences and Perspectives*. Information Science Publishing, Hershey, PA, USA, 2009, 273–288,
16. Shamma, D. A., Kennedy, L., and Churchill, E. F. 2009. Tweet the debates: understanding community annotation of uncollected sources. In *Proc. WSM '09*. ACM, New York, NY, 3-10.
17. Turkle, S. (2012). *Alone together: Why we expect more from technology and less from each other*. Basic Books.
18. Wohn, D. Y., and Na, E. K. (2011). Tweeting about TV: Sharing television viewing experiences via social media message streams. *First Monday*, *16* (3).

Documentscape: Intertextuality, Sequentiality, & Autonomy at Work

Lars Rune Christensen
Aalborg University Copenhagen
A.C. Meyers Vænge 15
2450 Copenhagen SV
Denmark
Lrc@learning.aau.dk

Pernille Bjørn
IT-University of Copenhagen
Rued Langaards Vej 7, 2300 Copenhagen S, Denmark
UCIrvine & Intel Center for Social Computing (ISTC)
Bren Hall, 6th Floor, Irvine, California, USA
pbra@itu.dk

ABSTRACT
On the basis of an ethnographic field study, this article introduces the concept of *documentscape* to the analysis of document-centric work practices. The concept of documentscape refers to the entire ensemble of documents in their mutual intertextual interlocking. Providing empirical data from a global software development case, we show how hierarchical structures and sequentiality across the interlocked documents are critical to how actors make sense of the work of others and what to do next in a geographically distributed setting. Furthermore, we found that while each document is created as part of a quasi-sequential order, this characteristic does not make the document, as a single entity, into a stable object. Instead, we found that the documents were malleable and dynamic while suspended in intertextual structures. Our concept of documentscape points to how the hierarchical structure, sequentiality, and authorless nature of documents serve as a constitutive platform for the development of iterative and emergent work practices, making it possible for highly distributed actors to collaborate with limited communication, as the documentscape serves as a vehicle of coordination.

Author Keywords
Documents; Documentscape; Global Software Development; Global Interaction

ACM Classification Keywords
K.4.3 [Organizational Impacts]: Computer-supported collaborative work

INTRODUCTION
In this article, we attempt to achieve a better understanding of how cooperative work is accomplished by collaborative actors through the creation and use of mutually constituted documents in document-centric work practices. Previous studies have focused on single documents (e.g., [14, 23]), and on collections of documents (e.g., [5, 20]). Building on this work, we explore how multiple documents are mutually constituted in a complex web of associations (e.g., [3, 5, 9, 20]), and what characterizes these associations in supporting distributed collaboration. Inspired by the work on mediascapes and technoscapes [1] in global work, we introduce the concept of *documentscape* as an analytical device to unpack how documents shape and are shaped by work practices. A series or an ensemble of documents may be said to form a documentscape when each document depends upon the wider ensemble for meaning as well as utility. Documents in the documentscape take their meaning from their position in an ensemble of documents used or produced in series or in parallel.

The study addresses the core HCI and CSCW problem of characterizing how artifacts partly constitute – and as such exert pressure on – human action. Analysing a hierarchy of artifacts (a documentscape) is part of this. The documentscape's interconnections provide scaffolding for the geographically distributed activities of global software development by providing hierarchy and sequentiality among the distributed documents (by way of intertextuality) to the otherwise emergent and continually changing documents that make up the project in progress. The structure of the documentscape, which is unfolded by the actors sequentially, yet iteratively, is what makes it possible for the distributed actors to take over the work of others with very limited direct communication and coordination. Note that situations where direct interaction and communication are absolutely required (e.g. in meetings) also exist. However, what this study highlights is that there are equally countless situations where the sequentiality and hierarchical intertextuality of the documentscape constitutes enough meaning and context for the competent actors to successfully perform their distributed work.

Our empirical data originate from a study of distributed document-centric work practices within global software development. In the process of software development, system architects, software developers, software testers,

ACM 978-1-4503-2473-1/14/04...$15.00.
http://dx.doi.org/10.1145/2556288.2557305

and project managers continuously create, use, and revise documents such as requirement specifications, system architecture descriptions, unit test cases, and source code. As such, software development practices are highly document-heavy practices. By carefully examining the document practices and how documents support the collaboration in global software development, we are able to characterize the associations that make the documents connect and form a whole. Such characterization is critical if we are to design collaborative systems supporting document-centric work.

The paper is structured as follows. First, we will revisit prior research on documents in general and create the theoretical basis for our concept of *documentscape*. Then, we will introduce the empirical case, followed by the analysis, where we unpack the documentscape of global software development practices, revealing how the documentscape is enacted in collaborative distributed practice. Finally, we discuss the characteristics of the associations that make the documentscape a constitutive part of document-centric work practices.

DOCUMENTS IN COLLABORATIVE WORK

The study of documents in cooperative work practice has become a central research topic within HCI and CSCW. Documents are used extensively in cooperative work for the execution of individual tasks as well as for the coordination of multiple tasks [10], and they may be said to manage the flow of information throughout the enterprise [5]. For this reason, researchers have long been studying the manner in which documents are used and produced in cooperative work practices. It is evident from this research that documents are woven into cooperative work activities as part and parcel of those activities, rather than as secondary tools where information is passively stored and retrieved [16]. Recent studies have pointed out that documents are *not* to be regarded as isolated artifacts, but rather as intertwined in heterogeneous networks of actors, activities, and other artifacts inherent to cooperative work practice (e.g., [3, 5, 9, 20]).

Documents have three main descriptive characteristics: multiplicity, materiality, and autonomy [7]. First, documents are multiplicities, meaning that although the signs they may hold are stable, the documents can take many different forms and ways to convey the same signs; thus they are dynamic [7]. For example, the same signs might be analog in some situations while digital in other situations. Second, documents have materiality – and materiality matters for the information content [7, 10]. The materiality of documents is closely related to their multiplicity, since the particular materiality of a particular document places particular affordances or constraints on what the document can do, and how it is enacted within practice. The materiality provides specific conditions for what role the documents can take. Finally, documents have autonomy, which means that in many cases documents can affect the world directly; they are not simply a medium for a particular author, and in many cases documents might be authorless and still have agency within the practices they take part in [7].

Hertzum's study of documents demonstrates how professionals use and manage their documents in situations where the context of the documents is left unsaid, because documents are being understood in terms of how they belong to certain on-going activities [10]. Schmidt & Wagner [20] provide an extensive and nuanced account of highly elaborate systems of titling and classification by which documents are ordered within architectural practice. They point to the nomenclature for document identification as well as the locally occasioned annotations, embellishments, and reworking, which make documents become part of the ordering system inherent to architectural work practice. Cabitza & Simone [5] concentrate on document-mediated awareness practices in a hospital, describing how awareness is partly mediated by conventions inherent to complex webs of documents. Their account shows how multiple documents can provide awareness in many forms, for example, awareness of the content of other documents, awareness of data (in)consistency between documents, awareness of accountability for task performance, and awareness of what tasks should be performed urgently.

According to Grinter [8], global software development projects are often decomposed into a number of activities that are then distributed among the global actors. This work of cutting the work into smaller pieces which then can be solved in isolation from the rest, also impact the role of documents. By decomposing the work, the links between the sub-tasks become essential to organize the work as well as to make sense of the task and context of each sub-task. In addition, when the sub-tasks are done, extra work of recomposing the sub-tasks back into one coherent whole emerges. Decomposition thus leads to recomposition activities, and all such work is handled through document-centric practices in e.g. global software development.

Building on the above-mentioned previous research on documents, we take a step further and focus on the continuous work of creating, maintaining, and collaborating within document-centric practices. However to understand the practices of decomposition and recomposition of tasks and sub-tasks, we need to understand the characteristics of the associations across documents as well as how the associations are handled in geographically distributed settings.

THE CONCEPT OF DOCUMENTSCAPE

We introduce the concept of documentscape as an analytical device to examine document-heavy collaborative practices. Adding the suffix *–scape* to the word *document* allows us to point to the fluid, irregular shapes that characterize this landscape of documents while indicating that the associations across the documents are perspectival constructs based upon the historical and linguistic situatedness of different actors. Documents in a documentscape take their meaning from their position in an ensemble of documents used or produced in series or in parallel. Here it is important to notice that when we refer to the use of documents in collaboration, we do not simply refer to people's interpretation of the documents [11]. Instead, we are interested in the practices and agency of documents that makes it possible for remote collaborators to continue working based upon what was inscribed by others in the documents. A series or an ensemble of documents may be said to form a documentscape when each document depends upon the wider ensemble for meaning as well as utility. In addition, digital documents have the special characteristic of being able to perform in dual stages dynamically, for example, by making it possible for several actors to collaborate through the document in stages of reading and writing simultaneously. This simultaneity of reading/writing is crucial when we think about documents in practice, and it is a process that has emerged with the increased digitalization of documents on the Internet in particular [24].

It is critical to note that a documentscape is not a stable entity, but continuously changes and gets transformed over time – each document contributing to the documentscape by its unique "life cycle" [9]. Documents in a documentscape may interlock in many different ways, and these links or associations may serve a variety of purposes, including making the individual document meaningful and useful. This raises an interesting question: How are the associations between documents achieved?

In the seminal work of Saussure [18], and following him Bakhtin & Volosinov [2] and subsequently Kristeva [13], texts or documents are to be treated semiotically; that is, language is a system of signs in which one sign implies the presence or absence of another sign [18]. This means that no document is "isolated"; rather, each document is linked to each and every other document through intertextuality, that is, through a practice of "presence and anticipated presence (absence)." The most crucial aspect of language, from this perspective, is that all language responds to previous utterances and to existing patterns of meaning and criteria of evaluation, but it also anticipates and seeks to promote future responses. One cannot create or even understand an utterance or a written work such as a document as if it was detached in meaning, unconnected to previous or future utterances or written works [2, p.72].

Inspired by literary theory, we will suggest that the main characteristic of the associations in a documentscape is intertextuality understood as (1) *presence* and (2) *anticipation*. *Presence* is when the creation and meaning of a document is dependent upon the presence of another document or series of other documents. Sometimes documents point directly to other texts by, for example, quote, reference or hyperlink, and other times the reference is more subtle. *Anticipation* is when the creation, meaning, and utility of a document are associated or dependent upon the anticipation of other documents. Without the anticipation of all these other documents, the requirements specification, for example, would lose it's meaning as we know it.

The two types of intertextuality may (partly) determine a document's position in the documentscape. The concept of documentscape highlights how intertextuality may draw the distributed use of documents together and provide structure and integration to highly distributed work practices such as global software development.

METHOD

To study the characteristics of associations within document-centric practices, we studied empirical data from an ethnographic study of global software development. The research was carried out as part of a larger 5-year research project: NexGSD (nexgsd.org), where we are collaborating with several industrial partners to study, for example, changes in work practices when initiating global work [17], strategic partnerships in global software development [21], and possible sources of miscommunications [12]. GlobalSoft (company anonymized) was one of the industrial partners who provided us with access to conduct ethnographic fieldwork in their geographically dispersed organization, with offices in Denmark and the Philippines, in the period from December 2010 until October 2013.

Three researchers (for the initial interview round we included a forth research assistant as well) carried out the empirical work. We conducted 25 audio-recorded interviews in both Denmark (19) and the Philippines (9), organized 4 workshops both in Denmark (2) and in the Philippines (2), and we did field observations at both locations. Importantly, we also collected a sample of the documents used and produced by the actors. Three researchers visited the Philippine location on four occasions (December 2010 to January 2011, July 2011, November 2011, and January 2012), accounting for approximately four months in total. One researcher spent 12 months following one project at the Danish location.

During this period the researcher spent approximately 1-4 days a week with the organization observing meetings and work practices, interviewing staff, etc. We finished a final round of interviews in the fall of 2013, where we re-interviewed key people (Danes and Filipinos) reflecting back on the period since December 2010.

The empirical case

The software development company is a supplier of customized software solutions for clients in Denmark and all over Europe. The company is based in Denmark and has approximately 1,500 employees, around 225 of whom are situated in offices outside Denmark, for example, in the Philippines. The office in Manila currently has 80 employees.

Globally distributed software development work is a document-centric practice, which means that most of the work in handled through various practices of documents. Each phase of the development process is associated with the production of several documents. In certain phases or activities, the main work product is a document. Of course, there are phases where the document is more a means to an end than an end in itself. Still, every phase or activity in the software development process is associated with the creation and/or use of documents. Examples of the documents are user requirements, product descriptions, and source code. We may say that there is sequentiality, with moments of iteration and backtracking, of course; nevertheless, a timeline along which documents get produced is apparent in our empirical case. In addition, most documents have a geographical origin. There is, then, a global distribution and quasi-sequential nature to authoring of the documentscape.

THE DOCUMENTSCAPE

Examining the association's that glue together the documentscape in our empirical case, we carefully examined all the documents and their connections within our empirical case. We will consider some key documents and, in particular, point to the characteristics of the associations between the documents.

Requirement specification

It is mainly the actors situated in the Copenhagen office that author the requirement specification. This document is a description of the intended behaviour of a proposed software system.

Concerning this document's place in the documentscape, we may say that by stipulating the requirements of the software in the making, the requirement specification anticipates a series of other documents, including the system architecture description, the software component description, the unit test cases, the source code, the binary machine code, and the test plan. These documents are all subservient to the requirement specification in the sense that they are all intended to comply with the requirements set forth in the document in various ways (it is *not* the other way around). The perhaps most obvious example is that the requirement specification document anticipates the writing of the software code in the sense that it describes the behaviour of the proposed software to be written or coded. Other anticipations are at work, too. For example, the requirement specification's section on the quality standards of the proposed system can be said to anticipate the creation of the test plan to be followed when testing the quality of the software. Yet another example is the system architecture description that acts as the overall technical blueprint of the requirements stated.

System architecture description

Actors situated in Copenhagen, as well as the Manila office, create the system architecture description. This text describes the system's components, and the relations between them, at a high level of abstraction.

In connection to this document's place in the documentscape, we may say it is created based on the presence of the requirement specification (that it is subservient to) and in anticipation of the source code text (that it takes prominence over). The system architecture description is subservient to the requirement specification in the sense that it may be regarded as the overarching technical blueprint of the solution to the requirements set forth in the former document. The system architecture description takes prominence over the many units or components of the source code making up the software system, as it stipulates the components and their interrelationships. For example, the system architecture description anticipates the creation of the source code text by containing a class diagram (i.e., a number of classes identified and grouped together that are to be implemented or coded). Although the system architecture is a critical main document created quite early on in the development process, it does not mean the document stays stable during the entire project. Instead, we saw examples where system architecture proposed applying a particular new technology to handle the issues of data security when working in a global setup. However, as it turned out, after several months in the project, the new technology did not provide the right kind of technical setup, and thus the system architects needed to re-think how to handle the data security, applying different types of technology. This meant that the system architecture document was changed, causing a ripple effect for other documents.

Component list

Actors situated in Copenhagen, as well as Manila, create the component list. The document is a list of all the software components that in combination are going to make up the proposed system.

With regard to this document's place in the documentscape, we may say it is created based on the presence of the requirement specification as well as the system architecture description (that it is subservient to) and in anticipation of the source code text (that it takes prominence over). The software component list is subservient to the requirement specification and the system architecture description in the sense that it is a list of the components making up the proposed system. The component list anticipates the implementation of the components (i.e., source code text) by listing them.

Unit test cases

The software developers at the Manila office write the unit test cases (before writing the actual code).

The creation of the unit test cases is based on the presence of not least the technical descriptions preceding it, that is, the system architecture document that describes the overall structure of the units, as well as the component list. The subject matter of a unit test case is a detailed description of a test that a particular piece or unit of software code must be able to pass. When software is developed using a test-driven approach, writing the unit test case may be a part of creating a detailed design specification for a software unit to be created. In this manner the unit test cases anticipate the source code text as well as the compiled machine code to be tested.

The position of a unit test case in the documentscape is such, then, that it takes prominence over the source code that must comply with it while being subservient to the system architecture document as well as the requirement specification.

Source code

The software developers at the Manila office write the majority of the source code.

With regard to the position of source code in the documentscape, we may say that the source code text builds on the presence of the requirement specification, the system architecture document, and, finally, the unit test cases. Often the ambition will be to write the simplest code that will pass the unit test for as given unit. For example, here is a source code that will pass a unit test case such as the ones mentioned above:

```
interface Multiplier {
  int multiply (int a, int b);
}
class MultiplierImpl implements Multiplier{
  int multiply (int a, int b) {
    return a * b;
  }
}
```

In this manner, a specific piece of source code will build on the presence of a unit test case. Furthermore, the source code anticipates the making of other texts, most notably, perhaps, the binary *machine code.*

Machine code

Software developers work with human-readable source code that is then translated or compiled into machine code in order to accommodate execution by a computer. The developers in the Manila office make the machine code.

The machine code is based on the presence of the source code text from which it is created (i.e., compiled) as well as, by association, the documents that the source code builds on (i.e., the unit tests cases, the system architecture description, and the requirement specification). Furthermore, the intertextual relationship of the machine code does not stop there, as it alludes to other documents, including the test plan, test reports, iteration reports, and the installation guide (here we will only mention a few).

Test plan and reports

The test manager at the Manila office writes the test plan in collaboration with the project manager in Copenhagen. This document entails a schedule for and stipulation of the test activities of the project. Testers located in the Manila office create the test reports, based upon the test plan.

With regard to the position of the test reports in the documentscape, we may say that the respective test reports allude to the presence of the overall test plan in the sense that they are all reports on testing done according to the test plan. As such, all test reports are subservient to the test plan. For example, a test report may state that the scope of the report is on "unit test," "build verification test," or "system integration test," all described in the test plan. As such, the test plan and the test report are meaningful as a consequence of their intertextual relationships (a test plan without a test report, and *vice versa*, does not make much sense in the context of software development, you might say). In addition, the test reports of course build on the presence of the code, source code as well as machine code, that is the object of the testing in its various forms. Furthermore, the test reports say something about the status of the project, that is, the quality of the software produced so far.

Technical documentation

It is the software developers located in the Manila office who write the technical documentation. This document has the purpose of capturing the design as well as the implementation of a module or series of modules. That is, this is a document that is based on the presence of the program code that it documents, for example, by providing a diagram of the modules as implemented. By extension, the detailed technical documentation is based on the presence of all the documents leading up to the creation of the source code text, including the unit test cases, the system architecture description, as well as the requirement specification. Furthermore, the document may be said to anticipate the iteration report in the sense that part of what must be reported on at the end of a development iteration is the status of the implementation accounted for in the technical documentation.

Iteration report

The iteration report is written by the project manager at the Copenhagen office.

The position of this text in the documentscape is given by virtue of its intertextual relations to the other documents of global software development. A given iteration report builds on the presence of the other documents of the documentscape in the sense that it is the status of the project, including the status of the documentscape, that is accounted for in the report – particularly the status of the implementation described in the technical documentation as well as the test reports. Just as the iteration report builds on the presence and status the documentscape, it anticipates the (re)making of parts of it in yet another development iteration. By accounting for what has yet to be done, a given iteration report may anticipate the making of new unit test cases, new source code text, new machine code, as well as new test reports. Furthermore, the status given in the iteration report may anticipate adjustments of the requirement specification and the system architecture description. As the project nears completion, the iteration report on the *final* iteration anticipates the installation guide.

At this juncture, it should be evident that documents are woven into global cooperative work activities as part and parcel of those activities rather than as secondary tools where information is passively stored and retrieved (see also [3, 5, 16, 20]). That is, documents are *not* to be regarded as isolated artifacts, but rather as forming *documentscapes* inherent to cooperative work practice.

THE DOCUMENTSCAPE AS CONSTITUTIVE OF PRACTICE

Above we have described the various interlinked documents that make up the documentscape of a global software development project. We will now focus on how a documentscape is enacted in practice.

Working with documents in global software development, then, is constitutive of the activities performed by the participants. We may say that software developers would not be software developers, and testers would not be testers, without the documentscape. The documentscape is not simply there to *support* the work; rather, we may say that the documentscape is *constitutive* of the work. That is, the performance of every individual or collaborative activity (almost always) involves some kind of document as an integral part of the work. Creating *documents is the work* in document-heavy practices such as global software development. Making documents, in our case, is not the taken-for-granted-background work that often gets neglected unless there is a breakdown [22]. The documentscape of global software development is not the "boring infrastructure" [22]. Instead, it is the center of attention, and making the documents is what makes the job positions such as tester, system analysts, or system architect.

However, while some of the documents are written as emails, memos, or minutes from meetings, others take on more significant (and sometimes official or legal) status and persist throughout the life of the project. It is the collection of these significant documents that makes up the documentscape.

While the above description of the documentscape illustrates the quasi-sequential and orderly structure that forms the documentscape, we also need to understand the documentscape practices and how these practices are emergent, iteratively, and continuously ongoing.

The most promising route towards understanding document-centric practices lies not in opposing the quasi-sequential and orderly to the emerging and situated or the complexity of global software development to the documentscape's limited representation of it, *but instead in seeing how the two different perspectival constructs (orderly versus situated) merge and interlock.* You might say that the quasi-sequential order of the documentscape opposes the emergent practices; however, we found that it is precisely the interlocking of the two that constitutes the collaborative work. We will now illustrate how the documentscape is constitutive of the practitioners' actions and, in particular, point to the *iterative*, *in-progress*, and *authorless* nature of the documentscape, while showing how the *intertextuality* of the documentscape is in part what makes it an enabler and a constitutive part of practice.

The emerging, authorless, and autonomous nature of the documentscape

One of the important purposes that the documentscape serves is representing the baseline of the project. The baseline is when the client and GlobalSoft formally agree on the scope, the cost, and the duration of the project at a particular point in time. Baseline activities are repetitive activities for the whole duration of the project. Now, in setting the baseline the documentscape plays a crucial part. Setting the baseline involves defining the scope and cost of the software project such that future changes in the scope will result in increases in cost, prolong time to deliver, or both. The baseline is always a compromise between partners, and when the baseline is agreed upon, neither partner can suddenly demand additional work without new negotiations. The *baseline is inscribed in the documentscape*, and all future work will have references back to the baseline documents. For example, future technical descriptions will have references back to the former product descriptions and detailed technical requirements – each document that becomes part of the documentscape under creation will be created with the anticipation that other documents are to come in the future and that these documents will be referring back to them. As a team leader in Manila put it during an interview:

"It's like you create your draft first, based on your understanding and of course based on the overview. And then as a developer, you're supposed to detail it further. And then you should meet the team leads, they're the ones who review the draft that you've created. After review, they'll just add additional comments and then you recreate it, update the document. And then it goes through a review process again. And then if it's already approved, it's sent to Denmark for approval." (Interview, Team Leader, July 12, 2011)

What is evident in the above quote is that creating the baseline by *freezing* the documentscape at a particular time does not mean that the documentscape becomes a stable entity. Instead, as the team leader is explaining in the above quote, the documentscape has a cyclic iterative nature, which might be 'frozen' at particular times, but it is still continually being configured, changed, and modified.

"Most of the time, they have these complete requirements. Let's say not complete in a sense that it's really complete. Sometimes we just need more information, and they just go back to the client and they wait for the client and the client takes time to answer. So, we move on to the other parts of the development. It's like that." (Interview, Team Leader, July, 2011)

There are several drafts of each document, which are reviewed by other parties and then later re-reviewed. In this way, the documentscape might be sequential and at times stable, but it is constantly re-opened in a cyclic process of reviews by all partners. We say all partners because it is not only the site responsible for the client interaction (in this case Denmark) who reviews the work of the offshore workers (in this case the Philippines). Instead, all relevant participants for the particular activity (e.g., system analysts, testers, system architects, etc.) review the work of each other to ensure alignment between the interpretations of the work.

"When Denmark gives us the requirement specifications or the product descriptions, what we do is we read through it and then come up with questions or scenarios or cases like: "what if the user does this and that?" And then I guess we become part of the workflow for the requirements since they [Danish site] would then ask the customer. Like, "Oh, we haven't asked that, so maybe we should ask the customer that." (Interview, System Analyst, July, 2011)

What this shows is that even though the requirement specification is mainly created with the client by the requirements specialist in Denmark, the system analyst based in the Philippines takes part in the creation of the document through reviewing and questioning the basic assumptions behind the requirements, which are then feedback into new revisions. What is particularly interesting here is how this cyclic process of reviewing has various impacts on the documentscape as a whole. First, it causes all documents to be in an almost endless state of "in-progress," and changes in one document may ripple changes to other documents within the documentscape. We should mention that the requirement specification might be taken up at a later stage in the process and, due to new information, be revised, even at a late stage. Changing the requirement specification also changes the baseline of the project. The documentscape even continues after the project has ended; however, the documents are much more stable. Second, the intertextual nature of the documentscape becomes extremely important in handling the ripples of change.

"The requirement text (the Word document) is translated and further broken down and detailed in the product description, which will turn into the screens and the wireframes. This together with the UX, which the designers have done in DK together with the client, will be turned into the prototype. Basically, the prototype just gives an impression of what the system will look like [...] We ask them [the Danish developers] to review it [the prototype and connected documents] and then they'll be given their feedback and then we will baseline it [the documents] again. It's just a cycle." (Interview, System Analyst, Manila, July, 2011)

Unpredicted issues and change requests will always emerge over the course of a large IT project, and in these situations the baseline, which is inscribed in the documentscape, becomes essential. The order of the documents within the documentscape is not horizontal. Instead, the order is hierarchical in structure, which is critical for how the documentscape can mediate the collaboration across developers, geography, and time zones. Also, we must notice that due to continuous revision of the documentscape, individual authors disappear. As a result, the documentscape becomes an *authorless entity*, with a multiplicity of authors who revise and change the documentscape over time based on the current state of the project. This structural element of the authorless documents can be seen as a strategy for reducing the complexity of the distributed nature of work [19] – a strategy where people can leave the project and others can enter the project without too much interruption for the project, since the documents all follow standards and structures that make it possible for newcomers to understand the project and task at hand. This might also be seen as the larger trend towards efficiency in global work; however, our point here is that who the authors of particular documents and codes are is less relevant for making collaborative work function. Relatedly, the documents of the documentscape may be said to have autonomy in the sense that in many cases documents can affect the world directly, and as such are not simply a medium for a particular author [7]. The documents are not vehicles for communicating meaning from particular authors; the documentscape is active and constitutive far beyond the immediate intentions or actions of the original author (to the extent that one can be identified).

"You must make the detailed specification in a way that the module is written down. So if you ever need to pass it down to another developer he can just read up on the detail specification and right there and then he understands how you created the software. And if ever he needed to extend or provide further details or features, he can just open up the code, check on the detailed specification, and 'this is the part where I need to change or extend.'" (Interview, Team Leader, July 2011)

What is critical for the utility of the documentscape is its ability to constitutively facilitate the collaboration between the many developers. For example, when one developer must pass the code on to another developer, the other developer must be able to understand the code based on the detailed specifications, which are created as part of the work. If there is, for example, an aspect of a module that is incomprehensible, the developer can then, by following the interlinked hierarchical structure organizing the documentscape, "zoom" in for more details. That is, by searching through the connections between the code, the detailed specifications, the product specifications, and the requirement specification, all part of the documentscape, the competent developer can continue the work based upon the work of others. This capability of the documentscape is critical to making global software development practices work. It is important here to note that we do not argue that direct communication is not needed in software development; evidently communication is critical. Instead our point is that in many situations, developers do continue work left by others without communication [6].

What enables the documentscape to form the backbone of the collaborative effort is partly the competent actors' familiarity with the order and nature of the documentscape. The competent actor has an (normative) image of the nature of the documentscape even before it has taken its (initial) form – this is due to her training and experience. That is, knowing how documents are (supposed to be) ordered, with documents building on each other in intricate modes of presence and anticipation, serves as a mechanism of interaction [see also 19]. By knowing the quasi-sequential order and associated links through the iterative, authorless practices and continuous in-progress state of documents, collaborators can refer to, identify, and locate important knowledge relevant for their individual tasks at hand without necessarily consulting other developers all the time. Having said that, it is important to note that performing relations between the documents is an achievement on the part of the actors, and these efforts may at times be fruitless. That is, achieving intertextuality between documents may fail, and documents may drift apart without forming a documentscape.

DISCUSSION

What are the characteristics of the associations that link together the documents in the documentscape? Documents may take their meaning from their position in an ensemble of documents, used or produced in series or in parallel, and usually by many people working together. The associations that position the documents in orderly structures are organized through intertextuality.

A documentscape is characterized by being a multiplicity of different co-exiting documents with various content (typically in form of texts), which have agency beyond the intentions of the collaborative authors. Authorless documents [7], such as the requirement specification, have direct impact on the creation of latter documents, such as source code, without the creator of the source code necessarily knowing the overall intentions of the authors of the requirement specification. Instead, such high dependencies were handled in the collaborative work by the intertextuality within the documentscape. The intertextuality creates the context, which makes it possible to link the status, meaning, and sub-activities of each document to the whole structure of the project.

In our case, the documentscape has a *prolonged state of incompletion* due to the diverse commitments of actors. The documentscape we studied existed and continued to evolve for the duration of the project. A documentscape is not a stable entity, but continuously changes and gets transformed over time – each document contributing to the documentscape by its unique life cycle [9]. The documentscape may be seen, then, as a constantly changing entity [24] that is constitutive of (i.e., not possible to detach from) the software project. When IT developers decompose the work into smaller sub-tasks to reduce complexity and delegate work across several locations [8], the associations within the documentscape ensure that the reintegration or recomposistion of the work can be done later by utilizing the intertextual links between documents. The author of each document can continue working not knowing the exact details of other people's work, but simply by knowing where in the ensemble the sub-task is connected.

Thinking of the documentscape as one coherent heterogeneous artifact, we can say that the documentscape comprises an artifactual multiplicity [4], since it takes many different shapes and forms and is the solo artifact which holds together all sub-processes and practices. No human actor in the software project has a complete overview of all documents and their relations. It is only the documentscape, which embodies all associations, that makes it possible for individuals to zoom in on particular interests, leaving out other interests, but without loosing relations. The diversity in the material forms of the various documents (e.g., natural language or source code) points to how the materiality of the documentscape shapes the collaboration. Whether a document is a Word document, a source file, or a compiled program matters for how the document takes its place within the documentscape. In particular, the materiality is important for how the relationships among the diverse sets of documents can come into being [7].

By embedding intertextuality among the documents, creating the documentscape can be characterized as a form of interactions between the collaborating actors and the documents that are created [11]. Documents that are part of a documentscape are constantly part of a reading/writing process somewhat similar to the one found in hypertext [15]. However, in contrast to hypertext, the documentscape is quasi-sequential and hierarchical in structure. That is, particular documents must follow or precede others in a temporal sense, and some documents are more pertinent and fundamental than others throughout large parts of the process.

CONCLUSION

The documents within a documentscape are characterized by being authorless, autonomous, iterative, and constantly in the state of in-progress while being organized through formal sequential and hierarchical structures that associate the documents through intertextuality. The documentscape is a multiplicity of different co-exiting materials that have agency beyond the intentions of the co-authors. The associations between the documents create the context, making authorless documents understandable without the creator of the document necessarily knowing the overall intentions of the authors of prior documents. Instead, high dependencies are handled by the intertextuality within the documentscape. The documentscape as an analytical concept helps us to illuminate the hierarchical and sequential nature of documents as they are created, revised, and continually change over the time of the project they are part of creating. The documentscape narrates the story of the project under creation, and how it evolves, transforms, and changes throughout the project. The documentscape is a malleable object that very much provides, and is the scaffold holding together, the global collaboration.

This study addresses the core HCI and CSCW problem of characterizing how artifacts partly constitute and as such exert pressure on human action - proposing a hierarchy of artifacts (a documentscape) is part of this. Power or pressure is inherent in an analysis of a documentscape, that is, pressure understood as normative pressure rather than causal determinism. The concept of a documentscape points to how hierarchical structures and sequentiality are constitutive of the iterative and emergent practices of distributed actors. The documentscape associations provide a scaffold for the globally distributed activities by providing hierarchy and sequentially (organized and handled via intertextuality) to the otherwise emergent and continually changing documents that make up the project in progress. We are arguing that the sequentiality of the documentscape structure in combination with the prolonged state of in-progress iterative documents is what makes it possible for distributed actors to take over the work of others with very limited direct communication and coordination. Here it is important to note that of course there will always be situations where communication and coordination is needed – articulation work in meetings, for example, is an everyday occurrence after all. However, the interesting part of our argument is that there are also many situations where the sequentiality and hierarchical intertextuality of the documentscape constitute enough meaning and context for the competent actors to make the collaboration work.

By embracing the characteristics of a documentscape as an analytical lens when designing systems to support document-heavy practices, such as global software development, we have to look beyond version control, coordination, and awareness features and instead include technological support for the authorless, prolonged nature of documents and their interlinked practice of sequentiality and intertextuality, which holds them together.

ACKNOWLEDGMENTS

This study was conducted within the context of the interdisciplinary and inter-organizational research project 'Next Generation Technologies for Global Software Development,' a research project that is financially supported by the National Council for Strategic Research, Ministry of Science, Innovation and Higher Education in Denmark. For further information, see www.nexgsd.org. Rasmus Eskild Jensen and Helle Storm took part in collecting the empirical data. A very warm thanks to our industrial partners for a fruitful collaboration, and lastly, thanks to the anonomys reviewers for their insightful comments and advice.

REFERENCES

1. Appadurai, A., *Disjuncture and Difference in the Global Cultural Economy.* Public Culture, 1990. **2**(2): p. 1-24.
2. Bakhtin, M.M. and V.N. Volosinov, *Marxism and the Philosophy of Language.* 1986, Cambridge MA and London.: Harvard University Press.
3. Bardram, J. and C. Bossen. *A web of coordinative artefacts: Collaborative work in a hospital ward.* in *GROUP.* 2005. Sanible Island: ACM.

4. Bjørn, P. and M. Hertzum, *Artefactual Multiplicity: A Study of Emergency-Department Whiteboards.* Computer Supported Cooperative Work (CSCW): An International Journal, 2011. **20**(1): p. 93.

5. Cabitza, F. and C. Simone, *"...and do it the usual way": Fostering awareness of work conventions in document-mediated collarboration*, in *ECSCW*2007, Springer: Limerick, Ireland. p. 119-138.

6. Christensen, L.R., *Practices of Stigmergy in Architectural Work.*, in *Proceedings of the 2007 international ACM conference on Supporting group work.*2007, ACM: Sanibel Island, Florida, USA. p. 11-20.

7. Frohmann, B., *Multiplicity, Materiality, and Autonomous Agency of Documentation*, in *A Document (Re)turn: contributions from a research field in transition*, R. Skare, N.W. Lund, and A.Varheim, Editors. 2007, Peter Lang GmbH: Frankfurt am Main p. 27-39.

8. Grinter, R., *Recomposition: Coordinating a web of software dependencies.* Computer Supported Cooperative Work (CSCW): An International Journal, 2003. **12**: p. 297-327.

9. Harper, R., *Inside The IMF: An ethnography of Documents, Technology and Organizational Action*1998, San Diego: Academic Press.

10. Hertzum, M. *Six Roles of Documents in Professionals' Work.* in *Sixth European Conference on Computer Supported Cooperative Work.* 1999. Copenhagen, Denmark, September 12-16: Kluwer Academic Publisher.

11. Jensen, C.B. and P. Lauritsen, *Reading digital Denmark: IT reports as material-semiotic actors.* Science, Technology & Human Values 2005. **30**(3): p. 352-373.

12. Jensen, R.E. and P. Bjørn, *Divergence and convergence in global software development: Cultural complextities as societal structures*, in *COOP: Design of cooperative systems*2012, Springer: France. p. 123-136.

13. Kristeva, J., *The Kristeva Reader*, ed. T.M. (ed.)1986, Oxford.: Blackwell.

14. Luff, P., C. Heath, and D. Greatbatch, *Tasks-in-interaction: Paper and Screen based Documentation in Collaborative Activity.*, in *Proceedings of the Conference on Computer Supported Cooperative Work.* 1992, ACM.

15. Lund, N.W., *Document theory.* Annual Review of Information Science and Technology, 2009. **43**(1): p. 1-55.

16. Malone, T., *How do people organize their desks? Implications for the design of office information systems.* ACM Transactioins on Information Systems, 1983. **1**: p. 99-112.

17. Matthiesen, S., P. Bjørn, and L.M. Petersen, *Figure Out How to Code with the Hands of Others: Recognizing Cultural Blind Spots in Global Software Development*, in *Computer Supported Cooperative Work (CSCW)*2014, ACM: Baltimore, USA.

18. Saussure, F.d., *Course in General Linguistics*1974, London: Fontana.

19. Schmidt, K. and L. Bannon, *Taking CSCW Seriously: Supporting Articulation Work.* Computer Supported Cooperative Work (CSCW). An International Journal., 1992. **1**(1-2): p. 7-40.

20. Schmidt, K. and I. Wagner, *Ordering systems: Coordinative practices and artifacts in architectural design and planning.* Computer Supported Cooperative Work (CSCW): The Journal of Collaborative Computing, 2004. **13**(5-6): p. 349-408.

21. Søderberg, A.M., S. Krishna, and P. Bjørn, *Global Software Development: Commitment, Trust and Cultural Sensitivity in Strategic Partnerships.* International journal of Management, 2013.

22. Star, S.L., *The ethnography of infrastructure.* American Behavioral Scientist, 1999. **43**: p. 377-391.

23. Xiao, Y., et al. *Cognitive properties of a whiteboard: A case study in a trauma centre.* in *Seventh European Conference on Computer Supported Cooperative work.* 2001. Bonn, Germany: Kluwer Academic Publisher.

24. Zacklad, M., *Documentarisation Processes in Documents for Action (DofA): The Status of Annotations and Associated Cooperation Technologies.* Computer Supported Cooperative Work, 2006. **15**(205): p. 205-228.

Cloudy Forecast: An Exploration of the Factors Underlying Shared Repository Use

Charlotte Massey
University of California at Santa Cruz,
High St, Santa Cruz, 95064.
cmassey@ucsc.edu

Thomas Lennig
Imimtek
Palo Alto, 94303.
thomas@imimtek.com

Steve Whittaker
University of California at Santa Cruz,
High St, Santa Cruz, 95064.
swhittak@ucsc.edu

ABSTRACT
Many teams are now adopting *shared repositories* for their work. Such adoption is paradoxical, however, as past research has repeatedly shown major *co-organizational barriers*; teams cannot agree a common organizational scheme, making it difficult to retrieve information organized by others. Another barrier is *email competition*; email provides a reliable alternative for distributing files that are then personally organized. To address this paradox, we explored how 27 participants actively using shared repositories overcome these barriers in a qualitative study. We found teams addressed co-organization using 4 strategies. First they create *ContentMaps* that provide explicit structure to organize shared information. Participants also co-organize using implicit strategies based on *task structure*, *expertise*, and *tool affordances*. Greater shared repository use also leads to a changed role for email. Versioning problems mean email is not used for distributing attachments, instead for task management. We present technical implications suggesting how new tools might be better integrated with email facilitating these continued email uses.

Author Keywords
Shared repositories; co-organization; email competition; ContentMaps; versioning.

ACM Classification Keywords
H.5.m. Information interfaces and presentation (e.g., HCI): Miscellaneous.

INTRODUCTION
People who collaborate usually generate shared digital content. But collaborators typically face a dilemma about how to *share* the information they create together. They need to choose between storing shared files in a *shared repository* (e.g. GoogleDrive) or sharing *email attachments* and then organizing them in personal repositories.

There are excellent intuitive arguments for using shared repositories rather than email. Relying on email involves all collaborators independently managing their own personal collection of relevant files, duplicating time and cognitive effort. Furthermore, email distribution leads to well-documented problems in retrieving and reconciling *different versions* of the same file [7,8,30]. Many organizations therefore have a policy of encouraging teams to use a common repository when sharing files [20].

Despite these arguments, the history of shared repositories has been one of repeated failure. The first such repositories were developed over 20 years ago [11,19]. They were unsuccessful initially and subsequent research continues to document outstanding problems. One commonly observed barrier to adoption is *co-organizational failure* when participants *cannot agree a shared organization* [11, 19, 24, 27]. Many studies describe disagreements arising from different organizational strategies among members of the collaborative team. One consequence of co-organizational failure is balkanization where individuals store information in their own private region of the common repository, undermining its function as a shared resource, and making it difficult for others to find that information [24].

A second problem with shared repositories is *email competition*. Successful collaboration depends on people being aware of coworker actions, allowing them to co-ordinate interdependent tasks. To avoid destructive co-edits and costly version reconciliation, interdependent tasks like collaborative document editing require that collaborators know which is the most recent draft, who is editing it, and when a draft is completed. One important limitation of early shared repositories was that participants had to *explicitly access* the repository to discover whether new versions had been created [11]. To avoid this, participants sent emails alerting others about version changes, sometimes including new files as attachments. Such attachments undermined the shared repository leading some collaborators to revert to email for sharing [20, 27].

New shared repositories like Dropbox and GoogleDrive provide potential solutions to versioning with features like alerting and concurrent editing. Nevertheless they have not overcome all outstanding problems. Indeed recent studies of modern repositories have identified additional problems, including *learning new conceptual models* [22].

CHI 2014, April 26 - May 01 2014, Toronto, ON, Canada

ACM 978-1-4503-2473-1/14/04..$15.00.
http://dx.doi.org/10.1145/2556288.2557042

Furthermore the proliferation of different shared repositories now means collaborators not only have to agree how to organize information *within* each tool, but also how information is to be distributed across multiple *different* tools [22, 27]. People now have to decide whether that document is in Drive, Dropbox, or on the shared fileserver.

Despite these problems, we have recently seen greater adoption of shared repositories. Dropbox reports 100 million active users who upload a billion files each day, and Drive reports 10 million users, although these numbers include private usage [1, 2]. This widespread adoption gives rise to a *paradox*. If shared repositories are being extensively deployed, how are users overcoming the many barriers documented in prior work?

One possible answer may be the use of *keyword search*, which potentially finesses the problems of co-organization. Keyword search may allow collaborators to overcome *co-organization problems*, supporting successful retrieval even when searchers don't know *exactly where* the information is stored [12, 25].

We address the *adoption paradox* for shared repositories, to determine how and why users are overcoming well-documented problems. We interview 27 people to determine success factors and characteristics of effective deployment. With greater uptake of these tools, we ask:

- What new factors promote successful adoption: *how* are users of new tools such as Drive and Dropbox *overcoming the co-organizational barriers* of older tools?
- How *successful are users at retrieving information* given that others may have organized this information? Do users rely on keyword search to avoid having to navigate others' organizational systems?
- What is the *relationship between shared repositories and email*? Are these in competition, or are they used synergistically?

We address *informal collaboration* rather than more formal processes, e.g. software engineering where teams often deploy dedicated versioning tools to handle collaborative problems. Another important characteristic of our study is that we examine shared repositories in *everyday work contexts*. Our participants talked about familiar shared files accessed on a daily basis and not long-term archives. This focus contrasts with much prior work that examined shared repositories in *academic research contexts*, where there are different demands for systematic organization to guarantee long-term access and retrieval [31].

RELATED WORK

Co-organizational Difficulties Within and Across Tools

Many studies have documented problems collaborators experience in agreeing a common organizational scheme for shared repositories [11, 19, 24]. Early work enumerated different personal organizational strategies (scruffies vs neats, savers vs purists...), and the problems that ensued when these incompatible personal schemes were applied to a shared research repository.

Personal Information Management (PIM) research examines how *individuals* organize information. One repeated PIM observation is large individual differences in how people organize information to promote later retrieval [10, 31]. People differ in how much information they keep, in the extent to which they organize, and in the different methods used to organize their information [9, 17, 31]. Similar individual differences in organization occur with physical files [21], email [7, 13] and web resources [3, 5, 17]. These organizational choices affect retrieval: people with shallow broad file hierarchies navigate to information faster than those with deeper, narrower structures [10].

Participants in *shared* repositories may therefore be motivated to use personal organization because they worry they will be unable to find information organized using someone else's framework [24]. [19] argues that "People adding and retrieving information in group information systems must mash their often idiosyncratic categories, indices, schema and information routines" (p. 243).

These problems are exacerbated with newer social media and cloud based tools [26, 27]. [22] describes how collaborators have incompatible and often incorrect models of how shared tools work, undermining their utility. Learning a new system represents a significant adoption barrier. If a single collaborator fails to learn the new shared repository this undermines its collaborative utility potentially leading participants to abandon it [16]. Other problems arise when individuals attempt to stratify their use of multiple tools according to different online identities or roles (e.g. work vs personal). Collaborators may be unaware of these personal decisions leading them to post information in unexpected places [27].

We explore the implications for shared repositories of these findings. How do people organize and access shared information when successful access to personal information often depends on exploiting idiosyncratic organizational schemes? We examine whether and how active users of new shared repositories are able to reconcile personal and collaborative organization.

Keyword Search, Organization and Retrieval

Keyword search has potential implications for shared repositories. If search is successful, users no longer have to navigate through file hierarchies to retrieve information, as they can search for it *without knowing exactly where it is* [12, 25]. Search is provided for Drive, and regular desktop search accesses the contents of shared repositories like Dropbox.

Although keyword search has not been widely studied in shared repositories, there is extensive work examining its use in *personal* repositories. Somewhat surprisingly, navigation through the file system is the preferred retrieval strategy [9]. Search is only used as a 'last resort' when people are unsure where information is located [9]. In this study we address whether search solves co-organization problems in shared repositories, allowing retrieval without knowing where information is stored.

Distribution, Versioning, and Co-Editing

Email has long been used as a tool for distributing shared materials [8, 30]. Its benefits for sharing include that it is simple, highly familiar and participants do not have to install or learn a new application. It also finesses the co-organizational problem because each participant organizes materials independently, allowing them to each organize information as they choose. However there are problems associated with using email in this way. Email is difficult to manage efficiently, especially when used for collaborative tasks [8, 30]. If multiple versions of a file are circulated in email, overloaded inboxes mean that collaborators may accidentally access and edit outdated versions. This in turn leads to complex reconciliation of different versions. While newer tools support collaborative task management in email [7,18], these remain research prototypes without widespread adoption.

In shared repositories, two main approaches address problems of versioning. The first allows concurrent edits on a single version, as in Drive or Sharepoint. In the second, peripheral alerts inform users when changes are made to a shared repository (e.g. in Dropbox). If two participants accidentally co-edit then different versions are saved leaving users to reconcile these. Even with shared repositories, email still plays an important role in task management. When participants use a shared repository, they often use email to describe new versions and to allocate workflow [8, 14]. This study explores how participants address versioning both in email and in shared repositories.

Organizational and Transactive Memory

Collaborative information management can be viewed as a form of *organizational memory* [4, 6]. Furthermore, *transactive memory* [28] describes how in collaborative settings, people delegate remembering to familiar others, who they know have superior recall in that domain. Thus one member of a couple might excel at remembering family birthdays, whereas the other might best remember passwords or bank account details. By playing to their strengths, they out-remember what they can achieve alone. We later explore whether transactive memory concepts apply to participants' attempts to co-organize shared files, with organizational tasks being delegated to familiar others with known areas of expertise.

METHOD

Participants and Their Work Settings

We interviewed 27 participants of whom 9 were females. Their ages ranged from 24-52. Our intention was to explore *successful usage strategies*, so we targeted people who incorporated shared repositories into day to day work tasks. They were recruited using convenience sampling in the San Francisco Bay Area and worked for multiple different organizations, with heterogeneous job types. See Table 1. None of the participants was an academic, a decision motivated by prior research suggesting that academics have rather specific strategies for managing personal information [31]. Companies ranged in size from individual consultants and small 3 person startups to massive multinationals.

Interviews

Two interviewers conducted semi-structured interviews that explored the following topics:

- *Co-organization*: how shared repositories were co-organized, who was responsible for their organization, as well as collective problems and or disagreements associated with creating the organization,
- *Retrieval*: how participants retrieved information from repositories, in particular whether participants relied on search, as this has implications for needing to organize,
- *Email*: the relationship between shared repositories and email, and perceived strengths and weaknesses of each.

Interviews were based around *collaborations*: we first asked participants to describe 3-5 current collaborations. Participants then talked about shared repositories used for each collaboration, including: the data kept in each tool, who creates that data, how the tool is organized, who organizes it and their finding strategies within the tool. We then explored the relationship between each shared repository and email.

Interviews were conducted over Skype using remote desktop sharing. There was one exception, (P12), who we interviewed face to face. Participants showed us each shared repository, illustrating how it was organized and used, and demonstrating various retrieval strategies used with that tool. We then probed participants' collaborative email practices, asking them to compare sharing using email attachments with shared repository use. Interviews lasted 45-60 minutes: they were audio recorded and transcribed. Participants typically talked about 1-3 different collaborations in depth, but also provided an overview of the entire set of shared repositories they used.

Data Analysis and Coding

Analysis involved four phases: identifying initial themes, reaching consensus, applying themes and reliability checks. Initial coding schemes were developed by two coders who independently analyzed 7 interviews, identifying themes, based on categories suggested by prior research [11, 22, 24, 27], and developing new themes. These two coders then reconciled their separate coding schemes, agreeing on key themes. One of the initial coders then coded the remaining interviews coding using the agreed themes. Finally two additional independent coders checked each interview to ensure reliability of coding. This process identified:

Table 1: Participants (N=27)

Total Participants	Participant Numbers	Job Type
2	P23, P24	CEO
1	P6	Startup Cofounder
1	P17	VP Marketing
1	P15	Sales Director
1	P9	Marketing Coordinator Project Manager
5	P1, P2, P5, P7, P14	Researcher - Manager
1	P3	Researcher
1	P11	Lead Software Engineer
3	P10, P19, P21	Software Engineer
1	P27	Presales Engineer
1	P16	QA Engineer
1	P8	Mechanical Engineer/Test Manager
1	P20	Junior Game Designer
1	P4	Junior Technical Writer
1	P26	IT Director
1	P13	Technology Integrator
1	P12	Technical Support
2	P18, P22	Teacher
1	P25	Contract Photographer

problems and solutions to co-organization, retrieval strategies, and email comparisons.

RESULTS

Teams address co-organization using 4 strategies. They created *ContentMaps* providing explicit structure to organize shared information. Participants also co-organized using implicit strategies based on *task structure*, *expertise*, and *tool affordances*. Greater shared repository use also led to a changed role for email.

Individuals Use Multiple Repositories

Consistent with other recent studies [22, 27] most participants used *multiple* shared repositories (e.g. Dropbox and Drive or a wiki and SharePoint). After we had eliminated a small number of repositories used for *personal* storage (e.g. personal backup or access from multiple devices), the mean number of shared repositories used by each participant was 2.48, with a minimum of one and a maximum of 5. Table 1 shows Dropbox and Drive were most frequently used, and most participants used both. People using just one repository used Dropbox or Drive. About a third of participants used shared network folders (i.e. intranet folders on an organizational server). Wikis and Sharepoint were less common, and there were a small set of tools used by just a single participant.

Table 2: Frequency of Use of Collaborative Tools (N=68)

Examples	Frequency
Dropbox	23
GoogleDrive: Gdocs, Gspreadsheet and Gslides	23
Shared Network Folders (Fileshare, Filezilla)	10
Wikis (Confluence, Communities)	5
SharePoint	4
Box	2
PRIM (in-house repository)	1

Reduced Attachments and Little Use of Search Imply Participants are Co-organizing

The active use of shared repositories implies participants are at least partially overcoming problems described in prior work. In addition participants reported reduced use of email for sharing attachments, which also suggests that shared repositories were becoming more successful. *Every single* participant acknowledged that they were less dependent on email for distributing attached versions.

(p11) E: Do people send you attachments in email?

P: If it's something basic, yes. But the majority of the time it's just a link to the drive or a link to Dropbox.

(p23) E: Would you say that email is primarily for communication or file sharing?

P: Communication. Like 95%. Because there are so many other ways to share documents so Dropbox, GoogleDrive.

A few participants even described frustration when they were forced to revert to using email attachments:

(p17) my [colleagues] will not send attachments; we are dead opposed to it. So if somebody is sending an attachment it's somebody that's not up to speed in that modern stuff.

(p24) [I don't use email] unless I'm forced to because the person that I'm collaborating with is a dinosaur. I don't email file attachments.

However actively using shared repositories and reduced attachment use may not mean that participants are successfully co-organizing. An alternative explanation is that participants are finessing co-organization by relying on *keyword search* for retrieval. Our data suggests that this is not the case; we asked each participant the most common way they retrieved information from shared repositories. Keyword search was used in 29% of retrieval cases:

(p3) I suppose if I really can't find something then I would search. But usually I find it faster to navigate than to search.

(p13) If need be, I'd use the search bar, but it's pretty well organized and pretty, with this at least I'm pretty anal about my folders, so I never really have trouble looking for stuff.

These results indicate that participants do not rely on search to avoid the need to co-organize. Prior work indicates people use desktop search as a 'last resort' when they don't know where information is located. The low search percentage reported indicates that participants feel they know where information is located. The use of keyword search alone cannot account for increased use of repositories, so participants seemed to be achieving co-organization.

Overcoming the Co-Organization Barrier: Explicit Strategies to Organize Shared Materials

Despite being explicitly asked, participants did not describe complex discussions to agree common organizational strategies for shared repositories. They also reported few difficulties in using shared repositories. How then were participants able to co-organize well enough to encourage tool adoption? Participants described *explicit* and *implicit strategies* used to collaboratively organize. They discussed 4 strategies to create shared structures allowing people to navigate to relevant collaboration materials. The first explicit strategy relies on *ContentMaps,* a term we use for a *structured description* of where those materials are located. There were also 3 implicit strategies relying on *Tasks, Expertise* and *Tools.*

ContentMaps: Explicit Information Structuring by Proactive Leadership

One way to address co-organization was for one person to generate a *ContentMap*, that provided *direct access* to collaboration materials via active links to the shared repository. Fourteen people described using ContentMaps to structure and share information. This could involve a *combination* of different collaborative tools. The most common instances of ContentMaps involved a 'Map' generated in a wiki, task management application or Googledoc. This Map also served as 'front end', pointing directly to underlying data in the shared repository. Maps contained a description with a set of active links to a shared repository such as Dropbox or Box, or links to other Googledocs. In other instances, structuring information was provided in a workflow application such as a task manager, (e.g. Jira, Asana). Of course ContentMaps do not remove the need for information structuring, but such organization is imposed by *the person organizing the tasks*, rather than resulting from a negotiated team discussion.

ContentMaps served to facilitate access to the contents of the repository. If active links weren't provided, the wiki, Googledoc or task manager would instead include an explanation of where key information was to be found and specify which new materials needed uploading to the repository. This description helped other collaborators ensure that they accessed the right versions of information, incorporating updated material into the appropriate places. Maps might also include who to contact about specific information, and occasionally a history of prior interactions. The map is updated as the repository grows in size.

Here a participant describes how his team's work is distributed via an email that contains a ContentMap ('the Tech List') consisting of a Googledoc with a series of links to different jobs for members of his team. Clicking on a link directly locates the relevant document in Drive, allowing him to edit it in place. He does not have the overhead of navigating the underlying structure of the collaborative archive; the materials he needs are accessed directly via links, without having to know how those documents are organized. Here he describes the format of the ContentMap, how it is shared and how linking removes the need for him to understand the repository structure.

(p16) Our QA manager usually creates the Tech Lists 90% of the time, and she'll just share it with us. She'll send an email with tasks, then we'll go to that master list, which is a Googledoc and we'll find what we need. We just open a link to a document that's stored on Drive straight from the email, it's like seamless and we'd just click on it goes straight into the doc, straight into editing it, so I don't even use that "My Drive," I hardly ever use that.

ContentMaps might also directly reference materials stored in Dropbox, ensuring that updates are carried out on the relevant version of the document:

(p4) you create a directory link inside of the document. And other people can just download them directly and import it over and copy it exactly. So you can put a pointer into the document itself and it'll reference it to this file, even if it is in Dropbox.

Using ContentMaps addresses some versioning problems experienced with email attachments. This participant uses Drive as a ContentMap for shared Dropbox files.

(p23) Our GoogleDrive will reference certain files. Particularly [XY] documents since they're all up on Dropbox so we'll have a Google Drive that says <u>this</u> particular file in <u>this</u> folder on Dropbox needs this done to it.

Using direct linking to reference materials avoids versioning problems, because the Map points to the exact document that needs to be modified via a shared editor.

(p15) we'll use links to GoogleDrive documents as opposed to full blown attachments. Because it helps us with version control.

The above examples involve combining *two tools*, one as the front end Map, and the other as the shared repository. A related method for successfully accessing shared documents without explicit co-organization involved creating a *single structured shared application* that both provided structure and allowed data entry. Participants here didn't combine multiple tools, but instead structured a *single* shared tool like a Google spreadsheet or document, so that others could contribute concurrently to it. The application was carefully organized to structure collaboration *within* the application itself. Tabs or fields in the shared document were clearly demarcated with task, worker or client names allowing collaborators to concurrently enter data. This allowed participants to simultaneously track complex responsibilities, enter data or post links. Shared applications therefore structured concurrent work, again without the overhead of managing multiple versions that follow from complex email interactions involving attachments. This marketing manager describes how his team appropriated and structured a Googledoc allowing them to subdivide, track and concurrently collate different client leads.

(p15) it's really important to us that we're not redundant [when following client leads]. And so we have this shared document which shows what date did we contact people, who is the rep, and our result. We kinda improvise the functionality with things like GoogleDrive. So you can see I hit up, you know, 18 people I wanted to meet up with last night. We color code it for [clients] that might be interested and we can either eliminate bad candidates or keep up to date with the state of our conversations with our good candidates using GoogleDrive.

Implicit Co-organization: Expertise, Tasks and Tools

However on other occasions multiple team members did co-organize common repositories, with different team members organizing different subparts. As we noted above, this was not done following complex discussions about organizational semantics, nor did participants describe problems with the resulting organization. How then was this co-organization achieved and how did participants know how to organize and find information within it?

Participants used 3 implicit co-organization strategies based around tasks, expertise and tools. Although these strategies seem somewhat obvious, they were effective to a large extent because participants shared *common knowledge* [4, 28] about shared tasks and information. Participants were intimately familiar with their daily work tasks, how these were organized, who was responsible to each subtask and what tools were generally used to carry these out. In contrast much prior work examined academic contexts where tasks are more open-ended, leading to disagreement about how research resources might be categorized. Instead our participants shared common knowledge [28] about their expertise and tasks, which they exploited to determine how information should be organized. They therefore deliberately delegated organization of specific areas of the shared repository to experts, rather than everyone contributing to the entire organizational scheme. Of course there were limits to this form of organization, participants working in large multinationals lacked knowledge about expertise within a large team. However in these contexts participants were usually not actively collaborating with a huge extended team, but instead publishing final versions of documents for others to consume.

Co-organization by Expertise: One very common implicit way to structure shared repositories was around *expertise* (reported by 11 participants). Although materials were shared, individual collaborators took responsibility for parts of the repository related to *personal job responsibilities or expertise.* People were aware of who had which expertise, and delegated organization to experts. This allowed materials to be exploited by all, without individuals contesting how different subareas ought to be organized. In unusual cases where responsibility was unclear then emails might be exchanged to determine where specific materials were located. The following participant describes his team's distributed expertise, stressing how each person controls different projects (Business/Marketing, Backend, FrontEnd). This shared knowledge about responsibilities makes the resulting organization 'very simple'.

(p6) we are each of us working on a specific problem area. I am working on Business and Marketing and my partner is working on [system] Backend and the other guy is working on the Frontend. When it comes to projects for Customers, there is a project file for all the projects we do. This represents the projects we do for our clients. We know the type of project and once we know from then on [the organization] is very simple.

Co-organization by High Level Task Structure: For predictable workflows e.g. documentation or client management, co-organization reflected *task structure.* Collaborators were each familiar with this structure, allowing them to anticipate where information should be placed to promote easy access for others. 16 participants described using this method to organize shared files. This participant talks about how shared materials are assembled around a simple high level structure when writing a book. Information is architected into a modular structure of chapters, graphics, and style guidelines. Note also that the resulting structure is deliberately designed to be shallow and 'flat' so collaborators don't have to learn a complex hierarchical system.

(p17) We try to be as flat as possible; the root directory is a folder for every project. The only live project is the XX book. And within the XX book there is a folder for chapters, folder for graphics which would be rich media, a folder for my YY press guidelines. it's a high level architecture and so you have logical groupings of content. As soon as the logical grouping you've exhausted the apparent top level topic then everything should be flat underneath.

Often one collaborator (a manager or domain expert) created high-level categories that fit the tasks that the team was carrying out. These categories were later individually populated by different members of the team who contributed new materials. This form of organization was described by multiple participants as 'organic', implying it was both natural and self-organizing. Notice again that this organization mirrors the expertise within the team:

(p15) we have a number of different folders in (Dropbox): Development, investors, competitors, marketing operations, photos, sales, it's loosely grouped into areas where different types of people have different relevancy. Like development, all the coders can go there, investors obviously, it's where you're going to be dealing with people who are going to capitalize the company. Competitors is a very sparse folder with pretty stark and limited look at who our competitors are, we don't have that many. ... this way if we want to go in to look at sales related things for example, it's pretty easy to go to that folder.

One important limitation to these implicit strategies was that organizational difficulty increased with repository size. This participant notes that the success of using simple strategies relies on maintaining only active files:

(p24) When you first start using it it's really straightforward and you only have five or six folders, but after you've used it for a couple of years it's just like any other repository. It does have to be managed, and you do have to have some sort of information architecture with how you're storing things, and you do have to maintain some control or governance over depreciation and deletion of content.

Co-organization by Tool Affordances: Similar implicit solutions were exploited to determine tool choice. Many collaborations used *multiple* repositories, so how did participants agree which of these repositories would contain particular information? Again we saw a reliance on implicit strategies. Different tools had clearly different affordances for collaborative tasks, allowing participants to *infer* which tool would contain that information. 12 participants described using this method.

(p5) I know that participant data is going to be on [a proprietary shared repository]. I know that things that require a visual representation are going to be in Googledocs and often I remember creating specifically that file or editing it. And everything else is going to be in Dropbox.

Participants mapped different collaborative tasks onto the perceived strengths of each shared tool, allowing them to infer where information would be. Participants expected low fidelity documents to be in GoogleDocs as this allows concurrent editing, but has unsophisticated formatting. In contrast external documents e.g. business plans, contracts or drawings, require professional formatting and access to dedicated applications. These were more likely to reside in DropBox, Shared Filesystems or Sharepoint, as these repositories allowed participants to use dedicated applications to generate higher production quality. Collaborators were aware of tool affordances, and they expected information would be located in the relevant tool.

(p6) in general we work with day to day documents we use Google Docs, for more advanced document sharing think about drawings, physical drawings, or any technical documents or official documents and presentations for work we use Dropbox.

Overall our participants were successful in incorporating shared repositories into their work tasks despite using relatively simple solutions to co-organize. This contrasts with previously documented difficulties. The difference could be explained by restating that these strategies rely on shared team knowledge about tasks, roles, and tools that allow co-organization to be accomplished in a typical work environment. Prior work has noted that in the academic contexts that have often been studied previously, roles, tasks and responsibilities are often far less clear [27].

Finding Materials In A Shared Repository is Usually Unproblematic

Our next question concerned *finding*. We have documented strategies for co-organizing shared repositories. However a critical question concerns how *effective* these strategies are in supporting retrieval. Prior work documents problems in retrieving information from shared repositories, in part because people do not understand where others have placed information [11, 24]. However, our participants did not often report such retrieval problems, even though we specifically asked them about this. Why was this? On some occasions, ContentMaps provided *direct links* to where information was located, removing the need to understand exactly how information was co-organized:

(p10) Usually what you have is a very specific file path that's in the Googledoc. So you don't really search for it or don't really browse for it, you just like put in a direct path and you go straight to it

Even when direct links weren't provided, the relatively simple organizational schemes we described above made collaborative access straightforward. As a result, participants described few problems in retrieving files. Organization reflected *current* work tasks with structures relating to that task or specific people: shared files were familiar and in frequently visited locations. A common retrieval strategy was therefore simply to *browse* common repositories like Dropbox. 17/18 participants who answered how they found items in Dropbox relied on simple navigation. This reliance on navigation suggests that participants knew where information was; as discussed above, prior work suggests people are more dependent on desktop or keyword search if they don't know where information is located [9]. Several participants described how navigation with the shared repository was straightforward, with relatively little use of complex subfolder structures:

(p17) I go direct to files. [Project X] is flat so there is only one subfolder and the reason there is a subfolder code, but other than that it's purely flat. So when I'm trying to find a document I will usually go by date modified, I know a range of date modified and I will know the exact name of the document that I want.

When a ContentMap is used in association with the shared repository, participants exploited explicit structure it provided to assist finding. This participant describes how a task management tool is used to index to underlying files:

(p9) I can navigate by which project, projects are kind of like folders and then there are different tags that we use.... you can see the tag shows me which folder it is in

We asked participants how they found information within each shared repository. Participants were slightly more likely to use keyword search in Drive than other repositories with 6/17 participants describing their finding behavior by saying that they 'usually' searched within Drive. But even in Drive, the majority of participants navigated to content, implying that they understood where information was located.

Overall participants are successful in finding. They exploit ContentMaps or locate familiar sets of files that are organized by tasks and expertise. The three participants who did experience occasional finding problems tended to be retrieving under rather unusual circumstances. They were looking for information that had been created several months previously by an independent team. However attempting to find such old, unfamiliar information was the exception rather than the rule. In most circumstances, for everyday information needs, ContentMaps and work-related implicit structure make access successful.

Back To The Future: Reduced Attachments But Email Still Critical For Alerts and Task Management

One possible implication is that successful practices around collaborative repositories, *reduce participants' dependence on email.* As we noted above, every single participant acknowledged less dependence on email for distributing attached versions. Although some still executed simple ad hoc collaborations by exchanging email attachments, for most this was not habitual for teamwork. Despite a reduced exchange of attachments, participants were still reliant on email in their collaborations. However they now used email for *different aspects of collaboration*: alerting, task management, commenting/discussion and social finding. This continued interdependence between collaborative tools and email is ironic given that a major initial motivation of collaborative tools was to reduce overall email traffic.

Alerting about Changes in the Shared Repository

A thorny, unresolved problem is how participants are *alerted* about changes in shared repositories, allowing people to react when new information or new tasks are posted. The two main approaches are *push*: where collaborators receive an *explicit notification* when there is a change, or *pull* where there is no alert and participants must *actively visit* the repository to see whether a change has occurred. Both have disadvantages. Explicit change alerts in email may overwhelm people, leading them to ignore notifications. On the other hand, relying on participants actively visiting the repository may lead them to be unaware of new versions.

Despite successfully using shared repositories, our participants were still dependent on email alerts. Only one participant wanted to actively access the repository to detect updates. People were aware that pushed alerts contribute to email overload but accepted this as the price they must pay for not overlooking important content.

Such email alerts did not contain attachments, as this would undermine the entire point of using shared repositories. Emails often contained *repository links* however. Accessing the repository rather than an isolated email attachment has very different consequences. Accessing the repository meant that people can see *all* recent versions allowing them to straightforwardly find the most recent version. This contrasts with email versioning involving collating multiple versions across different emails, hoping that an email search has exhaustively found all relevant materials.

(p27) Rather than sending the document itself, which the challenge of that is that document is a snapshot in time, I'll send a link to a document. And now once you've sent a link to a document the people have the updated version of it. Then if there's an updated version they'll be able to see the new version and the old version; The real problem [with email] is that, you know, for all intents and purposes email is transitory. I mean, yes, I have a saved copy of it, but, well, which version of it?

In some cases alerting was supplied automatically by the underlying collaborative tool. Dropbox provides screen alerts when shared folders change. Again however, with one exception, users erred on the side of caution and also explicitly posted email alerts. Of course a major problem with increasing email traffic this way is that overloaded inboxes may lead participants to *overlook* the alert, and we discuss this problem later.

Task Management Involving Shared Repositories

However we saw multiple cases of where simple email alerts were insufficient. It was not enough to email collaborators that the contents of the shared repository had changed. Often more explicit actions and responsibilities were included to describe outstanding tasks. This participant points to the target document and describes what actions need to be performed on it.

(p14) you write an email saying 'here is a link to the Google document and here is what you are supposed to do: number one do this number two do that'.

Task management emails might contain links or a ContentMap detailing tasks and responsibilities, as well as how to access relevant content. Even when teams used dedicated workflow applications for task management, collaborators sometimes still provided an additional email nudge or clarification. Here a participant talks about how an email conversation clarifies the status of an outstanding task that had been delegated via a task management system.

(p9) if somebody is not following up with something, if somebody didn't notice something in [the task management system], I'll just send them an email linking back to the [workflow] ticket saying 'hey did you see this I think this needs attention' and then they can let me know that 'I saw that, it's not a priority because of whatever reason or thanks I've been meaning to get to that or..' sometimes people need a little extra push.

Social Finding

Finally and rarely email was used as a last resort if people couldn't find information in the shared repository. As we noted above, refinding problems were uncommon, but when they occurred, one tactic was to exploit transactive memory and email someone likely to know where the information was. However we found just two examples of this in our participant set, and both agreed that this was an unusual situation. One participant who was uninvolved in an early phase of a project wanted to locate relevant data and so emailed another collaborator who collected that data:

(p1) I wasn't heavily involved in the data collection and analysis, so I would find someone who was and say, "Where is this data?" and then get a pointer to it and access to it.

So to conclude, while email is being used less for distributing attachments, it retains multiple interdependent functions with shared repositories. All of these functions share a common weakness however; an overloaded inbox may mean that collaborators overlook critical emails, and email search does not guarantee that all messages relevant to the collaboration are reliably retrieved. We suggest technical implications that partially address this in the following section.

DISCUSSION AND CONCLUSIONS

Our findings address a paradox. Prior research fails to explain increased collaborative repository adoption, instead documenting teams' problems in co-organizing and retrieving shared information. In contrast, we present new empirical findings that identify practices that allow people to circumvent these problems. We document novel practices that facilitate successful adoption of shared repositories, leading to a changed role for email. We explore the theoretical and technical implications of these new findings.

Strategies for Finessing Co-organization Problems

In contrast to prior work, we found that participants experienced few co-organizational problems. However our participants were not using keyword or desktop search to find information, even though this could potentially have removed the need to actively co-organize. How then were participants able to co-organize when prior studies show the opposite? We found they relied on strategies to co-organize including: *ContentMaps,* using other applications such as wikis, task management and Googledocs achieving co-organization by providing structured 'front ends' linking directly to shared materials. Other implicit strategies imposed predictable high-level structures based on expertise, task and tool affordances relying on shared knowledge between participants. Participants seemed to exploit transactive memory [28], being aware of coworkers' expertise, and delegating organizational tasks to experts rather than everyone contesting and being consulted on all aspects of organization. Furthermore both ContentMaps and implicit strategies seemed to be successful in promoting retrieval, with participants reporting few problems in accessing shared information.

How then can we explain these contrasts to prior work? There are at least two possibilities. The first is that prior studies looked at older tools *used in isolation*. In contrast in our work, participants addressed co-organization by *combining tools* in innovative ways, e.g. using wikis or task managers to structure information for their collaborators as ContentMaps. A second possibility is that we examined a different population carrying out very different tasks. Prior work looked at researchers often accessing long-term archival materials. In contrast, our participants were mainly focused on familiar short-term activities mediated by clear roles and responsibilities. It is interesting to note that the three exceptions in our sample who experienced finding problems were searching for long-term materials on projects that they had not been involved in directly. These observations and participant comments point to intriguing future questions about the scalability of current implicit strategies. Such strategies were used for relatively small active repositories, but it remains to be seen whether they can scale to larger, more complex settings.

The Changing Role of Email

Repository use was very closely tied to email practices and we also explored participants' use of email in collaboration. Consistent with prior work we found problems in using email for exchanging and locating multiple document versions. Greater use of repositories did not mean that email was abandoned, however. Instead it was used to *support* shared repositories. Email was used for alerting, task management and occasionally locating missing information. These uses of email are not problematic in terms of collaboration, as they provide social accountability, but they do exacerbate general email overload increasing the possibility that important collaboration-relevant emails get overlooked. We now explore ways of addressing this.

Design Implications

Our findings about synergies between tools and the changing role of email suggest several concrete ways that collaboration tools might be improved. We are aware that aspects of these solutions are available in enterprise contexts but not as standard features of common collaborative repositories like Dropbox or Drive. One approach would aim to improve access to, and management of, shared repositories, by making ContentMaps a standard repository feature. The power of ContentMaps was that participants saw task instructions and responsibilities linked directly to underlying content. ContentMaps are a useful way to reference shared content, so every repository could have a wiki-like structure describing repository content, along with direct links to that content.

We also saw the importance of implicit strategies using task or role information for organizing shared repositories. To support such strategies, tools like Dropbox, Drive, and shared folders might be modified to allow automatic tagging of files with roles or tasks. Tags could include derived metadata about content, including document creator, most recent editor, workflows and so forth. Although there are benefits to the simplicity of current tools, automatic tags could support enhanced views that extend simple folders (Dropbox) or flat lists (Drive) to mirror implicit strategies by showing tasks, owners and responsibilities.

Another important technical implication concerns improved integration of email and share repositories. One approach would be to modify email to support *active structured links* to repositories. We found that emails currently contain information about alerts, collaborative tasks, and pointers to shared content often using ContentMaps. Email clients might provide ContentMaps natively as a specific template. Templates could be automatically created containing links to shared content, making it easier for collaborators to share action plans about shared content. Such linking facilities are already provided in software development tools (IBM Rational Team Concert, MS Studio). Linking is also supported in a simplified fashion in Gmail, but regular email clients could be modified so that structured indexing is routine.

A different but complementary approach to email integration might be to populate shared repositories with communication information. Currently when you access Dropbox or Drive you don't see relevant email communications concerning that shared content. However such communications could be directly incorporated into the repository without having to leave it to access email or a task manager. Again such facilities are provided in some software development contexts and research prototypes [22]. Such integration could be a useful addition to shared repositories such as Dropbox, Drive, or shared file systems.

Limitations and Future Work

Limits of the work are that the participant set is relatively small and homogeneous. It also needs to be supplemented with direct observation of teams to triangulate how strategies are enacted. There are also outstanding questions about the effects of shared repositories on work practices. Our work analyzed relatively small teams, but do successful techniques scale when collaborators are less familiar with each other's expertise and job responsibilities? Can ContentMaps succeed when collaborators have less shared knowledge? Other questions concern email. How will email practices change as email is increasingly used for coordinating around repositories rather than distributing attachments? When do people choose to share attachments rather than use shared repositories? How important is active leadership in the successful implementation and adoption of these tools?

In conclusion we have shown how and why current shared repositories are beginning to address the classic co-organization barrier. We have reported new uses of collaboration tools in the forms of ContentMaps and implicit co-organization that allow participants to work together effectively without needing to explicitly agree on collaboration structures. We have also reported how this has changed uses of email, and suggested ways that new technologies might improve existing tools.

REFERENCES

1. http://reviews.cnet.com/8301-13970_7-57571513-78/dropbox-clears-1-billion-file-uploads-per-day/
2. http://techcrunch.com/2012/06/28/google-drive-now-has-10-million-users-available-on-ios-and-chrome-os-offline-editing-in-docs/
3. Abrams, D., Baecker, R., & Chignell, M. Information archiving with bookmarks. *Proc CHI,* ACM Press (1998) p. 41-48.
4. Ackerman, M. S., & Halverson, C. Organizational memory as objects, processes, and trajectories. *Proc CSCW, 13*(2) (2004) p. 155-189.
5. Aula, A., Jhaveri, N., & Käki, M. Information search and re-access strategies of experienced web users. In *Proc WWW*, ACM Press (2005) p. 583-592.
6. Bannon, L. and S. Bødker Constructing Common Information Spaces. *Proc CSCW*, ACM Press (1997) p. 81–96.
7. Bellotti, V., Ducheneaut, N., Howard, M., & Smith, I. Taking email to task. In *Proc. CHI 2003,* ACM Press (2003), 345-352.
8. Bellotti, V., Ducheneaut, N., Howard, M., Smith, I., & Grinter, R. E. Quality versus quantity: E-mail-centric task management and its relation with overload. *HCI, 20*(1) (2005) p 89-138.
9. Bergman, O., Beyth-Marom, R., Nachmias, R., Gradovitch, N., & Whittaker, S. Improved search engines and navigation preference in personal information management. *ACM TOIS*, 26(40) (2008).
10. Bergman, O., Whittaker, S., Sanderson, M., Nachmias, R., Ramamoorthy, A. The effect of folder structure on personal file navigation. *JASIST*, 61(12) (2010) p. 2426-2441.
11. Berlin, L.M., Jeffries, R., O'Day, V.L., Paepcke, A., & Wharton, C. Where did you put it? Issues in the design and use of a group memory. In *Proc. CHI 1993.* New York: ACM Press (1993) pp. 23–30.
12. Cutrell, E., Dumais, S. T., & Teevan, J. Searching to eliminate personal information management. *Communications of the ACM, 49*(1) (2006) p. 58-64.
13. Dabbish, L. A., & Kraut, R. E. Email overload at work: an analysis of factors associated with email strain. *In Proc CSCW*, ACM Press. (2006) p. 431-440.
14. Ducheneaut, N., & Bellotti, V. E-mail as habitat. *Interactions*, *8*(5) (2001) p. 30-38.
15. Dumais, S., Cutrell, E., Cadiz, J. J., Jancke, G., Sarin, R., & Robbins, D. C. Stuff I've seen: a system for personal information retrieval and re-use. In *Proc SIGIR*, ACM Press (2003) p. 72-79.
16. Grudin, J. Groupware and social dynamics: eight challenges for developers. *CACM, 37*(1) (1994) p. 92-105.
17. Jones, W. *Keeping Found Things Found.* Morgan Kaufmann, 2010.
18. Kushmerick, N., Lau, T., Dredze, M., & Khoussainov, R. (2006, July). Activity-centric email: A machine learning approach. In *Proc AAAI 21(2)* (2006) p. 1634.
19. Lutters, W.G., Ackerman, M.S., & Zhou, X. Group Information Management. In W. Jones & J. Teevan (Eds.), *Personal Information Management* Seattle: University of Washington Press. (pp. 236–248), 2007.
20. Mahmud, J., Matthews, T., Whittaker, S., Moran, T., & Lau, T. Topika: integrating collaborative sharing with email. In *Proc CHI,* ACM Press. (2011) p. 3161-3164.
21. Malone, T. How do people organize their desks? Implications for the design of office information systems. *ACM TOIS*, 1(1) (1983) p. 99-112.
22. Marshall, C., & Tang, J. C. That Syncing Feeling: Early user experiences with the cloud. In *Proc DIS*, ACM Press (2012) p. 544-553.
23. Nardi, B. A., Whittaker, S., Isaacs, E., Creech, M., Johnson, J., & Hainsworth, J. Integrating communication and information through ContactMap. *CACM, 45*(4) (2002) p89-95.
24. Rader, E. Yours, Mine, and (Not) Ours. *Proc CHI*, ACM Press *(2009)* 2095-2098.
25. Russell, D., & Lawrence, S. Search everything. *Personal information management*, (2007) 153-166.
26. Shami, N. S., Muller, M., & Millen, D. Browse and discover. *Proc CSCW,* ACM Press (2011) p. 295-304.
27. Voida, A., Olson, J. S. & Olson. G. M. Turbulence in the Clouds. In *Proc CHI* ACM Press (2013).
28. Wegner, D. M. Transactive memory: A contemporary analysis of the group mind. In *Theories of group behavior* (pp. 185-208). Springer New York. (1987)
29. Whittaker, S., & Sidner, C. Email overload: exploring personal information management of email. In *Proc CHI*, ACM Press (1996) p. 276-283.
30. Whittaker, S. Supporting collaborative task management in e-mail. *Human Computer Interaction*, *20*(1-2) (2005) p. 49-88.
31. Whittaker, S. Personal information management: from information consumption to curation. *ARIST*, *45*(2011)p3-62.

Designing Information Savvy Societies: An Introduction to Assessability

Andrea Forte, Nazanin Andalibi, Thomas Park, Heather Willever-Farr
College of Computing and Informatics
Drexel University, Philadelphia, PA, USA
{aforte, na477, tp352}@drexel.edu, hwilleverfarr@gmail.com

ABSTRACT
This paper provides first steps toward an empirically grounded design vocabulary for *assessable design* as an HCI response to the global need for better information literacy skills. We present a framework for synthesizing literatures called the Interdisciplinary Literacy Framework and use it to highlight gaps in our understanding of information literacy that HCI as a field is particularly well suited to fill. We report on two studies that lay a foundation for developing guidelines for assessable information system design. The first is a study of Wikipedians', librarians', and laypersons' information assessment practices from which we derive two important features of assessable designs: information provenance and stewardship. The second is an experimental study in which we operationalize these concepts in designs and test them using Amazon Mechanical Turk (MTurk).

Author Keywords
Credibility; information literacy; assessability; Wikipedia

ACM Classification Keywords
H.5.3 [Information Interfaces]: Group and Organization Interfaces – Collaborative computing, Computer-supported cooperative work, Web-based interaction

INTRODUCTION
Technologies can be designed to support human needs in different ways; for example, they can be designed using principles of usability [25], accessibility [30], ergonomics [29], or, as we suggest in this paper, *assessability*. We define assessability as the extent to which an interface helps people make appropriate assessments of information quality in a particular context of use. Thinking in terms of assessable design could change how designers approach the problem of creating environments where people search, produce, and access information.

Terms like "information overload," "drinking from the firehose," and "information pollution" have surfaced in scholarly and popular press to describe problems associated with unprecedented access to information. Barack Obama issued a presidential proclamation about the need for U.S. citizens to learn sophisticated information literacy skills to function in an information-rich democratic society [26] and global organizations such as the International Federation of Library Associations and Institutions (IFLA) and the United Nations Educational, Scientific and Cultural Organization (UNESCO) compile and publish information literacy materials from around the world [16].

Supporting the development of information literacy skills has largely been the domain of education and librarianship communities. This emphasis on education implicitly suggests that information production systems are features of the world within which people must adapt and learn. Yet, how people learn to act within systems is only half of the story. From a sociotechnical HCI perspective, it is clear that the technologies we use to find, access, and produce information are designed environments that can be modified and extended in response to and anticipation of social, cultural, and cognitive needs.

The need for an integrated HCI response to the problem of information literacy is particularly salient because of the proliferation of participatory information sources such as Wikipedia, Wikia sites, Reddit, and Ancestry.com, which are information sources produced and curated by numerous contributors using collaboration or aggregation platforms. Such systems mediate information production and access for millions of users.

In this paper, we introduce a framework to integrate HCI literature with literature from other disciplines that address information literacy to highlight complementary approaches and gaps. We then report on two studies that advance our understanding of designing systems to support information literacy practices: an interview study from which we derived potential features of assessable designs, and an experimental study in which we operationalized these proposed features as design elements in Wikipedia interface modifications and tested them using MTurk.

THE INTERDISCIPLINARY LITERACY FRAMEWORK
Innovations in information production, search, and access have attracted many researchers to problems associated with information literacy. It's an area that is important, complex, and ubiquitous, which makes it attractive to

CHI 2014 April 26 - May 01 2014, Toronto, ON, Canada. Copyright is held by the owner/author(s). Publication rights licensed to ACM.
ACM 978-1-4503-2473-1/14/04...$15.00.
http://dx.doi.org/10.1145/2556288.2557072

researchers of all stripes. Not surprisingly, information literacy research extends across many literatures, draws on diverse theoretical and disciplinary traditions, and encompasses overlapping vocabularies, some of which identify as research on media literacy, search, credibility, persuasion, and trust.

We synthesize these diverse vocabularies by introducing a framework that highlights two critical dimensions of information literacy: assumptions about the skills involved in literate practices, and approaches to transforming practice (See Figure 1).

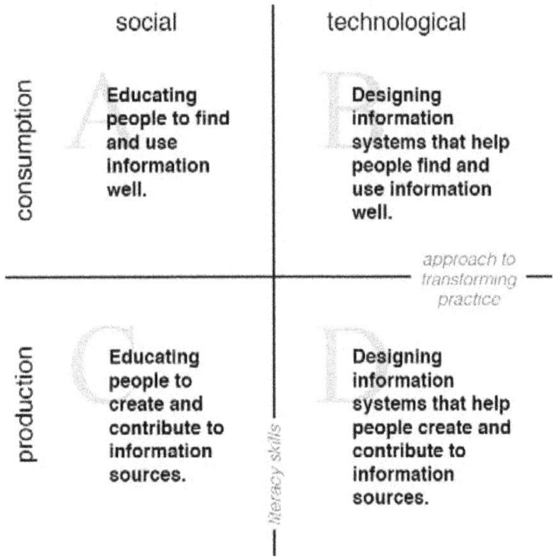

Figure 1: The Interdisciplinary Literacy Framework applied to the domain of information literacy.

Skills involved in literate practice. In order to measure literacy, researchers and educators must define what skills are common to literate individuals and develop methods of assessing these skills. These definitions and methods are based on a set of culturally informed assumptions about what literacy entails. We suggest that literacy entails both consumption and production skills; in traditional terms: both reading *and* writing. In terms of information literacy, on one end of the axis lie practices associated with consumption such as searching, browsing, accessing, and assessing information. Increasingly information literacy research also addresses the other end of the axis: producing and contributing to information resources.

Approach to transforming practice. A second set of assumptions concerns the ways in which these practices can be transformed. Information literacy research often includes a transformative agenda: researchers seek to understand practice in order to improve people's abilities to use and participate in systems of information production. On one end of this axis, social solutions to information literacy propose innovative education standards and interventions to help people develop more sophisticated literacy skills. On the other end, technological solutions aim to design information environments to make them more amenable to user participation and assessment.

By juxtaposing these dimensions, we can map the literature on information literacy onto four quadrants. What follows is not an exhaustive review, but integrates some of the most relevant HCI work with other disciplines to exemplify four types of approaches to information literacy research.

A. **Social approaches to encouraging better information consumption practices.** These approaches are by far the most abundant, for example, library instruction classes in which students are taught how to find and assess information resources or specialized programs such as Google search education [15]. Research that supports these approaches has sought to identify existing practices and ways of interpreting technologies [9, 22, 24], to evaluate educational approaches to modifying these practices [20], and to offer standards and guidelines for implementing such activities [2]. (Social approaches may include using educational technologies.)

B. **Technological approaches to designing for better information consumption practices.** Examples of these approaches include novel search engines designed to support credibility judgments [32, 41] and use of concepts like "information foraging" [31] to predict online information seeking behaviors [3]. In the domain of participatory information sources, WikiTrust [1] is computes a rating of reliability for Wikipedia text based on revision histories and Wikidashboard [18] is a system that exposes editing activity to readers.

C. **Social approaches to helping people become good contributors to information sources.** These approaches are often initiated to help communities attract contributors as socializing newcomers is a challenge for open collaboration communities [13]. People need to learn not only that they can contribute to information resources, but how to do so well. For example, through efforts like Wikipedia Academies[1], individuals from under-represented groups in the Wikipedia community can receive training. Similarly, projects have been launched to involve university students in the production of articles [8, 21]. Others have evaluated socialization tactics to identify factors that contribute to success [4]. The efforts above are usually framed as projects to support Wikipedia, not would-be learners of production skills.

D. **Technological approaches to designing for higher quality participation in information production.** Many tools have been developed to support experts as they negotiate complex interactions and production

[1] http://en.wikipedia.org/wiki/Wikipedia:Academy

activities. For example, SuggestBot helps Wikipedia editors find tasks they might enjoy and that need to be done [5]. Re:Flex is a system that creates visualizations of interactions among Wikipedia editors and content to support social translucence [23]. Despite research that documents newcomer practices in online production communities [27, 34] and a pervasive belief that interface features such as lack of WYSIWYG can hamper newcomer participation [40], design experimentation to support newcomers in participatory information systems is scarce.

A Critical Gap: Making People Smarter, Not Computers

The quadrants in the Interdisciplinary Literacy Framework do not represent mutually exclusive agendas; most research implicitly or explicitly involve elements of at least two even if it only emphasizes one. Many researchers have discussed the traversal of these axes, particularly as people move between consumption and production using participatory forms of media [17, 28]. Sormunen et al. used writing on a wiki as a context for learning both critical consumption and production skills in Swedish schools [35]. St. Jean et al. examined how content producers assess information they find [36]. Forte and Bruckman developed a wiki for high schools with specialized tools to support sharing citations in a bibiliographic database; they suggested that producing an information resource for others not only supports practicing writing, but also transforms strategies for finding and assessing information [12].

Looking ahead, we see a continued need for work that spans these quadrants, in particular where participatory information sources are concerned. Moreover, we see an important gap in quadrant B—an area that HCI is well-suited to fill. Although algorithmic approaches such as those behind credibility-based search results [32, 41] or content ratings in WikiTrust [1] can help deliver important information that support critical consumption, these methods rely on the designers of algorithms to define credibility. Our vision of assessable design is one in which designers support people in learning how information is produced so they can make informed assessments.

Kittur et al.'s early work with Wikidashboard is one of the few projects that has addressed this problem directly [18]. They used Amazon Mechanical Turk to demonstrate that showing people editing activity can affect their judgments of Wikipedia articles: more perceived volatility led to lowered trust and more perceived stability led to higher trust. More recently, Towne et al. [39] tested whether exposing content-related discussions would engender less trust in Wikipedia content by making the messiness of the process more visible; in fact, they discovered that viewing discussions generally lowered trust in a given article (especially when conflict was perceived), but participants *reported* that it raised their assessment both of the article and Wikipedia as a source. Towne et al. speculate this might be because viewing discussions engenders more confidence in one's ability to assess Wikipedia articles.

These findings suggest that understanding how information is produced informs not only how people assess information (information literacy skills) but also their self-efficacy (propensity to use and confidence in information literacy skills). This raises two questions. First, the findings that people feel more critical when they are exposed to conflict and that viewing visualizations of edit histories affect how people judge content both raise the question of how expert Wikipedians, who should be deeply familiar with production on the site, differ from others' in interpreting such information to inform their assessment strategies:

> RQ1. What strategies do expert Wikipedians use to assess articles and how do they differ from the strategies used by people with less knowledge of how information in Wikipedia is produced?

Second, if we can identify features of the site that give people insight into article quality, we want to capitalize on these and begin to develop a vocabulary for talking about assessable designs, using Wikipedia as a testbed.

> RQ2. Can we use expert Wikipedian strategies to help inform the design of assessable interface features that help inform non-Wikipedians' strategies?

We address these questions in the following two studies.

STUDY 1: DIARY AND INTERVIEW STUDY

In order to answer RQ1 and better understand interactions between different forms of expertise and assessment of Wikipedia articles, we recruited a strategic sample of individuals that represent a broad swath of information consumers for a diary and interview study:

- *Amateur experts.* Highly experienced Wikipedians, expert producers of a participatory information resource who are not professionally trained. Wikipedians were recruited through Wikimedia Foundation contacts and using snowball recruitment.
- *Librarians.* Librarians are formally trained to be discerning about the selection and assessment of information. We wanted to understand how this formal training influences information assessment strategies. Information professionals were recruited from local libraries using flyers and mailing lists.
- *Novices.* These are individuals who do not participate in information production and have no special training in assessing information, but who use Wikipedia. These were recruited from local undergraduate student populations using flyers and mailing lists.

Methods

We conducted phone or in-person interviews with 6 librarians, 3 Wikipedians, and 3 students for a total of 12 interviewees. Before the interview, participants completed a search diary for up to 7 days (average 5.2 days) in which they recorded details about Internet searches they had conducted. Interviews began with open-ended explorations of participants' experiences with participatory media, then included a semi-structured protocol [33] in which participants responded to specific questions about their search practices grounded in data from their diaries. Finally, in a think-aloud protocol [7], the participants were asked to examine two Wikipedia articles. The first article, on Apollo 9, was relatively short, tagged as needing more citations, and included primarily technical information; whereas the second article, about the moon, had attained the level of featured article by undergoing a rigorous process of community review. We asked participants to provide an assessment of them and verbally explain how they made judgments about the information. Both articles were saved to the first author's website before the interview study in order to ensure that all participants saw the same version.

Interview data were transcribed and coded using the software Dedoose to identify patterns of information assessment strategies within and across participant groups. After open coding yielded a catalog of assessment strategies used by participants, we examined, compared, and grouped these to identify higher-level concepts that describe important features of assessable participatory information sources. This process of open, axial, and selective coding is typical of a grounded theory approach to data analysis [14].

Findings

Our analysis yielded two concepts that describe important features of assessable designs: provenance and stewardship.

Information Provenance. Provenance is a concept that is familiar in disciplines such as history, archival studies, and the sciences and relates to metadata that make it possible to trace the ownership or origins of an artifact or dataset. This is a critical concept for people dealing with participatory information sources. *Where did this information come from?* The most simple technique for sourcing is a citation. In all populations, the source of information surfaced as an important element of assessment, although the ways people used that information varied. Knowing where information came from is related to the concept of verifiability.

All our participants demonstrated assessment strategies that relied on establishing provenance, but these strategies were informed by different understandings of Wikipedia and its interface. For example, compare the responses of a student, a librarian, and a Wikipedian to the presence of a warning posted at the top of the Apollo 9 article that suggested it was lacking citations:

> Student: It says it needs more citations for verification. That's important. So I'd probably want something that... Is this the only Apollo 9 article on Wikipedia?
> Interviewer: Yeah, this is the official one.
> Student: That's the official one? Well someone needs to work on this one, because I'm sure there's more information on it.
>
> Librarian: This article needs additional sources for verification. My response is, of course it does! It's crowd sourced, or it's user-generated content. It always probably will.
>
> Wikipedian: You know, the citation needed template at the top shows up too many places to actually be a good indicator of whether or not there is stuff that actually needs citations... One reason people are not good at judging the quality of Wikipedia articles is that Wikipedians are bad about tagging poor quality articles and I mean that to say that we tag too many of them.

The student took the warning at face value and it influenced his perception of the article's quality; once warned that the article did not sufficiently establish where its information came from he reflected that someone needed to work on it. He interpreted the warning as a reader and acknowledged it is a signal for attention from editors. The librarian had already committed to an assessment of Wikipedia as an information resource and, thus, the warning didn't affect her. She views Wikipedia articles as eternally in need of better sourcing. The Wikipedian uses his knowledge about the practice of tagging articles and suggests that the warning isn't reliable; he went on to offer his own assessment of the citations.

All participants mentioned citations as important features of source quality, not only in Wikipedia articles, but also in blogs or other information sources they encounter online. They most often noted the quantity of citations (the featured article, *Moon*, included over 150 citations); however, librarians and Wikipedians also noted characteristics like type, recency, publisher, or length of the resources cited.

Stewardship. It is often difficult to attribute authorship of—and thus responsibility for—any particular passage in participatory information sources to a specific author; however, the idea that many individuals share responsibility for maintaining the resource is a rationale that people used for trusting Wikipedia. Librarians and student participants understood that many people maintain Wikipedia; however, only Wikipedians used knowledge of stewardship processes to inform their assessments.

Expert Wikipedians use their knowledge of tools and practices on the site to determine how likely an article is to be well maintained; for example, by assessing whether an article is likely to have been worked on by many editors. One clear indication of this is the "featured article" status, which is signified by an unobtrusive star in the corner of the article. Wikipedian interviewees immediately noted that the moon article was featured and, when asked, explained that featured articles have been rigorously reviewed and are the best content on Wikipedia. Explained one Wikipedian, "it's very hard to get an article to featured status. I've got several of them, and I'm proud of them, and they're on my resume." None of the other participants noticed or could explain what the star meant without clicking on it.

Casual Wikipedia users likewise commented on the potential for many editors to create a robust article and for many eyes to catch mistakes:

> Student: There's a lot of subcategories and everything, which really leads me to think that a lot of different people went and looked at this. Because if you get one guy from NASA on the Apollo 9, but you don't have a physicist, then you're lacking some information. Like different fields get different information.

Like a Wikipedian, this student uses his general understanding of how Wikipedia works to assess the article at hand; however, later he explains that he doesn't know much about Wikipedia's rules. He knows *that* many people create and maintain Wikipedia, but he has never done it and doesn't know *how* this process is managed. In a couple of cases, casual Wikipedia users referred to the process of continuous refinement by multiple editors as "peer review," a term reserved by our librarian participants for traditional information production and stewardship processes that they typically held in contrast to that of Wikipedia.

In some cases, librarians' professional training was evident. Some librarians explained their assessments in terms of traditional information production processes that place trained professionals in the role of gatekeeper. For example, when asked about students using Wikipedia:

> Librarian: The web is great for students but at the same time they have to do so much more work. They have to do the selecting and then the verifying instead of some editorial board doing it for them… an editorial board has looked at this journal but then also the librarian who knows the most about the subject has also curated or looked through as well as looking at reviews.

Another librarian stated that Wikipedia is "a bibliographic aid or portal"—not a credible information source itself, but a list of places to look for information. "One day," she reflected, "maybe it could be considered more of a scholarly source, because it does have a lot of information in one place." At times librarians seemed to struggle with the conflicting sense that the articles were useful and a belief that stewardship on the site is non-existent or inferior to traditionally authored reference works.

Outcome: Proposed Features of Assessable Designs

Based on these findings, we propose that assessable designs will expose features of provenance and stewardship.

Although information provenance can be documented in multiple ways, for Wikipedia and other kinds of participatory information sources discussed by participants such as blogs, citations play a central role in informing their assessments. In particular where the citation list exceeded 150 items, people who wanted to assess the *quality* of citations struggled to do so. The "wall of citations" appeared to overwhelm many participants. It may be that a standard bibliographic list of citations, appropriate for scholarly publications whose readers are experts at reading and interpreting citations, is not the ideal presentation for a lay population. Our first design exploration of provenance will be an alternate representation of what's cited in a Wikipedia article.

Our data on how people interpret stewardship on the site suggest that people who haven't participated in editing articles aren't even aware that Wikipedia has processes for managing article quality. Thus, our first design exploration of stewardship will be a representation of Wikipedia's quality review process.

STUDY 2

In a follow-up study, we used Amazon Mechanical Turk (MTurk) to test our design explorations by measuring whether they affect assessments of Wikipedia articles and how participants interpret representations of information provenance and stewardship.

Experimental Design

To develop the different interface conditions, we selected three articles from Wikipedia that were of roughly comparable quality by searching for biology-related articles rated 'B-class' on the Wikipedia quality scale: Dengue Virus, Domestication, and Root. We lightly edited a local copy of these articles to be of similar length and include similar numbers of citations and images. We asked three experienced Wikipedians to compare the modified articles; all three rated them of similar quality.

We developed two types of visualizations to represent features of information provenance and stewardship (see Figure 2). To create different experimental conditions, we included one at the top of the otherwise unchanged articles. In the information provenance visualization, participants were shown a pie chart that gave information about what kinds of resources were cited in the article. This is intended not only to give people a heuristic for making assessments,

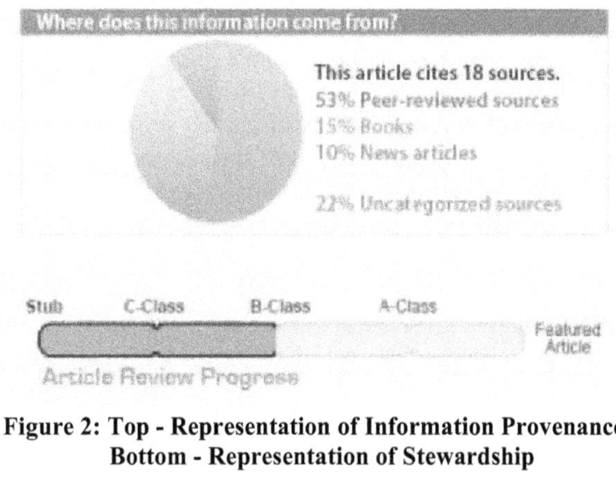

Figure 2: Top - Representation of Information Provenance Bottom - Representation of Stewardship

but also to suggest the importance of paying attention to where the information comes from. In the information stewardship visualization, participants were shown a thermometer chart that depicts how far the article has progressed from a stub-class article toward featured article. This is intended, again, not only to alert people to the article's status, but also to communicate the fact that Wikipedia has a review process and articles may be at different levels of quality.

Two versions of each representation were created: one for a lower quality condition and one for a higher quality condition. This yielded 5 total conditions in which the visualization depicted:

- REF: 75% uncategorized sources, 15% news, 10% peer-reviewed, and 5% books.
- REFA: 85% peer-reviewed sources, 10% books, and 5% uncategorized sources.
- REVIEW: article had reached B-class.
- REVIEWA: article had reached A-class.
- PLAIN: Control group with no visualization

We followed best practices for using Mechanical Turk for user studies [19, 39]. After completing a short demographic survey, each participant assessed a plain article, then two of the four visualizations. Participants were offered $0.50 for each article they assessed with an additional $0.10 for completing all three. We varied the order in which visualizations were presented so that half the participants saw REF before REVIEW, and half saw REVIEW before REF. Higher and lower quality conditions were paired. We included verification questions to ensure participants attended to articles. To control the order and number of tasks available to participants, we provided a link to a custom survey form on the first author's website where participants were asked to enter their MTurk worker ID. At the end of each task, participants were given a code to enter in MTurk to receive payment. Statistical analysis of responses was done using SPSS.

Measures

Quality. To measure quality, we included five survey items that asked to what extent participants agreed that each article was written well, accurate, a bad source of information, unbiased, and trustworthy on a 4-point scale (strongly disagree, somewhat disagree, somewhat agree, strongly agree). Because we were interested in comparing differences, not in measuring quality on an absolute scale, a symmetric four-point continuum was chosen as a forced measure. One item was presented negatively to ensure that the participants were attending to the task and was inverted for data analysis. A principle component analysis was conducted to verify these variables measured one construct. The Kaiser-Meyer-Olkin measure of sampling adequacy was 0.78, above the recommended value of 0.6, and Bartlett's test of sphericity was significant ($p<.01$). One component was extracted and the percentage of variance accounted for by that was 56.56%. The component loadings for writing, trustworthiness, accuracy, neutrality, and good information were 0.76, 0.86, 0.85, 0.67, and 0.56 respectively. Because these variables are measuring a single construct, the sum of these five variables was used as the overall quality variable for each article assessment.

Visualization Effect. This construct refers to the extent participants believed the visualizations of provenance and stewardship affected their assessment of the article. This survey item was included as a five-point scale on which participants indicated whether the visualizations [strongly lowered, somewhat lowered, did not affect, somewhat raised, strongly raised] their assessment of the article.

Global Visualization Effect. This construct refers to the extent participants believed the visualizations affected their assessment of Wikipedia as an information source. This survey item included the same five-point scale on which participants indicated whether the visualizations affected their assessment of Wikipedia as a source.

Visualization Interpretation. To support our interpretations and discussion of quality assessments, we included two prompts with free response answers: "Briefly describe what the infographic at the top of the article represents" and "Did you use the information in the infographic to answer the survey questions? If so, how? What did it mean to you?"

Participants

We conducted a pilot study with 20 participants to ensure that the plain article conditions were comparable and that the survey was understandable. With minor modifications, the final version of the study was run with 244 English-speaking participants, which yielded 682 article assessments. See Table 1 for participant demographics.

Using responses to verification questions in combination with free text responses and task completion time, we checked whether any participant had entered "junk" data and should be excluded. All participants were found to have participated in earnest.

Analysis and Findings

Before comparing the visualization conditions, we first confirmed that participants assessed PLAIN articles on root, dengue fever, and domestication to be of equal quality. A one-way ANOVA was conducted on article quality to compare each of the PLAIN conditions and demonstrated that there was no significant difference between them [$F(2, 230) = 2.718$, $p=.07$].

Comparing the Visualizations

Next we compared quality in the four visualization conditions. To compare each of the paired conditions, we used the Mann-Whitney U test, which is a non-parametric test that compares distributions of ranked data, making it appropriate for ordinal data. A Mann-Whitney test

		#	%
	Male	149	61%
	Female	93	38%
Education	High school	31	13%
	Some college	95	39%
	College degree	95	39%
	Graduate degree	22	9%
Reads Wikipedia	Never/Don't know	4	2%
	< Once per month	21	9%
	1-3 times per month	54	22%
	1-3 times per week	91	37%
	Most days	53	22%
	Multiple times per day	21	9%
Edits Wikipedia	Never/Don't know	185	76%
	> 10 times	54	22%
	10-300 times	3	1%
	300-5000 times	1	<1%
	Over 5000 times	0	-

Table 1: Participant Demographics
Not all sections add up to 244 because of four missing values.

confirmed that quality assessments were significantly higher for the REFA condition (Mean=17.6) than for the REF condition (Mean=16.4) [U=4209, p<.01, r=.25]. Likewise, participants rated REVIEWA (Mean=17.6) higher than REVIEW (Mean=16.1) [U=4022, p<.01, r=.3]. The *r* value (effect size) for the REVIEW visualization is larger than for the REF visualization, and therefore we can conclude that the REVIEW visualizations had a more powerful effect on quality ratings.

An analysis of Visualization Effect and Global Visualization Effect indicated that participants' perceptions of the visualizations' effects on their rating behaviors are aligned with their actual rating behaviors (See Figures 3 and 4). In the case of REF and REVIEW, nearly 35% of participants believed that the presence of the visualization lowered their assessment of the article. In the case of REFA and REVIEWA, perceptions shifted dramatically toward a belief that the visualizations raised assessments.

Comparing the Participants

We were interested in comparing Wikipedia editors and non-editors to see if editing experience affected perceptions of the visualizations. We hypothesized that experienced Wikipedians would be less affected by our visualizations since they represented features of Wikipedia that should already be familiar to frequent editors. Only four participants had significant Wikipedia editing experience, which made it impossible to carry out a meaningful statistical analysis. Although we believe editing fewer than 10 times is a weak signal of expertise, by collapsing participants who had ever edited into one group, we were able to run Mann-Whitney U tests on Visualization Effect in each condition and compare the results to those who had and had not edited Wikipedia.

For both editors and non-editors we found significant differences in all conditions. Among people who had edited Wikipedia, the difference between Visualization Effect ratings in the REVIEWA (Median=4.5) and REVIEW conditions (Median=4) was significant. [U=232.5, p=.01, r=.34]. Similarly, there were significantly higher effects for REVIEWA (Median=5) than for REVIEW (Median=4) [U=1807, p<.01, r=.43] among non editors. There were significantly higher effects for the REFA condition (Median=5) than for the REF condition (Median=4) [U=170.5, p<.01, r=.48] among those who had edited Wikipedia and those who had not edited Wikipedia also reported significantly higher Visualization Effects in the REFA condition (Median=5) than the REF condition (Median=4) [U=1592, p<.01, r=.46].

Table 2 provides a comparison of the effect sizes for these findings. The effect size for REF conditions is similar among editors and non-editors. This is not surprising since paying attention to citations is not something unique to Wikipedia editors. The effect sizes for REVIEW

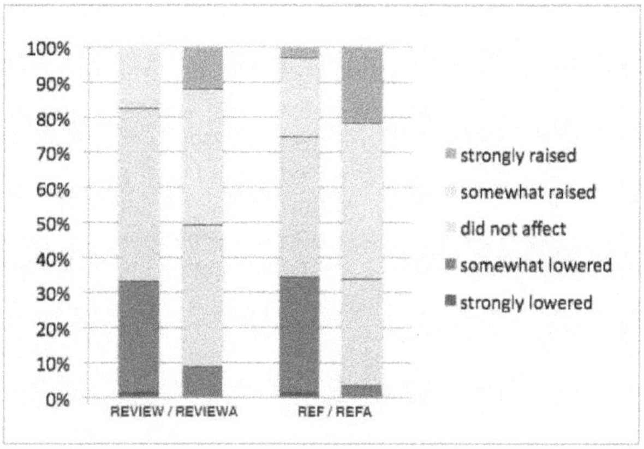

Figure 3: Visualization Effect as measured by the question "The infographic at the top of the article ___ my assessment of this article."

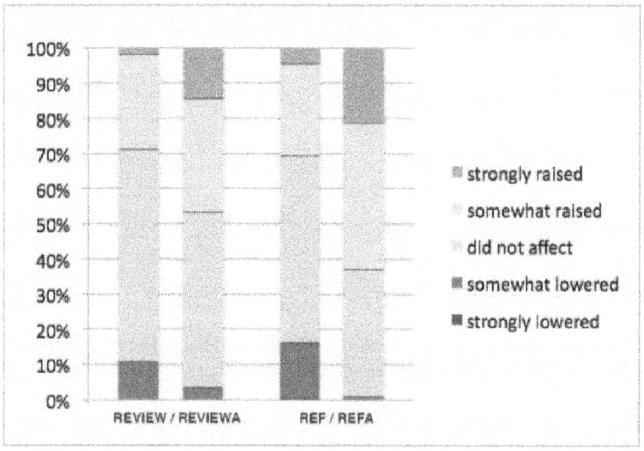

Figure 3: Global Visualization Effect as measured by the question "The infographic at the top of the article ___ my assessment of Wikipedia as an information resource."

conditions, however, are quite different. The effect size of the difference between REVIEW and REVIEWA is much higher for non-editors. This suggests that non-editors perceived information about information stewardship on Wikipedia as a stronger influence on their assessments than editors.

Effect size of difference between:	Edited	Not Edited
REF and REFA	.48	.46
REVIEW and REVIEWA	.34	.43

Table 2: Effect sizes for differences between VIZ and VIZA conditions for participants who had/had not edited Wikipedia

The visibility of formal training on librarians' assessment strategies in Study 1 prompted us to wonder whether participants with higher levels of education would be better able to use the information in our visualizations to inform their assessments. We hypothesized that people who had spent more years in school would be better trained to take note of things like the quality of sources or indication of a review process. To investigate this, we used a Mann-Whitney U test to compare the differences between visualization effect, global visualization effect, and quality ratings of REF and REFA, and REVIEW and REVIEWA by education level. With one exception, the mean values for REFA and REVIEWA conditions were equal or higher than for REF and REVIEW conditions respectively. Table 3 highlights statistically significant results and provides the difference between mean ratings to help readers interpret the data. (Quality is a composite represented by the sum of five ranked items whereas Viz Effect and Global Viz Effect are each measured using a single ranked item.)

		Graduate Degree	College	Some College	High School
Quality	REF	**4.1 p<.01**	1.85 p=.01	.78 p=.04	.06 p=.96
	REVIEW	.59 p=.5	**2.31 p<.01**	1.16 p=.01	.79 p=.86
Viz Effect	REF	**1.32 p<.01**	**.96 p<.01**	**.77 p<.01**	.76 p=.02
	REVIEW	.29 p=.44	**1.01 p<.01**	**.58 p<.01**	.41 p=.33
Global Viz Effect	REF	**1.23 p<.01**	**.61 p<.01**	**.52 p<.01**	.6 p=.04
	REVIEW	-.19 p=.28	.41 p=.01	.42 p=.01	.44 p=.26

Table 3: Differences between mean ratings for VIZ and VIZA conditions. p values < .05 and .01 are highlighted.

We found that the highest and lowest levels of education were associated with reduced impact of visualizations, particularly in the REVIEW conditions. REF visualizations consistently had an effect across education levels, with reduced impact among high school students. We speculate that advanced scholarship may yield effects similar to that observed in interviews with librarians: although people with advanced degrees are very familiar with and use citations to assess the articles, they are more likely to make their own judgments about the quality of Wikipedia, regardless of what the Wikipedia quality scale says.

We turned to free text Visualization Interpretation data to help us further understand these findings. These data confirmed that graduate students were able to correctly interpret the REVIEW visualizations but that they were making their own judgments independent of it. Wrote one, "This seems like a trustworthy and accurate article. The infographic suggests it is only average. That rating indicates Wikipedia has very high quality standards." His interpretation of the visualization was flawed; however, this participant separated his own assessment of the article (trustworthy and accurate) from the one he was given on the Wikipedia quality scale.

DISCUSSION

We have completed a few first steps toward an empirically grounded design vocabulary for assessability. So far, we have established that assessable designs help people understand something about:

- information provenance, where information came from,
- and information stewardship, how it is maintained.

The concepts we've identified and tested resonate with literature on credibility, which dates back millennia to Aristotelian logos (logic of content), pathos (appeal to emotion), and ethos (reputation of speaker/writer). Contemporary scholars in many fields use related concepts like trust, believability and expertise in sometimes inconsistent and overlapping ways to describe subjective and objective features of credibility. We define credibility as a perceptual, subjective experience, not a characteristic of information itself; provenance and stewardship are important features of information content and production insofar as they are perceived and understood by people.

Perceptions of content characteristics (such as the presence of citations) appear frequently in the literature on web credibility. Fogg's credibility grid [11] is a prime example of identifying online content features that can serve as credibility cues to information consumers. Stewardship surfaces less frequently. Sundar's MAIN model of credibility assessment [38] accounts for something like stewardship in its treatment of "agency." Provenance and stewardship are also closely related to but not precisely congruent with Flanagin and Metzger's message credibility and media credibility [10]. They differ in that media credibility refers to perceived credibility of a communication channel rather than the process by which information is produced and maintained.

Our dimensions of assessability also complement two important bodies of work in the HCI literature that were introduced earlier in this paper. By developing a visualization that allows readers to quickly see editing activity, WikiDashboard was developed to enhance editor accountability and "help users to identify interesting edit patterns in Wikipedia pages" [37] as an effort to improve social translucence and support assessment of "trustworthiness" [18]. This is a step toward communicating stewardship in that it helps readers perceive editing activity; however, although WikiDashboard exposes the activity itself in "interesting" ways, it does not provide guidance on interpreting these data to help readers perceive policy/quality control mechanisms familiar to Wikipedians.

More recently, Re:Flex is a set of interface components that was developed for Wikipedia atop a general system architecture (Re:Arch) that supports designing for social translucence [23]. This infrastructure has not been used to support assessabilty; however, McDonald et al. identify dimensions of social translucence including content, interaction, relations, and systemic states that could be used to expose important features of provenance and stewardship and develop robust assessable design prototypes.

Provenance and stewardship are not the only two concepts that will be important for designing assessable information environments, but they are a starting point grounded in user experiences. We can imagine explorations of assessable designs that help people know how the information has been used by others and in what contexts. References to reputation and social networks ties are absent in our interview data. One possible reason for this is that social information is not typically used for the tasks we studied and people neither expect it nor have developed a repertoire of strategies for using it for information assessment. Another explanation is that most people do not have ready access in their networks to the expertise necessary to vet the kind of information they need for the tasks we've studied.

We think it is important to note that Wikipedia is a remarkably conservative resource given its reputation as a renegade reference. Policies surrounding citation defer to well-established publishing processes like scientific peer review and traditional journalism and prohibit the production of personalized content. Studying informational sites with different characteristics, such as Twitter, Amazon, or Ancestry.com will broaden our understanding of assessability and help with next steps toward a robust design framework and guidelines.

We began this paper by suggesting that a vocabulary for assessability could change how designers think about information environments. Our inspiration for this vision is the literature on social translucence [6, 23, 37]. Erickson and Kellogg suggested that common forms of computer-mediated communication (CMC) provide little social information that can help people make choices about how to behave. The physical world is rich with social information that we use continuously, but "[i]n the digital world, we are socially blind" [6]. By analogy, Internet users suffer from information blindness. The content we encounter online is not often accompanied by clues about how it was created or where it came from that can help inform information behaviors. Search engines and aggregators exacerbate the problem by divorcing information from its original context of production.

The system properties of visibility, awareness, and accountability articulated in the social translucence literature do not dictate the form that social norms might take; rather, they provide a basis for making choices about how to behave. Likewise, our vision of assessable design is not to dictate what information is considered relevant, credible, useful or junk. Instead, designs should make features like information provenance and stewardship visible so that people can learn to make assessments themselves. Assessable design does not mean filtering information, sifting the wheat from the chaff, the credible from the suspicious; it is a vision for design that facilitates the development of sophisticated understandings about how information is produced in participatory environments and, by extension, perhaps how one might contribute.

ACKNOWLEDGMENTS

This work is supported by NSF (CISE IIS-1253302). We also thank members of Wikimedia Foundation and community for their feedback and assistance.

REFERENCES

1. Adler, B.T., Chatterjee, K., Alfaro, L.d., Faella, M., Pye, I., and Raman, V. Assigning trust to Wikipedia content. *WikiSym 2008*. ACM Press (2008), 1-12.
2. American Association of School Librarians, *Standards for the 21st-century learner in action.* American Association of School Librarians, Chicago, 2009.
3. Chi, E., Pirolli, P., and Pitkow, J. The scent of a site: a system for analyzing and predicting information scent, usage, and usability of a Web site. *CHI* (2000), 161-168.
4. Choi, B., Alexander, K., Kraut, R.E., and Levine, J.M. Socialization tactics in wikipedia and their effects. *CSCW*, ACM (2010), 107-116.
5. Cosley, D., Frankowski, D., Terveen, L., and Riedl, J. SuggestBot: using intelligent task routing to help people find work in wikipedia. in *Proceedings of the 12th international conference on Intelligent user interfaces.* ACM (2007), 32-41.
6. Erickson, T. and Kellogg, W.A., Social translucence: an approach to designing systems that support social processes. *ACM Trans. Comput.-Hum. Interact.*, *7*, 1, (2000), 59-83.
7. Ericsson, K. and Simon, H., *Protocol analysis: Verbal reports as data.* MIT Press, Cambridge, 1993.
8. Farzan, R. and Kraut, R.E. Wikipedia classroom experiment: bidirectional benefits of students' engagement in online production communities. *CHI.* ACM (2013), 783-792.

9. Flanagin, A. and Metzger, M., The role of site features, user attributes, and information verification behaviors on the perceived credibility of web-based information. *New Media and Society*, *9*, 2, (2007), 319-342.
10. Flanagin, A. and Metzger, M., Digital media and youth: unparalleled opportunity and unprecedented responsibility, in *Digital Media, Youth, and Credibility*, M. Metzger and A. Flanagin, Editors., MIT Press, Cambridge, MA, 2008, 5-28.
11. Fogg, B.J., Soohoo, C., Danielson, D.R., Marable, L., Stanford, J., and Tauber, E.R. How do users evaluate the credibility of Web sites?: a study with over 2,500 participants. *Proceedings of the 2003 conference on Designing for user experiences*. ACM (2003), 1-15.
12. Forte, A. and Bruckman, A., Citing, writing and participatory media: wikis as learning environments in the high school classroom. *International Journal of Learning and Media*, *1*, 4, (2009), 23-44.
13. Forte, A. and Lampe, C., Defining, Understanding and Supporting Open Collaboration: Lessons from the Literature. *Am Behav Scientist*, *57*, 5, (2013), 535-547.
14. Glaser, B. and Strauss, A., *The Discovery of Grounded Theory: strategies for qualitative research.* Transaction Publishers, New Brunswick, 1967.
15. Google. *Search Education.* [cited Jan 4, 2014]; http://www.google.com/insidesearch/searcheducation.
16. IFLA and UNESCO. *Information Literacy International Resources Dir*. http://infolitglobal.net/directory/en/.
17. Jenkins, H., Purushotma, R., Weigel, M., K., C., and Robinson, A.J., *Confronting the challenges of participatory culture: Media education for the 21st century.* MIT Press, Cambridge, MA, 2009.
18. Kittur, A., Chi, E., and Suh, B. Can you ever trust a wiki? Impacting perceived trustworthiness in Wikipedia. in *CSCW*, ACM (2008), 477-480.
19. Kittur, A., Chi, E.H., and Suh, B. Crowdsourcing user studies with Mechanical Turk. *CHI,*ACM,2008,453-456.
20. Kuiper, E., Volman, M., and Terwel, J., The Web as an Information Resource in K-12 Education: Strategies for Supporting Students in Searching and Processing Information. *Rev of Ed Research*, *75*, 3,(2005), 285-328.
21. Lampe, C., Obar, J., Ozkaya, E., Zube, P., and Velasquez, A. Classroom Wikipedia participation effects on future intentions to contribute. *CSCW*, ACM (2012), 403-406.
22. Lucassen, T. and Schraagen, J.M. Trust in wikipedia: how users trust information from an unknown source. in *Proceedings of the 4th workshop on Information credibility*. ACM (2010), 19-26.
23. McDonald, D.W., Gokhman, S., and Zachry, M. Building for social translucence: a domain analysis and prototype system. *CSCW*, ACM (2012), 637-646.
24. Menchen-Trevino, E. and Hargittai, E., Young Adults' Credibility Assessment of Wikipedia. *Information, Communication & Society*, *14*, 1, (2011), 24-51.
25. Nielsen, J., *Usability Engineering.* Morgan Kaufmann, San Diego, CA, 1993.
26. Obama, B. *National Information Literacy Awareness Month, A Proclamation*. 2009; Available from: http://www.whitehouse.gov/the_press_office/Presidential-Proclamation-National-Information-Literacy-Awareness-Month.
27. Panciera, K., Priedhorsky, R., Erickson, T., and Terveen, L. Lurking? cyclopaths?: a quantitative lifecycle analysis of user behavior in a geowiki. *CHI*, ACM (2010), 1917-1926.
28. Peppler, K. and Kafai, Y., From SuperGoo to Scratch: Exploring creative digital media production in informal learning. *Learning, Media and Tech*, *32*, 2, (2007), 17.
29. Peres, S.C., Nguyen, V., Kortum, P.T., Akladios, M., Wood, S.B., and Muddimer, A. Software ergonomics: relating subjective and objective measures. *CHI,* ACM (2009), 3949-3954.
30. Petrie, H. and Kheir, O. The relationship between accessibility and usability of websites. *CHI*, ACM (2007), 397-406.
31. Pirolli, P. and Card, S., Information Foraging. *Psychological Review*, *106*, 4, (1999), 32.
32. Schwarz, J. and Morris, M. Augmenting web pages and search results to support credibility assessment. *CHI*, ACM (2011), 1245-1254.
33. Seidman, I., *Interviewing as Qualitative Research: a guide for researchers in education and the social sciences.* Teachers College Press, New York, 2006.
34. Singh, V., Johri, A., and Mitra, R. Types of newcomers in an online developer community. *Proceedings of the ACM 2011 conference on Computer supported cooperative work.* ACM (2011), 717-720.
35. Sormunen, E., Eriksson, H., and Kurkipää, T., Wikipedia and wikis as forums of information literacy instruction in schools, in *The Road to Information Literacy: Librarians as facilitators of learning*, R. Gwyer, R. Stubbings, and G. Walton, Editors., International Federation of Library Associations and Institutions, 2012, 311-330.
36. St Jean, B., Rieh, S.Y., Yang, J.Y., and Kim, Y.Ä., How content contributors assess and establish credibility on the web. *ASIS&T*, *48*, 1, (2011), 1-11.
37. Suh, B., Chi, E., Kittur, A., and Pendleton, B.A. Lifting the veil: improving accountability and social transparency in Wikipedia with WikiDashboard. *CHI*, ACM (2008), 1037-1040.
38. Sundar, S.S., The MAIN model: A heuristic approach to understanding technology effects on credibility. *Digital media, youth, and credibility*, (2008), 73-100.
39. Towne, W.B., Kittur, A., Kinnaird, P., and Herbsleb, J. Your process is showing: controversy management and perceived quality in wikipedia. *CSCW*, ACM (2013), 1059-1068.
40. Wales, J. Opening Remarks. *Wikimania* (2006).
41. Yamamoto, Y. and Tanaka, K. Enhancing credibility judgment of web search results. *CHI*, ACM (2011), 1235-1244.

Addressing Misconceptions About Code with Always-On Programming Visualizations

Tom Lieber
MIT CSAIL
Cambridge, MA USA
tom@alltom.com

Joel Brandt
Adobe Research
San Francisco, CA USA
joel.brandt@adobe.com

Robert C. Miller
MIT CSAIL
Cambridge, MA USA
rcm@mit.edu

ABSTRACT
We present Theseus, an IDE extension that visualizes run-time behavior within a JavaScript code editor. By displaying real-time information about how code *actually* behaves during execution, Theseus proactively addresses misconceptions by drawing attention to similarities and differences between the programmer's idea of what code does and what it actually does. To understand how programmers would respond to this kind of an always-on visualization, we ran a lab study with graduate students, and interviewed 9 professional programmers who were asked to use Theseus in their day-to-day work. We found that users quickly adopted strategies that are unique to always-on, real-time visualizations, and used the additional information to guide their navigation through their code.

Author Keywords
Programming; debugging; code understanding

ACM Classification Keywords
D.2.5. Software Engineering: Debugging Aids

INTRODUCTION
Programmers are often wrong about what code actually does [4, 6, 8]. This causes them to generate incorrect hypotheses while reading, writing, and debugging code, to waste time and energy investigating false leads, and to introduce new bugs while modifying code [8, 18]. Unfortunately, code behavior is invisible in most programming environments because few debugging interfaces are designed to be left on and visible during all phases of programming. Instead, the programmer must request information explicitly, for example by opening an inspector, setting a breakpoint, or inserting a print statement. This means that a faulty mental model is corrected only by applying it during debugging. We believe that programmers would benefit substantially from tools that *proactively* work toward correcting misconceptions by displaying information about execution sooner.

Our solution is a code editor extension called Theseus (Figure 1). Theseus visualizes the program's run-time state using

Figure 1. Theseus shows call counts for every function, and an asynchronous call tree allows the user to see how functions interact. In the log below the code, users can see which call to `fetch` corresponds to the failure without adding any debugging-specific code or re-executing their program.

code coloring and marginal notes, allowing the programmer to perceive that information unobtrusively as they read the code. A function body that has not been executed at all is shown with a gray background, and functions that have been called repeatedly are labeled with the call count. The colors and call counts update in real time so that the user can watch them respond to the actions they take in their program. A program trace is collected so that clicking on one of those call counts can immediately add entries to a log showing the arguments and return values of every invocation. Theseus organizes the log entries into a call tree that accounts for asynchronous invocations (such as event handlers), allowing programmers to quickly answer many time-consuming reachability questions [8].

In order to test whether these tools would help correct misconceptions more quickly, we ran two studies and deployed Theseus as an extension to the Brackets IDE[1]. Participants in the first lab study performed programming tasks with and without Theseus. Theseus users identified the locations where chains of callbacks broke down more quickly (often

[1] `http://brackets.io`

CHI 2014, April 26–May 1, 2014, Toronto, ON, Canada.

ACM 978-1-4503-2473-1/14/04$15.00.
http://dx.doi.org/10.1145/2556288.2557409

within seconds of opening a file) than users with just a breakpoint debugger, and exhibited behaviors such as arranging their desktop so that they could see their code while interacting with their application. In the second study, professional software developers used Theseus in their day-to-day programming activities. We then interviewed them to see how Theseus fit into their programming workflow.

The contributions of this paper are:

- An open-source debugging interface called Theseus that answers reachability questions in the context of the programmer's source code and exemplifies the always-on design principle
- 2 studies of how Theseus affects programmers' behavior
- An open-source library called Fondue for collecting JavaScript traces in real-time for always-on interfaces

In this paper we will introduce related work, describe the interface and implementation, then discuss the results of our two studies.

RELATED WORK

A live programming interface provides feedback to the programmer after every change about the new program's behavior [20]. Many interface ideas have arisen from live programming research, such as McDirmid's probes and traces interface [12], Swift's live code annotations for temporal recursion [19], and Bret Victor's demonstrations of a programming environment with domain-specific visualizations [21]. Theseus shares aspects with all three of these interfaces, but is designed to work with JavaScript in non-live environments. Block-based programming environments like Scratch and Scheme Bricks highlight code as it is executed, which can help users draw correspondences between the code and program behavior, though that information does not persist, like Theseus's coloring and call counts [15, 5]. Theseus's coloring plays a similar role to continuous testing interfaces, which provide the programmer feedback on their progress by indicating which tests are passing and failing [16].

Reacher [9] answers reachability questions by presenting a compact graph representation of the interactions between several functions. Reacher uses static analysis to generate the graph, whereas Theseus visualizes execution that has actually occurred. Thus, Reacher can answer questions about what *can* happen, and Theseus can answer questions about what the user has just *seen* happen. Theseus's log and Reacher provide complementary views of the same kind of information and it would be fruitful to combine them.

Whyline [7] is a debugging interface that users can ask questions like, "Why is this widget blue?" Whyline answers this question by generating a slice of the program containing the UI events and branches that led to the widget being blue. Since Theseus visualizes the execution of individual functions (which is usually completely invisible), it opens up a world of information about which programmers could ask questions with an interrogative debugger such as Whyline.

The idea of adding edges to the call graph (such as those Theseus adds for asynchronous calls) to aid debugging goes back to ZStep [10], an omniscient step debugger. A ZStep user could step to the point when a given expression was evaluated, to the next time the GUI changed, or to when a particular screen element was drawn. IntelliTrace [14] is similar in that it allows users to index into a program trace by selecting an event, such as a button click or an exception. In addition, some effort has been made to generate JavaScript stack traces that cross event boundaries [17], and more generally across client-server boundaries [13].

Timelapse offers self-contained, fully-replayable traces of entire web pages [1]. Timelapse integrates tightly with WebKit browsers in order to apply low-level algorithms based on virtual machine record/replay. Theseus's instrumentation library, Fondue, is based on source rewriting. The overhead of collecting the trace is much worse than that of Timelapse, but Fondue is flexible and can be adapted to new contexts—such as instrumenting Node.js or creating an instrumenting proxy server—more easily as a result.

INTERFACE DESIGN

Theseus is designed to address three types of challenges that programmers face: 1) cost of information: the inefficiency of querying a debugger about program execution, 2) finding code/behavior correspondence: identifying which code is responsible for a particular program behavior, and 3) understanding asynchronous control flow.

These areas of focus come from research into the types of questions programmers ask while programming [8, 18], primarily the first three categories of questions identified by Sillito et al. (finding initial focus points, building on those points, and understanding a subgraph) and reachability questions over a call graph with asynchronous links.

In this section, we demonstrate how Theseus's always-on visualizations aid the programmer with these challenges by describing two sessions with Theseus.

Scenario: A Network Activity Indicator

In this scenario, Samantha is creating an animated widget to appear during network operations on an HTML page.

A sanity check

Samantha starts by sketching the functions she'll need: a constructor for the widget, and a callback function to instantiate one when the page loads. After writing only the definitions of those functions, Samantha opens the page in a browser.

As shown below, the way her code is displayed immediately changes in two ways: code that has not executed is given a gray background, and the number of times each function is called is displayed in the margin to the left of each function. From these cues, Samantha infers that her syntax was correct, that she registered her document-ready event handler correctly, and that no exception was thrown because none of the call counts are colored red.

```
0 calls   function Activity() {
          }

1 call    $(document).ready(function () {
          });
```

The Brackets IDE will automatically reload the browser after every save, so sanity checks like these are quick to make.

After writing some code to add the activity indicator to the DOM (Document Object Model), she saves the file and again gets immediate feedback that both functions were called and neither threw an exception.

Understanding timing

Some time later, Samantha wants to update the DOM periodically to create the animated effect. Even before adding any code to the function to update the page, she can judge whether the timer is appropriately configured by how quickly the call counts change in the sidebar.

```
1 call     function Activity() {
               var d = $("<div />");
               for (var i = 0; i < 10; i++) {
                   $("<span />").text(".").appendTo(d);
               }
56 calls       setInterval(function () {
               }, 300);
               return d;
           }
```

The call count which currently reads '56' increments by 1 every 300 milliseconds, making it easy to pick out code responsible for the animation.

Verify that the timer clears appropriately

Samantha adds a conditional statement that should cancel the timer when the activity indicator's DOM element is removed from the page. She verifies that it works correctly just by watching the call counts: when the timer stops, the call count for its handler will stop incrementing.

```
1 call     function Activity() [
               var d = $("<div />");
               for (var i = 0; i < 10; i++) {
                   $("<span />").text(".").appendTo(d);
               }
10 calls       var timer = setInterval(function () {
                   d.find("span:last").prependTo(d);
                   if (!$.contains(document, d[0])) {
                       clearInterval(timer);
                   }
               }, 300);
               return d;
           }

1 call     $(document).ready(function () {
               var indicator = Activity();
               $(document.body).append(indicator);
1 call         setTimeout(function () {
                   indicator.remove();
               }, 3000);
           });
```

After 3 seconds, the activity indicator was removed from the page and the timer's call count stopped at 10.

Discussion

Throughout the implementation of the widget, Samantha was able to verify the behavior of her code even before it had any output. The only time Samantha had to look at the web page was to verify its appearance. Samantha never had to interact with the debugger directly. No clicks or keystrokes were made solely for the sake of debugging. This greatly reduced the cost of the information she received, and made it easy to recognize that the code responsible for the timer was behaving as expected.

Retroactive Logging

In this scenario, Samantha is working on a Node.js program to count the total size of all the files in a directory.

She starts with a sanity check. She verifies that she is using `fs.readdir`—the function for listing directory entries—correctly by calling it with an empty callback. When she runs the program, she sees that the callback is called, and by clicking on the call count, the log is populated with the values of the arguments to the function. Convention dictates that the first argument is an object encapsulating an error if there is one (so it being null is a good sign), and expanding the array allows her to see that the files she expects to find are there.

```
1 call     function du(path, callback) {
1 call         fs.readdir(path, function () {
               });
           }

0 calls    du('./test-dir', function (size) {
               console.log('total size', size);
           });
```

Log

('readdir' callback) (du.js:4)	10:55:31.320	arguments[0] = null	arguments[1] = [Array:16] 0 = ".gitignore" 1 = "Gemfile" 2 = "Gemfile.lock" 3 = "README.rdoc" 4 = "Rakefile"

Samantha continues coding, running the program periodically to verify that the call counts make sense and that no exceptions are being thrown. She eventually notices a disparity: the `add` function, which gathers results, is being called fewer times (84) than the function that iterates over directory entries (91).

```
84 calls   var add = function (size) {
             totalSize += size;
             if (++count === totalCount)
               callback(totalSize);
           };
42 calls   fs.readdir(path, function (err, filenames) {
             totalCount = filenames.length;
91 calls     filenames.forEach(function (filename) {
               var childPath = path + '/' + filename;
91 calls       fs.stat(childPath, function (err, stats) {
                 if (stats.isDirectory()) du(childPath, add);
                 else if (stats.isFile()) add(stats.size);
               });
             });
           });
```

She is faced with a difficult reachability question: find calls to the filename iterator callback that do not result in a call to the `add` function—either directly, or asynchronously.

Breakpoints don't work here because she cannot step into the `fs.stat` callback, and anyway there would be 91 instances to step through. Naively adding log statements like `console.log("in iterator")` and `console.log("in add")` wouldn't work because it would be very difficult to find corresponding entries. Her solution is to use Theseus's log.

She clicks the call count next to the file entry iterator callback and the call count next to the `add` function. A log appears that looks like this:

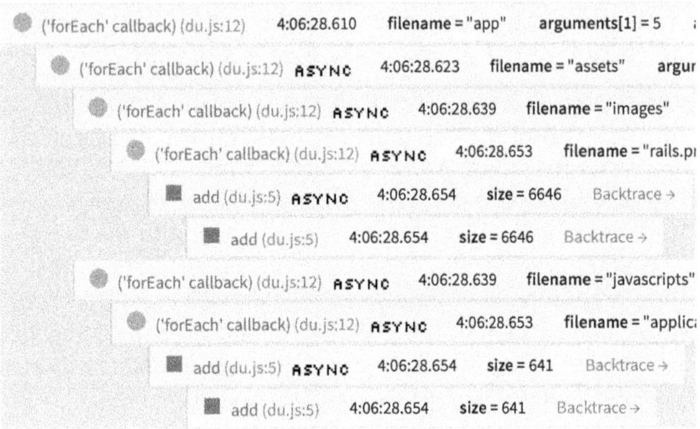

Finding calls to the iterator callback that don't eventually call the `add` function can now be done by skimming the log, using the glyphs' shapes or colors, the names of the functions, or the shapes of the log entries themselves (`add` takes fewer arguments, so its lines are shorter). The desired log entries happen to be clustered here:

They correspond to the empty sub-directories of the `tmp` directory of a Rails project. When she adds a check for empty directories, the `add` function's call count jumps to 140. She clicks the `du` callback function's call count to see the final answer.

Discussion

Samantha answered several more common programming questions (what are the arguments to this function? what are the values of the arguments at run-time? how is control (not) getting from here to here?), including a difficult-to-answer reachability question involving recursive asynchronous function calls.

In addition to answering questions, the always-on features of the interface provide information scent that Samantha uses for sanity checks and identifying a silent bug that would not have been otherwise caught without a test suite [3]. Though the information is always present, the ambient display heuristics of Mankoff, et al. do not indicate any obvious deficiencies of Theseus's always-on features and, as described in the coming evaluation section, programmers find a variety of ways to use that information [11].

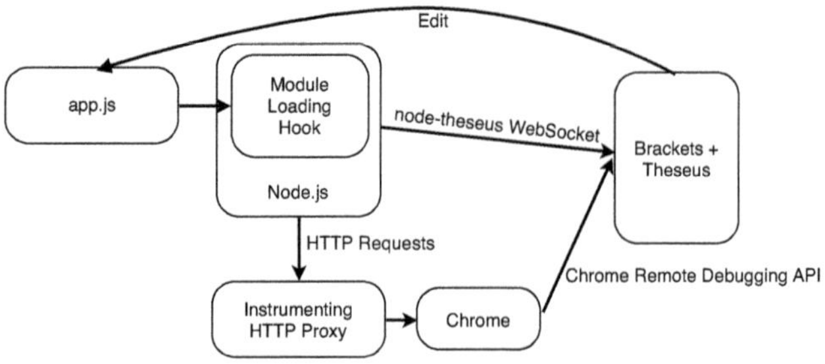

Figure 2. System overview. To instrument Node.js code, node-theseus hooks into the Node.js module loader to pre-process files with Fondue. To instrument code in the browser, HTTP requests are redirected to a proxy server. To read the Node.js trace and execute queries, node-theseus connects to Theseus via a WebSocket. Browser traces are read by connecting to Chrome using Chrome's Remote Debugging Protocol.

IMPLEMENTATION

Theseus consists of an extension for the Brackets editor, two modules that the extension uses to communicate with Chrome and Node.js, the JavaScript instrumentation library called "Fondue". See Figure 2 for a graphical overview. The components are described briefly in this section, and their complete source code is available online[2].

Fondue, the JavaScript instrumentation library

Fondue transforms JavaScript source code to record a trace of its execution to a global trace object. Functions are changed to report the arguments they receive, the values they return, and other information. This information is used to build a call graph as the code executes.

The call graph that Fondue builds also contains edges for asynchronous function calls. For example, in the code below, `foo` schedules `bar` to be executed 1,000 milliseconds later. There is no direct call chain connecting `foo` and `bar`, which is why a programmer could not step from `foo` into `bar` in most JavaScript debuggers.

```
function foo() {
    setTimeout(function bar() {}, 1000);
}
```

Fondue creates edges from an invocation of `foo` to every invocation of `bar` that results from it. To make this work, Fondue alters `bar`'s function definition so that when it is evaluated, the invocation at the top of the stack (in this case, `foo`) is recorded in the closure. That invocation is regarded as the function's asynchronous caller. Then, when no synchronous call chain connects `bar` to another function in the log, asynchronous call chains will be used instead if they exist. An

[2]Theseus: **https://github.com/adobe-research/theseus**
Fondue: **https://github.com/adobe-research/fondue**

'async' flag is displayed in the child entry in the log when this happens.

Mutability

Since objects in JavaScript are mutable, if the trace stored only a reference to function arguments or return values, their values might change by the time they were requested by the debugger. To protect against this, Fondue makes a shallow clone of all objects that it stores. Memory use and accuracy can be balanced by adjusting the depth of the copy operation, which is currently set to 1 for objects and 2 for arrays (so that objects within arrays will be cloned).

Querying the program trace

When Fondue rewrites JavaScript to add the instrumentation hooks, it also prepends the definition of a global object to receive the trace data. That global object contains methods for accessing information such as the locations of function definitions in all loaded files, the number of times that functions have been called, and the log entries corresponding to a given query. The functions are designed to be polled so that the consumer can control the refresh rate, which for Theseus is about 10 Hz. The simple JSON API and polling model make it easy to use Fondue in various contexts, such as those described in the next two sections.

Debugging server-side Node.js code

The user runs their code with the command `node-theseus app.js` instead of `node app.js`. node-theseus installs itself as a pre-processor of all JavaScript code that is loaded into that Node.js process. From then on, all code is instrumented with Fondue before being executed. node-theseus then opens a WebSocket server to listen for a debugging connection from Theseus. The WebSocket server simply applies the deserialized messages as arguments to functions on the trace object, then sends the return value back as JSON.

Debugging client-side code in Chrome

Theseus starts a web server that serves files from the user's project directory, using Fondue to process any JavaScript embedded in HTML or served as `.js` files. When the user opens a web page from that server, Theseus connects to that Chrome window using the Chrome Remote Debugging Protocol, which supports evaluation of arbitrary JavaScript expressions on the page and receiving the return values as JSON[3].

EVALUATION 1: LAB STUDY

We designed the first study to determine whether an effect on programmers' behavior using our interface could be discerned, and to observe how well programmers could use our always-on interface and log tool in a handful of typical programming scenarios. We anticipated that the call counts and reachability code coloring would allow users to find correspondences between code and program behavior quickly, and would allow users to tell at a glance where chains of callbacks were breaking down.

[3] `https://developers.google.com/chrome-developer-tools/docs/debugger-protocol`

Subject	Age	Gender	Prog. Ability	JS Ability	Uses JS
S1	24	M	••●••	••••●	Daily
S2	23	M	••●••	•••●•	Daily
S3	20	M	••●••	••●••	Few days/wk.
S4	29	M	••••●	•••●•	Few days/wk.
S5	24	M	••••●	•••●•	Few days/mo.
S6	21	M	••••●	••●••	Few days/mo.
S7	39	M	••••●	••●••	Not recently

Table 1. Participants of Evaluation 1. Programming Ability and JavaScript Ability are on a 5-point scale, with 1 on the left labeled "Novice", and 5 and the right labeled "Expert".

In this study, we focused on three research questions regarding three types of programming tasks:

RQ1. How would programmers find correspondences between code and program behavior with Theseus?

RQ2. How would programmers use Theseus to find where chains of callbacks break down?

RQ3. Would programmers use Theseus's log to sort through tangled control flow problems?

Methodology

We recruited 7 participants, described in Table 1, to a 90-minute lab study. Subjects were required to have JavaScript programming experience. They were given 5 programming tasks: two 20-minute tasks and three 5-minute tasks. To facilitate within-subjects comparison, each participant was assigned to the Theseus or control condition for each task independently (but always with 2 tasks in one condition and 3 in the other). They performed the tasks on a computer we provided while their screen was recorded and an observer took notes. Subjects completed all of their control tasks first using CDT (Chrome Developer Tools), then all of the Theseus tasks (during which CDT were disallowed). Although Theseus's functionality could not entirely replace CDT, we expected that programmers would use it exclusively if under time pressure and given the choice. Thus, we disallowed CDT in the experimental condition to maximize the available time to observe subjects using Theseus.

We put together five programming tasks which would allow us to test our hypotheses two of which were longer problems with more involved solutions, and three short tasks from which we had hoped to gather timing data:

A. Canvas Painter (20 minutes). Subjects were given the source code for a browser-based drawing site with approximately 2,000 lines of JavaScript spread across 8 files. They were asked to fix a bug where a line-painting operation worked if the user clicked the start and end points, but not if they dragged the mouse.

B. du (20 minutes). Subjects were given the skeleton for a Node.js command-line tool for calculating the total size of all files in a directory and asked to complete it. They were asked to use only the asynchronous filesystem API calls.

C. Laggy AJAX UI (5 minutes). Subjects were given a web page with 25 lines of JavaScript for a web page that down-

Subj.	A	B	C	D	E	Ease of Use	Would Use	Would Recom.
S2	•	•	✓	✓	✓	•••●•	●••••	●••••
S7	•	•	✓	•	✓	••●••	••●••	••••●
S5	•	•	✓	✓	✓	•••●•	••●••	••••●
S1	•	•	✓	✓	•	•••●•	•••●•	•••●•
S6	•	•	✓	•	•	••••●	••••●	•••●•
S3	✓	?	✓	•	✓	•••●•	••••●	••••●
S4	✓	✓	✓	✓	✓	•••●•	••••●	••••●

Table 2. Summary of study results. The cells in the columns labeled A–E contain ✓ if the subject successfully completed that task. The cells are shaded blue if the task was done with Theseus. The correctness of S3's solution for task B was unclear, so that cell contains a question mark. Ease of Use, Would Use, and Would Recommend are on a 5-point scale, with the lowest agreement rating of 1 on the left end and the highest agreement rating of 5 on the right end.

loaded JSON from the server and displayed it in a popup. Subjects were asked to determine why it took so long for the popup to appear. The solution was a delay hard-coded into the server.

D. Faulty Auto-Complete (5 minutes). Subjects were given the code for both the server (80 lines of Node.js) and client (63-line HTML file with embedded JavaScript) of a web page that showed auto-complete search results from an address book. Subjects were asked why the results never displayed. The problem was a logic error on the client while processing the results.

E. Real-Time Chat (5 minutes). Subjects were given the code for the server (33 lines of Node.js) and client (31 lines of JavaScript on a web page) of a real-time chat site. Subjects were asked why messages from one window did not appear in the other. The problem was that the message name on the client and server was mis-matched.

The source code for all tasks is available online[4].

All of the tasks except B required the user to discover correspondences between code and behavior on a web page. Because the code was broken in some way in tasks A, D, and E, users were forced to validate many assumptions they made about the code. Task B was chosen because it exemplified tangled asynchronous control flow. Task E was selected because it involved broken callback chains.

Each subject was given the At the conclusion of the study, we verbally asked five questions regarding their opinion of Theseus.

Results

The results of the study are summarized in Table 2. We found no statistically significant relationships between participants' success rates and the tools they used. A chi-squared test found no relationship between using Theseus and the participant's ability to complete the tasks successfully ($\chi^2(1, N = 34) = .119, p = 0.73$).

RQ1: How might programmers find correspondences between code and program behavior with Theseus?

[4]`https://github.com/alltom/theseus-lab-study-files`

Participants frequently sought code correspondences using Theseus by keeping the call counts and code coloring on the screen as they interacted with the program they were working on. They were pleased with how much information they could absorb this way, an experience S1 described like this: "[Theseus] feels really interactive. [As opposed to breakpoints], it's more of a 'watch and see what happens' thing, which I like." This behavior was not observed during Tasks B or E, likely because Task B involved writing a non-interactive command-line tool and the problem in Task E resided in the logic of a single function. However, during Task A, S1 and S3 used this strategy many times (6 times and 3 times, respectively) during the task. Four of the six participants used this strategy during Tasks C and D. The only participants who did not use this strategy on Tasks C and D were S2 and S4, likely because they spent their first 20 minutes with Theseus working on Task B, the non-interactive command-line tool.

There was some disagreement about whether the call counts were useful for finding correspondences when the user had no idea where to begin. S5 said, "how the call counts changed live when I interacted with the application ... was especially useful for Canvas Painter because it was a lot of source code and I didn't really know where to start." As a result, S5's rating of whether they would use Theseus outside the study depended on the size of the project: rated 4 out of 5 if the code base is large, but only 1 out of 5 if the code base is small. S1 had the opposite opinion, stating, "I felt like it was the least useful when I wasn't sure where the problem was. So in the canvas thing, I didn't know where the issue was, and there's not much of a global scope with Theseus. ... When I didn't know where to start, there was no way to find a global call stack and identify candidate starting points. ... [In short, Theseus is] more useful on a narrow scope, less useful on a global scope."

Participants were interested in the time at which the call counts changed if they were interacting with their application, but also the total number. A changing call count could alert the programmer to surprising or revealing information, such as when S3 watched the call counts during Task A. At one point, S3 thought aloud, "I get 2 mouse up actions [every time I click]. Huh." S5 noted that they had become fixated on a handful of functions while trying to narrow down the location of some strange behavior because "it seems weird to me that I get 2 mouse ups every time I click, while I only get 1 mouse down. ... I'd expect the call counts to be the same for both of them, but they're not." S4 and S6 also used the fact that a function was called 17 times as verification that it was being called once for each file in the directory during Task B, since they had checked that there were 17 files.

The call counts also turned out to be useful for verifying that a code change had had the desired effect. In S4's case, the fact that their change caused a function to be called a different number of times was encouraging. The call count seemed a reliable enough indicator for checking that the new behavior was correct that they performed no further tests.

RQ2: How might programmers use Theseus to find where chains of callbacks break down?

Finding where chains of callbacks break down is an important subtask of finding code correspondences. In JavaScript, functions typically cannot block while waiting for the result of an I/O operation, which forces the programmer to split computations into multiple callback functions, with no guarantee that control will flow successfully from one function to the other.

We noted several points during the study when participants using Theseus were able to quickly, sometimes immediately, locate the cause of a broken call chain, using the code coloring and call counts. In one instance, S4 opened a source file and was immediately drawn to a network event handler that had never been called, becoming suspicious because it looked like a handler that should have fired several times if the page had been working correctly. This was in contrast to S3's experience using a breakpoint debugger, in which they set breakpoints and reloaded the page three times before they finally determined how much of the code had actually executed.

RQ3: Would programmers use Theseus's structured log to sort through tangled control-flow problems?

S4 named the log as Theseus's most useful feature, saying that Theseus is most useful "if you have recursion problems," referring to Task B in which his solution involved recursive asynchronous operations. S3 dubbed the call counts "automatic silent breakpoints." S1 compared the log to typical log output, saying, "[Theseus] is a lot more focused ... with console.logs it's global. ... [With Theseus] you can pick the scope you want to look at on the fly." S4 summarized his opinion of the log like this: "It gives you what you would do if you were really careful and did console.log every function."

S4 would often click the call counts for several functions at once, saying, "all the time, the thing that I wanted to do first is select all the functions and then see the whole tree." Showing the asynchronous call tree for all the functions of interest in the file helped him to locate the points of interest. He cited the lack of a 'Select All Pills [call counts] in File' command as the reason he rated Theseus' ease of use as 4/5 instead of 5/5. S6 felt similarly, at one point saying aloud, "These are the four functions that are interacting," and without pausing, enabling the call counts for those four functions to see how they related.

Discussion

Users seemed to integrate the call counts and code coloring displays into their programming flow as was demonstrated by the widespread use of the side-by-side strategy. We did not see any clear evidence of whether call counts can help find code correspondences in a large, unknown code base, but users used them successfully in several different ways when the search space was small. We learned that the total number of calls, the differences in the total over time, and the relationships between call counts of different functions are all relevant to programmers, and observed situations in which each was used. We noted that participants had to memorize call counts that were separated by time or space, which software could have helped with. Participants also desired insight into activity throughout the project and not just the code that was visible on the screen.

Participants responded favorably to being able to add entries to the log without restarting their program, and used the log's call tree structure to see how several functions interact. The fact that asynchronous edges were used to build the call tree did not play a large role in participant's experiences.

EVALUATION 2: INTERVIEWS

Programmers in the last study seemed to perform about as well with Theseus as they did without, so we decided to look more closely at the behaviors we expected would contribute to their greater success when using Theseus, primarily usage of the increased information scent in the code, from which we expected an increased ability to draw code correspondences. We were also interested in whether programmers would adopt Theseus if they had more time to become better at using it.

Methodology

We recruited a team of nine professional JavaScript programmers who work on a code base of about 80,000 lines to participate in a week-long study. The participants were all male. Because they were professional programmers, the subjects in this study were significantly more experienced than the university students in the previous study. Subjects received $25 as compensation.

We introduced Theseus to the study participants at a group meeting and encouraged them to use Theseus for one week. We asked them to document a programming problem in the next week for which Theseus was or was not useful, and to save a snapshot of the code at that point in time. At the end of the week, we conducted hour-long semi-structured interviews with each participant. Each interview was comprised of two parts: First, we asked the participant to walk through the problem they documented, as well as their solution. Second, we asked partitipants to complete the Canvas Painter programming task from the previous study. Subjects were instructed to use whatever programming tools they were most comfortable with. However, if they did not choose to use Theseus on their own, we asked them near the end to continue working with Theseus instead of their preferred tool.

In this study, we evaluated two hypotheses about how always-on visualizations might aid programmers in debugging tasks:

H1. People will notice errors or oddities for investigation.

H2. People will locate the code responsible for a particular behavior more accurately/confidently.

Additionally, we evaluated three hypotheses regarding the overall perception of always-on displays:

H3. People will verify code behavior by running it, to take advantage of always-on displays that display runtime information.

H4. People will feel like they waste less time interacting with debugging tools with always-on displays active.

H5. People will want more always-on displays.

Theseus Use Pre-Interview (self-reported)	Participants
<15 minutes	S23, S26
<1.5 hours	S22, S25, S27
>3 hours	S20, S21, S24, S28

Table 3. Each subject's self-reported time spent using Theseus before the interview.

Finally, we were interested in gaining a qualitative understanding of *how* always-on displays fit into a programmer's workflow, namely 1.) the down-sides that programmers found, such as distraction and information overload, and 2.) the situations when they were found to be appropriate, helpful, or preferred.

A prompted think-aloud protocol was used, with the interviewer's prompts guided by the hypotheses. That is, when a subject seemed to be performing a relevant act, such as reading code, the interviewer would elicit the participant's justification for his current actions. We made a screen and audio recording of each interview. The audio was transcribed by one researcher. Then, the transcripts were coded for relevance to the above hypotheses by five researchers (one of whom was the interviewer).

The observer's notes from the interviews were broken into 1,611 fragments of about one sentence each. The fragments were loaded into Frenzy [2], a crowd work tool that the coders used to tag each fragment with the research questions to which it was relevant (if any). Each coder voted those tags up or down in the case that the fragment had already been categorized. The results sections were written by summarizing those categorized piles. Since coders did not work independently, inter-rater reliability was not measured.

Results

Subjects spent varying amounts of time using Theseus during the week between its introduction and their interview. The times are summarized in Table 3. The evidence related to each of the hypotheses is presented under each of the headings below.

H1. People will notice errors or oddities for investigation

Code coloring affected the reading process of the programmers. S24 was drawn to a particular section of unexecuted code and read it to figure out whether it should have executed, according to how he thought the code worked. S25 skipped reading portions of a file, saying, "Okay, nothing called in this." However, his attention was drawn to code that had been called even if it was not related to the code he was attempting to locate. S20 ignored the coloring and read code that Theseus marked as unexecuted to understand the behavior of the page, despite knowing that unexecuted code could not have had any effect.

During an explanation, S21 described how a certain situation could not occur because a certain function wasn't being called. He checked the source and discovered that actually the function *was* being called, which led to further exploration and a revised explanation.

Call counts were effective in revealing oddities or confirming correct behavior. S20, S21, S24, and S25 encountered instances where the absolute number of calls to a function drew their attention to a problem or an aspect of the code that they did not yet understand. S20 noticed a call count while forming a hypothesis about the code and used it to inform his thinking, saying, "Hmm, this is only called one time ... does that mean the ... clearing the drawing is not another drawing ..." S21 had his attention drawn to call counts that were surprisingly high, which allowed him to make a guess at what the code was for, saying "This was called a bunch, 319 times... maybe they're simulating dragging." S24 used Theseus on a project that loaded 100 images asynchronously and noted that "`img.onload` is stopping at 100. That's good, that's perfect."

The differences between call counts also proved important. S21 noticed that a callback was occurring twice every time he performed an action on the page, instead of only once as he had expected. Both S24 and S27 found bugs in their respective applications when they noticed that a pair of functions that should have been called the same number of times actually had different call counts. In S24's case it was the start and end of a callback chain, and for S27 it was a pair of mouse-down and mouse-up handlers.

The colors of the call counts were occasionally useful as well. S28 noticed the red coloring of a call count that indicated an exception in the function he was reading, and stated that he had not noticed the exception when it was printed to the console.

H2. People will locate the code responsible for a particular behavior more accurately & confidently

Subjects used total call counts, changes in call counts, and lack of calls to make informed guesses about what code was for. S21, S23, and S24 used the side-by-side technique to verify that they understood what the code they were looking at was responsible for the behavior they thought it was. S21 was satisfied with weak evidence in one case, saying, "So this was called 7 times. ... Seems about right. I didn't draw that many things." In the process of watching call counts change for one function, S21 noticed that the mouse-up handler nearby was being called more times than expected. S23 used the *lack* of changes to a call count to determine that they were incorrect about which handler was used for a particular action. When reading a screen full of potential handlers for an event, S20 used the code coloring to decide which was the one he was looking for—it was the only one that wasn't gray.

S26 adapted a trace comparison strategy he was used to using with log statements to the information available in Theseus. S26 wished to compare what happened in the code when he triggered the bug with what happened when he performed the same task in a way that did not trigger the bug. To do so, he reset the call counts by reloading, performed the task in one way, observed the counts, then repeated those steps with the alternate means. The process was tedious, but the difference in the call counts gave him an idea of where to look. S20 and S25 found that Theseus would have been more helpful with locating responsible code if it visualized activity at the project level.

H3: People will verify code behavior by running it instead of reading and guessing

Subjects did not activate a debugger or Theseus until they got stuck. Upon starting the Canvas Painter task, all subjects began by skimming the source code without the aid of any always-on displays. The task was to change the way the page reacted to mouse events (specifically the end of a drag), so subjects gravitated toward mouse-related code. S21 started by searching for 'click' but the rest just skimmed files that had suggestive names for code that looked like it contained mouse event handlers. 4 of the 9 subjects said something like "familiarize myself with where all the code is" for this step (S26's words). S22 went so far as to say, "I try to stay out of the debugger as much as possible because it's a time suck."

Three subjects eventually ran the code as part of the initial code location step. S23 used Chrome's event breakpoints to have the step debugger stop every time JavaScript code ran in response to a click event. S24 and S27 ran Theseus to tell which of several mouse handlers was the one they should be interested in. S27 explained that if he didn't have Theseus, he would probably spend more time just reading the code, since breakpoints interrupt streams of mouse events, and that adding log statements is tedious.

H4. People will feel they waste less time with always-on tools

The interviews revealed relatively little evidence about perceived or actual time-wasting. S20 observed that Theseus's ability to associate each callback with the invocation that created it was very hard to accomplish with other debuggers, and perceived it as a time-saver. S23 felt that the "biggest JavaScript debugging time suck" was determining why an event handler wasn't being called, and Theseus answered that question more efficiently than inserting log statements by hand. However, S23 and S25 had to wait for Theseus to render a large group of log statements once each.

H5. People will want more live displays

4 subjects (S22, S25, S27, and S28) expressed interest in more always-on displays, usually as extensions to Theseus's current interface. S22 wished for Theseus to show the time spent in every function, S22 and S25 wanted the file-level counterpart to the function-level call counts, and S27 and S28 wanted information about the state changes on individual lines.

Subjects S20 and S21 preferred step debuggers to Theseus. S20 felt strongly that breakpoint debuggers were more natural. S21 switched away from Theseus to Chrome's step debugger, saying "I can't quite see ... how that influences which conditional we're going down," and that the "[step debugger] mental model is easier to understand." S21 pointed out that with a step debugger, he could also watch the web page update as he stepped.

Downsides of always-on displays

Two subjects experienced information overload when interacting with the log. S23 said that showing all of the arguments and return values simultaneously made him unable to parse any of it. S25 simply noted that there was a lot of information which he did not need. On the other hand, S22 appreciated that the log showed a lot of data at once.

When do programmers find Theseus to be helpful?

Breakpoints interfered with reproducing bugs related to mouse gestures, but Theseus did not. S23 and S24 chose to use Theseus instead of breakpoints because of the way breakpoints would affect the behavior of the program. In S23's case, he feared that interacting with the step debugger would interfere with reproducing bugs on the web page with the mouse. S24's code involved downloading many files in parallel and the code that executed in the meantime, so stopping at breakpoints would affect the order that events occurred. S23 said that they had considered adding log statements as well, but that it was more tedious than using Theseus's log.

S20 chose to use breakpoints at first, but eventually switched to Theseus. S20 started by setting a breakpoint, then running the code but failing to hit the breakpoint. He repeated those steps 2 more times before saying, "I can see that this kind of thing might be a lot easier to see ... with Theseus." He activated Theseus and was able to see which functions were actually used during his mouse gesture.

However, S21 preferred using breakpoints to using Theseus. S21 thought that omniscience was the useful aspect of Theseus, saying that if his browser's breakpoint debugger were omniscient, he would use that instead of Theseus's log. He pointed out that breakpoints allowed him to view the entire state (including the contents of the web page) after every step.

S27 did not use Theseus because there would have been "a bunch of calls all over the place" and he feared that he wouldn't be able to see which were related to his bug. S28 discovered that Theseus introduced timing delays in his multi-threaded animations which changed the characteristic of the bug he was investigating.

Discussion

The programmers in this study seemed to think of Theseus as a debugger and not a tool to be left running all the time. Their feedback suggested that the overhead of instrumenting their entire project was too great, which may have been what kept in the as-needed category of tool. This would explain why only two programmers used Theseus to verify their initial focus points were correct.

Again, we observed users using live-updating call counts in the same variety of ways as in the lab study, although we also saw evidence that presentation may need to be improved to reduce errors such as S20 reading unexecuted code to find the source of a bug. Being able to watch call counts rise as they interacted was enough to know whether the code they were looking at corresponded to the behavior they thought it did, and to get a sense of how often the code was executed, both of which breakpoints turned out to be poorly suited for. However, it seems that breakpoints are still needed when the programmer wants to walk through the code, or when they want to inspect a lot of program state at a time.

S21's experience suggests that visualized data which merely supports a certain conclusion without proving it outright can be useful for making snap judgements without distracting programmers from their current task.

Four programmers wanted more visualizations with a similar presentation to the visualizations in Theseus, although not necessarily for them to be always on. The types of information desired were varied enough to suggest always-on display modes depending on the task. Users found problems such as the overhead of the instrumentation and information overload in the log, but call counts were used in a variety of ways, and the call counts and coloring turned out to be a good lightweight alternative to breakpoints for finding code correspondences and having "just enough" evidence to support a conclusion. The evaluations have revealed several avenues for improvement on a style of debugging interface whose time has come.

OPEN-SOURCE DEPLOYMENT

Theseus has been available as an extension for the Adobe Brackets editor since February 11, 2013. It can be installed from within Brackets, and the source code is available[5]. As of December 2013, Theseus has been installed approximately 2,500 times (users may choose not to send usage data) and 512 of those users have actively used Theseus on at least 2 separate days. 46 bug reports and feature requests have been filed.

CONCLUSION

This paper presented Theseus, an IDE extension that visualizes run-time behavior within a JavaScript code editor. Theseus visualizes the program's run-time state using code coloring for unreached functions, call counts for executed functions, and automatic retroactive logging of parameters and return values. A lab user study and a field deployment found that programmers enjoyed the availability of reachability coloring and call counts, and adopted new problem-solving strategies to take advantage of their strengths.

ACKNOWLEDGMENTS

This work was supported in part by Adobe, and by the National Science Foundation under award number SOCS-1111124. Any opinions, findings, conclusions, or recommendations in this thesis are the authors', and they do not necessarily reflect the views of the sponsors.

REFERENCES

1. Burg, B., Bailey, R., Ko, A. J., and Ernst, M. D. Interactive record/replay for web application debugging. UIST '13, ACM (New York, NY, USA, 2013), 473–484.
2. Chilton, L., Kim, J., André, P., Cordeiro, F., Landay, J., Weld, D., Dow, S., Miller, R., and Zhang, H. Frenzy: Collaborative Data Organization for Creating Conference Sessions. SIGCHI '14 (2014).
3. Fleming, S. D., Scaffidi, C., Piorkowski, D., Burnett, M., Bellamy, R., Lawrance, J., and Kwan, I. An information foraging theory perspective on tools for debugging, refactoring, and reuse tasks. *TOSEM 22*, 2 (2013), 14.
4. Gould, J. D. Some psychological evidence on how people debug computer programs. *International Journal of Man-Machine Studies 7*, 2 (1975), 151–182.
5. Griffiths, D. Scheme Bricks, Sept. 2013. `http://www.pawfal.org/dave/index.cgi?Projects/Scheme%20Bricks`.
6. Ko, A., Myers, B., and Aung, H. Six learning barriers in end-user programming systems. In *VL/HCC* (2004), 199–206.
7. Ko, A. J., and Myers, B. A. Designing the Whyline: A Debugging Interface for Asking Questions about Program Behavior. In *SIGCHI '04*, vol. 6 (2004).
8. LaToza, T. D., and Myers, B. A. Developers Ask Reachability Questions. In *Proc. ICSE 2010*, vol. 1, ACM Press (New York, New York, USA, 2010).
9. LaToza, T. D., and Myers, B. A. Visualizing Call Graphs. In *VL/HCC 2011* (Sept. 2011).
10. Lieberman, H., and Fry, C. Bridging the Gulf Between Code and Behavior in Programming. CHI '95 (1995).
11. Mankoff, J., Dey, A. K., Hsieh, G., Kientz, J., Lederer, S., and Ames, M. Heuristic evaluation of ambient displays. CHI '03, ACM (2003), 169–176.
12. McDirmid, S. Usable live programming. *SIGPLAN* (2013).
13. Meier, M. S., Miller, K. L., and Pazel, D. P. Experiences with Building Distributed Debuggers. In *Proc. SIGMETRICS 1996* (1996).
14. Microsoft. Debug Your App by Recording Code Execution with IntelliTrace. `http://msdn.microsoft.com/en-us/library/vstudio/dd264915.aspx`.
15. Resnick, M., Maloney, J., Monroy-Hernández, A., Rusk, N., Eastmond, E., Brennan, K., Millner, A., Rosenbaum, E., Silver, J., Silverman, B., et al. Scratch: programming for all. *Communications of the ACM 52*, 11 (2009), 60–67.
16. Saff, D., and Ernst, M. Reducing wasted development time via continuous testing. In *ISSRE '03* (2003), 281–292.
17. Schrock, E. Debugging AJAX in Production. *ACM Queue* (2009).
18. Sillito, J., Murphy, G. C., and De Volder, K. Questions programmers ask during software evolution tasks. SIGSOFT '06/FSE-14, ACM (2006), 23–34.
19. Swift, B., Sorensen, A., Gardner, H., and Hosking, J. Visual code annotations for cyberphysical programming. In *1st International Workshop on Live Programming (LIVE)* (2013).
20. Tanimoto, S. Towards a theory of progressive operators for live visual programming environments. In *IEEE Workshop on Visual Languages* (1990), 80–85.
21. Victor, B. Learnable Programming. `http://worrydream.com/#!/LearnableProgramming`, 2012.

[5]Theseus: `https://github.com/adobe-research/theseus`
Fondue: `https://github.com/adobe-research/fondue`

Emergent, Crowd-scale Programming Practice in the IDE

Ethan Fast[1], Daniel Steffee[1], Lucy Wang[1], Joel Brandt[2], Michael S. Bernstein[1]
Stanford University[1], Adobe Research[2]
{ethan.fast, dsteffee, lucywang, msb}@cs.stanford.edu, joel.brandt@adobe.com

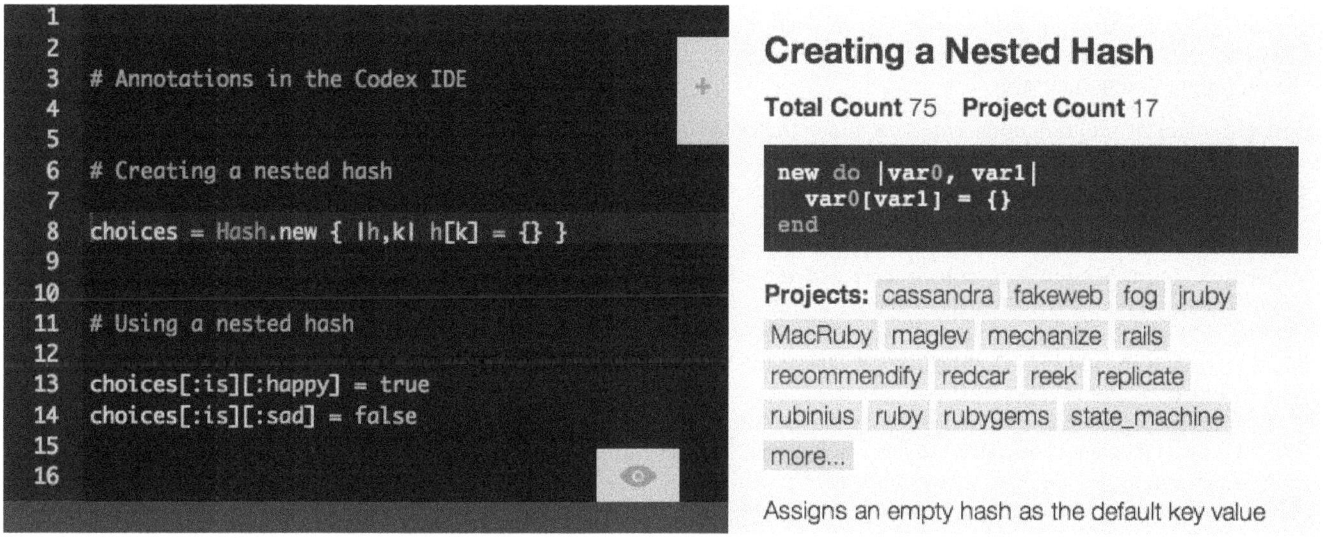

Figure 1. Codex draws on millions of lines of open source code to create software engineering interfaces that integrate emergent programming practice. Here, Codex's pattern annotation calls out popular idioms that appear in the user's code.

ABSTRACT
While emergent behaviors are uncodified across many domains such as programming and writing, interfaces need explicit rules to support users. We hypothesize that by codifying emergent programming behavior, software engineering interfaces can support a far broader set of developer needs. To explore this idea, we built Codex, a knowledge base that records common practice for the Ruby programming language by indexing over three million lines of popular code. Codex enables new data-driven interfaces for programming systems: *statistical linting*, identifying code that is unlikely to occur in practice and may constitute a bug; *pattern annotation*, automatically discovering common programming idioms and annotating them with metadata using expert crowdsourcing; and *library generation*, constructing a utility package that encapsulates and reflects emergent software practice. We evaluate these applications to find Codex captures a broad swatch of programming practice, statistical linting detects problematic code snippets, and pattern annotation discovers nontrivial idioms such as basic HTTP authentication and database migration templates. Our work suggests that operationalizing practice-driven knowledge in structured domains such as programming can enable a new class of user interfaces.

CHI 2014, April 26–May 1, 2014, Toronto, Ontario, Canada.

http://dx.doi.org/10.1145/2556288.2556998

Author Keywords
Programming tools, data mining

ACM Classification Keywords
H.5.2. Information Interfaces and Presentation: Graphical user interfaces

INTRODUCTION
The way people adapt to a system can be just as informative as its original design. In software engineering systems, user practice and designer intention differ across several levels of abstraction: programmers use library APIs in undocumented and unexpected ways [26], language idioms evolve over time [34], and programmers repurpose source code for new tasks [3, 9]. Norms emerge for programming systems that aren't codified in documentation or on the web. What is the best idiom or library to use for a task? Does my code follow common practice? How is a language being used *today*?

We can examine the ecosystem of open source software to find answers to these practice-driven questions. The informal rules and conventions of programming languages and libraries are implicitly present in open source projects, which, when analyzed, illuminate the ways people code that are too complex or uncommon to appear in official forms of documentation. We can operationalize this knowledge to support everyday programming practice.

Here we present *Codex*, a knowledge base that models practice-driven knowledge for the Ruby programming language. Codex provides a living corpus of how programmers write code, informed by popular open source Ruby projects. The system normalizes program abstract syntax trees (ASTs) to collapse similar idioms and identifiers, filters these idioms and annotates them using paid crowd experts, and then allows applications to query its database in support of new data-driven programming interfaces.

In the domain of programming, emergent practice develops at both the *high-level* of programming idioms, for example code that initializes a nested hash, and at the *low-level* of code syntax, for example blocks that return the result of an addition operation. Codex seeks to capture both higher-level patterns of reuseable program components and lower-level combinations and chains of more basic programming units. Through the *pattern finding* module, Codex identifies commonly reused Ruby idioms. This module uses typicality analysis to identify idioms (e.g., `Hash.new { |h,k| h[k] = {} }`, the most accepted way to initialize a nested hash table). Expert crowds then attach metadata to these idioms, such as a title, description, and measure of recommended usefulness. Alternatively, using the *statistical analysis* module, Codex can compute the frequencies of AST node combinations (e.g., the number of times one function has been chained with another), describing the uniqueness of syntatical patterns.

We present three applications that demonstrate how Codex supports programming practice and software engineering interfaces. First, *pattern annotation* automatically annotates Ruby idioms inside the IDE and presents these annotated snippets through a search interface. Second, *statistical linting* identifies problematic syntax by checking code features (e.g., the kinds of AST nodes used as function signatures or return values) against a large database of trusted and idiomatic snippets; more generally, these statistics give programmers a tool to quantify the uniqueness of their code. Finally, *library generation* pulls particularly common Ruby idioms into a new standard library — authored not by individual developers but by emergent software practice — helping programmers avoid the redefinition of common program components.

This paper makes the following primary contributions:

- Codex: a knowledge base that codifies how developers use programming languages in practice.
- An algorithm for finding common idioms using typicality analysis and expert crowdsourcing; an interface for calling out the idioms and metadata in the Codex IDE.
- *CodexLint*: an approach for *unlikely code* detection that identifies potentially undesirable syntax; an interface for displaying these warnings in the Codex IDE.
- *CodexLib*: An open source Ruby Gem that encapsulates common code patterns into a new library.

Codex enables new software engineering applications that are supported by large-scale programming behavior rather than sets of special-cased rules. While other projects have crowdsourced documentation for existing library functions [28, 8], mined code to enable query-based searching for patterns or examples [26, 33], or embedded example-finding tools into an IDE [5, 7, 15, 29], Codex augments traditional data mining techniques with crowds, presenting a broad data-driven window into programming convention. We demonstrate how these kinds of emergent behavior can inform new design opportunities for user interfaces.

RELATED WORK

Codex draws on techniques from software repository mining to extract patterns from a large body of open source code. Other researchers have mined code for software patterns and redundant code using code normalization or typicality [26, 3, 9, 20, 28, 8]. However, much of this research emphasizes the discovery of known design patterns and is oriented towards applications such as refactoring of duplicate code, while Codex discovers new patterns from the ground up. Further, Codex combines typicality analysis with expert crowdsourcing to build its database — an approach independant of any particular code normalization scheme.

Databases can also systematize knowledge about open source code. However, these databases are usually designed to enable specific forms of code search [35, 33], example-finding [22, 16, 29], or autocompletion [21], either query based or automatic. While tools designed for specific use cases may be highly optimized for their tasks, Codex enables a broader set of applications, including pattern annotation and detecting problematic code through statistical linting.

One of Codex's core applications is to help programmers avoid bugs. Much work has focused on tools for static and dynamic analysis [2, 10]. Other work has focused on helping users debug their programs through program analysis or crowdsourced aggregation of user activities [18, 1, 14, 24, 28]. Codex does not explicitly try to discover bugs in programs; rather, it notifies users when code violates convention. This is a subtle but important difference: code may be syntactically correct but semantically unusual and error-prone.

Codex takes inspiration from prior research on code example finding and reuse. Some of these tools rely on official forms of documentation [5] and others focus on real code from the web [29, 19, 32]. Codex generalizes this work — it covers a broader set of examples than manually curated datasets and can determine when an example is a one-off and when it represents more general practice. Codex also enables a more powerful search over examples through AST analysis, benefits from the human-powered filtering and annotation, and makes possible many applications besides example-finding.

Researchers have also addressed how programmers make use of example code, whether the code is copy-pasted [23] or foraged from documentation or online examples [7, 6, 15]. By formalizing embedded software practice, Codex is able to support programmers through a larger space of examples and lower-level conventions. Many of these idioms and code snippets may not have been formally discussed on the web.

Codex draws on insights from data-driven interfaces in non-programming domains. Users can gain much through querying and exploration. For example, Webzeigeist allows designers to query a large corpus of rendered web sites [25]. Crowd data also allows interactive systems to transform a partial sketch of the users intent into a complete state, for example matching a sung melody against a large database of music to produce an automatic backup band [31]. Algorithms can then identify patterns in crowd behavior and percolate them up to the interface, for example answering a wide variety of user queries, demonstrating how a given feature is used in practice [4, 11, 27], or predicting likely actions from past history [17]. Codex demonstrates that the more structured nature of programming languages provides a platform for more powerful interactive support such as error finding.

CODEX APPLICATIONS

To ground the opportunities that Codex creates, we begin by introducing three software engineering applications that draw on the Codex data model and high or low level code analysis. In general, Codex enables interfaces and applications that are supported by emergent programming behavior rather than a set of special-cased rules. Following this section, we discuss the techniques behind these applications in more detail.

Statistical Linting

Sometimes, developers program badly: they write code that performs in unexpected ways or violates language conventions. Poorly written code causes significant damage to software projects; bugs tax programmers' time and energy, and code written in an abstruse or non-idiomatic style is more difficult to maintain [30, 13]. Given the complexity of programming languages, rule-based linters can't catch much of this unusual or non-idiomatic code.

Codex operates on the insight that poorly written code is often syntactically different from well written code. For example, functions might be used in the wrong combination or order. So if we collect and index a set of code that is representative of best practices, bad code will often diverge syntactically from the code in this index. Not all syntactically divergent code is bad — the space of well written Ruby programs is very large — but by applying high-precision detectors to a few general AST patterns, Codex can detect syntactically divergent code that is likely to be problematic.

Function Chaining and Composition

Programmers frequently chain and compose functions and operators to create complex algorithmic pipelines, but chaining the wrong kinds of functions together will often cause subtle program bugs. For example, bugs might arise from functions chained in the wrong order, or variables added or assigned in ways they should not be. Codex helps programmers find potential bugs in function chains by identifying unlikely combinations of functions.

For example, if Ava is querying a database that has been normalized to lower case, she needs to convert a string held by the variable `name` to lower case form. She intends to assign the lower case variant of `name` to the variable `lower_case_name` and use this new varible in her query. The Ruby methods `downcase` and `downcase!` will both convert a string variable to lower case, and without thinking too deeply, Ava codes: `lower_case_name = name.downcase!`

Unfortunately, Ava has forgotten that `downcase!` has a side-effect: it changes the variable `name` in place and returns itself. The function she ought to have used is `downcase`, which returns a new lower cased string and does not change `name`. When Ava later uses `name` elsewhere in her program, it doesn't hold the value she expects.

Codex indicates that the line of code is statistically unlikely: `downcase!` is not commonly chained with an assignment statement (although such code is not technically incorrect). Codex notifies Ava that it has observed `downcase!` 57 times, and the abstraction `var = var.`*`any_method`* more than 100,000 times, but it has only encountered one variant of Ava's combined snippet. However, Codex has encountered variants of the correct snippet, `lower_case_name = name.downcase`, more than 200 times.

Block Return Value Analysis

Ruby programmers often manipulate data by passing blocks (lambda-like closures) to functions, but using the wrong kind of block, or passing a block to the wrong kind of function, can process data in unintended ways. Codex identifies unlikey pairings of functions and block return values.

For example, as part of data analysis pipeline, Ash wants to raise every number in a list to the power of 2. He tries to do this with a map block, but encounters a problem (he uses the operator `^` in place of `**`) and adds a `puts` (print) statement inside the map block to help him debug his mistake:

```
new_nums =
    nums.map do |x|
        x^2
        puts x
    end
```

In doing so, Ash has introduced another bug. The `puts` method returns `nil`, which means that `new_nums` will be a list of `nil`. When Ash runs his code, this new error complicates his old problem.

Codex returns a warning: most programmers do not return the method `puts` from a map block. We can anchor this concern in data: Codex has observed `map` blocks 4297 times and `puts` statements 5335 times, but it has never observed `puts` as the last line (an implicit return) of a `map` block. However, Codex observes that `puts` statements are a common return value of blocks that are predominantly used for control flow, like `each` (observed 272 times), so it produces a warning.

Function Type Analysis

Passing the wrong kinds of arguments to a function, or passing positional arguments in the wrong order, can lead to many subtle bugs — especially in duck typed languages like Ruby. However, by analyzing the kinds of AST nodes passed as positional arguments to functions, Codex can warn users about unlikely function signatures.

Figure 2. The Codex IDE calls out a snippet of unlikely code by a yellow highlight in its gutter. Warning text appears in the footer.

For example, Severian wants to divide a few hundred datapoints into ten buckets, depending on their id number. To do this, he needs to initialize an array of ten elements, where each element is a hash. Severian codes: `Array.new({},10)`.

Unfortunately, Severian doesn't often initialize arrays with specific lengths and values, and he has reversed the arguments of `Array.new`. When he executes his code, it fails with the error, "TypeError: can't convert Hash into Integer."

Codex could have told Severian that programmers don't often pass `Array.new` an argument list composed of a `string` and `integer`. While Codex observes `Array.new` 674 times, it has never observed `Array.new` with string and integer arguments. However, Codex observes the correct parameterization `Array.new(integer,string)` several times, which is the correct version of Severian's code.

Variable Name Analysis

Good variable names provide important signals about how a variable should be treated and lead to more readable code [30]. Likewise, badly named variables can lead to poor code readability and downstream program errors. By analyzing variable name associations with primitive values (e.g., Strings, Integers, Hashes), Codex can warn programmers about violations of naming conventions.

For example, Azazel is writing a complicated function to process a large dataset from a database call. He is collecting the data in an an `Array` called `array`. However, he later realizes that a hash would be simpler to manage and changes the variable type. In a rush, Azazel changes the variable's type but doesn't bother to change its name: `array = {}`. Later, Ash, who is Azazel's coworker, is looking elsewhere in the function and sees a line `array.keys { ... }`. He wonders, does an `Array` have `keys`? He hadn't thought so.

Instead, Codex notifies Azazel that most programmers do not initialize a variable named `array` with a `Hash` value. While Codex observes initializations to variables named `array` 116 times and variables assigned a `Hash` value many thousands of times, it has never observed the two together. Instead, Codex observes `array = []` 46 times.

It is not wrong to assign a `Hash` value to a variable named `array`, but code that does so is likely less readable and might lead to downstream errors. Codex can determine that such an assignment violates Ruby convention. Likewise, Codex would notice integers stored in `str` or common loop count iterators like `i` being initialized with other variable types.

The Codex IDE integrates CodexLint (Figure 2), allowing users to call up statistics about any line of code in the editor. The linter also runs behind the scenes during development, highlighting any unlikely code with a yellow overlay on the window gutter. When the cursor moves over a marked line, a small message appears on the lower bar of the Codex window, e.g., "We have seen the function split 30,000 times and strip 20,000 times, but we've never seen them chained together."

Pattern Annotation

Many valuable programming idioms are not collected in documentation or on the web. While users can access standard library documentation for core abstractions (e.g., for Ruby, **`http://ruby-doc.org/`**), and libraries often ship with similar kinds of documentation provided by their maintainers, the common idioms by which basic functions may be combined and extended often remain uncodified. Instead, these idioms live in the minds of programmers and — sometimes — on the message boards of communities and forums. Novice users of languages and libraries must "mind the gap" present in official forms of documentation.

Codex fills in gaps of practice-driven knowledge by detecting common idioms as it indexes code and sending them out to be filtered and annotated by a crowd of human experts. Codex finds these idioms by selecting snippets in its database with query parameters such as commonality and complexity. These selected snippets (e.g., that appear in a large number of unique projects and are sufficiently nontrivial) are primed for annotation and human filtering. For instance, over the course of its indexing, Codex identifies `inject { |x,y| x + y }` as a common snippet, occurring 15 times across 4 projects.

Next, Codex sends these snippets — strings of Ruby code, along with examples of them in use — to a Ruby expert on oDesk, a paid expert crowdsourcing platform. The worker annotates the snippet with a title (e.g., "sum all the elements in a list"), a description, and a vote of how useful the snippet would be for an everyday Ruby programmer. Codex stores these annotations in its index along with the original source snippet, making previously implicit knowledge explicit. Eventually, we envision a community of Ruby programmers that annotates snippets of interest.

The Codex IDE uses this annotated snippet information to provide higher-level interpretability to code. The annotations appear whenever a programmer opens a file containing the idiom. Users benefit from annotated code under many different scenarios: perhaps using code scavenged from a web tutorial;

Example Codex Annotated Snippets

HTTP Basic Auth

```
if var0.user
    var1.basic_auth(var0.user, var0.password)
end
```

Sets the basic-auth parameters (username and password) before making an HTTP request, perhaps using Net::HTTP [. . .]

Popping Options Hash from Arguments

```
if Hash === var0.last
    var0.pop
else
    {}
end
```

Pops the last element from the list 'var0' if it is a Hash. Gives an empty hash if the last element is not a Hash [. . .]

Raise StandardError

```
raise(StandardError.new("str0"))
```

Raise a StandardError exception using "str0" as exception message [. . .]

Configure action_controller to disable caching

```
config.action_controller.perform_caching=(false)
```

This will set a global configuration related to caching in action_controller to false [. . .]

Create a migration template

```
record do |var0|
  var0.migration_template("str0", "str1")
end
```

Create a migration template using "str0" as the source and "str1" as destination. Will create a database-migration [. . .]

Table 1. Codex identifies common programming snippets automatically, then feeds them to crowdsourced expert programmers for metadata such as the bolded title and descriptive text.

opening an unfamiliar file passed on by a collaborator; revisiting a segment of copy/pasted code; or trying to recall the use of an idiosyncratic library function.

Consider one such user, Morwenna, who is collaborating with a colleague on a Ruby on Rails application. Morwenna hasn't had much experience with Rails, so she begins navigating the many files of her colleague's code in an attempt to build familiarity with the framework. While visiting *config/application.rb*, Morwenna comes across the snippet `config.action_controller.perform_caching = false` and wonders what this means. Codex indicates the line has an annotation, so she asks to see it. The annotation reads, "Turns off default Rails caching."

The Codex IDE calls out and displays any available and relevant annotations (Figure 1). When the cursor moves over a line where annotations are avaiable, a user can call them forward into the sidebar window.

We present examples of these annotated snippets in Table 1. In general, Codex's annotation system uncovers higher-level connections between more basic program components. For instance, human workers can infer the relation of a snippet to some outside library, providing context that isn't explicitly present (e.g., `Net:HTTP` or Ruby on Rails). Similarly, Codex allows for the documentation of higher-level idioms,

Function	**Description**
`Array#sort_by_index(idx)`	Sort an array by the value at `idx`
`Array#convert_join(str)`	Converts each array element to a string then joins them all on `str`
`Array#upto_size`	Create a range, same size as the array
`String#capital_tokens(str)`	Capitalize all tokens in a string
`Hash.nested`	Create a hash with default value {}
`Hash#get(key)`	Retrieve based on :key or "key"
`File#try_close`	Close a file if it's open

Table 2. A sample of functions from CodexLib, detected in emergent programming practice and encapulated into a new standard library.

where programmers can find each component in documention but not the snippet itself, like the combination of `raise` and `StandardError.new`.

Querying for Understanding

In addition to the automatic idiom detection provided by the *pattern finding* module, users can query Codex directly to better understand community practices around a line or block of code. Queryable parameters include the type of AST node (e.g., a block, conditional, or function call), the body string of the normalized code associated with a node, the body string of original code, the amount of information contained in an AST node (i.e., a measure of code complexity), and the frequency of a node's occurrence across files and projects.

For instance, from a library-driven standpoint, suppose that programmers want to know more about how people use the `Net::HTTP` class. They can query for all blocks that contain `Net::HTTP.new`, sorting on the ones that occur most often. By the diversity of this result set, programmers gain a sense of the kinds of context in which `Net::HTTP` is used — even more so, if any of the results have been annotated by Codex's crowdsourcing engine. This is a more query-driven approach to example-driven development [5, 28].

Queries also have applications in other more IDE-specific components like auto-complete, where the IDE might attempt to find the most common completion for a snippet of code, given additional program context. For example, with the line `Hash.new` and an open block, Codex suggests the completion block `{ |h,k| h[k] = [] }`, which initializes the default value of a `hash` to a new empty `Array`.

Codex's user query system enables a broad set of functionalities including code search, auto-complete, and example discovery. The details of the query language are discussed in the *Codex* section.

Library Generation

Many of the Ruby snippets discovered by Codex are modular, reusable components. The recomposable nature of these snippets suggests that programmers might benefit from their encapsulation in a new standard library that reflects the "missing" functionality that Ruby programmers actually use. Programmers may sometimes engage in unnecessary work: both the mechanical work of typing out repetitive syntax, and also the mental work of caching task-oriented semantics in working memory.

Here we present *CodexLib*, a library created by emergent practice (Table 2). Unlike human language, which evolves over time (e.g., "personal computer" becomes "PC" and "smartphone" emerges to describe a new class of devices), programming languages and libraries often remain more static. CodexLib suggests programming libraries can similarly evolve based on actual usage.

Consider one common Ruby idiom, creating a new `Hash` object where its default lookup value is another empty `Hash`. This nested hash object allows programmers to write code in a matrix-like style, e.g., `hash[''Gaiman''][''Coraline''] = true`. Programmers usually create a nested hash with the snippet, `Hash.new { |h,k| h[k] = {} }`. The nested hash idiom is 22 characters long and involves some nontrivial tracking of syntactic details, yet it appears in 66 times in 12 projects. Programmers would likely benefit by the creation of a shorter library function. Using CodexLib, they can create a new nested hash with the code `Hash.nested`, which is only 10 characters long and has far fewer opportunities for error.

Alternatively, consider the Ruby idiom to capitalize each word token in a string, which occurs 10 times across 5 different projects:

```
var0.split(/str0/).map do |var1|
    var1.capitalize
end.join("str0")
```

This idiom is dense and not immediately self-descriptive; it contains four function calls and a block within three lines. The code splits `var0` on `str0` (in practice, usually " ") to produce an array, applies `capitalize` to each element in this array, the uses `join` to knit the array into a new string again using `str0`. Programmers might benefit from a simpler way to express this task. Using CodexLib they can achieve the same result with the shorthand code: `var0.capital_tokens(''str0'')`.

CodexLib is a layer on top of the Codex snippet database. To construct it, we extract the most popular idioms and their crowdsourced descriptions from the database. For this small number of functions, it is feasible to manually write function signatures and encapsulate them in new class methods for Hash, Array, String, Float, File, and IO (Table 2). Programmers can download this library as a Ruby gem at **http://hci.st/codexlib**.

CODEX

Norms of practice and convention emerge for software systems that aren't codified in documentation. Codex uncovers these norms by processing and aggregating millions of lines of open source code from popular Ruby projects on Github.

Indexing and Abstraction

To build its database, Codex indexes more that 3,000,000 lines of code from 100 popular Ruby projects on Github. It gathers these projects through the Github API by sorting all Ruby projects on the number of watchers and then selecting the 100 projects most watched by other Github users. Codex first breaks apart a project recursively into all constituent AST nodes and annotates these nodes with metadata; next, it normalizes all the AST nodes and collapses those that share a normalized form into a single generalized database entry. The unparsed representation of each of these normalized nodes is a Codex *snippet*.

Snippets of Ruby source code tend to be syntactically unique due to high variance in identifier names and primitive values. Pattern finding tools usually need to abstract away some properties if they are to find meaningful statistical patterns [18, 3, 9]. While we might implement normalization in many different ways, Codex groups together snippets that are functionally similar by standardizing the names of local variables and primatives. For some snippets (e.g., variable assignment) Codex also keeps track of the original identifiers to enable variable name analysis.

Specifically, Codex's normalization renames variable identifiers, strings, symbols, and numbers. The first unique variable in a snippet would be renamed `var0`, the next `var1`, the first string `str0`, and so on. Codex does not normalize class constants and function calls, as these abstractions provide information important to Codex's task-oriented search functionality and statistical linting. As programmers use many different variable names and primitive values when accomplishing a specific task, abstracting away these names helps Codex represent the core behavior of a snippet.

For instance, consider the Ruby snippet:

```
[:CHI, :UIST].map do |z|
    z.to_s + ''is a conference''
end
```

After normalization, this snippet will be:

```
[:sym1, :sym2].map do |var1|
    var1.to_s + ''str1''
end
```

Normalization works less well when such primitives (e.g., specific string or number values) are vital to the interpretation of a snippet. In the future, we will only normalize snippet variable names and identifiers if there is sufficient entropy in their definitions across similar snippets. Snippets with vital identifiers are likely to be more consistent. Other normalization schemes may succeed as well, but we find that this approach successfully collapses most similar snippets together.

Codex applies a map-reduce to the database, collapsing AST nodes with the same normalized form into a single AST entry. We collect additional parameters as part of the map-reduce step: *files*, a list of each file in which the snippet occurs; *projects*, a list of projects in which the snippets appears; *count*, the total number of times a snippet has appeared; *file_count*, the number of times a snippet has appeard in unique files; and *project_count*, the number of times a snippet has appeared in unique projects. Codex uses these parameters to enable the statistical and pattern finding modules.

Codex users the Parser and AST Ruby gems by *whitequark* for AST processing. We have deployed the Codex database on Heroku, using RethinkDB and MongoHQ.

Statistical Analysis Module

Codex has two modules that together enable both *high-level* and *low-level* pattern detection. First we describe the low-level module, which focuses on syntactical patterns that occur among AST nodes.

The statistical analysis module allows Codex to warn users when code is *unlikely*. Codex decides this likelihood using a set of statistics: the frequency of the snippet and also the frequencies of component forms of the snippet (e.g., `.to_s` and `.split` for `.split.to_s`). When a snippet's component forms are sufficiently common and the snippet itself is sufficienctly uncommon, Codex labels it unlikely; that is, a snippet s must have occurred fewer than t times and all its component pieces, c_i must have occurred at most t_i times.

Detecting Surprisingly Unlikely Code

Codex indexes many kinds of AST nodes (e.g., blocks, conditionals, assignment statements, function calls, function definitions), but it conducts syntactic analysis upon a subset of these nodes. The function by which a snippet of unlikely code is declared surprising differs based upon the type of node in question. We discuss four representative analyses we have built to demonstrate the system's power:

1. *Function Call Analysis*: This analysis checks how many times a function has been called with a given "type signature", which Codex defines as the kind of AST nodes passed as arguments (not the runtime type of the expression), relative to the number of times the function has been called with other kinds of signatures. If a sufficiently common function appears with a type signature that is very rarely observed by Codex, this may suggest problematic code. In `split(' ',2)`, s is `split(string,number)`; c_1 is the name of the function; c_2 is the function signature, e.g., `[string, number]`). Codex checks how many times `split` is called with string and integer arguments relative to other kinds of arguments.

2. *Function Chaining Analysis*: This analysis checks how many times one function has been chained with another; that is, the result of some first function is used as the caller of some second function. Here s is the function chain, e.g., `split.to_s`; c_1 is the first function, e.g, `split`; and c_2 is the second, e.g., `to_s`. Two functions that are often used but never chained together suggest unusual code.

3. *Block Return Value Analysis*: This analysis checks how many times a certain kind of block has returned a certain kind of value. For instance, it would be legal but unusual to write the code `things.each { |x| x.to_s }`, which does transform every element in the `things` list to a string, but does not alter `things` itself since `to_s` does not change the state of its caller (to change the values in `names`, a programmer might instead use the expression `x = x.to_s` inside the `each` block). Here s is a kind of block with a particular return type, e.g., a `each` block with return type of the `to_s` function; c_1 is a kind of block, e.g., an `each` block; and c_2 is a kind of block return type, e.g., blocks returning the `to_s` function.

4. *Identifier Analysis*: This analysis checks how many times a variable identifier has been assigned with a certain type of primitive. Often variable names suggest the type of the variable that they reference; this analysis allows Codex to warn programmers about misleading or unconventional variable names (e.g., `str = 0` or `my_array = {}`). Here s is the variable name as assigned to a particular type, e.g., `str = 0`; and c_1 is the variable name, e.g., `str`.

Pattern Finding Module

Whereas the statistical analysis module focuses on low-level syntactical structure, the pattern finding module detects a set of high-level Ruby idioms and example snippets commonly reused by programmers. By constructing an appropriate query over the normalized snippets in its database, Codex can find snippets that isolate common programming idioms. The pattern finding module also enables other specific kinds of queries based on context (e.g., searching for certain library methods called from within a map block.)

The general form of Codex's pattern finding consists of a single query that is applied to the database of abstracted snippets; we intend it to filter out snippets that programmers are less likely to find interesting or useful. The query has five parameters, corresponding to attributes stored in the database, and ordered here by their selectivity:

1. *Project Count*: the number of unique projects in which an abstracted snippet has occurred. A lower bound of 2% of the number of projects indexed by codex filters out snippets that tend to be longer and more idiosyncratic.

2. *Total Count*: the total number of times an abstracted snippet has occurred. An upper bound of the 90% percentile filters out overly trivial snippets (e.g., `var0 = var1`).

3. *File Count*: the total number of unique files in an abstracted snippet has occurred. An upper bound of 20% of the count of an abstracted snippet filters out snippets that are reused quite a bit within one or more files; these snippets tend to be overly domain specific.

4. *Token Count*: the number of unique variables, function calls, and primitives that occur in an abstracted snippet. An upper bound of the 80% percentile of all snippet token counts filters out overly domain specific code.

5. *Function Count*: the number of unique function calls in a snippet. A lower bound of 2 filters out trivial snippets.

These snippets are then passed to expert crowds, who attach metadata such as a title, description, and measure of recommended usefulness.

Together, these parameters produce 9,693 abstracted snippets from the Codex database, corresponding to 79,720 original snippets in the index. This query is designed to produce general purpose snippets; other queries might be constructed differently to produce more domain specific results.

EVALUATION

Codex hypothesizes that we can build new software engineering interfaces by using databases that model practice-driven

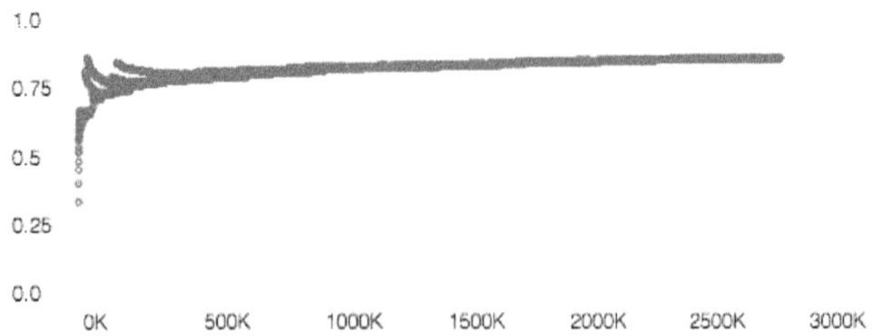

Figure 3. A plot of Codex's hit rate as it indexes code over four random samples of file orderings. The y-axis plots the database hit rate, and the x-axis plots the number of lines of code indexed.

knowedge for programming languages. In this section, we provide evidence for three claims:

1. *The 3,000,000 snippets in the Codex database are sufficient to characterize and analyze a broad swath of program behavior.* We measure the redundancy of AST nodes as Codex indexes increasing amounts of code.
2. *Codex captures a set of snippets that are recomposable and task-oriented.* We ask oDesk Ruby experts to describe and review a subset of the Codex patterns.
3. *Codex allows us to identify unlikely code, without too many false positives.* We evaluate the number and kinds of warnings that Codex throws across a test set of 49,735 lines of code.

The Codex Database

The Codex database is composed of more than 3,000,000 lines of open source code, indexed from 100 popular Ruby projects on Github. These projects come from a diverse set of application areas, including programming languages, plugins, webservers, web applications, databases, testing suites, and API wrappers.

We designed Codex to reflect programming practice. Programming is open ended — the number of valid strings of source code in most languages is infinite — so no database can hold information about every possible AST node or program. However, programming is also highly redundant when examined at a small enough level of granularity [12]. Of the approximately 7 million AST nodes that Codex has indexed, only 13% are unique after normalization. Among the more complex types of AST nodes we see variablity in this redundance. For example, among block nodes 74% are unique, and among class nodes 85% are unique (Table 3).

To evaluate the breadth of code that Codex knows about, we examine the overall *hit rate* of its database as it indexes more code. That is, when indexing N lines of code, what percentage of its normalized AST nodes have not been seen before as they are added to the database? We analyzed the raw Codex dataset for values ranging from 92 to 3,000,000 lines of code across four random samples of file ordering.

Codex's hit rate exceeds 80% after 500,000 lines of code (Figure 3), meaning that Codex had already observed 80% of the AST nodes after normalization. Different AST node types display slightly different curves, with the same overall shape.

Node Type	Percent Unique
Class definition	85%
Rescue statement	78%
Block statement	74%
Function definition	69%
If statement	66%
Interpolated string	29%
Function call	28%
Inlined hash	17%

Table 3. The percent of snippets that are unique after normalization for common AST node types.

Category	Percent of Snippets
Standard Library	76%
External Library	14%
Data or Control Flow	9%

Table 4. Programmers from an expert crowdsourcing market annotated Codex's idioms with their usage type. The vast majority concern the use of standard, built-in libraries.

Many of the nodes we are interested in for statistical analysis are more complex, and so they are less amenable to the leveling of this curve. However, were Codex to index more code, its hit rate would increase even futher.

Pattern Annotation

We asked professional Ruby programmers on the oDesk expert crowdsourcing marketplace to annotate 500 Codex snippets randomly sampled from the approximately 10,000 snippets that passed Codex's general pattern finding filter.

First, we asked crowdworkers to label each snippet with one of the categories: Data or Control Flow, Standard library, External library, and Other (Table 4). The majority of snippets address standard library tasks (76%), followed by external library tasks (14%), and tasks involving data or control flow (9%). None fell outside these categories (Other = 0%).

Next, we asked oDesk crowdworkers to answer: 1) Is this snippet a useful programming task or idiom? 2) Can this snippet be encapsulated into a seperate standalone function? 3) Is there a more common way to write this snippet?

The oDesk Ruby experts reported that 86% of the snippets queued for annotation are useful, 96% are recomposable, and 91% have no more common form. These statistics indicate that Codex's pattern finding module produces snippets that are generally recomposable and reflective of good programming practice.

Statistical Linting

Stastical linting relies upon the low-level properties of millions of lines of code to warn users about code that is unlikely. Codex defines a general approach for detecting unlikely code, on which it implements analyses for: type signatures, variable names, function chains, and block return types. Here we evaluate to what extent CodexLint's produces *false positives* through a training set of 49,735 lines of code.

As Codex seeks to identify unlikely code, and not program bugs, the distinction between true positives and false positives is largely subjective. Inevitably, some users will want to be warned about these properties, while others will not. Here we test the statistical linter against code known to be of high quality. Supposing the number of warnings CodexLint suggests is small, relative to the number of lines of code analyzed, this provides evidence that the statistical linting tool does not suggest too many false positives.

We based our CodexLint test set on 6 projects randomly sampled and witheld from the 100 repositories collected to build Codex's index. The test set projects contain a total of 49,735 lines of code, and all of these projects are popular and widely used, with more than 100 watchers on Gitub (as the case for all the projects selected for indexing by Codex). Since 90% of the snippets annotated through Codex's pattern finding module are found by crowdsourced experts to be idiomatic, and over 85% are rated as useful, we can safely assume that these projects generally *do* contain high-quality code — the null hypothesis would be the principle, "garbage in, garbage out." By treating each warning it throws as a false positive, we arrive at a conservative estimate of the error rate.

Running CodexLint against the test set, we find that it generates 1248 warnings over 49,735 lines of code; this suggests a conservate false positive rate of 2.5%.

The most common category of false positive involves functions and blocks that appear at least a few times across a number of projects, but that haven't been observed enough for Codex to appropriately model their behavior. For example, `nodes` and `uri` are part of a HTML parsing library that Codex has only seen used in a few files, and the system throws a warning about their combination, e.g., `nodes.uri`. We are working on a new technique to detect sparse functions based on library dependancies and additional program context that will handle them seperately in analysis.

The second most common false positive occurs when Codex observes two AST nodes, neither of them particularly uncommon, together in a new and valid way, e.g., `lambda` blocks returning a function call to `rand`, which did not appear at all in Codex's index. Programming is an open-ended task, and there will always be valid combinations of expressions that a system like Codex has not encountered.

Other false positives are more ambiguous. For example, one project passes the `map` function a string, which would usually produce an error. This project had overridden `map` to support new functionality. Similarly, another file assigns a variable named `@requests` an integer value, and Codex has only ever observed `@requests` as an array. Programmers might be well served by changing their code in response to these warnings.

Finally, this false positive rate will decrease as the size of Codex's index grows and fewer correct code paths surprise it. As the statistical linting algorithm is based upon probability thresholds, users can make the linter even more conservative by adjusting these thresholds — analogous to adjusting the parameters of traditional linters.

LIMITATIONS AND FUTURE WORK

The approach that Codex takes has limitations, many of which we plan to address with future work. First, while we have collected evidence that suggests Codex's index is large enough to encompass a broad swath of program behavior, it is likely that many applications — such as pattern annotation and statistical linting — would benefit from a larger index of code. We have tested Codex with indexes as large as ten million lines of code, with no significant difference in the kinds of nodes and statisitical properties it detects. However, as the size of the index grows, there will be fewer and fewer edge cases and false positives, and Codex will more easily detect idioms and make precise statistical statements about combinations of AST nodes. Codex must balance its desire for more coverage against the danger of indexing lower-quality code.

Second, many more kinds of program analyses can be defined beyond Codex's current abstractions. All the analyses tested in the current version of Codex rely upon local properties of AST nodes, and not the sourrounding program context. By incorporating more of this context into analyses, we might detect more complex properties (e.g., detecting that a user hasn't initialized a MySQL database wrapper).

Third, due to the subjective nature of CodexLint's warnings, we have not determined a precise rate of true positives and false positives. In future work, we might ask programmers to evaluate these warnings, to better determine how often they are useful. Moreover, this paper does not address the general question: do programmers really find it useful to know when they are violating convention? We can determine the answer more concretely through longitudinal study.

Finally, while Codex models practice-driven knowledge for the Ruby programming language, our techniques for processing AST nodes and generating statistics are applicable to any AST structure or language. For example, it might be feasible to generate a Codex database for JavaScript by crawling highly-trafficked web pages. Moreover, while we focused on a dynamic language due to its popularity and flexibility of naturalistic usage, static languages provide additional metadata that Codex could leverage. Extending Codex's analyses to these other languages remains future work.

CONCLUSION

Codex suggests that mining and codifying emergent programmer behavior can support a broad set of software engineering interfaces. By modeling how developers use programming languages in practice, Codex enables algorithms for finding common idioms and detecting unlikely code. In combination with human crowds, we use these algorithms to enable new applications like statistical linting, pattern annotation, and library generation.

More broadly, systems like Codex point towards a future of programming languages as living artifacts: where libraries self-update to use the latest, most common idioms, IDEs offer suggestions to programmers that suit evolving coding styles, and languages evolve to better support their users. In this way, the wisdom of the crowd can be fed back to make crowds themselves wiser.

ACKNOWLEDGEMENTS
Special thanks to our reviewers and colleagues at Stanford. This work is supported by Adobe Research.

REFERENCES
1. Ahmadzadeh, M., Elliman, D., and Higgins, C. An analysis of patterns of debugging among novice computer science students. *In Proc. ITiCSE 2005.*
2. Ayewah, N., et al. Using static analysis to find bugs. *In IEEE Software 2008.*
3. Baxter, I.D., et al. Clone detection using abstract syntax trees. *In Proc. ICSM 1998.*
4. Bernstein, M.S., et al. Direct answers for search queries in the long tail. *In Proc. CHI 2012.*
5. Brandt, J., Dontcheva, M., Weskamp, M., and Klemmer, S.R. Example-centric programming: integrating web search into the development environment. *In Proc. CHI 2010.*
6. Brandt, J., et al. Opportunistic programming: Writing code to prototype, ideate, and discover. *In IEEE Software 2009.*
7. Brandt, J., et al. Two studies of opportunistic programming: interleaving web foraging, learning, and writing code. *In Proc. CHI 2009.*
8. Buse, R.P.L. and Weimer, W. Synthesizing api usage examples. *In Proc. ICSE 2012.*
9. Ducasse, S., Rieger, M., and Demeyer, S. A language independent approach for detecting duplicated code. *In Proc. ICSM 1999.*
10. Engler, D., et al. Bugs as deviant behavior: a general approach to inferring errors in systems code. *In Proc. SOSP 2001.*
11. Fourney, A., Mann, R., and Terry, M. Query-feature graphs: bridging user vocabulary and system functionality. *In Proc. UIST 2011.*
12. Gabel, M. and Su, Z. A study of the uniqueness of source code. *In Proc. FSE 2010.*
13. Gamma, E., Helm, R., Johnson, R., and Vlissides, J. *Design Patterns: Elements of Reusable Object-Oriented Software*. 1994.
14. Goldman, M., Little, G., and Miller, R.C. Collabode: collaborative coding in the browser. *In Proc. CHASE 2011.*
15. Goldman, M. and Miller, R.C. Codetrail: Connecting source code and web resources. *In Proc. VL/HCC 2009J.*
16. Grechanik, M., et al. Exemplar: Executable examples archive. *In Proc. ICSE 2010.*
17. Greenberg, S. and Witten, I.H. How users repeat their actions on computers: Principles for design of history mechanisms. *In Proc. CHI '88.*
18. Hartmann, B., MacDougall, D., Brandt, J., and Klemmer, S.R. What would other programmers do: suggesting solutions to error messages. *In Proc. of CHI 2010.*
19. Hartmann, B., Wu, L., Collins, K., and Klemmer, S.R. Programming by a sample: rapidly creating web applications with d.mix. *In Proc. UIST 2007.*
20. Hindle, A., et al. On the naturalness of software. *In Proc. ICSE 2012.*
21. Holmes, R., Walker, R.J., and Murphy, G.C. Strathcona example recommendation tool. *In Proc. FSE 2005.*
22. Hummel, O., Janjic, W., and Atkinson, C. Code conjurer: Pulling reusable software out of thin air. *IEEE Software 2008.*
23. Kim, M., Bergman, L., Lau, T., and Notkin, D. An ethnographic study of copy and paste programming practices in oopl. *In Proc. ISESE 2004.*
24. Ko, A.J. and Myers, B.A. Designing the whyline: a debugging interface for asking questions about program behavior. *In Proc. the CHI 2004.*
25. Kumar, R., et al. Webzeitgeist: Design Mining the Web. *In Proc. CHI 2013.*
26. Mandelin, D., Xu, L., Bodík, R., and Kimelman, D. Jungloid mining: helping to navigate the api jungle. *In Proc. PLDI 2005.*
27. Matejka, J., Li, W., Grossman, T., and Fitzmaurice, G. CommunityCommands. *In Proc. UIST 2009.*
28. Mooty, M., Faulring, A., Stylos, J., and Myers, B.A. Calcite: Completing code completion for constructors using crowds. *In Proc. VL/HCC 2010.*
29. Sahavechaphan, N. and Claypool, K. Xsnippet: mining for sample code. *In Proc. OOPSLA 2006.*
30. Seacord, R.C., Plakosh, D., and Lewis, G.A. *Modernizing Legacy Systems: Software Technologies, Engineering Process and Business Practices*. 2003.
31. Simon, I., Morris, D., and Basu, S. MySong: automatic accompaniment generation for vocal melodies. *In Proc. CHI 2008.*
32. Stylos, J. and Myers, B.A. Mica: A web-search tool for finding api components and examples. *In Proc. VL/HCC 2006.*
33. Thummalapenta, S. and Xie, T. Parseweb: a programmer assistant for reusing open source code on the web. *In Proc. ASE 2007.*
34. Urma, R.G. and Mycroft, A. Programming language evolution via source code query languages. *In Proc. PLATEAU 2012.*
35. Ye, Y. and Fischer, G. Supporting reuse by delivering task-relevant and personalized information. *In Proc. ICSE 2002.*

Design Considerations for Parallel Performance Tools

Roman Atachiants, David Gregg, Kim Jarvis and Gavin Doherty
Lero@TCD
Trinity College Dublin
atachiar@tcd.ie, David.Gregg@tcd.ie, kjarvis@tcd.ie, Gavin.Doherty@tcd.ie

ABSTRACT

In recent years there has been a shift in microprocessor manufacture from building single-core processors towards providing multiple cores on the same chip. This shift has meant that a much wider population of developers are faced with the task of developing parallel software: a difficult, time consuming and expensive process. With the aim of identifying issues, emerging practices and design opportunities for support, we present in this paper a qualitative study in which we interviewed a range of software developers, in both industry and academia. We then perform a systematic analysis of the data and identify several cross-cutting themes. These analysis themes include the practical relevance of the probe effect, the significance of orchestration models in development and the mismatch between currently available tools and developers' needs. We also identify an important characteristic of parallel programming, where the process of optimisation goes hand in hand with the process of debugging, as opposed to clearer distinctions which may be made in traditional programming. We conclude with reflection on how the study can inform the design of software tools to support developers in the endeavour of parallel programming.

Author Keywords

many-core, multi-core; parallel programming; qualitative study;visualisation

ACM Classification Keywords

H.5.m. Information Interfaces and Presentation (e.g. HCI): Miscellaneous

INTRODUCTION

As computers become more prevalent in modern society, the tasks that computers may perform have also become increasingly complicated. In order to cope with this increasing complexity, programmers develop ever more computationally demanding algorithms and applications. Likewise the volume of data processed by computers has also increased enormously. These factors together have led to ever increasing demands on microprocessor performance. In order to cope with this increasing demand for computational power, hardware manufacturers continually increased the clock frequency of their central processing units (CPUs). However, this approach meant that the power consumption of each CPU also trended upwards. This strategy of increasing frequency eventually became less viable, as the power required to increase performance introduced a range of difficulties, such as excessive heat generation and current leakage.

An alternative strategy for increasing the number of instructions per second that a CPU can process is to put multiple processors (cores) on the same chip. Many modern personal computers now have two or more cores that enable multiple tasks (threads) to be executed simultaneously. This concerns not only servers and supercomputers, but also concerns any possible variety of a computer: from smart-phones and games consoles to desktops and tablets.

In the near future, computers are expected to have even more cores - the trend towards "many-core" computing. A many-core processor is a multi-core processor in which the number of cores is large enough that traditional multiprocessor techniques are no longer efficient. While with a small number of cores performance gains can be achieved simply by running different programs simultaneously, with many cores, performance gains will only be achieved through the use of parallel programming. On modern servers and supercomputers it is already common to have hundreds or even thousands of cores.

In order to take advantage of the multi-core and many-core hardware of today and tomorrow, programmers are faced with a need to parallelise their code and distribute work across multiple processors. This process of parallelisation is complex and requires application programmers to think about many possible outcomes and situations that may occur.

A programmer seeking to parallelise a program has to overcome the challenges of synchronisation, non-determinism and orchestration that a programmer writing an equivalent sequential program would not have to face. Additionally, the very process of parallelising may introduce bugs, deadlocks and race conditions into the program. On top of that, when looking at a program it is not necessarily obvious what its parallel performance will be.

For over two decades, a great deal of research effort has been directed at tools for improving the performance of parallel applications and over 200 now defunct, parallel-programming languages saw the light in the 1990s [29]. However, twenty years later, concurrency bugs are still extremely common and theoretical performance is often very difficult to realise [38].

CHI 2014, April 26–May 1, 2014, Toronto, Ontario, Canada.

ACM 978-1-4503-2473-1/14/04..$15.00.
http://dx.doi.org/10.1145/2556288.2557350

In this paper a qualitative study of parallel programming practices is presented. The goal of the study is to increase our understanding of the human factors and practices involved in parallel programming tasks. By doing so, we hope to shed light on some of the challenges which have been previously noted in the literature [19, 38]. We hope to gain a better understanding of the underlying techniques and processes the programmers of concurrent systems use in order to stay productive and inform the design of tools and visualisation systems that could help programmers in their endeavours.

Following a review of related work, we describe the methodology used for the study and present a qualitative analysis of the data. We propose a number of possible implications for the design of support tools, and look towards the development of a set of design guidelines based on the lessons gleaned from the interviews and analysis.

RELATED WORK

While the practice of parallel programming for ordinary developers has not been widely studied from a HCI perspective, the scientific computing and software engineering communities have grappled with the problems associated with parallel programming for some time.

That being said, over the past twenty years many studies have been carried out on novice programmers and identified good and bad aspects of today's programming systems [33]. While testing and debugging are two very complex areas for novice programmers, some researchers claim that programming tools should support source-level debugging with data visualisation to be more effective [4].

Using an appropriate concrete metaphor, a familiar analogy explaining how the programming system works, can have a positive effect on the usability [27] and also maximises transfer of knowledge if the metaphor is close to a real-world system [41].

Expert programming can be considered as an opportunistic activity [13], however some research indicates that expert programmers use intricate plans and strategies in order to schedule and prioritise their activities [1]. Planning is common among novice programmers and the absence of good planning strategy results in wrong assumptions and more bugs [3]. Programming tools should also consider locality; related components should be physically close [2] and hidden dependencies reduce understanding [13].

For both novice and expert programmers the ability to test partial solutions is an important feature [33]. Incremental running and testing, a programming strategy where the code is iteratively tested while new code is being written, have been found to be an effective debugging strategy [14], and it has been observed that developers perform better when such a strategy is adopted [12, 13].

In addition, there have been attempts to understand how programmers work from a sensemaking perspective, applying information foraging [35] to understand how developers debug [23, 34]. Various empirical studies and models have attempted to understand and help answer questions that developers' ask [20, 10]. These have used a variety of methodologies, including observations of pairs of programmers given sample tasks [39], and questionnaire based studies [22].

Prabhu et al. [36] present an extensive survey of software practices in computational science. They conclude that current programming systems and tools do not meet the requirements for scientific computing. They indicate that most tools assume that programmers would invest time and energy to learn and master a particular system, which turned out not to be the case with programmers wanting results immediately. They found that most of the scientists understand the importance of parallel programming in the context of scientific computing and many scientists spend a significant amount of time and energy programming. Despite this effort, most scientists seem to be unsatisfied with the performance of their programs and believe that the improvement of performance will significantly improve their research and, in some cases, allow larger experiments or enable fundamentally new research avenues. The survey concluded that overall the needs of computational scientists were underserved and new tools and techniques were needed to unlock the potential of high-performance computing.

In another study, Hannay et al. conducted an online survey of approximately two thousand scientists in order to study software engineering practices in the scientific community [16]. Their study found that for the concepts "software testing" and "software verification" scientists assign on average a higher level of importance to these concepts than they judge their level of understanding of these concepts. Scientists seem to care a great deal about the correctness of their code, but feel they lack knowledge of software engineering practices to verify it. Additionally, their findings suggest that informal learning from peers was more important to scientists than formal education at an academic institution or formal training at the work place, they postulate that this may be due to the lack of appropriate formal training. Their study also confirmed the hypothesis that the majority of scientists use desktop computers most of the time for developing and using scientific software as opposed to supercomputers or clusters.

A classroom study conducted across a number of universities compared different programming models across a variety of representative applications [18]. It is worth noting that most of these studies use novices as the study participants rather than experienced programmers. The study compared shared memory (multi-core) and message passing (distributed) implementations of two problems, written by novice programmers. They found that the message passing development effort, measured in lines of code, was statistically greater but resulted into more correct programs. On the other hand, shared memory programs were smaller and easier to write but were more error-prone.

Luff conducted an experiment comparing developers' performance using various parallel programming models (actor model, transactional memory and standard shared memory threading with locks) while keeping the programming language and environment (IDE) the same [25]. The results were inconclusive and showed no significant difference in any objective measurement between those models.

A study conducted by Eccles et al. [8] had novice and expert programmers both categorising different parallel algorithms, using a card sorting method. They found that novices and experts used a different classification scheme: novice programmers organised problems around the problem domain while expert programmers organised problems around communication granularity and overhead. This difference in classification could identify a set of concepts which delineate novices from experts [38]. They concluded that the best way of organising parallel programming material and libraries is around the expert classification scheme, and postulate that it would result in a more usable parallel software.

A wide variety of prior literature related to program maintenance focuses on debugging, with a particular emphasis on novice versus expert difference [28]. Most research agrees that reading and understanding code is the fastest debugging method [7, 43], although this is not always feasible for very large programs [21]. Fix et al. [9] found that experts had more sophisticated mental models than novices, and so were able to use them more effectively to debug programs.

A study by Pancake [32] attempted to determine a correlation between mental models and the effectiveness of visualisations for parallel debuggers. It demonstrated that it is possible to implement various conceptual models using any programming language, however program development becomes significantly easier and more reliable when the language has support for expressing the desired model. The same correlation applies to the debugger visualisation models.

Fleming [37] conducted an exploratory think-aloud study in which he observed 15 programmers debugging multithreaded server application which was seeded with a defect. He claimed that the programmers who succeeded used a previously undocumented failure-trace strategy while debugging, and using such a strategy made the programmers more likely to succeed. The strategy involved modelling interactions between various threads in the program in order to find a failure trace (i.e. the interaction that led to a failure). He also postulated that cognitive strain may have been an important barrier as the failure-trace strategy was modelled internally. In addition, it is claimed that the inherent concurrency of parallel programming makes managing hypotheses regarding the cause of a bug more difficult.

An important aspect of tool support for multi-core programming is understanding performance data. Given the volume and complexity of this data, visualisation is an important design direction as it leverages capacities and bandwidth of the visual system to quickly assess and understand large volumes of data. Visualising the behaviour of parallel programs is a very complex task, as the behaviour of the programs themselves is often complex. The area of effective visualisation techniques for parallel programs is still relatively unexplored within parallel programming research and has usability implications [38]. However, the need to form a scientific body of research, develop human-centered models, and target production level applications and their developers has been recognised [26]. A number of tools such as ParaGraph and ParaDyn have been developed to visualise behaviour [17, 30]; most of the tools that have been developed for the High-Performance Computing domain target distributed systems such as HPC clusters.

While previous work has identified a number of broad issues and goals for tools to support programmers in understanding the performance of their programs, only a relatively small proportion of the literature deals specifically with the problems faced in the construction of parallel programs. With regards to tools, existing systems can be seen as providing answers to two main issues: topological mapping, and synchronisation. The topology issue requires that spatial relationships in programs be understood. The synchronisation issue requires various events occurring within the processor, to be correlated [6]. While some existing visualisations are potentially useful, there is a need for analysis of how such tools can aid in the diagnosis of problems.

METHODOLOGY

A qualitative study was carried out to better understand how developers approach parallel programming, identify the issues that they are trying to address, and how software performance analytics systems could help them in their work. We conducted a range of interviews across various organisations including a large corporation producing operating systems, one of the largest B2B software corporations, universities, research laboratories and small to medium sized software companies. A broad spectrum of organisations was targeted in order to obtain a general overview of the field of parallel programming practices and problems.

Interview participants were practicing software developers, engineers and academics. All of the interviewees were practicing parallel programming in some way, including high performance computing (HPC), Graphics Processing Unit (GPU) accelerators, many-core and/or multi-core programming. The goal of the semi-structured interviews was to explore and understand the daily activities and challenges faced by programmers and, to explore the techniques they use in order to tackle those challenges. The interviewees were asked to describe the nature of their work and recent projects involving parallel programming.

Overall, 22 people were interviewed. 14 of them were recorded, resulting in over 8 hours of audio. Interviews were transcribed (around 47,000 words), open coded (582 open codes, unified into 252 codes), categorised in 8 major categories and sub-categorised in 23 sub-categories. Interview participants are summarised in Table 1.

Interviews were semi-structured, and interviewees were asked to talk about the challenges they had to overcome in their every day work related to parallel programming, the tools they had employed, and practices they used. While this analysis method has its roots in Grounded Theory [42], we would like to highlight that it was not our goal to build a holistic theory from the data. Following common practice in HCI [31], we used the approach as the foundation

Participant	Organisation	Activity	Years
P1, Male	Corporate	Engineering	0-5
P2, Male	Corporate	Engineering	0-5
P3, Female	Corporate	Engineering	5-10
P4, Male	Corporate	Engineering	5-10
P5, Male	Corporate	Engineering	10+
P6, Male	Corporate	Engineering	10+
P7, Male	Corporate	Engineering	10+
P8, Male	Corporate	Engineering	10+
P9, Male	Corporate	Engineering	10+
P10, Male	Corporate	Research	10+
P11, Male	Corporate	Research	10+
P12, Male	Corporate	Research	10+
P13, Male	SME	Consultancy	5-10
P14, Male	SME	Consultancy	5-10
P15, Male	SME	Consultancy	10+
P16, Male	SME	Engineering	5-10
P17, Female	SME	Engineering	10+
P18, Male	SME	Engineering	10+
P19, Male	University	Research	0-5
P20, Male	University	Research	5-10
P21, Male	University	Teaching	5-10
P22, Male	University	Teaching	5-10

Table 1. A table of participants with their years of experience, main activity and the type of organisation.

for a focussed analysis of the transcribed interviews. Interview questions along with the full set of codes are available at `https://www.scss.tcd.ie/ManyCore/`.

DEVELOPING PARALLEL SOFTWARE

During our study we identified three major poles of activity in a developers work. Developers attempt to: 1) Meet their own goals and the goals of their organisation, 2) Understand what is going on with the workers (threads, processes, machines). Where are they, what are they doing, are they performing well? 3) Orchestrate the group of 'workers' and make them work efficiently together. In the following subsections we examine these three poles.

Context for development

The developers interviewed were mostly based in industry and every organisation had their own unique set of constraints and concerns. Their working environments (both physical and virtual) are composed of various components such as software specifications, budgeting and deadlines, human resources, hardware and software constraints, programming languages, software architecture, the actual code, etc. An interesting aspect of the study is that the programmers interviewed didnt dwell on programming paradigms and talked about their experience across different programming languages. We know, however, that many were using imperative languages such C, C++, fortran or Java, and some used hybrid languages such as C# or Matlab.

Throughout the interviews, developers often talked about complexity, and specifically about the complexity of the software: large systems tend to become larger and ever more complex as new features are introduced. One developer, commenting on a major web search engine stated:

> Interviewee: *"When you have a 20 million line app, no one can fit it in the brain."*

The complexity of many of these systems is such that no one person understands every detail of the system. The knowledge is shared between people in the organisation, and distributed across various information systems.

While developers often worked with extensive tool support in the form of IDE's, this support does not extend specifically to debugging and optimising parallel software. As a result, developers tend to rely on intuition and resort to 'thinking really hard' about the problem. There are two aspects to reasoning about problems; on a conceptual level developers want to focus on the problematic elements of their program and abstract away elements not immediately relevant to the matter in hand. At a concrete level, there are also issues of experimental noise; they may wish to replicate the problem in the simplest possible form in order to clearly identify the source of the issue and test possible solutions.

> Interviewee: *"(...) sort of a test bench, where we just took that problem piece of code and then just on that algorithm, just enough of the code to be able to start that algorithm and run it or just enough of the code to run it to get the results and to be able to verify that they were accurate."*

However, developers are often confronted with various and sometimes unexpected problems. These problems can occur on different levels: in a particular function in their code, in an external library, on a particular machine or a cluster, or even on an abstract architectural level.

Most developers who develop parallel software do so in order to obtain better performance. Therefore, performance becomes a design requirement. In consequence, developers do not think of parallel performance optimisation as a separate process, but as a correctness issue, a particular type of bug. This contrasts with traditional software development where the two concerns are generally more easily separated.

> Interviewee: *"In the normal software development they usually forget about optimisation at the beginning and then look to optimise later. In HPC it is totally different approach: you design your code to be optimal."*

Understanding

In almost every interview, developers described methods they use which help them improve their understanding of the system they are working on, the environment or various problems occurring. There are numerous things they try to understand. For example, they may want to know which component is at fault (code path, thread, task), when and what caused the failure to occur. Alternatively, they may be interested in understanding the architecture of the software they are working on (patterns of communication, design patterns, dependancies, hardware).

In order to improve their understanding, developers use a range of techniques. Some of these techniques are only possible with very specific tools whereas in other cases they may simply ask other people.

Table 2 provides a non-exhaustive list of techniques that were mentioned or discussed to some extent during the interviews.

% of Participants	Technique
60%	Active Experimentation
47%	Verification
40%	Visualizing
33%	Tracing
27%	Abstracting the Complexity
20%	Benchmarking
20%	Chain of Events Analysis
13%	Deadlock Detection
13%	Documentation

Table 2. A non-exhaustive set of techniques for understanding and the percentage of interviewees who were talking about the subject.

In addition to this, there are various obstacles that they have to overcome in order to gain a better understanding. Obstacles mentioned include the overall complexity, non-determinism, incomplete information, incorrect assumptions and lack of documentation.

A developer in a large organisation commented:

> Interviewee: *"Some classes were written decades ago, then somebody puts it in another product, and then to another product. And suddenly someone says that we're going to use multiple threads to do that, and all of the sudden this legacy code has been dragged into the 21st century."*

In this case, the programmer used an external library (a piece of code) written by someone else some decades ago. The new developer made an erroneous assumption about thread-safety as relevant information was not available to him, resulting in a poorly performing and buggy program.

Inadequate Tools

The majority of developers we interviewed expressed dissatisfaction with available tools. Three developers we interviewed clearly stated that the tools were very poor a few years ago, but gradually getting better over time. Five of the interviewees asserted that they do not use any performance analysis tools at all.

> Interviewee: *" (...) Take the lock again, commit everything back. But the problem is, at least in C++ and C, there's no great tools or mechanisms to support that type of thing, or to even find out that you have those problems."*

In some cases, this discontent even results in a person, in the case of the next quote, a computer-science expert, not using tools and relying solely on intuition for the whole debugging and optimisation process.

> Interviewee: *"I think the only way I can do most of this debugging is stare at it and debug it in my head, which is the least effective way you can ever debug."*

There seems to be a gap between the results that performance analysis tools provide and the information that developers seek. Developers are usually interested in a specific issue that they wish to diagnose. They see a symptom of a performance issue and they attempt to figure out what caused it. This is a challenging, and often time consuming process. This process of understanding is still poorly understood and developers use various techniques. For example, they might experiment, putting traces in code, recompiling over and over again, they might try to go back to the whiteboard and create some hypotheses of which component is failing, or use tools that assist them. The whole process is usually a combination of all those things.

> Interviewee: *"But I spent, I don't know, maybe a week just staring at the thing, watching it god knows how many times."*

The Probe Effect

One of the most problematic barriers for understanding the performance of complex software systems, is the presence of the probe effect. The probe effect denotes an unintended change to the behaviour of a system caused by observing (measuring) that system [11, 24]. In order to measure something in the program, an automated tool or a person adds additional code to record features of interest. This approach is called program instrumentation.

> Interviewee: *"And then, there's a question of how to observe the parallelism. [...] An observation brings problems which wouldn't be there if we wouldn't observe."*

In order for a performance measurement system to be safe to use on production systems, it is generally considered that the performance analysis infrastructure should have zero probe effect when disabled and should not accidentally induce any errors when enabled [5]. However, most instrumentation techniques have a probe effect when enabled making it difficult to apply continuous monitoring of performance on production systems.

Developers are aware of the presence of potential probe effects and 27% highlighted the probe effect as an important issue, resulting in them not using any performance analysis tools on production systems. By slowing down the whole program, the behaviour of the program is altered and makes it difficult or impossible to track some performance issues such as race conditions. This is especially problematic when developers have to diagnose performance issues, as the instrumentation may slow down the whole program to the point where the performance problem is no longer observable.

> Interviewee: *"We had a number of interesting issues. The actual turning on the log it slowed everything down such as the problem would not be there with logging on."*

Information representation and resources

In order to cope with the complexity of software development, developers create abstract representations of the environment and contextualise the work they are performing. For example, interviewees talk about a global scope or a local scope. The scope represents a context in which they perform their tasks, allowing them to focus and reason on a particular level:

> Interviewee: *"So you have parallel programming at the GPU level, at the CPU level at cluster level, and then, you know, maybe deeper even."*

The global scope represents a 'big picture' of the system. For example, hardware, system and software architectures. The global scope thinking allows developers to think about the problem in more abstract way. The local scope represents a 'detailed picture' of a sub-system of the system the developers are working on. For instance, a developer might consider using a specific algorithm in order to optimise some part of a program.

As mentioned above, complexity can be overwhelming. Developers therefore use tools to offload knowledge into the world. For example, several developers reported using UML[1] or sketching tools, even pen and paper, in order to externalise their knowledge by 'charting' the environment in this way:

> Interviewee: *"The only tools I used [during the project] were UML analysis tools."*

However, while developers are focusing on a local scope, they may lack contextual information. For example, while with a modern integrated development environment (IDE), the developer may know what parameters are taken by a function they call, they usually do not know whether the function is thread-safe, what side-effects it produces or how well it performs. This is especially problematic in the case of functions or classes that are poorly documented. Developers stated that they rely heavily on documentation, augmenting available resources with internal wikis, and tend to use third party libraries that they know are well tested and perform well.

> Interviewee: *"I'll often look to use the Intel MKL[2] libraries, wherever possible. [...] But the documentation for it is really excellent. "*

Developers seek information relevant for the task at hand. For example, if a programmer designs a new feature which complements a bigger system, they need information about the existing elements of the system in order to achieve their goal. If the programmer develops a particular algorithm destined to work on particular hardware, they might need hardware specifications in order to create an optimal algorithm. The programmer needs information relevant to their task, but information is often fragmented and distributed across various sources (documentation, internal wiki, people).

Orchestration

The process of parallel programming is essentially a process of coordinating the efforts of different workers and balancing workload, which we can paraphrase as orchestration. The programmer attempts to distribute the workload across multiple worker nodes, to achieve optimal resource utilisation, maximise throughput, minimise response time, and avoid overhead. Programmers in different contexts will have different constraints and therefore might perform this orchestration differently. For example, a developer working alone in a small company, would want to reduce his costs in writing the software by reducing the time required to do so. On the other hand, a PhD researcher might concentrate more on the performance of their program, sacrificing time. This leads the developers to use different orchestration techniques, depending on the situation.

Orchestration Models

As mentioned above, programmers go through a process of orchestration, trying to find a solution that allows them to efficiently distribute the workload across multiple workers. In programming, as with many other crafts, reusable solutions for commonly occurring problems are often formalised. Some such solutions discussed during the interviews are also known, more formally, as design patterns. An advantage of such formalised design patterns is that they provide both a common conceptual model and a vocabulary for everyone who uses them, allowing programmers to reason about and solve problems more easily.

> Interviewee: *"The goal was to decouple an image processing part as much as possible in a pipeline and partition the tasks on the different resources [machines]."*

During the interviews, we asked people to talk about various challenges they encountered during their projects. They all gave at least one, high level explanation of the solution they implemented. The projects the programmers worked on were varied: from a small multiplayer game running on a single computer, to one of the biggest search engines in the world, running on thousands of computers. They talked about the way their program is orchestrated, about the architecture and about the high-level design.

Across these various projects and solutions that were put in place, similar orchestration patterns were applied. Surprisingly only some of the developers were familiar with formalised design patterns and named them. However, many developers we interviewed were essentially talking about a design pattern. Table 3 shows the percentage of developers we interviewed who were using knowingly or unknowingly a recognisable design pattern in their work.

Occurrences	Orchestration Model
40%	Producer / Consumer
33%	Active Object
27%	Scatter / Gather
20%	Pipes and Filters
20%	Futures and Promises

Table 3. A non-exhaustive set of orchestration models and the percentage of interviewees who were talking about the subject.

For example, one of most commonly mentioned design patterns is the Producer/Consumer, a design pattern that is used

[1]UML stands for Unified Modelling Language, a standardised general-purpose modelling language in the field of software engineering.

[2]MKL stands for Math Kernel Library, a set of routines which includes highly vectorised and threaded Linear Algebra, Fast Fourier Transforms (FFT), Vector Math and Statistics functions.

to decouple workers that produce and consume data at different rates. Such decoupling grants the programmer flexibility in how they partition the workload in a scalable manner. Another example of a widely used design pattern is the Active Object model. This pattern allows independent threads of execution to interleave their concurrent access to data modelled as a single object. This model allows the developers to simplify synchronisation complexity and transparently leverage available parallelism.

While design patterns are in part formally defined in the literature, in the context of parallel programming, their significance is in the way that they provide **orchestration models**. An easy metaphor to understand this, is to consider that a developer who writes parallel programs does not write recipes (as often taught to first year computer science students), but manages a project with several workers working for him. The developer attempts to orchestrate these workers in an optimal way, considering the available resources and tasks at hand. In the parallel programming context, such workers can be threads, processes, machines, domain-specific classes, etc.

> Interviewee: *"It's like seeing a team working. Sometimes the team works better when you have some people that work worse for some reason."*

Orchestration models are a type of design pattern employed in parallel programming, and they span different contexts (or scopes) on which developers are focusing. In software engineering design patterns are often related to reusable code skeletons for quick and reliable development of parallel applications [40]. In contrast, orchestration models are more abstract, spanning not only patterns related to software architecture, but hardware and system architectures as well.

Programmers tended to refer to specific orchestration models when describing the way they think about the design and implementation of concurrent systems.

Difficulties with Orchestration

While the orchestration models provide an initial basis for design, helping the programmers to reason about and implement their system, there are many issues associated with the process of orchestration. In this section we highlight some of the difficulties described by the developers.

To illustrate our point, we start by giving a couple of examples of problems the programmers encountered.

Problem: Novice programmers (computer science students) were implementing a concurrent game, running on a single multicore machine. They ran into critical deadlock and slowdown issues due to lock contentions.

Adopted Solution: Students were forced to reengineer the whole game and completely understand the interactions between components. By removing redundant locks and following a critical section pattern for every component, they achieved a correct and fast implementation. They drew a schema of interaction of various components, mainly in order to understand the activity of workers at any given moment, and the resource usage and sharing.

Problem: Expert developers were implementing a system, allowing them to perform computationally intensive tasks on a massively parallel GPU. They ran into a series of subtle problems, the most common being branch misprediction. Branch misprediction occurs when a processing unit (CPU or GPU) mispredicts the next instruction to execute, which impacts adversely on overall execution time.

Adopted Solution: They ran tests to identify which branches were taken most often and adapted the code accordingly.

Problem: Expert developers were implementing an equivalent of an OpenMP "parallel for" loop. They were building a library for other developers to use and ran into a problem where their implementation did not perform as well as expected in production, far below the theoretical performance. They had been very focused on the implementation and theoretical performance and did not consider the context, in this case, the influence of the operating system which negatively impacted on the performance.

Adopted Solution: They adopted a clever solution, where workers would steal work from other workers (work-stealing). This allowed them to have an implementation which was more dynamic in nature and could cope with the uncertainty introduced by the operating system.

In the examples above, as in many other instances observed during our interviews, developers implemented the system, but noticed a slower than expected performance or a critical bug during the verification phase. They encountered undesirable side effects of both a deterministic and non-deterministic nature.

> Interviewee: *"Because it just works most of the time, and you occasionally just see some corruption"*

Non-deterministic issues may manifest themselves in various forms, and, most importantly be unpredictable and difficult to reproduce. The programmer's job is to prune as much nondeterminism as possible. Moreover, in many cases, developers had to go back to the drawing board and reengineer, at least partially, their system.

"Optimal" solutions

Developers want to reach a working solution which is close to the best achievable result given their organisational constraints. Essentially, they are trying to find an orchestration model that allows them to build a system with satisfactory performance. The "optimal solution" in this context represents an ideal, a scalable and practically feasible solution that programmers strive to achieve (rather than theoretically optimal).

> Interviewee: *"There isn't an analysis tool in existence that helps to ensure that we're getting to an optimal solution."*

Picking an adequate orchestration model is not an easy task as it depends on various constraints. We have previously illustrated some of such constraints, including the correctness or performance, but an orchestration model, as opposed to a design pattern, can also have more general constraints, such as usability. To illustrate this, consider the following quote from an expert developer who worked on a "parallel for" loop abstraction, from the third example.

> Interviewee: *"Next thing we worked on is a parallel for. A parallel for by itself it's not terribly hard [to implement], but there is different types of workloads... So, analysing every workload and seeing how a parallel for would perform and what are the different jobs that a user could actually use. [It] turned out to be a herculean task, because most people use it for a very simple thing. For example: I have two arrays of numbers and I use parallel for to sum them. So now, there's work which is too small in every iteration, which means we can not introduce any overhead. But the same parallel for could be used to do much more complex problems: tons of work within every iteration. And, even worse, they could use it for raytracing, for which in every iteration the work is different."*

Essentially, the developer explained to us that in addition of having correct and fast implementation, their system had to be used in many different ways by developers, and thus being usable and flexible. Once again, they had to go back and reengineer a part of the system to cope with this requirement.

Summary

Whether explicitly or implicitly, developers are thinking about their programs in terms of orchestration models. The majority (60%) of developers we interviewed talked about load balancing and optimality. They want to orchestrate their programs in a efficient manner, coordinate workers and distribute resources. There is a clear need for tools that help developers to go 'back to the drawing board' and analyse the underlying architecture, the orchestration model, of a program upon encountering performance problems.

DISCUSSION

In this section, we consider and discuss potential implications of the study regarding parallel programming practices and the design of tools to support these.

Cover both correctness and performance - While our study initially intended to focus only on performance improvement, during the interviews it quickly became clear that that performance concerns cannot easily be separated from program correctness, as is the case in traditional programming tasks. This is due to the nature of the problem itself, as programmers write parallel code in order to leverage the resources and increase performance. Good performance thus becomes a design requirement.

This observation leads us to consider a range of implications. Firstly, tools that support parallel programming activity should consider both correctness and performance issues at the same time. This is different from traditional programming where we can see two major types of tools: profilers which are used for measuring and analysing the performance of a system, and debuggers used for diagnosing correctness problems. Secondly, this observation also means that it might be possible to apply research on debugging in software engineering to parallel performance problems, such as the information foraging perspective [23, 35].

Support active experimentation and tracing - Developers are not happy with currently available tools for parallel programming. At least one interviewed developer in five was not using any performance analysis tools at all and attempting to reason about the performance using tracing and active experimentation.

Therefore we suggest features supporting incremental running and testing of programs should be included in software performance analytics systems. It has been previously noted that such features help developers to be more productive during the debugging process [14, 13]. Hence, enhancing software performance analytics systems with immediate feedback and exploratory search could result in more productive performance analysis. As an example, consider a visualisation system of performance data that supports an exploratory search process, allowing developers to localise performance bottlenecks and hence narrow the range of possible causes. Moreover, such a visual analytics tool could aid program comprehension and help reduce bugs [12]. While this strategy is applicable to more traditional programming tasks, parallel programming introduces more parameters which might be varied, such as conducting multiple runs with different numbers of threads, or changing processor affinity.

Consider the environment and the context - Developers deal with very complex environments and create abstractions and contextualise the work they are doing. However, they seem to lack support for integration of various sources of information, even simple things such as a link to the page of the company's wiki explaining the architecture of a particular library or server configuration.

We suggest that developers of software performance analytics systems keep in mind that developers work in a highly interconnected system. The interviewees expressed concern about lack of context, bad documentation or legacy code. This can be solved by integrating contextualised knowledge into tools. For example, if a developer uses a particular library, it is useful for him to be able to have easy access to documentation, have it automatically checked for thread-safety, or present some information about performance of the piece of code they are about to include.

Consider the probe effect - Developers are concerned about the probe effect. Most tools rely on code instrumentation, and hence alter the behaviour of the program. In some cases, this leads to developers avoiding using any tools and relying solely on intuition. The probe effect also makes developers avoid using performance analysis tools for continuous monitoring of production systems. Once the system is deployed, developers desire maximum performance of the system and anything that might slow down or impair a deployed program is avoided. This makes it difficult to measure the performance, capture and diagnose performance issues on production servers, when it occurs. It is especially problematic with non-deterministic issues which may occur only rarely.

We suggest that probe effect issue must be considered from the beginning while building performance analysis tools. It may be possible to reduce or avoid the probe effect by using a combination of hardware counters and operating system events. While such approaches are less relevant from a HCI perspective, an important challenge is how to make this data meaningful to the programmer; it must be possible to relate the low-level data back to the structure of the program.

Make use of orchestration models - During the interviews, developers discussed a range of design patterns and architectures they used throughout their programs. An interesting design direction would hence be to leverage orchestration models in the design of software performance analysis tools. Developers seek to pick a suitable orchestration model for a particular scope. It can be a design pattern, a way to split an array in a function for a parallel loop, or even a cluster configuration. A good tool should help them in this endeavour of "thinking parallel", which is also the number one point on a recent list of challenges in parallel computing [26].

One can think of numerous ways to take advantage of orchestration models. One direction would be to design visualisations which are specific to particular design patterns, and which emphasise features of interest within these, illustrating the performance data with respect to the pattern. One example of such a visualisation can be found in Sutter [15], in which scalability of a given algorithm is charted for a range of different numbers of producer threads and consumer threads, within a producer-consumer orchestration model.

Provide support for scope exploration - We have noted that developers consider the notion of scope of their orchestration. Additionally, when faced with a challenge, developers must often go 'back to drawing board' and reconsider their orchestration model. This process requires them to look at the problem from different angles, essentially being able to consider orchestration models at various levels of abstraction. By providing the ability to developers to interactively change the scope (core, CPU, thread, and upwards) and re-sample measurement data accordingly, developers would have additional flexibility in the challenge of diagnosis and re-orchestration.

CONCLUSIONS

Parallel programming is an important, but very complex activity. In this paper we have identified and explored some of the challenges involved in parallel programming, in particular the challenge of parallel performance analysis.

As well as illustrating the way in which correctness and performance issues are interwoven in parallel programming, the way in which the probe effect influences their performance analysis and debugging behaviour, and the way issues surrounding the complexity of the task and environment, the study has looked at the role of orchestration models in parallel software development. While some of the issues identified are apply to more traditional software development, in all cases additional dimensions are introduced by parallel programming.

The study can help to inform the discussion on potential tool support for developers, and particularly the design of performance analysis tools. Future work will involve the design, implementation and evaluation of a performance tool, building on insights and requirements emerging from the study. There is also scope for further investigation of parallel programming practices using other methodologies.

Acknowledgements

This work was supported by supported, in part, by Science Foundation Ireland grant 10/CE/I1855.

REFERENCES

1. LJ Ball and TC Ormerod. Structured and opportunistic processing in design: A critical discussion. *International Journal of Human-Computer Studies*, 1995.

2. J. Bonar and B. Liffick. A visual programming language for novices. Technical report, 1987.

3. J. Bonar and E. Soloway. Preprogramming Knowledge: A Major Source of Misconceptions in Novice Programmers. *Human-Computer Interaction*, 1(2):133–161, 1985.

4. BD Boulay, T O'Shea, and J Monk. The black box inside the glass box: Presenting computing concepts to novices. *International Journal of Human-Computer Studies*, 51(2):265–277, 1999.

5. B Cantrill, MW Shapiro, and AH Leventhal. Dynamic Instrumentation of Production Systems. *USENIX Annual Technical Conference*, 2004.

6. T Casavant. Tools and Methods for Visualization of Parallel Systems and Computations Guest Editors Introduction, June 1993.

7. J. Gould; P. Drongowski. An Exploratory Study of Computer Program Debugging. *Human Factors*, 16:258–277, 1974.

8. R. Eccles and D. Stacey. Understanding the Parallel Programmer. *20th International Symposium on High-Performance Computing*, pages 12–12, 2006.

9. V. Fix, S. Wiedenbeck, and J. Scholtz. Mental representations of programs by novices and experts. In *Proc. INTERACT '93/ACM CHI '93*, pages 74–79, 1993.

10. T. Fritz and G.C. Murphy. Using information fragments to answer the questions developers ask. *Proc. ACM/IEEE ICSE 2010*, 1:175, 2010.

11. J. Gait. A probe effect in concurrent programs. *Software, practice & experience*, 16(3):225–233, 1986.

12. D.R. Goldenson and B.J. Wang. Use of Structure Editing Tools by Novice Programmers. In *Empirical Studies of Programming: Fourth Work*, pages 99–120, 1991.

13. T R G Green and M Petre. Usability Analysis of Visual Programming Environments: A 'Cognitive Dimensions' Framework. *Journal of Visual Languages and Computing*, 7(2):131–174, 1996.

14. L. Gugerty and G Olson. Debugging by skilled and novice programmers. In *Proc. ACM CHI '86*, number April, pages 171–174, 1986.

15. H. Sutter. Understanding Parallel Performance. *Dr. Dobb's Journal*, 2008.

16. J.E. Hannay, C. MacLeod, J. Singer, H.P. Langtangen, D. Pfahl, and G. Wilson. How do scientists develop and use scientific software? *2009 ICSE Workshop on Software Engineering for Computational Science and Engineering*, pages 1–8, May 2009.

17. MT Heath. Visualizing the performance of parallel programs. *IEEE Software*, pages 29–39, 1991.

18. Lorin Hochstein and Jeff Carver. Parallel programmer productivity: A case study of novice parallel programmers. *High Performance Networking and Computing*, pages 1–9, 2005.

19. G. Kammer, P.and Bolcer, R. Taylor, A. Hitomi, and M. Bergman. Techniques for Supporting Dynamic and Adaptive Workflow. *Computer Supported Cooperative Work*, 9(3-4):269–292, 2000.

20. AJ Ko and BA Myers. An exploratory study of how developers seek, relate, and collect relevant information during software maintenance tasks. *IEEE Transactions on Software Engineering*, 32(12):971–987, 2006.

21. J Koenemann and SP Robertson. Expert problem solving strategies for program comprehension. *Proc ACM CHI '91*, pages 125–130, 1991.

22. T.D. LaToza and B.A. Myers. Hard to answer questions about code. In *"Second Workshop on Evaluation and Usability of Programming Languages and Tools (PLATEAU'2010) at SPLASH/Onward!"*, 2010.

23. J. Lawrance, C. Bogart, M. Burnett, and R. Bellamy. How people debug, revisited: An information foraging theory perspective. *IEEE Transactions on Software Engineering*, 39(2):197–215, 2009.

24. CH LeDoux and DS Parker Jr. Saving Traces for ADA Debugging. *ACM SIGAda Ada Letters*, 1985.

25. M. Luff. Empirically investigating parallel programming paradigms: A null result. *Usability of Programming Languages and Tools*, (October), 2009.

26. T. Mattson and M. Wrinn. Parallel programming: can we PLEASE get it right this time? *Proc. 45th Annual Design Automation Conference*, pages 7–11, 2008.

27. R.E. Mayer. The Psychology of How Novices Learn Computer Programming. *ACM Computing Surveys*, 13(1):121–141, January 1981.

28. R. McCauley, S. Fitzgerald, G. Lewandowski, L. Murphy, B. Simon, L. Thomas, and C. Zander. Debugging: a review of the literature from an educational perspective. *Computer Science Education*, 18(2):67–92, June 2008.

29. P.E. McKenney, M. Gupta, M.M. Michael, Phil Howard, Joshua Triplett, and Jonathan Walpole. Is parallel programming hard, and if so, why? *Control*, 2002.

30. B.P. Miller, M.D. Callaghan, J.M. Cargille, J.K. Hollingsworth, R.B. Irvin, K.L. Karavanic, K. Kunchithapadam, and T. Newhall. The Paradyn parallel performance measurement tool. *Computer*, 28(11):37–46, 1995.

31. MJ Muller and S. Kogan. Grounded theory method in HCI and CSCW. *Cambridge: IBM Center for Social Software*, pages 1–46, 2010.

32. CM Pancake and S Utter. Models for visualization in parallel debuggers. In *Proc. ACM/IEEE conference on Supercomputing*, pages 627–636, 1989.

33. J Pane and B Myers. Usability issues in the design of novice programming systems. Technical Report August, 1996.

34. D. Piorkowski, S. Fleming, I. Kwan, M. Burnett, C. Scaffidi, R. Bellamy, and J. Jordahl. The whats and hows of programmers' foraging diets. *Proc. ACM CHI 2013*, pages 3063–3072, 2013.

35. P. Pirolli and S. Card. Information foraging in information access environments. *Proc. CHI '95*, pages 51–58, 1995.

36. P. Prabhu, Y. Zhang, S. Ghosh, D.I. August, J. Huang, S. Beard, H. Kim, T. Oh, T.B. Jablin, N.P. Johnson, M. Zoufaly, A. Raman, F. Liu, and D. Walker. A survey of the practice of computational science. *State of the Practice Reports on - SC '11*, page 1, 2011.

37. S. Fleming. *Successful Strategies for Debugging Concurrent Software: An Empirical Investigation*. PhD thesis, 2009.

38. C. Sadowski and A. Shewmaker. The Last Mile : Parallel Programming and Usability. *FOSER*, 2010.

39. J. Sillito, G.C. Murphy, and K. De Volder. Questions programmers ask during software evolution tasks. In *SIGSOFT'06/FSE-14: Proceedings of the 13th ACM SIGSOFT and 14th international symposium on Foundations of Software Engineering*, 2006.

40. S Siu, M De Simone, D Goswami, and A Singh. Design Patterns for Parallel Programming. *PDPTA*, 1996.

41. DC Smith, A Cypher, and J Spohrer. KidSim: programming agents without a programming language. *Communications of the ACM*, 37(7):54–67, June 1994.

42. A.L Strauss and J. Corbin. *Basics of Qualitative Research: Techniques and Procedures for Developing Grounded Theory*. Sage, 2nd edition, 1998.

43. I. Vessey. Expertise in Debugging Computer Programs: An Analysis of the Content of Verbal Protocols. *IEEE Transactions on Systems, Man, and Cybernetics*, 16(5):621–637, September 1986.

The Patchworks Code Editor: Toward Faster Navigation with Less Code Arranging and Fewer Navigation Mistakes

Austin Z. Henley
University of Memphis
Memphis, Tennessee, USA
azhenley@memphis.edu

Scott D. Fleming
University of Memphis
Memphis, Tennessee, USA
Scott.Fleming@memphis.edu

ABSTRACT

Increasingly, people are faced with navigating large information spaces, and making such navigation efficient is of paramount concern. In this paper, we focus on the problems programmers face in navigating large code bases, and propose a novel code editor, Patchworks, that addresses the problems. In particular, Patchworks leverages two new interface idioms—the patch grid and the ribbon—to help programmers navigate more quickly, make fewer navigation errors, and spend less time arranging their code. To validate Patchworks, we conducted a user study that compared Patchworks to two existing code editors: the traditional file-based editor, Eclipse, and the newer canvas-based editor, Code Bubbles. Our results showed (1) that programmers using Patchworks were able to navigate significantly faster than with Eclipse (and comparably with Code Bubbles), (2) that programmers using Patchworks made significantly fewer navigation errors than with Code Bubbles or Eclipse, and (3) that programmers using Patchworks spent significantly less time arranging their code than with Code Bubbles (and comparably with Eclipse).

Author Keywords

Integrated development environment (IDE); code editor; navigation; user study.

ACM Classification Keywords

D.2.6 Software Engineering: Programming Environments; H.5.m. Information Interfaces and Presentation (e.g. HCI): Miscellaneous.

INTRODUCTION

Increasingly, people are faced with navigating large information spaces. For example, foraging for information has been recognized as a key part of sensemaking in such domains as intelligence analysis [11] and end-user programming [13]. To aid people in such activities, researchers have sought methods to make navigation more efficient (e.g., [12]). In this paper, we focus specifically on the problem that programmers face in efficiently navigating source code. The navigation problem is particularly acute in programming, where modern programs may comprise millions of lines of code, organized into hundreds of thousands of interrelated modules.

CHI 2014, April 26–May 1, 2014, Toronto, Ontario, Canada.

http://dx.doi.org/10.1145/2556288.2557073

Traditionally, programmers main means of navigating code has been the *file-based code editor* (e.g., the Eclipse Java editor); however, there is growing concern about how much time programmers spend on navigation in such editors. For example, one study found that programmers spent 35 percent of their time on the mechanics of navigation [18]. Thus, a variety of approaches have been proposed to make navigation less time consuming.

One of the most common approaches is to augment a file-based editor with shortcuts that the programmer can use to instantly "jump" to locations in the code. Such approaches have explored a variety of ways to generate shortcuts, such as using structural relationships in code (e.g., [20]), programmers' natural language queries (e.g., [15]), collaborative tagging (e.g., [31]), and programmer interaction behavior (e.g., [26]). However, since these approaches support only certain types of navigations, they do not entirely free programmers from the inefficiencies of navigation in file-based editors.

To directly address the problems of file-based editors, researchers have proposed a new paradigm of *canvas-based code editors* (e.g., [3, 4, 9]). These editors aim to improve programmer navigation efficiency by enabling programmers to manipulate finer-grain fragments of code, as opposed to whole files, and by enabling them to arrange those fragments on a 2D canvas. Preliminary empirical evaluations of these canvas-based editors have been generally favorable: for example, one study found that programmers using Code Bubbles made, on average, nearly half the navigation actions per minute as programmers using the file-based editor, Eclipse [3]. However, opportunities to improve on the canvas-based editor concept may remain.

In particular, the 2D canvas idiom may be the source of several types of navigation inefficiency. Programmers seeking code fragments on a large 2D canvas, may tend to make navigation mistakes (i.e., navigating in the wrong direction) because of the large space of possible directions to navigate. Moreover, arrangements of fragments on the canvas may result in on-screen clutter, increasingly the likelihood that a programmer will fail to visually locate a fragment he/she seeks. Additionally, the 2D canvas idiom may lead programmers to spend extra time and effort on arranging fragments; however, such time may not be well spent if the programmer is not far enough along in the sensemaking process to choose effective arrangements, or if arrangements quickly become obsolete because the programmer's information needs change rapidly (as recent research suggests [26]).

To address these concerns about canvas-based editors, we propose a new editor concept, *Patchworks*. Patchworks seeks to maintain the efficiency gains of canvas-based editors, while reducing the number of navigation mistakes that programmers make and the time they spend arranging code. To achieve these goals, Patchworks employs two new interface idioms: the *patch grid* and *ribbon*. These features enable programmers to edit and juxtapose code at a finer level of granularity than file-based editors, while leaving less room for navigation mistakes than canvas-based editors, and disallowing many of the time-consuming window management activities encouraged by canvas-based editors.

To validate the benefits that Patchworks provides, we conducted an empirical evaluation that pitted Patchworks against a representative file-based editor, Eclipse, and a representative canvas-based editor, Code Bubbles. In particular, the evaluation investigated three research questions:

- RQ1: Do programmers using Patchworks navigate between fragments of code more quickly?
- RQ2: Do programmers using Patchworks make fewer navigation mistakes?
- RQ3: Do programmers using Patchworks spend less time arranging code fragments?

Our work makes several key contributions. First, we introduce a novel code-editor design for efficient code navigation, Patchworks. Second, we contribute a working prototype of Patchworks for Java programming. Third, we contribute the results of an empirical evaluation that show (1) that programmer navigation in Patchworks and in Code Bubbles was significantly faster than in Eclipse, (2) that programmers made significantly fewer navigation mistakes in Patchworks than in Eclipse or in Code Bubbles, and (3) that programmers spent significantly less time arranging code fragments in Patchworks and in Eclipse than in Code Bubbles.

BACKGROUND

How Programmers Navigate Code

Empirical studies have found that programmers spend considerable time navigating among fragments of code. For example, one study found that programmers spent, on average, 35 percent of their time navigating between relevant code fragments [18]. One reason for this navigation is that programmers spend a lot of time seeking information in their code environment. One recent study found that programmers spent 50 percent of their time foraging for information [28]. Similarly, another study found that information "scent" was a significant predictor of where programmers would navigate [21].

One reason for all this information foraging may be that a primary challenge in debugging or adding a feature to a piece of software is identifying all the code relevant to the task, which is called the programmer's *working set* [19]. The process of identifying this code typically involves traversing relationships between fragments of code (e.g., following control flow dependencies). However, programmers may spend considerable time inspecting irrelevant code, as one study found [18], or even "getting lost" in the code, as another found [8].

In addition to exploratory navigations for finding relevant code, programmers also navigate frequently within their working sets. For example, one study of predictive models of programmer navigation found that the strongest predictor of which method a programmer would click in next was how recently he/she had visited the method (more recently implies more likely) [27]. This finding agrees with another study of models of programmers' information foraging behavior that found that the foraging model that took recency into account was the strongest predictor [22]. Thus, the programmers tended to repeatedly revisit the same code fragments.

However, these recency results may also suggest that the code sought by a programmer evolves as the task progresses. In particular, navigation decisions may be tied to the programmer's evolving information goals during information foraging. One recent study supported this idea with the finding that using only the last (one) navigation to predict where a programmer would go next produced more accurate predictions than using his/her last ten navigations [26].

As programmers navigate to revisit code fragments, their *spatial memory* may affect how efficiently they locate the fragments. Spatial memory is the ability to remember the location or orientation of objects. It has been leveraged to improve users' navigation times in graphical user interfaces [10], web sites [5], file systems [12, 16], and source code [7]. For example, Code Thumbnails [7] aids programmers in building spatial memory of source code by giving them a zoomed-out visualization of code files, laid out on a 2D canvas.

File-Based Code Editors

At present, file-based editors are the dominant tool paradigm that programmers use to create, modify, and navigate source code, and the empirical evidence above is mostly based on programmers using such editors. Most modern development environments, including Eclipse, NetBeans, and Visual Studio, employ file-based editors. In this paper, we will focus on the Eclipse[1] code editor as an exemplar of this paradigm. A key characteristic of file-based editors is that for reading and editing, they present the code in units by file. For example, Fig. 1 shows an Eclipse editor with the contents of one file (*Buffer.java*) displayed. To open a file, environments typically provide features for navigating the file system and for exploring the hierarchy of code modules (e.g., Java packages, classes, and methods). Since the editors we will be discussing do not vary significantly in this regard, we will say little more about such features. To navigate among code fragments (such as methods) within a file, the main capability that file-based editors provide is vertical scrolling. To navigate among open files, editors typically employ tabs that the user can click or cycle through using keyboard shortcuts (Fig. 1B).

Given the considerable time that programmers spend navigating in Eclipse [18], several qualities of traditional file-based editors may hinder efficient navigation. First, because programmers' working sets may contain only a subset of the methods in a file, navigating between two such methods may involve scrolling back and forth over irrelevant code. In such

[1] `http://www.eclipse.org/`

Figure 1. Eclipse's file-based editor, including (A) a vertically scrollable file, (B) visible tabs, and (C) two elided tabs.

cases, the programmer must take care not to miss the method he/she seeks as the code scrolls by. Additionally, scrolling through text has been found to disrupt a person's spatial memory [24, 25].

Second, because a programmer's working set may contain methods from a variety of files, navigating between such methods may involve a combination of scrolling and tab switching. However, if the programmer has too many tabs open, editors will typically begin eliding tabs, as in Fig. 1C. This automatic eliding may also disrupt the programmer's spatial memory. Moreover, revealing the elided tabs and choosing one involves additional clicking, which takes time.

Third, if a programmer wants to navigate back and forth between two methods, it stands to reason that having both methods on screen at the same time (i.e., *juxtaposing* the methods) would be ideal; however, traditional file-based editors lack effective features for juxtaposing. For example, although Eclipse provides features for splitting the editor view so that two files can be viewed at once, programmers rarely use these features [3, 19]. Moreover, prior research suggests that programmers actually want to juxtapose code [1], but find doing so in file-based editors inconvenient [3, 19].

To address the inefficiencies of navigation using file-based editors, a number of approaches augment such editors by providing shortcuts (i.e., hyperlinks) to places in the code. One common approach is linking code elements in the editor to structurally related elements. For example, in Eclipse, a programmer can select a variable name in the editor, and in a single action, link to that variable's declaration. Other approaches have included searching based on natural language queries (e.g., [15]), enabling programmers to leave tags in the code and provide shortcuts to those tags (e.g., [31]), and using programmers navigation histories to infer and link to places in the code that might be relevant (e.g., [8, 26]). However, none of these approaches have superceded the file-based editor paradigm, and programmers still commonly use scrolling and tabbing features to navigate between fragments of code, and thus, experience the inefficiencies discussed above.

Canvas-Based Code Editors

To address the problems with file-based editors, researchers have proposed a new paradigm of canvas-based code editors that enable programmers to work with more fine-grain code

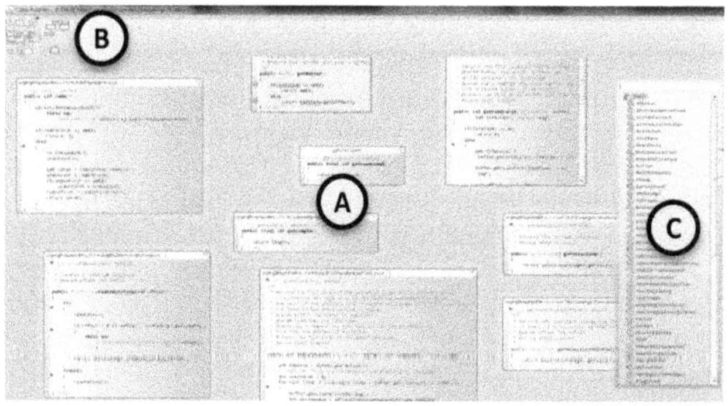

Figure 2. The Code Bubbles editor, including (A) a number of bubbles, (B) a workspace bar, and (C) a package explorer.

fragments and to arrange those fragments on a 2D canvas. This approach mitigates two key problems with file-based editors: First, it enables the programmer to focus only on relevant code fragments, rather than having to negotiate all the fragments in a file. Second, juxtaposing code fragments on a canvas is considerably more efficient than in file-based editors. Several tools have been proposed that follow this paradigm: the Self programming system [30], JASPER [4], Code Canvas [9], and Code Bubbles [2, 3]. In the remainder of the paper, we focus on Code Bubbles as a representative example of the canvas-based paradigm.

Fig. 2 depicts the Code Bubbles editor, which enables the programmer to view and edit code fragments at the granularity of methods (as well as whole files). It presents the fragments in resizeable "bubbles" (the green and red boxes in Fig. 2). The programmer can arrange the bubbles on a large 2D canvas that extends well beyond the visible area on screen. Code Bubbles also has features for grouping bubbles and for automatically drawing edges between bubbles that represent declaration relationships (neither of which are shown in the figure). Additionally, Code Bubbles has a workspace bar (Fig. 2B) that shows a bird's eye view of the canvas.

Although the canvas-based paradigm may address some problems of file-based editors, it may also introduce new ones. There are several potential problems with arranging fragments on the canvas. First, there are many more possible places to place a fragment on a 2D canvas than, for example, there are to put a tab in the tab list; however, at the time that a programmer is opening code, he/she may not have sufficient understanding of the program or task to make a quick, effective decision about where to place the fragment. For example, a recent study showed that people required a rich mental model of a topic before they could effectively structure (i.e., arrange/organize) information on the topic [17]. Second, if programmers' goals are rapidly changing (as per reactive information foraging [22, 26]), arrangements may be quickly rendered obsolete and not useful. Third, because it is common for fragments in canvas-based editors to automatically respace themselves, inserting a fragment near a group of fragments can cause those in the group to move in a cascading fashion. If the programmer does not see how the fragments have moved, it could undermine his/her ability to leverage spatial memory for navigation.

There may also be several issues with navigating about the 2D canvas. First, if there are too many fragments on screen, the programmer may have to resort to visual searching, which is relatively slower than spatial memory [14]. In fact, the creators of Code Bubbles specifically claim that it can show more code on screen than Eclipse, saying that it can fit, on average, 20 randomly selected methods from the JEdit project [2]. But if programmers place that much code on screen, the fragments may begin to all look alike, depriving the programmer of landmarks to spatially orient him/herself. Moreover, the programmer may be more likely to miss a sought method. Second, if the programmer must navigate to off-screen fragments, the large space of possible directions in which to navigate may increase the chance of navigation mistakes. Consider how this situation compares to a vertically scrolling file-based editor where the programmer has only two scrolling choices: up or down. However, in a 2D canvas, the programmer can pan in 360 degrees—considerably more room for navigational errors. Third, while navigating in the 2D canvas, the programmer may have difficulty identifying landmarks and orienting him/herself, which has been shown to be important for spatial memory [6], because of the potentially large number of similar-looking fragments.

PATCHWORKS

To overcome apparent issues with both traditional file-based editors and the canvas-based editors, we propose the Patchworks tool concept. Like the canvas-based editors, Patchworks allows the programmer to view and edit fine-grain code fragments (methods, in particular). However, Patchworks abandons the canvas idiom, and introduces instead two new idioms: the *patch grid* and the *ribbon*.

The Patch Grid

Fig. 3 depicts our Patchworks prototype. The main part of the editor consists of a 3×2 grid of *patches* (Fig. 3B). Each patch is an editor that can hold code fragments at a variety of granularities, including method, class, and file. For our initial prototype, we tentatively chose for the grid to have 6 patches, a decision based on working memory capacity (7±2) [23] as well as an attempt to optimize the use of screen space while avoiding visual clutter; however, we defer to future work the question of what the optimal number of patches might be.

A key design decision was to make the grid of patches fixed: the programmer can neither adjust the size of a patch nor the number of patches. In contrast to canvas-based editors, such as Code Bubbles, we intentionally restrict the ways in which programmers can arrange their code to discourage wasting effort on creating arrangements that provide little benefit. For example, Plumlee and Ware [29] argue that having users manage windows adds considerable complexity due to the time and attention of sizing and positioning them. Thus, Patchworks aims to alleviate this complexity by disallowing such window management. Moreover, because the patches are spatially in six fixed positions, the programmer may be less likely to miss fragments he/she is seeking and be able to scan more efficiently. Also, the patch titles always being in the same screen locations may be beneficial since it has been shown that labels enhance spatial memory [16].

Code fragments can be moved between patches in several ways. A code fragment can be opened in a patch by dragging an element from the package explorer (Fig. 3A) into the patch. The Patchworks package explorer is essentially equivalent to that of Eclipse and Code Bubbles. Fragments may be moved between patches by dragging from one patch to another. If there is an existing fragment in the destination patch, the contents of the patches are swapped.

Fig. 4 depicts the features of an individual patch. A patch consists of a title bar with the name of the fragment (Fig. 4A), a close button (Fig. 4B), and a code-fragment editor (Fig. 4C). The fragment name is based on the type of the fragment, so a method fragment gets the name of the method plus its parameters, a class gets the name of the class, etc. The fragment editor has common code-editor features, such as syntax highlighting and code folding. Clicking the close button removes the fragment from the patch, leaving the patch empty.

The Ribbon

Although the patch grid contains only six visible patches at a time, conceptually, the six patches constitute a view into a never-ending ribbon of patches. Fig. 5 depicts the ribbon concept. The visible patch grid can be shifted left or right along the ribbon via keyboard shortcuts or menu items. Patchworks animates left/right shifts to convey to the programmer the feeling of moving along the ribbon.

A key design decision was to make the ribbon extend out along one dimension, as opposed to, say, a 2D grid. By restricting the ribbon to one dimension, the programmer can slide in only two directions along the ribbon, left or right. In contrast to a 2D canvas, this considerably reduces the room for the programmer to make a navigation mistake (e.g., by navigating in the wrong direction). This idea is consistent with prior evidence comparing 2D and 3D interfaces. For example, one study of both physical and virtual 2D and 3D systems found that the participants' ability to locate information deteriorated as dimensionality increased, and that the participants reported the higher dimension systems to be more cluttered and less efficient [5].

Similar to Code Bubble's workspace bar, Patchworks has a *ribbon view* (Fig. 6) that presents a bird's eye view of the ribbon. The programmer can use the ribbon view to adjust the visible patch grid. In contrast to Code Bubbles, the ribbon view provides information about each patch, and the programmer can manipulate patches in the ribbon. Each fragment in the ribbon view includes a name (in a title bar), a thumbnail preview of its contents, and a close button. The programmer can use the ribbon view to add, move, swap, and close patches (via the same interactions as in the patch grid).

EVALUATION METHOD

To address our three research questions, we conducted a controlled study that compared our Patchworks editor to a traditional file-based editor, Eclipse, and a canvas-based editor, Code Bubbles. Thus, there were three treatments, one for each editor. To test a treatment, participants used the editor to perform tasks on a Java code base that involved opening and arranging methods (i.e., code fragments), and navigating to

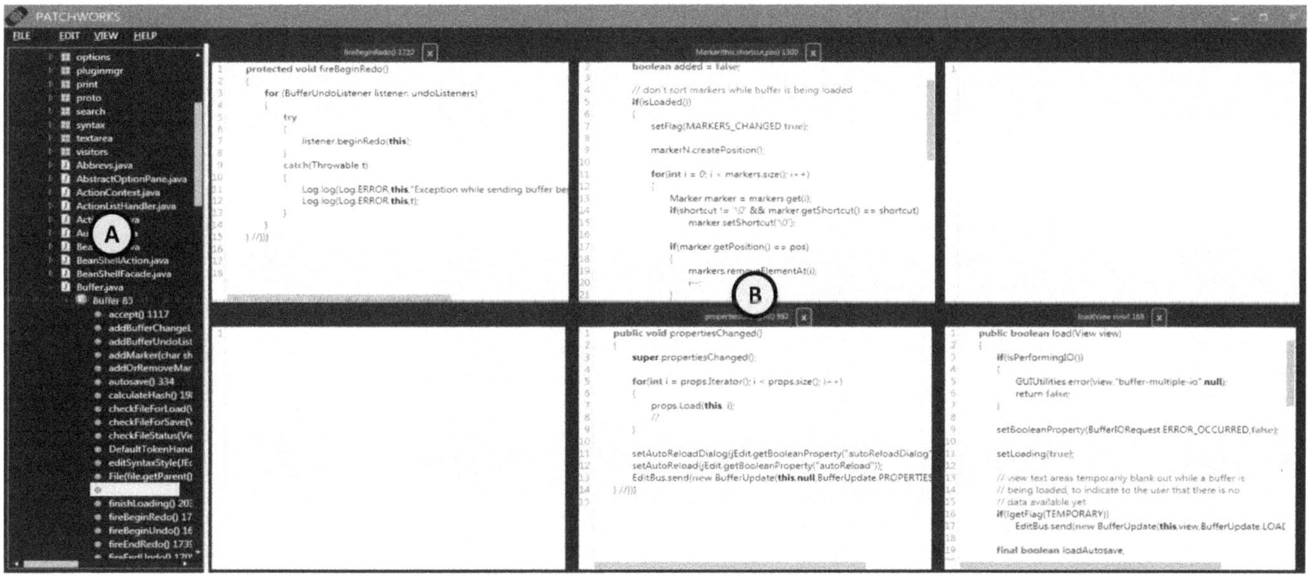

Figure 3. The Patchworks editor, including (A) a package explorer and (B) a 3×2 patch grid. Four of the patches contain code fragments and two are empty.

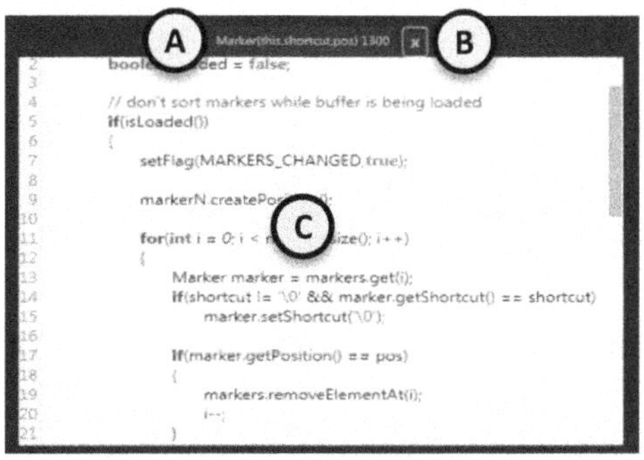

Figure 4. A patch, including (A) a title bar, (B) a close button, and (C) a code-fragment editor.

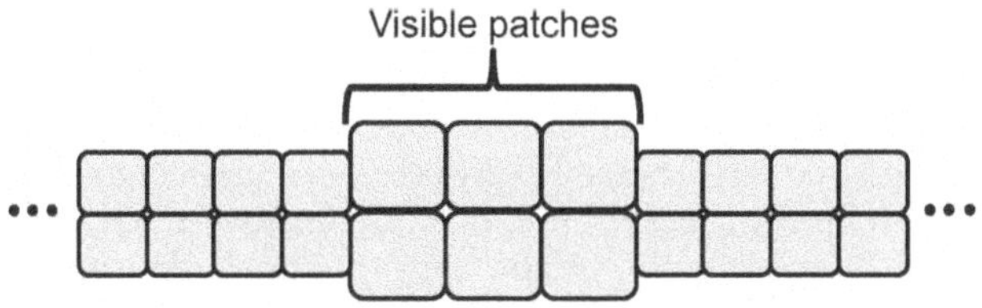

Figure 5. The conceptual ribbon of patches.

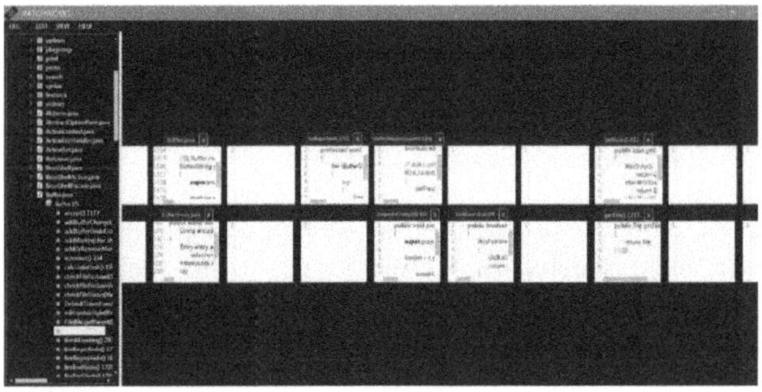

Figure 6. Patchworks' ribbon view, which provides a bird's eye view of the ribbon.

methods. Due to time constraints, each participant received only two of the treatments, randomly assigned, but balanced so that each treatment was tested equally. Since each participant tested two editors, there were two task sets, one for each editor. We blocked for two potential confounds: treatment order (due to learning effects) and task set. In addition to addressing our main RQs, we also assessed the participants' subjective opinions of the editors.

Participants

Our participants consisted of 15 university students (12 males, 3 females; 14 graduate, 1 undergraduate). They reported, on average, 4.9 ($SD = 2.6$) years of programming experience. All participants reported having at least 2 years of Java programming experience and some experience with Eclipse. None of the participants were familiar with Code Bubbles or Patchworks.

Subject Code Base

Each of the two task sets involved opening, arranging, and navigating code from the JEdit open-source text editor. We chose JEdit because it is a real-world software project, comprising 5876 Java methods and 98,718 lines of code. Each task set involved a different group of 30 methods. To enhance ecological validity, the methods in each group were all relevant to a particular concern. One of the concerns pertained to JEdit's autosave feature and the other pertained to text folding. We generated the groups using Suade [32], an automated software engineering tool for mapping methods to concerns.

Task Sets

Each task set had the following format, differing only in the concern code involved. First, the participant performed a method-opening and code-arranging task. He/she was given the list of 30 methods related to the concern, along with the reason why each method was included, and instructed to open all the methods and arrange them as he/she saw fit. The participant was also told that he/she could take as much time as he/she wanted to do this arranging. We did not reveal to the participant that we were timing this task. Next, the participant performed a series of 10 navigation tasks. For each navigation task, the participant was shown a card with the name of a method (as well as its package and class), and instructed to navigate to the method as quickly as possible. We asked participants not to use code-search features, because such features do not vary significantly among the editors, and were not the focus of this evaluation. The participant had to successfully complete each navigation task before beginning the next one, and we informed the participant that we were timing these tasks.

Procedure

Each participant's session took roughly 60 minutes. First, the participant filled out a background questionnaire, and was given an overview of the session format. Next, the participant performed the two task sets described above, each using a different tool. Before starting each task set, the participant was briefly introduced to the features of the tool he/she would be using. Last, the participant filled out a questionnaire regarding his/her opinions of the editors. If the participant used Patchworks, he/she also answered a set of Likert-scale questions regarding his/her opinion of Patchworks. In addition to the questionnaire responses and recorded times, the collected data comprised audio and video of each participant's task performance, including screen-capture video.

Analysis Method

Statistical Tests

Following standard practice, we tested the distributions of our data for normality to decide whether parametric or non-parametric statistical tests were appropriate. For RQ1 (navigation time) and RQ2 (number of mistakes), the Shapiro-Wilk test showed that for each treatment, the recorded times and counts were most likely not normally distributed ($p < 0.01$ for each), so we used the non-parametric Kruskal-Wallis rank sum test for those data. On the other hand, for RQ3 (arranging time), based on Shapiro-Wilk, we could not reject the null hypothesis that any of the recorded times were normally distributed ($p > 0.05$ for each treatment), so we used the parametric analysis of variance (ANOVA) test for those data.

Our clustering by participant might have violated the data independence assumption of our statistical tests; however, we found near 0 correlation between participant and navigation time (Spearman's $r_s = 0.06$), between participant and mistakes (Spearman's $r_s = -0.06$), and between participant and opening time (Pearson's $r = -0.03$). Thus, we conclude that participant had no significant effect on our response variables.

Navigation-Mistake Coding

To identify participants' navigation mistakes during their navigation tasks, we used the following objective criteria. We coded a navigation action as a mistake if the action moved the participant's view farther away from the target method. In our coding, we merged sequences of repeated mistakes into a single mistake. In Eclipse, scrolling in the wrong direction or selecting the wrong file tab constituted a navigation mistake. In Patchworks, shifting the view along the ribbon in the wrong direction constituted a navigation mistake.

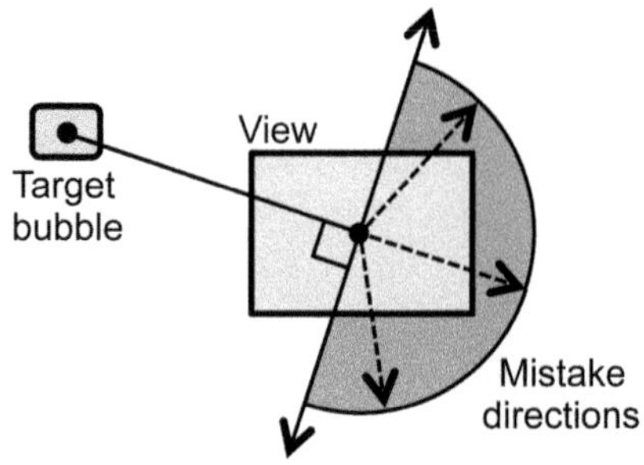

Figure 7. Method for coding navigation mistakes in Code Bubbles when the participant's target bubble is out of view.

In Code Bubbles, identifying mistakes was complicated by the 2D canvas. If the target bubble was *in view* (i.e., the majority of the bubble and its entire name were visible on screen), we coded a mistake if a navigation action caused the bubble to go *out of view* (i.e., majority off screen or name obscured). Fig. 7 illustrates how we coded mistakes if the target bubble was out of view. In such cases, we coded a mistake if the participant's navigation action caused the center of his/her view to move in any of the directions labeled *mistake directions*. To eliminate small unintentional moves and other artifacts of using a mouse, we counted only moves that resulted in bringing an out-of-view bubble (not necessarily the target) into view.

Additionally, we identified *misses*, that is, navigation mistakes in which participants had the target method in view, but failed to spot it. To count as a miss, the majority of the target method had to be in view, and the participant had to perform a navigation action that moved the method out of view.

RESULTS

RQ1 Results: Navigation Time

As Fig. 8 shows, the mean navigation times for participants using Code Bubbles and Patchworks were considerably lower than for those using Eclipse. In fact, participants' navigations in Eclipse took, on average, roughly double the time they did in Patchworks. Indeed, the results of a Kruskal-Wallis test revealed a significant effect of editor on navigation time ($\chi^2(2) = 12.1, p < 0.01$). Furthermore, a pairwise multiple-comparisons test showed that participants' navigation times with Eclipse were significantly greater than with Code Bubbles ($p < 0.05$) and with Patchworks ($p < 0.05$).

RQ2 Results: Navigation Mistakes

As Fig. 9 shows, participants made considerably fewer navigation mistakes using Patchworks than using Eclipse or Code Bubbles: Patchworks users make less than half the number of mistakes that Eclipse users and Code Bubbles users made. The results of a Kruskal-Wallis test showed a significant effect of editor on number of mistakes ($\chi^2(2) = 8.56$, $p = 0.01$). Looking at just the mistakes in which programmers failed to see a code fragment that was on screen (see the

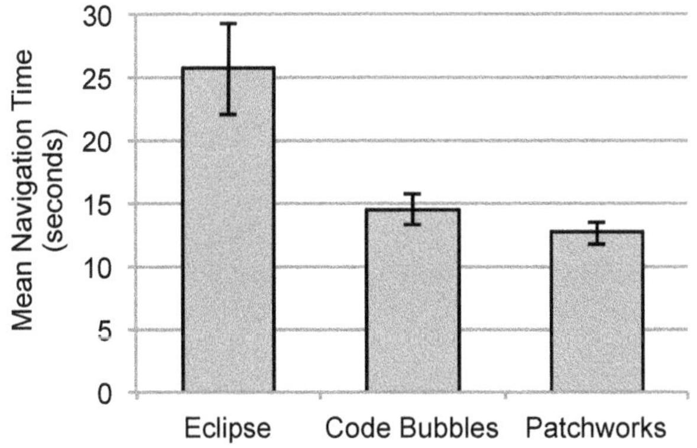

Figure 8. Participants' mean navigation times in Eclipse ($n = 99$), Code Bubbles ($n = 98$), and Patchworks ($n = 99$). Whiskers denote standard error.

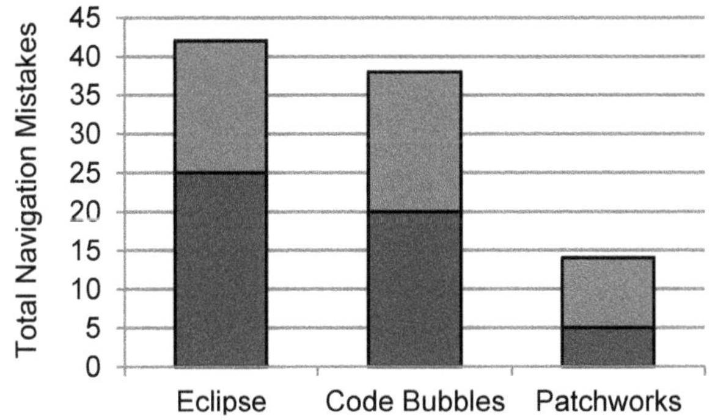

Figure 9. The number of navigation mistakes that participants made while navigating (out of 99 navigation tasks for Eclipse and Patchworks, and 98 for Code Bubbles). Inner bars show the subset of mistakes that were misses.

inner miss-mistake bars in Fig. 9), the effect of Patchworks was even stronger: Patchworks users missed code fragments one quarter or less of the number of times that they missed a fragment in Code Bubbles and Eclipse. Again, a Kruskal-Wallis test revealed a significant effect of editor on miss mistakes ($\chi^2(2) = 6.22, p = 0.04$).

RQ3: Time to Open/Arrange Code

As Fig. 10 shows, participants using Code Bubbles spent considerably more time opening and arranging their code than they did using Patchworks or Eclipse: for example, on average, Code Bubbles users took over 8 minutes longer than Patchworks users (who took 24 min on average). Indeed, an ANOVA test revealed a significant effect of editor on time ($F(2, 27) = 3.67, p = 0.04$). Delving deeper into the model, the regression coefficients, with Code Bubbles as intercept, showed a significant difference between Code Bubbles and both Eclipse ($p = 0.02$) and Patchworks ($p = 0.04$).

Participants' Subjective Opinions

As Table 1 shows, all participants reported positive opinions of Patchworks. Recall that each participant who used Patchworks completed a Likert-style opinion questionnaire (5 questions, each covering a different aspect of Patchworks). Based on their responses, participants found Patchworks particularly easy to learn and use, and they would use the patch grid and ribbon features if available in their IDE of choice.

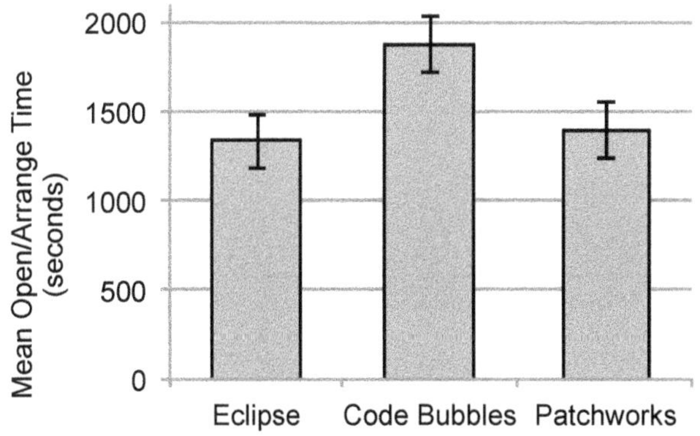

Figure 10. Mean time that participants took to open and arrange their code. Whiskers indicate standard error. $n = 10$ for each tool.

Question	Min	Mean (Std. Dev.)	Max
Easy/hard to learn?	6	6.63 (0.50)	7
Easy/hard to use?	5	6.27 (0.64)	7
Features help/hinder?	4	5.63 (0.92)	7
Like/dislike?	4	6.09 (0.83)	7
Would you use Patchworks?	5	6.27 (0.90)	7

Table 1. Results of Patchworks opinion questionnaire (on a 7-point likert scale from 7 = most favorable to 1 = least favorable).

When asked which of the tools they liked better and why, participants also favored Patchworks most often. They expressed preferring Patchworks 2:1 over Eclipse and 2:1 over Code Bubbles. Although they also preferred Code Bubbles over Eclipse, the margin was smaller at 3:2.

DISCUSSION

Summary of Results

Table 2 summarizes the results of our evaluation, and as the table shows, Patchworks matched or exceeded Eclipse and Code Bubbles on each of the evaluation criteria. As a result, Patchworks performed better overall (i.e., across all criteria) than the other editors. In particular, Patchworks was able to maintain the navigation speed gains of the canvas-based approach, Code Bubbles, but like the file-based Eclipse editor, Patchworks users spent less time arranging their code fragments. Moreover, Patchworks surpassed the other editors in helping programmers avoid navigation mistakes.

In the remainder of this section, we discuss these results with respect to our qualitative observations and the participants' comments on the questionnaire, and close with a discussion of our study's limitations.

Eclipse: Excessive Scrolling Leads to Missed Methods

Based on our qualitative observations, participants' long navigation times in Eclipse appeared largely due to time spent scrolling through files full of irrelevant code (as opposed to switching tabs), and failing to see the methods they wanted among that code. For example, P13 was searching for

Result	Eclipse	Code Bubbles	Patchworks
Fastest navigation		✔	✔
Fewest mistakes			✔
Least arranging	✔		✔
Most preferred			~

Table 2. Summary of results. A check indicates statistical evidence, and a tilde indicates evidence, but on a sample not amenable to statistics. Two checks in the same row indicate comparable results (i.e. a tie).

the method `updateStructureHighlight` within a file, *TextArea.java*, which was over 5500 lines long. In general, participants had no trouble navigating to the correct file: only two participants (P1 and P6) chose the wrong tab while navigating. P13 was no exception, and he rapidly navigated to the correct file tab; however, the editor had been previously scrolled to the middle of the file, and the target method was not in view. He began slowly scrolling toward the top of the file, scanning over methods as he went. But after passing a few methods, perhaps growing impatient, he suddenly began scrolling much more rapidly. He quickly arrived at the top of the file, having passed the target method without seeing it. He then began scrolling back down the file, this time more slowly; however, this slow pace did not last long. Again, he sped up, passing the target method a second time without seeing it, until finally arriving at the bottom of the file. He repeated this process several times before finally spotting his target. In total, he spent nearly 2 minutes scrolling, and passed the method without seeing it 5 times.

Because users of Code Bubbles and Patchworks were able to open code at the granularity of methods, they had the advantage of never having to scroll through code to reach their navigation targets. They had to search only through the 30 methods related to their current concern, which they navigated among by panning the view around the canvas in Code Bubbles, and sliding the view along the ribbon in Patchworks. Furthermore, Eclipse typically displayed only one or two methods at a time on screen, whereas Code Bubbles and Patchworks displayed substantially more methods, increasing the chances that the participant's target was already in view. One final possible advantage Code Bubbles and Patchworks users had was that the method names were clearly presented in bubble or patch title bars, as opposed to being embedded in blocks of text, as in the Eclipse editor.

Code Bubbles: More Organized, but Misses Still Common

Participants using Code Bubbles clearly invested more into the arrangement of their code fragments than Patchworks or Eclipse users. For example, when P3 performed the opening/arranging task using Code Bubbles, he first arranged his bubbles into four groups. However, apparently disatisfied with this arrangement, he spent an additional 16 minutes and 13 seconds reorganizing them into six groups. In total, this involved 270 bubble-moving actions. Similarly, P12 realized he was spending considerable time arranging his bubbles, and made several apologetic remarks: "sorry this is taking longer [compared to Patchworks]." He later commented about Code Bubbles being tougher to use than Patchworks: "the second one [Code Bubbles] took more time for me because the dragging and dropping those things [bubbles] around. . . "

In contrast, participants spent little time arranging the patches in Patchworks. In fact, only two participants moved a patch after he/she initially placed it. We observed that most participants placed the code along the ribbon in one direction. When asked what their strategy was for arranging the patches, several participants (P4, P7, P10, and P15) said they placed them sequentially along the ribbon. Other participants (P5, P11, P14) said they didn't have a strategy but P11 clarified that a strategy wasn't needed because of the ribbon view. Regardless of the strategy used, it was common for participants to leave empty columns of patches between groups, possibly as landmarks or separators.

Despite how much time Code Bubbles users spent arranging their bubbles, they still made numerous navigation errors (significantly more than Patchworks). A common mistake was for Code Bubbles users to revisit bubbles they had already seen while searching for a particular method. For example, P2 arranged his bubbles into four columns, grouped by class and function. On one of the navigation tasks, he started with the viewing area at the top of his third column. The target method, `requestFocus`, was on screen, but he failed to notice it. Instead, he panned to the bottom of the column slowly, and then back to the top. Still not seeing the method, he again panned downwards, but only halfway down the column, before going back to the top and finally noticing the method. P13 had a similar incident while performing a navigation. He had arranged his bubbles in a large square-like shape grouped by class. He started searching for the method `read` from the bottom left corner of the canvas and then panned around in a clockwise fashion, following the perimeter of his bubble cluster. Eventually, he reached the part of the cluster he had started from. He then panned around the perimeter of his cluster two more times, only this time going counter-clockwise. Finally, he spotted the method after having missed it a total of three times.

Perhaps, for the above reasons, participants made several critical comments regarding Code Bubbles. For instance, P9 preferred Code Bubble to Eclipse, but added the caveat that Code Bubbles is better only when the user is "cautious." On the other hand, P14 described Code Bubbles as "impressive," but still favored Eclipse.

Participant Feedback on Patchworks

In addition to the participants' positive Likert scores regarding Patchworks, a number of their questionnaire responses got at "why" they liked it. For instance, Participant P15 said that, compared to Eclipse, in Patchworks "It is much easier to navigate." Similarly, P13 described Patchworks as a "good way to organize methods and work switching between them," and P3 commented that Patchworks "definitely gives me an extra opportunity for quick navigation and for placing code side by side for easy viewing." P5 described Patchworks as "very fluid," and added "Eclipse is nice when only focusing on one file at a time (as I usually am doing), but Patchworks seems like a great tool for comparing and following code that may not be organized in a way that makes sense to me (ex: if I were viewing code someone else had written)." In comparing Patchworks and Code Bubbles, Participant P10 even indicated that the patch grid and ribbon features indeed overcame issues with canvas-based editors: "because it's easy to navigate through the grid rather than a canvas." These comments are encouraging and lend credence to the idea that Patchworks had successfully achieved its design objectives.

Participants also offered critical feedback and suggestions for improving Patchworks. Participant P4 wanted more lines of text in a patch, and P5 wanted more "zoom levels" for viewing the ribbon. P15 reported having difficulty finding the method names of patches. (This information was presented in a label at the top of each patch, but the font may have been too small for him to see.) P11 reported feeling "clumsy" using Patchworks, and preferred Eclipse because it was "more familiar." She also expressed wanting search features like Eclipse has, and support for multiple monitors (although she did not give specifics). Most of these concerns seem straightforward to address, and we will consider them in future work.

Limitations

Our study had several limitations that should be addressed in future work. First, from an ecological standpoint, the tasks that the participants performed were artificial, and were chosen to enable us to focus on our specific research questions. However, as a way to enhance ecological validity, we had them work with code from a real-world software project (JEdit), and we selected code fragments that were related to a shared concern. An open question that we will address in future work is how working with code over longer periods of time affects programmer navigation (e.g., because the programmer has more time to develop spatial memory). Second, all the participants in our study were students (mostly graduate), and it is an open question whether our results would hold for seasoned professional developers. Third, reactivity effects may have influenced participant performance/responses; however, we were careful not to tell participants which tool was ours or what comparisons we were making. Although participants certainly knew that Eclipse was not our tool, none were familiar with Code Bubbles or Patchworks. Fourth, the participants were using Code Bubbles and Patchworks for the first time, and it is an open question how experts with those tools might perform. However, it is encouraging that, despite being unfamiliar, participants navigated significantly faster with those tools than with the more familiar Eclipse.

CONCLUSION

In this paper, we have presented the novel Patchworks code-editor, with its two new interface idioms: the patch grid and the ribbon. Our aim was to help programmers navigate to fragments of code more quickly and with fewer navigation mistakes, and to help programmers spend less time arranging code fragments. The results of our user study show promising evidence that Patchworks fulfills these goals:

RQ1 (navigation time): Programmers using Patchworks navigated significantly faster than those using Eclipse (and comparably to those using Code Bubbles).

RQ2 (navigation mistakes): Programmers using Patchworks made significantly fewer mistakes than those using Eclipse and those using Code Bubbles.

RQ3 (arranging code): Programmers using Patchworks spent significantly less time arranging code than those using Code Bubbles (and a comparable amount of time to those using Eclipse).

These findings suggest several promising directions for future research. One open question is how programmers might best arrange fragments in the ribbon. For example, Participant P15 said that his strategy was to lay the fragments out sequentially, in the order he opened them. Scaling this strategy across time and tasks, a programmer could continually build as-needed clusters of patches in one direction along the ribbon, allowing obsolete clusters to accumulate as he/she goes. Having the patch clusters ordered by when they were accessed potentially enables the programmer to leverage a combination of temporal and spatial memory to locate patches. Building on this idea, the ribbon might be augmented with time-sequence information or even manual tagging. Another open question is how to support multiple monitors. The number of patches in the patch grid might simply be expanded to fill the available space, or alternatively, multiple patch grids might be provided, each with an independent view of the ribbon. In conclusion, answering these questions will represent a substantial step toward delivering programmers more fluid and less frustrating code navigation, and helping them regain the time they now lose to the tedious mechanics of navigation.

ACKNOWLEDGMENTS

We thank Dale Bowman Armstrong for her counsel on statistical methods. This material is based upon work supported by the National Science Foundation (NSF) under Grant No. 1302117. Any opinions, findings, and conclusions or recommendations expressed in this material are those of the authors and do not necessarily reflect the views of the NSF.

REFERENCES

1. Bragdon, A. Creating simultaneous views of source code in contemporary IDEs using tab panes and MDI child windows: A pilot study. Tech. Rep. CS-09-09, Brown Univ., 2009.
2. Bragdon, A., Reiss, S. P., Zeleznik, R., Karumuri, S., Cheung, W., Kaplan, J., Coleman, C., Adeputra, F., and LaViola, Jr., J. J. Code Bubbles: Rethinking the user interface paradigm of integrated development environments. In *Proc. 32nd ACM/IEEE Int'l Conf. Software Eng.*, ICSE '10 (2010), 455–464.
3. Bragdon, A., Zeleznik, R., Reiss, S. P., Karumuri, S., Cheung, W., Kaplan, J., Coleman, C., Adeputra, F., and LaViola, Jr., J. J. Code Bubbles: A working set-based interface for code understanding and maintenance. In *Proc. CHI '10* (2010), 2503–2512.
4. Coblenz, M. J., Ko, A. J., and Myers, B. A. JASPER: An Eclipse plug-in to facilitate software maintenance tasks. In *Proc. 2006 OOPSLA Workshop Eclipse Technology eXchange*, ETX '06, ACM (2006), 65–69.

5. Cockburn, A., and McKenzie, B. Evaluating the effectiveness of spatial memory in 2D and 3D physical and virtual environments. In *Proc. CHI '02* (2002), 203–210.
6. Darken, R. P., and Sibert, J. L. Wayfinding strategies and behaviors in large virtual worlds. In *Proc. CHI '96* (1996), 142–149.
7. DeLine, R., Czerwinski, M., Meyers, B., Venolia, G., Drucker, S., and Robertson, G. Code Thumbnails: Using spatial memory to navigate source code. In *Proc. IEEE Symp. Visual Languages and Human-Centric Computing*, VL/HCC '06 (2006), 11–18.
8. DeLine, R., Khella, A., Czerwinski, M., and Robertson, G. Towards understanding programs through wear-based filtering. In *Proc. 2005 ACM Symp. Software Visualization*, SOFTVIS '05 (2005), 183–192.
9. DeLine, R., and Rowan, K. Code Canvas: Zooming towards better development environments. In *Proc. 32nd ACM/IEEE Int'l Conf. Software Eng.*, ICSE '10 (2010), 207–210.
10. Ehret, B. D. Learning where to look: Location learning in graphical user interfaces. In *Proc. CHI '02* (2002), 211–218.
11. Evans, B., and Card, S. Augmented information assimilation: Social and algorithmic Web aids for the information long tail. In *Proc. CHI '08* (2008), 989–998.
12. Fitchett, S., Cockburn, A., and Gutwin, C. Improving navigation-based file retrieval. In *Proc. CHI '13* (2013), 2329–2338.
13. Grigoreanu, V., Burnett, M., Wiedenbeck, S., Cao, J., Rector, K., and Kwan, I. End-user debugging strategies: A sensemaking perspective. *ACM Trans. Comput.-Hum. Interact. 19*, 1 (May 2012), 5:1–5:28.
14. Hick, W. E. On the rate of gain of information. *Quarterly Journal of Experimental Psychology 4*, 1 (1952), 11–26.
15. Hill, E., Pollock, L., and Vijay-Shanker, K. Exploring the neighborhood with Dora to expedite software maintenance. In *Proc. 22nd IEEE/ACM Int. Conf. Automated Software Eng.*, ASE '07 (2007), 14–23.
16. Jones, W. P., and Dumais, S. T. The spatial metaphor for user interfaces: Experimental tests of reference by location versus name. *ACM Trans. Inf. Syst. 4*, 1 (Jan. 1986), 42–63.
17. Kittur, A., Peters, A. M., Diriye, A., Telang, T., and Bove, M. R. Costs and benefits of structured information foraging. In *Proc. CHI '13* (2013), 2989–2998.
18. Ko, A. J., Aung, H., and Myers, B. A. Eliciting design requirements for maintenance-oriented IDEs: A detailed study of corrective and perfective maintenance tasks. In *Proc. 27th Int'l Conf. Software Engineering*, ICSE '05 (2005), 126–135.
19. Ko, A. J., Myers, B. A., Coblenz, M. J., and Aung, H. H. An exploratory study of how developers seek, relate, and collect relevant information during software maintenance tasks. *IEEE Trans. Softw. Eng. 32*, 12 (Dec. 2006), 971–987.
20. Krämer, J.-P., Kurz, J., Karrer, T., and Borchers, J. Blaze: Supporting two-phased call graph navigation in source code. In *Ext. Abstracts CHI '12* (2012), 2195–2200.
21. Lawrance, J., Bellamy, R., and Burnett, M. Scents in programs: Does information foraging theory apply to program maintenance? In *Proc. IEEE Symp. Visual Languages and Human-Centric Computing*, VL/HCC '07 (2007), 15–22.
22. Lawrance, J., Burnett, M., Bellamy, R., Bogart, C., and Swart, C. Reactive information foraging for evolving goals. In *Proc. CHI '10* (2010), 25–34.
23. Miller, G. A. The magical number seven, plus or minus two: Some limits on our capacity for processing information. *Psychol. Rev. 63*, 2 (1956), 81–97.
24. O'Hara, K., and Sellen, A. A comparison of reading paper and on-line documents. In *Proc. CHI '97* (1997), 335–342.
25. O'Hara, K., Sellen, A., and Bentley, R. Supporting memory for spatial location while reading from small displays. In *Ext. Abstracts CHI '99* (1999), 220–221.
26. Piorkowski, D., Fleming, S., Scaffidi, C., Bogart, C., Burnett, M., John, B., Bellamy, R., and Swart, C. Reactive information foraging: An empirical investigation of theory-based recommender systems for programmers. In *Proc. CHI '12* (2012), 1471–1480.
27. Piorkowski, D., Fleming, S. D., Scaffidi, C., John, L., Bogart, C., John, B. E., Burnett, M., and Bellamy, R. Modeling programmer navigation: A head-to-head empirical evaluation of predictive models. In *Proc. IEEE Symp. Visual Languages and Human-Centric Computing*, VL/HCC '11 (2011), 109–116.
28. Piorkowski, D. J., Fleming, S. D., Kwan, I., Burnett, M. M., Scaffidi, C., Bellamy, R. K., and Jordahl, J. The whats and hows of programmers' foraging diets. In *Proc. CHI '13* (2013), 3063–3072.
29. Plumlee, M. D., and Ware, C. Zooming versus multiple window interfaces: Cognitive costs of visual comparisons. *ACM Trans. Comput.-Hum. Interact. 13*, 2 (June 2006), 179–209.
30. Smith, R. B., Maloney, J., and Ungar, D. The Self-4.0 user interface: Manifesting a system-wide vision of concreteness, uniformity, and flexibility. In *Proc. 10th Annu. Conf. Object-Oriented Programming Syst., Languages, and Applicat.*, OOPSLA '95 (1995), 47–60.
31. Storey, M.-A., Cheng, L.-T., Bull, I., and Rigby, P. Shared waypoints and social tagging to support collaboration in software development. In *Proc. Conf. Computer Supported Cooperative Work*, CSCW '06, ACM (2006), 195–198.
32. Warr, F. W., and Robillard, M. P. Suade: Topology-based searches for software investigation. In *Proc. 29th Int'l Conf. Software Eng.*, ICSE '07 (2007), 780–783.

A Novel Knee Rehabilitation System for the Home

Mobolaji Ayoade and Lynne Baillie
ITT Research Group, School of Engineering and Built Environment,
Glasgow Caledonian University, UK
{Mobolaji.ayoade, L.baillie}@gcu.ac.uk

ABSTRACT
In this paper, we describe the design and evaluation of an interactive home-based rehabilitation visualisation system used by a wide variety of ages (users in our studies were aged from 47-89) to undertake rehabilitation in the home following knee replacement surgery. We present the rehabilitation visualization system and the results of a randomized controlled study in which we investigated the usability and feasibility of the system in the home. We found that our users were able to use the system successfully for their rehabilitation with improved rehabilitation outcomes after 6 weeks when compared to the current rehabilitation care. Finally we highlight the lessons learned which will benefit prospective designers of home rehabilitation technology in ensuring successful home evaluations in clinical rehabilitation.

Author Keywords

User Design; Usability; Home Knee Rehabilitation; Inertial Sensors; Visualizations.

ACM Classification Keywords
H.5.2. Information interfaces and presentation: Miscellaneous.

INTRODUCTION
Osteoarthritis of the knee is a degenerative joint disease associated with ageing, characterised by excessive pain and disability of the knee. Knee replacement (KR) is an effective treatment for severe knee osteoarthritis where the worn knee joint is replaced with ceramic or metal implants. However to optimise functional recovery a period of physical rehabilitation is routinely prescribed [17]. Over 80,000 knee replacements are performed per year [1] in the UK and the bulk of the acute post-operative rehabilitation takes place in the patients' homes and not in the hospital or rehabilitation centres. As life expectancy is rising across the world, the population of older adults affected by osteoarthritis and needing home rehabilitation is set to increase. After surgery the patients use exercise handbooks and/or DVDs for their home rehabilitation. Patients are also often supported during their home rehabilitation with a phone call check up in the second week of their home rehabilitation. There is growing evidence that the exercises provided in the handbook and shown in the DVD's are less than ideal because they can be repetitive, boring [35] and lack a reasonable level of interactivity, which could lead to low adherence [23] and therefore poor rehabilitation outcomes. This is particularly problematic for KR because it can lead to: failure to recover suitable knee range of motion (ROM), lead to the inability to safely carry out activities of daily living [30]; or revision surgery and reduction in the lifespan of the new joint [21].

CHI 2014, April 26 - May 01 2014, Toronto, ON, Canada
Copyright 2014 ACM 978-1-4503-2473-1/14/04...$15.00.
http://dx.doi.org/10.1145/2556288.2557353

In order to improve the effectiveness of home rehabilitation, it has been suggested that the presence of a physiotherapist in the home or return visits to a community based rehabilitation centre could ensure the correct performance of the exercises and provide motivation to exercise [9]; however this method is less than optimal because it can be very expensive and time consuming for health professionals and patients. Thus there has been a growing interest in the development and evaluation of enabling rehabilitation technologies that could provide some form of feedback and motivation for various health conditions. These health conditions include but are not limited to stroke rehabilitation [26], falls prevention [34] and knee replacements [3, 33]. Some of these systems have been shown to motivate and promote enjoyment of rehabilitation activities but there is limited evidence supporting their clinical effectiveness [12].

Furthermore, the majority of the studies of home rehabilitation have been carried out in controlled environments, such as laboratories [8] or rehabilitation centers [24]. Only a few studies have focused on truly home-based systems [2]. In those home-based studies, health professionals have retained control over the system and supervised the exercise sessions with patients over the Internet [22]. This would result in extra workload for the therapists in countries like the UK where the patients have limited contact with therapists during the home rehabilitation period. The performance of these home-based systems in the home under the full control of patients over the full term of their rehabilitation has thus not been reported upon before. We designed a home-based system, which would be controlled by the patients themselves. We also evaluated the system in the home, as we believe that the true potential of home rehabilitation technology cannot be verified without testing it thoroughly in the home, which is the setting for knee rehabilitation. This placed strict constraints on us as designers to create a system that was capable of being used over a 6 week time period by the intended users' i.e. older people, with an average age of 68 years [28]. To our knowledge, this is the first reported study of the use of motion sensors, visualization and video conferencing by patients on their own in their homes to aid their rehabilitation after knee surgery. We present evidence of its effectiveness in improving rehabilitation outcomes, patient experiences, and communication with therapists. Finally we highlight the lessons learned which will benefit prospective designers of home rehabilitation technology in ensuring successful home evaluations in clinical rehabilitation.

RELATED WORK

In a survey, Zhou et al. [37] identified that seniors (> 65 years) have not adopted technology as part of their rehabilitation because most systems have complex set ups, are expensive, often have poor interactivity and may require large or fixed spaces which may not be available or wanted in people's current homes. There have however been recent developments in commercial video game technologies, gesture and motion sensors, which are cheap, require less space and are simpler to use allowing researchers to adapt these technologies for rehabilitation purposes [12]. The use of commercial gaming in rehabilitation has been shown to have the potential of improving motivation and adherence to rehabilitation programs by facilitating the enjoyability of physical activities, but they do not necessarily promote correct performance of rehabilitation exercises as the game controllers capture users' gestures or gross movement patterns [32].

Camera based systems such as Animal Feeder [6] Silver fit [24] and the Kinect allow easy full body interaction without the need to wear markers or sensors. However a knee replacement patient must sit or lie on a bed or chair in a comfortable position while performing the exercises and the cameras may not be able to separate the patient from the furniture causing the system to incorrectly show the users movement [13]. Other popular commercial game technology involving the use of hand held controllers such as the Nintendo Wii are unsuitable because of their inability to capture fine-grained movements [7], also they were not built to be body worn sensors and wearing two on one leg could be uncomfortable for the patients who has just undergone knee surgery.

Other types of sensing systems suitable for home use include smartphones with in-built motion sensors. For instance, Doyle et al. [8] used the accelerometer in an iPhone strapped to the body to provide visual feedback on correct pace and angle of motion and found that the visual feedback encouraged the correct performance of rehabilitation exercises. However this set up is unsuitable for knee rehabilitation because multiple phones would be required and interaction would be cumbersome. Another study used a self-contained wearable knee device for visualizing knee rehabilitation exercises that indicated how straight the knee is during exercises [2]. While this setup is suitable for knee rehabilitation, the amount of feedback provided was very limited and does not cover the full range of knee rehabilitation exercises. Another study used wireless motion sensors to provide real-time visual feedback during lower limb rehabilitation in a controlled setting [36] but the usability in an uncontrolled setting is yet to be evaluated. In this paper we report on the inertial sensors that we used to overcome the limitations posed by other motion sensing technologies. These sensors were found to be easy to use as well as comfortable for the user to wear [3].

The studies discussed above had relatively short evaluation durations of two days for investigating the effectiveness of their knee rehabilitation systems. The recommended duration for knee rehabilitation after knee surgery is six weeks; therefore two days could be viewed as too short a time to test such a system fully. Our study investigated the effectiveness of the Rehabilitation Visualisation System (RVS) over the entire period (6 weeks) of acute rehabilitation following knee replacement surgery.

Other longer-term studies in rehabilitation like Russell et al's. [25], have delivered supervised home-based therapy sessions over video calls. Yet after the sessions patients still have to continue in unsupervised sessions before the next supervised session. To overcome this, Piqueras et al [22] used wireless motion sensors for an interactive rehabilitation system that allows the patient to be monitored by therapists' in-between sessions. Their system was therapist centered and only limited feedback on progress was given to the user. Our system is patient centered requiring no intervention from the therapists, and we provide rich feedback on performance and progress in unsupervised exercise sessions. We integrated a video conferencing application to our system to help the patient discuss their rehabilitation progress with a therapist and get additional feedback on their performance.

Many studies on rehabilitation technology have employed user-centered approaches to the design of rehabilitation tools for seniors [11, 34]. The result has been more usable and acceptable applications, as identified by Kujala [15]. We also employed the principles of user-centered design throughout the phases of the development of the system.

The majority of the studies in rehabilitation technology have focused on usability metrics such as ease of use [10], effectiveness of visual feedback [2] and satisfaction of the target population [12]. However, it has been found that usability metrics alone will not cover the full extent of the users experience of rehabilitation over time [14]. We therefore wanted to explore some additional metrics such as quality of life and improved knee function that are meaningful to the patients and health professionals.

The first novel part of our work is in the combination of: the sensors, video conferencing, wedge (for correct sensor-body alignment calibration) and the user designed interfaces, which incorporated designs directly from people who had undergone knee surgery). The second novel part of our work was to go beyond the normal usability evaluation and in order to do this we needed to carefully ensure that our rehabilitation visualisation system could be used by patients to undertake their 6 week rehabilitation programme in their own home unsupervised. In the next section, we will describe the design process and evaluation protocol for the rehabilitation visualization system.

METHODS

Figure 1 shows all the steps leading up to the home study, which is reported in this paper.

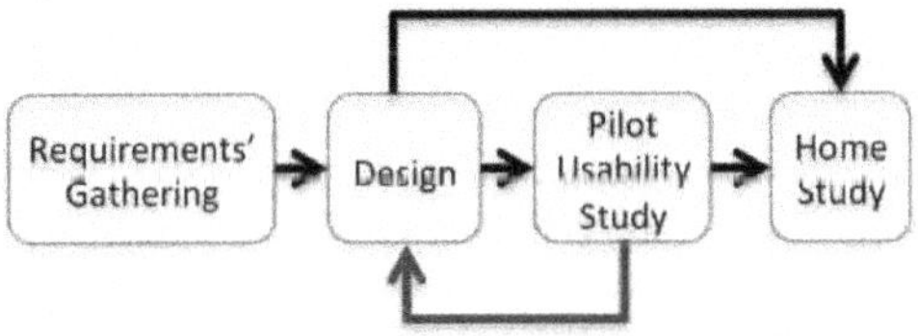

Figure 1. Research phases.

The study phases are established HCI practices in Participatory Design (PD). However, very few studies on rehabilitation technologies have gone further than the laboratory or controlled environments to real world contexts [4]. The home study was carried out in unsupervised settings and thus would provide valuable design insights for future rehabilitation systems.

User Requirement Gathering

The clinical pathways for knee replacement intervention in two hospitals were studied using semi-structured interviews and field observations/shadowing with 2 orthopedic surgeons and 2 physiotherapists in order to identify the requirements for effective knee rehabilitation in the home. We found that the exercises prescribed are aimed at restoring strength and range of motion of the operated leg. Most patients do these exercises on their own in their homes with the aid of a handbook. The list below summarizes initial requirements used in developing a low fidelity exploratory prototype.

- Patients require feedback on correctness of movement during exercises.
- Patients need to be motivated beyond the initial relief from excessive pain – which usually occurs almost immediately after surgery.
- Easy-to-use home technology that is suitable for frail seniors to setup and use on their own.

User Design Workshop

We undertook a design workshop that was published in [3] with eleven former knee replacement patients to explore user design requirements. The first prototype rehabilitation visualization system was presented to them and consisted of two inertial motion sensors and a low fidelity animation on a laptop. The workshop was structured around discussions on past rehabilitation experiences, the prototype rehabilitation visualization system and the participants design ideas for the visual elements. Figure 2 shows the user sketches for knee ROM. The participants wanted color-coded feedback on knee range of movements, a full body figure showing the appropriate posture of the exercises and a weekly progress screen.

Figure 2. User sketches (a) knee ROM (b) height of leg.

Additional requirements not shown in the Figure 2 include: a repetition counter, and a timer. All of the participants felt the use of the prototype rehabilitation visualization system was appropriate and relatively easy to use.

System Description

Rehabilitation Visualization Interface

We created the final design based on our findings from the design workshop and previous discussions with health professionals. Figure 3 shows a typical visualization for the knee replacement rehabilitation exercises. (A) is the guide mannequin that shows the user how to correctly perform the exercises at the optimum pace. This guide could be minimized at anytime. (B) is the real-time feedback on the user's movements. The whole body was used to provide guidance on correct posture.

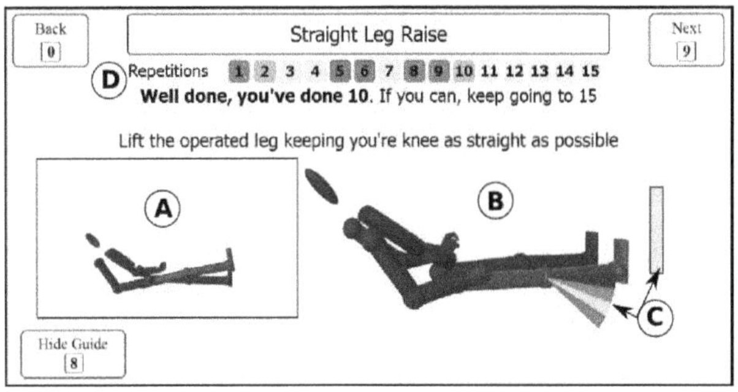

Figure 3. 'Straight leg raise' exercise visualization.

(C) is the graphic (fan) with changing gradient of colors (red to green) was used to show the users range of motion in real-time during each repetition: a deep green represented the recommended range of movement; a light green represented an 'almost there' range; a yellow indicated a minimum range and a red indicated a poor range. (D) Is a colored repetition counter bar that allows the user to see their performance for each repetition completed.

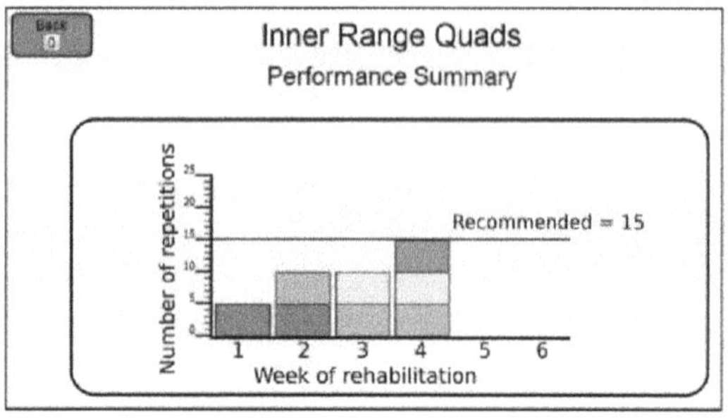

Figure 4. Progress chart.

Figure 4 shows a typical progress chart that tracks the users' quality and quantity of motion in the affected limb over an extended period of time. This way, the user could tell how much progress they had made with each exercise in terms of the ability to move the affected joint and the average number of repetitions completed per week. Both the target users and the health professionals suggested that progress should be shown on a weekly basis rather than a daily basis because not every exercise session will show progress.

Hardware Description

We built inertial motion sensors that could be easily attached to the thigh and leg with elastic Velcro straps. The sensors are charged over standard mini-USB ports. The sensors labels contain a text and an arrow showing the up direction for correct placement (Figure 5). An inertial sensor unit consists of three sensors a triple-axis gyroscope, triple-axis accelerometer, and triple-axis magnetometer.

Figure 5. Wireless inertial sensors.

The user's movement is wirelessly transmitted to a laptop running the rehabilitation software, previously described. For an inertial sensor to accurately track body movement the sensor-body offsets must be estimated and corrected using a calibration procedure [19]. We used a simple static calibration procedure that requires the user to place the knee on a wedge of a known angle (140 degrees).

Figure 6 shows a typical home setup. In a typical home set up the rehabilitation software runs automatically once the laptop is switched on and a user interacts with the rehabilitation software using either the keyboard or a remote control. To use the system, a patient sets up the laptop in any comfortable location in the house e.g. bedroom, wears the sensors and use the blue knee wedge as shown in Figure 6 while during home exercise sessions. The remote control was used because it would be difficult for knee patients to reach the laptop. Furthermore most seniors are familiar with a TV remote.

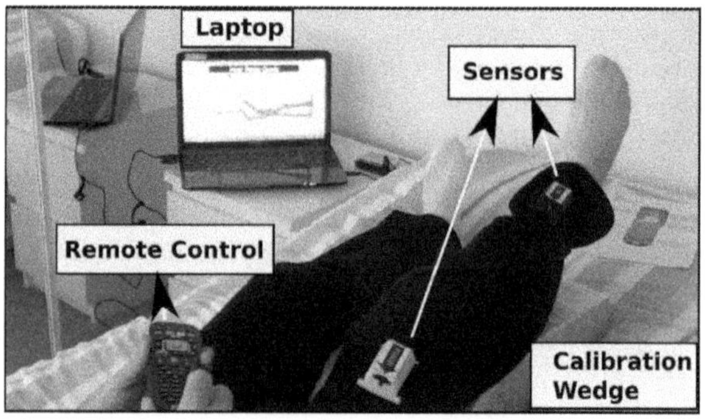

Figure 6. A typical home set up.

Pilot Usability Study

We carried out two pilot usability studies with six former knee replacement patients after we developed a working rehabilitation visualization system. One study was carried out in the laboratory so that the system could be evaluated in a controlled environment. The other study was carried out in participants' homes (the intended environment) [3]. We found that the rehabilitation visualization system enabled the participants to perform the exercises more correctly as they paid attention to the pace, range of movement and the number of repetitions completed. On the other hand, certain usability issues were identified with regards to the angular ranges we had adopted – the angles seemed to be too difficult for the users to achieve.

Randomized Controlled Home Study

The main focus of this paper is the randomized controlled home study we conducted with knee replacement patients in the acute phase of their post-operative rehabilitation for a period of six weeks. The objectives of the study were as follows:

1. To explore the user experiences of our rehabilitation visualization system following knee replacement surgery.
2. To investigate the effects of using our system compared to standard care following knee replacement surgery.
3. To explore the use of video conferencing, which is used in our system, as an alternative to the phone call checkup.

Ethical Approval and Recruitment

The NHS West of Scotland Research Ethics Committee 5 approved the study (Ref: 12/WS/0151). All patients scheduled to undergo their first unilateral total knee replacement at the hospital were eligible for inclusion into the study. Patients with severe visual or cognitive impairments (determined by the treating surgeon) and non-English speakers were excluded from the study. The surgeons screened the patients and provided a summary of the trial to the patients at the preoperative assessment clinic. They then signposted the patients to the researchers who answered any further questions the patient might have. The time between the preoperative assessment clinic and surgery varies between a few days to months. Informed consent was obtained from the patients when they arrived at the hospital a day before or the day of surgery or postoperatively before discharge.

Randomization

Baseline measures were obtained by the researchers just before a patient was discharged. The patients were randomized after the baseline measures had been obtained. The randomization was stratified on age (<69 or >69 years) and sex to ensure group comparability. The participants were randomly assigned into either the control group or the rehabilitation visualization system (RVS) group using an offsite computer generated randomization system. Both groups received the standard care handbook but only the RVS group received the system.

The Home Rehabilitation

Patients received the exercise handbook and DVD provided by the hospital as part of their standard care. In addition a therapist called each patient on a one off basis in the 2nd week from discharge to check up on rehabilitation progress. For participants in the RVS group, we setup the system within 10 days of their getting home. The setup procedure consists of a brief training session on how to use the various components of the system. The participants were advised to use the rehabilitation visualization system each time they exercised. The following are the steps involved in using the rehabilitation visualization system.

- Setup: switch on laptop and sensors, put on the sensors
- Select exercise from the exercise menu
- Calibrate the sensors using the wedge
- Undertake the exercise
- Select the next exercise
- Quit when session is completed.

The participants could also view their progress at the end of every week from the exercise menu. They received a video call in week 3 from the therapist and in the sixth week they returned to the hospital for a clinical checkup.

Outcome Measures

Functional Performance Assessments

Knee range of motion is an important clinical parameter following knee replacement surgery. It is a predictor of independence and safety of the patients when carrying out activities of daily living [16]. The active knee ROM was measured using a standard goniometer. Three measurements were recorded and the average used for analysis.

Health Surveys in Orthopedics

We used the Oxford knee score (OKS) - a self-reported condition specific measure that provides a measure of knee condition before and following knee replacement surgery. It consists of 12 items with 5 possible ratings and is widely used as an outcome measure following knee replacement surgery [20]. The scoring system ranges from 0 – 48, with 48 meaning no problem with the knee. We also measured the participants' general health using the short form health survey SF-12[1]. It consists of 12 questions with 5 response scales. We report the mental component summary (MCS) scores in this paper.

Rehabilitation Experience

Each participant completed a background questionnaire during the baseline measurement i.e. shortly before discharge from the hospital. Participants also completed an intrinsic motivation inventory[2] (IMI) at the end of the 2nd and 6th week. The Intrinsic Motivation Inventory (IMI) was used to assess participants' subjective experiences related to their home rehabilitation and was completed by all the participants. We selected interest/enjoyment, perceived competence, pressure/tension and effort subscales based on our research objectives.

Adherence to exercise program

A post study questionnaire was used to assess users' experiences in terms of adherence and compliance levels to rehabilitation program on a scale of 0 – "I did few or none" to 3 - "I did the recommended number daily". They were also asked to list the factors influencing their compliance to the rehabilitation program. We also captured any particular challenges the users might have faced using the system.

Usability

The System usability scale (SUS) was used as a self reported measure of perceived usability of the rehabilitation visualization system [27]. The SUS consists of 10 question and an answer rating on a 5 point Likert scale from 1-strongly disagree to 5-strongly agree.

RESULTS

The group difference was analyzed using the Mann-Whitney test for two independent samples.

Participants

Twenty-one participants started the home study. The demographic information is shown in Table 1.

Variable	Control	RVS
Median Age (Range)	71(47 - 85)	69 (50 - 78)
Female	5	6
Male	5	5
Novice user	5	2
Occasional user	2	4
Experienced user	3	5
Excluded		
• Dropouts	1	2
• Complications	2	1
Net Participants	7	8

Table 1. Baseline characteristics of both groups (RVS= Rehabilitation Visualization System).

[1] The SF12v2: *http://www.sf-36.org/tools/sf12.shtml.*
[2] *http://www.selfdeterminationtheory.org/questionnaires/*

However only data from 15 participants were included in the analysis. This was because three participants dropped out of the study while another three were excluded because they had medical complications.

User Experience Outcomes

Usability

The mean SUS score for the RVS group was 95.83 ($SD = \pm 6.12$). The 95% confidence interval is (91.13 – 100.54). However, 2 participants that dropped out of the study because of problems with the remote control as windows updates was interfering with the remote control script. Another participant had problems with the remote control but continued using the keyboard until the problem was fixed. A fourth participant encountered problems with the charging port for the sensors.

Some of the user comments on the different rehabilitation aids can be seen in Table 2.

Handbook/ DVD	*"When I'm sitting down and watching the TV, I'm reading the book. Handy"* *"Book explained what you were expected to achieve"*
	"Older people in DVD just didn't look right" *"Using the DVD made you feel like you were part of a group."*
RVS	*"It is easier and more interesting because you can watch your progress. It will be boring otherwise"* *"Encourages completion of 15 repetitions. It helped me to monitor my improvement"*

Table 2. User comments on the tools used.

From the user comments, it is evident that the rehabilitation visualization system made the home rehabilitation more engaging – actively encouraging better performance.

Motivation

The results of the average rating (maximum rating of 7) for the four subscales of intrinsic motivation inventory are shown in the Table 3. The values displayed are mean and standard deviation. On the interest/enjoyment subscale both groups had above average intrinsic motivation, but the control group had lower levels than the RVS group in week 2. In week 6, the trend was reversed with the control group having higher levels of intrinsic motivation. On the perceived competence subscale, the RVS group felt more competent than the control group in week 2. However by week 6, the control group felt a lot more competent while on the effort/importance subscale, both groups placed almost an equal amount of importance on the rehabilitation exercises in week 2. It is only the control group that reported increase in the effort/importance; the RVS group remained the same.

		Compe-tence	**Effort**	**Interest**	**Pressure**
Wk. 2	Control	5.8 ±1.1	6.5 ±0.8	5.9 ±1.1	2.8 ±1.5
	RVS	6.1 ±1.2	7.0 ±0.8	6.5 ±1.5	2.5 ±1.5
	P-value	**0.371**	**0.492**	**0.232**	**0.435**
Wk. 6	Control	7.0 ±0.8	7.0 ±0.6	7.0 ±1.1	1.0 ±1.4
	RVS	7.0 ±0.7	7.0 ±0.8	6.3 ±1.1	1.0 ±1.0
	P-value	**0.505**	**0.352**	**0.234**	**0.469**
Chan-ge	Control	0.3 ±0.9	0.0 ±0.6	0.8 ±0.5	-0.4±1.5
	RVS	0.8 ±1.2	0.0 ±0.1	-0.4 ±1.5	-0.8±1.0
	P-value	**0.438**	**0.195**	**0.079**	**0.411**

Table 3. Intrinsic motivation subscales.

The pressure subscale shows that both groups had similar levels of pressure, which reduced by the 6th week.

Adherence to Rehabilitation Program

The participants were asked to describe their average compliance to the recommendations of the health professionals – 4 times daily. Table 4 shows there were similarities in the compliance profile between the two groups.

Adherence Level	Control	RVS
I missed many days (< 60 %)	0	0
I missed a few days (60 - 80 %)	2	2
I did <4 times daily (80 – 90 %)	2	2
I did 4 times everyday (> 90 %)	3	4

Table 4. Adherence profile across both groups.

It seems the control group reported higher adherence to the exercises but not significantly different ($p = 0.379$). However, when we probed further by asking them to list the top 3 factors that influenced their adherence level, the following themes emerged:

- Exercise burden: 5 of the RVS group reported that 4 times a day was too much given the average exercise session of 40 minutes. Three of the control group expressed similar sentiments. A typical comment made by the participants was that *"... not enough time and you get exhausted"*.
- Family support: 3 of the participants felt they were able to undertake the exercises because of the family support they received as evidenced by this comment: *"My husband and son motivated me to go on"*
- Health: 4 of the participants that missed a few days cited poor health or pain as the reason for non-compliance while a participant attributed her good health as one of her factors for full compliance.

- Fitness: 4 of the participants wanted to get back to full fitness quickly so that they could either go back to work or independence. A typical comment *"the desire to get back to full fitness motivated me."*
- Commitments to: family such as holidays and funerals (n=1), the research (n=3) and the hospital staff (n=2) were also cited as motivators for various levels of compliance.

Communicating Progress
The therapist during the video call check up could observe the progress charts of the patients and see and talk to the patients. Most of patients reported that they felt more confident discussing their performance with the therapist because they could point out when they had achieved a green (good) performance. A typical conversation between the patient and therapist is shown in Figure 7.

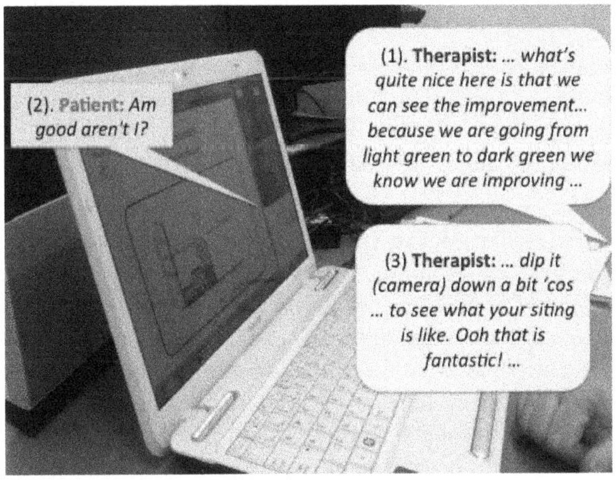

Figure 7. A therapist examines a user's progress.

The use of the video call and rehabilitation visualization system (RVS) during check up opened up new possibilities for effective check up as evidenced in the therapist's comments *"I could identify which exercises require more effort"* and *"previously patients had difficulty visualizing what constitutes 90 degrees of knee flexion"*.

Heath Outcomes

Improvements in knee function and general health
For the SF12 the mental component of health (MCS), RVS group had a percentage improvement of 9.8% compared to -1.4% for the control group. The absolute change and improvement from week 1 indicates that the RVS group had slightly better recovery in terms of their mental health (median change: Control = -2.8, *SD* = 10.2; RVS = 3.1, *SD* = 11.5; p = 0.140). The negative improvement for the control group implies that some participants recorded a decrease in the SF12 score after 6 weeks.

For the subjective knee function (measured by the Oxford Knee Score), both groups reported improvement in the knee score. The absolute change from week 1 by week 6 tended towards statistical significance (median: Control = 17, *SD* = 7.8; RVS = 23, *SD* = 8.7; p = 0.109).

For the knee flexion, the RVS group were significantly worse than the control group in Week 1 (median: Control = 81 degrees, *SD* = 11.9; RVS = 69 degrees, *SD* = 9.7; p = 0.047). However by week 6, both groups had comparable knee flexion (median: Control = 105 degrees, *SD* = 14.0; RVS = 96 degrees, *SD* = 8.9; p = 0.478). The RVS group had greater improvement compared to the control group as shown in Figure 8. This improvement suggests a trend toward significant improvement with a p-value of 0.06.

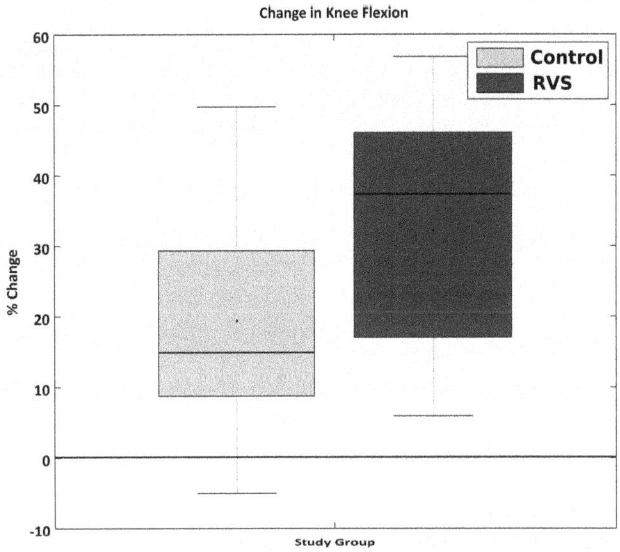

Figure 8. Boxplot of improvement in knee flexion.

It can also be seen that some of the control group had worse knee flexion than at the start (negative change) while none of the RVS group had worse knee flexion.

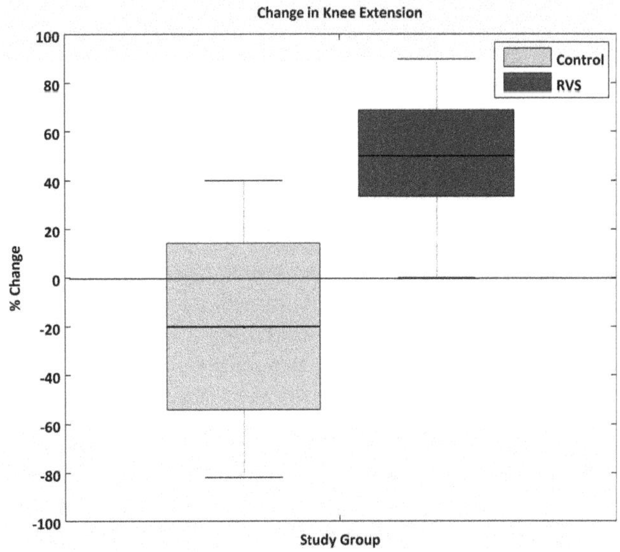

Figure 9. Preoperative and postoperative knee extension.

Similarly, for the knee extension assessments, it appeared the RVS group was worse off than the control group (P = 0.064) at the start in week 1. However at the end of the rehabilitation period, the RVS group had significantly greater improvement than the control group ($p = 0.002$) as shown in Figure 9. In addition, the negative improvement observed in Figure 9 in the control group indicates that most participants in the control group got worse (four out of seven). On the other hand, most of the participants in the experimental group improved (seven out of eight).

DISCUSSION

Challenges in designing rehabilitation technology

Our experiences show the complexity of designing rehabilitation systems that fits with both patients and therapists goals. We had engaged representative users in the design of the rehabilitation visualization system and most of the design decisions were made from their point of view. The following themes emerged from our work.

Safely encourage correct performance

The health professionals were concerned about the safety of using the rehabilitation visualization system for unsupervised home exercise sessions. Their desires were expressed through the emphasis placed on correct performance. We have demonstrated that seniors can safely use a rehabilitation visualization system designed to safely encourage correct performance by adopting relaxed angular targets suggested by the physiotherapists. No adverse effect was experienced by the users as a result of using the technology for their rehabilitation but seniors could be frustrated when things did not work as expected.

Motivation

Our findings show that the motivation to exercise following total knee replacement surgery could be higher than previously thought [38]. It could be concluded that for certain rehabilitation scenarios such as after surgery, patients could be more motivated than other non surgical settings like stroke rehabilitation [4]. The main requirements identified for post surgical rehabilitation was correct performance. However it was observed that motivation was improved with the use of the rehabilitation visualization system during the early stages. The motivation however decreased as recovery progressed but did not affect adherence. The reduction in motivation levels observed in the rehabilitation visualization system group might be connected to the safe targets adopted. Comments were made about the system becoming a bit easy for them as their recovery progressed. A possible solution would be to increase the difficulty of the targets as recovery progresses.

Usability

The high system usability scores demonstrate that the system and setup was generally acceptable to the seniors. Seniors successfully managed two inertial sensors and a laptop on their own i.e. charging, wearing and switching on/off. The calibration was considered simple and relatively accurate using the knee wedge. We found the therapist-measured knee ROM at the end of the rehabilitation period corresponds to the progress charts. Designers could improve the chances of adoption of technology by seniors, especially those without prior computer experience, if they include simple and robust interaction techniques such as a remote control – a familiar interface for seniors.

Role of rehabilitation technology

All the participants agreed that the visualization of home physiotherapy exercises helped ensure correct performance of the exercises.

Improve recovery

The rehabilitation visualization system group showed significant improvement in knee ROM when compared to the control group. This implies that home rehabilitation technology could improve rehabilitation outcomes. In all the other measures the rehabilitation visualization system group outperformed the control group. A minimally clinical significant difference of greater than 3 points [20] was observed in the OKS. Although not significantly ($p > 0.05$), these findings suggest that without the rehabilitation visualization system some patients got worse. Our findings provide evidence that patients benefit more from having an interactive rehabilitation visualization system at home as a result of the improved exercise quality [22].

Adherence to exercise program

The rehabilitation visualization system seemed to not have made seniors do more exercises. This is contrary to the findings of Yeh et al. [36] that such systems could increase the quality and quantity of exercises done after knee replacement. A possible explanation is that their study was done for a short time (2 days) and users behavior could change over a longer study duration. Another factor is the time it takes to complete an exercise session. It takes about 40 minutes to complete all the exercises using the rehabilitation visualization system as it enforces the correct performance and hold times, something not enforced by the booklet. This is an interesting point to note as we did find a significant difference with one of the outcome measures despite the control group reporting higher quantity of exercises. Hence designers should consider emphasizing and promoting in their design not just the quantity of rehabilitation exercises but also the quality.

Improve general health

An interesting result was found in the mental component of health SF12 MCS. The entire rehabilitation visualization system group had positive improvement whereas some of the control group declined. The visualization of rehabilitation exercises could possibly improve other areas of health in addition to the physical component related to exercise performance. Plausible reasons might include the mental gratification felt when targets were achieved and for some participants the learning of a new skill could have had a positive impact on their mental health.

Improve patient-therapist communication

The rehabilitation system and the video call check up proved to be quite useful to both patients and physiotherapists. The participants reported increased confidence when discussing their rehabilitation progress with physiotherapists. Being able to see their feedback during and after rehabilitation sessions provided reassurance, improved feelings of competence and reduced anxiety.

Design recommendations
The following design recommendations emerged from our study. First, design to promote correct performance e.g. a simple traffic light type real-time color-coded feedback with 3 - 4 levels on performance motivates users to want to achieve a better score. The appropriate levels should be defined by the rehabilitation goal and the measures of improvement expected over time. Secondly, the presence of a repetition counter that shows the target number of repetitions facilitated the completion of recommended repetitions for each exercise. Thirdly, always provide progress history. While caution must be taken in the frequency of and the period to show progress, we found that a weekly period worked very well for our participants. Fourthly, display the essential movement parameters at the right level of abstraction – colored fan and bars rather than numbers. Fifth, show ideal movement side by side with user's movement by inserting the ideal movement in a small portion of the screen compared to the users movement. This will ensure the patients are not forced to match the ideal pace and range of movement when they are still trying to recover their optimum movement in the early rehabilitation stages.

Lessons learned
Our strategy to obtain informed consent before surgery did not always work and we later changed the approach to anytime after surgery but before the patient was discharged. Most patients without previous experience with computing technology would decline to take part in the rehabilitation technology studies. It was also found that two participants would have benefited from multiple training sessions. Another reason for the low recruitment rate was that we had very strict inclusion and exclusion criteria. The use of stratified randomization helped promote baseline comparability between the two groups on age and sex distribution. Designing and evaluating rehabilitation systems are complex and multiple instruments should be used to capture the different facets of usability and health outcomes during long-term studies in uncontrolled settings.

CONCLUSION
This is the first time that we know of that a wireless motion capture based home rehabilitation visualization system has been used by users, unsupervised for their rehabilitation after surgery. By paying attention to the requirements for older adults with limited computer experience through our design workshops, pilot usability study and iterative design process, we have developed a rehabilitation visualization system that is (a) easy to use by seniors unsupervised (b) effective in ensuring correct performance of home knee exercises (c) motivates patients at the early rehabilitation phase (d) facilitates communication of rehabilitation progress with therapists (e) improve knee range of motion and accelerates functional recovery, and (f) improves the mental health of patients. Our results are limited by the small sample size so should be viewed as suggestive rather than conclusive.

ACKNOWLEDGMENTS
Funding for this study comes from the Medical research Council, UK, LLHW (Phase 2), Grant ID: 91021.

REFERENCES
1. 9th Annual Report 2012, National Joint Registry. http://www.njrcentre.org.uk/.
2. Ananthanarayan, S., Sheh, M., Chien, A., Profita, H. and Siek, K. Pt Viz: towards a wearable device for visualizing knee rehabilitation exercises. *Proc. CHI 2013,* ACM Press (2013), 1247–1250.
3. Ayoade, M., Uzor, S., and Baillie, L. The Development and Evaluation of an Interactive System for Age Related Musculoskeletal Rehabilitation in the Home. *Proc. INTERACT 2013,* 8120 (2013), 1-18.
4. Balaam, M., Rennick-Egglestone, S., Fitzpatrick, G., Rodden, T., Hughes, A. M., Wilkinson, A., Nind, T., Axelrod, L., Harris, E., and Ricketts, I. Motivating mobility: designing for lived motivation in stroke rehabilitation. *Proc. CHI 2011,* ACM Press (2011).
5. Bohannon, R. W. Reference values for the timed up and go test: a descriptive meta-analysis. *Journal of Geriatric Physical Therapy* 29, 2 (2006), 64-68.
6. Borghese, N.A., Pirovano, M., Mainetti, R. and Lanzi, P.L. An integrated low-cost system for at-home rehabilitation. In *Proc. VSMM 2012*, (2012), 553–556.
7. Celinder, D. and Peoples, H. Stroke patients' experiences with Wii Sports® during inpatient rehabilitation. *Scandinavian Journal of Occupational Therapy* 19, 5 (2012), 457–463.
8. Doyle, J., Bailey, C., Dromey, B. and Scanaill, C.N. BASE - An interactive technology solution to deliver balance and strength exercises to older adults. In *Proc. PervasiveHealth 2010,* (2010), 1–5.
9. Froimson, M.I. In-home care following total knee replacement. *Cleveland Clinic Journal of Medicine* 80, e-Suppl_1 (2013), 15–18.
10. Fung, V., Ho, A., Shaffer, J., Chung, E. and Gomez, M. Use of Nintendo Wii FitTM in the rehabilitation of outpatients following total knee replacement: a preliminary randomised controlled trial. *WCPT* 98, 3 (2012), 183–188.
11. Gerling, K.M., Livingston, I., Nacke, L.E., and Mandryk, R.L. Full-Body Motion-Based Game Interaction for Older Adults. *Proc, CHI 2012*, ACM Press (2012), 1873-1882.
12. Harms, M. Advancing technology in rehabilitation. *WCPT* 98, 3 (2012), 181–182.

13. Huang, J.-D. Kinerehab: a kinect-based system for physical rehabilitation: a pilot study for young adults with motor disabilities. *Proc. ACCETS 2011*, ACM Press (2011), 319–320.

14. Karapanos, E., Zimmerman, J., Forlizzi, J. and Martens, J.-B. User experience over time: an initial framework. In *Proc, CHI 2009*, ACM Press (2009), 729–738.

15. Kujala, S. User involvement: A review of the benefits and challenges. *Behaviour & Information Technology* 22, 1 (2003), 1–16.

16. Lavernia, C.J., D'Apuzzo, M., Rossi, M.D., Lee, D. Accuracy of knee range of motion assessment after total knee arthroplasty. *The Journal of Arthroplasty* 23, 6 (2008), 85–91.

17. Maclean, C., Deakin, A.H. and Picard, F. Is patient self-assessment of flexion after TKR able to identify risk of manipulation under anaesthesia? *Orthopaedics & Traumatology: Surgery & Research* 98, 6 (2012), 672.

18. Mizner R. L., Petterson S. C., Clements K. E., Zeni J. A., Irrgang J. J. and Snyder-Mackler L. Measuring functional improvement after total knee arthroplasty requires both performance-based and patient-report assessments. *The Journal of Arthroplasty* 26, 5 (2011),728–737.

19. Morton, L., Baillie, L., and Ramirez-Iniguez, R. (2013, October). Pose calibrations for inertial sensors in rehabilitation applications. *Proc. WiMob,* (2013), 204.

20. Murray, D.W., Fitzpatrick, R., Rogers, K., Pandit, H., Beard, D.J., Carr, A.J. and Dawson, J. The use of the Oxford hip and knee scores. *Journal of Bone & Joint Surgery, British Volume* 89-B, 8 (2007), 1010–1014.

21. Noble PC, Gordon MJ, Weiss JM, Reddix RN, Conditt MA, Mathis KB. Does total knee replacement restore normal knee function? *Clinical Orthopaedics and Related Research* 431, (2005), 157-165.

22. Piqueras, M., Marco, E., Coll, M., Escalada, F., Ballester, A., Cinca, C., Belmonte, R. and Muniesa, J. Effectiveness of an interactive virtual telerehabilitation system in patients after total knee arthoplasty: A randomized controlled trial. *Journal of Rehabilitation Medicine* 45, 4 (2013), 392–396.

23. Pisters, M.F., Veenhof, C., Schellevis, F.G., Twisk, J.W.R., Dekker, J. and De Bakker, D.H. Exercise adherence improving long-term patient outcome in patients with osteoarthritis of the hip and/or knee. *Arthritis Care & Research* 62, 8 (2010), 1087–1094.

24. Rademaker, A., Linden, S.V. der and Wiersinga, J. 2009. SilverFit, a virtual rehabilitation system. *Gerontechnology* 8, 2 (2009), 119.

25. Russell T. G., Buttrum P., Wootton R., Jull G.A. Internet-based outpatient telerehabilitation for patients following total knee arthroplasty: a randomized controlled trial. *J Bone Joint Surg* 93, 2 (2011),113–120.

26. Saposnik, G., Teasell, R., Mamdani, M., Hall, J., McIlroy, W., Cheung, D., Thorpe, K.E., Cohen, L.G., Bayley, M. Effectiveness of Virtual Reality Using Wii Gaming Technology in Stroke Rehabilitation: A Pilot Randomized Clinical Trial and Proof of Principle. *Stroke* 41, 7 (2010), 1477–1484.

27. Sauro, Jeff. Measuring Usability with the System Usability Scale (SUS). http://www.measuringusability.com/sus.php.

28. Scottish Arthroplasty Project Biennial Report 2012. www.arthro.scot.nhs.uk/Reports/sap_national_report_2012.pdf

29. SF Health Surveys, http://www.qualitymetric.com/WhatWeDo/SFHealthSurveys/tabid/184/Default.aspx

30. Silva M, Shepherd EF, Jackson WO, Pratt JA, McClung CD, Schmalzried TP. Knee strength after total knee arthroplasty. *J Arthroplasty* 18, 5 (2003), 605-611.

31. Stevens-Lapsley, J.E., Schenkman, M.L. and Dayton, M.R. Comparison of Self-Reported Knee Injury and Osteoarthritis Outcome Score to Performance Measures in Patients After Total Knee Arthroplasty. *Physical Medicine and Rehabilitation* 3, 6 (2011), 541 – 549.

32. Tanaka, K., Parker, J., Baradoy, G., Sheehan, D., Holash, J.R. and Katz, L. A Comparison of Exergaming Interfaces for Use in Rehabilitation Programs and Research. *Loading* 6, 9 (2012), 69–81.

33. Tousignant, M., Moffet, H., Boissy, P., Corriveau, H., Cabana, F. and Marquis, F. A randomized controlled trial of home telerehabilitation for post-knee arthroplasty. *J. of Telemedicine and Telecare*, 4 (2011).

34. Uzor, S., Baillie, L., and Skelton, D. Senior designers: empowering seniors to design enjoyable falls rehabilitation tools. *Proc. of CHI 2012*, ACM press (2012), 1179-1188.

35. Uzor, S., and Baillie, L.. Exploring & designing tools to enhance falls rehabilitation in the home. *Proc. CHI 2013*, ACM Press (2013), 1233-1242.

36. Yeh, S.-C., Chang, S.-M., Chen, S.-Y., Hwang, W.-Y., Huang, T.-C. and Tsai, T.-L. A lower limb fracture postoperative-guided interactive rehabilitation training system and its effectiveness analysis. *Proc. Healthcom 2012,* (2012), 149–154.

37. Zhou and Hu, H. Human motion tracking for rehabilitation—A survey. *Biomedical Signal Processing And Control* 3, 1 (2008), 1–18.

38. Carr, A. Barriers to the effectiveness of any intervention in OA. *Best Practices and Research in Clinical Rheumatology,* 15 (2001), 645-656.

GaitAssist: A Daily-Life Support and Training System for Parkinson's Disease Patients with Freezing of Gait

Sinziana Mazilu[1], Ulf Blanke[1], Michael Hardegger[1],
Gerhard Tröster[1], Eran Gazit[2], and Jeffrey M. Hausdorff[2,3]

[1]Wearable Computing Laboratory, ETH Zürich, Switzerland
[2]Laboratory of Gait and Neurodynamics, Tel Aviv Sourasky Medical Center, Israel
[3]Harvard Medical School, Boston, MA, USA
{mazilus, michahar, blankeu, troester}@ife.ee.ethz.ch, {erang, jhausdor}@tasmc.health.gov.il

ABSTRACT
Patients with Parkinson's disease often experience freezing of gait, which bears a high risk of falling, a prevalent cause for morbidity and mortality. In this work we present GaitAssist, a wearable system for freezing of gait support in daily life. The system provides real-time auditory cueing after the onset of freezing episodes. Furthermore, GaitAssist implements training exercises to learn how to handle freezing situations. GaitAssist is the result of a design process where we considered the input of engineers, clinicians and 18 Parkinson's disease patients, in order to find an optimal trade-off between system wearability and performance. We tested the final system in a user study with 5 additional patients. They reported a reduction in the freezing of gait duration as a result of the auditory stimulation provided, and that they feel the system enhanced their confidence during walking.

Author Keywords
Wearable Support; User-Centered; Gait Impairment; On-Body Sensors; Freezing of Gait.

ACM Classification Keywords
H.5.2 Information Interfaces and Presentation: Auditory feedback; Interaction Styles; User-centered design.

INTRODUCTION
Parkinson's disease (PD) is a degenerative neurological disorder characterized by postural instability, rigidity, reduced movement range, and tremor. Worldwide prevalence is estimated between 4 and 16.1 million people [24]. Current treatment is mainly pharmacological and focuses on relief of motor symptoms. Medication has significant positive effects on some of the motor symptoms; however, other symptoms are not very responsive to anti-parkinsonian medications. Many of these are related to one key deficit – the loss of the automaticity of movement. This loss implies that patients find it difficult to maintain movement amplitude, rhythm, and postural tone without consciously attending to it.

CHI 2014, April 26–May 1, 2014, Toronto, Ontario, Canada.

http://dx.doi.org/10.1145/2556288.2557278

A particular problem of PD patients is Freezing of Gait (FoG). FoG is a transient episode, lasting less than a minute, in which gait is halted [26] and the patient feels that her/his feet are glued to the ground. When the patient overcomes the motor block, walking can be performed relatively smoothly. The FoG phenomenon is common in PD, with approximately 70% of the patients developing FoG during the disease progress [13]. FoG often occurs in situations that involve special attention, e.g., turning, while passing narrow corridors, at gait initiation, or in cognitively demanding situations such as in dual-tasking. In the later disease stages, FoG can also occur spontaneously, even in open runway spaces. FoG does not only drastically increase the risk for falls and fall-related injuries [6], but also has a strong impact on the social life of affected patients [22].

Clinical studies show that attentional strategies such as external rhythmical cueing through visual or auditory stimulation, e.g., floor-projected lines or metronome ticking sounds, have beneficial effects on gait in PD in general [34], and in particular in case of FoG [9]. However, as the effect of this stimulation wears off with time, continuous cueing for PD patients in daily life is not advised. Instead, the cueing support should only be provided in critical situations or during FoG episodes. We use the term *FoG support system* for a system that uses body-worn sensors for FoG-aware cueing in daily life. We furthermore assume that strategies to make use of the stimulation can be learned and improved by patients.

In this work, we present the development, design and evaluation of GaitAssist, a wearable system to support PD patients with FoG. More specifically, GaitAssist aims at assisting patients in unsupervised environments, e.g., at home, where clinicians are not actively monitoring the patient. Our work lies at the crossroads of human-computer-interaction, machine learning, and clinical intervention, creating a *sense-act-react* loop targeting FoG rehabilitation in Parkinson's disease. In the *sense* part, the GaitAssist system captures the motor properties of the gait in real-time. The system then *acts* by giving an auditory cue to the patient, in case of an ongoing FoG event. Finally, the patient *reacts* to the system's cue by trying to resume gait.

GaitAssist is the result of a participatory design effort that took into account input from engineers, patients and clinicians. The contributions of our work are as follows:

(1) In a first step, we assess technical and usability requirements for the design and development of a fully wearable FoG support system. For this purpose, we arranged an exploratory data recording session with 18 PD patients and performed interviews with clinicians, engineers, and patients.

(2) Secondly, we present the resulting prototype system *GaitAssist*, an unobtrusive and robust daily-life system for reducing FoG. Besides operating as a wearable assistant, GaitAssist provides support for a set of FoG-training exercises defined by clinicians.

(3) Finally, we present the results of a preliminary evaluation of GaitAssist. For this purpose, 5 PD patients that did not participate in the design-phase used the system in controlled lab sessions, as well as in a real-life session. A final survey shows the patients' high satisfaction and a subjective trust in the system. Furthermore, preliminary results indicate a decrease of FoG duration during the study.

RELATED RESEARCH

In previous work, both auditory and visual cueing have been tested as modalities for decreasing FoG severity [3,12]. However, these studies rely on continuous cueing, and as shown in [25] the effect of continuous stimulation wears off with time. To mitigate this effect, other systems only provide the cue upon detection of FoG. These FoG-aware support systems use small trembling motions in the 3-8 Hz band that are present during freeze episodes for detection of FoG [15,23]. They use wearable motion sensors to detect this trembling and activate rhythmic auditory stimulation immediately when the power in the 3-8 Hz band exceeds a threshold. Bächlin et al. [4] present experiences in the development of a system for real-time FoG detection in lab settings, using wearable accelerometers. The focus of the paper is on the technical feasibility for detecting FoG in real-time, and not on the wearable technology choices or the interaction of the patient with the system. In our work, we are going further and aim at the development of a wearable assistant that patients can use in daily life without requiring any support. For this, we are taking into account the input from both clinicians and patients to build the system, and we study how it influences the user's gait. Methods to detect in real-time FoG episodes based on machine learning algorithms are presented in [20,36]. In this paper, we follow up on the findings from our previous research and use the same methods as in [20] to detect FoG.

While auditory cueing is beneficial for reducing FoG duration [9,25], the gait training effect on FoG severity with a wearable system was not investigated yet. Literature indicates that PD patients can improve motor functions thanks to performing rehabilitation exercises [35]. Espay et al. [10] present a visual gait training system tested by 13 PD patients. The study showed that there was a significant improvement of gait parameters after daily training with the system for 30min at home. We therefore develop our wearable FoG-assistant to also support gait training exercises in home settings.

As suggested in [32], the perception of a rehabilitation technology by the patient has a strong impact on the outcome of a treatment. While the previously listed papers investigated the technical and medical feasibility of FoG support and rehabilitation in PD, they did not study the acceptance of such assistants by patients. In this work, we also addressed the user acceptance of a PD gait support system, an often not considered aspect in the development of healthcare systems [5]. The following issues regarding wearable systems for support and rehabilitation are known from literature:

(1) Obtrusiveness: The weight, bulkiness, number and location of sensors attached to the body decide on how comfortable a sensor setup is [21,27]. In particular for people with motor deficits, the sensor attachment is also critical [38]: Sensors may be mounted with Velcro straps, belts, integrated into cloths or glued to the skin. In general, measurements are more reliable if sensors are fixed tightly to the body.

(2) Stigmatization: As indicated by [28], body-worn technologies that are visible to other people may lead to a feeling of stigmatization. This is a particular problem for sensor setups that are worn permanently, e.g., for monitoring or daily-life support as in our work.

(3) Feedback: [5,11] report that patients require regular feedback from the system, even if there is no medical reason for this. Feedback is necessary to assure the user of the system functionality and increase his trust in the system.

(4) Further issues that came up in the design of wearable sensor networks for healthcare are related to privacy, security, reliability and battery lifetime [2].

In practice, there is always a trade-off between these user-acceptance issues and the technical feasibility. As shown in [20], multiple sensors would lead to better FoG detection rates but at the same time, this increases the systems obtrusiveness. [33] indicates that the expectations regarding user acceptance by researchers and caregivers do not always agree with the actual perception by patients. Therefore, Uzor et al. [37] recommend involving users as passive participants at all stages of design process: They organized workshops during which elderly people could discuss past experiences with fall rehabilitation, play prototype games and outline own ideas. The inputs lead to improvements in later game versions. In a related example, Alankus et al. [1] showed that customization of games leads to a better patient-experience in stroke rehabilitation. These works proof that patients can provide valuable information on how to improve system features, and that they are able to develop own ideas and suggestions. These findings directly influenced the development methodology applied for GaitAssist: Given that PD patients are the final GaitAssist users, they can best decide on the system obtrusiveness they are willing to accept for optimal FoG support. Furthermore, they know when and where they experience FoG, and what strategies help to overcome the episodes. For all these reasons, and due to the success of other user-centered rehabilitation technologies, e.g., [7,18,37], we decided to adapt the user-participatory design principles for the development of GaitAssist.

A recent survey [28] concludes with the notion that wearable sensor systems have been successfully applied in various rehabilitation scenarios, e.g., back and upper limb, stroke rehabilitation. For this reason we also investigate possible training effects of GaitAssist.

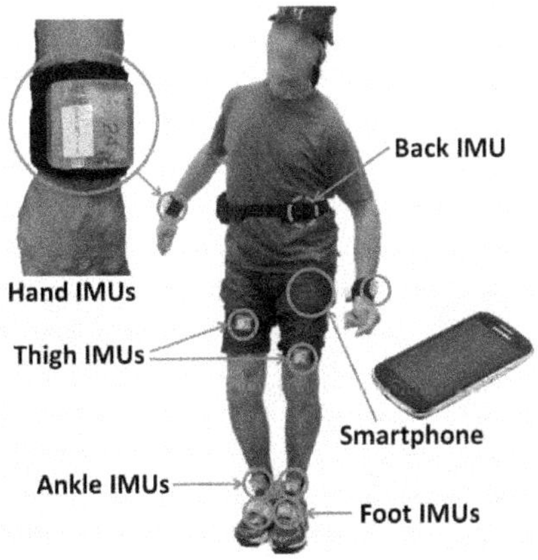

Figure 1. The pre-study system, used by healthy users and PD patients, in order to collect knowledge of how to build the GaitAssist system.

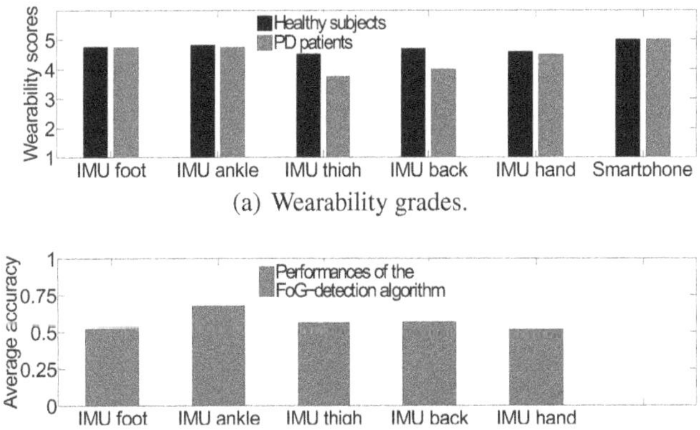

(a) Wearability grades.

(b) FoG detection performance.

Figure 2. Wearability grades versus FoG-detection performance for different on-body sensor positions in the pre-study.

RESEARCH QUESTIONS

To build a wearable FoG-support system that can be successfully deployed in unsupervised settings, we base our work on the following questions:

(1) How should a wearable assistant for at-home FoG support and training be designed to both enable robust FoG aware cueing, and be unobtrusive and well accepted by PD patients?

(2) What are the patients' experiences and opinions on the use of the resulting wearable system, and how does the system influence the patients' gait? What are the patients' reaction on the system feedback?

TECHNOLOGY

GaitAssist provides real-time cueing feedback to the PD patients whenever FoG occurs. We based our system on Inertial Motion Units (IMUs) and a smartphone as wearable computing platform. The smartphone processes data received from the sensors and triggers an audio feedback upon FoG detection. The system also provides support for gait-training exercises for FoG designed by the clinicians, and logs the number of FoG events and their duration. In the following, we discuss the design and development of the GaitAssist system, a collaborative effort between engineers and clinicians, taking into account the feedback received from healthy subjects and PD patients with FoG.

System Design

Previous studies [18, 20, 23] showed that on-body inertial sensors capture body-movements specific for FoG episodes. Critical for the system's performance is the number and placement of the body-worn sensors. To find a trade-off between technological requirements, i.e., achieving a high FoG-detection accuracy, while maintaining a low obtrusiveness to the patient, we performed participatory design sessions with clinicians, engineers and patients, as well as a data recording that involved 18 PD patients with FoG.

We recruited patients according to the following inclusion and exclusion criteria: patients with PD were included if they are (1) cognitively intact, (2) suffer from self-reported FoG, (3) have adequate vision and hearing abilities, and (4) live with a caregiver or a relative. Patients were excluded from the study if they (1) suffer from psychiatric co-morbidities, e.g., major depression, or (2) have a history of stroke, traumatic brain injury, brain tumor or other neurological disorders.

In the data recording session, we deployed a system with nine wearable IMUs attached to the feet, ankles, thighs, hands and the back of the patients, and a smartphone placed in the trouser pocket (Figure 1). We used the same setup previously describe in [19] where technical details about the sensors setup and overall flow of the experiment can be found. We chose these sensor placements after reviewing previous related studies [4, 14, 36], and based on discussions with clinicians. The pre-study was video recorded and synchronized with the sensing data [19]. We first tested the setup with 5 healthy subjects (2 females and 3 males with ages between 26 and 31 years), and then with a second group of 18 PD patients experiencing FoG (4 females and 14 males, aged between 49 and 89 years, with disease durations between 2 and 18 years). Both groups performed various gait exercises with the sensors attached. Each of the participants wore the system continuously for approximately 2 hours.

We define as a *FoG label* the period of time when the patient experiences FoG. The FoG labels were obtained from clinicians' annotations using stopwatch and videos, and later synchronized with the sensor datastream. Clinicians considered the moment of arrested gait pattern, i.e., stop in alternating left-right stepping, as start of a FoG episode, and the instant when the patient resumed a regular gait pattern as end. In total, clinicians coded 182 FoG episodes throughout the recording, with durations between 0.2s and 98.8s.

We evaluated the sensor positions in terms of obtrusiveness with questionnaires, as suggested in [17], and semi-structured interviews. We asked both healthy users and patients to rate the following statements on a scale from 1 (lowest score) to 5 (highest score): *(1) Attachment*: I can feel the device on my body, *(2) Harm*: The device is causing me some harm, *(3) Change*: I feel strange wearing the device, and *(4) Movement*: The device affects the way I move.

Figure 2(a) depicts the average wearability grades for all the sensor positions on the body. The users generally felt comfortable wearing the sensors, and the attachments did not affect their motor performance. Patients had a lower acceptance for certain on-body attachments, i.e., in particular the thigh position was rated low. These low scores are not only related to the age, but more with the motor problems associated with PD – for people with PD it is complicated to wear on-body accessories in daily life. Nevertheless, the *foot, ankle* and *smartphone* positions obtained similar scores from PD patients and healthy subjects. Patients often answered that they actually forgot that they were wearing these devices. The smartphone, the ankle and foot IMUs received the best scores.

We additionally organized discussions with the 18 patients, in which they could express their opinion regarding the GaitAssist system. Discussions were based on three main questions:

(1) At which locations would you prefer to have the sensors attached, if you would use a wearable system for FoG support and training in home settings?

(2) Would you put a smartphone in your pocket, if this helps to avoid or shorten FoG episodes?

(3) If yes, for how long would you be willing to wear it?

Patients chose the ankle as the best position to wear the sensors (5 patients), followed by foot (4), thigh (2), hand (2) and back (1). For 4 patients, the attachment location did not matter. All the patients answered positively regarding the possibility of using a smartphone as a wearable assistant. 16 patients would wear the system all day, while 2 of them prefer to wear it only for 2-3h, during periods of increased movement. Additional discussions with two clinicians and the PD patients gave us the following important social insights, related to the age and gender of the PD patients: *(1)* One patient said that he prefers the sensors to be below the trousers and therefore invisible to others. He associated the attachment with a surveillance system. *(2)* A female patient mentioned that she would wear the sensors only as a bracelet, for social reasons – she did not want to be seen with electronics attached to her lower body. This corresponds to the findings in other studies with wearable systems, e.g., [21, 27, 28]. Thus, for the GaitAssist wearable system, we needed to make sure that the IMU shape and attachment are not only comfortable, but also that they do not induce social exclusion feelings to the patients.

Furthermore, engineers analyzed the data collected from the 18 PD patients to identify the best IMU positions for FoG detection. We modeled detection as a machine learning problem [20], where the input is the sensing data from the IMUs. The FoG-detection chain is detailed further in the next subsection. The same detection algorithm was applied to sensor data from each of the 5 body positions. We evaluated the detection performance using average accuracy as measure, i.e., the output of the algorithm was compared against the ground-truth FoG annotations given by clinicians from videos. Results are plotted in Figure 2(b). The best performance was achieved with ankle-mounted IMUs. We also investigated the option of detecting FoG from the smartphones internal sensor data. However, the differences in placement and the sometimes loose attachment to the body across the participants resulted in noisy acceleration data. As a consequence, it was not possible to detect the typical, small trembling motions that are characteristic for FoG from smartphone sensors.

Given that ankle-mounted IMUs performed well in terms of FoG detection and were at the same time well accepted by the patients, we decided to base our system on up to two IMUs attached to the ankle of each leg.

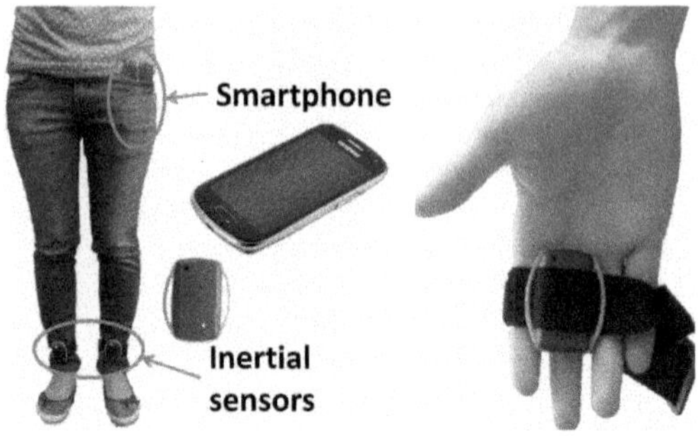

(a) (b)

Figure 3. GaitAssist system setup and sensor attachments.

Figure 3(a) shows the final GaitAssist setup. It comprises a Samsung Galaxy S3 mini as the wearable computer, and up to two wearable EXEL IMUs[1] that stream 3D acceleration, 3D gyroscope, and 3D magnetometer data at $N_f = 32Hz$ to the smartphone via Bluetooth. The sensors are attached with Velcro stripes as shown in Figure 3(b).

Software

The *GaitAssist* system has two aims: (1) to enable daily-life FoG-aware cueing, and thus to help patients resume gait at the occurrence of FoG, and (2) to support training with the FoG cueing through FoG-provoking exercises. As these two functionalities build upon each other, GaitAssist implements them in a single Android application. Subsequently, we describe the individual blocks of the application in detail.

FoG Detection. The main functionality of GaitAssist is the real-time detection of FoG episodes from the continuous motion data collected by the ankle-worn IMUs. To accurately detect FoG in real-time, we built a user-independent FoG-detection model using data from the 18 PD patients participating in the pre-study. For this purpose, we follow a machine learning approach. Raw 3D acceleration data is segmented in windows of $2s$, with an overlap of $0.25s$. These values were selected as a trade-off between FFT-based descriptive power of the human gait and the latency of the real-time FoG-detection. We compute the acceleration magnitude sequence for each window, and then extract features such as FFT-based features tailored to FoG detection [22], mean, standard deviation, and movement amplitude. Extracting features from the acceleration magnitude ensures invariance against orientation changes and sensor displacement during walking. Features are fed into a two-class C4.5 classifier with *FoG* and *normal gait* categories. Feature extraction and classification can be executed efficiently and in real-time on a smartphone, i.e., within at most $6ms$. This allows GaitAssist to run in real-time and leave sufficient resources and battery power for other phone activities. In a realistic usage setting, GaitAssist consumes less than 1% from the battery power per hour. However, the IMU batteries last for at most 4 hours. In future

[1] www.exelmicroel.com

Training	Task	Description	GaitAssist support
Gait initiation	Forward steps	The user has to step forward in response to a sound, then return to the start position	Beeps to signal that the person should step forward and RAS upon FoG
Gait initiation	Weight shifting	The person has to shift his weight while standing or stepping in place	Signals the beginning and end of the training, optional continuous RAS at the beginning of the exercise, and after this period and RAS upon FoG
Gait initiation	Cognitive load	The person should start walking only when a specific shape, e.g., a red circle, appears on the GaitAssist screen	Randomly shows different shapes and colors, with higher probability for red circles to appear; starts RAS upon FoG
Turning		The user is instructed to perform various turning movements, e.g., circles, figure eight, 180-degrees turns, 360-degrees turns	The system provides cueing upon FoG

Table 1. GaitAssist training exercises as designed by clinicians.

we will use new versions of EXEL IMUs, which will hopefully solve the battery issue.

Rhythmic Cueing Feedback. In response to the detection of a FoG event, we provide a cueing signal to the user. Previous studies [25] showed that auditory cueing is the most effective for improving gait in PD patients. We therefore chose to provide *Rhythmic Auditory Stimulation* (RAS) in the form of a metronome ticking sound at the onset of FoG episodes [30]. Clinicians and interviewed patients endorsed the metronome-based cueing. The FoG detection and RAS feedback generation together can be used for day-long FoG support, but are also essential for the training component.

Training Exercises. The implemented exercises of GaitAssist are designed by clinicians and should encourage the patient to practice the use of FoG-aware cueing in FoG-provoking situations. The exercises include typical movements which cause FoG and that are often performed in unsupervised environments. The system implements the support for performing these exercises. There are two classes of exercises: (1) gait initiation exercises, e.g., sit-to-stand, and (2) turning exercises, both with the additional option of dual-tasking. The GaitAssist user interface provides support for each of the tasks, such as signals to start and stop an exercise, as well as dual-tasking exercises that are displayed on the screen. Table 1 presents a brief review of the exercises supported by GaitAssist. If none of the exercises or additional options is selected, the system is in default FoG-support mode, and will start RAS upon FoG detection.

PROCEDURE

In the first part of the paper we showed how we designed the GaitAssist system together with patients, clinicians, and engineers. To study the efficacy and the user-acceptance of the system, we performed a study with new PD patients that were not involved in the design process. In a 3-day study we *(a)* investigated the effect of training with FoG-aware cueing on FoG duration and frequency, and *(b)* the user acceptance of the wearable assistant. In the first two days, the patients performed gait exercises, following the instructions of a physiotherapist and with GaitAssist providing cueing during FoG episodes. On the third day, the patients used the GaitAssist application in a real-life walking task.

A total of 5 PD patients suffering of FoG participated in this pilot study (2 females, and 3 males, mean age: 75.6 ± 4.7 years). Patients did not have knowledge about the GaitAssist system. We followed the same recruitment criteria as in the pre-study Four patients had moderate disease severity (Hohen and Yahr III) and one had mild disease severity (H&Y II) with a mean UPDRS [29] motor score of 26.8 ± 18.5 and mean disease duration of 8.8 ± 3.7 years. FoG severity varied between subjects with S#2 and S#5 experiencing FoG even during regular walking, and others experiencing FoG only during challenging conditions, in particular S#1 and S#4. This wide inclusion range allowed us to reflect on the potential utility of the system throughout the course of the disease.

Evaluation Protocol. Participants were invited to come to the hospital on three sessions during different days in one week, with each session lasting approximately 30 minutes. Subsequently, we attached the two IMUs of GaitAssist to the participant's ankle with soft Velcro belts. The application was started in support mode for FoG-aware cueing in daily-life, and the patient was asked to perform FoG-rehabilitation exercises. A clinician supervised the patient while performing the exercises. In the final use-case, the application outlines the same tasks and exercises to the patients as given by the clinician. It will therefore allow the patient to perform the same training routines at home.

The training exercises that the patients performed on the first two days were designed by clinicians, and include FoG-provoking tasks, as known from literature [26, 31]:

(1) The Ziegler protocol [39]: This protocol was designed to provoke FoG in PD patients in a clinical setting. It includes two 360-degrees turns, one 180-degrees turn, and passing through a narrow passage (Figure 4(a)).

(2) Figure eight: This task consisted of walking 10 figure eight shapes in a 3 m^2 area.

(3) Straight line walking with turns: The patients had to walk on a 10 m straight line, turn, and return.

(4) Turn around a chair (Figure 4(b)): The patients had to rise from sitting positing, walk 3 m towards a chair, walk in clockwise direction around the chair, then change the direction and circle it in counter-clockwise direction. Finally, patients had to return to the initial position and sit down.

Between the tasks, we included rest periods, and patients were free to ask for a break at any moment of the training.

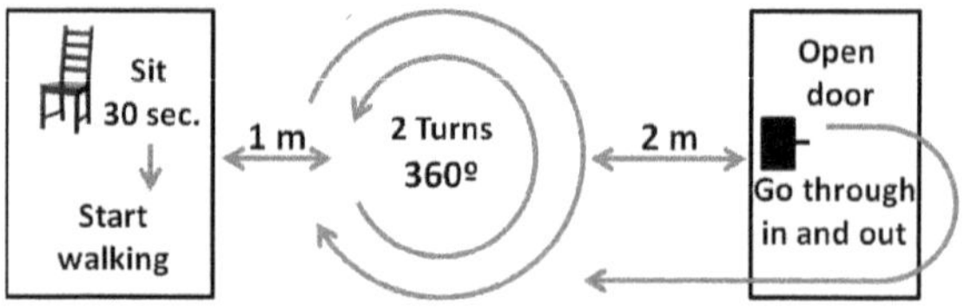

(a) The Ziegler protocol [39] exercise.

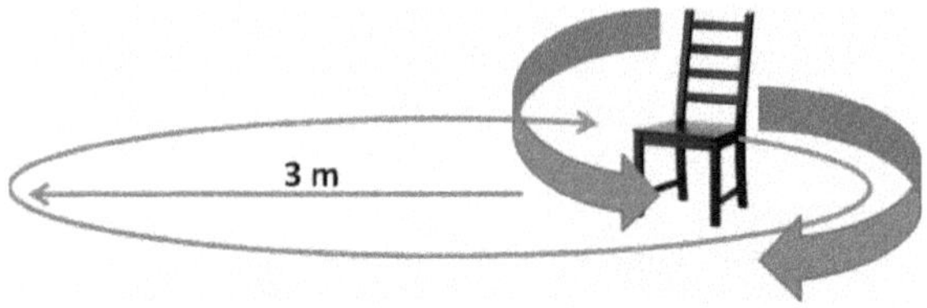

(b) The turn around the chair exercise.

Figure 4. Examples of tasks in the evaluation study.

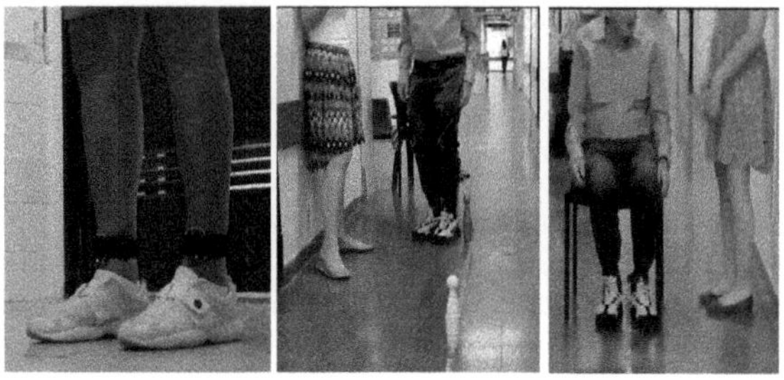

Figure 5. The GaitAssist system during assessment with Parkinson's disease patients. From left: sensor location, figure 8 task, Ziegler protocol.

On the first day, the tasks were executed without cognitive load. During the second day, we increased the task difficulty by adding cognitive load through (1) engaging the patients in conversation, (2) letting them execute serial subtractions while walking, and (3) combinations of these distractions. We included them as clinical literature reports that PD patients experience a higher number of FoGs during cognitive load tasks [26]. In the straight-line task, patients had to additionally pass through a narrow corridor, which increases the emotional and perceptual load, and is known to be particularly FoG-provoking. The training program as described above includes tasks that are known to provoke FoG in PD patients, e.g., turns, gait initiation and dual task conditions [31, 39]. We also included activities that often occur in daily life, e.g., rising from a chair, passing through narrow corridors, and are potential hazards for FoG in daily-life settings (Figure 5).

After the first two days, patients were familiar with the GaitAssist system. In the third day we asked them to use it in more realistic scenario during a hospital tour including a recurring walking (Figure 6). It included roaming the hospital's crowded hallways with involuntary stops to give way to other people, turns, changes of direction, entering cluttered environments such as bookshops, using the elevator, and walking through narrow spaces. In this session, the patients could evaluate the usefulness of the system in a more realistic situation. Synchronized video recordings with the GaitAssist system were taken during the sessions. Clinicians used the same FoG-annotation procedure as in the pre-study [19].

At the end of each trial day, we asked the patients to complete a feedback questionnaire regarding the system usability,

Figure 6. The hospital tour task. A representation of a possible tour including walking in a crowded busy hospital corridor and walking outdoors.

feasibility and comfort (Table 2). The structured questionnaire was based on other questionnaires for assessing technology [8], and adapted to the specifics of GaitAssist. Each statement was based on a 5-points Likert-scale. The first part of the questionnaire on usability assessed the participant's experiences with the audio feedback. The feasibility part inquired about the possible use of the GaitAssist system at home, and their motivation to use the system in daily life. In the final part of the questionnaire, we addressed the usage of the system from a technical point of view, and the user-friendliness of the software and sensor setup. Additionally, we performed informal discussions between a clinician and the patient to gather more detailed feedback than in the questionnaire.

RESULTS

System Functionality

Clinicians used the synchronized videos to identify and annotate 102 FoG events that occurred overall during the validation study. GaitAssist successfully detected 99 FoG episodes and started cueing in response, typically with a latency of $< 0.5s$ after the start of FoG. The 3 missed FoG events were shorter than 0.5 s, and therefore difficult to detect. 27 false alarms occurred in total during the study, meaning that GaitAssist started cueing at moments without a FoG in progress. This was often in response to unusual motions that resembled FoG, for example during gait festination, turning with very small steps, sudden stops, or during *sit-to-stand* and *stand-to-sit* movements. The latter ones were due to the lack of these types of movements in the training data.

The number of false alarms varied for each user, and was dependent on the patient's walking style. For example, S#1 had energetic walking, sometimes even dance-like walk, but sometimes she lost the balance, especially after sudden stops. For her, the false alarms started in response to these sudden stops. S#2 and S#5 had a calm walking style, but they tended to make rapid small steps during turns. For them, GaitAssist sometimes started cueing while they were performing turns. For S#3 and S#4, the RAS started also in response to an abrupt decrease of the step length. While these events are not FoG events as such, they often preceed FoG, and are generally challenging for patients.

#	Statement	Mean score
	Usability	**4.2**
1	The auditory feedback always turns on when FoG occurs	4.1
2	The auditory feedback always turns off at the end of the FoG event	4.2
	Feasibility	**3.9**
3	I can use the wearable system independently	3.9
4	In my opinion, the system is suitable for patients with Parkinson's disease	4.5
5	I feel safe when using the system	4.4
6	In my opinion, the feedback provided by the system can reduce the number of FoG events	2.6
7	In my opinion, the feedback provided by the system can reduce the duration of freezing events	**4.3**
8	I feel that the system may contribute to my independence	3.7
9	Using the system serves as a challenging training for me	3.8
	Comfort	**4.9**
10	The weight of the earphones does not interfere with the task performance	5.0
11	The auditory feedback is heard well	4.9
12	It is possible to wear the earphones independently	5.0
13	It is possible to take the earphones off independently	5.0

Table 2. The feedback questionnaire with the average grades reported by the 5 participants in the evaluation study.

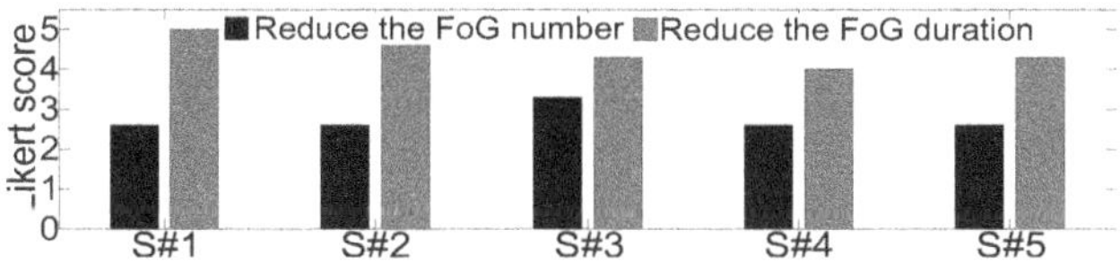

Figure 7. Participants individual feedback for questions #6 and #7.

Patient and Clinician Feedback

As previously mentioned, the patients filled in a questionnaire at the end of each day. In Table 2 we report the mean scores for all participants over the 3 trial days. In general, the patients were highly satisfied with the performance of the system. The average usability score for GaitAssist was 4.2 points (out of 5), the feasibility 3.9 points, and the comfort 4.9 points (out of 5). We subsequently summarize the participants' feedback on the different aspects of the system, i.e. the setting up of the system, wearing it, and performing the training exercises.

Usability and Comfort

Patients reported that they were satisfied with wearing GaitAssist and its performance. They enjoyed using the system and felt that it is reliable and accurate. Sensors did not malfunction and the system was easy to use. Clinicians confirmed that setting up the system could be done within 1-2 minutes, even without supervision. The sensor attachments did not bother the patients during walking, and subjects reported that they often forgot that they were wearing the sensors during the trials. Patients used only one earplug, so that they could hear also the ambient sounds (wearing both earplugs might cause problems in real-life scenarios such as when crossing a street or walking in the city). The audio feedback as played through earphones was perceived as easy to listen to, even in noisy environments. Participants reported that the auditory feedback was always triggered when a long FoG occurred.

Feasibility

All participants felt that they benefited from the GaitAssist support during freezing episodes. Figure 7 demonstrates their perception on whether the feedback provided by GaitAssist can reduce the number of freezing events and reduce the duration of FoG episodes. They reported that the FoG duration was shorter compared to their normal experience. They also felt that using the system will probably not decrease the number of FoG. Although RAS was provided in some cases without a FoG in progress, the patients reported that it may have prevented them from experiencing more FoGs.

Informative Feedback

Besides completing the questionnaire, the clinicians had informative interviews with the patients participating in the study after each trial day. During these discussions, patients had the possibility of giving their general opinion about the GaitAssist application. Table 3 lists the questions which formed the basis of the interviews. In a first part, we discussed with the patients about the wearability of the on-body system. Then we asked for further feedback about the auditory cueing provided by GaitAssist. We further give details about the feedback that we received from the participants.

Wearability. All the patients were comfortable with wearing sensors attached to the ankle, although they expressed the desire to wear the sensors below the trousers, so that they cannot be seen by other people. This confirms the previous findings from the pre-study with 18 patients. Bending down to attach the sensors to the legs was sometimes difficult, especially when the medication effect wears off. Patients also suggested a simpler attachment with the sensor directly integrated in a Velcro-band or belt strap (similar to sweat bands at the wrist of tennis players). A particular advantage was that the orientation and exact location of the sensors did not influence the application's performance. Regarding the smartphone, reactions varied. Not all of them wore clothes with pockets, and some had to hold the smartphone in the hand during the recording. This was perceived as uncomfortable and dangerous in case of falling. Patients therefore proposed to attach the phone to a special belt or a necklace. It was also suggested to have the possibility of disabling all other functionalities of the phone, as the multitude of smartphone usages may be distracting for the mostly elderly patients suffering from PD. While walking in crowded and noisy envi-

Wearability
1. Did you feel the sensors on the legs? Were they comfortable to wear? Would you like to wear them during the home exercises?
2. What is your opinion about using the phone? Is it comfortable to use?

Auditory Feedback
1. Did you feel that ticking sound started when there were gait problems? (e.g., when the FoG occurred, when not feeling sure while walking)
2. Did you have the feeling that the metronome ticking helps in resuming the gait? Improving the gait?
3. Is the metronome ticking too long, or too short?
4. Is the metronome sound annoying for you? Would you prefer other solutions (e.g., music)?
5. Do you think that the whole system will help in improving the gait, resume the gait after FoG events?

Table 3. Questions in the informative discussions with the patients.

ronment, the patients suggested they should wear one ear bud only. In that way, they could listen to the RAS and still hear environment sounds.

Auditory Feedback. In the discussion session, patients confirmed that the metronome ticking sound was played at the right time and with low response latency, i.e., less than 0.5-1 seconds, after the beginning of a FoG episode. This corresponds well with our measured latency of less than 0.5s. Patients usually change their walking pattern during the day in response to their medication cycle. An adjustable FoG-detection module could therefore improve the performance of GaitAssist in daily-life usage. All patients liked the ticking sound and they did not agree with playing music as an alternative. They stated that it is harder to get the rhythm from songs, and that a tune can get annoying after a short time. Two patients suggested that the RAS should continue for an extended period after the onset of FoG (>30s), as it takes some time for them to pick up the ticking rhythm.

At the end of the questionnaire we asked the users to describe in one phrase their overall experience regarding GaitAssist system. Final statements confirm the appreciation of the tool:

S#1: "I feel like I am not alone. This system is like someone that supports me in my way of walking. I can listen to the rhythm and walk according to the beatings."

S#2: "I would wear it all day long, as I think it reduces the FoGs duration, but it does not reduce the number of FoGs."

S#3: "It is a great system. I feel safe, and it might improve the gait pattern and reduce the FoG duration."

S#4: "It is very useful, as it reduces the FoG duration and reminds me of how to walk."

S#5: "Very good, I feel that it improves my gait."

Subjective Perception versus Measured Effect

We checked whether the subjective feeling of the patients corresponds to a quantitative assessment of the FoG duration, i.e., if the system's feedback upon FoG helps the patients to react to it, and thus supports them in resuming walk. For this purpose, we analyzed the FoG durations during each individual task of the three-day study. We compared the average FoG duration in the first half of each task, with the average FoG duration in the second half of the task. The idea behind this correlation is to see if the user learns to react to the feedback received from the system, and can better follow the cues during an exercise. We show the results of this analysis for S#2 and S#3 in Figure 8. Out of all 5 participants in the study, S#2 and S#3 experienced sufficient FoG episodes during the study for evaluating the performances of GaitAssist (S#2 experienced 44 FoG episodes in total, and S#3 41 FoG episodes). For the other subjects, the number of FoG during each task was not sufficient (i.e., during an exercise, the user experienced only one or none FoG).

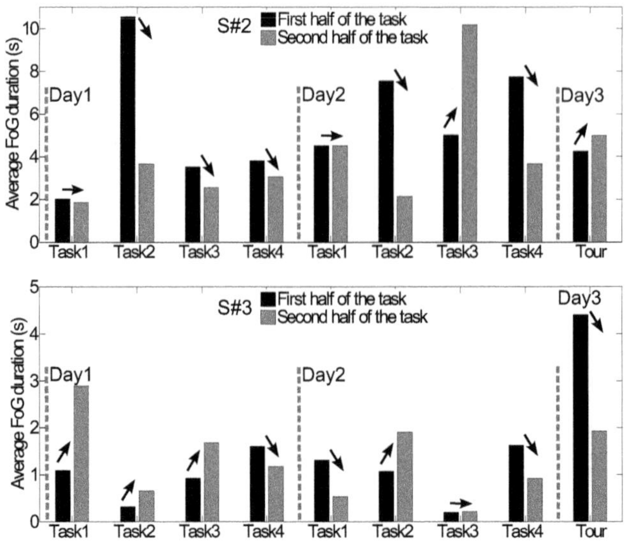

Figure 8. A comparison of the average FoG-duration for the first half and the second half of the tasks, for S#2 and S#3.

In case of S#2 (Figure 8), there was a significant decrease in FoG duration when comparing the first and second halves of the tasks on the first day. This is in line with the personal feeling of the patient, who stated that she mostly agrees (grade=4) that the system helps her in reducing the FoG duration. During the second day, when dual-task exercises were performed, she stated that she neither agrees nor disagrees (grade=3) with the same statement. The subjective grade is in line with the analysis (only 2 out of 4 sessions had a decrease in FoG duration). However, on the third day, when the patient tested GaitAssist in a real-life setting, she stated that the system helped her (grade=5) even though our technical analysis does not show a decrease in FoG duration throughout the session.

For S#3, the analysis indicates an increase in FoG duration during the first session, although the patient subjectively reported that the FoG duration decreased thanks to GaitAssist (grade=4). On the first day, the patient often stopped doing the exercise when the cueing started, instead of following the rhythm. In the next two days (second session of exercises and real-life session), the patient strongly agreed that the system helped in reducing FoG duration (grade=5), which is in line with the obtained measurements.

DISCUSSION

Our pilot study confirmed that GaitAssist provides FoG support at the right time, and that this support is perceived as helpful by patients. Furthermore, the decrease in average FoG duration over the three sessions, for subjects S#2 and S#3, suggests that patients react positively to the system's cueing feedback. With this regard, the subjective perception of patients as reported in questionnaires was in line with our measurements.

There are two main outcomes of the pilot, regarding the patient-system interaction: *(1)* only the duration and not the number of FoGs are affected by the FoG support system, and *(2)* what engineers count as false positive (FoG detection during motion difficulty) is actually perceived as helpful by users and clinicians. Patients stated that the feedback in these instances helped them to avoid a potential FoG episode. To conclude, a binocular view on the study, as in [37], confirms that subjective perception by users and measured FoG duration are in line.

As we took into account the feedback of 18 PD patients during the system design phase, GaitAssist was already well-adapted to the patients' needs at the time of the study. Our design procedure was similar to the one described in [37], with discussion sessions and pre-studies during which patients wore a prototype sensor setup. We considered issues regarding obtrusiveness and stigmatization that are common in body-worn systems [28] (small IMUs that can be placed below the trousers, standard smartphone) and, as a result, users did not give any negative feedback regarding this aspect. Overall, we experienced that the involvement of patients and clinicians at an early stage speeds up the design process and leads to a strong acceptance by end users. Nevertheless, the pilot study showed that there is still a need for improvements before widely deploying GaitAssist: simpler attachment of the sensors to the ankles; an attachment for the smartphone in case the person does not have trouser pockets.

The studies described in this paper are preliminary studies, and even though the tasks performed by the patients resemble at-home usage as we imagine it with GaitAssist, they took place in a hospital, with clinicians close-by. We further have to assess the adoption of GaitAssist in daily life and see whether patients are willing to wear GaitAssist outside of the study protocol [16]. For this we plan a clinical study with 40 PD patients in their homes, without any clinical supervision. Patients will use the system as support in gait training exercises, but also as an assistant when walking in unsupervised environments. The target is to analyze whether GaitAssist cueing has a long term effect in the rehabilitation of gait, but also to check the learning curve of the system adoption. Given the positive reactions of all 23 patients that participated in the pilot study and the design phase, we believe that GaitAssist will be well accepted, even outside of clinical settings.

CONCLUSIONS

We introduced GaitAssist, a wearable system for FoG support and training in unsupervised environments. The system consists of up to two ankle-mounted IMUs and a smartphone that collects and processes the sensor data. It reliably provides cueing in the form of a metronome ticking sound after the onset of FoG. In addition, GaitAssist provides exercises that the patients can perform at home for practicing the handling of cueing in FoG-provoking situations. GaitAssist was developed and adapted to the needs of patients through a participatory design process, and well-perceived in terms of wearability and effectiveness in supporting PD patients during daily-life activities. Overall, 23 PD patients with FoG participated in the design and testing of the GaitAssist system. Patients that tested the system reported a reduction in the FoG duration as a result of the auditory stimulation provided, and reported that the system was enhancing their confidence during walking. This must be further investigated in long-term studies with patients using the system at home, without the supervision of clinicians.

ACKNOWLEDGEMENTS

We thank to the anonymous reviewers and to our shepherd, Nadir Weibel, for their useful comments and guidance. The research leading to these results has received funding from the European Union - Seventh Framework Programme under grant agreement no 288516 (CuPiD project).

REFERENCES

1. G. Alankus, A. Lazar, M. May, and C. Kelleher. Towards customizable games for stroke rehabilitation. In *Proc CHI*, pages 2113–2122, 2010.
2. H. Alemdar and C. Ersoy. Wireless sensor networks for healthcare: A survey. *Comp Net*, 54:2688–2710, 2010.
3. N. Allen, C. Canning, C. Sherrington, et al. The effects of an exercise program on fall risk factors in people with pd: a randomized controlled trial. *Mov Disord*, 25:1217–1225, 2010.
4. M. Bächlin, M. Plotnik, D. Roggen, et al. Wearable assistant for Parkinson's disease patients with the freezing of gait symptom. *IEEE Trans on Inf Tech in Biomed*, 14:436–446, 2010.
5. J. Bergmann and A. McGregor. Body-worn sensor design: What do patients and clinicians want? *Annals of Biomed Eng*, 39:2299–2312, 2011.
6. B. R. Bloem, J. M. Hausdorff, J. Visser, and N. Giladi. Falls and freezing of gait in Parkinson's disease: A review of two interconnected, episodic phenomena. *Mov. Disord.*, 19:871–884, 2004.
7. S. Bodker and J. Buur. The design collaboratorium: a place for usability design. *ACM Trans Comput-Hum Interact*, 9:152–169, 2002.
8. L. Demers, R. Weiss-Lambrou, and B. Ska. Development of the Quebec User Evaluation of satisfaction with Assistive Technology (QUEST). *Assist Technol*, 8:3–13, 1996.
9. S. Donovan, C. Lim, N. Diaz, et al. Laserlight cues for gait freezing in Parkinson's disease: an open-label study. *Parkinsonism Relat Disord*, 17:240–245, 2011.

10. A. Espay, Y. Baram, A. Dwivedi, et al. At-home training with closed-loop augmented-reality cueing device for improving gait in patients with Parkinson disease. *J Rehabil Res Dev*, 47:573–581, 2010.
11. R. Fensli and E. Boisen. Human factors affecting the patients acceptance of wireless biomedical sensors. In *Biomed Eng Syst and Tech*, pages 402–412. 2009.
12. G. Frazzitta, G. Bertotti, D. Uccellini, and R. Maestri. Parkinson's disease rehabilitation: a pilot study with 1 year follow up. *Mov Disord*, 25:1762–1763, 2010.
13. M. Hely, W. Reid, M. Adena, et al. The Sydney multicenter study of Parkinson's disease: the inevitability of dementia at 20 years. *Mov Disord*, 23, 2008.
14. F. Horak and M. Mancini. Objective biomarkers of balance and gait for parkinson's disease using body-worn sensors. *Mov Disord.*, 28:1544–51, 2013.
15. E. Jovanov, E. Wang, L. Verhagen, M. Fredrickson, and R. Fratangelo. deFOG: A real time system for detection and unfreezing of gait of Parkinson's patients. In *Proc IEEE Eng Med Biol Soc*, pages 5151–4, 2009.
16. P. Klasnja, S. Consolvo, and W. Pratt. How to Evaluate Technologies for Health Behavior Change in HCI Research. In *Proc CHI*, pages 3063–72, 2011.
17. J. Knight, C. Baber, A. Schwirtz, and H. Bristow. The comfort assessment of wearable computers. In *Proc ISWC*, pages 65–72, 2002.
18. B. Lange, S. Flynn, R. Proffitt, et al. Development of an interactive game-based rehabilitation tool for dynamic balance training. *Topics Stroke Rehab*, 17:345–52, 2010.
19. S. Mazilu, U. Blanke, D. Roggen, et al. Engineers meet clinicians: augmenting Parkinson's disease patients to gather information for gait rehabilitation. In *Proc Augmented Human*, pages 124–7, 2013.
20. S. Mazilu, M. Hardegger, Z. Zhu, et al. Online Detection of Freezing of Gait with Smartphones and Machine Learning Techniques. In *Proc PervasiveHealth*, pages 123–30, 2012.
21. A. Milenkovic, C. Otto, and E. Jovanov. Wireless sensor networks for personal health monitoring: Issues and an implementation. *Comp Comm*, 29:2521–33, 2006.
22. O. Moore, C. Peretz, and N. Giladi. Freezing of gait affects quality of life of peoples with Parkinson's disease beyond its relationships with mobility and gait. *Mov Disord*, 22:2192–2195, 2007.
23. S. Moore, H. MacDougall, and W. Ondo. Ambulatory monitoring of freezing of gait in Parkinson's disease. *J Neurosci Methods*, 167:340–348, 2008.
24. W. Muangpaisan, A. Mathews, H. Hori, and D. Seidel. A systematic review of the worldwide prevalence and incidence of parkinson's disease. *J Med Assoc Thai*, 94:749–755, 2011.
25. A. Nieuwboer. Cueing for Freezing of Gait in patients with Parkinson's disease: A rehabilitation perspective. *Mov Disord*, 23:475–81, 2008.
26. J. Nutt, B. Bloem, N. Giladi, et al. Freezing of gait: moving forward on a mysterious clinical phenomenon. *Lancet Neurol*, 10:734–744, 2011.
27. A. Pantelopoulos and N. Bourbakis. A survey on wearable sensor-based systems for health monitoring and prognosis. *IEEE Trans on Syst, Man, and Cyber, Part C*, 40:1–12, 2010.
28. S. Patel, H. Park, P. Bonato, et al. A review of wearable sensors and systems with application in rehabilitation. *NeuroEng and Rehab*, 9:21, 2012.
29. C. Ramaker, J. Marinus, A. Stiggelbout, and B. Van Hilten. Systematic evaluation of rating scales for impairment and disability in Parkinson's disease. *Mov Dis*, 17, 2002.
30. T. C. Rubinstein, N. Giladi, and J. M. Hausdorff. The power of cueing to circumvent dopamine deficits: A review of physical therapy treatment of gait disturbances in Parkinson's disease. *Mov Disord*, 17:1148–60, 2002.
31. J. Schaafsma, Y. Balash, T. Gurevich, et al. Characterization of freezing of gait subtypes and the response of each to levodopa in Parkinson's disease. *Eur J Neurol*, 10:391–8, 2003.
32. D. Schuler and A. Namioka, editors. *Participatory design: Principles and practices*. Routledge, 1993.
33. A. Sponselee, B. Schouten, D. Bouwhuis, and C. Willems. Smart home technology for the elderly: Perceptions of multidisciplinary stakeholders. In *Constructing Amb. Intel.*, pages 314–326. 2008.
34. M. Suteerawattananon, G. Morris, B. Etnyre, et al. Effects of visual and auditory cues on gait in individuals with Parkinson's disease. *J Neurol Sci*, 19:63–9, 2004.
35. C. Tomlinson, S. Patel, C. Meek, et al. Physiotherapy versus placebo or no intervention in Parkinson's disease. *Cochrane Database of Systematic Reviews*, 8, 2012.
36. E. Tripoliti, A. Tzallas, M. Tsipouras, et al. Automatic Detection of Freezing of Gait Events in Patients with Parkinson's Disease. *Comp Met and Progr in Biomed*, 110(1):12–26, 2013.
37. S. Uzor and L. Baillie. Exploring and designing tools to enhance falls rehabilitation in the home. In *Proc CHI*, pages 1233–42, 2013.
38. C.-C. Yang and Y.-L. Hsu. A review of accelerometry-based wearable motion detectors for physical activity monitoring. *Sensors*, 10:7772–88, 2010.
39. K. Ziegler, F. Schroeteler, A. Ceballos-Baumann, and U. Fietzek. A new rating instrument to assess festination and freezing gait in parkinsonian patients. *Mov Disord*, 25:1012–18, 2010.

A Technology Probe of Wearable In-Home Computer-Assisted Physical Therapy

Kevin Huang[1], Patrick J. Sparto[2], Sara Kiesler[1], Asim Smailagic[3], Jennifer Mankoff[1], Daniel Siewiorek[1]

[1]HCII, Carnegie Mellon University, 5000 Forbes Ave., Pittsburgh, PA 15213, USA, khhuang@cs.cmu.edu, kiesler@cs.cmu.edu, jmankoff@cs.cmu.edu, dps@cs.cmu.edu,

[2]University of Pittsburgh Medical Center, 200 Lothrop St. Pittsburgh, PA 15213, sparpj@upmc.edu

[3]ICES, Carnegie Mellon University, 5000 Forbes Ave., Pittsburgh, PA, 15213, USA, asim@cs.cmu.edu

ABSTRACT
Physical therapists could make better treatment decisions if they had accurate patient home exercise data but today this information is only available from patient self-report. A more accurate source of data could be gained from wearable computing designed for physical therapy exercise support. Existing systems have been tested in the lab but we have little information about issues they may face in home settings. We designed a technology probe, SenseCap, and deployed it for seven days in ten physical therapy patients' homes. SenseCap is a wearable physical therapy support system that gathers patient exercise compliance and performance data and summarizes the data in charts on an iPad Dashboard for physical therapists to view when patients return to the clinic. In this paper, we present the results of our deployment, show in-home patient exercise data gathered by the probe, and make design recommendations based on patient and physical therapist responses.

Author Keywords
Technology probe, physical therapy, rehabilitation, quantifying, exercise, ubiquitous computing, mobile, wearable, iPod

ACM Classification Keywords
H.5.m. Information interfaces and presentation (e.g., HCI): Miscellaneous.

INTRODUCTION
Physical therapy is a key component of current treatment methods for many neurological and musculoskeletal problems, including balance disorders, spinal cord injuries, and joint mobility disorders. These disorders affect millions globally. In the U.S., up to 25% of the population experience balance disorders [1,12] and more than 20 million have knee osteoarthritis, suffer joint pain, weakening of quadriceps muscles, and restrictions in mobility [13].

Mobile technologies are promising for supporting home physical therapy exercises. Mobile sensors can be used to provide real-time analysis of physical movement and record exercise metrics for patients and physical therapists (PTs) to review. These metrics can allow PTs to make more informed decisions regarding treatment adjustments.

Researchers have explored the use of wearable sensors for supporting physical therapy, but these studies were done in controlled laboratory settings where researchers can oversee patient exercises and technicians can set up and monitor the technology. We lack information on how wearable physical therapy support systems would work in patients' homes where therapists are not present, context is uncontrolled and patients have no professional support. In this work, we bridge this gap by deploying a technology probe to examine how patients and PTs would use such a system in a real context.

Our technology probe, SenseCap, consists of an iPod Touch 4G fitted into a baseball cap. The physical therapy used in this probe study is a head-rotation exercise commonly prescribed to balance rehabilitation patients. Patients wear the hat when they exercise and take it off when they finish. SenseCap collects compliance and performance data and communicates them to PTs through an iPad-based PT Dashboard.

The contributions of this work are the lessons learned and the design recommendations derived from the in-home deployment of SenseCap to physical therapy patients. The findings and design guidelines focus on how to capture and communicate important data, as well as PT and patient needs that are important to consider.

BACKGROUND
Physical therapy treatment programs typically last several months and involve bi-weekly (or more) clinical visits with physical therapists (PTs) [16]. At the start of the treatment program, PTs diagnose conditions and prescribe home exercise regimes. In follow-up visits, PTs assess patients' progress and make decisions on how to adjust their exercise prescription, deciding which exercises to add or remove and how to adjust exercise frequency and difficulty.

CHI 2014, April 26 - May 01 2014, Toronto, ON, Canada
Copyright 2014 ACM 978-1-4503-2473-1/14/04...$15.00.
http://dx.doi.org/10.1145/2556288.2557416

Lack of Home Exercise Information

Because the exercises are performed at home, PTs cannot supervise patients and do not have quantitative exercise data indicating whether patients are compliant with the prescribed exercise frequency and whether they are performing the exercises correctly. Without this information, it is difficult for PTs to make informed decisions on treatment adjustments. For example, when patients do not show expected improvement, it is difficult to deduce whether the cause is ineffectiveness of the exercise, patient non-compliance with the exercise prescription – a significant issue in physical therapy [14], or incorrect patient performance of the exercises. To make informed decisions, PTs need to know how often patients exercise, the duration (or repetitions) of each session, the average velocities and ranges of motion in each session, the symptom levels (*e.g.* pain or dizziness) before and after exercise, and what mistakes patients make.

Technological Support for Physical Therapy

Many researchers have examined the use of computerized technology for supporting home physical therapy exercises, including infrastructure-based systems and mobile devices. Infrastructure-based systems include those that use the Kinect and Wii in conjunction with an output device such as a television. However, research has shown that infrastructure-based technologies may not be suitable for many patients. Axelrod & Fitzpatrick [2] showed that many elderly patients dislike technology that is complex to set up and maintain. In addition, their study and a study by Balaam and colleagues [3] showed that many patients do not like technology tethered to the living room.

Wearable technology may address the above preferences. Along with their potential to accurately measure body joint movements, wearable devices are portable and self-contained, making them potentially easier to set up and configure. They may be able to track movements unobtrusively while patients engage in their activities of interest. With the increasing ubiquity of mobile sensors (e.g. accelerometers and gyroscopes), many researchers have explored their use in-lab for supporting physical therapy treatment [5, 10, 11, 17, 18, 19]. These wearable systems range from simple (single sensor) to complex (multiple sensors, body area networks, and so forth).

Brutovsky and Novak [5] explored placing a tri-axial accelerometer sensor node on knee rehabilitation patients' legs during leg raise exercises. Visual and audio cues were delivered to the patient through a hand-held PDA to guide the patients. The system collected exercise metrics and generated compliance reports. Melzi and colleagues [10] proposed a wireless body-area network of accelerometers to capture exercise movements and quantify performances. The researchers used an ensemble of 2-axis accelerometers on various parts of users' arms during bicep curl exercises. As typical of physical therapy support systems, the number of repetitions, speed of performance and fluidity of movement were measured. Taylor *et al.* [17, 18] also explored using multiple body-worn accelerometers to measure the quality of knee rehabilitation exercises. They used machine learning to train models to distinguish between correct performances and errors. The performance data are then presented on a computer screen.

Because these systems have undergone tests in laboratory settings only, we lack information on actual in-home use by patients. What complications arise when patients use such systems in real homes? What do home exercise compliance data really look like (cf. [14])? Chandra and colleagues explored the needs of physiotherapy patients in the home, but the studies were done with storyboarding [6]. Deploying real systems into real patient homes can raise many issues not illuminated in a lab or hypothetical setting. In this paper, we present a technology probe deployed into ten patient homes to help answer these types of questions and provide design recommendations.

Technology Probe for In-Home Physical Therapy

As Hutchinson and colleagues argue [9], "a [technology] probe is an instrument that is deployed to find out about the unknown–to hopefully return with useful or interesting data." The technology probe's goal is to explore real-world usage in order to inform new designs.

Probes are typically simple and contain one main function, unlike prototypes, which may contain many layers of functionalities and address a range of needs [9]. The reason for limiting functionality is to aid ease of development and deployment. The goal of the probe is not to see how comprehensive in functionality the system can be, but to see how real stakeholders use the system in a real context in order to generate rich and informed design ideas.

In this vein, SenseCap contains the core functionality of gathering the patient exercise compliance and performance data for balance rehabilitation. We could have added many more functionalities such as a range of mistake detection and vocal feedback but we wanted to probe how patients currently perform the exercises at home before further complicating the system.

Balance Rehabilitation as a Test Domain

We chose balance rehabilitation as a probe domain because balance disorders have a high prevalence in the U.S., affecting approximately 69 million Americans [1].

Gaze Stabilization Exercise

Commonly prescribed to balance rehabilitation patients is a head-turn exercise, also called the Gaze Stabilization Exercise [4]. Patients fix their eyes on a target, such as a business card, placed three feet in front of them and rotate their head side-to-side (yaw direction) for typically 30 seconds. They repeat the exercise in the up-and-down (pitch) direction. These movements strengthen the vestibular function through neural stimulation [20].

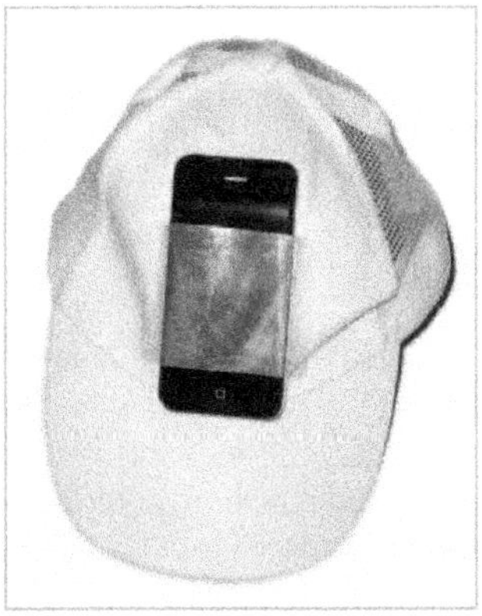

Figure 1. The SenseCap

SENSECAP

Patients wear SenseCap when they perform the head-turn exercise and take it off when they finish. SenseCap was co-created with our research collaborators at the Center for Balance Disorders at University of Pittsburgh Medical Center.

SenseCap Architecture

SenseCap has three components: an iPod Touch 4G, a cap with a sewn-in sleeve to hold the iPod (Figure 1), and a custom software application. Patients wear the cap when they perform the head rotation exercises. Since the iPod has a capacitive touch screen, it can be operated through the see-through sleeve.

The iPod Touch 4G contains a 3-axis accelerometer and a 3-axis gyroscope. With these sensors, it is possible to measure head rotation velocity (degrees/sec), frequency (rotations/sec) and range of motion (degrees).

SenseCap Metrics

SenseCap gathers the following quantitative patient exercise data, used for metrics useful to PTs.

Times of exercise each day – The application automatically timestamps the start and end of each session and allows PTs and patients to see number of exercises performed each day.

Exercise duration – For this exercise, PTs use duration rather than number of repetitions because the latter can become high and cumbersome to count (100+). A simple difference between start and end time of sessions is used to record the duration. The durations were rounded to the nearest 10 seconds at PTs' request.

Average head-turn velocity – The iPod provides the rotation velocity about its own X, Y and Z axes. We transformed the data into earth-fixed velocities to accurately measure the yaw (side-to-side) and pitch (up-and-down) rotations of the head.

Turns-per-second –We segmented the data to calculate the number of repetitions, which was then divided by the exercise duration to create turns per second.

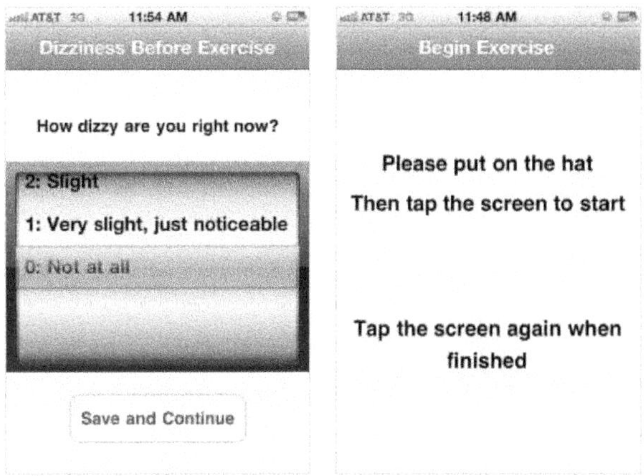

Figures 2.1 and 2.2 – SenseCap iPod user interfaces

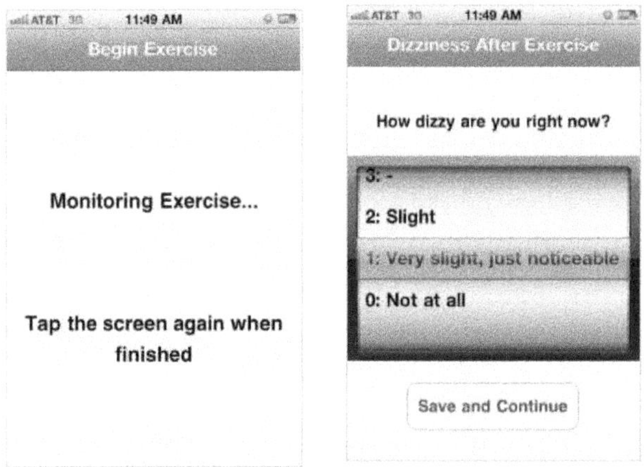

Figures 2.3 and 2.4 – SenseCap iPod user interfaces

Average head-turn range of motion – We integrated the velocity data to calculate range of motion for each repetition and averaged them for each session.

Dizziness before and after each session – Patients entered this dizziness rating (0 to 10) before and after each exercise (Figure 2.1). The scale was modeled after the paper rating scale used in the physical therapy clinic and requested by PTs. PTs want to know if patients are dizzy after exercising. For some conditions, the patients should be dizzier after the exercise to encourage recalibration of the patient's vestibular system.

SenseCap iPod User Interface

A series of simple displays on the iPod leads patients through the exercise (Figures 2.1 to 2.4). When patients first launch the SenseCap iPod application, they are prompted, via screen as well as voice prompt, to enter their current level of dizziness (Figure 2.1). Another dizziness rating is prompted after the exercise so that the difference can be measured.

After they enter their pre-exercise dizziness, patients put on the cap and tap the screen anywhere to start (Figure 2.2). Upon a tap, a voice announces "begin" and they begin their exercise. To assist with exercise timing, SenseCap

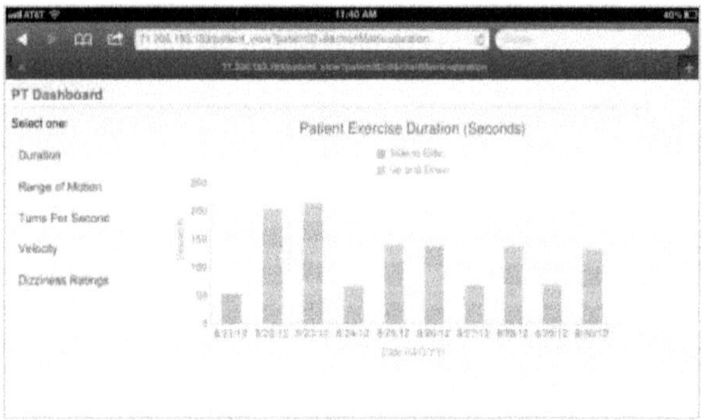

Figure 3. The iPad Dashboard

announced, through audio, the time elapsed every 10 seconds for up to 60 seconds.

When they finish, they tap on the screen again and a voice announces "finished" (Figure 2.3). A voice then asks them to take off the cap and enter their post-exercise dizziness rating (Figure 2.4). Because some patients had hand tremors, we implemented a 3-second threshold after the starting tap before the system would recognize the finishing tap.

After entering the post-exercise dizziness rating, patients are then asked whether they need to perform another exercise or finish and return the iPod to its charger. Patients may tap "Perform Another Exercise" to begin a second exercise. Finally, a summary screen is also available to patients to reassure them that the system is working in recording the exercises.

iPad PT Dashboard

The patient exercise data are stored on a web server and presented to PTs through a PT Dashboard on the iPad, as shown in Figure 3.

SENSECAP SENSOR VALIDATION

A technology probe will be of little value if the system's main function is defective. In this regard, SenseCap needed to capture patient exercise movements accurately. Therefore, we felt it necessary to validate this functionality of SenseCap.

Before conducting the in-home study with patients, we validated the head-referenced yaw and pitch velocity measurements of SenseCap against a commercially available magnetic field motion tracking system (Fastrak, Polhemus, Inc, Colchester, VT, RMS Static Accuracy 0.15 deg). Healthy control patients without a history of vestibular disease (six male, two female, age 18-50) performed head movements that are similar to those used in vestibular rehabilitation. While performing the head movements, patients wore a plastic rock-climbing helmet to which the motion tracker and iPod were rigidly attached. The iPod was tested in three pitch inclinations from the horizontal (0, 45 and 90 degrees).

We asked each participant to perform head movements for 30 seconds under varying conditions: orientation of iPod (0, 45, 90 degrees), frequency of head motion (0.25, 0.5, 1 Hz), direction of turning (pitch, yaw). We controlled the frequency of head turns by playing a metronome and asking the participants to move in synchrony with it. Each participant performed 18 trials to include all the combinations of the above, in randomized order. Each participant used one of three different iPods to test for consistency across iPods.

For each trial, a correlation coefficient was computed to determine the strength of association between the magnetic field motion tracker and iPod measurements of yaw and pitch velocity, using the entire time series. The correlations between the measurements were high and consistent across all experimental conditions. Across all patients and trials, the mean correlation was 0.99 (standard deviation 0.005). Furthermore, the average Root Mean Square error between the measurements was 3.4 deg/sec (SD 5.5 deg/sec), across a range of speeds from 58 to 178 deg/sec. We concluded that SenseCap measurements were valid.

TECHNOLOGY PROBE DEPLOYMENT

We deployed SenseCap for seven days in 10 clinical patient homes. Patients were recruited by vestibular rehabilitation PTs from the University of Pittsburgh Medical Center.

Method

All patients were given the head-turn exercise prescription by their PTs. We did not intervene in the prescription process. They were briefly instructed in SenseCap use by either the first author or the PT second author in the clinic after they received the exercise prescriptions. The patients took the SenseCap hat home and used it for seven days.

At the end of the seven-day trial, patients returned SenseCap and completed a questionnaire on its usability. They also were interviewed briefly about their experience.

Columns 1 through 4 of Table 1 show the patient demographics and their prescriptions. For example, patient 1 was prescribed a set of side-to-side and up-and-down exercises three times a day (6 exercises total), with each exercise being 30 seconds long. The gender range in the patient sample reflects the actual vestibular patient distribution. As can be seen in the table, the prescriptions varied in exercise duration and daily frequency prescribed for patients.

Next we present and discuss patient home-exercise compliance and performance data captured by SenseCap.

Compliance Results

Columns 6 through 12 of Table 1 show the actual exercise frequency of patients. Red cells with normal font are days where the patient was under-compliant, *i.e.* exercised less than prescribed. Green cells with italic font are days where the patient exercised the same amount as prescribed. Blue cells with bold font are days were the patient was above-compliant, *i.e.* exercised more than prescribed. For example, patient 1 was prescribed 3 sets of exercises, 30

Table 1. Compliance data of patients during probe. Red = Under-compliant (below prescribed exercise amount) Compliant (at prescribed exercise amount); Blue bold = Above-compliant (above prescribed exercise amount)

Patient	Gender	Age	Prescription	Direction	Day 1	Day 2	Day 3	Day 4	Day 5	Day 6	Day 7
1	F	59	3x30s	Yaw	1x60	1x60	1x60	1x60	1x60	1x60	Stopped *
				Pitch	0	1x60	1x60	1x60	1x60	1x60	
2	F	65	2x30s	Yaw	1x30	1x30	**3x30**	*2x30*	1x30	1x30	**3x30**
				Pitch	1x30	1x30	**3x30**	*2x30*	1x30	1x30	**3x30**
3	F	67	8x60s	Yaw	1x60	1x60	1x60	2x60	2x60	1x60	2x60
				Pitch	1x60	1x60	1x60	2x60	2x60	1x60	2x60
4	F	52	6x60s	Yaw	1x30	1x50	1x30	2x30	1x30	1x30	Returned early
				Pitch	0	1x50	1x30	0	1x30	1x30	
5	M	53	2x30s	Yaw	**2x60**	**4x60**	**4x60**	**4x60**	**4x60**	**4x60**	**4x60**
				Pitch	**2x60**	**4x60**	**4x60**	**4x60**	**4x60**	**4x60**	**4x60**
6	F	58	3x30s	Yaw	*3x30*	**6x30**	*3x30*	*3x30*	**5x30**	**6x30**	*3x30*
				Pitch	1x30	**5x30**	**4x30**	*3x30*	0	**6x30**	*3x30*
7	F	47	4x60s	Yaw	**5x60**	*4x60*	**4x90**	**4x90**	**4x120**	Returned early	
				Pitch	*4x60*	*4x60*	**4x90**	**4x90**	**4x120**		
8	F	28	6x60s	Yaw	**9x60**	**18x60**	**25x60**	**13x60**	iPod error **		
				Pitch	0	0	0	0			
9	M	54	3x30s	Yaw	2x30	*3x30*	*3x30*	1x30	2x30	2x30	1x30
				Pitch	0	*3x30*	*3x30*	1x30	2x30	2x30	1x30
10	M	36	5x60s	Yaw	4x60	**6x60**	**10x60**	*5x60*	*5x60*	iPod error **	
				Pitch	3x60	**7x60**	**10x60**	*5x60*	**7x60**		

* Patient stopped using the device for fear of acquiring brain cancer from iPod device.

** iPod contained a software bug which caused a crash when saving data; data from these sessions were lost.

secs each (3x30s), but on day 1, she only did 1 exercise for 60 secs (1x60), so she was under-compliant for that day.

Some patients returned the iPod early – before 7 days – because of their scheduling constraints. For two patients, the iPod application crashed due to a bug towards the end of the trial. In confirmation of survey studies, approximately half the patients were under-compliant. Sluijs et al surveyed 300 PTs of various domains about their patients' compliance rates; these rates were measured by patient retrospective self-report [14]. The study found that non-compliance rates might be as high as 70%. However, SenseCap gathered data that might not be captured in survey studies, *e.g.*, that five of the patients exercised more than prescribed. One patient (#8) exercised significantly more, peaking at 25 sets of horizontal exercises in one day compared to the prescribed six sets.

Patient Performance Results

Head movement metrics (range of motion and velocity), showed substantial variability, both inter-subject and intra-subject. Inter-subject variability was shown with the mean values of head velocity ranging from 98 to 204 deg/sec in the yaw direction. Intra-subject variability is exemplified by patient #3 who showed a range of 113 to 222 deg/sec throughout the trial. Similar variability was seen among the patients for range of motion, ranging from 20 to 124 degrees for yaw direction and 5 to 71 degrees for pitch direction. Documenting such variation is potentially of considerable importance in customizing exercises and prescriptions to patient needs.

Symptom Level Results

Another metric recorded by the device was dizziness ratings before and after each exercise. These daily ratings are important to PTs because they show the subjective effects of exercise. Physical therapists conventionally ask patients to provide dizziness ratings in paper diaries. PTs interviewed reported that this approach has a very low compliance rate, although exact numbers have not been documented. However, researchers have documented paper-diary compliance rates in other domains such as for pain patients. A study by Stone *et al.* showed that paper diaries had only an 11% compliance rate [15]. This study also showed that an electronic diary, such as the dizziness-rating logging function in our system, which can timestamp entries automatically, yielded a much higher compliance rate (94%). The study suggests that automatic time stamping discourages fake diary construction and motivates patients through accountability.

Patients in this study started with a low mean dizziness severity rating prior to performing the exercises, about level 2 (equated with "slight" dizziness). The lowest and highest values were 0.2 and 4.7. Immediately after the exercise was performed, yaw movements induced slightly more dizziness than pitch movements (increase of 0.6 points v. 0.3 points) on average.

Patient Critique

Comfort

When asked the question: "How comfortable was the cap to wear," with the options being: "Very comfortable", "comfortable", "neutral", "uncomfortable", and "very uncomfortable". Two patients reported "very comfortable", six patients reported "comfortable", and two patients reported "neutral".

One patient reported that he felt the weight of the iPod (101 grams, half the weight of a roll of quarters), though it did not interfere with the exercises.

Exercise Interference

For the question, "Did the hat interfere with your exercises," five patients reported "not at all" and five patients (IDs 1, 2, 6, 8, 10) reported "a little". Two types of interference were reported. The first type dealt with vision obstruction and the second type dealt with sizing and fit.

Some patients reported that when they performed the up-and-down exercises, the brim of the hat obstructed their vision of the OK sign in front of them. Some of these patients reported fixing this quickly by rotating the hat upwards so that the brim points higher. Others reported not being able to fix this particular issue and suggested a hat with a shorter brim or none at all.

Some patients reported that interference was caused by the cap being too loose, even at the tightest Velcro adjustment. This prompted them to hold on to the hat with one hand while doing the exercises. They suggested having different size hats for men and women to provide more accurate sizing.

Motivation Through Accountability

Patients reported an increase in their motivation and dedication during the interviews. Patients 2 and 8 stated:

> *"It was more motivating to do the exercise knowing that I was accountable...that it was going to record whether I did it or not. People should do it for all exercises; then they wouldn't skip so much."* – *Patient 2*

> *"I have a 2-year old... I'm running around all the time. With this, I felt more dedicated to doing it. I had to set aside time and be dedicated."* – *Patient 8*

COMMUNICATING PATIENT EXERCISE DATA TO PHYSICAL THERAPISTS

PTs have limited time for each clinical session, and an increase in time spent deciphering data means a decrease in time spent with patients. Thus, the patient in-home exercise data presented to PTs should be quickly and easily comprehensible as well as useful for treatment decision making.

We presented patient in-home exercise data to PTs using a series of charts (visualizations of the data) to gather their feedback on the data's importance and comprehensibility.

Method

We visualized the following exercise data components on an iPad PT Dashboard: Patient compliance, performance metrics, and symptom levels. The visualizations were created with our PT co-author.

We presented these data and their visualizations to four independent vestibular rehabilitation PTs who were not involved in the creation of SenseCap. They were shown hypothetical patient data as would be gathered with the system. We created this hypothetical patient data in order to intentionally insert problematic performances to see if the data and visualizations were effective in communicating these problems. Many of the inserted problems came from actual patient data. We named the hypothetical patient Sally.

Communicating Exercise Compliance

Compliance data are crucial as they quickly inform the PT if patients have adhered to the prescription. The key pieces of information are: how many times a day patients exercised and how long each exercise session lasted. (For other types of rehabilitation, such as knee osteoarthritis, repetition counts are often used instead of session duration.)

Since there are two types of exercises in this study (side-to-side and up-and-down), PTs also wanted to know the ordering of these exercises. Were patients doing all of the side-to-side exercises together or interleaving them with up-and-down exercises as instructed? To encode number of exercises, their durations, and the exercise order, we used a stacked bar chart as shown in Figure 4.

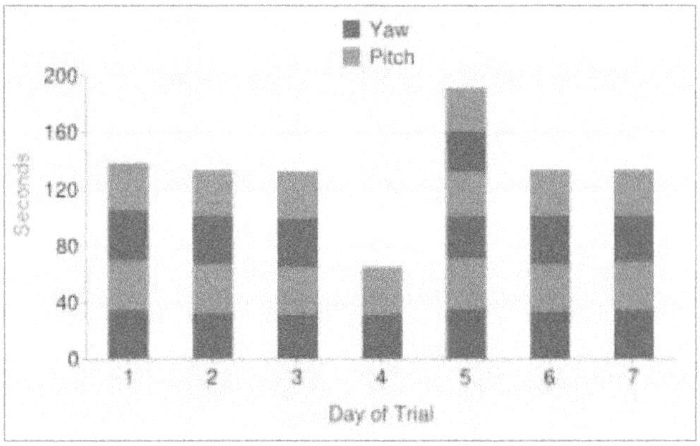

Figure 4. Patient Sally exercise compliance chart. Each block represents one exercise performed.

As can be seen from Sally's chart, the abnormality inserted was that the patient did four exercises on the first three days, but skipped two on the fourth day and then tried to make up for it by doing more on the fifth day.

PT Comments and Suggestions

PTs appreciated the concise nature of this data summary. They recognized the missing sessions on day four, but stated that it was an insignificant lapse and that the patient still showed good compliance overall. PTs found the compliance data to be important.

PTs suggested that they wanted to be able to see the time of day when patients were doing these exercises, e.g., were they doing them all in the morning, the evening, or more evenly spaced out (the last option being most beneficial). Thus, encoding exercise-time-of-day into the visualization would be important for future rehabilitation systems.

Communicating Exercise Performance Metrics

We presented data regarding head-turn velocity (degrees/sec), turns-per-second, and range of motion (degrees) to PTs. Figure 5 shows an example metric chart (range of motion).

Unlike the duration chart, we did not mix the two exercises into one since the blue and red dots may overlap and become indistinguishable. Thus, we separated the side-to-side and up-and-down exercises into a pair of charts, as shown in Figure 5. The dots are translucent and appear darker when overlapped by sessions with similar values.

PT Comments and Suggestions

PTs found the exercise metrics data valuable. One PT found the velocity metric, expressed in degrees per second, difficult to interpret. For example, she stated: "It's hard to get a sense of how fast say 52 degrees per second is..." She suggested having categories of "slow", "medium" and "fast." All of the PTs found the turns-per-second and range of motion metrics helpful.

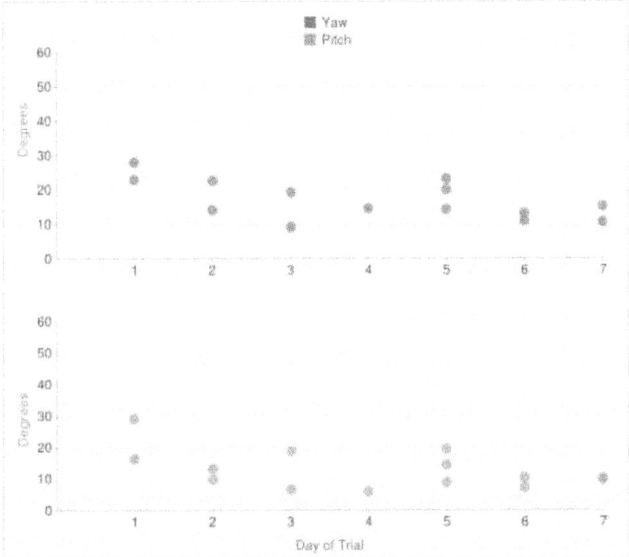

Figure 5. Patient range of motion chart. Each dot represents one exercise performed. Dots may overlap.

Communicating Pre-Post Exercise Symptom Levels

Pre and post exercise symptom levels are important information to PTs, whether they are dizziness ratings or pain ratings. They indicate the level of stimulation of the exercise. PTs usually try to find the right balance in prescribing exercises that are not too easy and not too difficult.

The pre and post exercise dizziness levels in this case posed unique challenges for summarizing in an easily interpretable format. PTs not only needed to know the exact ratings, but also to quickly understand their intra-session and inter-session patterns of change. We used a pair-point graph with connected lines, as shown in Figure 6. Each pair of points represent the before and after ratings of one session, and the line helps to connect them as well as visualize their direction of change (increase, decrease or plateau).

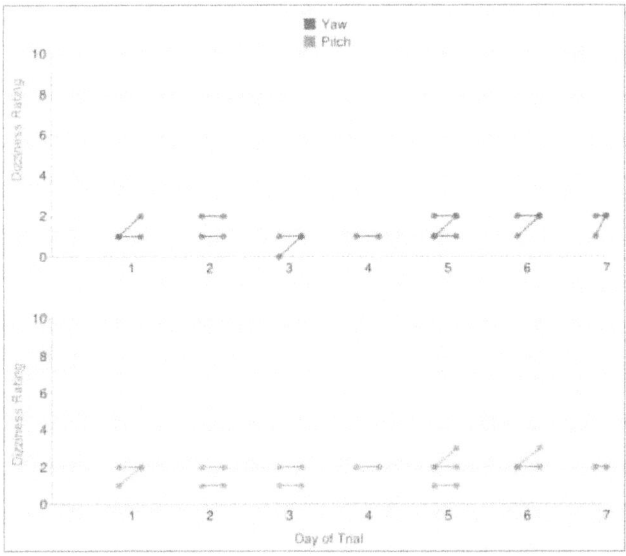

Figure 6. Pre and post-exercise dizziness levels. Each pair of dots, connected by a line, represents the pre- and post- dizziness of an exercise performed. Dots may overlap.

PT Comments and Suggestions

PTs appreciated this data component and recognized that many of the sessions involved plateaus in symptom levels. Given this information, PTs stated that they would increase the difficulty level by asking the patient to target faster turning speeds or a larger range of motion, or add more advanced exercises to the prescription.

PTs wanted more information regarding the reason for plateaus, increases, and decreases in symptom levels. They suggested having charts that allow them to easily see performances metrics associated with a certain dizziness rating. For example, if an exercise session were marked by a plateau in dizziness ratings, then they should be able to quickly check that session's average range of motion. If it is low, then it shows that the patient was not exercising rigorously enough to induce symptoms. If it is normal, then that suggests that the exercise has become too easy for the patient, and exercises that are more difficult should be introduced.

Because there are many components to patient home exercise data, PTs also reported a need for a summary screen. In our PT Dashboard, we provided the data components on separate screens, requiring the PTs to tap through them one by one. They stated that a summary screen which shows all of the metrics (exercise durations, range of motion, dizziness levels, and so forth) at once would allow for faster understanding of the big picture regarding patient home exercises. Errors and abnormalities can be highlighted here for more detailed investigation.

Although patients felt that SenseCap increased their motivation through accountability, the PTs interviewed about the patient data felt that SenseCap could increase patient motivation in another respect. They stated that one major reason for non-compliance in physiotherapy is pain and discomfort of the exercises. Vestibular patients are often debilitated by resulting dizziness after exercises. Not only is this uncomfortable but it can also be a major obstruction to their daily activities. To make the pain "worth it", they need to see benefits from the exercises. However, when progress is slow, it is difficult for them to see progress from day to day or at times week to week. This often leads to abandoning of exercise regime. Thus, PTs stated that being able to show incremental progress through SenseCap would be a significant motivating factor. PT 3 specifically states:

> *"That would be kind of helpful to me to be able to show them the differences, you know what I'm saying? I mean how much you couldn't move your head or how slowly you moved your head and now we are in week three and look how much better that is...Yes, motivational or you know what? Look at this week one and week three..."*

DESIGN RECOMMENDATIONS

In this section, we synthesize our findings, present additional lessons learned, and provide design implications for creating wearable physical therapy home exercise support systems. The discussion centers on two main topics: (1) what to capture and communicate about patient in-home exercises, and (2) patients' special needs and preferences.

Patient Exercise Data to Capture and Communicate

Because PTs have limited session-time and need to make rapid patient assessments, systems should allow PTs to glean the following key pieces of information quickly:

Exercise Compliance and Timing

Prior work in capturing patient compliance data typically records repetition counts or session durations. For example, Balaam *et al.* described a system that counted daily repetitions of a hand exercise for a stroke patient [3]. While repetition and duration are key pieces of information, our findings showed that PTs sought detailed information on exercise timing as well. Specifically, they needed information on exercise time-of-day (morning, afternoon, evening), and exercise ordering (*i.e.* whether patients did all of the side-to-side exercises together or interleaved them with up-and-down exercises). This information conveys not only compliance but also the spacing of the exercises, which can impact their effectiveness.

We thus recommend that visualization of compliance data also support rapid assessment of exercise time-of-day and ordering. A stacked bar chart can be used to visualize exercise duration and ordering together, as in Figure 4. When patients do the same exercise (e.g. side-to-side) several times in a row, a separator could be added to distinguish between contiguous bars of the same color. Exercise time-of-day could be encoded using patterns in addition to the colors, such as cross-stitch or horizontal lines for representing daytime and evening.

Above-Compliance of Exercises

Much focus of past physiotherapy-compliance research has been on non-compliance or under-compliance. For example, one survey by Sluijs *et al.* [14] asked patients "Did you manage to exercise regularly last week?" with the options of: "(1) not at all, (2) a little, (3) rather regularly, (4) very regularly."

However, our findings showed that five patients exhibited above-compliance, a phenomenon that has been less documented – perhaps partly due to the wording of questions such as the above which do not include an above-compliance option. PTs informed us that even though above-compliance can be a positive sign of motivation, excessive levels can worsen symptoms. Patient #8, peaking to 25 sets in one day (compared with her prescription of 6) was later asked to reduce her sets by her PT who was informed by the probe data.

We recommend that above-compliance as well under-compliance data be highlighted in visualizations as both information are important to PT decision making. In addition, systems with real-time feedback can caution the patient accordingly when detecting significant above-compliance.

Exercise Performance and Symptom Levels

Prior work on quantifying exercise performances focused on movement metrics such as velocity, frequency (repetitions per second) and range of motion [7, 18]. Similar metrics were sought by the PTs in our study.

In addition to these metrics, however, we discovered that the PTs considered symptom levels (dizziness in this case) to be just as important for informing treatment decisions. PTs used pre- and post-excise symptom levels as the bottom-line measurement of an exercise's effectiveness. In the case of this exercise, dizziness levels would ideally increase after an exercise (intra-session), signifying that the exercise has a stimulating effect, but decrease over time (inter-session), signifying gradual neural strengthening and adaptation.

Thus, systems should support the assessment of this rehabilitative process by: (1) encouraging patients to log their symptom levels before and after an exercise, (2) provide visualizations to view intra-session trends, and (3) provide visualizations to view inter-session trends. Figure 6 shows an example of a possible visualization to show both intra- and inter-session trends together.

Patients' Needs and Preferences to Support

Patients' Spatial Preferences

Axelrod & Fitzpatrick and Balaam *et al.* reported that patients strongly prefer certain home locations where they do their rehabilitation exercises [2, 3]. Our observations support and extend this finding. Patient 4, who suffered nerve damage through a brain inflammation, was too dizzy to drive to the clinic and needed home-visits to receive and return SenseCap. When interviewed her at home, she explained that the kitchen was an ideal place to compensate for her level of dizziness because she frequently needed something to hold on to. With the OK sign posted on her refrigerator, she could conveniently use her chairs for support. Thus, in addition to room preferences based on aesthetics and space availability, as shown by prior studies, we also recommend that system designers consider room preferences based on patients' needs for exercise scaffolding.

Supporting Patients with Cognitive Challenges

Some patients face cognitive challenges, including disorientation and forgetfulness. Patient 4 reported that her nerve damage caused her to experience confusion and memory lapses such as where she last put her pencil, or where she is in a public place such as a store. As a result, she reports that she often forgets either some exercise sessions, or an entire prescribed exercise altogether when given multiple exercises. Her exercise compliance for this study shows that she is very much under-compliant.

Another patient showed similar forgetfulness (Patient 8). Though she was very motivated to improve (performing many more side-to-side exercises than prescribed), she forgot to do up-and-down exercises entirely.

SenseCap did not include exercise reminder features, but these data confirm that it would be an important part of a physical therapy support system.

Supporting Patients with Physical Challenges

To reduce reliance on fine motor control, we allowed patients to tap the screen anywhere to begin monitoring exercise and tap anywhere when finished. However, we discovered a usability obstacle experienced by patients with hand tremors. These patients sometimes accidentally tapped the screen twice in rapid succession, causing the system to say "begin" and "finished" before they started exercising. As a solution, we added a 3-second threshold after the starting tap before the system would recognize the finishing tap. After this implementation, subsequent patients did not report the problem.

We recommend similar considerations for future systems when the same interface area is used for both the starting and stopping functions.

Adapting to Patient Variations in Sensor-Positioning

Another challenge we discovered was a variation in how patients wore their caps. We learned that cap positioning can vary not only along the pitch-axis (how high or low the brim was tilted), but also along the roll-axis which occurred when patients held on to a loose cap with one hand, causing one side of the hat to droop.

We initially used an algorithm for velocity transformation - from iPod velocities to earth-fixed velocities - that accounted for variations in the pitch axis. However, the unexpected variations in the roll-axis (horizontal slanting of the cap) created false errors during data analysis. It appeared as if the patients were moving out of plane and doing the exercises incorrectly.

After discovering this phenomenon through patient interviews and an analysis of the gravity vector data, which shows the slanting of the cap, we created a more robust algorithm to account for roll-axis variations as well. The validation data was re-run with the new algorithm, which did not affect its results since the validation test-patients wore the magnetic tracking helmet under supervision with only pitch-axis variations. When we re-ran the patient data using the new algorithm, the false errors disappeared.

We recommend that future systems take into account all possible shifting of position and orientation of worn sensors within and between exercise sessions so that data transformation produces consistent exercise metrics.

Motivating Patients

Motivation can play a significant role in a patient's recovery. Patients in our study appeared to have increased motivation because they felt more accountable for doing their exercises. To support patient motivation further, future systems could also highlight improvements from session to session, day to day, and week to week. These visualizations and highlights should be available to patients at any time and not just during clinical visits with PTs so that patients can get immediate and continuous motivational benefits.

In addition, the system could support goal setting, done collaboratively between PTs and patients. Goal-setting and information visualization has been used to motivate behavioral change in other domains such as sustainability [8]. Since exercise performance parameters are quantifiable in this setting, weekly target goals can be set to further track and motivate progress.

CONCLUSION AND FUTURE WORK

In this paper, we presented a technology probe for wearable physical therapy support systems. We deployed SenseCap into 10 patient homes for seven days. SenseCap consists of a white baseball cap fitted with an iPod Touch 4G and a custom application. Patients wear the hat when they exercise and remove it when they finish. The data are visualized on an iPad Dashboard to assist PT decision-making during clinical sessions.

Based on the probe, we presented lessons learned and design insights from both patient and PT perspectives for creating wearable systems for supporting physical therapy. The lessons and design insights focused on data that are important to capture and communicate and patients' special needs and preferences to consider.

For a future system, we plan to explore more interactivity features including real-time error recognition and guidance. We plan to implement several error-recognizers and types of corrective feedback (auditory and tactile) to the SenseCap probe to explore how patients respond to real-time coaching at home.

ACKNOWLEDGMENTS

We are grateful to the physical therapists of the Centers for Rehab Services who helped recruit and provided feedback about the system: Kathryn E. Brown, PT, MS, NCS, Pamela Dunlap, DPT, Sheri Fedor PT, DPT, Dana Hinderliter, PT, DPT, MS, Brooke Klatt, PT, DPT, NCS, Anne Mucha PT, DPT, MS, NCS, Tracy Spitz, MPT, CBIS, and Susan L. Whitney, PT, DPT, PhD, NCS, ATC, FAPTA. This material is based upon work supported by the National Science Foundation under Grant No. EEEC-0540865.

REFERENCES

1. Agrawal, Y., Carey J.P., Della, C.C., Schubert, M.C. and Minor, L.B. Disorders of balance and vestibular function in US adults. *Arch Intern Med*, 169, 10 (2009), 938-944.
2. Axelrod, L. and Fitzpatrick, G. The reality of homes fit for heroes: design challenges for rehabilitation technology at home. *Journal of Assistive Technology*, 3, 2 (2009), 35-43.
3. Balaam, M., Rennick, E.S., Fitzpatric, G., Rodden, T., Hughes, A.M., Wilkinson, A., Nind, T., Axelrod, L., Harris, E., Ricketts, I., Mawson, S., and Burridge, J. Motivating Mobility: Designing for lived motivation in stroke rehabilitation. In *CHI 2011*, 3073-3082.
4. Balance and Vestibular Rehabilitation Therapy http://www.tchain.com/otoneurology/treatment/rehab.html
5. Brutovsky, J. and Novak, D. Low-cost motivated rehabilitation system for post-operation exercises. *IEEE Engineering in Medicine and Biology Society 2006*, supplement, 6663-6666.
6. Chandra, H., Oakley, I. and Silva, H. Designing to support prescribed home exercises: Understanding the needs of physiotherapy patients. In *NordiCHI 2012*, 607-616.
7. Chen, P., Hsieh, W., Wei, S., and Kao, C. Interactive wiimote gaze stabilization exercise training system for patients with vestibular hypofunction. *Journal of NeuroEngineering and Rehabilitation*, 77, 9 (2012).
8. Consolvo, S., McDonald, D.W. and Landay, J. Theory driven design strategies for technologies that support behavior change in everyday life. In *CHI 2003*, 405-414.
9. Hutchinson, H., Mackay, W., Westerlund, B., Bederson, B.B., Druin, A., Plaisant, C., Beaudouin-Lafon, M., Conversy, S., Evans, H., Hansen, H., Roussel, N. and Eiderback, B. Technology probes: inspiring design for and with families. In *CHI*, 17-24.
10. Melzi, S., Borsani, L., and Cesana, M. The virtual trainer: Supervising movements through a wearable wireless sensor network. *In Sensor, Mesh, and Ad Hoc Communications and Networks Workshops 2009,* 1-3.
11. Milenkovic, M., Jovanov, E., Chapman, J., Raskovic, D. and Price, J. An accelerometer-based physical rehabilitation system. *In System Theory 2002*, 57-60.
12. Neuhauser, H. K., Radtke, A., von Brevern, M., Lezius, F., Feldmann, M. and Lempert, T. Burden of dizziness and vertigo in the community. *Archives of Internal Medicine.* 168, 19 (2008), 2118-2124.
13. Shiel Jr, W.C. Osteoarthritis (Degenerative Arthritis) Causes, Diagnosis, Symptoms. *MedicineNet, Inc, April 2008*. http://medicinenet.com/osteoarthritis/article.htm.
14. Sluijs, E.M., Kok, G.J. and van der Zee, J. Correlates of exercise compliance in physical therapy. *Phys Ther,* 73, 11 (1993), 771-786
15. Stone, A.A., Shiffman, S., Schwartz, J.E., Broderick, J.E. and Hufford, M.R. Patient compliance with paper and electronic diaries. *Control Clin Trials*, 24, 2 (2003), 182-99.
16. Szturm, T., Ireland, D.J. and Lessing-Turner, M. Comparison of different exercise programs in the rehabilitation of patients with chronic peripheral vestibular dysfunction. *J. Vestibular Research*, 4, 6 (1994), 461-79.
17. Taylor, P. E. Sensor-based assessment of the quality of human motion during therapeutic exercise. Dissertations 2012, Paper 200. http://repository.cmu.edu/dissertations/200
18. Taylor, P.E., Gustavo, J.M., Kanade, T. and Hodgins, J.K. Classifying Human Motion Quality for Knee Osteoarthritis Using Accelerometers. In. *Engineering in Medicine and Biology Society 2010*, 339-343.
19. Tseng, Y., Wu, C., Wu, F. and Huang, C. A wireless human motion capturing system for home rehabilitation. In *International Conference on Mobile Data Management 2009,* 359-360.
20. Whitney, S. L. and Sparto, P. J. Principles of vestibular physical therapy rehabilitation. *Neuroreabilitation*, 29, 2 (2011), 157-166.

Exploring the Acceptability of Google Glass as an Everyday Assistive Device for People with Parkinson's

Róisín McNaney[1], John Vines[1], Daniel Roggen[2], Madeline Balaam[1], Pengfei Zhang[1], Ivan Poliakov[1] and Patrick Olivier[1]

[1]Culture Lab,
School of Computing Science,
Newcastle University, UK
{r.mcnaney; john.vines}@ncl.ac.uk

[2]School of Engineering and Informatics,
University of Sussex
Brighton, UK
daniel.roggen@ieee.org

ABSTRACT

We describe a qualitative study investigating the acceptability of the Google Glass eyewear computer to people with Parkinson's disease (PD). We held a workshop with 5 PD patients and 2 carers exploring perceptions of Glass. This was followed by 5-day field trials of Glass with 4 PD patients, where participants wore the device during everyday activities at home and in public. We report generally positive responses to Glass as a device to instil confidence and safety for this potentially vulnerable group. We also raise concerns related to the potential for Glass to reaffirm dependency on others and stigmatise wearers.

Author Keywords

Google glass; Parkinson's disease; field trial; qualitative.

ACM Classification Keywords

H.5.m [Information interfaces and presentation (e.g., HCI)]: Miscellaneous;

INTRODUCTION

Parkinson's disease (PD) is a progressive neurological condition affecting up to 10 million people worldwide, with onset generally in those over 50 [9]. PD manifests itself in motor symptoms including rigidity, tremor and bradykinesia, or slowness of movement [2]. These affect balance, gait, arm and facial movements. Motor blocks (freezing) most commonly affect an individual's legs during walking and is generally referred to as freezing of gait. Speech and voice are also typically affected in terms of volume and clarity. People with PD can also be prone to transient and unpredictable "ON/OFF" cycles, wherein medication becomes less effective at treating symptoms, giving periods of effectively controlled symptoms (ON) and periods of severe symptoms (OFF). Aside from the physical signs of PD there are a myriad of emotional and social factors relating to loss of independence, self-confidence, embarrassment and stigma [7].

CHI 2014, April 26 - May 01 2014, Toronto, ON, Canada

ACM 978-1-4503-2473-1/14/04...$15.00.
http://dx.doi.org/10.1145/2556288.2557092

Prior work has explored the use of wearable technology to help the self-management of PD symptoms (e.g. [1, 8]) with further work primarily focusing on diagnostics and tremor classification e.g. [5]. One of the major recent wearable computing breakthroughs is Google's new 'eyewear computer', expected to be commercially available in 2014, referred to as *Glass* [6]. Eyewear computers are claimed to be the next evolution beyond smartphones. Glass is designed to resemble, as much as possible, normal off-the-shelf spectacles. Yet it is equipped with a miniature computer, a micro-display and contains many sensors: an inertial measurement unit (gyroscope, compass and accelerometer) to measure head movements, a microphone for ambient sound pickup, a capacitive touch sensor on the main housing and a front-facing camera. Interaction with Glass is through touch gestures on the side of the frame and spoken commands. Additionally, Glass can provide audio and visual information to a wearer through a bone conducting speaker and the translucent display filling a small region of the field of view. It can be connected via Bluetooth to a mobile phone to access its sensor data (e.g. GPS or additional motion sensors) or the Internet.

Glass opens a new space for exploring the design and development of wearable context-aware systems. As a commercial device it might avoid the stigma associated with devices designed specifically for people with a condition [8]. However, given the novelty of Glass, the expectations and possible acceptance of such devices are not yet known. We fill this void by presenting a qualitative study based on workshop discussions and an initial field trial of the Glass device with people with PD from the United Kingdom.

THE STUDY

First, we undertook a 'Hands on the Glass' workshop with 5 people with PD, representing a diverse range of typical symptoms, and 2 carers. Participants were aged between 46-70 and all were supportive of research and interested in the idea of Glass. The workshop gathered qualitative insights about how participants currently use technology both socially and in managing their condition and to gather initial reactions to the Google Glass technology. Second, we undertook a series of 5 day-long field trials of the Google Glass with 4 of the participants with PD, with daily phone interviews and an exit interview. The workshop and interviews were audio recorded, which were transcribed and anonymised for later analysis. We conducted an inductive thematic analysis [4] on transcribed data by coding it at the sentence to paragraph level and drawing out themes across the data set. The quotes used to describe themes illustrate themes drawn across all participants and data, with the exception of instances where we focus on individual differences (e.g. the 'Wearing the Glass out and about' section). Participant comments are denoted in the text as per; being Parkinson's or carer (P/C), gender (M/F) and participant number (1-7).

HANDS ON THE GLASS WORKSHOP

The 'Hands on the Glass' workshop lasted approximately 2 and a half hours. All 5 of the participants with PD who took part owned mobile phones and used the internet at home, with 3 using specific applications to manage their condition. One participant owned and used a Wii. The workshop began with open discussion about how participants used technology to support daily routines, social activities, and manage their PD. This revealed how many of the participants felt privileged by being able to leave their home and be independent. It was also clear that, while all the participants used mobile phones, they became deeply frustrated by an inability to manipulate them due to hand tremors. Following this discussion, a promotional video of Glass was played, highlighting the video calling, photo sharing, social media, street directions, and information searching features of the device. Following this a researcher gave a demonstration of Glass. Each participant was then given the opportunity to wear and use Glass for a short period of time. Group discussions were facilitated throughout, with the purpose of gathering views on what Glass could do 'out of the box' and encouraging participants to express ideas of alternative uses for the device. The thematic analysis of the workshop revealed 4 themes, discussed in the following.

Issues and Frustrations Relating to Technology Usage

Participants discussed issues they experienced with existing technologies at length. There were particular problems with smartphones specifically related to PD. Tremor and a loss of fine motor ability were identified as symptoms causing great difficulty with using touchscreens and a major source of frustration (PF6: *"the movements have to be quite precise with a touchscreen and if your hand is rigid and not moving very well it's no good really")*. This linked into discussion around needing to place the phone on a stable surface in order to use it (PF5: *"I have to put the phone down to use the touchscreen and it's very, very tricky"*). Participants therefore felt that having a voice activation system would be a huge benefit for them (PF5: *"definitely some kind of hands free - it's definitely the only option for someone with PD"*). Having this on an easily accessible platform such as Glass was perceived to be immensely advantageous when compared with a typical mobile phone based hands free systems.

However, voice command was not without its issues. Many people with PD experience severe problems with their speech and voice which can change with ON/OFF periods. PM3 in particular had marked difficulty producing intelligible speech, which often caused him to avoid certain situations or social interactions: *"This* [his voice] *is not right... It's frustrating. You can't get rid of this* [...] *Now it's really worse, so now I tend to wait for me to be better* [...] *There's no point in carrying on a conversation if you can't understand me"*). This led to concerns from PM3 and other participants that the spoken commands would not work unless highly personalised to specific vocal gestures. Following the 'trying on the Glass' activity, however, there was a high level of success experienced by the participants using the voice activation, including PM3, which incited a sense of encouragement.

Confidence and Safety

All PD participants explained how they had lost confidence as a result of the sudden physical changes associated with unpredictable OFF stages, e.g. PM2 experienced severe and frequent difficulties with freezing, causing him anxiety in crowds or when out alone. This would lead to situations where they were liable to fall or be unable to get required help from the public (PF6: *"well, you lose confidence because you can fall...people don't always understand what you're saying...your voice gradually wears out"*). Glass was immediately seen as something that could instil confidence for participants by providing a feeling of safety. Participants felt they could be independent and go out on their own in the knowledge they could quickly contact someone who could *"see where they are"* and offer instruction and support (PF6: *"It would give me confidence back. I would be more independent because I'm not allowed to be independent much at the moment. That would give anyone in that position the confidence back to be able to be on their own."*). Supporting increased confidence and safety would be two-way between patient and carer. Carers would also benefit from knowing their family member could be contacted as and when needed (CF7: *"Having that, that person can* [...] *see that you're fine and everything"* and PF6: *"the carer would have more confidence in the cared for and the person would have more confidence in themselves to be able to go out and about"*). However, there was also the consideration of burdens for the carer, who may not want to be looking over the person at all times (CM4: *"I wouldn't want to be watching your every move"*).

Security and Vulnerability

Concerns emerged over personal security and the potential that criminals would want to steal the device due to its expense ($1500 +) and rarity (PF5: *"I think at the moment while they're still so pricey I'd be worried that someone was going to whip them off me."*). Participants felt the constant visibility of Glass made them vulnerable, in the sense that it must be worn to be used. Feelings around security differed from those directed to mobile phones, which could be hidden and need not be on public display (PM1: *"You put the phone in your pocket* [...] *If you've got Glasses on here, they can be running past and have them away")*. However, despite these concerns there was an overwhelming sense that using the device could provide features that were worth potential security risks (PM1: *"it offers so much for you.* [...] *It's offering you more safety features than it's actually giving you a problem with"*).

Privacy

There was apprehension that video linking could be abused by overly concerned relatives, who might think they are helping but are instead using the device as a way to control family members with a medical condition. Participants felt that they would need full control over who was able to call them via video link in order to avoid this issue (PF6: *"I don't want my children watching every move I make. There is a potential there for saying, "Mum can't do this", or, "Mum shouldn't do that"."*). Concerns were also raised over *"always being available"*, in the sense that relatives would expect Glass to be easily accessible at all times. This was contrasted with a mobile phone where excuses could be made about why it was not answered (CF7: *"You cannot say, 'Oh, I haven't got my mobile with me'"*).

FIELD TRIALS

The second phase of the study was a series of field trials wherein 4 participants were provided with an operational Glass to use in their own time for 5 days. All participants had PD and had participated in the earlier workshop. PM1 and PM3 wore a black Glass while PM2 and PF5 wore blue. For the trials we provided participants with a boxed Glass, a Google Nexus 4 phone to tether it to, a basic instruction booklet on how to operate Glass, and cables for charging (Glass lasted approximately 5 hours with full charge). At the start of the trial a researcher demonstrated and explained how to use the device. Participants were informed that they could use Glass as much as they wished. However, in an attempt to encourage interactions with the device we provided a pack of 5 prompt cards with activities for participants to perform each day. This included: requesting and following directions, taking photos, creating videos, checking the calendar, and making to do lists.

Each evening a researcher phoned the participants for a brief interview. These interviews identified any significant problems in using the device and also gauged general usage of the device. At the end of the trial each participant took part in an exit interview. These interviews focused on; where they wore the device, what they enjoyed using it for, where they felt it could be improved and to identify whether perceptions towards Glass had altered since the workshop. Each device was then wiped of all content. We describe the themes from the field-trial in the following.

Wearing Glass while 'Out and About'

All of the participants used Glass daily at home as well as in outdoor settings, such as the shopping mall (PF5), when meeting with friends (all), while out driving (PM1, PF5) and during a hospital appointment (PM1, PM2, PM3).

PF5 wore Glass to a busy shopping mall and reported receiving a lot of fleeting attention: *"most people would kind of look and then, out of politeness or whatever, would not pursue it"*. She invited conversation from several service staff and was surprised to hear that they had perceived her as having a visual impairment: *"I went into the bank and the coffee shop, the person serving me* [...] *kept looking.* [...] *I explained what they were and both of them said 'oh, I thought you had some kind of visual impairment'"*. This did not however make her feel uncomfortable and she felt the attention was not excessive.

PM1 took a different approach while shopping. He attempted to provoke a reaction from others but found they *"took no notice"* of him. PM3 had a very different experience however, as he removed his Glass while shopping because he: *"felt people were looking at me. They were staring. I found it quite hostile, it was almost like 'you're up to something'"*. This contrasted with the experiences of his wife (also his carer), who had worn Glass while out for lunch with a friend and felt that *"no one noticed"*. PM3 stated *"it's different for you because your hair hides it"* indicating that he did not want Glass to draw undue attention to him. This possibly related to a lack of confidence PM3 feels in his daily life due to his poor speech, which sees him often avoid social interactions with people he does not know. He associated the unwanted attraction with a feeling of disability: "*people peer at you, it's almost like the blue* [disabled] *badge on the car - they peer inside to look at you as if to say 'what's wrong with you?' That's how I felt*". For PM3 the visibility of the device on his head was a source of stigma. Similar concerns were raised by PM2, who wore a light blue Glass during the trial: *"They should be black so people don't notice it"*. 3 out of 4 of the participants also reported that they would not wear Glass in particular settings due to concerns over their safety.

Frustrations when Interacting with Glass

All of the participants experienced usability issues with Glass. The voice recognition caused frustration amongst everyone (PF5: *"the fact that it wasn't recognising what I wanted was very irritating and very frustrating"*). For PM2 and PM3, who already have marked difficulties with their speech through PD, this proved deeply disheartening (PM3 *"my voice wasn't always working...it came up saying 'try again'"*; PM2's wife: *"he had to shout at it a few times because obviously his voice is very quiet"*). It was noted that, for PM1, *"the voice application is going to have to be re-engineered and made a bit easier"* in order for it to be usable for someone with PD. These difficulties contrasted with the relative successes these same participants had when testing Glass in the workshop.

The navigation gestures, namely tapping on the side of the device, were also problematic in everyday use. There was more success when using the swiping gesture to navigate menus however (PM1: *"I found that the tapping was quite difficult... your hand just keeps going"*). PM2 also found this to be a difficult gesture to master *"scrolling backwards and forwards wasn't too good at times, sometimes you went too far and it was hard to get back"*.

Appreciating Glass

There were a number of successes experienced when using the preinstalled apps on Glass both at home and outdoors. The SatNav system in particular was appreciated: (PM1: *"it was very good, it was the most interactive one I've had...so accurate it's unbelievable"*). When working correctly participants were struck by the speed at which searches could be performed: (PM2: *"the information it gave you was great...it was very quick"*). That they did not have to get a phone out and deal with the resulting physical interaction problems was also valued: (PM1: *"I can't do that with a mobile phone but other people can"*; PM2: *"it's better than a phone. With Parkinson's you can't text because you can't hit the buttons. With the glass you would just talk, you can see what you're doing, it's just instant"*).

GLASS-BASED SELF-MANAGEMENT FUTURES

Across the workshop and deployment phases of our study reactions to Glass were, on the whole, positive. Some of this was down to the novelty of the technology, particularly for PM1, but there was also a genuine appreciation that the device could transform the lives of those with PD. Our aim with this study was to elicit rich initial impressions of Glass based upon the existing, rather limited, selection of apps and functions the device provides. Based on our findings and participant comments, however, Glass also has alternative applications that could potentially help someone with PD self-manage their symptoms.

Contextual Reminders and Prompts: There is great potential to utilise the on-board sensors to detect, and respond to, oncoming OFF periods for someone with PD [PM1, PM2, PF5]. Clinical studies have already shown the potential of using sensors to detect ON/OFF motor fluctuations [3]. Context aware medication reminders and information logging capabilities could prove advantageous in the monitoring and management of medication use [PF5], providing both clinicians and the individual with PD an insight into how well their medications are working.

In-Sight Task Support: The sense of loss of ability, independence and self-confidence was palpable throughout the workshop, thus attempting to recover this in some small way could make a vast difference to the life of someone with PD. Glass allows for instant feedback and support during tasks through the translucent display. This feature could have a positive impact both on the confidence and independence of someone with PD, e.g., sharing what you see with a carer [PF6], or the SatNav system to aid oneself when out alone [PM1].

Cueing for Self-Management: Cueing for freezing has been shown to be successful for people with PD [1]. A person who is seemingly unable to move can be cued into initiation through having a simple visual cue in the form of someone's foot, a laser spot or a walking stick which they are then able to step over. Using a visual overlay displayed on Glass to provide a cue for people experiencing freezing episodes was suggested by several participants [PM1, PM2, PM3]. The cueing theme was extended with further ideas around situated cueing for posture correction, swallowing, blinking and speech [PM1, PF5].

CONCLUSION

Our study of Glass was with a small sample of PD patients and over a short trial period. However, initial impressions were very promising. Our findings show that there is worth in exploring the technical feasibility of applications for PD supporting reminding and prompting, in-sight task support and self-management cues. Future work will also need to address several of the basic functions of Glass, such as the voice recognition and navigation gestures, to ensure it can accommodate for usability issues caused by PD symptoms.

ACKNOWLEDGEMENTS

This research was supported by a Google Glass Research Award, the EPSRC Digital Economy theme Social Inclusion through the Digital Economy Research Hub (EP/G066019/1) and the Technology Strategy Board project 'SALT' (2377-25137).

REFERENCES

1. Bächlin, M et al. Wearable assistant for Parkinson's disease patients with the freezing of gait symptom. In *IEEE Trans Inf Technol Biomed, 14*, 2 (2010), 436 – 446, 2010.
2. Berardelli, JC et al. Pathophysiology of bradykinesia in Parkinson's disease. *Brain, 124*, 11 (2001), 2131-2146.
3. Bonato, P et al. Data mining techniques to detect motor fluctuations in Parkinson's disease, *IEEE EngMed Biol Soc,* 2 (2004), 4766-4769.
4. Braun, V, & Clarke, V. Using thematic analysis in psychology. *Qualitative research in psychology*, *3*, 2 (2006), 77-101.
5. Chen H, et al. An efficient diagnosis system for detection of Parkinson's disease using fuzzy k-nearest neighbor approach. *Expert Syst. Appl. 40*, 1 (2013) 263-271.
6. Google Glass. http://www.google.com/glass/start/
7. MacCarthy, B et al. Psychosocial factors in Parkinson's disease. *Brit J. Clin Psych, 28*, 1 (1989) 41-52.
8. McNaney, R et al. Cueing for swallowing in Parkinson's disease. In: *Proc. CHI '11*, (2011), 619-622.
9. Parkinson's Disease Foundation. Statistics on Parkinson's. http://www.pdf.org/en/parkinson_statistic

Non-Intrusive Tongue Machine Interface

Qiao Zhang, Shyamnath Gollakota, Ben Taskar, Rajesh P. N. Rao
University of Washington
{qiao, gshyam, taskar, rao}@cs.washington.edu

ABSTRACT
There has been recent interest in designing systems that use the tongue as an input interface. Prior work however either require surgical procedures or in-mouth sensor placements. In this paper, we introduce TongueSee, a non-intrusive tongue machine interface that can recognize a rich set of tongue gestures using electromyography (EMG) signals from the surface of the skin. We demonstrate the feasibility and robustness of TongueSee with experimental studies to classify six tongue gestures across eight participants. TongueSee achieves a classification accuracy of 94.17% and a false positive probability of 0.000358 per second using three-protrusion preamble design.

Author Keywords
Electromyography (EMG); Tongue Gesture Interface

ACM Classification Keywords
H.5.2 [User Interfaces]: Input devices and strategies

INTRODUCTION
Researchers have recently explored the feasibility of using the tongue as an assistive interface, to help millions of patients [2] suffering from conditions such as tetrapelgia and Amyotrophic Lateral Sclerosis. Prior approaches, however, require devices to be inserted within the mouth to directly sense the tongue motion. Solutions such as the Tongue Drive [1] extract rich tongue gestures by instrumenting the tongue with magnetic piercings; such solutions are however unlikely to extend to the general user base. Identifying this challenge, researchers have proposed detecting tongue gestures using optical sensors placed on a tongue retainer that is placed in the mouth [3].

We introduce TongueSee, a non-intrusive tongue gesture recognition system that requires neither surgical procedures nor inconvenient in-mouth sensor placements. TongueSee can achieve classification accuracies similar to, if not better than, prior sensor placement approaches [3]. TongueSee leverages the basic observation that different tongue movements often trigger slightly different electrical activity on the surface of the skin at the chin and the throat. TongueSee measures these signals non-intrusively using surface electromyography (sEMG) sensors that measure the gross electrical activity produced during muscular contractions.

The challenge, however, is that the muscles connecting the tongue to other structures in the mouth are hidden under facial muscles and blood vessels. Thus, sEMG sensors typically do not directly capture the electrical signals from the tongue muscles. Instead, they measure the EMG signals responsible for the minute jaw movements corresponding to the tongue gestures. As one would expect, a number of muscles at the lower face and throat are responsible for moving the jaw, and as a result, the sEMG sensors register the cumulative effect of all these muscles. To address this issue, we pick the sensor placement in a physiologically informed manner, to ensure that the sensors are in close proximity to certain muscles to maximize the signals from them. Table. 1 shows the tongue gestures and the corresponding muscle groups that are mainly involved, and the labels of the sEMG sensors covering them.

We are not the first to use EMG signals for gesture sensing. Saponas *et al.* [4] have demonstrated the feasibility of using EMG signals from the forearm to accurately classify finger gestures. Similarly, Sasaki *et al.* [5] use EMG signals to estimate tongue position and contact force, but they have to insert a mouthpiece at the roof of the mouth for training and feedback.

We make the following contributions:

- We introduce a non-intrusive tongue gesture system that classifies six tongue gestures – left, right, up, down, protrude, and rest, with an average accuracy of 94.17%.[1] To do this, we identify EMG sensor positions near the chin and throat, in a physiologically informed manner.
- We describe an anytime classification algorithm that provides a tradeoff between classification accuracy and the real-time responsiveness. We show how to achieve this without retraining the model for different response times.
- We build a TongueSee prototype using the the Biosemi ActiveTwo system, evaluate it across eight participants, and demonstrate its robustness with time. Further, we design a preamble mechanism that allows TongueSee to address the problem of false positive events.

Our work is also related to concurrent work [6] that has close parallels to TongueSee. In contrast, however, TongueSee takes a systematic approach that not only works with a larger gesture set but also addresses key challenges such as false

[1] TongueSee's classification accuracy for the four gestures in [3], is about 96%.

CHI 2014, April 26–May 1, 2014, Toronto, Ontario, Canada.

http://dx.doi.org/10.1145/2556288.2556981

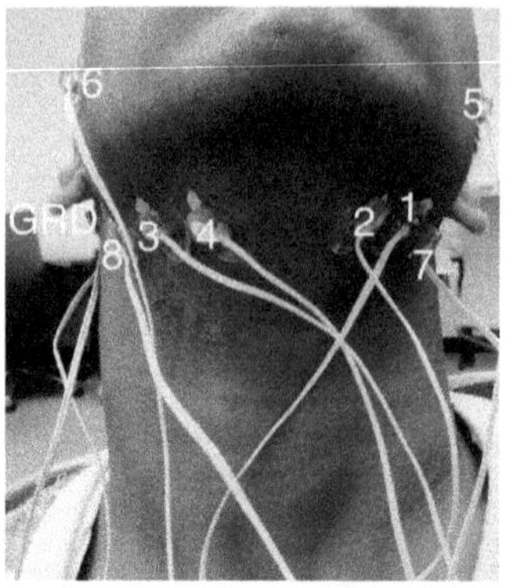

Figure 1. Sensor placements on an experimental participant

Gestures	*Muscle Group*	*Sensors*
Left	Masseter	5,6
Right	Masseter	5,6
Up	Mandibular, Digastric, Omohydroid	1,2,3,4,7,8
Down	Mandibular, Digastric, Omohydroid	1,2,3,4,7,8
Protrude	Digastric, Mylohyoid	1,3,5,6
Rest	-	-

Table 1. Tongue Gestures and Sensor Placements

positives and robustness across sessions, which are crucial in practice. Specifically, our system successfully classified a larger set of six instead of three voluntary gestures, which we achieved by carefully selecting our EMG sensors locations. Further, we design our system to work across sessions over long periods of time (our results show four hours of experiments). Finally, we introduce the preamble design and have determined the appropriate preamble gesture sequence that addresses the problem of false positives. We believe that the above contributions make the experiments, results and algorithmic designs in our paper a significant step towards making this line of work practical.

THE TongueSee SYSTEM

TongueSee leverages EMG signals to reliably classify tongue gestures without requiring any sensor placement in the mouth. We choose the left, right, up, down, protrude, and rest gestures since they are the basic building blocks in any computer input modality. As shown in Fig. 1, our system uses six EMG sensors along a thin strip below the jaw and two EMG sensors covering the Masseter muscles. TongueSee's anytime algorithm can return a classification result at any time (with a resolution of 0.0625 s); the algorithm achieves higher classification accuracies, the longer it runs.

Hardware Equipment and Setup

Our system uses the BioSemi ActiveTwo device to collect EMG signals from the sensor positions shown in Fig. 1. We sample at 2048 Hz from the eight sensors, and use two ground sensors placed behind the ear to reduce line noise and other types of noises. Experimental results are recorded using the BioSemi 2, DummySignalProcessing and StimulusPresentation modules in BCI2000 – BCI2000 is a data acquisition and processing system typically used with EMG signals. The signals are processed with a notch filter at 60 Hz to further remove the line noise and a high pass filter at a low frequency of 0.1 Hz to remove drifts seen in the captured signals.

Feature Extraction

TongueSee extracts two features from each sensor, for a total of 16 features across all the eight sensor locations. The first feature is the root-mean-square (RMS) value of a disjoint window of 128 samples from the sensor. The second is the RMS value of the signed difference between the signal value and mean signal value. Since the sampling rate is 2048 Hz, we get one training point every 0.0625 seconds. Note that our feature extraction mechanism requires minimal computation on the EMG signals, and hence has the advantage of being fast enough to enable real-time testing.

Classification

Our goal is to design an algorithm that can output classification results at any time, while the user performs the gesture. Such an algorithm can enable TongueSee to adapt with the interactivity requirements of the applications. Further, it would provide feedback to the users so that they can continue to perform the gesture until the system gets the classification right. Specifically, we train our multi-class SVM classifier with gaussian kernel using the features extracted from the EMG signals every 0.0625 seconds. However, since the tongue gestures are typically much longer than the above duration, TongueSee performs classification on the test data at coarser resolutions through majority voting. In particular, we divide the test data into non-overlapping intervals of 0.0625 seconds and use our SVM classifier to predict for each interval. To generate a tongue gesture prediction, we apply majority voting to combine the predictions at the fine time scale to coarser time resolutions. Our algorithm thus allows a tradeoff between the interactivity requirements of the application and classification accuracy. Further, our results show that majority voting can significantly increase the accuracy if we combine predictions over long enough durations.

EXPERIMENTS AND RESULTS

We run our experiments with eight volunteers from our research organization. The participants consist of 6 males and 2 females, with an average age of 24.4 ± 1.2, average height of 172.2 ± 9.9 cm, and an average BMI of 23.3 ± 2.8. They were previously inexperienced with EMG sensing technology. In our experiments, they are given a description for the sensor placements, and are instructed to put on the sensors themselves. The sensor placements are therefore approximate, yet effective as shown by our experimental results.

Feasibility of Tongue Gesture Recognition

First, we evaluate the feasibility of using TongueSee to detect and distinguish tongue gestures.

Experiments: We run experiments with all the participants performing six tongue gestures (left, right, up, down, protrude, and rest). Since the participants are unable to replicate sensor placements exactly, we collect the training and test data for each participant separately. In principle, one

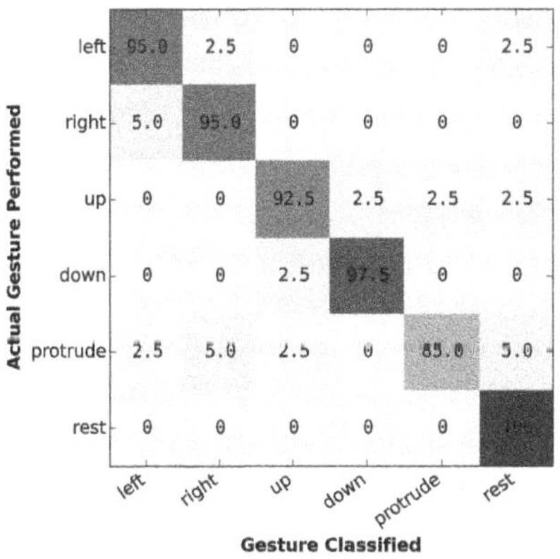

Figure 2. Confusion matrix for tongue gestures: The average accuracy across eight participants for all six tongue gestures is 94.17%. The matrix also shows that the rest action is unlikely to be misclassified.

could integrate the EMG sensors with a chin support band to achieve a more accurate sensor placement and avoid per-participant training; this however is not in the scope of this paper. We run experiments in blocks where each block consists of a sequence of six tongue gesture stimuli that are presented to the participant. Each stimulus consists of a caption shown visually in a 600×480-resolution window on the top left corner of the computer screen. At the beginning of each block, there is a three-second pause for the participants to adjust comfortably for data collection. Each stimulus is then presented for four seconds, with a four-second inter-stimulus pause. During the stimulus presentation, the participants are instructed to perform the appropriate tongue gesture as shown in the captions. They are also asked to hold their tongues in position during the stimulus presentation, and perform the tongue gestures as consistently as possible. During the inter-stimulus pause, the caption screen is blank and the participants are told to relax. We collect 20 blocks of data for each participant; the first 15 blocks are used for training and the last 5 blocks for testing.

Results: We classify the test gestures over a one-second duration using our majority voting mechanism. Fig. 2 plots the confusion matrix computed across participants and the six gestures. Each column of the matrix represents the instances in a predicted class, while each row represents the instances in an actual class. This matrix shows the extent to which one tongue gesture is mislabeled as another by TongueSee. Our findings are as follows:

- The average classification accuracy across eight participants for all six tongue gestures is $94.17\% \pm 7.29\%$. This is in comparison to an accuracy of 17% with random guesses for six gestures. The average accuracy and standard deviation for these gestures are 94.17% (90.83%) and 7.29% (7.72%) when using the first 15 (10) blocks for training and the last 5 (5) blocks for testing.
- Of the misclassifications, the rest action was the least likely to be confused as tongue gestures. This is expected, since in the absence of tongue motion, the EMG signals do not undergo significant changes and have a low value. As a result, the rest action has a distinct EMG signal pattern that is the farthest from actual tongue motions.

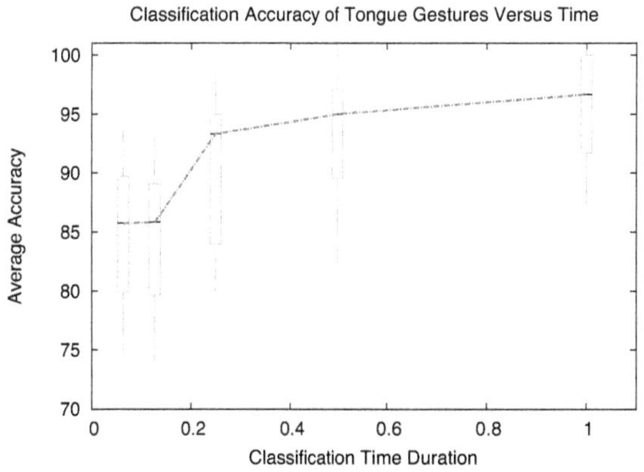

Figure 3. Boxplot of classification accuracy against time resolution for features. The horizontal axis shows the time duration over which the classification was performed. Each candlestick shows the accuracy averaged across all eight participants. The whisker of the box plot shows the error bar (one standard deviation), while the box itself extends from the first quartile to the third quartile of the accuracies. The median is marked in the box.

Next, we demonstrate the trade-off between accuracy and real-time responsiveness of our anytime classification algorithm. Specifically, we compute the average accuracy across the eight participants for different classification time durations. In Fig. 3, we plot the accuracy for six tongue gestures against the time duration over which the classification is performed on the test data. The plot shows an increase from 83.91% to 94.17% as the classification time duration increases from 0.0625s to one second. The trade-off for the increase in accuracy is that instead of detecting a tongue gesture every 0.0625 of a second, the system now detects a gesture every second. Hence, depending on the application, we can trade off classification accuracy for the optimal time responsiveness on the system.

TongueSee's Robustness

We next evaluate the robustness of TongueSee in classifying tongue gestures across time.

Experiment: Since TongueSee requires training per participant, it is crucial to ensure that training model is robust over time. To evaluate this, the participant performs the six tongue gestures across five test sessions that are separated in time. Specifically, the training session consists of 15 blocks, each consisting of a sequence of the six tongue gestures. After the training session, the participant performs 5 blocks for the first testing session. The participant then waits for an hour before the second test session of 5 blocks; the third, fourth and fifth sessions are performed, each after an hour gap and consists of 5 blocks each.

Results: Fig. 4 shows the average accuracy over time; the average is computed across the six tongue gestures for a single participant. Each plot in the figure shows the accuracies for six tongue gestures for different time durations over which

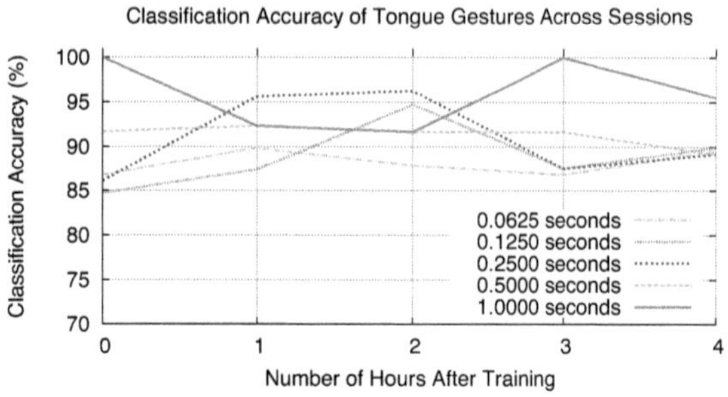

Figure 4. Classification accuracy on the test set is plotted against the number of hours after training for the left and the right tongue gestures. The accuracy is found to be fairly constant over a period of four hours.

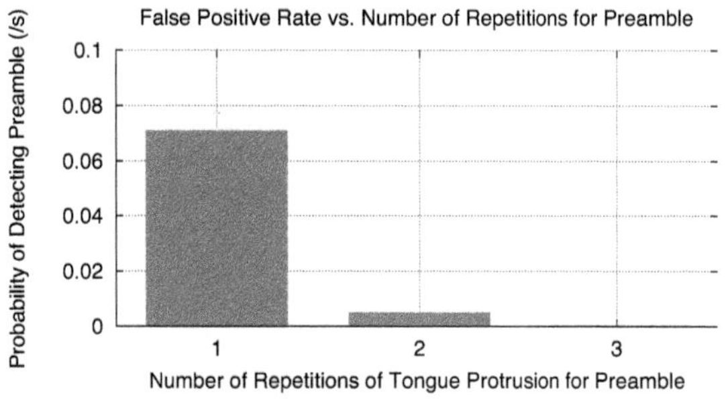

Figure 5. False positive rate. TongueSee uses a repetitive protrusion gesture sequence to gain access to the system. The false positive rate reduces as the number of repetitions in this sequence increases.

the majority voting for classification was performed. The figure shows that the classification accuracies are all above 85% for different time durations used for majority voting. The accuracies are above 90% when one second is used for majority voting. We also note that the one-second accuracies are as high as 100% for a smaller gesture subset, i.e., left and right gestures. The important trend however is that accuracy does not significantly change across time. This shows that TongueSee generalizes over time and is robust across sessions.

False Positives with TongueSee

In practice, users perform a number of involuntary tongue motions that can create false positives in our system. To address this problem, TongueSee uses a repetitive gesture sequence as a starting preamble. Specifically, in TongueSee, users perform a repetitive tongue gesture sequence to gain access to the system. Once TongueSee recognizes the repetitive sequence, the users can perform normal non-repetitive tongue gestures to interact with the device.

Experiments: We compute the false positive rate by running the experiment for a period of 90 minutes. Four participants perform 15 blocks of training, each consists of six tongue gestures. After the training session, the four participants wear the EMG sensors and perform normal activities such as eating, talking, moving his head, and working at the desk for the whole duration of the 90 minutes. Our preamble gesture consists of a repetition of the tongue protrusions. We classify the captured EMG signals for the whole duration to detect the repetitive preamble gesture. We compute the false positive rate as the probability of detecting the preamble gesture each second over the whole 90 minute duration.

Results: In Fig. 5, we plot the false positive rate as a function of the number of repetitions of the protrusion gesture in the preamble. The figure shows that the probability of detecting the preamble per second is 0.071 ± 0.0064, with a single protrusion gesture as the preamble. Using the multiplication rule in probability, the false positive rate decreases with the number of repetitions – it reduces to 0.000358 with three protrusion gestures. We note that if we use three up tongue gestures as the preamble, the false negative rate would be 0.540 ± 0.157 since users are far more likely to move their tongues up during normal activities. These results show that by using three tongue protrusions as the preamble gesture, TongueSee can significantly reduce the false positive rate.

CONCLUSION

We demonstrate the feasibility and robustness of a non-intrusive tongue machine interface that achieves comparable, if not better, classification accuracy for a rich set of six tongue gestures than prior work. Our proposed algorithm trains and classifies at a finer time scale but uses majority voting at a coarser scale, allowing us to maximizes the classification accuracy for different interactivity requirements. Our system can deliver high-fidelity tongue gesture recognition with the potential to help millions of patients.

ACKNOWLEDGEMENTS

We thank Sidhant Gupta, members of UW Networks and Wireless Lab, and the anonymous reviewers for their valuable feedback. We also thank Devapratim Sarma for helping with the experimental set-up. Finally, we thank the experiment participants from our department. This work was partially supported by NSF grant EEC-1028725 and ARO Award no. W911NF-11-1-0307.

REFERENCES

1. Krishnamurthy, G., and Ghovanloo, M. Tongue drive: A tongue operated magnetic sensor based wireless assistive technology for people with severe disabilities. In *Circuits and Systems, 2006. ISCAS 2006. Proceedings. 2006 IEEE International Symposium on*, IEEE (2006), 4–pp.
2. Lee, B., Cripps, R., Fitzharris, M., and Wing, P. The global map for traumatic spinal cord injury epidemiology: update 2011, global incidence rate. *Spinal cord* (2013).
3. Saponas, T. S., Kelly, D., Parviz, B. A., and Tan, D. S. Optically sensing tongue gestures for computer input. In *UIST '09* (2009), 177–180.
4. Saponas, T. S., Tan, D. S., Morris, D., and Balakrishnan, R. Demonstrating the feasibility of using forearm electromyography for muscle-computer interfaces (2008).
5. Sasaki, M., Arakawa, T., Nakayama, A., Obinata, G., and Yamaguchi, M. Estimation of tongue movement based on suprahyoid muscle activity (2011). 433–438.
6. Sasaki, M., Onishi, K., Arakawa, T., Nakayama, A., Stefanov, D., and Yamaguchi, M. Real-time estimation of tongue movement based on suprahyoid muscle activity. In *Engineering in Medicine and Biology Society (EMBC), 2013 35th Annual International Conference of the IEEE* (2013), 4605–4608.

Causing Commotion with a Shape-changing Bench - Experiencing Shape-Changing Interfaces in Use

Erik Grönvall
IT University of Copenhagen
Rued Langgaards Vej 7, 2300
Copenhagen S, Denmark
erig@itu.dk

Sofie Kinch
Aarhus School of Architecture
&The Alexandra Institute Ltd.
Nørreport 22, 8000 Aarhus,
Denmark
sofie.kinch@alexandra.dk

Marianne Graves Petersen, Majken K. Rasmussen
Aarhus University
Aabogade 34, 8200 Aarhus,
Denmark
{mgraves,denmike}@cs.au.dk

ABSTRACT
In this paper we describe results from testing coMotion, a shape-changing bench, in three different contexts: a concert hall foyer, an airport departure hall and a shopping mall. We have gathered insights from more than 120 people, with regard to how users experience and make sense of the bench's shape changing capability. The paper applies McCarthy and Wright's six different sense making processes (*anticipating, connecting, interpreting, reflecting, appropriating and recounting*) as an instrument to analyse people's experience with shape-changing furniture in the wild. The paper also introduces *exploring* as a seventh sense making process. Based on this analysis, the paper points to three relevant aspects when designing shape-changing artefacts for the wild, namely: 1) Affordance of shape-changing interfaces, 2) Transitions between background and foreground and 3) Interpreting physically dynamic objects.

Author Keywords
Shape-changing interface; user experience; in situ; design; interactive furniture; sense-making;

ACM Classification Keywords
H.5.2. User Interfaces

INTRODUCTION
Emerging shape-changing technologies pave the way for making seemingly everyday objects become physically dynamic and transform their shape through digitally controlled self-actuation. Shape-changing technologies allow computation to be literally interwoven with the fabric of everyday life. Visions depict how shape-changing interfaces can potentially make their way into for example our bathrooms, as shape-changing water taps [35], our living rooms as dynamic curtains [6], our pockets as shape-shifting mobile phones [14] or even into our streets as dynamic facades [18]. As the above-mentioned examples illustrate, shape-changing interfaces are slowly securing a foothold within the HCI community. However, despite the increasing amount of research in shape-changing interfaces, the focus is still primarily on their potentials and technical challenges, rather than on how people experience these types of interfaces [30]. We argue (in line with e.g. [30]) that this exploration must go hand in hand with the study of how humans can make use and make sense out of such dynamic objects and environments in everyday life.

Although researchers have begun seeking to understand how people experience shape-changing interfaces, this has primarily so far been done in the lab (e.g.[13,15]). The challenge of testing shape-changing interfaces in a lab setting is that people know that they are participating in some kind of experiment. While they might not be prepared to encounter a shape-changing interface, they are prepared to encounter something new. As a way to gather insights into how people actually experience the, as of yet, uncommon experience of shape-changing interfaces, we suggest taking them out of the lab and into the "wild". Testing in the "wild" is not a new approach [3], but as advocated by Rogers et al. [32] among many others, it offers a way to understand complexities of how users behave, understand and appropriate technologies on their own terms and in complex contexts and situations. User testing in the wild is generally conducted by introducing users to a piece of design and then letting them try out the design for a period of time [3]. However, we have deployed coMotion, a shape-changing bench, in the wild without instructing people about its functionality or purpose, while observing how people experienced the shape-changing ability of the bench, as they sat down to rest while shopping, waited for a plane or relaxed with a drink during a concert intermission. To get further insights into their experiences, people were approached and interviewed as they left the bench.

In this paper, we present related work on shape-changing interfaces and experience design. We present coMotion, a shape-changing bench, which has been designed to explore how people experience an encounter with a piece of shape-changing furniture and how shape-change can affect social behavior in-situ. We discuss insights gained from three user studies of coMotion 'in the wild' with regard to McCarthy

CHI 2014, April 26 - May 01, 2014, Toronto, ON, Canada.

http://dx.doi.org/10.1145/2556288.2557360

Figure 1. The coMotion bench in a shopping center.

and Wright's [24] framework for making sense of the experience of living with technology. We also present an additional category, namely *exploring,* to McCarthy and Wright's framework advocating the importance of embodied, exploratory actions in sense making. Furthermore, we discuss three topics of relevance when implementing shape-changing interfaces in the wild: affordance of shape-changing interfaces, their transition from background to foreground and user interpretation.

RELATED WORK

During recent years numerous shape-changing interfaces have been explored within both the science and art communities. Examples of shape-changing interfaces can be found in mobile phones [14], toys [19], and home appliances [35]. While most shape-changing interfaces are implemented at a scale relating to the hand or other isolated body parts, rather than the whole body, there are examples of larger shape-changing installations, such as Muscle Space [28], Textile Mirror [7] and ExoBuilding [33]. There exist a few examples of shape-change being implemented on a body-scale, allowing for a tactile as well as visual effect of the change. Examples include: Hebing's [11] interactive bench that changes its physical form based on the actions of the person sitting on it and Chalayan's [4] shape shifting garments.

Over the past decade, there has been a growing recognition that as interactive technology becomes an integral part of our everyday lives and environments we need to understand how users experience technology [2,20,24]. The developments of shape-changing interfaces have spurred a growing concern for the agendas and conceptualizations that guide their design, but they have yet to be studied more systematically from an experience perspective. We address these concerns from an experience-oriented perspective by acknowledging the complexity of experiences, as they are merging feelings, thoughts and actions. Koskinen and Battarbee [2], identify three broad approaches to apply and interpret user-experiences in HCI; First, the 'measuring approach' to develop and test how technology emotionally affects the user; Second, the 'empathic approach' to design products that are connected to an individual's needs, dreams and motivations; Third, the 'pragmatic approach' addresses user-experience as the basis of linking action and interaction to meaning. In this manner, the 'pragmatic approach' accounts for the situated unity of action, emotion and thought [ibid] and it emphasizes a focus on lived, everyday life experiences [24]. One example of this approach is McCarthy and Wright's work [ibid] on making sense of experience, which is further explored later in this paper. Based on the coMotion bench user studies we point towards unleashed potentials for people's sense making process through bodily action and engagement with shape-changing interfaces.

THE COMOTION BENCH

The coMotion bench (see Figure 1) is a shape-changing bench. CoMotion was designed as a probe to understand how people will experience shape-changing interfaces in their daily life, rather than as an outstanding, innovative design or as a future product. With the coMotion bench, we also sought to explore whether an unexpected shape-change in an everyday object could spark encounters between strangers. The bench was chosen as a medium for the experiment, as it is a typical artefact in public spaces, where strangers co-locate for periods of time, while rarely engaging with one another. While an unexpected event that make strangers talk with each other can be generated in many ways, for example by sound or street artists, the bench allowed us to explore how physical shape-change and the effects of bodily manipulation, can influence and potentially trigger social encounters in public spaces. The following sections provide a description of the design, and the methodological research approach.

The design

The coMotion bench has a simple rectangular form with neither back nor armrest and can comfortably accommodate six people. The bench is 2,5 meters long, 55 cm high and 40 cm wide. The height and angle of the bench seat can be altered by eight linear actuators (four pairs), which are hidden beneath the grey and black upholstery. The height of each actuator is controlled through instructions sent from the coMotion's main control board to control boards connected to each actuator. The main control board is equipped with an AVR ATMEGA 32 micro-controller and each motor control board uses an AVR ATMEGA 8 for controlling the communication and one actuator. The height-changing commands is sent to the main board either by a wireless remote control or is automatically generated by the main board based on input from six seat-sensors integrated in the surface of the bench that detect how people sit on it. The shape of the bench can be altered in three sections, making it possible to angle the seat, and altering the appearance of the bench, from a flat seating surface to an angled one. The bench moves at a slow place, which makes the movement almost imperceptible at first, in the three contexts, as the sound of the actuators could not be heard. Further technical descriptions can be found in [20] and a visual experience of the coMotion bench and our experiments can be found in the supplementary video material to this paper.

The form, material and color of the bench were designed to allow the bench to blend in, rather than stand out, in the three different environments where it was deployed. The digital properties of the bench was hidden, and there was only a few clues about the bench's shape-changing capabilities, such as the power-cord coming out of the bench, and the somewhat unconventional upholstery materials used (spandex and elastic). Consequently, people were not assisted in making sense of the functionality and how to control it, but had to interpret the form and movement of the bench themselves.

The methodological research approach

The coMotion bench was tested "in the wild", as it provided a possibility for people to experience the shape-change of the bench in their daily life. Deploying the coMotion bench in the "wild" enabled us to investigate some of the challenges facing users of ubiquitous computing systems when technology becomes invisible and disappears into the woodwork.

We deployed the coMotion bench in three different locations; a concert hall foyer, an airport departure hall and a shopping mall. We selected these contexts as each of these locations has different atmospheres and people from different walks of life. However, the locations still hold similar characteristics as public spaces that have a high flow of people [ibid]. We advocate that testing in different contexts secure a foothold, when analyzing people's experience of a new type of interfaces from a more general point of view. The key figures of our tests is illustrated in Table 1.

Location	Days	Seated minutes	Users
Concert hall foyer	2	125	47
Airport departure hall	2	80	54
Shopping mall	1	60	28
In total	5	265	129

Table 1. Data from the three test locations.

The three tests were divided into two phases; an explorative phase using the Wizard of Oz (WoO) method (i.e. using a wireless remote control to alter the bench's physical shape), conducted in the concert hall and the airport departure hall. The insights gained in the first two tests were used to inform the second phase (i.e. test three) where the coMotion bench was programmed with 'behavioral patterns' (i.e. to take on diverse physical expressions) depending on how people sat and used the bench in the first two tests. The programmed behavior of the bench was tested in the shopping mall (a description of the programmed behavior can be found in [20]). All three tests were video recorded from a distance. Users were not aware that they were participating in a test until they left the bench, where a researcher who conducted a short semi-structured interview approached them. As a consequence, the interviews also served to 'de-brief' people with a negative experience of the bench. Indeed, working with 'unaware users' put emphasis on the ethical aspect of our research. Each interview took on average five minutes and the questions focused on people's experience through investigating how people made sense of the bench, before, during and after their engagement with it. The interviews were voice recorded. During the tests there were two-three researchers present ensuring that multiple persons or groups could be interviewed when they left the bench simultaneously. A few people were missed due to getting lost in the crowd and a few of the interviews were rather brief as people were not interested in participating. The video recorded observations were eventually compared to the interviews and analyzed using the framework by McCarthy and Wright [24]. A seventh perspective was added to the framework as a result of this investigation.

MAKING SENSE OF THE EXPERIENCE

Few have provided frameworks, seeking to describe how users make sense of artifacts and experiences. However, Krippendorff [22] has presented a framework describing making sense, as a cognitively constructed relationship, where features of an object and features of its context (real or imagined) are selectively connected into a coherent unity. McCarthy and Wright [24] have presented a framework seeking to describe experience as well as how we *make sense* of an experience. The framework consists of four intertwined threads of experience: the sensual, the emotional, the compositional, and the spatio-temporal thread, alongside six different sense making processes; anticipating, connecting, interpreting, reflecting, appropriating and recounting. The six processes do not occur as a linear sequence of thought and action, but are intertwined and do not occur in a predefined sequence.

We have found McCarthy and Wright's framework a useful tool for directing attention during the analysis, as well as for articulating the different aspects of people's experience with coMotion, and to some extent it resonates well with the observations made throughout our study. We saw for example several instances where people's anticipation influenced the way they connected with the bench. Thus in the following, we present our analysis according to the six processes outlined by McCarthy and Wright [ibid]. The framework provides a structure for describing the different aspects of people's sense making processes, but also presents the challenge of disentangling the intertwined sense making processes and separating them into categories. Based on our experiments we propose an additional category, *exploring,* to the six sense making processes described by McCarthy and Wright. During the trial periods it was striking how people engaged in actively exploring the bench, physically and tactically, by looking down under it, trying to squeeze it, trying to lift up the textile, moving around on it etc. Paradoxically this sensorial rich part of the experience does not seem to be covered

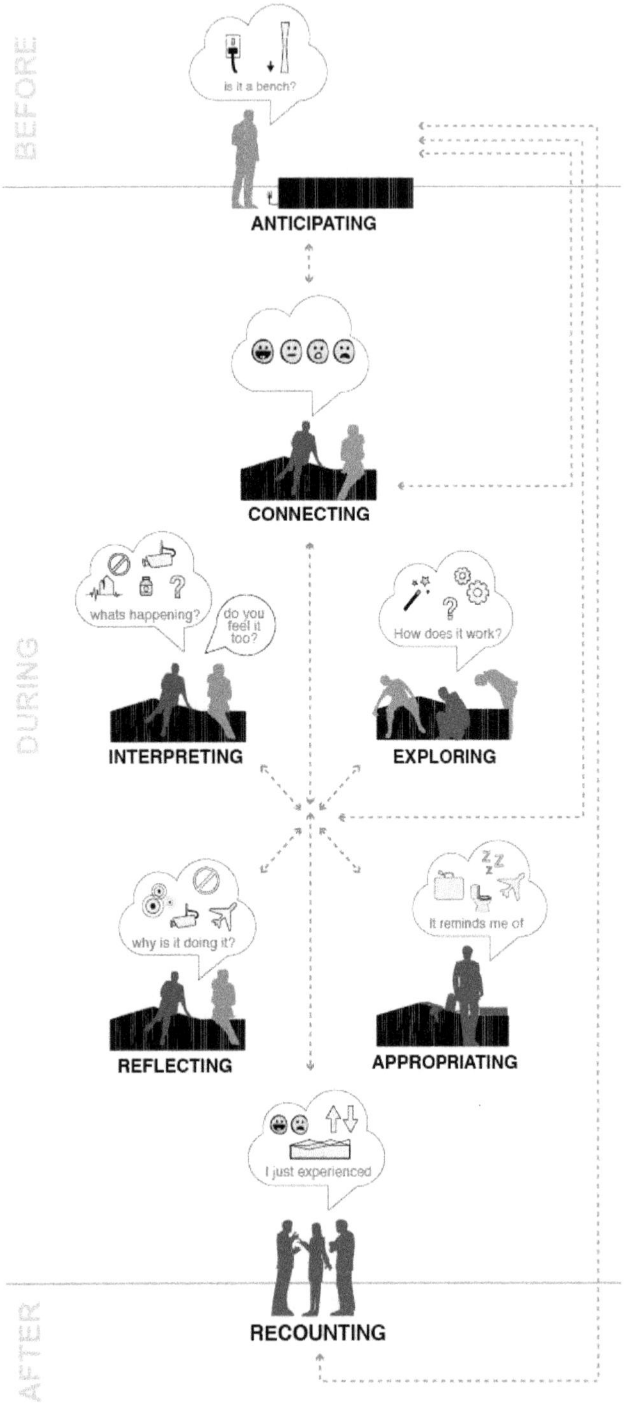

Figure 2. Making sense of the experience.

sufficiently by McCarthy and Wright's framework. Despite that the framework is based heavily on pragmatist philosophy, which emphasises that knowledge is participative, felt and sensed [25], McCarthy and Wright somehow understate this in their six processes, placing the emphasis on the mental reasoning about the experience. Figure 2 presents a visual account of the sense making processes, and their interconnectedness, as we interpreted them in the context of the coMotion bench.

Anticipating: Is it a bench or not?

McCarthy and Wright [24] indicate the need to extend the sense making of an experience beyond its starting point. Given that users do not arrive unprejudiced to an experience, but bring all sorts of expectations, prior experiences, and sense making strategies with them.

The majority of people seating themselves on the coMotion bench were not anticipating *an experience,* but just a place to meet, to wait, or simply to rest ones feet. Indeed, the design of the bench seeks to encourage users in anticipating an ordinary bench. However, while the design of the coMotion bench attempts to adhere to the familiar 'format' of a bench, with regard to seating height and the length, it still differs from the look-and-feel of the average public bench in terms of the materials, as spandex and elastic is used, rather than the familiar hardwearing materials, such as wood, metal and concrete.

The behavior of the bench also aims to support people's initial impression of it simply being an ordinary bench. The bench waits 30 seconds before it begins to alter its shape, allowing people to get seated, comfortable and thereby hopefully dispelling any doubts caused by the divergences from the prototypical bench in public spaces. Despite the attempts to design the coMotion bench in a way where it would blend into the different surroundings it was tested in, the design still caused people to be unsure about what to anticipate. The sense of uncertainty as to what to expect and whether it was a bench or not, was apparent in people's recounts of their experiences, such as *"In the beginning I was unsure whether one could sit on it or not"* - [female, 50's and *"I went off right away when it began to move. I thought, oh... this is not for seating"* - [male, 60's]. Another remarked *"I thought, what is that for a monstrosity? And then I saw that it was plugged in, and then I thought, why was that? Could it do something or what?"* - [female 70's]. The uncertainty could also be observed in peoples' actions. People often touched or poked the bench before sitting down, as if to test whether their assumption of it being a place to sit held true. In the shopping mall, the presence of other people on the bench in its static state, tended to attract more people to the bench. As if the fact that someone else was sitting on the bench helped with categorizing the structure as a bench, rather than something, which might be a bench, but that also might be something else.

Connecting: when sensation becomes emotional

Wright et al. [37] describe connecting, as the first sensuous impact of a situation, occurring as a pre-linguistic response, before we even begin giving meaning to the sensation. As such, connecting represents our immediate impression of for example a bench, and how this engenders a quick emotional response. We emphasize how connecting posits the unity of senses into an overall atmospheric experience situated in the contextual setting.

Due to the temporal aspect of the coMotion bench, two different experiences of connecting are created: one before and one after the shape change. Initially, as people seated themselves on the bench their senses were not subject to any unexpected experience, as they simply 'connected' with the common sensation of sitting down on any given bench. However, when the bench suddenly began to alter its shape, thus impacting on the occupant's senses in an (for most people) unexpected way, it immediately gave rise to a range of experiences, ranging from fright, to confusion, surprise, dizziness, and amusement.

The recorded video-material from the three test-sites provides direct and unfiltered reactions to the unexpected occurrence of the bench beginning to alter its shape. Through the video analysis it became evident the bench's shape-change was a bodily and often quite emotional experience People changed facial expressions, looked around, froze, stood up, walked away or even became afraid. A person said: "*I think it was confusing. I sat quite comfortable, but when it moved, it was like an underlying feeling of unease suffused my body. I was scared that somebody would come up from behind*" - [male, 50's].

Connecting addresses how the user's processes the bench experience from background awareness into focal attention. However, the shape change did not always cause the bench to be in focus. What was experienced as coMotion changed shape seems to be influenced by people's bibliography as well as their momentarily emotional state when sitting down. To give an example a man in the airport said: *"I just realized that I forgot my wallet and when the bench then moved, I felt unwell, like everything fell apart"* - [male, 60's]. Hence, his stressful mind seemed to influence his experience of the bench. In this situation, the bench's movement amplified the embodied state he was in, rather than alter it to become something different.

People's immediate reactions to the bench's movements differed in the three contexts. People in the concert hall smiled and laughed more, and reacted more relaxed towards the intrusion of the unexpected movements. However, in the other two contexts, the sudden movement caused more people to feel a sense of alarm and to become uncomfortable. The deployments in the three contexts indicate that even our immediate response to sensations, including the unexpected ones, can be affected by the context in which it is experienced.

Interpreting: what just happened?

McCarthy and Wright [24] describe interpreting as giving meaning to an unfolding experience, discerning what has happened and what is likely to happen, as well as determining the possibilities for action.

Interpreting the immediate sensation, caused by the bench altering its shape, was not a straightforward task for the occupants of the bench, as the initial sensation was often met with a sense of disbelief. Occupants on the bench often attributed the initial sensation, as something being wrong with themselves, rather than attributing it to the bench. Initially, the thought that the bench would begin to move seemed inconceivable. However, if the occupants remained seated on the bench, then the initial sense of disbelief was dispelled, as the source of the sensation gradually became evident with the increasing inclination of the seat. A couple in their 30's described the experience as: *"we thought it was defiantly entertaining"* - [male 30's], *"you were pretty annoyed when it just happened"* - [female 30's], *"but, that was because I didn't know what was happening"* - [male 30's]. The man continues: "*We didn't talk about it right away, I just had to comprehend what was going on ... is it the room or me? I thought that something was wrong here. The funny thing was I had a thought, isn't something happening, and then I thought, nothing is happening we are just sitting on a bench. I actuarially thought that it was funny that even though the room seemed to change, then I thought it must be my head that something is wrong with, until it became obvious that it just was the bench that was moving"* - [male, 30's]. Other people similarly attributed the experienced sensation to themselves, a woman in her twenties said *"initially I thought, I must be going crazy"* - [female, 20's]. However, the majority of people eventually attributed the sensation as being caused by the bench. Others did not remain seated long enough to rectify their initial interpretation of the sensation, as they left the bench rapidly, still believing the sensation to be attributed to something being wrong with themselves. A woman in the shopping mall left the bench in a hurry immediately after the bench began moving. The interviewing researcher caught up with her to ask her about her experience with the shape changing bench, which caused some confusion as she answered: *"Was it the bench that moved? I have just had a virus causing balance disorder, and I thought it was flaring. I wanted to go home straight away"* - [female, 60's].

People who sought to interpret the sensation proposed a varied spectrum of interpretations based on the shape-change of the bench. Many of the occupants interpreted the movements as a warning notifying them that they were not allowed to sit there. A woman noted, *"I thought I wasn't allowed to sit on it"* - [woman, 60's], while another got up to look at the bench after it moved, saying that *"I had to see what it was for a thing, I had to see if I had sat down too hard and something was broken... Then I decided that the guard, which was passing by would scold me if I wasn't allowed to sit here, but he just passed by, and then I thought it was okay to sit her"* - [male, 70's]. Others interpreted the movements as someone playing a trick on them: *"at first I thought it was hidden camera, or some kind of joke, or something else* (laughing)" - [male, 30's].

We observed how people's interpretations were often formed socially in a group, through discussing and recounting individual interpretations to the group.

Exploring: making sense through action

When surveying the sense making strategies and processes that people employed when attempting to make sense of the coMotion bench, a number of instances of peoples' actions and experiences did not seem to fit into the six sense making processes proposed by McCarthy and Wright [24]. What we term *exploring,* refers to the process of making sense through bodily action and engagement. This involves sensing the material and the physical resistance of the object, moving around it, and by trying to bodily approach it in different ways, e.g. lying on the bench, sitting on it, standing beside it. Exploring also holds a social aspect to it, as the physical exploration primarily happened when people were in pairs or groups. However, the exploration in some cases went outside the predefined groups. For a short while, two groups could for example, explore the bench together. An example of this is in the music hall where two pairs (two girl friends in their 20's and a couple in their 50's), together stated to joke and laugh about the bench after it had started to move. After a while all four people got up from the bench to look at it, before eventually sitting down on it again. The exploration also became social in the sense that people tried to physically explore it with others, to see how it would change when there is more than one person on it, when sitting close and far apart etc.

The abovementioned actions cannot be categorized as either interpreting or reflecting, but instead as trying to make sense through exploration and by sensing it.

Reflecting: What is the meaning of this?

McCarthy and Wright [24] describe reflecting as a sense making process, which can happen either *in* an experience or as reflection *on* an experience after it has run its course. Reflecting hence deals with the judgments made about an experience as it unfolds and whether a person can make sense of it. Reflection also deals with how a person feels about the situation and what value is placed on the experience. Reflecting often takes the form of a dialogue, either with oneself or with others.

Peoples' reflections on their experience with the coMotion bench, was generally wrought with confusion, curiosity, amusement, or even annoyance. The three locations seemed to influence how people felt about the situation. In the concert hall people had prepared themselves for entertainment, which seemed to affect their experience of the bench, reflected in statements such as: "*At one point we stood up; it was as if the ride was over*" - [couple, 40's]. Whereas the reflections in the airport seemed more influenced by the heighten sense of alertness, for example caused by entering through the security check and the stress of travelling.

The reflections recounted in the interviews, were mainly focused on reflecting upon why the bench acted in such an unordinary way. A dialogue between two friends was observed: as one of the two friends arrived back to the bench from a visit to the toilet, the other said "*I really don't know what's happening, all of a sudden it just stood up (…) It is really a very odd chair*" (she looks frustrated). An airport security guard passes by the bench, and one of the women asks *"Do you know what this is?*" to which the guard answers "*No, I have never seen it before*" and moves on. The girl replies back to the guard *"It is moving, you know"*. When approached by the researches, one of the women immediately asked: *"What is the meaning of this? (...) We have just been sitting and discussing what it was that we were sitting on. And we agreed that it must be a work of art. We really want to know what the meaning of it is"* - [female, 20's & 30's]. Although many of the occupants on the bench reflected upon their interpretation of the bench behaviour, and it's seemingly unwillingness to have people seated on it. Few sought to provide an explanation for the bench's odd behaviour. One reflected upon this as: *"...the idea could be that it was a clever way to say that you can rest here for a few minutes, but then you have to move on*" - [male, 40s]. Others pointed to that "*it could be a preparation for going flying. You know elderly people who have to sit in a plane for a long time, might benefit from a bit of exercise to get the blood circulation started"* - [female, 30s]. Some users also reflected upon the social situation created by the bench. One user pointed to wishing he had been seated the other way round on the bench, as he thought that, as the bench moved, he was sitting a little too close to the other occupants on the bench.

Although the bench had been designed to spark social encounters between strangers, only a few of the interviewed occupants reflected upon this. When asked about what the bench was designed for, one answered that: *"It could also just be furniture designed for exploring encounters between people"* - [male, 40s]. However, although people tended not to reflect upon the ability of the bench to foster social encounters, this often happened. The alteration in shape did often spark encounters between strangers as they sought to make sense of the experience. The encounter was generally initiated as means to seek confirmation that the bench, rather unexpectedly, was moving. This was done either simply by a movement of the head, flicker of the eyes, a smile, or a comment spoken out to the other occupants on the bench. As one of the men explained in the interview: "[…] *the other man said to me; I think it is moving"* - [male 60's]. Another person said: *"Indeed, we talked about what was happening; it was not that we talked about anything else than the bench, but we talked with all the others while sitting there"* - [male, 50's].

Appropriating: How does it become mine?

McCarthy and Wright [24] describe appropriating as making an experience our own, by relating it to both previous and future experiences and thereby giving the experience a more personal meaning to us.

Users appropriated the movements, the design and the unexpected occurrence of technology to their prior experiences. Especially in the deployment in the airport context, users related the coMotion bench to their previous experiences. In the airport the design caused people to relate it to different aspects of transportation, "*the elastics refer to the seatbelt, something about being fastened down*" - [female, 30's], she further remarked that "*The first thing I think of is that I am going flying. And the bench kind of refer to spreading our wings and taking off*". Another person also related it to the context "*It has an aviation feel about it...*" - [male, 40s]. In the concert hall a woman noted that that the bench reminds her of an experience being at a toilet in Japan that unexpectedly flushed upwards with water, played music and had a vibrating seat, which caused her to stand up to get a good look at what was happening - [female 60+]. For others it was rather the movement that sparked their memory, "*it reminds me of a massage chair*" - [female, 20's] or the effect of the movement, which made them relate the coMotion experience to other experiences: "*I started thinking about that I visited my neighbour last night, and he was suddenly saying that he felt dizzy... he is only 40-45 years old, and then he suddenly fell down. And then I thought, am I experiencing the same?* - [female, 60s].

Recounting: guess what I just experienced

McCarthy and Wright [24] describe recounting as being essentially dialogical, as the experience is recounted to ourselves and others. Recounting the experience enable us to savor the experience again, discover new possibilities and new meanings. As the experience is recounted it can be altered depending on the situation and the moment-to-moment response from others. When recounting an experience to others, we draw out their responses, which might in turn alter our own assessment of an experience.

The information used to recount the users' experience with the coMotion bench in the previous sections, is based both on what is observable in the video, as well at people's recounts of how they experienced the bench altering its shape underneath them. Therefore it is important to note that the majority of the quotes used in the sections above are derived from people recounting their experience. What has been recounted to the interviewer may thus not always be what was interpreted or reflected upon *in* the experience, but may be altered by new meanings and interpretations formed as the experience was recounted. Consequently, it is difficult to separate the "sense made" in the other sense making processes, from insights users gained during recounting their experiences. However, what seemed clear was that the questions asked during the interviews, led the users to a deeper reflection about the preceding experience.

What was interesting to note was that when users were presented with the opportunity to recount their experience to people, who had not yet experienced the unexpected movements of the bench, they often chose not to recount it. These instances often occurred when people had experienced the bench changing shape on their own, while waiting for friends or relatives. Users in this type of situation generally attempted to keep it quiet, seeing it as an opportunity for a good joke, where they were in on the prank while the others were not.

DISCUSSION

The coMotion bench exemplifies how shape-changing technologies can, in their static state, weave themselves almost imperceptible into the fabric of everyday life. However, people's interaction with the coMotion bench illustrates that the occurrence of movement is drastically and unexpected. The bench's transition from static to a dynamic object is not smooth, despite the slowness of the movement. The surprise, or even chock, caused by the transforming action of the bench becomes amplified when physically felt or experienced, rather than seen at a distance.

The deployment of the coMotion bench into everyday life settings illustrates that shape-changing technologies embedded in everyday life poses a number of challenges for the user, especially when the shape-changing capabilities are hidden. As the hidden shape-changing capabilities are revealed, objects that formerly were part of the background awareness, can suddenly force themselves into the foreground of peoples attention. Our work raises the question of, if we are to embed shape-changing capabilities imperceptibility into objects, then how do we deal with, for example: 1) changing affordances in shape-changing interfaces, 2) their transition from background to foreground and 3) user interpretation of shape-changing interfaces? We will now discuss perspectives that emerged from our early investigation of the abovementioned three topics. Hopefully this work will help to initiate a debate and provide questions for future work on shape-changing interfaces.

Affordance of shape-changing interfaces

Affordance has, since Gibson [9] coined the term and Norman [25] introduced it to the HCI community, been widely used by for example computer scientists, designers and psychologists. Gibson [9] defines affordance as the actionable properties between the world and an actor. Norman in turn described affordances as the "perceived and actual properties of the thing, primarily those fundamental properties that determine just how the thing could possibly be used" - [27, p.8].

The notion of affordances [9,25], and more specifically the potential for dynamic affordances has been widely mentioned within shape-changing research (e.g. [5,23,30]). Affordance, and especially dynamic affordances, has been used to boast about the potentials shape change hold, such as: "*learn to adapt to their different conditions of use and respond with just-in-time affordances*" - [5, p.3433], and "*in the case of shape-shifting materials these affordances exist over time, but not statically*" - [24, p.38]. However, despite the numerous references to affordances within shape-changing research, few use it to analyze their designs' or reflect on the users' ability to understand dynamic affordances. Shape-changing interfaces appropriate affordances in two ways; *static* and *dynamic*. Static refer to the static physical properties indicating an artifact's action possibilities and shape changing capabilities. Dynamic refer to the physical shape change indicating altered action possibilities or information embedded in the kinetic change itself.

In its static state, the coMotion bench affords 'sitting', and other uses of an everyday sturdy bench, such as 'laying down on top of it' or 'placing a heavy bag on it', all of which action that we observed performed on the bench. CoMotion deliberately does not provide the users with perceptual information about its shape-changing capabilities. Possible affordances that the bench can demonstrate through changing its shape are at this stage (and in Gaver's terminology [8]) hidden. As the bench begins to alter its shape, a user's original interpretation (i.e. based on the actions afforded by the static shape) is challenged. The bench no longer has a horizontal seating surface and the height of the bench no longer matchers the length of the occupants' legs. If the bench initially had this non-horizontal form, it would not have afforded 'sitting'. However, the majority of people remained seated after the transformation from the horizontal to the 'cracked up' or non-horizontal state, despite the uncomfortable seating position. At this point however, few people sat down on the bench, and those who did, either knew people sitting on the bench, or had observed the shape-change at distance.

The shape-changing capability of coMotion hence challenge the idea that the desired, relevant actions should be readily perceivable in a design [26]. In some cases it is in the discrepancy between the perceptual information provided to the user, and the actual capabilities, wherein the quality of the design lie, as it can be a source of engagement, curiosity and appropriation. However, as also pointed out by Jung et al. [16], if it is not the intention to surprise users, then designers should provide predictable cues, such as structural appearance or sound, which allow users to naturally foresee upcoming events. Having said this, designers must be mindful of, as seen in the case of coMotion that although some indicators (material and cord) provided the user with indicators of the bench's shape-changing possibilities, this was often not enough information for people to comprehend the capabilities of the bench. Furthermore, if movement had been used to indicate that the bench could change shape, then people might not have considered it to be a bench in the first place.

Consequently, providing cues of shape changing capabilities is not straightforward, especially when dealing with shape-changing furniture, as the change will often be felt, rather than seen. It raises the question of whether we need to define a new visual language to communicate shape-changing capabilities within consumer products, and common spaces to make people aware of such capabilities and their functions? How we can employ the notion of affordances to emphasize desired affordances and re-emphasize undesired ones [8]?

Transitions between background and foreground

The coMotion bench challenges the paradigm of the invisible computer and allows for exploring the experiential aspects of the ubiquitous vision in peoples' everyday lives. Building upon Weiser and Brown's notion of Calm Technology; *"a calming technology may be one that easily moves from center to periphery and back"* - [37, p.2], we address some ethical issues on the sense making of shape changing interfaces disturbing the calming effect.

Indeed, when people approach coMotion they are unaware that they are about to interact with a technology-augmented bench. Upon sitting down, the bench is generally positioned in peoples' background awareness as they are "only sitting on a common bench". However, when coMotion begins to move it immediately shift into people's focal attention. Instead of designing for calm transitions between background awareness and foreground attention, we accentuate the transitions, which promptly lead to strong emotional responses. From the field tests we observed how people tried to make sense out of a confusing situation, and how the experience influenced body posture, as it for example caused users to imitating each other's posture (both consciously and non-consciously) as a way to cope with the unknown.

Within the interaction design community, researchers have presented different perspectives on dealing with the transitions between background and foreground attention. With few exceptions (e.g. [32]), there seems to be a general tendency towards designing for calming effects. We elaborate upon Kinch and Hoejlund [21] who describe how the concept of 'embodied habituation' helps designers to gradually and through repetitive actions accustom the users background awareness to accomplish a given task. This is fruitful when for example designing for a stressful situation [ibid]. We acknowledge that the consequences of hiding the shape-changing capabilities in the coMotion bench, is an obstruction of the embodied habituation process. However, we will in the following turn towards some neglected potentials and experiential qualities of shifting peoples' collective mindset within a fraction of a second.

Derived from soundscape research, Augoyard and Torgue [1] propose a range of 'sonic effects' to articulate how to design for sonic experiences, which changes over time. To address peoples' unexpected experience of sitting on the coMotion bench, we point towards their proposed 'cut-out effect' that *"punctuates movement from one ambiance to another"* - [1, p29]. The 'cut-out effect' is best explained through an anecdote of a broken glass; *"Suspended for a moment, the murmurs of the hall resume. The timbre and rhythm change. People come back to tell their stories. We can feel the warmth of the place rising again. A consensus has been found again, as if the cards had been re-dealt"* - [1, p.158]. The quote points towards how collective shifts in awareness are incorporated in everyday life, thus we emphasize that transitions from background to foreground attention not only exist as calming, habituation processes [21], but may also be disrupted, leading to dis-habituation. Habituation and dis-habituation are both natural processes, which are mutually dependent on each other. When we design for dis-habituation, we propose that manipulating people's collective awareness scaffolds new types of experiences, which exists in the realm of the shifting from background to foreground awareness. Designing for inter-subjective and atmospheric experiences can foster social encounters, as illustrated by the coMotion bench [20]. However, social encounters are shaped differently according to the interaction modality, thus sound and visuals have other socializing effects [30], than the haptic modality investigated in this paper. The haptic sensation is one reason why people initially point towards the shape-change as something happening within them (i.e. a bodily experience). Consequently, the dis-habituation is reserved for those who are physically affected by the shape change.

Interpreting physically dynamic objects

Classic psychology experiments, for example by Heider and Simmel [12] and Scholl and Tremoulet [34], have illustrated how people tend to attribute motivations, intentions, and goals to individual rigid objects, based solely on the pattern of their movements. These studies show how proficient people are in detecting movements and deriving meanings from them.

The application of anthropomorphic or zoomorphic movement patterns has been used to design product movement patterns, and has had some success in getting people to interpret the intentions of the product movement (e.g. [15,16,17]). However, the movements of the coMotion bench did not lean on anthropomorphic or zoomorphic movement patterns, as has been a common approach when designing shape-changing interfaces. Rather than seeking to portray emotion or postures through form change and movements, the bench's shape change relied on the haptic effect on its occupants, caused by the altered angle of the seats. Consequently, people's interpretations focused on why the bench moved, such as: *"I thought I wasn't allowed to sit on it"*, or "*... to say that you can rest here for a few minutes, but then you have to move on*", rather than the character of the movement itself. This might be due to the lack of anthropomorphization of the movements, or that users' interpretation of the shape-change used in coMotion often relied more on interpreting the haptic sensation, rather than on visual information. Although users' reflections on the bench indicated that they did not personify the bench, as is often the case with shape-changing interfaces, they still often patted the bench or stroked it when it moved.

A parameter, which other studies of motion (e.g. [15,16,17]) have not taken into account, is the influence of context on people's interpretation of the shape change. The coMotion study indicated that people's interpretation was not only affected by the movement itself, but was affected by the context, the seated people's present activity and their emotional state. We wish to stress the importance of considering how the test-context influences the interpretation of a shape-changing artefact, and that a lab where (any) technology is tested is not a neutral place, but influences how people respond and interpret to shape change.

CONCLUSION

In order to fully exploit the potential of shape-changing interfaces, we need to study how they are experienced and adopted by people in real life and "in the wild". The presented study reports on lessons learnt from 129 people's encounter with a shape-changing bench in three different contexts. One lesson indicates that the coMotion bench promotes strong emotional responses, both positive and negative, which advocates the importance to 'debrief' people after their first encounter with coMotion. Another lesson indicates that designers of future shape-changing interfaces must be aware of both the mental and bodily effects shape-change may have on people.

The paper applies and develops McCarthy and Wright's framework for Making Sense of Experience to analyse and discuss people's experiences with the shape-changing bench. The authors found that the six sense making processes, as described by McCarthy and Wright worked well for this purpose. However, to complement the existing framework, this paper also introduced *exploring* as a seventh sense making process. Applying the seven processes, points to for example that aspects of affordances are critical to consider when designing shape-changing interfaces. Therefore, there might have to be developed a new visual language to assist people to comprehend and effectively use shape-changing artefacts. We illustrate how the context is highly influential upon how people interpret the meaning of shape-changing objects. With this work, we are only beginning to understand how shape-changing interfaces are experienced out there "in the wild" and we encourage the CHI community to help us further explore the issues outlined and discussed in this paper.

ACKNOWLEDGEMENTS

Center for Participatory IT (Aarhus University) contributed to funding this research. LINAK kindly supplied the bench actuators and Maria Stjernholm Svendsen helped us design the bench upholstery. Finally we thank all people who helped us by interacting with the coMotion bench.

REFERENCES

1. Augoyard, J.F. and Torgue, H. *Sonic Experience: A Guide to Everyday Sounds*. MQUP, 2006.
2. Battarbee, K. and Koskinen, I. Co-Experience: User Experience as Interaction. *Co-design, interdisciplinary journal of design 1*, 1 (2004), 5–18.
3. Brown, B., Reeves, S., and Sherwood, S. Into the wild: challenges and opportunities for field trial methods. *Proceedings of the SIGCHI Conference on Human*

Factors in Computing Systems, ACM (2011), 1657–1666.
4. Chalayan, H. *http://chalayan.com/collection/view/album/id/35*, 2007.
5. Coelho, M., Ishii, H., and Maes, P. Surflex: a programmable surface for the design of tangible interfaces. *CHI '08*, (2008), 3429.
6. Coelho, M. and Maes, P. Shutters: A Permeable Surface for Environmental Control and Communication. *TEI '09*, (2009), 13.
7. Davis, F., Roseway, A., Carroll, E., and Czerwinski, M. Actuating mood: design of the textile mirror. *TEI* (2013), 99–106.
8. Gaver, W.W. Technology affordances. *Proceedings of the SIGCHI Conference on Human Factors in Computing Systems*, ACM (1991), 79–84.
9. Gibson, J.J. *The Ecological Approach to Visual Perception*. Houghton Mifflin, Boston.
10. Hassenzahl, M. User Experience and Experience Design. *Encyclopedia of Human-Computer Interaction*, (2011).
11. Hebing, R. Bench. 2013. Retrieved from: http://www.robhebing.nl/?p=19.
12. Heider, F. and Simmel, M. An Experimental Study of Apparent Behavior. *The American Journal of Psychology 57*, 2 (1944), 243–259.
13. Hemmert, F., Hamann, S., Löwe, M., Wohlauf, A., Zeipelt, J., and Joost, G. Take me by the hand: haptic compasses in mobile devices through shape change and weight shift. *NordiCHI '10*, (2010), 671–674.
14. Hemmert, F., Hamann, S., Löwe, M., Zeipelt, J., and Joost, G. Shape-changing mobiles: tapering in two-dimensional deformational displays in mobile phones. *CHI EA '10*, (2010), 3075.
15. Hemmert, F., Löwe, M., Wohlauf, A., and Joost, G. Animate mobiles: proxemically reactive posture actuation as a means of relational interaction with mobile phones. *TEI* (2013), 267–270.
16. Jung, J., Bae, S.-H., and Kim, M.-S. Three Case Studies of UX with Moving Products. *UbiCom*, (2013), 509–518.
17. Jung, J., Bae, S.-H., Lee, J.H., and Kim, M.-S. Make it move: a movement design method of simple standing products based on systematic mapping of torso movements & product messages. *CHI*, (2013), 1279–1288.
18. Kahn, N. and UAP. Brisbane airport kinetic parking garage facade, Retrieved from: http://www.designboom.com/weblog/cat/10/view/23329/brisbane-airport-kinetic-parking-garage-facade-by-ned-kahn-uap.html.
19. Katsumoto, Y., Tokuhisa, S., and Inakage, M. Ninja track: design of electronic toy variable in shape and flexibility. *TEI* (2013), 17–24.
20. Kinch, S., Grönvall, E., Petersen, M.G., and Rasmussen, M.K. Encounters on a Shape-changing Bench: Exploring atmospheres and social behaviour in situ. *TEI'14*.
21. Kinch, S; Hoejlund, M.K. Kidkit Guides Children into Alarming Atmospheres -designing for embodied habituation in hospital wards. *DPPI*, (2013).
22. Krippendorff, K. On the Essential Contexts of Artifacts or on the Proposition That "Design Is Making Sense (Of Things)."*Design Issues 5*, 2 (1989), 9–39.
23. Lakatos, D. and Ishii, H. Towards Radical Atoms - Form-giving to transformable materials. *IEEE (CogInfoCom)*, (2012), 37–40.
24. McCarthy, J. and Wright, P. Technology as experience. *interactions 11*, 5 (2004), 42–43.
25. Norman, D.A. *The psychology of everyday things*. Basic Books, 1988.
26. Norman, D.A. Affordance, conventions, and design. *interactions 6*, 3 (1999), 38–43.
27. Norman, D.A. *The Design of Everyday Things*. Basic Books, 2002.
28. Oosterhuis, K. and Biloria, N. Interactions with proactive architectural spaces. *Communications of the ACM 51*, 6 (2008), 70.
29. Pallasmaa, J. *The Eyes of the Skin: Architecture and the Senses*. Academy Group Ltd, United Kingdom, 1996.
30. Rasmussen, M.K., Pedersen, E.W., Petersen, M.G., and Hornbæk, K. Shape-changing interfaces: a review of the design space and open research questions. *CHI '12*, ACM (2012), 735–744.
31. Rogers, Y. Moving on from Weiser's Vision of Calm Computing: Engaging UbiComp Experiences. In P. Dourish and A. Friday, eds., *UbiComp 2006: Ubiquitous Computing*. Springer Berlin Heidelberg, 2006, 404–421.
32. Rogers, Y. Interaction design gone wild: striving for wild theory. *interactions 18*, 4 (2011), 58–62.
33. Schnädelbach, H., Irune, A., Kirk, D., Glover, K., and Brundell, P. ExoBuilding: Physiologically Driven Adaptive Architecture. *ACM Trans. Comput.-Hum. Interact. 19*, 4 (2012), 25:1–25:22.
34. Scholl, B.J. and Tremoulet, P.D. Perceptual causality and animacy. *Trends in Cognitive Sciences 4*, 8 (2000), 299–309.
35. Togler, J., Hemmert, F., and Wettach, R. Living interfaces: The Thrifty Faucet. *TEI '09*, (2009), 43.
36. Weiser, M. and Brown, J.S. Designing Calm Technology. *POWERGRID JOURNAL 1*, (1996).
37. Wright, P., McCarthy, J., and Meekison, L. Making Sense of Experience. In M. Blythe, K. Overbeeke, A. Monk and P. Wright, eds., *Funology*. Springer Netherlands, 2005, 43–53.

Paddle: Highly Deformable Mobile Devices with Physical Controls

Raf Ramakers Johannes Schöning Kris Luyten
Hasselt University - tUL - iMinds
Expertise Centre for Digital Media
Diepenbeek, Belgium
firstname.lastname@uhasselt.be

ABSTRACT
We present the concept of highly deformable mobile devices that can be transformed into various special-purpose controls in order to bring physical controls to mobile devices. Physical controls have the advantage of exploiting people's innate abilities for manipulating physical objects in the real world. We designed and implemented a prototype, called Paddle, to demonstrate our concept. Additionally, we explore the interaction techniques enabled by this concept and conduct an in-depth study to evaluate our transformable physical controls. Our findings show that these physical controls provide several benefits over traditional touch interaction techniques commonly used on mobile devices.

Author Keywords: Deformable Interfaces; Tangible Interfaces; Mobile Devices

ACM Classification Keywords: H.5.2 [Information interfaces and presentation]: User Interfaces: Input devices and strategies

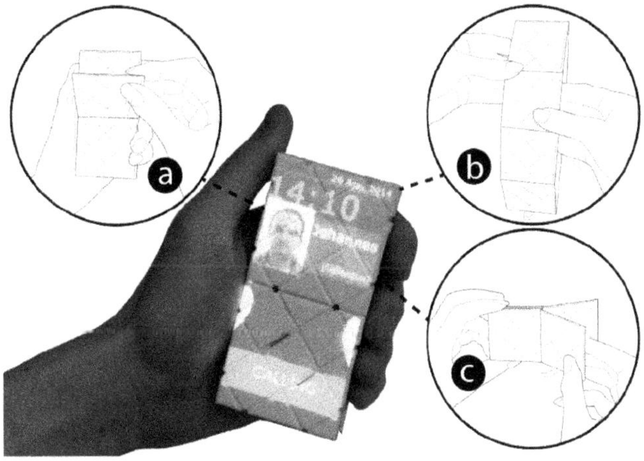

Figure 1. Paddle supports several physical controls, including (a) peeking, (b) scrolling, (c) leafing.

INTRODUCTION
Touch screens have been widely adopted in mobile devices. Although touch input is very flexible in that it can be used for a wide variety of applications on mobile devices, touch screens does not provide physical affordances [13], encourage eyes-free use [5] or utilize the full dexterity of our hands [18] due to the lack of physical controls. On the other hand, physical controls are often tailored to the task at hand [13], making them less flexible and therefore less suitable for general purpose use in mobile settings. In this paper, we show how to combine the flexibility of touch screens with the physical qualities that real world controls provide in a mobile context. We do so using a deformable device that can be transformed into various special-purpose physical controls. To demonstrate this concept, we present one possible implementation, called *Paddle* (Figure 1).

Researchers already explored how bending [17, 19] and folding [7, 15] interactions supported by deformable mobile devices can be used as physical controls. Compared to traditional tangibles and touch screens, however, these controls lack affordances in that it is often unclear how folds and bends map to actions [19].

When the number of possible deformations a device supports increases, there is a novel opportunity to transform these devices into differently shaped physical controls that provide clear physical affordances for the task at hand. Paddle is an early prototype of such a device and allows switching between various physical controls, including a window to peek at content (Figure 1-a), a ring to scroll through lists (Figure 1-b) and a book-like form factor to leaf through pages (Figure 1-c). Similar to other prototyped deformable devices [15, 16], Paddle bridges the gap between differently shaped mobile devices, such as phones, tablets and wristbands. Paddle's ability to transform to various physical controls, however, has to our knowledge not been investigated before.

When transforming a device to differently shaped physical controls, it should be possible to switch between these shapes in only a few steps. In contrast, earlier prototypes of deformable mobile devices [7, 15, 19] are paper-like and thus support an origami transformation model that often requires numerous transformations. As Paddle is based on engineering principles used in the design of 3D puzzles, the transformation model is superior to origami and allows switching between different shapes in only a few steps (e.g. two steps to change a small flat form factor (Figure 1-a) into a ring (Figure 1-b)).

CHI 2014, April 26 - May 01 2014, Toronto, ON, Canada

ACM 978-1-4503-2473-1/14/04...$15.00.
http://dx.doi.org/10.1145/2556288.2557340

Contribution

The main contribution of this paper is the concept of *highly deformable mobile devices that can be transformed into various special-purpose physical controls to bring physical controls to mobile devices.* We demonstrate this concept using one possible prototype, which we call *Paddle*. Additionally, we explore the novel interaction techniques enabled by Paddle. Finally, we report on an in-depth study showing that physical controls supported by Paddle have several benefits compared to traditional direct touch interactions on mobile devices.

PADDLE

The mechanical construction of our prototype, Paddle, is based on principles used in the design of the Rubik's magic puzzle, a folding plate puzzle (Figure 3). Tiny infrared reflective markers are attached to this device and tracked with an optical tracking system. This enables us to project on the device to provide visual output. Similarly, touch input is enabled by tracking the fingers of the user. In the future however, we envision Paddle devices to be self-contained using electronic connectors to track the topology of the device [8] and tiny integrated displays [23], as those used in Tilt displays [1] and Facet [22], for visual output.

Scenario

Figure 2 shows an example interaction that illustrates how Paddle can be used. (a) Adam gets a call from his close friend John on his Paddle, to see if he is in for a hike this week. (b-c) Adam answers the call by unfolding the compact device to a flip phone, which is more comfortable to hold while calling. (d) After a short chat Adam quickly transforms the device into a ring shape to scroll through the weather forecast of the next days. (e-f) On Wednesday and Thursday the weather looks perfect for a hike and Adam transforms the device into an agenda book through which he can leaf to see when he is available. (g) Both agree to hike on Tuesday and Adam unfolds his Paddle to see his schedule for that day. (h) Meanwhile, Adam can peek to check the status of the call or look for incoming emails. (i) Adam notices that he is only available in the afternoon and adds the appointment. (k) He unfolds his Paddle to a map on which he can plan a hike through the woods.(j) At the end of the call, John and Adam say goodbye and Adam folds his Paddle back in a compact form to fit inside his pocket.

BENEFITS AND LIMITATIONS

Highly deformable mobile devices that can be transformed into various physical controls have the following benefits compared to existing deformable devices and traditional mobile devices operated by touch:

(1) *Combining multiple special-purpose tangibles in a single mobile device.* Paddle abandons the idea of mobile devices having rigid, flat shapes with pointing as the sole interaction technique. Paddle therefore brings tangibles to mobile devices by introducing transformable physical controls. To switch between these controls quickly, Paddle's transformation model is superior to origami transformations. Paddle therefore allows to switch between completely different controls in a few steps.

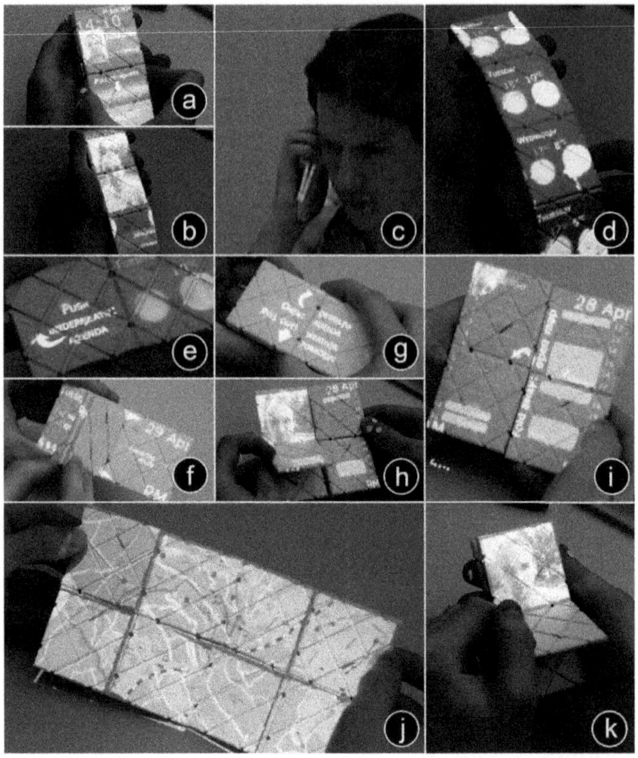

Figure 2. An example interaction that illustrates how Paddle could be used during a call.

(2) *Physical controls with clear affordances.* Bending and folding interactions supported by earlier prototypes of deformable devices, often lack affordances in that it is unclear how these controls map to actions [15, 19]. In contrast, the special-purpose physical controls supported by Paddle offer clear affordances, leaving no abiguity on how to perform an action.

(3) *Input and output in a single integrated space.* In contrast to traditional tangible user interfaces [9], Paddle makes input indistinguishable from its graphical output, integrating them in a single space. As a result, physical controls supported by Paddle provide *inherent feedback*, where feedback is a natural consequence of an action [4].

(4) *Bridging the gap between differently shaped mobile devices.* As a result of being highly deformable, a single Paddle can become a small phone to hold comfortably in your hand, a tablet for reading and an armband while running.

Paddle is also subject to two limitations. (1) The transformation model supported by Paddle might be unknown to the user, making it challenging to switch between form factors. Furthermore, users can always perform transformations that are not supported in a given context. These problems can be alleviated by providing visual help cues [2, 32] to show transformation possibilities. Although our scenario (Figure 2-a,e,g) demonstrates this idea, more generic visualizations are needed in the future. (2) Transforming a device can be time consuming, especially when interactions with a single form factor last for only a few seconds. In these situations, traditional touch interaction on one of the flat shapes supported by Paddle can be used at the expense of the benefits that the custom shape would provide. Alternatively, future Paddle interfaces can support the training of users' muscle memory to switch between shapes in less than a second after some practice. We also see potential in integrating actuators, such as shape memory alloys [25, 10] in our design to ease or even automatc transformations.

RELATED WORK

This paper is motivated by work on tangible user interfaces and paper-like interfaces.

Tangible User Interfaces

Researchers have proposed symbolic [5] as well as specialized physical controls [13] in order to encourage eyes-free use and bimanual interaction [5], reduce error [9] and enable physical affordances [13]. On the other hand, researchers noticed that the coupling of physical controls to digital content often reduces the feeling of engagement with digital content, which is more prominent when using direct touch [9].

One interesting approach to take advantage of touch interaction as well as our dexterity with handling physical controls in the real world, is to emulate the physical world on a touch screen. However, we seem to use multiple fingers [31] and hands [30] totally different on interactive screens. This suggests that simulating affordances and physics in a user interface may not be sufficient for encouraging interactions similar to those used for manipulating real world objects [30].

Paddle, however, takes the opposite approach and strengthens the coupling between physical form and digital content by integrating them in a single space. Similar approaches have been explored by other researchers for different purposes [12]. Examples include malleable surfaces for terrain modeling [24], shape displays for physical affordances [6] and tiltable displays to increase realism [1]. These approaches bridge the gap between the physical and digital world, but are often not suitable for general purpose mobile devices. Rudeck et al. [26], on the other hand, present a malleable touch pad to enable differently shaped touch controls on mobile devices. Paddle is different in that the dominant form of interaction is through real world controls instead of touch.

Paper-Like Interfaces

Our prototype can be transformed using folding interactions. Paddle therefore relates to research efforts to incorporate affordances of paper documents in the design of systems used in workplace environments [11] and mobile settings [28]. These flexible paper displays have been used to dynamically adjust screen size [16], navigate through documents by bending [33, 34] and to enable advanced interaction techniques with volumetric images, videos and virtual characters [29]. Lahey et al. [19] and Lee et al. [21] show how bending, folding and more free-form deformations with flexible displays can be used as physical controls in various applications, such as a

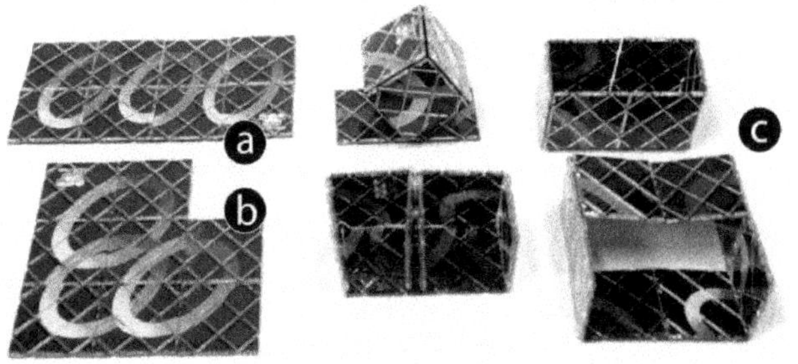

Figure 3. Paddle leverages engineering principles of the Rubik's Magic puzzle: (a) start configuration and (b) end configuration of Rubik's Magic, (c) some of the other supported shapes.

music player and e-reader. In contrast to the physical controls supported by Paddle, these bend and fold interactions often lack affordances, making it difficult for users to map these interactions consistently to actions [19]. Similar to our research, Foldme [15] demonstrates various folding interactions using a double sided display with predefined hinges. Paddle is different in that it is not based on an origami transformation model. This makes it possible to switch between very different shapes in only a few steps.

PADDLE PROTOTYPE

Mechanical design

While highly deformable mobile devices do not exist yet, we aim at prototyping devices that provide similar interaction styles. Our prototype, Paddle, is based on engineering principles used in creating 3D puzzles. 3D puzzles have already existed for centuries[1], thus capturing a vast amount of design knowledge in constructing compact mechanisms to enable complex transformations.

Our prototype leverages engineering principles of the Rubik's Magic design (Figure 3), a folding plate puzzle. The original goal of the puzzle is to transform the tiles until the pictures on the different tiles all line up and form an interconnection of rings (Figure 3-a,b).

The design of the puzzle consists of a loop of square sized tiles held together by wires. A special wiring technique, where every wire runs diagonally across the tiles, ensures that all tiles can hinge along two adjacent sides. The location of these hinges is different when a tile is on top or underneath another tile. This technique is an extension of the Jacobs Ladder folk toy principle. Although the puzzle can only be transformed piece-wise, the special engineering principles used in the hinges make it possible to transform the puzzle to various shapes (Figure 3). Figure 4 shows how the wires flip between the tiles to move a hinge from one side of a tile to another adjacent side, when going from a flat form factor (Figure 5-g) to a ring (Figure 5-a).

System Implementation

Paddle uses an eight-camera OptiTrack system to track the topology of Paddle and a projector to provide visual output.

[1] Scientific American, Volume 16 Nr. 15, 1889, page 227

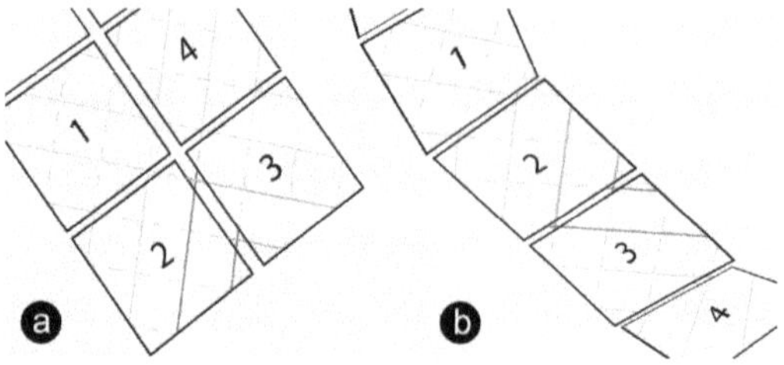

Figure 4. The wiring pattern used for the hinges in Paddle: (a) flat form factor, (b) ring form factor.

This makes our current prototype entirely passive. By attaching five tiny infrared reflective markers on both sides of every tile, we can track the position and rotation of every tile and distort every region of the projected user interface precisely. The Rubik's magic puzzle is painted white to make the projection clearly visible.

To enable touch interactions, markers are attached to the users' fingers. We calibrate every finger to get a precise estimate of the location of the markers on the fingers. When a finger touches our device, TUIO events are generated and translated into touch events using Multi-Touch Vista [2]. Our entire system is implemented in C#/WPF, making it possible to use the Microsoft Surface SDK[3] to have the same look-and-feel as traditional touch screens.

In the future, however, we envision devices similar to Paddle that are entirely self-contained, using electronic connectors to track the topology of the device [8] and tiny integrated displays [1, 22] for output. The wires necessary for interconnecting these displays and sensors can replace the wires used in the hinges to not interfere with transformation possibilities.

INTERACTIONS

Highly deformable mobile devices, such as Paddle, provide many new opportunities for interaction design. We explore this interaction space.

Paddle Transformations

The wide variety of transformations supported by Paddle (Figure 5) can be used for different purposes. Overall, we see three main purposes, which are also highlighted in the scenario (Figure 2):

1. *Shape fits digital content:* Similar to earlier prototypes of deformable devices [15, 16], Paddle can be enlarged to make additional data or tools available (Figure 6-b). Alternatively, the same content can take up a larger space as a way to zoom-in on data (e.g. text or maps). Oftentimes, it is also desirable to have a semantical zoom, providing a more detailed or concise version of the same content when Paddle changes in size. Finally, the size or shape of digital data can be reflected in the physical form of Paddle [20]. For example, in Figure 5 the tiles of configuration (a) can be used to display different elements of a list, (c) has the size of a traditional phone, (e) can fit a portable game console (Figure 6-a) and (g) matches the size of a paper sheet.

[2]http://multitouchvista.codeplex.com/

[3]http://msdn.microsoft.com/en-us/library/ff727815.aspx

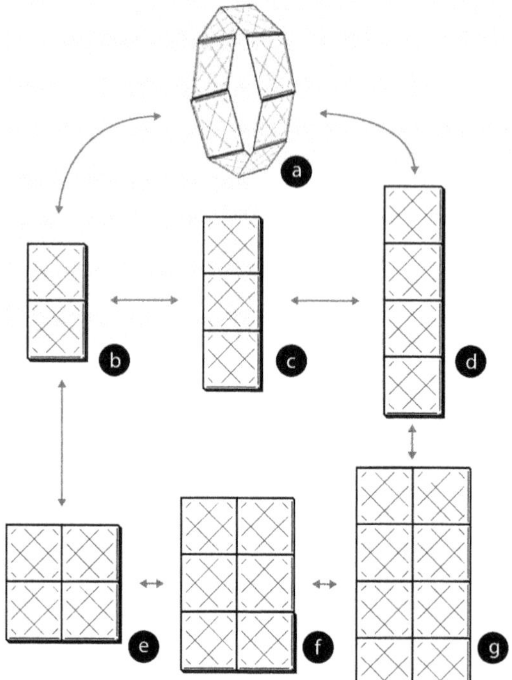

Figure 5. The transformations that are supported by Paddle. This is only a subset of the transformation model of the Rubik's magic puzzle, which is at the basis of our prototype.

Figure 6. Transformations supported by Paddle can be used for many purposes, for example, (a) a game controller, (b) opening a toolpalet.

2. *Ergonomics:* The shape of Paddle is highly related to the comfort that it provides. For example, it's more comfortable to read a text on a large device (e.g. Figure 5-g), while a device that can be supported entirely by the palm of the hand (e.g. Figure 5-b) provides more comfort (more normal force [3]) during touch interactions. As a result of the hinges used in Paddle, our device can be bended piece-wise to fit more comfortably in the hand or back pocket, to make a larger region accessible for thumb interactions or to position audio sensors closer to the mouth and ear to improve voice and sound quality during calls[4].
3. *Physical controls (i.e. Paddle controls):* Folds [15] and bends [19] have already been used as physical controls in user interfaces. As Paddle supports a lot more transformations, the device can be transformed into various special-purpose controls that provide better physical affordances. We elaborate on these Paddle controls in the next section.

[4]http://www.lgnewsroom.com/newsroom/contents/63988

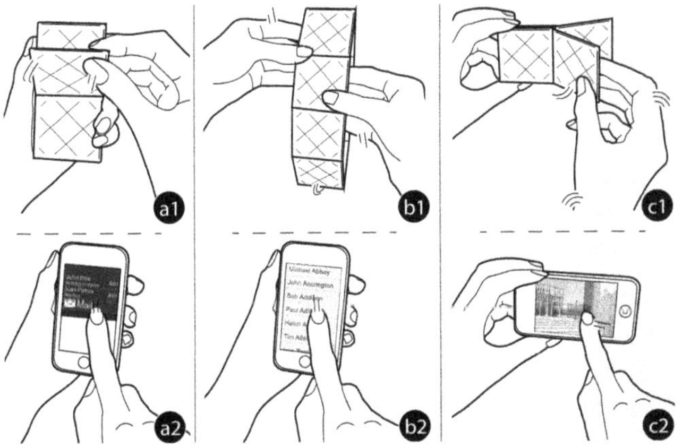

Figure 7. Paddle shows how physical controls (i.e. Paddle controls) for (a1) peeking, (b1) scrolling and (c1) leafing can be brought to mobile devices as alternatives for traditional touch interactions (a2,b2,c2).

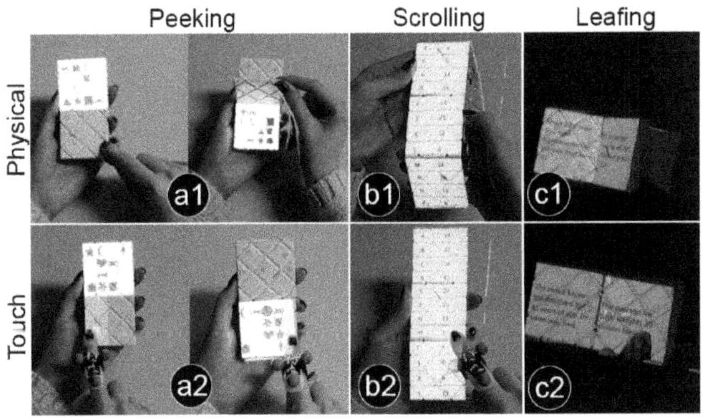

Figure 8. Our first study compares (1) physical to (2) touch interactions for (a) peeking, (b) scrolling and (c) leafing tasks.

In many situations, these purposes are not mutually exclusive. For example, the large flat shape shown in Figure 5-g can be a suitable shape to display a full page of text at once, but doing so also provides great comfort for reading [14].

To communicate the transformation possibilities at any moment, Paddle provides visual help cues to guide the user, as shown in our scenario (Figure 2-a,e,g). These cues are only displayed when the user places his fingers at predefined spots, visualized by virtual fingers (Figure 2-b,d). This approach (inspired by TouchGhosts [32]) reduces visual clutter and shows how to hold Paddle to perform different transformations. On the other hand, users can always choose to perform transformations that are not supported by the current form factor (Figure 5). In these situations, help cues are provided to backtrack to a supported configuration.

Paddle Controls

Deformable devices can be transformed for different purposes, as discussed in the previous section and demonstrated by earlier prototypes [15, 16, 19]. The potential of highly deformable devices to transform to various physical controls has to our knowledge not been investigated before. Although, FoldMe [15] and PaperPhone [19] show how bends and folds can be used as physical controls, they lack affordances compared to traditional tangibles [13] and touch screens, as it is often unclear how folds and bends map to actions [19]. In contrast, Paddle can be transformed to various physical controls (Figure 7), each providing customized physical affordances for the task at hand. Figure 5 shows how to switch between the physical controls supported by Paddle: configurations (b) and (e) support peeking (Figure 7-a), configuration (a) supports scrolling (Figure 7-b) and configuration (b) also supports leafing (Figure 7-c). In this last configuration, pages continuously flip from one side to the other to simulate an unlimited number of pages.

Paddle controls are different from traditional tangibles in that, similar to direct touch, Paddle combines input and output in a single space, making input indistinguishable from its graphical output [9]. Although direct touch and Paddle controls both offer clear affordances, the interaction styles they adopt are very different: direct touch relies on pointing as sole interaction technique whereas various grasps are used to interact with Paddle controls.

Below, we conduct an in-depth study to investigate the benefits one gets from the physicality of Paddle controls compared to traditional direct touch interactions on mobile devices.

STUDY 1: THE BENEFITS OF PADDLE CONTROLS

In a first experiment, we investigate the potential benefits of Paddle controls compared to traditional direct touch input typically used on mobile devices. We picked *peeking*, *scrolling* and *leafing*, as they are good representatives of Paddle controls and equivalent interactions are supported on many touch screens (Figure 7).

Tasks

Since we are interested in measuring differences in skills and the resulting cognitive effects when using Paddle controls, our tasks are based on best practices for measuring skill and motor behavior [27]. Various pilot studies were conducted to calibrate the difficulty of the task sets.

Peeking

For this task, 9 different symbols (out of a set of 17 different symbols e.g. a circle, triangle, star) are displayed at random positions in a grid (Figure 8-a). When performing a peeking interaction, all 9 symbols plus an additional symbol become visible at random locations on the window that is revealed (Figure 8-a). The original window then becomes invisible to encourage more peeking interactions. The task is completed when the user identifies the additional symbol. In the physical condition, the peeking window is located on the upper side of the device, while in the touch condition, the peeking window can be opened by dragging the window from left to right which reduces the effect of occlusions caused by the hand.

Scrolling

The main goal of the scrolling task is to encode a given word into a series of digits, as fast as possible, using the encoding list displayed on the device (Figure 8-b). The user can scroll through a look-up table that has 26 entries, one for every letter in the alphabet, using Paddle. Four entries of the encoding table are displayed on every tile of Paddle, leaving 1.5

tiles empty between the end and the starting point of the loop (Figure 8-b1). In the touch condition (Figure 8-b2), the loop is simulated, making it possible to scroll infinitely, similar to the physical condition. Different encoding tables are used for every word. Although words with the same length are used, different letter combinations require different amounts of scrolling. We compensate for this by generating encoding tables that requires the same amount of scrolling for every condition.

Leafing

For the leafing interaction, participants leaf through a book of 10 pages in which facts about various topics are shown on every page (Figure 8-c). Participants can leaf through the book and read the facts for 70 seconds. Afterwards, 4 facts are presented, but some of the facts have their details changed. Participant are asked if the fact is correct (distractor task) and have to estimate the page number of the fact in the book (main task).

Variables

For the peeking and scrolling task, we measure *task completion time* as the main measure of performance. For the peeking tasks we also measure the *number of peeks*. Since both tasks are feasible with a very low error rate (confirmed by the pilot studies) under all conditions, a new task was given in the rare occasions when participants failed to give the right answer. For the leafing task, the *error rate* for estimating page numbers and the *grade* (percentage) for detecting correct facts was measured.

Procedure

We recruited 16 participants (2 female, mean age 25) from our university campus. All were right-handed. The study used a within subjects design. For each of the three tasks, the physical and touch condition, were presented in a counterbalanced order. Additionally, the task sets were switched over the conditions to balance potential differences in task difficulty.

For every condition (physical, touch), the participant received instructions about how to perform the task. For the peeking and scrolling task, participants were instructed to complete the task as fast as possible. For the leafing task, we instructed participants to focus on the distractor task (correctly identifying wrong facts). Participants controlled a footswitch to start and end every task. Every condition started with a series of practice trials until the participant understood the interaction style and felt comfortable with the system. For the touch conditions, the participant's pointing finger was instrumented with markers to enable touch interaction on Paddle.

After every condition, a modified version of the ISO 9241-9 questionnaire with dependent rating scale for testing input devices was filled in, with only a single fatigue category and an additional "intuitiveness" category. All interactions were recorded on video. The average experiment completion time was approximately one hour. After a participant completed the experiment, there was an informal discussion during which the participant was asked to explain his interaction preferences.

Hypotheses

We expect that peeking using touch requires participants to focus on both the content in the peeking window and how the entire peeking window is moving when it is opened or closed. When using physical peeking, on the other hand, participants rely on tactile sensory feedback to interact with the peeking window and can thus better focus on the visual information that is presented (i.e. our symbol comparison task). We therefore hypothesize that:

H1: Physical peeking is faster than peeking using touch.

We expect that physical scrolling helps users to build up spatial memory and better uses sensory motor skills compared to touch. We therefore think that with physical scrolling, participants will immediately grasp at elements along the ring instead of scrolling through all elements, as is necessary with touch. We therefore hypothesize that:

H2: Physical scrolling is faster than scrolling using touch.

Physical leafing with Paddle is a more expressive way to navigate through a book compared to swipes using touch. We therefore expect that with physical leafing, participants are more aware of the position of the current page in the book at any time and are thus better at recalling the structure of this book. We therefore hypothesize that:

H3: Physical leafing results in more accurate estimates of page numbers.

Results

We collected 384 data points for the peeking tasks, 384 data points for the scrolling tasks and 512 data points for the leafing tasks. After removing error trials (respectively 3.1%, 2.1% and 0.2%) and outlier response times for the peeking and scrolling task (respectively 1.6% and 1.6%), we were left with respectively 366, 370 and 511 trials in this analysis. Trials were labeled as outliers for each condition when exceeding the mean by three standard deviations.

For every task, we aggregated the trials of every participant, and ran a repeated-measure ANOVA. For the peeking task, we found a significant difference between physical and touch (13.9s vs. 16.5s, $F_{1,15} = 5.75$, p=0.03), as shown in Figure 9-a. This confirms H1. Contrary to *H2*, we did not find a significant difference between physical scrolling and scrolling using touch (p=0.93) (Figure 9-b). As shown in Figure 9-c, we found a significant difference between physical leafing and leafing using touch, with the physical condition resulting in 46% more accurate page estimates ($F_{1,15}$ =62.97, $p<0.001$). This confirms H3. Although not included in our hypothesis, when physically leafing through pages, there are significantly fewer errors when participants were asked if the presented fact was correct (73.3% vs. 57.4%, $F_{1,15}$ = 25.79, $p<0.001$). Additionally, participants leafed significantly more in the physical condition (15.2 vs. 12.8 leafs, $F_{1,15} = 7.26$, p=0.02).

Subjective User Feedback

The comparative ISO 9241-9 questionnaire confirmed our quantitative results for the peeking interaction (H1). Participants reported that they found physical peeking significantly

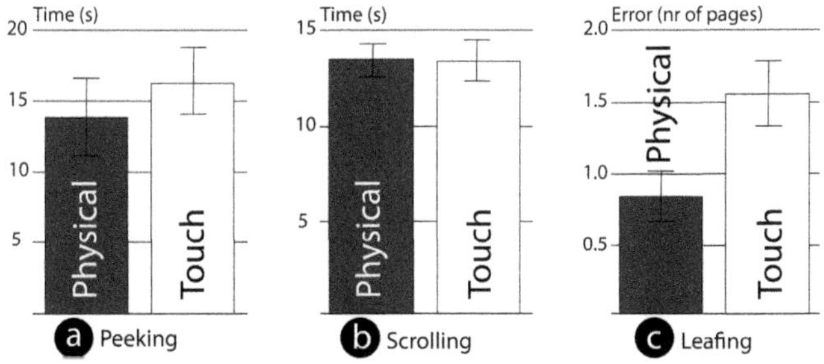

Figure 9. The results of study 1 comparing physical and touch for (a) peeking, (b) scrolling, (c) leafing.

better on the scale of force, intuitiveness, accuracy, speed, comfort, smoothness and overall operation. Physical peeking performed equally well as peeking using touch on the scales of effort and fatigue. Some noticeable comments during the interview also help to further explain our quantitative results: "When using touch, I have the feeling that my eyes are following my finger unconsciously.", "In the physical condition, you intuitively know how far to open the peeking window to reveal all content. In the touch condition, the peeking window can have any size.", "In the physical condition, the content does not move.", "Touch requires better targeting as one needs to stop at the border of the device to prevent losing track of the touch point."

Similar to the quantitative data, there was no clear preference in interaction style for scrolling (H2). However, participants agreed that physical scrolling requires significantly more effort than scrolling using touch. Contrary to H2, five participants mentioned during the interview that they did not know how many tiles to scroll with the physical ring to go to a specific letter. Two of these participants commented that they were confused because multiple items were displayed on a single tile. Four other participants mentioned that their performance in the physical condition could have been influenced by the latency of our system. This latency was much more noticeable when physically scrolling through the list, because the device moved a lot more.

Contrary to the quantitative results for the leafing task (H3), participants rated leafing using touch significantly better on the scales of force, effort, speed, comfort and smoothness. Physical leafing performed equally well as leafing using touch on the scales of intuitiveness, accuracy, overall operation and fatigue. When participants were asked during the interview which interaction style they preferred overall for the leafing task, the ratings of the questionnaires were confirmed, with 11 participants preferring touch, 3 preferring physical and 2 undecided. However, six of the participants who preferred touch, mentioned that they would prefer physical leafing if the leafing mechanism was more comfortable. Many of these participants commented that when leafing physically, the device was less comfortable to hold as pages have to flip back from behind in order to have a book with an unlimited number of pages. One participant mentioned that he felt more confident about the page numbers he gave when physically leafing through the book.

Discussion

Overall, hypotheses H1 and H3 were confirmed. Our study clearly shows that physicality provides benefits for leafing interactions. Participants could better recall the structure and content when physically leafing through the book.

Although we also measured a significant benefit for physical peeking compared to touch, it remains unclear if the direction for opening the peeking window in the touch condition played a significant role in the effect that we measured. As one participant correctly noticed, the direction in which the peeking window had to be pulled out in the touch condition might have slowed him down, because the end point of the dragging movement was near the border of the device, which introduces a speed-accuracy trade-off, known as Fitts' law. Additionally, our experiment did not confirm our second hypothesis, in that we did not measure a difference between physical scrolling and scrolling using touch.

We identified four factors that require further investigation in a second experiment, in order get a deeper understanding of the benefits of Paddle controls. Three factors focus on scrolling, for which we could not yet find any significant difference. The last factor focuses on peeking, for which we already found significant differences.

1. *Does the mapping of digital items to physical elements contribute to the efficiency of physical scrolling?* We observed that displaying multiple digital items (in our case 4 letters of the alphabet) on a single physical element (in our case a single tile of the physical ring) introduces a mismatch between tactile and visual information and confused participants, as they were not used to think in terms of groups of 4 items. To investigate this, we will compare physical scrolling to scrolling using touch with a list of 8 elements, one for every tile in the physical ring (Figure 10-b1,b2).
2. *Does visual realism contribute to the efficiency of physical scrolling?* A lack of visual realism in the physical scrolling condition, due to the latency of our prototype, might have influenced the performance of the physical scrolling condition more than the touch condition, as physical scrolling requires more and faster movements of the device. To measure this effect, we will compare a physical ring with 8 elements printed on it (Figure 10-b3) to the condition where 8 elements are projected on the ring (Figure 10-b2).
3. *Does the quality of scroll inertia contribute to the efficiency of scrolling using touch?* Although inertia was enabled on the scroll list in the touch condition, our prototype implementation could have influenced the performance of scroll inertia, as we tracked the position of the fingertip to the surface of our device, which can slightly vary over different hand/finger postures. To measure this effect, we will compare scrolling using touch on Paddle (Figure 10-b2) to scrolling using touch on a tablet on which exactly the same list is displayed (Figure 10-b4).
4. *Does homing towards a target near the border of a device when opening a peeking window, contribute to the efficiency of peeking using touch?* For this, we will evaluate touch and physical peeking in another direction, which eliminates precise targeting and similar to the previous ex-

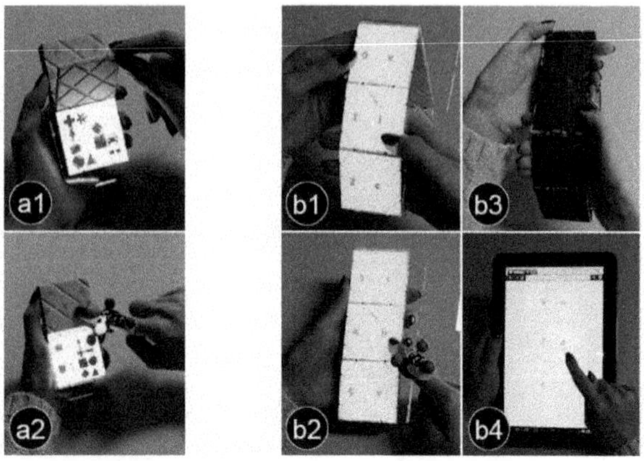

Figure 10. Our second study further investigates the factors contributing to the efficiency of Paddle controls and touch interaction for peeking and scrolling.

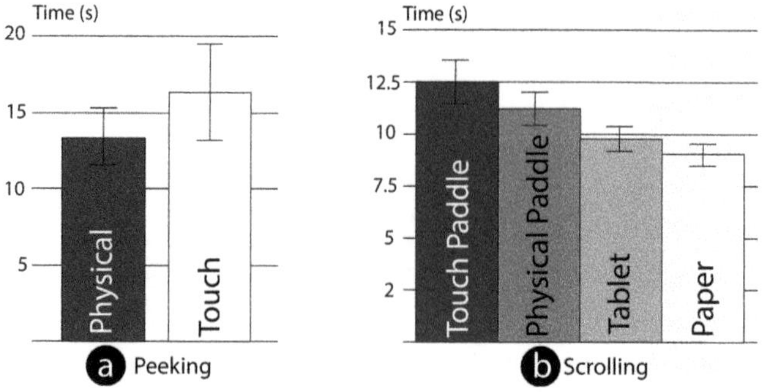

Figure 11. The results of study 2, investigating the factors contributing to the differences between physical and touch for (a) peeking and (b) scrolling.

periment, reduces the effects of occlusion by the hand to a minimum (Figure 10-a).

STUDY 2: CONTRIBUTING FACTORS

To understand the factors contributing to the differences between physical and touch for both our peeking and scrolling interaction, we conducted a second study. We evaluate the relative effect of the location of the target position when opening a peeking window using touch by evaluating peeking in another direction (Figure 10-a). For the scrolling task, we investigate the importance of mapping digital to physical items (Figure 10-a-b), the potential effects of visual realism for the physical condition (Figure 10-d) and scroll inertia for the touch condition (Figure 10-c).

Modifications to the tasks

For the peeking conditions, we used task sets similar to the ones used in our first experiment, but we displayed them on different regions of Paddle (Figure 10-a). For the scrolling conditions, the task sets were slightly adapted, as we now have lists consisting of only 8 elements (compared to 26 in the first study). We therefore generated new look-up tables, which translate 8 ordered numbers (0-7) to letters. The resulting word is nonexistent, which prevents participants of giving the answer before looking up all the numbers. Participants were also explicitly instructed to look up the numbers in the order in which they were displayed. We also increased the number of items that participants had to look up, from 4 in the previous study to 5, in order to encourage more scrolling and compensate for the shorter look-up tables.

Procedure

We recruited 16 participants (4 female, mean age 26), 8 of which were randomly chosen from our previous pool. All were right-handed. The study used a within subjects design. For the peeking task, the conditions were fully counterbalanced. The four scrolling conditions were presented in a counterbalanced order using a balanced Latin square. Additionally, the task sets were counterbalanced over the conditions for every task, in order to balance potential differences in task difficulty. The entire experiment lasted one hour on average, after which there was an informal discussion with the participant.

Hypotheses

H4: Physical peeking outperforms peeking using touch, independent of the location of the peeking window.

H5: Physical scrolling outperforms scrolling using touch when displaying exactly one digital element on every tile.

H6: Physical scrolling with the paper prototype outperforms physical scrolling with Paddle using projection.

H7: Scrolling on the tablet outperforms scrolling on Paddle using touch.

H8: Physically scrolling with the paper prototype outperforms scrolling on the tablet.

Results

We collected 384 data points for the peeking task and 768 data points for the scrolling task. After removing error trials (respectively 3.6% and 2.6%) and outliers (respectively 2.1% and 0.7%), we were left with 362 and 742 trials, respectively. We analyzed the results using repeated measures ANOVA. All post hoc comparisons used Bonferroni corrected confidence intervals.

Consistent with the findings of our first study, we found a significant difference between physical peeking and peeking using, touch as shown in Figure 11-a (13.4s vs. 16.4s, $F_{1,15} = 5.45$, $p=0.03$), confirming H4.

Figure 11-b shows the overall trend of our results for the scrolling tasks. There was a significant main effect ($F_{3,45} = 50.5$, $p<0.001$). Pairwise tests show that participants were significantly faster with physical scrolling than scrolling using touch on Paddle (11% faster, $p=0.02$). Furthermore, physically scrolling with the paper prototype outperformed physical scrolling with projection (20% faster, $p<0.001$). Scrolling on the tablet was significantly faster than scrolling on Paddle using touch (22% faster, $p<0.001$). Finally, physically scrolling with the paper prototype was significantly faster than scrolling using touch on the tablet (9% faster, $p=0.01$), confirming H5-H8.

Subjective User Feedback

Although all participants agreed that physical scrolling was more tiring than touch, 11 participants preferred physical scrolling with the paper prototype and only 3 participants preferred the tablet (2 participants were undecided). 13 participants agreed that they could easily remember the position of elements along the physical ring. Five participants even noticed that overshooting targets occurred more often on the tablet than when physically scrolling with the paper prototype.

FINDINGS OF STUDY 1 AND STUDY 2

Our two studies combined show that physical controls supported by Paddle have certain benefits compared to traditional direct touch interaction techniques.

Starting with the peeking interaction technique, our first and second study reveal that physical peeking is significantly faster and subjectively preferred compared to peeking using touch (H1+H4). We therefore conclude that physical peeking outperforms peeking using touch. Our results suggest that peeking using touch requires users to focus on both the content in the peeking window and how the window is moving. When using physical peeking, on the other hand, users rely mostly on tactile feedback to interact with the peeking window and can therefore better focus on the visual information presented in the task at hand.

For the leafing interaction, our first study shows that physical leafing is a slower and more tiring interaction compared to touch, but results in an improved recall of the structure and content of a book (H3). Similar results have been found in studies on paper vs. e-readers [14]. Their results were, however, motivated by the fact that paper books facilitate the process of picturing content on pages, as real books provide implicit cues (e.g. thickness) about where you are in the book. Our finding suggests that the physical leafing interaction itself is a large contributing factor to the benefits one gets from interacting with real books. So in addition to all efforts of making e-readers look and feel like real paper [33, 34], Paddle shows how certain benefits one experiences with real books can be brought to devices using physical controls.

For the scrolling interactions, our first study indicates that physical scrolling is more tiring than scrolling using touch. No other significant differences between these input modalities were found (H2). Our second study, however, shows that when displaying exactly one item of a list on every tile of the physical ring, participants were significantly faster with physical scrolling than scrolling using touch (H5). In the physical scrolling condition, users can locate elements very precisely and are thus able to directly grasp at elements further in the ring compared to the touch condition, in which scrolling through all elements is necessary. This suggests that users are better able to use their sensory motor skills and build up spatial memory when scrolling physically.

Our second study also shows that visual realism plays an important role when physically scrolling through lists. Physical scrolling with the paper prototype turns out to be significantly faster than both physical scrolling with Paddle with projection (H6) and a traditional tablet with scroll inertia enabled (H8). The latter result suggests that scrolling with future Paddle devices with perfect visual fidelity (i.e. with real displays) will result in faster acquisition of elements compared to traditional lists on touch screens with scroll inertia.

Physical scrolling through longer lists

Our first and second study only show significant benefits for physical scrolling when mapping every item of a list to a single physical element of our ring (i.e. same number of digital and physical items). It remains unclear how to efficiently support longer scrolling lists with Paddle. We therefore conduct a smaller final study in which we compare physical scrolling through longer lists using Paddle to scrolling through the same list on the tablet. The same tasks are used as in the second study, but now the look-up tables are twice as long. Instead of displaying multiple items of the scrolling list on a single physical element at the same time, as we did in the first study, we now wrap the scrolling list multiple times around the physical ring. We asked 8 participants to perform both conditions in a counterbalanced order. Our analysis is based on 185 valid trials.

Although our second study shows that scrolling using touch on the tablet was significantly faster than physically scrolling with projection, we did not find a significant difference between these two conditions when the list is twice as long (p=0.79). These results suggest that participants gained more benefits from physicality when the lists become longer. While users commented that physical scrolling is more tiring with longer lists, analyzing our video recordings clearly shows the dexterity that participants have when scrolling physically through the long lists. Even though participants noticed the latency of our system when physically scrolling using Paddle as in study 1 and 2, participants knew almost exactly how many times to turn the ring to get to a specific item. Our second study shows that visual realism is an important contributing factor for the efficiency of physical scrolling with Paddle. We therefore expect that for longer scrolling lists, future Paddle devices with perfect visual fidelity (i.e. with real displays), will also outperform direct touch.

CONCLUSION & FUTURE WORK

In this paper, we presented the concept of highly deformable devices that can be transformed into various special-purpose controls in order to bring physical controls to mobile devices. We demonstrated this concept by showing one possible implementation, called Paddle. This prototype was based on the design of the Rubik's magic puzzle. An in-depth study revealed that the physical controls supported by our prototype provide several benefits compared to touch supported by traditional mobile devices, such as being able to better utilize sensory motor skills, improved abilities to build up spatial memory and improved comprehension of content. Although Paddle is still a prototype, we believe that our findings can inform and encourage the design of future highly deformable devices and their abilities to bring physical controls to mobile devices. As future work, we plan to investigate how Paddle interfaces can be designed to help train users' muscle memory over time in order to switch between shapes more quickly.

ACKNOWLEDGMENTS

We thank Jo Vermeulen for the many useful discussions and help with the paper, Davy Vanacken, Brent Hecht and Mieke Haesen for their comments on the paper, Steven Maesen for the technical advice and Linsey Raymaekers for her help with the video. We also thank the study participants for their time and the reviewers for their valuable comments.

REFERENCES

1. Alexander, J., Lucero, A., and Subramanian, S. Tilt displays: designing display surfaces with multi-axis tilting and actuation. In *Proc. MobileHCI '12*, 161–170.
2. Bau, O., and Mackay, W. E. Octopocus: A dynamic guide for learning gesture-based command sets. In *Proc. UIST '08*, 37–46.
3. Dijkstra, R., Perez, C., and Vertegaal, R. Evaluating effects of structural holds on pointing and dragging performance with flexible displays. In *Proc. CHI'11*, 1293–1302.
4. Djajadiningrat, T., Overbeeke, K., and Wensveen, S. But how, donald, tell us how?: on the creation of meaning in interaction design through feedforward and inherent feedback. In *Proc. DIS '02*, 285–291.
5. Fitzmaurice, G. W., Ishii, H., and Buxton, W. A. S. Bricks: laying the foundations for graspable user interfaces. In *Proc. CHI '95*, 442–449.
6. Follmer, S., Leithinger, D., Olwal, A., et al. inform: Dynamic physical affordances and constraints through shape and object actuation. In *Proc. UIST '13*, 417–426.
7. Gallant, D. T., Seniuk, A. G., and Vertegaal, R. Towards more paper-like input: flexible input devices for foldable interaction styles. In *Proc. UIST '08*, 283–286.
8. Gorbet, M. G., Orth, M., and Ishii, H. Triangles: tangible interface for manipulation and exploration of digital information topography. In *Proc. CHI '98*, 49–56.
9. Hancock, M., Hilliges, O., Collins, C., Baur, D., and Carpendale, S. Exploring tangible and direct touch interfaces for manipulating 2d and 3d information on a digital table. In *Proc. ITS '09*, 77–84.
10. Hawkes, E., An, B., Benbernou, N. M., et al. Programmable matter by folding. *in Proc. NAS '10 107*, 28, 12441–12445.
11. Holman, D., Vertegaal, R., Altosaar, M., Troje, N., and Johns, D. Paper windows: interaction techniques for digital paper. In *Proc. CHI '05*, 591–599.
12. Ishii, H., Lakatos, D., Bonanni, L., et al. Radical atoms: beyond tangible bits, toward transformable materials. *interactions 19*, 1 (2012), 38–51.
13. Ishii, H., and Ullmer, B. Tangible bits: towards seamless interfaces between people, bits and atoms. In *Proc. CHI '97*, 234–241.
14. Jabr, F. Why the brain prefers paper. *Scientific American 309*, 5 (2013), 48–53.
15. Khalilbeigi, M., Lissermann, R., Kleine, W., and Steimle, J. Foldme: interacting with double-sided foldable displays. In *Proc. TEI '12*, 33–40.
16. Khalilbeigi, M., Lissermann, R., Mühlhäuser, M., and Steimle, J. Xpaaand: interaction techniques for rollable displays. In *Proc. CHI '11*, 2729–2732.
17. Kildal, J., Lucero, A., and Boberg, M. Twisting touch: Combining deformation and touch as input within the same interaction cycle on handheld devices. In *Proc. MobileHCI '13*, 237–246.
18. Klemmer, S. R., Hartmann, B., and Takayama, L. How bodies matter: five themes for interaction design. In *Proc. DIS '06*, 140–149.
19. Lahey, B., Girouard, A., Burleson, W., and Vertegaal, R. Paperphone: understanding the use of bend gestures in mobile devices with flexible electronic paper displays. In *Proc. CHI '11*, 1303–1312.
20. Lee, J. C., Hudson, S. E., and Tse, E. Foldable interactive displays. In *Proc. UIST '08*, 287–290.
21. Lee, S.-S., Kim, S., Jin, B., et al. How users manipulate deformable displays as input devices. In *Proc. CHI '10*, 1647–1656.
22. Lyons, K., Nguyen, D., Ashbrook, D., and White, S. Facet: a multi-segment wrist worn system. In *Proc. UIST '12*, 123–130.
23. Merrill, D., Kalanithi, J., and Maes, P. Siftables: Towards sensor network user interfaces. In *Proc. TEI '07*, 75–78.
24. Piper, B., Ratti, C., and Ishii, H. Illuminating clay: a 3-d tangible interface for landscape analysis. In *Proc. CHI '02*, 355–362.
25. Roudaut, A., Karnik, A., Löchtefeld, M., and Subramanian, S. Morphees: toward high "shape resolution" in self-actuated flexible mobile devices. In *Proc. CHI '13*, 593–602.
26. Rudeck, F., and Baudisch, P. Rock-paper-fibers: bringing physical affordance to mobile touch devices. In *Proc. CHI '12*, 1929–1932.
27. Schmidt, R. A., and Lee, T. *Motor Control and Learning, 5E*. Human kinetics, 1988.
28. Schwesig, C., Poupyrev, I., and Mori, E. Gummi: a bendable computer. In *Proc. CHI '04*, 263–270.
29. Steimle, J., Jordt, A., and Maes, P. Flexpad: highly flexible bending interactions for projected handheld displays. In *Proc. CHI '13*, 237–246.
30. Terrenghi, L., Kirk, D., Sellen, A., et al. Affordances for manipulation of physical versus digital media on interactive surfaces. In *Proc. CHI '07*, 1157–1166.
31. Tuddenham, P., Kirk, D., and Izadi, S. Graspables revisited: multi-touch vs. tangible input for tabletop displays in acquisition and manipulation tasks. In *Proc. CHI '10*, 2223–2232.
32. Vanacken, D., Alexandre, D., Luyten, K., and Coninx, K. Ghosts in the interface: Meta-user interface visualizations as guides for multi-touch interaction. In *Proc. IEEE TABLETOP '08*, 81–84.
33. Watanabe, J.-i., Mochizuki, A., and Horry, Y. Bookisheet: bendable device for browsing content using the metaphor of leafing through the pages. In *Proc. UbiComp '08*, 360–369.
34. Wightman, D., Ginn, T., and Vertegaal, R. Bendflip: examining input techniques for electronic book readers with flexible form factors. In *Proc. INTERACT '11*, 117–133.

Is my Phone Alive? A Large-Scale Study of Shape Change in Handheld Devices Using Videos

Esben W. Pedersen
Department of Computer Science
University of Copenhagen
esbenwp@diku.dk

Sriram Subramanian
Department of Computer Science
University of Bristol
sriram@cs.bris.ac.uk

Kasper Hornbæk
Department of Computer Science
University of Copenhagen
kash@diku.dk

ABSTRACT
Shape-changing handheld devices are emerging as research prototypes, but it is unclear how users perceive them and which experiences they engender. The little data we have on user experience is from single prototypes, only covering a small part of the possibilities in shape change. We produce 51 videos of a shape-changing handheld device by systematically varying seven parameters of shape change. In a crowd-sourced study, 187 participants watched the videos and described their experiences using rating scales and free text. We find significant and large differences among parameters of shape change. Shapes that have previously been used for notifications were rated the least urgent; the degree of shape change was found to impact experience more than type of shape change. The experience of shape change was surprisingly complex: hedonic quality were inversely related to urgency, and some shapes were perceived as ugly, yet useful. We discuss how to advance models of shape change and improve research on the experience of shape change.

ACM Classification Keywords
H5.2. Information interfaces and presentation (e.g., HCI): User Interfaces—Haptic I/O, Input Devices and strategies, Interaction styles.

General Terms
Experimentation; Human Factor; Measurement

Author Keywords
Shape-changing Interfaces; Shape Displays; Organic User Interfaces; Actuated Interfaces

INTRODUCTION
Handheld devices have become orders of magnitude smaller, more powerful, and higher-resolution compared to a few decades ago. Such devices used to be static in physical appearance, but that is changing. Shape-changing handheld devices are being discussed in workshops [1] and as industrial concepts (e.g., Nokia Kinetic [21]), and realized as commercial products (e.g., www.tactustechnology.com) or research prototypes (e.g., [8, 15, 32]). Examples of the latter include Morphees [32], a series of shape-changing handheld devices that are self-actuated and can adapt their shapes to offer better affordances, and Animated Mobiles [17], a device that reacts to the user's hand by moving so as to show affection or rejection. These devices are instances of what may be called shape-changing interfaces [7, 31], or organic interfaces [9].

CHI 2014, April 26 - May 01 2014, Toronto, ON, Canada
Copyright 2014 ACM 978-1-4503-2473-1/14/04... $15.00.
http://dx.doi.org/10.1145/2556288.2557018

Our current understanding of shape-changing handheld devices mostly rests on prototypes such as those mentioned above. Two important trends of research try to move beyond prototypes. One trend is to formulate more general models of shape change [30–32]. The paper on Morphees [32], for instance, listed 10 parameters of shape change and illustrated how they may be varied to produce markedly different handheld devices. Such models may be used to characterize shape-changing interfaces and to generate ideas for new, principled different prototypes. Another trend is to evaluate the user experience of shape-changing handheld devices. Hemmert et al. [15] showed that users could accurately detect changes in the angle of the backplate of a shape-changing mobile and that its attractiveness was rated highly. Not only do such evaluations help assess prototypes, they also give a sense of the type of experiences that shape-changing handheld devices may engender.

However, these two trends – modeling shape change and studying user experience – are hard to bridge. Models cannot be directly evaluated; when they are used to create prototypes, evaluations of those prototypes are rarely related back to parameters of the model. Whereas earlier models identified parameters such as curvature and amplitude (e.g., [32]), for instance, they did not suggest what users would find acceptable and useful ranges. Conversely, all evaluations of curvature that we are aware of are done on one design instance, which makes it difficult to obtain any general understanding of how different parameters of shape change are perceived and how they affect the user experience. The present paper attempts to bridge these trends.

We systematically vary the parameters in models of shape change to produce 51 videos of a shape-changing handheld device. We describe users' reactions to those videos using several measures and open-ended questions about user experience. The differences in experience that we find are then related back to parameters of the models used to create the videos. The key assumption of this approach is that users' reactions to videos capture at least some of how they would perceive actual devices. This assumption has been used both in HCI (e.g., in studying interactivity [27]), and outside (e.g., in studying physical designs [20], how intention behind actions are understood [18], and social robotics [4]).

We make three contributions. First, we describe experience over a wide range of shape parameters, rather than just with a point design or over one parameter of shape change. Second, we describe some boundaries of known shape models for handheld devices. Third, we show how the relation between model and experience may be used to reason about how a design may be changed to change experience. These contributions are primarily oriented toward researchers in shape-changing handheld devices, but have implications for designers of such devices as well.

RELATED WORK

We draw on three areas of research related to shape-changing handheld devices. First, we review papers describing prototypes of shape-changing handheld devices, then we discuss models of shape change, and finally we review user evaluations of shape-changing handheld devices.

Shape-changing Handheld Devices

Shape-changing handheld devices are a class of shape-changing interfaces with the ability to physically displace their surface through self-actuation, and which are small enough to fit in the palm of the user. Such interfaces may be divided into two groups: (a) conceptual prototypes [15, 16, 32], and (b) more developed prototypes that support both actuation and graphical output [2, 10]. In addition to these two categories, deformable, non-actuated handheld devices exist [25, 34], but are outside the scope of this paper.

The first group include Shape-Changing Mobiles by Hemmert et al. [15], a transparent, phone-sized box that can move the top and bottom half of the backplate independently to create both angular actuation and thickness actuation. This conceptual prototype was motivated by a desire to improve ergonomics and to provide navigational cues such as pointing towards a destination to support navigation. Dynamic Knobs [16] uses small bumps on the side of the device to notify the user of missed calls. The numbers of bumps indicate the number of missed calls and can both be seen and felt. The Morphee prototypes [32] explored different ways of designing shape-changing handheld devices and showed how different materials and actuation methods create devices with different affordances and shape-changing properties.

The second group of shape-changing handheld devices are the ones that support both actuation and graphical output. MorePhone [10] is a thin prototype of a phone that uses Shape-Memory Alloys (SMA) to bend the corners of its flexible e-ink display or bend the entire device. It does so to notify users about incoming calls, text messages, etc. Tilt Display [2] is a self-actuated handheld device with a display made of several individual displays, each of which can tilt along one or more axes and move up and down. This enables Tilt Display to show graphical content, like maps and videos, in 3D.

Models of Shape and Shape Change

The purpose of models of shape change is to generalize changes in shape and break them down into a set of shape primitives. These models help characterize similarities and differences among devices, inspire new designs, and provide a common vocabulary for researchers on shape change. The first model for shape change was presented by Parkes and Ishii [30]. In this model the authors focus on deconstructing shape changes into material properties (e.g., *skeletal*, *layered*) and mechanical properties (e.g., *hinge*, *fan*, *aperture*). They use these properties to describe the kinetic capabilities of devices.

In a review of 44 papers on shape-changing interfaces, Rasmussen et al. [31] distilled eight types of change occurring in shape-changing interfaces. Compared to the kinetic properties of Parkes and Ishii's model [30], the types of shape change found in the model of Rasmussen et al. are more high-level. The eight types of shape change are divided into changes that are topologically equivalent (*orientation*, *form*, *volume*, *texture*, *viscosity*, and *spatiality*) and not topologically equivalent (*adding/subtracting* and *permeability*).

Focusing on shape-changing surfaces, Roudaut et al. [32] presented a model with ten features that describe and help compare the deformation capabilities of shape-changing surfaces. The ten features are *area*, *granularity*, *porosity*, *curvature*, *amplitude*, *zero-crossing*, *closure*, *stretchability*, *strength*, and *speed*. The model, which is based on Non-uniform Rational B-splines, provides a classification of existing devices and a tool to compute specific values for the parameters for any shape-changing surface.

The models mentioned above all help clarify the parameters of shape change. However, they provide little understanding of how the various parameters affect the user's experience.

Evaluations of Shape-changing Handheld Devices

Research in shape-changing handheld devices has primarily been technology-driven and focused on exploring the design possibilities enabled by the advent of shape-changing materials. But this is starting to change. Researchers have begun doing empirical studies of shape-changing devices to understand how they affect user experience. A focus-group study of the Tilt Display [2] found that participants compared visual imagery in this display to a 3D image and found that movement of the display conveyed additional information.

Two studies have investigated the use of shape change in mobile phones to express emotion and intention. Hemmert et al. studied user reactions to a phone-sized transparent box that responded to the nearing hand of the user with five postures [17]. Their results show that, even though the device had no animal-like characteristics, participants tended to explain its behavior by using animal metaphors. The results also showed that the postures were interpreted inconsistently among participants and that more systematic evaluation is needed. The capability of shape change to convey emotions is supported by Dawson et al. in a study of DEVA [8]. DEVA is a gesturing phone that mimics breathing, crawling, and shivering. The evaluation of this prototype showed that shape changes in handheld devices are capable of expressing emotions of both valance and arousal.

A recent study of the MorePhone by Gomes et al. [10] focused on the use of shape change to display notifications. In a study with 14 participants, the authors investigated which events participants associated with different shape changes (i.e., fullscreen bend and corner bend) and how urgent participants perceived the shape notifications. Fullscreen bend was perceived as significantly more urgent than corner bends.

The above evaluations have provided many insights into user experience. However, the number of studies is limited and they often only evaluate one design instance. In addition, there is no link between those evaluations and more general models of shape change like those mentioned above.

OVERVIEW OF STUDY

Based on the review of related work, we want to systematically vary shape change to produce videos of shape-changing handheld devices. Using these videos we want to capture users' reactions to shape change by collecting user experience measures and answers to open-ended questions. We describe the study to do so in two parts. *Part 1* describes how the 51 videos that form the basis of our study were generated. *Part 2* describes the details of the empirical study.

PART 1: DESIGN OF VIDEOS

A key decision in our study is the videos presented to participants. From research on video prototyping, we know that the narrative and the context in which a technology is portrayed affect the intellectual and emotional responses elicited [29]. It is thus important to consider carefully how to represent the shape-changing handheld device, and how to communicate the user interaction and the device's response. Four decisions are involved in generating the videos: (a) the shape-changing handheld device shown, (b) how it is rendered, (c) which use scenarios it is shown in, and (d) which parameters of shape it changes. In the following we will describe our design choices. The movie accompanying this paper shows examples of the videos used in the study.

Shape-changing Handheld Device

The videos in our study use the smartphone shown in Figure 1. To make it readily visible that it is a smartphone, the size of the device and the aspect ratio of its screen is similar to current consumer models. The smartphone measures 160 x 90 mm and has a 6.9" display. This size is comparable with larger smartphones like the HUAWEI Ascend Mate and research prototypes like MorePhone [10].

The thickness of a device is known to be an important factor when users seek to guess the interactions afforded by shape-changing handheld devices [25]. We wanted a phone that signaled deformability and flexibility. Consequently, we chose a thickness of only 4 mm. This is thinner than current smartphones, but comparable to research prototypes [10, 25, 32].

Rendering Style

Research on video prototyping suggests that the responses generated by videos are influenced by whether a low fidelity prototype or a high fidelity prototypes is used [28]. Lo-fi prototypes generate more high-level comments, whereas comments on hi-fi prototypes tend to be less general and focus more on specifics (e.g., placement of buttons).

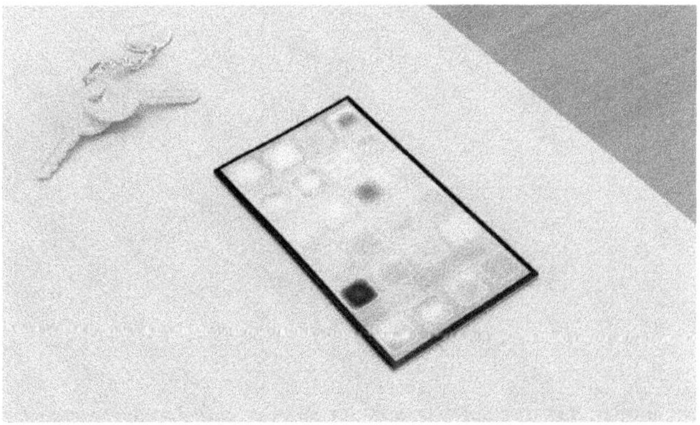

Figure 1. The smartphone shown in the videos. The phone measure 160x90x4 mm and has a 6.9" screen.

To find the best compromise between abstraction and detail, we tested three ways of rendering the smartphone and surroundings: A realistically rendering (Figure 2a), a sketchy rendering that made the animation look hand-drawn (Figure 2b), and a hybrid version with sketchy surroundings and a realistically rendered smartphone (Figure 2c). We pilot tested the rendering styles in an online video survey with 54 participants recruited from Amazon Mechanical Turk. 79.6% of participants preferred the realistic rendering style, 16.7% liked the mixed style the best, and only 3.7% preferred the sketchy rendering style. A typical argument for this preference was that *"the realistic rendering made it easier to think of it as me using the phone"*. As a consequence, we chose the realistic rendering style for the videos in the main study.

Use Scenarios

We find it highly likely that the use scenarios shown in the video clips will influence how participants react to shape changes. Whereas an increase in area might be practical when browsing, it may be unacceptable for displaying a notification. We therefore included two different use scenarios. The two use scenarios are explained below and are illustrated in Figure 3 with curvature as shape parameter. Although many other use scenarios could be imagined (see for instance other types of interaction in Rasmussen et al. [31]) – and many variations within the above types are possible – we wanted to restrict the number to keep down the total number of videos.

Notification

In the *notification* use scenario the smartphone is shown lying on a table with the screen turned off. Its display turns on as a

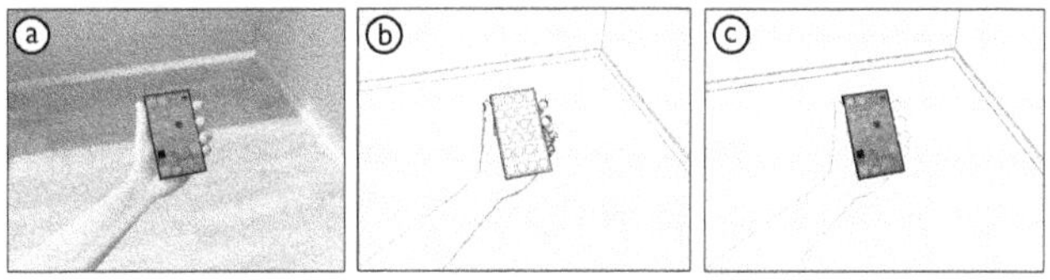

Figure 2. The three tested rendering styles of the device and surroundings: A realistically rendering (a), a sketchy rendering that made the animation look hand-drawn (b), and a hybrid version (c).

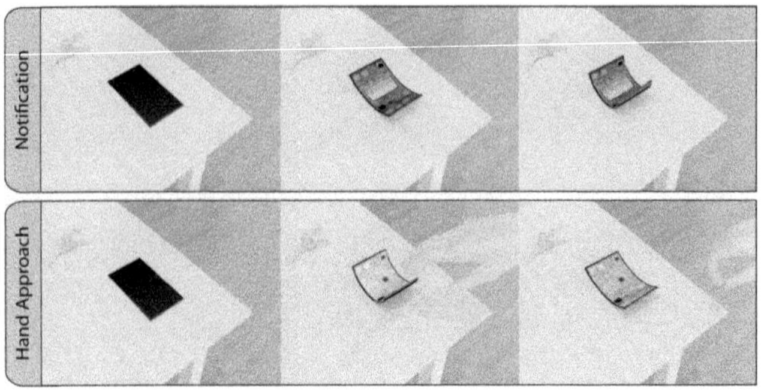

Figure 3. The two use scenarios investigated in the study: displaying a notification (top), and showing a reaction to a hand that approaches the smartphone (bottom).

notification is received and the smartphone changes shape to physically notify the user. We included this use scenario because shape change has previously been purposed as an ambient and expressive way of displaying information [6,22,31], and because the literature contains several hypotheses about how shape change may affect users' sense of urgency [10].

Hand Approach

In the *hand approach* use scenario, the phone is again shown lying on a table with the screen turned off. The hand of a user approaches the phone as if to grab it, and the smartphone reacts autonomously to the approaching hand by changing shape and turning on the screen. The user stops moving the hand for one second before removing the hand quickly. The phone reacts by changing its shape to the initial state (i.e., flat screen, turned off). We included this use scenario to investigate the use of shape change to portray emotions and intention. This is a frequent purpose of using shape change [8, 23, 35] and one that has recently been investigated with shape-changing handheld devices (e.g., [8, 17]).

Parameters of Shape Change Manipulated

To determine which shape parameters to change, we compared the available models of shape change [30–32], and found that the model of Roudaut et al. was the most suitable for generating shape changes on flat surfaces. Because participants can only observe shape changes visually in our study, and not feel or interact with the device, we only consider manipulating visual parameters from the model. We therefore distilled the 10 parameters of shape change to the following five: *Area*, *Curvature*, *Amplitude*, *Zero-crossing* and *Speed*. *Porosity, stretchability*, and *strength* are inherently tactile and thus hard to evaluate using video. In the case of shape-changing handheld devices, we can merge *closure* with *curvature* as they enable similar manipulations (i.e., curving the display to form an arc).

In this section we determine a low, medium, and high level of shape change for each of the five parameters. Where possible, we set the level based on the capabilities of existing shape-changing handheld devices. For the parameters of shape change that have not yet been explored in handheld devices, we have broadened our scope to include all shape-changing interfaces in order to determine suitable levels.

Area corresponds to the ability of a device to change its surface area. The only shape-changing handheld devices that change their area are the Shape-Changing Mobiles by Hemmert et al. [15]. By raising several levers an area increase of 3x is achieved in order to provide better form factor and navigational cues. Though not a mobile phone, the Inflatable Mouse is also capable of increasing its area by 5x by inflating a ballon inside the mouse.

Because few area-changing handheld devices exist, we have set the low increase in area as 1.5x ourselves. 3x is used as a medium increase (similar to [15]), and 5x is used as a high increase (similar to Inflatable Mouse [23]).

Curvature corresponds to the ability of the device to change the curviness of its surface. Curvature is computed by measuring the angle between 3 consecutive control points [32]. For example, MorePhone [10] curved a thin, e-ink display to indicate notifications. Its range goes from from flat (curvature 0) to a curvature of $-3\pi/5$ curvature. Other prototypes use a larger range. Morphee-forged [32] can change from the shape of a convex semicircle (curvature $\pi/2$) to a concave semicircle (curvature $-\pi/2$) using home-educated shape-memory alloy (SMA).

We use $-\pi/2$ (concave semicircle) as low curvature, $-3\pi/5$ as medium curvature (similar to MorePhone), and $\pi/2$ (convex semicircle) as high curvature.

Amplitude corresponds to the range of displacement of a point on the surface. It is calculated as the distance between the rest position of a point and the actuated position. MorePhone [10] and Hemmert's Shape-Changing Mobiles [15] can perform shape changes with an amplitude of 15 mm, whereas TiltDisplay has a maximum amplitude of 20 mm [2]. Of the hand-held devices, Morphee-motor [32] offer the largest amplitude of 60 mm.

Consequently, we used the vales 15 mm, 20 mm, and 60mm as low, medium, and high in our studies.

Zero crossing describes the capability of a shape to have wave-like patterns. It is calculated as the number of sign-changes between each pair of consecutive angles across the surface. The only shape-changing handheld device that is capable of creating wave-like patterns is the Morphee-couture [32], which can create 3 zero-crossings. To find interfaces capable of producing more zero-croossing, we must include larger devices with more actuators. Project FEELEX [19] is capable of creating 8 zero-crossings, whereas Relief [26] is capable of 14 zero-crossings.

In our study we use 3 as low number of zero-crossings (similar to Morphee-couture [32]), 8 as medium (similar to FEELEX [19]), and 14 as high (similar to Relief [26]).

Speed is defined as the minimum time required to move a control point from 0 to max. Many shape-changing handheld devices actuate using SMA that offer an organic, albeit slow change. MorePhone [10] moves at a speed of 15mm/sec, and Morphee-couture [32] moves at a speed of 13mm/sec. Motors allow for faster actuation but may result in more bulky prototypes. TiltDisplay [2] reports a speed of 20mm/sec, whereas the Shape-Changing Mobile by Hemmert et al. [15] move with a speed of 53mm/sec (speed was not specified in the paper, but calculated from the video of the prototype).

In our study we use 13mm/sec as low speed (representing the SMA-based prototypes) and 53mm/sec as high speed (representing the motor-based prototypes). To study speed, we cross it with all other parameters. We restrict speed to only two levels, in order to keep down the total number of videos. Speed is not used in the *hand approach* use scenario, as the speed of shape change in this use scenario is determined by the speed of the approaching hand.

In addition to the 5 parameters above, we included two specific instances of shape change, tapering and corner bend, that have previously been studied empirically [10, 17]. We do this in order to be able to compare our results to studies that used physical handheld devices.

Tapering is created by diminishing or reducing the thickness towards one end. This type of shape change, which is an instance of area change, was studied by Hemmert et al. [17] as a means of showing affection and aversion in a physical manner. The handheld device used in Hemmert's study performed 18 mm tapering away from and towards the user. We use these levels in our study.

Corner bend is created by bending the corner of the phone upwards. This type of shape change is an instance of curvature change and was recently studied by Gomes et al. [10] as a means creating physical notifications on a shape-changing mobile phone. They used 1-, 2-, and 3-corner bend with a height of 15 mm. We use the same number of corner bends in our study.

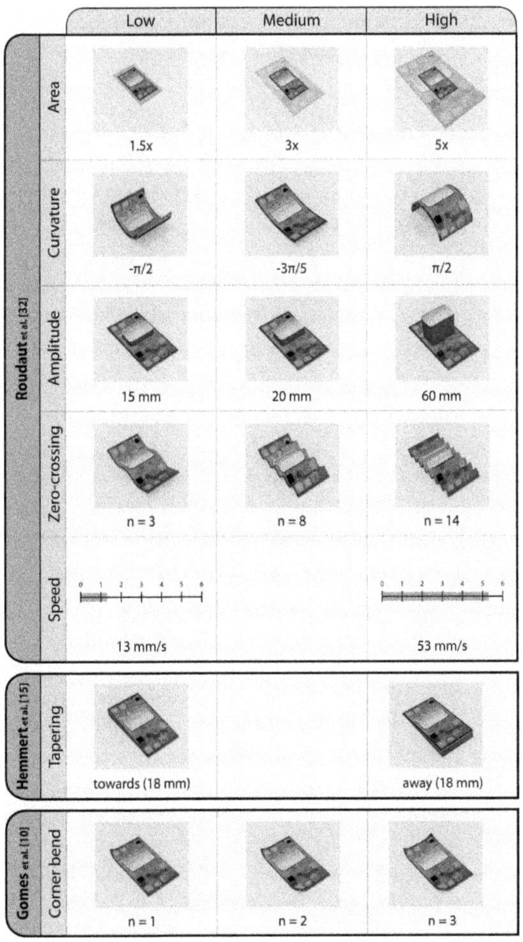

Figure 4. Seven parameters of shape change with two to three levels per parameter. Five parameters came from Roudaut et al. [32], one from Hemmert et al. [15], and one from Gomes et al. [10].

PART 2: EMPIRICAL STUDY

The videos described above allow us to assess users' experience of and reactions to seven parameters of shape change in two use scenarios. Experiences and reactions were obtained through crowd-sourcing the viewing and rating of videos on Amazon Mechanical Turk. Earlier work suggests that crowd-sourced evaluations yield similar results to laboratory studies [13, 24]. As noted, the empirical study has as premise that users react to and experience videos in a manner that can inform us about real use; this premise has also been assumed in much other work (e.g., [20, 27]).

Design

The study has two independent variables: shape parameters and use scenario. We varied shape parameters within subjects, and use scenario between subjects. Had we used a pure within-subjects design, each participant would have to rate many videos (a tedious and potentially unreliable task). Participants assessed one video at a time: 34 videos for the *notification* use scenario, 17 videos for the *hand approach* use scenario.

Dependent Variables and Open-ended Reponses

The main data collected were dependent variables about the experience and reactions to videos. For all videos we obtained a measure of *hedonic* and *pragmatic quality* using an eight-item abridged version of the AttrakDiff2 questionnaire [12]. AttrackDiff2 is a widely validated questionnaire on user experience that separates hedonic quality (e.g., tacky/stylish) from pragmatic quality (e.g., unpredictable/predictable). Finally, we obtained measures of *goodness* and *beauty*, also based on earlier work on user experience [11]. Goodness was measured as a seven-point semantic differential from bad to good; beauty as a differential from ugly to beautiful. These questions are supposed to capture an overall, evaluative assessment of the experience.

In addition to these general questions, we asked questions specific for each use scenario. These questions were based on earlier work. For the *notification* use scenario, we asked participants about *urgency*, which was measured as agreement on a five-step Likert scale with the following statement *"This shape indicates something urgent has happened that requires my immediate attention"* (as in [10]). Participants were also asked *"How would you respond to the message?"* and could answer *"attend to it"* or *"dismiss it"*.

For the *hand approach* use scenario, we obtained the following measures. We asked participants to *"describe what you just saw*". This question was intended to gauge participants' interpretation of the videos; it is similar to questions asked about MorePhone [10] and in classic experiments on the interpretation of visual scenes [14]. *Animacy* was rated using six items taken from research in social robotics [4]. Items were rated on a 10-point scale and included Mechanical/Organic and Apathetic/Responsive. The *hand approach* use scenario has been linked to particular emotional responses [8]. Therefore we asked participants about *valence* and *arousal* using the self-assessment mannequin, SAM [5]. SAM has been used in user experience research [3] and to study shape change [8].

Participants

We recruited participants through Amazon Mechanical Turk. Across tasks, 200 participants started watching and rating videos. Three verification videos were included among the other videos. In each of the verification videos one notable detail changed, and participants were required to textually describe the difference. Using these questions we excluded 2 participants for giving too few details in answers and for repeating earlier answers, 5 participants were removed because they completed the study too fast (<15 min), and 6 participants were removed because they indicated a non-optimal video playback. That leaves 187 participants.

The majority of participants were US residents (99.5%). The remaining 0.5% came from Brazil. 51% identified as men, and 49% as women. Participants ranged in age from 18 to 66 ($M = 31.0$, $SD = 9.7$). 56.4% of participants worked, 18.1% studied, and 25.5% were unemployed. 84% of participants had attended or graduated from college. Participants received 4 US dollars for completing the questionnaire. This corresponds to an hourly salary of 7.2 US dollars, given the average completion time of 33 minutes.

Procedure

Before participants started to assess videos, they viewed an instructional video that introduced them to the functionality of the website and explained the purpose of the study. Participants then viewed the videos one at a time in random order. Videos were shown at 640x480 pixel resolution with 1 mbit/s video encoding. If participants shifted away from the browser or attempted to fast-forward the video, it stopped. Only after having viewed the video uninterruptedly, participants could answer the questions shown next to the video. Upon completion, participants were debriefed and given a link for compensation.

RESULTS

In this section we report on the results of the two use scenarios. With the *notification* use scenario, we focus our analysis on the scales of user experience as well as urgency and the willingness to attend to a notification. With the *hand approach* use scenario we focus on participants' emotional responses, scales of animacy, and the open ended questions. All scales showed good internal consistency with Cronbach αs ranging from .79 to .96. Thus we merge the individual measures and treat hedonic quality, pragmatic quality, and animacy as single scales.

Notification Use Scenario

Table 1 summarizes the results for the *notification* use scenario. In the following, we investigate the effects of shape, level of change, and speed individually. In our analysis, we highlight the results for Corner Bend as this shape change has previously been used and studied for shape notifications [10].

Effects of Shape

A MANOVA found significant differences among shapes (Wilks' lambda = .372, $F_{30,1842} = 14.911, p < .001$) with no interaction effects. Individual ANOVAs showed that shape significantly affected all the six scales (Fs between 7.69 and 95.9, all ps below .001). Next, we analyze these effects in turn. We give the effect size (η^2) for the above mentioned F-tests when relevant; significant results mean Bonferroni-corrected post-hoc tests.

Shape had a large effect on pragmatic quality ($\eta^2 = .138$). Recall that pragmatic quality is made up by the qualities *structured*, *practical*, *predictabe*, and *simple*. Tapering was rated highest on pragmatic quality ($M = 4.85$), whereas participants scored Zero Crossing significantly lower than all other shapes ($M = 3.96$). Corner Bend was rated second lowest on pragmatic quality ($M = 4.48$).

Shape also affected hedonic quality, though not as strongly ($\eta^2 = .113$). Hedonic quality encompasses the qualities *captivating*, *stylish*, *premium*, and *creative*. Zero Crossing, which scored the lowest on pragmatic quality, was rated the highest of all shapes on hedonic quality ($M = 5.17$) – significantly higher than Area, Corner Bend, and Tapering. Likewise, Tapering was rated second lowest on hedonic quality ($M = 4.57$), even though it scored the highest on pragmatic quality. This suggests that participants find some shapes impractical but nice, and vice versa. Corner Bend was perceived as having the lowest hedonic quality of all shapes ($M = 4.14$) and was rated significantly lower than all other shapes, except Area.

Shape also affected goodness ($\eta^2 = .042$), with Tapering being most highly rated ($M = 4.75$) and significantly higher so than Corner Bend and Area. Perceived beauty is also affected by shape ($\eta^2 = .064$). Here, Curvature is rated significantly higher than all other shapes (except Tapering). Tapering is rated significantly higher than Amplitude and Corner Bend.

The largest observed effect in this use scenario was the effect that shape had on perceived urgency ($\eta^2 = .330$) and on the willingness to attend to a notification ($\eta^2 = .225$). Corner Bend was experienced as the least significant notification shape ($M = 2.89$). This is 27% lower than the ratings of shapes with the highest urgency (Amplitude, Area, Zero Crossing). Tapering was significantly lower on urgency ($M = 3.29$) than all other shapes except Corner Bend. Consistent with the urgency scale, participants were more likely to react to notifications with Amplitude, Area, Curvature, and Zero Crossing (ranging from 82% - 88%) compared to Tapering ($M = 68\%$) and Corner Bend ($M = 56\%$).

Effects of Levels of Change

A MANOVA found significant differences among the levels of shape change (Wilks' lambda = .481, $F_{24,1480}$ =

		N	Pragmatic	Hedonic	Goodness	Beauty	Urgency	Attend to?
Shape	Amplitude	564	4.56 (.11)	4.69 (.13)	4.37 (.15)	3.99 (.15)	3.95 (.07)	86% (3%)
	Area	564	4.65 (.11)	4.62 (.13)	4.22 (.15)	4.26 (.14)	3.98 (.08)	85% (3%)
	Corner bend	564	4.48 (.11)	4.14 (.14)	4.29 (.14)	4.06 (.14)	2.89 (.10)	56% (4%)
	Curvature	564	4.65 (.10)	5.04 (.12)	4.72 (.14)	4.72 (.14)	3.71 (.08)	82% (3%)
	Tapering	564	4.85 (.12)	4.57 (.15)	4.75 (.16)	4.51 (.15)	3.29 (.11)	68% (5%)
	Zero crossing	564	3.96 (.11)	5.17 (.12)	4.54 (.16)	4.29 (.16)	3.98 (.08)	88% (3%)
Level	Low	940	4.65 (.08)	4.79 (.10)	4.67 (.11)	4.49 (.11)	3.59 (.07)	79% (3%)
	Medium	940	4.53 (.09)	4.71 (.10)	4.44 (.11)	4.29 (.11)	3.61 (.07)	77% (3%)
	High	940	4.20 (.09)	4.69 (.11)	4.17 (.13)	4.01 (.13)	3.90 (.07)	82% (3%)
	Toward	188	5.05 (.17)	4.83 (.21)	5.08 (.21)	4.85 (.20)	3.41 (.16)	76% (6%)
	Away from	188	4.64 (.17)	4.31 (.21)	4.43 (.23)	4.17 (.22)	3.16 (.15)	61% (7%)
Speed	Slow	1598	4.52 (.07)	4.64 (.08)	4.49 (.09)	4.33 (.09)	3.64 (.07)	78% (2%)
	Fast	1598	4.50 (.06)	4.68 (.08)	4.44(.09)	4.25 (.09)	3.66 (.05)	79% (2%)

Table 1. Experience and urgency of shape change in the *notification* use scenario based on ratings of 3196 video clips. Parentheses give 95% confidence intervals.

$14.911, p < .001$), again with no interaction effects. Table 1 shows the differences across levels.

Because levels are related to the shape parameter, we first analyze the levels of low-medium-high. Justified by the MANOVA above, individual ANOVAs found significant differences among these three levels across all scales (Fs between 7.72 and 24.10, all ps below .001) except hedonic quality ($F_{2,186} = 2.98, p > .14$). The three levels significantly affects pragmatic quality ($\eta^2 = .328$), goodness ($\eta^2 = .188$), and beauty ($\eta^2 = .183$). For these three scales, pairwise comparisons between low, medium, and high show that measures of experience go significantly down as the size of shape change increases. This is clear for pragmatic quality, goodness, and beauty, which fall 10% -11% as the size of shape change increases from low to high. Hedonic quality also falls as level of shape change increases, but not significantly so: the difference between low and high is only a 2% fall in hedonic quality). Thus, from an experience point of view, smaller shape changes seem preferable to larger ones.

The three levels of shape change affected perceived urgency ($\eta^2 = .259$). The sense of urgency goes up as the size of shape change increases from low to high. From low shape change levels to high levels, urgency increases by 9%. As discussed above, this is the opposite effect of what was observed with the experience measures. Level also affects participants' willingness to attend to a notification, but only as a small effect ($\eta^2 = .033$).

Next, we turn to the levels of Tapering: moving away from or toward the user. Individual ANOVAs show significant differences among these two levels across all scales (Fs between 7.95 and 43.57, all ps below .001). This difference had a large effect on all measures of experience (PQ: $\eta^2 = .135$; HQ: $\eta^2 = .199$; Goodness: $\eta^2 = .166$; Beauty: $\eta^2 = .229$). In all cases, if the smartphone moves towards the user, all ratings increase significantly, ranging from a 16% increase in beauty to a 9% increase in pragmatic quality.

Moving away from or towards the user also affected urgency ($\eta^2 = .079$) and whether participants would attend to the notification ($\eta^2 = .144$). Moving towards the users gives an increase in 8% rating of urgency, compared to moving away from the user. Thus, the relation of movement to the viewpoint of the user seems to affect the experience strongly.

Effects of Speed

A MANOVA did not find a significant difference in the six scales based on speed of shape change (Wilks' lambda = .876, $F_{6,88} = 2.069, p > .06$). As Table 1 shows, the pattern is that experience measures are slightly higher for slow speeds than for fast speeds, but that these are small compared to the differences described above. Beauty, for instance, is 2% higher, whereas pragmatic quality is just 0.5% higher. For the urgency measures, the pattern is the opposite, but the differences here are also minuscule (urgency is rated 0.5% lower for slow videos than for fast ones).

Hand Approach Use Scenario

The purpose of the *hand approach* use scenario was to investigate the use of shape change to convey intentions or elicit emotions. A MANOVA found significant differences among shapes (Wilks' lambda = .713, $F_{15,1264} = 10.99, p < .001$). Individual ANOVAs showed that both the arousal, valence, and animacy differed significantly across shape (Fs between 5.97 and 7.60, all ps below .001).

Emotional Response

Figure 5 shows participants' emotional responses to the shape changes plotted on the circumplex model of affect [33]. As the figure shows, all parameters of shape change are near the center of model. This indicate that no shape change sparked extreme emotional responses.

Changes in Area evoked the strongest emotional response in terms of both pleasure and arousal and is the only shape parameter that is plotted in the first quadrant of the model. A post-hoc pairwise comparison confirmed the significance of this emotional difference. Changes in Area seem to create a mild feeling of delight or happiness. All other parameters made participants feel more calm than aroused with Corner Bend being the shape change that caused the lowest level of arousal. Interestingly, none of the shape parameters evoked the feelings that are associated with unpleasant arousal and belong to the second quadrant of the model (e.g, frustration, annoyance, anger).

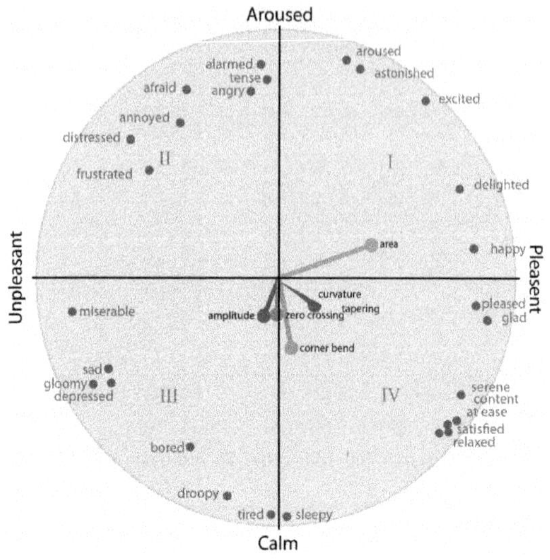

Figure 5. Shape parameters plotted on the circumplex model of affect.

Animacy

Figure 6 shows the average level of animacy by shape parameter. Generally, all shape changes where perceived as having a high level of animacy with scores from around 7 and above. Corner Bend was the shape change that was associated with the lowest level animacy (M = 6.93), and Area was associated with the highest level of animacy (M = 7.63). Interestingly, Corner Bend and Area also scored lowest and highest in terms of arousal. This indicates a link between the levels of animacy and the resulting level of arousal.

We found no significant affect of the level of shape change on the level of animacy ($F_{2,184} = 1.64, p > .05$).

Textual Answers

For each of the videos in the *hand approach* use scenario, participants were asked to *"describe what you just saw"*. In this section we report on the results of the 1581 textual descriptions total (17 descriptions from 93 participants). The descriptions were coded by one of the authors using the following four categories: *Purely matter-of-fact, phone is expressing intention, phone is expressing emotions*, and *shape change serves functional purpose*. As Table 2 shows, the majority of textual descriptions were purely objective and matter-of-fact (91.5%). Amplitude and Tapering generated most descriptions of intention. In contrast, changes in Area generated the lowest number of description of intention, but the highest number of descriptions of functional purposes.

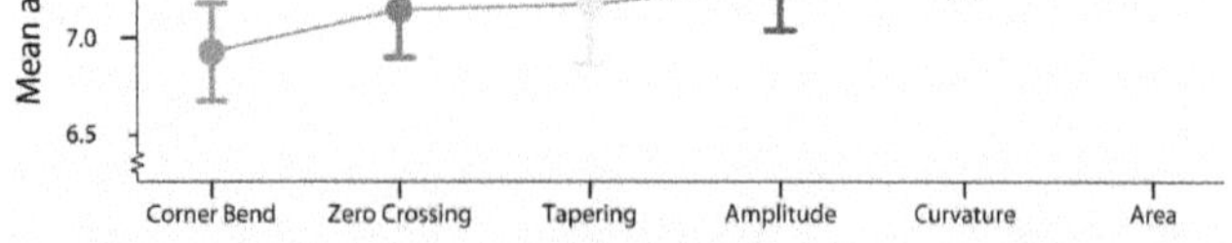

Figure 6. Animacy by shape parameters.

	Matter-of-fact	Intention	Emotion	Functional
Area	89.9%	1.1%	0.4%	8.7%
Curvature	88.8%	4.2%	2.8%	4.2%
Amplitude	89.2%	9.0%	0.0%	1.9%
Zero Crossing	97.8%	1.5%	0.0%	0.7%
Tapering	88.7%	9.2%	0.0%	2.2%
Corner Bend	94.5%	2.6%	0.4%	2.6%
Mean	91.5%	4.6%	0.6%	3.4%

Table 2. Distribution of the coding of the textual descriptions

In the following we report the most important trends in the descriptions. In addition to investigating the intentional, emotional, and functional purposes of shape change, we look at what words participants used to describe the shape changes.

The words associated with changes in Area were *"increased in size"*, *"grew"*, or *"got bigger"*. Changes in Area was the shape change that most participants perceived as having a functional purpose: 8.7% of the descriptions interpreted the increase in area as a practical feature that allowed the device to function both as a smartphone and as a tablet. This feature seemed very desirable to participants. One participant was particularly enthusiastic: *"If a phone could grow that big and then go back I would pay crazy amounts of money for it"*.

When describing changes in Curvature, participants used the words *"curved up"*, *"arched up"*, or *"bridged"*. Many descriptions ascribe animal qualities to the shape change: *"like someone arching their back"*, *"like a cat"*, or *"like a caterpillar"*. Descriptions of intention is split between inviting (*"standing on two legs waiting to be picked up"*) to aggressive (*"seeming to bite at the hand"*). The descriptions of functional purposes envisioned that this shape change would allow the phone to be worn on the wrist (*"like a watch"* or *"like a bracelet"*).

Changes in Amplitude were described mainly with the words *"bulge"*, *"bump"*, *"hill"*, or *"mountain"*. However, a few answers (1.8%) indicate that changes in Amplitude might also have sexual connotations. Some participants described the shape change as *"an erection"*, *"kind of phallic"*, or *"an aroused nipple"*. Participants perceived Amplitude as an effort to *"meet the approaching hand"* or to get the users attention (*"I want attention and you need to deal with me NOW!"*). A few descriptions perceived the shape change as a way to help the user select the desired icon.

Zero Crossing was described very differently from participant to participant. The most common words were *"crinkled up"*, *"zig-zagged"*, *"rippling effect"*, *"jagged"*, and *"pleat"*. Zero Crossing mainly generated matter-of-fact descriptions. Only 2.2% of the answers described an intention of a functional purpose. The change in Zero Crossing was primarily perceived as a message to *"leave the phone alone"*.

Participants described Tapering by saying that it *"lifted up"*, *"raised up"*, *"expanded"*, or *"got thicker"*. Regardless of whether the phone tapered away from or towards the hand, the shape change was interpreted as an inviting gesture (*"lifts up like it is sitting in a chair and kind of says hello"*). One participant described Tapering as a *"build-in stand"*.

DISCUSSION AND CONCLUSION

We have used videos of a shape-changing handheld device to collect measures of participants' experience, perception of urgency, animacy, and affect, and related them to parameters from models of shape change. Overall, the results show that manipulations of shape and the level of shape change had large effects on experience, perceived urgency, and emotions; the manipulation of speed had less effect. Next, we discuss these results in detail, outline some future work, and discuss limitations of the present paper.

Shape Change Parameters

We have several remarks on shape change parameters. First, compared to other shapes, Corner Bend did not perform well, resulting in low scores on hedonic and pragmatic quality, arousal, and perceived urgency. Yet, Corner Bend is one of the most studied types of shape change for notification (e.g., in MorePhone [10]). We speculate that better alternatives for notification than Corner Bend exist. Our results suggest Area and Zero Crossing as interesting shape parameters for this purpose. Our results confirm earlier findings that Curvature is perceived as more urgent than Corner Bend [10].

Second, Zero Crossing worked well for displaying notifications and engendering a strong hedonic response. It was not – perhaps unsurprisingly – perceived as practical. This suggest, as many of our other results, that different shape changes may be useful for entirely different functions. For instance, Animated Mobiles [17] may not have chosen the best shape to reach its goal: Tapering did not score high on animacy compared to other shapes, although Hemmert et al. [17] observed that users attributed animacy to their prototype.

In addition to specific shapes, level of shape change had a surprisingly strong impact on experience and perceived urgency. Our measures of effect size suggest that it is larger than manipulation of shape. For instance, the direction of tapering changed participants' experience, so that movements toward participants were rated higher. Hemmert et al. [17] speculated that such movement would impact experience and provided qualitative data supporting this speculation. Our results seem to resonate well with this speculation. Further, it was interesting to see that smaller shape changes were perceived as giving nicer experiences (though less urgent) than larger shape changes.

Speed did not have much effect on participants' experience: differences are only a few percent on most measures. This was surprising because earlier work has speculated that speed is important to shape change (e.g., [32]) and because the differences in speed we used were quite large.

Reactions to Video Clips

A key finding of this paper is that the effects of shape change are multi-dimensional. Zero Crossing was perceived as being nice but not practical; participants had strong reactions when describing changes in Area, but rated Area low on goodness. In some ways these effects are unsurprising, in other ways they highlight the need for richer, multi-facetted studies of user experience with shape-changing handheld devices (as argued by [31] for shape change in general). We believe that we have provided some rough, initial data on what shape changes may be used to which effect.

The textual descriptions from the *hand approach* use scenario showed that very few participants ascribed intentions or emotions to the shape changes when they were not explicitly asked to do so. Moreover, most descriptions of the shape change as a means to convey a message did not agree on the nature of the message. The convex curving of the phone was, for instance, perceived both as a gesture of greeting and one of defense. This suggests that it is difficult to convey unambiguous messages with shape change, given the limited shape vocabulary that current prototypes allow.

Limitations and Future Work

Our study leaves several open questions. We varied only a limited set of shape changes and, with the exception of speed, we did not cross them. We have established first ranges of levels of shape change (low, medium, and high, in particular). Although these were derived from the literature, they are clearly a snapshot that needs to be refined and extended in future work. Also, the shapes we manipulated has several confounds: the most important of these is that the area that moves varies with what we call shape change. We also note that existing models do not clearly separate speed as a distinct parameter that must be crossed with other dimensions (e.g., [31]) and if they do, they say little about levels of speed (e.g., [32]). We hope to address these issues in future work.

We have argued that video clips are valid for studying experience. However, it is also clear that real interactions with products might work differently, for instance because of the ability to physically touch and manipulate the device. In some cases our results seem to confirm earlier work. For instance, our results show good agreement with MorePhone [10] in their investigation of urgency. We aim to validate our results with a real prototype that is capable of performing the shape changes used in this paper.

ACKNOWLEDGEMENTS

This work has been supported by the EC within the 7th framework programme through the FET Open scheme under grant agreement no. 309191.

REFERENCES

1. J. Alexander, J. Kildal, K. Hornbæk, V. Aaltonen, A. Lucero, and S. Subramanian. Interaction with deformable displays. In *Proc. of MobileHCI '12*, pages 237–240, New York, NY, USA, 2012. ACM.
2. J. Alexander, A. Lucero, and S. Subramanian. Tilt displays: designing display surfaces with multi-axis tilting and actuation. In *Proc. of MobileHCI '12*, pages 161–170, New York, NY, USA, 2012. ACM.
3. J. A. Bargas-Avila and K. Hornbæk. Old wine in new bottles or novel challenges: a critical analysis of empirical studies of user experience. In *Proc. of CHI '11*, pages 2689–2698. ACM, 2011.
4. C. Bartneck, D. Kulić, E. Croft, and S. Zoghbi. Measurement instruments for the anthropomorphism, animacy, likeability, perceived intelligence, and perceived safety of robots. *Int. Journal of Social Robotics*, 1(1):71–81, 2009.

5. M. M. Bradley and P. J. Lang. Measuring emotion: the self-assessment manikin and the semantic differential. *Journal of behavior therapy and experimental psychiatry*, 25(1):49–59, 1994.
6. M. Coelho and P. Maes. Shutters: a permeable surface for environmental control and communication. In *Proc. of ITS '09*, pages 13–18, New York, NY, USA, 2009. ACM.
7. M. Coelho and J. Zigelbaum. Shape-changing interfaces. *Personal Ubiquitous Comput.*, 15(2):161–173, Feb. 2011.
8. J. Dawson, O. Schneider, J. Ferstay, D. Toker, J. Link, S. Haddad, and K. MacLean. It's alive! exploring the design space of a gesturing phone. In *Proc. of GI '13*, New York, NY, USA, 2013. ACM.
9. A. Girouard, R. Vertegaal, and I. Poupyrev. Special issue: Organic user interfaces. *Interacting with Computers*, 25(2):115–116, 2013.
10. A. Gomes, A. Nesbitt, and R. Vertegaal. Morephone: a study of actuated shape deformations for flexible thin-film smartphone notifications. In *Proc. of CHI '13*, pages 583–592, New York, NY, USA, 2013. ACM.
11. M. Hassenzahl. The interplay of beauty, goodness, and usability in interactive products. *Hum.-Comput. Interact.*, 19(4):319–349, Dec. 2008.
12. M. Hassenzahl, M. Burmester, and F. Koller. Attrakdiff: Ein fragebogen zur messung wahrgenommener hedonischer und pragmatischer qualität. In *Mensch & Computer 2003*, pages 187–196. Springer, 2003.
13. J. Heer and M. Bostock. Crowdsourcing graphical perception: using mechanical turk to assess visualization design. In *Proc. of CHI '10*, pages 203–212. ACM, 2010.
14. F. Heider and M.-A. Simmel. An experimental study of apparent behaviour. *American Journal of Psychology*, 57:243–259, 1944.
15. F. Hemmert, S. Hamann, M. Löwe, J. Zeipelt, and G. Joost. Shape-changing mobiles: tapering in two-dimensional deformational displays in mobile phones. In *Proc. of CHI EA '10*, pages 3075–3080, New York, NY, USA, 2010. ACM.
16. F. Hemmert, G. Joost, A. Knörig, and R. Wettach. Dynamic knobs: shape change as a means of interaction on a mobile phone. In *Proc. of CHI EA '08*, pages 2309–2314, New York, NY, USA, 2008. ACM.
17. F. Hemmert, M. Löwe, A. Wohlauf, and G. Joost. Animate mobiles: Proxemically reactive posture actuation as a means of relational interaction with mobile phones. In *Proc. of TEI '13*, New York, NY, USA, 2013. ACM.
18. M. Iacoboni, I. Molnar-Szakacs, V. Gallese, G. Buccino, J. C. Mazziotta, and G. Rizzolatti. Grasping the intentions of others with one's own mirror neuron system. *PLoS biology*, 3(3):e79, 2005.
19. H. Iwata, H. Yano, F. Nakaizumi, and R. Kawamura. Project feelex: adding haptic surface to graphics. In *Proc. of SIGGRAPH '01*, pages 469–476, New York, NY, USA, 2001. ACM.
20. W. Ju and L. Takayama. Approachability: How people interpret automatic door movement as gesture. *International Journal of Design*, 3(2):1–10, 2009.
21. J. Kildal, S. Paasovaara, and V. Aaltonen. Kinetic device: designing interactions with a deformable mobile interface. In *Proc. of CHI EA '12*, pages 1871–1876, New York, NY, USA, 2012. ACM.
22. H. Kim and W. Lee. Shade pixel. In *ACM SIGGRAPH 2008 posters*, SIGGRAPH '08, pages 34:1–34:1, New York, NY, USA, 2008. ACM.
23. S. Kim, H. Kim, B. Lee, T.-J. Nam, and W. Lee. Inflatable mouse: volume-adjustable mouse with air-pressure-sensitive input and haptic feedback. In *Proc. of CHI '08*, pages 211–224, New York, NY, USA, 2008. ACM.
24. S. Komarov, K. Reinecke, and K. Z. Gajos. Crowdsourcing performance evaluations of user interfaces. In *Proc. of CHI '13*, pages 207–216, New York, NY, USA, 2013. ACM.
25. B. Lahey, A. Girouard, W. Burleson, and R. Vertegaal. Paperphone: understanding the use of bend gestures in mobile devices with flexible electronic paper displays. In *Proc. of CHI '11*, pages 1303–1312, New York, NY, USA, 2011. ACM.
26. D. Leithinger and H. Ishii. Relief: a scalable actuated shape display. In *Proc. of TEI '10*, pages 221–222, New York, NY, USA, 2010. ACM.
27. Y.-k. Lim, S.-S. Lee, and K.-y. Lee. Interactivity attributes: a new way of thinking and describing interactivity. In *Proc. of CHI '09*, pages 105–108, New York, NY, USA, 2009. ACM.
28. W. E. Mackay, A. V. Ratzer, and P. Janecek. Video artifacts for design: bridging the gap between abstraction and detail. In *Proc. of DIS '00*, pages 72–82, New York, NY, USA, 2000. ACM.
29. C. Mancini, Y. Rogers, A. K. Bandara, T. Coe, L. Jedrzejczyk, A. N. Joinson, B. A. Price, K. Thomas, and B. Nuseibeh. Contravision: exploring users' reactions to futuristic technology. In *Proc. of CHI '10*, pages 153–162, New York, NY, USA, 2010. ACM.
30. A. Parkes and H. Ishii. Kinetic sketchup: motion prototyping in the tangible design process. In *Proc. of TEI '09*, pages 367–372, New York, NY, USA, 2009. ACM.
31. M. K. Rasmussen, E. W. Pedersen, M. G. Petersen, and K. Hornbæk. Shape-changing interfaces: a review of the design space and open research questions. In *Proc. of CHI '12*, pages 735–744, New York, NY, USA, 2012. ACM.
32. A. Roudaut, A. Karnik, M. Löchtefeld, and S. Subramanian. Morphees: toward high "shape resolution" in self-actuated flexible mobile devices. In *Proc. of CHI '13*, pages 593–602, New York, NY, USA, 2013. ACM.
33. J. A. Russell. A circumplex model of affect. *Journal of Personality and Social Psychology*, 39(6):1161–1178, Dec. 1980.
34. C. Schwesig, I. Poupyrev, and E. Mori. Gummi: a bendable computer. In *Proc. of CHI '04*, pages 263–270, New York, NY, USA, 2004. ACM.
35. J. Togler, F. Hemmert, and R. Wettach. Living interfaces: the thrifty faucet. In *Proc. of TEI '09*, pages 43–44, New York, NY, USA, 2009. ACM.

Evaluating the Effectiveness of Physical Shape-Change for In-pocket Mobile Device Notifications

Panteleimon Dimitriadis
School of Computing and Communications
Lancaster University, UK
pantelis.dimit@gmail.com

Jason Alexander
School of Computing and Communications
Lancaster University, UK
j.alexander@lancaster.ac.uk

ABSTRACT
Audio and vibrotactile output are the standard mechanisms mobile devices use to attract their owner's attention. Yet in busy and noisy environments, or when the user is physically active, these channels sometimes fail. Recent work has explored the use of physical shape-change as an additional method for conveying notifications when the device is in-hand or viewable. However, we do not yet understand the effectiveness of physical shape-change as a method for communicating in-pocket notifications. This paper presents three robustly implemented, mobile-device sized shape-changing devices, and two user studies to evaluate their effectiveness at conveying notifications. The studies reveal that (1) different types and configurations of shape-change convey different levels of urgency and; (2) fast pulsing shape-changing notifications are missed less often and recognised more quickly than the standard slower vibration pulse rates of a mobile device.

Author Keywords
Mobile devices; notifications; shape-change;

ACM Classification Keywords
H.5.2. Information interfaces and presentation (e.g., HCI): User Interfaces—Haptic I/O.

INTRODUCTION
The increasing array of applications available for mobile devices has resulted in a steady rise in the number and frequency of notifications pushed to users. Some of these notifications are urgent (incoming phone calls, diary appointments), while others are less worthy of immediate attention (application updates, game progression). Missing high-priority notifications is at best annoying, but can also lead to more serious consequences.

Current mobile devices use audio and vibrotactile channels to attract the user's attention. Unfortunately, many scenarios arise where these two channels collectively fail to alert the user. Typically this happens in noisy and busy environments (where the user fails to hear the audio notification) and/or when physically active (failing to feel the vibrotactile notification). Shape-change is one alternative for providing notifications, for example Hemmert et al's backplane tapering for in-hand information transfer [5]; Gomes et al's display bending for ambient (visual) notifications [4] and; Horev's actuated pixel matrices [6].

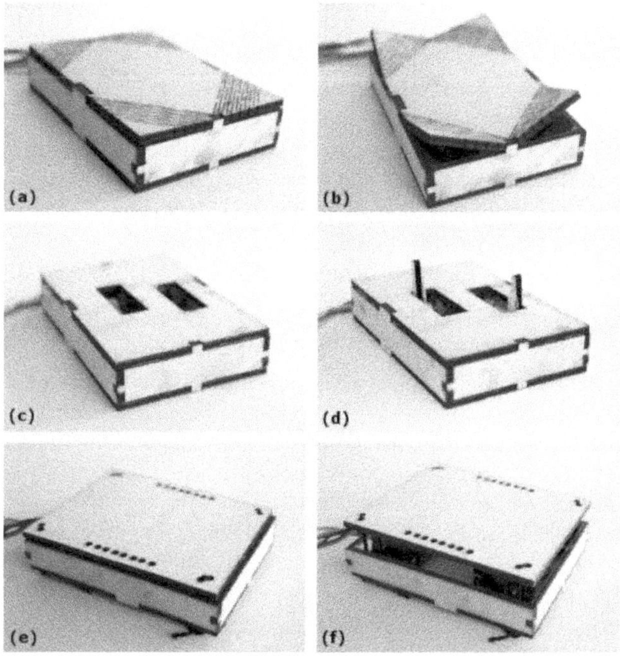

Figure 1: Shape-changing notification devices. (a) Inactive Corner Bending (b) Four corners bent (c) Inactive protrusion (d) Maximum protrusion (e) Inactive Volume Expansion (f) Full volume expansion

By augmenting audio feedback with shape-change (or, in silent mode, replacing vibrotactile feedback) mobile devices may provide more reliable event notifications. However, we do not yet understand the effectiveness of this new modality for attracting users' attention when the phone is in their trouser pockets (which is common among males [7]).

In this paper, we evaluate the effectiveness of three shape-changing devices for providing notifications. We implemented devices capable of delivering variable-urgency notifications while in the user's pocket (see Figure 1). Through two user studies we evaluate the efficiency of

CHI 2014, April 26 - May 01 2014, Toronto, ON, Canada
Copyright 2014 ACM 978-1-4503-2473-1/14/04...$15.00.
http://dx.doi.org/10.1145/2556288.2557164

shape-change for attracting a user's attention, understand factors that influence urgency, and compare our devices against traditional techniques. The primary contributions of this paper are: 1) The development of three shape-changing devices; 2) A user study evaluating the efficiency and urgency conveyed by different configurations of these devices and; 3) A user study comparing shape-change to vibration for notifications in noisy environments.

RELATED WORK

Mobile Device Notifications

Audio and vibrotactile channels are typically used to provide notifications on mobile devices. Audio provides 'public', attention-demanding notifications that are often perceived as inappropriate [8]. Vibrotactile notifications provide a personal (effectively silent) channel to alert the user, with Tactons defining a structure for non-visual communication using time- and intensity-based patterns [2]. Visual-only cues are typically not used as a primary alerting function as they are likely to be missed if the display does not have the user's full attention [9].

Mobile Shape-Changing Interfaces

There is growing interest in developing mobile-sized shape-changing interfaces to provide an additional information channel to the user. To describe such interfaces, Coelho categorised technological properties [3], Rasmussen et al. high-level shape-change descriptors [10] and Roudaut et al. a low-level shape-describing framework [11].

Several point-designs in this space already exist. Hemmert using back-plane tapering [5] for in-hand information transfer finding users could estimate the angle between the device's front and back planes. Horev [6] used a matrix of actuated pixels to convey in-pocket dynamic information. Several examples also combine visual displays with mobile shape-change. Alexander et al. [1] employed display module tilt to add an additional information channel; Gomes et al. [4] demonstrated that flexible display bending can successfully convey ambient notifications (with whole device bending considered more urgent than corner bending); and Roudaut et al. describe a range of actuation implementation strategies [11]. We use these previous designs as inspiration for deriving three shape-changing devices suitable for in-pocket notifications.

SHAPE-CHANGING NOTIFICATION DEVICES

We constructed three shape-changing devices suitable for in-pocket testing. They cover a range of prototypes suggested in the literature and implement four of Rasmussen et al's types of shape-change [10] (noted in brackets):

Protrusion (form, texture)

The protrusion device is conceptually based on Horev's actuated pixels [6]. A small arm protrudes from the device having the effect of physically 'poking' the user (Figure 1c–1d). The urgency and intensity of notifications are configured by adjusting: the protrusion height (10mm or 15mm) and the type of protrusion (static, slow pulse, or fast pulse). In static protrusion, the arm moves immediately to its final position (taking 200ms); slow pulses move to the protruded position (200ms), pause for 500ms, return to the rest position (200ms) and pause for a further 500ms before repeating and; fast pulses continually move between protruded and rest position. These terms are also used to describe the movement in the remaining devices.

Volume Expansion (volume)

Based on Hemmert et al's phone-tapering [5], the back-plate expands from the base to increase the device's volume (Figure 1e–1f). In full expansion mode, the whole back-plate moves away from the device; in tapering mode, one end moves away from the base. The urgency and intensity of notifications are configured by adjusting: the operation mode (full expansion or tapering), the height of the expansion (5mm or 10mm), and the type of expansion (static, slow pulse, fast pulse).

Corner Bending (orientation, form, volume, texture)

Drawing from MorePhone [4], Morphees [11] and Tilt Displays [1], each of the four corners of the device can individually, or in any combination, bend away from the base's corner (see Figure 1a–1b). Notifications are configured by adjusting: the number of corners actuating (1–4), the tip of the bend's height (8mm or 12mm), and the type of movement (static, slow pulse, fast pulse).

Our devices were constructed using laser cut 3mm wood, actuated by servo-motors, and controlled by an Arduino microcontroller. They were 70mm (W) × 105mm (L) × 20mm (H), approximately the size of a mobile device, meaning they could easily fit into participants' pockets (Volume Expansion was slightly larger, W = 85mm).

USER-STUDY 1: EVALUATING THE EFFICIENCY AND URGENCY OF SHAPE-CHANGING NOTIFICATIONS

To understand the influence of device configuration, we aimed to: (1) Determine the efficiency (recognition time, missed notifications) of in-pocket shape-change to gain the user's attention and; (2) Understand the urgency afforded by different types and configurations of shape-change.

Experimental Task

Tasks are conducted with one of the devices placed into the participant's preferred front trouser pocket with the shape-changing components facing their body. A notification on the device is randomly triggered within a 4sec window and the participant presses a physical button held in their dominant hand when they feel the device move, stopping a timer. The notification lasts for 10sec; if it's not recognised within this time it is deemed 'missed'. The participants then provide an urgency rating for that notification (1 = Not at all urgent, 5 = Very Urgent). If participants fail to recognise the notification within 10sec it is deemed 'missed' and the next task is then attempted.

Experimental Setup

We conducted a within-subjects study where each participant completed tasks with all three devices (previously described) in a variety of device-specific configurations. This allows us to form a greater understanding of the individual devices. The configurations tested were:

- Corner Bending: *number of corners* (1, 2, 3, 4), *expansion height* (8mm, 12mm) and *corner movement type* (static, slow, fast).
- Protrusion: *protrusion height* (10mm, 15mm) and *protrusion movement type* (static, slow, fast).
- Volume Expansion: *expansion type* (full expansion, tapered expansion), *expansion height* (5mm, 10mm) and *expansion movement type* (static, slow, fast).

To assess only the effectiveness of the notifications, participants stood still and wore headphones playing white-noise to avoid recognition through sound made by the device's servo motors. Participants used the devices in the above listed order, testing all possible configurations.

Participants

Sixteen volunteer participants (6 female, 10 male) between the ages of 22 and 33 (mean 24 years) took part in the study. Half of the participants wore jeans and the other half looser pants. They placed the devices in their preferred front trouser pocket: 10 in the left and 6 in the right.

Results

Corner Bending

Participants missed 33 of the 384 notifications. All occurred during the 8mm bending for a variety of corners and movement types. An ANOVA identified a significant difference in response time by factor *number of corners* ($F_{3,45} = 8.12$, $p < 0.01$). Bonferroni-corrected paired t-tests (evaluated at $\alpha = 0.002$) showed differences between corners (slowest listed first): 1 & 2 ($t(95) = 5.36$, $p < 0.001$), 1 & 3 ($t(95) = 3.54$, $p < 0.001$), and 1 & 4 ($t(95) = 5.31$, $p < 0.001$).

The larger 12mm corner expansion was recognised significantly faster (1.5sec) than 8mm (1.7sec, $F_{1,15} = 14.22$, $p < 0.05$). There was also a significant effect of movement type ($F_{2,30} = 93.77$, $p < 0.01$). A post-hoc Tukey test found an HSD of 665ms ($\alpha = 0.01$) showing slow pulsing movement (2.2sec) to take significantly longer for recognition than static (1.3sec) and fast pulsing movement (1.3sec).

Participants' urgency ratings did not show a difference between the number of corners used, but showed a significant difference between the larger 12mm extrusion (mean 4.0) and the smaller 8mm extrusion (mean 2.0, $\chi^2 = 178.3$, $p < 0.01$). Movement type also significantly impacted on urgency, with static movement least urgent (mean 2.5), followed by slow pulsing movement (3.0) and fast pulsing movement (3.6, $\chi^2 = 113.08$, $p < 0.01$).

Overall, the corner bending device effectively communicates urgent notifications using four corners, with a large extrusion in a fast pulsing manner. Using a small bend extrusion leads to missed notifications.

Protrusion

Participants recognised all 96 notifications from this device. ANOVA confirmed that the larger 15mm protrusions were recognised significantly faster (1.4sec) than the smaller 10mm protrusions (1.6sec, $F_{1,15} = 6.86$, $p < 0.05$). There was a further significant difference based on protrusion type ($F_{2,30} = 93.20$, $p < 0.001$). A post-hoc Tukey test gave an HSD of 338ms ($\alpha = 0.01$) indicating slow pulsing (2.1sec) is significantly slower than static (1.3sec) and fast pulses (1.2sec). There was no interaction between protrusion and speed. Participants' urgency rankings showed both high-speed pulses ($\chi^2 = 9.95$, $p < 0.05$) and larger protrusions ($\chi^2 = 46.02$, $p < 0.001$) to have higher urgency ratings.

Overall, the protrusion device creates reliable notifications, with low-urgency transmitted using small protrusions in a static position and high-urgency using high-frequency pulses of large protrusions.

Volume Expansion

In total, participants only missed 2 of the 192 notifications using this device. There was no significant difference in response time between full expansion and tapered expansion. An ANOVA confirmed 10mm expansion was recognised more quickly (1.5sec) than 5mm expansion (1.6sec, $F_{1,15} = 7.11$, $p < 0.05$). There was a significant different in recognition time based on movement type ($F_{2,30} = 145.43$, $p < 0.01$). A post-hoc Tukey test revealed an HSD of 359ms ($\alpha = 0.01$), indicating slow pulsing (2.1sec) was significantly slower than static (1.3sec) and fast pulsing (1.3sec). There were no further time-based interaction effects.

Participants' urgency rankings showed full expansion (mean 3.9) to be more urgent than tapered expansion (mean 3.2, $\chi^2 = 23.3$, $p < 0.01$); 10mm expansion (mean 4.25) more urgent than 5mm expansion (mean 2.8, $\chi^2 = 68.3$, $p < 0.01$); and urgency increasing from static (mean 2.8) to slow pulsing (mean 3.5) to fast pulsing (mean 4.25, $\chi^2 = 81.0$, $p < 0.01$).

Overall, Volume Expansion creates reliable notifications, with high-urgency transmitted using fast-pulsing, large-depth, full expansion. Less urgent notifications can use static, tapered expansion with a shallower depth.

Summary

All of the devices were successfully able to convey notifications, with different configurations conveying differing urgency. Greater protrusion and fast pulse rates created more quickly recognised and higher urgency notifications. Participants indicated their overall preferences as: Volume Expansion (8), Protrusion (7), and Corner Bending (1).

USER-STUDY 2: COMPARING SHAPE-CHANGE TO VIBRO-TACTILE FEEDBACK

Shape-change notifications are likely to be most effective when audio is not available (in 'silent' mode, or busy/noisy environments). To validate this assumption and to compare against the status-quo of vibrotactile feedback (the current best method for communicating non-audio, non-visual mobile notifications), we conducted a study where participants walked and were unable to hear the device's audio.

Notification Devices and Configurations

We choose the most efficient notification configuration of each of our three devices for comparison, as follows: (1) Protrusion, 15mm, fast pulses, (2) Volume Expansion, full expansion, 10mm, fast pulses, (3) Corner Bending, four corners, 12mm, fast pulses (4) Samsung Galaxy S3 default vibration mode (1.6sec pulse/pause cycle).

Experimental Setup and Participants

We conducted a within-subjects study with a single independent variable, *device,* with the four levels described above. Notifications were provided to simulate a phone call, so lasted for 20sec. To simulate a noisy/busy environment, users walked in a figure-of-eight with marker distances 2.3m apart and wore headphones playing white noise. Participants pressed a physical button whenever they felt a notification from the device in their pocket. Each device provided five notifications, with the order counterbalanced.

Ten participants (4 female, 6 male) between the ages of 22 and 27 (mean 24) took part in the study. Three wore tight jeans and the remainder wore looser pants. Half placed the devices in their right front pocket, the rest in the front left.

Results

Participants missed 25 of the 200 notifications (12.5%). 21of the missed notifications were from the mobile phone in vibration mode, the remainder from the Corner Bending device. There was a significant difference in response time between devices ($F_{3,27} = 24.471$, $p < 0.01$); a post-hoc Tukey test showed an HSD of 2.2sec ($\alpha = 0.01$), showing the vibration alert (6.3sec) was recognised significantly slower than the three shape-changing devices (Protrusion = 1.4sec, Volume Expansion = 1.7sec, Corner Bending = 2.0sec). There were no other differences between pairs.

DISCUSSION AND LIMITATIONS

Our studies established in-pocket shape-changing notifications are effective, complementing previous findings [4]. Real deployments would continue to also use audio for out-of-sight notifications. The biggest limitation to their deployment is power. Our shape-changing devices with multiple motors under load (i.e. when in a tight pocket) can require peak power of over 1A.

While we were able to simulate a noisy/busy environment with physical movement and white noise, a true 'in the wild' study is still required to prove their effectiveness over longer periods of time and under real-use conditions (including a variety of clothing styles). Further investigation is also needed to understand the influence of pulse rate when comparing vibrotactile and shape-change notifications.

CONCLUSION

We implemented three shape-changing devices and conducted two user studies to evaluate their effectiveness for in-pocket notifications. Shape-change can successfully alert the user and be configured to output a range of variable-urgency notifications. In busy/noisy environments, shape-change provides alerts that are missed less often and recognised faster than the traditional vibration of a mobile phone.

ACKNOWLEDGEMENTS

This work is partially funded by the EC's 7th Framework Programme, FET-Open scheme (grant no. 309191).

REFERENCES

1. Alexander, J., Lucero, A., and Subramanian, S. *Tilt Displays: Designing Display Surfaces with Multi-axis Tilting and Actuation.* in *MobileHCI '12*. 2012: ACM.
2. Brewster, S. and Brown, L.M. *Tactons: Structured Tactile Messages for Non-visual Information Display.* in *AUIC '04*. 2004. Australian Computer Society, Inc.
3. Coelho, M. and Zigelbaum, J., *Shape-changing Interfaces.* PUC, 2011. **15**(2): p. 161-173.
4. Gomes, A., Nesbitt, A., and Vertegaal, R. *MorePhone: a study of actuated shape deformations for flexible thin-film smartphone notifications.* in *CHI '13*. 2013: ACM.
5. Hemmert, F., Hamann, S., Löwe, M., Zeipelt, J., and Joost, G. *Shape-Changing Mobiles: Tapering in Two-dimensional Deformational Displays in Mobile Phones.* in *CHI EA '10*. 2010: ACM.
6. Horev, O. *Talking to the hand–The interactive potential of shape-behavior in objects and tangible interface.* in *DeSForM '06*. 2006.
7. Ichikawa, F., Chipchase, J., and Grignani, R. *Where's The Phone? A Study of Mobile Phone Location in Public Spaces.* in *MTAS* '05. 2005.
8. Ling, R., *One Can Talk about Common Manners! The Use of Mobile Telephones in Inappropriate Situations.* Telektronikk, 1998. **94**: p. 65-78.
9. McCrickard, D.S. and Chewar, C.M., *Attuning notification design to user goals and attention costs.* Commun. ACM, 2003. **46**(3): p. 67-72.
10. Rasmussen, M.K., Pedersen, E.W., Petersen, M.G., and Hornbæk, K. *Shape-Changing Interfaces: A Review of the Design Space and Open Research Questions.* in *CHI '12*. 2012: ACM.
11. Roudaut, A., Karnik, A., Löchtefeld, M., and Subramanian, S. *Morphees: Toward High "Shape Resolution" in Self-Actuated Flexible Mobile Devices.* in *CHI '13*. 2013: ACM.

Changibles: Analyzing and Designing Shape Changing Constructive Assembly

Anne Roudaut, Rebecca Reed, Tianbo Hao, Sriram Subramanian
Department of Computer Science, University of Bristol, UK
roudauta@gmail.com, {rr0743, th12120}@my.bristol.ac.uk, sriram@cs.bris.ac.uk

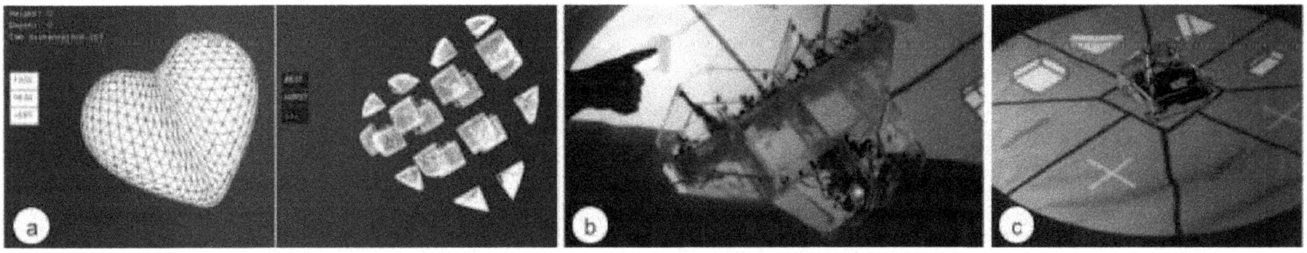

Figure 1: (a) Our analyzing tool helps the design of shape changing assemblies by indicating the forms that the units must take in order to create assemblies representing a set of given objects with the best accuracy. These units, that we called Changibles, are interactive wireless *units* that reshape themselves and can be composed to create a shape changing assembly, such as (b) a pulsing heart composed of several (c) independent shape changing units.

ABSTRACT
Advances in shape changing assemblies have been made in reconfiguration algorithms, hardware designs and interaction techniques. However no tools exist for guiding designers in building those modular devices and especially for choosing the shape of the units. The task becomes even more complex when the units themselves can change their shapes to animate the entire assembly. In this paper, we contribute with the first analysis tool which helps the designer to both choose the right subset of forms for the units and to create an assembly with maximum accuracy from the set of given objects. We introduce the concept of Changibles that are interactive wireless units that can reshape themselves and be attached together to create an animated assembly. We present a use case to demonstrate the use of our tool, with an instantiation of six Changibles that are used to construct a pulsing heart assembly.

Author Keywords
Shape changing object, Constructive assembly, Actuated display, Modular robot.

ACM Classification Keywords
D.2.2 Design Tools and Techniques: Computer-aided software engineering; H.5.2 User Interfaces.

INTRODUCTION
Constructive assemblies [10,11], actuated displays [9,12] and modular robots [2,4] are embodiments of the programmable matter vision [13,8,5] where small interactive *units* are automatically (or manually) put-together to create an interactive *assembly*. In each case the assembly is a collection of interactive units in the form of rods, tiles, cubes or more specific shapes that can be systematically manipulated to create the desired complex *objects*.

CHI 2014, April 26 - May 01 2014, Toronto, ON, Canada
Copyright 2014 ACM 978-1-4503-2473-1/14/04...$15.00.
http://dx.doi.org/10.1145/2556288.2557006

While current device designs rely on changing the *position* of the bits of matter (or unit) to transform, we focus on manipulating their *form*. We call this new type of shape-changing assembly units Changibles. Fig.1 illustrates our concept on a tabletop scenario: the user places a unit on the table and uses the contextual menu to change its form. By assembling units, the user creates a heart. The user can then choose an animation item in the contextual menu to animate the entire assembly that now becomes a pulsing heart.

Changible assemblies have advantages over non-morphing unit systems: (1) the number of units required is reduced as they can take many forms and thus serve as multi-functional units; (2) the accuracy of the assembly is higher, for example cubical units can change their curvature to create smooth edges; and (3) the assembly can reshape into new shapes without changing the position of units, for example creating the pulsing heart of Fig.1. In addition the assembly is portable and can provide haptic feedback by changing the form of a unit, e.g. its curvature to create buttons.

Starting from a set of objects we have little understanding of how to generate a set of units that can facilitate dynamic construction of any assembly from that set. A designer usually faces this problem, which is further compounded by Changibles where each unit can morph on their own. It is wishful thinking that one can create a small set of universal interactive units to cover the entire spectrum of possible objects an assembly can morph into. However, covering this entire spectrum is of a very high dimensionality and poses engineering challenges; even Lego® constantly creates new units to provide richer assemblies. To tackle this problem we created a software analysis tool that allows to import a set of objects in which an assembly shifts in and provides a tractable subset of forms for the units. We also contribute the concept of Changible and provide a use case with six wireless units controlled via an interactive surface.

AN ANALYSING TOOL FOR CHANGIBLES

We implemented a software tool (Fig.2) to help designers to build Changibles. It helps to choose the transformations required for the units to construct a set of given objects. We illustrate it with a walkthrough, and explain the algorithm.

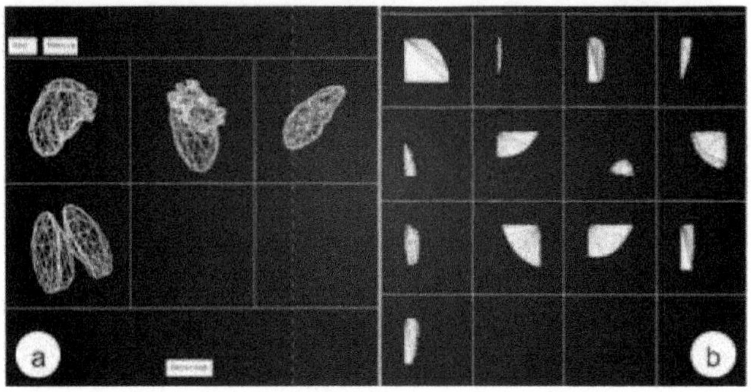

Figure 2. Our tool breaks (a) given objects into subdivisions and group them by similarity into *m* clusters. It then displays the (b) most representative subdivisions for each cluster, as well as a reconstitution of the initial objects where the initial subdivisions are replaced by their representative subdivisions (see Fig.1a).

Walkthrough

A designer wants to create an application for children in which an assembly morphs into organs. He navigates the database of objects and adds them to his workspace. Our tool breaks the objects into cube regions and extracts the forms (*subdivisions*) inside those regions. It analyses the similarity between subdivisions and organizes them into ***m*** clusters. The most representative subdivisions of each cluster are then displayed (see algorithm for more details). It also displays a reconstitution of the initial objects where the initial subdivisions are replaced by the representative subdivisions of the cluster they belong to (Fig.1a). The designer can thus see how close the assembly will be from the original objects if the Changibles reshape into the representative subdivisions. The designer can then start to design the physical units with a tractable set of forms.

The designer can go further by analyzing more parameters in order to have a feel for the best options before building the units. E.g. he wants the units to fit children's hands and considers building 4-9cm units. For that, our tool displays a graph that shows, for each unit size × cluster number, a *shape error* representing the level of resemblance in the cluster (Fig 3a). This is possible with a measure of similarity of the subdivisions. The designer then visualizes the representative subdivisions for a particular cluster number and unit size by clicking on the corresponding dot on the graph (Fig.3b). We also provide the histogram of subdivisions per cluster (Fig.3b). These combined graphs help the designer to know which forms the units must take.

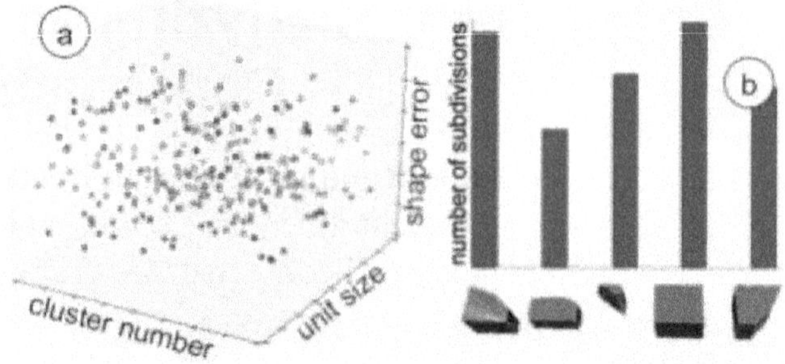

Figure 3. For each combination of unit size × cluster number, it displays (a) the shape error, a value indicating the level of resemblance in the cluster; (b) By clicking on a dot, it displays the distribution of subdivisions for a particular combination of unit size × cluster number.

Changibles with different roles

In our scenario, the designer creates units doing identical transformations. It is however possible that he wishes to create various categories of units, each taking care of certain transformations while others handle the rest. This is the case when no hardware solution is found to provide two transformations in the same unit. Another case is when some of the units cover different range of forms: e.g., in Fig.4a, the assembly can reconfigure into the four-color shapes of a card game using nine different types of Changibles, each of them responsible for a certain type of transformation. To inform the designer on which transformations need to happen in the same unit, our tool provides *links* that show the clusters that need to be linked and the one that does not (Fig.4b).

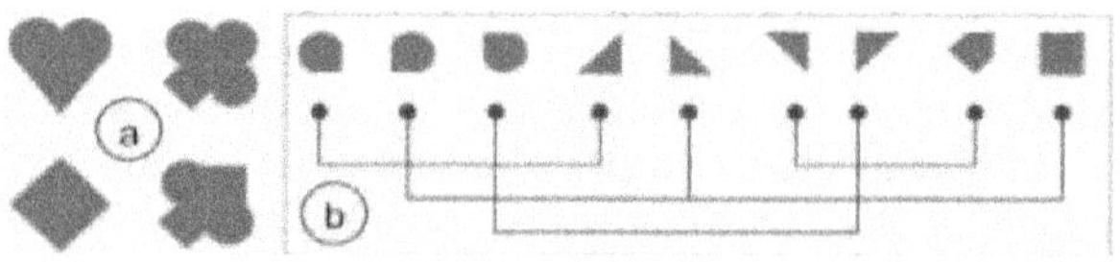

Figure 4. Changibles can have different roles, e.g. (a) to create an assembly that morphs into the four-color shapes of a card game. Our tool gives (b) links between clusters showing which transformations need to take place in the same unit.

Automatic vs. manual construction

Our tool allows designers to specify the type of link between objects: in the heart example, if the two hearts are linked *automatically* the pulsing animation is possible; otherwise the user must reconfigure the assembly *manually* to mold it into the given objects. The designer can use a combination of automatically and manually linked objects and use the *links* between clusters described earlier to know which transformation needs to take place in the same units. This functionality can be used to generate static units (like Lego's ®). In this case the designer can parameterize the tool to create the subdivisions using a rotation invariant algorithm as users can manually rotate the units.

Software

We implemented our software in OpenFramework C++ using OpenGL for the rendering. The software only works on objects with manifold geometry. On a Macbook 2.4Ghz dual core, our algorithm takes ~20s to create 1x1x1 cm units in a 4x4x4 cm object and ~40s to create 20 clusters.

Algorithm

Given a subdivision of objects, our goal is to find the optimal ***m*** and ***n*** so that (1). In the optimal case, both sides of the equation are the same and the error is zero, i.e. the assembly morphs perfectly into the given objects.

$$(1)\sum_{0}^{n} Cluster(m,Si) \rightarrow \sum_{0}^{n} Si$$

{S0, …, Sn} the n subdivisions of the objects
Cluster(m,Si) groups the Si subdivisions in m clusters, returns the representative subdivision of the cluster to which Si belongs.

Step1: Tiling the space

It centers the objects and decomposes the space into *tiles* whose shape is specified by the designer. Our current implementation only considers cubes but other shapes can be easily added such as a honeycomb, sphere or rod. Note that for mechanical reasons, it could be appropriate to consider tiles that fully tessellate (no empty space). To find the position of the tiles position, we use the ray-casting algorithm based on Jordan's Theorem [3].

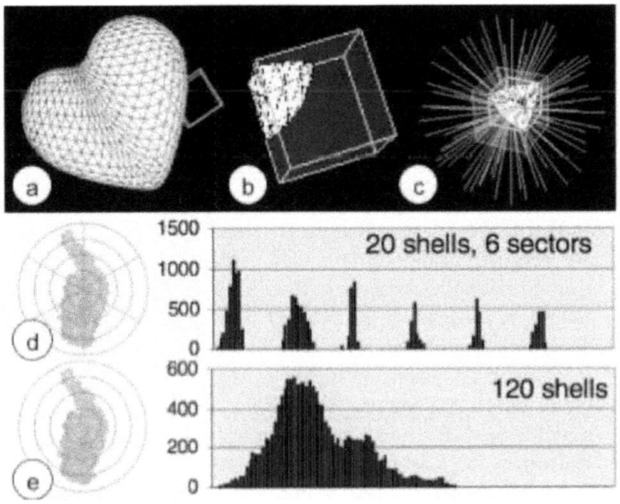

Figure 5. (a) A tile on the side of a heart and (b) its extracted subdivision; (c) Ray casting from the tile center to create a (d) histogram representing the space; (e) a rotation invariant version of this algorithm.

Step2: Subdividing the objects

It breaks the objects in *subdivisions* (Fig.5b) fitting the tiles (Fig.5a). For that, it does, for each tile, the Boolean intersection with the object being currently treated.

Step3: Encoding the subdivisions for similarity matching

It creates, for each subdivision, a vector of features that will serve to evaluate its similarity to other subdivisions. A lot of research has been focused on comparing shapes and shown that this is a hard challenge, especially for 3D shapes [14]. We choose *shape distribution* [1], which consists in decomposing the space into concentric *shells* and *sectors* that emerge from the centroid of the tiles. It then shoots rays from the center of the tiles to points placed uniformly on the surface of a sphere (Fig.5c). It then computes the radial distance and the polar angle to the ray intersections, and stores them into the appropriate bins (shells and sectors), thus creating a histogram of the points that immediately defines a decomposition of the subdivision (Fig 5d). When there is only one sector, the histogram is made of concentric shells, in turn creating a rotation independent model, i.e. any rotations of a subdivision around the center of the tiles results in the same histogram.

Step4: Clustering the subdivisions

It clusters the histograms previously generated using the k-means algorithm that partitions them into ***m*** clusters in which each observation belongs to the cluster with the nearest mean, serving as a representative of the cluster. This representative mean is used to find the representative subdivision to display for each respective cluster. In this step we also measure the cluster *shape error* as:

$$(2)\left(\sum_{0}^{r} d(R) - d(Sr)\right) / \|Sr\|$$

{S0,…, Sr} the r subdivisions in the cluster
R the representative subdivision for the cluster
d() the Euclidean distance

Step5: Linking the clusters

It generates the links between subdivisions belonging to objects being automatically linked, and propagates the links to the cluster representative subdivisions (by default objects are automatically linked to create a morphing assembly).

Step6: Generating data

Finally, it runs the last five steps on various values of unit size and cluster number in order to provide the comprehensive graphs for the designers (Fig.2, 3 and 4).

USE CASE: PULSING HEART

To validate our tool we built Changibles for the pulsing heart scenario. The designer has entered two hearts of different size in the software and has analyzed the graph showing the fidelity achieved depending on the number of units, their size and the number of clusters (Fig. 3). Fig.6 shows the results of the analysis, which he obtained for a unit size of 9cm. Now he must design a unit that can reproduce the full range of forms shown on the figure. He decides to go for units with a tilting top, which will approximately allow to reproduce these forms.

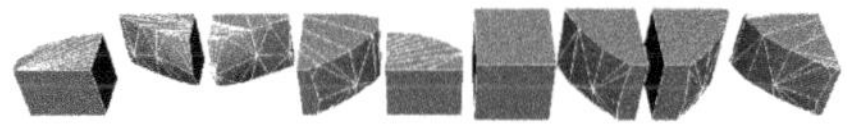

Figure 6. Pulsing heart results with 9 clusters × 9cm units.

Hardware

Our 9×9cm Changibles (Fig.7) have a movable top linked to two scissor jack mechanisms. This allows the unit to reshape into various forms by changing the length of two opposite sides in a similar fashion than Hemmert et al. phone [6]. In our case, we take advantage of the scissor mechanism to divide, by a factor>3, the height of the Changible (down to 3cm) thus allowing for a thin base for the electronic components. Note that additional arms can be added to the scissor jack mechanisms to make bigger units.

Changibles are attached using a set of permanent magnets that are freely moving inside circular pockets in the casing. As they can freely move, they naturally face other magnets when two units are close to each other, thus maintaining the connection between them. We embedded four of them on the top and bottom side and two on each side to constrain rotation between units. Each Changible is self-contained and controlled wirelessly using an x-OSC board. The board connects with two servos attached to the jack mechanisms, a 1000 mA lithium battery and a mini USB battery charger to recharge the battery without disassembling the unit.

Note that we choose this design because it allows for small units (large space to fit the board and the battery) but that other designs are possible to achieve the same motion.

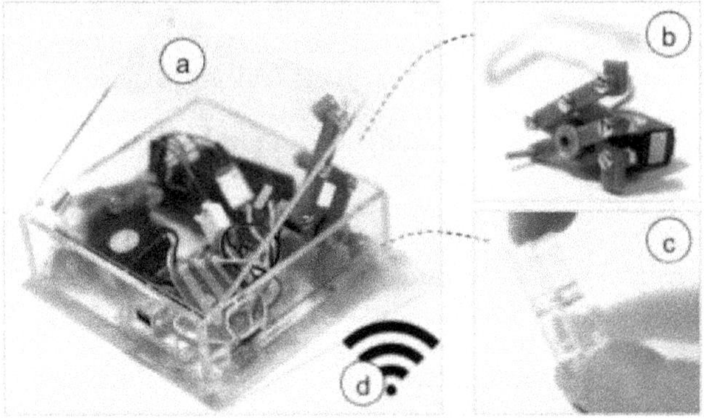

Figure 7. Our Changibles have a tilting top (a) linked to (b) scissor jacks. They reshape into various forms by changing the length of two opposite sides. They attach using (c) free moving magnets confined in the casing. They are self-contained and (d) controllable via WiFi.

Software

We implemented our code in C++. We use the oscpack library to send WiFi messages to the x-OSC boards. While the Changibles can be controlled in more than one manner, we implemented the user interface using a FTIR table combined with a Kinect to track the unit positions. When independent units are detected, contextual menus appear around them to let users change the form of each units. When an assembly is detected, the contextual menu appears around it to allow the selection of the shape of the assembly (e.g. to create the pulsing heart shown on Fig.1bc).

DISCUSSION FOR FUTURE WORK

On the software side, our tool could be extended to cover units that can change their scale, as well as units of different size (non identical tiles in the tessellation). There are also challenges to tackle on the hardware side such as shrinking the size of units, increasing the range of transformations that one unit can produce, or providing packaging solutions: e.g. a latex fabric could be added around our unit to cover the open sides. Informal tests show that such type of fabric is adapted to small units but reaches its limit of stretchability with larger ones. Another solution we found is to use Origami such as several Miura structures that extend vertically only without bending (Fig.8).

More importantly, our tool only provides the analyzing step in a design process, and designers must use additional tools for other steps (typically designing, building, evaluating). For example, to create the hardware of the units, one could use prototyping software in a similar fashion that [6]. We thus believe that the power of our tool can be increased by many manifolds by integrating it with fabrication tools such as CAD, prototyping software (and devices) and evaluation platforms in order to support the designers' working flow in all steps required to create advanced devices. This tool can help close the loop by feeding our analysis tool with insights from user experience evaluations.

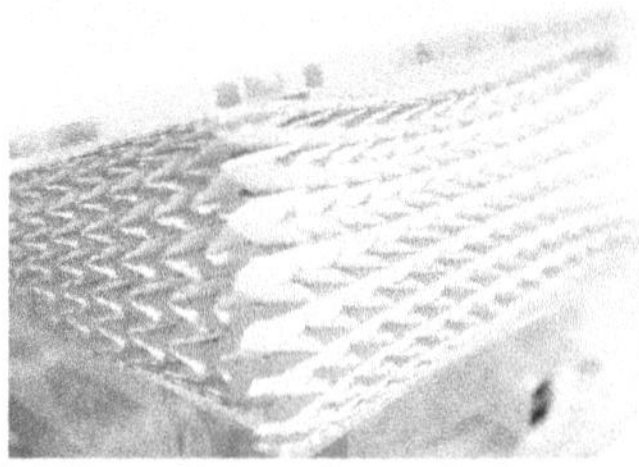

Figure 8. Miura Origami attached on each side of our Changibles to cover the openings.

ACKNOWLEGMENTS

We thank x-io Tech. Ltd for access to the x-OSC boards. This work is funded by the EC's 7th framework programme through the FET Open scheme (grant no. 309191) under the GHOST project (www.ghost-fet.com).

REFERENCES

1. Ankerst, M. Kastenmüller, G. Kriegel, H.P, Seidl, T., 3D Shape Histograms for Similarity Search and Classification in Spatial Databases. In Cs Vol.1651, 1999, 207-226
2. Christensen, D. J., Campbell, J. D. 2007. Locomotion of miniature catom chains: Scale effects on gait and velocity. In ICRA '07.
3. De Berg,M., Computational Geometry,1998, Computational Geometry in C, O'Rourke, 2005.
4. Gilpin, K., Koyanagi, K., Rus, D. 2011. Making self-disassembling objects with multiple components in the robot pebbles system. In ICRA'11 IEEE, 3614 –3621.
5. Goldstein, S. C., Mowry, T. C. 2004. Claytronics: A scalable basis for future robots. In RoboSphere 2004.
6. Hartmann, B., Klemmer, S.R., Bernstein, M., Abdulla, L., Burr, B., Robinson-Mosher, A., Gee, J. 2006. Reflective physical prototyping through integrated design, test, and analysis. UIST '06, 299-308.
7. Hemmert F., Hamann S., Löwe M., Zeipelt J., Joost G. Shape-changing mobiles: tapering in two-dimensional deformational displays in mobile phones. CHI EA'10.
8. Ishii, H., Lakatos, D., Bonanni, L., Labrune, J.-B. 2012. Radical atoms: beyond tangible bits, toward transformable materials. interactions 19, 1 (Jan.), 38–51.
9. Leithinger, D., Lakatos, D., DeVincenzi, A., Blackshaw, M., Ishii, H. 2011. Direct and gestural interaction with relief: a 2.5D shape display. UIST '11, 541-548.
10. Parkes, A., Ishii, H. 2010. Bosu: a physical programmable design tool for transformability with soft mechanics. DIS '10, 189-198.
11. Raffle, H.S, Parkes, A.J., and Ishii, H. Topobo: A Constructive Assembly System with Kinetic Memory. CHI'04, 647-654.
12. Roudaut, A., Karnik, A., Lochtefeld, M., Subramanian, S. 2013. Morphees: Toward high "shape resolution" in self-actuated flexible mobile devices. In CHI'13.
13. Sutherland, I. E. 1965. The ultimate display. In Proceedings of the IFIP Congress, 506–508.
14. Yang, M., Kpalma K. I., Ronsin, J. A survey of shape feature extraction techniques. Pattern Recognition, Peng-Yeng Yin (Ed.) (2008) 43-90, pages 43–90.

Expanding Touch Input Vocabulary by Using Consecutive Distant Taps

Seongkook Heo, Jiseong Gu, Geehyuk Lee
Department of Computer Science, KAIST
Daejeon, 305-701, South Korea
seongkook@kaist.ac.kr, jiseong.gu@kaist.ac.kr, geehyuk@gmail.com

ABSTRACT
In recent years, touch screens have emerged and matured as the main input interface for mobile and tablet computers calling for extended touch input possibilities. In this paper, we explore the use of consecutive distant taps to expand the touch screen input vocabulary. We analyzed time intervals and distances between consecutive taps during common applications on a tablet and verified that consecutive distant taps can be used conflict-free with existing touch gestures. We designed the two interaction techniques *Ta-tap* and *Ta-Ta-tap* that utilize consecutive distant taps. *Ta-tap* uses two consecutive distant taps to invoke alternative touch operations for multi-touch emulation, whereas *Ta-Ta-tap* uses a series of consecutive distant taps to define a spatial gesture. We verified the feasibility of both interaction techniques through a series of experiments and a user study. The high recognition rate of *Ta-tap* and *Ta-Ta-tap* gestures, the few conflicts with existing gestures, and the positive feedback from the participants assert the potential of consecutive distant taps as a new design space to enrich touch screen interactions.

Author Keywords
Ta-tap; *Ta-Ta-tap*; consecutive distant taps; command shortcut; touch screen

ACM Classification Keywords
H.5.2. Information interfaces and presentation (e.g., HCI): User Interfaces – Input devices and strategies

INTRODUCTION
Recently, touch screens have emerged as the dominating interface for mobile devices and tablet computers. However, a major downside of touch screen interfaces is their limited input vocabulary. Various touch gestures were designed to handle this problem. For example, touch-and-hold is a common gesture for alternative selections. Also,

CHI 2014, April 26 - May 01 2014, Toronto, ON, Canada

ACM 978-1-4503-2473-1/14/04···$15.00.
http://dx.doi.org/10.1145/2556288.2557234

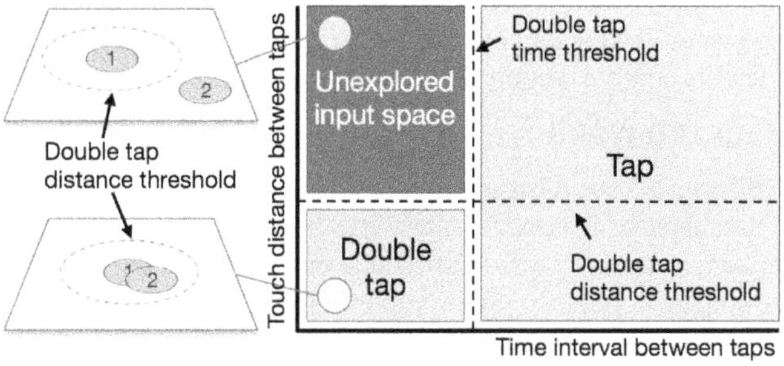

Figure 1. Input space of tap inputs and illustrative examples of double tap and unexplored input space. Gray circles with the numbers 1 and 2 indicate the first and the second taps.

multi-touch gestures such as a two-finger tap or a four-finger swipe are used for alternative selections or for switching between applications. More recent examples are attempts of using a finger's movement patterns to enable additional touch gestures as well as attempts of enhancing a touch input through additional modalities like the finger contact shape, the touch pressure, and the tapping velocity for a richer touch interaction. Such attempts, however, require additional sensors or signal processing.

We will identify and explore the underutilized gesture space of touch interactions. Although the set of touch gestures is greater than that of mouse inputs, many touch gestures resemble mouse inputs. For instance, tap and click, slide and drag, or double tap and double click are very similar to each other. Among mouse inputs, consecutive clicks, such as a double click and a triple click, are performed only at same locations since it is difficult to move a mouse cursor to a distant location in a short time interval (500 ms for the Microsoft Windows default setting [18]). This condition is different for a finger touch. A previous study revealed that a mouse is more accurate when selecting a small target, whereas a finger touch is faster regarding target selection [7, 16, 26]. In addition, when using two fingers, the target selection speed increases compared to the one-finger condition [17], whereas the use of two mice for a symmetric task does not lead to any performance improvement [7].

We anticipate that touch screen users will be able to perform a new set of touch gestures comprised of consecutive taps at distant locations as illustrated in Figure 1. Unlike the double tap gesture, which has only single triggered location information, a set of consecutive distant taps adds the information of the second tap's relative location. With the spatial arrangement of the distant taps, the new gesture can be used for triggering alternative touch operations for multi-touch emulation, or for invoking a large gesture set by drawing a dot path with multiple taps.

In this paper, we observe touch operations performed while using applications on a current touch screen device. Furthermore we define a consecutive distant tap and reveal that the consecutive distant tap is an available input space. We then describe two interaction techniques of using consecutive distant taps. We also verify the feasibility of the consecutive distant taps for several applications.

RELATED WORK

Enriching Touch Input with Touch Behaviors

The shape of a finger contact has been commonly utilized to augment touch information due to its application without adding any sensors. Such vision-based touch surfaces can detect the whole silhouette of a finger contact utilizing the size of a touch contact [2, 5] as well as the orientation of a touch [29, 30]. On a mobile device, the contact area of a thumb touch is utilized [4] to enable richer input for one-handed use.

Finger movement patterns have gained more attention than the shape information, because many mobile devices are equipped with a capacitive touch screen that can estimate the touch area only indirectly via capacitance distribution. For example, MicroRolls [24] has found that the movement of a touch point, while rolling a thumb on a touch surface, is different from that of an existing thumb gesture, such as a drag, swipe, or rub. Bezel swipe [23] uses a drag gesture starting from the bezel of a touch screen to distinguish the initial position of the bezel among similar drag gestures. Bonnet et al. [3] use a similar gesture to that of Benko et al. [2], which is a rocking movement of the thumb. The quick rolling down and up of a thumb is used as an alternative click. Heo and Lee [14] developed a shear force estimation method that utilizes micro-movements of a finger contact while applying shear force. Wagner et al. [28] designed a bimanual interaction technique for touch tablets. Thereby, users can change modes or trigger additional operations with the fingers of the holding hand.

Enriching Touch Input Using Additional Modalities

Nowadays, mobile devices are usually equipped with more sensors than desktop or laptop computers, such as an accelerometer, gyroscope, magnetometer, microphone, light intensity sensor, and location sensors like GPS. Some studies tried to combine sensor data from built-in sensors on a mobile device to expand the touch input vocabulary. Hinckley and Song [15] proposed the use of motion data obtained by an accelerometer and a gyroscope, and showed various interaction scenarios of using the combinations of motion and touch data. ForceTap [13] uses the built-in accelerometer to estimate the tapping force by calculating the sum of acceleration values caused by the movement of tapping. Serrano et al. [27] presented Bezel-Tap gestures, which consist of a first bezel tap detected by a built-in accelerometer and a following screen tap detected by a capacitive touch screen. Because the first bezel tap does not require touch sensing, Bezel-Tap can be used while a screen is turned off. GripSense [8] uses a built-in vibration motor and gyroscope to detect hand posture and touch pressure by measuring the vibration diminution of the hand. Harrison et al. [11] introduced TapSense, which recognizes finger parts or tools tapping the surface by analyzing the tapping sound.

Force is also a frequently used property. Blackberry storm 2 by Research in Motion [22] has four force sensors installed under the touch screen and measures the normal force to distinguish touch and press. GraspZoom by Miyaki and Rekimoto [19] utilizes normal force for continuous zooming and scrolling. Heo and Lee [12] presented gesture scenarios that use combinations of normal force, shear force, and touch movement. Harrison and Hudson [10] explored possible interaction scenarios to use shear force with touch input.

CONSECUTIVE DISTANT TAPS

Multiple tap gestures, including double taps and triple taps, are designed like multiple clicks on a mouse. Multiple clicks are usually performed without moving the pointer because moving to a certain location in a short amount of time is difficult, and the user has to rely on visual feedback. On the other hand, we rely on both the visual movement of a real finger, rather than the visual feedback displayed on a screen, and the kinesthetic sense of the finger when using a touch screen. We can switch fingers or use a finger of another hand to input consecutive taps that are not adjacent. However, except for the touch-typing tasks, only multiple taps at the same location are commonly used on a touch screen. A series of consecutive distant taps may open a new input space on a touch screen (Figure 1). In order to determine the possibility of using consecutive distant taps, we first observed the time interval and the distance between taps while using well-known tablet applications.

Time Interval and Distance between Taps

In order to analyze the taps made while using tablet applications, we had to choose representative applications. Müller et al. [20] studied the use of tablet computers to identify frequent activities or tablet-use contexts. In their result, checking emails, playing games, social networking, looking up information, and watching TV/videos were considered to be frequent uses of touch screen tablets by most participants. Because watching TV or videos does not require frequent interaction, we chose the activities of emailing, gaming, social networking, and looking up information using a web browser. Whereas other studies have mostly considered content consumption rather than content creation tasks, we also added a simple word-processing application. A 'jailbroken' Apple iPad was used in this experiment, and all touch events and the use of the touch screen keyboard while using the selected applications were logged. Twelve students with an average age of 21.1 years (6 female and 6 male) participated in the pilot study. All participants were experienced with touch screen devices, and eight of them were currently using a tablet. All participants reported that they did not experience any difficulties using the applications. Participants were compensated with approximately $7 for their time.

In the pilot test, participants were asked to use the selected applications freely for 5-10 minutes. For the emailing and content creation tasks, we asked participants to perform predefined tasks rather than to use them freely. While using the Mail app, which is a built-in email client on an iPad, we asked participants to browse and search through emails and draft a short reply to a specific email. For the web-browsing task, the participants were asked to freely browse and search web pages with the Safari app. The Facebook app was used as an example of a social networking scenario. Fruit Ninja and Juke Beat were used for the gaming scenarios. Both gaming applications require frequent touches; Fruit Ninja required frequent short slides, and Juke Beat required frequent taps for each beat in a song. For the content creation task, the participants were asked to make a copy of a sample document, which included a picture, normal, bold, and different-sized fonts, and aligned texts, using Apple Pages.

We collected 14,193 touch events in total. These touch events were grouped into four categories: tap, typing tap, slide, and multi-touch operations. Each category had 4400, 4479, 4908, and 406 touch operations. We analyzed the time interval and the distance between consecutive taps. Figure 2 shows the distributions of the time interval and the distance of non-typing taps and typing taps. The time interval axis was cropped to 3 s for better visualization of the short-interval taps, which were of interest to us. We found that the non-typing taps with a short time interval (<0.5 s) were adjacent to each other (<9.6 mm) and that there was no distant tap with a short time interval. This

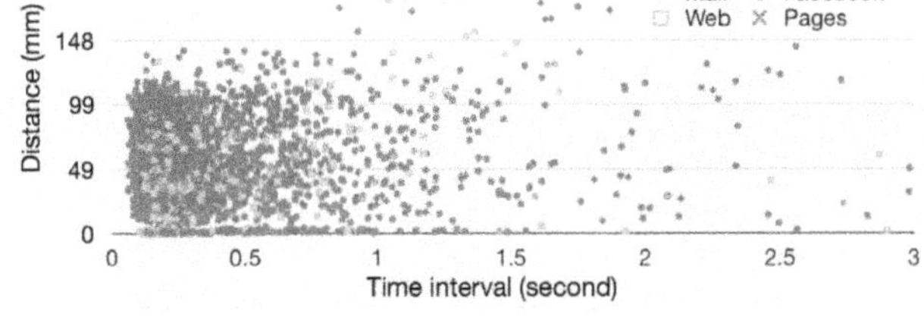

Figure 2. Time interval and distance distributions of (a) taps and (b) typing taps

resulted in an unused input space becoming annotated as shown in Figure 2a, and we called the taps in this area "consecutive distant taps." In contrast, 87.2% of the typing taps had a time interval of less than 0.5 s (Figure 2b). This revealed that the users were capable of making consecutive distant taps. Taps made from the Juke Beat application were spread throughout the entire area, including the short-interval distance area. However, the gaming applications were special cases that were difficult to generalize and touch operations frequently used in the games conflicted with double taps or multi-touch gestures. Thus, we omitted Juke Beat taps from the graph in order to emphasize the unexplored area. We also excluded Fruit Ninja taps because only a few number of taps, which were used for menu selections, occurred per person.

Using Consecutive Distant Taps

We verified that the consecutive distant taps belonged to an unused input space. The next step was designing interaction techniques with those consecutive distant taps. While there could be a continuum of application possibilities, we explored the two extreme ends. On the one extreme, we used two consecutive distant taps that we called *Ta-tap*. A *Ta-tap* can be used for defining two control points for a zooming or rotating operation. It may also be used for instantiating a GUI control that can be defined with two points such as a scroll wheel control or a pie menu. On the other extreme, we used an arbitrary number of consecutive distant taps to form a spatial gesture. For instance, we can make a constellation gesture based on key locations on a QWERTY layout. Numerous spatial tap gestures could be defined and used for invoking a command. We called such a spatial tap gesture *Ta-Ta-tap*. In the following two sections, we explore the possibility of the two extreme cases of *Ta-tap* and *Ta-Ta-tap*, respectively.

TA-TAP: USING CONSECUTIVE DISTANT TAPS FOR ONE-HANDED TOUCH SCREEN USE

We define a *Ta-tap* operation as a set of two consecutive distant taps. *Ta-tap* can be useful for a one-handed touch screen use because its performance does not require multiple fingers. As shown in Figure 3, *Ta-tap* consists of two stages: activation and manipulation. When two consecutive distant taps are detected, a GUI control that consists of two handles (circles) at the two taps is displayed on the screen. The users can then drag one of the handles to use the control. Because the manipulation is performed with a drag gesture, we modified *Ta-tap* to be activated with the touchdown of the second tap. A novice user can perform two taps to check the manipulation handle, and then perform the manipulation. With this modification, expert users can seamlessly perform manipulations with a drag gesture.

Ta-tap Use Scenarios

We developed three use scenarios of using *Ta-tap*, which are multi-touch emulation, virtual scroll wheel, and pie-menu invocation. In the first scenario, two consecutive distant taps are regarded as two touches. When a user performs *Ta-tap*, a handle with two circles at two tap locations appears on a screen as shown in Figure 4a. The user can move one of the circles to zoom or rotate an image or a map with an anchor point at another circle location. If a user performs drag instead of the second tap, the first tap location becomes an anchor and the drag location scales or rotates the picture. With this technique, users can perform multi-touch operations with a single thumb.

In the second scenario, users can make a virtual scroll wheel on a screen with a *Ta-tap*. As shown in Figure 4b, the first tap location defines the center of a scroll wheel, and the second tap location determines the radius of the wheel. Users then circularly move their finger on a wheel to continuously scroll a long content, without repeatedly flicking their finger. It is also possible for a user to preform a drag instead of a second tap, to access the scrolling function, instantly.

Ta-tap can also be used for invoking a pie-menu. Accessing the menu at the top or bottom of the screen can be hard for single-handed use and it becomes harder on larger touch screen devices. In contrast, invoking a pie-menu with *Ta-tap* allows users to run commands at the 'sweet spot' of the touch screen, the center area. As shown in Figure 4c, the first tap location sets the pie-menu location, and the second touch moves the handle to select a menu item. Users can cancel the pie-menu by locating the second touch handle to the pie-menu center.

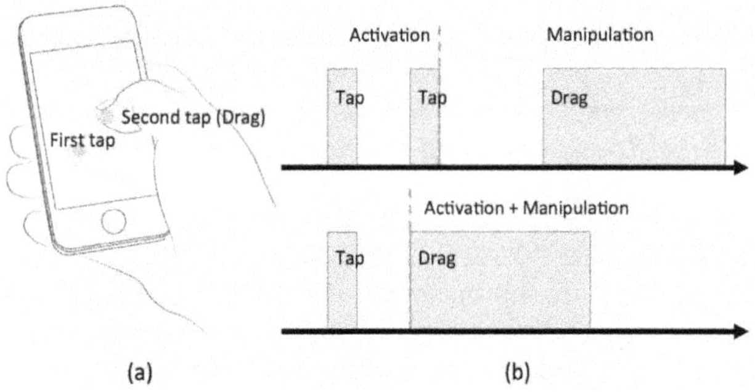

Figure 3. (a) Performing *Ta-tap*, (b) integration of *Ta-tap* and drag operation

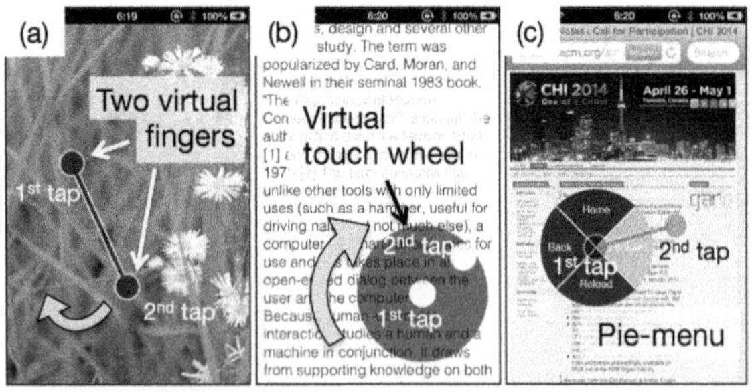

Figure 4. Using *Ta-tap* for (a) multi-touch zoom / rotate, (b) virtual scroll wheel, and (c) pie-menu invocation

Feasibility Test

We conducted an experiment to evaluate the feasibility of *Ta-tap*. The experiment was based on two questions:

- Can users perform consecutive distant taps within 500 ms?
- Can users distinguish between a double tap and a *Ta-tap*?

The first question is to check whether the 500 ms threshold, which is a time threshold for double tap detection for many systems, is enough for *Ta-tap* with a single thumb so that we can use *Ta-tap* without increasing the existing double tap detection delay. Even though a user can perform *Ta-tap*, it can be problematic if performing distant taps are too difficult to perform so that the taps are not far enough from each other to be discriminated from double tap. Thus, we checked whether *Ta-tap* is a gesture that can be differently performed by a user.

Task and Procedure

The experiment consisted of two tasks. The first and second tasks were designed to answer the first and second questions, respectively. Figure 5 shows the experimental setting and experimental program user interface. The first task was a consecutive tapping. When the experiment started, two circles were displayed at random locations as shown in Figure 5b. Two targets were located at more than 7.7 mm (50 pixels on iPhone) from each other, and number 1 and 2 were written to indicate the tapping sequence. The task consisted of five blocks and each block had 20 trials. The second task was a gesture-performing task. Before starting this task, we briefly introduced how to use two different gestures: double tap and *Ta-tap*. Participants could try two gestures for a while (< 3 min). The target gesture was displayed as an icon, double tap as two concentric circles and *Ta-tap* as two distant circles as shown in Figure 5c. Participants were asked to perform the displayed gesture anywhere on the screen. The recognized gesture was shown on the screen after the participant performed the gesture. Participants were asked to perform 20 trials in 5 blocks.

We recruited seven participants (6 male and 1 female) with an average age of 26.14 years. All participants were right-handed and were familiar with touch screen mobile devices. The participants received $5 each for their participation.

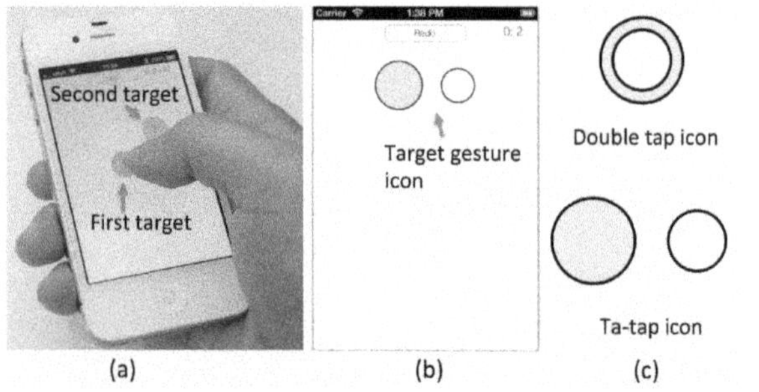

Figure 5. (a) Experiment settings and screen configurations of experiment 1 and (b) experiment 2. (c) Target gesture icons

The experimental program was implemented in Objective C, and runs on Apple iPhone 4S with a 3.5-inch display. All the participants completed the experiments while being seated, using the device with a thumb of a single hand.

Result

The results revealed that the interval between the two taps performed by all the participants was less than 500 ms, with an average of 231.1 ms and the maximum of 432 ms (see Figure 6). In the second experiment, the participants correctly performed 99.6% (3 errors/700 trials) of the double taps and *Ta-taps*. The three errors were attributed to the participants' mistakenly performing different gestures instead of the target gestures. As shown in Figure 6, the double taps and *Ta-taps* could be clearly distinguished by the distance threshold. The participants used three applications and were asked to comment on the usability of the new gesture. All participants answered that the new gesture was easy to learn and use. Multi-touch operations and the virtual scroll wheel scenarios were preferred among the three use scenarios. The participants commented that the multi-touch operation was natural and easy to understand and that it would be useful for one-handed use. For the virtual scroll wheel, the participants liked that they did not need to repeat the scroll with their thumb when scrolling a long page.

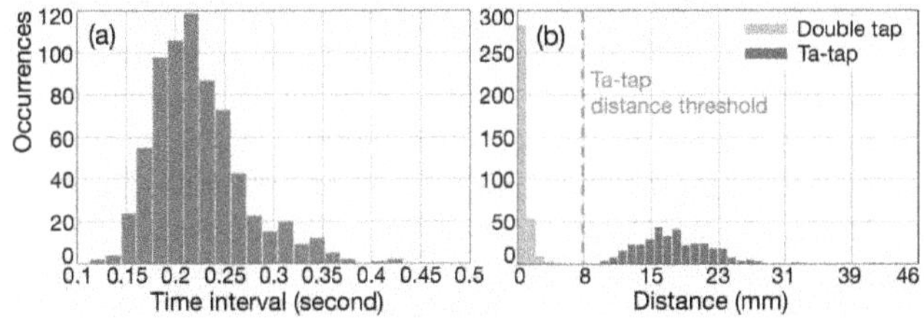

Figure 6. Histograms of (a) time intervals between two taps from the first task and (b) distances between two taps from the second task

TA-TA-TAP: USING CONSECUTIVE DISTANT TAPS AS COMMAND GESTURE

Another possible use of consecutive distant taps is to define a spatial gesture. We can define a constellation gesture with a series of consecutive distant taps. Numerous spatial tap gestures, that we call *Ta-Ta-tap*, can be defined this way and be used for invoking a command. The first two taps in *Ta-Ta-tap* should be at a distance to avoid conflict with double tap. While *Ta-Ta-tap* can open a huge input space, it poses a scalability problem for gesture designers and a learnability problem for users. It is not easy to come up with a distinct *Ta-Ta-tap* gesture for a new command. It is also difficult for users to remember numerous *Ta-Ta-tap* gestures.

As a means to handle the scalability and learnability problems, we decided to exploit the spatial knowledge that we are familiar with: QWERTY typing. Different from stroke gestures, words themselves have meanings, making it easier to learn them and to form a large set. Gustafson et al. [9] already showed that spatial knowledge is transferred from physical devices to an imaginary interface. Since QWERTY typing without visual cues was also investigated by Findlater et al. [6], we assume that the spatial information of the QWERTY layout and the sequence of typing could also be transferred to an invisible flat surface.

In order to design an algorithm of using consecutive distant taps on the QWERTY layout, it is necessary to observe the patterns of blind QWERTY typing on a tablet.

Investigation on Blind QWERTY Typing

In order to use the sequences of consecutive distant taps, the time threshold to change the operation mode to the consecutive distant tap detection mode should be defined. We conducted an experiment to measure the time interval between the first and the second tap while typing short commands to determine the time threshold. We chose 15 commands, namely save, load, left, right, center, font, color, bold, italic, zoom, copy, cut, paste, find, and replace. These commands were displayed on a screen in a random order, and all commands appeared five times each.

This experiment was performed with the previous pilot study on time interval and distance in the consecutive distant taps section, thus the same participants were recruited in this study. This study had a 2 × 2 between-subject design with two factors: key layout visibility and number of typing fingers. Half of the participants typed commands with a keyboard layout on a screen and the other half typed without keyboard layout. Six participants typed commands with two thumbs while holding the device. The remaining six typed with all fingers while placing the device on a table. The participants were not informed about the purpose of the experiment. Participants performed all tasks while seated and resting their arms on a table. Further, the Apple iPad 3 was used for the experiment.

Participants of the without-keyboard-overlay condition assumed that there is an on-screen keyboard. There was a keyboard-shaped overlay for the participants who performed the test under the with-keyboard-overlay condition. These participants were also told that the keyboard was not real, so they did not need to be accurate. The position and the timestamp of the taps were logged.

The time interval between the first and the second tap was important because the first two touches decided the mode changes. Figure 7 shows the histogram of the time interval between the first and the second taps. The average time interval was 234.9 ms when there was a keyboard overlay and 230.7 ms when there was no overlay. The value at 95% percentile was 399.9 ms for the keyboard-overlay condition and 333.2 ms for the no-overlay condition. Even though the keyboard overlay condition had a longer tail as we can see in Figure 7, most of the consecutive taps were closer than 400 ms. Thus, we set the threshold to 500 ms, which is a threshold of the double tap detection and is sufficiently long to detect typing-like taps.

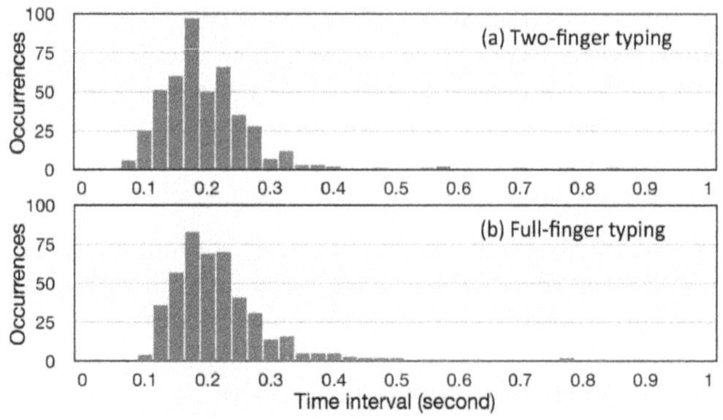

Figure 7. Time interval between first and second taps of (a) two-finger typing (b) full-finger typing

Gesture Recognizer

There has been intensive research on gesture recognition techniques. Gesture recognizer by Rubine [25] recognizes gestures based on statistical features and needs a large number of sample gestures for training. DTW [21] can recognize gestures independent of the time variance and exhibits high accuracy with a small set of templates; however, it requires a relatively long computation time. $1 gesture recognizer [31] provides a simple algorithm and exhibits high accuracy with a small number of templates. However, it still requires rotation and scaling to compensate for the individual differences.

Compared to gestures used in the aforementioned research, gestures made with consecutive distant taps have more constraints. When using a touch tablet, people assume the width of the screen to be the width reference of a screen keyboard, making the width fixed. Further, the tablet itself becomes the rotation reference as the conceptual model of an imaginary keyboard is horizontally aligned. Because the QWERTY layout is familiar to many people, their spatial knowledge of the keyboard is transferred to the imaginary keyboard. Since each vertex is made by a single tap, the resampling of in-between samples is not required. Thus, we can build a simpler gesture recognizer, which removes the resampling, translation, scaling, and rotation requirements from that developed by Wobbrock et al. [31]. Further, we can calculate the average distance d_i between the points of a consecutive distant tap sequence H and the ith point of templates T_i as follows:

$$d_i = \frac{\sum_{k=1}^{N} \sqrt{\left(H[k]_x - T[k]_x\right)^2 + \left(H[k]_y - T[k]_y\right)^2}}{N}$$

Gesture templates are essential for gesture recognizer systems, and the generation of templates is time consuming. Gesture templates for *Ta-Ta-tap* can be automatically generated on the basis of the position of each key on the QWERTY layout. When a word or a set of words is given, the first character becomes the origin and the locations of the following characters can be calculated with respect to the origin.

We implemented the proposed algorithm using Objective C. When a tap was detected, the system saved the current touch location and waited for the next tap for 500 ms. If the next tap was detected within 500 ms and the distance between the taps was larger than 50 pixels (9.6 mm on iPad and 7.7 mm on iPhone), the system entered the *Ta-Ta-tap* mode. In the *Ta-Ta-tap* mode, every relative tap location to the first touch location was added to the consecutive distant tap sequence.

We did not consider preventing false positives. In the real use, the algorithm can display command candidates to the user, and the user may select among the candidates or dismiss false positives (see Figure 12).

Experiment 1—Performance Evaluation

In this experiment, we evaluated the recognition performance and the computation time of the *Ta-Ta-tap* algorithm. We performed the experiment twice, once on the iPad and another time on the iPhone.

We recruited participants who can type QWERTY-layout keyboard blindly. Ten people (3 female, 7 male) with an average age of 22.8 years and eight people (5 female, 3 male) with an average age of 20.75 years were recruited in this experiment for iPad and iPhone, respectively. The participants were compensated approximately $5 for their effort. All participants were experienced with touch-typing on a mobile phone, and six participants for the iPad experiment were familiar with typing text on tablets. We also asked the preferred posture they used for typing text. All participants for the iPhone experiment preferred two-thumbs typing with their hand and eight over ten participants for the iPad experiment preferred ten-finger typing.

The experimental application was developed in Objective C and run on an Apple iPad 3 and an iPhone 4S. All participants performed the experiment while being seated and resting their arms on a table. Figure 8 shows the poses of the task execution. In the iPad experiment, half of the participants completed the tasks with two thumbs, and the other half typed with ten fingers. For the iPhone, all participants performed tasks only with two thumbs.

Task and Procedure

We collected 200 app names from the Apple App Store's Top Charts, 100 names of free apps and 100 of the paid apps. We then removed special characters and numbers from the app names because our algorithm only supports alphabetic characters and spaces. We also excluded app names that had many numerical characters. As a result, we had a total of 192 app names.

The experimental task was designed to be similar to that of Findlater et al.'s study [6]. The participants started the experiment right after a short instruction, without any practice. As shown in Figure 8a, a randomly chosen app name is displayed on the screen. When a participant tapped the screen, an asterisk feedback was shown to indicate the number of taps they entered. The participants proceeded to the next trial by tapping the button with the 'Next' label that was activated as soon as they completed entering the name without mistakes. When they had made a mistake, they could retype the word by tapping the 'Again' button. In order to prevent users from tapping the 'Next' button instead of 'Again' button accidentally, we enabled 'Next' button only when the number of taps matched the number of characters of the task word. The purpose of the experiment and the recognition results were hidden to the participants. Each participant performed 100 trials.

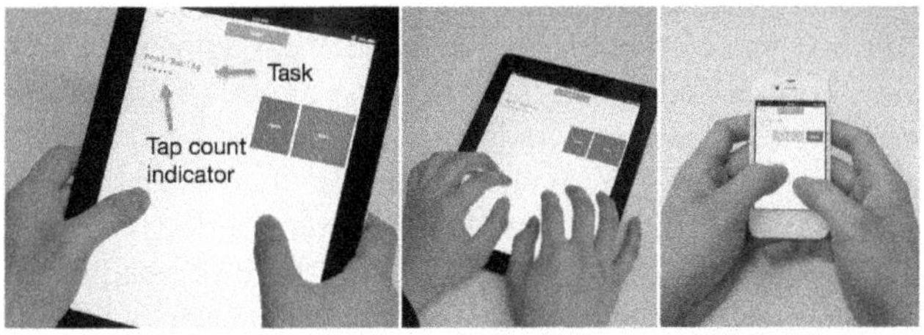

(a) On iPad, two thumbs (b) On iPad, all fingers (c) On iPhone, two thumbs

Figure 8. Tapping poses in the experiment

Result: Gesture Recognition Performance

The algorithm calculated the average of distances for every trial and every consecutive tap that exceeded a single tap. The recognition result is summarized in Table 1. In the case of the tablet use condition, 493 sets (98.6%) and 490 sets (98.0%) of *Ta-Ta-taps* over 500 trials matched to the gestures with a minimum average distance for two-thumbs and for all fingers conditions, respectively. Including gesture candidates with second-minimum average distances, the recognition rates for the two-thumb condition and full-finger condition increased to 99.6% and 98.4%, respectively. Recognition performance was similar with the iPhone use condition. Among 800 trials, the best-matched templates of 787 trials (98.4%) matched to the task word. The recognition ratio increased to 99.1% and 99.4% with candidates with including second-minimum average distances and candidates with including both second-minimum and third-minimum distances, respectively. The average computation time for matching one gesture was 33.6 ms on the iPad and 29.4 ms on the iPhone. This means that the algorithm could match 192 gestures 30 times per second, and it had a possibility of real-time processing.

Typing all letters may not be feasible in a real use scenario, because the names of some applications are longer than 20 characters. Hence, recommending commands as tapping is necessary. We measured the minimum required number of taps to be correctly classified. Figure 9 shows the histogram of the number of characters including spaces of app names used in the experiment, and the number of taps required to achieve the correct recognition. As a result, 82.3% of *Ta-Ta-taps* were correctly classified within four taps.

As shown in Figure 10, users could make a similar pattern for the same term without any keyboard layout visualization. Even though the absolute locations are different, the recognizer still could recognize patterns correctly.

Number of Candidates	1	2	3
Tablet, Two thumbs	98.6%	99.6%	99.6%
Tablet, All fingers	98.0%	98.4%	98.8%
Phone, Two thumbs	98.4%	99.1%	99.4%

Table 1. Recognition rate by the number of gesture candidates

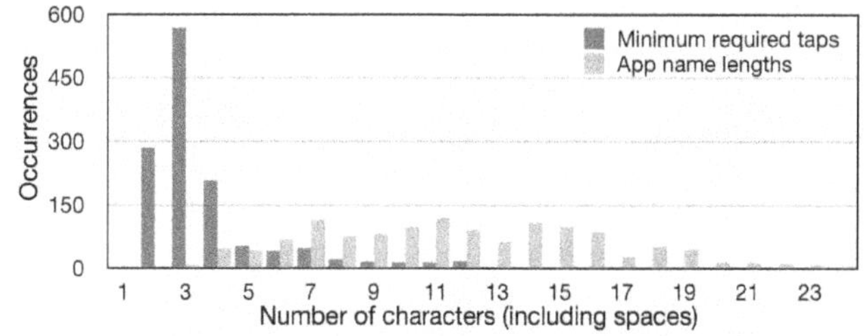

Figure 9. Histogram of app name lengths and minimum number of taps for correct recognition

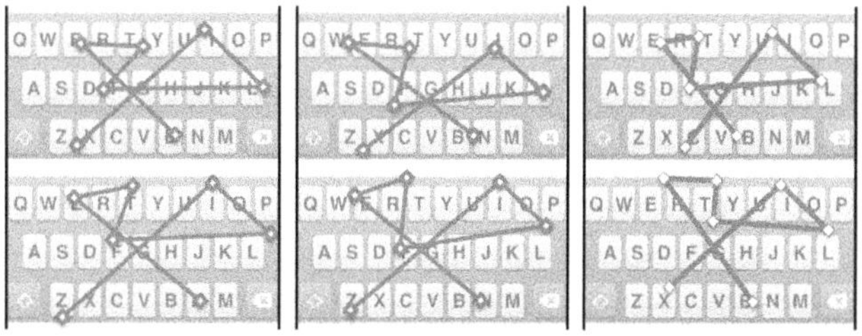

Figure 10. Gesture patterns of "Netflix" of four users from the iPhone experiment, which are all correctly recognized. We overlaid iPhone screen keyboard for better understanding.

Experiment 2—Gesture Conflict

Although we observed that the input space of consecutive taps is not being used on many applications, it is necessary to check whether they create a conflict with the other touch gestures. We conducted an experiment to check the conflict of the *Ta-Ta-tap* gesture with touch gestures, which are tap, double tap, and drag. Eight individuals (1 female) with an average age of 24.75 years participated in this experiment. The Apple iPad 3rd generation was used, and the experimental application was implemented in Objective C. All the participants completed the tasks while remaining seated; however, we did not ask the participants to assume a specific posture or to use a specific finger.

Task and Procedure

In this experiment, the participants were asked to perform touch gestures following a short instruction displayed on the screen. The tasks included tapping and double tapping a box, dragging an item, and typing a command using Ta-*Ta-tap*. The tasks were displayed in a random order. The experiment consisted of three blocks, and each block had 20 trials (5 trials for each gesture). The screen had 20 target boxes aligned in 5 rows and 4 columns, and all the target boxes responded to touch gestures. Hence, we could log all the gesture events.

Result

Among the 480 trials, a tap, three double taps (2.5% of 120 double taps), two *Ta-Ta-taps* (1.67%), and one drag (0.83%) were misclassified as other gestures. One tap and two *Ta-Ta-taps* were classified as drag gestures, which was attributed to the sliding of the finger when it touched the screen surface. Three double taps and a drag were classified as taps. No touch gesture was classified as *Ta-Ta-tap*, and the misclassification of *Ta-Ta-tap* was not higher than that of the other gestures.

Discussion

Ta-Ta-tap relies on the user's recall capability. Different from the recognition-based user interface, recall may cause difficulties remembering exact commands. For example, if a user who may want to add a meeting to her calendar should have typed 'Schedule' instead of entering the word 'Book'. Because the *Ta-Ta-tap* algorithm can make a gesture template based on the characters in a word, we can generate multiple gestures with synonyms for a single function.

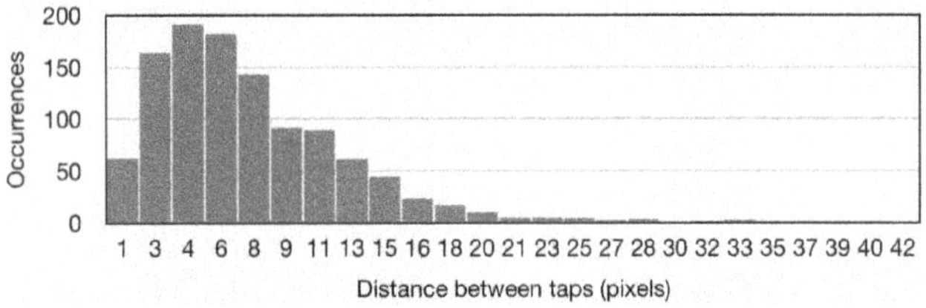

Figure 11. Histogram of double tap distances

Using *Ta-Ta-tap* on a small-sized touch screen can cause conflicts with double tap since the distances between adjacent keys are shorter (approx. 4.9 mm on the iPhone) than the double tap distance threshold (approx. 6.9 mm on iPhone, experimentally determined). We thought that the double tap distance could become shorter than the current setting. We had a brief study to determine the distance between two taps while performing double taps. 14 participants performed 100 double taps on randomly displayed targets. Figure 11 shows the histogram of distances between two taps performed by the participants. The result showed that more than 99% of the double taps have a distance between the taps that measures less than 3.9 mm. Thus, we can lower the double tap distance threshold for *Ta-Ta-tap* enabled controls on small-sized touch screen devices.

FOCUS GROUP

We conducted a focus group to receive usability feedbacks, to reveal usability issues, and to look for possible application scenarios. We recruited five undergraduate students (four male and one female), since the recommended number ranges from three to seven [1]. All participants were experienced users of touch screen mobile devices, and the four of the participants were familiar to touch tablets. At the beginning of the focus group interview, we gave a brief instruction on the consecutive distant tap input and demonstrated *Ta-tap* and *Ta-Ta-tap*. Then, participants were asked to test *Ta-tap* and *Ta-Ta-tap* with the selected applications of an image viewer with *Ta-tap* multi-touch emulation, a text reader with *Ta-tap* scroll wheel, and a web browser with *Ta-tap* pie-menu which are aforementioned in the *Ta-tap* section. We also developed a mock-up web browser with *Ta-Ta-tap* functionalities. Figure 12 shows the application. Users can type a command on a web page view. When two consecutive distant taps are detected, the system blocks the touch event delivery to web view control and enters the *Ta-Ta-tap* mode. In the *Ta-Ta-tap* mode, a dialog window with four buttons appears approximately 2 cm above the highest touch location. At every tap, the titles of three buttons from the left side on a dialog window changes to top three gesture candidates. Thus users do not have to type all letters but select when the intended command appears. The last button is to cancel the *Ta-Ta-tap* mode. Then, users may select a function by choosing a button. In our implementation, we applied a multi-stage command system. Users may type "scrap" and confirm to scrap the page. Users can type "run" to confirm, then type "youtube" and confirm to run the YouTube application. To make a reminder, they can type "new" and confirm, type "reminder" and confirm, then write down a reminder on a pop-up window. Participants used the *Ta-tap* applications on an iPhone and the *Ta-Ta-tap* application on an iPad.

After using the applications, we asked the participants to comment on the following questions: could you use the new interaction technique; did you have any difficulties using it; what were pros and cons; and are there other scenarios that this technique might be useful for. All participants answered that they could easily find how to use it and they felt that both *Ta-tap* and *Ta-Ta-tap* were intuitive to use. One participant answered that he may have had difficulties learning the techniques if there was only a text manual, and he commented that a short video manual would be better to understand. All participants also told that both techniques are useful. The preferred use scenarios using *Ta-tap* was different for each participant, and no scenario was significantly preferred. One participant commented that the use scenarios of *Ta-tap* were useful, but only one scenario could be performed at a time. For example, when using a web browser, users may want to zoom in a web page, scroll the page with a wheel, and perform shortcut menus with a pie menu. She suggested combining double tap and consecutive taps, which we can call as consecutive distant double taps, to add to the *Ta-tap* mode. Four participants liked and had no difficulties of using *Ta-Ta-tap*, but one participant reported that he failed to memorize the QWERTY layout so that he had difficulties using it.

The participants gave us many ideas for using new gestures. One participant suggested that the tapping locations might form a rectangle so that he can capture a screenshot of a selected area. Another participant told that the second tap of *Ta-tap* is usually manipulated with a drag and confirmed by a finger lift after the drag, making the location of the second tap less important. So she suggested using the relative location of the second tap to enable multiple mode *Ta-tap* operations. Other participants commented that the *Ta-tap* would be also useful for rate-controlled scrolling, with the relative position of the second tap to the first tap.

(a) Typing "new" (b) Confirm

Figure 12. Mockup web browser application with a *Ta-Ta-tap* interaction technique

DISCUSSION

To open up the unused input space of consecutive distant taps, working within 500 ms delay threshold is unavoidable. In fact, current tablet systems, such as an iPad, already have 500 ms of delay to detect double taps and the delay exists on double tap enabled controls. Apple tried to reduce the feeling of the delay by giving a visual feedback before triggering an action. For example, the Safari app uses a double tap gesture to zoom a paragraph on a web page. It has a delay to detect the double tap and triggers the tap gestures 500 ms after the gesture. The system shows a visual feedback indicating that a tap is performed when the first tap was detected so that the user can notice that his input has not been ignored. It may help users to experience a shortened delay. We use a similar approach. When a user taps a screen, a visual feedback shows a preview of a single tap operation.

As we observed in the pilot test, some game applications use consecutive taps at various locations. Thus, there can be conflicts between gameplay taps and consecutive distant tap gestures. It is an unavoidable limitation, while gameplay uses maximum input capabilities. The problem already exists with currently used gestures. Tap-and-hold and double tap gestures are also being used in many game applications. However, despite the limitations, we still perform well for most of the applications. With an option to enable or disable the consecutive tap gesture, the gesture potentially will be useful for many applications.

In the focus group interview, we learned that participants considered multiple mode *Ta-tap* operations to be better, to which we agreed. There can be three ways to add modes to the *Ta-tap* operations. First, we can use the relative position of two taps. As one participant commented in the focus group, the relative location of the second tap was not utilized. Previous work [32] also showed that utilizing the relative position of the pen stroke to the initial tap or stroke can increase the input vocabulary of marking menus. Thus, we may change modes through the relative direction of the second tap location or through the distance between two taps. Secondly, we can utilize the time to change a mode. Since we are already familiar with utilizing the time on a touch screen in a touch-and-hold gesture, adding the time factor to *Ta-tap* will be also feasible. Finally, we can use more taps. We introduced *Ta-tap* as the simplest way of using consecutive distant taps, but there can be slight modifications. In the *Ta-tap* use scenario, we emulated two-finger gestures with two consecutive distant taps. In a similar manner, three or four taps can emulate three- or four-finger gestures like the ones used on the iPad to switch applications. Two distant taps can be two distant double taps.

CONCLUSION

In this paper, we revealed an unused input space of consecutive distant tap gestures, and showed through a user study that the input space has not been used. We developed two interaction techniques utilizing consecutive distant taps, and verified their feasibility through a series of experiments. Participants reported that they could use consecutive distant taps with ease. The experiment also showed that the simple gesture recognizer for QWERTY-like consecutive distant tap gestures had a recognition rate of higher than 98% within approximately 30 ms of the average computation time. More than 82% of the 192 application names were recognized within four taps. The main contribution of the current study was to identify and utilize the unused design space of developing gestures that are not in conflict with existing operations. We did not consider comparing *Ta-Ta-tap* with other stroke-based gestures. Instead, we focused on showing how well the new techniques coexist with present operations, and how well users accept those new techniques. In addition to *Ta-tap* and *Ta-Ta-tap*, we expect that the general concept of using consecutive distant taps will enable many new interaction techniques to enrich the touch screen interface.

ACKNOWLEDGMENTS

This work was supported by the IT R&D program of MKE/KEIT. [KI10041244, SmartTV 2.0 Software Platform]

REFERENCES

1. Adams, A. and Cox, A. L. Questionnaires, in-depth interviews and focus groups. In P. Cairns and A.L. Cox, eds., *Research Methods for Human Computer Interaction.* Cambridge University Press (2008), 17–34.

2. Benko, H., Wilson, A., and Baudisch, P. Precise selection techniques for multi-touch screens. In *proc. CHI '06*, ACM (2006), 1263-1272.

3. Bonnet, D., Appert, C., and Beaudouin-Lafon, M. Extending the Vocabulary of Touch Events with ThumbRock. In *proc. GI '13*, ACM (2013).
4. Boring, S., Ledo, D., Chen, X., Marquardt, N., Tang, A., and Greenberg, S. The Fat Thumb: Using the Thumb's Contact Size for Single-Handed Mobile Interaction. In *proc. MobileHCI '12*, ACM (2012), 39-48.
5. Davidson, P.L. and Han, J.Y. Extending 2D object arrangement with pressure-sensitive layering cues. In *proc. UIST '08*, ACM (2008), 87-90.
6. Findlater, L., Wobbrock, J.O. and Wigdor, D. Typing on flat glass: examining ten-finger expert typing patterns on touch surfaces. In *proc. CHI '11*, ACM (2011), 2453-2462.
7. Forlines, C., Wigdor, D., Shen, C., and Balakrishnan, R. Direct-touch vs. mouse input for tabletop displays. In *proc. CHI '07*, ACM (2007), 647-656.
8. Goel, M., Wobbrock, J.O., and Patel, S.N. GripSense: Using Built-In Sensors to Detect Hand Posture and Pressure on Commodity Mobile Phones. In *proc. UIST '12*, ACM (2012), 545-554.
9. Gustafson, S., Holz, C., and Baudisch, P. Imaginary Phone: learning imaginary interfaces by transferring spatial memory from a familiar device. In *proc. UIST '11*, ACM (2011), 283-292.
10. Harrison, C. and Hudson, S. Using Shear as a Supplemental Two-Dimensional Input Channel for Rich Touchscreen Interaction. In *proc. CHI '12*, ACM (2012), 3149-3152.
11. Harrison, C., Schwarz, J. and Hudson, S.E. TapSense: enhancing finger interaction on touch surfaces. In *proc. UIST '11*, ACM (2011), 627-634.
12. Heo, S. and Lee, G. Force gestures: augmenting touch screen gestures with normal and tangential forces. In *proc. UIST '11*, ACM (2011), 621-626.
13. Heo, S. and Lee, G. ForceTap: extending the input vocabulary of mobile touch screens by adding tap gestures. In *proc. MobileHCI '11*, ACM (2011), 113-122.
14. Heo, S. and Lee, G. Indirect shear force estimation for multi-point shear force operations. In *proc. CHI '13*, ACM (2013), 281-284.
15. Hinckley, K. and Song, H. Sensor synaesthesia: touch in motion, and motion in touch. In *proc. CHI '11*, ACM (2011), 801-810.
16. Karat, J., McDonald, J.E., and Anderson, M. A comparison of menu selection techniques: touch panel, mouse and keyboard. *International Journal of Man-Machine Studies 25*, 1 (1986), 73–88.
17. Kin, K., Agrawala, M., and DeRose, T. Determining the benefits of direct-touch, bimanual, and multifinger input on a multitouch workstation. In *proc. GI '09*, Canadian Information Processing Society (2009), 119-124.
18. Microsoft MSDN, http://msdn.microsoft.com/en-us/library/windows/desktop/bb760404(v=vs.85).aspx
19. Miyaki, T. and Rekimoto, J. GraspZoom: zooming and scrolling control model for single-handed mobile interaction. In *proc. MobileHCI '09*, ACM (2009), 11:1-11:4.
20. Müller, H., Gove, J., and Webb, J. Understanding Tablet Use: A Multi-Method Exploration. In *proc. MobileHCI '12*, ACM (2012), 1-10.
21. Myers, C.S. and Rabiner, L.R. A comparative study of several dynamic time-warping algorithms for connected word recognition. *The Bell System Technical J. 60*, 7 (1981), 1389-1409.
22. Research In Motion™, SurePress™ Technology. http://us.blackberry.com/specifications/communication/surepress-touch-screen.html
23. Roth, V. and Turner, T., Bezel swipe: conflict-free scrolling and multiple selection on mobile touch screen devices. In *proc. CHI '09*, ACM (2009), 1523-1526.
24. Roudaut, A., Lecolinet, E., and Guiard, Y. MicroRolls: expanding touch-screen input vocabulary by distinguishing rolls vs. slides of the thumb. In *proc. CHI '09*, ACM (2009), 927-936.
25. Rubine, D. Specifying gestures by example. In *proc. SIGGRAPH '91*, ACM (1991), 329-337.
26. Sears, A. and Shneiderman, B. High precision touchscreens: design strategies and comparisons with a mouse. *International Journal of Man-Machine Studies 34*, 4 (1991), 593–613.
27. Serrano, M., Lecolinet, E., and Guiard, Y. Bezel-Tap gestures: quick activation of commands from sleep mode on tablets. In *proc. CHI '13*, ACM (2013), 3027-3036.
28. Wagner, J., Huot, S., and Mackay, W. BiTouch and BiPad: designing bimanual interaction for hand-held tablets. In *proc. CHI '12*, ACM (2012), 2317-2326.
29. Wang, F., and Ren, X. Empirical evaluation for finger input properties in multi-touch interaction. In *proc. CHI '09*, ACM (2009), 1063-1072.
30. Wang, F., Cao, X., Ren, X., and Irani, P. Detecting and leveraging finger orientation for interaction with direct-touch surfaces, In *proc. UIST '09*, ACM (2009), 23-32.
31. Wobbrock, J., Wilson, A., and Li, Y. Gestures without libraries, toolkits or training: a $1 recognizer for user interface prototypes. In *Proc. UIST '07*, ACM (2007), 159-168.
32. Zhao, S., Maneesh, A., and Hinckley, K. Zone and polygon menus: using relative position to increase the breadth of multi-stroke marking menus, In *Proc. CHI '06*, ACM (2006), 1077-1086.

LinearDragger: a Linear Selector for One-finger Target Acquisition

Oscar Kin-Chung Au
City University of Hong Kong
Hong Kong
kincau@cityu.edu.hk

Xiaojun Su
City University of Hong Kong
Hong Kong
xiaojun.su88@gmail.com

Rynson W.H. Lau
City University of Hong Kong
Hong Kong
rynson.lau@cityu.edu.hk

ABSTRACT
Touch input is increasingly popular nowadays, especially for mobile devices such as smartphones and tablet computers. However, the human finger has considerably large fingertip size and finger input is imprecise. As such, acquiring small targets on a touch screen is still a challenging task. In this paper, we present the *LinearDragger*, a new and integrated one-finger target acquisition technique for small and clustered targets. The proposed method has three advantages. First, it allows users to select targets in dense clustered groups easily with a single touch-drag-release operation. Second, it maps the 2D selection problem into a more precise 1D selection problem, which is independent of the target distribution. Third, it avoids finger occlusion and does not create visual distraction. As a result, it is particularly suitable for applications with dense targets and rich visual elements. Results of our controlled experiments show that when selecting small targets, *LinearDragger* takes about 70% and 30% less selection time than target acquisition without using any techniques and with the state-of-the-art target acquisition technique that involves a single touch operation, respectively, while maintaining a reasonable error rate.

Author Keywords
target acquisition; touch input; dense target selection.

ACM Classification Keywords
H.5.2 User Interfaces: Graphical user interfaces (GUI), Interaction styles; I.3.6 Methodology and Techniques: Interaction techniques

General Terms
Human Factors; Design

INTRODUCTION
Touch input is increasingly popular in the past decade due to the popularity of mobile devices, such as smartphones and tablet computers. Although it is extremely convenient and intuitive to use our finger, instead of a mouse, as an input device, it has one limitation. Human fingers have considerably large finger tip size, referred to as the "fat finger" problem [4], making it a challenging task for users to acquire small targets from dense target clusters due to two problems. First, the fat finger tip has low input precision. Second, it causes occlusion during target acquisition.

Several techniques have been introduced to address the input precision and occlusion problems in acquiring small targets. The snap-to-target technique [9, 18] partitions the entire screen space into tiles of selection regions using Voronoi tessellation, to ease small target acquisition. Although this method has been proven helpful in a sparse target layout, it shows little effect when the targets are clustered as there is no space to extend. Unfortunately, clustering of targets appears in many applications, such as selectable items in an online map (Figure 1(a)), clustered UI elements of a text editor (Figure 1(b)), crowds of characters in an online game (Figure 1(c)), and words and characters of document being selectable targets in a text editor (Figure 1(d)). To facilitate acquisition of clustered targets, *Starburst* [2] partitions the screen space by expanding clustered targets to form selectable regions. However, this often produces long and thin selectable regions, which may be difficult to acquire by the user. *Escape* [25] adopts both the contact positions and swiping directions to disambiguate the selection of targets in dense clusters. However both approaches require auxiliary visual elements as visual cues for target selection, leading to undesired visual distraction and potentially degraded performance in extremely dense target distributions (e.g., characters in a text document).

Several other techniques address the occlusion problem either by displaying the occluded local region or controlling the virtual cursor with different mapping methods. *Shift* [23] displays the local region occluded by the fingertip in a nearby empty space. The user may perform a precise control in the offset display to select small targets within the local region. Several virtual cursor techniques [20, 22, 11, 21] map the movement of the contact point to the virtual cursor motion, such that the user may control the cursor and select the desired target without occluding the target region. However all these techniques still require precise 2D touch control when working with small and clustered targets.

In this paper, we present the *LinearDragger*, an integrated one-finger target acquisition technique for small and clustered targets. Besides using only the contact point to determine the selected target, *LinearDragger* allows the user to select a target in a dense clustered group easily with a single touch-drag-release operation without the need to accurately point to the

CHI 2014, April 26–May 1, 2014, Toronto, Ontario, Canada.

http://dx.doi.org/10.1145/2556288.2557096

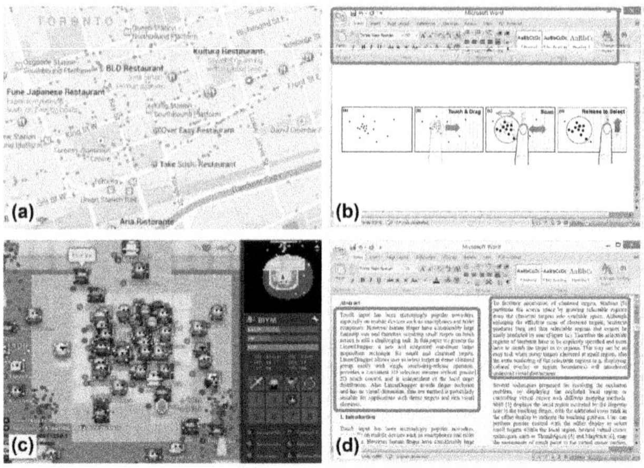

Figure 1. Non-uniform target distributions are common in many applications: (a) map application showing restaurants and stations, (b) menus and tool icons in a text editor, (c) crowds of characters in an online game, and (d) words and characters of a document in a text editor.

desired target. If the first contact point can unambiguously identify a single target, the user just lifts the contact finger to select the target, i.e., select by tapping. However if there are multiple items within the local region around the contact point, the user could simple drag the finger to explore and select the desired target as shown in Figure 2. All potential targets within the local region are ordered according to the finger moving direction, and are associated with effective regions of equal width. This converts the 2D selection problem into a 1D one, removing the need for precise 2D touch control. Hence, *LinearDragger* is independent of target distribution. In addition, as it does not have finger occlusion and introduces no auxiliary visual elements, it causes no visual distraction to the user. Thus, the proposed method is particularly suitable for applications with dense targets and rich visual elements. We have conducted a user study to evaluate the performance of *LinearDragger* under different conditions, and found that when selecting small targets, *LinearDragger* performs faster than *Escape* and *Shift* while having similar error rates.

RELATED WORK

Target Expansion

Target expansion is a common approach to facilitate small target acquisition with a pointing device. Methods of this approach include [24, 5], which adopt dynamic control-display ratio; [9, 15, 6], which increase the target's effective width by applying an area cursor; and [10, 19], which are based on zooming in the visual space.

On a touch screen, target expansion techniques [18, 2] enlarge the effective sizes of small targets by partitioning the screen space into tiles with each tile corresponding to a single target. The user may click anywhere inside a tile to select a target. In [18], Voronoi tessellation is used for screen partitioning such that the nearest target from the contact point is always selected. However, the performance of this approach is highly dependent on the distribution of the targets, with small tiles for clustered targets. This makes it difficult to acquire small targets. *Starburst* [2] partitions the screen space by extending the tiles of all clustered targets from the cluster to the surrounding empty space, resulting in thin and lengthy pathways. Hence, the selectable regions of *Starburst* have to be explicitly specified and the user has to visually trace the region of the target. This may not be an easy task when many targets are clustered in a tight area. In addition, the display of the selectable regions, drawn as colored overlay or region boundaries, introduces undesired visual distractions.

Zooming is another common approach in expanding the target sizes for easier exploration and selection. In [3], a precise pointing technique with two-handed interaction is proposed. With a secondary finger to help adjust the level of magnification, the primary finger may perform precise selection in the zoomed region. Similarly, in [16], a bimanual zooming method is proposed, with zooming being operated by tapping with a secondary finger. Recently, a multitouch technique called *FingerGlass* is introduced [12], in which the user defines a local region with the first two contact fingers and the magnified local region is popped up for precise selection using the second hand. Although all these methods provide intuitive interaction, two-handed operation is not practical in many situations, such as working with a handheld device.

There are also zooming techniques that involve only single-finger interactions. In [16], a rubbing gesture is introduced for zooming, which can be integrated with the panning operation using only a single finger. In [21], a two-stage selection method is proposed. The user first taps on the screen to popup a magnified viewport of the local area, and then taps again to select the target within this viewport. *Excentric Labeling* [7] is a technique to label a neighborhood of objects around the cursor, in a layout comfortable for human eyes. It can be transformed to a target acquisition technique using hierarchical operations. The main drawback of these techniques is that zooming and target selection have to be performed in separated steps. In constrast, *LinearDragger* integrates zooming and target selection into a single one-finger operation, which reduces operation complexity and is applicable in almost all selection scenarios.

Occlusion Avoidance

Occlusion is a common problem of touch screen interactions – due to the size of the finger tip, selectable objects can be easily occluded by the contact finger during target selection. The *Offset Cursor* technique [20] is one of the earlier notable works to address this problem. It places a displaced cursor above the actual contact point, and the item under the cursor is selected when the user releases the finger. In [22], a stabilization technique is proposed for the *Offset Cursor* to provide faster and more accurate selection of small targets. However, the main drawbacks of *Offset Cursor* are that the precise cursor position is unknown until the finger touches the screen and it is not possible to select targets at the bottom of the screen since the offset position is always above the finger. In [23], an improved technique, called *Shift*, is introduced. It displays a copy of the local region occluded by the finger at a nearby position. The selection hotspot remains under the fingertip. The user may select any small object under the finger while watching the offset display. Results of the user study show that *Shift* is more accurate than traditional

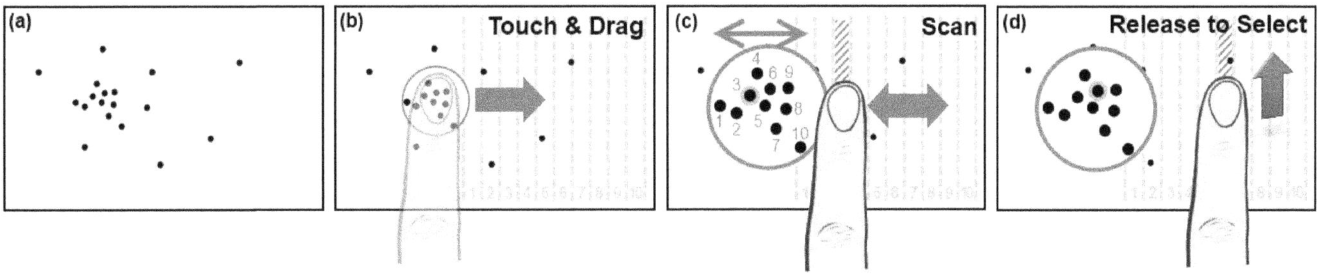

Figure 2. Overview of LinearDragger. (a) It is difficult to select a target from a clustered group of selectable objects. (b) LinearDragger is activated when the finger touches and drags on the touch screen. The contact position defines a region of interest (ROI), containing the user's desired target. (c) As the user continues dragging his finger, LinearDragger scans the potential targets within the ROI one by one. The scanning order is determined by the initial dragging direction. (d) The user just lifts the finger to select the desired target.

finger selection on small targets and faster than the original *Offset Cursor* on larger targets.

There are other virtual cursor techniques that involve complex mapping between finger gesture and cursor motion. In [3], an offset cursor located at the midpoint of two contact fingers is proposed. In [21], an occlusion avoidance method called *MagStick* is proposed. The user presses an arbitrary position on the screen to define a reference point and a virtual cursor. The virtual cursor will then be controlled by the dragging motion of the contact finger, such that the cursor motion is opposite to the dragging motion with respect to the reference point. In [18], a snap-to-target technique is applied to the virtual cursor to increase the target sizes in motion space. *Thumbspace* [11] is a technique to allow the user to reach a large screen space from a small input area using the thumb. It maps the input area to the whole screen and magnifies the user's finger motion in the input area to the mapped screen. Although *ThumbSpace* and *MagStick* resolve the occlusion problem, similar to the *Offset Cursor*, they require precise 2D touch control to acquire small targets.

Precision Refinement

Another problem of touch screen interactions is that the human finger has limited precision due to the fat finger tip. In order to acquire dense and small targets, precision refinement methods are proposed to ease target selection. In [1], *Cross-Lever* and *Precision-Handle* are introduced to increase the motion space of the virtual cursor on the touch screen. *Cross-Lever* involves controlling the intersection point between two crossed lines. It provides high precision control but is time consuming to use. *Precision-Handle* involves mapping a faction of the contact finger motion to the virtual cursor, thus enlarging the motor space and increasing the selection precision. Both techniques require separate operation steps for region selection, precise handle control and selection validation, which could potentially degrade selection performance and user experience.

In [25], a precision refinement technique called *Escape* is proposed. It allows user to select targets by swiping gestures, cued by both the target position and appearance. By swiping the fingertip in one of the predefined directions, the closest object specified with this swiping direction will be selected. In [14], the swiping gesture is applied to touch screen widgets to resolve ambiguity by assigning different swiping directions to adjacent widgets. The *Enhanced Area Cursor* [8] allows the user to first specify a coarse area and then selects the desired target within the area by invoking an angular menu with swiping gesture. However as these techniques have limited possible swiping orientations, ambiguity in swiping directions may not be completely avoided in cases of extreme dense target distributions. The swiping directions are further limited for targets near to the boundary of the screen, as the swiping gesture cannot go beyond the edge of the screen. To indicate the swiping directions of all selectable objects, a special color scheme and icon design are introduced. However, this leads to visual distractions and limits the usage of customized symbols and labels, such as the map application shown in Figure 1(a). SQUAD [13] is a progressive refinement technique for target acquisition in a 3D space. It resolves the problems of dense targets and occlusion in 3D target selection by applying a sequence of refinement operations to filter out the unwanted targets.

DESIGN AND IMPLEMENTATION

In this section, we first give an overview design of *LinearDragger* and then the implementation details.

LinearDragger is activated by dragging the finger away in any direction from the user's specified initial region (see Figure 2 and the accompanying video). A *region of interest* (ROI) is defined as the user's finger first touches the screen. We set the ROI as a circular area, with the center being the first contact point of the finger. The radius of the ROI is adjustable and its optimized value depends on the screen size and the average size of the finger tips of the user group. All selectable targets within the ROI are considered as the set of *potential targets*. We assume that one of these potential targets is the user's *desired target*.

The user drags the finger to linearly scan (and highlight) the potential targets one by one (Figure 2(b)). The order of scanning is determined by the moving direction of the contact finger. It starts from the opposite end and scans along the direction of the finger motion, as the user keeps dragging the finger away from the first contact point (Figure 2(c)). The user may select an highlighted target anytime by lifting the contact finger up (Figure 2(d)). Zooming of the ROI is invoked as the finger drags and leaves the ROI. This facilitates better visual feedback with small targets. To minimize visual distraction and avoid unnecessary focus switching, all the visual elements about the activation areas in Figures 2, 3 and 4 (i.e., the dashed lines, the shaded region and numbers) are for illustration purpose only; they are not shown on the screen.

The distance between the current position and the first contact point of the contact finger determines which of the potential targets is focused and highlighted. This essentially defines a uniform 1D mapping between the ordered list of potential targets and the moving distance of the contact finger from the first contact point. The user may intuitively scan through the potential targets one by one by dragging the contact finger in the scanning orientation. This 1D mapping provides a *constant effective width* for all potential targets and avoids the need for precise selection in a 2D space, which is required by methods such as *MagStick* [21] and *ThumbSpace* [11].

The user is free to move the contact finger in any direction to activate *LinearDragger*. The moving direction may depend on the user's preference or the location of the ROI on the screen. This allows the user to select any targets on the screen, including those located near to the boundary/corner of the screen (Figure 3(b)).

In general, *LinearDragger* has the following nice properties:

- **Single-handed one-finger interaction** – *LinearDragger* only requires one finger to operate, which is perfectly suitable for use in a small mobile device being held by one hand and operated with a single finger.
- **Single action** – It combines activation, selection and dismissal into a single touch action.
- **Intuitive to use** – By remapping the potential targets into a linear list, it provides a simple 1D selection paradigm.
- **Insensitive to target distributions** – The targets' effective widths are independent on target density and distribution. The user can easily acquire small and clustered targets without precise operation.
- **No finger occlusion** – The contact finger always drags away from the ROI, and hence no finger occlusion occurs.
- **No visual distraction** – It does not introduce any visual distraction as no extra widgets / elements are shown. (Note that the zoomed ROI may possibly lead to visual distraction, but this zooming feature is optional and does not affect the selection operation of *LinearDragger*.)
- **Adaptable to different screen sizes** – *LinearDragger* can be operated with any finger and different device holding gestures. Thus, it is applicable to large tablets or even wall-sized touch screens.

Cancellation Mechanisms

We provide two different mechanisms for the user to dismiss *LinearDragger* and cancel the selection. The first mechanism adopts an additional waiting step after the user has selected a potential target by lifting the contact finger. Within the waiting period, the user may tap the screen at any location to cancel the selection and dismiss the focusing ROI. In our study,

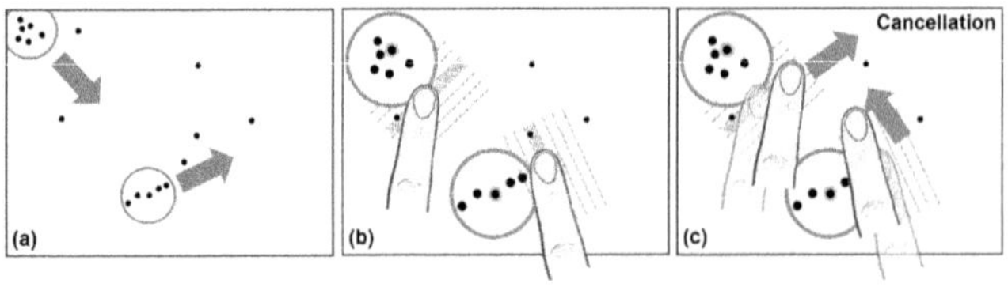

Figure 3. (a) The user may drag the finger in any direction to activate *LinearDragger*. (b) The zoomed ROI will be located within the screen, even if the original ROI may be located near to the screen boundary. (c) The user may cancel the selection and dismiss *LinearDragger* by moving the finger in the orthogonal direction to the original dragging direction.

we set the additional waiting period as 1 second, which is long enough for the user to confirm the selected target or to cancel the selection if necessary. However, these additional waiting period and tapping step introduce extra user interaction and longer operation time.

To achieve a better performance, we have designed another cancellation mechanism, which only requires a simple step to cancel the selection. After *LinearDragger* is activated, the user may cancel the selection and dismiss *LinearDragger* by moving the contact finger roughly in the *orthogonal direction* to the original dragging direction (Figure 3(c)). This design retains the feature of a simple touch-drag-release interaction.

We have conducted a preliminary user study on both cancellation mechanisms and found that the orthogonal dragging method gives better performance.

Integration with Target Expansion Techniques

LinearDragger can be easily integrated to existing target expansion techniques. In our experiments, we have integrated *LinearDragger* with the snap-to-target approach of the Bubble cursor [9], which continuously sets the selection focus to the target closest to the cursor location. This approach effectively partitions the screen space using Voronoi tessellation.

In our implementation, we adopt the Bubble Cursor approach such that for sparse regions, the user may directly select a target by tapping on it or the nearby space without ambiguity. For dense regions, the user may activate *LinearDragger* to help select a target by a simple dragging operation.

Implementation

LinearDragger maps the 1D movement of the contact finger to the focus switching of the potential targets. This is the key for the user to efficiently access all potential targets in the ROI with intuitive and controllable input. We have experimented two different mapping functions in our implementation. The first one uses a constant effective width, as described before. This is based on the assumption that all potential targets are equally important. The second one uses a linearly scaled effective width. It is based on the assumption that a potential target nearer to the first contact point is more likely to be the intended target.

The first mapping function uses a constant effective width, as shown in Figures 2 and 3. It allows easy control in target scanning. Specifically, it is formulated as:

$$k = \begin{cases} \lfloor (d - d_{min})/EW_{base} \rfloor + 1, & \text{if } d > d_{min} \\ 1, & \text{otherwise} \end{cases} \quad (1)$$

where k is the 1-based index of the current focused target. d is the projected distance from the current contact point to the first contact point. d_{min} is the minimal distance threshold. EW_{base} is the predefined effective width (see Figure 4(a)). The projected distance is defined as $d = (p - p_0) \cdot v$, where p and p_0 are the positions of the current contact point and the first contact point, respectively, and v is the normalized vector of the initial moving direction computed from the first few finger movement samples. The threshold distance, d_{min}, controls how long the finger should be dragged before the scanning is started, and depends on the size of the finger since the contact finger should not occlude the ROI during scanning and selection. In our experiments, we set $d_{min} = 100$ pixels (about $13.5mm$) for the main testing device, as this size is close to the average size of the finger tip.

The constant effective width gives a more predictable control. However, users may sometimes prefer the targets closer to the first contact point to be selected easier than others in the ROI. Hence, we also introduce the linearly scaled effective width, which associates different effective widths to different potential targets, with targets closer to the first contact point having larger effective widths, i.e., easier to be selected. Specifically, an extra expansion is added to the effective width of each target, such that the closest target received the maximum expansion of EW_{ex}, and the expansion reduces linearly along the two sides of the ordered list (Figure 4(b)).

We have conducted an informal preliminary study to evaluate how these two mapping methods affect the performance of *LinearDragger*. We have found that the constant effective width always gives better performance and all participants prefer this mapping method because of its predictable control. Since we hide the activation areas with no visualization support, users found it difficult to perform selection and were confused by the non-uniform size of activation areas with the linearly scaled mapping method.

To facilitate better visual feedback, a local expansion in the visual space of the ROI is optionally provided (Figures 2 and 3). The ratio of zooming is controlled by distance d (see Eq. 1), such that the magnified region will occupy the empty space between the current finger location and the original ROI. Specifically, the zooming ratio r is defined as:

$$\tilde{r} = \begin{cases} (d - d_{min})/s + 1, & \text{if } d > d_{min} \\ 1, & \text{otherwise} \end{cases} \quad (2)$$

$$r = \min(\tilde{r}, r_{max}) \quad (3)$$

where s determines the speed of zooming. r_{max} is the maximum zooming ratio. In our experiments, we set $r_{max} = 2.5$ and $s = d_{min}$.

If the orthogonal dragging method is adopted for cancellation of the selection, we need to determine when the user moves the contact finger in the orthogonal direction to the original dragging direction. We compare the magnitude of the orthogonal component of the movement vector with the pre-specified threshold: $|(p - p_0) \times v| > \tau$. In all our experiments, we set $\tau = 50$ pixels (or $6.75mm$).

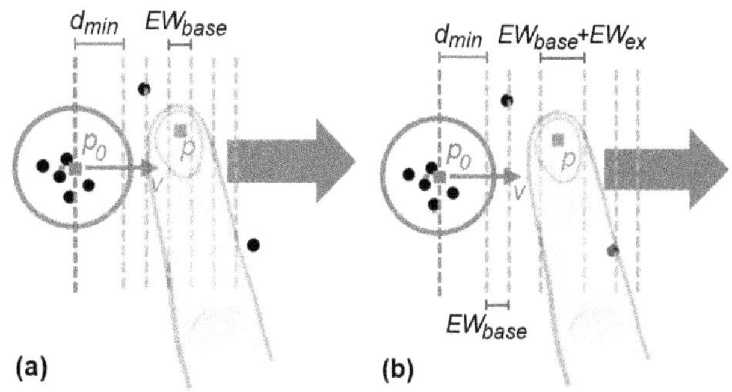

Figure 4. We have designed two mapping functions for mapping the finger motion to the scanning speed of the potential targets: (a) linear mapping with constant effective width, and (b) non-linear mapping that gives larger effective widths to targets closer to the initial contact point.

PRELIMINARY STUDY 1: SIZE OF THE ROI

Before comparing *LinearDragger* with other touch-based target acquisition techniques, we first conducted a preliminary study to evaluate how the size of the ROI affects the performance of the proposed method.

Apparatus

The experiment was conducted on an Acer W3-810 tablet computer, with an $8.1''$ ($20.6cm$) touch screen running MS Windows 8. The screen is of $17.5cm \times 11cm$ and has a resolution of 1280×800 (73.6 pixels/cm). Participants were free to hold the tablet in any way or to place it on a table. The experimental application was implemented using C# and .Net Framework, and displayed in full screen mode.

Participants

Eight participants (4 males and 4 females) between the age of 24 to 29 were recruited. They were mainly postgraduate students. All had experience with computers, touchscreen tablets and smart phones, and happened to be right handed. All participants were recruited from a university (recruitment posters were posted for open recruitment). Each of them was given a gift voucher of USD13 for participating in the user study.

Procedure and Design

At the beginning of the task, a button of $2cm \times 2cm$ was displayed at the middle-right of the screen. Once the participant tapped the button, 12 circular candidate targets of 12 pixels ($1.6mm$) in diameter were distributed randomly within a circular region of 100 pixels ($13.5mm$) in diameter, such that no targets overlap each other. In each task, participants were asked to select the desired target among the candidate targets as accurate and fast as possible. The desired target is highlighted in blue, while other candidate targets are filled in black color. Besides having the clustered targets within the circular region, 20 distracter targets of the same size as the clustered targets were placed randomly in the remaining empty space (Figure 5(a)). Each participant performed the experiment in two separate sessions. One session was divided into two ROI size configurations: 26 and 40 pixels (or $3.6mm$ and $5.4mm$) in diameter. Another session was divided into three ROI size configurations: 52, 66 and 80 pixels (or $7.2mm$, $9.0mm$ and $10.8mm$) in diameter. For each ROI size configuration, each participant was asked to perform fifty selection tasks. Each participant spent approximately one hour in total on the two sessions.

The sizes of the ROI were chosen based on the finding by [17] that objects should be at least $9.2mm \times 9.2mm$ in size in order to keep the selection error rates low. Hence, we adopted a ROI with a similar reference size ($9mm$ in diameter), plus a larger size and three smaller sizes (40% to 120% of the reference) in this experiment.

We recorded the duration between the user tapping the start button and when the target selection task was completed. The participants were allowed to use the orthogonal dragging mechanism to cancel a selection process. If a participant selected a wrong target or cancelled the selection before selecting the desired target, the task would be restarted until the correct target was selected and the recorded time would be accumulated. Before the experiment, we explained the details of the procedure and gave the participant a short duration of 5 to 10 minutes to get familiar with the interface. A total of $8 \times 5 \times 50 = 2,000$ selection tasks were performed in this experiment, with each participant completed 250 tasks.

Results

When the size of the ROI is set to 26, 40, 52, 66, and 80 pixels ($3.6/5.4/7.2/9.0/10.8mm$), the mean selection times were $3180ms$, $2740ms$, $2280ms$, $3230ms$, and $3520ms$, and the corresponding error rates were 12.1%, 9.3%, 4.6%, 11.3% and 13.7%, respectively. There was a significant effect on the mean selection time ($F_{(4,28)}$=25.32, p<0.001) and the error rate ($F_{(4,28)}$=5.71, p<0.001).

Discussion

We observe that both the selection time and the error rate are at the minimum when the size of the ROI is 52 pixels. This may due to the fact that a larger ROI size leads to more targets being included in the scanning. Thus, participants needed to look through more candidate targets, resulting in a longer selection time and a larger error rate. On the other hand, if the size of the ROI is too small, it is much harder for the participants to specify the ROI so as to include the desired target. Hence, the participants needed to redo the selection, which affected the overall performance. As such, we fixed the size of the ROI to 52 pixels ($7.2mm$) for the remaining experiments presented in the paper, unless specified otherwise.

PRELIMINARY STUDY 2: CANCELLATION MECHANISM

We also conducted another preliminary study to evaluate the two proposed cancellation mechanisms. Note that the diameter of the ROI was set to 52 pixels ($7.2mm$) as stated in preliminary study 1.

Apparatus and Participants

Same as those in preliminary study 1.

Procedure and Design

Participants were asked to perform two different types of tasks in this experiment.

In the first session, we evaluated the selection performance of both cancellation mechanisms. We used the same selection task as described in preliminary study 1, and asked participants to select the desired targets using the specified cancellation mechanisms. Recall that with the orthogonal dragging mechanism, only a single touch-drag-release operation is used for selection, while for the other mechanism, an additional waiting time is needed to validate the selection. Each participant performed two groups of 50 selection tasks in one session, each group using one cancellation mechanism.

The second session of the experiment is to evaluate the accuracy of the cancellation mechanisms. With the same setting as the first session, we asked the participants to cancel the selection with the specified cancellation method after focusing on the desired target. (Hence, the task was completed if the desired target was the last highlighted target before the cancellation was performed.) The whole experiment lasted for about an hour and as in preliminary study 1, after the detailed explanation provided in each session, participants could practice for a short duration. In this experiment, a total of $8 \times 2 \times 50 = 800$ selection tasks and $8 \times 2 \times 50 = 800$ cancellation tasks were performed. The completion times of all selection tasks and successful rates of the cancellation tasks were recorded.

Results

Experimental results show that the mean selection time using Orthogonal Dragging was $2310ms$ with a cancellation accuracy of 97.5%, while the mean selection time using Additional Tap was $3400ms$ with a cancellation accuracy of 99.4%. Repeated measures analysis of variance shows that different cancellation mechanisms have significant effect on selection time ($F_{(1,7)}=15.30, p<0.001$)) but no significant effect on cancellation accuracy.

Discussion

We can see that using Additional Tap was slower than using Orthogonal Dragging by around $1s$ for the target selecting tasks. This was mainly caused by the extra waiting time needed for the system to validate the target selection. Because of their similar accuracy but different performances, we chose to use Orthogonal Dragging as the cancellation mechanism in *LinearDragger* in the main experiment.

MAIN EXPERIMENT: PERFORMANCE COMPARISON

After determining the size of the ROI and the cancellation mechanism, we conducted the main experiment to quantitatively evaluate the performance of *LinearDragger*. We compared it with unaided touch pointing *DirectTouch*, which served as a baseline, the *Bubble* Cursor [9], which is a common target expansion approach for selecting small targets, *Shift* [23] and *Escape* [25], which are two alternative single-touch target selection techniques supporting high precision selection.

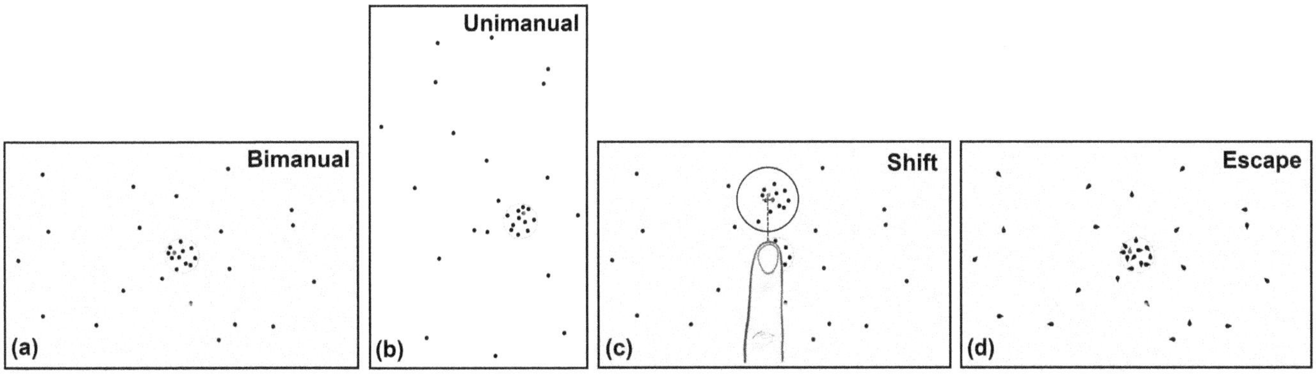

Figure 5. Cluster placements for different operation modes: (a) Bimanual mode and (b) Unimanual mode; and illustrations of the display style of two alternative selection techniques: (c) Shift [23] and (d) Escape [25].

The main reason for selecting *Shift*, *Escape* and *Bubble* as the methods for comparison is that all three methods, like *LinearDragger*, involve only single touch-drag-release operation. Note that when using *Bubble* on a touch input device, the user may drag the touching finger to highlight different targets (i.e., the target closest to the touch point), even though the highlighted target may be occluded by the touching finger. On the other hand, there are techniques that involve multiple operations, such as *TapTap* [21], which involves separated zooming and selection operation and is shown to outperform *Shift*. Although it would be interesting to compare *LinearDragger* with this type of methods, the main focus of this user study is to evaluate the performance of the target selection methods using the same touch-drag-release operation, and we leave this issue as a future work.

To better evaluate the performance in different operating scenarios, we also introduced the operation mode as one of the factors of the experiment. Participants were instructed to use both hands (bimanual mode) or single hand (unimanual mode) to perform the selection tasks. Specifically, in bimanual mode, participants need to hold the device with the non-dominant hand and perform selection with the dominant hand. In unimanual mode, participants need to hold the device and perform the tasks with the same hand. In both operation modes, participants were free to use any finger of the specified hand to complete the selection tasks.

Apparatus

Same as those in preliminary studies 1 and 2.

Participants

Twelve adult participants (8 females and 4 males) of age 24 to 29 were recruited. All participants happened to be right-handed and had experience in using computers, tablets and smart phones with touch screens. They were all recruited from a university (recruitment posters were posted for open recruitment). Each of them was given a gift voucher of USD13 for participating in the user study.

Procedure and Design

We followed the same general procedure as in preliminary study 1. Participants were required to select the desired target highlighted in blue from a cluster of candidate targets. We used parameter **Count** to control the total number of the clustered targets. The clustered targets were located within a circular region of 100 pixels ($13.5mm$) in diameter, such that no targets overlapped each other. The circular region was placed at the center of the touchscreen in the bimanual mode (Figure 5(a)) and at the bottom-right quarter ($35mm$ and $70mm$ from the right and bottom edges, respectively) in the unimanual mode (Figure 5(b)), in order to facilitate selection with the thumb of the holding hand. In addition, 20 distracter targets having the same size as the clustered targets were placed in the empty space outside the circular region.

Our experiment was a $5 \times 4 \times 3 \times 2$ within-participant design with the following factors: (1) Five techniques **TECH** for comparison: *LinearDragger*, *DirectTouch*, *Bubble*, *Escape* and *Shift*. (2) Four target sizes **Size**: 6, 12, 18 and 24 pixels ($0.8/1.6/2.4/3.2mm$). (3) Three numbers of clustered targets **Count**: 8, 12 and 16. (We set the maximum number of clustered targets to 16 because if we put too many targets into the clustered region of a diameter $13.6mm$, they would likely overlap and occlude each other.) (4) Two operation modes **Mode**: bimanual and unimanual.

Each participant performed the experiment in 2 sessions of different operation modes, each session was divided into 5 groups of different techniques. Each **TECH** group was further divided into 12 subgroups of different combinations of **Size** and **Count**. Within each subgroup, each participant needed to complete 20 selection tasks. In the experiment, **Mode** was counterbalanced, **TECH** (except *DirectTouch*) was ordered in a balanced Latin-square with *DirectTouch* always being used at the end, and the order of subgroups was randomized. A total of 28,800 selection tasks were included in the experiment. Similar to the preliminary studies, before using each operation mode and technique, participants were instructed and given a 5–10 minute warm-up session to get familiar with the technique and the tasks.

We implemented *Shift* [23] with the zero escalation time. This is because in each trial, all clustered targets were of the same small size (with a maximum size of $3.2mm$) packed within a small area. Hence, we assumed that the pop-up of the occluded area was always needed by the participants. However, no refinement or correction of the touching position was used as we would like to provide a consistent touching point precision and control among all techniques including *DirectTouch* and *Bubble*, which are very sensitive to the touching positions. *Escape* [25] was implemented with 8-directional beak-shape targets. Note that unlike the original design in [25], we did not apply any color scheme as visual cues, as we would like to have a similar display complexity and style for all tested techniques. (All targets were in black with the desired target in blue.) Figure 5(c) shows the pop-up local copy of the occluded area and Figure 5(d) shows the same set of clustered targets with the beak-shape indicators. For *LinearDragger*, we set the size of the ROI to 52 pixels ($7.2mm$) and used the Orthogonal Dragging cancellation mechanism. In order to have a fair evaluation on *LinearDragger*, we disabled the target expansion feature (i.e., the Bubble cursor approach) in the main experiment.

Results

Selection Time

Repeated measures analysis shows a significant main effect for **TECH** ($F_{(4,44)} = 32.4, p < 0.0001; F_{(4,44)} = 48.72, p < 0.0001$), **Size** ($F_{(3,33)} = 5.0, p = 0.0022; F_{(3,33)} = 7.91, p < 0.0001$) and **Count** ($F_{(2,22)} = 3.31, p = 0.0481; F_{(2,22)} = 3.35, p = 0.0371$) on both bimanual and unimanual modes, respectively. The mean selection time was $2557ms$ for *LinearDragger*, $8336ms$ for *DirectTouch*, $3989ms$ for *Bubble*, $4384ms$ for *Escape* and $3574ms$ for *Shift*. The following significant interactions are also observed: **TECH** × **Size** ($F_{(12,132)} = 2.72, p = 0.0021; F_{(12,132)} = 2.68, p < 0.0001$) and **TECH** × **Count** ($F_{(8,88)} = 2.54, p = 0.0113; F_{(8,88)} = 2.30, p = 0.0230$) for bimanual mode and unimanual mode, respectively.

Figures 6 and 7 show the mean selection times of different techniques grouped by **Size** and **Count**, using bimanual mode and unimanual mode, respectively. We can observe that *LinearDragger* had the shortest mean selection time in most of the cases. *DirectTouch* had the worst performance among all selection techniques, particularly when the target size was small. We found that it was almost impossible for participants to select targets in size of 6 pixels (0.8 mm) using *DirectTouch*. Hence, we added a maximum movement time for each selection task 30s in our setting) to ensure that participants could complete the sessions within a reasonable amount of time, and a task would be terminated if it could not be finish in time. Since more that 80% of the selection tasks using *DirectTouch* and with target size of 6 pixels ($0.8mm$) could not be finished successfully in time, we decided to skip this combination of *DirectTouch* in the computation of average movement time and error rate. This does not affect the overall evaluation as *DirectTouch* only served as the baseline in our experiment. To gain a thorough understanding of the measurement, the Tukey HSD post-hoc tests are conducted to evaluate the significance in the performance gaps. Post-hoc tests analysis the significance in the performance difference among different techniques. We present the post-hoc test result in the following manner. A technique, T_1, has a rank higher than that of another technique, T_2, if and only if the post-hoc test shows that T_1 significantly outperforms T_2 under the given scenario.

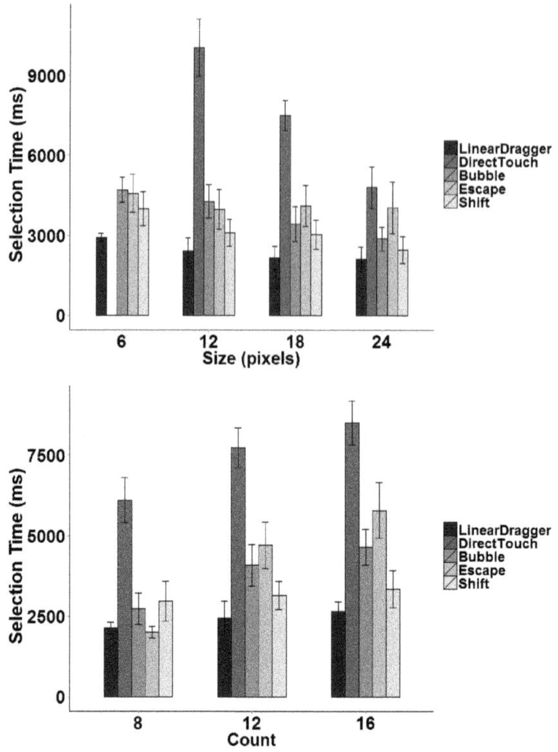

Figure 6. The selection times of different techniques grouped by Size (up) and Count (down), for the bimanual operation mode. The error bars are at the 95% confidential level.

The post-hoc test result shown in Table 1 reveals that *LinearDragger* was significantly faster than all other methods, for target sizes smaller than 18 pixels ($2.4mm$). When the target size was set to 24 pixels ($3.2mm$), there was no significant difference in the mean selection time among *LinearDragger*, *Bubble* and *Shift* in the bimanual operation mode. The post-hoc test result shown in Table 2 reveals that both *LinearDragger* and *Escape* performed the best and were significantly faster than *DirectTouch*, *Bubble* and *Shift* when **Count** was set to 8, in both operation modes. However, the performance of *Escape* degraded dramatically when **Count** increased.

Error Rate

Repeated measures analysis of variance shows that the error rate was significantly affected by **TECH** ($F_{(4,44)} = 8.31, p < 0.0001; F_{(4,44)} = 10.82, p < 0.0001$) for bimanual mode and unimanual mode, respectively. The mean error rate was 7.2% for *LinearDragger*, 35.3% for *DirectTouch*, 8.5% for *Bubble*, 29.1% for *Escape* and 9.7% for *Shift*. The significant interactions **TECH**× **Count**($F_{(8,88)} = 5.42, p < 0.0001; F_{(8,88)} = 4.93, p < 0.0001$) are also observed for bimanual and unimanual modes, respectively.

Discussion

By comparing Figures 6 and 7, we observe that target selection in unimanual mode took much more time than in bimanual mode. This can be easily explained as target selection us-

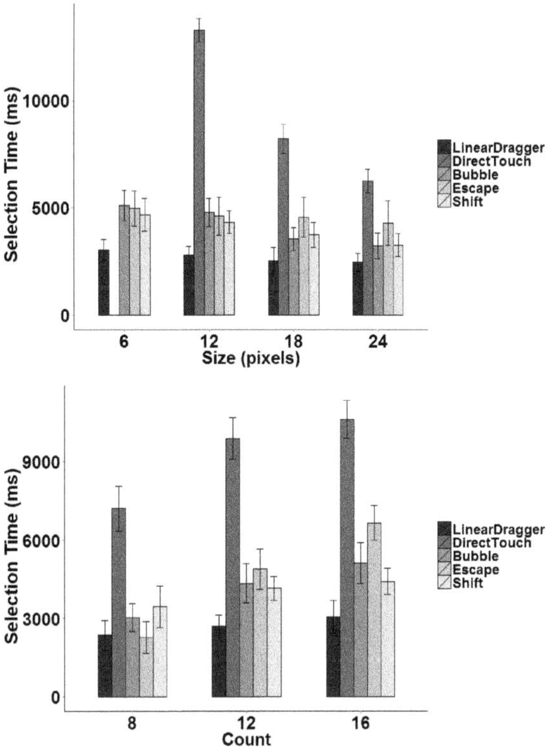

Figure 7. The selection times of different techniques grouped by Size (up) and Count (down), for the unimanual operation mode. The error bars are at the 95% confidential level.

ing both hands provides stabler control over the device than using a single hand. Besides, this effect is especially significant for *Shift* since it requires precise touch control while other techniques (except *DirectTouch*) can tolerate a noisier touch input.

From the post-hoc test result shown in Table 1, we observe that the performance of *Shift* is correlated with the target size – when the target size increased, the selection time of *Shift* decreased significantly. This is due to the fact that the operation of *Shift* is similar to *DirectTouch* but without the occlusion problem. Thus, its performance is directly related to the effective size of the target.

From the post-hoc test result shown in Table 2, we observe that *Escape* relies on assigning distinguishable swiping directions to the crowded targets. When **Count** becomes greater than the number of possible swiping directions, multiple targets in the cluster will be assigned with the same swiping direction, making them more difficult to be selected. On the other hand, as both *DirectTouch* and *Bubble* do not resolve the occlusion problem, they incurred a considerable amount of selection errors. As excepted, the performance of *Bubble* degraded with dense target distributions, since the targets' effective areas become smaller in denser cluster and are more often occluded by the finger tip.

Qualitative Results

Participants were asked to rank the techniques by subjective preference in a post-hoc questionnaire. Eight participants ranked *LinearDragger* as their preferred technique, while four ranked *Shift* as their preferred technique and *LinearDragger* as second. Most participants commented that they liked *Escape* for Count less than 8 but not very helpful for larger cluster sizes.

Tukey HSD test ($\alpha = 0.05$)						
Mode	Size	Rank				
		LG	DT	B	E	S
Bimanual	6	1	-	3	3	2
	12	1	4	3	3	2
	18	1	4	2	3	2
	24	1	3	1	2	1
Unimanual	6	1	-	2	2	2
	12	1	3	2	2	2
	18	1	4	2	3	2
	24	1	4	2	3	2

LG = *LinearDragger*, DT = *DirectTouch*, B = *Bubble*, E = *Escape*, S = *Shift*

Table 1. Significant differences on mean selection time among TECH by Size, for bimanual (top) and unimanual (bottom) modes.

Tukey HSD test ($\alpha = 0.05$)						
Mode	Count	Rank				
		LG	DT	B	E	S
Bimanual	8	1	3	2	1	2
	12	1	4	3	3	2
	16	1	4	3	3	2
Unimanual	8	1	3	2	1	2
	12	1	4	2	3	2
	16	1	5	3	4	2

LG = *LinearDragger*, DT = *DirectTouch*, B = *Bubble*, E = *Escape*, S = *Shift*

Table 2. Significant differences on mean selection time among TECH by Count, for bimanual (top) and unimanual (bottom) modes.

CONCLUSION

This paper introduces *LinearDragger*, a new one-finger target acquisition technique for small and clustered targets. Our key contribution is a mapping approach to convert the 2D targeting selection problem to a 1D selection problem, with a simple touch-drag-release operation. Our technique gives constant effective width for all candidate targets, which is independent of the target distribution. This leads to a predictable and controllable selection interface. Results of our controlled experiments show that *LinearDragger* is a promising target acquisition technique for touch devices, and performs better than existing popular selection techniques that involve a single-touch operation, in terms of both selection time and error rate.

Limitations

LinearDragger may suffer from three limitations. First, as it is designed for acquiring a target from a predefined set of discrete targets, it may not be able to support selection of arbitrary screen points in a continuous 2D space. This may be an interesting issue for further research. Second, as *LinearDragger* overwrites the original dragging operation, it may not naturally support object dragging in some applications. However this can be easily addressed by adopting a tap-and-a-half operation to enter the object dragging mode after an object is being selected. Third, it is difficult to apply *LinearDragger* at the OS level without modifying individual client applications. However, as most recent OSs support rich touch APIs and dynamic reflection of UI elements from client applications, we believe that the proposed method can be integrated to the applications by introducing an additional global touch event hooking at the OS level, to convert appropriate dragging events into selection operations.

Future Work

As a future work, we would like to compare *LinearDragger* with other techniques involving different genres of touch operations, such as *TapTap* [21], which involves multiple tapping operations and is shown to outperform *Shift*, and to study user preferences about touch operations and other aspects. We would like to apply and evaluate *LinearDragger* in other application scenarios, such as multiple object selections. We would also like to investigate the possibility of applying *LinearDragger* in context-aware applications, such as an integrated interface including context menus.

ACKNOWLEDGEMENTS

We thank all the reviewers of this paper for the insightful comments and constructive suggestions. The work described in this paper was partially supported by two grants from City University of Hong Kong (CityU Reference No.: 7003056 and 7004155), and two GRF grants from the RGC of Hong Kong (RGC Reference No.: CityU 116010 and CityU 115112).

REFERENCES

1. Albinsson, P.-A., and Zhai, S. High precision touch screen interaction. In *Proc. ACM SIGCHI* (2003), 105–112.
2. Baudisch, P., Zotov, A., Cutrell, E., and Hinckley, K. Starburst: a target expansion algorithm for non-uniform target distributions. In *Proc. Working Conference on Advanced Visual Interfaces* (2008), 129–137.
3. Benko, H., Wilson, A., and Baudisch, P. Precise selection techniques for multi-touch screens. In *Proc. ACM SIGCHI* (2006), 1263–1272.
4. Bi, X., Li, Y., and Zhai, S. Fitts law: Modeling finger touch with fitts' law. In *Proc. ACM SIGCHI* (2013), 1363–1372.
5. Blanch, R., Guiard, Y., and Beaudouin-Lafon, M. Semantic pointing: improving target acquisition with control-display ratio adaptation. In *Proc. ACM SIGCHI* (2004), 519–526.
6. Chapuis, O., Labrune, J.-B., and Pietriga, E. Dynaspot: speed-dependent area cursor. In *Proc. ACM SIGCHI* (2009), 1391–1400.
7. Fekete, J.-D., and Plaisant, C. Excentric labeling: Dynamic neighborhood labeling for data visualization. In *Proc. ACM SIGCHI* (1999), 512–519.
8. Findlater, L., Jansen, A., Shinohara, K., Dixon, M., Kamb, P., Rakita, J., and Wobbrock, J. Enhanced area cursors: reducing fine pointing demands for people with motor impairments. In *Proc. ACM UIST* (2010), 153–162.
9. Grossman, T., and Balakrishnan, R. The bubble cursor: enhancing target acquisition by dynamic resizing of the cursor's activation area. In *Proc. ACM SIGCHI* (2005), 281–290.
10. Gutwin, C. Improving focus targeting in interactive fisheye views. In *Proc. ACM SIGCHI* (2002), 267–274.
11. Karlson, A., and Bederson, B. Thumbspace: generalized one-handed input for touchscreen-based mobile devices. In *Proc. INTERACT*, Springer (2007), 324–338.
12. Käser, D., Agrawala, M., and Pauly, M. Fingerglass: efficient multiscale interaction on multitouch screens. In *Proc. ACM SIGCHI* (2011), 1601–1610.
13. Kopper, R., Bacim, F., and Bowman, D. Rapid and accurate 3D selection by progressive refinement. In *Proc.. IEEE Symp. 3D User Interfaces* (2011), 67–74.
14. Moscovich, T. Contact area interaction with sliding widgets. In *Proc. ACM UIST* (2009), 13–22.
15. Moscovich, T., and Hughes, J. Multi-finger cursor techniques. In *Proc. Graphics Interface* (2006), 1–7.
16. Olwal, A., Feiner, S., and Heyman, S. Rubbing and tapping for precise and rapid selection on touch-screen displays. In *Proc. ACM SIGCHI* (2008), 295–304.
17. Parhi, P., Karlson, A., and Bederson, B. Target size study for one-handed thumb use on small touchscreen devices. In *Proc. MobileHCI* (2006), 203–210.
18. Parker, J., Mandryk, R., Nunes, M., and Inkpen, K. Improving target acquisition for pointing input on tabletop displays. In *Proc. INTERACT* (2005), 80–93.
19. Pietriga, E., and Appert, C. Sigma lenses: focus-context transitions combining space, time and translucence. In *Proc. ACM SIGCHI* (2008), 1343–1352.
20. Potter, R., Weldon, L., and Shneiderman, B. Improving the accuracy of touch screens: an experimental evaluation of three strategies. In *Proc. ACM SIGCHI* (1988), 27–32.
21. Roudaut, A., Huot, S., and Lecolinet, E. Taptap and magstick: improving one-handed target acquisition on small touch-screens. In *Proc. Working Conference on Advanced Visual Interfaces* (2008), 146–153.
22. Sears, A., and Shneiderman, B. High precision touchscreens: design strategies and comparisons with a mouse. *International Journal of Man-Machince Studies 34*, 4 (Apr. 1991), 593–613.
23. Vogel, D., and Baudisch, P. Shift: a technique for operating pen-based interfaces using touch. In *Proc. ACM SIGCHI* (2007), 657–666.
24. Worden, A., Walker, N., Bharat, K., and Hudson, S. Making computers easier for older adults to use: area cursors and sticky icons. In *Proc. ACM SIGCHI* (1997), 266–271.
25. Yatani, K., Partridge, K., Bern, M., and Newman, M. Escape: a target selection technique using visually-cued gestures. In *Proc. ACM SIGCHI* (2008), 285–294.

Faster Command Selection on Tablets with FastTap

Carl Gutwin[1], Andy Cockburn[2], Joey Scarr[2], Sylvain Malacria[2], and Scott Olson[1]

[1]Computer Science, University of Saskatchewan
Saskatoon, Saskatchewan, Canada

[2]Computer Science, University of Canterbury
Christchurch, New Zealand

carl.gutwin,scott.olson@usask.ca andy,joey@cosc.canterbury.ac.nz, sylvain@malacria.fr

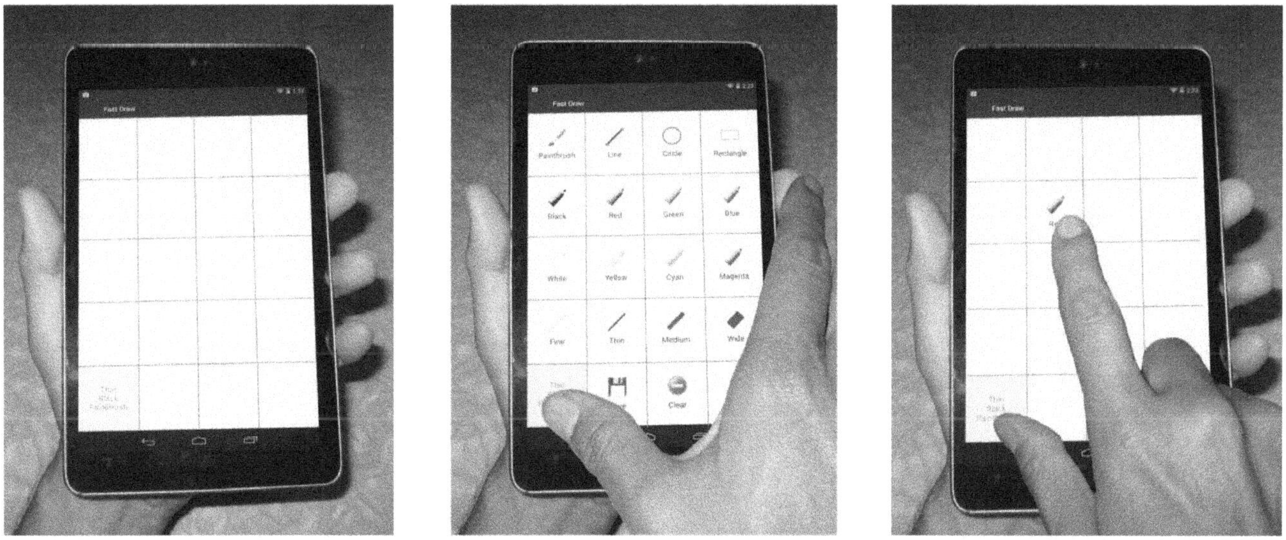

Figure 1. FastTap interface. Left: default state of the interface (gridlines enhanced). Center: FastTap grid overlay after touching the activation button. Right: FastTap selection by chording with the thumb and forefinger, without waiting for the overlay.

ABSTRACT

Touch-based tablet UIs provide few shortcut mechanisms for rapid command selection; as a result, command selection on tablets often requires slow traversal of menus. We developed a new selection technique for multi-touch tablets, called FastTap, that uses thumb-and-finger touches to show and choose from a spatially-stable grid-based overlay interface. FastTap allows novices to view and inspect the full interface, but once item locations are known, FastTap allows people to select commands with a single quick thumb-and-finger tap. The interface helps users develop expertise, since the motor actions carried out as a novice rehearse the expert behavior. A controlled study showed that FastTap was significantly faster (by 33% per selection overall) than marking menus, both for novices and experts, and without reduction in accuracy or subjective preference. Our work introduces a new and efficient selection mechanism that supports rapid command execution on touch tablets, for both novices and experts.

Author Keywords

Command selection; expertise; tablet UIs

CHI 2014, April 26–May 1, 2014, Toronto, Ontario, Canada.

ACM 978-1-4503-2473-1/14/04...$15.00.
http://dx.doi.org/10.1145/2556288.2557136

ACM Classification Keywords

H.5.2. Information interfaces (e.g., HCI): User Interfaces.

INTRODUCTION

Desktop interfaces often offer multiple ways to select the same command, and the different mechanisms can have very different performance characteristics. For example, selecting commands from menu hierarchies is slow when compared to keyboard shortcuts and toolbars, which provide access to commands with fewer actions. Having these types of shortcuts in an interface can substantially increase a user's efficiency over time, by allowing the user to learn quicker methods of invoking the commands they use most often.

On portable touch-based devices such as tablet computers, however, interface shortcuts are seldom available. The lack of a physical keyboard means that there are no keyboard shortcuts for quick selection, and limitations on screen real estate leave little or no room for always-visible components such as toolbars. Touch-based command interfaces, therefore, often take the form of tedious menu hierarchies, with no way of making a transition to an expert method of interaction. This greatly decreases the utility of touch devices for productivity tasks.

One widely-studied interface that supports expertise on touchscreens is the *marking menu*, a type of radial menu that allows visual inspection of menu items for novices, and rapid gestural interaction for expert users [12]. However, the contact-move-lift actions for marking menu gestures may take longer to perform than a simple tap action. With multi-touch capabilities widely available in modern tablet computers, there are opportunities for interfaces that support rapid command execution for experts, as well as smooth transitions from novice to expert use [3, 16, 23].

In this paper, we present FastTap, a new rapid-access interaction technique that allows fast command selection on multi-touch devices for both novice and expert users. As shown in Figure 1, FastTap uses the entire screen to present a spatially-stable grid of commands (based on the recent CommandMap interface [20]). The command overlay is hidden by default, and is shown when the user holds their thumb on the grid activation button. The interface can then be inspected, and commands can be selected with a finger; when the user lifts their thumb, the grid disappears.

Novices use the interface by showing the grid and visually searching for the commands they need. As users become familiar with commands, however, they remember item locations in the grid, leading to expert behavior – experts can select a command with a single 'chorded' tap using the thumb and forefinger, without waiting for the grid to appear. Similar to marking menus, this design follows Kurtenbach's principle that *'guidance should be a physical rehearsal of the way an expert would issue a command'* [15] – in other words, since the novice and expert interaction methods require similar motor actions, users can develop spatial and muscle memory of the action required for each command through natural use.

To assess the performance of FastTap, we carried out a controlled study comparing selection time and errors with FastTap and marking menus. Our study showed that selection time was significantly and substantially faster with FastTap (mean 1.6 seconds per selection) than with marking menus (mean 2.4 seconds). In addition, FastTap was significantly faster at all levels of expertise with the interface, and provided an additional speed benefit when multiple commands were carried out in sequence. We found no differences in terms of errors, effort, or preference.

Our work makes three main contributions. First, we introduce a new interaction technique for tablets that was significantly faster than marking menus in an initial study. Second, we further demonstrate the power of spatial memory as an organizing principle for visual interfaces, and demonstrate how spatial memory can be exploited together with multi-touch input to produce rapid command selection interfaces. Third, we provide empirical results about user performance with FastTap and marking menus.

DESIGN GOALS AND RELATED WORK

As shown in Figure 1, the FastTap interface works by displaying a CommandMap [20] over the main workspace when the user places their thumb on an on-screen activation area. In this section, we discuss the design goals behind FastTap and frame them in the context of related work.

Design Goal 1: Enable rapid command execution

Modern touch-screen applications typically use hierarchical menus and dialogs, with a few commands accessible on the main display, and others requiring several pointing actions that slow their selection.

Gesture-based systems, such as marking menus [12, 14], are one alternative to hierarchical linear menus, with some implementations appearing in commercial products (e.g., Autodesk Sketchbook Pro). Marking menus allow practiced users to traverse a radial menu hierarchy in a single gesture, speeding up interaction. However, navigating the hierarchy can still be slow, and marking menus are inherently limited in terms of the number of items that can appear at each hierarchical level (see Design Goal 3 for extensions to marking menus that can reduce this problem).

Multi-touch technology has created new opportunities for designing efficient command selection interfaces that exploit the higher bandwidth available with multiple concurrent contacts. For example, Wu and Balakrishnan [24] describe multi-finger and whole-hand interaction techniques for tables, including a selection mechanism that posts a toolglass with the thumb, allowing selection with another finger. Similar techniques are used and studied in Wagner et al.'s BiTouch system [23], but with a focus on handheld tablets where the thumb of the non-dominant hand is used to post interface components.

Multitouch marking menus [16] and finger-count menus [3] both allow users to specify a menu category by changing the number of fingers used to touch the screen (thus reducing the number of levels that must be traversed). Other techniques parallelize the hierarchy traversal: for example, Banovic et al.'s multi-finger pie menu [4] allows users to post the menu with one finger and select an item with another; Kin et al.'s two-handed marking menus [10] allow users to draw the marks for different menu levels simultaneously, by using both thumbs. However, these higher-bandwidth techniques do not always improve performance, since a more-complex control action may take more time to retrieve and execute [10].

Techniques utilizing device features other than the touch-screen have also been implemented. Jerktilts [1] allow quick selection of one of eight commands by quickly tilting the mobile device. Bezel Tap [22] uses the accelerometer to detect taps on the edge of the device, allowing shortcuts to commands while the device is asleep.

One key characteristic that determines whether a command selection interface is efficient is the number of separate actions needed to navigate to an item. Reducing this number is a main design goal of Scarr et al.'s CommandMap [20] technique, which uses a full-screen overlay to display as many commands as possible at once. These commands can be selected with a single action, which is faster than the multiple navigational steps needed for hierarchical menus and ribbons. Scarr et al. also showed that navigational errors (e.g., choosing the wrong menu) substantially increased the time needed for hierarchical organizations. In this work, we adapt the CommandMap's flat and spatially stable design to work with mobile devices.

Design Goal 2: Support a transition to expertise

One of the primary advantages of marking menus is the way in which they support a smooth and rapid transition to expert use [12]. After activating a marking menu, a novice user can wait for a short time to see a labeled radial menu appear, from which they make their selection with a touch gesture; an expert user can make the same gesture without waiting for the menu to appear. Since the motor actions for the novice and expert uses of the menu are identical, users learn the expert gestures through normal interaction.

This principle of *rehearsal* is extremely important to the development of user expertise. FastTap is therefore designed to support rehearsal during novice use. In a similar manner to marking menus, the command grid only appears on-screen after a delay; users with spatial or muscle memory of the interface can interact instantly without waiting for the visual display, using the exact physical action they used as novices; intermediate users suspecting the desired command location but unwilling to execute it without confirmation can also benefit from FastTap, by anticipating the location of the target, positioning their finger over it while waiting for the grid to appear, and selecting the command after visual confirmation.

Design Goal 3: Support a large number of commands

While marking menus are generally limited to eight or twelve commands per level [14], various extensions significantly increase this limit. Polygon menus [25] and flower menus [2] both allow more commands by increasing the types of gestures available. More recently, Roy et al. [19] developed Augmented Letters, a system whereby users draw the first letter of a command on the screen, then select from a radial menu of resulting candidate commands. OctoPocus [5] recognizes gestures by shape, and provides visual suggestions for the remaining gesture based on the initial movements. While these systems increase the number of commands that marking menus can support, they still rely on gesture-based interaction.

Rapid execution is our priority for FastTap, but we also intend that it will support a wide command vocabulary. In FastTap, the number of items at each level is limited only by the size of the screen; our prototype uses a 5x4 grid, with one cell being used as the FastTap activation button. However, this number can be increased through the use of different activation buttons, or command tabs, which can be arranged along the bottom of the screen. We consider these design possibilities further in the Discussion.

STUDY: SELECTION PERFORMANCE

The aim of the study was to assess the performance of FastTap for command selection on tablets. We compared FastTap to marking menus [15], which allow fast command selection for experts and support a smooth transition to expertise. We compared the two interfaces in a controlled experiment where participants selected a set of commands over several repeated blocks, allowing us to examine both novice and more expert selection behavior.

Experimental Conditions

Both FastTap and marking menus were implemented in a functional multi-touch drawing application (see Figure 2).

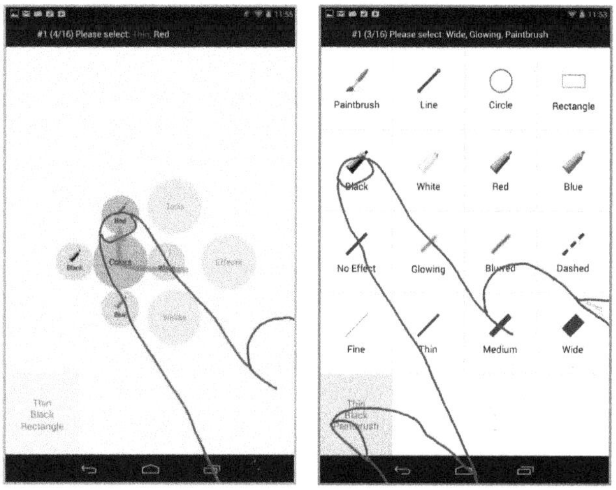

Figure 2. Study UIs. Left: marking menu (arrow shows gesture path). Right: FastTap. Cue appears at top of screen.

FastTap. As described above, FastTap provides modal access to a grid of command buttons. Selections are made by pressing a command button, either after invoking the grid display, or simultaneously with the invocation button (i.e., by chording). There is no difference in the selection mechanism for novice or expert use – experts who know the item locations simply tap the command before the interface is shown. After a chorded selection, feedback on the selected command is given by displaying the command icon for 500ms (Figure 1, right). The interface used in the experiment contained sixteen command buttons in a 4x4 grid , of which eight were used as study targets. The sixteen commands were organized into four rows that grouped similar commands together (see Figure 2).

Marking menus. We implemented a 16-item marking menu with a two-level hierarchy, adapted from Kurtenbach's previous work [15]. Once again, only eight of the 16 items were used as study targets. Upon invocation of the menu (described below), users move a finger towards one of four categories shown on screen (Shapes, Colors, Line Style, Line Width), and then to one of the items in that category (see Figure 2, left). The items in each category were the same as the row groups used in FastTap (Figure 2). We used a hierarchy because previous research indicates that selection errors increase significantly for menu levels containing more than eight items [15]. We chose commands for the study that fit well with the four categories, to reduce the chance that participants would select the wrong category. The categories are only needed when participants are new to the menu, however; as users become familiar with item locations in the marking menu, they can shift to expert interaction simply by drawing the gesture that uniquely indicates an item (e.g., up-right).

Marking menus also need an invocation mechanism, and we used the same activation button as in the FastTap condition (see Figure 2). Users invoked the menu by touching the activation button with their thumb, then touching their finger on the screen to instantly post the menu. Moving the finger in one of the four directions then opens the corresponding submenu, and moving again selects one of four items. Some implementations of marking menus use a 'press timeout' invocation, but to avoid disadvantaging the menu condition, we chose a method that was equally fast to the invocation of FastTap.

Procedure

Participants completed a demographics questionnaire, and then performed a sequence of selections in a custom study system with both marking menus and FastTap. For each trial, a command stimulus (consisting of one, two, or three command names) was displayed at the top of the screen; the participant then selected the command(s) using the interface provided. Trials involved selecting a combination of one, two, or three individual tools and properties that could be used within the drawing application (e.g., 'Red', 'Red Line', 'Red Thin Line'). Trials were timed from the appearance of the stimulus until all targets were successfully selected. In the case of multiple-command targets, command names in the stimulus were crossed out as they were selected, and participants could select commands in any order. Participants were instructed to complete tasks as quickly as possible, and were told that errors could be corrected simply by selecting the correct item. Completion times included the time for correcting errors.

Of the sixteen commands in each interface, only eight were used as stimuli, in order to allow faster development of spatial memory and expertise for both interfaces. Two commands were used from each interface category (Shape, Color, Line Style, Line Width). Multiple-command targets were also composed from these eight commands.

For each interface, selection trials were organized into blocks of sixteen selections (eight one-command targets, four two-command targets, and four three-command targets). Participants first performed one practice block of sixteen trials (data discarded) to ensure that they could use the interfaces successfully. They then carried out 10 blocks of sixteen selections. Targets were presented in random order (sampling without replacement) for each block. Short rest breaks were given between blocks.

After each interface, participants filled out a NASA-TLX questionnaire [8]; at the end of the study, they also answered summary questions about their preferences.

Participants and Apparatus

Sixteen participants were recruited from a local university (8 female; mean age 26.2 years). The study was conducted on a Nexus 7 Android tablet (7-inch screen, 1280x800 resolution). The software was written in Java, and recorded all experimental data including selection times and errors.

Design and Hypotheses

The study used a 2×3×10 within-participants RM-ANOVA with factors *Interface* (FastTap, MarkingMenu), *NumberOfCommands* (1, 2, or 3 commands per trial), and *Block* (1-10). Dependent measures were command selection time, and errors per command selection. Interface was counterbalanced between participants. Hypotheses were:

H1. Mean selection times for *FastTap* will be faster than for *MarkingMenu*.
H2. *FastTap* will be faster than *MarkingMenu* both for novices and for experts.
H3. *FastTap* will show an added speed benefit for two- and three-command targets.
H4. There will be no evidence of a difference in error rates between the two interfaces.
H5. There will be no evidence of a difference in perception of effort for the two interfaces.
H6. Users will prefer *FastTap* over *MarkingMenu*.

Results

For significant ANOVA results, we report partial eta-squared (η^2) as a measure of effect size (where .01 should be considered small, .06 medium, and > .14 large [5]).

Selection Time per Command

We calculated the selection time for each command by dividing the total trial time by the number of commands in that trial. As shown in Figure 3 (rightmost bars), mean selection times were about 0.8 seconds faster per command with *FastTap* (1.60s, s.d. 0.52s) than with *MarkingMenu* (2.39s, s.d. 0.65s), giving a significant main effect of *Interface* ($F_{1,15}$=84.37, p<.0001, η^2=0.85). We therefore accept **H1** – FastTap selections were 33% faster overall than the marking menu.

Figure 3 also shows selection time by the number of commands per trial. ANOVA showed a significant main effect of *Number of commands* ($F_{2,30}$=3.7, p<.05, η^2=0.20), and also an interaction with *Interface* ($F_{2,30}$=6.69, p<0.005, η^2=0.31). As suggested by Figure 3, both effects can be attributed to *FastTap* permitting faster selections when commands are joined into groups of two or three. Post-hoc t-tests (Bonferroni corrected) show a significant difference between the two interfaces for each number of commands (all p<.0001). We therefore accept **H3**.

Learning Effects

As shown in Figure 4, selection times decreased across trial blocks; ANOVA showed a significant main effect of *Block* ($F_{9,135}$=17.49, p<.0001, η^2=0.54). There was no interaction with *Interface* ($F_{9,135}$=1.43, p=.183) or with *NumberOfCommands* ($F_{18,270}$=1.29, p=.194).

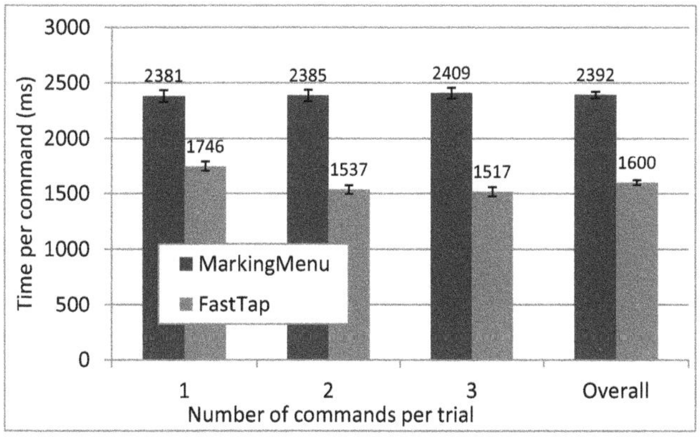

Figure 3. Mean selection times by Interface and Number.

We also analysed the performance difference between interfaces at each block. Bonferroni-corrected t-tests showed that *FastTap* was faster than *MarkingMenu* at all levels of expertise (all p<.001). Since the advantage of FastTap over marking menus is consistent across trial blocks, we accept **H2.**

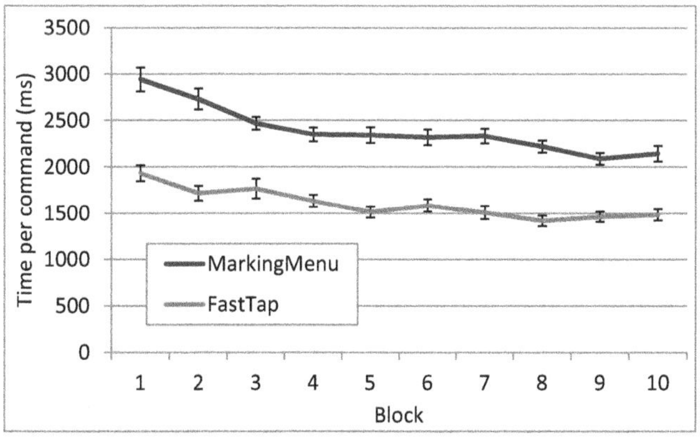

Figure 4. Mean trial times by Interface and Block.

Errors

As with selection time, we analysed errors per command, dividing the number of errors in a trial by the number of commands in that trial. Errors were counted as any incorrect selection (note that multiple-command trials could be carried out in any order). ANOVA showed no effect of *Interface* on errors, with *FastTap* at 0.10 errors/command, s.d. 0.13, and *MarkingMenu* at 0.08 errors/command, s.d. 0.11 ($F_{1,15}$=2.96, p=.11). We therefore accept **H4** (errors are considered further in the discussion section).

There was also no effect of *Block* ($F_{9,135}$=0.41, p=.93) or *NumberOfCommands* ($F_{2,30}$=0.51, p=.61) on errors per command; there were no interactions between any factors.

Subjective Responses: Effort and Preferences

User response was positive to both interfaces, but with no strong differences in NASA-TLX scores (compared using the Friedman test; see Table 1). No significant differences were found on any effort question, and the mean scores were close in all cases; therefore, we accept **H5**.

	FastTap	Marking Menu	χ^2_r	p
Mental demand	5.3 (2.2)	5.1 (2.0)	0.25	.62
Physical demand	3.8 (2.0)	4.4 (1.8)	0.25	.62
Temporal demand	4.6 (2.0)	4.7 (1.7)	0.0	1.0
Success	6.6 (1.3)	6.5 (1.4)	0.0	1.0
Hard work	5.3 (1.8)	5.5 (1.5)	0.25	.62
Frustration	3.6 (1.8)	3.5 (1.6)	0.0	1.0

Table 1. Mean (s.d.) NASA-TLX scores (0-9 scale, low to high).

We also asked participants which interface they preferred in terms of several qualities (see Table 2). As with the effort scores, counts were very close with no quality showing a significant difference. When asked about overall preference, seven participants preferred FastTap, eight preferred marking menus, and one had no preference. We therefore cannot accept **H6**.

	FastTap	Equal	Marking Menu	χ^2_r	p
Speed	8	2	6	0.071	.79
Accuracy	6	1	9	0.26	.61
Memorization	6	2	8	0.071	.79
Expert mode	5	3	8	0.31	.58
Comfort	8	1	7	0.0	1.0
Overall	7	1	8	0.0	1.0

Table 2. Counts of participant preferences.

Participant Comments

Like the preference results, participant comments were about evenly divided between the two selection techniques, and participants often mentioned the characteristic features of the designs when explaining their preferences. For example, participants made several comments about how spatial stability and quick activation helped the speed of FastTap: one person commented on *"the simple and stable location of each icon"*; another said *"the grid is faster because it only requires a two finger tap, with one finger always in the same place. The menu, however, demands specific movements (swipes) which expend a few milliseconds more time."*

It was also clear that some participants liked the semantic categories of the Marking Menu, and others liked FastTap's access to all commands at once. In favour of marking menus, participant comments included *"the menu compartmentalized the options much better"*; *"the menu required less memory"*; and *"visually a grid with all available options is not as easily navigable as a menu with divisible submenus."* In favour of FastTap, comments included: *"the options are all available at one time which makes it easier to pick, and memorization also helps a lot in the grid"*; *"it is easier to see the items that you want to select"*; and *"there is only one level to be memorized, where [the marking menu] has two levels."*

Some of the participants were initially concerned with the number of commands in FastTap, but ultimately preferred it: *"after a while, the grid became easier to remember"*; *"I was able to catch on much quicker [with FastTap] and be able to visualize where everything was."*

Finally, one participant also mentioned that the sliding motions needed for the marking menu could present problems on a touch surface, and that FastTap's tapping action did not have this problem: *"sliding over a surface can be impeded by many factors like moisture [on the] hand and friction over the surface. [...] I feel the tapping action in the grid is more comfortable."*

ADDITIONAL INFORMAL USAGE OBSERVATIONS

To gather additional information about whether FastTap would work outside of a study setting, we developed a simple multi-touch painting application with a FastTap interface and showed the system to five people in an informal test. We were interested in whether people would hold the device in a way that allowed correct FastTap operation (building on the work of Wagner et al. [23]), whether people would be able to use the interface with a minimum of instruction, and whether people would take initial steps toward expert selection behavior.

The five participants used the interface in a variety of settings (an office, an undergraduate lab, and three homes), and we asked them to play with the interface and to recreate a printed picture three times (to simulate increasing familiarity with a set of commands).

Holding the device. Wagner et al. [23] looked at the ways that people held an iPad, in order to determine whether the non-dominant hand could be used for bimanual input (e.g., to show toolbars or other interface elements). They observed several common postures involving the non-dominant palm or forearm. We also saw several different handholds in our informal sessions, some of which were seen by Wagner – for example, the tablet held in the left palm, with the FastTap activation button pressed by the non-dominant thumb. However, several other people held the device by gripping it between their left thumb and fingers – which was not possible in Wagner's study due to the size of the iPad, but which was possible with our seven-inch Nexus tablet. This grip-based hold allowed operation of FastTap with the thumb and fingers of the dominant hand, which matched our intention in designing the method.

Novice and more expert behaviour. In our informal sessions, people found it easy to use FastTap – their hands fit the interface reasonably well, and people did not have any difficulty finding the commands that they wanted. On a few occasions, however, people inadvertently drew rather than selecting. In the short time of these sessions, we saw only a few uses of expert chording behaviour; however, it was clear that all users were gaining spatial memory of frequently-used commands. For example, people moved their selection finger towards or over the target even before displaying the grid, showing that they had an idea about where the desired command was located.

These preliminary observations are limited, but provide initial evidence that FastTap can work in natural use.

DISCUSSION

Our investigation of FastTap provides four main results:

- Selection with FastTap was significantly faster overall than with marking menus (0.8s per selection, more than 33%), and it was faster throughout the learning curve;
- Making multiple selections allowed a speedup of about 200ms in selection time for FastTap, which did not occur with marking menus.
- There was no significant difference in errors between FastTap and marking menus, although FastTap had a slightly higher error rate (0.10 errors/selection compared to 0.08 for Marking Menu);
- Participants were evenly divided between the two interfaces for perceived effort and overall preference; some participants particularly liked each interface;
- In limited usage observations, we saw that people were able to hold the device appropriately for FastTap, were able to find commands easily, and appeared to quickly build memory of command locations.

The following sections provide explanations for these findings, address design issues for real-world use of FastTap, and discuss its generalizability.

Explanation and Interpretation of Results

Why did FastTap work well for both novices and experts?
Our experiment showed that FastTap improved (by 33%) on a well-known technique (marking menus) for selecting commands on tablets; in addition, FastTap was faster at all stages of learning.

The performance advantage of FastTap can be explained through an analysis of the steps required for command selection, in both novice and expert cases. For novices, there are three steps required: activating the command mode, searching for the desired command, and executing a selection action. Activating the command mode was the same in both interfaces, but the interfaces differed in the second and third steps. Searching for a command in FastTap involves only visual search over all of the concurrently displayed items, whereas search in marking menus involves first choosing and selecting a semantic category (Colours, Tools, etc.) and then searching in a much smaller set of items. Although some participants found the semantic categories helpful, previous research has shown that the decision and selection time costs of traversing the hierarchy can exceed that of a broader visual search [20]. The visual search needed for FastTap could take longer initially, since there are more items to inspect, but the rapid development of spatial memory means that novice users will quickly make a transition from full visual search to remembering where items are located. The third step – execution of the selection action – is faster in FastTap, since a tapping action can be carried out more quickly than the sliding motion of a marking menu.

For experts, selection requires only two steps: retrieval of the command action (either a location or a gesture) from memory, and execution of that action. The performance advantage for expert use of FastTap most likely arises from the speed of execution, since the memory-retrieval step is similar for both techniques. Execution of a thumb-and-finger tapping is a faster action than a drawn gesture, leading to a performance advantage for FastTap.

Why were multiple selections faster than single selections?
Multiple commands selected with FastTap were each about 200ms faster than single commands. We believe that this speed-up is due to people's ability to visualize multiple command locations within FastTap's grid interface, and optimize their movements for multiple selections. For example, we observed participants re-ordering the selections to reduce finger movement (e.g., ordering the selections by grid row allowed people to move their finger in a straighter line). With the marking menu, there is less opportunity for optimization (e.g., re-ordering the commands does not reduce overall movement).

Does FastTap lead to more errors?
Error rates were high overall in both techniques (10% and 8% for FastTap and marking menus). This high error rate is probably an artifact of our experimental protocol, which explicitly instructed participants to select items as quickly as possible, while noting that errors could be corrected afterwards. Although FastTap had a slightly higher mean error rate (10%) than marking menus (8%), the difference was not statistically significant (p=.11). However, if we assume that effect of higher errors with FastTap is actually a reliable one, we see three candidate explanations. First, the quick execution of a selection action in FastTap may have encouraged participants to view errors as amenable to rapid correction, thereby encouraging users towards a 'guess and correct' mode of operation. Second, participants may have found the post-selection visual feedback in FastTap more clearly communicative of the selected item than the marking menu, again encouraging faster but more error prone selections. Third, it is possible that people's memory of an item's spatial location was imperfect, and so participants may have experienced 'near misses' more often than with marking menus. Further work is needed to determine whether the difference in error rates is reliable, and to properly explain its cause if it is.

FastTap and Marking Menus with Larger Item Sets
Our study tested FastTap and marking menus with a small command set (sixteen items), and it is worth considering how the two approaches would compare in the case of a larger interface. The main performance differences between FastTap and marking menus are in initial visual search (novice behavior) and the number of actions needed for a learned item (expert behavior). These differences arise due to the properties of FastTap's single-level presentation, compared with marking menu's hierarchical organization.

With a larger command set, it seems likely that FastTap will require more visual search than marking menus – provided the hierarchical organization of the marking menu items is clear (which can be a non-trivial design problem [20]). However, several prior studies suggest that the novice period of use is relatively short (e.g., [20, 21]) and users will soon be interacting with commands that they are familiar with. In this case, FastTap selection time will be similar to that observed in our study – since only a single invocation and selection action is needed, regardless of the size of the command set. Marking menus, however, must create hierarchies because they use less space, and so experts must continue to execute multiple navigational steps (even if these are executed as marks).

Recent work on multi-touch marking menus [3, 10, 16] suggests ways that these navigation interactions can be speeded up – e.g., by encoding top-level menu categories with different finger postures [16], or by parallelizing the execution of navigational marks [10]. Although we believe that FastTap will continue to compare well against other selection techniques as command sets increase in size, further work is needed to explore the potential differences between the spatial-memory approach of FastTap and the gesture-memory approach of marking menus.

Design issues for FastTap
In the following sections we consider issues likely to arise if deploying FastTap in real-world tablet interfaces.

How many commands can the interface accommodate?
Our drawing interface contained 19 commands in a 5×4 grid, but this is not the limit for the FastTap approach. In general, the number of commands in the interface is limited by the size of the device, the minimum desired size of the targets, and the size of the user's hand (to facilitate chording). Using the average width of an adult index finger (16-20mm [7]) as a guideline, it would be possible to have a grid of up to 40 buttons in an 8×5 layout on a 7-inch tablet. If we consider Parhi et al.'s recommendation that touch targets be no smaller than 9.6mm [17], a maximum density of 150 items in a 15×10 arrangement is possible. However, this size guideline is debatable – larger button sizes have been shown to provide higher success and satisfaction rates [17, 18], yet much smaller targets can also be used, as demonstrated by smartphone virtual keypads (which can be operated substantially eyes-free with sufficient practice). There are interesting research questions around users' ability to form spatial and motor memories for varying numbers of targets at different target densities.

Importantly, however, the possibilities for adapting FastTap to high functionality applications, or to small displays, is not necessarily limited to the 'all commands at once' designs examined in this paper. The capacity of the interface to display candidate targets can be multiplied through the use of multiple trigger buttons, or 'tabs', which organize the commands into multiple categories – each trigger button would then show a separate set of commands (see mockup in Figure 5). As discussed under Design Goal #3, this technique requires the allocation of additional trigger-button regions in the bottom row of the grid. Further research is required to determine how well people can remember these two-finger combinations.

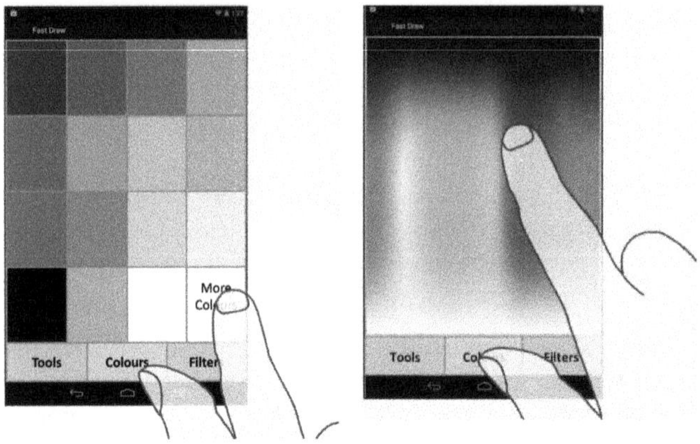

Figure 5. Left: FastTap UI with three tabs. Right: A color picker converted to work with FastTap.

Finally, it is also possible that if the grid interface cannot accommodate all of the application's commands, it could still function as a 'hotbox' [13] for frequently-used items.

FastTap with different size factors
Our experiments were conducted on a device equipped with a 7-inch touchscreen. We used this relatively small size factor because tablets with screens smaller than 8 inches are the main proportion of the current tablet market, and this proportion is forecast to increase by 2017 [9]. We conducted pilot studies on several smaller touch-screen devices (e.g., Nexus 4, Galaxy S3), mostly testing the drawing system. The systems worked well, although the command buttons were smaller overall, which may have accuracy implications for expert users.

Porting FastTap to tablets with *larger* screens also raises interesting questions, especially whether the designer should use the full screen to fit more commands. If not, the FastTap interface can be limited to a comfortable size for the user's hand. Using the full screen, however, would permit more commands to be displayed, but it would also create problems for single-handed operation due to hand-span limitations. A different triggering mechanism might be used for commands that are further away than a hand span – such as the bimanual thumb technique used in Wagner's BiTouch system [23].

Issues regarding device orientation
Mobile devices such as tablet computers can be used in different orientations, which changes the aspect ratio of the screen. There are three possibilities to accommodate orientation changes. First, the grid could maintain its overall aspect ratio and scale to fit the smaller dimension of the new orientation, requiring that users adapt to a different-scale interface. Second, the grid could change its aspect ratio to fill the new orientation, requiring that users adapt to a stretched version of the grid. As shown by Scarr et al. [20], these two transformations would cause only a minor disruption to spatial selections. Finally, the grid could maintain its size regardless of the orientation, fitting the most constraining orientation.

Biomechanical constraints
Some of our participants cited difficulties with the hand positions required to select commands with FastTap. Specifically, participants noted that targets were more difficult to acquire when they were close to or far away from the trigger button, or when they were at the lower-right side of the grid. People with long fingernails had particular difficulty maintaining registered contact with the display when selecting targets near to the trigger button, (the natural posture for such selections involves the fingers being nearly perpendicular to the display, causing nails to lift fingers off the touch screen).

In all cases, however, problems with hand positions were addressed in two ways. First, users could re-orient the device with the holding hand in order to present a better presentation of the trigger and target buttons. For example, to more easily tap a target in the lower right part of the grid, the user could turn the device slightly anticlockwise with their holding hand, so that the target button (finger) was above and to the right of the trigger button (thumb). Second, users did not have to use the thumb and forefinger to make selections, and could use a combination that simplified the particular selection. For example, many users used their first and second fingers for the bottom row of commands instead of their thumb and first finger.

It would also be possible to change from a grid-based command organization to one that better matches the ergonomics of the hand. However, it is not clear whether a non-rectilinear grid would make it more difficult to acquire targets in expert mode (i.e., with no visual feedback).

FastTap and advanced interfaces
Modern UIs generally include widgets more advanced than push-buttons. For example, sliders or color spectrum pickers can be used to provide a finer degree of control over application parameters. These widgets can easily be converted to work with FastTap, as shown in Figure 5. FastTap provides quick access to these widgets and allows users to perform rapid and coarse slider positioning that can instantly be adjusted without having to switch modes.

Modal interface and occlusion of the document
All in-place interfaces (including marking menus) occlude parts of the document, but the overlay presentation of FastTap's interface is different in that it completely fills the screen. In most cases, this is unlikely to cause a problem for the user, for three reasons: first, the grid is partially transparent and so the main visual elements of the document can be seen through the FastTap overlay; second, the overlay does not appear at all in expert mode, so there is no occlusion problem for experienced users; third, it is easy for the user to control the presence of the overlay (by lifting their thumb from the activation button), allowing rapid switching back and forth from the document to the UI.

One case where the overlay presentation requires a design solution is the situation where the user has selected an object on the screen, and wants to see previews of a command's effects on that object (e.g., what it looks like in different colours). Although it is possible to simply select different colours using the standard FastTap process (expert mode makes this fast and easy), other designs could reduce the problem – such as placing a floating copy of the selected object above the grid, or fading out the overlay whenever the user's finger stops moving across the grid.

Last, the visual presence of the activation button is another potential cause of occlusion. This button is also partially transparent, and could easily increase in transparency level as the user becomes more experienced (although this does not happen in our current prototype).

Multiple simultaneous selection
Normal expert selection in FastTap involves two digits (normally the thumb and one finger; but sometimes two different fingers). This combination selects one command; however, there is no reason why additional commands cannot be selected simultaneously in the same chorded tap. For example, the user could select "black paintbrush" with the three-finger chord shown in Figure 6.

These kinds of selections already work in our prototype application. Added-finger selections work well only for certain combinations (because of constraints on positioning the fingers); therefore, if these are to be used in interface design, further work must determine which fingers combinations are possible, and which command combinations are desirable.

Error rates in memory-based UIs
Above we discussed error rates with FastTap and marking menus. However, a more general question concerns the errors that will always occur with a memory-based means for interaction. Errors are inherent in any memory-based technique, particularly in the transition from novice to expert use, since users must at some point depend on their memory rather than on visual feedback. This issue affects marking menus, keyboard shortcuts, and FastTap.

In general, there are several issues that must be considered when designing for the possibility of errors: the destructiveness of a command, the ease with which the error can be identified, the time that the command takes to execute, and the time required to correct the error. For non-destructive and instantaneous commands such as the property-setting commands of a drawing program (colour, line style, etc.), selection errors are a minor problem. If feedback on the selection is given (as it is in our implementation, even in expert mode), users are likely to realize their error and simply correct it.

For commands that take a long time to construct or execute (e.g., a complicated image filter), commands should be easily interruptible to avoid problems of erroneous selection. For destructive commands (e.g., deletions), systems may need a confirmation step or a well-designed 'undo' facility. It is possible that memory-based techniques like FastTap or marking menus could be reserved for lighter-weight commands, with destructive or time-consuming commands accessed through a different mechanism (e.g., a traditional application menu).

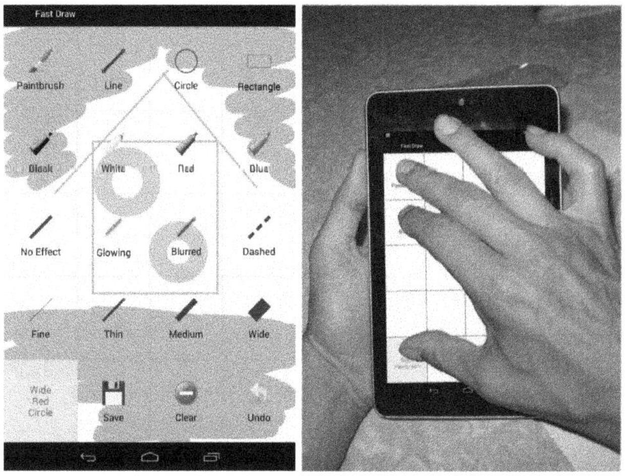

Figure 6. Left: transparent grid with drawing behind. Right: three-finger chord that selects two commands.

Single-handed use
Although we developed FastTap on a tablet that would be difficult or impossible to use with one hand, several people have noted that phone-sized mobile devices are often used in a one-handed fashion. The ideas underlying FastTap can be used in a one-handed context, providing some or all of the benefits of the interface. The spatial-memory advantages of FastTap could be achieved even without multi-touch chorded taps; a two-tap version of the interface would bring up the interface with one tap, and then allow selection with a second tap. For most single-handed operation, the user touches the screen with their right thumb, which means that the activation button would have to be moved to the right side of the screen.

It would also be possible to place an activation button somewhere else on the device to accommodate chording with one-handed use (e.g., on the back of the device, or on the bezel under one of the other fingers, although these would require hardware changes). Similarly, the activation functionality that currently uses a multi-touch selection could be changed to another modality – for example, double-tapping on a grid location could be a method for specifying both activation (the double tap) and selection (the location) with a single finger.

CONCLUSIONS AND FUTURE WORK

Although multi-touch tablets are now common, and are starting to be used for productivity work, there are few techniques for these devices to support rapid command selection. In this paper, we presented a new selection technique for multi-touch tablets called FastTap that uses thumb-and-finger touches to show and choose from a grid-based overlay interface. FastTap allows novices to view and inspect the full interface, but once item locations are known, FastTap also allows people to select commands with a single quick thumb-and-finger tap. The interface helps users move toward expert use, since the motor actions carried out in novice mode rehearse the expert behavior. A controlled study with 16 participants showed that FastTap was significantly faster (0.8 sec/selection, 33%) than marking menus, both for novices and experts, and without reduction in accuracy or subjective preference.

Our research thus far with FastTap gives us strong initial results, and future work will continue in three directions. First, we will continue development of the drawing application and release a fully-functional version of the app, in order to gather real-world usage and performance data from a wide audience. Second, we will develop new prototypes that explore some of the design issues described above, including tabbed command sets, complex interface widgets, and interface scaling for larger devices. Third, we will develop FastTap prototypes for other applications that could benefit from fast access to commands and shortcuts (e.g., contacts and response options in a mail client, or favourites and page actions in a web browser). Our experience with FastTap suggests that the underlying ideas of spatial-memory-based expertise and quick tap-based access can be successfully and broadly applied across several application domains.

ACKNOWLEDGMENTS

This work was supported by the NSERC SurfNet Research Network and the GRAND NCE, and by the Royal Society of New Zealand Marsden Grant 10-UOC-020.

REFERENCES

1. Baglioni, M., Lecolinet, E. and Guiard, Y. JerkTilts: using accelerometers for eight-choice selection on mobile devices. *Proc. ICMI 2011*, 121-128.
2. Bailly, G., Lecolinet, E. and Nigay, L. Flower menus: a new type of marking menu with large menu breadth, within groups and efficient expert mode memorization. *Proc. AVI 2008*, 15-22.
3. Bailly, G., Müller, J. and Lecolinet, E. Design and Evaluation of Finger-Count Interaction: Combining Multitouch gestures and Menus. *IJHCS* 70(12):673-689.
4. Banovic, N., Li, F., Dearman, D., Yatani, K. and Truong, K. Design of unimanual multi-finger pie menu interaction. *Proc. ITS 2011*, 120-129.
5. Bau, O., and Mackay, W., OctoPocus: a dynamic guide for learning gesture-based command sets. *Proc. UIST 2008*, 37-46.
6. Cohen, J. Eta-squared and partial eta-squared in communication science. *Human Communication Research* 28(56):473-490.
7. Dandekar, K., Raju, B. and Srinivasan, M. 3-D finite-element models of human and monkey fingertips to investigate the mechanics of tactile sense. *Journal of Biomechanical Engineering*, 125, 5, 2003, 682-691.
8. Hart, S. and Staveland, L. Development of NASA-TLX (Task Load Index): Results of Empirical and Theoretical Research. in Hancock, P. and Meshkati, N. eds. *Human Mental Workload*, 1988, 139-183.
9. IDC. IDC Forecasts Worldwide Tablet Shipments to Surpass Portable PC Shipments in 2013, www.idc.com/getdoc.jsp?containerId=prUS24129713, 2013.
10. Kin, K., Hartmann, B., and Agrawala, M., Two-Handed Marking Menus for Multitouch Devices. *ToCHI* 18(3): article 16.
11. Kurtenbach, G. and Buxton, W. Issues of Combining Marking and Direct Manipulation Techniques. *Proc. UIST 1991*, 137-144.
12. Kurtenbach, G. and Buxton, W. User Learning and Performance with Marking Menus. *Proc. CHI 1994*, 258-264.
13. Kurtenbach, G., Fitzmaurice, G., Owen, R. and Baudel, T. The Hotbox: efficient access to a large number of menu-items. *Proc. CHI 1999*, 231-237.
14. Kurtenbach, G., Sellen, A. and Buxton, W. An Empirical Evaluation of Some Articulatory and Cognitive Aspects of Marking Menus. *Human-Computer Interaction* 8(1):1-23.
15. Kurtenbach, G.P. *The design and evaluation of marking menus*, PhD Thesis, University of Toronto, 1993.
16. Lepinski, G., Grossman, T. and Fitzmaurice, G. The design and evaluation of multitouch marking menus *Proc. CHI 2010*, 2233-2242.
17. Parhi, P., Karlson, A. and Bederson, B. Target size study for one-handed thumb use on small touchscreen devices. *Proc. Mobile HCI 2003*, 203-210.
18. Park, Y., Han, S., Park, J. and Cho, Y. Touch key design for target selection on a mobile phone *Proc. Mobile HCI 2008*, 423-426.
19. Roy, Q., Malacria, S., Guiard, Y., Lecolinet, E. and Eagan, J. Augmented letters: mnemonic gesture-based shortcuts *Proc. CHI 2013*, 2325-2328.
20. Scarr, J., Cockburn, A., Gutwin, C. and Bunt, A. Improving command selection with CommandMaps *Proc. CHI 2012*, 257-266.
21. Scarr, J., Cockburn, A., Gutwin, C. and Malacria, S. Testing the Robustness and Performance of Spatially Consistent Interfaces. *Proc. CHI 2013*, 3139-3148.
22. Serrano, M., Lecolinet, E. and Guiard, Y. Bezel-Tap gestures: quick activation of commands from sleep mode on tablets *Proc. CHI 2013*, 3027-3036.
23. Wagner, J., Huot, S., and Mackay, W. BiTouch and BiPad: Designing bimanual interactions for hand-held tablets. *Proc CHI 2012*, 2317-2326.
24. Wu, M., and Balakrishnan, R. Multi-finger and whole hand gestural interaction techniques for multi-user tabletop displays. *Proc. UIST 2003*, 193-202.
25. Zhao, S., Agrawala, M. and Hinckley, K. Zone and Polygon Menus: Using Relative Position to Increase the Breadth of Multi-Stroke Marking Menus. *Proc. CHI 2006*, 1077-1086.

Crossing-Based Selection with Direct Touch Input

Yuexing Luo, Daniel Vogel
Cheriton School of Computer Science
University of Waterloo, CANADA
{y57luo, dvogel}@uwaterloo.ca

ABSTRACT
Fundamental performance results for crossing-based selection tasks with direct touch input are presented. A close adaptation of Accot and Zhai's indirect stylus crossing experiment reveals similar trends for direct touch input: touch crossing task time is faster or equivalent to touch pointing; continuous selection of large orthogonal crossing targets is most effective; and continuous selection of small collinear targets is least effective. Unlike indirect stylus and mouse crossing, not every kind of direct touch pointing performance is modeled accurately with standard Fitts' law. Instead, "FFitts" law, used previously for touch pointing with small targets, is used to more accurately model discrete touch crossing with a directionally constrained target. In addition, visual touch feedback is shown to have a strong effect on absolute accuracy. Our work empirically validates touch crossing as a practical and efficient selection technique, and motivates the exploration of novel forms of expressive multi-touch crossing.

Author Keywords
Crossing; goal crossing; pointing; target selection; touch input; multi-touch; stylus input; pen input; Fitts; FFitts;

ACM Classification Keywords
H.5.2 [Information Interfaces and Presentation]: User Interfaces - Input devices and strategies;

INTRODUCTION
Selecting targets by crossing a boundary "goal" instead of pointing inside a perimeter has been theoretically investigated [2,3,4,12,14,26] and practically applied to interaction techniques for mouse and stylus input [5,6,13]. With the increased popularity of direct touch input, this *crossing paradigm* has also been applied to touch screen interaction techniques [8,20,21,23,27]. However, unlike stylus and mouse input, there is no generalizable, controlled empirical support for the application of crossing to touch input. Studies of conventional touch input have noted unique characteristics compared to other input [7,15,17,18,22], some which might affect crossing performance — like increased friction from skin rubbing on the display when dragging with touch [10,11].

CHI 2014, April 26 - May 01 2014, Toronto, ON, Canada

http://dx.doi.org/10.1145/2556288.2557397

Our work contributes new controlled empirical evidence and theoretical results that provide fundamental support for crossing-based interaction techniques in direct touch interfaces. We adapt Accot and Zhai's indirect stylus crossing experiment [3] to direct touch input, and find that with directionally constrained targets, continuous touch crossing is faster than touch pointing, and discrete crossing performs similar to pointing. Our results suggest a minimum crossing target width of 12.7mm will reduce error rates to 4% or less. We also confirm a trend observed for stylus input: the selection of large directionally constrained crossing targets is most effective and continuous selection of small collinear targets is least effective. For a continuous crossing task with direction constraint, direct touch is approximately 37% faster than indirect stylus, and 58% faster than direct stylus crossing in a similar study by Forlines and Balakrishnan [14].

We found that standard Fitts' law accurately models all crossing tasks except discrete crossing with a direction constraint. To address this, we utilize "FFitts law" [9], a formulation of Fitts' law for finger touch tapping input which takes into account the contribution of absolute touch precision independent of the speed-accuracy tradeoff effect. In a second experiment, we measure absolute touch precision with crossing and demonstrate the applicability of FFitts law for improved modeling of discrete crossing with a direction constraint. Continuous crossing with a direction constraint is modeled equally well with FFitts law, though not as well as with Fitts' law. Our second experiment also controls for visual touch feedback and demonstrates its pronounced affect on absolute touch precision.

RELATED WORK
Almost all empirical evaluations of elementary crossing performance use stylus or mouse input. Crossing with a stylus can be faster and less error prone than pointing [3,14], so techniques using stylus crossing are easily justified. Conversely, a well-controlled study found that crossing with a mouse is sub-optimal compared to pointing [26]. In spite of the ubiquity of mouse input, this may be why few applications use mouse crossing. The problem is that although there are multiple examples of touch crossing interaction techniques, there is no controlled, generalizable empirical evidence to justify them.

Crossing-Based Selection with Stylus Input

Accot and Zhai's performed an early crossing-based selection experiment which they referred to as a "goal passing task" [1]. This formed the first step in the development of their Steering Law, but also led to their subsequent thorough examination crossing [2]. In this thorough crossing study, Accot and Zhai compared crossing to pointing with indirect stylus input using six different task conditions. We use the same six tasks in our study with direct touch input (Figure 1), but name them with the refined task terminology of Apitz et al. [4].

In the Accot and Zhai study and our study, two tasks require pointing selection and four require crossing selection. For both kinds of selection, the orientation of the precision constraint for a goal or target can be collinear to movement, so that controlling movement *amplitude* is most important, or it can be orthogonal to movement, so that controlling movement *direction* is most important. When crossing, the continuity of contact may by *continuous* when the stylus remains on the surface between targets, or *discrete* when it must lift to avoid distractors.

With indirect stylus input, Accot and Zhai found that pointing and continuous crossing with a *direction* precision constraint (DP and C\DC) were at least 10% faster than all other tasks. In contrast, continuous crossing with an *amplitude* precision constraint (C\AC) was slower than all other tasks. All tasks except C\AC had error rates close to, or lower, than 7.8%, the error rate for pointing. In addition, Fitts' law modeled all tasks extremely well (all r^2 greater than 0.975). Their study provides evidence that crossing can be substituted for pointing with no decrease in performance, however this can only be confidently stated for an indirect stylus device with absolute mapping.

Forlines and Balakrishnan [14] also use Accot and Zhai's six tasks to study direct and indirect stylus input with tactile feedback. They report no difference in task time between direct and indirect stylus input when pointing, but when crossing, direct stylus input is 16% faster. They also report a surprising interaction between input device and continuity of contact. Discrete crossing tasks are 11% faster with direct stylus input, but 15% slower with indirect stylus input. This nuanced performance emphasizes the need to test and validate crossing performance across input modalities. Perhaps due to the inclusion of a small 0.7 mm target, they report a mean error rate of 20% for crossing, much higher than Accot and Zhai's work.

Motivated by potential benefits of crossing selection in parameter selection dialog boxes, Dixon et al. [12] test crossing target density and orientation. Using a direct stylus input device they find crossing is faster than pointing for dialog boxes, and also remain spatially efficient. Apitz and Guimbretiere's [5] CrossY is fully crossing-based drawing application using direct stylus input. It illustrates many crossing-based widgets and interaction techniques. Although no formal study was conduced with CrossY, the empirical evaluations of elementary crossing performance with stylus justify the design.

Crossing-Based Selection with Mouse Input

Using a mouse and trackball, Wobbrock and Gajos [26] compare pointing and crossing with able-bodied people and those with motor impairments. Although not the primary focus of their work, the data from able-bodied participants in 15 controlled combinations of distances and widths provide evidence that crossing with a mouse is sub-optimal. A detailed study of different crossing configurations like those done for the stylus should be done with mice. At present, the results suggest that techniques like Dragicevic's [13] Fold-and-Drop and Baudisch's Toggle Maps [6] may be better suited for stylus input.

Crossing-Based Selection with Touch Input

In spite of no controlled, generalizable empirical evidence to justify them, multiple crossing-based applications and interaction techniques have been proposed for touch input. Benko et al. designed a crossing-based menu for a multi-touch tabletops [8]. Sulaiman and Olivier's Attribute Gates [23] use crossing for attribute selection. Roth and Turner's Bezel Swipe [21] is crossing with one side of a smartphone bezel as the goal. Yoshikawa et al.'s HandyWidgets [27] create implicit crossing goals defined by hand position on a multi-touch tabletop. Nakamura et al. [20] create a new interaction technique called double-crossing and claim improvements on both selection time and error rate.

These examples of touch crossing are exciting, but to our knowledge, the only comparison of touch pointing and crossing is Guerreiro et al.'s study with 15 tetraplegic participants using a smartphone [16]. They use single, circular crossing targets larger than 7 mm and did not control for distance. Due to impairment, participants did not necessarily use a finger to touch. The paper reports tapping and crossing performance as similar, which is encouraging. However, the study lacks experimental controls for key factors used in Accot and Zhai's work, and the exclusive use of motor impaired participants makes generalizing these results beyond their intended purpose problematic.

It would be convenient to simply justify touch crossing by referring to empirical evidence for direct stylus crossing, but investigations into properties of touch reveal many subtle and not so subtle differences. The fat finger problem is one pronounced difference [24], and achieving high accuracy is challenging without rethinking the centroid touch point model [17] or using advanced fingerprint sensors [18]. Cockburn et al. [11] test many facets of touch input and note the problem with friction between fingers and the surface when dragging. This problem has been noted in studies with indirect touch as well [10], and seems likely to influence the performance of touch crossing. Benko and Wigdor's overview of touch input problems [7] enumerates issues problems with precision, occlusion, capture, and physical constraints.

The extensive empirical work available to guide and validate touch pointing does not exist for designers and researchers exploring touch crossing as an alternative or complementary interaction technique. To remedy this situation, we conducted a controlled experiment to explore and validate performance characteristics of touch crossing.

EXPERIMENT 1: TOUCH CROSSING PERFORMANCE

This experiment is a very close adaptation of Accot and Zhai's indirect stylus crossing experiment [3,4]. It has also been used by Forlines and Balakrishnan [14] for direct stylus input. Our adaption of Accot and Zhai's experiment is described in detail below, but the main changes are:

- All target distances and sizes are scaled by a ratio so the maximum distance would fit within a typical touch tablet. By using a ratio, task IDs remain unchanged.
- The largest target width is removed and a smaller width inserted to focus our evaluation on relatively high ID tasks with practical dimensions.

By closely following an established design, the validity of the experiment is stronger and direct comparisons with previous results for direct and indirect stylus are possible.

Participants

Twelve right-handed participants were recruited (8 female), ranging in age from 22 to 34. All reported experience with touch screen devices.

Apparatus

The experiment was performed on a 3M M2256PW capacitive touch display. The 513.2 × 337.8 mm display has a resolution of 1680 × 1050 px resolution creating an effective density of 3.3 px/mm (90 DPI). This display was selected due to its very low 6 ms latency. The display was laid on a standard table, tilted at an angle of 10° towards the participant. Participants sat in a standard office chair.

Our experiment code is written in Java using the Multitouch For Java (MT4j) library. It runs on a Phenom 9950 Quad-Core 2.6 GHz Processor with 8 GB ram. All touch input events and experiment events are logged at approximately 60 Hz with no noticeable user interface lag.

Tasks and Stimuli

The primary independent variable is TASK type. We use the same six tasks as Accot and Zhai, but we follow the revised terminology introduced in Apitz et. al. [4]. Pointing and crossing tasks differ by a target precision constraint (amplitude or direction), and crossing tasks also differ by the nature of the action (discrete or continuous). There are two reciprocal pointing tasks, AP and DP, and four reciprocal crossing tasks, D/AC, D/DC, C/AC, C/DC which are illustrated in Figure 1 and described below:

***AP:** Amplitude* constrained *Pointing*. This is a traditional one-dimensional Fitts' tapping task [19]. The "infinite" vertical dimension of two rectangular targets imposes a precision constraint along the movement amplitude. In other words, since the smallest dimension of the rectangular

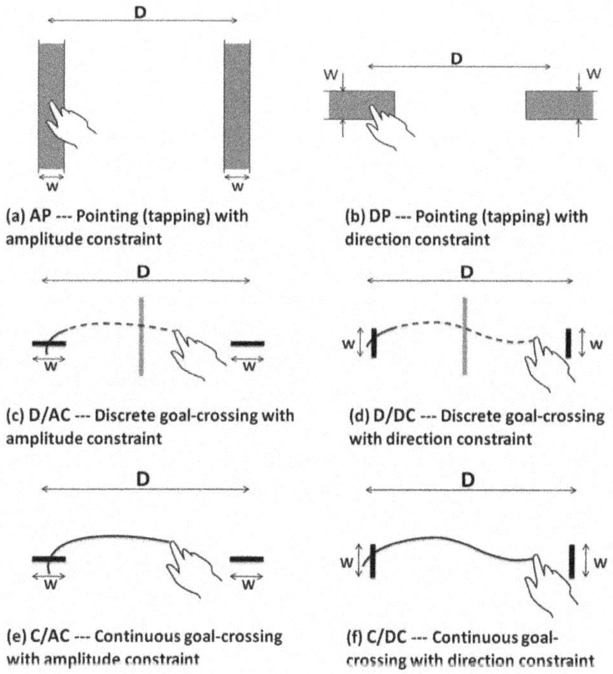

(a) AP --- Pointing (tapping) with amplitude constraint
(b) DP --- Pointing (tapping) with direction constraint
(c) D/AC --- Discrete goal-crossing with amplitude constraint
(d) D/DC --- Discrete goal-crossing with direction constraint
(e) C/AC --- Continuous goal-crossing with amplitude constraint
(f) C/DC --- Continuous goal-crossing with direction constraint

Figure 1. The six TASK conditions

target is parallel to the movement path, it requires the movement distance (called 'amplitude' in Fitts' law studies) to be more precise than the movement direction. We refer to the size of the precision constraint as the target width W. The distance between the midpoints of the targets is D.

***DP:** Directional* constrained *Pointing*. Tapping is the selection action, but the rectangular targets are rotated to be "infinite" horizontally. This imposes a precision constraint W along the approach direction of the movement path. In other words, since the smallest target dimension is orthogonal to the movement path, it requires the movement direction to be more precise than the movement amplitude. The distance between targets is D.

***D/AC:** Discrete, Amplitude-constrained Crossing*. Instead of pointing, the task is to cross two horizontal goals of width W with midpoints separated by distance D. Each goal is crossed with a downward stroke in a reciprocal pattern. A barrier between targets makes each goal crossing discrete (the finger must lift to pass over the barrier, or an error tone sounds).

***D/DC:** Discrete, Direction-constrained Crossing*. Two vertical goals of width W are each crossed left-to-right in a reciprocal pattern. A barrier makes the task discrete.

***C/AC:** Continuous, Amplitude-constrained Crossing*. The same task as D/AC, but no barrier and the finger must remain in continuous contact with the display throughout the reciprocal task, or else an error tone sounds.

C/DC: *Continuous, Direction-constrained Crossing*. The same task as D/DC, but with continuous finger contact throughout the reciprocal task.

Each task required 9 target or goal selections, each selection alternating between right and left target. The next target to select is shown in green and the other target orange. The time duration between two serial target selections creates one measurable data point, resulting in 8 measurable data trials. Participants were instructed to perform all tasks as quickly and accurately as possible.

To keep participants focused on accuracy, an error tone sounds when a target/goal is missed and that target/goal has to be completed before continuing. This produced extra tapping or crossing trials. We removed the error trials in the time analysis. A crossing was successful if the line segment formed between two successive touch points intersects with the line describing the crossing target. An error tone sounded when the line segment formed between two successive touch points intersected with the infinite line collinear with the crossing target.

Most tablet operating systems provide no cursor-like feedback for touch points, so we initially used no feedback as well. However, a 6 person pilot study with no feedback had very poor performance (a comparison to this pilot data is in our discussion). Cursor feedback for touch has been shown to be important [25]. For the main experiment, we used simple cursor feedback in the form of a gray dot at the touch position with a radius 4.6 mm transparent circle outlined in a 1 px blue stroke.

Distance and Width Combinations

To enable direct comparison with previous work, we choose values for independent variables W and D to approximately reproduce six out of seven task index of difficulties (ID) tested by Accot and Zhai [3] and four out of eight IDs tested by Forlines and Balakrishnan [14]. We accomplish this by applying a scaling ratio to previous W and D values.

For applicability to tablets, we constrain the maximum D value to be less than 203 mm, the display width of a 245 mm (10") 4:3 tablet. The maximal D must leave reasonable landing and takeoff space for crossing trajectories [12]. To estimate landing and takeoff space, we conducted a pilot experiment with 12 people, all right-handed. Participants crossed a single, centered 30.5 mm vertical crossing goal 50 times from the left, then another 50 times from the right in rapid succession. We found a mean landing area of 290.86 mm and mean takeoff area of 217.21 mm. This is a highly unconstrained task, so these means are more representative of upper bounds.

Using this additional distance constraint, we establish the largest distance as D = 203 mm, or 666 px. Given Accot and Zhai's largest distance of 1024 px, this creates a scaling ratio of 0.65 resulting in two distances, D = 203 and 50.8 mm. However, Accot and Zhai's smallest 8 px target width[1] scales to 1.6 mm (5 px) on our device, well below recommended touch target sizes [18]. Early pilots confirmed that very small crossing targets had high error rates, so we remove the smallest 1.6 mm. The remaining scaled target/goal widths are W = 3.2, 6.4, 12.7, and 25.4 mm. We insert a fifth W = 5.0 mm to provide additional ID data points and access to mobile-sized applications, since 5mm is the key width of the touchscreen keyboard on Galaxy Nexus. Across all D-W combinations, the ID range is 1.6 to 6.0.

Design and Protocol

The experiment design is within-subjects, repeated measures, and full factorial. For each of the six TASKS, participants performed 1 full practice block and 2 consecutive measurement BLOCKS of 10 sets of D-W trials. Each set of trials covered one D-W combination and required 9 reciprocal selections of targets or goals to create 8 measured trials between successive selections. TASK order was counterbalanced using a Latin Square and the order for the set of D-W trials was randomized.

A short instruction and demonstration block was presented at the beginning of each TASK with three sets of trials for one D-W combination (D = 121mm, W = 30mm, ID = 2.32). Short rest breaks were enforced at the end of each task and encouraged after each block. The experiment took 45 minutes on average. In summary:

6 TASKS (AP, DP, D/AC, D/DC, C/AC, C/DC) ×
2 BLOCKS ×
2 distances D (203.8, 50.8 mm) ×
5 widths W (3.2, 5.0, 6.4, 12.7, 25.4 mm) ×
8 measured target selections
= 960 data points per participant

Results

Although we intended the first block to function as a practice block, since it was a full block we can use it to test for leaning effects. Including the practice block, we found no significant effects for BLOCK or BLOCK × TASK (Figure 2) confirming no learning effects were present.

Selection Time

Selection time is the mean duration of each measured selection. There is a main effect of TASK on selection time ($F_{5,55}$=13.91, p<0.0001). Post hoc analysis[2] found that C/DC is significantly different than D/AC, D/DC, and C/AC (all p<0.001). Continuous crossing tasks are significantly different from pointing tasks (all p<0.01). Among them, C/AC was slowest (743ms, 198 STD) and C/DC fastest (464ms, 190 STD). There are no significant differences between AP (610ms, 87 STD), DP (615ms, 136 STD), D/AC (689ms, 198 STD), or D/DC (718ms, 148 STD).

[1] An 8 px target translates to 1.0 mm in motor space on the 7.9 px/mm indirect stylus tablet used by Accot and Zhai. Forlines and Balakrishnan use an even smaller 0.7 mm target. These target sizes are small even for stylus input.

[2] All post hoc tests use the TukeyHSD adjustment.

As predicted by previous work, movement distance D significantly affected time ($F_{1,11}$=222.4, p<0.0001). The time to select targets at the long distance was 764 ms (188 STD), 46% slower than the short distance (Figure 3). Target width W also had a significant effect on selection time ($F_{4,44}$=113.5, p<0.0001). Post hoc analysis indicated that all widths were significantly different with each other (all p<0.04). (Figure 4). The mean time for W = 3.2mm is 934 ms (260 STD), 59% slower than the mean time of all other widths, and more than twice the mean completion time W = 25.4mm at 426 ms (120 STD).

Error

There is a main effect of TASK on error ($F_{5,55}$=2.535, p=0.039). But given high probably type I error, post hoc analysis found no differences. Task error rates are similar (AP 12%, DP 15%, D/AC 15%, D/DC 13%, C/AC 17%, C/DC-12%). Our error rates are higher than Accot and Zhai, but lower than Forlines and Balakrishnan for all tasks except D/AC (see discussion and Figure 7). Note that our smallest w = 3.6 mm is small for touch input [18] and Forlines and Balakrishnan tested extremely small targets, so higher error rates are expected.

There is main effect of W on error ($F_{4,44}$=11.75, p<0.0001). Post hoc tests reveal that all pairs of widths are significantly different (all p < 0.0001), except for W=5.0mm with W=6.4mm, and W=12.7mm with W=25.4mm. The significance and quantity of errors for widths remained the same even if only crossing tasks were analyzed. Given that error increases from 4% for W=12.7mm to 16% for W=6.4mm, we recommend touch crossing targets no smaller than 12.7mm without further investigation.

There is also a main effect for D on error ($F_{1,11}$=34.94, p<0.001). Post hoc tests found error rates are marginally higher for D = 203.3mm (16%) compared to D = 50.8mm are (12%). We believe that the longer distance encourages a higher velocity and this reduces crossing accuracy.

Post-experiment Questionnaire

A post-experiment questionnaire collected subjective participant opinion of touch crossing and tapping. Interestingly, 8 out of 12 participants said tapping was easier, but 8 out of 12 said crossing is more accurate. 10 out of 12 participants said targets with a directional constraint were easier and more accurate.

Fitts' Law Modeling

Five tasks are modeled well with Fitts' Law with high fitness values (Table 1). However, the model for D/DC achieves only r^2=78%. This unexpected result encourages us to seek a more accurate predictive model for this task condition. Inspired by FFitts Law, a stronger model for touch pointing interactions with small targets, we designed Experiment 2 and tested the predictive power of FFitts Law on touch crossing interactions.

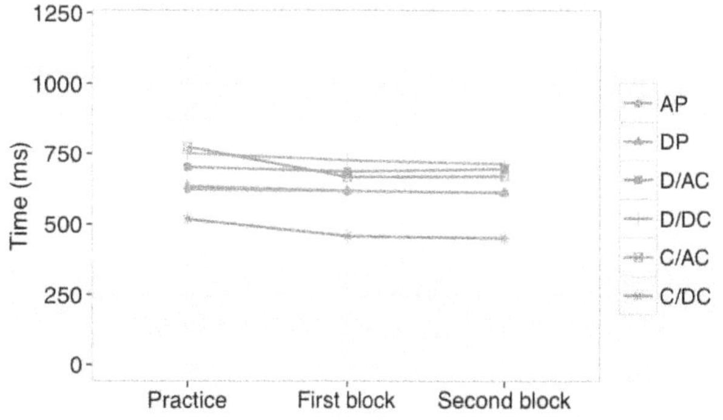

Figure 2. Effect of BLOCK on task time

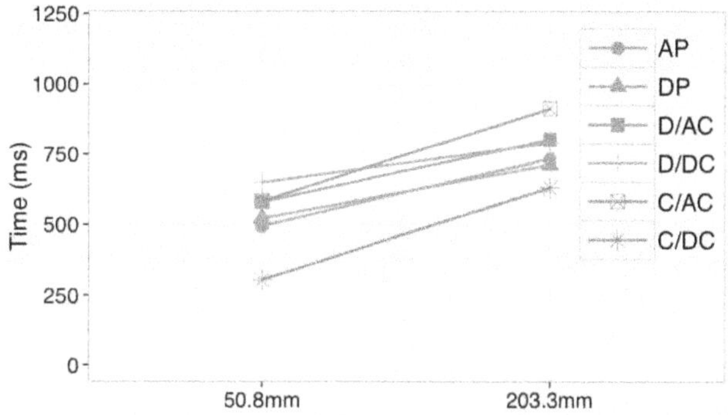

Figure 3. Effect of D on task time

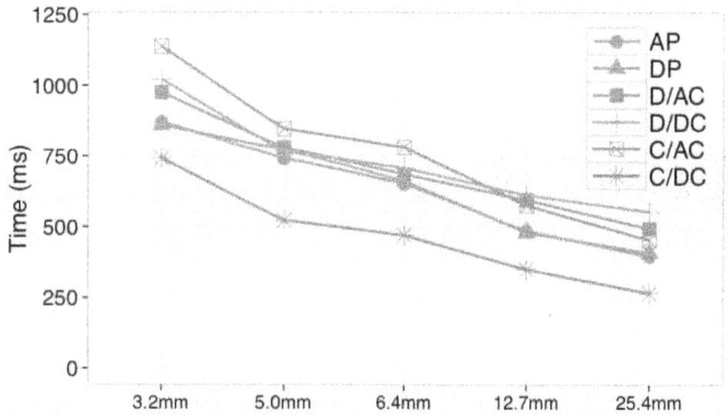

Figure 4. Effect of W on task time

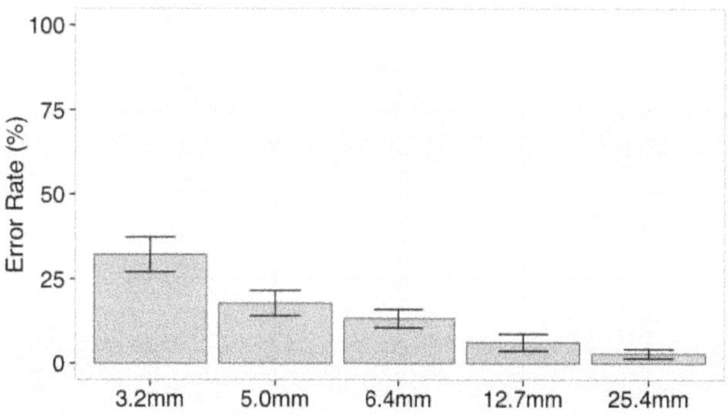

Figure 5. Error rates by width for crossing tasks (all error bars in figures are 95% CI)

AP:	$T = 24.45 + 158.12 \times ID$	$r^2 = 96.48\%$
DP:	$T = 75.29 + 147.16 \times ID$	$r^2 = 91.87\%$
D/AC:	$T = 141.03 + 147.62 \times ID$	$r^2 = 93.53\%$
D/DC:	$T = 247.81 + 126.89 \times ID$	$r^2 = 77.79\%$
C/AC:	$T = -51.98 + 211.39 \times ID$	$r^2 = 94.54\%$
C/DC:	$T = -195.39 + 173.92 \times ID$	$r^2 = 95.81\%$

Table 1. Fitts' law models for all tasks

Discussion

The subjective results from our questionnaire align with our main quantitative finding: in terms of time and error rate, touch crossing is as good, or better, than pointing with directionally constrained targets. Orthogonal targets also had the highest performing in the Accot and Zhai and Dixon et al. stylus crossing studies [3,12]. Considering only orthogonal targets, continuous crossing is 33% faster than pointing in our experiment.

Comparison of Touch Crossing to Stylus Crossing

To contextualize touch crossing performance, we can make direct comparisons with stylus crossing performance for indirect stylus in Accot and Zhai [3] and direct stylus in Forlines and Balakrishnan [14]. This is possible because our experiment and Forlines and Balakrishnan's experiment are near replications of Accot and Zhai's original study. Our comparison uses quantitative results determined by analyzing figures in both papers, so quantities are approximate. In addition, recall that we reproduce 6 out of 8 task IDs used in Accot and Zhai and 4 out of 8 IDs from Forlines and Balakrishnan. We removed higher ID tasks to accommodate known limitations of touch input, but we also inserted an additional medium high ID. Our intention is to contextualize rather than make definitive conclusions.

Task time for touch crossing compares favorably with both indirect stylus crossing and direct stylus crossing (Figure 6). While indirect stylus and touch have a similar performance trend across tasks (with C/DC performing fastest), the trend for direct stylus favors crossing with amplitude targets. Error rates are lower for indirect stylus in all cases, but touch crossing error rates are lower than all direct stylus crossing tasks except D/AC.

Cursor Feedback Visualization

Because touch cursor feedback is rarely used in commercial devices, we originally ran a version of Experiment 1 without any cursor feedback. After 6 participants (3 female), we found error rates were extremely high. Participants were frustrated and some "gave up." We abandoned this approach and considered this a "no feedback pilot" for Exper-

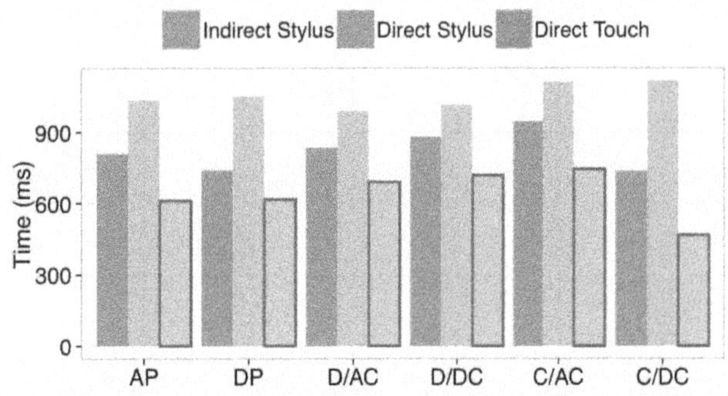

Figure 6. Time comparison with previous work: Accot and Zhai *indirect stylus* [3]; Forlines and Balakrishnan *direct stylus* [14]; our experiment 1 *direct touch*

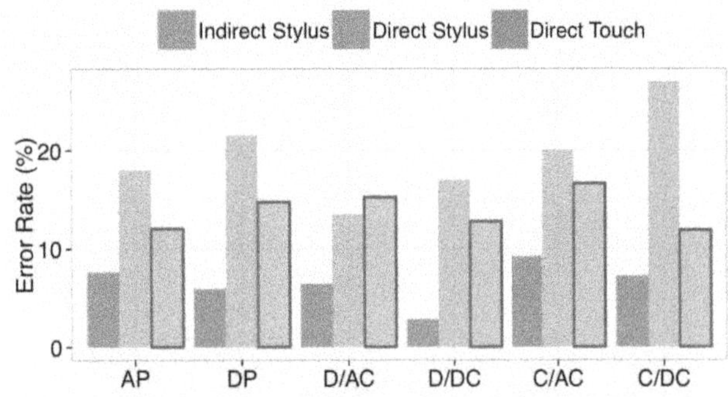

Figure 7. Error comparison with previous work: Accot and Zhai *indirect stylus* [3]; Forlines and Balakrishnan *direct stylus* [14]; our experiment 1 *direct touch.*

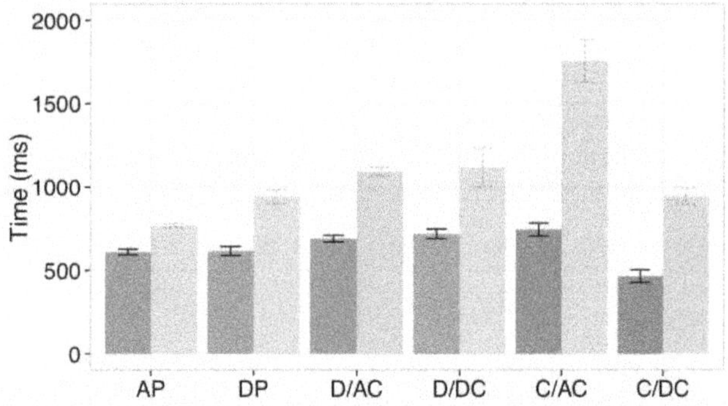

Figure 8. Comparison of time by TASK type: experiment 1 data *with* feedback (dark colours); data from a pilot evaluation *without* feedback (light colours).

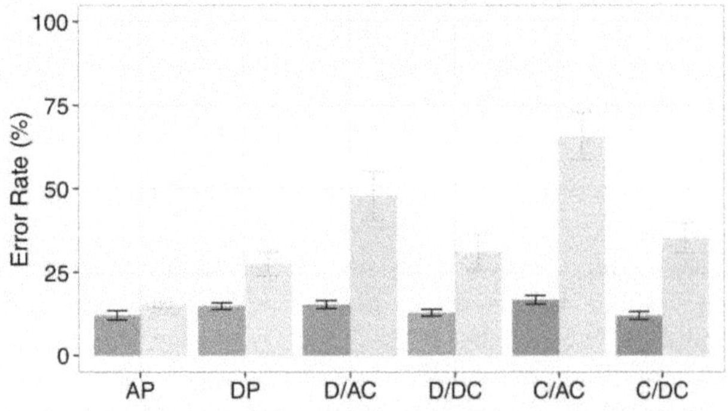

Figure 9. Comparison of error rate by TASK type: experiment 1 data *with* feedback (dark colours); data from a pilot evaluation *without* feedback (light colours).

iment 1. However, this data enables us to compare the time and error rates between the no feedback pilot and main experiment using the circular cursor visualization Adding the circle cursor feedback decreases time and decreases errors (Figure 8, Figure 9), but it remains unclear if other types of feedback are also effective.

Poor Fitts' Law Model for D/DC

Discrete crossing is practically necessary for any crossing interaction. A discrete crossing action must be performed at the start and end of all crossing interactions, even when crossing multiple goals in a continuous action. So the poor modeling with Fitts' law is a concern. In the next experiment we apply Bi et al.'s FFitts law [9] to D/DC.

EXPERIMENT 2: FFITTS LAW FOR CROSSING

Our primary goal is to apply Bi et al.'s FFitts law [9], a modification of Fitts' law [19] to directionally constrained crossing to attain a better model for D/DC. Our motivation is that FFitts law explicitly considers precision with touch input, and this is a possible reason for the poor fit of D/DC with Fitts' law. In addition, since cursor feedback affected performance in Experiment 1, we also examine the effect of different types of feedback in more detail.

Fitts' law and FFitts law

Fitts' law models the tradeoff between speed and accuracy in human performance using a single distribution of selection endpoints. This distribution is a function of the nominal target distance D and the effective target width W_e, where $W_e = \sqrt{2\pi e}\sigma$and σ is the empirically observed variability of selection endpoints. However, when using an input modality like touch, a portion of endpoint variability is due to the absolute precision of the finger. This is a second distribution independent of the relative speed accuracy tradeoff distribution modeled by Fitts' law.

FFitts law breaks σ into two endpoint distributions: one resulting from the relative speed-accuracy tradeoff σ_R and the other resulting from absolute accuracy σ_A. Assuming central distributions, these are related as $\sigma^2 = \sigma_R^2 + \sigma_A^2$ and the FFitts index of difficulty is expressed as:

$$ID_f = \log_2\left(\left(D/\sqrt{2\pi e(\sigma^2 - \sigma_A^2}\right) + 1\right)$$

To apply FFitts law, we use the empirically measured distributions of endpoints σ from Experiment 1 and we calculate σ_A for directionally constrained crossing using this controlled experiment. Bi et al. used a similar controlled experiment design to find σ_A for touch tapping.

Participants

Twelve right-handed participants were recruited (6 female), ranging in age from 19 to 29. All reported experience with touch screen devices.

Apparatus

The same apparatus as Experiment 1 was used.

Task and Stimuli

We tailor the "Finger Calibration Task," used by Bi et al.'s Experiment 1, to directionally constrained crossing. A single 0.6mm crossing target is shown at the center of the display with no distance amplitude specified. This target size follows Bi et al.'s recommendations: it is very small, but still legible (2 px on our display) and it requires the highest possible precision to achieve. Two vertical bars placed 10 px to either side of the small target reminded participants to cross horizontally, and they were asked to cross left to right to be consistent with the directionally constrained tasks in Experiment 1.

In each trial, the participant first tapped a larger start button to force a break, and then crossed the small target. We asked participants not to rush and focus on accuracy: measuring σ_A is not about speed [9]. A magnified view of vertical deviation from the target was shown and an error sound played if the target was missed. Both were intended to help participants focus on accuracy. Errors were determined in the same way as Experiment 1.

Cursor Feedback Type

We tested four types of cursor FEEDBACK (Figure 10). FEEDBACK C is a gray dot at the touch position with a radius 4.6mm transparent circle outlined in a 1 px blue stroke. This is the same cursor visualization used in Experiment 1. FEEDBACK T is a 1 px thick blue line representing the trail of 35 recent touch points. FEEDBACK CT combined the circle cursor and trail stroke. FEEDBACK N has no feedback.

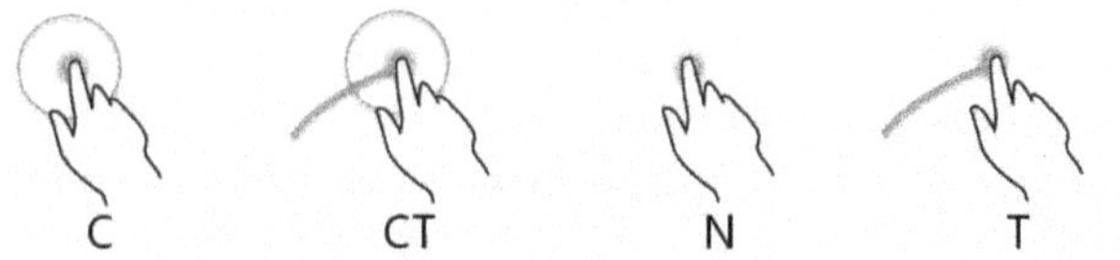

Figure 10. Cursor FEEDBACK type: C for cursor only; CT for cursor and trail; N for none; T for trail only.

Procedure and design

The experiment design is within-subjects, repeated measures, and full factorial. For each of the four cursor FEEDBACKs presented in randomized order, participants performed 10 practice trials and then 10 measured trials. A post-experiment questionnaire asked participants to rank the four FEEDBACK types in terms of ease-of use and accuracy. The experiment took 10 minutes on average.

Results

4.4% (20 out of 453) data points more than three standard deviations from the mean were removed as outliers.

Absolute Precision Distribution (σ_A)

The distribution of deviations from target center, called σ_A, is the standard deviation of all intersection points between the touch path and the vertical line through the target. Smaller σ_A values reflect higher absolute accuracy.

There is a main effect of FEEDBACK on σ_A ($F_{3,33}$=0.003, p=3.416). However post hoc analysis found no significant differences in means (Table 2). During the experiment participants in the N condition appeared to cause appreciably more audible error tones than the rest. An analysis of error rate showed a main effect of FEEDBACK on error rate ($F_{3,33}$=16.53, p=0.005). Post hoc analysis found the error rate of N (85.8%) was significantly different and was higher than all other feedback types, while no difference has been found between C, CT and T. In the post-experiment questionnaire, ten out of twelve participants said N was most difficult and least accurate.

FEEDBACK	σ_A (mm)	Errors (%)	Speed (m/s)
C	1.12	38.3	0.22
CT	0.96	32.5	0.16
N	1.59	85.8	0.23
T	1.03	35	0.16

Table 2. σ_A, error rate, speed by FEEDBACK type.

The selection deviation distributions for each feedback type provide more insight into reasons why N has such a high error rate, but more reasonable σ_A (Figure 11). C, CT, and T have modes near the target center, so distributions are in the target. The mean of N is below the target, so the distribution σ_A does not fall within the target. This consistent offset is similar to Holz and Baudisch's observation of perceived versus actual input positions with touch tapping [18].

FFitts Law for Directionally Constrained Crossing

We apply FFitts Law to the data from the two directionally constrained tasks in Experiment 1, D/DC and C/DC, using Bi et al.'s procedure [9]. Our intent is to improve the D/DC model, but we include C/DC for completeness. We use the σ_A value for C feedback since it was used in Experiment 1. We calculate σ values using the same method as σ_A, but on the actual target widths in Experiment 1.

At first, modeling with FFitts Law was very poor for D/DC with r^2=58.53%, but reasonable for C/DC with r^2=84.31% albeit lower than Fitts' Law (Figure 13). On closer inspection of the D/DC data, we noted that the highest error rate (30%) and longest time was for ID = 6.1, the combination of W = 3.2 mm and D = 203.3 mm. Looking at the distribution of crossing points for W = 3.2 mm revealed a slight bimodal distribution, not seen with W = 3.2 mm and the short distance D = 50.8 mm (Figure 12). FFitts law assumes a unimodal distribution of selection points, so it is not surprising that it did not work well with this point.

To test our hypothesis, we removed the unusual ID = 6 points and re-ran the regression with FFitts law. This time the r^2 for D/DC fitness improved from 75.26% with standard Fitts' law to 84.3% with FFitts law. The fit for C/DC remained similar at r^2 = 85.9 (Figure 13). Admittedly, a higher r^2 value is desirable, but our exercise provides evidence for the applicability of FFitts law to crossing.

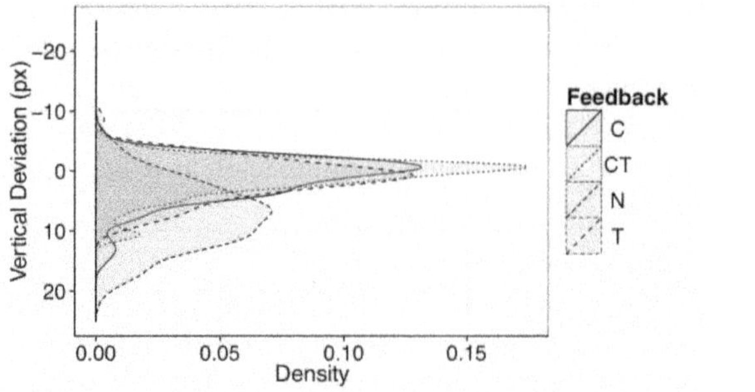

Figure 11. Distribution of crossing points, by FEEDBACK

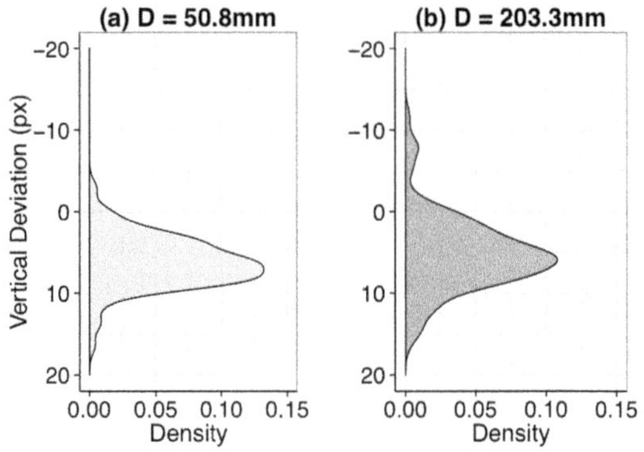

Figure 12. Crossing point distributions for D/DC with W = 3.2 mm for the two distances

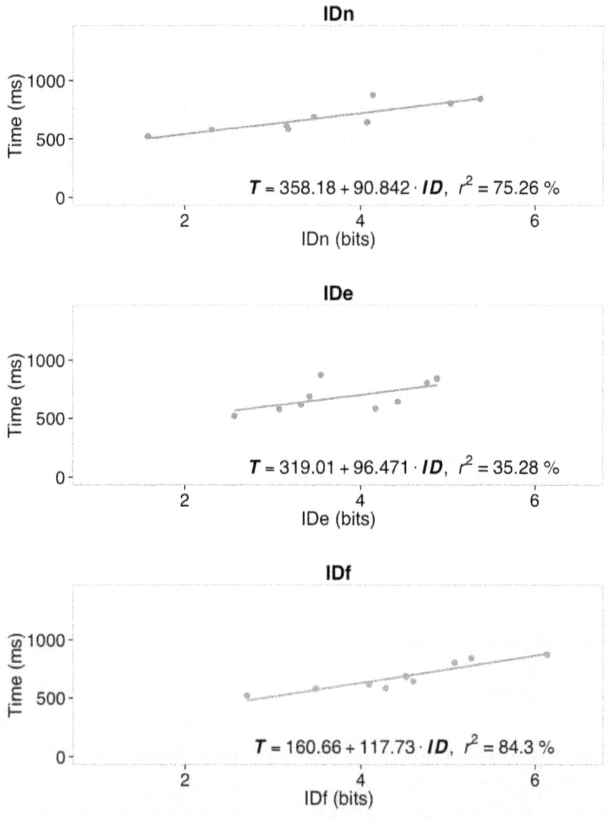

Figure 13. Modeling D/DC using: (IDn) Fitts' law; (IDe) Fitts' law with effective width; (IDf) FFitts law.

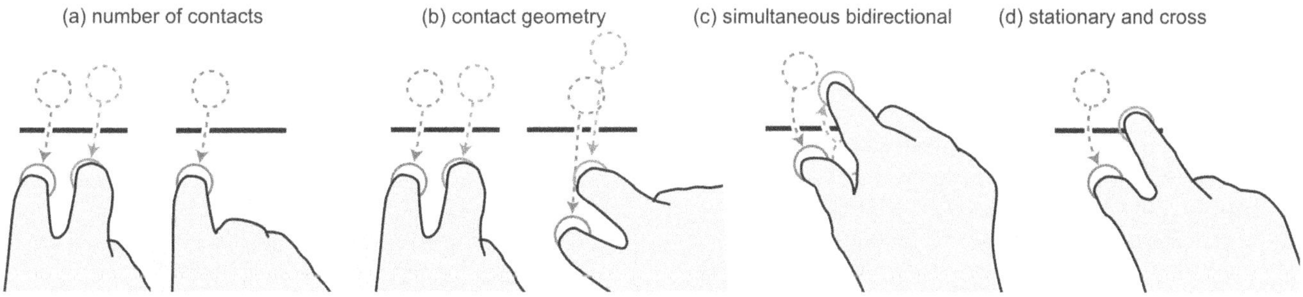

Figure 14. Examples of expressive multi-touch crossing: (a) different crossing actions depending on number of contacts; (b) different crossing actions by changing the crossing contact geometry; (c) simultaneous bidirectional crossing of two contacts similar to a 'finger snap'; (d) keep one contact stationary while crossing with another contact

IMPLICATIONS FOR DESIGN

Designers creating crossing interfaces for direct touch can use these basic guidelines based on our empirical data:

- The minimum recommended touch crossing target width is 12.7 mm.
- Like pen input, crossing targets should be positioned orthogonal to the direction of movement (directionally constrained) when possible.
- Continuous touch crossing is better than pointing, but if many discrete crossing actions, the benefit is lost.
- With discrete crossing, the combination of small targets and long distances introduces some abnormal behavior.
- We have evidence that a perceived input location [18] applies to touch crossing.

More Expressive Multi-touch Crossing

With touch crossing empirically validated as a practical and efficient selection technique, we can explore other novel forms of touch crossing. For example, Accot and Zhai [3] present an idea for bi-directional target crossing, where crossing in one direction triggers one command, and crossing in the other direction triggers another command. CrossY [5] implements this idea with crossing goals that perform an action in one direction but make it easy to instantly undo that action when crossed back from the other direction. Accot and Zhai cite bidirectional crossing as just one example of the richer semantics possible when crossing compared to pointing, stating "in some sense crossing is a step from pointing towards free gesturing…". With multi-touch input, crossing semantics can be even richer than with pen or mouse.

A simple extension of bidirectional crossing is to assign a different action according to the number of fingers used to cross (Figure 14a). Wider goals are needed to reliably cross with multiple touch points which seems like a disadvantage, but this also means that five smaller goals could be combined to one large goals and the same five actions still possible using crossing with 1 to 5 contacts.

With two or more contacts, the geometric relationship between contacts and the goal during crossing enables even more variations in triggered actions. For example, the line segment between two touch points can be orthogonal or collinear with the crossing goal, with each triggering a different action (Figure 14b).

There is no requirement that multiple touch points cross a goal from the same side. Placing the thumb and index finger on either side of a goal, then making a snapping movement while maintaining contact, creates a simultaneous crossing from both sides (Figure 14c). This movement can be further differentiated when performed in the reverse directions. A similar action can be made with the index and middle finger.

There is also no reason why both fingers must cross. One contact can remain stationary while the other crosses (Figure 14d). The stationary finger could even activate crossing targets for neighboring fingers to cross. This could pack more crossing targets in a small area by activating them only when a button is pressed or overload a standard touch event without resorting to dwell time.

Combining touch input with crossing may provide a way to further increase touch expressivity and help close the performance gap when abandoning mouse and keyboard.

CONCLUSION AND FUTURE WORK

Our work serves to validate crossing performance for touch and demonstrates a new application of FFitts law. This new empirical evidence provides necessary support for crossing-based interaction techniques in touch interfaces.

Future empirical work includes reproducing and validating Dixon et al.'s [12] direct stylus crossing dialog experiments with touch input, but our results already suggest more work on crossing application for people with motor impairments, building on [16], examining one handed thumb crossing with smartphones and designing touch crossing only interfaces like CrossY [5]. Most of all, our results provide a confident footing to implement and evaluate the more expressive multi-touch crossing ideas described above.

REFERENCES

1. Accot, J. and Zhai, S. Beyond Fitts' law: models for trajectory-based HCI tasks. *Proc. of the SIGCHI conference on Human factors in computing systems*, ACM (1997), 295–302.
2. Accot, J. and Zhai, S. Scale effects in steering law tasks. *Proc. of the SIGCHI conference on Human factors in computing systems*, ACM (2001), 1–8.
3. Accot, J. and Zhai, S. More than dotting the i's --- foundations for crossing-based interfaces. *Proceedings of the SIGCHI conference on Human factors in computing systems*, ACM (2002), 73–80.
4. Apitz, G., Guimbretière, F., and Zhai, S. Foundations for designing and evaluating user interfaces based on the crossing paradigm. *ACM Trans. Comput.-Hum. Interact. 17*, 2 (2008), 9:1–9:42.
5. Apitz, G. and Guimbretière, F. CrossY: a crossing-based drawing application. *Proceedings of the 17th annual ACM symposium on User interface software and technology*, ACM (2004), 3–12.
6. Baudisch, P. Don't click, paint! Using toggle maps to manipulate sets of toggle switches. *Proc. of the 11th annual ACM symposium on User interface software and technology*, ACM (1998), 65–66.
7. Benko, H. and Wigdor, D. Imprecision, Inaccuracy, and Frustration: The Tale of Touch Input. In C. Müller-Tomfelde, ed., *Tabletops - Horizontal Interactive Displays*. Springer London, 2010, 249–275.
8. Benko, H., Wilson, A.D., and Baudisch, P. Precise selection techniques for multi-touch screens. *Proc. of the SIGCHI conference on Human Factors in computing systems*, ACM (2006), 1263–1272.
9. Bi, X., Li, Y., and Zhai, S. FFitts law: modeling finger touch with fitts' law. *Proc. of the SIGCHI Conference on Human Factors in Computing Systems*, ACM (2013), 1363–1372.
10. Buxton, W.A.S., Hill, R., and Rowley, P. Issues and techniques in touch-sensitive tablet input. *SIGGRAPH Comput. Graph 19*, 3 (1985), 215–224.
11. Cockburn, A. Understanding performance in touch selections: Tap, drag and radial pointing drag with finger, stylus and mouse. *International Journal of Human - Computer Studies 70*, 3 (2012), 218–233.
12. Dixon, M., Guimbretière, F., and Chen, N. Optimal parameters for efficient crossing-based dialog boxes. *Proc. of the SIGCHI Conference on Human Factors in Computing Systems*, ACM (2008), 1623–1632.
13. Dragicevic, P. Combining crossing-based and paper-based interaction paradigms for dragging and dropping between overlapping windows. *Proc. of the 17th annual ACM symposium on User interface software and technology*, ACM (2004), 193–196.
14. Forlines, C. and Balakrishnan, R. Evaluating tactile feedback and direct vs. indirect stylus input in pointing and crossing selection tasks. *Proc. of the twenty-sixth annual SIGCHI conference on Human factors in computing systems*, ACM (2008), 1563–1572.
15. Forlines, C., Wigdor, D., Shen, C., and Balakrishnan, R. Direct-touch vs. mouse input for tabletop displays. *Proc. of the SIGCHI conference on Human factors in computing systems*, ACM (2007), 647–656.
16. Guerreiro, T., Nicolau, H., Jorge, J., and Gonçalves, D. Towards accessible touch interfaces. *Proc. of the 12th international ACM SIGACCESS conference on Computers and accessibility*, ACM (2010), 19–26.
17. Holz, C. and Baudisch, P. The generalized perceived input point model and how to double touch accuracy by extracting fingerprints. *Proc. of the SIGCHI Conference on Human Factors in Computing Systems*, ACM (2010), 581–590.
18. Holz, C. and Baudisch, P. Understanding touch. *Proc. of the SIGCHI Conference on Human Factors in Computing Systems*, ACM (2011), 2501–2510.
19. MacKenzie, I.S. Fitts' Law as a Research and Design Tool in Human-Computer Interaction. *Human-Computer Interaction 7*, 1 (1992), 91–139.
20. Nakamura, T., Takahashi, S., and Tanaka, J. Double-Crossing: A New Interaction Technique for Hand Gesture Interfaces. *Proc. of the 8th Asia-Pacific conference on Computer-Human Interaction*, Springer-Verlag (2008), 292–300.
21. Roth, V. and Turner, T. Bezel swipe: conflict-free scrolling and multiple selection on mobile touch screen devices. *Proc. of SIGCHI Conf. on Human Factors in Computing Systems*, ACM (2009), 1523–1526.
22. Sasangohar, F., MacKenzie, I.S., and Scott, S.D. Evaluation of Mouse and Touch Input for a Tabletop Display Using Fitts' Reciprocal Tapping Task. *Proc. of the Human Factors and Ergonomics Society Annual Meeting 53*, 12 (2009), 839–843.
23. Sulaiman, A.N. and Olivier, P. Attribute gates. *Proc. of the 21st annual ACM symposium on User interface software and technology*, ACM (2008), 57–66.
24. Vogel, D. and Baudisch, P. Shift: a technique for operating pen-based interfaces using touch. *Proc. of the SIGCHI conference on Human factors in computing systems*, ACM (2007), 657–666.
25. Wigdor, D., Williams, S., Cronin, M., et al. Ripples: utilizing per-contact visualizations to improve user interaction with touch displays. *Proc. of the 22nd annual ACM symposium on User interface software and technology*, ACM (2009), 3–12.
26. Wobbrock, J.O. and Gajos, K.Z. Goal Crossing with Mice and Trackballs for People with Motor Impairments: Performance, Submovements, and Design Directions. *ACM Trans. Access. Comput. 1*, 1 (2008), 4:1–4:37.
27. Yoshikawa, T., Shizuki, B., and Tanaka, J. HandyWidgets: local widgets pulled-out from hands. *Proc. of the 2012 ACM international conference on Interactive tabletops and surfaces*, ACM (2012), 197–200.

Easy Does It: More Usable CAPTCHAs

Elie Bursztein
Google
elieb@google.com

Angelika Moscicki
Google
moscicki@google.com

Celine Fabry
contact@celine.im

Steven Bethard
University of Alabama at Birmingham
bethard@uab.edu

John C. Mitchell
Stanford University
jcm@cs.stanford.edu

Dan Jurafsky
Stanford University
jurafsky@stanford.edu

ABSTRACT
Websites present users with puzzles called CAPTCHAs to curb abuse caused by computer algorithms masquerading as people. While CAPTCHAs are generally effective at stopping abuse, they might impair website usability if they are not properly designed.

In this paper we describe how we designed two new CAPTCHA schemes for Google that focus on maximizing usability. We began by running an evaluation on Amazon Mechanical Turk with over 27,000 respondents to test the usability of different feature combinations. Then we studied user preferences using Google's consumer survey infrastructure. Finally, drawing on the insights gleaned during those studies, we tested our new captcha schemes first on Mechanical Turk and then on a fraction of production traffic. The resulting scheme is now an integral part of our production system and is served to millions of users. Our scheme achieved a 95.3% human accuracy, a 6.7% improvement.

Author Keywords
Security; CAPTCHA; World Wide Web; Empirical Methods; Quantitative Usability Testing and Evaluation; User Studies;

ACM Classification Keywords
K.6.5. Management of computing and information systems: Security and Protection

Introduction
Distinguishing computers from humans is a central issue for website security. For example, GMail must prevent abuse by automated spammers, eBay must stop bots from flooding its site with scams, and Facebook must block the proliferation of fake profiles used to send spam and cheat at games.

CHI 2014, April 26–May 1, 2014, Toronto, Ontario, Canada.

ACM 978-1-4503-2473-1/14/04..$15.00.
http://dx.doi.org/10.1145/2556288.2557322.

Captchas [18] [1] allow websites to make this distinction automatically. Captchas usually take the form of distorted or rotated sequences of characters that are easy for humans to recognize, but are hopefully difficult for computers to process. Over the last years at Google, in collaboration with Stanford University, we have been working on designing usable and yet effective captchas schemes using a systematic design approach.

This work focuses on designing a high usability captcha for use in cases with low risk, where the captcha is used primarily as a means to elicit an interactive engagement with the end user. As with any security mechanism, captcha design involves a tradeoff between security and usability. An easier captcha can be used when the impact of abuse is low, or when it has been verified by other means that the user is unlikely to be an attacker (e.g., from a trusted IP address). However, even in the low risk case, designing a usable captcha is still a challenge.

We ran an extensive study of visual features that are used in captchas (e.g., adding a line) and how they interact in order to understand how they affect the difficulty of the captcha, and alter user perception. Our user preference study shows that these two are not in fact the same.

Based on the insights gleaned during this study, we were able to devise a new captcha scheme that increased our users' pass rate by 6.7% over our previous scheme. We were able to do this without compromising the security of our system, but our system does not rely on captchas in isolation.

We began by identifying a set of distinctive security features that are common across the thirteen most widely used captcha schemes [5, 6] or mentioned in previous work on captcha usability [8]. We supplemented them with visual features described in human legibility and readability litterature [3,14,17]. Our feature set includes basic text features such as character set, font size and color, anti-segmentation techniques such as overlapping characters, and anti-recognition techniques such as character rotation. We implemented an open source generator (`http://goo.gl/ZPejcY`), that allows us to create new captchas based on combinations of features.

[1] We write this acronym in lower case for readability.

We conducted our study by presenting our generated captchas to users and measuring how the different features influenced solving time and accuracy. We examined the effects of each feature in isolation and analyzed the interaction between features by varying multiple features at the same time.

To conduct this study on a scale large enough to obtain meaningful results, we built an application for Amazon's Mechanical Turk[2] (AMT) and used it to record human performance on nearly a million captchas. To our knowledge, this study is the first large scale systematic study of captcha features.

Our work confirms some of the findings of previous work [8] on a large scale and in real-world conditions, while also expanding the set of features tested. We also explored how computer hardware (namely screen resolution) impacts human accuracy and solving time. We find that screen resolution does not have a significant impact on captcha accuracy or solving time.

Besides studying features in isolation, our study is also the first to systematically analyze how feature combinations (in particular pairwise interactions) affect user accuracy and solving time. We uncovered an important limit to systematic design: predicting the effect of interactions between features is currently intractable. Our analysis reveals that this limitation stems from the fact that the effect on accuracy of many feature interactions, 20.7% of the pairwise interactions, requires a nonlinear function to be described and there is no clear pattern to which interactions are nonlinear. This means that we can't reliably predict the outcome of a specific feature combination using statistical analysis or machine learning.

This led us to use an iterative approach with human testing to reach our final design. We offer multiple examples of how unexpected interactions impact accuracy, demonstrating how important iterative HCI methods are to the field.

Finally, our study of user preferences about captcha schemes reveals that perceived captcha difficulty is not necessarily aligned with their real difficulty. For instance, when words are used, the meaning and frequency of the words greatly affects user perception of difficulty. Negative words and low frequency words are perceived as harder to complete, whereas positive or high frequency words are perceived to be easier.

The accuracy we observed on AMT (97%) turned out to be very close to the accuracy we observed in production (95.3%), confirming that AMT is an effective way to approximate real world results. On the other hand, deploying our scheme on real world traffic allowed us to discover very subtle usability issues due to feature interactions that are only observable on extremely large sample size. This led us to conclude that AMT is a great tool for rapid iteration but it needs to be supplemented with large scale A/B testing on real traffic to polish captcha design.

The remainder of the paper is organized as follows: first we present our AMT experimental setup, then we report accuracy and solving time for each feature in isolation. Next we analyze feature combinations, and show why predicting feature interaction outcomes is currently intractable. Then we report the result of our user preferences study, and discuss how user perception of difficulty differs from the measured accuracy and solving time. Finally we discuss how we used what we learned to design Google's new captcha schemes, and conclude by discussing the lessons learned throughout this study and how they generalize beyond captchas.

[2] `http://www.mturk.com`

BACKGROUND AND RELATED WORK

The most similar previous work [8] mainly focused on testing a specific set of security features in a laboratory setting on a small population (76 participants). The authors studied the impact of a subset of the features studied in this paper, but they did not examine character collapsing, which is the most common security feature used today [6], or any aesthetic features. They also did not consider the interactions between features. In [2], the authors studied the usability of a specific captcha scheme called ScatterType, where parts of the characters are erased and the fragments are separated. They examined in a lab setting how different fonts affect solving accuracy. They also studied easily confusable characters such as 'c' and 'e' impact usability. In [4] the authors look at the usability issues in presenting audio captchas to humans and in [22] the authors study the effect of page aesthetics and feedback when running captcha tasks.

In [25], the authors discuss the usability of image-based captchas but didn't perform a user study. In [13] the authors study how to balance security and usability for video-based captchas. More recently, [23] revisited this topic and extended it to all sort of moving captchas. In [7], human performance on captchas was considered for both humans and computers but only for single-character recognition.

CAPTCHA FEATURES STUDY

The main goal of this study was to understand how each feature used in captchas affects user accuracy and solving time, both in isolation and in combination. First we established a baseline by measuring how well users solve captchas where the fonts, colors, etc. were all set to common web browser defaults. Then we measured how users responded to changes in individual features in isolation. Finally, we measured user response to variation in pairs of features. This set of experiments was run on AMT.

Users. We recruited participants for our study from Amazon's Mechanical Turk (AMT) [12], an online marketplace providing workers who solve Human Intelligence Tasks (HITs). We chose AMT primarily because it gave us access to a large number of participants, suitable for the scale of our study. AMT has also been used successfully for user studies in related fields [12, 19]. In all of our experimental settings, we presented AMT workers (colloquially,"Turkers") with a survey of basic demographic information like age, language, and education. Turkers were paid $.30 to solve a series of 20 captchas, one at a time, before answering the survey.

Turkers typed in their guesses for each captcha and we recorded their responses and solving time. 27,422 Turkers participated in the study according to Amazon's count.

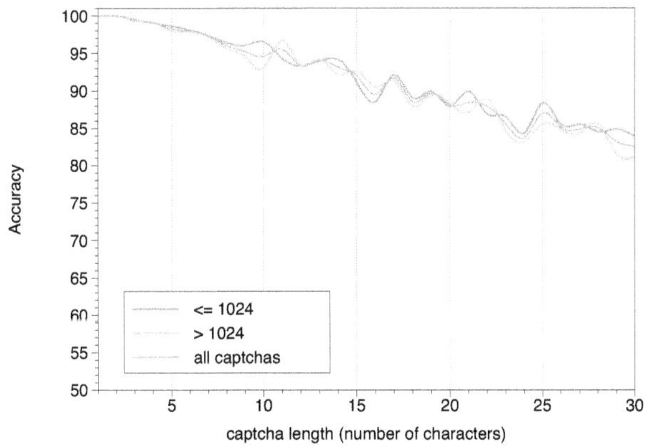

Figure 1. The non-impact of screen resolution on captcha solving accuracy.

As in previous studies using AMT [5, 19], most of our participants were between ages 18 and 35 (51%), though participants as old as 78 were reported. Many of our participants (35%) were also between the ages of 26-35, and the remaining participants were older than 36. Tamil was the most common native language of our participants (49%), with English a distant second (18%). There was a wide variety of other native languages reported. In order from most prevalent to least prevalent we observed: Malayalam, Hindi/Urdu, Telugu, Kannada, Marathi, Gujarati, and Bengali. About 7% of our participants reported native languages other than these. Finally, for most of our participants (58%) the maximum education level was a bachelors degree, though there were a moderate number of participants with only a high school education (20%), and a moderate number of participants with a masters degree (19%). Overall, these demographics are comparable to those observed in [5]. We do note that our Turker group is slightly younger and more Indian centric than in [19].

The non-impact of hardware. We were concerned by the impact of screen resolution, as captcha solving is a visual task. To understand whether screen resolution introduced a bias, we ran an experiment with Turkers solving our baseline captchas with length from 1 to 30 characters (1,000 samples for each length; 30,000 captchas total). We captured screen resolution programmatically using JavaScript.

We found that screen resolution did not impact the accuracy or the solving time of our participants. Figure 1 shows that the accuracy is similar for resolutions both greater than and less than 1024 by 768 pixels.

Captcha features

We identified a set of features based on the thirteen most widely used captcha schemes mentioned in [5] and from previous work [11] done in a small lab experiment. We divided our features into three categories:

1. *visual features* unrelated to security but relevant to usability such as text size and font color.

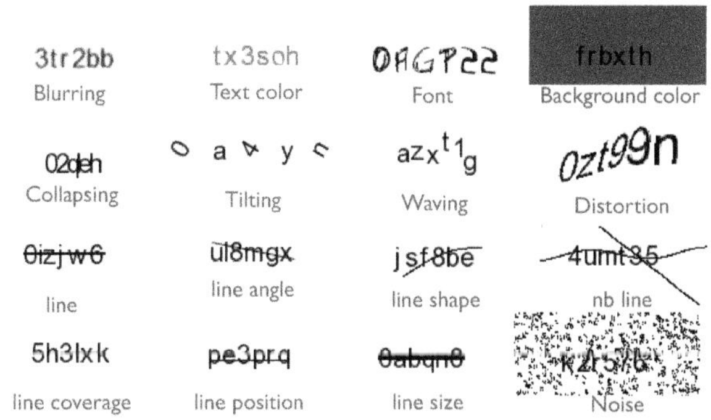

Figure 2. Main set of captcha security features produced by our captcha generator.

2. *anti-segmentation features* used to prevent programs from automatically separating the captcha into individual letters such as adding a line, collapsing characters.
3. *anti-recognition features* used to impede recognition of individual letters such as character rotation.

Visual features. The *visual* features are familiar parameters that can be relevant to usability but that are generally unimportant for automated captcha solvers.

- *Character sets*: lowercase letters (*a-z*), uppercase letters (*A-Z*), digits (*0-9*), lowercase letters and digits (*a-z0-9*), uppercase letters and digits (*A-Z0-9*), letters (*a-zA-Z*), letters and digits (*a-z0-9*), non-confusable letters and digits (*a-z0-9, except for 0, o, 1, l, i, 9 and g*), non-confusable letters (*a-z, except for o, l, i, g*), words (*a-z, but must be a valid English word*) and pseudo-words (*a-z, but derived from a character bigram model trained on English words*). Note that unlike the other character sets, for words and pseudo-words characters are not generated uniformly - there is a bias towards English-like character distributions.
- *Character counts*: between *4* and *15*. This matches the range of lengths observed for captchas in the wild.
- *Font sizes*: between *6px* and *36px*, in 2px increments.
- *Font families*: *Arial, Verdana, Times, Aescrawl, AfterShock, Atlandsketchesbbreg, BleedingCowboys, CardiffRegular, CrashcourseBBreg, DoktorTerror, Erthqake, FutureSallow, Grandesignneueserif, GreaseBalls, Imitation, Incubus, Jag, JaggaPoint, Jellykaestryahandwriting, Justusoldstyle, Phandv2, Slammertag, SlicedIron, Under, WhiteLineFever3D100.*
- *Foreground colors*: *black, white, gray, pink, red, orange, yellow, green, cyan, blue, purple*. The foreground color was used both for the font and for the defenses (e.g. lines, random noise) – using different colors would make the captcha insecure as the non-text color could be easily stripped away.
- *Background colors*: the same as foreground colors.

Anti-segmentation features. Some captcha features are specifically designed to make it more difficult for machines to automatically determine where characters begin and end. Preventing segmentation is central for captcha security. It has been shown in [24] that most of the captcha security comes from the inability of machines to segment captchas into individual characters. We refer to such features as *anti-segmentation* features, and consider the following variants:

- *Character overlaps*: gaps of *-15px* to *+5px* between successive characters.
- *Random dot sizes*: between *2px* and *10px*.
- *Random dot counts*: between *500* and *12,000* dots per captcha, in 500 dot increments.
- *Line types*: ***straight*** or ***wavy***. Wavy lines are generated by randomly picking adjacent points.
- *Line counts*: between *1* and *10* lines.
- *Line widths*: between *1px* and *10px*.
- *Line positions*: lines start to the left of the first character, allowing the vertical position of the start to range from 10% below the first character to *10%* above, at 10% intervals. Similarly, lines end to the right of the last character, again allowing the vertical position of the endpoint to range from 10% below to 10% above.
- *Similar foreground/background colors*: the background color is selected by moving from the foreground color in small steps in each possible direction in RGB space.

Anti-recognition features. Some features are designed to make it more difficult for attackers to recognize individual characters after segmentation. We refer to such features as *anti-recognition* features and consider the following variants:

- *Rotated character counts*: between *1* and *6* characters are rotated
- *Rotated character degrees*: between *10* and *350* degrees, at 10 degree increments. All characters are rotated the same amount.
- *Vertical shifting sizes*: between *5px* and *60px* at 5px increments. How much the character is shifted within the defined range is selected at random.
- *Character size variations*: differences from the previous character size between *2px* and *20px*, in 2px increments.
- *Character distortions*: based on attractor points, the basic idea is to pick two random points on the image to create a distortion field. Random perturbations to the field are added to make sure the deformation is not predictable and then the field is used to stretch and translate pixels based on their position in the field.

Experimental setup

We ran several rounds of experiments, summarized in Table 1. We began by establishing a baseline, intended to characterize the least obtrusive captcha that looks as much like regular browser text as possible. The baseline captcha consisted of 6 lowercase letters and digits in 20 pixel (15 point) black Arial font on a white background, with no anti-segmentation or anti-recognition techniques. We had 1,000 different captchas annotated so that we could measure accuracy with 0.1% precision.

Next we considered the effects of individual features in isolation. We enumerated 496 possible variations of our feature set. For example, a variation might be a captcha containing one line. Another variation might be a captcha containing 3 lines, or 7 lines, etc., all with the same character set, length, font, and colors as the baseline. We had 200 captchas annotated for each variation in order to achieve 0.5% precision in our results. The order in which the captchas were presented was randomized in order to avoid a prediction bias.

Then we tested variations of two to four features simultaneously. This is intended to capture the observation in [5] that captchas in the wild rarely exhibit more than one or two anti-segmentation features and one or two anti-recognition features. There were too many possible feature combinations to test the space exhaustively, so we took a random sample of 110,950 combinations out of 115,315,858 possible combinations.

Finally, we used our insights to settle on a single captcha design, and ran a last round of tests to validate the quality of our design before testing on production traffic. A subsequent section is dedicated to this experiment and our production deployment results.

Individual feature analysis

We evaluated participant performance on captchas in two ways: solving accuracy and solving time. For solving accuracy, we compared the answers given by participants to the text from which we generated the captcha, ignoring differences in case or spacing. Solving time was measured using JavaScript by recording the time between when participants were presented with a captcha and when they submitted their response.

We filtered out our experiment results by removing responses that were done too slowly or too quickly using 3 standard deviations, and ones that took less than 4 seconds (19.8% of all responses). Measuring times on AMT can result in high variance because many Turkers do other things on their computer at the same time even if we explicitly ask them to work as fast as possible. Still, by averaging over large numbers of participants, we can get an idea of which captchas take more or less time.

We claim that Turkers' behavior closely reflects real user attention patterns while surfing, for example, from home in front of the TV, which makes Turkers a more accurate subject pool than students or manually recruited subject for Internet behavior related studies. This claim is supported by the fact, as reported later in the paper, that the accuracy results obtained with AMT match very closely the results we got on real world traffic

Round	Task	N possible	N sampled	N tests per sample	Total tests
1	Preliminary Experiment	30	30	1000	*30000*
2	Baseline ("Control")	1	1	1000	*1000*
3	Features in isolation	496	496	200	*99200*
4	Feature interactions	115315858	110950	5-10	*804750*
5	new scheme design testing	8	8	2000	*16000*
	Total				*950.550*

Table 1. Overview of the experimentation rounds.

when we deployed our new capcha schemes and analyzed the results of tens of millions of captchas solved.

Character sets. Table 2 shows how participants performed on different character sets. Pseudo-words, words, and simple character sets like all digits, all lowercase letters and all uppercase letters were the easiest, with accuracies of *97%* or higher. Mixing letters, digits or uppercase and lowercase letters dropped accuracy down into the 80s, except in the case where we explicitly removed the easily confused letters.

Timing for the most part mirrored these trends, with words being the fastest, solved on average in only 4.3 seconds. While these results suggest that words and pseudo-words are the best choice, as we will discuss in the user preference study, word meaning and frequency greatly affect user perception and therefore should be used with caution. We note that *a-z0-9* can be used with minimal loss of speed or accuracy, as long as the confusable letters like *l, 1, o and O* are removed. However, as discussed in [6], using a larger key space does not increase captcha security, hence there is not a good reason to use a complex character set.

Number of characters We found that there is a slight decline in accuracy as more characters are presented. There is about a *1.5%* absolute drop for each additional character, and a moderate increase in time, about *1.0s* for each additional character. Thus, captcha designers can for the most part freely adjust the length of the captchas to achieve the desired level of security without harming the accuracy of their users, though there will be an additional time requirement.

Character Overlap Figure 3 shows that non-negative gap widths, including gaps of 0px, where characters touch all other characters, resulted in similar accuracies to the baseline *90-95%* range. Any amount of negative gap width however, caused dramatic drops in accuracy.

Charset	Time (s)	StdDev (s)	Accuracy
pseudo-word	5.0	2.2	99%
a-z	6.6	2.8	97%
0-9	6.1	2.5	98%
a-z0-9 (non-confusable)	6.6	2.6	97%
word	4.3	1.9	98%
a-z0-9	7.6	3.1	93%
a-zA-Z	8.2	3.6	88%
a-zA-Z0-9	8.3	3.4	82%

Table 2. Accuracy and solving time for various character sets

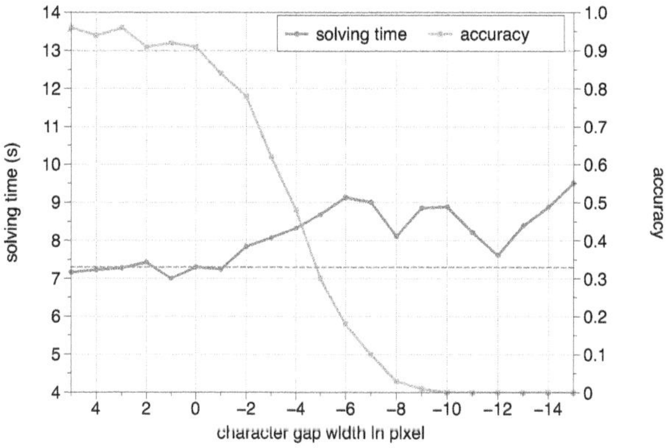

Figure 3. Accuracy and solving time vs. character overlap.

These results suggest that there is a hard limit to how much overlap between characters can be used to prevent captcha segmentation by automated solvers and still retain a tolerable user accuracy.

Font Size Participants performed similarly across different font sizes, with an accuracy standard deviation of only *1.7%*, and a time standard deviation of only *1.2s*. Thus, captcha designers can freely select whatever font size best fits their security design, without worrying about human performance issues.

Font Family Performance varied widely across fonts, with participants being most accurate on Arial and Verdana fonts, *97%* and *94%* respectively. There area some extreme differences between the other fonts – from an accuracy of *89%* on Grandesign Neue Serif to *1%* on Jellyka Estrya's Handwriting. This makes the choice of font family difficult without user testing.

Foreground and Background Color Like font size, varying the foreground and background colors generally had only a minimal effect, with an accuracy mean of *91.5%* and standard deviation of *3.5%*. Timing had a mean of *8.2s* and a standard deviation of *1.0s*. The two noticeably worse combinations were yellow-on-white (*84%* accuracy and *8.5s*) and white-on-yellow (*79%* accuracy and 9.8s). So colors may be tuned for the most part as desired, except for a few bad combinations.

Random Dots Participant performance was no worse than baseline with up to 2,000 random 1 pixel dots. However, for every additional 1,000 dots after that, accuracy declined about *6%* and solving time increased by *0.7s*. Thus, the random dot noise can be tuned a bit, but after more than 2,000 dots, human performance will suffer.

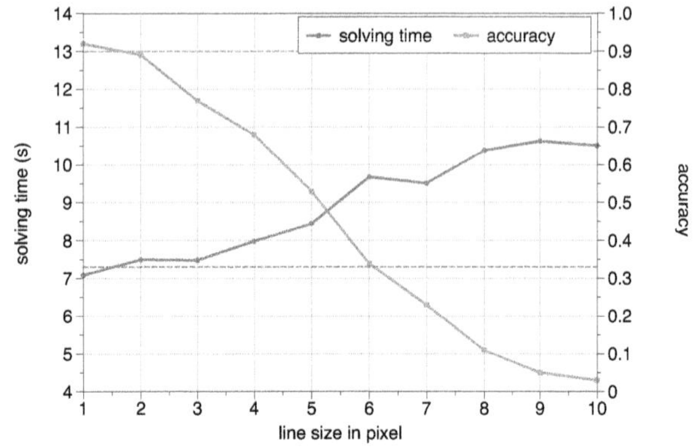

Figure 4. Accuracy and solving time vs. line size

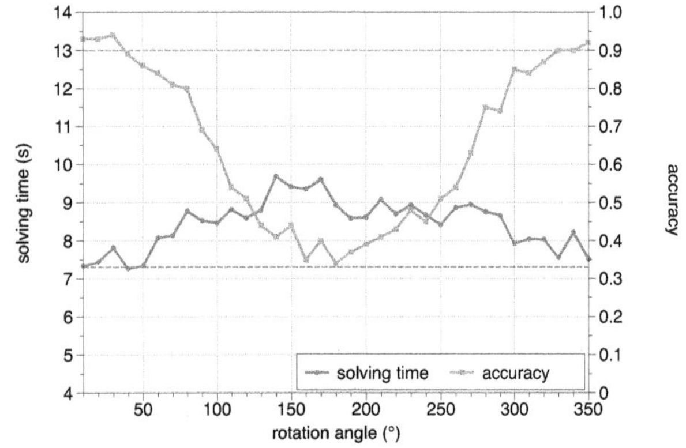

Figure 5. Accuracy and solving time vs. rotation angle

Lines We found that with up to three straight 1 pixel lines, participant performance was similar to that of no lines. Every additional straight line cost about 6.0% in accuracy and 0.5s in time. We also found that 1 or 2 pixel wide lines did not impair human performance, but thicker lines quickly hurt in both accuracy and time. See Figure 4. Wavy lines always impaired performance (figure not shown). These results suggest that a small number (1-3) of thin (1-2px) straight lines in any orientation can be added to captchas without noticeably impairing human performance.

Rotated Characters Angles of rotation within approximately 30 degrees of vertical had minimal effect on accuracy and solving time, as shown in Figure 5. The worst accuracies and slowest responses occurred with fully inverted characters (180 degrees). These results suggest that humans can tolerate small character rotations with minimal impact on performance. However, a larger rotation can have a much more dramatic impact on human accuracy.

Vertically Shifted Characters Shifting characters up and down in the captcha generally had only a small effect, and then only after shifts of 50 pixels or more. It is unclear how effective such shifting is as a security measure, but at least doing so has only a minimal effect on the readability of the captcha.

Character Size Variation Similar to vertically shifting characters, varying the size of characters generally did not impair our participants unless there was more than a 12 pixel difference in character size.Thus, character size variation is a reasonably safe feature to tune.

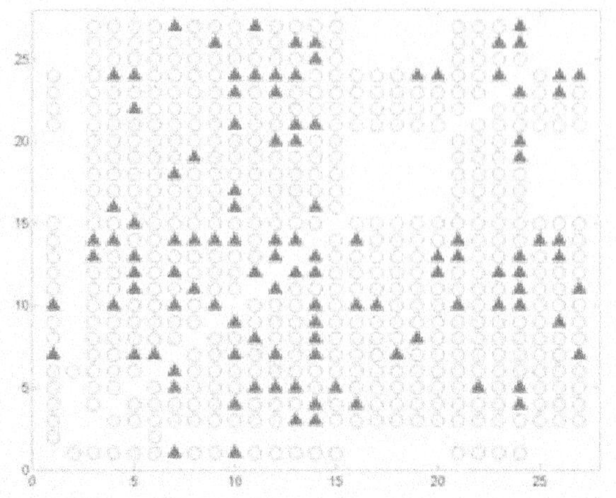

Figure 6. Scatter plot representing the type of interaction of pair-wise features (2d) accuracy. X and Y axis are features.

Feature Interactions

It turns out that many features are not wholly independent, thus it is also important to understand how features interact. One of our hopes was that we might be able to build a model to predict the accuracy and solving time of a captcha scheme given its features. However, in our experiments with various machine learning algorithms (e.g. SVM with various type of kernels) we were never able to beat the baseline.

Puzzled by how ineffective machine learning algorithms were on our dataset we shifted our goal to characterize the complexity of interactions between features. We used a function-fitting approach [16] that to find the simplest known function that explains a data distribution. For each pairwise interaction, we used the least squares method [20] and tested multiple functions: *additive, convolutive, exponential, logarithmic, square root, and polynomial (orders* 2 *to* n*)*. We kept the simplest one that had an overall error .001 or less. This is consistent with the Occam's razor principle that the best explanation is the simplest one.

We plotted the results of this procedure to show the types of functions needed to explain the resulting accuracy (Figure 6) for the various pairwise interactions. On this scatter plot the *blue circles* represent interactions that need a linear function to be explained. The *red triangles* represent the interactions that require a higher-order function to be explained. Typically this was the exponential function or a high order polynomial function. White space represents feature interactions that are meaningless as they create impossible to solve captchas, for example, black text on black background. Similar results were obtained for solving time. Figure 6 highlights two essential properties of our dataset that explain why it is so difficult to apply machine learning algorithms on it. First, higher order functions are needed to explain at least 20% of the feature

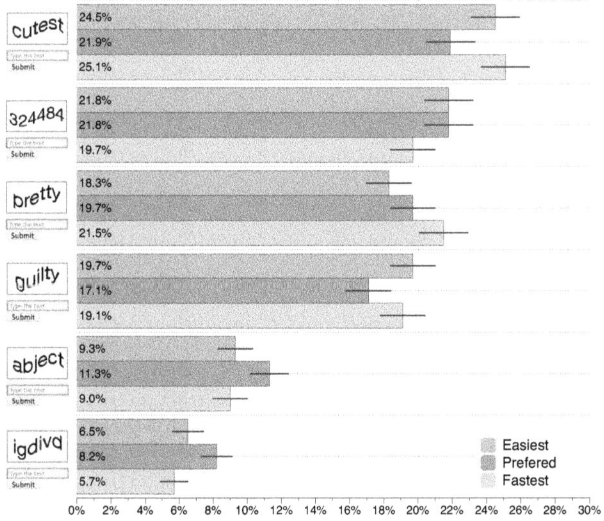

Figure 7. Word preferences

interactions (112/582 interactions for accuracy, 122/582 for solving time). Secondly, there is no discernible pattern that can be used to partition the set into features that require higher order functions and those that only need a linear function. As a result, building a predictive model that can explain this dataset accurately requires an extremely high order kernel function, which makes this problem intractable in practice. Remember here that we only analyzed pairwise interactions and that higher order interactions will require even larger higher order functions to be explained.

While there is still the possibility that deep belief networks or higher order machine learning algorithms might one day be able to predict the result of feature interaction, for now we are bound to rely on user testing and iterative design to validate captcha schemes.

USER PREFERENCES

We ran two Google consumer surveys [10] to understand how user perceived difficulty is related to solving time and accuracy. In each survey, we asked 5,000 respondents in the United States to answer three preference questions. We note that the Google consumer survey infrastructure ensures that the respondent population is representative of the US population [15]. The survey results are publicly available at `http://goo.gl/rkp4bZ`, `http://goo.gl/uYLaIj`.

Each question consisted of a handpicked set of captchas. In the first survey we show side by side 3 captchas where each captcha exhibits a distinct anti-segmentation feature: moderate noise, a single wavy line, and moderate character collapsing. The second survey consisted of 6 captchas with different character sets. Respondents were asked which captcha out of the group they thought was the *fastest*, which one was *easiest*, and which one they *preferred to solve*. The order in which the captchas were presented was randomized in order to avoid positional sampling artifacts.

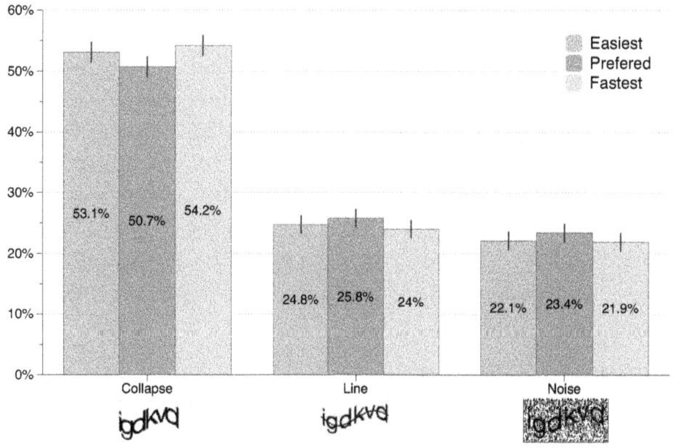

Figure 8. Security feature preferences

We found that word connotations play an important role in user perception. We chose the word *pretty* as an example of a high frequency positive word, and *cutest* as a low frequency positive word. Google search returned approximately 1.1 billion results for *pretty* and about 36 million results for *cutest*. We chose *guilty* as a high frequency negative word, and *abject* as a low frequency negative word. These words had 150 million and 4 million Google search results, respectively. Figure 7 shows a clear preference for positive words over negative words. It also suggests that low frequency words negatively impact user perception. The unconscious bias introduced by words led us to reject using words in our captcha schemes, since this bias makes it impossible to generate hundreds of millions of captchas with consistent user sentiment.

The lowercase meaningless string of letters is significantly ranked last in all three metrics considered, whereas strings of digits is users' second most preferred captcha, and second in terms of easiness, even though the result are not statistically significant when compared to positive words. We therefore chose to use digits as our character set.

The second survey reveals that users' preferences among-anti segmentation techniques, summarized in figure 8, align with their relative security strengths. According to [6], character collapsing is more secure than lines, which is in turn more secure than noise. That is, users happen to prefer more secure techniques. A possible explanation for this alignment is that users are more exposed to stronger security techniques used by prominent captcha schemes and are therefore more familiar with them.

These surveys show that accuracy and solving time are not good predictors of user preference. For example, our AMT results report in table 2 indicate that English words are solved the quickest and most accurately, whereas users perceive digits to be both faster and easier than words with negative connotations. Similarly, random lowercase strings have the same performance characteristics as random strings of digits, but users perceive digits to be faster, easier, and more likable.

PUTTING IT ALL TOGETHER: HOW WE DESIGNED OUR NEW CAPTCHA SCHEME

In this section we relate how we designed and deployed new, highly usable captcha schemes for Google using the knowledge gathered during our experiments and the guidelines for creating secure captchas devised in [6]. Overall our newly deployed captcha improved user accuracy by 6.7% (95.4% up to 88.5%). We also recount how the complexity of feature interaction caught us off guard several times and how we eventually overcame it.

Recall that our designs are for captchas for use in low risk situations, e.g., where they are combined with a comprehensive anti-abuse system. Therefore, we make design tradeoffs that aim to improve the user experience, and include only as many security features as are possible while still maintaining a very high accuracy rate.

Design choices

We decided to design two different schemes rather than just one; a main one, and a backup one in case the main one is broken.

For the main scheme we chose to retain as many visual features as possible from our current captcha in order to give users a sense of continuity. We kept the captcha size, the text color (black) and the background color (white).

We used a different font though, for reasons recounted in the next subsection. We also simplified the character set by moving from lowercase letters to digits. This decision was motivated by the data in [6] which shows that a complicated character set does not increase security, since machine learning algorithms are equally good on all common character sets. On the other hand, as discussed above, humans are more accurate on simpler character sets. While humans are also very good with words, we chose to avoid them due to the sensitivity of user perception to word meaning as discussed in the user preference section.

Anti-segmentation techniques. Line and character overlap are the two recommended, but imperfect, techniques to make captchas resistant to automated attacks [6]. Following the insights provided by the user preference study, we decided to use character overlap for the main scheme and combine it with a line for the backup scheme. This strategy also fits well with our wish to maintain continuity with our previous captcha scheme which also used character collapsing.

Extra security features. To thwart state-of-the-art attacks against overlap and line-based defenses [1, 6], we added the following extra security features to our captcha schemes:

- **Length randomization**: We randomize the length of the captcha between 6 and 8 to prevent the attacker from knowing how many segments are present [6]. As discussed earlier, longer captchas have little impact on actual difficulty.
- **Text-size randomization**: Similarly we randomize the character size to prevent the attacker from guessing how many characters there are in the captcha by looking at its width [6].

Original	Mturk v1	Mturk v2	1% test	New
88.6%	89.2%	97%	94.3%	95.4%
	82.6%	92.2%		93.2%

Figure 9. Comparison between our previous captcha, the AMT experiments we conducted (v1 and v2) and our new scheme (1% test and current one). The accuracy is reported at the bottom of the figure. As shown in the v1 column, when the collapsing and waving features are combined with the digit-charset the 1 and 7 are easily confused.

- **Tilting**: We also randomly tilt each character up to 20 degrees to provide a third layer of defense against length guessing attacks.
- **Waving**: Finally we use sinusoidal based waving to prevent the attack where the segmentation is inferred by looking at various shape invariants (such as the S pattern) as explained in [1].

While none of these features guarantee that our captcha scheme is secure against highly sophisticated attacks [9], they ensure that our captcha is not trivially breakable and that it fulfills its role of keeping unsophisticated attackers at bay.

Early Experiments

As digit character set measured accuracy is 98% (table 2), we were expecting close to that number for our main scheme. Based on our experiments, we were also anticipating the backup captcha to be around 5% less accurate than the main one because of the line addition.

Similar to the previous experiment, we used AMT to quickly test our new designs before running a field trial on a small fraction of our production traffic. We asked Turkers to solve 2,000 captchas of our two new schemes. As reported in Figure 9, accuracy results did not live up to our expectations.

After reviewing Turkers' answers, it became clear that the poor performance was due to the unexpected interaction between digits, overlap and waving: in many cases it was impossible to tell apart 7 and the 1 as shown in Figure 9. To address this issue, we decided to use a font that had an extra bar on the 7. We ended up testing using the sans-serif open fonts *tenor-sans* that included a bar on the 7. We achieved an accuracy pretty close to what we expected from our earlier experiments: 97% accuracy for the main scheme and 92.7% for the backup one. This anecdotally supports the conclusion of our feature interaction analysis: feature interactions are nonlinear and therefore can lead to unpredictable effects. We confirmed that our performance issue was due to the confusion between 1 and 7 by re-testing with another font that didn't have a bar on the 7 and ended up with results that were even worse than our baseline font (Arial): 86.2% accuracy.

Real world results

We decided to deploy the main scheme on a small fraction of production traffic in a series of field trials on a particular Google web page. We note that Google's captcha is used in many other places than the page we consider in this paper. Each trial consisted of approximately 100,000 captchas. We chose to use a version of the *Oxygen-Mono* font that we modified by adding bars on the 7 and 0 glyphs to avoid the confusion identified in the earlier AMT experiment. We excluded empty responses from the results reported in this section, and responses that contained the word 'captcha' (we noticed an interesting phenomenon where users type in what the image semantically is).

As reported in figure 9, we were able to achieve a 94.3% accuracy rate with our main scheme. This is slightly lower than the AMT experiment, but within a reasonable margin of error. To our knowledge, this is the first large scale empirical verification where results obtained via AMT are reproducible in real world conditions. Analysis of the errors that users made revealed another unintended interaction of combining features that was not detected in our AMT screening: users infrequently confused 0 with 8 due to the distortion combination. To further improve accuracy, we removed 1, 7, and 0 from our character set and repeated the experiment. We improved the accuracy to 95.3%. We believe that the confusion between 0 and 8 did not appear in the AMT screening due to its low prevalence - less than 1% of captchas - and therefore requires a very large sample to clearly stand out. Overall however, we found that AMT (or any other crowd computing service) is a very valuable tool to iterate quickly on captcha design and get it mostly right before experimenting on production traffic. Finally, we also field tested the backup variant that includes a varying width curve drawn across the digits. We found that adding this line cost 2.2% accuracy.

Following these experiments, we fully deployed our main scheme on production traffic in early September 2013. Since then we have not observed a significant change in abusive activity. However, our anti-abuse defenses do not solely rely on captchas, so our results in this regard may not generalize to other companies. Overall we observed a consistent 95.3% accuracy rate over a sample of approximately 20 million captchas. This is a 6.7% improvement over an equivalent traffic sample taken immediately prior to the new scheme.

Our captcha infrastructure also has a feature for users to skip difficult captchas and get new ones. Since deployment, we observe that users request new captchas 55% less often. This, combined with the accuracy improvement, resulted in approximately 20% fewer incorrect captcha solutions submitted to the page.

LESSONS LEARNED

Balancing security and usability. Captchas were originally intended to solve a security problem: automatic verification of humanity. As automatic text recognition software (OCR) improves, solving this problem with distorted text in isolation is becoming increasingly difficult, as well as burdensome for users. While captchas are still an effective security tool [21], we find that it is much more effective to use the captcha as a medium for engagement with the end user, and examine the interaction holistically. We believe that this is a positive development for usability, as shifting the security burden away from the captcha image itself makes it possible to use less aggressive distortions. Deploying the new captcha scheme did not result in decreased security at Google, but as mentioned earlier, captchas are just one component of Google's anti-abuse system. It may be interesting future work to extend the analysis of captcha features by acquiring captcha breaking software and measuring the break rate for each feature along side the usability.

MTurk results generalize to real world. Some of the results in this work are applicable beyond designing new captcha schemes. In particular one of our key results is the first large scale empirical verification that results obtained via AMT are reproducible in real world conditions with the caveat that fine-tuning at very large scale is still necessary. Overall the accuracy of our new scheme is very close (1.4%) to what our MTurk experiments predicted. On the other hand, our MTurk evaluation failed to reveal infrequent confusion between 0 and 8, due to the relatively low prevalence of captchas where the confusion might occur (< 1%). Exposing such infrequent biases may be prohibitively expensive using paid services like AMT.

User perception of the task difficulty is affected by unrelated variables. Another lesson learned is that user perception of a task difficulty is significantly influenced by cues (e.g content) that is unrelated to the actual task difficulty. The difficulty of solving the captchas in figure 7 is technically identical - they are all the same length, same character set (except digits), distorted the same way. Yet, users preferred the top example over two and a half times more than the bottom one (21.9% vs. 8.2%).

CONCLUSION

In this work we recount how we designed new captcha schemes for Google using a systematic design approach. We deployed it in production without adversely affecting security, and achieved a 95.3% accuracy, which is a 6.7% improvement over the previous captcha scheme.

To design these new schemes we first selected a comprehensive list of features used in captchas from prominent real world captcha schemes and previous work. We then produced captchas with different combinations of those features, and ran a usability study on Amazon's Mechanical Turk on nearly a million captchas. This allowed us to identify the limits of how much distortion users can process and maintain a tolerable accuracy. A key finding was that results obtained on AMT generalize well to the real world; the user accuracy measured on AMT is very close to our production result. Another key finding is the nonlinearity of interactions between features, which prevents using machine learning or statistical models to predict the accuracy of a given capcha scheme design. This finding emphasizes the importance of using an iterative approach to remove unexpected feature interactions that may hurt accuracy.

We also ran a user perception study to understand which factors influence perception of captcha difficulty. The study revealed that user sentiment towards captcha schemes is not aligned with real difficulty. In particular user perception is highly sensitive to the connotation and frequency of the content of the captcha.

REFERENCES

1. A. S. E. Ahmad, J. Yan, and M. Tayara. The robustness of google captchas. Technical report, New Castle, 2011.
2. H. S. Baird and T. P. Riopka. Scattertype: a reading captcha resistant to segmentation attack. In *Electronic Imaging 2005*, pages 197–207. International Society for Optics and Photonics, 2005.
3. M. Bernard, C. H. Liao, and M. Mills. The effects of font type and size on the legibility and reading time of online text by older adults. In *CHI '01: CHI '01 extended abstracts on Human factors in computing systems*, pages 175–176, New York, NY, USA, 2001. ACM.
4. J. P. Bigham and A. C. Cavender. Evaluating existing audio captchas and an interface optimized for non-visual use. In *ACM Conference on Human Factors in Computing Systems*, 2009.
5. E. Bursztein, S. Bethard, J. C. Mitchell, D. Jurafsky, and C. Fabry. How good are humans at solving captchas? a large scale evaluation. In *Security and Privacy*, 2010.
6. E. Bursztein, M. Martin, and J. Mitchell. Text-based captcha strengths and weaknesses. In *Proceedings of the 18th ACM conference on Computer and communications security*, pages 125–138. ACM, 2011.
7. K. Chellapilla, K. Larson, P. Simard, and M. Czerwinski. Computers beat humans at single character recognition in reading based human interaction proofs (hips). In *CEAS*, 2005.
8. K. Chellapilla, K. Larson, P. Simard, and M. Czerwinski. Designing human friendly human interaction proofs (hips). In *Proceedings of the SIGCHI conference on Human factors in computing systems*, pages 711–720. ACM, 2005.
9. C. Cruz-Perez, O. Starostenko, F. Uceda-Ponga, V. Alarcon-Aquino, and L. Reyes-Cabrera. Breaking recaptchas with unpredictable collapse: heuristic character segmentation and recognition. In *Pattern Recognition*, pages 155–165. Springer, 2012.
10. Google. Google consumer surveys. `http://www.google.com/insights/consumersurveys/home`.
11. P. S. K Chellapilla, K Larson and M. Czerwinski. Designing human friendly human interaction proofs. In ACM, editor, *CHI05*, 2005.
12. A. Kittur, E. H. Chi, and B. Suh. Crowdsourcing user studies with mechanical turk. In *CHI '08: Proceeding of the twenty-sixth annual SIGCHI conference on Human factors in computing systems*, pages 453–456, New York, NY, USA, 2008. ACM.
13. K. A. Kluever and R. Zanibbi. Balancing usability and security in a video captcha. In *SOUPS '09: Proceedings of the 5th Symposium on Usable Privacy and Security*, pages 1–11, New York, NY, USA, 2009. ACM.
14. K. Larson, M. van Dantzich, M. Czerwinski, and G. Robertson. Text in 3d: some legibility results. In *CHI '00: CHI '00 extended abstracts on Human factors in computing systems*, pages 145–146, New York, NY, USA, 2000. ACM.
15. P. McDonald, M. Mohebbi, and B. Slatkin. Comparing google consumer surveys to existing probability and non-probability based internet surveys. Technical report, Google, 2012.
16. H. Motulsky and L. Ransnas. Fitting curves to data using nonlinear regression: a practical and nonmathematical review. *The FASEB journal*, 1(5):365–374, 1987.
17. T. Mustonen, M. Olkkonen, and J. Hakkinen. Examining mobile phone text legibility while walking. In *CHI '04: CHI '04 extended abstracts on Human factors in computing systems*, pages 1243–1246, New York, NY, USA, 2004. ACM.
18. M. Naor. Verification of a human in the loop or identification via the turing test. Available electronically: `http://www.wisdom.weizmann.ac.il/~naor/PAPERS/human.ps`, 1997.
19. J. Ross, L. Irani, M. Silberman, A. Zaldivar, and B. Tomlinson. Who are the crowdworkers?: shifting demographics in mechanical turk. In *CHI'10: 28th international conference on Human factors in computing systems*, pages 2863–2872. ACM, 2010.
20. T. Strutz. *Data Fitting and Uncertainty: A Practical Introduction to Weighted Least Squares and Beyond.* Vieweg and Teubner, 2010.
21. K. Thomas, D. McCoy, C. Grier, A. Kolcz, and V. Paxson. Trafficking Fraudulent Accounts: The Role of the Underground Market in Twitter Spam and Abuse. In *Proceedings of the USENIX Security Symposium*, August 2013.
22. M. Toomim, T. Kriplean, C. P
"ortner, and J. Landay. Utility of human-computer interactions: toward a science of preference measurement. In *Proceedings of the 2011 annual conference on Human factors in computing systems*, pages 2275–2284. ACM, 2011.
23. Y. Xu, G. Reynaga, S. Chiasson, J.-M. Frahm, F. Monrose, and P. van Oorschot. Security and usability challenges of moving-object captchas: Decoding codewords in motion. In *Usenix Security*, 2012.
24. J. Yan and A. S. E. Ahmad. A low-cost attack on a microsoft captcha. `http://bit.ly/nfpEis`, 2008.
25. J. Yan and A. S. El Ahmad. Usability of captchas or usability issues in captcha design. In *SOUPS '08: Proceedings of the 4th symposium on Usable privacy and security*, pages 44–52, New York, NY, USA, 2008. ACM.

Using Personal Examples to Improve Risk Communication for Security and Privacy Decisions

Marian Harbach, Markus Hettig, Susanne Weber, Matthew Smith
Usable Security and Privacy Lab, Leibniz University Hannover, Germany
{harbach,smith}@dcsec.uni-hannover.de, {hettig, suey}@stud.uni-hannover.de

ABSTRACT
IT security systems often attempt to support users in taking a decision by communicating associated risks. However, a lack of efficacy as well as problems with habituation in such systems are well known issues. In this paper, we propose to leverage the rich set of personal data available on smartphones to communicate risks using personalized examples. Examples of private information that may be at risk can draw the users' attention to relevant information for a decision and also improve their response. We present two experiments that validate this approach in the context of Android app permissions. Private information that becomes accessible given certain permissions is displayed when a user wants to install an app, demonstrating the consequences this installation might have. We find that participants made more privacy-conscious choices when deciding which apps to install. Additionally, our results show that our approach causes a negative affect in participants, which makes them pay more attention.

Author Keywords
Android; Consequences; Examples; Permissions; Personalization; Privacy; Risks; Usable Security.

ACM Classification Keywords
H.5.2. Information Interfaces and Presentation (e.g. HCI): User Interfaces

INTRODUCTION
Communicating the risk pertaining to certain actions is a long-standing problem in human-computer interactions. A large amount of previous research has looked at how to effectively communicate security risks in general [7], for example arising from insecure SSL connections [23] or phishing [11]. Many IT security systems use a decision dialogue to provide the user with information about potential risks or privacy implications. However, recent research has repeatedly demonstrated that such dialogues are often ineffective and quickly ignored [6, 10] or provide information that is hard to understand for the user [14]. In contrast, Rader et al. found that informal stories influence security behavior and thinking as they are being relayed from one user to the next [21]. These stories offer concrete examples of good or bad things that happened to people which a user can relate to. Blackwell et al. [3] previously posited that abstract information in software causes a gap between system designers and users.

As smartphones gain popularity, they also get more important in many peoples daily life, managing a large variety of personal information, including emails, pictures, call logs, and text messages. On Android, this information is protected from unauthorized access using permissions. The user gets to decide whether or not he or she agrees to the capabilities an app will have and which information on the phone will be accessible by that app after it has been installed. The most important prerequisite for such permission systems to be useful and secure in general is that the user can understand and decide which (sets of) permissions are okay to grant for an app and which might be harmful in a given context. Since apps can harvest and send out private information on the first launch, we believe that current trial-and-error app installation behavior is critical from a privacy perspective. Previous research of Felt et al. has shown that only 17 % of Android smartphone users are consciously aware of the specific permissions an app demands during installation [13].

To overcome the abstract nature of the existing dialogue, we show the user personalized, concrete examples of capabilities the app would get and which information it can access, using personal information present on the phone. Our goal is to raise awareness and make users more cautious while installing apps. For example, such a personalized example during app installation can say: *"If you install this app, it will be able to access and delete the following of your photos"*, followed by a sample of the user's actual photos contained on the device. Thus, the communicated risks address a concrete, personal piece of information while listing a known cause as well as concrete consequences that a user can easily imagine. This can then allow users to judge whether or not a risk is acceptable or not: I may trust an anti-virus app to possibly delete some infected files in order to protect me from malware. Yet, I do not trust a random game to have access to text messages from my partner.

We emphasize that while users are probably aware of the private information they have on their devices and which apps they have installed, the individual relationship between an app's permissions and the concrete pieces of personal and private information that can then be accessed is never explicitly clarified. Our approach aims to enable users to make in-

CHI 2014, April 26–May 01, 2014, Toronto, ON, Canada

ACM 978-1-4503-2473-1/14/04..$15.00.
http://dx.doi.org/10.1145/2556288.2556978

formed decisions about the risks that apps pose to their private information by actually demonstrating which pieces of information can be accessed.

This paper makes the following main contributions to the HCI community:

- We explore the effect of personalized security decision dialogues on the Android app installation process, leveraging the rich set of personal information available on smartphones.
- We show how to design decision dialogues with personal examples and present a prototype of this approach.
- We provide and discuss the results of two user studies, demonstrating the effectiveness of our approach compared to the standard dialogue.

Our results shows that we are able to cause a considerable amount of users to rethink an app selection because of risks arising from permissions, even after an installation decision has already been made. Additionally, users who saw the modified permissions dialogue payed significantly more attention to an app's permissions in our experiments. We also found that a negative affect can increase attention. In the following, we will outline related work, introduce and motivate our concept before presenting the results, a discussion and future directions.

RELATED WORK

On the theoretical side, the HITL framework [8] and the C-HIP model [24], which HITL is based on, are general information transmission models which describe the process of sending an information through a channel to the human receiver. After receiving the concrete information, attention must be shifted to this information before the comprehension process starts and eventually an appropriate reaction follows. It has been shown [2, 25] that a personalization of decision dialogues can support this process.

According to De Paula et al. [9], the central problem of human interaction with IT security systems is that users should be able to make informed decisions without further help. Additionally, Bravo-Lillo et al. [4] state that such dialogues should "inform clearly about the consequences of the actions" and about the risks involved and emphasize that it is important to inform about whether an action is safe or not right before the user ultimately decides. Bravo-Lillo et al. [5] also investigated the behavior of novice users confronted with situations in which they should make security decisions. It was shown that those users are not aware of the sensitivity of their data and mostly started to worry after deciding to allow access. They found that novice users often act with a "let's-see-what-happens" attitude without thinking about possible consequences.

Blackwell et al. [3] discussed the influence of abstract representations in computational tasks and suggests to center a user's understanding of a system around task completion to overcome abstractness. Similarly, Inglesant et al. [16] and Karat et al. [17] find that the use of natural language to create access control policies is beneficial for their quality. Also, Raja et al. [22] found that users have improved mental models of firewall operation when using metaphors to embed security decisions into an application context.

Egelman [10] recently investigated Facebook Connect security decision dialogues. The central finding was that habituation caused most users to ignore the content of the dialogue, even though it was modified. Showing users personal information from their personal profiles, such as gender, name, or relationship status and sexual orientation, which would actually be accessed by the third-party website, did not improve the dialogue's efficacy in their study. In contrast to this work, the displayed information was already disclosed to at least one online service and the pieces of information cited in the dialogues were not very abstract or technical.

All of the above approaches argue for more concrete and graspable information in decision dialogues. Concrete examples of undisclosed private information have, however, not been used to highlight risks and possible consequences to support the decision demanded from the user. To the best of our knowledge, this is the first evaluation of personalized decision dialogues that leverages the large amount of personal information contained on smarpthones.

Permissions

A large body of work on Android permissions was compiled by Felt et al. (e. g., [12, 13]), investigating how permissions are used, how users perceive permissions, their attitudes towards potential risks as well as additional models applicable to ask for permission on smartphones. Most relevantly, they found that only very few users (3 %) actually understood which assets were protected by a given permission.

Pandita et al. [20] investigated to what extent a user's expectations of permissions match the actually requested set of permissions using natural language processing. They propose to automatically extract justifications for permissions from app descriptions and flag those apps where not all requested permissions are justified in the description. They postulate that this can help users to make informed decisions.

Recently, Kelley et al. [18] argued for the need of privacy as part of the app decision making process. They inserted an overview of the private information an app will be able to access into the overview page of Google's Play Store. Their results show that they were able to influence the user's decisions compared to the existing permissions display. Their goal was to make privacy part of the decision process by abstracting permissions into a summary table.

In contrast, we attempt to improve risk communication by making permission risks graspable and hence understandable. We want to enable users to take an ultimate decision if he or she is willing to trust a certain app and its developer with access to personal information. Using only the approach of Kelley et al., a user might just count the checkmarks in their Privacy Facts display and therefore make a privacy-aware choice. However, an app with only two permissions can already cause great harm if the app has malicious intent. We believe that more information is necessary to clarify the risks pertaining to certain permission sets than can be fitted on an overview page. Our approach is hence complementary to the Privacy Facts display of Kelley and colleagues.

DESIGN

To leverage the power of personal examples as security decision dialogues for app installation, this information needs to be presented to the user in a concise and appealing fashion. Additionally, it is paramount that the permission dialogue is able to make the user question an app selection that was already made. This is necessary since the permissions will be displayed on a separate dialogue, which only becomes visible after a button labeled "Install" has already been pressed and therefore a choice for an app has been made. In this section, we will present the design of our modified permission dialogue for Google's Play Store and discuss its rationale. During the development of the UI, we ran pilot studies to test prototype efficacy.

Permissions Visualization

The current permission dialogue of Google's Play Store by default only shows a small number of the 79 permissions[1] which are deemed to be most important. The remaining permissions which an app requests can be displayed by unfolding a hidden panel. As Felt et al. already reported in 2011, the Android OS defines a large number of permissions of which many are rarely used [12]. Therefore, we wanted to choose a representative set of permissions for our evaluation.

To find the most common permissions, we crawled the 34,875 most popular apps on Google's Play Store in early 2013 and counted which permissions are requested. From the top 20 of the set of requested permissions, we picked ten (see Table 1) that can affect private information.

Permission	Rank #	Requested By
full network access	1	82 %
modify external storage	3	56 %
read phone status and identity	5	42 %
view Wi-Fi connections	8	26 %
precise location	9	23 %
find accounts on the device	12	16 %
take pictures and videos	14	8 %
read contacts	15	7 %
read call log	17	6 %
retrieve running apps	18	6 %

Table 1. The permissions selected for our evaluation, their rank in the top 20 of permissions, and how many of the 34,875 crawled apps requested them.

To visualize each of these, several random examples are selected from the data that this permission allows access to and displayed alongside a concrete, one-sentence description mentioning the user's actual data. Choosing random examples for each permission can prevent habituation, as different content is visible each time the dialogue is shown. Additionally, not every example drawn from the available information on the phone is considered equally private and displaying multiple examples shows the user a cross-section of the private information available on the phone.

[1]Google does not specify the actual number. According to Au et al. [1], Android 4.0 offers 79 permissions that can be requested by a third-party app.

Three of the permissions are notable exceptions: *full network access*, *take pictures and videos* and *location* do not allow access to existing data but can be used to exfiltrate information from the device or eavesdrop on the user's actions or surroundings. In these cases, we only used a description for the *full network access* permission or used the actual camera view for the *take pictures and videos* permission and the current location for the *location* permission.

We used the same general layout, fonts and headlines as in the existing permissions dialogue for all visualizations to match the look-and-feel of the original store. We slightly increased the size of the headlines for each permission from 18 dp (density-independent pixels) to 20 dp to make them stand out more clearly from the examples themselves.

Each of the permissions and its visualization are shown in Figure 1. We changed the descriptive text to mention real data and showed pieces of this data where possible. For example, for *full network access*, the user would be warned that this permission can be used to download malware to his or her phone or upload private information. Similarly, *modify external storage* showed a different picture from all the pictures taken with the phone and accessible via the storage permission each 1.5 seconds and stated that this app would be able to delete those. The phone's IMEI number and a statement that this number could be used for tracking or abused by malware were presented when the *read phone status and identity* permission was present. The remaining permissions gave examples of the information that could be accessed by this app alongside a statement saying "This app can see ..." or "This app has access to ...". The display would then show a selection of three contacts, three previous calls, three accounts configured on the device, three currently running apps, three nearby Wi-Fi networks and the current location on a Google Maps satellite image. In each case, we explicitly mentioned that the app to be installed will be able to interact with the concrete piece of data, in order to create a graspable connection between the app and the private information.

Overall, our permissions display was modified to include a different descriptive text more related to real data and a personal example of that personal data where possible. Additionally, the headline font size was slightly increased.

In a pilot study, we monitored participants' reactions to each of the permission visualizations and ordered them so that those deemed most relevant would be shown first. Contacts, call log and photos received the most attention and reactions from participants. More technical permissions such as access to the IMEI number and a list of Wi-Fi networks were therefore moved to the end of the list.

The remaining permissions were not part of our visualization but could be displayed as a fold-out panel at the bottom of our modified permissions display, similar to the existing approach. The choice of which permissions to display and which examples to use potentially influences the efficacy of our approach. We will discuss possible implications in the *General Discussion* section after presenting the results of our evaluation.

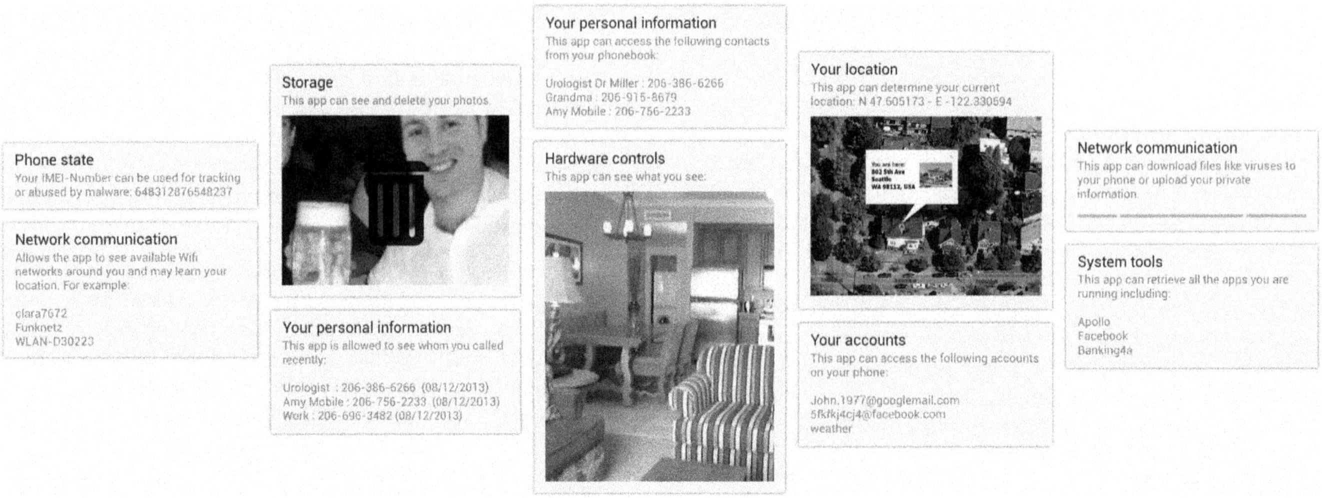

Figure 1. Overview of all permission visualizations created for our study.

Play Store Integration

As already argued above, we chose to replace the existing Play Store permissions dialogue, which acts as an ultimate decision before the actual installation. Figure 2 shows a comparison of the old and our modified permissions display. We created a working Android app simulating the existing Play Store, serving as a prototype for the evaluation.

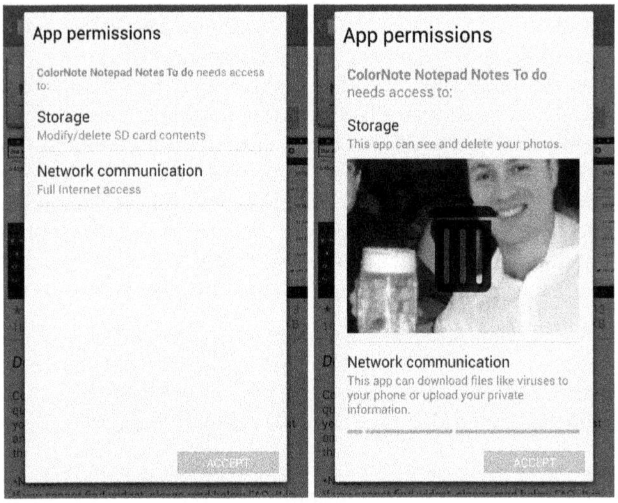

Figure 2. Comparison of the existing permissions dialogue on the left and our modified version on the right.

LAB STUDY

After piloting our prototype with several users, we set up a lab study to evaluate our approach and gain some further insights into how users select apps and perceive the risks pertaining to an app's permissions. Our methodology is based on the work of Kelley et al. [18]. To improve ecological validity, we let participants use their personal smartphones in this study and therefore base our evaluation on real private information.

Method

We invited owners of smartphones running Android 4.0 or newer from a university-wide study participation list to attend a lab study on app selection in the Google Play Store. We used limited deception by not mentioning the study's focus on permissions to prevent bias and recruited only Android users to prevent side effects from unfamiliarity with smartphones, apps or the Play Store. The invitation offered 8 Euros of compensation for a 30 minute study and stated that we would be installing a test app on users' personal device during the lab session. In the lab, each participant was introduced to the study and signed a consent form before installing our prototype app. Participants were informed that the app would be collecting usage data but no personal information and that we would transfer this information from their devices once the study was completed.

They were then instructed to complete six tasks, asking them to role-play the selection and installation of apps from a certain category that fit a certain purpose they were in need of. Participants were also asked to think aloud while making their decisions. Within each category, participants ultimately had to choose between installing one of two apps with different sets of permissions (see below). They were also instructed that they may choose not to install any app in each category, if none of the available options suited their personal needs. We added the "none" option to cater for the fact that users can normally abort an app choice process at any time without installing an app. In terms of study design, both, ours as well as the approach of Kelley et al. have drawbacks. Adding the "none" option allows participants to ignore a difficult choice, while forcing a decision may not represent realistic behavior. After finishing the tasks, participants completed a questionnaire on general app installation behavior as well as their perception of permissions. At the end, we debriefed participants about the true purpose of the study, clarified that our Play Store app was only a mockup and no apps were installed, removed all traces of the app from the participants' phones and gave them an opportunity to ask further questions.

The study used a between-subjects design with respect to the permissions dialogue and we compensated for effects of fatigue and learning by randomizing the task order. The task order assignment was based on latin squares.

Test App

To run this test, we implemented a mockup of the Google Play Store app as mentioned above. The mockup would either display the conventional representation of permissions as text or our representation using personal examples (cf. Figure 1). Before displaying the permissions, users were able to navigate through the Play Store as usual, compare several apps in the list view and look at app details, screenshots, and ratings. Each participant was provided with six tasks that asked them to find, select, and install an app with a certain purpose from a certain category of the Play Store. Our mockup app measured the time participants spent looking at each app description and the respective permission screens.

Apps

Each category contained two apps that actually fit the given purpose for the respective task. Within each category, we included padding apps to create a more realistic Play Store mockup. All apps and their names, descriptions, screenshots, permissions, and ratings were taken from the real Play Store and the 12 relevant apps (cf. Table 2) were selected to have similar functionality, average rating, and visual appeal. Similar to Kelley et al. [18], we also displayed one 2- or 3-star rating, one 4-star and one 5-star rating for each app. We selected apps that were likely to be unknown to our participants. We also included two app categories to test additional factors, rating and brand, to allow for assessing the influence of ratings and brand recognition on risk perception. Therefore, one photo app had a medium rating of 3.4 and another a high rating of 4.7. In another category, the well-known *Google Search* app was available with the *Quick Search* app. Concerning other properties the apps were again as similar as possible.

We also largely preserved the existing permissions for the apps. Yet, we wanted to have a larger variety of permission differences between the apps to see if there is a threshold of difference in terms of permission sets that is necessary for our approach to work. We therefore added or removed one or two permissions in four apps (cf. Table 2). Most notably, we made the Tetrity app not request any permissions and PicsArt, in addition to having a high rating, request all but one permission.

Mockup Store

To offer an experience as realistic as possible, the mockup store completely imitated the functionality of the real Play Store except for three differences. First, all app listings only included seven apps to not frustrate participants or have them spend too much time going through all available apps. Apps that did not fit the purpose of the task were not selectable. Second, there also was no search function, since our pilot study showed that participants would get frustrated searching for apps they already knew but were not included in this test. Instead, we instructed them to navigate using the categories.

App Name	Network Access	Ext. Storage	Phone State	WiFi Connections	Location	Find Accounts	Take Pictures	Read Contacts	Read Call Log	Running Apps	**Total**
EasyMoney		●	●				●				3
CWMoney	●	●	●		●		●	○			6
ColorNote	●	●									2
CatchNotes	●	●	●		●	●	●	●	●		8
Tetrity	⊖		⊖								0
Traris Deluxe	●		●	●	●						4
Weather	●			⊖	●						2
Eye in the Sky	●	●		●	●						4
PhotoEffects	●	●		●							3
PicsArt (rating)	●	●	●	●	●	●	●	○		●	9
Quick Search	●			●							2
Google (brand)	●	●		●	●	●		●	●		7

Table 2. The apps used in our studies and their respective permissions. A ○ indicates an added permission and a ⊖ indicates a removed permission. Two apps were part of a particular category (upper apps always requested less permissions) and participants were asked to choose one of those or none.

Third, the apps that suited the respective tasks would be randomly displayed as first or second item in the "Top Free" list to facilitate discovery and again make the tasks less frustrating without creating a bias for one app due to its position.

Participants and Results

After pilot testing our experimental setup, $n = 36$ participants completed the study. Sessions lasted between 15 and 30 minutes including the task, the questionnaire and the debriefing. Participant demographics can be found in Table 3. For the Westin index, we used the most recent set of question from Westin's 2001 Internet Privacy survey [19]. We did not find any significant differences in the measured data based on these demographic properties, including privacy inclination.

N	36	
age	19 – 30 years	
	median 23 years	
gender	12	female
	23	male
	1	N/A
IT experience	7	with professional or educational IT experience
	2	students of computer science
Westin Index	18	privacy fundamentalists
	17	privacy pragmatists
	1	privacy unconcerned
Incidents	17	previously victims of online dangers
	3	unsure

Table 3. Participants demographics for the lab study.

The left hand side of Table 4 details the results of our lab experiment, providing installation counts for each app. Across all six choices, more participants opted to install no app of the available two with the modified permissions dialogue when compared to the existing Android permissions. Yet, as shown in Table 4, the effect is only significant in half of the app choices. Also, in four cases participants tended to install the less-requesting app or no app rather than the over-requesting app. The well-known brand and higher rating of two of the over-requesting apps did not diminish this effect. Similarly, we did not observe any effects for the Tetrity app, requesting no permissions. The PicsArt app, however, requesting almost all permissions, had the greatest reduction of installation counts (yet not quite significant). Participants became aware of the large number of permissions requested, even though this app's rating was considerably higher than for the alternative. This is also a notable difference to the results obtained using the Privacy Facts display of Kelley et al., where the rating was actually more important than the privacy facts.

Participants only spent an average of 3.1 seconds (median 1.0s) looking at the old permissions and 7.6 seconds (median 2.4s) on the modified version. While these values differ significantly between the two permission displays (repeated measures ANOVA across apps, permission dialogue as between-subjects factor, omnibus $F(1, 34) = 4.98$, two-tailed $p = .03$), the time spent on each permissions dialogue is still very brief.

Installation Behavior

We also asked participants about their installation behavior with free apps. 19 (52.8 %) stated that they usually look at several apps and then install one of them. An additional 11 (30.6 %) said they would install multiple apps, try them and then uninstall apps that did not suit their needs. 5 participants said that they would use a mix of the previous strategies. One participant stated to just install a number of apps and trying them without paying much attention to any descriptions. We then asked participants to rate how similar their usual selection behavior is to their behavior in the study. All but four participants selected 5 or more on a scale from *not similar at all* (1) to *very similar* (7). This suggests that the observed app choices are a suitable approximation of real behavior.

We also asked our participants to state how frequently they have not installed an app because of several factors (cf. Figure 3). Most participants said to not have installed an app because of the rating or the cost of an app, while the number of requested permissions or improper permissions only caused about a third of the participants to not install an app more than five times. This underlines the small amount of time users spend viewing the permission display. Additionally, most participants did not see many risks arising from malicious apps in the Play Store: they gave an average rating of 3.4 (median of 3) on a scale from "very low risk" (1) to "very high risk" (7). However, there was a slightly higher concern for the amount of danger for private information arising from smartphone apps in general: participants gave a mean and median rating of 5.0 on a scale from "no danger at all" (1) to "great danger" (7).

Qualitative Insights

Relevant comments users gave while thinking aloud during the app selection tasks were collected by the interviewer. Most interestingly, many participants indicated to trust Google to curate the Play Store or to trust the community of Android users to flag malicious apps. This confirms the slightly better rating for risks arising from Play Store apps compared to apps in general presented in the previous section. Furthermore, several participants justified simply accepting any set of permissions without checking based on this view. Similarly, many participants stated to have "*nothing to hide*" or to be "*too uninteresting*" for anyone to attack them. Other participants also said that they do not put sensitive private information on their smartphone, because "*Google can see everything anyway*" or because existing protection mechanisms "*do not pose serious problems for hackers*".

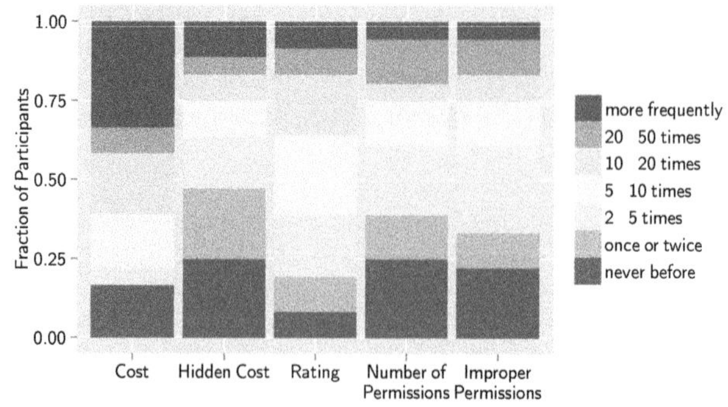

Figure 3. Frequency of not installing an app because of different factors from the lab study.

We queried those participants who had seen the new permission dialogue about which of the private information contained in the dialogue was most sensitive. Those participants mostly referred to the pictures as being undesirable for others to have access to but also found that phone book, call log, and location can be sensitive. One participant said "*there are contacts in my phone book for which I would not like others to know that I am in contact with those*". Several participants hinted at a negative affect ("*I felt very alarmed which data can be accessed by apps*") or were very surprised how far access can go ("*I would not have thought that it can see or even delete all these things!*").

Discussion

The lab study yielded encouraging results. Our modified permission dialogue was able to generate a significant effect on the participants' installation behavior. The participants' comments support that seeing examples of their personal data encouraged reflection about possible consequences and whether or not they are ready to trust the developer and accept the risks. However, participants' comments and questionnaire responses also indicate that many other factors compete with permissions for the installation decision. A certain amount of the variation found in the results presented above is therefore accountable to users' different tastes in apps, as the baseline installs show. Several participants also stated to completely ignore permissions, because they don't feel that their personal data is threatened by apps or that they have nothing to hide. It was not our aim to make these users mind their privacy if they don't have an interest in it. However, we hope that concretizing the risks can influence some users' views of privacy.

The users' choices during the study also showed that, while we chose the four sets of apps with equal functionality, rat-

	Lab Study				Online Study			
App Name	Existing Permissions Dialogue (n=18)	Personalized Permissions Dialogue (n=18)	Δ_l	p-value	Existing Permissions Dialogue (n=157)	Personalized Permissions Dialogue (n=175)	Δ_o	p-value
EasyMoney	77.8 %	33.3 %	-44.5 %		36.3 %	33.7 %	-2.6 %	
CW Money	5.6 %	22.2 %	+16.6 %		49.7 %	28.6 %	**-21.1 %**	
none	16.7 %	44.4 %	+27.7 %	**.028**	14.0 %	37.7 %	**+23.7 %**	< **.0001**
ColorNotes	88.9 %	50.0 %	-38.9 %		79.0 %	57.7 %	-21.3 %	
CatchNotes	11.1 %	11.1 %	± 0 %		12.7 %	13.1 %	+.4 %	
none	0.0 %	38.9 %	+38.9 %	**.006**	8.3 %	29.1 %	**+20.8 %**	< **.0001**
Tetrity	61.1 %	55.6 %	-5.5 %		49.1 %	68.0 %	+18.9 %	
Traris Deluxe	38.9 %	27.8 %	-11.1 %		44.6 %	22.9 %	**-21.7 %**	
none	0.0 %	16.7 %	+16.7 %	.28	6.4 %	9.1 %	+2.7 %	**.0002**
Weather	66.7 %	77.8 %	+11.1 %		75.8 %	70.9 %	-4.9 %	
Eye in the Sky	27.8 %	5.6 %	-22.2 %		17.8 %	15.4 %	-2.4 %	
none	5.6 %	16.7 %	+11.1 %	.2	6.4 %	13.7 %	+7.3 %	.081
PhotoEffects	16.7 %	33.3 %	+16.6 %		19.8 %	28.0 %	+8.2 %	
PicsArt (rating)	83.3 %	50.0 %	-33.3 %		71.3 %	49.1 %	-22.2 %	
none	0.0 %	16.7 %	+16.7 %	.068	8.9 %	22.9 %	**+14.0 %**	< **.0001**
Quick Search	27.8 %	27.8 %	±0.0 %		15.9 %	20.6 %	+4.7 %	
Google (brand)	72.2 %	44.4 %	-27.8 %		83.4 %	64.6 %	-18.8 %	
none	0.0 %	27.8 %	+27.8 %	**.041**	.6 %	14.9 %	**+14.3 %**	<**.0001**

Table 4. Installation count results of both, lab and online study. The table shows the percentage of participants that chose to install either one of two apps from each category or none, with the bottom app requesting more and unnecessary permissions than the top app within each group of two. Bold typesetting indicates significant contributions to the χ^2 value (standardized residual $>$ 1.96) and significant p-values according to Fisher's exact test on the respective 3 (choice) $\times$ 2 (type of permission dialogue) cross-table.

ing and potential for visual appeal, some apps were already clearly preferred in the baseline condition. However, in the cases where the over-requesting app was preferred, the permissions dialogue still had an impact and was able to make users rethink their choice (cf., for example, the Weather or ColorNotes app in Table 4). Additionally, the effect we found on the rating-category underlines that we are indeed able to overlay decisions already made, even when some factors are strongly in favor of the more dangerous option.

Furthermore, the examples of private information displayed to communicate the risks of installing a particular app appeared to be making many participants understand the extent of what a permission allows an app to do. Even though all participants had been using Android smartphones for several months and had installed several new apps, seeing the permissions displayed in this new fashion gave them a better idea of what permissions really entail. Participants that came in contact with the new permission dialogue stated that they would "*pay more attention to these things in the future*".

ONLINE STUDY

To confirm the effects observed in our lab experiment on a limited population, we went on to evaluate our approach with a more diverse population. Since the lab study showed large individual differences in the way apps are selected and installed, a larger sample would be required to obtain more reliable results. Also, students are often considered to interact differently with technology than the general population and may have therefore biased our lab results. Additionally, we wanted to investigate to what extent our approach caused participants to be afraid of misuse of their private information. Such a negative affect could be a key motivation for less risky installation decisions. The questionnaire in this study therefore included questions that elicited how afraid of misuse of private information participants felt as well as how aware participants were of an app's control over personal data through the use of the permissions dialogue.

Method

We planned the online study to largely resemble the lab study. To access a diverse population, we decided to use Amazon's Mechanical Turk service to run the experiment. While MTurk also does not provide a sample that is representative of the general population, this service is commonly used to access a population that is more diverse than usually available. The task was framed as the common role-play of helping a good friend (previously applied in e. g. [5, 18]), who just bought a smartphone and does not know which apps to install. We showed participants a description of the scenario, including a picture of the friend John and his family to create a feeling of familiarity. Participants were asked to imagine that John gave them his phone and a list of activities he could use an app for. They were presented with the two suitable apps for each of the six activities. The order of the app choices was again randomized to control for effects of learning and fatigue. After finishing the selection process, participants completed a questionnaire as in the lab study and were compensated with \$ 1.50. We asked participants to only participate if they use a phone running on Android 4.0 or newer in their daily life to have similar levels of familiarity and habituation with smartphones and app installations. We asked participants to specify their Android version in the questionnaire and excluded participants who specified a lower version.

As Amazon's TOS do not allow us to ask MTurk workers to install applications, we recreated the tasks in the browser.

Participants were presented with two side-by-side screenshots of the same apps for each of the same six tasks as in the lab study. Again, we chose a setup based on the work of Kelley et al. [18]. They were then asked to decide whether they would want to install any of the two apps. Again, they had the option to install none of the two. If participants chose to install an app, they were presented with a screenshot of the respective app's permissions dialogue (cf. Figure 2 and Table 2) and asked whether they want to continue with the installation or return to the app overview. Half of the participants were randomly assigned to our modified permission dialogue, which contained artificial private information of John (cf. Figure 2 and Figure 1). After each choice, participants were asked to explain the reasons for their selection.

Participants and Results

332 MTurk workers successfully and validly completed our task. We included attention check questions in the questionnaire and the tasks, which we used to exclude 49 participants answering inconsistently or specifying an Android version less than 4.0. Table 5 provides an overview of online study demographics. We found no differences in our measured variables with respect to these properties, except that participants indicating previous professional IT experience chose the Google app significantly more frequently (Fisher's exact test, $p = .035$, odds ratio .51).

N	332	
Age	18 – 64 years	
	median 27 years	
Gender	38.6 %	female
	61.4 %	male
Occupation	50.6 %	full-time employees
	19.3 %	students
	10.2 %	part-time workers
	7.9 %	self-employed
	7.0 %	Homemaker
	4.3 %	Unemployed or retired
IT Experience	27.1 %	have worked in or studied IT
Smartphone Use	18	months (median)
Westin Index	29.8 %	privacy fundamentalists
	52.1 %	privacy pragmatists
	18.1 %	privacy unconcerned
Incidents	38.9 %	previously victims of online dangers
	6.3 %	unsure

Table 5. Participants demographics for the online study.

During the app choice tasks, participants again were significantly less likely to install the over-requesting apps when using the permission dialogue with personalized examples as opposed to the baseline regular Android permission dialogue. The right hand side of Table 4 gives an overview of the results in comparison with the results from the lab. Again, brand and rating did not diminish the effect. The online study hence confirms the effect we found in the lab.

The Weather app was again so popular in the baseline condition, that we did not find significant effects in this case. However, this also suggests that we did not blindly scare users into not installing any app at all: the permission set of the Weather app was apparently reasonable enough to be accepted for its purpose. This is also mirrored in the participants' reasoning about this choice: *"The only permission it needed was my location. That makes sense." "It need [sic] permissions which I would expect from this kind of app"*. In other tasks, users responded differently: *"Both apps had permissions that I wasn't comfortable accepting"*. Furthermore, we found that 88.6 % of online participants with the new permission dialogue installed three or more apps each.

Similar to the lab results, the permission dialogue had a significant overall effect on the time spent viewing the permissions (repeated-measures ANOVA across apps, permissions dialogue as between-subjects factor, $F(1, 330) = 53.98$, $p < .001$). Yet, Bonferroni-Holm-corrected pairwise comparisons only yielded significant results for the PicsArt and Quick Search Widget apps. However, the time spent looking at permissions was still short with 5.6 seconds (median 2.5s) in the baseline condition and 8.5 seconds (median 5.3s) in the modified condition. It is important to note that these values contain network and rendering delays, as they were collected on the server-side.

Again, we asked participants about their installation behavior with free apps. Similar to the lab, 208 (62.7 %) stated to examine several and then install one, 88 (26.5 %) try multiple apps and then uninstall those that did not suit their needs, and 31 (9.3 %) just try several apps without paying much attention to descriptions. 5 participants (1.5 %) said that they would use a mix of the previous strategies, while also considering external information sources as well as the required permissions. 89.4 % of participants again indicated to have behaved similarly in the online study, answering with 5 or more on a scale from *no similarity* (1) to *great similarity* (7). Online participants were also slightly more concerned about malicious apps in Google's Play Store (mean rating 3.96, median rating 4; 7=highest concern, see lab results) but slightly less concerned about the amount of danger for private information arising from smartphone apps (mean rating 4.2, median rating 4; 7=great danger).

Concerning participants' awareness of an app's control over personal data after completing the task, we found that the modified permissions dialogue had a significant effect: more than twice as many participants compared to the existing dialogue (87 vs. 40) chose the highest rating on a scale from *not aware* (1) to *very aware* (7) (odds ratio 2.88, Fisher's exact test, $p < .0001$). To assess how afraid people felt after seeing permissions, we asked them to rate to what extend the display of app permissions caused them to be afraid of John losing personal data or information. Similar to the general awareness, four times as many participants (13 vs. 57) indicated the highest rating on the provided scale from *not afraid at all* (1) to *very afraid* (7) (odds ratio 5.32, Fisher's exact test, $p < .0001$).

Most interestingly, we also found a significant effect of the above rating on the time spent viewing the permissions (repeated-measures ANOVA across apps, permissions dialogue and highest fear rating as between-subjects factor, $F(1, 328) = 124.3$, $p < .0001$). Participants that were very afraid to have John's private information compromised spent

5.4 seconds longer looking at both versions of the permissions dialogue. This is a twofold increase. Additionally, there was no significant interaction between the two between-subjects variables, such that we did not find differences in being afraid and paying more attention with regard to which permissions dialogue participants saw ($F(1, 328) = .007, p = .8$).

Discussion

Even though the setup of the online study differed from our lab study and did not allow us to use participants' actual private information to personalize the permission dialogue, the results show that the approach was still effective. Participants were more likely to choose an installation option that requested less permissions. Furthermore, the Weather app showed that reasonable sets of permissions were recognized and accepted if they fit the app's purpose. The online study also suggests that communicating risk to users with examples created more awareness in participants and instilled a negative affect which caused them to pay more attention to the permissions. We therefore believe that this approach to risk communication can more easily override choices already made than existing approaches, especially when important information on the risk can only be presented afterwards.

GENERAL DISCUSSION

The two studies have shown that we can leverage personalized, more concrete examples and descriptions in security decision dialogues to increase their efficacy. We were able to significantly impact the choice of apps in the Google Play Store, given that some apps were a greater risk to participants' privacy than others. The results also demonstrate that using personal examples in these dialogues can leverage users' affect to increase attention. While the modified dialogue may have caused some users to shy away from installing any apps in our study, it will also make them consider the privacy-tradeoff they are about to enter as it actually is. We might also be scaring users into choosing conservatively, but users were not completely oblivious to what happens, as in many cases, an app was still installed. Users that didnt install an app during the one try they had in the study, would probably try to find another one at a later point or when they have more options as they still have a need for the desired functionality.

For this exploration, we used a mix of drastic and more neutral scenarios in our permissions display. It is, for instance, rather unlikely that an app will simply delete images while it is more plausible for an app to access and possibly upload contacts from the address book. Since it is not possible to automatically determine what actions an app actually can or does take, it is up to future work to determine which intensity of descriptions and which visualizations can work best in which situations. We posit that a balance between intensity and frequency of displaying the dialogue needs to be found, since it is likely that if the most extreme examples are routinely used, they will lead to a fatigue effect if the examples shown never happen.

The concrete choice of examples is also likely to be an additional factor for the efficacy of the risk-communication-by-example approach. Displaying photos of one's cat or a random landscape from some city the person has visited probably causes less of an emotional reaction than a portrait of one's partner or child. Since we only displayed random examples in this initial exploration, selecting specific and more private examples can potentially further increase the efficacy of personalized security decision dialogues.

Furthermore, the comments users gave during the experiments indicated that using our prototype only for a short amount of time already caused them to consider changing their general attitude towards permissions (*"I think I will pay more attention to those permissions in the future."*). Using personalized examples may therefore also be a suitable tool for an initial or recurring education campaign in systems that can serve to make users understand the risks present in this system.

The prototype we implemented for our evaluation assumes a single-user environment for the device. While this is reasonable in many cases, personalized decision dialogues may also be desirable in situations where a device is shared by multiple users. While a shared device, such as a tablet, will probably yield less information that is especially private to one of its users, a system would need to make sure that the personalized dialogues do not create a privacy issue themselves by disclosing private information to others. For mobile devices, this is an important and unsolved problem concerning many other aspects of the app model as well and is the subject of ongoing work (e. g., [15]).

Similarly, app installation may take place in public and hence cause privacy issues by displaying private information in the permission dialogue. To avoid this, users who frequently install apps in public should be able to opt out of using personal information or have the information displayed only after pressing a button.

Limitations

The study presented in this paper is a first contact study and thus the novelty of the dialogue itself may have increased the effects we observed. Additionally, we made the design decision to slightly increase headline size to separate the examples better, as well as to change the descriptive text of each permission to be less abstract and better fit the personalized context. These two changes may have confounded our results even though participants' qualitative reactions mainly concerned the personal information contained in the dialogues. Additionally, while we attempted to choose a set of apps which were not too well known, users may have already been familiar with some of the apps in our experiments, influencing their installation decision. Determining how each of these factors contributed to our results is the subject of future work.

As stated above, habituation can also occur with our personalized permission display. However, the displayed examples are chosen randomly and hence the dialogue changes between each app installation and therefore at least has a chance of countering habituation, especially since the users regularly create more personal data (e. g. new photos, contacts, and call log entries). This naturally needs to be investigated with a long term study before any reliable statements can be made.

CONCLUSION AND FUTURE WORK

In this paper, we have demonstrated the value of leveraging personalized examples to improve risk communication for security and privacy decisions, using the Android app installation process as an example. Two experiments with diverse populations have shown that users make more risk-aware app choices when presented with concrete examples of the information at risk from undesirable permissions. Furthermore, we found that when decision dialogues get personal, a negative affect was created in users which increased attention.

Thus, in future work, we would like to evaluate the long-term effects of this novel approach, especially with respect to habituation and general changes in behavior with respect to privacy. Since every interaction process uses a random selection of personalized information, our approach has the potential to counter habituation effects. Security decision dialogues with personalized examples can also be a valuable tool for other scenarios, including SSL warning messages, software installation on desktop computers or posting on social network sites. We also believe that personalized decision dialogues can serve as an educational tool, that may also work retrospectively. A user could be confronted with examples of private information, such as sent or received emails, that has been transmitted without proper privacy protection or encryption to see whether or not this causes more privacy risk awareness or a demand for better security measures.

REFERENCES

1. Au, K. W. Y., Zhou, Y. F., Huang, Z., and Lie, D. PScout: Analyzing the Android Permission Specification. In *Proc. CCS* (2012).
2. Besmer, A., Lipford, H. R., Shehab, M., and Cheek, G. Social Applications: Exploring A More Secure Framework. In *Proc. SOUPS* (2009).
3. Blackwell, A. F., Church, L., and Green, T. The Abstract is 'an Enemy'. In *Proc. Psychology of Programming Interest Group (PPIG) Workshop* (2008).
4. Bravo-Lillo, C., Cranor, L., Downs, J., and Komanduri, S. What Is Still Wrong With Security Warnings: A Mental Models Approach. In *Proc. SOUPS* (2010).
5. Bravo-Lillo, C., Cranor, L., Downs, J., and Komanduri, S. Bridging the Gap in Computer Security Warnings: A Mental Model Approach. *Security Privacy, IEEE 9*, 2 (2011), 18–26.
6. Bravo-Lillo, C., Cranor, L. F., Downs, J., Komanduri, S., Reeder, R. W., Schechter, S., and Sleeper, M. Your Attention Please: Designing Security-Decision UIs to Make Genuine Risks Harder to Ignore. In *Proc. SOUPS* (2013).
7. Bravo-Lillo, C., Cranor, L. F., Downs, J., Komanduri, S., and Sleeper, M. Improving Computer Security Dialogs. In *Proc. INTERACT* (2011).
8. Cranor, L. A Framework for Reasoning About the Human in the Loop. *UPSEC* (2008).
9. De Paula, R., Ding, X., Dourish, P., Nies, K., Pillet, B., Redmiles, D., Ren, J., Rode, J., et al. Two Experiences Designing for Effective Security. In *Proc. SOUPS* (2005).
10. Egelman, S. My Profile Is My Password, Verify Me! The Privacy/Convenience Tradeoff of Facebook Connect. In *Proc. CHI* (2013).
11. Egelman, S., Cranor, L. F., and Hong, J. You've Been Warned: An Empirical Study of the Effectiveness of Web Browser Phishing Warnings. In *Proc. CHI* (2008).
12. Felt, A. P., Chin, E., Hanna, S., and Wagner, D. Android Permissions Demystified. In *Proc. CCS* (2011).
13. Felt, A. P., Ha, E., Egelman, S., Haney, A., Chin, E., and Wagner, D. Android Permissions: User Attention, Comprehension, and Behavior. In *Proc. SOUPS* (2012).
14. Harbach, M., Fahl, S., Yakovleva, P., and Smith, M. Sorry, I Don't Get It: An Analysis of Warning Message Texts. In *Proc USEC* (2013).
15. Hayashi, E., Riva, O., Strauss, K., Brush, A. J. B., and Schechter, S. Goldilocks and the Two Mobile Devices: Going Beyond All-Or-Nothing Access to a Device's Applications. In *Proc. SOUPS* (2012).
16. Inglesant, P., Sasse, M. A., Chadwick, D., and Shi, L. L. Expressions of Expertness. In *Proc. SOUPS* (2008).
17. Karat, C.-M., Karat, J., Brodie, C., and Feng, J. Evaluating Interfaces for Privacy Policy Rule Authoring. In *Proc. CHI* (2006).
18. Kelley, P. G., Cranor, L. F., and Sadeh, N. Privacy as Part of the App Decision-Making Process. In *Proc. CHI* (2013).
19. Kumaraguru, P., and Cranor, L. F. Privacy indexes: A Survey of Westin's Studies. Tech. Rep. CMU-ISRI-5-138, Carnegie Mellon University, 2005.
20. Pandita, R., Xiao, X., Yang, W., Enck, W., and Xie, T. WHYPER: Towards Automating Risk Assessment of Mobile Applications. In *Proc. USENIX Security Symposium* (2013).
21. Rader, E., Wash, R., and Brooks, B. Stories as Informal Lessons About Security. In *Proc. SOUPS* (2012).
22. Raja, F., Hawkey, K., Hsu, S., Wang, K., and Beznosov, K. A Brick Wall, a Locked Door, and a Bandit: A Physical Security Metaphor for Firewall Warnings. In *Proc. SOUPS* (2011).
23. Sunshine, J., Egelman, S., Almuhimedi, H., Atri, N., and Cranor, L. F. Crying Wolf: An Empirical Study of SSL Warning Effectiveness. In *Proc. USENIX Security Symposium* (2009).
24. Wogalter, M., Dejoy, D. M., and Laughery, K. R. A Consolidated Communication-Human Information Processing (C-HIP) Model. *Warnings and Risk Communication* (1999), 15–23.
25. Wogalter, M. S., Racicot, B. M., Kalsher, M. J., and Noel Simpson, S. Personalization of Warning Signs: The Role of Perceived Relevance on Behavioral Compliance. *International Journal of Industrial Ergonomics 14*, 3 (1994).

"My religious aunt asked why I was trying to sell her viagra": Experiences with account hijacking

Richard Shay
Carnegie Mellon University
Pittsburgh, PA, USA
rshay@cmu.edu

Iulia Ion, Robert W. Reeder, & Sunny Consolvo
Google
Mountain View, CA, USA
{iuliaion, rreeder, sconsolvo}
@google.com

ABSTRACT
With so much of our lives digital, online, and not entirely under our control, we risk losing access to our communications, reputation, and data. Recent years have brought a rash of high-profile account compromises, but account hijacking is not limited to high-profile accounts. In this paper, we report results of a survey about people's experiences with and attitudes toward account hijacking. The problem is widespread; 30% of our 294 participants had an email or social networking account accessed by an unauthorized party. Five themes emerged from our results: (1) compromised accounts are often valuable to victims, (2) attackers are mostly unknown, but sometimes known, to victims, (3) users acknowledge some responsibility for keeping their accounts secure, (4) users' understanding of important security measures is incomplete, and (5) harm from account hijacking is concrete *and* emotional. We discuss implications for designing security mechanisms to improve chances for user adoption.

Author Keywords
Security; authentication; online accounts; account hijacking; account compromise; attackers; survey; microsurvey; Mechanical Turk; Google Consumer Survey

ACM Classification Keywords
H.5.m. Information interfaces and presentation (e.g., HCI): Miscellaneous, K.6.5. Security and protection

INTRODUCTION
"In the space of one hour, my entire digital life was destroyed," wrote Mat Honan, technology writer and editor for Wired magazine [19]. In his widely read 2012 narrative, Honan describes how he lost access to his Google, Twitter, and AppleID accounts, had a year's worth of photos, documents, and emails deleted, and had racist messages posted to his Twitter feed. Honan was *"mad," "sad,"* and *"shocked."* Ultimately, he was able to restore access to his accounts and much of the data that had been lost, though at considerable cost, time, and effort on his part [20]. When one of the attackers contacted him, Honan was able to ask why the attacker had done this damage – it was to access Honan's coveted 3-letter Twitter handle, "mat"; the data destruction was just *"collateral damage."*

Honan's article is gripping not only as a story about his experiences, but also as a cautionary tale. With so much of our lives now digital, online, and not entirely under our control, we can easily imagine losing access to our communications, reputation, and data, with little recourse. Recent years have brought a rash of other stories of high-profile account hijackings. For example, U.S. Vice Presidential candidate Sarah Palin's email account was compromised in 2008 [7], the personal email account of a Twitter executive's wife was compromised in 2009 [34], the group *Anonymous* broke into accounts of executives at a security firm in 2011 [9], and attackers broke into the Twitter accounts of numerous media outlets, including the Associated Press [29], the Financial Times [26], the Guardian [3], and the Onion [27] in 2013.

Account hijacking is hardly limited to high-profile accounts; anecdotal evidence suggests that it is widespread and can be devastating. In response, service providers continue to improve authentication, compromise detection, and account recovery mechanisms. However, the design space for these systems is vast, and they often require user participation, which is notoriously hard to get for security-related tasks [38]. A better understanding of the hijacking problem – and how to motivate users to take action against it – should help improve the design of such systems.

To gain a better understanding of the hijacking problem from the user's perspective, we surveyed 294 people about their experiences with and attitudes toward email and social network account hijacking. We confirm that the problem is, in fact, widespread; 30% of our 294 participants reported that at least one of their email or social networking accounts had been accessed by an unauthorized party.

We also highlight five themes that emerged from our results:

CHI 2014, April 26–May 01, 2014, Toronto, Canada.
ACM 978-1-4503-2473-1/14/04.
http://dx.doi.org/10.1145/2556288.2557330

(1) **Compromised accounts are often valuable to victims:** In our study, most hijacked accounts were for personal communication and used daily.
(2) **Attackers are unknown *and* known to victims:** Guarding against remote, anonymous attackers is most important, but it would be a mistake to ignore attacks from people close to victims.
(3) **Users acknowledge some responsibility:** Users seem to believe that they share responsibility for keeping their accounts secure.
(4) **Users' understanding of important security measures is incomplete:** Users are aware of malware, phishing, and third-party password database breaches as the most prevalent ways accounts are compromised. However, they emphasize password management measures for preventing account compromise and seem less aware of anti-phishing and anti-malware measures.
(5) **Harm from hijacking is concrete *and* emotional:** Concrete harm is usually minimal, though it can sometimes be severe. Even when it is minimal, users experience strong feelings of anger, fear, and embarrassment about the compromise.

We discuss implications for designing security mechanisms into large, modern Web services in ways that improve chances for users to adopt those mechanisms.

RELATED WORK

Our work fits into the space of research about people's experiences with and attitudes toward online security. In this section, we highlight key related work in that space.

One area of research has focused on models of how people think about security. For example, Camp proposed five mental models that were derived from a review of the literature [11]. Her models – *physical security, medical, criminal, warfare,* and *market* – represent a broad view of how people think about privacy and security and how they frame security decisions. Camp points out that people's understandings tend to rely too strongly on their own past experiences. For example, if a person has previously engaged in a risky computer activity without negative consequences, then that person may underestimate the risk of that activity and continue to engage in it.

Wash provides another view of how people think about computer security based on interviews with 33 people [37]. He identified several "folk models" that describe how people think about malware and attackers (e.g., *"viruses cause mischief," "viruses support crime,"* and *"hackers are criminals who target big fish"*). Similar to Camp, Wash points out how shortcomings in these models can lead people to misidentify threats. For example, those who think attackers would not bother going after them personally might not be aware of the threat posed by botnets.

Other researchers have explored how people make specific security-related decisions. For example, Mazurek et al. interviewed 33 people about how they made data sharing and trust decisions with devices in their homes [23]. The researchers found that interviewees often applied their own understandings of real-world physical security when making access-control decisions.

Another line of research has explored how people react to security incidents or changes in security policies. For example, in a survey of 301 undergraduate students, Rader, Wash, and Brooks investigated how stories that people tell about security incidents that they or others have experienced resonate with people and, in turn, are translated into security-related beliefs [30]. The researchers found that respondents encapsulated and transmitted security lessons in the form of stories and that these stories can affect behavior and understanding. In another example, Shay et al. surveyed 470 people on a university campus that had recently transitioned to a stricter password policy [35]. The researchers found that while respondents tended to be annoyed, they also felt more secure and were neutral about reverting to the previous policy. And finally, Harbach et al. investigated why users were slow to adopt a new German ID system with added security features [18].

This related work suggests that by identifying shortcomings in users' understanding, designers might be able to correct misunderstandings and encourage users to practice better security-related behaviors. The work presented in this paper fits into this space by helping to describe how users experience and perceive account hijacking so that we and others can figure out how to encourage users to make decisions and practice behaviors that help prevent their accounts from being compromised. To the best of our knowledge, this is the first such study on this topic.

METHODOLOGY

In July 2013, we conducted an online survey of people in the U.S. who use a personal email or social networking account at least once per month. In this section, we describe the survey – including supplemental data that we collected from an additional microsurvey, the participants' demographics, and how we analyzed the qualitative data.

The Survey

The online survey had two main branches: one branch was administered to people who had experienced the compromise of a personal email or social networking account (N=89) and the other was administered to people who had not (N=205). We recruited participants from the Amazon Mechanical Turk crowdsourcing service (MTurk). When we recruited, we did not mention that our survey was about account hijacking; rather, our posting proposed, "Answer a survey about your email or social networking account." Participants were assigned to one of the branches based on their response to the question: "As far as you know, has anyone ever broken into any of your personal email or online social networking accounts?" Those who answered "Yes, only once" or "Yes, more than once" continued with the branch for people who had experienced an account compromise, and those who responded "No" or "I don't know" continued with the other branch. Both branches included open- and close-ended questions.

We collected data over three hours on the evening of Friday, July 26, 2013. Each participant could only take the survey once and received $1 as compensation.

Those who had experienced a compromise (N=89)
Participants who had experienced the compromise of an email or social networking account were asked about their experience (N=89). If participants indicated having experienced more than one such compromise, they were instructed to answer the questions about "the most upsetting" episode. We asked about their account, how the compromise happened, who they thought did it, its consequences, and whose responsibility it was to prevent their accounts from being compromised.

Those who had not experienced a compromise (N=205)
Participants who had not experienced the compromise of an email or social networking account were instructed to think about either their primary personal email (N=111) or social networking (N=94) account throughout the survey. Those having only one or the other were asked about that one; otherwise we asked about one at random. We asked about whom participants were concerned about breaking into their accounts, how they thought accounts were compromised, what they thought an attacker would do if he or she broke into the participants' accounts, and whose responsibility it was to prevent their accounts from being compromised.

Survey Development
To develop the survey, we conducted five semi-structured interviews with a convenience sample of friends and family of our extended research team who had experienced an account compromise. Results from the interviews provided us with insight for creating the survey. After drafting the survey, it was reviewed by experts from our institution, revised, and then piloted with a convenience sample of six people from our institution who were not from our research team. After subsequent improvements, we launched a pilot on MTurk with 20 people. After we made minor adjustments from that pilot, we launched the final survey. We do not report data collected from these pilot studies.

We received 300 completed surveys and discarded six that were duplicates or did not meet our criteria for participation, such as if a participant did not have a personal email or social networking account that was checked at least once per month.

Mechanical Turk as a Recruiting Platform
MTurk, which has been used in prior usable security research (e.g., [6,14]), allowed us to collect data from a large number of diverse participants. MTurk has also been used by Kittur, Chi, and Suh to investigate how well "Turkers" (i.e., the people who complete tasks on MTurk) assessed the quality of Wikipedia articles [21]. The researchers were impressed with how well the Turkers' ratings compared to those of experts. Buhrmester et al. found that the MTurk population was more diverse than that found on a typical college campus and that using MTurk could result in high-quality data [10]. Paolacci et al. conducted a survey on the demographics of U.S. Turkers [28]. They found Turkers to be more female than male, and average 36 years with more education than the general U.S. populace. They also found evidence of MTurk resulting in data comparable in quality to surveying on a university campus.

Mechanical Turk Quality Control
Although MTurk has been shown to be a trustworthy platform for past user studies, it is possible to get low-quality responses. As with any online survey, participants on MTurk can cheat to receive incentives by answering all required questions as quickly as possible and providing junk data in the process. We took three measures to guard against such junk data in our results. First, we required that the Turkers who responded to our survey have a task approval rate of 95% or better, and have completed at least 100 tasks, so we expected to have a relatively high-quality pool of participants. Second, one member of the research team reviewed all responses to the open-ended questions to ensure that responses were on topic and determined that they all were. Finally, we had three trap responses to our multiple-choice questions – responses that were obviously wrong, and we expected no participant who was paying attention would choose. We found that six participants did choose trap responses. However, no participant chose more than one, and those participants did provide valid responses to open-ended questions. Thus, we assume the few trap responses we received were errors due to misreading or misclicking rather than cheating, and we include these participants' data in our analysis.

Confirming the rate of account compromises
We ran a separate one-question survey (or "microsurvey") with a different survey service (Google Consumer Surveys (GCS) [16]), and thus a different population, to confirm our finding about the rate of account compromises. Web users respond to microsurveys from GCS in order to access premium Web content [24,36]. We used GCS's "multiple choice, single answer" microsurvey format to ask, "As far as you know, has anyone ever broken into any of your personal email or online social networking accounts?" (i.e., the same question and set of response options that we used to branch participants in the main MTurk survey). We set the "audience sample" feature to target the general population in the U.S., and we collected data from 1,501 participants from Tuesday, July 30 through Thursday, August 1, 2013.

Participant Demographics (N=294)
Participants in our MTurk survey skewed slightly male and young: 58.8% male, 40.5% female, and 0.7% preferred not to answer; 34.4% were between the ages of 18-24, 40.5% were 25-34, 11.9% were 35-44, 6.1% were 45-54, 5.1% were 55-64, 1.7% were 65 or over, and one preferred not to

answer. As to their highest level of education, just over a third had Bachelor's degrees and another third had some college. The remaining third was spread over a broad range of from some high school (1.7%) to having a Master's or doctorate (8.8%).

Just over 70% of the participants were employed full- or part-time or were self-employed (37.1% full-time, 19.6% part-time, and 13.6% self-employed). 19.7% were students, some of whom were also employed, and 16.3% were unemployed or looking for work. Participants represented a broad range of occupations, including customer service representative, sign fabricator, human resources assistant, retired teacher, piano mover, biologist, lawyer, day trader, youth development professional, video editor, filmmaker, administrative assistant, web developer, construction worker, homemaker, writer, and lead programmer.

Data Analysis Approach

To mitigate priming and learn from participants in their own words, we asked open-ended questions. Participants who had experienced the compromise of an email or social networking account were asked five open-ended questions, and the other participants were asked one. For each question, we created a codebook to interpret responses. Coding categories were developed from our review of the responses and related work.

Two coders independently categorized each response using the codebooks. We validated the codebooks through pre- and post-discussion coding, measuring agreement with Cohen's Kappa [22]. Prior to discussion, the Kappa values show agreement ranging from "Fair" (0.373) to "Almost Perfect" (0.857). After discussion, the coders were in "Almost Perfect" agreement on responses from every question (with Kappa values ranging from 0.927 to 1) [22].

RESULTS

In this section, we review details of the compromises that participants experienced as well as who participants think is responsible for keeping their accounts safe and the role they think passwords have in account protection and recovery. We refer to participants who experienced an account hijacking as H1, ... , H89 and participants who did not as NH1, ... , NH205.

Compromise rates, account importance, & attackers

At the beginning of the survey, all participants were asked, "As far as you know, has anyone ever broken into any of your personal email or online social networking accounts?" Of our 294 participants, 89 (30.3%) answered that one or more such accounts had been compromised.

In our supplemental GCS microsurvey (N=1501), 15.6% of participants indicated that they had experienced one or more account compromises. Though less than our MTurk sample, it still represents a meaningful portion of the Web population experiencing account compromises. Moreover, GCS participants were more likely than MTurk participants to answer "I don't know" (18.7% versus 4.1%, respectively) rather than simply "No," for which the proportions were almost the same (65.8% and 65.6%, respectively). While we cannot account precisely for the difference in MTurk and GCS responses, we note that the motivations for completing surveys may be different; Turkers set out to complete a survey, while GCS participants are trying to get to premium Web content. Differences in the responses may be due to this motivational difference or to other demographic differences, but we note that account compromises are reported at high levels and seem to be a common experience. Our findings are consistent with a 2013 study from the Pew Research Center, which found that 21% of Internet users have had an email or social networking account compromised [31].

How important were the hijacked accounts?

Of the 89 participants who reported experiencing an account compromise, 73 (82.0%) used their accounts at least once a week, and 53 (59.5%) used their accounts daily. When we asked participants for the main reasons they used their accounts, 69 (77.5%) indicated "Personal communication," which we take to be an important use, compared with options such as "Receiving deals or coupons" or "Receiving updates or newsletters."

Who broke into the accounts?

We asked the 89 participants who had experienced a compromise, "Who do you think was behind the break-in?" and offered three response options:

- Someone you didn't know at the time of the break-in,
- Someone you knew but didn't live with at the time of the break-in, and
- Someone you lived with at the time of the break-in.

We followed that by asking for participants' confidence level about who broke in. Just over half (46; 51.7%) indicated they were "Not at all" confident about who broke in, but of the 35 who were at least moderately confident, 30 (85.7%) indicated it was someone they did not know. Of the remainder who expressed at least moderate confidence, three were extremely confident it was someone they knew but did not live with, and two indicated it was someone they lived with. Of those who expressed they were "Slightly" or "Not at all" confident, 51 (96.2%) indicated it was someone they did not know, and only two (3.8%) indicated it was someone they knew but did not live with.

What harm came from the compromise?

In this section, we provide a summary of the harms reported by participants as a result of the compromise.

Hundreds of my emails had been deleted

Most of the compromises reported by the 89 participants did not result in very harmful consequences. Many participants (33; 37.1%) reported having spam emails sent from their accounts to their contacts (e.g., H80 explained, *"I had spam emails sent to people on my contact list."*).

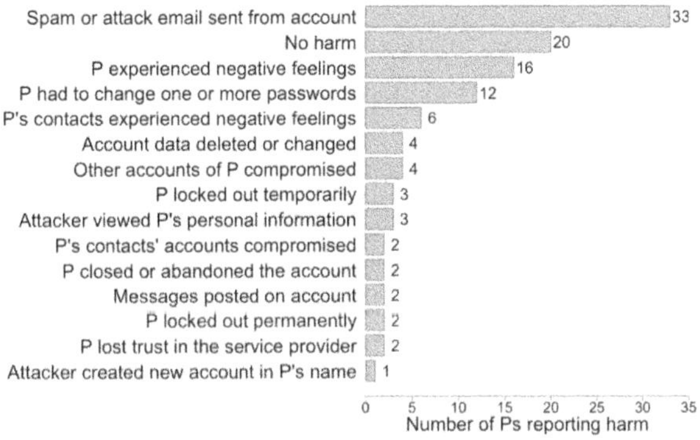

Figure 1. Categories of harm that participants (Ps) experienced as a result of their account compromises (from an open-ended question). Responses were coded into the categories shown; the data show the number of participants who reported each harm (N=89).

Twenty-two participants (24.7%) downplayed the harm (e.g., *"No harm, except for..."*); and 20 (22.5%) indicated that no harm at all resulted from the compromise. Sixteen participants (18.0%) reported experiencing a negative feeling, such as *"It was frustrating, but not harmful"* (H73).

However, for some, the harm was more substantial. Five participants reported being locked out of their accounts, two of whom never regained access. We note that in a later multiple-choice question, 25 (28.1%) of the 89 participants reported that they were locked out of their accounts at least temporarily; however, only five mentioned it as a harm in the earlier open-ended question. Four participants reported having other accounts hijacked as a result of the compromise, one of which was financially related: "*my amazon account [was] hacked and purchases were made*" (H47). Four reported that data in their account was altered or deleted (e.g., "*my personal information was changed*" (H20) and *"hundreds of my emails had been deleted"* (H83)). Two participants believed that accounts belonging to their contacts were compromised as a result, two others closed their accounts after the compromise, and two more lost trust in their service provider (e.g., H36 wrote *"Well, my friends no longer trust my email account and neither do I. We had to find another form of communication."*). See Figure 1 for a breakdown of the open-ended responses.

The harm was mental

Although most participants reported no substantial harm, when asked *how they felt* when they learned their account had been compromised, all but seven expressed strong negative feelings, such as "*I was mad,*" *"violated,"* or "*angry*." For example, though H50 reported, *"No harm came from it. It was just a nuisance,"* he nevertheless reported feeling *"angry"* and *"upset."* The most prominent feelings, each reported by over a quarter of participants, were anger (e.g., *"angry," "mad,"* or *"enraged")* and fear (e.g., *"afraid"* or *"paranoid"*). H48 explained: *"It also made me afraid as I realize how vulnerable electronic information is."* The next dominant emotion was annoyance. Furthermore, some participants felt "*violated,*" *"frustrated,"* or *"vulnerable."*

For some, the emotional damage persisted because they could not fully gauge the consequences. H5 explained,

> *"The harm was mental because I was afraid that the email hacking may have also allowed a computer bug to infiltrate [the] system."*

H72 continues to worry about potential future fraud: *"So far I have [not] noticed any thing* [sic] *like credit fraud yet, but I'm still nervous."*

It made a bad impression of me

Participants didn't just feel annoyed or afraid; a few were also *"embarrassed."* H19 reported,

> *"A lot of my friends and colleagues had received spam emails from [me] and it made a bad impression of me to them."*

Overall, six participants indicated that the compromise caused bad feelings for their contacts, making their contacts *"annoyed"* with the spam or *"a little upset."* H48 expressed the harm in terms of damage to his reputation: *"Rumors were spread, and people might look at me differently because of it."* The embarrassment sometimes was caused by the inappropriate content of the spam messages. For example, H52 explained, *"My religious aunt asked why I was trying to sell her viagra* [sic]."

However, the social implications were not all negative. When asked what good came of the compromise, H62 stated, *"I knew my friends cared! They warned me and asked if I was alright."*

Lock you out of your account

To understand what the 205 participants who had not experienced an account compromise believed might happen in a compromise, we asked, "If someone you don't know broke into your account, how likely is he or she to do the following?" Response options, which participants ranked from "Not at all likely" to "Extremely likely," were:

- Break into your other accounts,
- Send spam to your contacts,
- Find things to blackmail you with,
- Find things to blackmail your contacts with,
- Try to trick your contacts into sending him or her money,
- Lock you out of your account,
- Delete your account,
- Delete stuff in your account, and
- Impersonate you (i.e., identity theft).

Popular responses were that the attacker would impersonate the victim, send spam to the victim's contacts, or lock the victim out of the account. However, these participants were

Who is Responsible	Had a break-in (N=89)	Had no break-in (N=205)
User	**37.1%**	**38.0%**
Service Provider	13.5%	5.9%
Both, User & SP equally	**40.4%**	**40.0%**
Both, User more than SP	4.5%	11.2%
Both, SP more than User	0.0%	3.4%
Didn't mention User or SP	4.5%	1.5%

Table 1. Participants tended to split responsibility for preventing break-ins between the user and the service provider. Each participant is represented exactly once.

not very concerned about their accounts being hijacked. More than 70% were only slightly to not at all concerned (41.5% and 30.7%, respectively), while fewer than 8% were very or extremely concerned (3.4% and 4.4%).

Who is responsible?

In an open-ended question, we asked all 294 participants "Whose responsibility is it to prevent your account from being broken into?" Below, we discuss the responsibilities that participants mentioned for different stakeholders.

Participants acknowledge some responsibility

Most participants indicated that they alone were responsible for preventing break-ins (e.g., H52 explained, *"It is my responsibility to prevent my account from being broken into"*), or that they share responsibility with the service provider. Table 1 summarizes the results. Only 11 (3.7%) mentioned an entity other than the user or service provider, of which five (1.7%) indicated the attacker. We found no significant difference in responses between participants who had or had not experienced a compromise.

Some participants (10; 3.4%) indicated that the responsibility depends on the type of compromise. As NH116 explained: *"It depends, if someone breaks into Facebook and steals my password from them it's their fault. Otherwise its* [sic] *mine."* Furthermore, several participants stated clear responsibilities for users and service providers, such as users being responsible for following good password practices and service providers being responsible for providing a secure website or system.

I need to have a strong password that isn't easy to crack

Seventy-six participants (25.9%) indicated specific responsibilities for users, of which 61 (20.7% of the 294) mentioned something about password management. Responses varied, with most mentioning the need for strong passwords (38; 12.9%). For example, NH107 said, *"I need to have a strong password that isn't easy to crack."* Others mentioned that it is their responsibility to keep passwords secret (15; 5.1%), change passwords frequently (10; 3.4%), and not reuse passwords (9; 3.1%). For example, NH86 explained, *"it's my job to use secure passwords and not use the same password for multiple accounts."* Other user responsibilities included using only trusted websites (6; 2%), avoiding malware (5; 2%), using anti-virus software (4; 1%), logging out of their accounts when done (3; 1%), avoiding unsecured networks (3; 1%), keeping software up-to-date (1; 0.3%), and generally *"being cautious"* (5; 2%).

The provider needs to maintain a secure website

When asked who is responsible for preventing account compromises, 173 (59% of 294), said the service provider is at least partially responsible. Of these 173, 26 (8.8% of 294) indicated that the service provider was responsible for general security. For example, H73 said, *"It is the provider's responsibility to make sure the system is as hack-proof as possible."* Furthermore, 22 (7.5%) mentioned that providers need to keep their systems secure. For example, NH185 wrote, *"The provider needs to maintain a secure website and keep up to date on security threats,"* whereas NH6 mentioned that providers are responsible for *"keeping password databases secure."*

They should be able to tell if an account has been hacked

A few participants stated that the service provider has a duty to prevent the attacker from breaking in, detect suspicious activity, inform the user of the compromise, and help the user get back into the account. NH121 explained, *"They should be able to tell if an account has been hacked, and have a way to contact me."* H31 reported how being notified about the compromise by the service provider increased her trust in them, *"I trusted gmail* [sic] *because they notified me immediately"* (H31).

In a check-all-that-apply question, we asked the 89 participants who had experienced an account compromise, "How did you discover that your account was broken into?" Participants chose from:

- I got locked out because my password didn't work,
- Someone told me about something suspicious from my account (e.g., a strange email or post),
- I was notified by the service provider (e.g., Facebook, Google, LinkedIn),
- I noticed things happening in my account that I didn't do, and
- Other (with a write-in response).

Twenty-six (29.2%) were informed by their account's service provider. However, the most common response was that someone told them about something suspicious from their account (45; 50.6%). Twenty-seven (30.3%) noticed things happening in their account that they didn't do, and fifteen (16.9%) couldn't log in to their account.

The role of passwords in account protection & recovery

Participants not only reported that passwords played a role in their responsibility for preventing account compromises, but they also thought that passwords played an important role in keeping accounts secure in general.

Using a strong password

We asked all 294 participants the check-all-that-apply question, "Which of the following would help prevent your account from being broken into?" Participants chose from:

- Changing passwords often,
- Changing your computer wallpaper,
- Upgrading your web browser,
- Using two-factor authentication (e.g., 2-Step Verification),
- Deleting your web browser cookies,
- Using a strong password,
- Installing photo editing software,
- Avoiding logging in on public computers (such as a library or hotel),
- Avoiding using the same password on different accounts,
- Locking your computer or device screen,
- Signing out when you're done checking your account,
- Using your username as your password,
- None of these, and
- Other (with a write-in response).

The most common responses were password-related: "Using a strong password" (266; 90.5%); "Changing passwords often" (259; 88.1%); and "Avoiding using the same password on different accounts" (239; 81.3%).

Someone, somehow, found out my password

We asked the 89 participants who had experienced a compromise the open-ended question, "How do you think your account was broken into?" Many (28 of 89; 31.5%) believed that passwords were the source of the attack. Passwords were either brute-forced (6 participants), weak (5), guessed (5), reused (5), simply *"found out"* (4), shared (1), shoulder-surfed (1), or reset (1). H67 explained, *"I used the same username and password for everything,"* whereas H37 did not know how her password was stolen, *"Someone, somehow, found out my password. Which seems humanly impossible. Maybe they used a 'password cracking' machine."*

Besides compromised passwords, there was no other popular explanation for how participants thought the compromise occurred. Thirty participants (33.7%) indicated not knowing or being unsure about how their accounts were compromised; nine (10.1%) attributed it to phishing or a malicious link; seven (7.9%) blamed it on viruses or other malware; and five (5.6%) thought the compromise was a result of the service provider being hacked.

How are accounts broken into?

We asked the 205 participants who had not experienced a compromise the check-all-that-apply question, "Which of the following do you think are the most common ways that someone might try to break into your account?" The most popular option (166 of 205; 81%) was "Installing a virus or other program on your computer." Other popular choices were "Tricking you into typing your password on a website that's impersonating another site" (135; 65.9%), and "Stealing your password from another website where you used the same password" (113; 55.1%). Finally, 77 (37.6%) selected "Stealing your computer or device," and 79 (38.5%) chose "Stealing your web browser cookies."

I started using more secure passwords

We asked the 89 participants who had experienced a break-in, "What good, if any, came as a result of the break-in?" More than two thirds reported something positive from the experience, most often a heightened awareness or improved security-related behavior. For example, H74 said that the compromise *"gave me a wake up call about my password security."* The most popular response (reported by 34 participants; 38%) was changing the account password or improving password management. For example, H60 said,

> *"It made me realize that I need a more secure password and now I have the hardest password in the world."*

H72 also *"started using more secure passwords."* Overall, 23 participants (25.8%) reported changing the password for their account, with nearly half expressing that they had created a stronger password than before. Ten (11.2%) mentioned better password behavior not only for the account that was broken into, but also for other accounts. In contrast, having to change their account's password was mentioned as a harmful outcome by 12 participants (13.5%), as H79 explained, *"I had to change my password that I've used for a long time."* Furthermore, 13 participants (14.6%) provided a general statement about being more mindful or better about online security. H86 explained,

> *"I developed smarter habits. I change my passwords often. I also am careful about clicking on things I'm not sure about."*

Other participants reported a change in their account-related behavior. Five (5.6%) mentioned switching to another email provider as a positive, and three (3.4%) listed deleting or abandoning the account as a positive outcome.

DISCUSSION

Modern Web services that host millions of accounts can take a wide variety of measures to prevent account compromises. For system designers who are responsible for the security of these services, the set of design possibilities and tradeoffs is vast and often difficult to navigate. For example, password-based authentication can potentially be made more secure in a variety of ways: perhaps with a policy that prohibits easily guessed passwords; by serving content securely over HTTPS rather than over HTTP; or by using two-factor authentication (i.e., using a password plus another factor, such as a single-use code obtained from the user's mobile phone). Each candidate solution has costs and risks. Costs may include a learning curve for users and implementation and operational costs for the service provider. Potential risks include increased user lockout, increased friction for users, and low adoption rates. A system designer might ask which solutions are worth pursuing. Even after a service implements a solution, the designer is faced with choices about how to educate users about the new solution and how to motivate adoption.

Our results bring some data to bear on the difficult design tradeoffs that designers face. We discuss our results with an eye toward their implications for the secure design of large, modern Web services. With this perspective, we see five important themes emerging from our results:

(1) Compromised accounts are often valuable to victims;
(2) Attackers are unknown *and* known to victims;
(3) Users acknowledge some responsibility;
(4) Understanding of security measures is incomplete;
(5) Harm from hijacking is concrete *and* emotional.

Compromised accounts are often valuable to victims

Users place different values on their various digital accounts [16,33]. Some may be unimportant, such as accounts users set up merely to try out a new service that they soon abandon; others may be very important, such as a daily-use email or social-networking account. Our results suggest that most of our participants' compromised accounts were frequently used, and a primary use of those accounts was personal communication. Designers should acknowledge that many of today's vulnerable accounts are important, and that users might be willing to invest more effort into protecting them *if* users better understood the risks and outcomes of having their accounts compromised.

Attackers are both unknown *and* known to their victims

Different security mechanisms have strengths and weaknesses in protecting against different kinds of attacks, so it is valuable for system designers to understand the common forms of attack. Over 90% of the 89 participants who experienced a compromise believed their attackers to be unknown to them. Still, attacks by people close to the account holder occur and should not be ignored. If designers must make resource tradeoffs, our results suggest focusing on unknown attackers, but that known attackers should also be considered.

These results can help inform the cost-benefit tradeoff of using authentication systems like social authentication [32], which may provide some security against people unknown to the account holder, but may leave them vulnerable to people known to the account holder.

These results also suggest that two simple password memorability techniques that can help users use unique passwords for their different accounts – (1) writing passwords down at home; and (2) using a password manager on a home computer – are likely to be secure against the most common attackers. Password managers on a home computer also have the added benefit of being secure against phishing, since they provide passwords only to the correct domains. System designers might update advice and training to include recommendations for using these simple password memorability techniques.

Users acknowledge some responsibility

Given the literature indicating limited patience and cooperation of users for security measures [2,4,38], we were surprised that a large majority of participants indicated that they alone were responsible for keeping their accounts safe, or that they shared that responsibility with the service provider – 82% and 89% of compromised and non-compromised participants, respectively. These high rates at which participants acknowledged some responsibility suggest – though they do not guarantee – that users may be open to additional security features, such as two-factor authentication or social-based account recovery, that provide greater security at the cost of somewhat increased friction. Certainly, there are numerous barriers to adoption for such features [12], but our data suggest that at least one barrier – user attitudes – may be overcome.

Understanding of security measures is incomplete

When asked about the common ways accounts are compromised, participants selected malware ("Installing a virus or other program on your computer"), phishing ("Tricking you into typing your password on a website that's impersonating another site"), and third-party password database breaches ("Stealing your password from another website where you used the same password") as the top ways. This indicated a surprising (to us) awareness of the most common ways accounts are compromised.[1]

Nevertheless, when asked what they did or would do if their account were compromised, more participants mentioned password-related measures, such as using stronger passwords or unique passwords for each service, than anti-malware or anti-phishing measures. In particular, 90.5% of our participants selected "Using a strong password" as a way to prevent their account from being broken into, and in open-ended responses, participants emphasized the importance of "secure" and "strong" passwords. We note that "secure" or "strong" passwords are commonly interpreted to mean passwords with a variety of characters or with random-looking patterns. However, such passwords only mitigate some instances of one class of attack – password cracking. Even "Avoiding using the same password on different accounts," a response selected by 81.3% of our participants, only mitigates against third-party breaches and other reuse attacks, but not against phishing and malware. Guarding against phishing and malware attacks requires users to put other preventive measures in place. As others have argued, service providers might wish

[1] Though we are unaware of any published precise data on account compromise methods, evidence such as breach reports [27,31,34] and existence of phishing sites, malware, and database breaches [1,5,8,13,15,25] point to these as the top methods.

to focus efforts on encouraging users to take steps to guard against the most prevalent forms of attack [15,17].

Users may emphasize password management measures because they are a commonly communicated message in many account set-up processes, security training, and in the press; or because users may view password management as a relatively easy, actionable step they can take. Either way, it seems security mechanisms that focus on easily messaged and easily actionable steps are likely to have a chance at user acceptance. In fact, there are simple steps users can take against malware and phishing, such as updating their browser to the latest version, ensuring that automatic updates are enabled, and using a password manager. Simple steps like these could be more widely and clearly communicated through advice and training.

Harm from hijacking is both concrete *and* emotional

Our results suggest that the concrete harm that users experience from an account compromise is often minimal, though it can sometimes be severe. But even when concrete harm is minimal, users experience strong negative feelings such as anger, fear, and embarrassment. Designers who are trying to motivate users to adopt enhanced security mechanisms might try emotional appeals about the harms of compromised accounts to gain users' attention and interest. As one idea on this theme, designers might try using stories about the potential effects of account compromise. In fact, Rader, Wash, and Brooks found that stories are a prevalent and effective way for users to learn about security [30].

LIMITATIONS

This exploratory study has limitations with the population that we surveyed as well as with the methodology that we employed. We used MTurk as our recruiting platform and limited our population to Turkers in the U.S. who were over 18 years of age. As described above, MTurk has known biases, but allowed us to conduct this research quickly and in a reasonably cost-effective manner; we discussed several quality control mechanisms that we used to mitigate the biases. We used the GCS platform to compare our MTurk population to a more broad Web population, but the GCS platform comes with its own limitations.

As to our method, we relied on self-report data collected online. Such data is unconfirmed, and can be impacted by biases such as recall, social desirability, and lack of understanding. For example, participants may have been more likely to recall or even notice the compromise of an important account; therefore, such accounts may be disproportionately reported as compromised. Further, our survey of participants who had not experienced an account compromise often asked them to speculate.

Future work should validate and expand on our results, for example, by considering the experiences of and attitudes toward account hijacking in other countries, for other types of accounts, with different age groups, and by using other methods to investigate these issues.

CONCLUSION

In this paper, we presented results of a survey about people's experiences with and attitudes toward the compromise of a personal email or social networking account. We confirm that the problem is widespread; 30% of our 294 participants reported that at least one of their email or social networking accounts had been compromised. We highlighted five themes that emerged from our results: (1) compromised accounts are often valuable to victims, (2) attackers are unknown *and* known to their victims, (3) users acknowledge some responsibility for keeping their accounts safe, (4) users' understanding of security measures is incomplete, and (5) harm from account hijacking is concrete *and* emotional. We discussed implications for designing security mechanisms into large, modern Web services in ways that we hope will improve chances for user adoption.

ACKNOWLEDGMENTS

Our sincere thanks go out to Adrienne Porter Felt, Allison Woodruff, Anna Avrekh, Antonio Fuentes, Borbala Benko, Cindy Yepez, Diana Smetters, Ed Chi, Eddie Chung, Elie Bersztein, Jay Nancarrow, Kathy Baxter, Martin Ortlieb, Mayank Upadhay, Nadja Blagojevic, Noam Bernstein, Roberto Ortiz, Steve Gribble, Susan Gentile, Tadek Pietraszek, and the many other family, friends, colleagues, participants, and reviewers who have contributed to this work.

REFERENCES

1. Aaron, G. & Rasmussen, R., "Global Phishing Survey: Trends and Domain Name Use in 2H2012," *Anti-Phishing Working Group*, (2013).
2. Adams, A., & Sasse, M.A., "Users are not the enemy, *Communications of the ACM, 42(12),* (Dec 1999), 40-6.
3. The Associated Press, "Twitter feeds of UK's Guardian newspaper hacked," (Apr 29, 2013).
4. Beautement, A., Sasse, M.A., & Wonham, M., "The compliance budget: managing security behaviour in organisations." *Proceedings of the Workshop on New Security Paradigms*, (2008).
5. Bonneau, J., "The Gawker hack: how a million passwords were lost," *Light Blue Touchpaper Blog,* (Dec 15, 2010).
6. Bravo-Lillo, C., Cranor, L.F., Downs, J., Komanduri, S., & Sleeper, M., "Improving Computer Security Dialogs," *Proceedings of INTERACT '11*, (2011), 18-35.
7. Bridis, T., "Hacker impersonated Palin, stole e-mail password," *Associated Press*, (Sep 18, 2008).
8. Bright, P., " 'Military Meltdown Monday': 90K military usernames, hashes released," *arstechnica*, (Jul 12, 2011).
9. Bright, P., "Anonymous speaks: the inside story of the HBGary hack," (Feb 15, 2011).
10. Buhrmester, M., Kwang, T., & Gosling, S.D., "Amazon's Mechanical Turk A New Source of Inexpensive, Yet High-Quality, Data?," *Perspectives on Psychological Science*, *6(1)*, (2011), 3-5.

11. Camp, L.J., "Mental Models of Privacy and Security," *IEEE Technology & Society*, (2006).
12. Cranor, L.F., "A Framework for Reasoning About the Human in the Loop," *Proceedings of the Conference on Usability, Psychology, & Security: UPSEC '08*, (2008).
13. Doyle, K., "Second LulzSec hacker sentenced," *ITWeb*, (Aug 12, 2013).
14. Egelman, S., Sotirakopoulos, A., Muslukhov, I., Beznosov, K., & Herley, C., "Does My Password Go up to Eleven? The Impact of Password Meters on Password Selection," *Proceedings of the Conference on Human Factors in Computing Systems: CHI '13*, (2013), 2379-88.
15. Florencio, D. & Herley, C., "Where do security policies come from?" *Proceedings of the Symposium on Usable Privacy & Security: SOUPS '10*, (2010).
16. Google Consumer Surveys, http://www.google.com/insights/consumersurveys/how.
17. Grosse, E. & Upadhay, M., "Authentication at Scale." *IEEE Security and Privacy,* vol. 11, (Jan/Feb 2013), 15-22.
18. Harbach, M., Fahl, S., Rieger, M., & Smith, M., "On the Acceptance of Privacy-Preserving Authentication Technology: The Curious Case of National Identity Cards," *Privacy Enhancing Technologies, volume 7981 of Lecture Notes in Computer Science*, Springer Berlin Heidelberg, (2013), 245-64.
19. Honan, M., "How Apple and Amazon Security Flaws Led to my Epic Hacking," *Wired*, (Aug 6, 2012).
20. Honan, M., "Mat Honan: How I Resurrected My Digital Life After an Epic Hacking," *Wired*, (Aug 17, 2012).
21. Kittur, A., Chi, E.H., & Suh, B., "Crowdsourcing User Studies With Mechanical Turk," *Proceedings of the Conference on Human Factors in Computing Systems: CHI '08*, (2008), 453-6.
22. Landis, J.R. & Koch, G.G., "The measurement of observer agreement for categorical data," *Biometrics 33*, (1977), 159-74.
23. Mazurek, M.L., Arsenault, J.P., Bresee, J., Gupta, N., Ion, I., Johns, C., Lee, D., Liang, Y., Olsen, J., Salmon, B., Shay, R., Vaniea, K., Bauer, L., Cranor, L.F., Ganger, G.R., & Reiter, M.K., "Access control for home data sharing: Attitudes, needs and practices," *Proceedings of the Conference on Human Factors in Computing Systems: CHI '10,* (Apr 2010), 645-54.
24. McDonald, P., Mohebbi, M., & Slatkin, B., "Comparing Google Consumer Surveys to Existing Probability and Non-Probability Based Internet Surveys," Google Whitepaper, Retrieved from http://www.google.com/insights/consumersurveys/static/consumer_surveys_whitepaper.pdf.
25. Microsoft, *Microsoft Security Intelligence Report*, Vol. 14, (2012), Retrieved from http://www.microsoft.com/security/sir/default.aspx.
26. O'Mahony, J., "Financial Times hacked by Syrian Electronic Army," (May 17, 2013).
27. Onion Inc.'s Tech Team. "How the Syrian Electronic Army Hacked The Onion," (May 8, 2013).
28. Paolacci, G., Chandler, J., & Ipeirotis, P., "Running experiments on Amazon Mechanical Turk," *Judgment & Decision Making*, *5*(5), (2010), 411-9.
29. Perlroth, N. & Shear, M.D., "In Hacking, A.P. Twitter Feed Sends False Report of Explosions," *The New York Times: The Caucus*, (Apr 23, 2013).
30. Rader, E., Wash, R., & Brooks, B., "Stories as Informal Lessons about Security," *Proceedings of the Symposium on Usable Privacy and Security: SOUPS '12*, (2012).
31. Rainie, L., Kiesler, S., Kang, R., & Madden, M., "Anonymity, Privacy, and Security Online," *Pew Research Center*, (Sep 2013).
32. Schechter, S., Egelman, S., and Reeder, R.W., "It's Not What You Know, but Who You Know: A Social Approach to Last-Resort Authentication," *Proceedings of the Conference on Human Factors in Computing Systems: CHI '09*, (2009).
33. Schechter, S., & Reeder, R.W., "1 + 1 = You: Measuring the Comprehensibility of Metaphors for Configuring Backup Authentication," *Proceedings of the Symposium on Usable Privacy & Security: SOUPS '09,* (2009).
34. Schonfeld, E., "Twitter's @Ev Confirms Hacker Targeted Personal Accounts; Attack Was 'Highly Distressing,'" (Jul 14, 2009).
35. Shay, R., Komanduri, S., Kelley, P.G., Leon, P.G., Mazurek, M.L., Bauer, L., Christin, N., & Cranor, L.F., "Encountering stronger password requirements: user attitudes and behaviors." *Proceedings of the Symposium on Usable Privacy & Security: SOUPS '10*, (2010).
36. Sosik, V.S., Bursztein, E., Consolvo, S., Huffaker, D., Kossinets, G., Liao, K., McDonald, P., & Sedley, A., "Online Microsurveys for User Experience Research," *CHI '14 Extended Abstracts on Human Factors in Computing Systems*, (2014—to appear).
37. Wash, R., "Folk Models of Home Computer Security," *Proceedings of the Symposium on Usable Privacy & Security: SOUPS '10*, (2010).
38. Whitten, A. & Tygar, J.D. "Why Johnny Can't Encrypt: A Usability Evaluation of PGP 5.0," *Proceedings of the USENIX Security Symposium,* (1999).

Experimenting At Scale With Google Chrome's SSL Warning

Adrienne Porter Felt
Robert W. Reeder
Google Inc.
felt, rreeder@google.com

Hazim Almuhimedi
Carnegie Mellon University
hazim@cs.cmu.edu

Sunny Consolvo
Google Inc.
sconsolvo@google.com

ABSTRACT
Web browsers show HTTPS authentication warnings (i.e., SSL warnings) when the integrity and confidentiality of users' interactions with websites are at risk. Our goal in this work is to decrease the number of users who click through the Google Chrome SSL warning. Prior research showed that the Mozilla Firefox SSL warning has a much lower click-through rate (CTR) than Chrome. We investigate several factors that could be responsible: the use of imagery, extra steps before the user can proceed, and style choices. To test these factors, we ran six experimental SSL warnings in Google Chrome 29 and measured 130,754 impressions.

Author Keywords
Browser security warnings; SSL warnings; interruptive warnings; active warnings; interstitials

ACM Classification Keywords
H.5.2 Information Interfaces and Presentation (e.g. HCI): User Interfaces; K.6.5 Management of Computing and Information Systems: Security and Protection

INTRODUCTION
Web users rely on SSL for the privacy and security of their data. For journalists and dissidents, SSL can be the difference between safety and physical harm. Browsers show SSL warnings when they cannot establish a well-authenticated HTTPS connection to a website. When these warnings appear, it is up to the user to decide whether to proceed.

Our goal is to decrease the number of users who click through (i.e., ignore) Google Chrome's SSL warnings. Clicking through an SSL warning can be a safe choice if the user is confident that the warning is due to a benign server misconfiguration. However, it is often difficult or impossible to differentiate between server misconfigurations and attacks. Separate efforts are needed to improve the precision of SSL warnings, but we focus on nudging users in the direction of a lower CTR. We aim for a lower CTR because (a) it's safer to err on the side of caution, and (b) we hope that low CTRs will encourage developers to adopt valid SSL certificates.

CHI 2014, April 26 - May 01 2014, Toronto, ON, Canada
Copyright 2014 ACM 978-1-4503-2473-1/14/04 $15.00.
http://dx.doi.org/10.1145/2556288.2557292

Usable security researchers have studied web browser security warnings for years [4, 8, 2]. However, the difficulty of creating ecologically valid laboratory studies of warnings has impeded warning research. Participants may behave unnaturally in a laboratory setting [7]. Even when some idiosyncracies of laboratory studies are mitigated, experimenters still have to use contrived designs to direct participants toward sites where warnings will appear.

The most natural way to study SSL warnings is to measure reactions to real warnings on users' computers. We measured user reactions to experimental warnings encountered during everyday browsing in Google Chrome. In this paper, we present findings from 130,754 warning impressions. We implemented six experimental warnings in Google Chrome 29 that are designed to test several hypotheses about how users respond to warning design manipulations.

Akhawe and Felt showed that Firefox's SSL warning has a considerably lower CTR than Chrome's (33% vs. 70%) [1]. We tested the hypothesis that it is the warning's design — rather than the characteristics of Firefox or its user population — that leads to Firefox's lower CTR. We further tested whether any design advantages of the Firefox warning were due to: its requirement of an extra step to proceed through the warning; its distinctive, non-commercial styling; or its use of a human image with its gaze directed at the user.

Contributions. We make the following contributions:

- We show that warning design can drive users towards safer decisions. Design accounted for between a third and half of the difference in CTRs between Chrome and Firefox.
- Warning design did not account for the remaining difference between browsers. This means that other factors influence the CTR.
- Several design variations, such as images of watching eyes, had little to no effect on behavior.
- To our knowledge, we are the first to publish a field experiment on the effects of browser warning design under realistic conditions.

METHODOLOGY
We deployed six experimental SSL warnings and one matched control as part of Google Chrome 29. We measured user reactions to the default Chrome SSL warning (Condition 1), three versions of the Chrome SSL warning with new images (Conditions 2-4), and a replica of the Firefox SSL warning with two variants (Conditions 5-7).

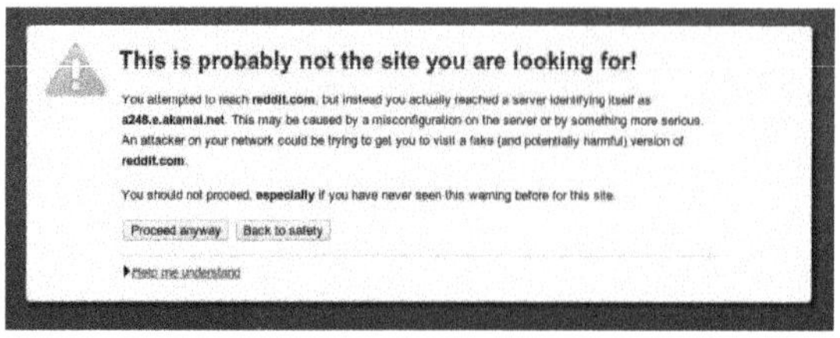

Figure 1. The default Chrome SSL warning (Condition 1).

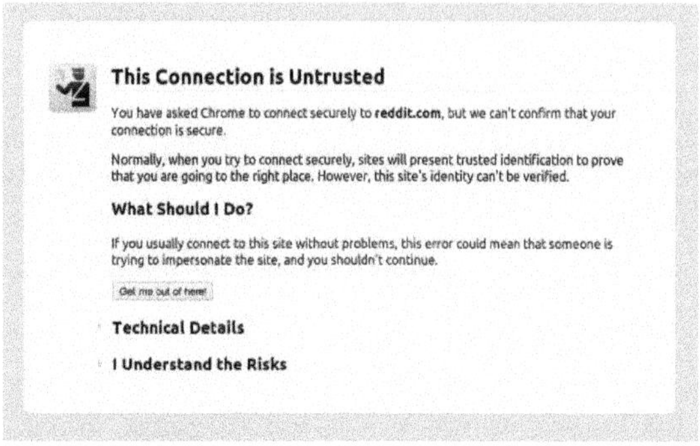

Figure 2. The mock Firefox SSL warning (Condition 5).

Hypotheses and Conditions

Firefox Warning Appearance

Hypothesis: The visual design of the Firefox SSL warning is the reason for the lower CTR in Firefox.

Akhawe and Felt found that Firefox's SSL warning has a CTR of 33% whereas Google Chrome has a CTR of 70% [1]. To test the impact of visual design on the CTR, we implemented a replica of the Mozilla Firefox SSL warning in Google Chrome.[1] Figure 1 shows the default Chrome SSL warning (Condition 1), and Figure 2 shows the mock Firefox SSL warning (Condition 5). Demographics, browsing habits, and other non-appearance factors are held constant because they were both tested in Google Chrome.

Our mock Firefox warning is identical to the actual Firefox warning in all ways but two. First, we replaced the name "Firefox" with "Chrome" in the warning text. Second, proceeding through the actual Firefox warning yields a secondary pop-up dialog that asks whether the browser should permanently remember the user's decision to proceed. Google Chrome did not support this feature at the time of this experiment, so there is no secondary dialog.

Steps to Proceed Past the Warning

Hypothesis: An extra step will *decrease* the CTR.

Some designers add extra steps to warnings with the intention of reducing the CTR. For example, Firefox users need to take three steps to proceed through the Firefox SSL warning: (1) click on "I Understand the Risks," (2) click on the (now unhidden) button to proceed, (3) click through a final pop-up dialog that appears in a separate window.

Sunshine et al. showed that the extra steps in the Firefox SSL warning make it difficult for users to proceed through the warning [8]. However, they conjectured that this would only work until users learn how to work around it. Akhawe and Felt studied the Firefox SSL warning and found that the third step discourages 15% of users from proceeding further, but they did not collect data on the earlier steps [1].

To bypass Conditions 5, 6, and 7, participants must: (1) click on "I Understand the Risks" to reveal the proceed button, (2) click the proceed button. We recorded how many participants clicked on both steps so that we could see how many participants changed their minds due to the extra step.

[1]With approval from the author of the Firefox warning.

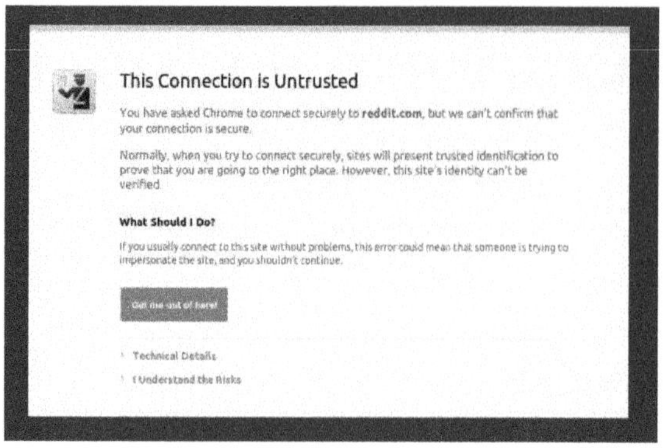

Figure 3. The Firefox SSL warning with Google styling (Condition 7).

Corporate Style Guidelines

Hypothesis: Applying corporate style guidelines to a warning will *increase* the CTR.

We hypothesize that warnings that resemble corporate products will have higher CTRs because they do not stand out as unusual. To test this, we created a Google-styled version of the Firefox SSL warning. Condition 5 is a faithful replica of the Firefox SSL warning, with a gray palette and unstyled buttons and links (Figure 2). A Google designer created another version by applying Google's corporate style guidelines to the warning (Condition 7). Condition 7 uses Google's palette, Google-styled buttons, and Google-styled links (Figure 3). We kept the text and layout constant between the two versions. Although Condition 7 could have been made to look more like a Google product if we had altered the text and layout, we wanted to control for these factors.

Images of Watching People

Hypothesis: Including an image of a human in a warning will *decrease* the CTR.

Studies have found that people behave in a more socially conscious manner when they are near images of watching eyes [5, 6]. Detecting a human face in an image activates the "social brain," which encourages pro-social and cooperative behavior [6]. We hypothesize that this physiological effect would lead to a lower warning CTR.

The Firefox warning (Condition 5, Figure 2) contains a black image of a human figure on a yellow-orange background. Although this figure does not have eyes or a face, it should still create the sensation of being watched because its posture indicates that it is looking at the viewer [3]. For comparison, Condition 6 is the same warning without the image.

Figure 4. The three images used in Conditions 2-4.

We added two images of human faces to the Chrome SSL warning: a policeman (Condition 2) and a criminal (Condition 3). Their eyes stare directly at the viewer. The images are drawings, which prior work has shown to be sufficient to activate the social brain [5]. For comparison, Condition 4 includes a red traffic light; the traffic light conveys the same "stop" message, but without a human face. Figure 4 shows the three images, which were the same height as the first paragraph of the Chrome warning (Figure 1).

Field Study Deployment

We modified Google Chrome 29 to include our experimental versions of the warnings. The first time a Google Chrome 29 client begins to load an SSL warning, our field trial code pseudorandomly assigns the client to a condition and loads the appropriate version of the warning. For each condition there was a 1.4% chance that the client would be assigned to it. A given client could be assigned to only one condition. The remaining 90.2% of the population received the default behavior and was not part of the study.

Google Chrome's opt-in metrics allow us to measure reactions to security warnings. During installation, Chrome users are asked whether they would like to send "crash reports and statistics" to Google. If they choose to participate, Chrome periodically sends statistical reports to Google. Each report includes whether the user has recently seen or clicked through an SSL warning, and this data is tagged with the appropriate condition. This lets us correlate CTRs with our experimental conditions. The reports are pseudonymous and, once stored, cannot be traced back to the sending client.

Our study ran from August 22 to 31, 2013. We report data from Google Chrome 29 (stable). Our data is from English (U.S.) clients on Windows, Mac, Chrome OS, and Linux.

Experimental Ethics

We relied on Google Chrome's opt-in metrics to measure click-through rates. We did not collect any sensitive or personal information about participants (e.g., no browsing history). We followed our internal review processes for field trial design quality and privacy.

One concern was that our experiment could increase the CTR, thereby putting users at greater risk. The study was first deployed on a small scale to developer versions of Chrome in May 2013, and we monitored the CTRs of the conditions. If any of the conditions had yielded adverse effects, we would have halted those conditions; however, they did not.

Limitations

Our sample is limited to participants in Google Chrome's metrics program. Since this is an opt-in program, it is possible that there is selection bias in our sample. However, even if they are not representative of the whole population, they still constitute a notable minority.

#	Condition	CTR	N
1	Control (default Chrome warning)	67.9%	17,479
2	Chrome warning with policeman	68.9%	17,977
3	Chrome warning with criminal	66.5%	18,049
4	Chrome warning with traffic light	68.8%	18,084
5	Mock Firefox	56.1%	20,023
6	Mock Firefox, no image	55.9%	19,297
7	Mock Firefox with corporate styling	55.8%	19,845

Table 1. Click-through rates and sample size for conditions.

Although we restricted each client to receiving only one condition, it is possible that participants with multiple computers experienced multiple conditions.

RESULTS AND IMPLICATIONS

We observed CTRs ranging from 55.8% to 68.9% for the six conditions and control. Table 1 contains an overview of the conditions and CTRs. In the following section, we correct for multiple testing by lowering our overall $\alpha = 0.05$ to $\alpha = 0.0083$ using Bonferroni's adjustment.

Firefox Warning Appearance

We find that visual appearance accounts for between a third and half of the 37-point (70%-33%) difference between Chrome' and Firefox's CTRs. We calculate this as follows:

- Participants clicked through 67.9% of default Chrome warnings (Condition 1) and 56.1% of mock Firefox warnings (Condition 5). Since all other factors were held constant, differences in the warnings' appearances are responsible for 12 of 37 points.

- Firefox users see a pop-up confirmation dialog after experiencing the real warning. 15% of the time that users see this dialog, they turn back [1]. If we were to implement this dialog in Chrome, it might have reduced the CTR by another 15%. This would make the warning as a whole responsible for an additional 8 points (15% $\times$ 56.1%).

Novelty could potentially bias participants' responses to the mock Firefox warning. Participants might have been startled or intrigued by an unfamiliar warning, leading to a lower CTR. However, the overall CTR remained steady for the duration of the study, and the CTR for participants with repeat impressions did not vary. Either ten days is insufficient for novelty to wear off, or novelty did not contribute to the CTR.

The control condition yielded a CTR of 67.9%, whereas Akhawe and Felt previously reported a CTR of 70% for Chrome [1]. A small amount of the difference could be attributed to fluctuation over time.

We therefore estimate that the design of the warning and pop-up dialog together account for between 12 and 20 points (i.e., 32% to 54%) of the difference between the two browsers' CTRs. This demonstrates that design can influence users' security decisions. The remaining difference must be due to other factors. Different demographics[2] might have different risk tolerances or preferences. Other aspects of the user experience might also change how users perceive warnings.

Steps to Proceed Past the Warning

For Conditions 5, 6, and 7, participants had to click twice to proceed past the warning. The second step did not serve as a meaningful deterrent: for all three conditions, 98% of participants who performed the first step also completed the second step. This demonstrates that the addition of a very simple extra step may not have a notable effect on the CTR. However, Akhawe and Felt reported that only 85% of users clicked through Firefox's third step (a pop-up dialog with more technical information), which means the third step is a bigger deterrent [1]. Combined with our finding, this suggests that the effectiveness of an extra step may depend on its complexity.

Corporate Style Guidelines

Applying Google's corporate style guidelines to the mock Firefox warning did not increase the CTR. The Google-styled version of the warning (Condition 7) performed slightly better than the unmodified mock Firefox warning (Condition 5), which is the opposite of what we predicted. However, the difference is very small (56.1% vs. 55.8%). We interpret this result to mean that tweaks to the color and style – e.g., updating an old warning with a newer style guide – may not have an effect on the CTR.

We held the layout and wording constant between Conditions 5 and 7 to avoid potential confounds. It is possible that changing the layout and wording to look more like a commercial product would yield the anticipated effect.

Images of Watching People

The brain's social response to human images is instinctive, and it should occur for even a hint of a human face [6, 5]. If the feeling of being watched were to influence how users react to warnings, all of the conditions with human images should have lower CTRs. However, we did not find this.

- Removing the human figure from the mock Firefox warning did not have an effect (56.1% vs. 55.9%) [1-tail z-test of proportions, $p = .3485$].
- The policeman (Condition 2) performs slightly worse than the imageless default warning (Condition 1): 67.9% vs. 68.9%, which was the opposite of our hypothesis.
- The criminal (Condition 3) had a lower CTR than the control (Condition 1) by a statistically significant amount [1-tail z-test of proportions, $p = 0.0025$], but the effect size is very small (67.9% vs. 66.5%). It also had a lower CTR than the red traffic light, which served as a secondary control [1-tail z-test of proportions, $p < 0.0001$].

Although ignoring an SSL warning can have social implications (e.g., leaking others' social media posts), this may not occur to participants when they are viewing warnings. Thus, triggering the social portion of the brain may not influence their decisions. The criminal may have yielded a very slight improvement through a different mechanism: fear arousal.

Other Design Differences

We found that the design of the Mozilla Firefox warning without the pop-up accounts for a third of the difference between the two browsers. What makes it more effective? We have ruled out the image of a human, the first additional step, and the styling as the cause. We therefore hypothesize that the Firefox warning's text, layout, and/or default button choice are responsible. The Firefox warning appears to follow warning design guidelines from prior work. The warning avoids technical jargon, identifies ways to mitigate the risk under "What Should I Do?" [9], hides technical details by default [4], and has a clear default choice [4, 2].

ACKNOWLEDGEMENTS

We thank Johnathan Nightingale for allowing us to replicate Firefox's warnings; Roberto Ortiz and Sebastien Gabriel for designing the new SSL artwork; and Melissa Bateman and Ross Anderson for discussing the use of human images.

REFERENCES

1. Akhawe, D., and Felt, A. P. Alice in Warningland: A Large-Scale Field Study of Browser Security Warning Effectiveness. In *USENIX Security Symposium* (2013).
2. Egelman, S., Cranor, L. F., and Hong, J. You've been warned: an empirical study of the effectiveness of web browser phishing warnings. In *Proceedings of CHI* (2008).
3. Emery, N. The eyes have it: the neuroethology, function and evolution of social gaze. *Neuroscience and Biobehavioral Reviews 24* (2000).
4. Nodder, C. Users and trust: A Microsoft case study. *Security and Usability: Designing Secure Systems that People Can Use* (2005), 589–606.
5. Rigdon, M., Ishii, K., Watabe, M., and Kitayama, S. Minimal social cues in the dictator game. *Journal of Economic Psychology 30* (June 2009).
6. Senju, A., and Johnson, M. H. The eye contact effect: mechanisms and development. *Trends in Cognitive Science* (March 2009).
7. Sotirakopoulos, A., Hawkey, K., and Beznosov, K. On the Challenges in Usable Security Lab Studies: Lessons Learned from Replicating a Study on SSL Warnings. In *Proceedings of SOUPS* (2011).
8. Sunshine, J., Egelman, S., Almuhimedi, H., Atri, N., and Cranor, L. F. Crying Wolf: An Empirical Study of SSL Warning Effectiveness. In *USENIX Security Symposium* (2009).
9. Wogalter, M. S., Conzola, V. C., and Smith-Jackson, T. L. Research-based guidelines for warning design and evaluation. *Applied Ergonomics 33*, 3 (2002).

[2] http://elie.im/blog/web/survey-internet-explorer-users-are-older-chrome-seduces-youth/

Betrayed By Updates: How Negative Experiences Affect Future Security

Kami Vaniea, Emilee Rader, Rick Wash
Department of Telecommunication, Information Studies, and Media
Michigan State University
{vaniea, emilee, wash}@msu.edu

ABSTRACT
Installing security-relevant software updates is one of the best computer protection mechanisms. However, users do not always choose to install updates. Through interviewing non-expert Windows users, we found that users frequently decide not to install future updates, regardless of whether they are important for security, after negative experiences with past updates. This means that even non-security updates (such as user interface changes) can impact the security of a computer. We discuss three themes impacting users' willingness to install updates: unexpected new features in an update, the difficulty of assessing whether an update is "worth it", and confusion about why an update is necessary.

Author Keywords
Software Updates; Human Factors; Security

ACM Classification Keywords
D.2.7 Software Engineering: Distribution, Maintenance, and Enhancement; H.5.2 Information Interfaces and Presentation: User interfaces—*user-centered design*; K.6.5 Management of Computing and Information Systems: Security and Protection

INTRODUCTION
Software companies regularly release updates that are intended to improve previously installed programs. These improvements can range from invisible but necessary changes, like small bug fixes and security patches, to significant feature changes that affect user workflow. Security updates are particularly important because they are one of the primary mechanisms users have to protect their computers from malicious software. Symantec and Microsoft have observed that the majority of computers are compromised using vulnerabilities for which a security update was available but had not yet been installed [?, ?], making timely installation of security updates important for computer security.

CHI 2014, April 26 - May 01 2014, Toronto, ON, Canada
Copyright 2014 ACM 978-1-4503-2473-1/14/04$15.00.
http://dx.doi.org/10.1145/2556288.2557275

Additionally, some updates combine security and non-security components, and it is not always clear to users which updates will improve security and which updates might make other changes. Some software updates are *technically* cumulative: all prior updates must be installed before the latest update can be installed. This means that security updates cannot be installed until the user decides to install earlier, non-security updates. This lack of differentiation, and the decisions companies make about how to roll out non-security updates, combined with the decisions users make about whether to install these updates, can potentially affect the overall security of users' computers.

We interviewed Windows users about their opinions and beliefs concerning software updates, to understand what makes people not want to update software. We found that respondents avoided updates that caused unexpected user interface changes. They also felt less inclined to update software they perceived as currently functional, or that they rarely used. These attitudes were learned over time from previous experiences with software updates, and stemmed from a desire to avoid risky actions with the potential to interfere with their workflow. The number of "apps" installed by end users is also on the rise [?] resulting in more and more update requests being shown to users. This presents a new challenge for software update authors, who should no longer assume that update compliance occurs in a vacuum.

METHOD
We recruited 37 non-expert Windows 7 users to participate in a study about software updates by sending an email through the Registrar of Michigan State University to a random sample of non-technical graduate students. Respondents were screened to ensure they used Windows 7 and had no prior experience in Computer Science or professional Windows management. Respondents ranged from 21 to 57 years old, with a mean age of 31; 17 were male and 20 were female. Three respondents used a Mac with Windows 7 in a virtual machine.

Software updates occur intermittently, and often while users are otherwise occupied; we therefore used retrospective, semi-structured interviews based around a set of hypothetical scenarios to elicit stories about past software update experiences. The interviewer asked participants to imagine how they would respond to: being prompted to restart an internet browser mid-task, seeing that a large number of urgent Windows updates were available, reading a news article about a virus, a software program that costs money to update, and a slow computer with lots of warnings. In each scenario the participant was asked what they would do, and if they had ever encountered a similar situation. A "browser" was mentioned in the first scenario and Windows 7 was explicitly mentioned in the second and fifth scenarios. All other software mentioned in this work was brought up by participants.

Interview sessions lasted around one hour, and respondents were compensated $25. Interviews were recorded, transcribed, and scrubbed to remove any personally identifying information. Each respondent was assigned a pseudonym, and we refer to individuals by their pseudonyms below. One member of the research team analyzed the interviews using an open, inductive approach, starting with an initial list of themes identified by the interviewers. The research team held regular meetings in which we discussed and iterated on the codes that emerged, and then expanded and modified the codes as additional team members read through transcripts. In later stages of the analysis, high-level themes emerged as we made connections between codes and participants [**?**].

FINDINGS

Our respondents talked about three overall themes for reasons they did not install software updates: trepidation about surprise new features in an update; the difficulty of assessing whether an update is "worth it" given uncertainty about what a program does and why it is needed; and confusion about why an update is necessary, if the program seems to be working fine. We discuss each theme in the context of a commonly mentioned piece of software that illustrates both the reason for not updating and the security implications.

Surprise UI Changes: "Just, like, leave it alone..."

User interface changes were disruptive for respondents' workflows, and were commonly mentioned. They found new interfaces "annoying" to learn, and reported that they avoided updating software that had a history of frequently changing the user interface. Nick discussed how new user interfaces were hard to learn and made him reluctant to update:

> "I just hate the idea of having to just relearn everything, where everything is, how to access 'help', something as basic as that. And when the new Office suite came along with Excel especially. Word, bad; Excel, worse, as far as just being completely different, counterintuitive. I try to stick with what I know rather than just take the time to relearn a whole new system."

User interface changes were perceived to have an immediate, negative impact on productivity. Kim talked about how she had "been working with these programs for 15 years. I know them like the back of my hand." To interact with the programs quickly Kim learned the hot keys, specific combinations of keyboard keys that can be used instead of clicking buttons. However, "every now and again, you get a new version and they change the hot keys."

The impact of interface changes on respondents' willingness to install updates was particularly highlighted by changes Apple made in version 11 of iTunes, their multimedia player. In version 10.7 the user interface had a navigation sidebar permanently visible on the left side of the screen. However, version 11 removed the navigation, and the user interface became modal with different available actions depending on the type of content being viewed.

The version 11 iTunes update was very unpopular with our respondents. Ashley expressed a common reaction: "all of a sudden, like, *Where did my things go?*" Respondents installed the update not realizing the user interface was going to change, and then became upset when it did. This caused some respondents to become wary of iTunes updates in general. Amber said that she had "ignored [iTunes updates] quite a few times because I'm like: *I don't need that update*." Rachel expressed worry about future iTunes updates:

> "I also always worry that everything is gonna get screwed up, especially for iTunes updates or things like that because they're always reconfiguring the layout of stuff, and I'm like, 'I don't want you to do that. Just, like, leave it alone...'"

Some respondents had learned from past experiences to check technology blogs and forums as a way of finding out what new updates might do before installing them. Melissa learned that the iTunes update would change the interface and explained that she had waited to update iTunes because she "was not ready to get used to [the new interface]." Chris talked about deciding not to update iTunes after reading that other people didn't like the new interface.

> "One of the prior iterations of iTunes, it just wasn't well received and there were some... A lot of complaints about the new version. People saying, 'Don't update'. I'm like, okay, I won't update."

Other respondents had less foresight and installed an unwanted iTunes update. In Lauren's case, an update disabled her ability to manage her old iPod and caused her to start refusing all iTunes updates because she was "mad at them."

> "You can't update it and and you can't change the songs because the new version of iTunes is like, 'Even though you took really good care of your machinery, we don't want you to have that one anymore.'"

On the surface, iTunes might not seem like it would be associated with security issues, and none of our respondents mentioned any concern about security in relation to it. However, software that displays web pages (HTML/Javascript) is the most common vector for compromise on Windows computers [**?**] and iTunes displays web pages as part of the iTunes store. In its version 10.7 release of iTunes, Apple patched 163 vulnerabilities, the majority of which involved the web page display functionality. Most users don't browse the web using iTunes; rather, they use a web browser. But when they click on specially formatted links it can cause iTunes to automatically launch and attempt to display the web content as part of the iTunes store. If a user running the 10.6 version of iTunes were to click the wrong link it could be used to install any software on the user's computer[1].

[1]http://www.zdnet.com/google-helps-close-163-security-vulnerabilities-in-itunes-7000004186/

Respondents talked about the need to update web browsers like Firefox, and Chrome as a way of protecting themselves from dangers on the internet. But they reported thinking about iTunes as a multimedia player that plays their songs, videos and interacts with their Apple devices. Their update choices were based on how they wanted to interact with the software and the functions they needed.

I Don't Understand It, so I Won't Update It

Respondents differentiated between programs they used regularly and programs they used infrequently, or not at all. They were more inclined to update software they used frequently because they recognized that doing so would bring them the latest features and make it easier to interact with other people who were running updated versions of software. They were less inclined to update rarely used software without a good reason. If a program stopped being used entirely, they tended to either stop updating it or uninstall it completely. Brandon talked about how update prompts caused him to either remove the program, or find a way to turn off updates.

> If I'm not using the program . . . either the software update will prompt me to go remove the program because I'd say, "I am not using and just get rid of it." Or, somehow turn off the preferences to say "Don't remind me to update this" 'cause I am not using the program.

Java in particular was problematic for our respondents, because they didn't understand what it was, and they didn't think they used it. Java is a program that provides functionality to other programs installed on a computer. Users rarely, if ever, directly interact with Java even though they may frequently use programs that need Java to function. Amy's experience highlights the confusion:

> "It's annoying and I don't think I need Java, so I just deleted the program. However, when I visit some website they asked me to install Java. 'Okay. I will install it, but if you ask me to update again, I will delete you.'"

To correct several serious security issues, four Java updates were released in six weeks in the beginning of 2013 just before our study. Typically Java releases updates about once every two months, and this escalation may have contributed to our respondents' irritation. Some respondents had formed a general animosity against Java because of the constant requests for updates. They reported feeling that Java wanted to update "all the time" and was really annoying. Lauren didn't understand why she needed Java, and got irritated by the repeated requests to update:

> "I don't know why the hell I need a Java so I ignore it... I'm just pissed off and I think I have a tendency then, when like I see Java pop up in the corner, I'm like, 'Fuck you, Java.'"

When respondents became confused by repeated requests for Java updates they said they went online and attempted to understand what the updates were doing. Because Java is well known as being vulnerable to security compromise some online forms advise uninstalling it. However, it is necessary for many programs to function correctly, so other forums recommend updating it regularly. Respondents searching for information on Java encountered conflicting discussions similar to the rhetoric described above and became confused about what to do. Ashley talked about such an event:

> "I started to think there was a problem, and so then I started looking more, and actually reading to try to decide, do I wanna install the update? You know, some things, [you should] install the update because it will make it better. Other things are like... Just take it off your computer completely."

Because it runs invisibly in the background, our respondents only saw that Java updates cost them time. They did not understand that updating Java made other programs potentially run better, or that not updating Java made them vulnerable to attackers. Java is the second most common source of security compromise on Windows computers, and one of the least updated programs with only 6% of Windows computers running the latest version [?].

If it Ain't Broke, Don't Fix It!

Respondents explained that if their software was working and fulfilling their needs, they saw no need to make changes. They were reluctant to expend effort and risk problems just to change the behavior of functional software.

As described above, respondents felt updating software is potentially fraught with uncertainty. Most updates provide little to no information to end users about what will occur when they click the "Install" button. In addition to the risk of user interface changes, there is also a risk that a needed feature will be removed from the software, or that the software will stop functioning entirely. When faced with the choice to update users have three options: blindly accept, research, or deny. Accepting the update carries the potential cost of installing an update that has unwanted components, and researching the updates costs time and mental energy, so some respondents chose the least risky option of deny.

Respondents talked about using software until it became non-operational, and then either updating the program or deleting it. Andrew talked about not updating software:

> "Many times I do not update. Just for regular software unless I feel that this software now is not working properly. Otherwise, I'll keep it simple."

Respondents also made a distinction between "regular" software which didn't need to be updated and security software such as anti-virus. Nick talked about how he kept security software up-to-date, but avoided other updates:

> "I feel like if I'm really used to the software I'm using and I think it's meeting my needs I won't upgrade the software. But if it is really important like anti-virus it has to be upgraded."

AdobeReader, a PDF viewer, was an excellent example mentioned by our respondents of a utilitarian software program that had a single clear function, and no obvious link to security. Respondents were puzzled about why AdobeReader needed to be updated at all. Justin explained that he never updated AdobeReader because there was no need to do so:

"I just don't see what an update to [AdobeReader] can do. I mean it's PDF files. Its viewing them..." David explained how he didn't "listen" to AdobeReader update requests, because the current version met his requirements: "Adobe, current version helps me to read. And so that's how I decided my requirements." Respondents saw AdobeReader as fulfilling a specific function, and if it was still functioning they saw no reason to change it.

Respondents talked about updating AdobeReader when it stopped functioning. Part of Mike's job involved downloading PDF files from websites and modifying them. If he did not have the latest version of AdobeReader he could have issues: "If I try and download something that is from a more advanced version, it won't accept it. It'll just die." Nicole also discussed not updating programs like AdobeReader, but when the program stopped opening files she would find and download a new program that wasn't broken.

Document viewers, and AdobeReader in particular, are the third most common source for computer compromises on Windows computers [?]. Respondents thought of document viewers as simply displaying static information; however, they are actually similar to web browsers in that they change the stored information into something visible to the user—a process which can result in security issues.

IMPLICATIONS

Prior work tells us that users don't install updates from all software equally [?, ?]. Our findings show that the decision to not update particular applications is sometimes an intentional one for end users and can leave computers and their users vulnerable to malicious attackers.

We have identified an additional challenge for software updates: people learn from past updates and apply that knowledge when deciding about future updates. When users update a piece of software and have a bad experience, they learn that updates to that software (and possibly updates in general) can have bad effects. Consequently, they may be less inclined to update in the future. Similar to behavior observed by Rader et al. [?], users also look to other people, and particularly blogs and forums, to learn about updates.

Many software updates are *technically* cumulative: you cannot install a future update until all past updates are installed. Our findings suggest that many software updates are also *user* cumulative: once a user decides not to install an update, they frequently will avoid future updates for that same piece of software. Also, once a user has a negative experience with an update, they are much less likely to install future updates.

Cumulative updates, due to technical requirements or to user decisions, create problems for security because security-related updates are sometimes avoided—not installed—for non-security-related reasons. For example, when respondents disliked the iTunes 11 interface change, they stopped installing all updates for iTunes, including security patches.

One obvious solution is to technically disentangle security updates from other types of updates. If users could install security updates without risking their user interface, features, or being forced to reboot, they might be more inclined to keep software up-to-date. However, most users do not currently distinguish between security updates and feature updates; all updates look the same, and have the same risks. Even if we removed the technical dependency between updates, unless users can clearly distinguish the two, the cumulative dependency for updates will remain due to user decisions.

The software ecosystem is moving toward a model where apps rather than software suites are the norm, and software created by individuals is difficult to distinguish from programs created by large companies with quality assurance departments. Apps bombard users with update notifications, but app updates occasionally introduce new software bugs (such as the Google Authenticator bug[2]) that should rightly be avoided, and regularly introduce user interface changes or feature additions. The burden on users to evaluate software updates and decide what to do is increasing. All decisions about updates should be treated as security-relevant, since they will have an important impact on device security.

ACKNOWLEDGMENTS

We thank Zack Girouard and Michelle Rizor for their assistance with data collection and early analysis. We thank everyone associated with the BITLab at MSU for helpful discussions and feedback. This material is based upon work supported by the National Science Foundation under Grant No. CNS-1116544 and CNS-1115926.

[2]https://support.google.com/accounts/answer/3376859

Understanding Sustained Community Engagement: A Case Study in Heritage Preservation in Rural Argentina

Mara Balestrini[1], Jon Bird[2], Paul Marshall[3], Alberto Zaro[4] and Yvonne Rogers[3]

[1]Intel ICRI Cities, University College London, UK, M.Balestrini@cs.ucl.ac.uk

[2]Department of Computer Science, City University London, UK, jon.bird@city.ac.uk

[3]UCL Interaction Centre, University College London, UK, {paul.marshall, y.rogers}@ucl.ac.uk

[4]Proyecto Intemperie, Arequito, Argentina, laiconosfera@gmail.com

ABSTRACT

HCI projects are increasingly evaluating technologies in the wild, which typically involves working with communities over extended periods, often with the goal of effecting sustainable change. However, there are few descriptions of projects that have been successful in the long-term. In this paper we investigate what factors are important for developing long lasting community ICT interventions. We do this by analysing a successful action research project and provide five recommendations for facilitating sustained community engagement. CrowdMemo aimed to preserve local heritage in a town in rural Argentina and the project was set up so that it could be continued by the community once researchers had left. Participants created videos about personal memories of the town and over 600 people attended the premiere where they were first screened. The impact has not just been short-term and there has been sustained engagement with the project by stakeholders in the town and wider region: the local school integrated digital storytelling into its curriculum; the approach has been adopted by two nearby towns; and the project has influenced regional government educational policy.

Author Keywords

Community engagement; research in the wild; action research; digital storytelling; HCI4D

ACM Classification Keywords

H.5.m. Information Interfaces and Presentation (e.g. HCI): Miscellaneous

INTRODUCTION

As HCI research moves out of the lab and into the wild [29, 11], there has been much discussion of the issues involved in engaging communities of users [8]; how to enable the appropriation of technologies by stakeholders [10]; and the difficulties that can arise after community projects finish and researchers leave the field [16, 33]. In particular, Taylor et al. [33] have discussed a number of challenges that researchers face as they collaborate with communities, in particular: the need to manage expectations and the challenge of maintaining and supporting novel technologies.

CHI 2014, April 26–May 1, 2014, Toronto, Ontario, Canada.

ACM 978-1-4503-2473-1/14/04 ...$15.00.
http://dx.doi.org/10.1145/2556288.2557323.

Figure 1. School children interview an older member of the community.

A recent TOCHI special issue on 'The Turn to The Wild in HCI' has raised issues regarding the methodological and ethical challenges of working with communities in situ [11], the tensions between innovation and scalability in technology interventions [1], and the benefits of sustained (years, not just a few weeks) large-scale engagement with whole communities [7, 24, 3]. However, apart from valuable examples such as the Blacksburg Electronic Village, which studied community engagement for more than two decades [7], there are very few descriptions of HCI projects that demonstrate long-term community engagement.

This paper extends previous work by investigating factors underlying sustained community engagement with ICT interventions. Our analysis focuses on CrowdMemo, an action research project where a group of researchers and members of a rural town in the Argentine Pampa designed and deployed a technology intervention to preserve local heritage: both tangible (buildings and public spaces) and intangible (personal memories of community members). Rapid development in the region due to expansion of soy bean production has led to significant changes in and around the town: for example, several old buildings have been replaced by modern ones. CrowdMemo uses digital storytelling as a vehicle to

Figure 2. QR codes installed on the facade of the sports club.

record and share community stories. The approach was to train local children in digital video production so they could interview and record the memories of older community members (Figure 1). These videos could be accessed by scanning QR codes (Figure 2) placed on buildings throughout the town and via Google Maps. As heritage preservation is a long-term goal, the project was set up so that the community could continue to contribute after the researcher had left. Significantly, 18 months after the intervention, the project has been successfully sustained by the local community as well as appropriated by other neighbouring communities; in addition, it has inspired public policy changes and further efforts towards heritage preservation.

By using CrowdMemo as a case study, we contribute to the understanding of how communities can harness the potential of technology to promote collective action and how such actions can be sustained after the initial technology deployment. We propose five recommendations for HCI researchers and practitioners who are conducting community technology projects. They are most applicable to action research projects but are also relevant considerations when designing and evaluating innovative technology prototypes in the wild.

RELATED WORK

A growing number of HCI researchers are collaborating with communities in the wild both to create novel technology interventions and/or to address social issues through ICT and effect sustainable change. In these studies, researchers usually adopt participatory approaches, such as action research [16], where the stakeholders engage in processes of design, deployment, iteration and observation to draw knowledge from their experience [9, 16, 17]. Taylor and Cheverst [32] collaborated with an English rural community to investigate how public displays may support social interactions at a local level. They adopted a set of user-centric and participatory methods, inspired by action research, to design and deploy the Wray Photo Display, a public situated display for community-generated photography. Crabtree et al. [10] used action research, ethnography and agile systems design to create PlaceBooks, a mobile toolkit aimed at enabling people in rural areas to create and share digital multimedia books. They found that participatory approaches, where the community is involved from the outset, are crucial to the development of innovative interventions in situ, that foster sustained community engagement and facilitate the use and appropriation of technologies. Following a similar approach, Chamberlain et al. [8] worked with a rural community to design a web portal for a farmers market. They highlighted key factors for generating user engagement, such as: building trust; fitting in with the day-to-day life of the stakeholder and demonstrating understanding of the context; working with local community groups (even involving politicians); and using methods that focus on action. Other studies that have developed ICT interventions with communities have stressed the importance of creating skills to facilitate the uptake of the resulting technologies and foster the sustainability of the projects [25, 33].

A number of projects addressing heritage preservation have demonstrated how community engagement can contribute to their success. A notable example is the Cassiar project (http://www.cassiar.ca), where a community of Facebook users helped preserve the intangible heritage of an abandoned mining town in Canada by annotating photographs in a collection of over 4000 historical images.

Storytelling has also been used as a vehicle for heritage preservation. Digital storytelling usually refers to the creation of audio-visual narratives, normally by amateurs, who use digital technologies ranging from cameras to mobile phones. These stories tend to be distributed online, of a short duration and biographical [22]. Myriad projects have blended technology and storytelling to enable communities to reflect on their identity and preserve their heritage. Bidwell et al. [2] worked with a rural community in a Xhosa tribal region of South Africa's Eastern Cape to design a mobile storytelling tool. Their goal was to enable users without access to personal computers to preserve, reflect on and share their life experiences using digital media. They found that the Western approach to storytelling differs from practices in rural Africa and that a participatory design approach was beneficial to inform the development of digital storytelling technologies for that context. In Australia, Klaebe et al. [20] worked with a community in Brisbane to develop History Lines, a project where citizens used digital tools to create and geotag stories. They found that effectively mediated historical narratives can contribute to identity, authenticity and creating a sense of belonging among community members. In Voice of Kibera citizens of a slum in Nairobi used handheld portable devices and OpenStreetMap to map their neighbourhood and geolocate stories about their daily lives. Hagen concluded that these practices have the potential to represent community opinions and a collective version of truth [15].

Empowering stakeholders who have typically been underrepresented by mainstream media has also inspired the work of activists and artists. Since 2003, Tisselli and Abad have collaborated on a series of community memory projects (available at megafone.net) to work with groups of citizens to create and distribute online media representations of themselves. They have collaborated with taxi drivers in Mexico City, displaced people in Colombia, and young Saharawi refugees in the Algerian Sahara, among others. Their participants use a mobile application that allows them to publish pictures and audio files directly from the device to an online platform. They define this practice as *"a medium for record-*

ing and archiving information relevant to a commons that is managed by a community and for diffusing this information among members or communicating it to those threatening the commons and thus the community" [31, p. 23]. There are three main benefits of using community memories and digital storytelling in a community project: it empowers under-represented groups by giving them a voice [30, 20]; it provides a medium for the preservation of memories [31]; and it has been successfully used as a teaching tool [5].

There is evidence that interactions between older and younger people can improve children's motivation for learning, and increase their awareness of personal and community culture [26]. Druin et al. [13] and Bonsignore et al. [3] have applied participatory design methods to design and develop mobile applications for intergenerational storytelling where community elders can play a role in educating the next generation of children. In formal learning settings like schools, digital storytelling has been adopted by many teachers because it combines interesting learning opportunities for students, including: learning how to operate digital tools; working creatively with others in the production of a story; and understanding how visual and textual content may blend to communicate a message. Some authors have referred to this set of knowledge as 'Media Literacy' or '21st Century Literacy' [18, 5].

An ultimate goal for action research is to achieve long-term change. This not only requires the community to engage with the project during its initial phases but also when the researchers have left: *"Once research facilitators leave, the community partners should be able to maintain the positive changes that have been made"* [16, p.13] . However, in HCI there have been few descriptions of ICT interventions that have successfully engaged communities over the long-term. The contribution of this paper is to reflect on CrowdMemo and highlight the factors that were important in sustaining (ongoing) community engagement in the hope that this analysis may benefit other HCI researchers and practitioners who are conducting technology projects with communities.

PROJECT CONTEXT

Rural communities in northeastern Argentina have experienced radical socioeconomic and cultural changes over the last three decades. In the Argentine Pampa, between 1985 and 2010, soybean production increased from 7.1 to 52.7 million tons per year and the cultivated area expanded roughly from 3 to 18 million hectares [6]. This expansion of soybean production was the result of an increase in the price of this commodity on the international market and the introduction of genetically modified seeds.

Arequito, a town of 6,000 inhabitants in the state of Santa Fe, is known as the 'Soybean Capital'. Like other towns in the Pampa, Arequito's landscape has changed dramatically in the last three decades. As a consequence, some members of the community have a growing concern that failure to document and preserve the architectural heritage of the town could weaken the sense of community and even threaten the preservation of the local identity. Furthermore, many adults worry about the legacy that they will pass on to the younger generation. A member of a local photography collective, working on a project documenting the architectural heritage of Arequito, contacted the first author and enquired about the possibility of her running a digital storytelling workshop to address these concerns.

CROWDMEMO

CrowdMemo is a growing collection of user generated microdocumentaries that present stories about places that are significant to the community in Arequito. These documentaries are created by school children and comprise interviews with elderly people who share their memories about those places. They are edited and uploaded to YouTube and can be seen both online and in situ: commemorative plaques containing QR codes associated with each documentary have been embedded on the facades of the places that they refer to (Figure 2). The project website includes a Google Map of all these geotags.

CrowdMemo was orchestrated collaboratively by the first author (who is also referred to as 'the researcher' in this paper) and two local stakeholders groups in Arequito. First, the elementary school of the town which has 260 students aged from 6 to 12 who are divided into 7 grades. There are 22 teachers, a headmaster and deputy headmaster, and at the time of the deployment three visiting ICT trainers from the Ministry of Education of the Province of Santa Fe who were invited by the school to document the project. The second stakeholder group was a photography collective who have been working on documenting the architectural heritage of Arequito for many years.

This paper presents the reflection stage of one action research cycle, which has consisted of planning action, taking action, evaluating and reflecting [9] and has an overall duration of 18 months. The planning phase was conducted over email and Skype and lasted four months. Within the first two months the stakeholders agreed that the main objective of the intervention was to engage the community and encourage it to reflect on and preserve its heritage using locally available technologies. In addition to this overarching goal, CrowdMemo had to meet the different objectives and expectations of the stakeholder groups and provide value for each of them: i. the school management's goal was to offer a learning experience to its teachers and students, mainly focused on digital literacy; ii. the teachers' goal was to learn how to use mobile phones and low cost cameras for the production of videos, as they thought it would motivate their students to take an active role in innovative educational activities; iii. the students' goal was to learn how to use handheld devices to produce short films at school; iv. the photography collective wanted to initiate a process for documenting the architectural heritage of the town, mainly driven by children; and v. as researchers, our goal was to understand the factors leading to sustained community engagement and how HCI research can foster long-term impact in a community through the use of off-the-shelf technologies and a range of engagement strategies.

It is important to emphasise the very active role that the stakeholder groups took in the project. Not only did they initiate the project, but representatives from the local school and the photography collective raised the funds to support CrowdMemo by persuading local enterprises, the town council and individuals to finance it. This was not planned by the researcher but rather instigated by the stakeholders who voluntarily decided to pay for the intervention in the absence of external funding. Furthermore, even though a film premiere was planned within the first stage of the cycle to launch the project, stakeholder groups have been responsible for organising other public events associated with CrowdMemo: 'Cafe Literario' and 'Encuentro en la Llanura' (which we describe in more detail later).

In the next sections we give a detailed account of the CrowdMemo approach in three different phases: conception and initiation; deployment and piloting; and project launch.

Project conception and initial training

During the first four months of CrowdMemo, we followed the action research approach of involving stakeholders in conceiving the project by organising online and offline workshops [14]. First, we conducted a framing and design workshop on Skype where a representative from the photography collective, the teachers, the headmaster and deputy headmaster and the first author discussed the goals of the project and the deployment strategy. We defined a roadmap for the execution of the initial training phase of CrowdMemo.

In two workshops in Arequito, teachers explained the project to students and led discussions about the history of the town and the places that are important to the community. As homework students were asked to discuss with their parents what places are significant for the community and learn about their history.

In a third workshop, two representatives from the photography collective taught students the theory and practice of using low cost cameras. They also presented a slide show showing how Arequito had changed over the last century.

In a last workshop teachers worked with students to select the locations that each grade was going to document in their videos. For several weeks they conducted research about the history of those places and found out which members of the community could share memories and anecdotes about them. The output of this process was a selection of nine locations, a list of people to be interviewed and photos, songs, videos and other media related to those places. Students then created one script for each selected location.

Deployment

The first author visited Arequito for the week long deployment phase. Before each class filmed their script they received an additional half day workshop, conducted by the first author, where they learnt how to film documentaries using mobile phones and low cost digital cameras. Nine microdocumentaries were filmed following the scripts devised in the previous phase. The students from the first and second grades did not film documentaries but participated by creating their own videos. Below, we present the titles and descriptions of some of the documentaries produced by students, each of which involved interviewing elderly people in the town:

- **The Rossini theatre** (5th grade) The Cine Teatro Rossini was opened in 1932 and was considered one of the most important theaters in the province for its architecture, its dimensions and the wonderful acoustics. During the deployment of CrowdMemo the theatre was temporarily out of use.
- **The history of our riverside resort** (7th grade) The Balneario Arequito riverside resort used to hold social gatherings every summer. It has been abandoned for decades.
- **A wagon full of memories** (6th grade) The first train arrived in Arequito in 1887 but stopped being used by passengers many years ago. The documentary explains how the train changed people's lives.
- **The aquarium of Mr Marmol** (4th grade) Mr Marmol created an aquarium in his backyard and it now contains thousands of fish species from all over the world. In the documentary Mr Marmol explains how he started his aquarium and shows hundreds of species of fish that he takes care of.

Project launch and blog

CrowdMemo was launched at a public film premiere that was advertised in the media. Refreshments were served and all nine micro documentaries were shown on a big screen and over 600 people attended the event.

During the premiere we also displayed the QR codes which enabled the videos to be watched online. Because many people in the town did not have previous experience with this technology, a group of community members volunteered to train people in how to download QR code scanners on their phones and teach them how to use them to view the videos. Children were also very keen to teach adults how to access the documentaries by scanning the codes. Many elderly people were moved when their stories appeared on the screens.

We created a blog (CrowdMemo.org) that was regularly updated during the process of deployment. This online resource allowed the community to track the evolution of the intervention and see pictures of the interviews and documentary locations. It gave students and other stakeholders an opportunity to leave comments. Importantly, it also increased awareness of CrowdMemo outside of Arequito which led to the appropriation of the project by other communities. Because one of our objectives was to understand how HCI research can foster long-term impact in communities through the use of off-the-shelf technologies and engagement strategies, we encouraged the appropriation of CrowdMemo. In the blog we deliberately described the project as being 'open source' and 'a common' that could be freely replicated and modified by others. We also provided step-by-step instructions on how other communities could set up similar projects.

DATA GATHERING METHODS AND ANALYSIS

The process of evaluation was conducted in collaboration with the stakeholders. We adopted a qualitative approach, combining participatory observations, questionnaires with closed and open ended questions and interviews covering all the phases of the intervention. In addition, we carried out a debriefing session with the school teachers, headmaster and deputy headmaster, representatives of the photography collective and two of the ICT trainers from the Ministry of Education of the Province of Santa Fe who had visited the school.

The questionnaires and interviews were designed to gather information about participants' experiences and opinions with regards to: i. the deployment of CrowdMemo, in particular the strengths and weaknesses of its different phases; ii. community engagement; iii. reflection and awareness about heritage preservation; and iv. sustainability of the project. They were answered by 22 participants from the school, the photography collective, the Ministry of Education and members of the community who took part in the project, 12 months after the researchers left the field. We also interviewed the coordinator of the first external appropriation of CrowdMemo, which took place in a neighbouring town, Pujato. We continued the evaluation through emails and discussed the results iteratively. All interviews where conducted in Spanish and quotes from the respondents have been translated to English.

We analysed participants' answers to the open ended questions by using thematic analysis [4]. Themes emerging from the analysis were discussed with stakeholders until reaching consensus. We identified two overarching themes: impact indicators and engagement. Quantitative data extracted from the field notes have been used to further validate the analysis.

RESULTS

In this section we present the findings from the thematic analysis following the two emergent themes introduced above. Speakers are identified by initials and role in the project.

Impact indicators

The community has kept the project going since the researchers left the field, renaming it 'Natives and immigrants at the 202 of Arequito' in reference to the cooperation between children (digital natives) and old people (digital immigrants) and the name of the school (202). We describe a number of other indicators that demonstrate the sustained impact of CrowdMemo.

Media coverage

The project launch received media coverage in the local newspaper, a radio station and on regional TV. A few months after the intervention, there was a local TV show about the story of the town and its characters building on the interviews created during CrowdMemo.

Attendance at public events

CrowdMemo was launched at a public premiere organised by the school, which over 600 people attended, a large proportion of the town, filling the venue to capacity: *"the day we organised the premiere everyone was there!"*[S.A.G., school teacher]. Many attendees found the event surprisingly moving: *"The emotion, the tears and other samples of appreciation were unexpected. We didn't imagine that this project would be so moving to people"* [M.J.G., school teacher].

After the intervention, the school and the photography collective organised two social gatherings around the problem of heritage preservation: the 'Cafe Literario' (seven months after), attended by 400 people; and the 'Encuentro en la Llanura' (14 months later), attended by 250. In both cases, the community discussed CrowdMemo and its legacy: *"Participants continued to talk about the process and about the premiere at the Cafe Literario...about the huge number of people who came together that day!"* [M.M., school teacher].

External appropriation

CrowdMemo's impact extended beyond Arequito and the project's approach has been appropriated by other communities in the state of Santa Fe. An ICT facilitator from the Ministry of Education explained *"This project has been a real 'social mobiliser', as it not only captured the collective memory of the town but it also inspired other projects within the local school and other external institutions"*. For example, a few months after the deployment, Pujato, located 43 km away, launched 'Replay' (nuestroreplay.wordpress.com/) their own version of CrowdMemo. School 227 of Pujato was celebrating its 125 year anniversary and invited people to the school to be interviewed by the students following the CrowdMemo approach. As well as capturing digital stories, they also created an ebook and a photography exhibition and organised a public event where the microdocumentaries were shared as well as showing them at different science fairs in the province. This appropriation was led by a member of the community who learnt about CrowdMemo through the project's website. Their initiative is also being sustained by the community with regular blog postings and creation of new microdocumentaries. In addition, in San Jose de la Esquina, a rural community 30 km away from Arequito, the local school is currently working on appropriating CrowdMemo to commemorate the 150th anniversary of the founding of their town.

Recognition by state government and impact on public policy

CrowdMemo was awarded 'project of interest' recognition by the Chamber of Deputies of the province of Santa Fe [12]. Furthermore, during the deployment, three ICT trainers from Santa Fe Ministry of Education visited the school to observe the project. They reported on the techniques used to train the school community in digital storytelling. As a result the Ministry of Education created a new training course called 'Make and narrate with ICT', which has so far been delivered to 1,500 teachers and students from 288 institutions across the state [23]. When interviewed, the coordinator for ICT in the Ministry of Education explained: *"It will be difficult to replicate the experience of CrowdMemo but we are trying to spread it in different ways"*.

Impact on architectural heritage preservation

Three of the locations captured in digital stories in CrowdMemo have undergone, or are about to undergo, refurbishment as a result of the project. First, the Cine Teatro Rossini has been restored and is now open to the community. Second, the local council launched an initiative to collaborate with students at the Faculty of Architecture (National University of Rosario, Santa Fe) in order to redesign the Balneario Arequito riverside resort. The council has received five project proposals and is now carrying out a technical assessment to choose and develop one. Third, restoration works are being carried out at the train station. Finally, one of the members of the photography collective is currently working on a research project named 'Conformation of the Historical Centre of Arequito'. The aim is to investigate whether Arequito can be recognised as having a historical centre in accordance with the UNESCO norms of Quito [27].

Integration into the school curriculum

Teachers and students have continued using mobile and low cost cameras phones to film new content: *"At school they use the short movies for reflective coursework and they still use the mobile phones"* [M.B., school teacher]; *"This year, 5th grade created a blog and students in 7th grade filmed interviews with mobile phones and little cameras for their language course"* [M.M., school teacher]; *"Fourth grade students continued with the project and we presented a short film with interviews honouring seamstresses from the town along with an exhibition that shows how fashions have evolved and a parade with bridal gowns made by dressmakers from different years"* [J.R., school teacher].

Engagement

One of the key factors leading to the sustained success of CrowdMemo was the strong engagement that it generated among the different groups involved in the project. One piece of evidence for this engagement is the positive emotions expressed by individuals from all of the stakeholder groups when they describe their experience of CrowdMemo [19]: *"To see the students, teachers and a lot of people from the town conversing, remembering worthy anecdotes about the town...their faces, voices, expressions and even silences denoted the strong emotional impact that the project generated"* [G.F., photography collective]; *"The excitement, tears and hugs of thanks [by members of the community] was something we did not expect. We did not think that it would affect people so much"* [J.R., school teacher]; *"...this project allowed for the participation of the community, which was full with emotion"* [deputy headmaster]; *"We had fun, we learnt and made really nice works"* [group comment by students on the project blog].

A second piece of evidence for engagement was the reflection CrowdMemo engendered about belonging to the community: *"I felt that the whole community was engaged with the project and that we were all working to transcend the walls of the school"* [A.M.C., school teacher]; *"The community's response was wonderful, all the people were talking about what the students were developing. The response was incredible, very positive! I learned a lot and the students have shown great interest, participation, emotion, habits, behaviours, vocabulary. It has been a wonderful project, an excellent motivator to get to know the history, architecture, and people in our town"* [C.B., school teacher]. A group of students commented: *"It was really nice to learn anecdotes about our town and those stories that are not written in any books"*.

We have identified three factors underlying the strong engagement of the stakeholders with CrowdMemo: recognition and pride; social encounters; and technology and skills.

Recognition and pride

A key factor in the community's engagement with the project was that they felt recognised and valued. This recognition came from both inside and outside the community.

Being interviewed engaged elderly members of the community in the project: *"People who were interviewed by the students expressed enthusiasm and excitement because they were being recognised again for what they had done"* [J.R., school teacher]. Having their stories recorded and shared led to their contributions being appreciated by the wider community: *"It allowed me to better value what we have and what our grandparents, mainly immigrants, built, their work ethic and perseverance"* [T.Z., member of the photography collective]. The community also valued the fact that their personal histories would persist as digital stories: *"Knowing that people I know are and will always be portrayed telling our story fills us up with pride!"* [M.A.V., school teacher].

Other respondents clearly expressed how seeing the digital stories led them to appreciate other members of the community: *"the community was surprised to know about the experience of neighbours. It was great to remember those events and learn about the places in our town from a different perspective"* [school deputy headmaster]. Memories are imbued with features of the local identity and publicly displaying them led to reflection on locations in the town and why they are relevant to the community's heritage: *"[CrowdMemo] made me reflect on the history of the local community but from a novel perspective. It's not only about our material achievements but through learning our ways of having fun, our achievements as a human group through our stories (...) It's not about some texts and paragraphs put together by a historian, it's about the testimony of those who gave life to many of the situations [in our heritage]."* [T.Z., member of the photography collective].

One source of outside recognition was the wide media coverage, which the community frequently discussed: *"In the town people are still talking about CrowdMemo, the local TV channel created a show telling the story of the town and its characters"* [C.B., school teacher]. Others were the award from the Chamber of Deputies of the State of Santa Fe and the creation of the course 'Narrate and make with ICT' by the Ministry of Education (mentioned in the 'Impact indicators' section): *"I think this novel experience gave a lot of prestige to our institution ... I feel very proud of my school and the school principals because they are always looking for positive innovation for our community...I am thankful to have been part of it"* [M.A.V., school teacher]; *"Those involved have been very excited and grateful to have contributed to the reconstruction of those stories. Everybody spoke about the impact of the project both here and in nearby towns"* [school deputy headmasterl]. Finally, the fact that the researcher came from Europe to Arequito to participate in the deployment was a source of community pride.

The main consequences for the community of these different forms of recognition were a sense of 'having their voice heard' and more generally feeling pride in the project, both of which resulted in sustained engagement. Another key factor leading to engagement was the opportunity for social encounters engendered by CrowdMemo.

Social encounters

CrowdMemo generated social encounters in three ways, each of which strengthened community engagement with the project and contributed to the sustainability of the project: i. enabling interactions between children and the elderly; ii. organising public events that fostered shared experiences among members of the community; and iii. creating triggers for conversation in public spaces.

According to 90 per cent of the participants, enabling conversation between children and older people was one of the most valuable aspects of CrowdMemo: *"People interviewed were emotionally engaged because they could revisit and transmit their experiences to the youngsters"* [S.A.G., school teacher]; *"Seeing my father in law and my son together remembering the old days, in front of the church and next to the old family car. Emotion and pride at the same time!"* [A.M.C., school teacher].

The public events created opportunities for members of the community to have face-to-face social encounters: *"I think that CrowdMemo was useful because it enabled dialogue between different community members about the town's heritage. Each group of participants visited the places where their stories had taken place...At the premiere and the Cafe Literario people were very excited to converse and reveal their memories to others'* [school deputy headmaster].

Public events also enabled sustained reflection. When asked about what happened in the 12 months after the deployment, respondents explained: *"Participants continued to talk about the process and the premiere at the Cafe Literario: about the huge number of people who came together on the day of the premiere!"* [M.M., school teacher].

The QR code plaques on the building facades facilitated conversation in public spaces: *"People who come to the town ask about the QR codes"* [school deputy headmaster]; *"We use them as a tool for cultural promotion available at all times for locals and visitors. TV programs show those places and interview the people who have been related to them"* [T.Z., member of the photography collective]. We now describe how the other technologies deployed in the project facilitated engagement.

Technology and skills

The combination of mobile phones, digital storytelling and QR codes represent a novel assemblage of technologies, rarely used in Argentinian schools. Participants often referred to the novelty of the technological approach, which generated a positive attitude to the project: *"The community feels motivated by this type of activity as it contributes to an innovative education"* [M.N.M., school teacher].

The project also created opportunities for teachers and students to learn new technical skills, which they found to be valuable and engaging: 70 percent of the respondents agreed that one of the most important aspects of CrowdMemo was that students learnt how to produce content using mobile phones. Students commented on the blog that they had fun learning how to film with phones and were grateful for having acquired such skills.

However, lack of time for a more extensive training phase was seen by teachers as the main limitation of CrowdMemo. Half of them thought that the limited training time was a consequence of the education system: for example, *"I think this weakness is related to the times of the school, which does not allow us to do everything we plan."* [M.M., school teacher].

DISCUSSION

This paper has presented CrowdMemo, an action research project that aimed to preserve the heritage of a town in rural Argentina by training members of a community to create digital stories from their personal memories. Our goal was to create sustained community engagement to ensure long-term heritage preservation. The project has been successful in this regard: two locations in the town have already been refurbished (the theatre and the train station) and there are plans to do the same with the riverside resort. Since the deployment, there have been two public events independently organised by the community that have sustained interest in heritage preservation in Arequito. The novel ways of using mobile phones and low cost cameras, as well as the skills learnt during the deployment, have been integrated into the local school curriculum and students regularly use digital storytelling at school. Furthermore, CrowdMemo has had a wider impact: it has been appropriated by two neighbouring towns which were not initially involved in the project; it has been recognised by the regional government; and it has influenced regional educational policy. This level of sustained engagement with a technology-enabled community project has rarely been described in the HCI literature. We now abstract from our results in order to understand what contributed to this success and propose a set of five recommendations for HCI researchers and practitioners who are conducting community technology projects. We finish by considering some of the limitations of these recommendations: they are most applicable to action research projects but we argue that they are also relevant considerations when evaluating innovative technology prototypes in the wild.

i. facilitate valued ownership by following action research principles: involve community stakeholders in the conception and running of the intervention and ensure that the project provides value for each stakeholder

Taylor et al. have identified that a crucial part of sustainably integrating technologies into community life is encouraging the community to feel a sense of ownership of the project [33]. People in Arequito involved with CrowdMemo had a strong sense of ownership, which was a consequence of several factors: they instigated the project by contacting the first author with a request to collaborate; the stakeholders were involved from the outset in the organisation and logistics of the project and they not only set the goals of the intervention in collaboration with the researcher, but also organised interviews between children and old people, as well as public social events such as the premiere. The importance of a participatory approach for sustained engagement has been recognised in the action research and HCI literature [16, 10]. Significantly, the community also raised all of the funds to support the project which enhanced their sense of ownership.

However, although necessary, ownership is not sufficient for sustained engagement. For example, many people own a technology that they do not use because it no longer has value for them, such as an old mobile phone left in a drawer or a forgotten gadget at the back of the kitchen cupboard. Importantly, CrowdMemo provided value for all of the stakeholder groups that were involved. Children were excited about using the technologies and curious about the stories they were told by the old people they interviewed. Elderly participants felt valued and useful and enjoyed sharing their memories with the children and having them preserved as digital stories. Members of the photography collective valued CrowdMemo because it encouraged the community to reflect about the architectural heritage of Arequito. Teachers valued learning new technology skills that enhanced their classroom practice. The school management found value in being able to play a significant role at the heart of the community.

ii. where possible use off-the-shelf technologies in novel ways rather than novel technologies

CrowdMemo facilitated a number of different technology encounters that deepened community engagement: students with mobile phones; teachers with digital storytelling tools; and townspeople and visitors with QR codes. Importantly, the technologies themselves were off-the-shelf rather than prototypes but the way they were used was novel. For example, in Argentina there were more than 50 million active mobile phones in 2012, among the highest rate in Latin America [28] and many students own a handset. However, they are usually banned from classrooms as they can be distracting. CrowdMemo legitimised mobile phone use at school by training students to use them, along with low cost cameras, to produce digital stories. Students were excited about this opportunity to use them in a new way. Kolb [21] highlights that a benefit of introducing mobile devices into the classroom is that most students not only know how to use them but enjoy using them. Furthermore, they enable teachers to plan technology-based activities that can take place outside the classroom. CrowdMemo introduced teachers to using mobile phones for digital storytelling. They learned new skills in order to create content using low cost devices, simple video editing software and QR codes. Using digital tools to produce pedagogical material allowed them to innovate their classroom practices.

We think it is significant that participants owned the technologies that were used in the project and were trained in the skills necessary to use them in novel ways, for example, making digital stories with mobile phones. These skills were embedded in the community through their incorporation in the school curriculum. As discussed by Taylor et al. [33], using off-the-shelf technologies bypasses many of the challenges associated with handovers of experimental technology prototypes to communities. Specifically, off-the-shelf technologies, such as mobile phones, and established infrastructures, such as 3G networks, are far more robust than research prototypes, generally require less maintenance, and if they do fail can easily be fixed or replaced. Furthermore, many people in the community are familiar with, and have the basic skills to use, off-the-shelf technologies like mobile phones and low cost cameras. CrowdMemo built on these existing skills, for example, by training community members in how to install and use QR code readers. Merkel el al. have also identified the importance of developing participatory processes that take advantage of a community's skills in order to develop and sustain an intervention [25].

iii. facilitate a range of face-to-face social encounters which can lead to discussion and ongoing engagement with the project

A key reason underlying the community's sustained interest in CrowdMemo was that it facilitated a range of social encounters which led to face-to-face conversations between different community members and thereby increased their engagement with project. The encounter between children and the elderly members of the community was identified by interviewees as one of the most important aspects of the project. The digital stories produced by the children meant that the old people knew that their life stories were recognised and valued by the community. The children also benefited from finding out about their heritage and by playing an important role in a project that was widely valued by their community. Steels and Tisselli [33] argue that face-to-face meetings between community members are essential to the success of an intervention because they create the necessary trust and engagement for collective action.

A second type of social encounter was facilitated by the three public events: the premiere; 'Cafe Literario'; and the 'Encuentro en la Llanura'. At these gatherings community members could share experiences and discuss the digital stories, and more generally the heritage of the town, in a group context. Previous studies have highlighted the importance of celebrating milestones [16] and capitalizing on public events [7] to engage participants in a project.

iv. design for appropriation by: first, providing clear instructions on how to conduct the project; and second, using off-the-shelf technologies which are readily available to participants and which many will have the necessary skills to use

CrowdMemo was designed to be open source in the widest sense. Our approach was to use widely available and low cost off-the-shelf technologies, provide clear step-by-step instructions on the project website, and explicitly encourage appropriation. For these reasons, CrowdMemo provided an attractive opportunity for other schools striving for ICT training and learning activities using readily available technologies.

Furthermore, the openness and low cost were crucial factors in the Ministry of Education's decision to scale up the digital storytelling aspect and train large numbers of teachers in this technique.

v. aim for broad media coverage of the project as positive external recognition leads to community pride and engagement

Both local media coverage and the project blog raised awareness of the project outside of Arequito. For example, CrowdMemo was appropriated by schools in the towns of Pujato and San Jose de la Esquina, neither of whom were initially involved with the project. This external recognition, as well as the local government recognising CrowdMemo as a 'project of interest' generated community pride in the project which in turn facilitated sustained engagement.

Limitations

In recent years, the HCI community has increasingly explored new research domains outside the laboratory [16, 33]. In these in the wild projects, researchers face a number of challenges when working with communities in diverse environments, either to address community issues using existing technologies or to develop new technologies that can augment the everyday experience of people [29]. CrowdMemo differs from many of these projects in a number of ways and this may limit the applicability of our findings.

One of the primary reasons for the success of CrowdMemo is that it used locally available everyday technologies. However, many in the wild projects are concerned with developing and evaluating novel prototypes. This makes it challenging for these projects to achieve the long-term sustainability that we have described in this paper (cf. Taylor et al. [33]). If prototypes are used then there should be an emphasis on ensuring they are robust and that stakeholders are provided with training so that they are able to use and maintain the technologies. In order to engage stakeholders in this training, and more generally motivate their sustained engagement in the project, it is important that they can see value in using the technology.

CrowdMemo also differs from most research projects in that it was instigated by the community, rather than a researcher. This meant that the community had a strong sense of ownership from the outset. A sense of ownership can be facilitated in projects that are research- rather than community-led by following an action research approach that aims to involve the community in the conception and running of the project.

Another distinctive aspect of CrowdMemo was that it was funded by the community itself. This is unlikely to be the case in research-led projects. Unless a community has instigated a project then requesting them to contribute to the running costs is more likely to disengage the community than engage them.

CONCLUSION

In this paper we have described CrowdMemo, an action research project for heritage preservation in rural Argentina that not only had short term impact, but has successfully engaged the local and wider community over a prolonged period (18 months) and continues to do so. In this paper our goal was to investigate the factors that made this project a success. Previous studies had identified some of the challenges faced by researchers when collaborating with communities in the wild, such as: the need to manage expectations; the challenge of maintaining and supporting novel technologies [33]; and how to facilitate the appropriation of technologies by stakeholders [10].

We have proposed a set of five guidelines in the hope of helping researchers in the field to overcome some of these issues. We found that creating a sense of valued ownership in all of the project stakeholders, using off-the-shelf technologies owned by participants, facilitating a range of social encounters, designing for appropriation and aiming for broad media coverage were positively related to sustained long-term engagement in CrowdMemo.

We are not claiming that following these recommendations is a recipe for guaranteed sustained community engagement; currently, we can't say which of these factors are necessary and sufficient. However, CrowdMemo does demonstrate that if researchers adopt a participatory approach that aims to empower communities, then a project can be appropriated in unanticipated ways and result in positive long-term impact.

ACKNOWLEDGMENTS

We thank all the participants in CrowdMemo, School 202 of Arequito, the collective enlaintemperie and those who appropriated CrowdMemo and harnessed the potential of locally available technologies to transform their realities. Special thanks to Martin Inderbitzin for his support during the intervention.

REFERENCES

1. Adams, A., Fitzgerald, E., and Priestnall, G. Of catwalk technologies and boundary creatures. *TOCHI 20*, 3 (2013), 15:1–15:34.

2. Bidwell, N. J., Reitmaier, T., Marsden, G., and Hansen, S. Designing with mobile digital storytelling in rural Africa. In *Proc. of the CHI 2010*, ACM (2010), 1593–1602.

3. Bonsignore, E., Quinn, A. J., Druin, A., and Bederson, B. B. Sharing stories 'in the wild': A mobile storytelling case study using StoryKit. *TOCHI 20*, 3 (2013), 18:1–18:38.

4. Braun, V., and Clarke, V. Using thematic analysis in psychology. *Qualitative research in psychology 3*, 2 (2006), 77–101.

5. Brown, J., Bryan, J., and Brown, T. Twenty-first century literacy and technology in K-8 classrooms. *Innovate Journal of Online Education 1*, 3 (2005).

6. Calvo, S., Salvador, M. L., Giancola, S., Iturrioz, G., Covacevich, M., and Iglesias, D. Causes and consequences of the expansion of soybean in Argentina. *ODR Las Palmas, EEA Colonia Benítez, CR Chaco-Formosa.* (2011).

7. Carroll, J. M., and Rosson, M. B. Wild at home: The neighborhood as a living laboratory for HCI. *TOCHI 20*, 3 (2013), 16:1–16:28.

8. Chamberlain, A., Crabtree, A., and Davies, M. Community engagement for research: Contextual design in rural CSCW system development. In *Proc. Int. Conf. on Communities and Technologies*, ACM (Munich, Germany, 2013), 131–139.

9. Coghlan, D., and Brannick, T. *Doing action research in your own organization*. Sage Publications, 2009.

10. Crabtree, A., Chamberlain, A., Davies, M., Glover, K., Reeves, S., Rodden, T., Tolmie, P., and Jones, M. Doing innovation in the wild. In *Proc. of the Biannual Conference of the Italian Chapter of SIGCHI*, ACM (2013), 25.

11. Crabtree, A., Chamberlain, A., Grinter, R. E., Jones, M., Rodden, T., and Rogers, Y. Introduction to the special issue of 'The Turn to The Wild'. *TOCHI 20*, 3 (2013), 13:1–13:4.

12. Cámara de Diputados de Santa Fe, Sesión Extraordinaria 22/03/2012. http://www.diputadossantafe.gov.ar/index.php/actividad-parlamentaria/sintesis-de-sesion/item/47-sesi%C3%B3n-extraordinaria-n%C2%B0-6-periodo-129-22-03-2012.

13. Druin, A., Bederson, B. B., and Quinn, A. Designing intergenerational mobile storytelling. In *Proc. Int. Conf. on Interaction Design and Children*, ACM (2009), 325–328.

14. Foth, M., and Axup, J. Participatory design and action research: Identical twins or synergetic pair? In *Proc. Participatory Design* (2006), 93–96.

15. Hagen, E. Mapping change: Community information empowerment in Kibera. *Innovations 6*, 1 (2011), 69–94.

16. Hayes, G. R. The relationship of action research to human-computer interaction. *TOCHI 18*, 3 (2011), 15.

17. Hearn, G. N., and Foth, M. Action research in the design of new media and ICT systems. *Topical issues in communications and media research issues in comms. and media research* (2005), 79–94.

18. Hull, G. A. At last: Youth culture and digital media: New literacies for new times. *Research in the Teaching of English 38*, 2 (2003), 229–233.

19. Kahn, W. A. Psychological conditions of personal engagement and disengagement at work. *Academy of management journal 33*, 4 (1990), 692–724.

20. Klaebe, H. G., Foth, M., Burgess, J. E., and Bilandzic, M. Digital storytelling and history lines: Community engagement in a master-planned development. In *Int.Conf. on Virtual Systems and Multimedia (VSMM'07)* (2007).

21. Kolb, L. Adventures with cell phones. *Educational Leadership 68*, 5 (2011), 39–43.

22. Lambert, J. *Digital Storytelling: Capturing Lives, Creating Community*. Routledge, 2013.

23. Aprenden a contar historias con celulares, cámaras y netbooks. http://www.ellitoral.com/index.php/diarios/2012/10/16/educacion/EDUC-01.html.

24. Memarovic, N., Langheinrich, M., Cheverst, K., Taylor, N., and Alt, F. P-LAYERS – a layered framework addressing the multifaceted issues facing community-supporting public display deployments. *TOCHI 20*, 3 (2013), 17:1–17:34.

25. Merkel, C. B., Xiao, L., Farooq, U., Ganoe, C. H., Lee, R., Carroll, J. M., and Rosson, M. B. Participatory design in community computing contexts: Tales from the field. In *Proc. PDC 2004*, vol. 1, ACM (2004), 1–10.

26. Ogozalek, V. The Worcester State College 'Elder Connection': Facilitating intergenerational education with information technology and multimedia. In *Sociomedia*, E. Barrett, Ed. MIT, 1994.

27. Final Report of the Meeting on the Preservation and Utilization of Monuments and Sites of Artistic and historical Value held in Quito, Ecuador. http://www.icomos.org/en/charters-and-texts/179-articles-en-francais/ressources/charters-and-standards/168-the-norms-of-quito.

28. Retegui, L. M., and Perea, R. G. Telecomunicaciones: Acceso, políticas y mercado. El caso de la telefonía móvil en la Argentina. *Question 1*, 35 (2012), 433–446.

29. Rogers, Y. Interaction design gone wild: Striving for wild theory. *Interactions 18*, 4 (2011), 58–62.

30. Skuse, A., Fildes, J., Tacchi, J. A., Martin, K., and Baulch, E. *Poverty and digital inclusion: Preliminary findings of finding a voice project*. UNESCO, 2007.

31. Steels, L., and Tiselli, E. Interfaces for community memories. In *Proc. Int. User Interface Conference IUI-2008 (Workshop)*, ACM (2008), 23–28.

32. Taylor, N., and Cheverst, K. Social interaction around a rural community photo display. *International Journal of Human-Computer Studies 67*, 12 (2009), 1037–1047.

33. Taylor, N., Cheverst, K., Wright, P., and Olivier, P. Leaving the wild: Lessons from community technology handovers. In *Proc. CHI 2013* (2013), 1549–1558.

Human Values in Curating a Human Rights Media Archive

Abigail Durrant, David S. Kirk and Stuart Reeves*

Culture Lab
Newcastle University, UK
{abigail.durrant; david.kirk}@newcastle.ac.uk

School of Computer Science*
University of Nottingham, UK
stuart@tropic.org.uk

ABSTRACT

Cultural institutions, such as museums, often curate politically and ethically sensitive materials. Increasingly, Internet-enabled, digital technology intersects with these curatorial practices offering new opportunities for public and scholarly engagement. We report on a case study of human rights media archiving at a genocide memorial centre in Rwanda, motivated by our interests in ICT support to memorialisation practices. Through an analysis of our discussions with staff about their work, we report on how accounts of the Rwandan Genocide are being captured and curated to support the centre's humanitarian agenda and associated values. We identify transferable curatorial concerns for human rights media communication amongst scholarly networks and public audiences worldwide, elucidating interaction design challenges for supportive ICT and contributing to HCI discourses on Value Sensitive Design and cultural engagement with sensitive materials.

Author Keywords

Human Rights Media; Rwanda; Genocide; Memorial; Curation; Value Sensitive Design.

ACM Classification Keywords

H.5.m. Information interfaces and presentation (e.g., HCI): Miscellaneous.

INTRODUCTION

Interest in cultural institutional settings has grown in recent years in the Human Computer Interaction (HCI) field, as networked digital technology increasingly intersects with the curatorial practices of these institutions, within a global frame [4, 17]. In parallel, increased attentiveness has been shown to the *human values* being supported by and implicated in the design of such technologies, including their ethical, legal and political dimensions, and transnational, multigenerational, cross-cultural spheres of operation [5, 6, 10, 21, 24, 25, 30]. In this paper, we contribute to these discussions on cultural engagement, diversity and value in HCI, by reporting on a study with a genocide memorial centre in Rwanda [18] about archiving human rights media for worldwide audiences [11].

CHI 2014, April 26 - May 01 2014, Toronto, ON, Canada

ACM 978-1-4503-2473-1/14/04...$15.00.
http://dx.doi.org/10.1145/2556288.2557196.

Our study formed part of a UK-based research project to understand how Information and Communications Technology (ICT) is being used to support practices associated with visiting and managing memorials in an international context, to deliver socio-cultural and technical insights on the participation of memorial centres as *sustainable* institutions in a global economy [12].

Herein, we report on our recent case study of the Kigali Genocide Memorial (KGM) [18] and its genocide archive (which is partially online [11]). Part of this case study – and the analytic focus of this paper – was to understand how accounts of the 1994 Rwandan Genocide are being captured and represented through KGM's media archiving practices, supported by technology, and what values are expressed by the KGM staff members when describing their work. We further aimed to highlight voiced curatorial concerns for those working with sensitive materials at KGM to support public and scholarly communication.

In the following, we provide background information on Rwanda and its 1994 Genocide, to set KGM's founding in context, focusing on the ethical and political values that direct its work. With KGM's institutional remit in focus, we position our study objectives in relation to work in HCI and related fields. We describe our method and analytic process, and discuss our key findings. In concluding, we elucidate transferable insights about curatorial concerns for supporting the communication of human rights media for international public and scholarly audiences, and describe interaction design challenges in this endeavour, contributing to HCI discourses about design for human values and cultural engagement with sensitive materials.

Background on Rwanda

Rwanda is a small East African country, one of the poorest in Africa [8]. Yet through heavy investment in IT infrastructure and following a national plan [28], Rwanda aims to become the 'IT Hub' for the East African economic zone. This plan is part of reconstruction efforts to transform the country after the 1994 Genocide, in which some 800,000+ Tutsis, Twa and Hutu moderates were massacred, under the instigation of the Government of the time [26].

It is widely accepted that the extent of this atrocity was due in no small part to inaction by the United Nations (UN), with peace being eventually restored by rebel Tutsis, of the Rwandan Patriotic Front (RPF). The RPF has remained in power since, stabilising Rwanda largely through President Kagame. However, some people have alleged that activities such as political oppression and enacting anti-genocide ideology and anti-divisionist laws – in the face of genocide deniers and those who would actively contest historical accounts – have led to subsequent human rights violations [14]. Now, 20 years following the Genocide, its discussion remains difficult for Rwandans – emotionally, politically, and legally; many remain guarded about it. Nonetheless, the country enters a period of national mourning each year for 100 days to commemorate the victims.

KGM and the Documentation Centre (KGM-DC)

KGM was established in 2004 as a national focal point for memorialising the Rwandan Genocide, with the support of the Rwandan government and the Aegis Trust, a UK-based charity and NGO [2]. Aegis created the UK's Holocaust Centre and memorial [31], which Kigali City Council members visited after the 1994 Genocide, leading to an invitation for Aegis to help them develop what would become KGM. Consequently, an Anglo-Rwandan dialogue heavily informed the founding of KGM, and KGM's institutional remit echoes that of Aegis: to promote the prevention of genocide to international audiences [2].

KGM constitutes a mass grave (with 250,000+ Genocide victims interred), a museum exhibition presenting a curated historical narrative of the genocide events, memorial gardens that have been designed to reflect the curation of the exhibition, and a recently launched Documentation Centre (KGM-DC). KGM-DC contains an archiving facility and library, and the archive incorporates a *physical* collection of genocide-related media (e.g. photos, letters and print publications) and a collection of digital resources.

At the time of our study, KGM pursued its humanitarian cause through three departments, Education, Social Enterprise, and Documentation, and activities including: an in-house extracurricular education programme for Rwandan schoolchildren; an international tourism service (Discover Rwanda), and not-for-profit enterprise initiatives that aim to sustain the centre; a social programme that financially supports genocide survivors in their everyday living; and the KGM-DC. It is the *documentation* work of the KGM-DC that is the focus of our analysis in this paper.

The staff members at KGM-DC work with a politically and ethnically contested history, and with material that is both emotive and visceral; herein we frame this as *sensitive archive material*. Given the socio-political complexities of discussing the Rwandan Genocide, KGM also strives explicitly to work beyond the influence of the Rwandan Government, using international connections to foster *independence*, support their *international outreach*, and to remain entirely *self-funding* as a cultural institution [18].

RELATED WORK

We now contextualise our study within prior related work, addressing research of relevance to HCI researchers about the archiving of sensitive digital materials in relation to human rights media, within cultural institutions that have a global reach. It is this specific focus that sets our case study apart from the study of cultural institutions per se.

Some recent work in HCI and related fields has begun to address issues around working with politically and ethically sensitive materials. For example, memorialisation practices and 'end of life' issues have been explored in a variety of different settings [23]. Also emerging is work on post-conflict settings in which memorialisation and processes of reconciliation may play a part; indeed, this has been explored specifically in the Rwandan context [e.g. 24, 25, 34]. Other work has explored reconciliation around personal sensitive materials in a domestic-familial context [7]. Connecting these areas of focus is a broader developing concern within HCI to design for enduring *human values* [10]. This foregrounding of values is a complex endeavour that has raised critical reflection on issues of cultural specificity and stakeholder 'voice' in the research process [5]. We are mindful of such issues as we approach our work herein; in our case we consider how these issues are addressed not just within our research process (i.e. reflexively) but also within the organisational practices of KGM-DC, to inform HCI discourses on value in design and cultural engagement with sensitive materials.

Our study has also been informed by wider literatures on museum and cultural studies describing the curatorial challenges of speaking to multiple audiences about sensitive materials within international contexts. For example, complex issues of representation and authorial voice have been actively considered at the long-established holocaust memorial Yad Vashem in Jerusalem [19] and in relation to the Holocaust exhibition at the Imperial War Museum, London [13]. Within such literatures, questions about digital media representations of genocide, and the potential for providing online access to archival content, have also been addressed, for example, at centres such as the Shoah Foundation Institute in California [29].

Studies on the types of sensitive media content being handled by genocide archives also inform our work. We have reflected significantly on Yoo and colleagues' [34] exploration of potential user responses to genocide archives (e.g. The Voices from the Rwanda Tribunal project), and their consideration of the design challenges for such archives from a multi-generational perspective. Relatedly, KGM-DC also deals with sensitive video data. The core of the KGM-DC work is the production and representation of *survivor video testimony* (as opposed to external judicial perspectives in the aforementioned project [34]). Survivor video testimony is a genre of human rights media communication that is understood and reproduced globally [22], and which captures individual first-hand witness accounts for authenticity and the fostering of empathetic response in viewers [ibid]. Since its founding in 2004, KGM has produced original survivor testimony accounts in digital video format, and KGM's use of this media genre has been to no small degree informed by the established organisational practices of the Aegis Trust and the Shoah Foundation, alongside another institution that KGM works in partnership with, University of Texas Libraries (UTL) [17]. The particular archiving challenges presented by human rights documentation have been recently reported as insights from the KGM-UTL collaboration, focused around the UTL Human Rights Documentation Initiative (HRDI) [ibid]. These relate to the *preservation* of 'fragile' media from physical deterioration or political attack and associated trust and legacy issues that affect *access* [ibid]. Lack of expertise, infrastructure and economic resource reportedly present other challenges that shape the everyday archiving strategies being explored by KGM-UTL.

As Kelleher and colleagues point out [ibid], such organisational challenges reflect the wider growing importance of managing archives that employ digital representations of cultural artefacts. Debate within library and information studies has also sought to question the changing nature of archives, with concern for collection, management, access, and scholarly communication, within an international context and impacted by developments in digital networked technologies [29, 32]. For many institutions, digital resources and the endeavour to share broadly (often initially for scholarly purposes [32]) pose new problems of Digital Rights Management (DRM) yet to be adequately addressed [9]. Responses to this are an issue picked up by McLagan [22] who highlights the complex politics of 'branding' digital human rights media. But currently under-explored by Kelleher and others, is detail about *how* the appropriation of digital tools and resources by cultural institutions like KGM is actually being carried out to serve the humanitarian *values* of the institution.

In framing our study, we further highlight that KGM is a cultural institution currently *developing* its archiving practices, with support from key stakeholders: Aegis Trust and scholarly partners Shoah Foundation and UTL. We position KGM's archiving endeavour within a Rwandan socio-political agenda of reconciliation and transformation, mediated by technology development encapsulated in the Rwanda Vision 2020 report [27].

This positioning of KGM in dialogue with worldwide public audiences and scholarly networks means that our study findings may inform a discourse within HCI on ICT development and use in the context of transnational interactions and global processes [e.g. 6, 15, 21, 28]. Methodological critique within this discourse raises concern for 'Western' researchers' positioning with respect to working with participants in 'other' parts of the world such as Africa, and conceptual issues of cultural difference-making and spatial categorisation (e.g. Here and There, East and West, Global North and South) that may influence the study of phenomena like technology appropriation [21, 30]. Our study design and analysis has been informed by this critique, as we explain in the sections to follow.

APPROACH

We now describe our study design, the nature of the data we collected, and our analytic method for addressing the following research questions:

(1) *How is the Rwandan Genocide being captured and represented through KGM-DC's everyday archiving practices, supported by technology?*

(2) *What values are expressed through the work of the KGM-DC staff, supported by technology?*

Our objective through addressing these questions was to understand current practices at KGM-DC and how these were motivated and shaped by institutional values and endeavours, to identify *transferable* insights about working with human rights media in cultural institutions, and curatorial concerns for human rights media communication to public audiences and scholarly networks worldwide. In this paper, we use these insights to frame interaction design challenges for developing ICT to support these concerns.

Study Design

Our interdisciplinary project team, at the University of Nottingham, held diverse skills in computer science, interaction design, social psychology, economics, and genocide education. A teacher amongst our team had worked with KGM for many years, and visited the staff there on several prior occasions. Both KGM and Aegis had previously partnered with our University on research projects, and our study design was grounded by a scoping visit to KGM by a subset of the team, carried out six months prior (Mar. 2010), to make observational studies and to hold planning meetings with KGM staff. KGM was particularly motivated to partner with us because they were launching the KGM-DC at the time, and were keen to gain, in their words, an '*outsider perspective*', to help evaluate their developing work practices. Akin to the framing of their other 'international facing' partnerships with academic institutions (e.g. [17]), ours was also positioned as mutually beneficial, whereby deliverables included *pragmatic*, constructive results for real-world impact, and *reflexive* understandings for scholarship and learning. Mindful of the critical discourse on researchers' cultural positioning [e.g. 6, 15, 21], we made sense of stakeholder cultural dynamics within the particular communities of practice of KGM and our University. We were also aware of the ethical concerns of working with participants in a complex socio-political environment and reflexively examined the values implicated in their participation.

In many ways our approach echoes and is inspired by Friedman and colleagues' concerns for Value Sensitive Design (VSD) [5, 10]. VSD is a 'theoretically grounded approach to the design of technology that accounts for human values in a principled and comprehensive manner throughout the design process' [10, p. 348], placing analytic focus on: the values of research stakeholders, designers;

values that may be embedded in a given technology; understanding individuals as they live and act as citizens within society; and the pragmatic, ethically-sensitive goal of designing technology to better support human endeavour. These concerns were shared in our study but in alignment with a different methodological orientation: Experience-Centred Design (ECD) [33]. ECD is similarly phenomenological and pragmatic, but distinctly interpretative and exploratory, guided by an emphasis on empathic engagement and dialogical (i.e. self-other) interaction within the functioning of human relationships.

Recruiting at KGM

In consultation with Aegis and KGM directors about our aims (Dec. 2010), we were recommended to liaise with KGM managers of the three key departments (introduced above). All of our communications were in English as many of the KGM staff members had a good working knowledge of the language. We conducted introductory discussions with each of these managers via Skype (Jan.-Feb. 2010); they then facilitated communication with their departmental teams. Together with these contacts, we designed three focus groups to take place at KGM in Kigali, each relating to a department and attended by associated staff, at which our emerging understanding of KGM practices could be explored in depth. During our consultation process, the managers recommended we also conduct interviews with the KGM Director along with local representatives from a pan-African telecoms company to gain additional perspectives. The Documentation manager (Director of KGM-DC) also recommended a 'tour' of the facility for staff to discuss their work *in situ*.

Participants interviewed (for this paper) were all Rwandan nationals, aged 18-35, all Rwandan University graduates and members of the Genocide survivor community, except for the KGM-DC Archivist, a Canadian visitor with a background in Photography and Curation, and the British Aegis Director. All names reported below are pseudonyms.

Visiting KGM

Three members of our project team (the three authors of this paper) organised to visit KGM in Kigali for a week in March 2011, at a time to fit with KGM's preparations for the national commemoration period. We conducted three focus groups (Education team, n=4, 3hrs; Social Enterprise team n=3, 3hrs; Documentation team, n=12, 4hrs), a guided tour of the KGM-DC (n=5, 3hrs) and three face-to-face interviews (n=4, 2hrs each). We also spent several hours every day observing KGM visitors and staff and visited other memorials outside Kigali to contextualise (within national memorialisation activities) our experiences of visiting KGM. We each wrote field notes capturing our personal experiences in Rwanda, and collected video recordings of the focus groups and tour, along with photographs of the setting, media artefacts published by Aegis-KGM, and internal strategy documents. Following our visit we conducted a further interview with an Aegis director at the UK's Holocaust Centre [31] (n=1, 3hrs), to discuss our initial insights on the data collected at KGM.

On KGM-DC: Data Collection and Analysis

In this paper, we focus specifically on data collected during the KGM-DC tour and focus group. The way in which the KGM-DC team wished to engage with our research team, inviting the tour to take place alongside the focus group, was significant for how we chose to collect our data. For the tour, the staff members chose to present their archiving practices in the form of a workflow that engaged *individuals* at various points, each member describing what aspect of the workflow they were involved in and how. The focus group that followed engaged the wider KGM-DC team. Our participants sat alongside us on chairs in one of the meeting rooms at the centre, making for an informal setting in which we structured the discussion with open questions from a semi-structured interview schedule.

We used Interpretative Phenomenological Analysis (IPA) to make sense of our data [20]. This involved our individual coding of video recordings and interview transcripts for analysing: (i) the participants' voiced experiences and (ii) researcher-participant dialogue in the context of the study; and eliciting phenomenological themes. We then each selected data excerpts, representative of the themes relevant to our research questions, for further group analysis. We discussed multiple researcher interpretations to establish consensus, deriving higher-level themes illustrated with excerpts. Our emerging collective insights were grounded by insight from the previous KGM visit and other aspects of the broader study (e.g. other interviews). We now turn to report findings from our analysis, supported by data excerpts and incorporating accounts of some but not all of the KGM staff we engaged.

FINDINGS

This section is structured around three distinct but interdependent phenomenological themes, generated in our analysis, reflecting the curatorial concerns and values expressed to us by centre staff. We open with a description of the observed and reported practices at KGM-DC, to clarify contextual details within our account to follow.

Overview of the KGM-DC Practices

At the time of our visit, the KGM-DC video archive contained some 1800 records, of which only a small subset had been digitised and made available online. Staff explained how KGM-DC primarily films, produces and archives video testimony of Rwandan Genocide survivors. This collection is complemented by film (including VHS and reel-to-reel tapes) about the Genocide collected from elsewhere, and other physical materials (e.g. propaganda and letters) stored in a custom-built, climate-controlled facility – some of which is also being digitised.

Staff described the process of collecting video testimony. Categories of testimony had been iteratively developed (e.g. Victims, Perpetrators, Liberators, Children, Women) as the archive developed and in response to local need. Schedules for collection were systematically developed and then participants sought. Participants were often provided by local survivor associations, and screened for suitability by KGM-DC staff. Staff members were then sent to record testimony, often in a person's home or workplace.

Following testimony collection, the DV tapes were brought back to KGM-DC to be systematically logged and processed. Video was digitised, edited, tagged with meta-data (e.g. time and date of recording) and then comprehensively categorised and indexed with archival search terms. Once processed, the testimony was added to a Glifos Media Wiki content management system and made available online. The DV tapes were systematically packaged and sent to UTL for repeat hard copy backup, before being returned to be stored on site. The web hosting of the online archive was also served from UTL, to ensure preservation and maintenance of the online archive (with high-speed local access to the wiki served at KGM-DC).

In parallel, the physical archivist systematically processed physical media collected for or donated to the archive. She cleaned materials, asset-tagged and logged them, then systematically digitised them to sit alongside the videos on the media wiki, before safely storing all physical materials.

Legitimisation through personal testimony

We now consider the values held in, and experiences of, the activities and processes framed above. The first of our analytic themes reflects the considerable value placed upon using first hand accounts for structuring *authentic representations* of the genocide.

Producing quality testimony

KGM-DC staff member Simon described the screening process used to select suitable testimony candidates.

> "If you get 20 survivors, we can't go straight and start encoding, we have to go to see which one will give us a testimony, according to the quality or the content. After talking to someone who will give us a testimony, you can understand the quality of a testimony from him."

Discussion raised the assessment of 'quality testimony'. It was further suggested that quality might rest on a geographical basis: 'The quality of the testimony we can get from Murambi is not the same as we can get from say one sector in Kigali' (Simon), with areas such as Murambi being 'A key area where genocide has taken intensity' (Jean). Maurice argued that, for him, 'Each testimony is good quality', but then went on to point out how one might *need* to find thematically relevant testimonies. When asked how candidates were prioritised, the KGM-DC Director gave more detail on the processes that had driven data collection since KGM's founding: 'At the beginning we just said "Let's collect some oral testimonies" - we had a simple choice of those who wanted to share their testimonies'. He explained how selection had effectively been snowballed, by knowing something happened at a specific site and then *looking for* testimonies there, adding: 'We want *balance* and to make sure we are *covering the history* as much as possible, so that we see we are at least *covering different areas*'. In achieving this 'coverage' and 'balance' in the collection, the Director explained *how* some thematic choices were made. These could be driven by specific temporal events.

> "For example if we had a women's commemoration then we'd want to get different types of experiences. When we were collecting, we were saying 'Can we get some testimonies of widows, adults and children, can we get women who have lost children but still have a husband?' So we try to look at what would be the experiences among women."

Such events provided opportunities to develop the archive in diverse ways, broadening the scope of its representations and reflecting multiple aspects of survivor experience. This richer picture, staff explained, also made for the perceived quality of the archive. In describing a methodical testimony collection, staff expressed how 'quality' is about validity, which in turn concerned capturing the witnessing of authentic experience. They emphasised that understanding 'who' is *providing* the testimony and 'where they come from' is *as* important for determining quality as understanding 'who' is *producing* the testimony and *how*.

This sense of accountability in capturing content was carried through to the use of video-editing tools. When Jeremy talked about his editing work, he explained trying to make minimal edits to address production quality rather than reconstructing content: 'I do not cut pictures, just small things like if he is talking about something which is not corresponding with the video' or 'if the image is not good'. Editing was presented as a qualitative process required of Jeremy with significant implications for the archive's function within the wider institution, as the KGM Director conveyed when putting KGM-DC practices in the context of the top-level endeavours and departments.

> "Which is important? Which is not? What should we remove from this testimony, what should remain? What is teaching more? Which message do people like or will have most impact on our other things?"

Whilst Jeremy's video-editing process might imply the imposition of narrative, what emerged as significant in our discussions was staff desires to convey the importance of being *transparent* in their approach, and beyond question in their representation of the genocide experience whilst retaining maximum impact from the materials.

Subjectivity and staff commitment

The KGM Director described staff motivations for working at KGM-DC and the role of *survivors* in the curation process, framing the relationship of staff to the material.

> "People who are working on the archive - so heavy, heavy to them, they're - 80 per cent are survivors themselves, what other survivors talk about is their own experience, and this is not an easy job to do."

Given the difficult nature of the work, the Director was keen to highlight the value of having 'a team which is committed, which we really appreciate'. He suggested that staffing the KGM-DC with survivors had implications for the moral *weight* they'd feel to sustain the archiving work.

> "To sustain this project, there's an element of commitment. We are [as survivors] already victims of it. We care about it - we say, 'in order to

shape the *future of our children*, we have to remember, it's a commitment'. We are talking about genocide but we're also talking about their families, we are talking about them: they have seen it."

Not only did this personal connection bind staff to the complex and 'heavy' work they were doing, it seemingly lent an *authority* or legitimisation to their role in processing the archive material. On multiple levels then, survivor voice was presented as essential for communicating, representing, and memorialising the genocide. This was the case both in terms of the *content* and also the *staff*, positioned as survivors offering a personal, sustained 'commitment' to sensitively handling records. One might argue that such records are inherently subjective, but in this case personal experience was used to demonstrate the authenticity and veracity of the testimonial accounts.

To summarise, the theme on legitimisation to emerge from our study was embedded in expressed concerns for authenticity, veracity, commitment and expert management of materials, in a team with a strong collective identity.

Professionalism in an international scholarly network

Through the tour and discussions with staff, we gained insight into how the sensitive materials were indexed, stored and displayed. This archiving work was found to be *highly collaborative*, involving *considerable interpretation* of content by subject experts and *dialogical understanding* between the KGM-DC team and their scholarly partners.

Collaboration within a specialist team

KGM-DC staff described being intentionally cross-trained so as to better understand the *specialist collective process* of archiving the sensitive materials. Most staff supported and took part in others' job roles: 'everyone has something they *specialise* in but everyone tries to have an awareness of what everyone else does' (Canadian archivist, Robyn). One task that required an interesting combination of specialist input and collaboration was the work of indexing the video testimonies, as Jean demonstrated, showing us his process of indexing the testimony of a woman.

"We have here a thesaurus that we are using to ask topics, the keywords. At five minutes and 36 seconds she is talking about 'Discrimination and Persecution'. I listen to the content she is talking about and then I use those topics. 'Roadblocks' is a sub-topic, embedded within 'Discrimination and Persecution'."

Jean described how understanding the context in Kinyarwanda (the Rwandan language) was critical and this translation alongside the development of index terms was an ongoing process engaged through dialogue with Rwandan linguists, UTL and The Shoah Foundation. Pointing to a document on his desktop, Jean elaborated on the *active* interpretation involved in practice, *on his part*, by introducing a new term within the indexing job.

"This is a new term. This is it in Kinyarwanda [points], and then we will have to translate it in English and French as well. If it is better to use the keywords from UTL then it is okay, but if it is a context which is matching the new term we use the new term."

We found that ongoing dialogue between KGM-DC and international expert partners aimed to produce new shared understandings of the media content within a transnational and scholarly frame of reference. Jean said that this teamwork was being standardised through the development of a guideline document, which he would have checked by others: 'I will have to submit the draft to those guys at the Shoah Foundation.' The impact of employing such terms for structuring genocide representations is not to be underestimated, as stated in the draft guideline itself: 'Those terms shall be the real reflection of the events'. Overall, a strong theme to emerge from our discussions was that the processing of archive media was *entrusted* to a specialised team and its established partners. The KGM-DC Director was clear on the relationship with Aegis, UTL and Shoah as external partners: 'We approached them'.

Reaching for 'international standards'

Staff members were keen to demonstrate their professionalism and desire to conform to international standards, for engaging in scholarly communication worldwide. This endeavour was couched within a learning process as KGM-DC staff member, André, explained.

"Day to day we struggle to reach standards. So we may find that one of the videos is not very well done and then we have to work with it again, or we may find that one of the corresponding documents is missing some data and then we have to work on it again. So I think we are in this process of trying to improve, to reach the standard."

This 'reaching for standards' was addressed through the interest and respect with which staff oriented to international scholarly partners including UTL and Shoah, showing an openness to learn from their expertise. Jean conveyed this, emphasising day-to-day team collaboration in the learning trajectory: 'We have always to call on UT archivists to help us because they are more experienced than us; over time we have been receiving supportive comments from UT; and we support each other to make a significant improvement'. Adoption of tools such as Glifos and Final Cut Pro, recommended by these experts but adopted and appropriated at KGM-DC, were supporting professional development to achieve digital literacy and self-empowerment, as Jeremy conveyed: 'I believe that by using those tools we are getting aware that we can do more'. As Jean added: 'Our ability to use those kinds of technologies has been evolving over time'. Robyn pointed out that developing this archive presented a new challenge for all involved, including partners, to pioneer ways of working: 'basically we started out with new staff, new technology, new concepts; as our collection grew so did our knowledge of what we were doing'.

We further observed, through descriptions of the systematic media back-ups on their partners' servers, that the process of international standardisation connected with KGM's endeavour to remain independent and sustainable within Rwanda. André clarified how UTL's remote access from abroad helped secure data storage: 'They can enter our network; whenever there is a problem we can give them access to our network'. Overall, the endeavour to *store* and *sustain* the media archive was being achieved through international networks and shared standards of scholarship.

Making human contact through digital resources

The third theme to emerge from our analysis centred on the core KGM endeavour, to promote genocide prevention to global audiences, using the KGM-DC media on Internet-enabled platforms to engage 'as many people as possible' (KGM Director) with the humanitarian cause. We now discuss the value that KGM-DC staff placed on Internet-enabled media communication when describing their work.

Web media communication to promote and sustain KGM

The KGM website [18] and related genocide archive [11] were described to us as important and effective means of communicating with international public audiences, including scholars, public interest groups and the Rwandan diaspora. In Maurice's words: 'It's good to have technology to reach out to people who are far away from us'. And Simon: 'There is an advantage in the website of letting people around the world "visit", to help them know about what happened in Rwanda'.

Engaging public audiences at a distance was found also to be an important mechanism for *sustaining the archive*, keeping KGM-DC operating. The reach of the web presence helped the centre gain forms of charitable support and visibility from outside Rwanda that, in turn enabled other humanitarian endeavours to be economically sustained *at the centre* (e.g. social enterprise, genocide education), coordinated within the Aegis partnership. As Maurice said of the audiences: 'We want people to commit'. One example of this is a web-based international student network, Aegis Students [1], that organises charitable work *in Rwanda* (Discover Rwanda) alongside campaigning for donations; on this site, KGM-DC media was being used to galvanise this student community into social action in Rwanda. Such social enterprises were described as having a significant local impact within survivor communities, and galvanising long-term commitment and interest from international visitors.

Indeed, whilst valuing the web presence, we found the unanimous staff view was that online visitor *engagement* was not 'complete' until people physically visited the centre. Simon said: 'There is a big difference; someone who visits the centre can feel more emotion, can talk with us about the archive face-to-face'. Staff personally placed greatest value on *face-to-face* interaction for fostering empathetic understanding about survivor experiences. Thus, remote, virtual engagement was considered to be a prompt to visiting Rwanda to experience, first hand, the impact of the genocide events *as the Rwandan people present them, live them, and memorialise them*.

Robyn foregrounded tensions on framing interpretation for online audiences.

> "One of the issues with this publically accessible website and this type of material is the type of context with which you're accessing it. Being around the Documentation Centre and the team here gives people a more comprehensive understanding of the history."

André explained that, at the time of our study, the KGM-DC actually received 'very few visitors in person'. Reflecting on this, he highlighted the potential role of the online media to encourage *more* visiting in person.

We found a desired close link between the endeavour to sustain engagement through web resources, and endeavours to sustain local survivor communities and the genocide prevention message worldwide. The KGM Director emphasised that, as members of the survivor community, his staff had a *personal* stake in this.

> "You can stop genocide physically, but, from my experience, genocide from survivors is given to children, like trauma is transmitted. We are already victims. So this is why *we* should teach the world this message."

Hence the local-global outlook on human rights media curation at KGM-DC is linked to: the expressed value in creating online communities of interest for promoting awareness and social action; and the central importance of human contact for 'complete' understanding and impact.

Tensions on public, Internet-enabled dialogue

This sense of the incompleteness of 'remote visiting' expressed by staff was found to raise questions about the public accessibility of the archive and its processes for display, and to what extent aspects of the archiving work should be opened up to involve those outside of the specialist KGM-DC team.

The role of the online archive for *financially sustaining* the centre remained a tricky issue, as Robin explained, raising a question about public 'openness' online: 'Whilst it's currently open to everyone it may not stay that way; whilst the collection is important for everyone, it's a very specialised collection'; as a point of comparison, 'look at the Shoah Foundation's collection, you can't just access it'.

On the one hand, dialogue with the Internet-enabled public was valued for developing tools and curatorial practices. Maurice explained why staff welcomed emails from website visitors and were 'open' to their thoughts.

> "It's always good and meaningful to interact with our visitors, to know their questions and impressions. This is all new to us. We are open to everything: comments, questions, critique. It is very sensitive data we are making online. We always have to be careful."

Maurice implied that this email dialogue was important for 'carefully' gauging the sensitivities of others. He explained that his team were recording statistics about their web audiences and inviting feedback, as part of their endeavour to develop best practices: 'Of course we are interested to see where people come from, and know the feedback from them to help improve our job and output'.

On the other hand, the suggestion of *live* public dialogue within a web forum was met with considerable trepidation. This was explicitly because of the sensitive nature of the materials being presented and the complex socio-political environment of Rwanda, as Robyn further explained.

> "A public forum is not possible with this kind of subject matter, that can get very complicated very quickly. There are a lot of people out there who have wrong intentions. If you're talking about narrative and

discourse, there are different perspectives on Rwandan history. People could misuse the information."

Concern was expressed about this kind of dynamic dialogue and the misappropriation of the sensitive material.

Similar concerns were expressed when considering opening up media *classification* to those outside the team, especially those with local knowledge. Robyn described the *potential* of this for assisting the challenging work of interpreting photographic material in the physical archive: 'At the moment it's just us doing it, however with the website we're going to encourage people to submit information if they recognise the place or people, or when it was taken, or if they took it'. But further discussion revealed tensions; some staff members were against the idea of the public classifying this media because of, again, complexities associated with the risk of malicious misappropriation.

The sense of legitimacy associated with the personal identities of archive workers also carried with it implications for opening up the task of *capturing* archive data to others who do not work at the KGM-DC, and different processes of collection. Conscious that the centre had started associating digital media with GPS information indicating 'where' a photographic referent was captured [11], we asked the KGM-DC team what they thought about further leveraging location-based computing to input data into the archive *in-situ*. Jean immediately pointed to potential problems of 'controlling' this data and its subsequent use: 'Who has control over who uploads?' 'What control do you have on that picture about who can see that picture?' Simon added: 'We can have people who add information in a *negative* way'. Maurice advocated this kind of tool for exclusive use by the KGM-DC team.

"I think the problem my colleagues raised, is mainly about making our system open and dynamic. But I think it could be interesting if we use it *within* the Documentation Centre as a team. If we send people around the country to go where mass killings happened during the genocide, and take a nice smart--phone, take pictures, write some description, and immediately associate that point with those data, it can really work and be really helpful. But, at this stage in our history, we don't know if we can make it *open* and *dynamic*."

In turn, we asked the team how they felt instead about 'displaying' the material at the site of its capture. Robyn replied: 'I think that's much more applicable'.

To summarise: in balancing the desires for outreach with trust and control, in terms of both communicating the humanitarian message and collecting and handling material for the archive, there was much tension amongst KGM-DC staff around the notion of public involvement.

DISCUSSION

We now turn to reflect upon our findings (mindful of our 'outsider perspective' and the ethical weight of the subject matter), to address our research objectives and to make sense of our participants' voiced curatorial concerns for HCI researchers interested in working with cultural institutions on archiving sensitive materials within a global frame. We open with an interpretative summary of how value and meaning is attributed in the KGM-DC archiving work, as voiced by the staff. This serves to contextualise two further discussion points, on how key archiving endeavours are pursued. In this discussion, we reflect on issues of cultural specificity and stakeholder voice to inform HCI discourses on Value Sensitive Design and cultural engagement with sensitive materials, and to frame interaction design challenges for supportive ICT.

The Currency of Witnessing in Human Rights Media

Our research team reflected that the personal identity of KGM-DC workers as survivors, and the team's collective identity as a survivor community, was integral to the *identity of the archive*. Survivor identity and experience was found to have great currency, not only within the testimony genre, but also in terms of its production. This afforded the team the ability to approach and empathise with testimony subjects in their communities, and know how to recruit to capture and represent survivors' voices. This empathetic 'closeness' to the subject was found to centrally inform the myriad of value judgments and decisions on the production process, largely making up the team's specialist expertise to understand what makes for 'quality testimony' and deliver impactful human rights media. Moreover, the staff members' survivor experience *legitimised* them in their effort, and afforded them a sense of authorial control over the archive in its development.

We have used this understanding to help frame the team's voiced curatorial concerns for two digitally mediated endeavours: (i) *Dialogue with scholarly experts*; and (ii) *Dialogue with public audiences*.

Trusted Human Relationships in the Scholarly Network

We found that the KGM-DC staff greatly valued their collaborations with external scholarly experts (e.g. Shoah, UTL), for understanding how to develop their archive to meet international standards. We have conceptualised these partnerships in terms of a dialogue through which shared understandings are generated about how to construct a genocide archive that is accessible to multiple audiences worldwide. We relate this endeavour to Thorin's notion of scholarly communication: dialogue encompasses 'the processes by which scholars communicate with each other as they create new knowledge' [32, p. 221]. Developing the KGM-DC archive presented a *unique*, transnational context for the creation of new knowledge, requiring original and highly specialised processes to be *pioneered*. KGM-DC staff developed a *trust relationship* with their partners over time as they adopted, appropriated and developed skills and resources. Networked IT systems afforded this dialogical process of developing the archive to take place at a distance as an active, ongoing endeavour.

Making sense of these scholarly processes, we note that the network of developing knowledge is necessarily small and closed. Furthermore, the *human relationship* in the network seems to be of crucial importance; KGM required the development of a secure, trusted scholarly community for bringing shared values and ethics to the handling of sensitive materials. We suggest that this requirement may, at times, sit *in tension* with the institutional aspirations to foster international collaborations and connections for visibility, accessibility, and financial sustainability. Thorin emphasises that in the uncertain landscape of digital archiving and curation, research communities need to find 'trusted and enduring organizations' to 'preserve' data and make it 'available', mindful that, with what technology affords them, 'scholars are now beginning to expect that they will be able to move these digital materials into their own digital surroundings and modify them for use in their research and teaching' [32, p. 238]. Networked systems afford easy access and the potential for rapid dissemination and re-appropriation of media (e.g. channelisation); in relation to sensitive archive materials this then requires that curatorial control reside in the *trusted human contact*.

This reflection frames a broader interaction design challenge to address how cultural institutions handling sensitive materials may extend their scholarly network within the 'transnational imagination' [21] whilst managing the pragmatics of multi-site curation. This may involve considering how web technologies are leveraged by archivists to support the development of trusted networks of collaborators, for dynamically developing best practices between cultural institutions that may be operating in different countries or at a distance. Reflecting on this challenge also prompts consideration of DRM [9] and models of data storage that enable the virtualisation of archive records and their mirroring to facilitate sharing through trusted networks, whilst ensuring the maintenance and longevity of collections. We may ask: How could interfaces to these networked systems be designed to reflect and leverage the significance of the trusted human contact?

Guardianship of Archive and Humanitarian Message

As a survivor community, the KGM-DC team's collective identity arguably extends to incorporate the archive. In our observations, the team oriented to the archive more as *guardians* than curators, to facilitate the communication of the preserved archive materials rather than reinterpret them. It appeared that, for the staff, there were very real and emotive risks of working in a post-conflict setting with a fragile stability and a cultural preoccupation with a living and contested history. Fears about others misappropriating archive materials mean that approaches to opening up the archive to public audiences (in terms of consumption and production) are met with trepidation. At the same time, the benefits of engaging with multiple audiences worldwide to sustain the archive and spread the humanitarian message are held as core institutional endeavours. This tension raises broader curatorial challenges, such as how to support public dialogue around sensitive archive materials whilst keeping the curated message intact.

Such concerns point to an interesting interaction design challenge around the use of web platforms to support public engagement with sensitive archive materials whilst fostering and supporting empathetic connection to the cause, to do the contextualisation work that face-to-face contact has traditionally been used for. A key design challenge is that this may need to be done without disrupting other endeavours (such as creating visitor footfall to the institution) that may be valued. An intriguing additional challenge is to consider how designers may leverage empathetic engagement with curators online to directly encourage face-to-face contact rather than replace it, as this may be considered crucial for 'proper' communication and cultural engagement with the materials.

We also further reflected upon how we, as UK researchers, had positioned the voice of our participants in our analysis, and felt that this positioning had relevance for the VSD agenda within HCI research. Recent HCI research on sensitive archive materials in the Rwandan context has suggested developing systems to *support diverse cultural values* and accommodate the appropriation of materials by different cultural groups [34]. In part this stance seems to suggest a tendency towards the 'universal' value principles critiqued by Borning and Muller [5]. Borning and Muller's position appears to be one of pluralism, suggesting that at times the interaction designer must choose and respond to a set of values amongst competing alternatives. Sensitised by our ECD approach [33], we present herein an empirical example of this kind of instance – and choice point – for design. In the context of handling sensitive materials at KGM-DC, given the relationship between the staff as members of the survivor community and the archive materials, it seems problematic to suggest that diverse cultural values could be supported through ICT design for this institution, when the potential for appropriation of materials by those with differing and potentially opposing values is considered to be of serious concern. Interaction designers working with this community to develop ICT support to the archive would need to acknowledge the specificity of the cultural values at play within it.

CONCLUSION

In this paper we have reported on a case study of human rights media archiving at KGM-DC in Rwanda, motivated by our interest in ICT support to memorialisation practices and focusing herein on curatorial concerns for establishing public and scholarly communication around sensitive materials. Identifying as researchers in a scholarly partnership with centre staff, we have utilised our 'outsider perspective' to make sense of how the Genocide is being captured and represented, and what values are expressed by the staff in describing their work. We have been judicious in our account to respect sensitivities surrounding discussion of this Genocide and to emphasise our interpretative stance, elucidating transferable insights relevant for CHI about curatorial concerns and interaction design challenges to support the communication of human rights media for global public and scholarly audiences.

Significantly, we have framed two potential challenges for interaction design: (1) to support the development of trusted networks of partners at a distance that centre on and leverage human capital and human dialogue; (2) to develop web platforms that enhance cultural engagement with an archive's contents by supporting empathetic interaction with its 'guardians' in furtherance of contextualising sensitive materials to enhance curatorial control.

In exploring this subject matter, our paper has also sought to reflect on and contribute to an HCI discourse on Value Sensitive Design (VSD), by offering an empirical case example that illustrates tensions on the universal versus pluralistic positioning of ICT designers about 'value', in efforts to support forms of community and cultural engagement that may be ethically and politically sensitive.

ACKNOWLEDGMENTS

This work was funded by RCUK through the Horizon Digital Economy Research grant (EP/G065802/1). We wish to sincerely thank our partners the Aegis Trust and KGM for their support, our participants for their invaluable time and insight, and Rolf Wiesemes, Tom Rodden, Derek McAuley and Bob Anderson for their helpful advice.

REFERENCES

1. Aegis Students. http://www.aegisstudents.org
2. Aegis Trust. http://www.aegistrust.org
3. Appadurai, A. *Globalisation and the research imagination.* Oxford: Blackwell, 1999.
4. Bell, G. *Making sense of museums: the museum as a cultural ecology*. Intel Corp. Technical Report, 2002.
5. Borning, A. and Muller, M. Next steps for value sensitive design. In *Proc. CHI 2012*, ACM Press (2012), 1125-1134
6. Burrell, J. and Anderson, K. I have great desires to look beyond my world: trajectories of information and communication technology use among Ghanians living abroad. *New Media Society* (2008), 10:203.
7. Clarke, R., Wright, P., Balaam, M., et al. Digital Portraits: Photo-sharing after Domestic Violence. In *Proc. CHI 2013*, ACM Press (2013), 429-438.
8. Countries by GDP per capita http://bit.ly/193E8H
9. Fetsherein, M. Present State and Emerging Scenarios of Digital Rights Management Systems. *The Int. Journal on Media Management*. 4, 3 (2002), 164-171.
10. Friedman, B., Kahn, P. H., Borning, A. Value Sensitive Design and Information Systems. In Zhang, P. and Galletta, D. (Eds) *Human-Computer Interaction in Management Information Systems: Foundations*. M.E. Sharpe, Inc: NY (2006) 348—372.
11. Genocide Archive Rwanda. http://www.genocidearchiverwanda.org.rw
12. Global Development Horizons 2011: Multi-polarity – The New Global Economy. *World Bank Publications*. http://econ.worldbank.org
13. Hoskins A. Signs of the Holocaust: exhibiting memory in a mediated age. *Media, Culture and Society*, (2003) 25: 7–22
14. Human Rights Watch. Law and Reality: Progress in Judicial Reform in Rwanda. *Human Rights Watch Reports*. (2008) http://bit.ly/16eD2os
15. Irani, L., Vertesi, J., Dourish, P. et al. Postcolonial computing: a lens on design and development. In *Proc. CHI 2010*, ACM Press (2010) 1311-1320.
16. Keene, S. Digital collections: museums and the information age. Oxford: Routledge, 1998.
17. Kelleher, C., Sangwand, T., Wood, K. et al. The Human Rights Documentation Initiative at the University of Texas Libraries. *New Review of Information Networking* 15: (2010), 94-109.
18. Kigali Genocide Memorial. http://www.kigalimemorialcentre.org
19. Krakover, S. The Holocaust Remembrance Site of Yad Vashem Welcomes Visitors. *Int. Research in Geographical and Environmental Education*. 11:4 (2002), 359-362.
20. Langdridge, R. *Phenomenological Psychology: Theory, Research and Method.* London: Pearson, 2007.
21. Lindtner, S., Anderson, K. and Dourish, P. Cultural appropriation: information technologies as sites of transnational imagination. In *Proc. CSCW 2012*. ACM Press (2012), 77-86.
22. McLagan, M. Principles, Publicity, and Politics: Notes on Human Rights Media. *American Anthropologist* 105(3): (2003), 605-612.
23. Massimi, M., Odom, W., Banks, R. et al. Matters of life and death: locating the end of life in lifespan-oriented HCI research. In *Proc. CHI 2011*. ACM Press (2011), 987-996.
24. Nathan, L. P. and Friedman, B. Interacting with Policy in a Political World: Reflections from the Voices from the Rwanda Tribunal Project. *interactions* 17, 5, (2010) 56-59.
25. Nathan, L. P., Lake, M., Carden Grey, N., et al. Multi-lifespan Information System Design: Investigating a New Design Approach in Rwanda. In *Proc. iConference 2011*. ACM Press (2011), 591-597.
26. Prunier, G. *The Rwanda Crisis: History of a Genocide*. New York: Columbia University Press, 1995.
27. Rwanda Vision 2020. http://bit.ly/niwUQW
28. Sriram, C. L., King, J.C., Mertus, J.A., et al. (Eds.) *Surviving Field Research: working in violent and difficult situations.* New York: Routledge, 2000.
29. Solanilla, L. The Internet as a Tool for Communicating Life Stories: a New Challenge for 'Memory Institutions'. *Int. Journal of Intangible Heritage*. 3 (2008) 103-116.
30. Taylor, A. S. Out there. In *Proc. CHI 2011*. ACM Press (2011) 685-694.
31. The Holocaust Centre. http://holocaustcentre.net
32. Thorin, S. Global Changes in Scholarly Communication. In H. S. Ching, P. W. T. Poon and C. McNaught (Eds.), *eLearning and Digital Publishing,* (2006) 221–240.
33. Wright, P. & McCarthy, J. *Experience-centred Design: Designers, Users and Communities in Dialogue*. San Rafael: Morgan and Claypool, 2010.
34. Yoo, D., Lake, M., Nilsen, T. et al. Envisioning Across Generations: A Multi-lifespan Information System for International Justice in Rwanda. In *Proc. CHI 2013.* ACM.

Protibadi: A Platform for Fighting Sexual Harassment in Urban Bangladesh

Syed Ishtiaque Ahmed,
Steven J. Jackson
Information Science
Cornell University, Ithaca, NY
{sa738, sjj54}@cornell.edu

Nova Ahmed
ECE, North South University
Dhaka, Bangladesh
nova@northsouth.edu

Hasan Shahid Ferdous,
Md. Rashidujjaman Rifat,
A.S.M Rizvi,
Shamir Ahmed,
Rifat Sabbir Mansur
CSE, BUET
Dhaka, Bangladesh
help.protibadi@gmail.com

ABSTRACT
Public sexual harassment has emerged as a large and growing concern in urban Bangladesh, with deep and damaging implications for gender security, justice, and rights of public participation. In this paper we describe an integrated program of ethnographic and design work meant to understand and address such problems. For one year we conducted surveys, interviews, and focus groups around sexual harassment with women at three different universities in Dhaka. Based on this input, we developed "*Protibadi*", a web and mobile phone based application designed to report, map, and share women's stories around sexual harassment in public places. In August 2013 the system launched, user studies were conducted, and public responses were monitored to gauge reactions, strengths, and limits of the system. This paper describes the findings of our ethnographic and design-based work, and suggests lessons relevant to other HCI efforts to understand and design around difficult and culturally sensitive problems.

Author Keywords
Sexual Harassment; ICTD; HCI4D; Bangladesh; Ethnography; Postcolonial Computing; Design

ACM Classification Keywords
H.1.2. Human Factors

INTRODUCTION
The sexual harassment of women is an extensively investigated and intensively treated social problem around

CHI 2014, April 26 - May 01 2014, Toronto, ON, Canada

ACM 978-1-4503-2473-1/14/04…$15.00.
http://dx.doi.org/10.1145/2556288.2557376

the globe [26, 28, 30]. It occurs in multiple forms and locations, from domestic violence inside the home to more generalized patterns of harassment in public places. Street harassment constitutes a form of sexual discrimination and violence that includes verbal and nonverbal behaviors ranging from whistles, leers, and winks to unwanted physical contact, catcalls, and sexually suggestive remarks [18, 38]. The experience of street harassment undermines women's security and well-being along with freedoms of choice, action, and participation in public life that are core to the basic civil and political rights of every human being [4]. It also has potentially important group-level effects: by limiting or discouraging access to public space, street harassment can serve as an additional mechanism by which women's voices and participation are silenced. While much literature and media attention has focused on more extreme forms of sexual violence (rape, domestic abuse, etc.), a growing body of work [11, 18, 23] suggests that the chronic and pervasive effects of street harassment can be just as damaging to women's security, freedom, and participation in public life.

Because the causes, effects, and basic cultural understandings of street harassment differ radically around the world, it is hard to reliably estimate its prevalence or effects. This is particularly true in locations like urban Bangladesh, where interpretations of sexual harassment are diverse and highly contested, and where few reliable mechanisms for the reporting of street harassment exist. According to local crime reports, 4,853 incidents of violence against women took place in Dhaka from October 2011 to September 2012, including 993 recorded incidents of rape. This almost certainly vastly understates the problem however, as anecdotal evidence from local newspapers [12], international media reports [36], comparative experience and our own ethnographic work suggests that incidents of sexual violence are routinely underreported, perhaps especially in the pervasive culture of shame that surrounds such incidents in Bangladesh. Indeed, many of the forms of street harassment targeted here are not considered crimes and reportable to Police in the Bangladeshi context. But these incidents can make a very deep psychological and social impact upon the victims, and can lead to isolation, depression, and even suicide, as found in a recent study by *Nahar et al.* [24].

Designing technology-based interventions services for a developing country like Bangladesh is often challenged by limited public access to electronic devices and the Internet, as previously reported in the ICTD literature [5, 21]. In recent years however Bangladesh has seen one of the fastest growing cellular networks in the world, with more than 96% of the population now under mobile coverage. The number of Internet users is also growing fast, the largest portion of whom use cell phones to access the Internet [2]. This suggests that mobile phone based applications might contribute to ameliorate deep-seated problems of gender violence, discrimination, and inequality in Bangladesh today. In this paper we report our experience in designing and developing mobile phone and web-based applications to support women experiencing and fighting street harassment in urban Bangladesh. We also reflect on broader challenges confronting HCI efforts to understand and design around difficult and culturally sensitive problems in the gender and ICT for development space.

BACKGROUND AND LITERATURE REVIEW

A growing body of HCI work has explored the nature of computational practice and design in non-western and post-colonial contexts. Much of this work – identified sometimes under the HCI for Development ('HCI4D') or Information and Communication Technology for Development ('ICT4D') labels – has followed an interventionist and design-oriented agenda, seeking to apply new computational tools and approaches to a series of social problems (poverty, hunger, inequality, governance, public health, etc.) confronting targeted programs of social and economic change, often in 'developing country' contexts. In many instances, such interventions target widely shared and relatively uncontroversial collective goals (even where preferred avenues to change may vary). As a low cost and increasingly prevalent system of communication, mobile phone technologies have been central and promising players in many of these interventions, supporting a wide and growing range of design interventions targeted at the problems of vulnerable individuals and communities, ranging from urban sex workers and taxi drivers, to homeless young people and farmers [9, 26, 27, 29, 32, 39].

But these early forays have also revealed, sometimes by tripping on them, a number of distinct challenges facing design-based HCI work in this space. 'Universal' principles of design may turn out to be anything but conflicting with locally held aesthetics, metaphors, and assumptions [22]. Taken for granted infrastructures ranging from reliable power supply to stable systems of law and governance may be absent, undermining design or project-level efforts [10]. Expectations around user or community engagement may differ, dictating new modes of engaging local actors. And the fault lines and divisions of local culture and power may be misunderstood, leading to non-adoption, suspicion, or simple indifference to HCI design and system-building efforts [17].

These complexities only multiply when the matters of collective concern at the heart of HCI interventions are themselves unsettled and subject to ongoing processes of cultural negotiation, contestation, and dissent. Under such conditions, HCI work confronts a deeply agonistic field in which basic cultural propositions are being worked out in conjunction with the design and use of tools and systems themselves, and the deeply value-laden nature of HCI intervention emerges with particular force and clarity. As discussed later, this complicates the process while raising the stakes of ethnographic fieldwork and design, and poses challenging questions around the positionality of HCI research and researchers vis-à-vis the worlds they engage.

Such insights are central to a growing body of theoretical work in the feminist [3, 6, 18] and post-colonial [17] HCI space, along with several of the specific design methodologies (e.g., adversarial design [10]) meant to reflect and accommodate these principles. As this work makes clear, design and ethnographic interventions often (always?) occur against the backdrop of cultural currents that run deeper than our typical instruments for producing understanding and explanations of the world we engage can plumb. This fact becomes all the more true as we move towards interventionist modes of engagement, and towards spaces of deep cultural contestation and dissent. Responsibility in this space cannot be discharged or avoided behind a simple instrumentalist stance. Nor can it be decided by reassuring reference to a world of user or system needs decided 'out there,' according to reliable and uncontroversial social processes from which we remain somehow disconnected. Rather, the fields of feminist and critical HCI4D are likely to occupy fundamentally agonistic spaces, in which HCI researchers are necessarily implicated. In such a world, the principles of pluralism, participation, advocacy, embodiment, self-disclosure and ecological awareness characterizing feminist and many post-colonial research stances become simultaneously more important and more complicated to practice [3, 17, 18].

Beyond such theoretical insights, our project also learned from design-based HCI interventions that have sought to deal with problems of gender violence and discrimination through the development of systems and applications designed to improve women's safety, security, and freedom of movement in public space. Work by *Satchell et al.*, for example, has investigated the potential for mobile technology to help users manage their personal safety concerns in the city at night [33, 34]. They found that mobile devices may provide users with a sense of security and real time protection via connectivity to closely co-located persons, and that mobile social networking systems are not only integral for bringing people together, they can help in the process of users safely dispersing as well.

Other works have sought to raise awareness around problems of public sexual harassment similar to the ones tackled here. One such initiative is "*Hollaback!*" [16], an initiative to raise awareness through grassroots photo-blogging and public documentation of harassment (and harassers). Through the system, now operating in 25 countries and in 12 different languages, users post photographs and narrative accounts of individual encounters with offenders. Another noteworthy initiative is "*Harassmap*" [14], a volunteer-based initiative with a mission to end the social acceptability of sexual harassment in Egypt. In this system, women can report of any harassment they experience or observe around them through mobile phones or the website. There are still other mobile applications that have been built to offer support to victims or potential victims of sexual harassment. For example, the app "*Circle of Six*" [6], allows women to call friends with pre-programmed texts, which can alert them in real-time to problems or incidents that may be occurring. "*On Watch*" [25] forwards a GPS coordinate to friends if a situation goes bad.

Our study builds on these insights and design approaches while extending them to problems of public sexual harassment in Bangladesh. The paper that follows describes our efforts to understand the forms, prevalence, and experiences of public sexual harassment in urban Bangladesh. We communicated with university-aged women through written and online questionnaires and face-to-face interviews and focus groups in order to better understand the prevalence and impact of public sexual harassment, and source the women's own ideas about possible systems and applications that might help. On the basis of this input, we designed "*Protibadi*" (a Bangla word meaning "one who protests"), a system that allows women to quickly inform emergency contacts when situations of harassment occur, document the location and nature of incidents, and enter descriptive blogs and narratives that share the experience of sexual harassment in a collective way. We conclude with reflections on distinctive challenges confronting HCI research and design interventions around culturally sensitive problems in the gender and ICT for development space.

FIELD STUDY

We began our work with a three-part field study designed to develop a better understanding of the prevalence, severity, and consequences of sexual harassment among female university students in Dhaka. Our choice of university women was dictated by three basic factors. First, most of them had access to technology like mobile phones and Internet, and so were more obvious first targets for an experimental system that made use of such tools. Second, in large part because of their education and socioeconomic standing, university women in Dhaka are often more attuned to problems of gender discrimination and sexual harassment, and more receptive to systems that combat it. Finally, as the inclusion of university-educated women in public life is often identified as a step towards gender participation and equality more generally, their exclusion from public space and participation through instances of harassment may be particularly insidious and damaging to the broader goals of gender equity and participation in public life. The decision to focus the study in this way poses obvious limits to the generalizability of the findings and designs that result. We hope to address these through additional study and future iterations of the system.

Online Survey

At the outset of our study, we wanted to develop a broad understanding of the forms and prevalence of sexual harassment as experienced by our target group. We made and circulated a small online questionnaire for university students asking if they had any direct or indirect experience of being harassed in a public place, and if they had witnessed such events. The participants could respond to this survey anonymously. We shared the link to this survey through the Facebook groups of three different universities and requested students to participate in the survey. We received 121 responses, including from 51 women and 42 men (the remainder did not disclose their gender). Following the survey, 7 women and 2 men contacted the investigators individually and shared additional information via email, telephone conversation, or face-to-face meetings. Every female respondent reported direct or indirect experience of being harassed in public places, with 32 saying they had experienced such harassment more than once. All of the participants said that they had seen women harassed before them in public places. Broken down by location, 72 participants reported incidents of harassment that took place in public vehicles (e.g., buses), 21 reported harassment while walking on public streets, and 30 reported incidents that took place in public gatherings such as rallies or concerts. All of the respondents identified public sexual harassment as a common and damaging experience of contemporary life in urban Bangladesh. As one woman wrote,

"You *will hardly find any Bangladeshi girl who traveled on the streets and has not experienced sexual harassment. Some women are brave enough to talk about it, while others remain silent for many reasons.*"

Another respondent explained the impact of such activities:

"Everyday I walk in the park. My mother often comes with me but at a much slower pace. When I am alone, some boys at the park laugh at me, tease me. I say nothing. I want to keep walking. Sometimes I can ignore them, sometimes I cry alone at my room. It's not my dress – I wear a hijab (Islamic head scarf), it's just me being a female."

Focus Group Discussion

Next we arranged a focus group discussion conducted by a female faculty member at one of our three participating universities. To organize this, we sought help from a volunteer organization named "*Community Action*", which issued invitations to female students at the three universities to participate. The discussion took place in a closed room in one of these three universities. Thirteen women participated in the focus group, which lasted for about three hours.

The women in the discussion shared their difficulties and deep feelings of anger and vulnerability around sexual harassment, and identified three public situations in which they found themselves most vulnerable: i) public buses, ii) crowds in markets and concerts, and 3) lonely or isolated places after dark. Although it was an oral discussion, some women found it too difficult to speak about these experiences, and preferred instead to write them down, which were then handed to the female faculty member who was conducting the discussion. One of the women, for example, shared the following experience:

"*The more I was moving towards the window in a public bus, the more that man beside me was pushing me with his legs and then he put his hand on my lap. I asked him to behave several times. He was not listening to me and was pushing me more and at that point, I slapped him.*"

The women described not only how badly they were treated in public places, but also spoke about painful incidents in which relatives or friends had harassed them. This brought out strong feelings of shame, sadness, and regret, but also defiance, anger, and a strong resolve towards change. As one participant explained, *"My mother taught me to stay quiet. But I will ask my daughter to carry a knife."*

One-on-One Interviews

Next we conducted semi-structured interviews of women at the three universities. Due to participant sensitivity, the interviews were conducted in private in the offices of female faculty members associated with the study. The interviewers asked the women about their understandings and experiences of sexual harassment, and their priorities for any design intervention that might address such problems. Participants were invited through paper flyers posted on university notice boards, and through advertisements at different student groups on Facebook. A total of 11 women responded, 9 opting to speak with the faculty member at their own university and 2 requesting an interviewer from a university other than their own.

Ten women participated from two of the three universities, five from each. Only one woman participated from the third university before the study was halted there for reasons described below. In general, however, participation was low across all three universities. Many women responded and set up a time for the interviews, but did not show up. In some cases, the women came and started talking to the interviewers, but then became uncomfortable and left in the middle of the interview. In such instances and at the request of the participants, notes and recordings were destroyed and no further record was retained. In one case, two women came together and one helped the other to tell her story. In some instances, participants refused to be audio-recorded, so the interviewers took hand-notes. In one case, a participant agreed to be interviewed and recorded, but asked that recordings and notes from the session not be shared with male members of the study team. All such requests were honored, and recorded interviews were subsequently translated, transcribed and analyzed by two independent coders, both of them native Bangla speakers.

Our participants offered different definitions of sexual harassment, some very broad and others more precise. One participant explained for example that

"*By 'Sexual Harassment' I understand any sort of activities or words that force me to feel that I am a girl even before I am a human being. It can also be true for boys, too. In these cases, we get a stronger feeling of being 'boys' or 'women' than being human beings. When these feelings are created inside me in a negative way – that is sexual harassment.*"

In contrast, another participant defined sexual harassment simply as, "*Physically abusing someone without permission*."

The participants shared stories of harassment that they had either experienced themselves or had directly witnessed. The public places where such incidents had occurred included public buses, crowded concerts, crowded market places, lonely streets, and while riding on rickshaws. The harassments ranged in form from catcalls, leering, staring, ridiculing, and making faces, to incidents of following, stalking, and touching. All of the participants said that there was no single time or place that they could mark as absolutely safe, though eight of them mentioned feeling more insecure in dark and isolated places. However, they all said that harassments are very common at crowded places.

Many participants described both immediate and enduring sense of fear associated with experiences of public harassment. One woman, for example, shared the following story:

"*The incident happened while I was returning home. A boy blocked my way. He then started talking about some big brother who liked me. So, he was not letting me go. Then, I slapped him in the face. He also raised his hand on me. It was near the Penaung restaurant. I quickly left the place and returned home. I almost ran half of the way. Later I made a General Report at the police station about this incident. But I didn't see those guys afterwards. After this incident, I always took rickshaw on that route, as I had to cross that place to reach my university. So, I stopped walking and always took a rickshaw after that incident.*"

Others spoke of the feelings of powerlessness that

harassment produced. As one participant recounted,
"My parents used to escort me to my school. So, I didn't notice any particular teasing or harassing incident when my parents were around. But then I started going to college by myself. Sometimes, I noticed some boys were singing at me. The songs were intended to me in a bad way. But there was nothing I could gain by challenging them. Noticing them would only give them more importance."

Beyond the immediate pain and difficulty caused by these experiences, women also reported direct and negative consequences on ability or willingness to navigate public spaces following the incident, whether self-chosen or imposed by family members. As one participant explained to us,

"It definitely causes confinement. If something happens to you then you will want to avoid those places afterwards. Like the incident that happened to me during shopping ... I do not want to go there again in order to avoid those incidents happening again. Besides, it is really very irritating to take the local buses. And going outside after 9pm/10pm is really impossible."

While all of the participants reported feeling better after having shared their experiences with others, they also described deep embarrassment, anguish, and senses of shame attached to the telling of their stories (including with family members and sometimes friends); this sense of shame and embarrassment was indeed described as one of the most serious and pervasive consequences of the sexual harassment experience (and contributes directly to public silence and underreporting of the issue as described above and returned to in the discussion section below). One participant told us that;

"I shared these stories with my family only a long time after the incident. After one and half year ... I could not share that much with friends either because I was not sure how they would think about me after hearing these ... But finally I had to share these with one of my friends, because I wanted to live my life."

DESIGN AND DEVELOPMENT

From the online survey, interviews, and focus group discussions, we came to understand that incidents of sexual harassment are a widespread and consequential problem in contemporary Dhaka. Although many women experience harassment every day, these incidents remain generally silenced within the social context of Bangladesh. However, the impacts of harassment may be severe and painfully felt, both by individual women and for the wider problem of women's participation in public space and the public sphere. To address these problems, informants in individual interviews and focus group discussions identified three potential features or attributes of any prospective design intervention in this space.

Help on the spot: In many cases, women pointed to the need for on-the-spot help to avoid, escape, or reduce the severity of harassment. All the women in our study reported feeling insecure in public places, and noted that the ability to alert bystanders to current incidents would make them more secure. One participant reported an incident in which her struggle with a perpetrator went unnoticed by bystanders at some distance away. Another reported an incident in which the perpetrator disappeared after seeing other people coming to the spot. These informants argued for some sort of alarm function that could call on help from nearby strangers when situations of harassment emerged. Others, however, spoke against this kind functionality, arguing that they would feel ashamed and embarrassed to become the center of attention in this way. As one explained,

"If you call people, they will start making fun of it. They will start asking you questions like "How did that happen?", "Where exactly did he touch?", and so on ... it is even more embarrassing. It is like being harassed for the second time. This is why most of the women do not want to share their harassment experiences."

Reaching friends when needed: All of the women said that they would feel better if they could reach their friends when they were in trouble. Although all of the participants had mobile phones, it was hard to make phone calls from the spot to all friends and seek help. Six of our participants said that they would not like it if their family members knew about their current location, but would feel better if their friends could be alerted to their location. As one participant explained this preference,

"I do not want my mom to know where I am going all the time. I am a grown-up woman and I do not like my parents tracking me. I know I can face danger on the street, and I have my friends to help me. If needed, they can inform my family."

Sharing Experiences with Others: All of our participants emphasized the need for a platform where they could share their experiences with others anonymously and get support. Participants described a double benefit to such a platform. First, victims could get support from other women and feel better. Second, by sharing experiences other women could learn about the incidents and make strategic choices to take precautions. As one participant explained,

"I could avoid these incidents if I knew boys always wait in that street to harass women. I would have my friends with me."

Others connected the sharing of stories to wider problems of public visibility. As one explained,

"I would definitely say that all women should know about these incidents. They would understand that being harassed is not their fault, but it is a crime and the perpetrators should be punished. In our country the victims hide

themselves from the society while the perpetrators move around proudly in the broad daylight."

These three needs became the central design principles guiding our subsequent development of the Protibadi system, a web and mobile-phone based platform designed to provide timely support, access to friends and contacts, and the sharing and public visibility of harassment experiences.

The Mobile Phone Application

The mobile phone application is built for android supported devices, and contains three basic tabs. The first tab has the "Save Me" button that serves the purpose of a Panic Button. The women can use this button whenever they feel uncomfortable in a public place. Upon pressing this button a loud sound is emitted from the mobile phone's speakers to draw the attention of other people around. At the same time, a text message will be sent to each of the emergency contacts of the user's profile. The text message contains the location of the user (if available through GPS) and allows the receiver to know that the user is in trouble. In the second tab, the user can add, delete, or edit the emergency contact details. In the third tab, the user can report incidents of harassment that she experiences or observes.

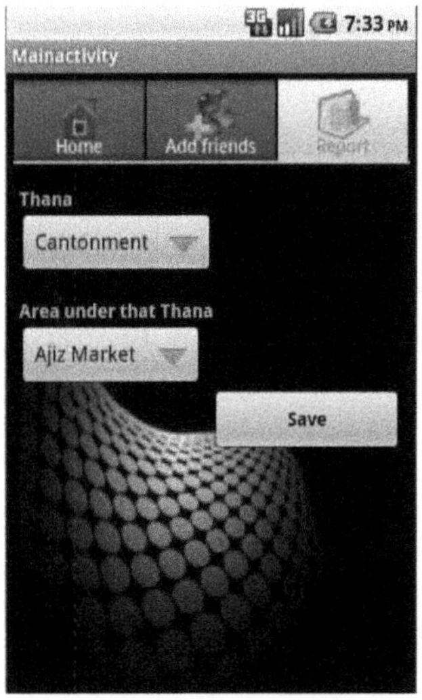

Figure 1. Screenshot of the reporting tab of mobile phone application.

Such reports are then stored in the system's webserver, and displayed on the "Protibadi" website described below.

The Website

The website consists of several components. A user can issue a request to register on the "*Protibadi*" system, which is subsequently reviewed and approved by the administrators of the website. Once registered, users can enter reports and blogs, and comment on the (anonymized) reports entered by other users. All reports are open for viewing to non-registered users.

When creating a new report, users are required to enter time and location data. This can be entered manually on the website, or sent directly from the mobile phone application entering the area or 'Thana' (district) in which the incident occurred. The system supports reporting in both English and Bangla. More generalized commentary blogs can be entered in similar ways, but don't require time and place information. Users can also mark a report as "serious" or "suspicious" by clicking the corresponding buttons added to that post. The system then superimposes reports and associated comments on a periodically refreshed map of the Dhaka urban area, as shown in Figure 2.

Figure 2. Screenshot of the homepage of the website.

The Protibadi website (www.protibadi.com) and mobile application were launched publicly in August 2013, and advertised via the Facebook pages of student groups at local universities. A corresponding Facebook page (https://www.facebook.com/protibadi) was subsequently created which system administrators periodically update with reports and blogs generated by Protibadi users.

While the system described above draws ideas and inspiration from past HCI applications in the sexual harassment space, there are also important differences between these systems and our own. *Hollaback* [16], *Harassmap* [14], *ComfortZones*, and *Safetipin* allow users to share experiences of harassment with friends, neighbors, family or social media, but contain no support for emergency help at the spot. *CircleOf6* [6] and *Fightback* [12] offer emergency help, but do not provide opportunities to share and report on incidents of harassment. Based on needs identified through our ethnographic fieldwork, Protibadi combines these functions in a single unified platform. Additionally, because we wanted to produce a system built with community participation and input from the ground up, it was important *not* to simply import systems developed elsewhere (though we learned from those systems in developing our own).

USAGE, FEEDBACK AND PUBLIC RESPONSES

Three months after releasing the website, there were 110 registered users on the site, 20 self-identified as men and the rest women. Users had entered 24 reports from different parts of Dhaka city, and a total of 618 people subscribed to the Facebook page, with posts viewed by more than 350 users on average. Reports described a range of harassment experiences shared by users of the system, with the following a fairly typical example:

"yesterday i was going by rickshaw. it was going through a crowdy road. because of the crowd the rickshaw was going slowly. suddenly i felt that someone grabbed my thigh. i was shocked, i tried to find out who it was, then i saw a figure rushing towards the crowd. it was totally unexpected and really horrible..it happened near shyamoli area."

Users had also made 12 blog posts, many of which spoke about issues of harassment in a more general sense (rather than reporting or describing a specific incident). For example, one user posted a blog titled, "*Eve Teasing-Primal Instincts Coming to Surface?*", where she wrote,

"Bangladesh is a society in transition where centuries old cultures, practices, and social beliefs are undergoing transformation. It is a tumultuous time, a stormy phase. Yet despite these changes, one fact remains consistent and true: Sexual violence and harassment of women exists, and it is rampant as a disease even in our current times."

User studies:

To understand early experiences and responses to the system beyond content and basic usage data, we conducted semi-structured interviews with 10 Protibadi users (contacted by site administrators via Facebook messages and conducted by female interviewers) regarding their experience of using the website and the mobile phone application. General responses to the system were positive, with several respondents noting the deep need and value for such a system (though also noting that it represented a small and limited intervention in relation to the pervasive problem of public sexual harassment). Six of the ten respondents cited the value and comfort provided by the instant messaging system, and the sense of security provided by one-touch access to emergency contacts. As one participant explained,

"The SMS system is very useful, because your information along with your location is instantly sent to an emergency contact person. Now you know you can get help anytime you are in trouble."

Participants also praised the reporting function, and mentioned the blog entries of other users as important sources of learning, sharing, and publicizing incidents of harassment. Users reported being generally happy with the overall aesthetics and usability of both the mobile phone and web-based system components.

Other of our design interventions were less successful or received more mixed reviews. None of our participants for example had used the "Save me" button at the time we conducted the interviews. Six of them said that they would have used this if they faced any such situation, while four of them (echoing findings in the earlier focus group and interview studies) said that they would never use this since it would only attract public attention and embarrassment. One respondent criticized the lack of integration of the site into systems of Police crime reporting, arguing that better integration with systems of enforcement would enhance women's motivation and willingness to contribute. Another argued that the site's primary focus on incidents of street harassment should be expanded to address other forms of sexual harassment, including the growing problems of stalking and harassment through social media. As this user explained,

"Eve teasing is not limited to the physical level anymore. It has started even virtually. There are pages on Facebook, where bad comments and pictures about women are posted. Often times one's pictures are being used in a very abusive manner without one's permission. So, events like this should also be reported on the website and awareness about it should be made."

Still another participant urged us to integrate the site more directly with Facebook (as opposed to manually porting system content to Facebook as described above), as this was the one social media site that she and her friends routinely and actively engaged.

This user feedback suggests a number of immediate design recommendations moving forward. First, though interested in and supportive of our system in general, users were reluctant to add yet another site to their regular social media routine. Accordingly, users were more responsive in reading and commenting on reports and blog posts when shared over Facebook than when on the original website.

Second, while supporting the system's general information sharing and awareness functions, users also described wanting to see some kind of immediate reaction to their posts. Especially in case of reporting, the victims often wanted to get support, or see the offender punished through their action. Mere sharing of the information was not always a strong motivation for users to report. Connecting the system to law-enforcement agencies or human-rights groups might therefore extend functionality and enhance motivation for site users (though we note that many of the harassment incidents reported through the site do not meet existing categories of offense under Bangladeshi law).

Third, users reported not wanting to limit themselves to reporting only sexual harassment in public places, and preferred instead a platform where they could talk about any sort of harassment or discrimination in general. This indicates the fact that this system is actually supporting an emotion of the users that is spread across a wide range of feelings they have. Hence, the users should be given the liberty to disclose all those feelings here and the users will not appreciate any restriction applied to that.

Public controversies:
Beyond the confines of our user study, some deeper issues around our design were reflected in a series of more public reactions to the site, including a number of controversies and debates that played out through the project's associated Facebook page. In one case, a user reported that she felt bad when an unknown man on the street asked her and her friend to cover their heads during the holy month of Ramadan. When this report was picked up on the Facebook page, a number of subscribers to the page reacted. They argued that the man did the right thing by asking two Muslim women to cover their heads, because that was what Islam suggested. One member said in his comment,

"... *Any person can say to another woman to wear hijab and veil becoz it's farz for women. If you don't admit it, then it's your mental problem*". ["*farz*" means "must do" in Islam]

Other followers responded to defend the original post, and the debate continued across a total of 34 comments, some defending the man and his actions, and others the original commenter's position.

In another example, the user expressed her frustration around the way staff and male passengers had behaved on a public bus, demanding full fare from the female students but only half from the male students. She also discussed situations in which male passengers took advantage of crowded buses to touch women inappropriately in public. In response, one member commented,

"*Islam says there must be a place preserved for women in any kinda vehicle where men aren't allowed. there must be a rigid partition to separate males and females. and all the fair must be collected from her mahram male companion (as women aren't allowed to go to and fro freely without mahram males) or in special case if the girl is alone ,fare must be taken outside of the partition. so why r u fussing around with your so called faminism without rules of Shari'ah*?" ["*mahram*" to a girl means the person who is not allowed to marry her]

In a third more sympathetic but also challenging example, a commenter pointed out that:

"This is a great initiative, but there is a weakness in their intention. They are making this so that women can avoid the places where eve teasing takes place. If this continues we have to keep the women inside an almirah after a few days. They should instead post the pictures and profiles of the perpetrators."

Next steps and future directions:
At the time of writing, the Protibadi system remains a work in progress. The site retains a small but active group of users, with a somewhat larger and more mixed audience through its associated Facebook page. The design team is working to weigh and incorporate some of the design considerations stemming from early stage usage and user feedback. Responsibility for long-term maintenance and development of the system is also in process of being transitioned to a local women's rights organization who have approached the research team to support and maintain the site over time, and potential interest in expanding it to support forms of harassment reporting among female workers in the textiles industry – a dominant and reputedly problematic employer in this regard. A second non-governmental organization has initiated discussions around modifying the system to support forms of harassment reporting in rural parts of the country (possibly building on Grameen Bank-inspired models of local system contacts after the 'village phone lady' model). In December 2013, the Protibadi system was featured in a report on national television and has attracted growing levels of attention since then.

DISCUSSION

But these immediate questions of system design and immediate project trajectory represent only a part (and arguably the smaller part) of potential lessons and implications that can be drawn from the wider Protibadi experience. At the most immediate level, ethnographic portions of our study make clear the seriousness and consequences of sexual harassment in Dhaka today. While our study can make no claim to statistical representativeness (and there are obvious selection effects that may shape people's elective participation and non-participation in the study), it was striking to us the ease with which experiences of harassment could be called up by all members of our survey, interview, and focus group studies. As our participants accounts made clear, experiences of harassment as detailed here are part of the real and regular experience of university-aged women in Dhaka today.

This is important because many of the public and academic debates around gender violence and discrimination in contemporary Bangladesh have tended to focus on rural parts of the country, have addressed the effects of social or cultural institutions like marriage, economy or the state, or have been built around the more 'extreme' forms of gender violence (rape, incest, etc.) that women also sometimes face [1]. As our study shows, forms of violence and discrimination can also be rooted in the conditions of everyday life, can be just as real and insidious in their effects, and are powerfully present even within the relatively cosmopolitan areas of Dhaka and among the comparatively empowered group that constitutes university women. These effects are both personal and political. Incidents of sexual harassment as reported by our informants can produce powerful experiences of fear, shame, and isolation (all the more so since it can be difficult or dangerous to share these experiences with friends and family members). But they also cause women to navigate the city differently, limiting or curtailing access to public space (markets, buses, etc.) and enforcing forms of conduct and expression that may further limit effective participation in public life. In this way, "small" incidents of harassment may produce "large" cultural consequences: mechanisms, as well as effects, of larger systems of gender discrimination and inequality.

Methodologically, our study raises important questions around the challenges of doing HCI design and ethnographic work around socially and culturally sensitive issues – a topic relevant to work in "HCI4D" or "post-colonial computing," but also the field more broadly. This showed up in painful and immediate form in challenges experienced in both the ethnographic and system building portions of our work. As noted earlier, it was difficult to get participants for focus group discussions and face-to-face interviews. Even after posting the flyers repeatedly in different places in the university campuses and inviting people on Facebook, participation remained low. By the same token, adoption of the system remained comparatively low, even where current and potential users spoke to the need and many positives of the system arrived at. This stands in stark contrast to the professed need and potential contribution of design interventions in this space.

Some of these effects may no doubt be attributed to limits in design, both of the ethnographic work and the subsequent system design. Others may be attributed to the relative newness of the system (an interpretation bolstered by recent signs of interest stemming from NGO and local media engagement). A more complete and challenging explanation however – and one offered by several of the participants in our study – may be found in the deep and long-standing culture of shame and fear surrounding sexual harassment in Bangladesh, whose weight (like all matters of deep cultural concern) will inevitably dwarf the comparatively brief and light interventions that HCI researchers are likely to make in this space.

As these examples make clear, public perceptions and even basic definitions of sexual harassment (what constitutes it, why it happens, etc.) live within a large and shifting field of cultural politics, which is no more settled in Bangladesh than anywhere else. In such a space, design interventions are likely to share and absorb the controversies of the topics they touch, with no obvious or irrefutable standpoint of truth. This brings to the fore the inevitably "agonistic" character of HCI design [10], in particular as it moves outwards from narrowly instrumental or functional concerns towards the larger interventionist ambitions that often characterize the HCI4D and feminist HCI space. Such circumstances open up ethnographic and design work to a series of ambivalences and unintended consequences, including the very real concern noted by our third commenter that calling out spaces of harassment may in fact exacerbate tendencies to avoid places marked as dangerous, and so further restrict women's navigation of public space (even while giving them new informational tools to make these judgments on a case-by-case basis). Given the depth and complexity of the cultural politics at play here, such ambivalences and unintended consequences may be a regular feature of ethnographic and design interventions around difficult, contested, and culturally sensitive problems of the sort addressed here.

They also necessarily implicate the positionality and security of HCI researchers themselves. Beyond the challenges faced by our study participants, the study also raised challenges and occasionally threats for female members of the research team. As mentioned earlier, research activities in one of our study sites was suspended after the interviewer, a faculty member at the university, started being harassed herself on the basis of her participation in the study. The faculty member was ridiculed by a number of office assistants while posting the flyers. She also received emails from unknown people who told her to advise the women to cover themselves according to the rules of Islam in order to avoid sexual harassment. At that point, the interviewer felt unsafe and the study at that university was suspended. Under such conditions, it becomes difficult to conduct research at all.

CONCLUSION

In this paper, we described an ethnographic study designed to understand the problem of sexual harassment in the public places of Dhaka city. We developed a specific design intervention, "*Protibadi*", intended to support women experiencing and fighting harassment. And we described initial responses to our system, as gathered through preliminary user studies and more public responses to our system.

We also discussed problems of HCI intervention more generally, including as the field engages deeply contested and unsettled cultural issues of the sort addressed here. Such complexities are likely only to intensify as the feminist and HCI4D projects within HCI grow and mature. More and careful work in this space, of both theoretical and empirical varieties, may cast further light on the dynamics and challenges described here. Such work may also enhance the impact and responsibility of the field.

ACKNOWLEDGEMENTS

We would like to thank the stuff, faculty, and students of Bangladesh University of Engineering and Technology (BUET), North South University, and BRAC University for their cooperation in our research. Research for this paper was supported by funding provided under the Intel Science and Technology Center for Social Computing and International Fulbright Science and Technology Fellowship.

REFERENCES

1. Alam N, Roy S.K., Ahmed T., Sexually harassing behavior against adolescent girls in rural Bangladesh: implications for achieving millennium development goals. *Interpersonal Violence*; 25(3), 443–56, 2010.
2. Bangladesh telecommunication Regulatory Commission Report, 2013.
3. Bardzell, S. Feminist HCI: taking stock and outlining an agenda for design. *In Proc. CHI '10,* pp. 1301–1310.
4. Bowman, C, L. A. Rudman, Street harassment and the informal ghettoization of women, *Harvard Law Review*, 106(3), 517–580, 1993.
5. Brewer, E., Demmer, M., Du, B., Ho, M., Kam, M., Nedevschi, S., Pal, J., Patra, R., Surana, S., Fall, K. The case for technology in developing regions, *Computer*, 38(6), 25–38, 2005.
6. Clarke, R., Wright, P., Balaam, M., & McCarthy, J. (2013, April). Digital portraits: photo-sharing after domestic violence. *In Proc. CHI '13*, pp. 2517–2526.
7. *Circleof6* website: http://www.circleof6app.com/
8. *ComfortZone Checkin:* http://www.comfortzonecheckin.com/
9. DeRenzi, B., Lesh, N., Parikh, T., Sims, C., Mitchell, M., Maokola, W., Chemba, M., Hamisi, Y., Schellenbe, D., Borriello, G. e-IMCI: Improving Pediatric Health Care in Low-Income Countries. *In Proc. CHI '08*, pp. 753–762.
10. DiSalvo, C. *Adversarial Design*, MIT Press, 2012.
11. Fairchild, KM., Rudman, LA, "Everyday stranger harassment and women's objectification", *Social Justice Research*, 21(3), 338–357, 2008.
12. Fightback App: http://www.comfortzonecheckin.com/
13. Hasan, O. "Street Harassment is Still Serious: The violation of women in Dhaka's public realm". The Daily Star, Forum, 5:11, 2011.
14. *Harassmap* website: http://harassmap.org/en/
15. Haque, M., Kawsar, F., Adibuzzaman, M., Ahamed, S., Love, R., Dowla, R., Roe, D., Hossain, S., and Selim S. Findings of e-ESAS: a mobile based symptom monitoring system for breast cancer patients in rural Bangladesh. *In Proc. CHI '12*, pp. 899–908.
16. *Hollaback!* website: http://www.ihollaback.org/
17. Irani, L., Vertesi, J., Dourish, P., Philip, K., and Grinter, B. 2010. Postcolonial Computing: A Lens on Design and Development. *In Proc. CHI '10*, pp. 1311–1320.
18. Kannabiran, G., Bardzell, J., and Bardzell, S. How HCI talks about sexuality: discursive strategies, blind spots, and opportunities for future research. *In Proc. CHI '10*, pp. 695–704.
19. Lahsaeizadeh, A., and Yousefinejad, E., Social Aspects of Women's Experiences of Sexual Harassment in Public Places in Iran, *Sexuality & Culture* (16), 17-37, 2012.
20. Luk R., Ho M., and Aoki M. P. Asynchronous remote medical consultation for Ghana. *In Proc. CHI '08*, pp. 743–752.
21. Madu, C. N. Transferring technology to developing countries—Critical factors for success, *Long Range Planning*, 22(4), 115–124, 1989.
22. Marcus, A. and Gould, E.W. Crosscurrents: cultural dimensions and global Web user-interface design. *Interactions* 7(4), 32–46, 2000.
23. Mitchell, M., Lesh, N., Crammer, H., Fraser, H., Haivas, I. Wolf, K. Improving Care – Improving Access: The Use of Electronic Decision Support with AIDS patients in South Africa. *Intl. J. of Healthcare Technology and Management*. 10(3), 156–168, 2009.
24. Nahar, P., Reeuwijk, M., and Reis, R., Contextualising sexual harassment of adolescent girls in Bangladesh. *Reproductive Health Matters*, 21(41), 78–86, 2013.
25. *OnWatch* website: http://www.onwatchoncampus.com/
26. Patel, N., Shah, K., Savani, S. R. Klemmer, P. Dave, and T. S. Parikh. Power to the peers: authority of source effects for a voice-based agricultural information service in rural India. *In Proc. ICTD '12*, pp. 169–178.
27. Patel, N., Chittamuru, D., Jain, A., Dave, P., and Parikh, T. 2010. Avaaj Otalo: a field study of an interactive voice forum for small farmers in rural India. *In Proc. CHI '10*, 733–742.
28. Pryor, J. B., Giedd, J. L., and Williams, K. B. A social psychological model for predicting sexual harassment. *Journal of Social Issues*, 51(1), 1995.
29. Richard, H. Sexism, sexual harassment and sexual assault: Toward conceptual clarity. Report submitted to *Defense Equal Opportunity Management Institute*, 2007.
30. Safetipin App: http://safetipin.com/
31. Sambasivan, N., Weber, J., and Cutrell, E. Designing a phone broadcasting system for urban sex workers in India. *In Proc. CHI '11*, pp. 267–276.
32. Sambasivan, N., Cutrell, E., Toyama, K., and Nardi. Intermediated technology use in developing communities. *In Proc. CHI '10*, pp. 2583–2592.
33. Satchell, C., and Foth, M. Welcome to the jungle: HCI after dark. *In Proc. CHI '11*, pp.753–762.
34. Satchell, C., and Foth. M. Fear and danger in nocturnal urban environments. *In Proc. CHI '10*, pp. 380–383.
35. Shimira, K., Mukasa, O., Schellenberg, A. J., Manzi, F., John, D., Mushi, A., Mrisho, M., Tanner, M., Mshinda, H., Schellenberg, D. The use of personal digital assistants for data entry at the point of collection in a large household survey in southern Tanzania. *Emerging Themes in Epidemiology* (2007), 4:5.
36. UNICEF Report: "UNICEF supports efforts to end sexual harassment of girls and women in Bangladesh", July 21, 2010.
37. Walker, LE., Psychology and domestic violence around the world, *American Psychologist*, 54, 21–29, 1999.
38. William, O. *Sexual harassment: Theory, research, and treatment*. Allyn & Bacon, 1997.
39. Woelfer, J. P., Iverson, A., Hendry, D. G, Friedman, B., and Gill, B. Improving the safety of homeless young people with mobile phones: values, form and function. *In Proc. CHI '11*, pp. 1707–1716.

How Technology Supports Family Communication in Rural, Suburban, and Urban Kenya

Erick Oduor[1], Carman Neustaedter[1], Tejinder K. Judge[2], Kate Hennessy[1], Carolyn Pang[1], and Serena Hillman[1]

School of Interactive Arts and Technology[1]
Simon Fraser University
250-13450 102nd Avenue, Surrey BC, Canada
[firstname_secondname]@sfu.ca

Google Inc. [2]
1900 Charleston Rd,
Mountain View, CA, 94043, USA
tkjudge@google.com

ABSTRACT
Much ICTD research for sub-Saharan Africa has focused on how technology related interventions have aimed to incorporate marginalized communities towards global economic growth. Our work builds on this. We present results from an exploratory qualitative study on the family communication practices of family members who communicate both within and between rural, suburban, and urban settings in Kenya. Our findings reveal that family communication focuses on economic support, well-being, life advice, and everyday coordination of activities. We also outline social factors that affect family communication, including being an eldest child, having a widowed sibling, and having reduced access to technology because of gender, literacy, or one's financial situation. Lastly, we discuss new opportunities for technology design and articulate the challenges that designers will face if creating or deploying family communication technologies in Kenya.

ACM Classification Keywords
H.5.3 [Information interfaces and presentation]: Group and Organization Interfaces - Computer Supported Cooperative Work

Author Keywords
ICT4D, family communication, awareness, mobile devices

INTRODUCTION
There exists a growing amount of research on communication practices in developing countries (e.g., [16,21,25,27,31]) with a specific emphasis on the effects of poverty, educational levels, and a lack of technological infrastructure. Our focus is on understanding the use of technology in Kenya for family communication. Within this space, we have seen studies that have explored how Kenyans living abroad use technology to communicate with their families who are 'back home' in Kenya [33], how technologies are used in different ways than in developed countries [36], how gender impacts cellphone adoption [7,21], and how rural–urban migration [1] and rural access of technology by women [16] affects communication.

CHI 2014, April 26–May 1, 2014, Toronto, Ontario, Canada.

http://dx.doi.org/10.1145/2556288.2557277

Overall, this research provides a solid foundation for understanding technology usage in developing countries. Yet we see less research in terms of how technology supports family communication, in particular, from a Human-Computer Interaction perspective, largely focused on understanding technology design and its usage. Our research builds on the existing literature to address this gap.

Specifically, we explore how Kenyans from rural, suburban, and urban settings share information within family structures even in the midst of challenges that result from continuous rural-urban migration [1]. To do this, we conducted an exploratory study involving in-depth interviews with 24 participants living in various regions of Kenya. Our goal was to uncover family communication practices that were technology-based and understand how families adopted the use of technology in rural, suburban, and urban areas when faced with infrastructure limitations. We also aimed to understand when technology was used and why, and what social factors affected this usage. This moves beyond infrastructure-related issues such as a lack of connectivity or electricity, which have already been reported (e.g., [33 - 36]).

To foreshadow, our results show that communication over technology between distributed family members was primarily for coordinating economic and subsistence support for relatives, obtaining updates about family members' well-being, providing advice about life, and coordinating everyday family activities (albeit this depended on the setting). We also uncovered social practices that: created pressure for the eldest children in families to be nearly constantly available, required a brother-in-law of widowed women to take on additional communication, and led to an imbalance in terms of access to technology. The latter relates to gender issues, finances, and literacy. Together, these results illustrate the complexity of designing for family communication practices in Kenya. Rather than present design implications that suggest *how* to create family communication technology for Kenya, which may easily be speculative at best, we focus our discussion on broadening the focus of technology in Kenya and illustrate what social challenges designers will need to carefully think through when creating or deploying family communication technologies in Kenya.

RELATED WORK

ICTD studies have highlighted the importance of understanding the dynamics and needs of local communities in developing countries before designing technology for them [29]. For example, Liu et al. [17] report on how rural Chinese families embraced the use of mobile phone entertainment. Rangaswamy & Sambasivan [24] documented the local practices of individuals in Bangalore, India, and reported that ownership or use of technology could either be single or collective. Sambasivan et al. [25] reported on how the roles of women in slums in India shaped their selection and use of technology through intermediated interactions where 'digitally skilled users' helped those who lack technical skills. Sambasivan et al. [26] also described how technology supported social networks in Indian slums where a group of industry laborers living together used multiple ringtones to distinguish call recipients for a shared mobile phone. Even in cases of "social, technical, and environmental obstacles," motivation was found to be the driving force for the adoption and use of technology in developing areas [27].

Studies of family life in Jamaica [12] found that a significant number of low-income families depended on remittances from abroad, which were discussed over mobile phones [11,12]. Another study showed that El Salvadorian immigrants in North America used mobile phones to communicate with distributed family members back 'home' to discuss topics related to their kinship [30].

Several studies have looked at the use of cellphones and the use of callback in rural African communities. Burrell [5] found that gender segregation of space, social policing and economic dependence on husbands negatively impacted women's cellphone usage in Uganda. A considerable number did not have access to a cell phone unless they used their husband's or were gifted one. Husbands were typically concerned about 'secret' activities by their wives in case they (the wives) had a mobile phone. In a study conducted in the Mankosi region of South Africa, the interactions with an Audio Repository (AR) prototype showed that rural Africans preferred voice in cell-phone usage [3]. The authors suggest that researchers should aim to situate designs in 'local ways' so as to enrich the potential for asynchronous voice communication. Studies also showed that people prefer to use callback free messaging services rather than SMS because of its affordability and accessibility; this contrasts other services such as 'buzzing' that do not record missed calls on low end phones [4]. In post war Liberia, users saw their cellphones as productivity enhancers and means of connectivity to family and friends that could also be used as sources of personal security [2]. The idea of the phone as a stylish object was not considered to be important especially in rural areas [2]. Namibians reported the use of Facebook not only to share religious and political views, but also to share posts about death which are considered private and taboo by North Americans [22].

There also exist several studies focusing specifically on technology use in Kenya. Agesa and Kim [1] reported on split migration that occurs when a household head moves from a rural to an urban area for search of work. Eriksson [7] showed that cell phones bridged the gap between cities and rural areas in Kenya by providing job seekers with an opportunity to be reachable. Kwake and Adigun [16] looked at the use and access of Information and Communication Technologies (ICTs) amongst rural women in Kenya. Besides the marked correlation between the respondents' level of education, type of ICTs accessed and information needs and purposes, they observed that ICTs alone are insufficient for the emergence of significant benefits to rural women. Murphy and Priebe [21] provide an analysis of a census on the usage of cellphones in Bungoma, Kenya and describe how women often rely on borrowing a phone from someone or being gifted one. This reflects typical household hierarchies, which are dominated by men. While related to our work, this study does not explore how gender affects family communication practices. Instead, it presents a high-level overview of mobile phone access.

Research has also shown that expatriates who worked and lived in Nairobi creatively 'got around' issues of limited connectivity and power by preplanning their communications before accessing the Internet [35]. Some Kenyans have adopted social media despite infrastructural challenges. Facebook usage focuses on connecting with friends [36], but, perhaps more importantly, around income generation, such as finding a job [32]. Challenges with the use of Facebook included the costs of using a 'free' service (e.g., paying for connectivity), mobile phone battery power, and low bandwidth [36]. We also see the value of mobile phones for promoting trade, regional cooperation and development within East Africa based on education levels, poverty, and fears of technology [19].

Similar to our study, Wyche et al. [33] conducted a study with Kenyan migrants living in the United States and found they had difficulties connecting with their family members in Kenya because of the technological and infrastructure limitations [33]. They also found that many family members who moved away from Kenya to more developed countries still engaged in domestic activities in their home villages related to the remittance of money [33]. Mobile phones dominated communication routines and they described the use of 'beeping' [6] to notify remote family members to call them back [33]. Our work builds on this study by focusing on how people *within* Kenya connected with family members who were distributed across the country in a mixture of rural, suburban, and urban settings. Overall, our work builds on the related literature to focus specifically on family communication practices where we identify how and why technology is used and what social factors affect this communication.

Figure 1. Migori: a rural home surrounded by land for subsistence cultivation.

STUDY METHODOLOGY

We conducted an interview-based study to understand: 1) how and why Kenyans used technologies to communicate with family members in rural, urban, and suburban areas, and 2) what social factors affected communication.

Participants and Recruitment

We recruited 24 people across three regions of Kenya. Participants were between 19 and 59 years of age.

Study Site 1: Migori (Rural)

Eleven participants (6 women) were from rural Migori, Our participants from this setting lived in Awendo, a rural part of the larger Migori District that lies 360 km from Nairobi with a population of ~47,000 [18]. Figure 1 shows a typical home in the rural part of Migori consisting of two or more huts built within the same compound and enclosed by a fence. Families in this region cultivate tobacco and plant sugarcane as cash crops while families that do not own large parcels of land engage in subsistence farming of maize, beans, coffee, groundnuts and vegetables. Polygamy is also practiced in this region. Education levels of our participants varied from no schooling to high school graduates. We also had a community leader, a woman who sold medicine without proper medical training as a chemist and a kindergarten teacher.

Study Site 2: Kisumu (Suburban)

Four participants (2 women) were from suburban Kisumu. Kisumu is a port city in western Kenya with a population of ~400,000 [15]. Kisumu is the major commercial center in Western Kenya. Fishing, agriculture (both large scale and subsistence sugar and rice cultivation), textile and fish processing industries are located in this city. Several offices of NGO's and commercial banks servicing the entire western Kenya region are also found here. Our participants from Kisumu included a businessman, a senior civil servant, and two recent university graduates.

Study Site 3: Githurai (Urban)

Nine participants (5 women) were from Githurai, a multilingual mixture of slums and suburbs that lies in the eastern part of Nairobi with a population of over 300,000 [10]. According to a World Bank report on Kenya, 47% of the population lives below the poverty line characterized by lack of proper housing, poor infrastructure, poor access to health care facilities and lack of quality education [23]. Figures 2 and 3 show the range of homes of our participants in Githurai. On one hand, Figure 2 shows a home of a participant who was selling fish by the roadside to make ends meet. Figure 3 shows the living and dining room in the home of a senior civil servant in a suburban area. People living in Githurai engage in merchandise sales in small retail shops, open air cloth stores, welding, carpentry, formal employment in the nearby Kenyatta University, and low-level administrative duties in government offices.

Figure 2. Githurai: a low income home.

Figure 3. Githurai: a sitting room in a suburban setting with a laptop on a desk in the background.

Recruitment

Three participants from Githurai and two from Kisumu were recruited through posts on Facebook and Twitter. The remaining participants from both regions were recruited through posters that were placed in small retail shops and by word-of-mouth. Our selection was iterative where we reached out to people of different occupations as we continuously learned about family practices.

In the rural settings, the community leader and chemist participants assisted us in identifying rural interviewees who had limited education. Participants were recruited through word-of-mouth and notices and posters that we displayed on the local village chief's office notice board and on the chemist shop entrance. After identifying our participants, the first author requested permission from the elders of the homes that we were to visit in cases where women were to be interviewed while their husbands were away or had passed on. This action was important since the elders had to be informed why the interviewer would spend time in the company of one's wife or a widow.

The first author has his ancestral roots in this community. As such, participants described wanting to have sustained involvement with the principal investigator's research.

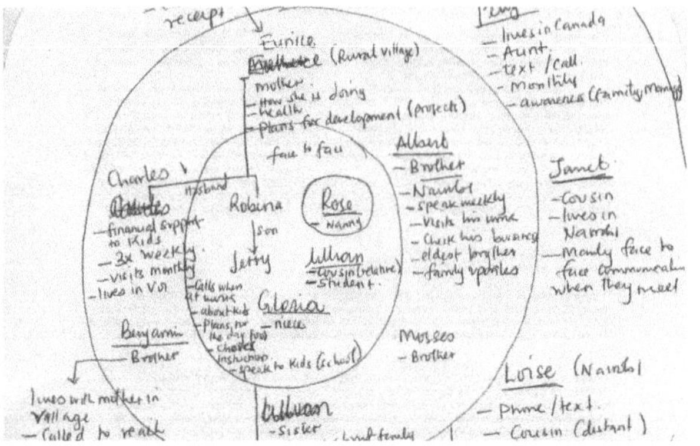

Figure 4. A participant's communication 'map'.

Household Composition
Eighteen participants lived with immediate family. Within this group, three participants lived with both immediate and distant family members under the same roof (one from the urban region and two from suburban regions) and two participants (from the rural setting) had two wives who both had young children aged between one to 10 years. The remaining six participants were either single or living alone.

Technology Ownership
Seventeen participants (10 rural, 5 urban and 2 suburban) owned a single mobile phone. On the other hand, seven participants (2 rural, 2 suburban and 3 urban) reported the ownership of more than one mobile phone where each phone was used for a different purpose. For example, one participant had a phone that he used to call family members and a second one dedicated for non-family related discussions. One rural participant owned a desktop computer that was kept in storage. Four suburban participants owned one laptop and two owned desktop computers. Three urban participants owned a laptop and six owned two laptops. Thus, we see only suburban and urban participants owned a form of computer, while rural participants relied primarily on mobile phones.

Interviews and Home Visits
We conducted semi-structured interviews with participants over the course of two visits. Each visit lasted between 45 and 60 minutes. During the first visit, the interviewer conducted an in-depth interview with the participant about his or her family and communication practices. Participants were provided with a sheet of paper and asked to draw their family communication networks. The investigator used information about kinship charts [12] to provide guidance. Participants filled in the type of technology and kind of information that was exchanged with their kin. Figure 4 shows a portion of a drawing created by a participant. Participants were then asked a series of questions about their communication routines with their family members. This included questions about when and how often a participant contacted each remote family member and what type of technology was used. The second visit happened approximately one week after the first visit where the investigator discussed findings from the first interview and asked follow-up questions.

Rural participants were interviewed within their homes while urban and suburban participants were interviewed either at their workplace or homes. One suburban participant was interviewed at his business premises, the senior civil servant at his home, while the university graduates were interviewed in their relatives' homes. Participants spoke in a range of dialects and languages, which were all understood (and later translated) by the first author who had lived in our study areas in the past. Overall, our participant selection gave insight into the family communication practices of five different tribes.

Data Collection & Analysis
All interviews were audio-recorded and handwritten notes were kept. Our findings are based on 24 transcribed interviews, 69 photographs (depicting participants' homes and areas of communication) and 92 pages of field notes. We analyzed our interview transcriptions and notes using open, axial, and selective coding [28].

Our results are organized into two main sections. First, we outline the reasons participants used technology to communicate with immediate and extended family members. Second, we describe the social situations that influenced family communication routines and activities. All participant names have been anonymized.

REASONS FOR COMMUNICATION WITH TECHNOLOGY
Participants described communication routines with their immediate family (parents, spouses, children, and siblings) and extended family (nieces, nephews and cousins). The family members were either co-located or remotely located in other parts of the country (rural, suburban or urban).

In rural areas, family communication was focused around in-person exchanges and technology was used only occasionally to communicate with the people that one lived with. While out working in places such as the farms, most participants did not communicate with their family members unless there was an important message to discuss. Mobile phones would then be used to coordinate urgent matters.

In the suburban and urban regions, family members had more frequent opportunities for exchanges of information throughout the day through the use of technology. Across these three areas, we found that technology-based communication generally focused on four topics: *economic support, life advice, well-being*, and, sometimes, *family coordination.* We describe each next.

Economic Support
Like findings from previous studies [1,8,9,12,13,19,33], our participants reported that the most important reason for communication with technology was for economic support. This occurred frequently where people living in rural areas would communicate with their suburban and urban family members. This included situations such as parents receiving financial assistance through MPesa (also documented in [13])

from their adult children who were working away from home. There were cases where participants were supporting a niece or a nephew through payment of fees (also found in [20]) and even others where siblings and cousins were supported with money to sustain subsistence farming of small scale business endeavors. The use of MPesa to send money to aged and unemployed parents living in the villages was reported by seven participants (2 from suburban and 5 from the urban areas).

Moving beyond other study's findings, we also found that family members who were considered wealthy were more likely to have communication focus around economic support. This sometimes created feelings of obligation or emotional struggles because conversations tended to overly-focus on economic support at the expense of other topics. For example, a successful suburban businessman explained to us that he felt obligated to financially assist both his immediate and extended family members.

"Most of my family members see that I have a successful business, they always call me whenever they need financial assistance. Sometimes I call them too, but most of the discussions will end up on some sort of money needed somewhere. Because I am able to assist them most of the time, I do not have a problem with this. However, I do not remember one person who called me just to know how I am doing over the past four months." – Bosire

Life Advice and Guidance

Communication between rural and urban family members also focused on parents providing advice to children and siblings and close friends encouraging each other about the challenges of life. This was especially the case for parents of adult children who had moved away from home. For example, one participant who was a retired teacher explained to us that, together with his wife, they called their children who worked and lived in other urban regions around the country to provide advice on how to face marriage and life's challenges and problems. They also provided parental advice to their children on the importance of Christian fellowship to build a united family.

"This is because as parents, we feel obliged to make sure that they live respectable lives in whichever part of the world that they are in." – Chumah

In another situation, Lavender, a housewife living in rural Migori, described how she called her mother, sister and her childhood friend to discuss their marital challenges and difficulties.

"I communicate a lot about family life and express my love to both my mother and sister who lived away from me. I also do the same with my husband while I am away from home while visiting my mother, sister or other close relatives. We talk about the wellbeing of the kids and private family issues over the phone if there is need to do so. I also talk to my sister and close friends who are all married to discuss issues within our respective marriages over the phone. This helps us to get encouragement that will enable us to overcome our marital challenges." – Lavender

As a tailor, Lavender could not afford to spend much money on calling. She would reach out to her relatives and friends occasionally when she received extra income from repairing clothes in addition to finances that her husband would provide for family upkeep. Thus, her calls greatly depended on the availability of funds after ensuring that basic housing needs such as food, children's medicine, and school equipment such as books and pens for her children had been purchased. Her family and friends would also call her occasionally to know how she was faring on. She would call her friend to set up a meeting so that they could discuss the strains of marriage that resulted from adultery suspicion of their husbands, abuse and alcoholism, which was a pertinent issue in most young families in rural settings.

Well Being

We also found that family members used technology to communicate about the well-being of others. For example, two rural participants reported calling their children in urban areas of Kenya as well as in other countries abroad with a focus on understanding their well-being, e.g., troubling times, health issues. This also occurred for six urban participants. Thus, this practice was limited and only occurred for people who were considered to be in a better economic situation. It was also more secondary in terms of importance when compared to communication around economic support.

"Apart from my wife, the next important person that I talk to is my mother who lives in the village. She will always give me updates on how immediate family members are generally doing ... I also call my siblings every other time to check on the well-being of their families. I tend to call the others often since I am the eldest in the family."- Athanas

Coordinating Family Activities

For households containing multiple individuals, it was important to coordinate the daily activities of family members. Face-to-face interaction was the widely used mode of communication between such families. While rarer, there were specific cases where technology was used for coordination purposes.

In rural settings, technology was not widely used for family coordination because it was too costly or simply not needed (since family members would see each other in person in the morning and evening). Instead, only people who had specific jobs that required them to use a mobile phone for work would do so. For example, George used his mobile phone while conducting his motorcycle taxi business to run small errands for his family members who lived in the village with him. He received calls from either of his two wives (whoever had enough credit for calling), his mother or his siblings (or their wives) who lived in the village while driving customers on his motorcycle. They would ask him to buy commodities such as bathing soap or sugar packs while taking customers to or from Awendo. He would then purchase the requested commodity and bring it home if he was dropping a customer off close to his home.

Second, suburban and urban participants who lived with other family members used technology more often for coordinating family activities in comparison to the rural participants. Parents reported using technology to get in touch with their children for shopping, dinner planning, and household chores. For example, Alice lived in the slums of Githurai and sold fish in the evenings after 5 pm to those returning home from work in the city and its environs. This meant that she would be at her stall while her teenage children returned home from school. Her eldest daughter owned a phone and would beep her since she did not have phone credits to actually place the call. Alice would then call back. Phone conversations focused on instructions to the children about what to do around the home, such as purchasing food for dinner and cooking it.

In another example, a suburban participant and senior civil servant was constantly travelling for training across the country. He bought mobile phones for all of the adults in his household so that whenever he called he could reach his children (age 10 to 16). In these cases, he wanted to ensure that the children were working on their school assignments or chores that had been assigned by their mother.

SOCIAL SITUATIONS AND CHALLENGES

Like other research [33], we found communication was often timed based on cheap calling time periods, when lots of family members would be present, an individual's economic situation, and electricity availability. We also saw instances of beeping, 'please call me texts,' and a focus on conversation brevity [33,34]. Beyond these practices, we also learned about various social situations, described next, that affected family communication routines ranging from being the eldest child, to supporting the families of deceased siblings (different than in [22]), to gender.

Eldest Children

Generally, parents were in charge of coordinating family activities. However, the dynamics of this situation changed when adult children moved away from the rural areas and migrated to suburban or urban areas. In these situations, parents would entrust the eldest children with the duty of passing information to their siblings who were also working or studying away from the rural villages.

For example, four participants (one female) who reported to be the eldest in their families were always prepared to communicate with any member of their family in case an emergency or important issue arose. Issues ranged from holding discussions aimed at solving an economic problem that needed financial intervention or even engaging in a serious discussion to solve family disputes and quarrels. Because of this, the eldest children (from our participant pool) who all lived in Githurai often felt obligated to have their mobile phones on as much as possible in order to receive information from their rural village and then share the same with dispersed family members. If the eldest child worked at a job that did not allow them to be constantly available, messages would then be shared through other family members. But seniority in terms of age, would dictate who was expected to handle sharing such messages.

"As the eldest in my family, my phone must always have credit because I have to keep in touch with my parents who live upcountry. I am always the first one they will contact if there is any information that needs to be sent to my brothers and sisters who live away from home. I also receive calls at any time from my siblings and extended family. My phone must be on all the time to ensure that I am able to receive all information and then pass any important ones to other family members."- Julia

Sometimes this created additional monetary burdens on the eldest children. If cases arose where one of the adult children was more financially well off than the eldest child, the obligation as 'information hub' moved to this child. For example, in one case, a civil servant participant who was seen to be financially well off in comparison to her eldest brother was expected to disperse information from her mother in the village to her siblings who lived in Nairobi.

Death and its Effects on Communication

We were also told about ways in which surviving relatives who worked away from home would use scarce financial resources to communicate with the families of their deceased siblings left behind in rural homes. This was a cultural obligation described by our participants.

For example, a participant named Opana who was in his early fifties was the only surviving male out of his entire family. His parents and siblings had all passed away and he lived in Githurai with his wife and six children. Opana was a low income clerical civil servant and lived on a very tight budget. He had to take out loans to meet his financial obligations and also engaged in a small tailoring business in the evening after work and during the weekends to make ends meet. Despite this, Opana was still culturally responsible to communicate with his siblings' widows to ensure the smooth running of the rural home as the surviving eldest male in his extended family.

Opana purchased mobile phone credits worth $0.60 (Kshs 50) to make phone calls whenever his siblings' widows from the village beeped him or sent him a please call me message. He would then call between 8 pm and 6 am when the special Telkom service provider rates could allow him at least 20 minutes worth of 'talk time' for this amount of money. To get the best value out of the discussion using the little phone credit available, he would let the eldest widow briefly explain the issue at hand before quickly giving his opinion and advice over the matter. This happened at least once or twice a month unless there were other pressing issues that required continuous consultation such as planning to attend a relative's funeral. In such cases, there would be a brief exchange of updates every now and then in an attempt to coordinate issues.

Gender

We also found that gender affects family communication practices. First, we found that women often had to rely on their husbands for access to mobile phones; Murphy and Priebe [21] also report this finding. Building on their work, we saw how husbands and wives created workarounds in order facilitate communication.

First, we found that husbands often used their male siblings as communication 'intermediaries' when they wanted to initiate communication with their wives. In cases where one's wife did not have a phone in their possession, the husband would contact his other male siblings in order to reach his wife. Thus, gender played a dominating role in *who* would be contacted as an intermediary in order to connect with one's wife. For example, two male participants in the rural setting reported that their wives did not own mobile phones. In one case, the participant and his wife would share one phone, though it routinely stayed with the husband. Thus, he claimed 'ownership' over the device. The other participant reported that in addition to sharing his phone with his wife, he would occasionally call his siblings to reach his wife in case he was away from home for casual work. This meant that rather than being able to directly contact his wife to converse, he relied on other people, specifically his male siblings.

"When I am away from home and need to speak to my wife on the phone, I will call my brother and ask him if he is able to pass his phone to my wife so that I can speak to her in private. Once our discussion is finished, she will return the phone and thank my brother." – Atandi

Second, we learned that some women would purchase SIM cards to enable them to call family members. SIM cards were cheaper than mobile phones and easier to conceal from husbands, if needed. For example, one female participant told us that she kept a SIM card with a small amount of phone credit on it (e.g., Kshs 20) in case she needed to contact a relative. She would borrow her husband's phone to call her female family members (e.g., sisters). This sometimes included sharing information about her husband to a close family member without the husband's knowledge. Her husband was aware that she kept her own SIM card and would occasionally ask to use it if he did not have enough credit on his own phone. In case her husband was out with his phone and the participant needed to make a call, she would walk for about 20 minutes to borrow a handset from her brother in-law's wife. This example reveals the ability to have communication access without the need to have a phone *per se*. Instead, one can use shared phones and a personally owned SIM card. It also reveals the lengths and 'workaround' strategies that women might go to in order to communicate with other female family members to gain life advice.

Third, we found that female participants who lived in urban or suburban areas were more likely to own mobile phones on their own. In some low income families, they often had to conceal their use of it from their husbands. For example, a female participant who was running a small scale fish selling business told us about the use of her mobile phone for discussing financial discussions with her sister. Her sister would supply her with fish from their rural home, and then deliver the fish overnight by a bus to Githurai. What was interesting about this case was that all communications between the participants and her sister had to be done without the participant's husband knowing.

"When I need to discuss my business progress with my sister, I have to make sure that my husband is not around the house if I have to make that call." – Rose

She explained that this secrecy was necessary because if her husband overheard communication related to profits, he would stop providing money for use within the house and let her take care of such expenses. This could result in her business 'going under' since she made little profit which was mainly used to support poor family members who lived in the village. Thus, she delicately negotiated the unequal relations of economic power with her husband through economic discussions without his knowledge.

Phone Sharing and Connecting through Intermediaries

Like other research [27,34], we also found that rural participants shared phones because of a lack of ownership, loss of service network, and a lack of battery power. On the other hand, urban and suburban participant did not report sharing of phones because of better infrastructure and ability to purchase additional phones. This finding is different from [27], where factory workers shared phones in urban areas mainly due to lack of cellphone ownership in urban India. In our case, Phone sharing created several interesting social situations.

First, shared phones created additional obligations on others to pass along messages. For example, we found that, in some cases, if a person being sought after was not available, the receiver would take the information over the call and then share it with the relevant family member later. This information had to be remembered or written down and later shared. If the information was private and only intended for the recipient, the caller would ask the owner of the mobile phone to alert him through a "please call me" message or a beep whenever the intended recipient of the message was located. This created additional work for the owner of the phone who would then receive replies to the "please call me" and have to transfer the information to call back the original caller.

Second, urban participants reported that they frequently faced network problems while trying to reach their relatives in rural areas. Some participants said they would keep trying until they were able to connect. Another practice was to try calling other family members, starting from immediate family including siblings and then progressively moving out to cousins and other relatives until a person was reached. Once they got a hold of someone, they asked them to tell the person being sought to get in touch with the individual calling from the urban area. Again, this created additional work beyond simply contacting one individual. Such behaviors were reported by seven urban and two suburban participants. The idea of calling people and asking them to pass on information was a practice that all the rural participants engaged in and understood to be the norm.

Computer Literacy and Finances

All participants communicated with their family members by calling on mobile phones. Urban and rural participants did not typically use text messages for communicating with one another because, in most cases, an immediate response was required due to a heavy focus on economic support. As a result they relied on voice communication. Illiterate participants also relied on voice communication because they simply could not read or write text messages.

We also found that one's financial situation affected what technologies were owned and used. While mobile phones were certainly the most popular communication tool, some urban participants also used computers, social media, and video conferencing to communicate with remote family members. This was because they were typically more financially well off than their rural family members. It also meant that computer-based communication did not occur between urban and rural areas because those in rural regions could often not afford computer technology and, even if they could, infrastructure issues and a lack of electricity, would create usage problems. Instead, computers were primarily used to connect with family members living abroad. For example, five urban and four suburban participants used their own laptops to connect to the Internet to send emails and use social media such as Facebook for chatting. This occurred either in their home or workplace and communication was mainly with family living outside of Kenya. Two suburban graduates reported the use of social media on their phones in addition to laptops to chat with their sibling, cousins and friends who lived within the country and abroad.

Computer literacy varied amongst our participants. Four urban participants and eight rural participants reported that they did not know how to use computers either due to lack of education or lack of motivation, while four rural participants mentioned that they had basic experience with computers. The distance to cyber cafes from rural areas (~20 km) made it difficult for computer literate participants to access the Internet (also reported in [33]). Other low-income participants would have been willing to gain knowledge in using computers but other economic related challenges seemed more important at present. Similar observations were also made in the outskirts of the urban areas where older participants who did not have prior experience with using technology thought it was not worth spending time to learn something that would not improve their lives economically.

DISCUSSION AND CONCLUSIONS

The goal of our study was to articulate the family communication practices of our participants with a focus on understanding when technology was used and why, and what social factors affected this usage. In this section, we point to design implications. We caution, however, that our implications are not focused on presenting guiding ideas for how to design technologies. We feel that any such discussion would be preliminary and speculative at this point. Instead, we suggest areas that present further design opportunities which move beyond the suggestions of previous work. We also outline the social challenges that designers will need to carefully think through when creating or deploying family communication technologies in Kenya.

The Focus of Communication

Technology-based family communication in the areas of Kenya that we studied focused largely on four main areas: providing and discussing economic support, life advice and guidance, maintaining an awareness of well-being, and, sometimes, the coordination of everyday family life. At a surface level, these results illustrate the areas where technology design for family communication in Kenya should be targeted.

Other research has suggested the coupling of financial transactions with communication [36] as a starting point for family communication design. Our results shed light on the idea that while economic support was critical to life in Kenya for most of our participants, they also found value and participated in communication exchanges on other topics that helped create a sense of well-being and allowed them to discuss, gain advice, and come to terms with life challenges (sometimes even related to their own spouses). This suggests a broader understanding of what family communication practices may be important for Kenyans. Solely focusing technology design on providing economic support may neglect the 'human' need of connecting with others for less utilitarian purposes. Certainly Kenyans need to earn money and negotiate financial help from remote family members, but they also have inherent human needs that need to be filled through the connection with others.

Social Challenges

We also found that a variety of social situations affect how families communicated using technology. First, we found that additional pressures are placed on the eldest children in the family and the siblings of widows to connect with family members. In these situations, Kenyans were socially and culturally obligated to stay aware of the activities of additional family members and coordinate the exchange of information. This presents results that move beyond past work that shows the obligations faced by those family members who are considered to be more 'well off' financially [33] to show what additional social factors affect cultural obligations.

This brings forward the idea that new technology designs will be used differently by users depending on their social role within a family. It also suggests design opportunities based on social roles. For example, the eldest children in a family may need technologies that allow them to easily be available on a continuous basis, while not being overwhelmed by such connectivity. Such technologies could be focused around the user as an information hub who frequently receives and sends-on information about a wide variety of family members. In another situation, the eldest males in a family containing widowed in-laws may value technologies that provide awareness information about the well being of the widows. Technologies for users who are not in these more demanding social roles may need to support less frequent information exchange between family members.

Second, we found that access to technology and usage will differ between men and women, those with different literacy rates and computer experience, and those with different levels of technology access due to connectivity and finances. This illustrates that technology cannot be designed with a 'one size fits all' mentality. Moreover, designers should consider how any future designs might affect these social and cultural issues. For example, one would need to carefully navigate the delicate gender balance and cultural norms related to social hierarchies in families. In this case, while it may seem beneficial to design technologies specifically for women, doing so could easily create an undesired shift in the traditional male-female roles found in Kenyan families. Gender is a very complex subject with many subtleties and certainly this aspect requires additional research.

We also found a contrast in computer accessibility, use, and knowledge between participants in rural and urban regions. Thus, our study draws attention to a 'digital divide' within Kenya. In rural areas, a large number of participants did not have knowledge about computers. This was partly because they were occupied with subsistence farming and small-scale income generating activities that were barely enough to support gaining knowledge about computers. On the other hand, the working class (civil servants and business men), college graduates and, to some extent, low income individuals living in urban areas were already using more advanced communication technologies (e.g., Facebook, Skype).

The challenge is that the rural and urban areas have different technological infrastructure, education, and understanding of computers. There will continue to be a disparity that needs to be designed around if family members are to easily communicate between rural and urban areas. Currently, mobile phones support this because they are simple to use. Yet as technology advances, in particular in the cities, designs may move away from mobile phones to other devices such as computers. This could easily create a new challenge for family communication in Kenya. Even though the family communication routines we uncovered in our study were specifically tied to mobile phones, it is likely that existing practices (e.g., a focus on economic support) will stay consistent as new technologies are introduced and developed in Kenya. This is because they are culturally specific and reflect the ways in which Kenyans need to communicate when separated by distance. This creates a challenge where researchers and designers of technologies will need to understand how to translate the cultural practices of Kenyans to the next wave of technological advancements to continue to create technologies that are uniquely Kenyan and balance disparities in education levels, income, electricity, and connectivity.

It is also likely that the future will hold new opportunities for the design of applications in Kenya that utilize the Internet and may even mean the creation and further adoption of social networking sites and rich communication systems such as video chat. However, it is not necessarily the case that such technologies will migrate from developed countries to developing countries on the simple basis of improved infrastructure where the use of these technologies is the same in Kenya as other developed countries. Instead, we feel that one should think carefully about the ways in which Kenyans are likely to need and use communication technologies and specifically design for such situations.

Study Limitations

We recognize that while valuable, our study results do come with their limitations. Our work should certainly be complemented by additional studies in other developing countries around the world. We focused on a country that is highly multicultural with many different ethnicities and village types. Other areas of Kenya beyond which we studied have different economic foci that do not contain subsistence farming. For example, some regions engage in fishing, hunting, pastoral work, etc. Other areas of Kenya also do not contain polygamy as a cultural practice. We also only investigated Kenyans from five tribes (out of a potential 42) [14], mainly drawn from western Kenya. Thus, the communication practices that we found may differ for these areas. This suggests additional investigations into family communication routines in other parts of the country and with additional tribes. Such studies will enrich our knowledge in understanding the dynamic family communication needs of a larger representation of similarly marginalized communities.

We will continue to explore this design space where we plan to prototype technologies that will provide our participants with opportunities to engage in audio, text, and, to some extent, video communication with their distributed relatives. We aim to understand how such avenues will support our participants in their communication routines.

ACKNOWLEDGMENTS

We thank NSERC and the GRAND NCE for funding this research. We also thank past reviewers for their helpful comments on revising this paper.

REFERENCES

1. Agesa, R.U. and Kim, S., "Rural to urban migration as a household decision: Evidence from Kenya," Review of Development Economics 5, 1 (2001), 60-75.
2. Best, M., Smyth, T. N, Etherton, J. & Wornyo, E. Uses of Mobile Phones in Post-Conflict Liberia. Inf. Tech. & Int'l Development Vol 6, (2) (2010), 91-108.
3. Bidwell, N.J. & Siya, M.J. Situating Asynchronous Voice in Rural Africa. Proc. INTERACT, Springer, (2013), 36–53.
4. Bidwell, N.J., Lalmas, M., Marsden, G., Dlutu, B., Ntlangano, S.,Manjingolo, A., Tucker, W.D., Jones, M., Robinson, R., Vartiainen, E., Klampanos, I. Please call ME.N.U.4EVER: Designing for 'Callback' in Rural Africa. Proc. IWIPS'11, (2011), 117-138.
5. Burrell, J., Evaluating Shared Access: social equality and the circulation of mobile phones in rural Uganda, Journal

of Computer-Mediated Communication, 15(2), (2010), 230-250.

6. Donner, J., "The Rules of Beeping: Exchanging messages via intentional "missed calls" on mobile phones, Journal Computer Mediated Communication, 13 (1), ACM Press (2008), 1-22.
7. Eriksson, E., A Case Study About Cell Phone Use by People in Rural Keyna, Vaxjo University, School of Mathematics and Systems Engineering Bachelor's Degree Thesis, Apr 2008,IV9003.
8. Francis, E., (2000) Making a Living: Changing Livelihoods in Rural Africa. Routledge, London.
9. Ginsburg, F. Rethinking the Digital Age, in Global Indigenous Media: Cultures, Poetics, and Politics, Wilson, P. and Stewart, M. (Eds.), Duke University Press (2008).
10. Githurai Community. A Kenyatta University-Githurai Partnership http://www.ku.ac.ke/Githurai/index.html.
11. Horst, H. Blessings and burdens of communication: cell phones in Jamaican transnational social fields, Global Networks, 6, 2, (2006), 143-159.
12. Horst, H. and Miller, D. From Kinship to Link-up: Cell Phones and Social Networking in Jamaica, Current Anthropology, 46, 5, (2005), 755-778.
13. Hughes, N. and Lonie, S., M-PESA: Mobile Money for the 'Unbanked' Turning Cellphones into 24-Hour Tellers in Kenya, Innovations: Technology, Governance, Globalization 2, 1-2 (2007), 63-81.
14. Tribes in Kenya http://www.kenyanview.com/ Kenyan tribes/kenyaweb.htm
15. Kisumu. http://en.wikipedia.org/wiki/Kisumu
16. Kwake, K. and Adigun, M., Analyzing ICT use and access amongst rural women in Kenya, International Journal of Education and Development using Information and Communication Technology (IJEDICT), 2008, Vol. 4, Issue 4, pp. 127-147.
17. Liu, J., Liu, Y., Rau, P.-L.P., Li, H., Wang, X. and Li, D., How Socio-Economic Structure Influences Rural Users' Acceptance of Mobile Entertainment, Proc. CHI, ACM Press (2010), 2203-2212.
18. MigoriTown.com http://migoritown.com/
19. Mimbi, L., Bankole, F., and Kyobe, M. Mobile Phones and Digital Divide in East African Countries, Pr.c SAICSIT, ACM Press (2011).
20. Morawczynski, O., and Pickenism, M-PESA: More Than Money Transfer, www.mobilepaymentsworld.com /m-pesa-more-than-money-transfer-by-olga-morawczy nski-and-mark-pickens/. Mobile Payments World, Accessed 9th September 2013.
21. Murphy, L and Priebe, A. 'My co-wife can borrow my mobile phone!': gender geographies of cellphone usage and significance for rural Kenyans, Gender Technology and Development, March 2011, Vol 15, No 1, 1-23.
22. Peters, A., Oren, M. and Bidwell, N., Namibian and American Cultural Orientations Toward Facebook, Proc. CHI, ACM Press (2012).
23. Poverty Overview, http://www.worldbank.org/en/topic/ poverty/overview.
24. Rangaswamy, M. and Sambasivan, N. Cutting Chaai, Jugaad and Here Pheri: towards UbiComp for a global community, Personal and Ubiquitous Computing, 15(6), Springer (2011).
25. Sambasivan, N., Cutrell, E., Toyama, K., and Nardi, B. Intermediated Technology Use in Developing Communities. Proc. CHI, ACM Press (2010).
26. Sambasivan, N., Rangaswamy, N, Cutrell, E., and Nardi, B. Ubicomp4D: Infrastructure for International Development–the case of Urban Indian Slums. Proc. CSCW, ACM Press (2009).
27. Smyth, T., Kumar, S., Medhi, I. and Toyamo, K., Where There's a Will There's a Way: Mobile Media Sharing in Urban India, Proc. CHI, ACM Press (2010). 753-762.
28. Strauss, A. and Corbin, J., Basics of Qualitative Research, 2nd Edition, Sage Publications (1998).
29. Taylor, A., Out There, Proc. CHI, ACM Press (2011).
30. Vertovec, S. Cheap Calls: The Social Glue of Migrant Transnationalism. Global Networks 4, 2, (2004).
31. Williams, A., Anderson, K., and Dourish, P. Anchored Mobilities: Mobile Technology and Transnational Migration. Human Factors, Proc. DIS, ACM Press (2008), 323-332.
32. Wyche, S., Forte, A. and Yardi, S. Hustling Online: Understanding Consolidated Facebook Use in an Informal Settlement in Nairobi, Proc. CHI, ACM Press (2013).
33. Wyche, S. and Grinter, R. "This is How We Do it in My Country": A Study of Computer-Mediated Family Communication Among Kenyan Migrants in the United States, Proc. CSCW, ACM Press (2012).
34. Wyche, S. and Murphy, L. "Dead China-Make'' Phones Off the Grid: Investigating and Designing for Mobile Phone Use in Rural Africa, Proc. DIS, ACM Press (2012).
35. Wyche, S.P., Smyth, T.N., Chetty, M., Aoki, P.M. and Grinter, R.E., Deliberate Interactions: Characterizing Technology Use in Githurai, Kenya, Proc. CHI, ACM Press (2010), 2593-2602.
36. Wyche, S., Yardi, S., and Forte, A. "Facebook is a Luxury": An Exploratory Study of Social Media Use in Rural Kenya, Proc. CSCW, ACM Press (2013).

www.ingramcontent.com/pod-product-compliance
Ingram Content Group UK Ltd.
Pitfield, Milton Keynes, MK11 3LW, UK
UKHW051418290926
15471UKWH00009B/1668

9 781450 332897